Description of French economic problems and the membership of France in the European Union *(Chapter 12)*

Examination of the effects of global competition on the German economy and lifestyle *(Chapter 19)*

Discussion of price reform in the former Soviet Union as an illustration of economic shocks *(Chapter 18)*

Discussion of Chinese imports and trade protections *(Chapter 36)*

Y0-AGR-984

Asia

Europe

Discussion of the role of the national government in Japan's economy *(Chapter 5)*

Examination of the Thai financial crisis of 1997, showing the interconnectedness of the world's economies *(Chapter 19)*

Africa

Examination of Pakistan's informal financial markets *(Chapter 13)*

Australia

Description of foreign aid to Somalia as an example of bilateral aid *(Chapter 18)*

"The California Debacle" *(Chapter 27)*
"Why Aren't Cows and Chickens on the Endangered Species List?" *(Chapter 28)*
"Stock Market Booms and Busts" *(Chapter 31)*
"Country Bond Ratings" *(Chapter 31)*
"The World Is Aging" *(Chapter 33)*
"Health-Care Spending in Various Nations" *(Chapter 33)*
"Economic Development and Happiness" *(Chapter 34)*
"The Dutch Disease" *(Chapter 35)*
"Smoot-Hawley Tariff" *(Chapter 36)*
"The IMF and the World Bank" *(Chapter 37)*

Economics

Economics

SIXTH EDITION

William Boyes
Arizona State University

Michael Melvin
Arizona State University

Houghton Mifflin Company   Boston   New York

To Melissa, Katie, and Lindsey
W. B.

To Bettina, Jason, and Jeremy
M. M.

Publisher: Charles Hartford
Editor in Chief: George Hoffman
Sponsoring Editor: Ann West
Associate Editor: Julie Hassel
Editorial Associate: Tonya Lobato
Project Editor: Paula Kmetz
Senior Production/Design Coordinator: Carol Merrigan
Senior Manufacturing Coordinator: Marie Barnes
Marketing Manager: Todd Berman

Cover image © Ian McKinnell/Photographer's Choice

PHOTO CREDITS

(Text Credits follow the Index.)

p. 2, © Tom Stewart/Corbis; p. 4, © AFP/Corbis; p. 24, © Mary Kate Denny/PhotoEdit; p. 34, © AFP/Getty Images; p. 40, © Marc Romanelli; p. 42 (top), © Dante Busquets-Sordo; p. 42 (bottom), © Oliver Benn/Stone/Getty Images; p. 56, © Norm Rowan/The Image Works; p. 72, AP/Wide World Photos; p. 85, © Jeff Greenberg/The Image Works; p. 98, © Porter Gifford/Getty Images; p. 103, © A. Ramey/PhotoEdit; p. 113, © David Simson/Stock Boston; p. 122, © Paul Chesley/Stone/Getty Images; p. 133, © Rainer Grosskopf/Stone/Getty Imagaes; p. 146, © J. Van Hasselt/Corbis Sygma; p. 155, © William Whitehurst/Corbis; p. 162, Arnold Cedric/Corbis Sygma; p. 167, © Margaret Bourke-White/Life Magazine/Getty Images; p. 170, © Danny Lehman/Corbis; p. 188, AP/Wide World Photos; p. 203, © Tim Boyle/Getty Images; p. 216, © Keith Dannemiller/Corbis Saba; p. 218, © James Nelson/Stone/Getty Images; p. 233, © Billy E. Barnes/PhotoEdit; p. 248, © Bill Bachman/PhotoEdit; p. 261, © Keith Dannemiller/Corbis Saba; p. 276, © Sandra Baker; p. 280, © AFP/Corbis; p. 302, © Hugh Sitton/StoneGetty Images; p. 326, AP/Wide World Photos; p. 332, © Najlah Feanny/Stock Boston; p. 354, © Michael J. Doolittle/The Image Works; p. 374, © Owen Franken/Stock Boston; p. 375, © Reuters NewMedia Inc./Corbis; p. 382, © Johannes Eisele/AFP/Getty; p. 400, © AFP/Corbis; p. 408, © Reuters NewMedia Inc./Corbis; p. 414, © Spencer Grant/PhotoEdit; p. 422, © Penny Tweedie/Stone/Getty Images; p. 433, © Chung Sung-Jun /Getty Images; p. 436, © AFP/Corbis; p. 439, © Sean Gallup/Getty Images; p. 441, AP/Wide World Photos; p. 452, © Reuters NewMedia Inc./Corbis; p. 453, © AFP/Corbis; p. 460, © Jose Fuste Raga/Corbis; p. 474, © Dick Doughty/HAGA/The Image Works; p. 476, © Tony Savino/The Image Works; p. 487, © Junko Kimura/Getty Images; p. 498, © Tim Boyle/Getty Images; p. 510, © David McNew/Getty Images; p. 524, © Michael Rosenfeld/Stone/Getty Images; p. 529, © Schiller/The Image Works; p. 552, © Steve Raymer/Corbis; p. 555, © Andy Sacks/Stone/Getty Images; p. 570, © Paula Bronstein/Stone/Getty Images; p. 579, © Bill Gillette/Stock Boston; p. 590, © Keren Su/Corbis; p. 594, © Jacksonville Journal-Courier/The Image Works; p. 610, © Caroline Parsons; p. 613, © Norbert Schwerin/The Image Works; p. 617, © Stephen Chernin/Getty Images; p. 634, © Bob Daemmrich/Stock Boston; p. 649, © Syracuse Newspapers/Dick Blume/The Image Works; p. 660, © Michael Newman/PhotoEdit; p. 669, © Gideon Mendel/Corbis; p. 688, © David Young-Wolff/PhotoEdit; p. 691, © S P/Corbis; p. 710, © Kevin Fleming/Corbis; p. 717, © Andy Freeberg; p. 727, AP/Wide World Photos; p. 736, © Paul A. Souders/Corbis; p. 762, © Kim Heacox/Stone/Getty Images; p. 768, © Lester Lefkowitz/Corbis; p. 774, © Syracuse Newspapers/The Image Works; p. 785, © Mike Greenlar/The Image Works; p. 796, © Mary Wolf/Stone/Getty Images; p. 802, © M. Vertinetti/Photo Researchers; p. 811, © M. Grecco/Stock Boston; p. 824, © Christian Lagereek/Stone/Getty Images; p. 828, © Jean-Leo Dugast/Corbis Sygma; p. 844, © Fred R. Palmer/Stock Boston; p. 856, © Bob Daemmrich/Stock Boston; p. 864, © AFP/Corbis.

Printed in the U.S.A.

Library of Congress Control Number: 2003109915

ISBN: 0-618-37252-0

3 4 5 6 7 8 9 —DOW— 08 07 06 05

Preface

I n the first edition of *Economics* we integrated the global perspective with the traditional economic principles to give students a framework to understand the globally developing economic world. Events since then have made this approach even more imperative. The Soviet Union has disintegrated, newly independent nations have emerged, and markets have been established where none had existed before. Students and instructors embraced the idea that the economies of countries are interrelated and that this should be made clear in the study of economics. *Economics* gives students the tools they need to make connections between the economic principles they learn and the now-global world they live in.

Students often wonder why they need to study economics. The sixth edition begins with a discussion of "Why Study Economics?" and provides information on what economists do and what majoring in economics means.

In this sixth edition, we continue to refine and improve the text as a teaching and learning instrument while expanding its international base by updating and adding examples related to global economics.

Changes in the Sixth Edition

The sixth edition of *Economics* has been thoroughly updated and refined. A detailed account of all the additions, deletions, and modifications can be found in the Transition Guide in the *Instructor's Resource Manual* and on the website at: college.hmco.com. We mention some of the highlights below.

Revised Macroeconomic Coverage

The most notable change in the macroeconomic chapters is the addition of a new chapter, 19, on globalization, which addresses the costs and benefits of the process by which the world's economies become more closely integrated. Although some of this material had been discussed in Chapter 17 of the fifth edition,

("Macroeconomic Links Among Countries"), this new chapter has significantly extended the coverage of globalization and the controversies surrounding it. Other noteworthy changes include: discussion in Chapter 7 that relates the balance of payments current account deficit to the national income accounting identities; new material in Chapter 8 on how the NBER defines and identifies a recession; a new figure and discussion in Chapter 10 on the actual long-run U.S. consumption function; and a new Global Business Insight box on Islamic banking in Chapter 13, along with a new section on informal financial markets in developing countries. Chapter 14 now contains a new section on inflation targeting, and Chapter 17 provides a new discussion of the role of computers in enhancing productivity as well as a new section on the role of financial market development in economic growth. Discussion of the effect of corruption on development has been added to Chapter 18. Chapter 37 has been completely revised and is now titled "Exchange Rates and Financial Links Between Countries." The chapter discusses how countries are linked via interest rates, exchange rates, and prices.

The macroeconomic chapters have all been updated to include the latest available economic statistics. In many chapters, numerical examples have been revised to provide greater clarity in the graphical presentations, and many of the Economically Speaking boxes and commentaries have been revised or replaced with more current examples of economic activity around the world.

Revised Microeconomic Coverage

The principal objective of the microeconomic material is to enable students to see the forest while wandering around in the trees, to learn the fundamentals while seeing the applicability to current events. "Financial Markets: Institutions and Recent Events" (Chapter 31), has been introduced in the sixth edition for two reasons. First, it enables discussion of stocks, bonds, mutual funds, and other financial instruments and the markets in which they are traded, including recent developments.

Second, it reinforces the applicability of economics to business. Chapter 27, "Antitrust and Regulation" provides the context for the financial markets chapter and includes economic regulation, social regulation, and financial markets regulation. The recent scandals in the stock market and the Sarbannes-Oxley Act are discussed. A new chapter, "Government and Market Failure" (Chapter 28), follows the market structure chapters ("Perfect Competition," "Monopoly," "Monopolistic Competition and Oligopoly"). Placing all the arguments regarding market failures in one chapter enables instructors to delve as deeply as they wish into the role of government in the economy. This chapter looks at the circumstances under which markets might fail—externalities, public goods, lack of private property rights, and asymmetric information—and discusses approaches to solving the problems created.

Successful Features Retained from the Fifth Edition

In addition to the considerable updating and revising we've done for the sixth edition, there are several features preserved from the previous edition that we think instructors will find interesting.

Enhanced Student Relevance

With all the demands on today's students, it's no wonder that they resist spending time on a subject unless they see how the material relates to them and how they will benefit from mastering it. We incorporate features throughout the text that show economics as the relevant and necessary subject we know it to be.

Real-World Examples   Students are rarely intrigued by unknown manufacturers or service companies. Our text talks about people and firms that students recognize. We describe business decisions made by McDonald's and Pizza Hut, by Kodak and Fuji, and by the local video store or café. We discuss the policies of George W. Bush and other world leaders. These examples grab students' interest. Reviewers have repeatedly praised the use of novel examples to convey economic concepts.

Economic Insight Boxes   These brief boxes bring in contemporary material from current periodicals and journals to illustrate or extend the discussion in the chapter. By reserving interesting but more technical

sidelights for boxes, we lessen the likelihood that students will be confused or distracted by issues that are not critical to understanding the chapter. By including excerpts from articles, we help students learn to move from theory to real-world examples. And by including plenty of contemporary issues, we guarantee that students will see how economics relates to their own lives. New topics covered in the fifth edition include features of the new $20 bill and why wages don't fall in recessions.

Economically Speaking Boxes   The objective of the principles course is to teach students how to translate to the real world the predictions that come out of economic models and to translate real-world events into an economic model in order to analyze and understand what lies behind the events. The Economically Speaking boxes present students with examples of this kind of analysis. Students read an article that appears on the left-hand page of a two-page spread at the end of each chapter. The commentary on the right-hand page shows how the facts and events in the article translate into a specific economic model or idea, thereby demonstrating the relevance of theory. Nearly two-thirds of the articles and commentaries are new to the sixth edition, covering such current events as the underground economy, the record U.S. trade deficit, and budget deficits in the European Union.

Global Business Insight Boxes   These boxes link business events and developments around the world to the economic concepts discussed in the main text of the chapters. A map is used to highlight the area of the world under discussion and to provide a geographic context for the economic issues examined. Topics include such basic micro- and macroeconomic issues as global competition, resource pricing, and foreign exchange.

An Effective and Proven System of Teaching and Learning Aids

This text is designed to make teaching easier by enhancing student learning. Tested pedagogy motivates students, emphasizes clarity, reinforces relationships, simplifies review, and fosters critical thinking. And, as we have discovered from reviewer and user feedback, this pedagogy works.

In-Text Referencing System   Sections are numbered for easy reference and to reinforce hierarchies of ideas. Numbered section heads serve as an outline of the chapter, allowing instructors flexibility in assigning reading, and making it easy for students to find topics to review. Each item in the key terms list and summary at the end of the chapter refers students back to the appropriate section's number.

The section numbering system appears throughout the Boyes/Melvin ancillary package; the *Test Banks, Study Guides,* and *Instructor's Resource Manual* are organized according to the same system.

? Fundamental Questions These questions help to organize the chapter and highlight those issues that are critical to understanding. Each related fundamental question also appears in the margin by the text discussion and, with brief answers, in the chapter summaries. A fuller discussion and answer to each of these questions may be found in the *Study Guides* available as supplements to this text. The fundamental questions also serve as one of several criteria used to categorize questions in the *Test Banks.*

Preview This motivating lead-in sets the stage for the chapter. Much more than a road map, it helps students identify real-world issues that relate to the concepts that will be presented.

RECAP **Recaps** Briefly listing the main points covered, a recap appears at the end of each major section within a chapter. Students are able to quickly review what they have just read before going on to the next section.

Summary The summary at the end of each chapter is organized along two dimensions. The primary organizational device is the list of fundamental questions. A brief synopsis of the discussion that helps students to answer those questions is arranged by section below each of the questions. Students are encouraged to create their own links among topics as they keep in mind the connections between the big picture and the details that make it up.

Comments Found in the text margins, these comments highlight especially important concepts, point out common mistakes, and warn students of common pitfalls. They alert students to parts of the discussion that they should read with particular care.

Key Terms Key terms appear in bold type in the text. They also appear with their definition in the margin and are listed at the end of the chapter for easy review.

All key terms are included in the Glossary at the end of the text.

Friendly Appearance

Economics can be intimidating; this is why we've tried to keep *Economics* looking friendly and inviting. The one-column design and ample white space in this text provide an accessible backdrop. Over 300 figures rely on well-developed pedagogy and consistent use of color to reinforce understanding. Striking colors were chosen to enhance readability and provide visual interest. Specific curves were assigned specific colors, and families of curves were assigned related colors.

Annotations on the art point out areas of particular concern or importance. Students can see exactly which part of a graph illustrates a shortage or a surplus, a change in consumption or consumer surplus. Tables that provide data from which graphs are plotted are paired with their graphs. Where appropriate, color is used to show correlations between the art and the table, and captions clearly explain what is shown in the figures and link them to the text discussion.

The color photographs not only provide visual images but make the text appealing. These vibrant photos tell stories as well as illustrate concepts, and lengthy captions explain what is in the photos, again to draw connections between the images and the text discussion.

Thoroughly International Coverage

Students understand that they live in a global economy; they can hardly shop, watch the news, or read a newspaper without stumbling on this basic fact. International examples are presented in every chapter but are not merely added on, as is the case with many other texts. By introducing international effects on demand and supply in Chapter 3 and then describing in a nontechnical manner the basics of the foreign exchange market and the balance of payments in Chapter 7, we are able to incorporate the international sector into the economic models and applications wherever appropriate thereafter. Because the international content is incorporated from the beginning, students develop a far more realistic picture of the national economy; as a result they don't have to alter their thinking to allow for international factors later on. The three chapters that focus on international topics at the end of the text allow those instructors who desire to delve much more deeply into international issues to do so.

The global applicability of economics is emphasized by *using traditional economic concepts to explain international economic events and using international events to illustrate economic concepts that have traditionally been illustrated with domestic examples.* Instructors need not know the international institutions to introduce international examples since the topics through which they are addressed are familiar, for example, price ceilings, price discrimination, expenditures on resources, marginal productivity theory, and others.

Uniquely international elements of the macroeconomic coverage in the text include:

- The treatment of the international sector as one of the economic participants and the inclusion of net exports as early as Chapter 4

- The early description of the foreign exchange market and the balance of payments in Chapter 7

- International elements in the development of aggregate demand and supply

- An extended treatment of macroeconomic links between countries in Chapter 37

- An entire chapter devoted to globalization

Unique international elements of microeconomic coverage in the text include:

- The introduction of exchange rates as a determinant of demand and supply in Chapter 3

- Extensive analyses of the effects of trade barriers, tariffs, and quotas

- An examination of strategic trade

- An examination of dumping as a special case of price discrimination

- The identification of problems faced by multinational firms

- A comparison of behavior, results, and institutions among nations with respect to consumption, production, firm size, government policies toward business, labor markets, health care, income distribution, environmental policy, and other issues

Modern Macroeconomic Organization and Content

Macroeconomics is changing and textbooks must reflect that change. We begin with the basics—GDP, unemployment, and inflation. These are the ongoing concerns of any economy, for they have a significant influence on how people feel. These are the issues that don't go away.

Added to these core topics is an easy-to-understand, descriptive introduction to the foreign exchange market and the balance of payments. We provide a critical alternative for those instructors who believe that it is no longer reasonable to relegate this material to the final chapters, where coverage may be rushed.

Armed with these basics, students are ready to delve into the richness of macroeconomic thought. Macro models and approaches have evolved over the years, and they continue to invite exciting theoretical and policy debates. The majority of instructors we asked voiced frustration with the challenge of pulling this rich and varied material together in class and stressed that a coherent picture of the aggregate demand and supply model was critical. We have structured the macro portion to allow for many teaching preferences while assuring a clear delineation of the aggregate demand/aggregate supply model.

To help instructors successfully present a single coherent model, we present aggregate demand and aggregate supply first, in Chapter 9, immediately following the chapter on inflation and unemployment. This sequence allows for the smooth transition from business cycle fluctuations to aggregate demand/aggregate supply (*AD/AS*). The Keynesian income and expenditures model is presented in full in Chapters 10 and 11 as the fixed-price version of the *AD/AS* model (with a horizontal aggregate supply curve). Those who want to use the *AD/AS* model exclusively will have no problem moving from the Chapter 9 presentation of it to the fiscal policy material in Chapter 12. The policy chapters rely on the *AD/AS* model for analysis.

The macroeconomic policy chapters begin with a thorough presentation of fiscal policy, money and banking, and monetary policy, with international elements included. Chapter 15 covers contemporary policy issues, and various schools of thought are treated in Chapter 16, when students are ready to appreciate the differences and can benefit from a discussion of new Keynesian and new classical models as well as of their precursors.

Part Four, "Economic Growth and Development," brings together the concepts and issues presented in the core macro chapters to explain how economies grow and what factors encourage or discourage growth. Most of the world's population live in poor countries. Growth and development are critical to those people. The material in these chapters also addresses issues of importance to industrial countries, such as the determinants of productivity growth and the benefits and costs of globalization.

Modern Microeconomic Organization and Content

Instructors often face a quandary when teaching microeconomic material. They want students to understand the basic theory of economics and the powerful intuition that thinking like an economist can provide, but they also want to enlist students' attention with real-life, current issues. In *Economics,* Sixth Edition, the theory is never far away from applications. Students can see why environmental issues such as pollution and the razing of rain forests occur and can learn about the costs and benefits of various proposed solutions to these problems. Students can see why incomes are unequal within a country and among countries and can learn about the costs and benefits of attempting to reduce inequality. Students can see why collusion occurs among competing firms and what the costs and benefits are of minimizing such behavior through antitrust action or regulation.

Part Five presents basic concepts such as elasticity, consumer behavior, and costs of production. Parts Six and Seven both begin with overview chapters (Chapter 23 on product markets and Chapter 29 on resource markets). These overviews give students a chance to look at the big picture before delving into details they often find confusing. Chapter 23, for instance, gives students an intuitive overview of the market structures before they explore each type of structure in more detail in succeeding chapters. Chapter 23 lightens the load that the more-detailed chapters have to bear, easing students into the market structure material. The traditional topics are covered in the separate market structure chapters, Chapters 24 to 26, but the coverage is also modern, including such topics as strategic behavior, price discrimination, nonprice competition, and the economics of information. Having fought their way first through the cost curves and then the market structures, students often complain that they do not see the relevance of that material to real-world situations. The intuitive overview chapter alleviates some of that frustration.

A Complete Teaching and Learning Package

In today's market no book is complete without a full complement of ancillaries. Those instructors who face huge classes find good PowerPoint slides to be critical instructional tools. Others may find that computer simulations and tutorials are invaluable. Still others use Internet resources and Web-based teaching and learning tools. All of these are available. And to foster the development of consistent teaching and study strategies, the ancillaries pick up pedagogical features of the text—like the fundamental questions—wherever appropriate.

Boyes/Melvin Student Support Package The Boyes/Melvin Student Support Package is bundled with all new texts and is also available for sale separately. The package includes:

- **Interactive Tutorial/Simulation CD-ROM.** The Boyes/Melvin interactive graphing software provides an opportunity for students to review concepts and models for each text chapter and to test themselves on what they have learned. In each tutorial, students are guided through a series of interactive lessons that allow them to change data and immediately see how curves shift. A glossary and context-sensitive help are always available. The simulation component of the software includes over 70 years of data on more than 20 key economic indicators, allowing students to plot data, compare various measurement instruments, and print out the results in table or graph form.

- **Smarthinking™ Online Tutoring Service.** This live, online tutoring service provides access to trained, qualified "e-structors" from wherever students are, whenever they need help. Students may interact live online with an experienced Smarthinking "e-structor" (online tutor) between 2:00 and 5:00 P.M. and between 9:00 P.M. and 1:00 A.M. EST, every Sunday through Thursday. Smarthinking provides state-of-the-art communication tools, such as chat technology and virtual whiteboards designed for easy rendering of economic formulas and graphs, to help your students practice key concepts and learn to think like an economist.

- **Detachable Study Card.** This handy review card includes key macroeconomic and microeconomic equations, a key to curve and variable names, and visual reminders to help students study or quickly review material before tests and for class assignments.

Study Guides Janet L. Wolcutt and James E. Clark of the Center for Economic Education at Wichita State University have revised the *Macroeconomics* and *Microeconomics Study Guides* to give students the practice they need to master this course. Initially received by students and instructors with great enthusiasm, the guides maintain their warm and lively style to keep students on the right track. For each chapter:

- Fundamental questions are answered in one or several paragraphs. For students who have trouble formulating their own answers to these questions after reading the text, the *Study Guides* provide an invaluable model.

- Key terms are listed.

- A Quick Check Quiz is organized by section, so any wrong answers send the student directly to the relevant material in the text.

- Practice Questions and Problems, which is also organized by section, includes a variety of question formats—multiple choice, true/false, matching, and fill in the blank. They test understanding of the concepts and ask students to construct or perform computations.

- Thinking About and Applying . . . uses newspaper headlines or some other real-life applications to test students' ability to reason in economic terms.

- A Homework page at the end of each chapter contains five (two factual, two applied, and one synthesis/analysis) questions that can be answered on the sheet and turned in for grading. Answers are included in the *Instructor's Resource Manual.*

- Sample tests appear at the end of each *Study Guide* part and consist of 25 to 50 questions similar to *Test Bank* questions. Taking the sample tests helps students determine whether they are prepared for exams.

- Answers are provided for all questions except the Homework questions. Students are referred back to the relevant sections in the main text for each question.

Instructor's Resource Manual (*IRM*) Patricia Diane Nipper has produced a manual that will streamline preparation for both new and experienced faculty. Preliminary sections cover class administration, alternative syllabi, and an introduction to the use of cooperative learning in teaching the principles of economics.

The *IRM* also contains a detailed chapter-by-chapter review of all the changes made in the sixth edition. This Transition Guide should help instructors more easily move from the use of the fifth edition to this new edition.

Each chapter of the *IRM* contains:

- Overview and objectives that (1) describe the content and unique features of the chapter and (2) provide a list of concrete objectives that students will need to master in order to succeed with later chapters.

- The fundamental questions

- The key terms

- A lecture outline with teaching strategies—general techniques and guidelines, essay topics, and other hints to enliven your classes

- Opportunities for discussion

- Answers to every end-of-chapter exercise

- Answers to *Study Guide* homework questions

- Active learning exercises

Test Banks Test Banks for both *Macroeconomics* and *Microeconomics* are available. More than 8,000 test items, approximately 30 percent of which are new to this edition, provide a wealth of material for classroom testing. Features include:

- Multiple choice, true/false, and essay questions in every chapter

- Questions new to this edition are marked for easy identification

- An increased number of analytical, applied, and graphical questions

- The identification of all test items according to topic, question type (factual, interpretive, or applied), level of difficulty, and applicable fundamental question

- A *Study Guide* section of the test that includes five test items taken directly from the *Study Guide* and five test items that parallel *Study Guide* questions, for the instructor who is interested in rewarding students for working through the *Study Guide*

Computerized Test Bank A new sophisticated and user-friendly program called HMTesting is available to help instructors quickly create tests from over 7,000 test bank items according to various selection criteria, including random selection. The program prints graphs as well as the text part of each question. Instructors can scramble the answer choices, edit questions, add their own questions to the pool, and customize their exams in various other ways. HMTesting provides a complete testing solution, including classroom administration and online testing features in addition to test generation. This program is available for Windows and Macintosh users.

HMClassPrep CD-ROM This supplement contains all the resources you need to prepare lessons based on the sixth edition of the text, including lecture outlines and teaching strategies, chapter overviews and objectives, in-class discussion ideas and PowerPoint slides. This wealth of resources is organized by chapter and resource type for easy reference and class planning. The computerized testing program, HMTesting, is also included on this CD (see above description).

PowerPoint Slides Figures, tables, key equations from the text, lecture outlines, and other resources that extend the text are provided on electronic slides created for Microsoft's popular *PowerPoint* presentation software. *PowerPoint* allows instructors to create customized lecture presentations that can be displayed on computer-based projection systems. The slides are produced as a complete presentation, but using *Power-Point,* presenters can also insert their own slides into the presentation or use specific slides in sets that they create themselves.

Website The sixth edition website provides an extended learning environment for students and a rich store of teaching resources for instructors. To locate the Boyes text site, go to *college.hmco.com,* choose *Instructor* or *Student,* go to the economics discipline or course area homepage, and then select Boyes 6/e from the Principles of Economics textbook sites. Instructors will need a username and password (available from their Houghton Mifflin sales representative) to get onto the password protected parts of the site. Included are key economic links for every chapter, extended Web-based assignments, and online quizzes—all intended to help students test their mastery of the chapter content. The instructor site contains economic and teaching resource links, teaching tips, links to current economic articles, answers to end-of-chapter exercises, and access to demonstrations of other components of the teaching package.

WebCT e-Pack and Blackboard Course Cartridge These resources provide text-specific student study aids in customizable, Internet-based education platforms. Both platforms provide a full array of content delivery and course management features for instructors who wish to incorporate educational technology in their traditional classrooms or for those who are creating distance learning courses.

EduSpace EduSpace is an online teaching and learning environment that offers the same course management features as Blackboard but is enhanced with the addition of valuable text-specific content for both students and instructors. Instructors will find pre-designed homework assignments and tests as well as a wide array of teaching resources—all designed with Web-based education in mind. Instructors can also create their own tests from pools of questions corresponding to each chapter and section of the sixth-edition textbook. Students will find review content, self-testing quizzes, and other engaging study aids, such as chapter tutorials with interactive graphs.

Acknowledgments

Writing a text of this scope is a challenge that requires the expertise and efforts of many. We are grateful to our friends and colleagues who have so generously given their time, creativity, and insight to help us create a text that best meets the needs of today's students.

We'd especially like to thank the many reviewers of *Economics* listed on the following pages. Their comments have proved invaluable in revising this text. In particular, we wish to thank Les Manns of Doane College and Eugenio Dante Suarez of Trinity University, who reviewed the text for accuracy in the last stages of production.

Unsolicited feedback from current users has also been greatly appreciated. We'd like to thank Nancy Roberts and Elmer Gooding of Arizona State University, Calvin M. Hoy of County College of Morris, and John Somers of Portland Community College for their very useful feedback.

Thanks go to Eugenio Dante Suarez and Kenny Christianson of Binghamton University for their work on the *Test Banks* for this edition. Thanks also to Bob Cunningham of Alma College and Davis Folsom and Rick Boulware of University of South Carolina, Beaufort, who reviewed the *Test Banks* for accuracy. The important contributions of Melissa Hardison on the third edition *Test Banks,* Bettina Peiers and Karen Thomas-Brandt on the second edition *Test Banks,* and Michael Couvillion on the first edition *Test Banks* must also be acknowledged.

We would also like to thank James E. Clark and Janet L. Wolcutt of Wichita State University for their continued contributions to the *Study Guides* and Patricia Diane Nipper of Southside Virginia Community College for her work on the sixth and previous editions of the *Instructor's Resource Manual*. Thanks also to Chin-Chyuan Tai of Averett College for reviewing this important supplement as well as the student tutorial CD. Thanks, too, go to Paul S. Estenson of Gustavus Adolphus College and Edward T. Merkel of Troy State University for their contribution in preparing the second edition *Instructor's Resource Manual*.

We want to thank the many people at Houghton Mifflin Company who devoted countless hours to making this text the best it could be, including Ann West, Julie Hassel, Paula Kmetz, Carol Merrigan, Marie Barnes, and Tonya Lobato. We are grateful for their enthusiasm, expertise, and energy.

Finally, we wish to thank our families and friends. The inspiration they provided through the conception and development of this book cannot be measured but certainly was essential.

Our students at Arizona State University continue to help us improve the text through each edition; their many questions have given us invaluable insight into how best to present this intriguing subject. It is our hope that this textbook will bring a clear understanding of economic thought to many other students as well. We welcome any feedback for improvements.

W. B.   M. M.

Reviewers

Okechukwu Dennis Anyamele
Jackson State University
Jackson, MS

David Black
University of Toledo
Toledo, OH

Gary Bogner
Baker College-Muskegon
Muskegon, MI

Rick Boulware
University of South Carolina,
Beaufort
Beaufort, SC

Bradley Braun
University of Central Florida
Orlando, FL

William S. Brewer
Genesee Community College
Batavia, NY

Gregory Brown
Martin Community College
Williamston, NC

Kristin Carrico
Umpqua Community College
Roseburg, OR

Jill L. Caviglia
Salisbury State University
Salisbury, MD

Mitch Charkiewicz
Central Connecticut State University
New Britain, CT

Kenny Christianson
Binghamton University
Binghamton, NY

Valerie A. Collins
Colorado Mountain College
Glenwood Springs, CO

Wilfrid W. Csaplar, Jr.
Southside Virginia Community
College
Keysville, VA

Bob Cunningham
Alma College
Alma, MI

Steven R. Cunningham
University of Connecticut
Storrs, CT

Stephen B. Davis
Valley City State University
Valley City, ND

Lynne Pierson Doti
Chapman University
Orange, CA

Raymond J. Egan
WA
(Retired formerly at Pierce
College), Lakewood, WA

Martha Field
Greenfield Community College
Greenfield, MA

Fred Fisher
Colorado Mountain College
Glenwood Springs, CO

Davis Folsom
University of South Carolina,
Beaufort
Beaufort, SC

Kaya V. P. Ford
Northern Virginia Community
College
Alexandria, VA

Bradley Garton
Laramie County Community
College
Laramie, Wyoming

Omer Gokcekus
North Carolina Central University
Durham, NC

R.W. Hafer
Southern Illinois University
Edwardsville, IL

Michael Harsh
Randolph-Macon College
Ashland, VA

Arleen Hoag
Owens Community College
Toledo, OH

Calvin Hoy
County College of Morris
Randolph, NJ

James Johnson
Black Hawk College
Moline, IL

Jeff Keil
J. Sargeant Reynolds Community
College
Richmond, VA

Donna Kish-Goodling
Muhlenberg College
Allentown, PA

Ali Kutan
Southern Illinois University
Edwardsville, IL

Nikiforos Laopodis
Villa Julie College
Stevenson, MD

John D. Lathrop
New Mexico Junior College
Hobbs, NM

Paul Lockard
Black Hawk College
Moline, IL

Glenna Lunday
Western Oklahoma State College
Altus, OK

Leslie Manns
Doane College
Crete, NE

Dan Marburger
Arkansas State University
Jonesboro, AR

Buddy Miller
Carteret Community College
Morehead City, NC

Stan Mitchell
McLennan Community College
Waco, TX

Charles Okeke
Community College of Southern
Nevada
Las Vegas, NV

Robert Payne
Baker College
Port Huron, MI

John C. Pharr
Cedar Valley College
Lancaster, TX

Dick Risinit
Reading Area Community College
Reading, PA

Rose M. Rubin
University of Memphis
Memphis, TN

Robert S. Rycroft
Mary Washington College
Fredericksburg, VA

Charles Saccardo
Bentley College
Waltham, MA

Charles Sackrey
Bucknell University
Lewisburg, PA

Karen Rapp Schultes
University of Michigan
Dearborn, MI

Gerald Scott
Florida Atlantic University
Boca Raton, FL

J. Richard Sealscott
Northwest State Community
College
Archbold, OH

Steve Seteroff
Chapman University College
Silverdale, WA

James R. Shemwell
Mississippi County Community
College
Blytheville, AR

Richard Skolnik
SUNY-Oswego
Oswego, NY

Scott F. Smith
University at Albany
State University of New York
Albany, NY

Thom Smith
Hill College
Hillsboro, TX

John Somers
Portland Community College,
Sylvania
Portland, Oregon

John P. Speir Jr.
The University of Hartford
West Hartford, CT

John J. Spitzer
State University of New York
College at Brockport
Brockport, NY

Chin-Chyuan Tai
Averett University
Danville, VA

Rob Verner
Ursuline College
Pepper Pike, OH

Michele T. Villinski
DePauw University
Greencastle, IN

Mark E. Wohar
University of Nebraska
Omaha, NE

Edward M. Wolfe
Piedmont College
Athens, GA

Darrel A. Young
University of Texas
Austin, TX

Girma Zelleke
Kutztown University of
Pennsylvania
Kutztown, PA

Brief Contents

Contents

CHAPTER 4 The Market System and the Private Sector   72

CHAPTER 5 The Public Sector   98

Contents

Contents

CHAPTER 18   Development Economics   422

CHAPTER 19   Globalization   452

PART FIVE   Product Market Basics   472

CHAPTER 20   Elasticity: Demand and Supply   474

CHAPTER 21 Consumer Choice — 498

APPENDIX TO CHAPTER 21 Indifference Analysis — 516

CHAPTER 22 Supply: The Costs of Doing Business — 524

PART EIGHT   Issues in International Trade and Finance   822

Suggested Outlines for One-Term Courses

Macroeconomic Emphasis	Microeconomic Emphasis	Balanced Micro-Macro
1. Economics: The World Around You	1. Economics: The World Around You	1. Economics: The World Around You
2. Choice, Opportunity Costs, and Specialization	2. Choice, Opportunity Costs, and Specialization	2. Choice, Opportunity Costs, and Specialization
3. Markets, Demand and Supply, and the Price System	3. Markets, Demand and Supply, and the Price System	3. Markets, Demand and Supply, and the Price System
4. The Market System and the Private Sector	4. The Market System and the Private Sector	4. The Market System and the Private Sector
5. The Public Sector	5. The Public Sector	5. The Public Sector
6. National Income Accounting	20. Elasticity: Demand and Supply	6. National Income Accounting
7. An Introduction to the Foreign Exchange Market and the Balance of Payments	21. Consumer Choice	7. An Introduction to the Foreign Exchange Market and the Balance of Payments.
8. Unemployment and Inflation	22. Supply: The Costs of Doing Business	8. Unemployment and Inflation
9. Macroeconomic Equilibrium: Aggregate Demand and Supply	23. Profit Maximization	9. Macroeconomic Equilibrium: Aggregate Demand and Supply
10. Aggregate Expenditures	24. Perfect Competition	12. Fiscal Policy
11. Income and Expenditures Equilibrium	25. Monopoly	13. Money and Banking
12. Fiscal Policy	26. Monopolistic Competition and Oligopoly	14. Monetary Policy
13. Money and Banking	27. Antitrust and Regulation	20. Elasticity: Demand and Supply
14. Monetary Policy	28. Government and Market Failure	21. Consumer Choice
15. Macroeconomic Policy: Trade-offs, Expectations, Credibility, and Sources of Business Cycles	29. Resource Markets	22. Supply: The Costs of Doing Business
16. Macroeconomic Viewpoints: New Keynesian, Monetarist, and New Classical	30. The Labor Market	23. Profit Maximization
17. Economic Growth	31. Financial Markets: Institutions and Recent Events	29. Resource Markets
18. Development Economics	32. The Land Market and Natural Resources	34. Income Distribution, Poverty, and Government Policy
19. Globalization	33. Aging, Social Security, and Health Care	35. World Trade Equilibrium
35. World Trade Equilibrium	34. Income Distribution, Poverty, and Government Policy	
36. International Trade Restrictions	35. World Trade Equilibrium	
37. Exchange Rates and Financial Links Between Countries	36. International Trade Restrictions	

Economics

Part One

Introduction to the Price System

CHAPTER 1

Economics: The World Around You

1. **Why study economics?**

2. **What is economics?**

3. **What is the economic way of thinking?**

Americans today are more educated than ever. According to the 2000 Census, 30.7 percent of Americans aged 25 and older hold a college (bachelor's or associate's) degree, whereas twenty years ago, only 19 percent of Americans held a similar degree. Nearly 15.5 million Americans (5 percent of the population) are currently attending college; over 50 percent of Americans aged 18 to 22 are currently enrolled in a degree program.

Why has college attendance increased so much? College has not gotten any cheaper—indeed, the direct expenses associated with college have risen much more rapidly than average income. Perhaps it is because college is more valuable today than it was in the past. Technological change and increased international trade have placed a premium on a college education; more and more jobs require the skills acquired in college. As a result, the wage disparity between college-educated and non-college-educated workers is rising fairly rapidly. Over their lifetimes, college-educated people earn nearly twice as much as people without college degrees.

Why are you attending college? Perhaps you've never really given it a great deal of thought—your family always just assumed that college was a necessary step after high school; perhaps you analyzed the situation and decided that college was better than the alternatives. Whichever approach you took, you were practicing economics. You were examining alternatives and making choices. This is what economics is about.

The objective of economics is to understand why the real world is what it is. This is not an easy proposition, for the real world is very complex. After all, what happens in the real world is the result of human behavior, and humans are not simple creatures. Nonetheless, there are some fundamental regularities of human behavior that can help to explain the world we observe.

One such regularity is that people behave in ways that make themselves and those they care about better off and happier. Even without knowing that having a college education means that your income will be higher than if you do not earn a college degree, you and your family knew or suspected that the college degree would mean a better lifestyle and a more secure or more prestigious job for you. However, what makes one person happy may not make others happy.

To study economics is to seek answers not only for why people choose to go to college but also for why economies go through cycles, at times expanding and creating new jobs and at other times dipping into recessions; for why some people are thrown out of jobs to join the ranks of the unemployed while others are drawn out of the ranks of the unemployed into new jobs; for why some people live on welfare; for why some nations are richer than others; for why the illegal drug trade is so difficult to stop; for why health care is so expensive; or, in general, for why the world is what it is.

This chapter is the introduction to our study of economics. In it we present some of the terminology commonly used in economics and outline what the study of economics is.

1. Why study economics?

1. Why Study Economics?

Why are you studying economics? Is it because you are required to, because you have an interest in it, or because you are looking for a well-paying job? All of these are valid reasons. The college degree is important to your future living standards; economics is a fascinating subject, as you will see; and an economics degree can lead to a good job.

1.a. The Value of a College Degree

What is the difference between a high school diploma and a medical degree? About $3.2 million (U.S.), says the U.S. Census Bureau. Someone whose education does not go beyond high school and who works full time can expect to earn about $1.2 million between the ages of 25 and 64. Graduating from college and earning advanced degrees translate into much higher lifetime earnings: an estimated $4.4 million for doctors, lawyers, and others with professional degrees; $2.5 million for those with a master's degree; and $2.1 million for college graduates. These are average figures and do not take into account the value of different majors. In fact, there aren't too many majors that provide a higher income than economics. Among the business fields, economics ranks below accounting and information management but above marketing, management, and human resources in terms of starting salaries. Economics is the highest-paying social science, higher than sociology, psychology, and others. The median base salary of business economists in 2000 was $83,000, with benefits and other income bringing the median compensation to over $90,000 per year. The highest salaries are earned by those who have a Ph.D.

A bachelor's degree in economics prepares you for a career in any number of occupations—in business, banking, the nonprofit sector, journalism, international relations, education, or government. An economics degree is also excellent preparation for graduate study—in the law, business, economics, government, public administration, environmental studies, health-care administration, labor relations, urban planning, diplomacy, and other fields.

1.b. What Is Economics?

The reason that studying economics can be so useful is that there is a certain logic to economics that enables the economist to solve complex problems that are of great importance to society. Economists are concerned with why the world is what it is. They examine how individuals and firms make decisions about work, consumption, investment, hiring, and pricing goods and services. They study how entire economies work and how they work together; why recessions occur at times and why economies grow at other times; why some countries have much higher living standards than other countries; why some people are poor and others rich. They examine why baseball players earn multi-million-dollar salaries while teachers earn less than $50,000. Economics may not provide a student with a specific trade, like accounting or nursing, but it provides a broad base of skills to build on. Economics

Why do the citizens of different countries have different standards of living? Why is the difference between rich and poor much greater in emerging nations than it is in the industrial nations? Answers to questions like these emerge in your study of economics. In this photo, a shantytown is shown next to new, modern apartment buildings and other structures in the Philippines.

sheds light on how the world, and corporations, work, and, more importantly, it teaches a student how to think.

An old and tired joke about economists is that if you laid all the economists head to toe across the country, they still wouldn't reach an agreement. Another joke along the same lines is the one about Truman's wanting a one-handed economic adviser because economists were always saying, "On the one hand this result and on the other hand that result." It is true that the general public often has the idea that economists don't agree about anything, and thus that the subject has nothing of importance to say. The problem is that economists don't talk much in public about what they agree on, which is almost everything involving the logic of economics, but instead emphasize their disagreements. Understandably, the public—and government officials—concludes that since the professionals can't agree, their own instincts are as good as anyone else's. So the public and governments generalize from personal experience, which often leads them to come to erroneous conclusions.

Economics is often counterintuitive. In fact, economics is probably best defined as the study of unintended consequences. When you study economics, you learn that there are costs to everything—"there is no free lunch." This is the logic of economics that is often lost on the general public and on government ministers and representatives. The logic for the individual is obvious: If you spend more on one thing, you have less to spend on something else. The logic for nations should be just as obvious: If the United States or Mexico or any other country is going to spend more on the military, it has to give up spending more on something else. Why, then, do countries seemingly spend more on the military without giving up anything else? You will answer this question during your study of economics.

The environmentalists who organized protests at international meeting such as that in Seattle in 2002 argue that the world is being overrun by greedy corporations that destroy the environment, create global warming, and destroy rain forests. They argue that there should be no pollution and no harvesting of trees in the rain forests. Perhaps their arguments have some validity, but they forget the unintended consequences—there are costs to these policies. People are thrown out of jobs, standards of living decline, the poor are made even poorer, and so on. It is up to the economist to point out these consequences. People with good intentions pointed out that asbestos can be damaging to health. Thus, the government imposed strict rules regarding the use and removal of asbestos. These rules were supposed to save ten lives each year. The cost of the rules per life saved is about $144 million. The general public might say that a life is worth an infinite amount of money, but the economist would point out that spending $1,440 million to reduce asbestos damage each year has other consequences. In fact, the consequences of that expenditure may harm society more than the expenditure helps it. That money has to come from somewhere, and that means that spending on other things, such as safer cars, better health care, and leisure activities, has to be reduced. More people could die as a consequence than the spending on asbestos removal and restriction of use would save. Many people argue that wealthy nations need to provide more aid to poorer nations, that such aid will save many destitute people from starvation and disease. The economist has to say, "Let's look at the costs and benefits of this policy. Such aid could have unintended consequences."

Your study of economics will be interesting and challenging. It will challenge some beliefs you now hold. It will also help you build skills that will be of value to your life and in whatever occupation you choose.

2. The Definition of Economics

People have unlimited wants—they always want more goods and services than they have or can purchase with their incomes. Whether they are wealthy or poor, what they have is never enough. Since people do not have everything they want, they must use their limited time and income to select those things that they want most and forgo, or relinquish, the rest. The choices they make and the manner in which these choices are made explain much of why the real world is what it is.

2.a. Scarcity

Neither the poor nor the wealthy have unlimited time, income, or wealth, and both must make choices in order to use these limited items in a way that best satisfies their wants. Because wants are unlimited and incomes, time, and other items are not, scarcity exists everywhere. **Scarcity** of something means that there is not enough of that item to satisfy everyone who wants it; it means that if a good has no cost, that is, at a zero price, the amount of the good that people want is greater than the amount that is available. Anything for which this condition holds is called an **economic good.** An economic good refers to *goods and services*—where goods are physical products, such as books or food, and services are nonphysical products, such as haircuts or golf lessons.

> **scarcity:** the shortage that exists when less of something is available than is wanted at a zero price
>
> **economic good:** any item that is scarce

If there is enough of an item to satisfy wants, even at a zero price, the item is said to be a **free good.** It is difficult to think of examples of free goods. At one time people referred to air as free, but with air pollution control devices and other costly activities directed toward the maintenance of air quality standards, "clean" air, at least, is not a free good, as noted in the Global Business Insight "'Free' Air?"

> **free good:** a good for which there is no scarcity

If people would pay to have less of an item, that item is called an **economic bad.** It is not so hard to think of examples of bads: pollution, garbage, and disease fit the description.

> **economic bad:** any item for which we would pay to have less

Some goods are used to produce other goods. For instance, to make chocolate chip cookies, we need flour, sugar, chocolate chips, butter, our own labor, and an oven. To distinguish between the ingredients of a good and the good itself, we call the ingredients **resources.** (Resources are also called **factors of production** and **inputs;** the terms are interchangeable.) The ingredients of the cookies are the resources, and the cookies are the goods.

Economists have classified resources into three categories: land, labor, and capital.

> **resources, factors of production,** or **inputs:** goods used to produce other goods, i.e., land, labor and capital
>
> **land:** all natural resources, such as minerals, timber, and water, as well as the land itself
>
> **labor:** the physical and intellectual services of people, including the training, education, and abilities of the individuals in a society
>
> **capital:** products such as machinery and equipment that are used in production

1. **Land** includes all natural resources, such as minerals, timber, and water, as well as the land itself.

2. **Labor** refers to the physical and intellectual services of people, including the training, education, and abilities of the individuals in a society.

3. **Capital** refers to products such as machinery and equipment that are used in production. Capital is a manufactured or created product used solely for the production of the goods and services that are consumed by individuals. You will often hear the term *capital* used to describe the financial backing for some project or the stocks and bonds used to finance some business. This common usage is not incorrect, but it should be distinguished from the physical entity—the machinery and equipment and the buildings, warehouses, and factories. Thus we refer to the stocks and bonds as *financial capital* and to the physical entity as capital.

People obtain income by selling their resources or the use of their resources. Owners of land receive *rent*; people who provide labor services are paid *wages*; and owners of capital receive *interest*.

"Free" Air?

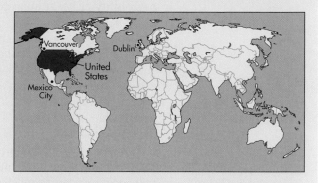

Although air might be what we describe as a free good, quality, breathable air is not free in many places in the world. In fact, breathable air is becoming a luxury in many places. Consider the Opus Hotel in Vancouver, British Columbia. It is the first North American hotel to offer hand-held oxygen dispensers in every room. These oxygen canisters are small enough to fit into a purse or briefcase and hold enough air for twelve minutes of breathing time. Breathing oxygen is said to increase energy, improve cognitive performance, and reduce the effects of hangovers. Opus charges $9.40 for the use of the canisters.

An oxygen bar where you can inhale 95 percent pure O_2 is the latest craze to hit Dublin, Ireland and other large cities around the world. Sniffing concentrated, flavored oxygen is a big hit in the United States.

Although these "luxury" purchases of oxygen are increasing, less developed countries find their sales of oxygen to be more a matter of necessity. In Mexico City, clean, breathable air is hard to find. In this city of 19 million people and over 3 million cars, dust, lead, and chemicals make the air unsafe to breathe more than 300 days a year. Beijing is no different. A few entrepreneurs have opened oxygen boutiques, where someone strolling along the walkway can drop in and for a few pesos or RMB (renminbi) breathe some clean oxygen.

The income that resource owners acquire from selling the use of their resources provides them with the ability to buy goods and services. And producers use the money received from selling their goods to pay for the resource services.

2.b. Choices

Scarcity means that people have to make choices. People don't have everything they want; they do not have the time or the money to purchase everything they want. When people choose some things, they have to give up, or forgo, other things. *Economics is the study of how people choose to use their scarce resources to attempt to satisfy their unlimited wants.*

2.c. Rational Self-Interest

2. What is economics?

rational self-interest: the means by which people choose the options that give them the greatest amount of satisfaction

Rational self-interest is the term economists use to describe how people make choices. It means that people will make the choices that, at the time and with the information they have at their disposal, will give them the greatest amount of satisfaction.

You chose to attend college although many in your age group chose not to attend. All of you made rational choices based on what you perceived was in your best interest. How could it be in your best interest to do one thing and in another person's best interest to do exactly the opposite? Each person has unique goals and attitudes and faces different costs. Although your weighing of the alternatives came down on the side of attending college, other people weighed similar alternatives and came down on the side of not attending college. Both decisions were rational because in both cases the individual compared alternatives and selected the option that the *individual* thought was in his or her best interest.

It is important to note that rational self-interest depends on the information at hand and the individual's perception of what is in his or her best interest. People will make different choices even when facing the same information. Even though the probability of death in an accident is nearly 20 percent less if seat belts are worn, many people choose not to use them. Are these people rational? The answer is yes. Perhaps they do not want their clothes wrinkled, or perhaps seat belts are just too inconvenient, or perhaps they think the odds of getting in an accident are just too small to worry about. Whatever the reason, these people are choosing the option that at the time gives them the greatest satisfaction. *This is rational self-interest.* Economists sometimes use the term *bounded rationality* to emphasize the point that people do not have perfect knowledge or perfect insight. In this book we simply use the term *rational* to refer to the comparison of costs and benefits.

Economists think that most of the time most human beings are weighing alternatives, looking at costs and benefits, and making decisions in a way that they believe makes them better off. This is not to say that economists look upon human beings as androids who lack feelings and are able only to carry out complex calculations like a computer. Rather, economists believe that the feelings and attitudes of human beings enter into people's comparisons of alternatives and help determine how people decide that something is in their best interest.

Human beings are self-interested, *not selfish.* People do contribute to charitable organizations and help others; people do make individual sacrifices because those sacrifices benefit their families or people they care about; soldiers do risk their lives to defend their country. All these acts are made in the name of rational self-interest.

RECAP

1. Scarcity exists when people want more of an item than exists at a zero price.
2. Goods are produced with resources (also called factors of production and inputs). Economists have classified resources into three categories: land, labor, and capital.
3. Choices have to be made because of scarcity. People cannot have or do everything they desire all the time.
4. People make choices in a manner known as rational self-interest; people make the choices that at the time and with the information they have at their disposal will give them the greatest satisfaction.

?

3. What is the economic way of thinking?

3. The Economic Approach

Economists often refer to the "economic approach" or to "economic thinking." By this, they mean that the principles of scarcity and rational self-interest are used in a specific way to search out answers to questions about the real world.

3.a. Positive and Normative Analysis

In applying the principles of economics to questions about the real world, it is important to avoid imposing your opinions or value judgments on others. Analysis that does not impose the value judgments of one individual on the decisions of others is called **positive analysis.** If you demonstrate that unemployment in the automobile

positive analysis: analysis of what is

industry in the United States rises when people purchase cars produced in other countries instead of cars produced in the United States, you are undertaking positive analysis. However, if you claim that there ought to be a law to stop people from buying foreign-made cars, you are imposing your value judgments on the decisions and desires of others. That is not positive analysis. It is, instead, **normative analysis.** *Normative means "what ought to be"; positive means "what is."* If you demonstrate that the probability of death in an automobile accident is 20 percent higher if seat belts are not worn, you are using positive analysis. If you argue that there should be a law requiring seat belts to be worn, you are using normative analysis.

normative analysis:
analysis of what ought to be

Conclusions based on opinion or value judgments do not advance one's understanding of events.

3.b. Common Mistakes

Why are so many items sold for $2.99 rather than $3? Most people attribute this practice to ignorance on the part of others: "People look at the first number and round to it—they see $2.99 but think $2." Although this reasoning may be correct, no one admits to such behavior when asked. A common error in the attempt to understand human behavior is to argue that other people do not understand something or are stupid. Instead of relying on rational self-interest to explain human behavior, ignorance or stupidity is called on.

fallacy of composition: the mistaken assumption that what applies in the case of one applies to the case of many

Another common mistake in economic analysis, called the **fallacy of composition,** is the error of attributing what applies in the case of one to the case of many. If one person in a theater realizes that a fire has broken out and races to the exit, that one person is better off. If we assume that a thousand people in a crowded theater would be better off behaving exactly like the single individual, we would be committing the mistake known as the fallacy of composition. For example, you reach an intersection just as the light switches to yellow. You reason that you can make it into the intersection before the light turns red. However, others reason the same way. Many people enter the intersection with the yellow light; it turns red, and traffic is congested in the intersection. The traffic going the other way can't move. You correctly reasoned that you alone could enter the intersection on the yellow light and then move on through. But it would be a fallacy of composition to assume that many drivers could enter the intersection and pass on through before the intersection is congested.

association as causation:
the mistaken assumption that because two events seem to occur together, one causes the other

The mistaken interpretation of **association as causation** occurs when unrelated or coincidental events that occur at about the same time are believed to have a cause-and-effect relationship. For example, the result of the football Super Bowl game is sometimes said to predict how the stock market will perform. According to this "theory," if the NFC team wins, the stock market will rise in the new year, but if the AFC team wins, the market will fall. This bit of folklore is a clear example of confusion between causation and association. Simply because two events seem to occur together does not mean that one causes the other. Clearly, a football game cannot cause the stock market to rise or fall. For another example, on Gobbler's Knob, Punxsutawney, Pennsylvania, at 7:27 A.M. on February 2, Punxsutawney Phil saw his shadow. Six more weeks of winter followed. However, whether the sun was or was not hidden behind a cloud at 7:27 A.M. on February 2 had nothing to do with causing a shortened or extended winter. Groundhog Day is the celebration of the mistake of attributing association as causation.

3.c. Microeconomics and Macroeconomics

Economics is the study of how people choose to allocate their scarce resources among their unlimited wants and involves the application of certain principles—scarcity, choice, rational self-interest—in a consistent manner. The study of economics is usually separated into two general areas, microeconomics and macroeconomics. **Microeconomics** is the study of economics at the level of the

microeconomics: the study of economics at the level of the individual

macroeconomics: the study of the economy as a whole

individual economic entity: the individual firm, the individual consumer, and the individual worker. In **macroeconomics,** rather than analyzing the behavior of an individual consumer, we look at the sum of the behaviors of all consumers together, which is called the consumer sector, or household sector. Similarly, instead of examining the behavior of an individual firm, in macroeconomics we examine the sum of the behaviors of all firms, called the business sector.

RECAP

1. The objective of economics is to understand why the real world is what it is.
2. Positive analysis refers to what is, while normative analysis refers to what ought to be.
3. Assuming that others are ignorant, the fallacy of composition, and interpreting association as causation are three commonly made errors in economic analysis.
4. The study of economics is typically divided into two parts, macroeconomics and microeconomics.

Summary

? Why study economics?

1. The objective of economics is to understand why the real world is what it is. *Preview*
2. The study of economics may be the road to a better job and will add skills that have value in your life and in your occupation. *§1*
3. Economics is interesting; it might be called the study of unintended consequences. *§1.b*

? What is economics?

4. The resources that go into the production of goods are land, labor, and capital. *§2.a*
5. Economics is the study of how people choose to allocate scarce resources to satisfy their unlimited wants. *§2.b*
6. Scarcity is universal; it applies to anything people would like more of than is available at a zero price.

Because of scarcity, choices must be made, and these choices are made in a way that is in the decision-maker's rational self-interest. *§2.a, 2.b, 2.c*

7. People make choices that, at the time and with the information at hand, will give them the greatest satisfaction. *§2.c*

? What is the economic way of thinking?

8. Positive analysis is analysis of what is; normative analysis is analysis of what ought to be. *§3.a*
9. Assuming that others are ignorant, the fallacy of composition, and interpreting association as causation are three commonly made errors in economic analysis. *§3.b*
10. The study of economics is typically divided into two parts, macroeconomics and microeconomics. *§3.c*

Key Terms

scarcity *§2.a*
economic good *§2.a*
free good *§2.a*
economic bad *§2.a*

resources, factors of production, or inputs *§2.a*
land *§2.a*
labor *§2.a*
capital *§2.a*

rational self-interest *§2.c*
positive analysis *§3.a*
normative analysis *§3.a*
fallacy of composition *§3.b*

association as causation *§3.b*
microeconomics *§3.c*
macroeconomics *§3.c*

Exercises

1. Which of the following are economic goods? Explain why each is or is not an economic good.

   a. Steaks
   b. Houses
   c. Cars
   d. Garbage
   e. T-shirts

2. Many people go to a medical doctor every time they are ill; others never visit a doctor. Explain how human behavior could include such opposite behaviors.

3. Erin has purchased a $35 ticket to a Dave Matthews concert. She is invited to a sendoff party for a friend who is moving to another part of the country. The party is scheduled for the same day as the concert. If she had known about the party before she bought the concert ticket, she would have chosen to attend the party. Will Erin choose to attend the concert? Explain.

4. It is well documented in scientific research that smoking is harmful to our health. Smokers have higher incidences of coronary disease, cancer, and other catastrophic illnesses. Knowing this, about 30 percent of young people begin smoking and about 25 percent of the U.S. population smokes. Are the people who choose to smoke irrational? What do you think of the argument that we should ban smoking in order to protect these people from themselves?

5. Indicate whether each of the following statements is true or false. If the statement is false, change it to make it true.

   a. Positive analysis imposes the value judgments of one individual on the decisions of others.
   b. Rational self-interest is the same thing as selfishness.
   c. An economic good is scarce if it has a positive price.

   d. An economic bad is an item that has a positive price.
   e. A resource is an ingredient used to make factors of production.

6. Are the following statements normative or positive? If a statement is normative, change it to a positive statement.

   a. The government should provide free tuition to all college students.
   b. An effective way to increase the skills of the work force is to provide free tuition to all college students.
   c. The government must provide job training if we are to compete with other countries.

7. In the *New York Times Magazine* in 1970, Milton Friedman, a Nobel Prize-winning economist, argued that "the social responsibility of business is to increase profits." How would Friedman's argument fit with the basic economic model that people behave in ways they believe are in their best self-interest?

8. Use economics to explain why men's and women's restrooms tend to be located near each other in airports and other public buildings.

9. Use economics to explain why diamonds are more expensive than water, when water is necessary for survival and diamonds are not.

10. Use economics to explain why people leave tips (a) at a restaurant they visit often and (b) at a restaurant they visit only once.

11. Use economics to explain why people contribute to charities.

12. Use economics to explain this statement: "Increasing the speed limit has, to some degree, compromised highway safety on interstate roads but enhanced safety on noninterstate roads."

ACE

Take the ACE Practice Test for this chapter to review the important concepts and get immediate feedback with answers.

economics.college.hmco.com/students

Choice of Major, Years of College Influence Student Debt

While a college degree and debt are becoming synonymous, it's degree choices that might be affecting how high that debt will be.

More than half of U.S. college majors graduate students with debts higher than lenders recommend, according to a study co-authored by a former Wichita State University accounting professor.

"In the U.S., educational loans are driven at least partially by choice of major, race and the amount of time necessary to complete a degree," says Steven Harrast, an assistant professor in the W. Frank Barton School of Business' School of Accountancy at the time of this study. He conducted the study with a former colleague, Gary Donhardt from the University of Memphis, and presented the findings this summer at a conference in Vienna, Austria.

To analyze the amount of debt a student could handle at graduation, Harrast and Donhardt figured it's necessary to analyze salary and debt by major.

Previous studies into student debt have typically ignored the differences that a choice of major can make.

They found 56 percent of all majors are graduating students with debts that exceed lender recommendations. Lenders usually recommend that less than 8 percent of an individual's gross income should be spent on student loan repayments.

Harrast and Donhardt found those getting engineering, nursing, special education or other technology-related degrees are generally within lender-recommended debt levels and have higher salaries at graduation.

Some majors don't lend themselves well to paying off loans, Harrast says.

Individuals getting degrees in the arts, liberal arts and social sciences find themselves with a lot more excess debt when compared to their salaries. The worst off were art history majors, who had debt levels that nearly triple lender recommendations. . . .

Debt among new college graduates and the rate of defaults on student loans is growing. In Texas, for example, the average indebtedness of college borrowers almost tripled in one decade from 1989–99. Default claims on student loans have reached into the billions.

"The cost of higher education is increasing at about three times the rate of inflation," Harrast says. "And often the cost of education increases when the economy is doing poorly because tax revenues decrease and funding for universities is therefore decreased. And we increase tuition, like we do now, to compensate for the loss in state revenues. Pell grants [a federal program] haven't kept pace so where's the money coming from? Well, students are borrowing. Pell grants used to pay a much larger portion of education. They pay only a small fraction now. If a family doesn't have resources to pay for an education, you've got to find it somewhere and most students have had to borrow."

According to Harrast's presentation, 64 percent of students borrowed money from the federal government during 1999–2000. And even those who seem to have the resources are borrowing: Forty-four percent of students from families earning $100,000 or more borrowed money for their education.

"A degree should further someone's situation in life, and it can't do that if you graduate with a ton of debt and end up in bankruptcy over credit card debt," Harrast says. "Then who can say you were better or worse off?"

Harrast says this study wasn't meant to discourage anyone from pursuing a field they are interested in.

"What we want to let people know is that if they choose a low-paying area of study, they need to make sure they minimize their debt when going through school so they don't have that burden once they get out."

Source: Copyright 2002 AScribe Inc.

AScribe Newswire/October 16, 2002

Economics is the study of human behavior, so it ought to be able to explain why people would take on such huge debts in order to go to college. Moreover, it should explain why people choose the majors they do when it is so clear which fields provide the greatest future incomes.

Economists argue that decisions are the result of comparing costs and benefits. In this article, two major decisions are discussed, going to college and selecting a major. The first decision compares the future income and quality of living that a college degree will offer with the costs of obtaining that college degree. What is the cost of the degree? It is the expense of college—what many students take out loans to pay. It is also the forgone income—that is, the income that you would have earned had you not gone to college. Someone who takes four or five years to complete college would have paid tuition, purchased books and materials, and paid for room and board over those years. Those costs range from a bare minimum of $20,000 to well over $100,000. You may have worked part time while you were attending college, but if you had not been attending college, you could have worked full time. The difference for the years of college would have been about $50,000. Thus, the cost of college could have been $150,000 or more.

The article notes that the amount of debt a student has at the end of college depends on the major chosen. If you choose to be an art history major, you should not take out much debt and should hurry through school. Why does it matter if one is pre-med or an art history major? The major you choose will influence your future income. A medical doctor earns on average about $4.5 million more than an art history major during their lifetimes. Clearly the medical doctor is able to pay off more debt and live better than the art history major.

Selecting a major involves a comparison of costs and benefits. As we just mentioned, different majors mean different amounts of future income. If a choice of major were only a matter of comparisons of future income, there would be fewer art history majors and more medical doctors. But it is not only income that enters into one's benefit calculations. Interest in the subject, living styles, amount of leisure time, and other aspects of life enter into one's choice of a college major.

Working with Graphs

According to the old saying, one picture is worth a thousand words. If that maxim is correct, and, in addition, if producing a thousand words takes more time and effort than producing one picture, it is no wonder that economists rely so extensively on pictures. The pictures that economists use to explain concepts are called *graphs*. The purpose of this appendix is to explain how graphs are constructed and how to interpret them.

1. Reading Graphs

The three kinds of graphs used by economists are shown in Figures 1, 2, and 3. Figure 1 is a *line graph*. It is the most commonly used type of graph in economics. Figure 2 is a *bar graph*. It is probably used more often in popular magazines than any other kind of graph. Figure 3 is a *pie graph*, or *pie chart*. Although it is less popular than the bar and line graphs, it appears often enough that you need to be familiar with it.

1.a. Relationships Between Variables

Figure 1 is a line graph showing the ratio of the median income of people who have completed four or more years of college to the median income of those who have completed just four years of high school. The line shows the value of a college education in terms of the additional income earned relative to the income earned without a college degree on a year-to-year basis. You can see that the premium for completing college has risen in recent years.

Figure 2 is a bar graph indicating the unemployment rate by educational attainment. The blue refers to high school dropouts, the red refers to those with four years of high school, and the green refers to those with four or more years of college. One set of bars is presented for males and one set for females. The bars are arranged in order, with the highest incidence of unemployment depicted first, the next highest second, and the lowest located third. This arrangement is made only for ease in reading and interpretation. The bars could be arranged in any order. The graph illustrates that unemployment strikes those with less education more than it does those with more education.

Figure 3 is a pie chart showing the percentage of the U.S. population completing various years of schooling. Unlike line and bar graphs, a pie chart is not actually a picture of a relationship between two variables. Instead, the pie represents the

FIGURE 1

Ratio of Median Incomes of College- to High School–Educated Workers

Figure 1 is a line graph showing the ratio of the median income of people who have completed four or more years of college to the median income of those who have completed four years of high school. The line shows the income premium for educational attainment, or the value of a college education in terms of income, from year to year. The rise in the line since about 1979 shows that the premium for completing college has risen. *Source:* U.S. Statistical Abstract, 2001, *U.S. Census Bureau, www.census.gov.*

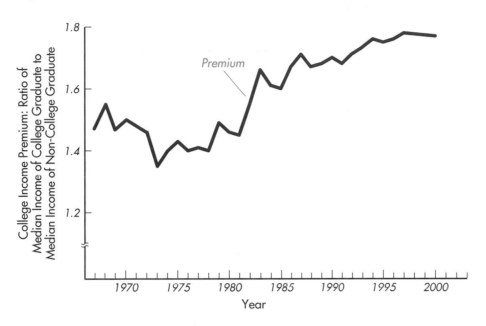

FIGURE 2

Unemployment and Education

Figure 2 is a bar graph indicating the unemployment rate by educational attainment. The blue refers to high school dropouts, the red refers to those with four years of high school, and the green refers to those with four or more years of college. One set of bars is presented for males and one set for females. The bars are arranged in order, with the highest incidence of unemployment shown first, the next highest second, and the lowest third. This arrangement is made only for ease in reading and interpretation. The bars could be arranged in any order. *Source: U.S. Census Bureau; www.census.gov/population.*

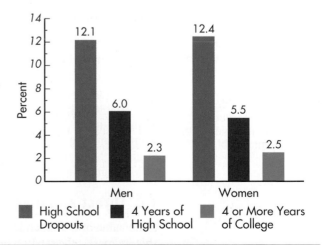

FIGURE 3

Educational Attainment

Figure 3 is a pie chart showing the percentage of the U.S. population completing various years of schooling. Unlike line and bar graphs, a pie chart is not actually a picture of a relationship between two variables. Instead, the pie represents the whole, 100 percent of the U.S. population in this case, and the pieces of the pie represent parts of the whole—the percentage of the population completing one to four years of elementary school only, five to seven years of elementary school, and so on, up to four or more years of college.
Source: U.S. Census Bureau, Sept. 15, 2000; www.census.gov/population.

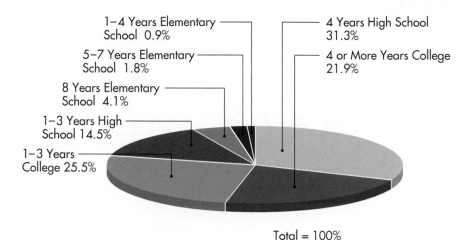

Total = 100%

whole, 100 percent of the U.S. population, and the pieces of the pie represent parts of the whole—the percentage of the population completing one to four years of elementary school only, five to seven years of elementary school, and so on, up to four or more years of college.

Because a pie chart does not show the relationship between variables, it is not as useful for explaining economic concepts as line and bar graphs. Line graphs are used more often than bar graphs to explain economic concepts.

1.b. Independent and Dependent Variables

independent variable: a variable whose value does not depend on the values of other variables

dependent variable: a variable whose value depends on the value of the independent variable

Most line and bar graphs involve just two variables, an **independent variable** and a **dependent variable.** An independent variable is one whose value does not depend on the values of other variables; a dependent variable, on the other hand, is one whose value does depend on the values of other variables. The value of the dependent variable is determined after the value of the independent variable is determined.

In Figure 2, the *independent* variable is the educational status of the man or woman, and the *dependent* variable is the incidence of unemployment (percentage of group that is unemployed). The incidence of unemployment depends on the educational attainment of the man or woman.

1.c. Direct and Inverse Relationships

If the value of the dependent variable increases as the value of the independent variable increases, the relationship between the two types of variables is called a **direct,**

direct, or **positive, relationship:** the relationship that exists when the values of related variables move in the same direction

inverse, or **negative, relationship:** the relationship that exists when the values of related variables move in opposite directions

or **positive, relationship.** If the value of the dependent variable decreases as the value of the independent variable increases, the relationship between the two types of variables is called an **inverse,** or **negative, relationship.**

In Figure 2, unemployment and educational attainment are inversely, or negatively, related: as people acquire more education, they are less likely to be unemployed.

2. Constructing a Graph

Let's now construct a graph. We will begin with a consideration of the horizontal and vertical axes, or lines, and then we will put the axes together. We are going to construct a *straight-line curve.* This sounds contradictory, but it is common terminology. Economists often refer to the demand or supply *curve,* and that curve may be a straight line.

2.a. The Axes

It is important to understand how the *axes* (the horizontal and vertical lines) are used and what they measure. Let's begin with the horizontal axis, the line running across the page. Notice in Figure 4(a) that the line is divided into equal segments. Each point on the line represents a quantity, or the value of the variable being measured. For example, each segment could represent one year or 10,000 pounds of diamonds or some other value. Whatever is measured, the value increases from left to right, beginning with negative values, going on to zero, which is called the *origin,* and then moving on to positive numbers.

A number line in the vertical direction can be constructed as well, and this is also shown in Figure 4(a). Zero is the origin, and the numbers increase from bottom to top. Like the horizontal axis, the vertical axis is divided into equal segments; the distance between 0 and 10 is the same as the distance between 0 and -10, the distance between 10 and 20, and so on.

In most cases, the variable measured along the horizontal axis is the independent variable. This isn't always true in economics, however. Economists often measure the independent variable on the vertical axis. Do not assume that the variable on the horizontal axis is independent and the variable on the vertical axis is dependent.

Putting the horizontal and vertical lines together lets us express relationships between two variables graphically. The axes cross, or intersect, at their origins, as shown in Figure 4(a). From the common origin, movements to the right and up, in the area—called a quadrant—marked I, are combinations of positive numbers; movements to the left and down, in quadrant III, are combinations of negative numbers; movements to the right and down, in quadrant IV, are negative values on the vertical axis and positive values on the horizontal axis; and movements to the left and up, in quadrant II, are positive values on the vertical axis and negative values on the horizontal axis.

Economic data are typically positive numbers: the unemployment rate, the inflation rate, the price of something, the quantity of something produced or sold, and so on. Because economic data are usually positive numbers, the only part of the coordinate system that usually comes into play in economics is the upper right portion, quadrant I. That is why economists may simply sketch a vertical line down to the origin and then extend a horizontal line out to the right, as shown in Figure 4(b). Once in a while, economic data are negative—for instance, profit is negative when costs exceed revenues. When data are negative, quadrants II, III, and IV of the coordinate system may be used.

FIGURE 4

The Axes, the Coordinate System, and the Positive Quadrant

Figure 4(a) shows the vertical and horizontal axes. The horizontal axis has an origin, measured as zero, in the middle. Negative numbers are to the left of zero, and positive numbers are to the right. The vertical axis also has an origin in the middle. Positive numbers are above the origin, and negative numbers are below. The horizontal and vertical axes together show the entire coordinate system. Positive numbers are in quadrant I, negative numbers in quadrant III, and combinations of negative and positive numbers in quadrants II and IV.

Figure 4(b) shows only the positive quadrant. Because most economic data are positive, often only the upper right quadrant, the positive quadrant, of the coordinate system is used.

(a) The Coordinate System

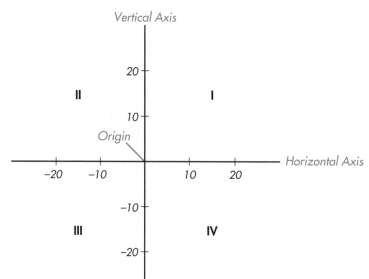

(b) The Positive Quadrant

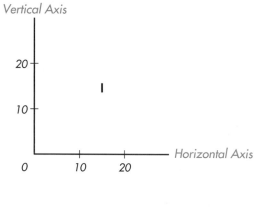

2.b. Constructing a Graph from a Table

Now that you are familiar with the axes, that is, the coordinate system, you are ready to construct a graph using the data in the table in Figure 5. The table lists a series of possible price levels for a personal computer (PC) and the corresponding number of PCs that people choose to purchase. The data are only hypothetical; they are not drawn from actual cases.

The information given in the table is graphed in Figure 5. We begin by marking off and labeling the axes. The vertical axis is the list of possible price levels. We begin at zero and move up the axis at equal increments of $1,000. The horizontal axis is the number of PCs sold. We begin at zero and move out the axis at equal increments of 1,000 PCs. According to the information presented in the table, if the price is $10,000, no one buys a PC. The combination of $10,000 and 0 PCs is point A on the graph. To plot this point, find the quantity zero on the horizontal axis (it is at the origin), and then move up the vertical axis from zero to a price level of $10,000. (Note that we have measured the units in the table and on the graph in thousands.) At a price of $9,000, there are 1,000 PCs purchased. To plot the combination

FIGURE 5

The information given in the table is graphed below. We begin by marking off and labeling the axes. The vertical axis is the list of possible price levels. The horizontal axis is the number of PCs purchased. Beginning at zero, the axes are marked at equal increments of 1,000. According to the information presented in the table, if the price level is $10,000, no PCs are purchased. The combination of $10,000 and 0 PCs is point *A* on the graph. At a price of $9,000, there are 1,000 PCs purchased. This is point *B*. The final step in constructing a line graph is to connect the points that are plotted. When the points are connected, the straight line slanting downward shows the relationship between the price of PCs and the number of PCs purchased.

Point	Price per PC (thousands of dollars)	Number of PCs Purchased (thousands)
A	$10	0
B	9	1
C	8	2
D	7	3
E	6	4
F	5	5
G	4	6
H	3	7
I	2	8
J	1	9
K	0	10

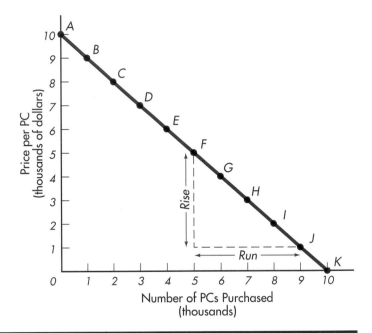

of $9,000 and 1,000 PCs, find 1,000 units on the horizontal axis and then measure up from there to a price of $9,000. This is point *B*. Point *C* represents a price of $8,000 and 2,000 PCs. Point *D* represents a price of $7,000 and 3,000 PCs. Each combination of price and PCs purchased listed in the table is plotted in Figure 5.

 The final step in constructing a line graph is to connect the points that are plotted. When the points are connected, the straight line slanting downward from left to right in Figure 5 is obtained. It shows the relationship between the price of PCs and the number of PCs purchased.

2.c. Interpreting Points on a Graph

Let's use Figure 5 to demonstrate how points on a graph may be interpreted. Suppose the current price of a PC is $6,000. Are you able to tell how many PCs are being purchased at this price? By tracing that price level from the vertical axis over to the curve and then down to the horizontal axis, you find that 4,000 PCs are purchased. You can also find what happens to the number purchased if the price falls from $6,000 to $5,000. By tracing the price from $5,000 to the curve and then down to the horizontal axis, you discover that 5,000 PCs are purchased. Thus, according to the graph, a decrease in the price from $6,000 to $5,000 results in 1,000 more PCs being purchased.

FIGURE 6

Shift of Curve

An increase in income allows more people to purchase PCs at each price. At a price of $8,000, for instance, 4,000 PCs are purchased rather than 2,000.

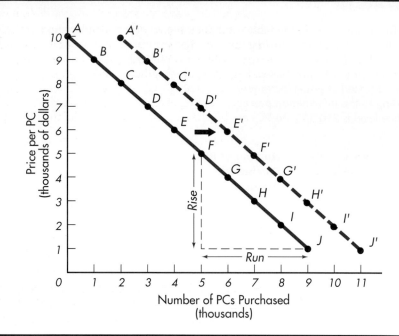

2.d. Shifts of Curves

Graphs can be used to illustrate the effects of a change in a variable that is not represented on the graph. For instance, the curve drawn in Figure 5 shows the relationship between the price of PCs and the number of PCs purchased. When this curve was drawn, the only two variables that were allowed to change were the price and the number of computers. However, it is likely that people's incomes determine their reaction to the price of computers as well. An increase in income would enable more people to purchase computers. Thus, at every price more computers would be purchased. How would this be represented? As an outward shift of the curve, from points *A, B, C,* etc., to *A', B', C',* etc., as shown in Figure 6.

Following the shift of the curve, we can see that more PCs are purchased at each price than was the case prior to the income increase. For instance, at a price of $8,000, the increased income allows 4,000 PCs to be purchased rather than 2,000. The important point to note is that if some variable that influences the relationship shown in a curve or line graph changes, then the entire curve or line changes—that is, it shifts.

3. Slopes

A curve may represent an inverse, or negative, relationship or a direct, or positive, relationship. The slope of the curve reveals the kind of relationship that exists between two variables.

3.a. Positive and Negative Slopes

slope: the steepness of a curve, measured as the ratio of the rise to the run

The **slope** of a curve is its steepness, the rate at which the value of a variable measured on the vertical axis changes with respect to a given change in the value of the variable measured on the horizontal axis. If the value of a variable measured on one axis goes up when the value of the variable measured on the other axis goes down, the variables have an inverse (or negative) relationship. If the values of the variables rise or fall together, the variables have a direct (or positive) relationship. Inverse relationships are represented by curves that run downward from left to right; direct relationships, by curves that run upward from left to right.

Slope is calculated by measuring the amount by which the variable on the vertical axis changes and dividing that figure by the amount by which the variable on the horizontal axis changes. The vertical change is called the *rise,* and the horizontal change is called the *run.* Slope is referred to as the *rise over the run:*

$$\text{Slope} = \frac{\text{rise}}{\text{run}}$$

The slope of any inverse relationship is negative. The slope of any direct relationship is positive.

Let's calculate the slope of the curve in Figure 5. Price (P) is measured on the vertical axis, and quantity of PCs purchased (Q) is measured on the horizontal axis. The rise is the change in price (ΔP), the change in the value of the variable measured on the vertical axis. The run is the change in quantity of PCs purchased (ΔQ), the change in the value of the variable measured on the horizontal axis. (The symbol Δ means "change in"—it is the Greek letter delta—so ΔP means "change in P" and ΔQ means "change in Q.") Remember that slope equals the rise over the run. Thus the equation for the slope of the straight-line curve running downward from left to right in Figure 5 is

$$\text{Slope} = \frac{\Delta P}{\Delta Q}$$

As the price (P) declines, the number of PCs purchased (Q) increases. The rise is negative, and the run is positive. Thus, the slope is a negative value.

The slope is the same anywhere along a straight line. Thus, it does not matter where we calculate the changes along the vertical and horizontal axes. For instance, from 0 to 9,000 on the horizontal axis—a change of 9,000—the vertical change is a negative $9,000 (from $10,000 down to $1,000). Thus, the rise over the run is −9,000/9,000, or −1. Similarly, from 5,000 to 9,000 in the horizontal direction, the corresponding rise is $5,000 to $1,000, or −$4,000, so that the rise over the run is −4,000/4,000, or −1.

Remember that direct, or positive, relationships between variables are represented by lines that run upward from left to right. Figure 7 is a graph showing the number of PCs that producers offer for sale at various price levels. The curve represents the relationship between the two variables number of PCs offered for sale and price. It shows that as price rises, so does the number of PCs offered for sale. The slope of the curve is positive. The change in the rise (the vertical direction) that comes with an increase in the run (the horizontal direction) is positive. Because the graph is a straight line, you can measure the rise and run using any two points along the curve and the slope will be the same. We find the slope by calculating the rise that accompanies the run. Moving from 0 to 4,000 PCs gives us a run of 4,000. Looking at the curve, we see that the corresponding rise is 2,000. Thus, the rise over the run is 2,000/4,000, or .50.

3.b. Equations

Graphs and equations can be used to illustrate the same topics. Some people prefer to use equations rather than graphs, or both equations and graphs, to explain a

FIGURE 7

Personal Computers Offered for Sale and Price

Figure 7 is a graph showing the number of PCs offered for sale at various price levels. The curve shows that as price rises, so does the number of PCs offered for sale. We move from 0 to 4,000, giving us a run of 4,000. The corresponding rise is 2,000. Thus, the rise over the run is 2,000/4,000, or .50.

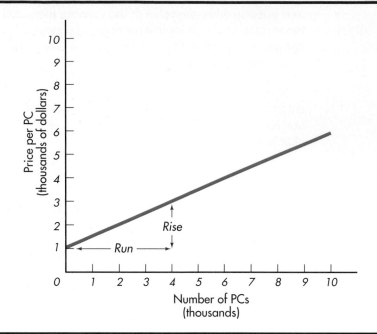

concept. Since a few equations are used in this book, we need to briefly discuss how they demonstrate the same things as a graph.

The general equation of a straight line has the form $Y = a + bX$, where Y is the dependent variable, X is the independent variable, a defines the intercept (the value of Y when $X = 0$), and b is the slope. If b is negative, the line slopes downward. If b is positive, the line slopes upward. In the case of Figure 5, the price, P, is the independent variable, and the number of PCs purchased, Q, is the dependent variable. The number of PCs purchased depends on the price. In equation form, substituting Q for Y and P for X, the relationship between price and PCs purchased is $Q = a + bP$. We already know that the slope, b, is negative. For each \$1,000 decline in price, 1,000 more PCs are purchased. The slope, b, is -1. The value of a represents the value of Q when P is zero. When the price is zero, 10,000 PCs are purchased. Thus, $a = 10,000$. The equation of Figure 5 is $Q = 10,000 - 1P$.

This equation can be used to tell us how many PCs will be purchased at any given price. Suppose the price is $P = \$4,000$. Substituting \$4,000 for P in the equation yields

$$Q = 10,000 - 1(4,000)$$
$$= 6,000$$

Summary

1. There are three commonly used types of graphs: the line graph, the bar graph, and the pie chart. *§1.a*

2. An independent variable is a variable whose value does not depend on the values of other variables. The values of a dependent variable do depend on the values of other variables. *§1.b*

3. A direct, or positive, relationship occurs when the value of the dependent variable increases as the value of the independent variable increases. An indirect, or negative, relationship occurs when the value of the dependent variable decreases as the value of the independent variable increases. *§1.c*

4. Most economic data are positive numbers, and so only the upper right quadrant of the coordinate system is often used in economics. *§2.a*

5. A curve shifts when a variable that affects the dependent variable and is not measured on the axes changes.

6. The slope of a curve is the rise over the run: the change in the variable measured on the vertical axis over the corresponding change in the variable measured on the horizontal axis. *§3.a*

7. The slope of a straight-line curve is the same at all points along the curve. *§3.a*

8. The equation of a straight line has the general form $Y = a + bX$, where Y is the dependent variable, X the independent variable, a the value of Y when X equals zero, and b the slope. *§3.b*

Key Terms

independent variable *§1.b*

dependent variable *§1.b*

direct, or positive, relationship *§1.c*

inverse, or negative, relationship *§1.c*

slope *§3.a*

Exercises

1. On the right are two sets of figures: the total quantity of Mexican pesos (new pesos) in circulation (the total amount of Mexican money available) and the peso price of a dollar (how many pesos are needed to purchase one dollar). Values are given for the years 1987 through 2002 for each variable.

   a. Plot each variable by measuring time (years) on the horizontal axis and, in the first graph, pesos in circulation on the vertical axis and, in the second graph, peso price of a dollar on the vertical axis.

   b. Plot the combinations of variables by measuring pesos in circulation on the horizontal axis and peso prices of a dollar on the vertical axis.

   c. In each of the graphs in parts a and b, what are the dependent and independent variables?

   d. In each of the graphs in parts a and b, indicate whether the relationship between the dependent and independent variables is direct or inverse.

2. Plot the data listed on the right:

   a. Use price as the vertical axis and quantity as the horizontal axis and plot the first two columns.

   b. Show what quantity is sold when the price is $550.

   c. Directly below the graph in part a, plot the data in columns 2 and 3. Use total revenue as the vertical axis and quantity as the horizontal axis.

   d. What is total revenue when the price is $550? Will total revenue increase or decrease when the price is lowered?

Year	Pesos in Circulation (billions)	Peso Price of a Dollar
1987	12,627	1.3782
1988	21,191	2.2731
1989	29,087	2.4615
1990	47,439	2.8126
1991	106,227	3.0184
1992	122,220	3.0949
1993	143,902	3.1156
1994	145,429	3.3751
1995	150,572	6.4194
1996	206,180	7.5994
1997	276,281	8.5850
1998	331,537	9.9680
1999	371,322	9.4270
2000	499,507	9.6420
2001	705,236	9.2850
2002	793,698	9.5270

Price	Quantity Sold	Total Revenue
$1,000	200	200,000
900	400	360,000
800	600	480,000
700	800	560,000
600	1,000	600,000
500	1,200	600,000
400	1,400	560,000
300	1,600	480,000
200	1,800	360,000
100	2,000	200,000

CHAPTER 2

Choice, Opportunity Costs, and Specialization

? Fundamental Questions

1. **What are opportunity costs? Are they part of the economic way of thinking?**

2. **What is a production possibilities curve?**

3. **Why does specialization occur?**

4. **What are the benefits of trade?**

In the previous chapter, we learned that scarcity forces people to make choices. There are costs involved in any choice. As the old saying goes, "There is no free lunch." In every choice, alternatives are forgone, or sacrificed.

All choices have both costs and benefits. This chapter explains how to calculate these costs and benefits and what they imply for the behavior of individuals and society as a whole. ■

1. Opportunity Costs

A choice is simply a comparison of alternatives: to attend college or not to attend college, to change jobs or not to change jobs, to purchase a new car or to keep the old one. An individual compares the costs and benefits of each option and chooses the option that is expected to provide the most happiness or net benefit. Of course, when one option is chosen, the benefits of the alternatives are forgone. When you choose not to attend college, you forgo the benefits of attending college; when you buy a new car, you forgo the benefits of having the money to use in other ways. *Economists refer to the forgone opportunities or forgone benefits of the next best alternative as* **opportunity costs**—the highest-valued alternative that must be forgone when a choice is made.

opportunity costs: the highest-valued alternative that must be forgone when a choice is made

Opportunity costs are part of every decision and activity. Your opportunity costs of reading this book are whatever else you could be doing—perhaps watching TV, talking with friends, working, or listening to music. Your opportunity costs of attending college are whatever else you could be doing—perhaps working full-time or traveling around the world. Each choice means giving up something else.

1.a. The Opportunity Cost of Going to College

Suppose you decided to attend a college where the tuition and other expenses add up to $4,290 per year. Are these your total costs of attending college? If you answer yes, you are ignoring opportunity costs. Remember that you must account for forgone opportunities. If instead of going to college you could have worked full-time and earned $20,800, the actual cost of college is the $4,290 of direct expenses plus the $20,800 of forgone salary, or $25,090. This calculation assumes that you do not work part-time or during the summer.

1.b. Tradeoffs and Decisions at the Margin

Life is a continuous sequence of decisions, and every single decision involves choosing one thing over another or trading off something for something else. A **tradeoff** means giving up one good or activity in order to obtain some other good or activity. Each term you must decide whether to register for college or not. You could work full-time and not attend college, attend college and not work, or work part-time and attend college. The time you devote to college will decrease as you devote more time to work. You trade off hours spent at work for hours spent in college; in other words, you compare the benefits you think you will get from going to college this term with the costs of college this term. When you have completed one term, you must decide whether to attend the next term. Each time, you compare the benefits of another term to the costs of attending another term. We say that people compare the **marginal costs** and the **marginal benefits.** *Marginal* means "change," so a decision involves the comparison of a change in benefits and a change in costs—in this case, the costs of one more term and the benefits of one more term.

tradeoff: the giving up of one good or activity in order to obtain some other good or activity

marginal cost: additional cost

marginal benefit: additional benefit

1.c. The Production Possibilities Curve

Societies, like individuals, face scarcities and must make choices. And societies, like individuals, forgo opportunities each time they make a particular choice and must compare the marginal costs and marginal benefits of each alternative.

The tradeoffs facing a society can be illustrated in a graph known as the **production possibilities curve (PPC).** The production possibilities curve shows the

production possibilities curve (PPC): a graphical representation showing the maximum quantity of goods and services that can be produced using limited resources to the fullest extent possible

maximum quantity of goods and services that can be produced using limited resources to the fullest extent possible. Figure 1 shows a production possibilities curve based on information (see the table in Figure 1) about the production of defense goods and services and nondefense goods and services by a nation such as the United States. Defense goods and services include guns, ships, bombs, personnel, and so forth, that are used for national defense. Nondefense goods and services include education, housing, and food that are not used for national defense. All societies allocate their scarce resources in order to produce some combination of defense and nondefense goods and services. Because resources are scarce, a nation cannot produce as much of everything as it wants. When it produces more health care, it must forgo the production of education or automobiles; when it devotes more of its resources to the military area, fewer are available to devote to health care.

If we could draw or even visualize many dimensions, we could draw a PPC that had a specific good measured along the axis in each dimension. Since we can't, we

---

FIGURE 1

The Production Possibilities Curve

With a limited amount of resources, only certain combinations of defense and nondefense goods and services can be produced. The maximum amounts that can be produced, given various tradeoffs, are represented by points A_1 through E_1 Point F_1 lies inside the curve and represents the underutilization of resources. More of one type of goods could be produced without producing less of the other, or more of both types could be produced. Point G_1 represents an impossible combination. There are insufficient resources to produce quantities lying beyond the curve.

Point	Defense Goods and Services (millions of units)	Nondefense Goods and Services (millions of units)
A_1	200	0
B_1	175	75
C_1	130	125
D_1	70	150
E_1	0	160
F_1	130	25
G_1	200	75

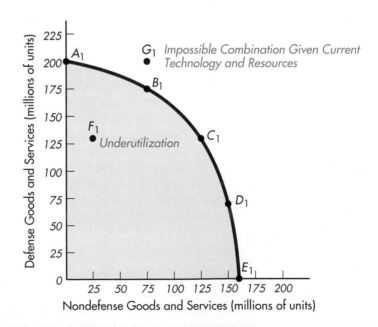

---

typically just draw a two-dimensional graph and thus can have just two classes of goods. In Figure 1, the two classes are defense-type goods and nondefense-type goods. But we could just as easily draw a PPC for health care and all other goods or for education and all other goods. These PPCs would look like Figure 1 except that the axes would measure units of health care and other goods or units of education and other goods.

A production possibilities curve shows that more of one type of good can be produced only by reducing the quantity of other types of goods that are produced; it shows that a society has scarce resources; and it shows what the marginal costs and marginal benefits of alternative decisions are. In what way does the PPC show these things? We can answer that question by looking more carefully at Figure 1. In this figure, units of defense goods and services are measured on the vertical axis, and units of nondefense goods and services are measured on the horizontal axis. If all resources are allocated to producing defense goods and services, then 200 million units can be produced, but the production of nondefense goods and services will cease. The combination of 200 million units of defense goods and services and 0 units of nondefense goods and services is point A_1, a point on the vertical axis. At 175 million units of defense goods and services, 75 million units of nondefense goods and services can be produced (point B_1). Point C_1 represents 125 million units of nondefense goods and services and 130 million units of defense goods. Point D_1 represents 150 million units of nondefense goods and services and 70 million units of defense goods and services. Point E_1, a point on the horizontal axis, shows the combination of no production of defense goods and services and 160 million units of nondefense goods and services.

The production possibilities curve represents the maximum, or the outer limit, that can be produced.

The production possibilities curve shows the *maximum* output that can be produced with a limited quantity and quality of resources. The PPC is a picture of the tradeoffs facing society. Only one combination of goods and services can be produced at any one time. All other combinations are forgone.

1.c.1. Points Inside the Production Possibilities Curve
Suppose a nation produces 130 million units of defense goods and services and 25 million units of nondefense goods and services. That combination, Point F_1 in Figure 1, lies inside the production possibilities curve. A point lying inside the production possibilities curve indicates that resources are not being fully or efficiently used. If the existing work force is employed only 20 hours per week, it is not being fully used. If two workers are used when one would be sufficient—say, two people in each Domino's Pizza delivery car—then resources are not being used efficiently. If there are resources available for use, society can move from point F_1 to a point on the PPC, such as point C_1. The move would gain 100 million units of nondefense goods and services with no loss of defense goods and services.

1.c.2. Points Outside the Production Possibilities Curve
Point G_1 in Figure 1 represents the production of 200 million units of defense goods and services and 75 units of nondefense goods and services. Point G_1, however, represents the use of more resources than are available—it lies outside the production possibilities curve. Unless more resources can be obtained and/or the quality of resources improved so that the nation can produce more with the same quantity of resources, there is no way that the society can currently produce 200 million units of defense goods and 75 million units of nondefense goods.

1.c.3. Shifts of the Production Possibilities Curve
If a nation obtains more resources, points outside its current production possibilities curve become attainable.

Suppose a country discovers new sources of oil within its borders and is able to greatly increase its production of oil. Greater oil supplies would enable the country to increase production of all types of goods and services.

Figure 2 shows the production possibilities curve before (PPC_1) and after (PPC_2) the discovery of oil. PPC_1 is based on the data given in the table in Figure 1. PPC_2 is based on the data given in the table in Figure 2, which shows the increase in production of goods and services that results from the increase in oil supplies. The first combination of goods and services on PPC_2, point A_2, is 220 million units of defense goods and 0 units of nondefense goods. The second point, B_2, is a combination of 200 million units of defense goods and 75 million units of nondefense goods. C_2 through F_2 are the combinations shown in the table in Figure 2. Connecting these points yields the bowed-out curve PPC_2. Because of the availability of new supplies of oil, the nation is able to increase production of all goods, as shown by the *shift* from PPC_1 to PPC_2. A comparison of the two curves shows that more goods and services for both defense and nondefense are possible along PPC_2 than along PPC_1.

FIGURE 2

A Shift of the Production Possibilities Curve

Whenever everything else is not constant, the curve shifts. In this case, an increase in the quantity of a resource enables the society to produce more of both types of goods. The curve shifts out, away from the origin.

Combination	Defense Goods and Services (millions of units)	Nondefense Goods and Services (millions of units)
A_2	220	0
B_2	200	75
C_2	175	125
D_2	130	150
E_2	70	160
F_2	0	165

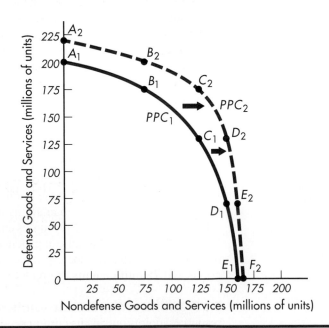

The outward shift of the PPC can be the result of an increase in the quantity of resources, but it also can occur because the quality of resources improves. For instance, a technological breakthrough could conceivably improve the way in which communication occurs, thereby requiring fewer people and machines and less time to produce the same quantity and quality of goods. The work force could become more literate, thereby requiring less time to produce the same quantity and quality of goods. Each of these quality improvements in resources could lead to an outward shift of the PPC.

The outward shift of the PPC illustrates that the capacity, or potential, of the economy has grown. However, being able to produce more of all goods doesn't mean that a society will do that. A society might produce at a point on the PPC or inside the PPC, or even attempt to produce at a point outside the PPC.

Knowing that the opportunity costs include the entire PPC plus the forgone production of those resources that are not fully or efficiently used, why would a society produce at a point inside the PPC? Almost as puzzling is why a society might try to produce beyond its capacity, something it cannot sustain, when the opportunity costs include not only the entire PPC but the possible damage to the society's "internal organs" as a result of overheating. The answers to these questions are far from straightforward; in fact, a significant part of macroeconomics is devoted to answering them.

RECAP

1. Opportunity costs are the benefits that are forgone as a result of a choice. When you choose one thing, you must give up—forgo—others.

2. Opportunity costs are an individual concept but can be used to demonstrate scarcity and choice for a society as a whole.

3. The production possibilities curve represents all combinations of goods and services that can be produced using limited resources efficiently to their full capabilities.

4. Points inside the production possibilities curve represent the underutilization or inefficient use of resources—more goods and services could be produced by using the limited resources more fully or efficiently.

5. Points outside the production possibilities curve represent combinations of goods and services that are unattainable given the limitation of resources. More resources would have to be obtained, or a more efficient means of production through the development of technology or innovative management techniques would have to be discovered, to produce quantities of goods and services outside the current production possibilities curve.

2. Specialization and Trade

No matter which combination of goods and services a society chooses to produce, other combinations of goods and services are forgone. The PPC illustrates what these forgone combinations are.

2.a. Marginal Opportunity Cost

The shape of the PPC illustrates the ease with which resources can be transferred from one activity to another. If it becomes increasingly more difficult or costly to

marginal opportunity cost:
the amount of one good or service that must be given up to obtain one additional unit of another good or service, no matter how many units are being produced

move resources from one activity to another, the PPC will have the bowed-out shape of Figure 1. With each successive increase in the production of nondefense goods, we see that some amount of defense goods has to be given up. The incremental amounts of defense production given up with each increase in the production of nondefense goods are known as marginal opportunity costs. **Marginal opportunity cost** is the amount of one good or service that must be given up to obtain one additional unit of another good or service, no matter how many units are being produced.

The bowed-out shape shows that for each additional nondefense good, more and more defense goods have to be forgone. According to the table and graph in Figure 3, we see that moving from point *A* to point *B* on the PPC means increasing nondefense production from 0 to 25 million units and decreasing defense production from 200 million to 195 million units, resulting in a marginal opportunity cost of 5 million units of defense goods and services for each 25 million units of nondefense goods and services. Moving from point *B* to point *C* means increasing nondefense production from 25 to 50 million units, decreasing defense production from 195 to 188 million units, and creating a marginal opportunity cost of 7 million units. Moving from point *C* to point *D* causes an increase in nondefense production from 50 to 75 million units, a decrease in defense production from 188 million to 175 million units, and a marginal opportunity cost of 13 million units. As you can see from the table for Figure 3, marginal opportunity costs increase with each successive increase in nondefense production. In other words, it gets more and more costly to produce nondefense goods. The increased marginal opportunity costs occur as a result of specialization. The first resources switched from defense to nondefense production are those that are least specialized in the production of defense goods. Switching these resources is less costly (less has to be given up) than switching the specialists. An accountant can do accounting in either defense- or nondefense-related industries equally well; an expert rocket physicist cannot work as efficiently in health care as in the defense area. But as more and more nondefense goods are produced, the more specialized resources have to be switched as well. This means higher opportunity costs, and increasing amounts of defense goods have to be forgone.

2.b. Specialize Where Opportunity Costs Are Lowest

?

3. Why does specialization occur?

Individuals, firms, and nations select the option with the lowest opportunity costs.

Because we cannot do everything, it is just common sense that we tend to devote our time and efforts to *those activities that require us to give up the smallest amount of other things*; in other words, we specialize where costs are lowest. A plumber does plumbing and leaves teaching to the teachers. The teacher teaches and leaves electrical work to the electrician. A country such as Grenada, which has abundant rich land suitable for the cultivation and production of nutmeg and other spices, specializes in spice production. If we specialize, however, how do we get the other things that we want? The answer is that we trade or exchange goods and services.

2.b.1. Trade By specializing in the activities in which opportunity costs are lowest and then trading, each country or individual will end up with more than if each tried to produce everything. Consider the simple hypothetical example given in Figure 4, which concerns two countries, Haiti and the Dominican Republic, that share an island. Assume that Haiti and the Dominican Republic must decide how to allocate their resources between food production and health care. Haiti's daily production possibilities curve is plotted using the data in columns 2 and 3 of the table. If Haiti were to devote all of its resources to health care, then it would be able to provide 1,000 people with adequate care each day but would have no resources with which to produce food. If it were to devote half of its available resources to each

FIGURE 3

The Production Possibilities Curve and Marginal Opportunity Costs

With a limited amount of resources, only certain combinations of defense and nondefense goods and services can be produced. The maximum amounts that can be produced are represented by point A through H. With each increase in nondefense production, marginal opportunity costs increase. This occurs as a result of specialization. The first resources switched from defense to nondefense production are those that are least specialized in the production of defense goods. But as more and more nondefense goods are produced, the more specialized resources have to be switched as well. This means higher opportunity costs; increasing amounts of defense goods have to be forgone.

Combination	Defense Goods and Services (millions of units)	Marginal Opportunity Costs (defense units forgone per 25 units of nondefense units gained)	Nondefense Goods and Services (millions of units)
A	200		0
B	195	5	25
C	188	7	50
D	175	13	75
E	155	20	100
F	125	30	125
G	75	50	150
H	0	75	160

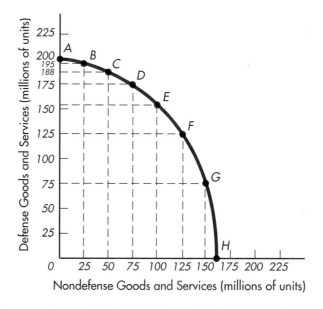

activity, then it would provide 500 people with adequate health care and produce 7 tons of food. Devoting all of its resources to food production would mean that Haiti could produce 10 tons of food but would have no health care. The Dominican Republic's production possibilities curve is plotted using the data in columns 4 and 5 of the table. If the Dominican Republic were to devote all of its resources to health care, it could provide adequate care to 500 people daily but would be unable to produce any food. If it were to devote half of its resources to each activity, then it could provide 300 people with health care and produce 5 tons of food; and if it were to devote all of its resources to food production, it could produce 10 tons of food but no health care.

FIGURE 4

The Benefits of Trade

The trade point of providing health care to 500 people and 2 tons of food is beyond the Dominican Republic's PPC; similarly, the trade point of providing health care to 500 people and 8 tons of food is beyond Haiti's PPC. However, through specialization and trade, these points are achieved by the two nations.

Allocation of Resources to Health Care	Haiti		Dominican Republic	
	Health Care (no. of people provided care)	Food (tons)	Health Care (no. of people provided care)	Food (tons)
100%	1,000	0	500	0
50	500	7	300	5
0	0	10	0	10

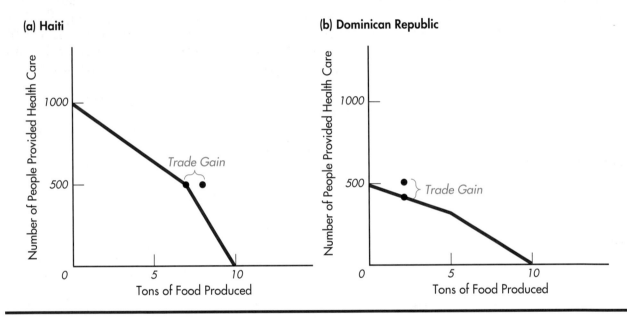

(a) Haiti

(b) Dominican Republic

Suppose that Haiti and the Dominican Republic each want 500 people per day provided with adequate health care. By itself, the Dominican Republic would be unable to grow any food if it devoted its resources to health care for 500 people. However, if the Dominican Republic and Haiti could agree to some type of exchange, perhaps the Dominican Republic could get some food and give the 500 people health care. But who produces what? The answer depends on opportunity costs. If the Dominican Republic decides to provide health care to 500 people, it must forgo 10 tons of food; Haiti, on the other hand, must forgo only 3 tons of food if it decides to provide health care to 500 people. Haiti's opportunity cost for devoting its resources to providing 500 people with health care, 3 tons of food, is lower than the Dominican Republic's, 10 tons. Conversely, if the Dominican Republic produces 10 tons of food, it forgoes providing health care for only 500 people, while Haiti forgoes health care for 1,000 people. Clearly, the Dominican Republic's opportunity costs of producing food are lower than Haiti's.

Given the differences in opportunity costs, it would make sense for Haiti to devote its resources to health care and for the Dominican Republic to devote its resources to food production. In this case, Haiti would provide 1,000 people health care and produce no food, and the Dominican Republic would produce 10 tons of food but no health care. The two nations would then trade. The Dominican Republic might give 8 tons of food to Haiti in exchange for health care for 500 people. Under this scheme, where each country gets health care for 500 people, the Dominican Republic would be better off by the 2 tons of food it would also get, while Haiti would be better off by the 8 rather than 7 tons of food it would get if it provided the 500 people with health care using its own resources. Each country is made better off by specialization and trade.

Specialization and trade enable nations to acquire combinations of goods that lie beyond their own resource capabilities. This is shown in Figure 4: the trade point of 500 people being provided with health care and 2 tons of food is beyond the Dominican Republic's PPC. Similarly, the trade point of 500 people being provided with health care and 8 tons of food is beyond Haiti's PPC. The same result applies to individuals and firms. Even though one person, one firm, or one nation is limited to the combinations of goods it can produce using its own resources along or inside its own PPC, through specialization and trade more goods can be acquired. This is why people, firms, and nations trade; this is why there are buyers and sellers.

2.c. Comparative Advantage

We have seen that the choice of which area or activity to specialize in is made on the basis of opportunity costs. Economists refer to the ability of one person or nation to do something with a lower opportunity cost than another as **comparative advantage.** In the example shown in Figure 4, the Dominican Republic had a comparative advantage in food production and Haiti had a comparative advantage in health-care provision. Devoting all of its resources to health care, Haiti can provide 1,000 people with health care, while the Dominican Republic can provide only 500 people with health care. Devoting all of their resources to food production, both Haiti and the Dominican Republic can produce 10 tons of food. Clearly, Haiti is better at health care and no worse at food production. Haiti's comparative advantage is in producing health care—it gives up 3 tons of food for providing 500 people with health care, while the Dominican Republic gives up 10 tons of food for providing 500 people with health care. Conversely, the Dominican Republic has a comparative advantage in food production. It gives up providing 500 people with health care if it produces 10 tons of food, while Haiti gives up providing 1,000 people with health care if it produces 10 tons of food. Haiti has a *comparative advantage* in health care, and the Dominican Republic has a *comparative advantage* in food production. It is the relative amount given up, not the absolute amount that can be produced, that determines comparative advantage. Even if Haiti could produce 11 tons of food while the Dominican Republic could produce only 10, the Dominican Republic's comparative advantage would be in food production.

Comparative advantage applies to every case of trade or exchange. You may be better at both computer programming and literature than your roommate, but you may be much better at computer programming and only slightly better at literature. You, then, have a comparative advantage in computer programming. Your roommate has a comparative advantage as well, in literature. Remember, comparative advantage depends on opportunity costs. Just because you are better than your roommate at both activities does not mean that you have the same opportunity costs in both.

comparative advantage: the ability to produce a good or service at a lower opportunity cost than someone else

Software companies in industrial nations have been employing citizens of India rather than comparably trained citizens of their own countries. The reason stems from comparative advantage; India has the comparative advantage of people trained in information technology. Because of the low opportunity costs of obtaining training in information technology for Indian citizens, a large number of well-trained individuals exist.

Like Haiti and the Dominican Republic, you and your roommate are better off specializing and then trading (helping each other) than if both of you do all the studying all by yourselves. You both get better grades and have more time to devote to other activities.

Tiger Woods and Anika Sorenstam specialize in golf and then buy (trade for) everything else. They have a comparative advantage in playing golf.

2.d. Specialization and Trade Occur Everywhere

(?)

4. What are the benefits of trade?

Individuals specialize in the activity in which their opportunity costs are lowest.

Each of us will specialize in some activity, earn an income, and then trade our output (or income) for other goods and services that we want. Specialization and trade ensure that we are better off than we would be if we did everything ourselves. *Specialization according to comparative advantage followed by trade allows everyone to acquire more of the goods they want.*

RECAP

1. Marginal opportunity cost is the amount of one good or service that must be given up to obtain one additional unit of another good or service.
2. The rule of specialization is: the individual (firm, region, or nation) will specialize in the production of the good or service that has the lowest opportunity cost.
3. Comparative advantage exists whenever one person (firm, nation) can do something with lower opportunity costs than some other individual (firm, nation) can.
4. Specialization and trade enable individuals, firms, and nations to get more than they could without specialization and trade.

Summary

? What are opportunity costs? Are they part of the economic way of thinking?

1. Opportunity costs are the forgone opportunities of the next best alternative. Choice means both gaining something and giving up something. When you choose one option, you forgo all others. The benefits of the next best alternative are the opportunity costs of your choice. *§1*

? What is a production possibilities curve?

2. A production possibilities curve represents the trade-offs involved in the allocation of scarce resources. It shows the maximum quantity of goods and services that can be produced using limited resources to the fullest extent possible. *§1.c*

3. The bowed-out shape of the PPC occurs because of specialization and increasing marginal opportunity costs. *§2.a*

? Why does specialization occur?

4. Comparative advantage accounts for specialization. We specialize in the activities in which we have the lowest opportunity costs, that is, in which we have a comparative advantage. *§2.c*

? What are the benefits of trade?

5. Specialization and trade enable those involved to acquire more than they could if they did not specialize and engage in trade. *§2.d*

Key Terms

opportunity costs *§1*

tradeoff *§1.b*

marginal cost *§1.b*

marginal benefit *§1.b*

production possibilities curve (PPC) *§1.c*

marginal opportunity cost *§2.a*

comparative advantage *§2.c*

Exercises

1. In most presidential campaigns, candidates promise more than they can deliver. Both Democrats and Republicans promise better health care, a better environment, only minor reductions in defense, better education, and an improved system of roads, bridges, sewer systems, water systems, and so on. What economic concept do candidates ignore?

2. Janine is an accountant who makes $30,000 a year. Robert is a college student who makes $8,000 a year. All other things being equal, who is more likely to stand in a long line to get a concert ticket?

3. Back in the 1960s, President Lyndon Johnson signed legislation that increased expenditures for both the Vietnam War and social problems in the United States. Since the U.S. economy was operating at its full employment level when President Johnson did this, what economic concept did he appear to be ignoring?

4. The following numbers measure the tradeoff between grades and income.

Total Hours	Hours Studying	GPA	Hours Working	Income
60	60	4.0	0	$ 0
60	40	3.0	20	$100
60	30	2.0	30	$150
60	10	1.0	50	$250
60	0	0.0	60	$300

a. Calculate the opportunity cost of an increase in the number of hours spent studying in order to earn a 3.0 grade point average (GPA) rather than a 2.0 GPA.

b. Is the opportunity cost the same for a move from a 0.0 GPA to a 1.0 GPA as it is for a move from a 1.0 GPA to a 2.0 GPA?

c. What is the opportunity cost of an increase in salary from $100 to $150?

5. Suppose a second individual has the following trade-offs between income and grades:

Total Hours	Hours Studying	GPA	Hours Working	Income
60	50	4.0	10	$ 60
60	40	3.0	20	$120
60	20	2.0	40	$240
60	10	1.0	50	$300
60	0	0.0	60	$360

a. Define comparative advantage.

b. Does either individual (the one in exercise 4 or the one in exercise 5) have a comparative advantage in both activities?

c. Who should specialize in studying and who should specialize in working?

6. A doctor earns $250,000 per year while a professor earns $40,000. They play tennis against each other each Saturday morning, each giving up a morning of relaxing, reading the paper, and playing with their children. They could each decide to work a few extra hours on Saturday and earn more income. But they choose to play tennis or to relax around the house. Are their opportunity costs of playing tennis different?

7. Plot the PPC of a nation given by the following data.

Combination	Health Care	All Other Goods
A	0	100
B	25	90
C	50	70
D	75	40
E	100	0

a. Calculate the marginal opportunity cost of each combination.

b. What is the opportunity cost of combination C?

c. Suppose a second nation has the following data. Plot the PPC and then determine which nation has the comparative advantage in which activity. Show whether the two nations can gain from specialization and trade.

Combination	Health Care	All Other Goods
A	0	50
B	25	40
C	50	25
D	75	5
E	100	0

8. A doctor earns $200 per hour, a plumber $40 per hour, and a professor $20 per hour. Everything else the same, which one will devote more hours to negotiating the price of a new car?

9. Perhaps you've heard of the old saying "There is no such thing as a free lunch." What does it mean? If someone invites you to a lunch and offers to pay for it, is it free to you?

10. You have waited 30 minutes in a line for the Star Tours ride at Disneyland. You see a sign that says, "From this point on your wait is 45 minutes." You must decide whether to remain in line or to move elsewhere. On what basis do you make the decision? Do the 30 minutes you've already stood in line come into play?

11. The university is deciding between two meal plans. One plan charges a fixed fee of $600 per semester and allows students to eat as much as they want. The other plan charges a fee based on the quantity of food consumed. Under which plan will students eat the most?

12. Evaluate this statement: "You are a natural athlete, an attractive person who learns easily and communicates well. Clearly, you can do everything better than your friends and acquaintances. As a result, the term *specialization* has no meaning for you. Specialization would cost you rather than benefit you."

13. During China's Cultural Revolution in the late 1960s and early 1970s, many people with a high school or college education were forced to move to farms and work in the fields. Some were common laborers for eight or more years. What does this policy say about specialization and the PPC? Would you predict that the policy would lead to an increase in output?

14. In elementary school and through middle school, most students have the same teacher throughout the day and for the entire school year. Then, beginning in high school, different subjects are taught by different teachers. In college, the same subject is often taught at different levels—freshman, sophomore, junior-senior, or graduate—by different faculty. Is educa-

tion taking advantage of specialization only from high school on? Comment on the differences between elementary school and college and the use of specialization.

15. The top officials in the federal government and high-ranking officers of large corporations often have chauffeurs to drive them around the city or from meeting to meeting. Is this simply one of the perquisites of their position, or is the use of chauffeurs justifiable on the basis of comparative advantage?

ACE ✔ *Practice Test*

Take the ACE Practice Test for this chapter to review the important concepts and get immediate feedback with answers.

economics.college.hmco.com/students

Economically Speaking

Guns and Butter

As a decorated soldier, when it came to guns, Hermann Göring certainly knew his stuff. Judging by his corpulent 280-pound frame, it's a fair bet that the Nazi Reichsmarschall knew a thing or two about fatty foods, too. Though his expertise in neither helped him much in the end—he died both obese and defeated—the rest of us still benefit from Goring's 1936 address to the German people: "Guns will make us powerful; butter will only make us fat."

Faced with that compelling logic, all of Germany quickly signed up for the Wehrmacht Diet—citizens starved while the Nazis devoted resources to conquering Europe. Ever since, the guns versus butter example has earned a place as a staple economic theory, a useful illustration of the opportunity-cost conundrum that all states confront: the more you spend on your military, the greater the toll on your domestic front, while every dollar going to farmers or highways is one more chink in the national armor. But there's no having it both ways.

And that's got the US administration perched on a dilemma. President George W. Bush has been steadfast in his assurances to his fellow Americans that the nation's defence is his top priority. Last year, US forces smashed the terrorist hives of Afghanistan. This year, given Saddam Hussein's opposition to weapons inspections and his continued sponsorship of terror, Bush has a hankering for a regime change in Iraq. While that may be welcome news to most Americans (and no doubt a lot of Iraqis, too), it could be a costly move. In the highest estimate yet for the price tag of a war against Iraq, Lawrence Lindsey, head of the President's National Economic Council, has reckoned the cost at somewhere between US$ 100 billion and US$ 200 billion. That's roughly twice as much as the past Gulf War—and most of that battle's US$ 60-billion tab was picked up by other countries. Since Dubya's vowed to take out Iraq alone if need be, the net drain on the US economy could be 1% to 2% of GDP.

Can the US afford to go to war? Many argue it can't afford not to. But while they ready for battle, Americans have so far refused to cut out the cholesterol. With midterm elections in November, the domestic butter is being spread on thick. One day before the first anniversary of Sept. 11, the Democratic Senate voted for almost US$ 6 billion in drought aid to farmers and ranchers. Despite Bush's reputation as a fiscal conservative, the Cato Institute, a conservative Washington, DC–based think tank, has estimated that this administration's discretionary spending next year will exceed what former president Bill Clinton had proposed for fiscal 2003 by US$ 124 billion. "Bush keeps making these threats to Congress to keep spending down," says Chris Edwards, Cato's director of fiscal policy. "But in the meantime he's for big farm bills, big prescription drug bills; he's absolutely exploded spending in the education department in the past few years—there are no areas he wants to cut." Even so-called emergency supplemental bills passed by Congress to expedite crisis funds to the war on terror have been loaded with hidden domestic lard, including highway projects, subsidies for fishermen and AIDS funding. While it may be money well spent, there's not enough to pay for all of it. Washington is looking at deficits "as far as the eye can see," says Edwards. . . .

KEVIN LIBIN

Source: Copyright 2002 CB Media Limited.

Canadian Business/October 14, 2002

Commentary

This article was written just prior to the U.S. invasion of Iraq in March 2003. It teaches us a valuable lesson today: that a country can't have both "guns and butter." What does this mean? Societies must make tradeoffs between military spending and spending on other things. If a society decides to increase military spending, then it must reduce spending elsewhere. This is shown by a production possibility curve. The curve shows the combinations of guns and butter that a society can produce given its current resources and technology.

We'll use this figure to represent the situation the United States faced in October 2002. The United States was producing the combination of guns and butter at point *A*. As President Bush increased military spending in preparation for a war in Iraq, the United States moved to point *B*. It couldn't move to point *C*, only to point *D*, since it did not have enough resources to move beyond its production possibilities curve and *D* was not enough military spending. Thus, the move from *A* to *B* meant that the United States could spend less on health care, the environment, leisure activities, or anything else. As the article notes, in the past, trying to move to point *C* rather than point *B* has spelled trouble. In the late 1960s, President Lyndon Johnson tried fighting the Vietnam War and the War on Poverty at the same time. The result was that the United States faced inflation and economic stagnation at home. Trying to run your car in the red zone will burn out the engine; similarly, trying to run the economy at a point beyond its PPC will burn out the economy.

The article notes that perhaps George W. Bush will be able to show economists that it is possible to move beyond the PPC. The author of the article is absolutely wrong here; it is not possible to move outside the PPC no matter how much one wants to. This is not just basic economics, it is physical law. You cannot do more than you are able to do with your resources.

So what will have to be given up in terms of "butter" in order to be able to produce more "guns"? Something must be given up. The government may decrease spending on Medicare and social security, on the war on drugs, on the environment, or on anything else it spends money on. If the U.S. government refuses to decrease its spending on other programs at the same time it increases military spending, then either inflation will result or the public will be forced to pay higher taxes. Either of these events will reduce the public's ability to purchase the goods and services that it wants.

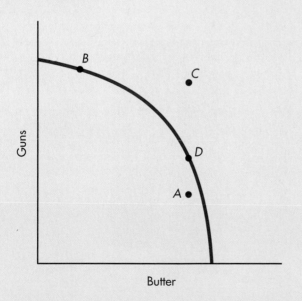

CHAPTER 3

Markets, Demand and Supply, and the Price System

? Fundamental Questions

1. What is a market?

2. What is demand?

3. What is supply?

4. How is price determined by demand and supply?

5. What causes price to change?

6. What happens when price is not allowed to change with market forces?

People (and firms and nations) can get more if they specialize in certain activities and then trade with one another to acquire the goods and services that they desire than if they do everything themselves. But how are the specialized producers to get together or to know who specializes in what? We could allow the government to decide, or we could rely on first-come, first-served, or even simply on luck. Typically it is the market mechanism—buyers and sellers interacting via prices—that we rely on to ensure that gains from trade occur. To see why, consider the following situation and then carry out the exercise.

I. At a sightseeing point, reachable only after a strenuous hike, a firm has established a stand where bottled water is sold. The water, carried in by the employees of the firm, is sold to thirsty hikers in 6-ounce bottles. The price is $1 per bottle. Typically only 100 bottles of the water are sold each day. On a particularly hot day, however, 200 hikers each want to buy at least one bottle of water. Indicate what you

think of each of the following means of distributing the water to the hikers by responding to each allocation approach with one of the following five responses:

a. Agree completely
b. Agree with slight reservation
c. Disagree
d. Strongly disagree
e. Totally unacceptable

1. Increasing the price until the quantity of water bottles that hikers are willing and able to purchase exactly equals the number of water bottles available for sale
2. Selling the water for $1 per bottle on a first-come, first-served basis
3. Having the local authority (government) buy the water for $1 per bottle and distribute it according to its own judgment
4. Selling the water for $1 per bottle following a random selection procedure or lottery

The following is a similar situation but involves a different product.

II. A physician has been providing medical services at a fee of $100 per patient and typically sees thirty patients per day. One day the flu bug has been so vicious that the number of patients attempting to visit the physician exceeds sixty. Indicate what you think of each of the following means of distributing the physician's services to the sick patients by responding with one of the following five answers:

a. Agree completely
b. Agree with slight reservation
c. Disagree
d. Strongly disagree
e. Totally unacceptable

1. Raising the price until the number of patients the doctor sees is exactly equal to the number of patients who are willing and able to pay the doctor's fee
2. Selling the services for $100 per patient on a first-come, first-served basis
3. Having the local authority (government) pay the physician $100 per patient and choose who is to receive the services according to its own judgment
4. Selling the physician's services for $100 per patient following a random selection procedure or lottery.

How did you answer the exercises? Did you notice that in fact, each allocation mechanism is unfair in the sense that someone gets the good or service and someone does not? With the market system, it is those without income or wealth who must do without. Under the first-come, first-served system, it is those who arrive later who do without. Under the government scheme, it is those not in favor or those who do not match up with the government's rules who do without. And, with a random procedure, it is those who do not have the lucky ticket or correct number who are left out.

Since each allocation mechanism is in a sense unfair, how do we decide which to use? One way might be by the incentives each creates.

With the first-come, first-served allocation scheme, the incentive is to be first. You have no reason to improve the quality of your products or to increase the value of your resources. Your only incentive is to be first. Supply will not increase. Why would anyone produce when all everyone wants is to be first? As a result, growth

A market arises when buyers and sellers exchange a well-defined good or service. In stock markets, buyers and sellers exchange their "goods," or stocks, solely through electronic connections. Shoppers at a flower market can examine the day's assortment and make their choices.

will not occur and standards of living will not rise. A society based on first-come, first-served would die a quick death.

A government scheme provides an incentive either to be a member of government and thus help determine the allocation rules or to perform according to government dictates. There are no incentives to improve production and efficiency, to improve quantities supplied, and thus no reason for the economy to grow. We have seen how this system fared with the collapse of the Soviet Union.

The random allocation provides no incentives at all; simply hope that manna from heaven falls on you.

With the market system, the incentive is to acquire purchasing ability—to obtain income and wealth. This means that you must provide goods that have high value to others and provide resources that have high value to producers—to enhance your worth as an employee by acquiring education or training and to enhance the value of the resources you own.

The market system also provides incentives for quantities of scarce goods to increase. In the case of the water stand in scenario I, if the price of the water increases and the owner of the water stand is earning significant profits, others may carry or truck water to the top of the hill and sell it to thirsty hikers; the amount of water available thus increases. In the case of the doctor in scenario II, other doctors may think that opening an office near the first might be a way to earn more; the amount of physician services available increases. Since the market system creates the incentive for the amount supplied to increase, economies grow and expand and standards of living improve. The market system also ensures that resources are allocated to where they are most highly valued. If the price of an item rises, consumers may switch over to another item, or another good or service, that can serve about the same purpose. When consumers switch, production of the alternative good rises and thus resources used in its production must increase as well. The resources then are reallocated from lower-valued uses to higher-valued uses. ■

1. Markets

1. What is a market?

The supermarket, the stock market, and the market for foreign exchange are similar in that well-defined goods and services are exchanged. A market may be a specific location, such as the supermarket or the stock market, or it may be the exchange of particular goods or services at many different locations, such as the foreign exchange market.

1.a. Market Definition

market: a place or service that enables buyers and sellers to exchange goods and services

A **market** makes possible the exchange of goods and services. A market may be a formally organized exchange, such as the New York Stock Exchange, or it may be loosely organized like the market for used bicycles or automobiles. A market may be confined to one location, as in the case of a supermarket or the stock market, or it may encompass a city, a state, a country, or the entire world. The market for agricultural products, for instance, is international, but the market for labor services is mostly local or national.

1.b. Barter and Money Exchanges

The purpose of markets is to facilitate the exchange of goods and services between buyers and sellers. In some cases money changes hands; in others only goods and services are exchanged. The exchange of goods and services directly, without money, is called **barter.** Barter occurs when a plumber fixes a leaky pipe for a lawyer in exchange for the lawyer's work on a will or when a Chinese citizen provides fresh vegetables to a U.S. visitor in exchange for a pack of U.S. cigarettes.

barter: the direct exchange of goods and services without the use of money

double coincidence of wants: the situation that exists when A has what B wants and B has what A wants

Most markets involve money because goods and services can be exchanged more easily with money than without it. When IBM purchases microchips from Yakamoto of Japan, IBM and Yakamoto don't exchange goods directly. Neither firm may have what the other wants. Barter requires a **double coincidence of wants:** IBM must have what Yakamoto wants, and Yakamoto must have what IBM wants. The transaction costs (the costs associated with making an exchange) of finding a double coincidence of wants for barter transactions are typically very high. Money reduces these transaction costs. To obtain the microchips, all IBM has to do is provide dollars to Yakamoto. Yakamoto is willing to accept the money, since it can spend it to obtain the goods that it wants.

1.c. Relative Price

When people agree to trade or exchange, they must agree on the rate of exchange, or the price. The price of an exchange is a **relative price**—the price of one good expressed in terms of the price of another good. In a barter exchange, a relative price is established between the goods traded. When the lawyer exchanges 2 hours of work for 1 hour of the plumber's work, the relative price established is 2/1. In a money exchange, the relative price is more implicit. You pay a money price of $1 for a carton of milk. But, with that purchase you are forgoing everything else you could get for that dollar. Thus, the carton of milk is worth 1/3 of a $3 box of Quaker Oats 100% Natural cereal, 1/200 of a $200 used Diamond Back mountain bike, 20 sticks of $.05/stick Trident gum, and so on. These are the relative prices of the milk.

Relative prices are a measure of what you must give up to get one unit of a good or service and are, therefore, a measure of opportunity costs. Since opportunity costs are what decisions are based on, when economists refer to the price of something, it is the relative price that they have in mind.

RECAP

1. A market is not necessarily a specific location or store. Instead, the term *market* refers to buyers and sellers communicating with each other regarding the quality and quantity of a well-defined product, what buyers are willing and able to pay for a product, and what sellers must receive in order to produce and sell a product.

2. Barter refers to exchanges made without the use of money.

3. Money makes it easier and less expensive to exchange goods and services.

4. The price of a good or service is a measure of what you must give up to get one unit of that good or service.

---

2. Demand

Demand and supply determine the price of any good or service. To understand how a price level is determined and why a price rises or falls, it is necessary to know how demand and supply function. We begin by considering demand alone, then supply, and then we put the two together. Before we begin, we discuss some economic terminology that is often confusing.

Economists distinguish between the terms **demand** and **quantity demanded.** When they refer to the *quantity demanded,* they are talking about the amount of a product that people are willing and able to purchase at a *specific* price. When they refer to *demand,* they are talking about the amount that people would be willing and able to purchase at *every possible* price. Demand is the quantities demanded at every price. Thus, the statement that "the demand for U.S. white wine rose after a

quantity demanded: the amount of a product that people are willing and able to purchase at a specific price

300 percent tariff was applied to French white wine" means that at each price for U.S. white wine, more people were willing and able to purchase U.S. white wine. And the statement that "the quantity demanded of white wine fell as the price of white wine rose" means that people were willing and able to purchase less white wine because the price of the wine rose.

2.a. The Law of Demand

Consumers and merchants know that if you lower the price of a good or service without altering its quality or quantity, people will beat a path to your doorway. This simple truth is referred to as the **law of demand.**

According to the law of demand, people purchase more of something when the price of that item falls. More formally, the law of demand states that the quantity of some item that people are willing and able to purchase during a particular period of time decreases as the price rises, and vice versa.

law of demand: the quantity of a well-defined good or service that people are willing and able to purchase during a particular period of time decreases as the price of that good or service rises and increases as the price falls, everything else held constant

The more formal definition of the law of demand can be broken down into five phrases:

1. The quantity of a well-defined good or service that
2. people are willing and able to purchase
3. during a particular period of time
4. decreases as the price of that good or service rises and increases as the price falls,
5. everything else held constant

The first phrase ensures that we are referring to the same item, that we are not mixing different goods. A watch is a commodity defined and distinguished from other goods by several characteristics: quality, color, and design of the watch face, to name a few. The law of demand applies to the well-defined good, in this case, a watch. If one of the characteristics should change, the good would no longer be well defined—in fact, it would be a different good. A Rolex watch is different from a Timex watch; Polo brand golf shirts are different goods from generic brand golf shirts; Mercedes-Benz automobiles are different goods from Saturn automobiles.

The second phrase indicates that people must not only *want* to purchase some good, they must be *able* to purchase that good in order for their wants to be counted as part of demand. For example, Sue would love to buy a membership to the Paradise Valley Country Club, but because the membership costs $35,000, she is not able to purchase the membership. Though she is willing, she is not able. At a price of $5,000, however, she is willing and able to purchase the membership.

The third phrase points out that the demand for any good is defined for a specific period of time. Without reference to a time period, a demand relationship would not make any sense. For instance, the statement that "at a price of $3 per Happy Meal, 13 million Happy Meals are demanded" provides no useful information. Are the 13 million meals sold in one week or one year? Think of demand as a rate of purchase at each possible price over a period of time—2 per month, 1 per day, and so on.

The fourth phrase points out that price and quantity demanded move in opposite directions; that is, as the price rises, the quantity demanded falls, and as the price falls, the quantity demanded rises.

Demand is a measure of the relationship between the price and quantity demanded of a particular good or service when the determinants of demand do not

determinants of demand:
factors other than the price of the good that influence demand—income, tastes, prices of related goods and services, expectations, and number of buyers

demand schedule: a table or list of the prices and the corresponding quantities demanded of a particular good or service

change. The **determinants of demand** are income, tastes, prices of related goods and services, expectations, and the number of buyers. If any one of these items changes, demand changes. The final phrase, everything else held constant, ensures that the determinants of demand do not change.

2.b. The Demand Schedule

A **demand schedule** is a table or list of the prices and the corresponding quantities demanded of a particular good or service. The table in Figure 1 is a demand schedule for video rentals (movies). It shows the number of videos that a consumer named Bob would be willing and able to rent at each price during the year, everything else held constant. As the rental price of the videos gets higher relative to the prices of other goods, Bob would be willing and able to rent fewer videos.

At the high price of $5 per video, Bob indicates that he will rent only 10 videos during the year. At a price of $4 per video, Bob tells us that he will rent 20 videos during the year. As the price drops from $5 to $4 to $3 to $2 and to $1, Bob is willing and able to rent more videos. At a price of $1, Bob would rent 50 videos during the year, nearly 1 per week.

FIGURE 1

Bob's Demand Schedule and Demand Curve for Videos

The number of videos that Bob is willing and able to rent at each price during the year is listed in the table, or demand schedule. The demand curve is derived from the combinations given in the demand schedule. The price-quantity combination of $5 per video and 10 videos is point *A*. The combination of $4 per video and 20 videos is point *B*. Each combination is plotted, and the points are connected to form the demand curve.

Combination	Price per Video (constant-quality units)	Quantity Demanded per Year (constant-quality units)
A	$5	10
B	$4	20
C	$3	30
D	$2	40
E	$1	50

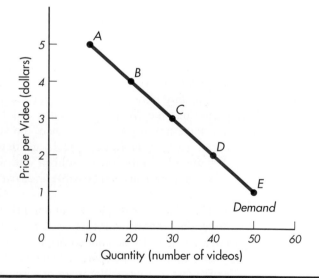

2.c. The Demand Curve

demand curve: a graph of a demand schedule that measures price on the vertical axis and quantity demanded on the horizontal axis

A **demand curve** is a graph of the demand schedule. The demand curve shown in Figure 1 is plotted from the information given in the demand schedule. Price is measured on the vertical axis, and quantity per unit of time on the horizontal axis. The demand curve slopes downward because of the inverse relationship between the rental price of the videos and the quantity an individual is willing and able to purchase (rent). Point *A* in Figure 1 corresponds to combination *A* in the table: a price of $5 and 10 videos demanded. Similarly, points *B, C, D,* and *E* in Figure 1 represent the corresponding combinations in the table. The line connecting these points is Bob's demand curve for videos.

When speaking of the demand curve or demand schedule, we are using constant-quality units. The quality of a good does not change as the price changes along a demand curve.

All demand curves slope down because of the law of demand: as price falls, quantity demanded increases. The demand curves for bread, electricity, automobiles, colleges, labor services, and any other good or service you can think of slope down. You might be saying to yourself, "That's not true. What about the demand for Mercedes-Benz cars or Gucci bags? As their price goes up, they become more prestigious and the quantity demanded actually rises." To avoid confusion in such circumstances, we say "everything else held constant." With this statement we are assuming that tastes don't change and that, therefore, the goods *cannot* become more prestigious as the price changes. Similarly, we do not allow the quality or the brand name of a product to change as we define the demand schedule or demand curve. We concentrate on the one quality or the one brand; so when we say that the price of a good has risen, we are talking about a good that is identical at all prices.

2.d. From Individual Demand Curves to a Market Curve

Bob's demand curve for video rentals is plotted in Figure 1. Unless Bob is the only renter of the videos, his demand curve is not the total, or market demand, curve. Market demand is the sum of all individual demands. To derive the market demand curve, then, the individual demand curves of all consumers in the market must be added together. The table in Figure 2 lists the demand schedules of three individuals, Bob, Helen, and Art. Because in this example the market consists only of Bob, Helen, and Art, their individual demands are added together to derive the market demand. The market demand is the last column of the table.

Bob's, Helen's, and Art's demand schedules are plotted as individual demand curves in Figure 2(a). In Figure 2(b) their individual demand curves have been added together to obtain the market demand curve. (Notice that we add in a horizontal direction—that is, we add quantities at each price, not the prices at each quantity.) At a price of $5, we add the quantity Bob would buy, 10, to the quantity Helen would buy, 5, to the quantity Art would buy, 15, to get the market quantity demanded of 30. At a price of $4, we add the quantities each of the consumers is willing and able to buy to get the total quantity demanded of 48. At all prices, then, we add the quantities demanded by each individual consumer to get the total, or market quantity, demanded.

2.e. Changes in Demand and Changes in Quantity Demanded

When one of the determinants of demand—income, tastes, prices of related goods, expectations, or number of buyers—is allowed to change, the demand for a good or service changes as well. What does it mean to say that demand changes? Demand is the entire demand schedule, or demand curve. When we say that demand changes, we are referring to a change in the quantities demanded at each and every price.

For example, if Bob's income rises, then his demand for video rentals rises. At each and every price, the number of videos Bob is willing and able to rent each year

FIGURE 2

The Market Demand Schedule and Curve for Videos

The market is defined to consist of three individuals: Bob, Helen, and Art. Their demand schedules are listed in the table and plotted as the individual demand curves shown in Figure 2(a). By adding the quantities that each demands at every price, we obtain the market demand curve shown in Figure 2(b). At a price of $1 we add Bob's quantity demanded of 50 to Helen's quantity demanded of 25 to Art's quantity demanded of 27 to obtain the market quantity demanded of 102. At a price of $2 we add Bob's 40 to Helen's 20 to Art's 24 to obtain the market quantity demanded of 84. To obtain the market demand curve, for every price we sum the quantities demanded by each market participant.

	Quantities Demanded per Year by			
Price per Video	Bob	Helen	Art	Market Quantity Demanded
$5	10 +	5 +	15 =	30
$4	20	10	18	48
$3	30	15	21	66
$2	40	20	24	84
$1	50	25	27	102

(a) Individual Demand Curves

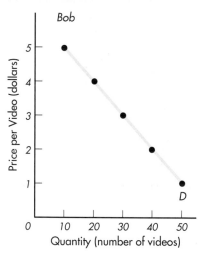
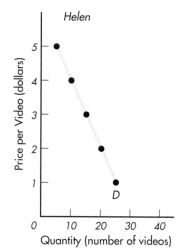
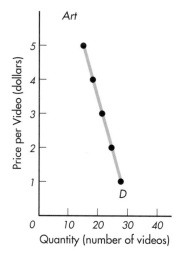

(b) Market Demand Curve

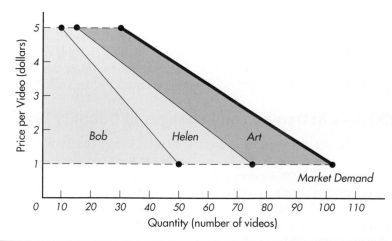

FIGURE 3

A Change in Demand and a Change in the Quantity Demanded

According to the table, Bob's demand for videos has increased by 5 videos at each price. In Figure 3(a), this change is shown as a shift of the demand curve from D_1 to D_2. Figure 3(b) shows a change in the quantity demanded. The change is an increase in the quantity that consumers are willing and able to purchase at a lower price. It is shown as a movement along the demand curve from point A to point B.

Price per Video	Quantities Demanded per Year	
	Before	After
$5	10	15
$4	20	25
$3	30	35
$2	40	45
$1	50	55

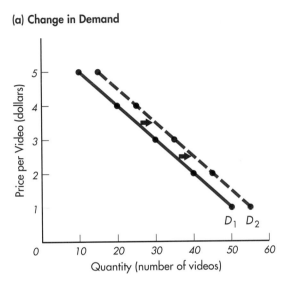

(a) Change in Demand

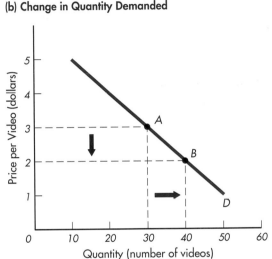

(b) Change in Quantity Demanded

rises. This increase is shown in the last column of the table in Figure 3. A change in demand is represented by a shift of the demand curve, as shown in Figure 3(a). The shift to the right, from D_1 to D_2, indicates that Bob is willing and able to rent more videos at every price.

When the price of a good or service is the only factor that changes, the quantity demanded changes but the demand curve does not shift. Instead, as the price of the rentals is decreased (increased), everything else held constant, the quantity that people are willing and able to purchase increases (decreases). This change is merely a movement from one point on the demand curve to another point on the same demand curve, not a shift of the demand curve. *Change in the quantity demanded* is the phrase that economists use to describe the change in the quantities of a particular good or service that people are willing and able to purchase as the price of that good or service changes. A change in the quantity demanded, from point A to point B on the demand curve, is shown in Figure 3(b).

The demand curve shifts when income, tastes, prices of related goods, expectations, or the number of buyers changes. Let's consider how each of these determinants of demand affects the demand curve.

2.e.1. Income

The demand for any good or service depends on income. For most goods and services, the higher someone's income is, the more that person can purchase at any given price. These are called **normal goods.** The increase in Bob's income causes his demand to increase. This change is shown in Figure 3(a) by the shift to the right from the curve labeled D_1 to the curve labeled D_2. Increased income means a greater ability to purchase goods and services. At every price, more videos are demanded along curve D_2 than along curve D_1.

For some goods and services, however, the amount demanded declines as income rises. The reason could be that these are goods or services that people use only when their incomes are declining—such as bankruptcy services. In addition, people might not like the good or service as well as they like a more expensive good or service, so when their income rises, they purchase the more expensive items. These types of items are called **inferior goods.**

2.e.2. Tastes

The demand for any good or service depends on individuals' tastes and preferences. For decades, the destination of choice for college students in the East and Midwest during spring break was Fort Lauderdale, Florida. Since the early 1990s, many students have decided that Mexico offered a more exciting destination than Fort Lauderdale. Regardless of the prices of the Fort Lauderdale and Mexican vacations, tastes changed so that more students went to Mexico. The demand curve for the Mexican vacation shifted to the right while that for the Fort Lauderdale vacation shifted to the left.

2.e.3. Prices of Related Goods and Services

Goods and services may be related in two ways. **Substitute goods** can be used for each other, so that as the price of one rises, the demand for the other rises. Bread and crackers, BMWs and Acuras, video rentals and theater movies, universities and community colleges, electricity and natural gas are, more or less, pairs of substitutes. As the price of cassette tapes rises, everything else held constant, the demand for CDs will rise and the demand curve for CDs will shift to the right. As the price of theater movies increases, the demand for video rentals will rise and the demand curve for the videos will shift to the right.

Complementary goods are goods that are used together, and so as the price of one rises, the demand for the other falls. Bread and margarine, beer and peanuts, cameras and film, shoes and socks, CDs and CD players, video rentals and VCRs are examples of pairs of complementary goods. As the price of cameras rises, people tend to purchase fewer cameras, but they also tend to purchase less film. As the price of VCRs rises, people tend to purchase fewer VCRs, but they also demand fewer video rentals. The demand curve for a complementary good shifts to the left when the price of the related good increases.

2.e.4. Expectations

Expectations about future events can have an effect on demand today. People make purchases today because they expect their income level to be a certain amount in the future, or they expect the price of certain items to be higher in the future.

2.e.5. Number of Buyers

Market demand consists of the sum of the demands of all individuals. The more individuals there are with income to spend, the greater the market demand is likely to be. For example, the populations of Florida and Arizona are much larger during the winter than they are during the summer. The demand for any particular good or service in Arizona and Florida rises (the demand curve shifts to the right) during the winter and falls (the demand curve shifts to the left) during the summer.

1. According to the law of demand, as the price of any good or service rises (falls), the quantity demanded of that good or service falls (rises), during a specific period of time, everything else held constant.

2. A demand schedule is a listing of the quantity demanded at each price.

3. The demand curve is a downward-sloping line plotted using the values of the demand schedule.

4. Market demand is the sum of all individual demands.

5. Demand changes when one of the determinants of demand changes. A demand change is a shift of the demand curve.

6. The quantity demanded changes when the price of the good or service changes. This is a change from one point on the demand curve to another point on the same demand curve.

7. The determinants of demand are income, tastes, prices of related goods and services, expectations, and number of buyers.

3. What is supply?

3. Supply

Why is the price of hotel accommodations higher in Phoenix in the winter than in the summer? Demand AND supply. Why is the price of beef higher in Japan than in the United States? Demand AND supply. Why did the price of the dollar in terms of the Japanese yen rise in 1999? Demand AND supply. Both demand and supply determine price; neither demand nor supply alone determines price. We now discuss supply.

3.a. The Law of Supply

supply: the amount of a good or service that producers are willing and able to offer for sale at each possible price during a period of time, everything else held constant

quantity supplied: the amount sellers are willing and able to offer at a given price during a particular period of time, everything else held constant

law of supply: the quantity of a well-defined good or service that producers are willing and able to offer for sale during a particular period of time increases as the price of the good or service increases and decreases as the price decreases, everything else held constant

Just as demand is the relation between the price and the quantity demanded of a good or service, supply is the relation between price and quantity supplied. **Supply** is the amount of the good or service producers are willing and able to offer for sale at each possible price during a period of time, everything else held constant. **Quantity supplied** is the amount of the good or service producers are willing and able to offer for sale at a *specific* price during a period of time, everything else held constant. According to the **law of supply,** as the price of a good or service rises, the quantity supplied rises, and vice versa.

The formal statement of the law of supply consists of five phrases:

1. The quantity of a well-defined good or service that

2. producers are willing and able to offer for sale

3. during a particular period of time

4. increases as the price of the good or service increases and decreases as the price decreases,

5. everything else held constant

The first phrase is the same as the first phrase in the law of demand. The second phrase indicates that producers must not only *want* to offer the product for sale but be *able* to offer the product. The third phrase points out that the quantities producers will offer for sale depend on the period of time being considered. The fourth phrase

determinants of supply: factors other than the price of the good that influence supply—prices of resources, technology and productivity, expectations of producers, number of producers, and the prices of related good and services.

supply schedule: a table or list of prices and corresponding quantities supplied of a particular good or service

supply curve: a graph of a supply schedule that measures price on the vertical axis and quantity supplied on the horizontal axis

points out that more will be supplied at higher than at lower prices. The final phrase ensures that the **determinants of supply** do not change. The determinants of supply are those factors other than the price of the good or service that influence the willingness and ability of producers to offer their goods and services for sale—the prices of resources used to produce the product, technology and productivity, expectations of producers, the number of producers in the market, and the prices of related goods and services. If any one of these should change, supply changes.

3.b. The Supply Schedule and Supply Curve

A **supply schedule** is a table or list of the prices and the corresponding quantities supplied of a good or service. The table in Figure 4 presents MGA's supply schedule for videos. The schedule lists the quantities that MGA is willing and able to supply at each price, everything else held constant. As the price increases, MGA is willing and able to offer more videos for rent.

A **supply curve** is a graph of the supply schedule. Figure 4 shows MGA's supply curve for videos. The price and quantity combinations given in the supply schedule correspond to the points on the curve. For instance, combination A in the table corresponds to point A on the curve; combination B in the table corresponds to point B on the curve, and so on for each price-quantity combination.

The supply curve for MGA slopes upward. This means that MGA is willing and able to supply more at higher prices than it is at lower prices. Recall from Chapter 2 that as society puts more and more resources into the production of any specific item, the opportunity cost of each additional unit of production rises because

---

FIGURE 4

MGA's Supply Schedule and Supply Curve for Videos

The quantity that MGA is willing and able to offer for sale at each price is listed in the supply schedule and shown on the supply curve. At point A, the price is $5 per video and the quantity supplied is 60 videos. The combination of $4 per video and 50 videos is point B. Each price-quantity combination is plotted, and the points are connected to form the supply curve.

Combination	Price per Video (constant-quality units)	Quantity Supplied per Year (constant-quality units)
A	$5	60
B	$4	50
C	$3	40
D	$2	30
E	$1	20

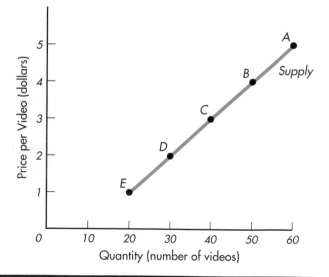

more-specialized resources are transferred to activities in which they are relatively less productive. So MGA finds that as it increases production, the opportunity costs of additional production rise. Hence, the only way that MGA, or any producer, will be willing and able to produce more is if the price rises sufficiently to cover these increasing opportunity costs.

3.c. From Individual Supply Curves to the Market Supply

To derive market supply, the quantities that each producer supplies at each price are added together, just as the quantities demanded by each consumer are added together to get market demand. The table in Figure 5 lists the supply schedules of three video rental stores: MGA, Motown, and Blockmaster. For our example, we assume that these three are the only video rental stores. (We are also assuming that the brand names are not associated with quality or any other differences.)

The supply schedule of each producer is plotted in Figure 5(a). Then in Figure 5(b) the individual supply curves have been added together to obtain the market supply curve. At a price of $5, the quantity supplied by MGA is 60, the quantity supplied by Motown is 30, and the quantity supplied by Blockmaster is 12. This means a total quantity supplied in the market of 102. At a price of $4, the quantities supplied are 50 by MGA, 25 by Motown, and 9 by Blockmaster, for a total market quantity supplied of 84. The market supply schedule is the last column in the table. The plot of the price and quantity combinations listed in this column is the market supply curve. The market supply curve slopes up because each of the individual supply curves has a positive slope. The market supply curve tells us that the quantity supplied in the market increases as the price rises.

3.d. Changes in Supply and Changes in Quantity Supplied

A change in the quantity supplied is a movement along the supply curve. A change in the supply is a shift of the supply curve.

When we draw the supply curve, we allow only the price and quantity supplied of the good or service we are discussing to change. Everything else that might affect supply is assumed not to change. If any of the determinants of supply—the prices of resources used to produce the product, technology and productivity, expectations of producers, the number of producers in the market, and the prices of related goods and services—changes, the supply schedule changes and the supply curve shifts.

3.d.1. Prices of Resources If labor costs—one of the resources used to produce video rentals—rise, higher rental prices will be necessary to induce each store to offer as many videos as it did before the cost of the resource rose. The higher cost of resources causes a decrease in supply, meaning a leftward shift of the supply curve, from S_1 to S_2 in Figure 6(a).

Two interpretations of a leftward shift of the supply curve are possible. One comes from comparing the old and new curves in a horizontal direction; the other comes from comparing the curves in a vertical direction. In the vertical direction, the decrease in supply informs us that sellers want a higher price in order to produce any given quantity. Compare, for example, point A on curve S_1 with point C on curve S_2. Points A and C represent the same quantity but different prices. Sellers will offer 66 videos at a price of $3 per video according to supply curve S_1. But if the supply curve shifts to the left, then the sellers want more ($3.50) if they are to supply 66 units.

In the horizontal direction, the decrease in supply means that sellers will offer less for sale at any given price. This can be seen by comparing point B on curve S_2 with point A on curve S_1. Both points correspond to a price of $3, but along curve S_1, sellers are willing to offer 66 units for rent, whereas curve S_2 indicates that sellers will offer only 57 videos for rent.

FIGURE 5

The Market Supply Schedule and Curve for Videos

The market supply is derived by summing the quantities that each producer is willing and able to offer for sale at each price. In this example, there are three producers: MGA, Motown, and Blockmaster. The supply schedules of each are listed in the table and plotted as the individual supply curves shown in Figure 5(a). By adding the quantities supplied at each price, we obtain the market supply curve shown in Figure 5(b). For instance, at a price of $5, MGA offers 60 units, Motown 30 units, and Blockmaster 12 units, for a market supply quantity of 102. The market supply curve reflects the quantities that each producer is able and willing to supply at each price.

Price per Video	Quantities Supplied per Year by			Market Quantity Supplied
	MGA	Motown	Blockmaster	
$5	60 +	30 +	12 =	102
$4	50	25	9	84
$3	40	20	6	66
$2	30	15	3	48
$1	20	10	0	30

(a) Individual Supply Curves

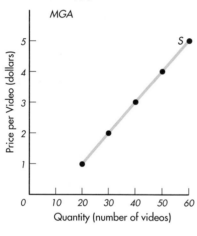
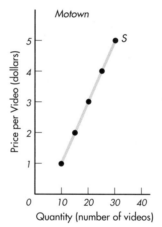
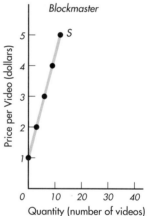

(b) Market Supply Curve

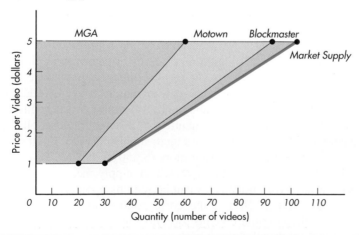

FIGURE 6

A Shift of the Supply Curve

Figure 6(a) shows a decrease in supply and the shift of the supply curve to the left, from S_1 to S_2. The decrease is caused by a change in one of the determinants of video supply—an increase in the price of labor. Because of the increased price of labor, producers are willing and able to offer fewer videos for rent at each price than they were before the price of labor rose. Supply curve S_2 shows that at a price of $3 per video, suppliers will offer 57 videos. That is 9 units less than the 66 videos at $3 per video indicated by supply curve S_1. Conversely, to offer a given quantity, producers must receive a higher price per video than they previously were getting: $3.50 per video for 66 videos (on supply curve S_2) instead of $3 per video (on supply curve S_1).

Figure 6(b) shows an increase in supply. A technological improvement or an increase in productivity causes the supply curve to shift to the right, from S_1 to S_2. At each price, a higher quantity is offered for sale. At a price of $3, 66 units were offered, but with the shift of the supply curve, the quantity of units for sale at $3 apiece increases to 84. Conversely, producers can reduce prices for a given quantity—for example, charging $2 per video for 66 units.

(a) Decrease in Supply

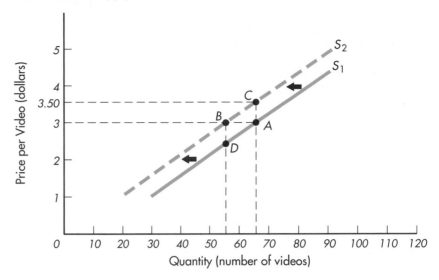

(b) Increase in Supply

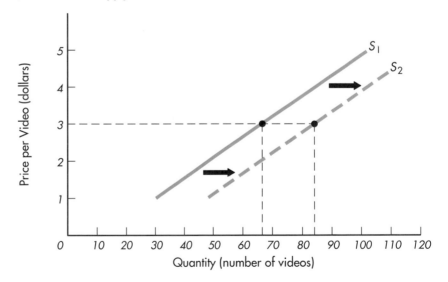

If resources are used more efficiently in the production of a good or service, more of that good or service can be produced at the same cost. In this photo, new technology is being applied to water desalinization, making the process of converting salt water to fresh water more economical. Thus, the supply of fresh water in areas such as Yuma, Arizona, where this desalinization plant is located, will increase.

If resource prices declined, then supply would increase. That combination would be illustrated by a rightward shift of the supply curve. If a firm purchases supplies from other nations, exchange-rate changes can affect the firm's costs and thus its supply curve. For instance, suppose a U.S. firm purchases lumber from Canada. At an exchange rate of 1 Canadian dollar per 1 U.S. dollar, 1,000 Canadian dollars worth of supplies costs 1,000 U.S. dollars. In 1998, with the Canadian dollar worth only .6992 U.S. dollars, the supplies worth 1,000 Canadian dollars cost only 699.20 U.S. dollars. Since the cost of supplies has declined for the U.S. firm, its supply curve shifts out.

3.d.2. Technology and Productivity

If resources are used more efficiently in the production of a good or service, more of that good or service can be produced for the same cost, or the original quantity can be produced for a lower cost. As a result, the supply curve shifts to the right, as in Figure 6(b).

The move from horse-drawn plows to tractors or from mainframe computers to personal computers meant that each worker was able to produce more. The increase in output produced by each unit of a resource is called a *productivity increase*. **Productivity** is defined as the quantity of output produced per unit of resource. Improvements in technology cause productivity increases, which lead to an increase in supply.

productivity: the quantity of output produced per unit of resource

3.d.3. Expectations of Producers

Sellers may choose to alter the quantity offered for sale today because of a change in expectations regarding the determinants of supply. A supply curve illustrates the quantities that suppliers are willing and able to supply at every possible price. If suppliers expect something to occur to resource supplies or the cost of resources, then suppliers may alter the quantities they are willing and able to supply at every possible price. The key point is that the supply curve will shift if producers expect something to occur that will alter the anticipated profits at every possible price, not just a change in one price. For instance, the expectation that demand will decline in the future does not lead to a shift of the supply curve; it leads instead to a decline in quantity supplied as the new demand curve intersects the supply curve at a lower level of prices and output.

3.d.4. Number of Producers   When more people decide to produce a good or service, the market supply increases. More is offered for sale at each and every price, causing a rightward shift of the supply curve.

3.d.5. Prices of Related Goods or Services   The opportunity cost of producing and selling any good or service is the forgone opportunity to produce any other good or service. If the price of an alternative good changes, then the opportunity cost of producing a particular good changes. This could cause the supply curve to change. For instance, if the video store can offer videos or arcade games with equal ease, an increase in the price of the arcade games could induce the store owner to offer more arcade games and fewer videos. The supply curve of videos would then shift to the left.

A *change in supply* occurs when the quantity supplied at each and every price changes or there is a shift in the supply curve—like the shift from S_1 to S_2 in Figure 7(a). A change in one of the determinants of supply brings about a change in supply.

When only the price changes, a greater or smaller quantity is supplied. This is shown as a movement along the supply curve, not as a shift of the curve. A change in

---

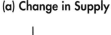 **FIGURE 7** ───

A Change in Supply and a Change in the Quantity Supplied

In Figure 7(a), the quantities that producers are willing and able to offer for sale at every price decrease, causing a leftward shift of the supply curve from S_1 to S_2. In Figure 7(b), the quantities that producers are willing and able to offer for sale increase, due to an increase in the price of the good, causing a movement along the supply curve from point A to point B.

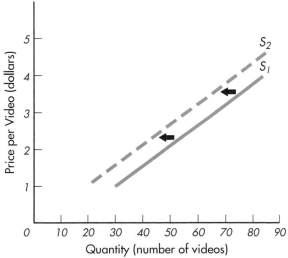

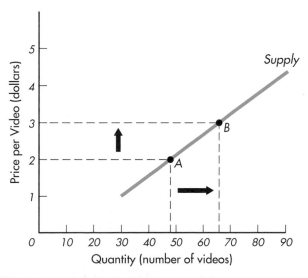

---

price is said to cause a *change in the quantity supplied.* An increase in quantity supplied is shown in the move from point *A* to point *B* on the supply curve of Figure 7(b).

4. Equilibrium: Putting Demand and Supply Together

equilibrium: the price and quantity at which quantity demanded and quantity supplied are equal

The demand curve shows the quantity of a good or service that buyers are willing and able to purchase at each price. The supply curve shows the quantity that producers are willing and able to offer for sale at each price. Only where the two curves intersect is the quantity supplied equal to the quantity demanded. This intersection is the point of **equilibrium.**

4.a. Determination of Equilibrium

4. How is price determined by demand and supply?

disequilibrium: a point at which quantity demanded and quantity supplied are not equal at a particular price

surplus: a quantity supplied that is larger than the quantity demanded at a given price; it occurs whenever the price is greater than the equilibrium price

Figure 8 brings together the market demand and market supply curves for video rentals. The supply and demand schedules are listed in the table and the curves are plotted in the graph in Figure 8. Notice that the curves intersect at only one point, labeled *e,* a price of $3 and a quantity of 66. The intersection point is the equilibrium price, the only price at which the quantity demanded and quantity supplied are the same. You can see that at any other price the quantity demanded and quantity supplied are not the same. These are called **disequilibrium** points.

Whenever the price is greater than the equilibrium price, a **surplus** arises. For example, at $4, the quantity of videos demanded is 48 and the quantity supplied is 84. Thus, at $4 per video there is a surplus of 36 videos—that is, 36 videos are not rented. Conversely, whenever the price is below the equilibrium price, the quantity demanded is greater than the quantity supplied and there is a **shortage.** For instance, if the price is $2 per video, consumers will want and be able to pay for more videos than are available. As shown in the table in Figure 8, the quantity demanded at a price of $2 is 84 but the quantity supplied is only 48. There is a shortage of 36 videos at the price of $2.

Neither a surplus nor a shortage will exist for long if the price of the product is free to change. Producers who are stuck with videos sitting on the shelves getting brittle and out of style will lower the price and reduce the quantities they are offering for rent in order to eliminate a surplus. Conversely, producers whose shelves are

FIGURE 8

Equilibrium

Equilibrium is established at the point where the quantity that suppliers are willing and able to offer for sale is the same as the quantity that buyers are willing and able to purchase. Here, equilibrium occurs at the price of $3 per video and the quantity of 66 videos. It is shown as point e, at the intersection of the demand and supply curves. At prices above $3, the quantity supplied is greater than the quantity demanded, and the result is a surplus. At prices below $3, the quantity supplied is less than the quantity demanded, and the result is a shortage. The area shaded tan shows all prices at which there is a surplus—where quantity supplied is greater than the quantity demanded. The surplus is measured in a horizontal direction at each price. The area shaded blue represents all prices at which a shortage exists—where the quantity demanded is greater than the quantity supplied. The shortage is measured in a horizontal direction at each price.

Price per Video	Quantity Demanded per Year	Quantity Supplied per Year	Status
$5	30	102	Surplus of 72
$4	48	84	Surplus of 36
$3	66	66	Equilibrium
$2	84	48	Shortage of 36
$1	102	30	Shortage of 72

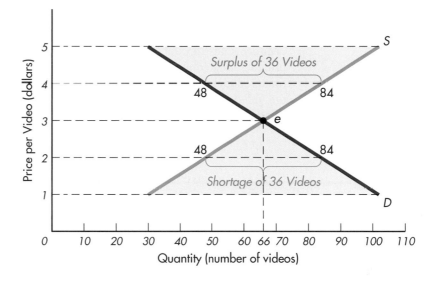

shortage: a quantity supplied that is smaller than the quantity demanded at a given price; it occurs whenever the price is less than the equilibrium price

empty while consumers are demanding videos will acquire more videos and raise the rental price to eliminate a shortage. Surpluses lead to decreases in the price and the quantity supplied and increases in the quantity demanded. Shortages lead to increases in the price and the quantity supplied and decreases in the quantity demanded.

Note that a shortage is not the same thing as scarcity. A shortage exists only when the quantity that people are willing and able to purchase at a particular price is more than the quantity supplied *at that price*. Scarcity occurs when more is wanted at a zero price than is available.

4.b. Changes in the Equilibrium Price: Demand Shifts

Equilibrium is the combination of price and quantity at which the quantities demanded and supplied are the same. Once an equilibrium is achieved, there is no incentive for producers or consumers to move away from it. An equilibrium price changes only when demand and/or supply changes—that is, when the determinants of demand or determinants of supply change.

Let's consider a change in demand and what it means for the equilibrium price. Suppose that experiments on rats show that watching videos causes brain damage. As a result, a large segment of the human population decides not to rent videos. Stores find that the demand for videos has decreased, as shown in Figure 9 by a leftward shift of the demand curve, from curve D_1 to curve D_2.

Once the demand curve has shifted, the original equilibrium price of $3 per video at point e_1 is no longer equilibrium. At a price of $3, the quantity supplied is still 66, but the quantity demanded has declined to 48 (look at the demand curve D_2 at a price of $3). There is, therefore, a surplus of 18 videos at the price of $3.

With a surplus comes downward pressure on the price. This downward pressure occurs because producers acquire fewer videos to offer for rent and reduce the rental price in an attempt to rent the videos that are sitting on the shelves. Producers continue reducing the price and the quantity available until consumers rent all copies of the videos that the sellers have available, or until a new equilibrium is established. That new equilibrium occurs at point e_2 with a price of $2.50 and a quantity of 57.

FIGURE 9

The Effects of a Shift of the Demand Curve

The initial equilibrium price ($3 per video) and quantity (66 videos) are established at point e_1, where the initial demand and supply curves intersect. A change in the tastes for videos causes demand to decrease, and the demand curve shifts to the left. At $3 per video, the initial quantity supplied, 66 videos, is now greater than the quantity demanded, 48 videos. The surplus of 18 units causes producers to reduce production and lower the price. The market reaches a new equilibrium, at point e_2, $2.50 per video and 57 videos.

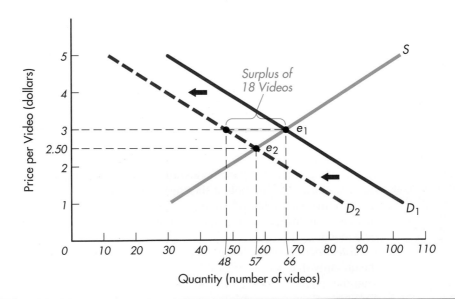

The decrease in demand is represented by the leftward shift of the demand curve. A decrease in demand results in a lower equilibrium price and a lower equilibrium quantity as long as there is no change in supply. Conversely, an increase in demand would be represented as a rightward shift of the demand curve and would result in a higher equilibrium price and a higher equilibrium quantity as long as there is no change in supply.

4.c. Changes in the Equilibrium Price: Supply Shifts

The equilibrium price and quantity may be altered by a change in supply as well. If the price of relevant resources, technology and productivity, expectations of producers, the number of producers, or the prices of related products change, supply changes.

Let's consider an example. Petroleum is a key ingredient in videotapes. Suppose the quantity of oil available is reduced by 40 percent, causing the price of oil to rise. Every video manufacturer has to pay more for oil, which raises the cost of videos. The higher cost means that the rental stores are going to have to pay more for each videotape. To purchase the videos and offer them for rent, the rental stores must receive a higher rental price in order to cover their higher costs. This is represented by a leftward shift of the supply curve in Figure 10.

The leftward shift of the supply curve, from curve S_1 to curve S_2, leads to a new equilibrium price and quantity. At the original equilibrium price of $3 at point e_1,

---

FIGURE 10

The Effects of a Shift of the Supply Curve

The initial equilibrium price and quantity are $3 and 66 units, at point e_1. When the price of oil increases, suppliers are willing and able to offer fewer videos for rent at each price. The result is a leftward (upward) shift of the supply curve, from S_1 to S_2. At the old price of $3, the quantity demanded is still 66, but the quantity

supplied falls to 48. The shortage is 18 videos. The shortage causes suppliers to acquire more videos to offer for rent and to raise the rental price. The new equilibrium, e_2, the intersection between curves S_2 and D, is $3.50 per video and 57 videos.

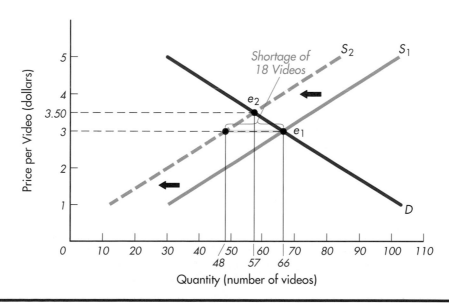

66 videos are supplied. After the shift in the supply curve, 48 videos are offered for rent at a price of $3 apiece, and there is a shortage of 18 videos. The shortage puts upward pressure on price. As the price rises, consumers decrease the quantities that they are willing and able to rent, and sellers increase the quantities that they are willing and able to supply. Eventually, a new equilibrium price and quantity is established at $3.50 and 57 videos at point e_2.

The decrease in supply is represented by the leftward shift of the supply curve. A decrease in supply with no change in demand results in a higher price and a lower quantity. Conversely, an increase in supply would be represented as a rightward shift of the supply curve. An increase in supply with no change in demand would result in a lower price and a higher quantity.

4.d. International Effects

The law of demand says that the amount of a good or service that people are willing and able to purchase during a particular period of time falls as the price rises and rises as the price falls. It does not indicate whether those people are residents of the United States or of some other country. The demand for a product that is available to residents of other countries as well as to residents of the United States will consist of the sum of the demands by U.S. and foreign residents. However, because nations use different monies or currencies, the demand will be affected by the rate at which the different currencies are exchanged. As pointed out in the Global Business Insight "The Foreign Exchange Market," an **exchange rate,** the rate at which monies of different countries are exchanged, can be thought of as the price of one country's money in terms of another country's money. If the exchange rate changes, then the foreign price of a good produced in the United States will change. To illustrate this, let's consider an example using Levi's blue jeans sold to both U.S. and Japanese customers. The Japanese currency is the yen (¥). In March 2003, it took 118 yen to purchase one dollar. Suppose that a pair of Levi's blue jeans is priced at $20 in the United States. That dollar price in terms of yen is 2,360. The exchange rate between the yen and the dollar means that ¥2,360 converts to $20; ¥2,360 = $20 × 118/$. In July of 1999 the exchange rate was ¥124 per dollar. If the U.S. price of the blue jeans was $20, in Japan, the yen value of the blue jeans would be $20 × ¥124/$ = ¥2,480. The blue jeans were less expensive in Japan because of the exchange rate change, even though the U.S. price of blue jeans did not change. The demand for U.S. blue jeans would have risen from July 1999 to January 2003 simply because of the exchange rate change. Thus, changes in exchange rates can affect the demand for goods. At constant U.S. prices, demand curves for U.S. goods will shift around as exchange rates change and foreign purchases fluctuate.

Many firms purchase supplies from other nations, or even locate factories and produce in other nations. Events in other parts of the world can influence their costs and thus the amounts they are willing to supply. Nike purchases its shoes from manufacturers in other parts of the world, particularly Asia. Suppose the manufacturing costs in Malaysia are 78 ringgit. In 1997 the exchange rate was .3150 U.S. dollars to the ringgit, so that manufacturing costs in terms of dollars were $24.57 (.3150 × 78). In March 2003, the exchange rate had fallen to .380 U.S. dollars to the ringgit. With the same manufacturing costs of 78 ringgit, the dollar costs had risen to $29.64 (.380 × 78). Thus, the costs to Nike had risen over the years without any changes in production. This means the supply curve of Nike shoes had shifted in.

exchange rate: the rate at which monies of different countries are exchanged

The Foreign Exchange Market

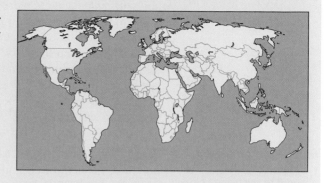

Most countries have their own national currency. England has the pound sterling, Japan the yen, the United States the dollar, and so on. The citizens of each country use their national currency to carry out transactions. For transactions among nations to occur, however, some exchange of foreign currencies is necessary.

Americans buy Toyotas and Nissans from Japan, while U.S. computer companies sell pocket calculators to businesses in Mexico. Some Americans open bank accounts in Switzerland, while U.S. real estate companies sell property to citizens in England. These transactions require the acquisition of a foreign currency. An English business that wants to buy property in the United States will have to exchange pounds sterling for dollars. A U.S. car distributor that imports Toyotas will have to exchange dollars for yen in order to pay the Toyota manufacturer.

The exchange of currency and the determination of the value of national currencies occur in the foreign exchange market. This is not a tightly organized market operating in a building in New York. Usually, the term *foreign exchange market* refers to the trading that occurs among large international banks. Such trading is global and is done largely through telephone and computer communication systems. If, for example, a foreign exchange trader at First Chicago Bank calls a trader at Bank of Tokyo to buy $1 million worth of Japanese yen, that is a foreign exchange market transaction. Banks buy and sell currencies according to the needs and demands of their customers. Business firms and individuals largely rely on banks to buy and sell foreign exchange for them.

The price of one currency expressed in terms of another currency is called a *foreign exchange rate*, or just *exchange rate*. You can think of an exchange rate as the number of dollars it costs to purchase one unit of another country's currency. For instance, how many dollars does it take to purchase one unit of Japan's currency, the yen? One yen (¥) costs about $.008, or eight-tenths of a cent. The list that follows shows the number of U.S. dollars it took to purchase one unit of several different nations' currencies in March 2003.

Number of U.S. Dollars Needed to Purchase One . . .	
Australian dollar	.6087
Canadian dollar	.6742
Euro	1.0804
Japanese yen	.00847
Russian ruble	.03169
Swedish krona	.1187
Swiss franc	.7398
United Kingdom pound	1.5731

6. What happens when price is not allowed to change with market forces?

4.e. Equilibrium in Reality

We have examined a hypothetical (imaginary) market for video rentals in order to represent what goes on in real markets. We have established that the price of a good or service is defined by an equilibrium between demand and supply. We noted that an equilibrium could be disturbed by a change in demand, a change in supply, or simultaneous changes in demand and supply. The important point of this discussion is to demonstrate that when not in equilibrium, the price and the quantities demanded and/or supplied change until equilibrium is established. The market is always attempting to reach equilibrium.

Looking at last year's sweaters piled up on the sale racks, waiting over an hour for a table at a restaurant, finding that the VCR rental store doesn't have a copy of the movie you want to rent in stock, or hearing that 5 or 6 percent of people who are willing and able to work are unemployed may make you wonder whether equilibrium is ever established. In fact, it is not uncommon to observe situations where quantities demanded and supplied are not equal. But this observation does not cast doubt on the usefulness of the equilibrium concept. Even if not all markets clear, or reach equilibrium, all the time, we can be reasonably assured that market forces are operating so that the market is moving toward an equilibrium. The market forces exist even when the price is not allowed to change, as illustrated in the following section.

price floor: a situation in which the price is not allowed to decrease below a certain level

4.e.1. Price Ceilings and Price Floors   A **price floor** is a situation in which the price is not allowed to decrease below a certain level. Consider Figure 11, representing the market for sugar. The equilibrium price of sugar is $.10 a pound, but because the government has set a price floor of $.20 a pound, as shown by the solid yellow line, the price is not allowed to move to its equilibrium level. A surplus of 250,000 pounds of sugar results from the price floor. Sugar growers produce 1 million pounds of sugar and consumers purchase 750,000 pounds of sugar.

We saw previously that whenever the price is above the equilibrium price, market forces work to decrease the price. The price floor interferes with the functioning of the market; a surplus exists because the government will not allow the price to drop. How does the government ensure that the price floor remains in force? It has to purchase the excess sugar. The government must purchase the surplus so that its price floor of $.20 per pound remains in force.

What would occur if the government had set the price floor at $.09 a pound? Since at $.09 a pound a shortage of sugar would result, the price would rise. A price floor only keeps the price from falling, not rising. So the price rises to its equilibrium level of $.10. Only if the price floor is set above the equilibrium price is it an effective price floor.

FIGURE 11

A Price Floor

The equilibrium price of sugar is $.10 a pound, but because the government has set a price floor of $.20 a pound, as shown by the solid yellow line, the price is not allowed to move to its equilibrium level. A surplus of 250,000 pounds of sugar results from the price floor. Sugar growers produce 1 million pounds of sugar and consumers purchase 750,000 pounds of sugar.

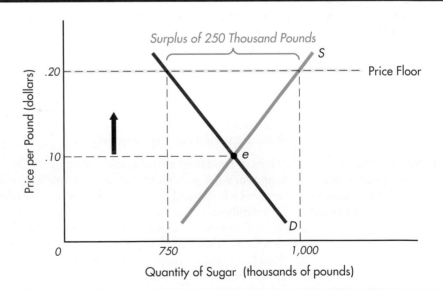

FIGURE 12

Rent Controls

A demand and supply graph representing the market for apartments in New York City is shown. The equilibrium price is $3,000 a month. The government has set a price of $1,500 a month. The government's price ceiling is shown by the solid yellow line. At the government's price, 3,000 apartments are available but consumers want 6,000. There is a shortage of 3,000 apartments.

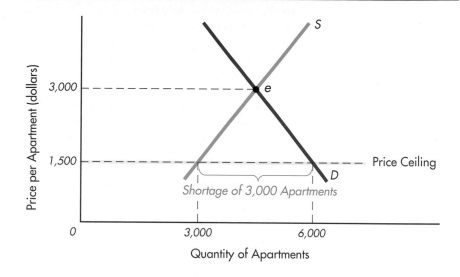

price ceiling: a situation in which the price is not allowed to rise above a certain level

A **price ceiling** is the situation in which a price is not allowed to rise to its equilibrium level. Los Angeles, San Francisco, and New York are among over 125 U.S. cities that have *rent controls*. A rent control law places a ceiling on the rents that landlords can charge for apartments. Figure 12 is a demand and supply graph representing the market for apartments in New York. The equilibrium price is $3,000 a month. The government has set a price of $1,500 a month as the maximum that can be charged. The price ceiling is shown by the solid yellow line. At the rent control price of $1,500 per month, 3,000 apartments are available but consumers want 6,000 apartments. There is a shortage of 3,000 apartments.

The shortage means that not everyone who is willing and able to purchase an apartment will be allowed to. Since the price is not allowed to ration the apartments, something else will have to. It may be that those who are willing and able to stand in line the longest get the apartments. Perhaps bribing an important official might be the way to get an apartment. Perhaps relatives of officials or important citizens will get the apartments. Whenever a price ceiling exists, a shortage results and some rationing device other than price will arise.

Had the government set the rent control price at $4,000 per month, the price ceiling would not have had an effect. Since the equilibrium is $3,000 a month, the price would not have risen to $4,000. Only if the price ceiling is below the equilibrium price will it be an effective price ceiling.

Price ceilings are not uncommon in the United States or in other economies. China had a severe housing shortage for 30 years because the price of housing was kept below equilibrium. Faced with unhappy citizens and realizing the cause of the shortage, officials began to lift the restrictions on housing prices in 1985. The shortage has diminished. In the former Soviet Union, prices on all goods and services were defined by the government. For most consumer items, the price was set below equilibrium; shortages existed. The long lines of people waiting to purchase food or clothing were the result of the price ceilings on all goods and services. In the United States, price ceilings on all goods and services have been imposed at times. During the First and Second World Wars and during the Nixon administration of the early

1970s, wage and price controls were imposed. These were price ceilings on all goods and services. As a result of the ceilings, people were unable to purchase many of the products they desired. The Organization of Petroleum Exporting Countries (OPEC) restricted the quantity of oil in the early 1970s and drove its price up considerably. The U.S. government responded by placing a price ceiling on gasoline. The result was long lines at gas stations—shortages of gasoline.

Price floors are quite common in economies as well. The agricultural policies of most of the developed nations are founded on price floors—the government guarantees that the price of an agricultural product will not fall below some level. Price floors result in surpluses, and this has been the case with agricultural products as well. The surpluses in agricultural products in the United States have resulted in cases where dairy farmers dumped milk in the river, where grain was given to other nations at taxpayer expense, and where citrus ranchers picked and then discarded thousands of tons of citrus, all to reduce huge surpluses.

There are many reasons other than price ceilings and price floors why we observe excess supplies or demands in the real world. In most cases, the excess demands or supplies are due to the difficulty of changing prices rapidly or to the desires of either the demanders or suppliers not to have prices change rapidly. We shall consider many such cases in the text. The important part of the discussion in this chapter is to keep in mind that unless the price is not allowed to change, surpluses and shortages will put pressure on the price to move to its equilibrium level.

RECAP

1. Equilibrium occurs when the quantity demanded and quantity supplied are equal: it is the price-quantity combination where the demand and supply curves intersect.

2. A price that is above the equilibrium price creates a surplus. Producers are willing and able to offer more for sale than buyers are willing and able to purchase.

3. A price that is below the equilibrium price leads to a shortage, because buyers are willing and able to purchase more than producers are willing and able to offer for sale.

4. When demand changes, price and quantity change in the same direction—both rise as demand increases and both fall as demand decreases.

5. When supply changes, price and quantity change, but not in the same direction. When supply increases, price falls and quantity rises. When supply decreases, price rises and quantity falls.

6. When both demand and supply change, the direction of the change in price and quantity depends on the relative sizes of the changes of demand and supply.

7. The exchange rate is a determinant of demand when a good is sold in both the United States and other countries. It is also a determinant of supply because it affects the costs of producing goods.

8. A price floor is a situation in which a price is set above the equilibrium price. This creates a surplus.

9. A price ceiling is a case in which a price is set below the equilibrium price. This creates a shortage.

Summary

❓ What is a market?

1. A market is where buyers and sellers trade a well-defined good or service. *§1*

❓ What is demand?

2. Demand is the quantities that buyers are willing and able to buy at alternative prices. *§2*

3. The quantity demanded is a specific amount at one price. *§2*

4. The law of demand states that as the price of a well-defined commodity rises (falls), the quantity demanded during a given period of time will fall (rise), everything else held constant. *§2.a*

5. Demand will change when one of the determinants of demand changes, that is, when income, tastes, prices of related goods and services, expectations, or number of buyers change. A demand change is illustrated as a shift of the demand curve. *§2.e*

❓ What is supply?

6. Supply is the quantities that sellers will offer for sale at alternative prices. *§3.a*

7. The quantity supplied is the amount that sellers offer for sale at one price. *§3.a*

8. The law of supply states that as the price of a well-defined commodity rises (falls), the quantity supplied during a given period of time will rise (fall), everything else held constant. *§3.a*

9. Supply changes when one of the determinants of supply changes, that is, when prices of resources, technology and productivity, expectations of producers, the number of producers, or the prices of related goods or services change. A supply change is illustrated as a shift of the supply curve. *§3.d*

❓ How is price determined by demand and supply?

10. Together, demand and supply determine the equilibrium price and quantity. *§4*

❓ What causes price to change?

11. A price that is above equilibrium creates a surplus, which leads to a lower price. A price that is below equilibrium creates a shortage, which leads to a higher price. *§4.a*

12. A change in demand or a change in supply (a shift of either curve) will cause the equilibrium price and quantity to change. *§4.b, 4.c*

13. The exchange rate affects the price of foreign-produced goods and services because both demand and supply are affected by the rate at which the different currencies are exchanged. *§4.d*

❓ What happens when price is not allowed to change with market forces?

14. Markets are not always in equilibrium, but forces work to move them toward equilibrium. *§4.e*

15. A price floor is a situation in which a price is not allowed to decrease below a certain level—it is set above the equilibrium price. This creates a surplus. A price ceiling is a case in which a price is not allowed to rise—it is set below the equilibrium price. This creates a shortage. *§4.e*

Key Terms

market *§1.a*

barter *§1.b*

double coincidence of wants *§1.b*

transaction costs *§1.b*

relative price *§1.c*

demand *§2*

quantity demanded *§2*

law of demand *§2.a*

determinants of demand *§2.a*

demand schedule *§2.b*

demand curve *§2.c*

normal goods *§2.e.1*

inferior goods *§2.e.1*

substitute goods *§2.e.3*

complementary goods *§2.e.3*

supply *§3.a*

quantity supplied *§3.a*

law of supply *§3.a*

Exercises

1. Illustrate each of the following events using a demand and supply diagram for bananas.

   a. Reports surface that imported bananas are infected with a deadly virus.
   b. Consumers' incomes drop.
   c. The price of bananas rises.
   d. The price of oranges falls.
   e. Consumers expect the price of bananas to decrease in the future.

2. Answer true or false, and if the statement is false, change it to make it true. Illustrate your answers on a demand and supply graph.

   a. An increase in demand is represented by a movement up the demand curve.
   b. An increase in supply is represented by a movement up the supply curve.
   c. An increase in demand without any changes in supply will cause the price to rise.
   d. An increase in supply without any changes in demand will cause the price to rise.

3. Using the following schedule, define the equilibrium price and quantity. Describe the situation at a price of $10. What will occur? Describe the situation at a price of $2. What will occur?

Price	Quantity Demanded	Quantity Supplied
$1	500	100
$2	400	120
$3	350	150
$4	320	200
$5	300	300
$6	275	410
$7	260	500
$8	230	650
$9	200	800
$10	150	975

4. Suppose the government imposed a minimum price of $7 in the schedule of exercise 3. What would occur? Illustrate.

5. In exercise 3, indicate what the price would have to be to represent an effective price ceiling. Point out the surplus or shortage that results. Illustrate a price floor and provide an example of a price floor.

6. A common feature of skiing is waiting in lift lines. Does the existence of lift lines mean that the price is not working to allocate the scarce resource? If so, what should be done about it?

7. Why don't we observe barter systems as often as we observe the use of currency?

8. A severe drought in California has resulted in a nearly 30 percent reduction in the quantity of citrus grown and produced in California. Explain what effect this event might have on the Florida citrus market.

9. The prices of the Ralph Lauren Polo line of clothing are considerably higher than those of comparable-quality lines. Yet, this line sells more than a J. C. Penney brand line of clothing. Does this violate the law of demand?

10. In December, the price of Christmas trees rises and the quantity of trees sold rises. Is this a violation of the law of demand?

11. In recent years, the price of artificial Christmas trees has fallen while the quality has risen. What impact has this event had on the price of cut Christmas trees?

12. Many restaurants don't take reservations. You simply arrive and wait your turn. If you arrive at 7:30 in the evening, you have at least an hour wait. Notwithstanding that fact, a few people arrive, speak quietly with the maitre d', hand him some money, and are promptly seated. At some restaurants that do take reservations, there is a month wait for a Saturday evening, three weeks for a Friday evening, two weeks for Tuesday through Thursday, and virtually no wait for Sunday or Monday evening. How do you explain these events using demand and supply?

13. Evaluate the following statement: "The demand for U.S. oranges has increased because the quantity of U.S. oranges demanded in Japan has risen."

14. In December 1992, the federal government began requiring that all foods display information about fat content and other ingredients on food packages. The displays had to be verified by independent laborato-ries. The price of an evaluation of a food product could run as much as $20,000. What impact do you think this law had on the market for meat?

15. Draw a PPC. Which combination shown by the PPC will be produced? Does the combination that is produced depend on how goods and services are allocated?

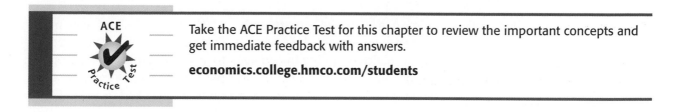

ACE

Practice Test

Take the ACE Practice Test for this chapter to review the important concepts and get immediate feedback with answers.

economics.college.hmco.com/students

A Sleuth for Landlords with Eviction in Mind

The silver Cadillac trolled by the stately red brick home a few times and then stopped in front. Two men in black suits and sunglasses stepped out of the car, drawing nervous glances from a crew of gardeners silently pruning bushes in an exclusive Westchester County neighborhood overlooking Long Island Sound.

After fishing something out of the trunk, one of the men, the stocky, bald fellow with the handlebar mustache, began walking toward the house. A private investigator named Vincent Parco, he wasn't playing games. His client wanted results, not excuses.

Suddenly, he reached into his bulging coat pocket. He pulled out a small video camera. He began filming the house, zooming in on the number on the mailbox and the license plates on the minivan in the driveway.

Mr. Parco is not the kind of P.I. who snaps photographs of married men in love nests with women who are not their wives. His specialty is getting the goods on people who two-time their landlords.

The owner of the house, he said, also had a rent-controlled apartment on East 83rd Street in Manhattan. The landlord of that building hired Mr. Parco in hopes of proving that the tenant has no right to remain in the apartment at below-market rent. Under state and city rent laws, those who benefit from rent regulation must use their apartments as their primary residences. Basically, that means they must live there at least half the time. . . .

In the case of an occupied apartment, if a landlord can prove in Housing Court that a tenant is spending less than 183 nights per year in the apartment, the landlord has a chance of evicting the tenant. Or he may simply have enough leverage to persuade the tenant to accept a modest buyout offer.

Then the landlord can try to deregulate the place and convert it to a condominium or co-op, or put it on the open rental market, often for many times the previous rent. . . .

Some landlord groups estimate that 20 percent of those who lease rent-regulated apartments do not use the apartment as their primary residence. These include the pied-a-terre set as well as tenants illegally subletting, those with suspected connections to prostitution, gambling and drugs, and those who use the apartments for commercial or professional purposes. . . .

COREY KILGANNON

New York Times/March 26, 2000

Rent controls, at their simplest, can be represented as a price ceiling (see figure, below left). A rent control could be represented as a maximum, or ceiling price, of P_m, which is less than the equilibrium price P_1. This price ceiling creates a shortage: At the rent-control price P_m, the quantity of housing units demanded is Q_d while the quantity of housing units supplied is only Q_s. The difference, $Q_d - Q_s$ is the number of families who are willing and able to rent a house at price P_m but for whom there are no homes available.

How is this excess demand resolved? Two things occur. One is that something other than price serves as the allocator. Common replacements for price are: first-come, first-served; preferences of the landlord; or black market or under-the-table payoffs. The second is that the landlord decreases the maintenance on the existing rentals, and new rental units are not brought to the market. As the landlord experiences a lower return on the rental housing, he or she has a lower incentive to devote resources to the upkeep of the unit. As a result, the quality of the housing deteriorates. Unable to secure what he or she considers a fair return, the landlord has no incentive to make improvements or maintain the property.

Not only does rent control lead to deterioration, but the lower return on the rental housing means that some landlords may convert their units to condominiums or to commercial properties and sell them. Over time, the supply of rental housing declines. The supply curve shifts in, to S_2 in the figure, below right, creating greater excess demand.

In the case of rent controls in New York, the inability of price to do the rationing of scarce apartments has created a cottage industry—the market for sleuths who discover tenants who are not using the rent-controlled apartment as specified by law. This industry would not exist if there were no rent controls. The cost of the industry is initially borne by the landlords whose costs of doing business rise, and thus, the supply curve shifts in further, driving rents even higher.

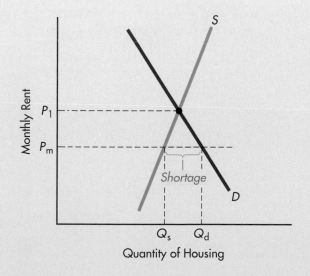

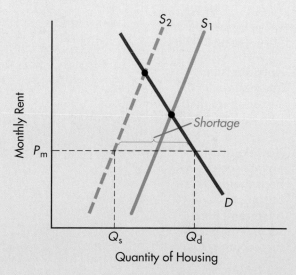

CHAPTER 4

The Market System and the Private Sector

Fundamental Questions

1. **In a market system, who decides what goods and services are produced and how they are produced, and who obtains the goods and services that are produced?**

2. **What is a household, and what is household income and spending?**

3. **What is a business firm, and what is business spending?**

4. **How does the international sector affect the economy?**

5. **How do the three private sectors—households, businesses, and the international sector—interact in the economy?**

You decide to buy a new Toyota, so you go to a Toyota dealer and exchange money for the car. The Toyota dealer has rented land and buildings and hired workers in order to make cars available to you and other members of the public. The employees earn incomes paid by the Toyota dealer and then use their incomes to buy food from the grocery store. This transaction generates revenue for the grocery store, which hires workers and pays them incomes that they then use to buy groceries and Toyotas. Your expenditure for the Toyota is part of a circular flow. Revenue is received by the Toyota dealer, who pays employees, who, in turn, buy goods and services.

Of course, the story is complicated by the fact that the Toyota is originally manufactured and purchased in Japan and then shipped to the United States before it can be sold by the local Toyota dealer. Your purchase of the Toyota creates revenue for the local dealer as well as for the manufacturer in Japan, who pays Japanese autoworkers to produce Toyotas. Furthermore, when you buy your Toyota, you must pay a tax to the government, which uses tax revenues to pay for police protection, national defense, the legal system, and other services. Many people in different areas of the economy are involved.

An economy is made up of individual buyers and sellers. Economists could discuss the neighborhood economy that surrounds your university, the economy of the city of Chicago, or the economy of the state of Massachusetts. But typically it is the national economy, the economy of the United States, that is the center of their attention. To clarify the operation of the national economy, economists usually group individual buyers and sellers into three sectors: households, businesses, and government. Omitted from this grouping, however, is an important source of activity, the international sector. Since the U.S. economy affects, and is affected by, the rest of the world, in order to understand how the economy functions, we must include the international sector.

We begin this chapter by examining the way that buyers and sellers interact in a market system. The impersonal forces of supply and demand operate to answer the following questions: Who determines what is produced and how it is produced? Who gets the output that is produced? The answers are given by the market system and involve the private-sector participants: households, business firms, and the international sector. Government also plays a major role in answering these questions, but we leave government and its role for the next chapter.

Following the discussion of the market system, we examine basic data and information on each individual sector with the objective of answering some general questions: What is a household, and how do households spend their incomes? What is a business firm, and how does a corporation differ from a partnership? What does it mean if the United States has a trade deficit?

After describing the three sectors that make up the private sector of the national economy, we present a simple economic model to illustrate the interrelationships linking all the individual sectors into the national economy. ▪

1. In a market system, who decides what goods and services are produced and how they are produced, and who obtains the goods and services that are produced?

1. The Market System

As we learned in Chapter 2, the production possibilities curve represents all possible combinations of goods and services that a society can produce if its resources are used fully and efficiently. Which combination, that is, which point on the PPC, will society choose? In a price or market system, the answer is given by demand and supply.

1.a. Consumer Sovereignty

In recent years, time-starved Americans spent about as much time eating out as they did eating at home. In the 1950s and 1960s, this trend was just beginning. Consumers wanted more and more restaurants and fast-food outlets. As a result, McDonald's, Wendy's, Big Boy, White Castle, Pizza Hut, Godfather's Pizza, and other fast-food outlets flourished. The trend toward eating away from home reached fever pitch in the late 1970s, when the average number of meals per person eaten out (excluding brown-bag lunches and other meals prepared at home but eaten elsewhere) exceeded one per day.

In the 1980s, people wanted the fast food but didn't want to go get it. By emphasizing delivery, Domino's Pizza and a few other fast-food outlets became very successful. In the 1990s, the takeout taxi business—where restaurant food is delivered to homes—grew 10 percent per year, and it remains very popular today. However, the star of this story is not Domino's, Pizza Hut, or other restaurants. It is the consumer. In a market system, if consumers are willing and able to pay for more restaurant meals, more restaurants appear. If consumers are willing and able to pay for food delivered to their homes, food is delivered to their homes.

Why does the consumer wield such power? The name of the game for business is profit, and the only way business can make a profit is by satisfying consumer wants. The consumer, not the politician or the business firm, ultimately determines what is to be produced. A firm that produces something that no consumers want will not remain in business very long. **Consumer sovereignty**—the authority of consumers to determine what is produced through their purchases of goods and services—dictates what goods and services will be produced. Supermarkets and grocery stores are responding to the consumer as well, by putting fast-food restaurants, like Pizza Hut and Taco Bell, inside their stores.

consumer sovereignty: the authority of consumers to determine what is produced through their purchases of goods and services

1.b. Profit and the Allocation of Resources

When a good or service seems to have the potential to generate a profit, someone with entrepreneurial ability will put together the resources needed to produce that good or service. An individual with entrepreneurial ability aims to earn a profit by renting land, hiring labor, and using capital to produce a good or service that can be sold for more than the sum of rent, wages, and interest. If the potential profit turns into a loss, the entrepreneur may stop buying resources and turn to some other occupation or project. The resources used in the losing operation would then be available for use in an activity where they would be more highly valued.

To illustrate how resources get allocated in the market system, let's look at the market for fast foods. Figure 1 shows a change in demand for meals eaten in

A Demand Change in the Market for in-Restaurant Food

In Figure 1(a), the initial market-clearing price (P_1) and market-clearing quantity (Q_1) are shown. In Figure 1(b), the market-clearing price and quantity change from P_1 and Q_1 to P_2 and Q_2 as the demand curve shifts to the left because of a change in tastes. The result of decreased demand is a lower price and a lower quantity produced.

(a) Restaurant Market

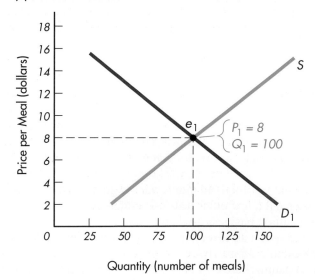

(b) The Effect of a Change in Tastes

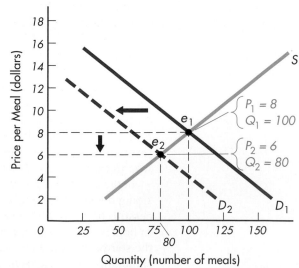

FIGURE 2

A Demand Change in the Market for Delivered Food

n Figure 2(a), the initial market-clearing price (P_1) and quantity (Q_1) are shown. In Figure 2(b), the demand for delivered food increases, thus driving up the market- clearing price (P_2) and quantity (Q_2), as the demand curve shifts to the right, from D_1 to D_2.

(a) Delivery Market

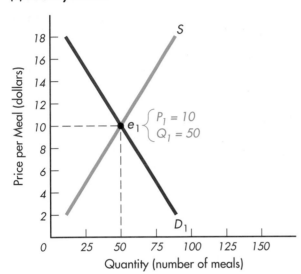

(b) The Effect of a Change in Tastes

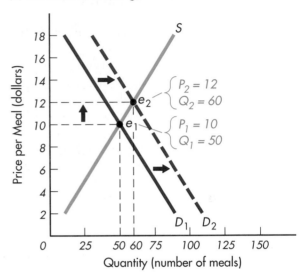

restaurants each month. The initial demand curve, D_1, and supply curve, S, are shown in Figure 1(a). With these demand and supply curves, the equilibrium price (P_1) is \$8, and the equilibrium quantity (Q_1) is 100 units (meals). At this price-quantity combination, the number of meals demanded equals the number of meals sold; equilibrium is reached, so we say the market clears (there is no shortage or surplus).

The second part of the figure shows what happened when consumer tastes changed, and people preferred to have food delivered to their homes. This change in tastes caused the demand for restaurant meals to decline and is represented by a leftward shift of the demand curve, from D_1 to D_2, in Figure 1(b). The demand curve shifted to the left because fewer in-restaurant meals were demanded at each price. Consumer tastes, not the price of in-restaurant meals, changed first. (A price change would have led to a change in the quantity demanded and would be represented by a move *along* demand curve D_1.) The change in tastes caused a change in demand and a leftward shift of the demand curve. The shift from D_1 to D_2 created a new equilibrium point. The equilibrium price (P_2) decreased to \$6, and the equilibrium quantity (Q_2) decreased to 80 units (meals).

While the market for in-restaurant food was changing, so was the market for delivered food. People substituted meals delivered to their homes for meals eaten in restaurants. Figure 2(a) shows the original demand for food delivered to the home. Figure 2(b) shows a rightward shift of the demand curve, from D_1 to D_2, representing increased demand for home delivery. This demand change resulted in a higher market-clearing price for food delivered to the home, from $10 to $12.

The changing profit potential of the two markets induced existing firms to switch from in-restaurant service to home delivery and for new firms to offer delivery from the start. Domino's Pizza, which is a delivery-only firm, grew from a one-store operation to become the second largest pizza chain in the United States. Pizza Hut, which at first did not offer home delivery, had to play catch-up; and by 1992, about two-thirds of Pizza Hut's more than 5,000 restaurants were delivering pizza.

As the market-clearing price of in-restaurant fast food fell (from $8 to $6 in Figure 1), the quantity of in-restaurant meals sold also declined (from 100 to 80) because the decreased demand, lower price, and resulting lower profit induced some firms to decrease production. In the delivery business, the opposite occurred. As the market-clearing price rose (from $10 to $12 in Figure 2[b]), the number of meals delivered also rose (from 50 to 60). The increased demand, higher price, and resulting higher profit induced firms to increase production.

Why did the production of delivered foods increase while the production of meals at restaurants decreased? Not because of government decree. Not because of the desires of the business sector, especially the owners of restaurants. The consumer—consumer sovereignty—made all this happen. Businesses that failed to respond to consumer desires and failed to provide the desired good at the lowest price failed to survive.

1.c. The Flow of Resources

After demand shifted to home-delivered food, the resources that had been used in the restaurants were available for use elsewhere. A few former waiters, waitresses, and cooks were able to get jobs in the delivery firms. Some of the equipment used in eat-in restaurants—ovens, pots, and pans—was purchased by the delivery firms; and some of the ingredients that previously would have gone to the eat-in restaurants were bought by the delivery firms. A few former employees of the eat-in restaurants became employed at department stores, at local pubs, and at hotels. Some of the equipment was sold as scrap; other equipment was sold to other restaurants. In other words, the resources moved from an activity where their value was relatively low to an activity where they were more highly valued. No one commanded the resources to move. They moved because they could earn more in some other activity.

Adam Smith described this phenomenon in his 1776 treatise *The Wealth of Nations,* saying it was as if an invisible hand reached out and guided the resources to their most-valued use. That invisible hand is the self-interest that drives firms to provide what consumers want to buy, leads consumers to use their limited incomes to buy the goods and services that bring them the greatest satisfaction, and induces resource owners to supply resource services where they are most highly valued. (There is more about Smith in the Economic Insight "Adam Smith.")

Competitive firms produce in the manner that minimizes costs and maximizes profits.

Firms produce the goods and services and use the resources that enable them to generate the highest profits. If one firm does this better than others, then that firm earns a greater profit than others. Seeing that success, other firms copy or mimic the first firm. If a firm cannot be as profitable as the others, it will eventually go out of business or move to another line of business where it can be successful. In the process of firms always seeking to lower costs and make higher profits, society finds that the goods and services buyers want are produced in the least costly manner. Consumers not only get the goods and services they want and will pay for, but they get these products at the lowest possible price.

Adam Smith

Adam Smith was born in 1723 and reared in Kirkcaldy, Scotland, near Edinburgh. He went to the University of Glasgow when he was 14, and three years later began studies at Oxford, where he stayed for six years. In 1751, Smith became professor of logic and then moral philosophy at Glasgow. From 1764 to 1766, he tutored the future duke of Buccleuch in France, and then he was given a pension for the remainder of his life. Between 1766 and 1776, Smith completed *The Wealth of Nations.* He became commissioner of customs for Scotland and spent his remaining years in Edinburgh. He died in 1790.

Economists date the beginning of their discipline from the publication of *The Wealth of Nations* in 1776. In this major treatise, Smith emphasizes the role of self-interest in the functioning of markets, specialization, and division of labor.

According to Smith, the fundamental explanation of human behavior is found in the rational pursuit of self-interest. Smith uses it to explain how men choose occupations, how farmers till their lands, and how leaders of the American Revolution were led by it to rebellion. Smith did not equate self-interest with selfishness but broadened the definition of self-interest, believing that a person is interested "in the fortune of others and renders their happiness necessary to him,

though he derives nothing from it, except the pleasure of seeing it." On the basis of self-interest, Smith constructed a theory of how markets work: how goods, once produced, are sold to the highest bidders, and how the quantities of the goods that are produced are governed by their costs and selling prices. But Smith's insight showed that this self-interest resulted in the best situation for society as a whole. In a celebrated and often-quoted passage from the treatise Smith says:

> But man has almost constant occasion for the help of his brethren, and it is in vain for him to expect it from their benevolence only. He will be more likely to prevail if he can interest their self-love in his favour, and show them that it is for their own advantage to do for him what he requires of them. . . . It is not from the benevolence of the butcher, the brewer, or the baker, that we can expect our dinner, but from their regard to their own interest.

Source: *An Inquiry into the Nature and Causes of the Wealth of Nations,* edited and with an introduction, notes, marginal summary, and index by Edwin Cannan (Chicago: University of Chicago Press, 1976). Reprinted by permission of the University of Chicago Press.

1.d. The Determination of Income

Consumer demands dictate *what* is produced, and the search for profit defines *how* goods and services are produced. *For whom* are the goods and services produced, that is, who gets the goods and services? In a price or market system, those who have the ability to pay for the products get the products. Your income determines your ability to pay, but where does income come from? Income is obtained by selling the services of resources. When you sell your labor services, your money income reflects your wage rate or salary level. When you sell the services of the capital you own, you receive interest; and when you sell the services of the land you own, you receive rent. A person with entrepreneurial ability earns profit as a payment for services. Thus, we see that buyers and sellers of goods and services and resource owners are linked together in an economy: the more one buys, the more income or revenue the other receives. In the remainder of this chapter, we learn more about the linkages among the sectors of the economy. We classify the buyers and the resource owners into the household sector: the sellers or business firms are the business sector; households and firms in other countries, who may also be buyers and sellers of this country's goods and services, are the international sector. These three sectors—households, business firms, and the international sector—constitute the

Ownership of resources determines who gets what goods and services in a market system.

private sector: households, businesses, and the international sector

public sector: the government

private sector of the economy. In this chapter we focus on the interaction among the components of the private sector. In the next chapter we focus on the **public sector,** government, and examine its role in the economy.

R E C A P

1. In a market system, consumers are sovereign and decide by means of their purchases what goods and services will be produced.

2. In a market system, firms decide how to produce the goods and services that consumers want. In order to earn maximum profits, firms use the least-cost combinations of resources.

3. Income and prices determine who gets what in a market system. Income is determined by the ownership of resources.

?

2. **What is a household, and what is household income and spending?**

household: one or more persons who occupy a unit of housing

2. Households

A **household** consists of one or more persons who occupy a unit of housing. The unit of housing may be a house, an apartment, or even a single room, as long as it constitutes separate living quarters. A household may consist of related family members, like a father, mother, and children, or it may comprise unrelated individuals, like three college students sharing an apartment. The person in whose name the house or apartment is owned or rented is called the *householder.*

2.a. Number of Households and Household Income

There are more than 104 million households in the United States. The breakdown of households by age of householder is shown in Figure 3. Householders between 35

FIGURE 3

Age of Householder, Number of Households, and Median Household Income in the United States

The graph reveals that householders aged 35 to 44 make up the largest number of households, and householders aged 45 to 54 earn the highest median annual income.
Source: U.S. Department of Commerce, Statistical Abstract of the United States, 2002.

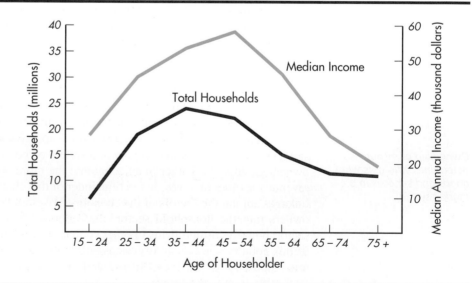

FIGURE 4

Size Distribution of Households in the United States

As the pie chart illustrates, two-person households make up a larger percentage of the total number of house-holds than any other group, a total of 33 percent. Large households with seven or more persons are becoming a rarity, accounting for only 1 percent of the total number of households.
Source: U.S. Department of Commerce, Statistical Abstract of the United States, 2002.

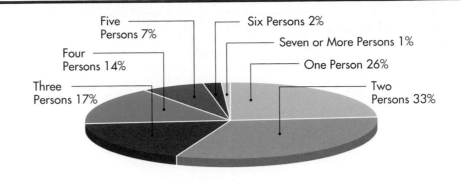

Five Persons 7%
Six Persons 2%
Four Persons 14%
Seven or More Persons 1%
Three Persons 17%
One Person 26%
Two Persons 33%

and 44 years old make up the largest number of households. Householders between 45 and 54 years old have the largest median income. The *median* is the middle value—half of the households in an age group have an income higher than the median, and half have an income lower than the median. Figure 3 shows that house-holds in which the householder is between 45 and 54 years old have a median income of about $58,217, substantially higher than the median incomes of other age groups. Typically, workers in this age group are at the peak of their earning power. Younger households are gaining experience and training; older households include retired workers.

The size distribution of households in the United States is shown in Figure 4. Thirty-three percent of all households are two-person households. The stereotypical household of husband, wife, and two children accounts for only 14 percent of all households. There are relatively few large households. Of the more than 104 million households in the country, only 1 percent have seven or more persons.

In the United States, the average number of people per household is 2.2. Worldwide, average household size in high-income countries (those with average per capita incomes over $9,000 per year) is near that of the United States; that of middle- and low-income countries is more than twice as large.

2.b. Household Spending

consumption: household spending

Household spending is called **consumption.** Householders consume housing, trans-portation, food, entertainment, and other goods and services. Household spending (also called *consumer spending*) per year in the United States is shown in Figure 5, along with household income. The pattern is one of steady increase. Spending by the household sector is the largest component of total spending in the economy—rising to over $6.7 trillion in 2000.

FIGURE 5

Household Spending and Income

Household spending (consumption) and income each year from 1959 to 2002 are shown. Both show a pattern of steady increase. *Source: U.S. Department of Commerce (Bureau of Economic Analysis); www.census.gov.*

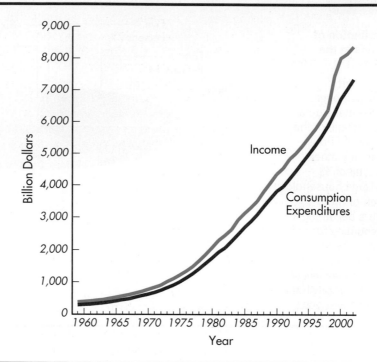

RECAP

1. A household consists of one or more persons who occupy a unit of housing.
2. An apartment or house is rented or owned by a householder.
3. As a group, householders between the ages of 45 and 54 have the highest median incomes.
4. Household spending is called *consumption*.

?

3. What is a business firm, and what is business spending?

3. Business Firms

A **business firm** is a business organization controlled by a single management. The firm's business may be conducted at more than one location. The terms *company, enterprise,* and *business* are used interchangeably with *firm.*

3.a. Forms of Business Organizations

business firm: a business organization controlled by a single management

sole proprietorship: a business owned by one person, who receives all the profits and is responsible for all the debts incurred by the business

Firms are organized as sole proprietorships, partnerships, or corporations. A **sole proprietorship** is a business owned by one person. This type of firm may be a one-person operation or a large enterprise with many employees. In either case, the owner receives all the profits and is responsible for all the debts incurred by the business.

A **partnership** is a business owned by two or more partners who share both the profits of the business and responsibility for the firm's losses. The partners could be individuals, estates, or other businesses.

partnership: a business with two or more owners who share the firm's profits and losses

corporation: a legal entity owned by shareholders whose liability for the firm's losses is limited to the value of the stock they own

multinational business: a firm that owns and operates producing units in foreign countries

A **corporation** is a business whose identity in the eyes of the law is distinct from the identity of its owners. State law allows the formation of corporations. A corporation is an economic entity that, like a person, can own property and borrow money in its own name. The owners of a corporation are shareholders. If a corporation cannot pay its debts, creditors cannot seek payment from the shareholders' personal wealth. The corporation itself is responsible for all its actions. The shareholders liability is limited to the value of the stock they own.

Many firms are global in their operations even though they may have been founded and may be owned by residents of a single country. Firms typically first enter the international market by selling products to foreign countries. As revenues from these sales increase, the firms realize advantages by locating subsidiaries in foreign countries. A **multinational business** is a firm that owns and operates producing units in foreign countries. The best-known U.S. corporations are multinational firms. Ford, IBM, PepsiCo, and McDonald's all own operating units in many different countries. Ford Motor Company, for instance, is the parent firm of sales organizations and assembly plants located around the world. As transportation and communication technologies progress, multinational business activity undoubtedly will grow.

3.b. Business Statistics

In the United States, there are far more sole proprietorships than partnerships or corporations. The great majority of sole proprietorships are small businesses, with revenues under $25,000 a year. Similarly, over half of all partnerships also have revenues under $25,000 a year, but only 23 percent of the corporations are in this category.

The 68 percent of sole proprietorships that earn less than $25,000 a year account for only about 9 percent of the revenue earned by proprietorships. The 0.4 percent of proprietorships with revenue of $1 million or more account for about 19 percent. The figures for partnerships and corporations are even more striking. The 58 percent of partnerships with the smallest revenue account for only 0.4 percent of the total revenue earned by partnerships. At the other extreme, the 5 percent of partnerships with the largest revenue account for 88 percent of total partnership revenue. The 23 percent of corporations in the smallest range account for less than 0.1 percent of total corporate revenue, while the 18 percent of corporations in the largest range account for 94 percent of corporate revenue.

Thus, big business is important in the United States. There are many small firms, but large firms and corporations account for the greatest share of business revenue. Although there are only about one-third as many corporations as sole proprietorships, corporations have more than fifteen times the revenue of sole proprietorships.

3.c. Firms Around the World

Big business is a dominant force in the United States. Many people believe that because the United States is the world's largest economy, U.S. firms are the largest in the world. Figure 6 shows that this is not true. Of the ten largest corporations in the world (measured by sales), four are foreign. Big business is not just a U.S. phenomenon.

3.d. Entrepreneurial Ability

The emphasis on bigness should not hide the fact that many new firms are started each year. Businesses are typically begun as small sole proprietorships. Many of them are forced to go out of business within a year or two. Businesses survive in the long run only if they provide a good or service that people want enough to yield a

FIGURE 6

The World's Ten Largest Public Companies

As shown in the chart, large firms are not just a U.S. phenomenon. Note: This list is accurate as of the end of 2002. Enron is no longer on the list of largest companies. *Source: Fortune Global 500, © 2003 Time Inc. All rights reserved.*

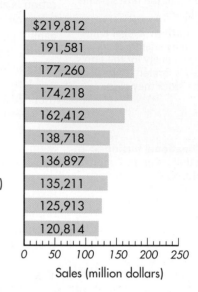

Rank	Firm (country)	Sales (million dollars)
1	Wal-Mart Stores (U.S.)	$219,812
2	Exxon Mobil (U.S.)	191,581
3	General Motors (U.S.)	177,260
4	BP (U.K.)	174,218
5	Ford Motor (U.S.)	162,412
6	Enron (U.S.) [defunct 2003]	138,718
7	DaimlerChrysler (Germany/U.S.)	136,897
8	Royal Dutch/Shell Group (Netherlands)	135,211
9	General Electric (U.S.)	125,913
10	Toyota Motor (Japan)	120,814

profit for the entrepreneur. Although there are fabulous success stories, the failure rate among new firms is high. Thorough research of the market and careful planning play a large part in determining whether a new business succeeds but so can luck, as the Economic Insight "The Successful Entrepreneur" confirms.

That many new businesses fail is a fact of economic life. In the U.S. economy, anyone with an idea and sufficient resources has the freedom to open a business. However, if buyers do not respond to the new offering, the business fails. Only firms that satisfy this "market test" survive. Entrepreneurs thus try to ensure that as wants change, goods and services are produced to satisfy those wants.

3.e. Business Spending

investment: spending on capital goods to be used in producing goods and services

Investment is the expenditures by business firms for capital goods—machines, tools, and buildings—that will be used to produce goods and services. The economic meaning of *investment* is different from the everyday meaning, "a financial transaction such as buying bonds or stocks." In economics, the term *investment* refers to business spending for capital goods.

Investment spending in 2002 was $1,588 billion, an amount equal to roughly one-fourth of consumption, or household spending. Investment spending between 1959 and 2002 is shown in Figure 7. Compare Figures 5 and 7 and notice the different patterns of spending. Investment increases unevenly, actually falling at times and then rising very rapidly. Even though investment spending is much smaller than consumption, business expenditures are an important factor in determining the economic health of the nation. For instance, investment spending declined from 1999 to 2002, causing the U.S. and world economies to grow very slowly or even decline.

The Successful Entrepreneur (Sometimes It's Better to Be Lucky Than Good)

Entrepreneurs do not always develop an abstract idea into reality when starting a new firm. Sometimes people stumble onto a good thing by accident and then are clever enough and willing to take the necessary risk to turn their lucky find into a commercial success.

In 1875, a Philadelphia pharmacist on his honeymoon tasted tea made from an innkeeper's old family recipe. The tea, made from sixteen wild roots and berries, was so delicious that the pharmacist asked the innkeeper's wife for the recipe. When he returned to his pharmacy, he created a solid concentrate of the drink that could be sold for home consumption.

The pharmacist was Charles Hires, a devout Quaker, who intended to sell "Hires Herb Tea" to hard-drinking Pennsylvania coal miners as a nonalcoholic alternative to beer and whiskey. A friend of Hires suggested that miners would not drink anything called "tea" and recommended that he call his drink "root beer."

The initial response to Hires Root Beer was so enthusiastic that Hires soon began nationwide distribution. The yellow box of root beer extract was a familiar sight in homes and drugstore fountains across the United States. By 1895, Hires, who started with a $3,000 loan, was operating a business valued at half a million dollars (a lot of money in 1895) and bottling ready-to-drink root beer across the country.

Hires, of course, is not the only entrepreneur clever enough to turn a lucky discovery into a business success. In 1894, in Battle Creek, Michigan, a sanitarium handyman named Will Kellogg was helping his older brother prepare wheat meal to serve to patients in the sanitarium's dining room. The two men would boil wheat dough and then run it through rollers to produce thin sheets of meal. One day they left a batch of the dough out overnight. The next day, when the dough was run through the rollers, it broke up into flakes instead of forming a sheet.

By letting the dough stand overnight, the Kelloggs had allowed moisture to be distributed evenly to each individual wheat berry. When the dough went through the rollers, the berries formed separate flakes instead of binding together. The Kelloggs toasted the wheat flakes and served them to the patients. They were an immediate success. In fact, the brothers had to start a mail-order flaked-cereal business because patients wanted flaked cereal for their households.

Kellogg saw the market potential for the discovery and started his own cereal company (his brother refused to join him in the business). He was a great promoter who used innovations like four-color magazine ads and free-sample promotions. In New York City, he offered a free box of corn flakes to every woman who winked at her grocer on a specified day. The promotion was considered risqué, but Kellogg's sales in New York increased from two railroad cars of cereal a month to one car a day.

Will Kellogg, a poorly paid sanitarium worker in his mid-forties, became a daring entrepreneur after his mistake with wheat flour led to the discovery of a way to produce flaked cereal. He became one of the richest men in America because of his entrepreneurial ability.

Source: *Entrepreneurs* by Joseph and Suzy Fucini. Hall and Company, 1985.

RECAP

1. Business firms may be organized as sole proprietorships, partnerships, or corporations.
2. Large corporations account for the largest fraction of total business revenue.
3. Many new firms are started each year, but the failure rate is high.
4. Business investment spending fluctuates widely over time.

FIGURE 7

U.S. Investment Spending

Business expenditures on capital goods have been increasing erratically since 1959. *Source:* Economic Report of the President, 2003.

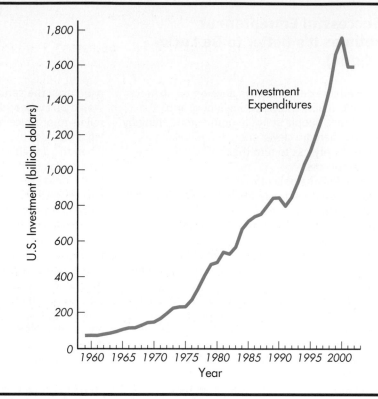

4. The International Sector

4. How does the international sector affect the economy?

Today, foreign buyers and sellers have a significant effect on economic conditions in the United States, and developments in the rest of the world often influence U.S. buyers and sellers. We saw in Chapter 3, for instance, how exchange-rate changes can affect the demand for U.S. goods and services.

4.a. Types of Countries

The nations of the world may be divided into two categories: industrial countries and developing countries. Developing countries greatly outnumber industrial countries (see Figure 8). The World Bank (an international organization that makes loans to developing countries) groups countries according to per capita income (income per person). Low-income economies are those with per capita incomes of $755 or less. Middle-income economies have per capita annual incomes of $756 to $9,265. High-income economies—oil exporters and industrial market economies—are distinguished from the middle-income economies and have per capita incomes of greater than $9,266. Some countries are not members of the World Bank and so are not categorized, and information about a few small countries is so limited that the World Bank is unable to classify them.

It is readily apparent from Figure 8 that low-income economies are heavily concentrated in Africa and Asia. Countries in these regions have a low profile in U.S. trade, although they may receive aid from the United States. U.S. trade is concentrated with its neighbors Canada and Mexico, along with the major industrial powers. Nations in each group present different economic challenges to the United States.

4.a.1. The Industrial Countries

The World Bank uses per capita income to classify twenty-three countries as "industrial market economies." They are listed in the bar chart in Figure 9. The twenty-three countries listed in Figure 9 are among the wealthiest countries in the world. Not appearing on the list are the high-income oil-exporting nations like Libya, Saudi Arabia, Kuwait, and the United Arab Emirates. The World Bank considers those countries to be "still developing."

The economies of the industrial nations are highly interdependent. As conditions change in one country, business firms and individuals may shift large sums of money between countries. As the funds flow from one country to another, economic conditions in one country spread to other countries. As a result, the industrial countries, particularly the major economic powers like the United States, Germany, and Japan, are forced to pay close attention to each other's economic policies.

4.a.2. The Developing Countries

The developing countries provide a different set of issues for the United States from that posed by the industrial countries. In the 1980s, the debts of the developing countries to the developed nations reached tremendous heights. For instance, at the end of 1989. Brazil owed foreign creditors $111.3 billion, Mexico owed $95.6 billion, and Argentina owed $64.7 billion. In

"The best and brightest are leaving." Statements like this are heard in many nations throughout the world. The best trained and most innovative people in many countries find their opportunities greater in the United States. As a result, they leave their countries to gain citizenship in the United States. But it is not easy for people to move from one country to another. The flow of goods and services among nations—international trade— occurs more readily than does the flow of workers.

FIGURE 8

World Economic Development

The colors on the map identify low-income, middle-income, and high-income economies. Countries have been placed in each group on the basis of GNP per capita and, in some instances, other distinguishing economic characteristics. *Source: World Bank, http://nebula. worldbank.org/website/ GNIwdi/viewer.htm.*

Low-income economies
$755 or less

Lower-middle-income economies
$756 to $2,995

Upper-middle-income economies
$2,996 to $9,265

High-income economies
$9,266 or more

No data

each case, the amounts owed were more than several times the annual sales of goods and services by those countries to the rest of the world. The United States had to arrange loans at special terms and establish special trade arrangements in order for those countries to be able to buy U.S. goods.

The United States tends to buy, or *import,* primary products such as agricultural produce and minerals from the developing countries. Products that a country buys from another country are called **imports.** The United States tends to sell, or *export,* manufactured goods to developing countries. Products that a country sells to another country are called **exports.** The United States is the largest producer and exporter of grains and other agricultural output in the world. The efficiency of U.S. farming relative to farming in much of the rest of the world gives the United States a comparative advantage in many agricultural products.

imports: products that a country buys from other countries

exports: products that a country sells to other countries

4.b. International-Sector Spending

Economic activity of the United States with the rest of the world includes U.S. spending on foreign goods and foreign spending on U.S. goods. Figure 10 shows how U.S.

trade surplus: the situation that exists when imports are less than exports

trade deficit: the situation that exists when imports exceed exports

net exports: the difference between the value of exports and the value of imports

exports and imports are spread over different countries. Notice that two countries, Canada and Japan, account for roughly one-third of U.S. exports and more than one-third of U.S. imports. Trade with the industrial countries is approximately twice as large as trade with the developing countries, and U.S. trade with eastern Europe is trivial.

When exports exceed imports, a **trade surplus** exists. When imports exceed exports, a **trade deficit** exists. Figure 10 shows that the United States is importing much more than it exports.

The term **net exports** refers to the difference between the value of exports and the value of imports: net exports equals exports minus imports. Figure 11 traces U.S. net exports over time. Positive net exports represent trade surpluses; negative net exports represent trade deficits. The trade deficits (indicated by negative net exports) starting in the 1980s were unprecedented. Reasons for this pattern of international trade are discussed in later chapters.

FIGURE 9

The Industrial Market Economies

The bar chart lists some of the wealthiest countries in the world. *Source: World Bank,* World Development Report, 2003; *http://devdata. worldbank.org/data_query.*

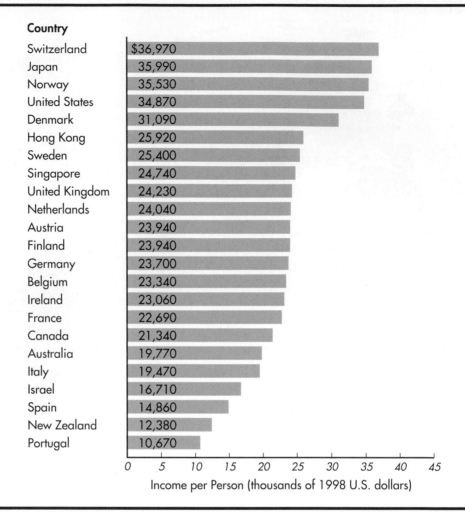

Country

Country	Income
Switzerland	$36,970
Japan	35,990
Norway	35,530
United States	34,870
Denmark	31,090
Hong Kong	25,920
Sweden	25,400
Singapore	24,740
United Kingdom	24,230
Netherlands	24,040
Austria	23,940
Finland	23,940
Germany	23,700
Belgium	23,340
Ireland	23,060
France	22,690
Canada	21,340
Australia	19,770
Italy	19,470
Israel	16,710
Spain	14,860
New Zealand	12,380
Portugal	10,670

Income per Person (thousands of 1998 U.S. dollars)

RECAP

1. The majority of U.S. trade is with the industrial market economies.
2. Exports are products sold to foreign countries: imports are products bought from foreign countries.
3. Exports minus imports equal net exports.
4. Positive net exports signal a trade surplus: negative net exports signal a trade deficit.

5. How do the three private sectors—households, businesses, and the international sector—interact in the economy?

5. Linking the Sectors

Now that we have an idea of the size and structure of each of the private sectors—households, businesses, and international—let's discuss how the sectors interact.

FIGURE 10

Direction of U.S. Trade

This chart shows that a trade deficit exists for the United States, since U.S. imports greatly exceed U.S. exports. The chart also shows that trade with western Europe, Japan, and Canada accounts for about half of U.S. trade.
Source: Economic Report of the President, 2003; *www.census.gov/foreign_trade.*

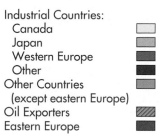

Industrial Countries:
  Canada
  Japan
  Western Europe
  Other
Other Countries
  (except eastern Europe)
Oil Exporters
Eastern Europe

U.S. Exports to:

$684

U.S. Imports from:

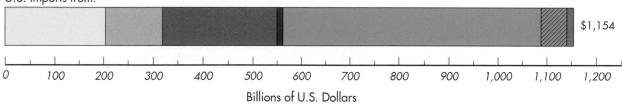

$1,154

0   100   200   300   400   500   600   700   800   900   1,000   1,100   1,200

Billions of U.S. Dollars

FIGURE 11

U.S. Net Exports

Prior to the late 1960s, the United States generally exported more than it imported and had a trade surplus. Since 1976, net exports have been negative, and the United States has had a trade deficit. *Source:* Economic Report of the President, 2003; *www.census.gov/foreign_trade.*

U.S. Net Exports

U.S. Net Exports (billion dollars)

Year

5.a. Households and Firms

Households own all the basic resources, or factors of production, in the economy. Household members own land and provide labor, and they are the entrepreneurs, stockholders, proprietors, and partners who own business firms.

Households and businesses interact with each other by means of buying and selling. Businesses employ the services of resources in order to produce goods and services. Business firms pay households for their resource services.

Households sell their resource services to businesses in exchange for money payments. The flow of resource services from households to businesses is shown by the blue-green line at the bottom of Figure 12. The flow of money payments from firms

---

FIGURE 12

The Circular Flow: Households and Firms

The diagram indicates that income is equal to the value of output. Firms hire resources from households. The payments for these resources represent household income. Households spend their income for goods and services produced by the firms. Household spending represents revenue for firms. Households save some of their income. This income reenters the circular flow as investment spending. Financial intermediaries like banks take in the saving of households and then lend this money to business firms for investment spending.

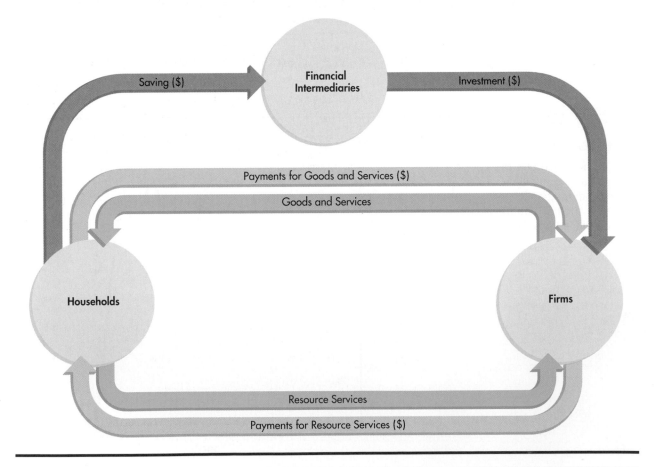

Part One Introduction to the Price System

to households is shown by the gold line at the bottom of Figure 12. Households use the money payments to buy goods and services from firms. These money payments are the firms' revenues. The flow of money payments from households to firms is shown by the gold line at the top of the diagram. The flow of goods and services from firms to households is shown by the blue-green line at the top of Figure 12. There is, therefore, a flow of money and goods and services from one sector to the other. The payments made by one sector are the receipts taken in by the other sector. Money, goods, and services flow from households to firms and back to households in a circular flow.

Households do not spend all of the money they receive. They save some fraction of their income. In Figure 12, we see that household saving is deposited in **financial intermediaries** like banks, credit unions, and saving and loan firms. A financial intermediary accepts deposits from savers and makes loans to borrowers. The money that is saved by the households reenters the economy in the form of investment spending as business firms borrow for expansion of their productive capacity.

The **circular flow diagram** represented in Figure 12 indicates that income is equal to the value of output. Money flows to the household sector are the sum of the payments to the resource owners, including the payments to entrepreneurs. Money flows to firms are the revenue that firms receive when they sell the goods and services they produce. Revenue minus the costs of land, labor, and capital is profit. Profit represents the payment to entrepreneurs and other owners of corporations, partnerships, and sole proprietorships. In this simple economy, household income is equal to business revenue—the value of goods and services produced.

5.b. Households, Firms, and the International Sector

Figure 13 includes foreign countries in the circular flow. To simplify the circular flow diagram, let's assume that households are not directly engaged in international trade and that only business firms are buying and selling goods and services across international borders. This assumption is not far from the truth for the industrial countries and for many developing countries. We typically buy a foreign-made product from a local business firm rather than directly from the foreign producer.

A line labeled "net exports" connects firms and foreign countries in Figure 13, as well as a line labeled "payments for net exports." Notice that neither line has an arrow indicating the direction of flow as do the other lines in the diagram. The reason is that net exports of the home country may be either positive (a trade surplus) or negative (a trade deficit). When net exports are positive, there is a net flow of goods from the firms of the home country to foreign countries and a net flow of money from foreign countries to the firms of the home country. When net exports are negative, the opposite occurs. A trade deficit involves net flows of goods from foreign countries to the firms of the home country and net money flows from the domestic firms to the foreign countries. If exports and imports are equal, net exports are zero because the value of exports is offset by the value of imports.

Figure 13 shows the circular flow linking the private sectors of the economy. This model is a simplified view of the world, but it highlights the important interrelationships. The value of output equals income, as always; but spending may be for foreign as well as domestic goods. Domestic firms may produce for foreign as well as domestic consumption.

financial intermediaries: institutions that accept deposits from savers and make loans to borrowers

circular flow-diagram: a model showing the flow of output and income from one sector of the economy to another

FIGURE 13

The Circular Flow: Households, Firms, and Foreign Countries

The diagram assumes that households are not directly engaged in international trade. The flow of goods and services between countries is represented by the line labeled "net exports." Neither the net exports line nor the line labeled "payments for net exports" has an arrow indicating the direction of the flow because the flow can go from the home country to foreign countries or vice versa. When the domestic economy has positive net exports (a trade surplus), goods and services flow out of the domestic firms toward foreign countries and money payments flow from the foreign countries to the domestic firms. With negative net exports (a trade deficit), the reverse is true.

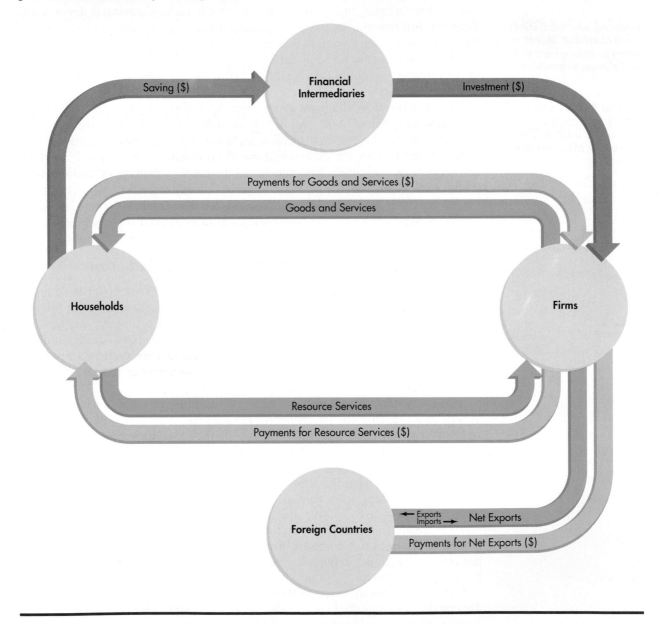

1. The circular flow diagram illustrates how the main sectors of the economy fit together.
2. The circular flow diagram shows that the value of output is equal to income.

Summary

? In a market system, who decides what goods and services are produced?

1. In a market system, consumers are sovereign and decide by means of their purchases what goods and services will be produced. *§1.a*

? How are goods and services produced?

2. In a market system, firms decide how to produce the goods and services that consumers want. In order to earn maximum profits, firms use the least-cost combinations of resources. *§1.c*

? Who obtains the goods and services that are produced?

3. Income and prices determine who gets what in a market system. Income is determined by the ownership of resources. *§1.d*

? What is a household, and what is household income and spending?

4. A household consists of one or more persons who occupy a unit of housing. *§2*
5. Household spending is called *consumption* and is the largest component of spending in the economy. *§2.b*

? What is a business firm, and what is business spending?

6. A business firm is a business organization controlled by a single management. *§3*

7. Businesses may be organized as sole proprietorships, partnerships, or corporations. *§3.a*
8. Business investment spending—the expenditure by business firms for capital goods—fluctuates a great deal over time. *§3.e*

? How does the international sector affect the economy?

9. The international trade of the United States occurs predominantly with the other industrial economies. *§4.a*
10. Exports are products sold to the rest of the world. Imports are products bought from the rest of the world. *§4.a.2*
11. Exports minus imports equal net exports. Positive net exports mean that exports are greater than imports and a trade surplus exists. Negative net exports mean that imports exceed exports and a trade deficit exists. *§4.b*

? How do the three private sectors—households, businesses, and the international sector—interact in the economy?

12. The resources combined to produce goods and services are also known as factors of production. *§5.a*
13. The total value of output produced by the factors of production is equal to the income received by the owners of the factors of production. *§5.a*

Key Terms

consumer sovereignty *§1.a*

private sector *§1.d*

public sector *§1.d*

household *§2*

consumption *§2.b*

business firm *§3*

sole proprietorship *§3.a*

partnership *§3.a*

corporation *§3.a*

multinational business *§3.a*

investment *§3.e*

imports *§4.a.2*

exports *§4.a.2*

trade surplus *§4.b*

trade deficit *§4.b*

net exports *§4.b*

financial intermediaries *§5.a*

circular flow diagram *§5.a*

Exercises

1. What is consumer sovereignty? What does it have to do with determining what goods and services are produced? Who determines how goods and services are produced? Who receives the goods and services in a market system?

2. Is a family a household? Is a household a family?

3. What is the median value of the following series? 4, 6, 8, 3, 9, 10, 10, 1, 5, 7, 12

4. Which sector (households, business, or international) spends the most? Which sector spends the least? Which sector, because of volatility, has importance greater than is warranted by its size?

5. What does it mean if net exports are negative?

6. Why does the value of output always equal the income received by the resources that produced the output?

7. Total spending in the economy is equal to consumption plus investment plus government spending plus net exports. If households want to save and thus do not use all of their income for consumption, what will happen to total spending? Because total spending in the economy is equal to total income and output, what will happen to the output of goods and services if households want to save more?

8. People sometimes argue that imports should be limited by government policy. Suppose a government quota on the quantity of imports causes net exports to rise. Using the circular flow diagram as a guide, explain why total expenditures and national output may rise after the quota is imposed. Who is likely to benefit from the quota? Who will be hurt?

9. Draw the circular flow diagram linking households, business firms, and the international sector. Use the diagram to explain the effects of a decision by the household sector to increase saving.

10. Suppose there are three countries in the world. Country A exports $11 million worth of goods to country B and $5 million worth of goods to country C; country B exports $3 million worth of goods to country A and $6 million worth of goods to country C; and country C exports $4 million worth of goods to country A and $1 million worth of goods to country B.

    a. What are the net exports of countries A, B, and C?
    b. Which country is running a trade deficit? A trade surplus?

11. Over time, there has been a shift away from outdoor drive-in movie theaters to indoor movie theaters. Use supply and demand curves to illustrate and explain how consumers can bring about such a change when tastes change.

12. Figure 3 indicates that the youngest and the oldest households have the lowest household incomes. Why should middle-aged households have higher incomes than the youngest and oldest?

13. The chapter provides data indicating that there are many more sole proprietorships than corporations or partnerships. Why are there so many sole proprietorships? Why is the revenue of the average sole proprietorship less than that of the typical corporation?

14. List the four sectors of the economy along with the type of spending associated with each sector. Order the types of spending in terms of magnitude and give an example of each kind of spending.

15. The circular flow diagram of Figure 13 excludes the government sector. Draw a new version of the figure that includes this sector with government spending and taxes added to the diagram. Label your new figure and be sure to include arrows to illustrate the direction of flows.

ACE

Take the ACE Practice Test for this chapter to review the important concepts and get immediate feedback with answers.

economics.college.hmco.com/students

Report: Ramsey Friend Sold Information to *National Enquirer*

A confidant of John and Patsy Ramsey said she sold handwriting samples and interrogation transcripts from their daughter's murder investigation to a supermarket tabloid for $40,000.

Susan Bennett, 51, of Hickory, N.C., told the Rocky Mountain News she sold the material to the *National Enquirer* because she believed that its publication would prove the Ramseys' innocence.

It was used in the tabloid's Dec. 3 edition in a 31-page story headlined: "JonBenet Secret Video Evidence: New Clues Expose Mom & Dad!," on newsstands Friday. Ramsey attorney L. Lin Wood said the couple feels betrayed that a friend would sell information. Wood said tabloids have cast suspicion on the parents throughout six years of reporting on the unsolved case.

"It's horribly naive to believe that the tabloids are going to fairly and accurately report on any issue or piece of evidence as it pertains to John and Patsy Ramsey," Wood said.

Wood said the information sold to the *Enquirer* was part of a discovery order in a federal libel lawsuit brought against the Ramseys by Chris Wolf, who the Ramseys called a suspect in a book they wrote about the murder.

Wood said Wolf's lawyer, Darnay Hoffman of New York, denied providing Bennett with the material. Hoffman was unavailable for comment.

Bennett, befriended by the former Boulder couple through her advocacy of their innocence, said she sold a transcript from an April 1997 police interrogation of the Ramseys, videotapes of a June 1998 police interrogation and handwriting samples from Patsy Ramsey.

"People make it sound as though I turned on the Ramseys," Bennett said. "I still believe 100 percent they are innocent."

JonBenet Ramsey was found beaten and strangled in the family's Boulder home on Dec. 26, 1996. No arrests have been made, but JonBenet's parents have remained under suspicion.

David Perel, editor of the *National Enquirer,* did not confirm the source of the information in his publication. He said the *Enquirer* is planning to publish a book about the case next year.

Wood said Bennett does not face legal action, but said he will investigate to see if she obtained the information in violation of a court order, and if the source of that information can be prosecuted for it.

"John and Patsy will no longer communicate with Ms. Bennett and will not share any information with her," Wood said.

The Ramseys previously sued American Media, publisher of the *National Enquirer,* over a story about their son, Burke, and won a settlement.

Source: The Associated Press State & Local Wire.

Associated Press/November 28, 2002

While standing in line at the grocery store, you notice the headlines on the tabloid, "Aliens Take Body of Britney Spears and Exchange It with Roseanne" and you wonder how anyone could pay for these ridiculous papers. Some people not only wonder about that but think that these tabloids are invading citizens' privacy. As the article notes, "It is terribly naive" to think that the tabloids will be fair or will try to provide a balanced viewpoint. Why then do these papers exist? Who determines whether these newspapers and magazines are appropriate, and who defines whether what they report is accurate or fair?

In a market system, it is consumers who determine whether these magazines and newspapers exist. If the producers of the newspapers and magazines cannot cover their costs with their revenues from sales and advertisements, then the producers will change what they do. They will either alter the coverage or presentation of stories or get out of the business altogether.

In a market system, products are provided if they result in a profit to producers. This means the customer must be willing and able to pay for them. If stories about baseball have no interest to readers, then consumers will not purchase magazines that focus on baseball. As a result, magazines will have to alter what they do present in order to attempt to retain their sales. *Sports Illustrated* would have to have stories about other sports, swimsuits, and other topics instead of baseball.

If people do not want to read tabloids and are unwilling to purchase the newspapers, then the tabloids will not exist. Only if people are willing and able to pay a price sufficient for the newspaper publishers to make a profit will the newspapers be published. No one is forcing anyone to read the tabloids.

Suppose that the market for tabloids is represented in the demand and supply diagram shown below. Suppose that for some reason, perhaps the tragedy of JonBenet Ramsey's death, that the willingness to purchase tabloids decreases. This is illustrated by an inward shift of the demand curve, from D_1 to D_2. The magazine and newspaper prices will decline, from P_1 to P_2. In addition, fewer magazines and newspapers are purchased—quantity sold falls from Q_1 to Q_2.

A decline in sales of the tabloids is not necessarily a good or a bad thing. All it really is, is a change in tastes and preferences and a shift of the demand curve. For some reason, people are not willing and able to purchase as many of the tabloids as they did before. There is no "good" or "bad" to this fact. It is simply a positive statement.

The lesson here is that the consumer does reign supreme in a market system. No profit-maximizing firm will ignore customer desires. Firms may try new cost-reducing approaches or revenue-enhancing techniques, but whether the tabloids are published depends on whether customers are willing and able to buy them.

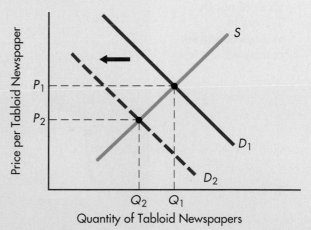

Chapter 4 The Market System and the Private Sector

The Public Sector

1. How does the government interact with the other sectors of the economy?

2. What is the economic role of government?

3. Why is the public sector such a large part of a market economy?

4. What does the government do?

5. How do the sizes of public sectors in various countries compare?

From conception to death, we are affected by the activities of the government. Many mothers receive prenatal care through government programs. We are born in hospitals that are subsidized or run by the government. We are delivered by doctors who received training in subsidized colleges. Our births are recorded on certificates filed with the government. Ninety percent of us attend public schools. Many of us live in housing that is directly subsidized by the government or whose mortgages are insured by the government. Most of us at one time or another put savings into accounts that are insured by the government. Virtually all of us, at some time in our lives, receive money from the government—from student loan programs, unemployment compensation, disability insurance, social security, or Medicare. Twenty percent of the work force is employed by the government. The prices of wheat, corn, sugar, and dairy products are controlled or strongly influenced by the government. The prices we pay for cigarettes, alcohol, automobiles, utilities, water, gas, and a multitude of other goods are directly or indirectly influenced by the government. We travel on public roads and publicly subsidized or controlled air-

lines, airports, trains, and ships. Our legal structure provides a framework in which we all live and act; the national defense ensures our rights of citizenship and protects our private property. By law, the government is responsible for employment and the general health of the economy.

According to virtually any measure, government in the United States has been a growth industry since 1930. The number of people employed by the local, state, and federal governments combined grew from 3 million in 1930 to over 19 million today; there are now more people employed in government than there are in manufacturing. Annual expenditures by the federal government rose from $3 billion in 1930 to approximately $628 billion today, and total government (federal, state, and local) expenditures now equal about $1.2 trillion annually. In 1929, government spending constituted less than 2.5 percent of total spending in the economy. Today, it is around 20 percent. The number of rules and regulations created by the government is so large that it is measured by the number of telephone-book-sized pages needed just to list them, and that number is more than 67,000. The cost of all federal rules and regulations is estimated to be somewhere between $4,000 and $17,000 per U.S. household each year, and the number of federal employees required to police these rules is about 125,000.

There is no doubt that the government (often referred to as the *public sector*) is a major player in the U.S. economy. But in the last few chapters we have been learning about the market system and how well it works. If the market system works so well, why is the public sector such a large part of the economy? In this chapter we discuss the public sector and the role government plays in a market economy. ◾

1. The Circular Flow

1. How does the government interact with the other sectors of the economy?

Government in the United States exists at the federal, state, and local levels. Local government includes county, regional, and municipal units. Economic discussions tend to focus on the federal government because national economic policy is set at that level. Nevertheless, each level affects us through its taxing and spending decisions, and laws regulating behavior.

To illustrate how the government sector affects the economy, let's add government to the circular flow model presented in the previous chapter. Government at the federal, state, and local levels interacts with both households and firms. Because the government employs factors of production to produce government services, households receive payments from the government in exchange for the services of the factors of production. The flow of resource services from households to government is illustrated by the blue-green line flowing from the households to government in Figure 1. The flow of money from government to households is shown by the gold line flowing from government to households. We assume that government, like a household, does not trade directly with foreign countries but obtains foreign goods from domestic firms that do trade with the rest of the world.

Households pay taxes to support the provision of government services, such as national defense, education, and police and fire protection. In a sense, then, the household sector is purchasing goods and services from the government as well as from private businesses. The flow of tax payments from households and businesses to government is illustrated by the gold lines flowing from households and businesses to government, and the flow of government services to households and businesses is illustrated by the purple lines flowing from government.

FIGURE 1

The Circular Flow: Households, Firms, Government, and Foreign Countries

The diagram assumes that households and government are not directly engaged in international trade. Domestic firms trade with firms in foreign countries. The government sector buys resource services from households and goods and services from firms. This government spending represents income for the households and revenue for the firms. The government uses the resource services and goods and services to provide government services for households and firms. Households and firms pay taxes to the government to finance government expenditures.

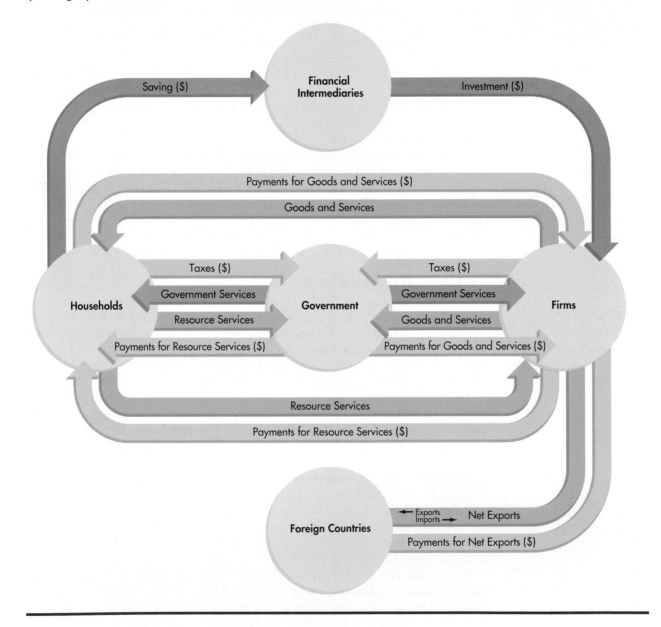

The addition of government brings significant changes to the model. Households have an additional place to sell their resources for income, and businesses have an additional market for goods and services. The value of *private* production no longer equals the value of household income. Households receive income from government in exchange for providing resource services to government. The total value of output in the economy is equal to the total income received, but government is included as a source of income and a producer of services.

RECAP

1. The circular flow diagram illustrates how the main sectors of the economy fit together.
2. Government interacts with both households and firms. Households get government services and pay taxes; they provide resource services and receive income. Firms sell goods and services to government and receive income.

2. The Role of Government in the Market System

2. **What is the economic role of government?**

We have learned that consumers use their limited incomes to buy the goods and services that give them the greatest satisfaction, that resource owners offer the services of their resources to the highest bidder, and that firms produce the goods and services and use the resources that enable them to generate the highest profits. In other words, everyone—consumers, firms, resource suppliers—attempts to get the most benefits for the least cost.

This apparently narrow, self-interested behavior is converted by the market into a social outcome in which no one can be made better off without making someone else worse off. Any resource allocation that could make someone better off and no one any worse off would increase efficiency. When all such allocations have been realized, so that the *only* way to make one person better off would harm someone else, then we have realized the best allocation society can achieve. As Adam Smith noted in 1776, self-interested individuals, wholly unaware of the effects of their actions, act as if driven by an *invisible hand* to produce the greatest social good.

2.a. Government as the Guardian of Efficiency

economic efficiency: a situation where no one in society can be made better off without making someone else worse off

technical efficiency: producing at a point on the PPC

Economic efficiency is the name given to the events described by Adam Smith. Efficiency can mean many things to many different people. Even within economics there are different definitions of efficiency. We have already talked about the production possibilities curve and efficiency; operating at a point on the PPC is called *productive* or **technical efficiency.** A firm is said to be operating efficiently when it produces a given quantity and quality of goods at the lowest possible cost. Consumers are said to be efficient when they are getting the greatest bang for the buck, using their scarce resources to get the greatest benefits. *Economic efficiency* encompasses all of these definitions of efficiency. When *one person cannot be made better off without harming someone else,* then we say economic efficiency prevails.

Somewhat amazingly, economic efficiency occurs in a market system simply through the self-interested individual actions of participants in that system. Efficiency is not the result of some despot controlling the economy and telling people what they can and cannot do. The market system results in efficiency because people own their resources and goods and will exchange their goods or resources for others only if the exchange makes them better off. The higher profits go, the more income is earned by people with entrepreneurial ability. In order to earn profits, entrepreneurs have to provide, at the lowest possible cost, the goods and services that consumers want and are able to buy. This means that the least-cost combination of resources is used by each firm, but it also means that resources are employed in their most highly valued uses. Any reallocation of resources results in a situation that is worse—some resources will not be used where they are most highly valued, and some consumers will be less satisfied with the goods and services they can purchase.

As we saw in the beginning of this chapter, the government plays a significant role in the U.S. economy; governmental influence is even larger in other market economies and is especially large in a socialist economy like Cuba. Why, if the actions of individuals in the market system result in the best social outcome, does the government play such a large role?

There are two justifications given for the government's role in a market economy beyond ensuring private property rights. One is based on cases where the market may not always result in economic efficiency. The second is based on the idea that people who do not like the market outcome use the government to change the outcome. Sections 2.b through 2.f are brief discussions of some cases where the market system may fail to achieve economic efficiency. Section 2.g is a brief discussion of cases where people manipulate the market outcome.

?

3. Why is the public sector such a large part of a market economy?

2.b. Information and the Price System

As you learned in Chapters 3 and 4, a market is a place or service that allows buyers and sellers to exchange information on what they know about a product, what buyers are willing and able to pay for a product, and what sellers want to receive in order to produce and sell a product. A market price is a signal indicating when more or less of a good is desired. When the market price rises, buyers know that the quantity demanded at the prior equilibrium price exceeded the quantity supplied.

A market price is only as good an indicator as the information that exists in the market. It takes time for people to gather information about a product. It takes time to go to a market and purchase an item. It takes time for producers to learn what people want and bring together the resources necessary to produce that product. Thus, people are not likely to be perfectly informed, nor will everyone have the same information. This means that not all markets will adjust instantaneously or even at the same speed to a change in demand or supply. It also means that some people may pay higher prices for a product than others pay. Some people may be swindled by a sharp operator, and some firms may fail to collect debts owed them.

market imperfection: a lack of efficiency that results from imperfect information in the marketplace

When information is not perfect, **market imperfections** may result. As a result of market imperfections, least-cost combinations of resources may not be used, or resources may not be used where they have the highest value. Often in such cases, people have argued for the government to step in with rules and regulations concerning the amount of information that must be provided. The government requires, for example, that specific information be provided on the labels of food products, that warning labels be placed on cigarettes and alcohol products, and that statements about the condition of a used car be made available to buyers. The government also declares certain actions by firms or consumers to be fraudulent or illegal. It also tests and licenses pharmaceuticals and members of many professions—medical doctors, lawyers, beauticians, barbers, nurses, and others.

Government plays an active role in regulating some professions. Physicians and other health professionals are licensed by the government with the intent to ensure that health-care providers are properly trained.

2.c. Externalities

The market system works efficiently only if the market price reflects the full costs and benefits of producing and consuming a particular good or service. Recall that people make decisions on the basis of their opportunity costs and that the market price is a measure of what must be forgone to acquire some good or service. If the market price does not reflect the full costs, then decisions cannot reflect opportunity costs. For instance, when you drive, you don't pay for all of the pollution created by your car. When you have a loud, late-night party, you don't pay for the distractions you impose on your neighbors. When firms dump wastes or radioactive by-products freely, they don't pay the costs. When homeowners allow their properties to become rundown, they reduce the value of neighboring properties but they don't pay for the loss of value. Not all such side effects of actions are negative. When society is educated, it costs less to produce signs, ballots, tax forms, and other information tools. Literacy enables a democracy to function effectively, and higher education may stimulate scientific discoveries that improve the welfare of society. When you acquire an education, however, you do not get a check in the amount of the savings your education will create for society. All these side effects—some negative, some positive—that are not covered by the market price are called **externalities.**

externalities: the costs or benefits of a transaction that are borne by someone not directly involved in the transaction

Externalities are the costs or benefits of a market activity borne by someone who is not a direct party to the market transaction. When you drive, you pay only for gasoline and car maintenance. You don't pay for the noise and pollutants that your car emits. You also don't pay for the added congestion and delays that you impose on other drivers. Thus, the *market* price of driving understates the *full* cost of driving to society; as a result, people drive more frequently than they would if they had to pay the full cost.

The government is often called upon to intervene in the market to resolve externality problems. Government agencies, such as the Environmental Protection Agency, are established to set and enforce air quality standards, and taxes are imposed to obtain funds to pay for external costs or subsidize external benefits.

Thus, the government provides education to society at below-market prices because the positive externality of education benefits everyone.

2.d. Public Goods

The market system works efficiently only if the benefits derived from consuming a particular good or service are available only to the consumer who buys the good or service. When you buy a pizza, only you receive the benefits of eating that pizza. What would happen if you weren't allowed to enjoy that pizza all by yourself? Suppose your neighbors had the right to come to your home when you had a pizza delivered and share your pizza. How often would you buy a pizza? There is no way to exclude others from enjoying the benefits of some of the goods you purchase. These types of goods are called **public goods,** and they create a problem for the market system.

public good: a good whose consumption by one person does not diminish the quantity or quality available for others

Radio broadcasts are public goods. Everyone who tunes in a station enjoys the benefits. National defense is also a public good. You could buy a missile to protect your house, but your neighbors, as well as you, would benefit from the protection it provided. A pizza, however, is not a public good. If you pay for it, only you get to enjoy the benefits. Thus, you have an incentive to purchase pizza. You don't have that incentive to purchase public goods. If you and I both benefit from the public good, who will buy it? I'd prefer that you buy it so that I receive its benefits at no cost. Conversely, you'd prefer that I buy it. The result may be that no one will buy it.

Fire protection provides a good example of the problem that occurs with public goods. Suppose that as a homeowner you have the choice of subscribing to fire protection services from a private firm or having no fire protection. If you subscribe and your house catches fire, the fire engines will arrive as soon as possible and your house may be saved. If you do not subscribe, your house will burn. Do you choose to subscribe? You might say to yourself that as long as your neighbors subscribe, you need not do so. The fact that your neighbors subscribe means that fires in their houses won't cause a fire in yours, and you do not expect a fire to begin in your house. If many people made decisions in this way, fire protection services would not be available because not enough people would subscribe to make the services profitable.

private property right: the limitation of ownership to an individual

The problem with a public good is the communal nature of the good. No one has a **private property right** to a public good. If you buy a car, you must pay the seller an acceptable price. Once this price is paid, the car is all yours and no one else can use it without your permission. The car is your private property, and you make the decisions about its use. In other words, you have the private property right to the car. Public goods are available to all because no one individual owns them or has property rights to them.

free ride: the enjoyment of the benefits of a good by a producer or consumer without having to pay for the good

When goods are public, people have an incentive to try to obtain a **free ride**—the enjoyment of the benefits of a good without paying for the good. Your neighbors would free-ride on your purchases of pizza if you didn't have the private property right to the pizza. People who enjoy public radio and public television stations without donating money to them are getting free rides from those people who do donate to them. People who benefit from the provision of a good whether they pay for it or not have an incentive not to pay for it.

Typically, in the absence of private property rights to a good, people call on the government to claim ownership and provide the good. For instance, governments act as owners of police departments and specify how police services are used. The Global Business Insight "Government Creates a Market for Fishing Rights" provides one example of government specifying private property rights.

Government Creates a Market for Fishing Rights

There is no practical way to establish ownership rights for ocean fish stocks. Traditionally, fish have been free for the taking—a common pool resource. Theory teaches that such underpricing leads to overconsumption. In the halibut fisheries off Alaska, fishing fleets caught so many halibut that the survival of the stock was threatened. No single fishing boat had an incentive to harvest fewer fish, since the impact on its own future catch would be minimal and others would only increase their take. This is an example of what is known as "the tragedy of the commons."

Countries claim fishing rights to the ocean water off their shores to a certain distance. But this just confines the problem to overfishing by domestic boats. The example of the Alaskan halibut fishery is valuable for all nations to consider.

Officials tried limiting the length of the fishing season. But this effort only encouraged new capital investment, such as larger and faster boats with more effective (and expensive) fishing equipment. In order to control the number of fish caught, the season was shortened in some areas from 4 months to 2 days by the early 1990s. Most of the halibut caught had to be frozen rather than marketed fresh, and halibut caught out of season had to be discarded.

In late 1992, the federal government proposed a new approach: assigning each fisherman a permit to catch a certain number of fish. The total number of fish for which permits are issued reflects scientific estimates of the number of fish that can be caught without endangering the survival of the species. Also,

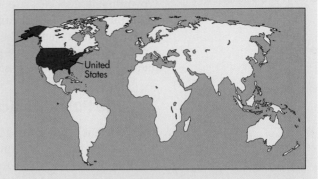

the permits are transferable—they can be bought and sold. By making the permits transferable, the system in effect creates a market where one did not exist previously. The proposed system encourages the most profitable and efficient boats to operate at full capacity by buying permits from less successful boats, ensuring a fishing fleet that uses labor and equipment efficiently. Moreover, the transferable permits system establishes a market price for the opportunity to fish—a price that better reflects the true social cost of using this common resource.

Today, the fishing season for halibut is 245 days. This results in much greater availability of fresh rather than frozen fish. Consumers receive a higher-quality product, and the survival of the halibut is protected.

Sources: *Economic Report of the President, 1993,* p. 207; www.lobsterconservation.com/halibutfq/.

2.e. Monopoly

If only one firm produces a good that is desired by consumers, then that firm might produce a smaller amount of the good in order to charge a higher price. In this case, resources might not be used in their most highly valued manner, and consumers might not be able to purchase the goods they desire. A situation where there is only one producer of a good is called a **monopoly.** The existence of a monopoly can imply a lack of economic efficiency. The government is often called on to regulate the behavior of firms that are monopolies or even to run the monopolies as government enterprises. The government also encourages competition through antitrust laws that limit the ability of firms to engage in anticompetitive policies.

monopoly: a situation where there is only one producer of a good

2.f. Business Cycles

People are made better off by economic growth. Economic growth increases the number of jobs and draws people out of poverty and into the mainstream of economic progress. Economic stagnation, on the other hand, throws the relatively poor out of their jobs and into poverty. These fluctuations in the economy are called **business cycles.** People call on the government to protect them against the periods of economic ill health and to minimize the damaging effects of business cycles. Government agencies are established to control the money supply and other important parts of the economy, and government-financed programs are implemented to offset some of the losses that result during bad economic times. The U.S. Congress requires that the government promote economic growth and minimize unemployment. History has shown that this is easier said than done.

business cycles: fluctuations in the economy between growth and stagnation

2.g. The Public Choice Theory of Government

The efficiency basis for government intervention in the economy discussed in sections 2.b through 2.f implies that the government is a cohesive organization functioning in much the same way that a benevolent dictator would. This organization intervenes in the market system only to correct the ills created by the market. Not all economists agree with this view of government. Many claim that the government is not a benevolent dictator looking out for the best interests of society but is instead merely a collection of individuals who respond to the same economic impulses we all do—that is, the desire to satisfy our own interests.

Economic efficiency does not mean that everyone is as well off as he or she desires. Economic efficiency merely means that someone or some group cannot be made better off without harming some other person or group of people. People always have an incentive to attempt to make themselves better off. If their attempts result in the transfer of benefits to themselves and away from others, however, economic efficiency has not increased. Moreover, the resources devoted to enacting the transfer of benefits are not productive; they do not create new income and benefits but merely transfer existing income and benefits. Such activity is called **rent seeking.** Rent seeking refers to cases where people devote resources to attempting to create income transfers to themselves. Rent seeking includes the expenditures on lobbyists in Congress, the time and expenses that health-care professionals devote to fighting nationalized health care, the time and expenses farmers devote to improving their subsidies, and millions of other examples.

rent seeking: the use of resources simply to transfer wealth from one group to another without increasing production or total wealth

A group of economists, referred to as **public choice** economists, argue that government is more the result of rent seeking than of market failure. The study of public choice focuses on how government actions result from the self-interested behaviors of voters and politicians. Whereas the efficiency justification of government argues that it is only in cases where the market does not work that the government steps in, public choice theory says that the government may be brought into the market system whenever someone or some group can benefit, even if efficiency is not served.

public choice: the study of how government actions result from the self-interested behaviors of voters and politicians

According to the public choice economists, price ceilings or price floors may be enacted for political gain rather than because of market failure; government spending or taxing policies may be enacted not to resolve a market failure but instead to implement an income redistribution from one group to another; government agencies such as the Food and Drug Administration may exist not to improve the functioning of the market but to enact a wealth transfer from one group to another. Each such instance of manipulation leads to a larger role for government in a market economy. Moreover, government employees have the incentive to increase their role and importance in the economy and therefore transfer income or other benefits to themselves.

The government sector is far from a trivial part of the market system. Whether the government's role is one of improving economic efficiency or the result of rent seeking is a topic for debate, and in later chapters we discuss this debate in more detail. For now, it is satisfactory just to recognize how important the public sector is in the market system and what the possible reasons for its prevalence are.

RECAP

1. The government's role in the economy may stem from the inefficiencies that exist in a market system.

2. The market system does not result in economic efficiency when there are market imperfections such as imperfect information or when the costs or benefits of the transaction are borne by parties not directly involved in the transaction. Such cases are called externalities. Also, the market system may not be efficient when private ownership rights are not well defined. The government is called upon to resolve these inefficiencies that exist in the market system.

3. The government is asked to minimize the problems that result from business cycles.

4. The public choice school of economics maintains that the government's role in the market system is more the result of rent seeking than of reducing market inefficiencies.

3. Overview of the United States Government

4. What does the government do?

When Americans think of government policies, rules, and regulations, they typically think of Washington, D.C., because their economic lives are regulated and shaped more by policies made there than by policies made at the local and state levels. Who actually is involved in economic policymaking? Important government institutions that shape U.S. economic policy are listed in Table 1. This list is far from inclusive, but it includes the agencies with the broadest powers and greatest influence.

Economic policy involves macroeconomic issues like government spending and control of the money supply and microeconomic issues aimed at providing public goods like police and military protection, correcting externalities like pollution, and maintaining a competitive economy.

3.a. Microeconomic Policy

Government provides public goods to avoid the free-rider problem that would occur if private firms provided the goods.

One reason for government's microeconomic role is the free-rider problem associated with the provision of public goods. If an army makes all citizens safer, then all citizens should pay for it. But even if one person does not pay taxes, the army still protects this citizen from foreign attack. To minimize free riding, the government collects mandatory taxes to finance public goods. Congress and the president determine the level of public goods needed and how to finance them.

Government taxes or subsidizes some activities that create externalities.

Microeconomic policy also deals with externalities. Activities that cause air or water pollution impose costs on everyone. For instance, a steel mill may generate air pollutants that have a negative effect on the surrounding population. A

TABLE 1

U.S. Government Economic Policymakers and Related Agencies

Institution	Role
Fiscal policymakers	
President	Provides leadership in formulating fiscal policy
Congress	Sets government spending and taxes and passes laws related to economic conduct
Monetary policymaker	
Federal Reserve	Controls money supply and credit conditions
Related agencies	
Council of Economic Advisers	Monitors the economy and advises the president
Office of Management and Budget	Prepares and analyzes the federal budget
Treasury Department	Administers the financial affairs of the federal government
Commerce Department	Administers federal policy regulating industry
Justice Department	Enforces legal setting of business
Comptroller of the Currency	Oversees national banks
International Trade Commission	Investigates unfair international trade practices
Federal Trade Commission	Administers laws related to fair business practices and competition

microeconomic function of government is to internalize the externality—that is, to force the steelmaker to bear the full cost to society of producing steel. In addition to assuming the costs of hiring land, labor, and capital, the mill should bear the costs associated with polluting the air. Congress and the president determine which externalities to address and the best way of taxing or subsidizing each activity in order to ensure that the amount of the good produced and its price reflect the true value to society.

Another of government's microeconomic roles is to promote competition. Laws to restrict the ability of business firms to engage in practices that limit competition exist and are monitored by the Justice Department and the Federal Trade Commission. Some firms, such as public utilities, are monopolies and face no competition. The government defines the output, prices, and profits of many monopolies. In some cases, the monopolies are government-run enterprises.

Government regulates industries where free market competition may not exist and polices other industries to promote competition.

3.b. Macroeconomic Policy

The focus of the government's macroeconomic policy is monetary and fiscal policy. **Monetary policy** is policy directed toward control of money and credit. The major player in this policy arena is the Federal Reserve, commonly called "the Fed." The

monetary policy: policy directed toward control of money and credit

Federal Reserve: the central bank of the United States

fiscal policy: policy directed toward government spending and taxation

Government has the responsibility of minimizing the damage from business cycles.

Federal Reserve is the central bank of the United States. It serves as a banker for the U.S. government and regulates the U.S. money supply.

The Federal Reserve System is run by a seven-member Board of Governors. The most important member of the board is the chairman, who is appointed by the president for a term of four years. The board meets regularly (from ten to twelve times a year) with a group of high-level officials to review the current economic situation and set policy for the growth of U.S. money and credit. The Federal Reserve exercises a great deal of influence on U.S. economic policy.

Fiscal policy, the other area of macroeconomic policy, is policy directed toward government spending and taxation. In the United States, fiscal policy is determined by laws that are passed by Congress and signed by the president. The relative roles of the legislative and executive branches in shaping fiscal policy vary with the political climate, but usually it is the president who initiates major policy changes. Presidents rely on key advisers for fiscal policy information. These advisers include Cabinet officers such as the secretary of the Treasury and the secretary of state as well as the director of the Office of Management and Budget. In addition, the president has a Council of Economic Advisers made up of three economists—usually a chair, a macroeconomist, and a microeconomist—who, together with their staff, monitor and interpret economic developments for the president. The degree of influence wielded by these advisers depends on their personal relationship with the president.

FIGURE 2

Federal, State, and Local Government Expenditures for Goods and Services

In the 1950s and early 1960s, federal government spending was above state and local government spending. In 1970, state and local expenditures rose above federal spending and have remained higher ever since. *Source: Data are from the* Economic Report of the President, 2003.

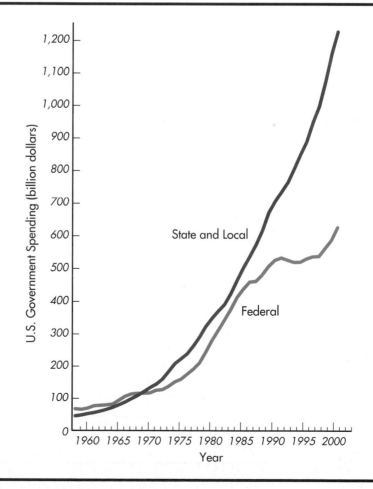

Chapter 5 The Public Sector

3.c. Government Spending

Federal, state, and local government spending for goods and services is shown in Figure 2. Except during times of war in the 1940s and 1950s, federal expenditures were roughly similar in size to state and local expenditures until 1970. Since 1970, state and local spending has been growing more rapidly than federal spending.

Combined government spending on goods and services is larger than investment spending but much smaller than consumption. In 2002, combined government spending was about $1,973 billion, investment spending was about $1,593 billion, and consumption was about $7,302 billion.

Besides government expenditures on goods and services, government also serves as an intermediary, taking money from some taxpayers and transferring this income to others. Such **transfer payments** are a part of total government expenditures, so the total government budget is much larger than the expenditures on goods and services reported in Figure 2. In 2002, total expenditures of federal, state, and local government for goods and services were about $1,973 billion. In this same year, transfer payments paid by all levels of government were about $1,253 billion.

The magnitude of federal government spending relative to federal government revenue from taxes has become an important issue in recent years. Figure 3 shows that the federal budget was roughly balanced until the early 1970s. The budget is a

transfer payment: income transferred by the government from a citizen, who is earning income, to another citizen

---

FIGURE 3

U.S. Federal Budget Deficits

The budget deficit is equal to the excess of government spending over tax revenue. If taxes are greater than government spending, a budget surplus (shown as a negative deficit) exists. *Source: Data are from the* Economic Report of the President, 2003.

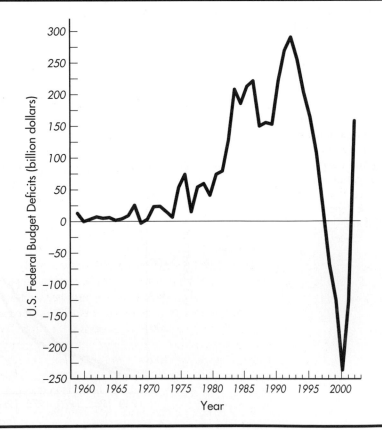

---

measure of spending and revenue. A balanced budget occurs when federal spending is approximately equal to federal revenue. This was the case through the 1950s and 1960s. If federal government spending is less than tax revenue, a **budget surplus** exists. By the early 1980s, federal government spending was much larger than revenue, so a large **budget deficit** existed. The federal budget deficit grew very rapidly to about $290 billion by the early 1990s before beginning to drop and turning to surplus by 1998. After four years of surpluses, a deficit was again realized in 2002. When spending is greater than revenue, the excess spending must be covered by borrowing, and this borrowing can have effects on investment and consumption as well as on economic relationships with other countries.

budget surplus: the excess that results when government spending is less than revenue

budget deficit: the shortage that results when government spending is greater than revenue

RECAP

1. The microeconomic functions of government include correcting externalities, redistributing income from high-income groups to lower-income groups, enforcing a competitive economy, and providing public goods.

2. Macroeconomic policy attempts to control the economy through monetary and fiscal policy.

3. The Federal Reserve conducts monetary policy. Congress and the president formulate fiscal policy.

4. Government spending is larger than investment spending but much smaller than consumption spending.

5. When government spending exceeds tax revenue, a budget deficit exists. When government spending is less than tax revenue, a budget surplus exists.

5. How do the sizes of public sectors in various countries compare?

centrally planned economy: an economic system in which the government determines what goods and services are produced and the prices at which they are sold

4. Government in Other Economies

The government plays a role in every economy, and in most the public sector is a much larger part of the economy than it is in the United States. In some economies, referred to as **centrally planned,** or nonmarket, economies, the public sector is the principal component of the economy. There are significant differences between the market system and the centrally planned systems. In market economies, people can own businesses, be private owners of land, start new businesses, and purchase what they want as long as they can pay the price. They may see their jobs disappear as business conditions worsen, but they are free to take business risks and to reap the rewards if taking these risks pays off. Under centrally planned systems, people are not free to own property other than a house, a car, and personal belongings. They are not free to start a business. They work as employees of the state. Their jobs are guaranteed regardless of whether their employer is making the right or wrong decisions and regardless of how much effort they expend on the job. Even though they might have money in their pockets, they may not be able to buy many of the things they want. Money prices are often not used to ration goods and services, so people may spend much of their time standing in lines to buy the products available on the shelves of government stores. Waiting in line is a result of charging a money price lower than equilibrium and imposing a quantity limit on how much a person can buy. The time costs, along with the money price required to buy goods, will ration the limited supply.

FIGURE 4

The Economic Systems

The closer a country is to a market economy without a public sector, the closer to the lower-left area of the diagram it is placed. Conversely, the more the country is a centrally planned economy, the closer to the upper-right area of the diagram it is placed.

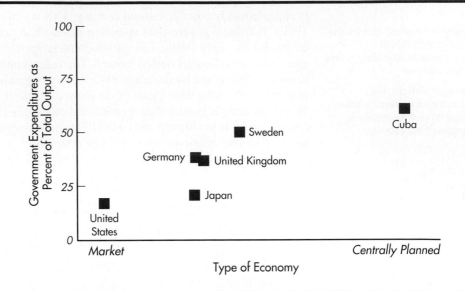

The Soviet Union implemented a centrally planned economy in the 1920s, following its October 1917 revolution. During, and especially following, World War II, the Soviet system expanded into eastern Europe, China, North Korea, and Vietnam. At the peak of Soviet influence, about one-third of the world's population lived in countries generally described as having centrally planned economic systems. The 1980s and 1990s ushered in a new world order, however. The Soviet Union's economy failed and ultimately led to the fall of the Communist governments in eastern Europe, the disintegration of the Soviet Union, the end of the Cold War, and the reunification of West and East Germany.

4.a. Overview of Major Market Economies

Figure 4 shows the size of government and the type of economy for several countries. The United States is representative of nations that are market economies with relatively small public sectors. Cuba is representative of nations that are primarily centrally planned. Germany and Japan are market economies, but the public sector plays a larger role than it does in the United States.

When one thinks of the richest countries in the world, the countries that come to mind are all market economies. The incentives for efficient production provided by markets create the high incomes enjoyed by residents of these countries. Yet it is important to realize that not all these countries are alike. Some have larger roles for government activity than others.

For instance, the role of the public sector in the United Kingdom is significant but not exceptional by European standards. Great Britain is an island economy with a land area slightly greater than that of the state of Minnesota and a population of just over 59 million persons. The resource base of the economy is quite limited, and the British economy is tied very closely to other economies. Government spending is about 40 percent of total output in the United Kingdom.

In Germany, the public sector owns few businesses, but it intervenes a great deal to foster social programs. For instance, the government regulates business hours, supports minimum prices for brand-name articles, imposes rent controls, regulates the

In Germany, the telephone company, Deutsche Telekom, is owned by private stockholders as well as the German government. When Telekom was "privatized" a few years ago, the government sold shares of stock to the public but retained a big share for itself. Such government involvement in seemingly private enterprise occurs in many industrial as well as developing countries.

hiring and firing of employees, regulates vacations, and has passed a series of other laws protecting workers and renters. State expenditures are about 40 percent of total output. The unification of the East and West German economies and the merging of two different types of systems led to additional government intervention.

Japan is a capitalist economy whose postwar rate of economic growth is the highest among the major industrialized countries. Japan is a small country with adequate labor but generally limited supplies of natural resources and land. Like Great Britain, Japan is an island economy. With a population of approximately 127 million and a land area slightly smaller than that of the state of California, Japan is densely populated. The public sector appears on the surface to have a relatively small role in the Japanese economy: Government spending as a percent of total output is only about 20 percent. But this statistic understates the reality. The public sector plays a very important role through the Japanese industrial families known as *keiretsu*. The government wields its influence on the keiretsu through various ministries. For example, the Ministry of International Trade and Industry (MITI) is responsible for international trade, domestic production, and domestic industrial structure. The MITI guides and influences economic decisions by promoting key sectors of the economy and carefully phasing out other, low-productivity sectors. The MITI uses government funds for research and development and to provide assistance for organizational change, such as mergers. Economic planning has not been an important element in the Japanese economy. Japan has had a planning agency since the late 1940s and has assembled numerous plans, but the plans are neither binding nor involuntarily implemented.

The Swedish economic system and its performance are of interest because Sweden is viewed as a system that has been able, over an extended period of time, to sustain economic progress through the efficiency of the market while at the same time ensuring that incomes are equally distributed. Sweden is a relatively small but highly industrialized country. It has a total area of roughly 450,000 square kilometers (somewhat larger than the state of California) and a population of about 8.9 million. Foreign trade is of vital importance to Sweden, accounting for more than

80 percent of its total output. The Swedish economy looks like a market economy in the production of goods and services, but the government accounts for nearly 50 percent of total purchases in Sweden.

RECAP

1. No economy is purely private. The public sector plays a role in every economy.

2. A market economy relies on prices and individual actions to solve economic problems. In centrally planned economies, the government decides what is produced, how it is produced, and who gets what.

Summary

❓ How does the government interact with the other sectors of the economy?

1. The circular flow diagram illustrates the interaction among all sectors of the economy—households, businesses, the international sector, and the public sector. *§1*

❓ What is the economic role of government?

2. The market system promotes economic efficiency. Economic efficiency means that in an economy one person cannot be made better off without harming someone else. *§2.a*

3. The market system does not result in economic efficiency when there are market imperfections, externalities, or public goods. Market imperfections occur when information is imperfect. *§2.b–2.g*

❓ Why is the public sector such a large part of a market economy?

4. Two general reasons are given for the government's participation in the economy: The government may resolve the inefficiencies that occur in a market system, or the government may be the result of rent seeking. *§2.b–2.g*

5. Economic efficiency means that some people cannot be made better off without others being made worse off. Some people do not like the result of the market outcome and want to alter it. In such cases, resources are devoted to creating a transfer of income. This is called rent seeking. *§2.g*

❓ What does the government do?

6. The government carries out microeconomic and macroeconomic activities. The microeconomic activities include resolving market imperfections, externalities, and public goods problems. The macroeconomic activities are directed toward monetary and fiscal policies and minimizing disruptions due to business cycles. *§3*

7. Governments often provide public goods and services such as fire protection, police protection, and national defense. Governments place limits on what firms and consumers can do in certain types of situations. Governments tax externalities or otherwise attempt to make price reflect the full cost of production and consumption. *§3.a*

8. Governments carry out monetary and fiscal policies to attempt to control business cycles. In the United States, monetary policy is the province of the Federal Reserve, and fiscal policy is up to the Congress and the president. *§3.b*

❓ How do the sizes of public sectors in various countries compare?

9. Market systems rely on the decisions of individuals. Centrally planned systems rely on the government to answer economic questions for all individuals. *§4*

10. The size and influence of the public sector ranges from the market economies of the United States and Canada to the centrally planned economy of Cuba. *§4.a*

Key Terms

economic efficiency *§2.a*

technical efficiency *§2.a*

market imperfection *§2.b*

externalities *§2.c*

public goods *§2.d*

private property right *§2.d*

free ride *§2.d*

monopoly *§2.e*

business cycles *§2.f*

rent seeking *§2.g*

public choice *§2.g*

monetary policy *§3.b*

Federal Reserve *§3.b*

fiscal policy *§3.b*

transfer payment *§3.c*

budget surplus *§3.c*

budget deficit *§3.c*

centrally planned economy *§4*

Exercises

1. Illustrate productive or technical efficiency using a production possibilities curve. Can you illustrate economic efficiency? Are you able to show the exact point where economic efficiency would occur?

2. Why would an externality be referred to as a market failure? Explain how your driving on a highway imposes costs on other drivers. Why is this an externality? How might the externality be resolved or internalized?

3. What is the difference between a compact disk recording of a rock concert and a radio broadcast of that rock concert? Why would you spend $12 on the CD but refuse to provide any support to the radio station?

4. "The American buffalo disappeared because they were not privately owned." Evaluate this statement.

5. Which of the following U.S. economic policies are the responsibility of the Federal Reserve? Congress and the president?

   a. An increase in the rate of growth of the money supply
   b. A decrease in the rate of interest
   c. An increase in taxes on the richest 2 percent of Americans
   d. A reduction in taxes on the middle class
   e. An increase in the rate of growth of spending on health care

6. "The Department of Justice plans to file a lawsuit against major airlines, claiming they violated price-fixing laws by sharing plans for fare changes through a computer system, officials said Friday." Is this a microeconomic or macroeconomic policy?

7. People sometimes argue that imports should be limited by government policy. Suppose a government quota on the quantity of imports causes net exports to rise. Using the circular flow diagram as a guide, explain why total expenditures and national output may rise after the quota is imposed. Who is likely to benefit from the quota? Who will be hurt? Explain why the government would become involved in the economy through its imposition of quotas.

8. Most highways are "free" ways: There is no toll charge for using them. What problem does free access create? How would you solve this?

9. In February 2003 the City of London imposed a £5 (British pounds; this is equal to about $8) per day fee for driving in central London between the hours of 7 a.m. and 6:30 p.m. Monday through Friday. The goal is to reduce traffic congestion in the central city. Respond to the following criticisms of the London policy:

   a. The rate charged (£5 per day) can't be the equilibrium price, as surely traffic is heavier at certain times of day than at other times and the equilibrium price should fluctuate with the varying demand for the scarce road space. Charging a constant price seems inefficient, as it will create a shortage of road space at some times and a surplus at other times.
   b. The toll charged is unfair. Only rich people will now drive in London, and the poor will have to ride buses or take the subway.
   c. Instead of charging a toll for all drivers, a better plan would be to regulate who is allowed to drive.

All personal vehicles should be banned and only taxis, buses, delivery trucks, and emergency vehicles be permitted.

10. The Global Business Insight in this chapter discussed creating a market for fishing rights to ensure that overfishing and depletion of fish do not occur. What other areas are subject to a "tragedy of the commons" where a lack of private property rights creates overutilization? Give three examples. How could one "create a market" for these activities to help decrease the overutilization?

11. Explain why the suggested government action may or may not make sense in each of the following scenarios.

    a. People purchase a DVD player with a guarantee provided by its maker, only to find that within a year the company has gone out of business. Consumers demand that the government provide the guarantee.

    b. Korean microchip producers are selling the microchips at a price that is below the cost of making the microchips in the United States. The U.S. government must impose taxes on the Korean microchips imported into the United States.

    c. The economy has slowed down, unemployment has risen, and interest rates are high. The government should provide jobs and force interest rates down.

    d. Fully 15 percent of all United States citizens are without health insurance. The government must provide health care for all Americans.

    e. The rising value of the dollar is making it nearly impossible for U.S. manufacturers to sell their products to other nations. The government must decrease the value of the dollar.

    f. The rich are getting richer at a faster rate than the poor are getting richer. The government must increase the tax rate on the rich to equalize the income distribution.

    g. The AIDS epidemic has placed such a state of emergency on health care that the only solution is to provide some pharmaceutical firm with a monopoly on any drugs or solutions discovered for HIV or AIDS.

12. Many nations of eastern Europe are undergoing a transition from a centrally planned to a market economic system. An important step in the process is to define private property rights in countries where they did not exist before. What does this mean? Why is it necessary to have private property rights?

13. Using the circular flow diagram, illustrate the effects of an increase in taxes imposed on the household sector.

14. Using the circular flow diagram, explain how the government can continually run budget deficits, that is, spend more than it receives in revenue from taxes.

15. Suppose you believe that government is the problem, not the solution. How would you explain the rapid growth of government during the past few decades?

16. The government intervenes in the private sector by imposing laws that ban smoking in all publicly used buildings. As a result, smoking is illegal in bars, restaurants, hotels, dance clubs, and other establishments. Is such a ban justified by economics?

17. In reference to exercise 16, we could say that before a ban is imposed, the owners of businesses owned the private property right to the air in their establishments. As owners of this valuable asset, they would ensure that it is used to earn them the greatest return. Thus, if their customers desired nonsmoking, then they would provide nonsmoking environments. How then does the ban on smoking improve things? Doesn't it merely transfer ownership of the air from the business owners to the nonsmokers?

Take the ACE Practice Test for this chapter to review the important concepts and get immediate feedback with answers.

economics.college.hmco.com/students

A Big "Nein" to Deutsche Telekom; Telecommunications: Germany Still Doesn't Have a Completely Open Market

Deutsche Telekom has become crazed over spending the loose change in its pockets. A few weeks ago, the company was reported to be considering an acquisition of Sprint. This week, Deutsche Telekom announced that it was buying VoiceStream Wireless for a deal valued at $50.5 billion.

This deal makes no sense financially: VoiceStream had a net loss last year of $455 million on revenue of $475 million. To acquire VoiceStream's 2.3 million wireless subscribers, Deutsche Telekom will pay more than $20,000 per subscriber. A return of 10% on this investment over 10 years would require a yearly profit of more than $3,200 per wireless customer. This is impossible, particularly for VoiceStream, which has losses nearly as large as its revenues. Wishful thinking, hopes for the future and faith are fine for religion, but are no way to run a business, as Deutsche Telekom soon will learn if this deal goes through. But if the Germans want to throw away their money, let them.

There are policy reasons, however, to oppose this acquisition because Deutsche Telekom is, in effect, a subsidiary of the German government and is actively expanding and acquiring other telecommunication firms in Germany and around the globe. These acquisitions are being done in the name of globalization, but that is simply a politically correct term for the colonialism and imperialism of the past.

Many countries have claimed to privatize the former government monopolization of telecommunications. Yet much of the stock of the "privatized" telecommunication firms is owned by the government. In the case of Germany, more than half of the stock of Deutsche Telekom is owned by the government. This is partial privatization.

One problem with partial privatization is that it is in the best interests of the government to maximize the value of the stock of the partially owned telecommunications company. This means that the partially privatized company is treated favorably by the government. Another problem is that governments are reluctant to sell their remaining ownership and totally privatize, since such a massive sale would decrease the value of all the shares on the open market. Thus, governments are motivated to manipulate the value of such stocks. The stock of Deutsche Telekom thus is overvalued, since much of it is held by the German government and is not on the open market. It is this overvalued stock that will fund the proposed acquisition of VoiceStream.

Even partial privatization is to be preferred to the old system of complete government ownership and control of telecommunications. Yet the solution to the evils of partial privatization is total privatization, such as what happened with British Telecom. But France, Germany, Japan and Sweden are dragging their feet in achieving complete privatization of their former government monopolies of telecommunications. In the meantime, they should not be allowed market entry into countries that are completely privatized.

Partial privatization is not consistent with open markets and competition. Until Germany completely privatizes Deutsche Telekom, the company should not be allowed to have dominant ownership of any telecommunications firm in the United States—even if it [is] about to lose its lederhosen in this deal.

A. MICHAEL NOLL

Source: *Los Angeles Times,* July 26, 2000, p. 9. Copyright 2000 Times Mirror Company.

Los Angeles Times/July 26, 2000

Commentary

Chapter 5 indicated that there is a legitimate role for government in a market economy. In particular, government is justified to be involved in the production of products involving market imperfections like externalities. However, in many countries, government has operated firms that could be better operated by private business. As a result, in recent years there has been a trend toward the *privatization* of such firms. The privatization of government-owned enterprises is generally intended to increase efficiency by providing the activity being privatized the same incentives that private business firms face. The outcome of such privatization is expected to minimize the costs of production for a given level and quality of output.

The article indicates that the German telephone company, Deutsche Telekom, has been *partially* privatized but that the German government still owns more than half of the company's stock. So private ownership does not exist in the usual sense of the term. This policy of partial privatization has been followed in many countries where privatization is politically controversial. Why should the government retain ownership of a substantial portion of a seemingly private firm? Politics is the short answer. Those who have benefited from the government control of the firm usually have an interest in maintaining government control, and if the government owns more than half of the firm's outstanding stock, then the government exercises majority control of the firm. Perhaps labor unions fear that private ownership will mean fewer jobs at lower wages. In the case of Telekom, there may have been some services that were provided at less than the true cost of production, and those households and/or firms that received service at a subsidized rate fear privatization may end their subsidy. Such groups provide political support for less than full privatization.

Privatization is likely to continue around the world as more and more governments seek to minimize their role in the economy and allow private business to respond to free market incentives in the production of goods. This article reminds us that partial privatization, where government retains some ownership of formerly government-operated enterprises, is not without controversy. The partially privatized firm may not have to compete with other firms on an equal basis but may be given favorable treatment by the government that increases its market value beyond that of a fully privatized firm.

This outcome is not a certainty, however, as the shares that are sold to the public may be worth less in a partially privatized firm than in a fully privatized firm if the public believes that the government involvement will hinder the efficiency of the firm and its ability to earn profits. The author assumes that the ownership of more than half of Deutsche Telekom by the German government has increased the value of the outstanding stock held by the public beyond what a fully privatized firm would have reached. While that may or may not be true in this case, it certainly will not be a general rule that will always occur. After all, how many people would believe that government can do a better job of running a business than private citizens—managers and employees—who will be compensated on the basis of the firm's performance and profitability?

Part Two

Macroeconomic Basics

CHAPTER 6

National Income Accounting

? **Fundamental Questions**

1. How is the total output of an economy measured?

2. Who produces the nation's goods and services?

3. Who purchases the goods and services produced?

4. Who receives the income from the production of goods and services?

5. What is the difference between nominal and real GDP?

6. What is a price index?

The Korean economy grew at an average rate of about 7 percent per year from 1980 to 2001. This compares with an average rate of about 3 percent per year for the United States over the same period. Still, the U.S. economy is much larger than the Korean economy and larger than the economies of the fifty largest developing countries combined. The *size* of an economy cannot be compared across countries without common standards of measurement. National income accounting provides these standards. Economists use this system to evaluate the economic condition of a country and to compare conditions across time and countries.

A national economy is a complex arrangement of many different buyers and sellers—of households, businesses, and government units—and of their interactions with the rest of the world. To assess the economic health of a country or to compare the performance of an economy from year to year, economists must be able to measure national output and real GDP. Without these data, policymakers cannot evaluate their economic policies. For instance, real GDP fell in the United States in 1980, 1981, and 1982, and again in 1990–1991 and 2001. This drop in real GDP was

accompanied by widespread job loss and a general decline in the economic health of the country. As this information became known, political and economic debate centered on economic policies, on what should be done to stimulate the economy. Without real GDP statistics, policymakers would not have known there were problems, let alone how to go about fixing them. ■

1. Measures of Output and Income

1. How is the total output of an economy measured?

national income accounting: the framework that summarizes and categorizes productive activity in an economy over a specific period of time, typically a year

In this chapter we discuss gross domestic product, real GDP, and other measures of national productive activity by making use of the **national income accounting** system used by all countries. National income accounting provides a framework for discussing macroeconomics. Figure 1 reproduces the circular flow diagram you saw in Chapter 5. The lines connecting the various sectors of the economy represent flows of goods and services, and money expenditures (income). National income accounting is the process of counting the value of the flows between sectors and then summing them to find the total value of economic activity in an economy. National income accounting fills in the dollar values in the circular flow.

National income accounting measures the output of an entire economy as well as the flows between sectors. It summarizes the level of production in an economy over a specific period of time, typically a year. In practice, the process *estimates* the amount of activity that occurs. It is beyond the capability of government officials to count every transaction that takes place in a modern economy. Still, national income accounting generates useful and fairly accurate measures of economic activity in most countries, especially wealthy industrial countries that have comprehensive accounting systems.

1.a. Gross Domestic Product

The most common measure of a nation's output is GDP.

Modern economies produce an amazing variety of goods and services. To measure an economy's total production, economists combine the quantities of oranges, golf balls, automobiles, and all the other goods and services produced, into a single measure of output. Of course, simply adding up the number of things produced—the number of oranges, golf balls, and automobiles—does not reveal the *value* of what is being produced. If a nation produces 1 million more oranges and 1 million fewer automobiles this year than it did last year, the total number of things produced remains the same. But because automobiles are much more valuable than oranges, the value of output has dropped substantially. Prices reflect the value of goods and services in the market, so economists use the money value of things to create a measure of total output, a measure that is more meaningful than the sum of units produced.

gross domestic product (GDP): the market value of all final goods and services produced in a year within a country

The most common measure of a nation's output is gross domestic product. **Gross domestic product (GDP)** is the market value of all final goods and services produced in a year within a country's borders. A closer look at three parts of this definition—*market value, final goods and services,* and *produced in a year*—will make clear what the GDP does and does not include.

Market Value The *market value* of final goods and services is their value at market price. The process of determining market value is straightforward where prices are known and transactions are observable. However, there are cases where prices

FIGURE 1

The Circular Flow: Households, Firms, Government, and Foreign Countries

The value of national output equals expenditures and income. If the domestic economy has positive net exports (a trade surplus), goods and services flow out of the domestic firms toward the foreign countries and

money payments flow from the foreign countries to the domestic firms. If the domestic economy has negative net exports (a trade deficit), just the reverse is true.

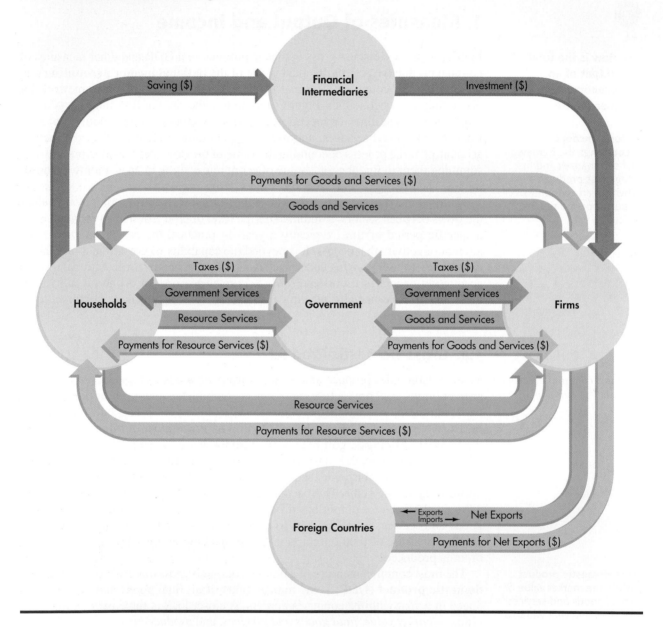

are not known and transactions are not observable. For instance, illegal drug transactions are not reported to the government, which means they are not included in GDP statistics. In fact, almost any activity that is not traded in a market is not included. For example, production that takes place in households, such as homemakers' services, is not counted, nor are unreported barter and cash transactions. For instance, if a lawyer has a sick dog and a veterinarian needs some legal advice, by trading services and not reporting the activity to the tax authorities, each can avoid taxation on the income that would have been reported had they sold their services to each other. If the value of a transaction is not recorded as taxable income, it generally does not appear in the GDP. There are some exceptions, however. Contributions toward GDP are estimated for *in-kind wages,* nonmonetary compensation like room and board. GDP values also are assigned to the output consumed by a producer—for example, the home consumption of crops by a farmer.

Final Goods and Services   The second part of the definition of GDP limits the measure to *final goods and services,* the goods and services available to the ultimate consumer. This limitation avoids double-counting. Suppose a retail store sells a shirt to a consumer for $20. The value of the shirt in the GDP is $20. But the shirt is made of cotton that has been grown by a farmer, woven at a mill, and cut and sewn by a manufacturer. What would happen if we counted the value of the shirt at each of these stages of the production process? We would overstate the market value of the shirt.

intermediate good: a good that is used as an input in the production of final goods and services

Intermediate goods are goods that are used in the production of a final product. For instance, the ingredients for a meal are intermediate goods to a restaurant. Similarly, the cotton and the cloth are intermediate goods in the production of the shirt. The stages of production of the $20 shirt are shown in Figure 2. The value-of-output axis measures the value of the product at each stage. The cotton produced by the farmer sells for $1. The cloth woven by the textile mill sells for $5. The shirt manufacturer sells the shirt wholesale to the retail store for $12. The retail store sells the shirt—the final good—to the ultimate consumer for $20.

Remember that GDP is based on the market value of final goods and services. In our example, the market value of the shirt is $20. That price already includes the value of the intermediate goods that were used to produce the shirt. If we add to it the value of output at every stage of production, we would be counting the value of the intermediate goods twice, and we would be overstating the GDP.

value added: the difference between the value of output and the value of the intermediate goods used in the production of that output

It is possible to compute GDP by computing the **value added** at each stage of production. Value added is the difference between the value of output and the value of the intermediate goods used in the production of that output. In Figure 2, the value added by each stage of production is listed at the right. The farmer adds $1 to the value of the shirt. The mill takes the cotton worth $1 and produces cloth worth $5, adding $4 to the value of the shirt. The manufacturer uses $5 worth of cloth to produce a shirt it sells for $12, so the manufacturer adds $7 to the shirt's value. Finally, the retail store adds $8 to the value of the shirt: It pays the manufacturer $12 for the shirt and sells it to the consumer for $20. The sum of the value added at each stage of production is $20. The total value added, then, is equal to the market value of the final product.

Economists can compute GDP using two methods. The final goods and services method uses the market value of the final good or service; the value-added method uses the value added at each stage of production. Both methods count the value of intermediate goods only once. This is an important distinction: GDP is not based on

FIGURE 2

Stages of Production and Value Added in Shirt Manufacturing

A cotton farmer sells cotton to a textile mill for $1, adding $1 to the value of the final shirt. The textile mill sells cloth to a shirt manufacturer for $5, adding $4 to the value of the final shirt. The manufacturer sells the shirt wholesale to the retail store for $12, adding $7 to the value of the final shirt. The retail store sells the final shirt to a consumer for $20, adding $8 to the value of the final shirt. The sum of the prices received at each stage of production equals $38, which is greater than the price of the final shirt. The sum of the value added at each stage of production equals $20, which equals the market value of the shirt.

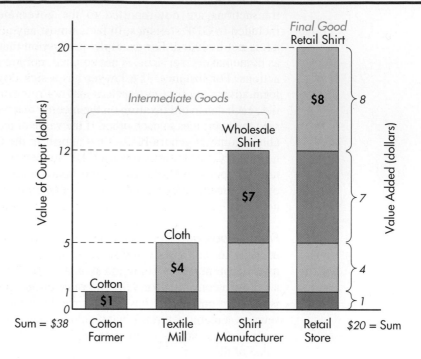

the market value of *all* goods and services, but on the market value of all *final* goods and services.

Produced in a Year GDP measures the value of output *produced in a year.* The value of goods produced last year is counted in last year's GDP; the value of goods produced this year is counted in this year's GDP. The year of production, not the year of sale, determines allocation to GDP. Although the value of last year's goods is not counted in this year's GDP, the value of services involved in the sale is. This year's GDP does not include the value of a house built last year, but it does include the value of the real estate broker's fee; it does not include the value of a used car, but it does include the income earned by the used-car dealer in the sale of that car.

inventory: the stock of unsold goods held by a firm

To determine the value of goods produced in a year but not sold in that year, economists calculate changes in inventory. **Inventory** is a firm's stock of unsold goods. If a shirt that is produced this year remains on the retail store's shelf at the end of the year, it increases the value of the store's inventory. A $20 shirt increases that value by $20. Changes in inventory allow economists to count goods in the year in which they are produced, whether or not they are sold.

Changes in inventory can be planned or unplanned. A store may want a cushion above expected sales (*planned inventory changes*), or it may not be able to sell all the goods it expected to sell when it placed the order (*unplanned inventory changes*). For instance, suppose Jeremy owns a surfboard shop, and he always wants to keep 10 surfboards above what he expects to sell. This is done so that in case business is surprisingly good, he does not have to turn away customers to his competitors and lose those sales. At the beginning of the year, Jeremy has 10 surfboards and then builds as many new boards during the year as he expects to sell. Jeremy *plans* on having an inventory at the end of the year of 10 surfboards. Suppose Jeremy expects to sell 100 surfboards during the year, so he builds 100 new boards. If business is surprisingly poor and Jeremy sells only 80 surfboards, how do we count the 20 new boards that he made but did not sell? We count the change in his inventory. He started the year with 10 surfboards and ends the year with 20 more unsold boards, for a year-end inventory of 30. The change in inventory of 20 (equal to the ending inventory of 30 minus the starting inventory of 10) represents output that is counted in GDP. In Jeremy's case, the inventory change is unplanned, since he expected to sell the 20 extra surfboards that he has in his shop at the end of the year. But whether the inventory change is planned or unplanned, changes in inventory will count output that is produced but not sold in a given year.

2. Who produces the nation's goods and services?

GDP is the value of final goods and services produced by domestic households, businesses, and government.

1.a.1. GDP as Output

The GDP is a measure of the market value of a nation's total output in a year. Remember that economists divide the economy into four sectors: households, businesses, government, and the international sector. Figure 1 shows how the total value of economic activity equals the sum of the output produced in each sector. Figure 3 indicates where the U.S. GDP is actually produced.[1] Since GDP counts the output produced in the United States, U.S. GDP is produced in business firms, households, and government located within the boundaries of the United States.

Not unexpectedly in a capitalist country, privately owned businesses account for the largest percentage of output: In the United States, 84 percent of the GDP is produced by private firms. Government produces 11 percent of the GDP, and households 5 percent.

Figure 3 defines GDP in terms of output: GDP is the value of final goods and services produced by domestic households, businesses, and government units. Even if some of the firms producing in the United States are foreign owned, their output produced in the United States is counted in U.S. GDP.

3. Who purchases the goods and services produced?

1.a.2. GDP as Expenditures

The circular flow in Figure 1 shows not only the output of goods and services from each sector but also the payment for goods and services. Here we look at GDP in terms of what each sector pays for the goods and services it purchases.

The dollar value of total expenditures—the sum of the amount each sector spends on final goods and services—equals the dollar value of output. In Chapter 4 you learned that household spending is called *consumption*. Households spend their income on goods and services to be consumed. Business spending is called *investment*. Investment is spending on capital goods that will be used to produce other

---

[1]Due to rounding, percentages and dollar amounts in the next three figures will not add exactly to the totals given.

FIGURE 3

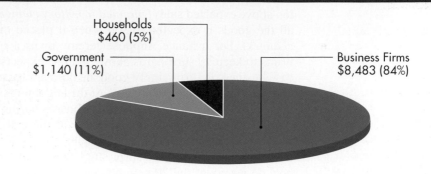

U.S. Gross Domestic Product by Sector, 2001 (billion dollars)

Business firms produce 84 percent of the U.S. GDP. Government produces 11 percent; households, 5 percent. *Source:* Economic Report of the President, 2003.

Households $460 (5%)

Government $1,140 (11%)

Business Firms $8,483 (84%)

goods and services. The two other components of total spending are *government spending* and *net exports.* Net exports are the value of *exports* (goods and services sold to the rest of the world) minus the value of *imports* (goods and services bought from the rest of the world).

$$\text{GDP} = \text{consumption} + \text{investment} + \text{government spending} + \text{net exports}$$

GDP = C + I + G + X

Or, in the shorter form commonly used by economists,

$$\text{GDP} = C + I + G + X$$

where X is net exports.

Figure 4 shows the U.S. GDP in terms of total expenditures. Consumption, or household spending, accounts for 69 percent of national expenditures. Government spending represents 18 percent of expenditures, and business investment, 16 percent. Net exports are negative (-3 percent), which means that imports exceeded exports. To determine total national expenditures on domestic output, the value of imports, spending on foreign output, is subtracted from total expenditures.

?

4. Who receives the income from the production of goods and services?

1.a.3. GDP as Income   The total value of output can be calculated by adding up the expenditures of each sector. And because one sector's expenditures are another's income, the total value of output also can be computed by adding up the income of all sectors.

Business firms use factors of production to produce goods and services. Remember that the income earned by factors of production is classified as wages, interest, rent, and profits. *Wages* are payments to labor, including fringe benefits, social security contributions, and retirement payments. *Interest* is the net interest paid by businesses to households plus the net interest received from foreigners (the interest they pay us minus the interest we pay them). *Rent* is income earned from selling the use of real property (houses, shops, farms). Finally, *profits* are the sum of corporate profits plus proprietors' income (income from sole proprietorships and partnerships).

Figure 5 shows the U.S. GDP in terms of income. Notice that wages account for 58 percent of the GDP. Interest and profits account for 6 and 7 percent of the

FIGURE 4

U.S. Gross Domestic Product as Expenditures, 2001 (billion dollars)

Consumption by households accounts for 69 percent of the GDP, followed by government spending for 18 percent, investment by business firms for 16 percent, and net exports for −3 percent.
Source: Economic Report of the President, 2003.

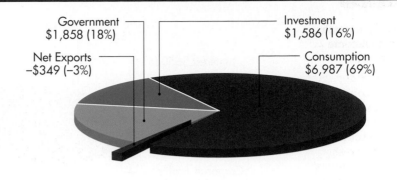

Government $1,858 (18%)

Investment $1,586 (16%)

Net Exports −$349 (−3%)

Consumption $6,987 (69%)

GDP, respectively. Proprietors' income accounts for 7 percent. Rent (2 percent) is very small in comparison. *Net factor income from abroad* is income received from U.S.-owned resources located in other countries minus income paid to foreign-owned resources located in the United States. Since U.S. GDP refers only to income earned within U.S. borders, we must deduct this kind of income to arrive at GDP (−.2 percent).

Figure 5 includes two income categories that we have not discussed: capital consumption allowance and indirect business taxes. **Capital consumption allowance** is not a money payment to a factor of production; it is the estimated value of capital goods used up or worn out in production plus the value of accidental damage to capital goods. The value of accidental damage is relatively small, so it is common to hear economists refer to capital consumption allowance as **depreciation.** Machines and other capital goods wear out over time. The reduction in the value of capital stock due to its being used up or worn out over time is called depreciation. A depreciating capital good loses value each year of its useful life until its value is zero.

Even though capital consumption allowance does not represent income received by a factor of production, it must be accounted for in GDP as income. Otherwise the value of GDP measured as output would be higher than the value of GDP as income. Depreciation is a kind of resource payment, part of the total payment to the owners of capital. All of the income categories—wages, interest, rent, profits, and capital consumption allowance—are expenses incurred in the production of output.

The last item in Figure 5 is indirect business taxes. **Indirect business taxes,** like capital consumption allowances, are not payments to a factor of production. They are taxes collected by businesses that then are turned over to the government. Both excise taxes and sales taxes are forms of indirect business taxes.

For example, suppose a motel room in Florida costs $80 a night. A consumer would be charged $90. Of that $90, the motel receives $80 as the value of the service sold; the other $10 is an excise tax. The motel cannot keep the $10; it must turn it over to the state government. (In effect, the motel is acting as the government's tax collector.) The consumer spends $90; the motel earns $80. To balance expenditures and income, we have to allocate the $10 difference to indirect business taxes.

capital consumption allowance: the estimated value of depreciation plus the value of accidental damage to capital stock

depreciation: a reduction in the value of capital goods over time due to their use in production

indirect business tax: a tax that is collected by businesses for a government agency

FIGURE 5

U.S. Gross Domestic Product as Income Received, 2001 (billion dollars)

The largest component of income is wages, at 58 percent of the GDP. Profits represent 7 percent, interest 6 percent, proprietors' income 7 percent, and rent 2 percent. Capital consumption allowance (13 percent) and indirect business taxes (8 percent) are not income received but still must be added; net factor income from abroad must be subtracted (−.2 percent). (Note: Percentages do not always equal 100 percent.)
Source: Data from Bureau of Economic Analysis.

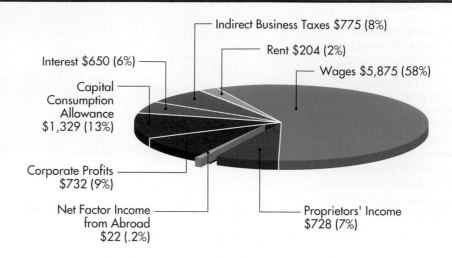

Indirect Business Taxes $775 (8%)
Rent $204 (2%)
Wages $5,875 (58%)
Interest $650 (6%)
Capital Consumption Allowance $1,329 (13%)
Corporate Profits $732 (9%)
Net Factor Income from Abroad $22 (.2%)
Proprietors' Income $728 (7%)

The GDP as income is equal to the sum of wages, interest, rent, and profits, less net factor income from abroad, plus capital consumption allowance and indirect business taxes.

To summarize, GDP measured as income includes the four payments to the factors of production: wages, interest, rent, and profits. These income items represent expenses incurred in the production of GDP. From these we must subtract net factor income from abroad and then add two nonincome items—capital consumption allowance and indirect business taxes—to find real GDP.

$$\text{GDP} = \text{wages} + \text{interest} + \text{rent} + \text{profits} - \text{net factor income from abroad} + \text{capital consumption allowance} + \text{indirect business taxes}$$

The GDP is the total value of output produced in a year, the total value of expenditures made to purchase that output, and the total value of income received by the factors of production. Because all three are measures of the same thing—GDP—all must be equal.

1.b. Other Measures of Output and Income

GDP is the most common measure of a nation's output, but it is not the only measure. Economists rely on a number of others in analyzing the performance of components of an economy.

1.b.1. Gross National Product

gross national product (GNP): gross domestic product plus receipts of factor income from the rest of the world minus payments of factor income to the rest of the world

Gross national product (GNP) equals GDP plus receipts of factor income from the rest of the world minus payments of factor income to the rest of the world. If we add to GDP the value of income earned by U.S.

residents from factors of production located outside the United States and subtract the value of income earned by foreign residents from factors of production located inside the United States, we have a measure of the value of output produced by U.S.-owned resources—GNP.

Figure 6 shows the national income accounts in the United States. The figure begins with the GDP and then shows the calculations necessary to obtain the GNP and other measures of national output. In 2001, the U.S. GNP was $10,104.1 billion.

FIGURE 6

U.S. National Income Accounts, 2001 (billion dollars)

Gross domestic product plus receipts of factor income from the rest of the world minus payments of factor income to the rest of the world equals gross national product. Gross national product minus capital consumption allowance equals net national product. Net national product minus indirect business taxes equals national income. National income plus income currently received but not earned (transfer payments, personal interest, dividend income) minus income currently earned but not received (retained corporate profits, net interest, social security taxes) equals personal income. Personal income minus personal taxes equals disposable personal income. *Source: Data from Bureau of Economic Analysis.*

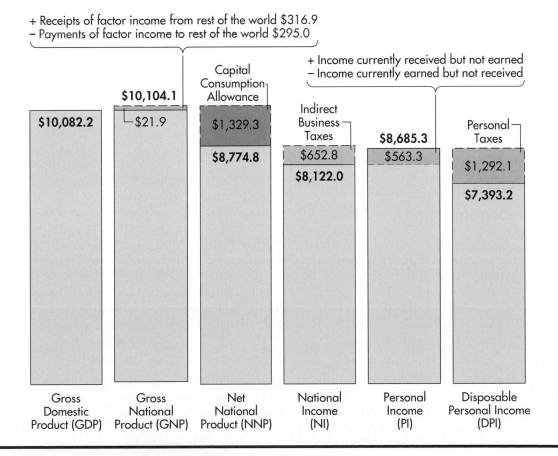

net national product (NNP): gross national product minus capital consumption allowance

1.b.2. Net National Product

Net national product (NNP) equals GNP minus capital consumption allowance. The NNP measures the value of goods and services produced in a year less the value of capital goods that became obsolete or were used up during the year. Because NNP includes only net additions to a nation's capital, it is a better measure of the expansion or contraction of current output than is GNP. Remember how we defined GDP in terms of expenditures in section 1.a.2:

$$\text{GDP} = \text{consumption} + \text{investment} + \text{government spending} + \text{net exports}$$

gross investment: total investment, including investment expenditures required to replace capital goods consumed in current production

net investment: gross investment minus capital consumption allowance

The investment measure in GDP (and GNP) is called **gross investment.** Gross investment is total investment, which includes investment expenditures required to replace capital goods consumed in current production. The NNP does not include investment expenditures required to replace worn-out capital goods; it includes only net investment. **Net investment** is equal to gross investment minus capital consumption allowance. Net investment measures business spending over and above that required to replace worn-out capital goods.

Figure 6 shows that in 2001, the U.S. NNP was $8,774.8 billion. This means that the U.S. economy produced over $8 trillion worth of goods and services above those required to replace capital stock that had depreciated. Over $1 trillion in capital was "worn out" in 2001.

national income: net national product minus indirect business taxes

1.b.3. National Income

National income (NI) equals the NNP minus indirect business taxes, plus or minus a couple of other small adjustments. The NI captures the costs of the factors of production used in producing output. Remember that GDP includes two nonincome expense items: capital consumption allowance and indirect business taxes (section 1.a.3). Subtracting both of these items from the GDP leaves the income payments that actually go to resources.

Because the NNP equals the GNP minus capital consumption allowance, we can subtract indirect business taxes from the NNP to find NI, as shown in Figure 6. This measure helps economists analyze how the costs of (or payments received by) resources change.

personal income (PI): national income plus income currently received but not earned, minus income currently earned but not received

transfer payment: income transferred by the government from a citizen, who is earning income, to another citizen

1.b.4. Personal Income

Personal income (PI) is national income adjusted for income that is received but not earned in the current year and income that is earned but not received in the current year. Social security and welfare benefits are examples of income that is received but not earned in the current year. As you learned in Chapter 5, they are called **transfer payments.** Transfer payments represent income transferred from one citizen, who is earning income, to another citizen, who may not be. The government transfers income by taxing one group of citizens and using the tax payments to fund the income for another group. An example of income that is currently earned but not received is profits that are retained by a corporation to finance current needs rather than paid out to stockholders. Another is social security (FICA) taxes, which are deducted from workers' paychecks.

disposable personal income (DPI): personal income minus personal taxes

1.b.5. Disposable Personal Income

Disposable personal income (DPI) equals personal income minus personal taxes—income taxes, excise and real estate taxes on personal property, and other personal taxes. DPI is the income that individuals have at their disposal for spending or saving. The sum of consumption spending plus saving must equal disposable personal income.

All final goods and services produced in a year are counted in the GDP. For instance, the value of a horseback excursion through the Grand Canyon is part of the national output of the United States. The value of the trip would be equal to the amount that travelers would have to pay the guide company in order to take the trip. This price would reflect the value of the personnel, equipment, and food provided by the guide company.

RECAP

1. Gross domestic product (GDP) is the market value of all final goods and services produced in an economy in a year.

2. The GDP can be calculated by summing the market value of all final goods and services produced in a year, by summing the value added at each stage of production, by adding total expenditures on goods and services (GDP = consumption + investment + government spending + net exports), and by using the total income earned in the production of goods and services (GDP = wages + interest + rent + profits), subtracting net factor income from abroad, and adding depreciation and indirect business taxes.

3. Other measures of output and income include gross national product (GNP), net national product (NNP), national income (NI), personal income (PI), and disposable personal income (DPI).

National Income Accounts

GDP = consumption + investment + government spending + net exports

GNP = GDP + receipts of factor income from the rest of the world
　　　　− payments of factor income to the rest of the world

NNP = GNP − capital consumption allowance

NI = NNP − indirect business taxes

PI = NI − income earned but not received
　　　　+ income received but not earned

DPI = PI − personal taxes

2. Nominal and Real Measures

5. What is the difference between nominal and real GDP?

The GDP is the market value of all final goods and services produced within a country in a year. Value is measured in money terms, so the U.S. GDP is reported in dollars, the German GDP in euro, the Mexican GDP in pesos, and so on. Market value is the product of two elements: the money price and the quantity produced.

2.a. Nominal and Real GDP

nominal GDP: a measure of national output based on the current prices of goods and services

real GDP: a measure of the quantity of final goods and services produced, obtained by eliminating the influence of price changes from the nominal GDP statistics

Nominal GDP measures output in terms of its current dollar value. **Real GDP** is adjusted for changing price levels. In 1980, the U.S. GDP was $2,795 billion; in 2001, it was $10,082.2 billion—an increase of 260 percent. Does this mean that the United States produced 260 percent more goods and services in 2001 than it did in 1980? If the numbers reported are for nominal GDP, we cannot be sure. Nominal GDP cannot tell us whether the economy produced more goods and services, because nominal GDP changes when prices change *and* when quantity changes.

Real GDP measures output in constant prices. This allows economists to identify the changes in actual production of final goods and services: Real GDP measures the quantity of goods and services produced after eliminating the influence of price changes contained in nominal GDP. In 1980, real GDP in the United States was $4,900.9 billion; in 2001, it was $9,214.5 billion, an increase of just 88 percent. The 260 percent increase in nominal GDP in large part reflects increased prices, not increased output.

Since we prefer more goods and services to higher prices, it is better to have nominal GDP rise because of higher output than because of higher prices. We want nominal GDP to increase as a result of an increase in real GDP.

Consider a simple example that illustrates the difference between nominal GDP and real GDP. Suppose a hypothetical economy produces just three goods: oranges, coconuts, and pizzas. The dollar value of output in three different years is listed in Figure 7.

As shown in Figure 7, in year 1, 100 oranges were produced at $.50 per orange, 300 coconuts at $1 per coconut, and 2,000 pizzas at $8 per pizza. The total dollar value of output in year 1 is $16,350. In year 2, prices are constant at the year 1 values, but the quantity of each good has increased by 10 percent. The dollar value of output in year 2 is $17,985, 10 percent higher than the value of output in year 1. In year 3, the quantity of each good is back at the year 1 level, but prices have increased by 10 percent. Oranges now cost $.55, coconuts $1.10, and pizzas $8.80. The dollar value of output in year 3 is $17,985.

Notice that in years 2 and 3, the dollar value of output ($17,985) is 10 percent higher than it was in year 1. But there is a difference here. In year 2, the increase in output is due entirely to an increase in the production of the three goods. In year 3, the increase is due entirely to an increase in the prices of the goods.

Because prices did not change between years 1 and 2, the increase in nominal GDP is entirely accounted for by an increase in real output, or real GDP. In years 1 and 3, the actual quantities produced did not change, which means that real GDP was constant; only nominal GDP was higher, a product only of higher prices.

Figure 8 plots the growth rate of real GDP for several of the industrial countries. One can see in the figure that the countries show somewhat different patterns of real GDP growth over time. For instance, real GDP grew at a slower pace in Japan over the period beginning in the mid-1990s than in other countries. Most of the countries had GDP grow at fairly fast rates in the late 1990s, only to experience a falling growth rate in 2001 and 2002.

FIGURE 7

Prices and Quantities in a Hypothetical Economy

In year 1, total output was $16,350. In year 2, prices remained constant but quantities produced increased by 10 percent, resulting in a higher output of $17,985. With prices constant, we can say that both nominal GDP and real GDP increased from year 1 to year 2. In year 3, quantities produced returned to the year 1 level but prices increased by 10 percent, resulting in the same increased output as in year 2, $17,985. Production has not changed from year 1 to year 3, however, so though nominal GDP has increased, real GDP has remained constant.

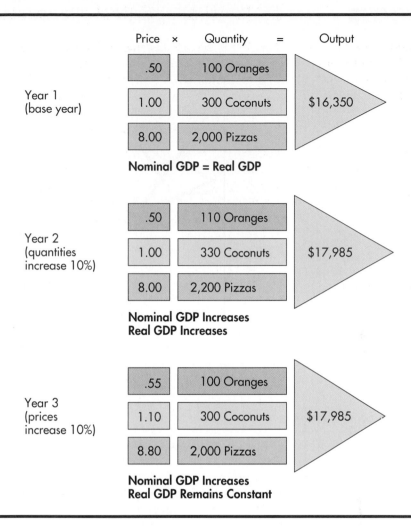

Price	×	Quantity	=	Output

Year 1 (base year)

.50	100 Oranges	
1.00	300 Coconuts	$16,350
8.00	2,000 Pizzas	

Nominal GDP = Real GDP

Year 2 (quantities increase 10%)

.50	110 Oranges	
1.00	330 Coconuts	$17,985
8.00	2,200 Pizzas	

**Nominal GDP Increases
Real GDP Increases**

Year 3 (prices increase 10%)

.55	100 Oranges	
1.10	300 Coconuts	$17,985
8.80	2,000 Pizzas	

**Nominal GDP Increases
Real GDP Remains Constant**

---

6. What is a price index?

2.b. Price Indexes

The total dollar value of output or income is equal to price multiplied by the quantity of goods and services produced:

$$\text{Dollar value of output} = \text{price} \times \text{quantity}$$

By dividing the dollar value of output by price, you can determine the quantity of goods and services produced:

$$\text{Quantity} = \frac{\text{dollar value of output}}{\text{price}}$$

price index: a measure of the average price level in an economy

In macroeconomics, a **price index** measures the average level of prices in an economy and shows how prices, on average, have changed. Prices of individual goods can rise and fall relative to one another, but a price index shows the general trend in prices across the economy.

FIGURE 8

Real GDP Growth in Some Industrial Countries

Real GDP grew at a fast pace in the late 1990s in most countries depicted in the figure, only to fall dramatically in 2001 and 2002. Japan has experienced slower growth of real GDP over this period than the other countries.

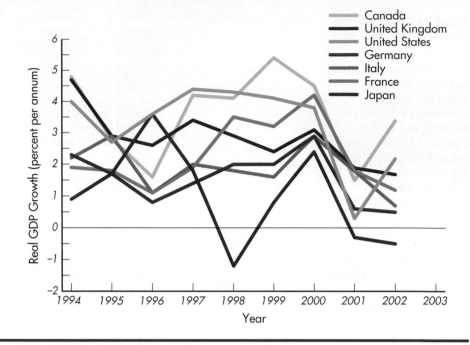

2.b.1. Base Year

base year: the year against which other years are measured

The example in Figure 7 provides a simple introduction to price indexes. The first step is to pick a **base year,** the year against which other years are measured. Any year can serve as the base year. Suppose we pick year 1 in Figure 7. The value of the price index in year 1, the base year, is defined to be 100. This simply means that prices in year 1 are 100 percent of prices in year 1 (100 percent of 1 is 1). In the example, year 2 prices are equal to year 1 prices, so the price index also is equal to 100 in year 2. In year 3, every price has risen 10 percent relative to the base-year (year 1) prices, so the price index is 10 percent higher in year 3, or 110. The value of the price index in any particular year indicates how prices have changed relative to the base year. A value of 110 indicates that prices are 110 percent of base-year prices, or that the average price level has increased 10 percent.

The value of the price index in any particular year indicates how prices have changed relative to the base year.

Price index in any year

= 100 + (or −) percentage change in prices from the base year

Beginning in 1995, the U.S. Department of Commerce has calculated the growth of real GDP using a "chain-type" price series instead of the old method of calculating a "constant-dollar" real GDP.

The old constant-dollar real GDP was calculated by picking a base year and then using prices in the base year to value output in all years. Over time, a constant-dollar real GDP will suffer from "substitution bias." This bias occurs because as prices of some goods rise faster than those of other goods, buyers will substitute away from the higher-priced goods and buy more of the lower-priced goods. Such substitutions will cause output to grow faster in the industries with relatively low

TABLE 1

Constant-Dollar and Chain-Type Real GDP Growth

Year 1			
	Quantity	Price	Expenditures
Apples	300	$1	$300
Bread	100	$2	$200
			$500

Year 2			
	Quantity	Price	Expenditures
Apples	200	$2	$400
Bread	200	$2.50	$500
			$900

Constant-Dollar Real GDP Growth Using Year 1 as Base Year:

(expenditures in year 2 using year 1 prices)/(expenditures in year 1 using year 1 prices) − 1

$$= \frac{(200 \text{ apples} \times \$1) + (200 \text{ bread} \times \$2)}{(300 \text{ apples} \times \$1) + (100 \text{ bread} \times \$2)} - 1 = \frac{\$600}{\$500} - 1$$

$$= 1.2 - 1.0 = 0.2, \text{ or } 20\%$$

Constant-Dollar Real GDP Growth Using Year 2 as Base Year:

(expenditures in year 2 using year 2 prices)/(expenditures in year 1 using year 2 prices) − 1

$$= \frac{(200 \text{ apples} \times \$2) + (200 \text{ bread} \times \$2.50)}{(300 \text{ apples} \times \$2) + (100 \text{ bread} \times \$2.50)} - 1 = \frac{\$900}{\$850} - 1$$

$$= 1.06 - 1.00 = 0.06, \text{ or } 6\%$$

Chain-Type Real GDP Growth:

[(expenditures ratio with year 1 base year + expenditures ratio with year 2 base year)/2] − 1 = [(1.2 + 1.06)/2] −1 = 1.13 − 1 = 0.13, or 13%

---

price increases. Because prices in these industries were relatively high in the base year, their growth will be overstated and constant-dollar real GDP will overestimate the true growth in the economy.

The computer industry provides a good example of substitution bias at work. Prices of computers have fallen since the 1996 base year used for estimating constant-dollar real GDP. By using the 1996 prices of computers in calculating real GDP, the substantial increase in the output of computer equipment is given too much weight. If evaluated at the falling prices actually occurring, the growth of both the computer industry and the overall economy would be lower.

chain-type real GDP growth: the mean of the growth rates found using beginning and ending year prices

Chain-type indexes of real GDP correct for this bias that is included in constant-dollar real GDP. A chain-type real GDP index utilizes prices in two years to calculate the percentage change in real GDP between the two years. Then an index of real GDP is created based on the estimated percentage growth. Table 1 illustrates the creation of a chain-type real GDP index compared to a constant-dollar index.

Table 1 illustrates a simple economy that only produces two goods: apples and bread. Note that total spending on food is $500 in year 1 and $900 in year 2. How should we compute real GDP to best measure how real output of goods has changed? First, let's see what a constant-dollar measure would yield and then compare this to a chain-type index measure as now being used to measure output in the United States. Using year 1 as the base year, we would construct real GDP in each year using year 1 prices associated with quantities. Valuing the quantities purchased in each year at year 1 prices results in a ratio of year 2 expenditures to year 1 expenditures of 1.2. This gives us a 20 percent increase in real GDP. Alternatively, we can use year 2 prices to value quantities in each year. Valuing the quantities purchased each year at year 2 prices results in a ratio of year 2 expenditures to year 1 expenditures of 1.06. This gives us a 6 percent increase in real GDP. Moving the base year forward in time has (and actually had) the impact of reducing the estimated growth of constant-dollar real GDP because the goods whose quantities increased the most are those whose prices increased, relatively, the least. So using the old prices gives too much weight to the rapidly growing sectors of the economy where prices are growing relatively slowly.

The chain-type index is calculated by taking an average of the growth rates found with the beginning and ending year prices. The actual average used by the Department of Commerce is a *geometric mean,* but an arithmetic mean will serve our purpose well here. So the growth of real GDP measured by the chain-type index is found by averaging the two expenditures ratios and then subtracting 1. So we sum the year 1 and year 2 expenditures ratios to get $1.2 + 1.06 = 2.26$. Then we divide this by 2: $2.26/2 = 1.13$. Finally, we subtract 1: $1.13 - 1 = 0.13$. We then find that real GDP growth is 0.13, or 13 percent. The term *chain-type index* indicates that the growth rate from one year to another is being estimated by "chaining together" the growth rates estimated using both the first and second year prices to value quantities rather than arbitrarily picking one period's prices.

Once the percentage changes in real GDP are estimated, then an index number for real GDP is created by picking some arbitrary year to equal 100 (1996 is the year currently used in the United States) and then increasing or decreasing the real GDP index for every other year by the percentage change found from the chain-type measure. We should note that the level of such a real GDP index has no meaning or interpretation apart from the percentage changes from year to year. The value of nominal GDP has a clear interpretation, since it is the observable dollar value of expenditures on output. But to say that the level of the chain-type real GDP index equals 109 in 1998 has no meaning other than as a comparison to other years. If the real GDP index equals 113.4 in 1999, then we can find the growth rate of real GDP from 1998 to 1999 of 4.0 percent ($[113.4/109.0] - 1 = .040$, or 4.0 percent).

2.b.2. Types of Price Indexes

The price of a single good is easy to determine. But how do economists determine a single measure of the prices of the millions of goods and services produced in an economy? They have constructed price indexes to measure the price level; there are several different price indexes used to measure the price level in any economy. Not all prices rise or fall at the same time or by the same amount. This is why there are several measures of the price level in an economy.

The price index used to estimate constant-dollar real GDP is the **GDP price index (GDPPI),** a measure of prices across the economy that reflects all of the categories of goods and services included in GDP. The GDP price index is a very broad

GDP price index: a broad measure of the prices of goods and services included in the gross domestic product

The Consumer Price Index

The CPI is calculated by the Department of Labor using price surveys taken in 87 U.S. cities. Although the CPI often is called a *cost of living index,* it is not. The CPI represents the cost of a fixed market basket of goods purchased by a hypothetical household, not a real one.

In fact, no household consumes the market basket used to estimate the CPI. As relative prices change, households alter their spending patterns. But the CPI market basket changes only every 2 years. This is due in part to the high cost of surveying the public to determine spending patterns. Then, too, individual households have different tastes and spend a different portion of their budgets on the various components of household spending (housing, food, clothing, transportation, medical care). Only a household that spends exactly the same portion of its income on each item counted in the CPI would find the CPI representative of its cost of living.

The Department of Labor surveys spending in eight major areas. The figure shows the areas and the

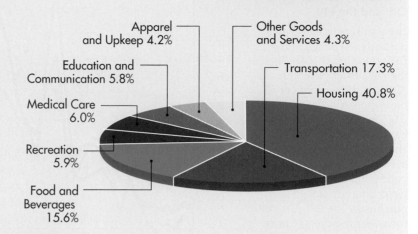

percentage of the typical household budget devoted to each area. If you kept track of your spending over the course of several months, you probably would find that you spend much more than the typical household on some items and much less on others. In other words, the CPI is not a very good measure of *your* cost of living.

Source: Data from Bureau of Labor Statistics.

---

measure. Economists use other price indexes to analyze how prices change in more specific categories of goods and services.

consumer price index (CPI): a measure of the average price of goods and services purchased by the typical household

Probably the best-known price index is the **consumer price index (CPI).** The CPI measures the average price of consumer goods and services that a typical household purchases. (See the Economic Insight "The Consumer Price Index.") The CPI is a narrower measure than the GDPPI because it includes fewer items. However, because of the relevance of consumer prices to the standard of living, news reports on price changes in the economy typically focus on consumer price changes. In addition, labor contracts sometimes include provisions that raise wages as the CPI goes up. Social security payments also are tied to increases in the CPI. These increases are called **cost of living adjustments (COLAs),** because they are supposed to keep nominal income rising along with the cost of items purchased by the typical household.

cost of living adjustment (COLA): an increase in wages that is designed to match increases in prices of items purchased by the typical household

producer price index (PPI): a measure of average prices received by producers

The **producer price index (PPI)** measures average prices received by producers. At one time this price index was known as the *wholesale price index* (WPI). Because the PPI measures price changes at an earlier stage of production than the CPI, it can indicate a coming change in the CPI. If producer input costs are rising, we can expect the price of goods produced to go up as well.

FIGURE 9

The GDP Price Index, the CPI, and the PPI

The graph plots the annual percentage change in the GDP price index (GDPPI), the consumer price index (CPI), and the producer price index (PPI). The GDPPI is used to construct constant-dollar real GDP. The CPI measures the average price of consumer goods and services that a typical household purchases. The PPI measures the average price received by producers; it is the most variable of the three because fluctuations in equilibrium prices of intermediate goods are much greater than for final goods. *Source:* Economic Report of the President, 2003.

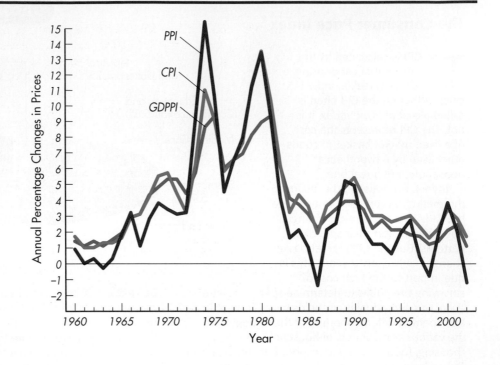

Figure 9 illustrates how the three different measures of prices changed between 1965 and 2001. Notice that the PPI is more volatile than the GDPPI or the CPI. This is because there are smaller fluctuations in the equilibrium prices of final goods than of intermediate goods.

RECAP

1. Nominal GDP is measured using current dollars.
2. Real GDP measures output with price effects removed.
3. Chain-type real GDP growth equals the mean of the growth rates found with beginning and ending year prices.
4. The GDP price index, the consumer price index, and the producer price index are all measures of the level of prices in an economy.

3. Flows of Income and Expenditures

GDP is both a measure of total expenditures on final goods and services and a measure of the total income earned in the production of those goods and services. The idea that total expenditures equal total income is clearly illustrated in Figure 1.

The figure links the four sectors of the economy: households, firms, government, and foreign countries. The arrows between the sectors indicate the direction of the flows. Gold arrows with dollar signs represent money flows; blue-green arrows without dollar signs represent flows of real goods and services. The money flows are both income and expenditures. For instance, household expenditures for goods and services from business firms are represented by the gold arrow at the top of the diagram. Household income from firms is represented by the gold arrow flowing from firms to households at the bottom of the diagram. Because one sector's expenditures represent another sector's income, the total expenditures on goods and services must be the same as the total income from selling goods and services, and those must both be equal to the total value of the goods and services produced.

RECAP

1. Total spending on final goods and services equals the total income received in producing those goods and services.
2. The circular flow model shows that one sector's expenditures represent the income of other sectors.

Summary

? How is the total output of an economy measured?

1. National income accounting is the system economists use to measure both the output of an economy and the flows between sectors of that economy. *§1*

2. Gross domestic product (GDP) is the market value of all final goods and services produced in a year in a country. *§1.a*

3. The GDP also equals the value added at each stage of production. *§1.a*

? Who produces the nation's goods and services?

4. The GDP as output equals the sum of the output of households, business firms, and government within the country. Business firms produce 84 percent of the U.S. GDP. *§1.a.1*

? Who purchases the goods and services produced?

5. The GDP as expenditures equals the sum of consumption plus investment plus government spending plus net exports. In the United States, consumption accounts for roughly two-thirds of total expenditures. *§1.a.2*

? Who receives the income from the production of goods and services?

6. The GDP as income equals the sum of wages, interest, rent, profits, proprietors' income, capital consumption allowance, and indirect business taxes less net factor income from abroad. Wages account for about 60 percent of the total. *§1.a.3*

7. Capital consumption allowance is the estimated value of depreciation plus the value of accidental damage to capital stock. *§1.a.3*

8. Other measures of national output include gross national product (GNP), net national product (NNP), national income (NI), personal income (PI), and disposable personal income (DPI). *§1.b*

? What is the difference between nominal and real GDP?

9. Nominal GDP measures output in terms of its current dollar value, including the effects of price changes; real GDP measures output after eliminating the effects of price changes. *§2.a*

? What is a price index?

10. A price index measures the average level of prices across an economy. *§2.b*

11. The GDP price index is a measure of the prices of all the goods and services included in the GDP. *§2.b.2*

12. The consumer price index (CPI) measures the average price of goods and services consumed by the typical household. *§2.b.2*

13. The producer price index (PPI) measures average prices received by producers (wholesale prices). *§2.b.2*

14. Total expenditures on final goods and services equal total income. *§3*

Key Terms

national income accounting *§1*

gross domestic product (GDP) *§1.a*

intermediate good *§1.a*

value added *§1.a*

inventory *§1.a*

capital consumption allowance *§1.a.3*

depreciation *§1.a.3*

indirect business tax *§1.a.3*

gross national product (GNP) *§1.b.1*

net national product (NNP) *§1.b.2*

gross investment *§1.b.2*

net investment *§1.b.2*

national income (NI) *§1.b.3*

personal income (PI) *§1.b.4*

transfer payment *§1.b.4*

disposable personal income (DPI) *§1.b.5*

nominal GDP *§2.a*

real GDP *§2.a*

price index *§2.b*

base year *§2.b.1*

chain-type real GDP growth *§2.b.1*

GDP price index *§2.b.2*

consumer price index (CPI) *§2.b.2*

cost of living adjustment (COLA) *§2.b.2*

producer price index (PPI) *§2.b.2*

Exercises

1. The following table lists the stages required in the production of a personal computer. What is the value of the computer in the GDP?

Stage	Value Added
Components manufacture	$ 50
Assembly	$ 250
Wholesaler	$ 500
Retailer	$1,500

2. What is the difference between GDP and each of the following?

   a. Gross national product
   b. Net national product
   c. National income
   d. Personal income
   e. Disposable personal income

3.

	Year 1		Year 2	
	Quantity	Price	Quantity	Price
Oranges	100	$3	150	$3
Pears	100	$3	75	$4

   a. What is the growth rate of constant-dollar real GDP using year 1 as the base year?
   b. What is the growth rate of constant-dollar real GDP using year 2 as the base year?
   c. What is the chain-type real GDP growth rate between years 1 and 2?

4. Why do total expenditures on final goods and services equal total income in the economy?

5. Why don't we measure national output by simply counting the total number of goods and services produced each year?

6. Why isn't the CPI a useful measure of *your* cost of living?

Use the following national income accounting information to answer exercises 7–11:

Consumption	$400
Imports	$ 10
Net investment	$ 20
Government purchases	$100
Exports	$ 20
Capital consumption allowance	$ 20
Indirect business taxes	$ 5
Receipts of factor income from the rest of the world	$ 12
Payments of factor income to the rest of the world	$ 10

7. What is the GDP for this economy?

8. What is the GNP for this economy?

9. What is the NNP for this economy?

10. What is the national income for this economy?

11. What is the gross investment in this economy?

12. Indirect business taxes and capital consumption allowance are not income, yet they are included in order to find GDP as income received. Why do we add these two nonincome components to the other components of income (like wages, rent, interest, profits, and net factor income from abroad) to find GDP?

13. Why has nominal GDP increased faster than real GDP in the United States over time? What would it mean if an economy had real GDP increasing faster than nominal GDP?

14. We usually discuss GDP in terms of what is included in the definition. What is *not* included in GDP? Why are these things excluded?

15. If a surfboard is produced this year but not sold until next year, how is it counted in this year's GDP and not next year's?

16. Constant-dollar real GDP may suffer from a "substitution bias." Explain how this can occur and give an example. How does the use of chain-type real GDP reduce this bias?

Take the ACE Practice Test for this chapter to review the important concepts and get immediate feedback with answers.

economics.college.hmco.com/students

Hiding in the Shadows: The Growth of the Underground Economy

A factory worker has a second job driving an unlicensed taxi at night; a plumber fixes a broken water pipe for a client, gets paid in cash but doesn't declare his earnings to the tax collector; a drug dealer brokers a sale with a prospective customer on a street corner. These are all examples of the underground or shadow economy—activities, both legal and illegal, that add up to trillions of dollars a year that take place "off the books," out of the gaze of taxmen and government statisticians.

Although crime and shadow economic activities have long been a fact of life—and are now increasing around the world—almost all societies try to control their growth, because a prospering shadow economy makes official statistics (on unemployment, official labor force, income, consumption) unreliable. Policies and programs that are framed on the basis of unreliable statistics may be inappropriate and self-defeating. . . .

Also called the underground, informal, or parallel economy, the shadow economy includes not only illegal activities but also unreported income from the production of legal goods and services, either from monetary or barter transactions. Hence, the shadow economy comprises all economic activities that would generally be taxable were they reported to the tax authorities.

Estimating the size of the shadow economy is difficult. After all, people engaged in underground activities do their best to avoid detection. But policymakers and government administrators need information about how many people are active in the shadow economy, how often underground activities occur, and the size of these activities, so that they can make appropriate decisions on resource allocation.

Table 1 shows average estimates for the three main country groups—developing countries, transition economies, and 21 advanced economies, the last all members of the Organization for Economic Cooperation and Development (OECD). The comparisons among countries remain somewhat crude because they are based on different estimation methods.

Countries with relatively low tax rates, fewer laws and regulations, and a well-established rule of law tend to have smaller shadow economies.

Macroeconomic and microeconomic modeling studies based on data for several countries suggest that the major driving forces behind the size and growth of the shadow economy are an increasing burden of tax and social security payments, combined with rising restrictions in the official labor market. Wage rates in the official economy also play a role. . . .

Shadow economies tend to be smaller in countries where government institutions are strong and efficient. Indeed, some studies have found that it is not higher taxes per se that increase the size of the shadow economy, but ineffectual and discretionary application of the tax system and regulations by governments.

Source: Friedrich Schneider with Dominik Enste, *Hiding in the Shadows: The Growth of the Underground Economy, Economic Issues,* No. 30, International Monetary Fund, March 2002.

TABLE 1

Shadow Economy as Percent of Official GDP, 1988–2000

Country Group	Percent of GDP
Developing	35–44
Transition	21–30
OECD	14–16

The ranges reflect the different estimation methods used by different sources.

International Monetary Fund/March 2002

In this chapter we learned about different measures of macroeconomic performance. It is important to have accurate measures in order to formulate appropriate policy. Bad data on economic performance could result in policymakers attempting to fix problems that don't really exist or failing to address problems that have not been identified. However, it is not easy to measure the performance of an economy. This article indicates a particular type of problem that exists in every economy: the underground economy.

The presence of a large and active underground economy indicates that official GDP is missing much of the economic activity that occurs. As indicated in the article, this is more than just illegal activity, like dealing in illicit drugs. Perfectly legal activities that are conducted "off the books" are missed in the official GDP accounting. So if a carpenter performs work for someone, is paid in cash, and never reports the transaction as income to be taxed, this activity is part of the underground economy. While the carpenter was engaged in productive activity, it will not be counted, and so the official GDP measure will underestimate the true amount of production undertaken in a year.

This article serves as a reminder that, while government officials may do the best job they can at counting economic activity, they will never be able to count everything. As shown in Table 1 of the article, the problems are worse for the developing countries and those countries that are in transition from socialism than for the industrial countries (referred to as OECD countries in the table). Yet even the industrial countries are estimated to have between 14 and 16 percent of GDP take place in the underground economy.

CHAPTER 7

An Introduction to the Foreign Exchange Market and the Balance of Payments

? Fundamental Questions

1. **How do individuals of one nation trade money with individuals of another nation?**

2. **How do changes in exchange rates affect international trade?**

3. **How do nations record their transactions with the rest of the world?**

In Chapter 6, you learned that gross domestic product equals the sum of consumption, investment, government spending, and net exports (GDP = $C + I + G + X$). Net exports (X) are one key measure of a nation's transactions with other countries, a principal link between a nation's GDP and developments in the rest of the world. In this chapter, we extend the macroeconomic accounting framework to include more detail on a nation's international transactions. This extension is known as balance of payments accounting.

International transactions have grown rapidly in recent years as the economies of the world have become increasingly interrelated. Improvements in transportation and communication, and global markets for goods and services have created a community of world economies. Products made in one country sell in the world market, where they compete against products from other nations. Europeans purchase stocks listed on the New York Stock Exchange; Americans purchase bonds issued in Japan.

Different countries use different monies. When goods and services are exchanged across international borders, national monies also are traded. To make buying and selling decisions in the global marketplace, people must be able to compare prices across countries, to compare prices quoted in Japanese yen with those quoted in Mexican pesos. This chapter begins with a look at how national monies are priced and traded in the foreign exchange market. ■

1. The Foreign Exchange Market

1. How do individuals of one nation trade money with individuals of another nation?

foreign exchange: currency and bank deposits that are denominated in foreign money

foreign exchange market: a global market in which people trade one currency for another

Foreign exchange is foreign money, including paper money and bank deposits like checking accounts that are denominated in foreign currency. When someone with U.S. dollars wants to trade those dollars for Japanese yen, the trade takes place in the **foreign exchange market,** a global market in which people trade one currency for another. Many financial markets are located in a specific geographic location. For instance, the New York Stock Exchange is a specific location in New York City where stocks are bought and sold. The Commodity Exchange is a specific location in New York City where contracts to deliver agricultural and metal commodities are bought and sold. The foreign exchange market is not in a single geographic location, however. Trading occurs all over the world electronically and by telephone. Most of the activity involves large banks in New York, London, and other financial centers. A foreign exchange trader at Citigroup in New York can buy or sell currencies with a trader at Barclays Bank in London by calling the other trader on the telephone or exchanging computer messages.

Only tourism and a few other transactions in the foreign exchange market involve the actual movement of currency. The great majority of transactions involve the buying and selling of bank deposits denominated in foreign currency. A bank deposit can be a checking account that a firm or individual writes checks against to make payments to others, or it may be an interest-earning savings account with no check-writing privileges. Currency notes, like dollar bills, are used in a relatively small fraction of transactions. When a large corporation or a government buys foreign currency, it buys a bank deposit denominated in the foreign currency. Still, all exchanges in the market require that monies have a price.

1.a. Exchange Rates

exchange rate: the price of one country's money in terms of another country's money

An **exchange rate** is the price of one country's money in terms of another country's money. Exchange rates are needed to compare prices quoted in two different currencies. Suppose a shirt that has been manufactured in Canada sells for 20 U.S. dollars in Seattle, Washington, and for 25 Canadian dollars in Vancouver, British Columbia. Where would you get the better buy? Unless you know the exchange rate between U.S. and Canadian dollars, you can't tell. The exchange rate allows you to convert the foreign currency price into its domestic currency equivalent, which then can be compared to the domestic price.

Table 1 lists exchange rates for March 10, 2003. The rates are quoted in U.S. dollars per unit of foreign currency in the second column, and units of foreign currency per U.S. dollar in the last column. For instance, the Canadian dollar was selling for $.6825, or a little more than 68 U.S. cents. The same day, the U.S. dollar was selling for 1.4652 Canadian dollars (1 U.S. dollar would buy 1.4652 Canadian dollars).

Active Trading Around the World

It is often said that the foreign exchange market never closes, since trading can take place in different parts of the world as time passes. However, people in each region tend to work certain normal business hours, and so each major foreign exchange trading location has fairly regular hours during which active trading occurs. The figure below shows the normal hours of active trading in each major trading region. The times are *Greenwich Mean Time,* or *GMT,* which is the time in London. For instance, we see that active trading in London is shown to open at 0800. This is 8 A.M. in London. Active trading stops in London at 1600, which is 4 P.M. in London. In many parts of the world, a 24-hour clock registers time from 0000 to 1200 in the morning, where 1200 is noon. Then in the afternoon, time starts to count up from 1200. So 1 P.M. is 1300, 2 P.M. is 1400, and so on.

The figure shows trading in New York as opening at 1200, or noon in London. Eastern time in the United States is 5 hours behind London time (as seen by the −5 for that region of the world at the bottom of the figure), so that when it is noon in London, it is 5 hours earlier, or 7 A.M., in New York. Note that active trading in London closes at 1600 and New York opens at 1200, so London and New York trading overlap for 4 hours each day. Similarly, the figure shows that trading in New York also overlaps with trading in Frankfurt, Germany. However, there is no overlap of trading in North America with trading in Asia, as Asian trading centers open after trading has ended in North America and close before trading begins in North America. There is a short overlap of Asian trading with European trading. This figure reminds us that the world of foreign exchange trading, and business in general, tends to be conducted during regular business hours in each region.

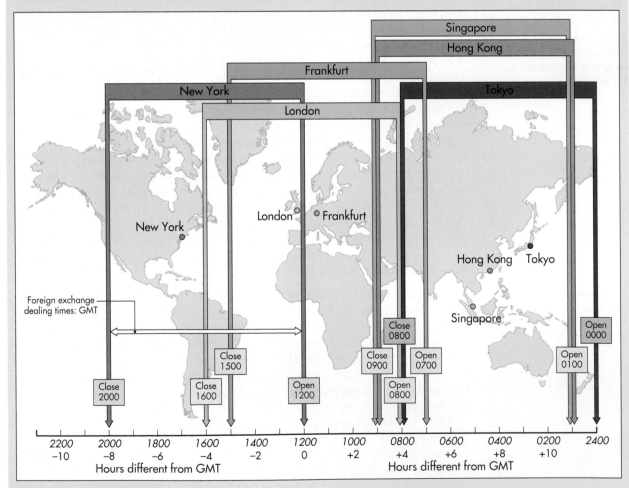

TABLE 1

Exchange Rates,
March 10, 2003

Country	U.S.$ per Currency	Currency per U.S.$
Argentina (peso)	.3190	3.1348
Australia (dollar)	.6148	1.6265
Britain (pound)	1.6019	.6243
Canada (dollar)	.6825	1.4652
China (renminbi)	.1208	8.2781
Israel (shekel)	.2062	4.8497
Japan (yen)	.00856	116.85
Mexico (peso)	.0904	11.0644
New Zealand (dollar)	.5591	1.7886
Russia (ruble)	.0317	31.556
Singapore (dollar)	.5761	1.7358
Switzerland (franc)	.7547	1.3250
EU (euro)	1.1058	.9043

Note: The second column lists U.S. dollars per foreign currency, or how much one unit of foreign currency is worth in U.S. dollars. On March 10 you could get about 68 U.S. cents for 1 Canadian dollar. The third column lists foreign currency per U.S. dollar, or how much 1 U.S. dollar is worth in foreign currency. On the same day, you could get about 1.47 Canadian dollars for 1 U.S. dollar.

Find the reciprocal of a number by writing it as a fraction and then turning the fraction upside down. In other words, make the numerator the denominator and the denominator the numerator.

If you know the price in U.S. dollars of a currency, you can find the price of the U.S. dollar in that currency by taking the reciprocal. To find the reciprocal of a number, write it as a fraction and then turn the fraction upside down. Let's say that 1 British pound sells for 2 U.S. dollars. In fraction form, 2 is 2/1. The reciprocal of 2/1 is 1/2, or .5. So 1 U.S. dollar sells for .5 British pound. The table shows that the actual dollar price of the pound was 1.6019. The *reciprocal exchange rate*—the number of pounds per dollar—is .6243 (1/1.6019), which was the pound price of 1 dollar that day.

Let's go back to comparing the price of the Canadian shirt in Seattle and in Vancouver. The International Standards Organization (ISO) symbol for the U.S. dollar is USD. The symbol for the Canadian dollar is CAD. (Table 2 lists the symbols for a number of currencies.) The shirt sells for USD20 in Seattle and CAD25 in Vancouver. Suppose the exchange rate between the U.S. dollar and the Canadian dollar is .8. This means that CAD1 costs .8 U.S. dollars, or 80 U.S. cents. To find the domestic currency value of a foreign currency price, multiply the foreign currency price by the exchange rate:

Domestic currency value = foreign currency price × exchange rate

In our example, the U.S. dollar is the domestic currency:

U.S. dollar value = CAD25 × .8 = USD20

If we multiply the price of the shirt in Canadian dollars (CAD25) by the exchange rate (.8), we find the U.S. dollar value ($20). After adjusting for the exchange rate, then, we can see that the shirt sells for the same price when the price is measured in a single currency.

TABLE 2

International Currency Symbols, Selected Countries

Country	Currency	ISO Symbol
Australia	Dollar	AUD
Canada	Dollar	CAD
China	Yuan	CNY
Denmark	Krone	DKK
India	Rupee	INR
Iran	Rial	IRR
Japan	Yen	JPY
Kuwait	Dinar	KWD
Mexico	Peso	MXP
Norway	Krone	NOK
Russia	Ruble	RUB
Saudi Arabia	Riyal	SAR
Singapore	Dollar	SGD
South Africa	Rand	ZAR
Sweden	Krona	SEK
Switzerland	Franc	CHF
United Kingdom	Pound	GPB
United States	Dollar	USD
Venezuela	Bolivar	VEB
European Union	Euro	EUR

The *euro* is the common currency of the following western European countries: Austria, Belgium, Finland, France, Germany, Greece, Ireland, Italy, Luxembourg, Netherlands, Portugal, and Spain. In midyear 2002 the former currencies of each of these countries, like the German mark, French franc, and so on, were eliminated and the euro replaced them all. The Global Business Insight "The Euro" provides more discussion.

1.b. Exchange Rate Changes and International Trade

2. How do changes in exchange rates affect international trade?

Because exchange rates determine the domestic currency value of foreign goods, changes in those rates affect the demand for and supply of goods traded internationally. Suppose the price of the shirt in Seattle and in Vancouver remains the same, but the exchange rate changes from .8 to .9 U.S. dollars per Canadian dollar. What happens? The U.S. dollar price of the shirt in Vancouver increases. At the new rate, the shirt that sells for CAD25 in Vancouver costs a U.S. buyer USD22.50 (CAD25 × .9).

A currency appreciates in value when its value rises in relation to another currency.

A rise in the value of a currency is called *appreciation.* In our example, as the exchange rate moves from USD.8 = CAD1 to USD.9 = CAD1, the Canadian dollar appreciates against the U.S. dollar. As a country's currency appreciates, international demand for its products falls, other things equal.

The Euro

The euro began trading in January 1999 and for more than three years circulated jointly with the national currencies of the 12 countries that adopted the euro. The countries and their former currencies are Austrian schilling, Belgian franc, Finnish markka, French franc, German mark, Greek drachma, Irish pound, Italian lira, Luxembourg franc, Netherlands guilder, Portuguese escudo, and Spanish peseta. Prior to the beginning of the euro, the value of each of the "legacy currencies" of the euro area was fixed in terms of the euro. For instance, 1 euro was equal to 40.3399 Belgian francs or 1.95583 German marks. In February 2002, the former monies of each of the euro-area countries were withdrawn from circulation, and now only the euro is used in the 12-country area.

Euro coins are available in the following denominations: 1, 2, 5, 10, 20, and 50 cents and 1 and 2 euros. One side of each coin has an image that is common in all euroland countries. The other side has a design that is individualized for each country. For instance, a 2-euro coin has a common side with a big number 2 placed over a map of Europe. But the reverse side differs across countries. In Germany, the 2-euro coin has an eagle surrounded by a ring of stars, while in Spain, the 2-euro coin has a portrait of the Spanish king, Carlos I. However, even though each

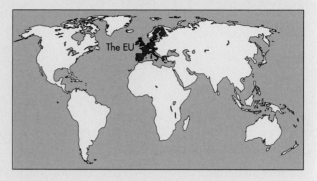

country can issue its own coins, the coins are all usable in any euroland country. You could receive French coins in Paris and then spend them in Rome. Euro currency or banknotes are available in the following denominations: 5, 10, 20, 50, 100, 200, and 500 euros. The paper money is identical in all countries.

At the time the text was being revised for this edition, three member countries of the European Union had not adopted the euro and still maintained their own currencies and monetary policies. The three countries were Denmark, Sweden, and the United Kingdom. It remains to be seen when, and if, these countries become part of "euroland."

A currency depreciates in value when its value falls in relation to another currency.

Suppose the exchange rate in our example moves from USD.8 = CAD1 to USD.7 = CAD1. Now the shirt that sells for CAD25 in Vancouver costs a U.S. buyer USD17.50 (CAD25 × .7). In this case, the Canadian dollar has *depreciated* in value relative to the U.S. dollar. As a country's currency depreciates, its goods sell for lower prices in other countries and the demand for its products increases, other things equal.

When the Canadian dollar is appreciating against the U.S. dollar, the U.S. dollar must be depreciating against the Canadian dollar. For instance, when the exchange rate between the U.S. dollar and the Canadian dollar moves from USD.8 = CAD1 to USD.9 = CAD1, the reciprocal exchange rate—the rate between the Canadian dollar and the U.S. dollar—moves from CAD1.25 = USD1 (1/.8 = 1.25) to CAD1.11 = USD1 (1/.9 = 1.11). At the same time that Canadian goods are becoming more expensive to U.S. buyers, U.S. goods are becoming cheaper to Canadian buyers.

In later chapters we look more closely at how changes in exchange rates affect international trade and at how governments use exchange rates to change their net exports.

1. The foreign exchange market is a global market in which foreign money, largely bank deposits, is bought and sold.
2. An exchange rate is the price of one money in terms of another.
3. Foreign demand for domestic goods decreases as the domestic currency appreciates and increases as the domestic currency depreciates.

3. How do nations record their transactions with the rest of the world?

balance of payments: a record of a country's trade in goods, services, and financial assets with the rest of the world

2. The Balance of Payments

The U.S. economy does not operate in a vacuum. It affects and is affected by the economies of other nations. This point is brought home to Americans when newspaper headlines announce a large trade deficit and politicians denounce foreign countries for running trade surpluses against the United States. In such times, it seems as if everywhere there is talk of the balance of payments.

The **balance of payments** is a record of a country's trade in goods, services, and financial assets with the rest of the world. This record is divided into categories, or accounts, that summarize the nation's international economic transactions. For example, one category measures transactions in merchandise; another measures transactions involving financial assets (bank deposits, bonds, stocks, loans). Balance of payments data are reported quarterly for most developed countries.

Once we understand the various definitions of the balance of payments, there remains the issue of why we should care. One important reason is that balance of payments issues are often hot political topics. One cannot make sense of the political debate without an understanding of balance of payments basics. For instance, the United States is said to have a large deficit in its merchandise trade with the rest of the world. Is this bad? Some politicians will argue that a large trade deficit calls for government action, as they assert that it is harmful for a nation to buy more than it sells in trade with the rest of the world. The economics of the balance of payments allows us to judge the value of such arguments. Some policymakers, labor leaders, and businesspeople will argue that it is bad if a county has a balance of trade deficit with another single country. For instance, if the United States has a trade deficit with Japan, it is common to hear calls for policy aimed at eliminating this *bilateral* trade deficit. Once again, an understanding of the economics of the trade deficit allows a proper evaluation of calls for policy aimed at eliminating bilateral trade imbalances. We will encounter references to policy issues related to the balance of payments in later chapters.

2.a. Accounting for International Transactions

double-entry bookkeeping: a system of accounting in which every transaction is recorded in at least two accounts and in which the debit total must equal the credit total for the transaction as a whole

The balance of payments is an accounting statement based on **double-entry bookkeeping,** a system in which every transaction is recorded in at least two accounts. Suppose a U.S. tractor manufacturer sells a $50,000 tractor to a resident of France. The transaction is recorded twice: once as the tractor going from the United States to France, and then again as the payment of $50,000 going from France to the United States.

Double-entry bookkeeping means that for each transaction there is a credit entry and a debit entry. *Credits* record activities that bring payments into a country; *debits* record activities that involve payments to the rest of the world. Table 3 shows the

TABLE 3

Balance of Payments Entries for the Sale of a U.S. Tractor to a French Buyer

Activity	Credit	Debit
U.S. firm exports tractor and receives $50,000 from French buyer	$50,000	
French buyer imports tractor and transfers $50,000 from U.S. bank account to U.S. firm		$50,000
	$50,000	$50,000

entries in the U.S. balance of payments to record the sale of a $50,000 U.S. tractor to a French importer. The sale of the tractor represents a $50,000 credit entry in the balance of payments because U.S. exports earn foreign exchange for U.S. residents. To complete the record of this transaction, we must know how payment was made for the tractor. Let's assume that the French buyer paid with a $50,000 check drawn on a U.S. bank. Money that is withdrawn from a foreign-owned bank account in the United States is treated as foreign exchange moved out of the country. So we record the payment as a debit entry in the balance of payments. In fact, the money did not leave the country; its ownership was transferred from the French buyer to the U.S. seller.

The sum of total credits must equal the sum of total debits so that the two columns of the balance of payments always balance.

The tractor sale is recorded on both sides of the balance of payments. There is a credit entry, and there is a debit entry. For every international transaction, there must be both a credit entry and a debit entry. This means that the sum of total credits and the sum of total debits must be equal. Credits always offset, or balance, debits.

2.b. Balance of Payments Accounts

current account: the sum of the merchandise, services, income, and unilateral transfers accounts in the balance of payments

The balance of payments uses several different accounts to classify transactions (Table 4). The **current account** is the sum of the balances in the merchandise, services, income, and unilateral transfers accounts.

Merchandise   This account records all transactions involving goods. The exports of goods by the United States are merchandise credits; its imports of foreign goods are merchandise debits. When exports (or credits) exceed imports (or debits), the

TABLE 4

Simplified U.S. Balance of Payments, 2002 Third Quarter (million dollars)

Account	Net Balance
Merchandise	−$123,176
Services	$12,315
Income	−$2,959
Unilateral transfers	−$13,221
Current account	−$127,041
Financial account	$172,653
Statistical discrepancy	−$45,612

Source: Data from Bureau of Economic Analysis.

surplus: in a balance of payments account, the amount by which credits exceed debits

deficit: in a balance of payments account, the amount by which debits exceed credits

balance of trade: the balance on the merchandise account in a nation's balance of payments

merchandise account shows a **surplus.** When imports exceed exports, the account shows a **deficit.** The balance on the merchandise account is frequently referred to as the **balance of trade.**

In the third quarter of 2002, the merchandise account in the U.S. balance of payments showed a deficit of $123,176 million. This means that the merchandise credits created by U.S. exports were $123,176 million less than the merchandise debits created by U.S. imports. In other words, the United States bought more goods from other nations than it sold to them.

Services This account measures trade involving services. It includes travel and tourism, royalties, transportation costs, and insurance premiums. In Table 4, the balance on the services account was a $12,315 million surplus.

Income Both investment income and employee compensation are included here. The income earned from investments in foreign countries is a credit; the income paid on foreign-owned investments in the United States is a debit. Investment income is the return on a special kind of service: It is the value of services provided by capital in foreign countries. Compensation earned by U.S. workers abroad is a credit. Compensation earned by foreign workers in the United States is a debit. In Table 4, there is a deficit of $2,959 million in the income account.

Unilateral Transfers In a unilateral transfer, one party gives something but gets nothing in return. Gifts and retirement pensions are forms of unilateral transfers. For instance, if a farmworker in El Centro, California, sends money to his family in Guaymas, Mexico, this is a unilateral transfer from the United States to Mexico. In Table 4, the unilateral transfers balance is a deficit of $13,221 million.

The current account is a useful measure of international transactions because it contains all of the activities involving goods and services. The **financial account** is where trade involving financial assets and international investment is recorded. In the third quarter of 2002, the current account showed a deficit of $127,041 million. This means that U.S. imports of merchandise, services, investment income, and unilateral transfers were $127,041 million greater than exports of these items.

financial account: the record in the balance of payments of the flow of financial assets into and out of a country

If we draw a line in the balance of payments under the current account, then all entries below the line relate to financing the movement of merchandise, services, investment income, and unilateral transfers into and out of the country. Credits to the financial account reflect foreign purchases of U.S. financial assets or real property like land and buildings, and debits reflect U.S. purchases of foreign financial assets and real property. In Table 4, the U.S. financial account showed a surplus of $172,653 million.

The *statistical discrepancy* account, the last account listed in Table 4, could be called *omissions and errors.* Government cannot accurately measure all transactions that take place. Some international shipments of goods and services go uncounted or are miscounted, as are some international flows of financial assets. The statistical discrepancy account is used to correct for these omissions and errors. In Table 4, measured credits were less than measured debits, so the statistical discrepancy was $45,612 million.

Over all of the balance of payments accounts, the sum of credits must equal the sum of debits. The bottom line—the *net balance*—must be zero. It cannot show a surplus or a deficit. When people talk about a surplus or a deficit in the balance of payments, they actually are talking about a surplus or a deficit in one of the balance of payments accounts. The balance of payments itself by definition is always in balance, a function of double-entry bookkeeping.

Because different countries use different currencies, international business requires the exchange of monies in the foreign exchange market.

2.c. The Current Account and the Financial Account

The current account reflects the movement of goods and services into and out of a country. The financial account reflects the flow of financial assets into and out of a country. In Table 4, the current account shows a deficit balance of $127,041 million. Remember that the balance of payments must *balance*. If there is a deficit in the current account, there must be a surplus in the financial account that exactly offsets that deficit.

What is important here is not the bookkeeping process, the concept that the balance of payments must balance, but rather the meaning of deficits and surpluses in the current and financial accounts. These deficits and surpluses tell us whether a country is a net borrower from or lender to the rest of the world. A deficit in the current account means that a country is running a net surplus in its financial account. And it signals that a country is a net borrower from the rest of the world. A country that is running a current account deficit must borrow from abroad an amount sufficient to finance that deficit. A financial account surplus is achieved by selling more bonds and other debts of the domestic country to the rest of the world than the country buys from the rest of the world.

In Chapter 6, we learned that the value of a nation's output, GDP, is equal to the sum of consumption, investment, government spending, and net exports, or $GDP = C + I + G + X$. We could rewrite this equation in terms of X as $X = GDP - C - I - G$. The X in total spending is net exports involving trade in goods and services. As can be seen in Table 4, this is the largest component of the current account. Thus, a country that is running a current account deficit will have a negative X. Since

$X = \text{GDP} - C - I - G$, one can see that negative net exports or a current account deficit is consistent with domestic spending in excess of domestic production. A country running a current account deficit is spending more than it produces. Such a country must borrow to cover this difference between production and spending.

Figure 1 shows the annual current account balance in the United States. The United States experienced large current account deficits in the 1980s and then again from the mid-1990s to the present. Such deficits indicate that the United States consumed more than it produced. This means that the United States sold financial assets and borrowed large amounts of money from foreign residents to finance its current account deficits. This large foreign borrowing made the United States the largest debtor in the world. A *net debtor* owes more to the rest of the world than it is owed; a *net creditor* is owed more than it owes. The United States was an international net creditor from the end of World War I until the mid-1980s. The country financed its large current account deficits in the 1980s by borrowing from the rest of the world. As a result of this accumulated borrowing, in 1985 the United States became an international net debtor for the first time in almost 70 years. Since that time, the net debtor status of the United States has grown steadily.

A net debtor owes more to the rest of the world than it is owed; a net creditor is owed more than it owes.

RECAP

1. The balance of payments is a record of a nation's international transactions.
2. Double-entry bookkeeping requires that every transaction be entered in at least two accounts, so that credits and debits are balanced.
3. In the balance of payments, credits record activities that represent payments into the country, and debits record activities that represent payments out of the country.

FIGURE 1

The U.S. Current Account Balance

The current account of the balance of payments is the sum of the balances in the merchandise, services, income, and unilateral transfers accounts. The United States experienced very large current account deficits in the 1980s, and again more recently.
Source: Economic Report of the President, 2003.

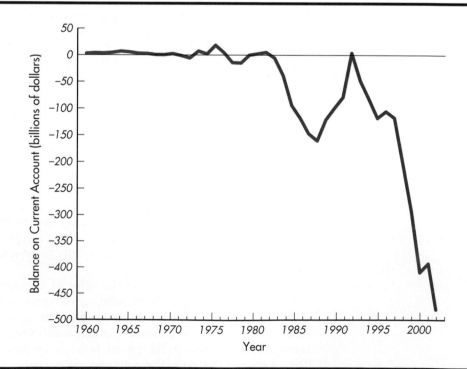

Part Two Macroeconomic Basics

4. The current account is the sum of the balances in the merchandise, services, income, and unilateral transfers accounts.

5. A surplus exists when credits exceed debits; a deficit exists when credits are less than debits.

6. The financial account is where the transactions necessary to finance the movement of merchandise, services, income, and unilateral transfers into and out of the country are recorded.

7. The net balance in the balance of payments must be zero.

8. A deficit in the current account must be offset by a surplus in the financial account. It also indicates that the nation is a net borrower.

Summary

? How do individuals of one nation trade money with individuals of another nation?

1. Foreign exchange is currency and bank deposits that are denominated in foreign currency. §1

2. The foreign exchange market is a global market in which people trade one currency for another. §1

3. Exchange rates, the price of one country's money in terms of another country's money, are necessary to compare prices quoted in different currencies. §1.a

4. The value of a good in a domestic currency equals the foreign currency price times the exchange rate. §1.a

? How do changes in exchange rates affect international trade?

5. When a domestic currency appreciates, domestic goods become more expensive to foreigners and foreign goods become cheaper to domestic residents. §1.b

6. When a domestic currency depreciates, domestic goods become cheaper to foreigners and foreign goods become more expensive to domestic residents. §1.b

? How do nations record their transactions with the rest of the world?

7. The balance of payments is a record of a nation's transactions with the rest of the world. §2

8. The balance of payments is based on double-entry bookkeeping. §2.a

9. Credits record activities that bring payments into a country; debits record activities that take payments out of a country. §2.a

10. In the balance of payments, the sum of total credits and the sum of total debits must be equal. §2.a

11. The current account is the sum of the balances in the merchandise, services, income, and unilateral transfers accounts. §2.b

12. In a balance of payments account, a surplus is the amount by which credits exceed debits, and a deficit is the amount by which debits exceed credits. §2.b

13. The financial account reflects the transactions necessary to finance the movement of merchandise, services, income, and unilateral transfers into and out of the country. §2.b

14. The net balance in the balance of payments must be zero. §2.b

15. A deficit in the current account must be offset by a surplus in the financial account. §2.c

16. A country that shows a deficit in its current account (or a surplus in its financial account) is a net borrower. §2.c

Key Terms

foreign exchange §1

foreign exchange market §1

exchange rate §1.a

balance of payments §2

double-entry bookkeeping §2.a

current account §2.b

surplus §2.b

deficit §2.b

balance of trade §2.b

financial account §2.b

Exercises

1. What is the price of 1 U.S. dollar in terms of each of the following currencies, given the following exchange rates?

   a. 1 euro = $.90
   b. 1 Chinese yuan = $.12
   c. 1 Israeli shekel = $.30
   d. 1 Kuwaiti dinar = $3.20

2. A bicycle manufactured in the United States costs $100. Using the exchange rates listed in Table 1, what would the bicycle cost in each of the following countries?

   a. Argentina
   b. Britain
   c. Canada

3. The U.S. dollar price of a Swedish krona changes from $.1572 to $.1730.

   a. Has the dollar depreciated or appreciated against the krona?
   b. Has the krona appreciated or depreciated against the dollar?

Use the information in the following table on Mexico's 1999 international transactions to answer exercises 4–6 (the amounts are the U.S. dollar values in millions):

Merchandise imports	$141,975
Merchandise exports	$136,391
Services exports	$16,644
Services imports	$31,526
Income receipts	$ 4,952
Income payments	$18,035
Unilateral transfers	$ 6,313

4. What is the balance of trade?

5. What is the current account?

6. Did Mexico become a larger international net debtor during 1999?

7. How reasonable is it for every country to follow policies aimed at increasing net exports?

8. How did the United States become the world's largest debtor nation in the 1980s?

9. If the U.S. dollar appreciated against the Japanese yen, what would you expect to happen to U.S. net exports with Japan?

10. Suppose the U.S. dollar price of a British pound is $1.50; the dollar price of a euro is $1; a hotel room in London, England, costs 120 British pounds; and a comparable hotel room in Hanover, Germany, costs 200 euro.

    a. Which hotel room is cheaper to a U.S. tourist?
    b. What is the exchange rate between the euro and the British pound?

11. Many residents of the United States send money to relatives living in other countries. For instance, a Salvadoran farmworker who is temporarily working in San Diego, California, sends money back to his family in El Salvador. How are such transactions recorded in the balance of payments? Are they debits or credits?

12. Suppose the U.S. dollar price of the Canadian dollar is $.75. How many Canadian dollars will it take to buy a set of dishes selling for $60 in Detroit, Michigan?

13. Why is it true that if the dollar depreciates against the yen, the yen must appreciate against the dollar?

14. Why does the balance of payments contain an account called "statistical discrepancy"?

15. Use the national income identity GDP = $C + I + G + X$ to explain what a current account deficit (negative net exports) means in terms of domestic spending, production, and borrowing.

ACE Practice Test

Take the ACE Practice Test for this chapter to review the important concepts and get immediate feedback with answers.

economics.college.hmco.com/students

Economically Speaking

High Gas Prices, Weak Euro Result in Room Availability, Less-Crowded Facilities at Popular U.S. National Parks

DENVER (BUSINESS WIRE)— The early-summer surge in gasoline prices and a strong U.S. dollar-to-euro exchange rate have resulted in higher-than-expected room availability and less-crowded facilities at many popular U.S. national parks, according to Amfac Parks & Resorts. Amfac is the largest park and resort management company in the country.

This trend began to appear shortly after Memorial Day when gasoline prices skyrocketed, said Andy Todd, president and CEO of Amfac Parks & Resorts. Gasoline prices have since begun to return to normal levels just when the traditional European holiday season is reaching its peak.

"The timing of these two factors has created a summer of opportunity in our national parks," said Todd. "Travelers typically make lodging arrangements at national parks far in advance, so people assume rooms are difficult to obtain on short notice. This year, however, spontaneous travelers and walk-ins will find a very welcome atmosphere, particularly in those parks that have traditionally appealed to international visitors."

A similar situation occurred in 1998 because of the Asian economic crisis. "People who assumed the parks would be full suddenly found room availability and more options," said Todd. . . .

Associated Press/July 24, 2000

Commentary

Why were there more vacant rooms and unfilled facilities in popular U.S. national parks in the summer of 2000? The article says it has to do with a strong U.S. dollar.

There are two components involved in determining the price of an internationally traded good: the price in terms of the home currency of the country where the good is produced and the exchange rate. With constant-dollar prices of U.S. goods, if the euro depreciates in value against the dollar, U.S. goods will become more expensive to European buyers, as emphasized in the article.

When the euro began to be used in January 1999, the euro price of 1 U.S. dollar was .84 euro per dollar. By May of 2000, 1 dollar cost more than 1.09 euro. This was an increase of about 30 percent. So even if the prices of goods and services in the United States did not change at all, the euro price to visitors from Europe increased by 30 percent.

Suppose in the fall of 1999, a European resident was planning a trip to visit the Grand Canyon in Arizona during summer 2000. In fall 1999, 1 dollar cost about .90 euro. Suppose one night at a hotel at the Grand Canyon costs $100. At an exchange rate of .90 euro per dollar, the hotel cost the European visitor 90 euro. But by the summer of 2000, when it is time to make the trip, the euro had depreciated in value to 1.09 euro per dollar, so the $100 hotel room now costs 109 euro. With the cost of visiting the United States rising so much (over 20 percent) from the time the U.S. vacation was planned to the time the trip was to occur, it is not surprising that many Europeans decided to cancel their U.S. vacation plans in 2000.

This brief article reminds us how interdependent countries are. The story of the decrease in foreign visitors to U.S. national parks in the summer of 2000 is a good example of how the exchange rate between currencies is one of the key variables linking countries together.

CHAPTER 8

Unemployment and Inflation

1. **What is a business cycle?**

2. **How is the unemployment rate defined and measured?**

3. **What is the cost of unemployed resources?**

4. **What is inflation?**

5. **Why is inflation a problem?**

I f you were graduating from college today, what would your job prospects be? In 1932, they would have been bleak. A large number of people were out of work (about one in four workers), and a large number of firms had laid off workers or gone out of business. At any time, job opportunities depend not only on the individual's ability and experience, but also on the current state of the economy.

Economies follow cycles of activity: periods of expansion, where output and employment increase, are followed by periods of contraction, where output and employment decrease. For instance, during the expansionary period of the 1990s and 2000, 4 percent of U.S. workers had no job by 2000. But during the period of contraction of 1981–1982, 9.5 percent of U.S. workers had no job. When the economy is growing, the demand for goods and services tends to increase. To produce those goods and services, firms hire more workers. Economic expansion also has an impact on inflation. As the demand for goods and services goes up, the prices of those goods and services also tend to rise. By 2000, following several years of economic growth, consumer prices in the United States were rising by about 3 percent a year. During

periods of contraction, as more people are out of work, demand for goods and services tends to fall and there is less pressure for rising prices. During the period of the Great Depression in the 1930s in the United States, consumer prices fell by more than 5 percent in 1933. Both price increases and the fraction of workers without jobs are affected by business cycles in fairly regular ways. But their effects on individual standards of living, income, and purchasing power are much less predictable.

Why do certain events move in tandem? What are the links between unemployment and inflation? What causes the business cycle to behave as it does? What effect does government activity have on the business cycle—and on unemployment and inflation? Who is harmed by rising unemployment and inflation? Who benefits? Macroeconomics attempts to answer all of these questions. ▪

1. Business Cycles

?

1. What is a business cycle?

In this chapter we describe the business cycle and examine measures of unemployment and inflation. We talk about the ways in which the business cycle, unemployment, and inflation are related. And we describe their effects on the participants in the economy.

The most widely used measure of a nation's output is gross domestic product. When we examine the value of real GDP over time, we find periods in which it rises and other periods in which it falls.

1.a. Definitions

business cycle: fluctuations in the economy between growth (expressed in rising real GDP) followed by stagnation (expressed in falling real GDP)

This pattern—real GDP rising, then falling—is called a **business cycle.** The pattern occurs over and over again, but as Figure 1 shows, the pattern over time is anything but regular. Historically the duration of business cycles and the rate at which real GDP rises or falls (indicated by the steepness of the line in Figure 1) vary considerably.

Looking at Figure 1, it is clear that the U.S. economy has experienced up-and-down swings in the years since 1959. Still, real GDP has grown at an average rate of approximately 3 percent per year over the long run. While it is important to recognize that periods of economic growth, or prosperity, are followed by periods of contraction, or **recession,** it is also important to recognize the presence of long-term economic growth—despite the presence of periodic recessions, in the long run the economy produces more goods and services. The long-run growth in the economy depends on the growth in productive resources, like land, labor, and capital, along with technological advance. Technological change increases the productivity of resources so that output increases even with a fixed amount of inputs.

recession: a period in which real GDP falls

Figure 2 shows how real GDP behaves over a hypothetical business cycle and identifies the stages of the cycle. The vertical axis on the graph measures the level of real GDP; the horizontal axis measures time in years. In year 1, real GDP is growing; the economy is in the *expansion* phase, or *boom* period, of the business cycle. Growth continues until the *peak* is reached, in year 2. Real GDP begins to fall during the *contraction* phase of the cycle, which continues until year 4. The *trough* marks the end of the contraction and the start of a new expansion. Even though the economy is subject to periodic ups and downs, real GDP, the measure of a nation's output, has risen over the long term, as illustrated by the upward-sloping line labeled "Trend."

If an economy is growing over time, why do economists worry about business cycles? Economists try to understand the causes of business cycles so that they can learn to moderate or avoid recessions and their harmful effects on standards of living.

FIGURE 1

U.S. Real GDP

The shaded areas represent periods of economic contraction (recession). The table lists the dates of business-cycle peaks and troughs. The peak dates indicate when contractions began; the trough dates, when expansions began. *Source: Data from Economic Report of the President, 2003 and http://www.nber.org/cycles.*

Peaks	Troughs
April 1960	February 1961
December 1969	November 1970
November 1973	March 1975
January 1980	July 1980
July 1981	November 1982
July 1990	March 1991
March 2001	November 2001

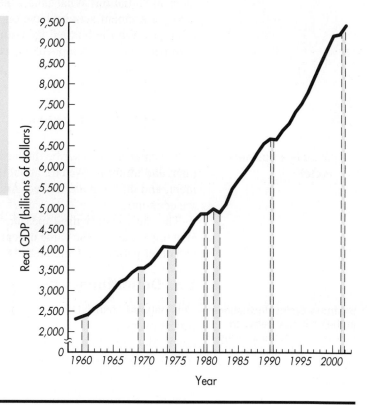

FIGURE 2

The Business Cycle

The business cycle contains four phases: the expansion (boom), when real GDP is increasing; the peak, which marks the end of an expansion and the beginning of a contraction; the contraction (recession), when real GDP is falling; and the trough, which marks the end of a contraction and the beginning of an expansion.

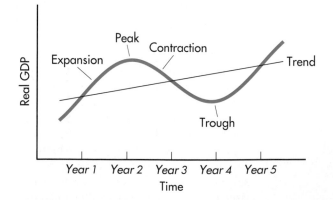

1.b. Historical Record

The official dating of recessions in the United States is the responsibility of the National Bureau of Economic Research (NBER), an independent research organization. The NBER has identified the shaded areas in the graph in Figure 1 as recessions and the unshaded areas as expansions. Recessions are periods between cyclical peaks and the troughs that follow them. Expansions are periods between cyclical troughs and the peaks that follow them. There have been thirteen recessions since 1929. The most severe was the Great Depression. Between 1929 and 1933, national output fell by 25 percent; this period is called the Great Depression. A **depression** is a prolonged period of severe economic contraction. The fact that people refer to "the Depression" when speaking about the recession that began in 1929 indicates the severity of that contraction relative to others in recent experience. There was widespread suffering during the Depression. Many people were jobless and homeless, and many firms went bankrupt.

depression: a severe, prolonged economic contraction

The NBER defines a recession as "a period of significant decline in total output, income, employment, and trade, usually lasting from six months to a year, and marked by widespread contractions in many sectors of the economy." People sometimes say that a recession is defined by two consecutive quarters of declining real GDP. This informal idea of what constitutes a recession seems to be consistent with the past recessions experienced by the United States, as every recession through the 1990s has had at least two quarters of falling real GDP. However, this is not the official definition of a recession. The business cycle dating committee of the NBER generally focuses on monthly data. Close attention is paid to the following monthly data series: employment, real personal income less transfer payments, the volume of sales of the manufacturing and wholesale–retail sectors adjusted for price changes, and industrial production. The focus is not on real GDP, because it is measured only quarterly and does not permit the identification of the month in which business-cycle turning points occur.

On November 26, 2001, the NBER announced that March 2001 was the most recent business-cycle peak. It always takes some time for the committee that dates business cycles to have enough evidence to be convinced that the data identify the turning point in the business cycle. On July 17, 2003, the NBER announced that the recession had ended in November 2001. It took more than 1.5 years to identify the trough that marked the end of the most recent recession.

1.c. Indicators

We have been talking about the business cycle in terms of real GDP. There are a number of other variables that move in a fairly regular manner over the business cycle. These variables are classified in three categories—leading indicators, coincident indicators, and lagging indicators—depending on whether they move up or down before, at the same time as, or following a change in real GDP (see Table 1).

leading indicator: a variable that changes before real output changes

Leading indicators generally change before real GDP changes. As a result, economists use them to forecast changes in output. Looking at Table 1, it is easy to see how some of these leading indicators could be used to forecast future output. For instance, new building permits signal new construction. If the number of new permits issued goes up, economists can expect the amount of new construction to increase. Similarly, if manufacturers receive more new orders, economists can expect more goods to be produced.

TABLE 1

Indicators of the
Business Cycle

Leading Indicators	
Average workweek	New building permits
Unemployment claims	Delivery times of goods
Manufacturers' new orders	Interest rate spread
Stock prices	Money supply
New plant and equipment orders	Consumer expectations

Coincident Indicators	Lagging Indicators
Payroll employment	Labor cost per unit of output
Industrial production	Inventories to sales ratio
Personal income	Unemployment duration
Manufacturing and trade sales	Consumer credit to personal income ratio
	Outstanding commercial loans
	Prime interest rate
	Inflation rate for services

Leading indicators are not infallible, however. The link between them and future output can be tenuous. For example, leading indicators may fall one month and then rise the next, while real output rises steadily. Economists want to see several consecutive months of a new direction in the leading indicators before forecasting a change in output. Short-run movements in the indicators can be very misleading.

coincident indicator: a variable that changes at the same time that real output changes

Coincident indicators are economic variables that tend to change at the same time that real output changes. For example, as real output increases, economists expect to see employment and sales rise. The coincident indicators listed in Table 1 have demonstrated a strong tendency over time to change along with changes in real GDP.

lagging indicator: a variable that changes after real output changes

The final group of variables listed in Table 1, **lagging indicators,** do not change their value until after the value of real GDP has changed. For instance, as output increases, jobs are created and more workers are hired. It makes sense, then, to expect the duration of unemployment (the average time workers are unemployed) to fall. The duration of unemployment is a lagging indicator. Similarly, the inflation rate for services (which measures how prices change for things like dry cleaners, veterinarians, and other services) tends to change after real GDP changes. Lagging indicators are used along with leading and coincident indicators to identify the peaks and troughs in business cycles.

RECAP

1. The business cycle is a recurring pattern of rising and falling real GDP.
2. Although all economies move through periods of expansion and contraction, the duration of the periods of expansion and recession varies.
3. Real GDP is not the only variable affected by business cycles; leading, lagging, and coincident indicators also show the effects of economic expansion and contraction.

As real income falls, living standards go down. This 1937 photo of a Depression-era breadline indicates the paradox of the world's richest nation, as emphasized on the billboard in the background, having to offer public support to feed able-bodied workers who were out of work due to the severity of the business-cycle downturn.

2. How is the unemployment rate defined and measured?

2. Unemployment

Recurring periods of prosperity and recession are reflected in the nation's labor markets. In fact, this is what makes understanding the business cycle so important. If business cycles signified only a little more or a little less profit for businesses, governments would not be so anxious to forecast or to control their swings. It is the human costs of lost jobs and incomes—the inability to maintain standards of living—that make an understanding of business cycles and of the factors that affect unemployment so important.

2.a. Definition and Measurement

unemployment rate: the percentage of the labor force that is not working

The **unemployment rate** is the percentage of the labor force that is not working. The rate is calculated by dividing the number of people who are unemployed by the number of people in the labor force:

$$\text{Unemployment rate} = \frac{\text{number unemployed}}{\text{number in labor force}}$$

This ratio seems simple enough, but there are several subtle issues at work here. First, the unemployment rate does not measure the percentage of the total population that is not working; it measures the percentage of the *labor force* that is not working. Who is in the labor force? Obviously, everybody who is employed is part of the labor force. But only some of those who are not currently employed are counted in the labor force.

The Bureau of Labor Statistics of the Department of Labor compiles labor data each month based on an extensive survey of U.S. households. All U.S. residents are potential members of the labor force. The Labor Department arrives at the size of the actual labor force by using this formula:

Labor force = all U.S. residents
− residents under 16 years of age
− institutionalized adults
− adults not looking for work

So the labor force includes those adults (an adult being someone sixteen or older) who are currently employed or actively seeking work. It is relatively simple to see to it that children and institutionalized adults (for instance, those in prison or in long-term care facilities) are not counted in the labor force. It is more difficult to identify and accurately measure adults who are not actively looking for work.

A person is actively seeking work if he or she is available to work, has looked for work in the past four weeks, is waiting for a recall after being laid off, or is starting a job within 30 days. Those who are not working and who meet these criteria are considered unemployed.

2.b. Interpreting the Unemployment Rate

Is the unemployment rate an accurate measure? The fact that the rate does not include those who are not actively looking for work is not necessarily a failing. Many people who are not actively looking for work—homemakers, older citizens, and students, for example—have made a decision to do housework, to retire, or to stay in school. These people rightly are not counted among the unemployed.

But there are people missing from the unemployment statistics who are not working and are not looking for work, yet would take a job if one were offered. **Discouraged workers** have looked for work in the past year but have given up looking for work because they believe that no one will hire them. These individuals are ignored by the official unemployment rate even though they are able to work and may have spent a long time looking for work. Estimates of the number of discouraged workers indicate that in 2003, 1.6 million people were not counted in the labor force yet claimed that they were available for work. Of this group, 28 percent, or 450,000 people, were considered to be discouraged workers. It is clear that the reported unemployment rate underestimates the true burden of unemployment in the economy because it ignores discouraged workers.

discouraged workers: workers who have stopped looking for work because they believe that no one will offer them a job

Discouraged workers are one source of hidden unemployment; underemployment is another. **Underemployment** is the underutilization of workers—employment in tasks that do not fully utilize their productive potential—including part-time workers who prefer full-time employment. Even if every worker has a job, substantial underemployment leaves the economy producing less than its potential GDP.

underemployment: the employment of workers in jobs that do not utilize their productive potential

The effect of discouraged workers and underemployment is an unemployment rate that understates actual unemployment. In contrast, the effect of the *underground economy* is a rate that overstates actual unemployment. A sizable number of the officially unemployed are actually working. The unemployed construction worker who plays in a band at night may not report that activity because he or she wants to avoid paying taxes on his or her earnings as a musician. This person is officially unemployed but has a source of income. Many officially unemployed individuals have an alternative source of income. This means that official statistics overstate the true magnitude of unemployment. The larger the underground economy, the greater this overstatement.

We have identified two factors, discouraged workers and underemployment, that cause the official unemployment rate to underestimate true unemployment. Another factor, the underground economy, causes the official rate to overestimate the true rate of unemployment. There is no reason to expect these factors to cancel one another out, and there is no way to know for sure which is most important. The point is to remember what the official data on unemployment do and do not measure.

2.c. Types of Unemployment

Economists have identified four basic types of unemployment:

Seasonal unemployment A product of regular, recurring changes in the hiring needs of certain industries on a monthly or seasonal basis

Frictional unemployment A product of the short-term movement of workers between jobs and of first-time job seekers

Structural unemployment A product of technological change and other changes in the structure of the economy

Cyclical unemployment A product of business-cycle fluctuations

In certain industries, labor needs fluctuate throughout the year. When local crops are harvested, farms need lots of workers; the rest of the year, they do not. (Migrant farmworkers move from one region to another, following the harvests, to avoid seasonal unemployment.) Ski resort towns like Park City, Utah, are booming during the ski season, when employment peaks, but need fewer workers during the rest of the year. In the nation as a whole, the Christmas season is a time of peak employment and low unemployment rates. To avoid confusing seasonal fluctuations in unemployment with other sources of unemployment, unemployment data are seasonally adjusted.

Frictional and structural unemployment are always present in a dynamic economy.

Frictional and structural unemployment exist in any dynamic economy. In terms of individual workers, frictional unemployment is short term in nature. Workers quit one job and soon find another; students graduate and soon find a job. This kind of unemployment cannot be eliminated in a free society. In fact, it is a sign of efficiency in an economy when workers try to increase their income or improve their working conditions by leaving one job for another. Frictional unemployment is often called *search unemployment* because workers take time to search for a job after quitting a job or leaving school.

Frictional unemployment is short term; structural unemployment, on the other hand, can be long term. Workers who are displaced by technological change (assembly line workers who have been replaced by machines, for example) or by a permanent reduction in the demand for an industry's output (cigar makers who have been laid off because of a decrease in demand for tobacco) may not have the necessary skills to maintain their level of income in another industry. Rather than accept a much lower salary, these workers tend to prolong their job search. Eventually they either adjust their expectations to the realities of the job market or enter the pool of discouraged workers.

Structural unemployment is very difficult for those who are unemployed. But for society as a whole, the technological advances that cause structural unemployment raise living standards by giving consumers a greater variety of goods at lower cost.

Cyclical unemployment is a product of recession.

Cyclical unemployment is a result of the business cycle. As a recession occurs, cyclical unemployment increases, and as growth occurs, cyclical unemployment decreases. It is also a primary focus of macroeconomic policy. Economists believe that a greater understanding of business cycles and their causes may enable them to find ways to smooth out those cycles and swings in unemployment. Much of the analysis in future chapters is related to macroeconomic policy aimed at minimizing

Agricultural harvests, like this chili-pepper harvest in Mexico, create seasonal fluctuations in the employment of labor. During the harvest period, workers are hired to help out. When the harvest has ended, many of these workers will be temporarily unemployed until the next crop requires their labor.

business-cycle fluctuations. In addition to macroeconomic policy aimed at moderating cyclical unemployment, other policy measures—for example, job training and counseling—are being used to reduce frictional and structural unemployment.

2.d. Costs of Unemployment

3. What is the cost of unemployed resources?

The cost of being unemployed is more than the obvious loss of income and status suffered by the individual who is not working. In a broader sense, society as a whole loses when resources are unemployed. Unemployed workers produce no output. So an economy with unemployment will operate inside its production possibilities curve rather than on the curve. Economists measure this lost output in terms of the *GDP gap:*

$$\text{GDP gap} = \text{potential real GDP} - \text{actual real GDP}$$

potential real GDP: the output produced at the natural rate of unemployment

natural rate of unemployment: the unemployment rate that would exist in the absence of cyclical unemployment

Potential real GDP is the level of output produced when nonlabor resources are fully utilized and unemployment is at its natural rate. The **natural rate of unemployment** is the unemployment rate that would exist in the absence of cyclical unemployment, so it includes seasonal, frictional, and structural unemployment. The natural rate of unemployment is not fixed; it can change over time. For instance, some economists believe that the natural rate of unemployment has risen in recent decades, a product of the influx of baby boomers and women into the labor force. As more workers move into the labor force (begin looking for jobs), frictional unemployment increases, raising the natural rate of unemployment. The natural rate of unemployment is sometimes called the "nonaccelerating inflation rate of unemployment," or NAIRU. The idea is that there would be upward pressure on wages and prices in a tight labor market in which the unemployment rate fell below the NAIRU. We will see macroeconomic models of this phenomenon in later chapters.

Potential real GDP measures what we are capable of producing at the natural rate of unemployment. If we compute potential real GDP and then subtract actual real GDP, we have a measure of the output lost as a result of unemployment, or the cost of unemployment.

Because frictional and structural unemployment are always present, the term full employment *is misleading. Today economists use the term* natural rate of unemployment *instead.*

The GDP gap in the United States from 1975 to 2002 is shown in Figure 3. The gap widens during recessions and narrows during expansions. As the gap widens (as the output not produced increases), there are fewer goods and services available, and living standards are lower than they would be at the natural rate of unemployment. Figure 3(b) is a graph of the gap between potential and real GDP, taken from Figure 3(a). During the strong expansion of the late 1990s, the gap went to zero.

FIGURE 3

The GDP Gap

The GDP gap is the difference between what the economy can produce at the natural rate of unemployment (potential GDP) and actual output (actual GDP). When the unemployment rate is higher than the natural rate, actual GDP is less than potential GDP. The gap between potential and actual real GDP is a cost associated with unemployment. Recession years are shaded to highlight how the gap widens around recessions.

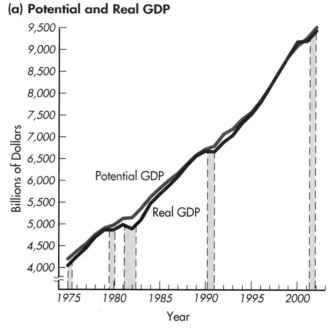

(a) Potential and Real GDP

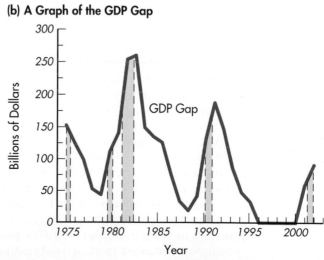

(b) A Graph of the GDP Gap

Chapter 8 Unemployment and Inflation

Until recently, economists used the term *full employment* instead of *natural rate of unemployment.* Today the term *full employment* is rarely used because it may be interpreted as implying a zero unemployment rate. If frictional and structural unemployment are always present, zero unemployment is impossible; there must always be unemployed resources in an economy. *Natural rate of unemployment* describes the labor market when the economy is producing what it realistically can produce in the absence of cyclical unemployment.

What is the value of the natural rate of unemployment in the United States? In the 1950s and 1960s, economists generally agreed on 4 percent. By the 1970s, that agreed-on rate had gone up to 5 percent. In the early 1980s, many economists placed the natural rate of unemployment in the United States at 6 to 7 percent. By the late 1980s, some had revised their thinking, placing the rate back at 5 percent. In the late 1990s, one could have said that 4 percent could be chosen. In fact, economists do not know exactly what the natural rate of unemployment is. It varies over time within a range from around 4 percent to around 7 percent. It will also vary across countries, as labor markets and macroeconomic policies differ.

2.e. The Record of Unemployment

Unemployment rates in the United States from 1951 to 2002 are listed in Table 2. Over this period, the unemployment rate for all workers reached a low of 2.9 percent in 1953 and a high of 9.7 percent in 1982. The table shows some general trends in the incidence of unemployment across different demographic groups:

In most years, the unemployment rate for women is higher than it is for men. Several factors may be at work here. First, during this period, a large number of women entered the labor force for the first time. Second, discrimination against women in the workplace limited job opportunities for them, particularly early in this period. Finally, a large number of women moved out of the labor force on temporary maternity leaves. The most recent years indicate that women now have lower unemployment rates than men. Whether this is just related to the recent recession remains to be seen.

Teenagers have the highest unemployment rates in the economy. This makes sense because teenagers are the least-skilled segment of the labor force.

Whites have lower unemployment rates than nonwhites. Discrimination plays a role here. To the extent that discrimination extends beyond hiring practices and job opportunities for minority workers to the education that is necessary to prepare students to enter the work force, minority workers will have fewer opportunities for employment. The quality of education provided in many schools with large minority populations may not be as good as that provided in schools with large white populations. Equal opportunity programs and legislation are aimed at rectifying this inequality.

Although exact comparisons across countries are difficult to make because countries measure unemployment in different ways, it is interesting to look at the reported unemployment rates of different countries. Table 3 lists unemployment rates for seven major industrial nations. The rates have been adjusted to match the U.S. definition of unemployment as closely as possible.

Knowing their limitations, we can still identify some important trends from the data in Table 3. In the late 1970s and early 1980s, both U.S. and European unemployment rates increased substantially. But in the mid-1980s, while U.S.

TABLE 2

Unemployment Rates in the United States

	Unemployment Rate, Civilian Workers[1]					
Year	All Civilian Workers	Males	Females	Both Sexes 16–19 Years	White	Black and Other
1951	3.3	2.8	4.4	8.2	3.1	5.3
1953	2.9	2.8	3.3	7.6	2.7	4.5
1955	4.4	4.2	4.9	11.0	3.9	8.7
1957	4.3	4.1	4.7	11.6	3.8	7.9
1959	5.5	5.2	5.9	14.6	4.8	10.7
1961	6.7	6.4	7.2	16.8	6.0	12.4
1963	5.7	5.2	6.5	17.2	5.0	10.8
1965	4.5	4.0	5.5	14.8	4.1	8.1
1967	3.8	3.1	5.2	12.9	3.4	7.4
1969	3.5	2.8	4.7	12.2	3.1	6.4
1971	5.9	5.3	6.9	16.9	5.4	9.9
1973	4.9	4.2	6.0	14.5	4.3	9.0
1975	8.5	7.9	9.3	19.9	7.8	13.8
1977	7.1	6.3	8.2	17.8	6.2	13.1
1979	5.8	5.1	6.8	16.1	5.1	11.3
1980	7.1	6.9	7.4	17.8	6.3	13.1
1981	7.6	7.4	7.9	19.6	6.7	14.2
1982	9.7	9.9	9.4	23.2	8.6	17.3
1983	9.6	9.9	9.2	22.4	8.4	17.8
1984	7.5	7.4	7.6	18.9	6.5	14.4
1985	7.2	7.0	7.4	18.6	6.2	13.7
1986	7.0	6.9	7.1	18.3	6.0	13.1
1987	6.2	6.2	6.2	16.9	5.3	11.6
1988	5.5	5.5	5.6	15.3	4.7	10.4
1989	5.3	5.2	5.4	15.0	4.5	10.0
1990	5.6	5.7	5.5	15.5	4.8	10.1
1991	6.8	7.2	6.4	18.7	6.1	11.1
1992	7.5	7.9	7.0	20.1	6.6	12.7
1993	6.9	7.2	6.6	19.0	6.1	11.7
1994	6.1	6.2	6.0	17.6	5.3	10.5
1995	5.6	5.6	5.6	17.3	4.9	9.6
1996	5.4	5.4	5.4	16.7	4.7	9.3
1997	4.9	4.9	5.0	16.0	4.2	8.8
1998	4.5	4.4	4.6	14.6	3.9	7.8
1999	4.2	4.1	4.3	13.9	3.7	7.0
2000	4.0	3.9	4.1	13.1	3.5	6.7
2001	4.8	4.8	4.7	14.7	4.2	7.7
2002	5.8	5.9	5.6	16.5	5.1	9.2

[1]Unemployed as a percentage of the civilian labor force in the group specified.
Source: *Economic Report of the President, 2003.*

TABLE 3

Unemployment Rates in Major Industrial Countries

	Civilian Unemployment Rate (percent)						
Year	United States	Canada	France	Italy	Japan	United Kingdom	Germany
1975	8.5	6.9	4.2	3.4	1.9	4.6	3.4
1976	7.7	7.2	4.6	3.9	2.0	5.9	3.4
1977	7.1	8.1	5.2	4.1	2.0	6.4	3.4
1978	6.1	8.4	5.4	4.1	2.3	6.3	3.3
1979	5.8	7.3	6.1	4.4	2.1	5.4	2.9
1980	7.1	7.3	6.5	4.4	2.0	7.0	2.8
1981	7.6	7.3	7.6	4.9	2.2	10.5	4.0
1982	9.7	10.6	8.3	5.4	2.4	11.3	5.6
1983	9.6	11.5	8.6	5.9	2.7	11.8	6.9
1984	7.5	10.9	10.0	5.9	2.8	11.7	7.1
1985	7.2	10.2	10.5	6.0	2.6	11.2	7.2
1986	7.0	9.2	10.6	7.5	2.8	11.2	6.6
1987	6.2	8.4	10.8	7.9	2.9	10.3	6.3
1988	5.5	7.3	10.3	7.9	2.5	8.6	6.3
1989	5.3	7.1	9.6	7.8	2.3	7.2	5.7
1990	5.6	7.7	9.1	7.0	2.1	6.9	5.0
1991	6.8	9.8	9.5	6.9	2.1	8.8	5.6
1992	7.5	10.6	9.9	7.3	2.2	10.1	6.7
1993	6.9	10.8	11.3	10.2	2.5	10.4	8.0
1994	6.1	9.5	11.8	11.2	2.9	9.5	8.5
1995	5.6	8.6	11.3	11.8	3.2	8.7	8.2
1996	5.4	8.8	11.9	11.7	3.4	8.1	9.0
1997	4.9	8.4	11.8	11.9	3.4	7.0	9.9
1998	4.5	7.7	11.3	12.0	4.1	6.3	9.3
1999	4.2	7.0	10.6	11.5	4.7	6.0	8.6
2000	4.0	6.1	9.1	10.7	4.8	5.5	8.1
2001	4.8	6.4	8.5	9.6	5.1	5.1	8.0

Source: *Economic Report of the President, 2003.*

unemployment began to fall, European unemployment remained high. The issue of high unemployment rates in Europe has become a major topic of discussion at international summit meetings and is addressed in the Global Business Insight "High Unemployment in Europe." Japanese unemployment rates, like those in Europe, were much lower than U.S. and Canadian rates in the 1970s and 1980s. However, by the late 1990s, Japanese rates began to approach those of the United States.

High Unemployment in Europe

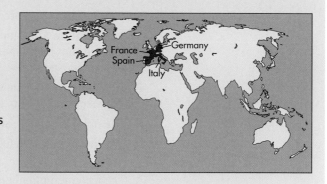

The data in Table 3 indicate that European countries tend to have higher unemployment rates than other industrial countries. This is not true for all European countries, but it is certainly true for the biggest: France, Germany, Italy, and Spain. One factor that contributes to the higher unemployment rates in these countries is government policy with regard to the labor market. Countries that have policies that encourage unemployment should be expected to have more unemployed workers. In a recent speech, a British scholar gave his analysis of why Europe has such high unemployment. One story he told illustrates how government policy aimed at protecting citizens against unemployment can create the very unemployment that is the focus of its concern. In Italy, laws require parents to support their adult children who do not work, even if the children are entirely capable of working. The story goes as follows:

> The Italian Court of Cessation ruled that a professor at Naples University, separated from his family, must continue to pay his 30-year-old son €775 per month until he can find himself suitable employment. This despite the fact that the son owns a house and possesses an investment trust fund worth €450,000. The judges said that an adult son who refused work that did not reflect his training, abilities and personal interests could not be held to blame. In particular the judges said, "You cannot blame a young person, particularly from a well-off family, who refuses a job that does not fit his aspirations." By contrast, under UK law, a separated father would only have to support his children until they completed full-time education. (Nickell, 2002)

The government requirement that parents support unemployed adult children encourages those children to remain unemployed.

Among men of prime working age (age 25–54), there are more who are inactive and not participating in the labor force than there are who are unemployed. The majority of these men are receiving benefits from the government, claiming disability or illness. In the 1970s, there were many fewer disabled or ill workers as a fraction of the population. But as social benefits were increased and the eligibility rules were relaxed, the number of people claiming to suffer from such problems increased also. The unfortunate truth of human nature is that as you provide better support for those who truly need help, there will be more and more who do not truly need it, yet claim a need. The experience of Denmark is instructive in this regard. Denmark has generous unemployment benefits. But in the 1990s, Danish eligibility requirements were tightened, creating greater incentives for the unemployed to look for work. Danish unemployment rates fell dramatically as a result.

Yet another factor contributing to higher unemployment rates in some countries is restrictions on the ability of firms to terminate workers and the requirement that firms pay high separation costs to workers whom they do fire. The more difficult it is for firms to adjust their labor force in the face of economic fluctuations, the less likely firms are to hire new workers. If you own a business and your sales increase, you are likely to hire extra employees to meet the increased demand for your product. However, you cannot be sure that your sales will be permanently higher, so you would be very conservative about hiring new workers if you would have to pay terminated workers a large amount of money if sales fell and you needed to lay off some of your employees. Such labor market rigidities, aimed at protecting workers from losing their jobs, create incentives against hiring so that those who would like to work cannot get hired.

The lesson from large European countries is that government policies aimed at protecting workers from unemployment may create a bigger unemployment problem. Then the costs imposed on the economy in the form of taxes and reduced labor market flexibility may exceed the benefits to those who keep their jobs or receive unemployment compensation because of the programs.

Sources: Stephen Nickell, "A Picture of European Unemployment: Success and Failure," speech given to CESifo Conference in Munich, December 2002, and Lars Ljungqvist and Thomas Sargent, "The European Unemployment Dilemma," *Journal of Political Economy,* 1998.

RECAP

1. The unemployment rate is the number of people unemployed as a percentage of the labor force.

2. To be in the labor force, one must either have or be looking for a job.

3. By its failure to include discouraged workers and the output lost because of underemployment, the unemployment rate understates real unemployment in the United States.

4. By its failure to include activity in the underground economy, the U.S. unemployment rate overstates actual unemployment.

5. Unemployment data are adjusted to eliminate seasonal fluctuations.

6. Frictional and structural unemployment are always present in a dynamic economy.

7. Cyclical unemployment is a product of recession; it can be moderated by controlling the period of contraction in the business cycle.

8. Economists measure the cost of unemployment in terms of lost output.

9. Unemployment data show that women generally have higher unemployment rates than men, that teenagers have the highest unemployment rates in the economy, and that blacks and other minority groups have higher unemployment rates than whites.

4. What is inflation?

inflation: a sustained rise in the average level of prices

3. Inflation

Inflation is a sustained rise in the average level of prices. Notice the word *sustained.* Inflation does not mean a short-term increase in prices; it means that prices are rising over a prolonged period of time. Inflation is measured by the percentage change in price level. The inflation rate in the United States was 1.6 percent in 2002. This means that the level of prices increased 1.6 percent over the year.

3.a. Absolute Versus Relative Price Changes

In the modern economy, over any given period, some prices rise faster than others. To evaluate the rate of inflation in a country, then, economists must know what is happening to prices on average. Here it is important to distinguish between *absolute* and *relative* price changes.

Let's look at an example using the prices of fish and beef:

	Year 1	Year 2
1 pound of fish	$1	$2
1 pound of beef	$2	$4

In year 1, beef is twice as expensive as fish. This is the price of beef *relative* to fish. In year 2, beef is still twice as expensive as fish. The relative prices have not changed between years 1 and 2. What has changed? The prices of both beef and fish have doubled. The *absolute* levels of all prices have gone up, but because they have increased by the same percentage, the relative prices are unchanged.

Inflation measures changes in absolute prices. In our example, all prices doubled, so the inflation rate is 100 percent. There was a 100 percent increase in the prices of

5. Why is inflation a problem?

beef and fish. In reality, inflation does not proceed evenly through the economy. Prices of some goods rise faster than others, which means that relative prices are changing at the same time that absolute prices are rising. The measured inflation rate records the *average* change in absolute prices.

3.b. Effects of Inflation

To understand the effects of inflation, you have to understand what happens to the value of money in an inflationary period. The real value of money is what it can buy, its *purchasing power:*

$$\text{Real value of \$1} = \frac{\$1}{\text{price level}}$$

The purchasing power of a dollar is the amount of goods and services it can buy.

The higher the price level, the lower the real value (or *purchasing power*) of the dollar. For instance, suppose an economy had only one good—milk. If a glass of milk sold for $.50, then $1 would buy two glasses of milk. If the price of milk rose to $1, then a dollar would only buy one glass of milk. The purchasing power, or real value, of money falls as prices rise.

Table 4 lists the real value of the dollar in selected years from 1946 to 2002. The price level in each year is measured relative to the average level of prices over the 1982–1984 period. For instance, the 1946 value, .195, means that prices in 1946 were, on average, only 19.5 percent of prices in the 1982–1984 period. Notice that as prices go up, the purchasing power of the dollar falls. In 1946 a dollar bought five times as much as a dollar bought in the early 1980s. The value 5.13 means that one could buy 5.13 times as many goods and services with a dollar in 1946 as one could in 1982–1984.

TABLE 4		
The Real Value of a Dollar		
Year	**Average Price Level**[1]	**Purchasing Power of a Dollar**[2]
1946	.195	5.13
1950	.241	4.15
1954	.269	3.72
1958	.289	3.46
1962	.302	3.31
1966	.324	3.09
1970	.388	2.58
1974	.493	2.03
1978	.652	1.53
1982	.965	1.04
1986	1.096	.91
1990	1.307	.77
1994	1.482	.67
1998	1.630	.61
2002	1.799	.56

[1]Measured by the consumer price index as given at http://data.bls.gov/cgi-bin/surveymost.
[2]Found by taking the reciprocal of the consumer price index (1/CPI).

Prices have risen steadily in recent decades. By 2002, they had gone up more than 79 percent above the average level of prices in the 1982–1984 period. Consequently, the purchasing power of a 2002 dollar was lower. In 2002, $1 bought just 56 percent of the goods and services that one could buy with a dollar in 1982–1984.

If prices and nominal income rise by the same percentage, it might seem that inflation is not a problem. It doesn't matter if it takes twice as many dollars now to buy fish and beef than it did before, if we have twice as many dollars in income available to buy the products. Obviously, inflation is very much a problem when a household's nominal income rises at a slower rate than prices. Inflation hurts those households whose income does not keep up with the prices of the goods they buy.

In the 1970s in the United States, the rate of inflation rose to near-record levels. Many workers believed that their incomes were lagging behind the rate of inflation, so they negotiated cost-of-living raises in their wage contracts. The typical cost-of-living raise ties salary to changes in the consumer price index. If the CPI rises 8 percent over a year, workers receive an 8 percent raise plus compensation for experience or productivity increases. As the U.S. rate of inflation fell during the 1980s, concern about cost-of-living raises subsided as well.

It is important to distinguish between expected and unexpected inflation. *Unexpectedly high inflation* redistributes income away from those who receive fixed incomes (like creditors who receive debt repayments of a fixed amount of dollars per month) toward those who make fixed expenditures (like debtors who make fixed debt repayments per month). For example, consider a simple loan agreement:

Maria borrows $100 from Ali, promising to repay the loan in one year at 10 percent interest. In one year, Maria will pay Ali $110—principal of $100 plus interest of $10 (10 percent of $100, or $10).

Unexpectedly high inflation redistributes income away from those who receive fixed incomes toward those who make fixed expenditures.

When Maria and Ali agree to the terms of the loan, they do so with some expected rate of inflation in mind. Suppose they both expect 5 percent inflation over the year. In one year it will take 5 percent more money to buy goods than it does now. Ali will need $105 to buy what $100 buys today. Because Ali will receive $110 for the principal and interest on the loan, he will gain purchasing power. However, if the inflation rate over the year turns out to be surprisingly high—say, 15 percent—then Ali will need $115 to buy what $100 buys today. He will lose purchasing power if he makes a loan at a 10 percent rate of interest.

Economists distinguish between nominal and real interest rates when analyzing economic behavior. The **nominal interest rate** is the observed interest rate in the market and includes the effect of inflation. The **real interest rate** is the nominal interest rate minus the rate of inflation:

nominal interest rate: the observed interest rate in the market

real interest rate: the nominal interest rate minus the rate of inflation

$$\text{Real interest rate} = \text{nominal interest rate} - \text{rate of inflation}$$

If Ali charges Maria 10 percent nominal interest and the inflation rate is 5 percent, the real interest rate is 5 percent ($10\% - 5\% = 5\%$). This means that Ali will earn a positive real return from the loan. However, if the inflation rate is 10 percent, the real return from a nominal interest rate of 10 percent is zero ($10\% - 10\% = 0$). The interest Ali will receive from the loan will just compensate him for the rise in prices; he will not realize an increase in purchasing power. If the inflation rate is higher than the nominal interest rate, then the real interest rate is negative—the lender will lose purchasing power by making the loan.

Real interest rates are lower than expected when inflation is higher than expected.

Now you can see how unexpected inflation redistributes income. Borrowers and creditors agree to loan terms based on what they *expect* the rate of inflation to be over the period of the loan. If the *actual* rate of inflation turns out to be different from what was expected, then the real interest rate paid by the borrower and received by the lender will be different from what was expected. If Ali and Maria both expect a 5 percent inflation rate and agree to a 10 percent nominal interest rate for the loan, then they both expect a real interest rate of 5 percent (10% − 5% = 5%) to be paid on the loan. If the actual inflation rate turns out to be greater than 5 percent, then the real interest rate will be less than expected. Maria will get to borrow Ali's money at a lower real cost than she expected, and Ali will earn a lower real return than he expected. Unexpectedly high inflation hurts creditors and benefits borrowers because it lowers real interest rates.

Figure 4 shows the real interest rates on U.S. Treasury bills from 1970 through 2001. You can see a pronounced pattern in the graph. In the late 1970s, there was a period of negative real interest rates, followed by high positive real rates in the 1980s. The evidence suggests that nominal interest rates did not rise fast enough in the 1970s to offset high inflation. This was a time of severe strain on many creditors, including savings and loan associations and banks. These firms had lent funds at fixed nominal rates of interest. When those rates of interest turned out to be lower than the rate of inflation, the financial institutions suffered significant losses. In the early 1980s, the inflation rate dropped sharply. Because nominal interest rates did not drop nearly as fast as the rate of inflation, real interest rates were high. In this

---

FIGURE 4

The Real Interest Rate on U.S. Treasury Bills

The real interest rate is the difference between the nominal interest rate (the interest rate actually observed) and the rate of inflation over the life of the bond. The figure shows the real interest rate in June and December for each year. For instance, in the first observation, for June 1970, a six-month Treasury bill paid the holder 6.91 percent interest. This is the nominal rate of interest. To find the real rate of interest on the bond, we subtract the rate of inflation that existed over the six months of the bond's life (June to December 1970), which was 5.17 percent. The difference between the nominal interest rate (6.91 percent) and the rate of inflation (5.17 percent) is the real interest rate, 1.74 percent. Notice that real interest rates were negative during most of the 1970s and then turned highly positive (by historical standards) in the early 1980s.

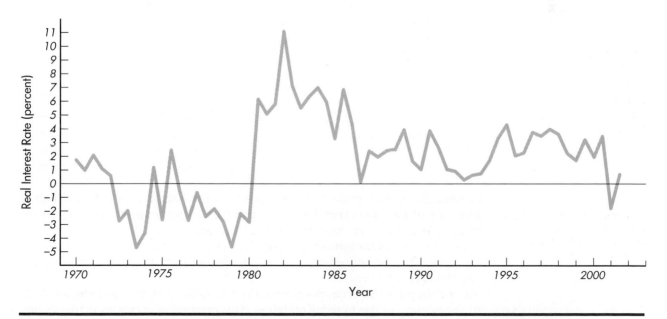

period many debtors were hurt by the high costs of borrowing to finance business or household expenditures.

Unexpected inflation affects more than the two parties to a loan. Any contract calling for fixed payments over some long-term period changes in value as the rate of inflation changes. For instance, a long-term contract that provides union members with 5 percent raises each year for five years gives the workers more purchasing power if inflation is low than if it is high. Similarly, a contract that sells a product at a fixed price over a long-term period will change in value as inflation changes. Suppose a lumber company promises to supply a builder with lumber at a fixed price for a two-year period. If the rate of inflation in one year turns out to be higher than expected, the lumber company will end up selling the lumber for less profit than it had planned. Inflation raises costs to the lumber company. Usually the company would raise its prices to compensate for higher costs. Because the company contracted to sell its goods at a fixed price to the builder, however, the builder benefits at the lumber company's expense. Again, unexpectedly high inflation redistributes real income or purchasing power away from those receiving fixed payments to those making fixed payments.

One response to the effects of unexpected inflation is to allow prices, wages, or interest rates to vary with the rate of inflation. Labor sometimes negotiates cost-of-living adjustments as part of new wage contracts. Financial institutions offer variable interest rates on home mortgages to reflect current market conditions. Any contract can be written to adjust dollar amounts over time as the rate of inflation changes.

3.c. Types of Inflation

Economists often classify inflation according to the source of the inflationary pressure. The most straightforward method defines inflation in terms of pressure from the demand side of the market or the supply side of the market:

> *Demand-pull inflation* Increases in total spending that are not offset by increases in the supply of goods and services and so cause the average level of prices to rise
>
> *Cost-push inflation* Increases in production costs that cause firms to raise prices to avoid losses

Sometimes inflation is blamed on "too many dollars chasing too few goods." This is a roundabout way of saying that the inflation stems from demand pressures. Because demand-pull inflation is a product of increased spending, it is more likely to occur in an economy that is producing at maximum capacity. If resources are fully employed, in the short run it may not be possible to increase output to meet increased demand. The result: Existing goods and services are rationed by rising prices.

Some economists claim that rising prices in the late 1960s were a product of demand-pull inflation. They believe that increased government spending for the Vietnam War caused the level of U.S. prices to rise.

Cost-push inflation can occur in any economy, whatever its output. If prices go up because the costs of resources are rising, the rate of inflation can go up regardless of demand.

For example, some economists argue that the inflation in the United States in the 1970s was largely due to rising oil prices. This means that decreases in the oil supply (a shift to the left in the supply curve) brought about higher oil prices. Because oil is so important in the production of many goods, higher oil prices led to increases in prices throughout the economy. Cost-push inflation stems from changes in the supply side of the market.

Cost-push inflation is sometimes attributed to profit-push or wage-push pressures. *Profit-push pressures* are created by suppliers who want to increase their profit margins by raising prices faster than their costs increase. *Wage-push pressures* are created by labor unions and workers who are able to increase their wages faster than their productivity. There have been times when "greedy" businesses and unions have been blamed periods of inflation in the United States. The problem with these "theories" is that people have always wanted to improve their economic status and always will. In this sense, people have always been greedy. But inflation has not always been a problem. Were people less greedy in the early 1980s, when inflation was low, than they were in the late 1970s, when inflation was high? Obviously, we have to look to other reasons to explain inflation. We discuss some of those reasons in later chapters.

3.d. The Inflationary Record

Many of our students, having always lived with inflation, are surprised to learn that inflation is a relatively new problem for the United States. From 1789, when the U.S. Constitution was ratified, until 1940, there was no particular trend in the general price level. At times prices rose, and at times they fell. The average level of prices in 1940 was approximately same as it was in the late eighteenth century.

Since 1940, prices in the United States have gone up markedly. The price level today is eight times what it was in 1940. But the rate of growth has varied.

Annual rates of inflation for several industrial and developing nations in the 1990s are shown in Table 5. Look at the diversity across countries: rates range from 0.0 percent in Japan to 328 percent in Turkmenistan.

hyperinflation: an extremely high rate of inflation

Hyperinflation is an extremely high rate of inflation. In most cases hyperinflation eventually makes a country's currency worthless and leads to the introduction of a new money. Argentina experienced hyperinflation in the 1980s. People had to carry large stacks of currency for small purchases. Cash registers and calculators ran out of digits as prices reached ridiculously high levels. After years of high inflation, Argentina replaced the old peso with the peso Argentino in June 1983. The government set the value of 1 peso Argentino equal to 10,000 old pesos (striking four zeros from all prices). A product that sold for 10,000 old pesos before the reform sold for 1 new peso after. But Argentina did not follow up its monetary reform with a noninflationary change in economic policy. In 1984 and 1985, the inflation rate exceeded 600 percent each year. As a result, in June 1985, the government again introduced a new currency, the austral, setting its value at 1,000 pesos Argentino. However, the economic policy associated with the introduction of the austral lowered the inflation rate only temporarily. By 1988, the inflation rate was over 300 percent, and in 1989 the inflation rate was over 3,000 percent. The rapid rise in prices associated with the austral resulted in the introduction of yet another currency, again named peso Argentino, in January 1992 with a value equal to 10,000 australes. This new peso was fixed at a value of 1 peso per 1 U.S. dollar, and this exchange rate lasted for about 10 years due to reasonably stable inflation in Argentina. In late 2001, Argentina experienced another financial crisis brought on by large government budget deficits; the fixed rate of exchange between the peso and the dollar ended, but the peso remained the currency of Argentina.

The most dramatic hyperinflation in modern times occurred in Europe after World War I. The price level in Germany rose to incredible levels between 1914 and

TABLE 5

Rates of Inflation for Selected Countries, 1990–2001

Country	Inflation Rate (percent)
Selected Industrial	
Canada	1.4
Germany	1.9
Italy	3.6
Japan	0.0
United Kingdom	2.8
United States	2.0
Selected Developing	
Botswana	8.9
Brazil	168.1
Chile	6.8
Egypt	7.7
Hong Kong, China	3.3
India	7.7
Israel	10
Mexico	18.2
Philippines	8.2
Poland	21.4
South Africa	9.3
Turkmenistan	328

Note: Data are average annual percentages. Changes in the GDP price index as reported in the World Bank, *World Development Report, 2003.*

1924 in relation to prices in 1914. By 1924, German prices were more than 100 trillion times higher than they had been in 1914. At the height of the inflation, the mark was virtually worthless.

Table 6 provides data on the most recent cases of hyperinflation. These episodes range in duration from only 3 months in Turkmenistan, when prices rose by 291 percent, to 58 months in Nicaragua, when prices rose an astounding 11,895,866,143 percent. Hyperinflation is often associated with crises that lead to new governments, new economic policies, and new monies that replace the essentially worthless old money.

In later chapters, we will see how high rates of inflation generally are caused by rapid growth of the money supply. When a central government wants to spend more than it is capable of funding through taxation or borrowing, it simply issues money to finance its budget deficit. As the money supply increases faster than the demand to hold it, spending increases and prices go up.

| | | **TABLE 6** | | |

TABLE 6

Recent Hyperinflations

Country	Dates	Months Duration	Cumulative Inflation (percent)
Angola	Dec. 94–Jun. 96	19	62,445
Argentina	May 89–Mar. 90	11	15,167
Armenia	Oct. 93–Dec. 94	15	34,158
Azerbaijan	Dec. 92–Dec. 94	25	41,742
Bolivia	Apr. 84–Sep. 85	18	97,282
Brazil	Dec. 89–Mar. 90	4	693
Congo, Dem. Rep.	Nov. 93–Sep. 94	11	69,502
Georgia	Sep. 93–Sep. 94	13	76,219
Nicaragua	Jun. 86–Mar. 91	58	11,895,866,143
Serbia	Feb. 93–Jan. 94	12	156,312,790
Tajikistan	Aug. 93–Dec. 93	9	3,636
Turkmenistan	Nov. 95–Jan. 96	3	291
Ukraine	Apr. 91–Nov. 94	44	1,864,715

Source: Stanley Fischer, Ratna Sahay, and Carlos A. Vegh, "Modern Hyper- and High Inflations," *Journal of Economic Literature,* September 2002, pp. 837–880.

RECAP

1. Inflation is a sustained rise in the average level of prices.
2. The higher the price level, the lower the real value (purchasing power) of money.
3. Unexpectedly high inflation redistributes income away from those who receive fixed-dollar payments (like creditors) toward those who make fixed-dollar payments (like debtors).
4. The real interest rate is the nominal interest rate minus the rate of inflation.
5. Demand-pull inflation is a product of increased spending; cost-push inflation reflects increased production costs.
6. Hyperinflation is a very high rate of inflation that often results in the introduction of a new currency.

Summary

❓ What is a business cycle?

1. Business cycles are recurring changes in real GDP, in which expansion is followed by contraction. *§1.a*
2. The four stages of the business cycle are expansion (boom), peak, contraction (recession), and trough. *§1.a*
3. Leading, coincident, and lagging indicators are variables that change in relation to changes in output. *§1.c*

❓ How is the unemployment rate defined and measured?

4. The unemployment rate is the percentage of the labor force that is not working. *§2.a*
5. To be in the U.S. labor force, an individual must be working or actively seeking work. *§2.a*

6. Unemployment can be classified as seasonal, frictional, structural, or cyclical. *§2.c*

7. Frictional and structural unemployment are always present in a dynamic economy; cyclical unemployment is a product of recession. *§2.c*

? What is the cost of unemployed resources?

8. The GDP gap measures the output lost because of unemployment. *§2.d*

? What is inflation?

9. Inflation is a sustained rise in the average level of prices. *§3*

10. The higher the level of prices, the lower the purchasing power of money. *§3.b*

? Why is inflation a problem?

11. Inflation becomes a problem when income rises at a slower rate than prices. *§3.b*

12. Unexpectedly high inflation hurts those who receive fixed-dollar payments (like creditors) and benefits those who make fixed-dollar payments (like debtors). *§3.b*

13. Inflation can stem from demand-pull or cost-push pressures. *§3.c*

14. Hyperinflation—an extremely high rate of inflation—can force a country to introduce a new currency. *§3.d*

Key Terms

business cycle *§1.a*

recession *§1.a*

depression *§1.b*

leading indicator *§1.c*

coincident indicator *§1.c*

lagging indicator *§1.c*

unemployment rate *§2.a*

discouraged workers *§2.b*

underemployment *§2.b*

potential real GDP *§2.d*

natural rate of unemployment *§2.d*

inflation *§3*

nominal interest rate *§3.b*

real interest rate *§3.b*

hyperinflation *§3.d*

Exercises

1. What is the labor force? Do you believe that the U.S. government's definition of the labor force is a good one—that it includes all the people it should include? Explain your answer.

2. List the reasons why the official unemployment rate may not reflect the true social burden of unemployment. Explain whether the official numbers overstate or understate *true* unemployment in light of each reason you discuss.

3. Suppose you are able-bodied and intelligent, but lazy. You'd rather sit home and watch television than work, even though you know you could find an acceptable job if you looked.
   a. Are you officially unemployed?
   b. Are you a discouraged worker?

4. Can government do anything to reduce the number of people in the following categories? If so, what?
   a. Frictionally unemployed
   b. Structurally unemployed
   c. Cyclically unemployed

5. Does the GDP gap measure all of the costs of unemployment? Why or why not?

6. Why do teenagers have the highest unemployment rate in the economy?

7. Suppose you are currently earning $10 an hour. If the inflation rate over the current year is 10 percent and your firm provides a cost-of-living raise based on the rate of inflation, what would you expect to earn after your raise? If the cost-of-living raise is always

granted on the basis of the past year's inflation, is your nominal income really keeping up with the cost of living?

8. Write an equation that defines the real interest rate. Use the equation to explain why unexpectedly high inflation redistributes income from creditors to debtors.

9. Many home mortgages in recent years have been made with variable interest rates. Typically, the interest rate is adjusted once a year on the basis of current interest rates on government bonds. How do variable interest rate loans protect creditors from the effects of unexpected inflation?

10. The word *cycle* suggests a regular, recurring pattern of activity. Is there a regular pattern in the business cycle? Support your answer by examining the duration (number of months) of each expansion and contraction in Figure 1.

11. Using the list of leading indicators in Table 1, write a brief paragraph explaining why each variable changes before real output changes. In other words, provide an economic reason why each indicator is expected to lead the business cycle.

12. Suppose 500 people were surveyed, and of those 500, 450 were working full-time. Of the 50 not working, 10 were full-time college students, 20 were retired, 5 were under sixteen years of age, 5 had stopped looking for work because they believed there were no jobs for them, and 10 were actively looking for work.

    a. How many of the 500 surveyed are in the labor force?

    b. What is the unemployment rate among the 500 surveyed people?

13. Consider the following price information:

	Year 1	Year 2
Cup of coffee	$ .50	$1.00
Glass of milk	$1.00	$2.00

    a. Based on the information given, what was the inflation rate between year 1 and year 2?

    b. What happened to the price of coffee relative to that of milk between year 1 and year 2?

14. Use a supply and demand diagram to illustrate:

    a. Cost-push inflation caused by a labor union successfully negotiating for a higher wage

    b. Demand-pull inflation caused by an increase in demand for domestic products from foreign buyers.

15. During the Bolivian hyperinflation in the 1980s, Bolivians used U.S. dollars as a substitute for the domestic currency (the peso) for many transactions. Explain how the value of money is affected by hyperinflation and the incentives to use a low-inflation currency like the dollar as a substitute for a high-inflation currency like the Bolivian peso.

16. Suppose the government raises the benefits available to unemployed workers and then discovers that the number of unemployed workers has increased substantially, although there has been no other change in the economy. How can government policies aimed at helping the unemployed actually create more unemployment?

ACE

Take the ACE Practice Test for this chapter to review the important concepts and get immediate feedback with answers.

economics.college.hmco.com/students

Economically Speaking

Things Really Are Tight at Most Levels of Job Market

This is how bad the job market has gotten in Colorado: On a recent Monday morning, many of my colleagues and I received spam—an indiscriminate, mass e-mailing—in the form of a resume from a man looking for a tech job in the Colorado Springs area.

Now, perhaps this unusual method of job search simply shows an extreme lack of tact. Or perhaps we should just give this guy the benefit of the doubt and assume he's just extremely desperate.

Our resume spammer isn't alone. Sure, the statistics will tell you that Colorado's unemployment rate isn't that high, at least compared with states like Oregon and Washington. But economists are still worried. One big problem, they say, is that too many people have lost high-paying jobs in Colorado's once-booming tech and telecom sector, and now can't find a comparable job—or can't find a job at all.

Of course, an unemployed telecom manager is better off than an unemployed fast-food worker. But, economists say, long-term unemployment among the state's better-paid residents can have a worrisome ripple effect on those lower-wage workers, and the economy as a whole.

When they go from highly paid to unemployed, these people may no longer buy new clothes or cars, or go to fancy restaurants, pinching retailers. They may put off pricey remodeling projects or expensive ski vacations, meaning lost revenue and jobs in those industries.

But perhaps most devastating, with their better qualifications, laid-off tech workers may take lower-paying, less-skilled jobs away from other workers, in turn making it harder for poorer people to find work.

"It's a drain on everyone," said Shepard Nevel, executive director of the Mayor's Office of Workforce Development, which provides job placement help.

It's tough to say how many people are facing long-term unemployment, since the state does not track that. But there are plenty of indications that the job market has gotten tougher.

In 2001, the Labor Department said the average worker eligible for unemployment benefits collected them for about 12 weeks. In 2002, the average increased to 15 weeks.

Also, the state Labor Department said, the computer and data processing industry lost about 9,300 jobs from December 2001 to December 2002, a 13 percent drop. The communications industry, which includes telecom firms, lost 6,400 jobs during that time, nearly 12 percent of jobs in that sector.

When Littleton resident Matt Mannino quit his job at Nextel in April 2001, he said he wasn't worried about losing his $45,000 salary. After all, he'd nearly completed a master's degree in information technology management, and that should have put him in high demand for an even better-paying tech job.

Nearly two years later, Mannino, 32, is still looking for work.

"Any (job) search possible I have done, and I've had zero interviews over the the course of the past two years," he said.

Mannino has gone from applying for IT jobs to applying for just about anything. When he circulated his applications to retailers such as at Costco and REI, "I even downplayed my skills and education," he said.

Mannino occasionally has gotten work delivering books for the Jefferson County Library, which paid $10 an hour, but lately even that has dried up.

By now, Mannino says he's depleted most of his savings, doesn't have medical insurance and is putting off his wedding because he can't afford it.

For some, losing a job after the frenetic pace of the go-go years offers a good breather—for a while. When Duncan McCloud, 37, was laid off from an IT manager job at Autoliv in September, he said it provided an opportunity for "some self-examination and reflection" about what he really wanted to do with his life.

But five months later, McCloud also is dealing with some harsh realities. He worries he'll have to take a pay cut or move his family out of state to find work. "I'm just hoping that I can find something," he said.

ALLISON LINN

***Rocky Mountain News*/March 1, 2003**

Commentary

The rise in unemployment of the early 2000s turned things upside down in the labor market. After the boom years of the 1990s, when jobs were plentiful and employers often could not find enough workers to hire, as more and more workers lost their jobs in the early 2000s, workers could not find enough job opportunities. The article says that many laid-off tech workers may take lower-paying, less-skilled jobs. Why would anyone take a job below the level of his or her past job? The answer lies in the type of knowledge that workers possess that may make them attractive to certain employers.

Many newly unemployed workers have worked for many years and earned higher salaries than they can expect to earn in other jobs. This, of course, is the problem. If they could simply find another job that offered them comparable pay, they would not be so devastated by the prospect of losing their jobs. This raises an interesting question: If someone is highly valued at one firm and paid accordingly, why isn't that person as valuable to other companies who could now hire her or him? In fact, it is often the case that laid-off workers with successful job histories at one firm are unable to meet entry-level requirements at other jobs.

We can better understand the causes of the plight of many laid-off industrial workers if we consider the determinants of people's wages. Economic theory suggests that people's wages are tied to the amount they contribute to their firm, which implies that wages increase with people's skills. We can think of two broad categories of skills; general skills that make people valuable to any firm and more specialized skills that make people valuable to certain firms. Examples of general skills include welding, bookkeeping, and an ability to manage people. Skills that are useful to only one firm are those that are specifically tied to the product or structure of that firm. Specific knowledge of this second type is not transferable to other firms.

People who work in a particular firm for an extended period learn both general skills that make them valuable to any similar company and specific skills that make them valuable to their company only. Experienced workers who are seeking new jobs must possess or else learn general skills that make them attractive in an economy with rapid technological change.

The article talks about massive layoffs in the communications industry. Someone who has spent years working for a telecom firm will have many skills that were highly valued by the former firm and, perhaps, by other firms in the telecom industry. However, the skills that were so valuable in the telecom firm may not be highly valued by an employer in another field. The fact that many unemployed workers must find work in a new field suggests the need for an educational system that can accommodate the needs of the experienced worker who needs to invest in his or her skills to find a good job in a new industry.

The distinction between general and firm-specific skills also suggests why the workers who are least likely to benefit from retraining are those within a few years of retirement. Older workers who must undergo on-the-job training will not be able to use their new firm-specific skills for as many years as younger workers. It is not worthwhile for firms to hire and train workers who are near retirement.

Structural change is an integral part of a dynamic, growing economy. Dislocations are probably inevitable when large-scale structural change occurs, and these dislocations benefit some people while hurting others. Although retraining helps mitigate some of the effects of the upheaval that accompanies structural change, unfortunately it cannot solve all the problems that arise. For the economy as a whole, such change is necessary. Unfortunately, some people are always harmed when the economy undergoes structural change.

CHAPTER 9

Macroeconomic Equilibrium: Aggregate Demand and Supply

Total output and income in the United States have grown over time. Each generation has experienced a higher living standard than the previous generation. Yet, as we learned in Chapter 8, economic growth has not been steady. Economies go through periods of expansion followed by periods of contraction or recession, and such business cycles have major impacts on people's lives, incomes, and living standards.

Economic stagnation and recession throw many, often those who are already relatively poor, out of their jobs and into real poverty. Economic growth increases the number of jobs and draws people out of poverty and into the mainstream of economic progress. To understand why economies grow and why they go through cycles, we must discover why firms decide to produce more or less and why buyers decide to buy more or less. The approach we take is similar to the approach we followed in the first five chapters of the text using demand and supply curves. In Chapters 3, 4, and 5, demand and supply curves were derived and used to examine questions involving the equilibrium price and quantities demanded and supplied of a single good or service. This simple yet powerful microeconomic technique of

analysis has a macroeconomic counterpart—aggregate demand and aggregate supply, which are used to determine an equilibrium price level and quantity of goods and services produced for the *entire economy.* In this chapter we shall use aggregate demand and supply curves to illustrate the causes of business cycles and economic growth. ▨

1. Aggregate Demand, Aggregate Supply, and Business Cycles

What causes economic growth and business cycles? We can provide some answers to this important question using aggregate demand (*AD*) and aggregate supply (*AS*) curves. Suppose we represent the economy in a simple demand and supply diagram, as shown in Figure 1. Aggregate demand represents the total spending in the economy at alternative price levels. Aggregate supply represents the total output of the economy at alternative price levels. To understand the causes of business cycles and inflation, we must understand how aggregate demand and supply cause the equilibrium price level and real GDP, the nation's output of goods and services, to change. The intersection between the *AD* and *AS* curves defines the equilibrium level of real GDP and level of prices. The equilibrium price level is P_e, and the equilibrium level of real GDP is Y_e. This price and output level represents the level of prices and output for some particular period of time, say 2003. Once that equilibrium is established, there is no tendency for prices and output to change until changes occur in either the aggregate demand curve or the aggregate supply curve. Let's first consider a change in aggregate demand and then look at a change in aggregate supply.

1.a. Aggregate Demand and Business Cycles

An increase in aggregate demand is illustrated by a shift of the *AD* curve to the right, like the shift from AD_1 to AD_2 in Figure 2. This represents a situation in which

FIGURE 1

Aggregate Demand and Aggregate Supply Equilibrium

The equilibrium price level and real GDP are determined by the intersection of the *AD* and *AS* curves.

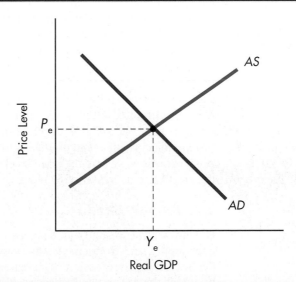

FIGURE 2

Effects of a Change in Aggregate Demand

If aggregate demand increases from AD_1 to AD_2, the equilibrium price level increases to P_{e2} and the equilibrium level of real GDP rises to Y_{e2}. If aggregate demand decreases from AD_1 to AD_3, the equilibrium price level falls to P_{e3} and the equilibrium level of real GDP drops to Y_{e3}.

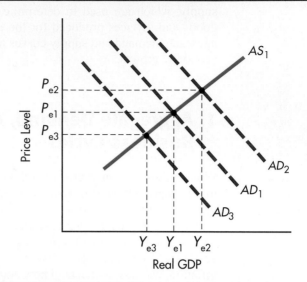

buyers are buying more at every price level. The shift causes the equilibrium level of real GDP to rise from Y_{e1} to Y_{e2}, illustrating the expansionary phase of the business cycle. As output rises, unemployment decreases. The increase in aggregate demand also leads to a higher price level, as shown by the change in the price level from P_{e1} to P_{e2}. The increase in the price level represents an example of **demand-pull inflation,** which is inflation caused by increasing demand for output.

If aggregate demand falls, like the shift from AD_1 to AD_3, then there is a lower equilibrium level of real GDP, Y_{e3}. In this case, buyers are buying *less* at every price level. The drop in real GDP caused by lower demand would represent an economic slowdown or a recession, when output falls and unemployment rises.

demand-pull inflation: inflation caused by increasing demand for output

1.b. Aggregate Supply and Business Cycles

Changes in aggregate supply can also cause business cycles. Figure 3 illustrates what happens when aggregate supply changes. An increase in aggregate supply is illustrated by the shift from AS_1 to AS_2, leading to an increase in the equilibrium level of real GDP from Y_{e1} to Y_{e2}. An increase in aggregate supply comes about when firms produce more at every price level. Such an increase could result from an improvement in technology or a decrease in the costs of production.

If aggregate supply decreased, as in the shift from AS_1 to AS_3, then the equilibrium level of real GDP would fall to Y_{e3} and the equilibrium price level would increase from P_{e1} to P_{e3}. A decrease in aggregate supply could be caused by higher production costs that lead producers to raise their prices. This is an example of **cost-push inflation**—where the price level rises due to increased costs of production and the associated decrease in aggregate supply.

cost-push inflation: inflation caused by rising costs of production

1.c. A Look Ahead

Business cycles result from changes in aggregate demand, from changes in aggregate supply, and from changes in both AD and AS. The degree to which real GDP declines during a recession or increases during an expansion depends on the amount by which the AD and/or AS curves shift. The degree to which an expansion involves

FIGURE 3

Effects of a Change in Aggregate Supply

If aggregate supply increases from AS_1 to AS_2 the equilibrium price level falls from P_{e1} to P_{e2} and the equilibrium level of real GDP rises to Y_{e2}. If aggregate supply decreases from AS_1 to AS_3, the equilibrium price level rises to P_{e3} and the equilibrium level of real GDP falls to Y_{e3}.

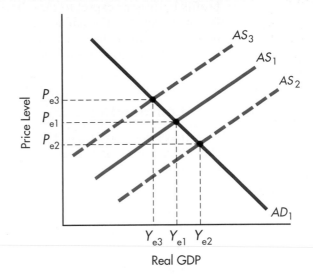

output growth or increased inflation depends on the shapes of the AD and AS curves. We need to consider why the curves have the shapes they do, and what causes them to shift.

The comparison we made earlier, between aggregate demand, aggregate supply, and their microeconomic counterparts, the supply and demand curves, is only superficial. As we examine the aggregate demand and supply curves, you will see that the reasons underlying the shapes and movements of AD and AS are in fact quite different from those explaining the shapes and movements of the supply and demand curves.

RECAP

1. Aggregate demand (AD) represents the total spending in the economy at alternative price levels.

2. Aggregate supply (AS) represents the total output of the economy at alternative price levels.

3. The intersection between the AD and AS curves defines the equilibrium level of real GDP and the level of prices.

4. Business cycles result from changes in AD and/or AS.

1. What factors affect aggregate demand?

2. Factors That Influence Aggregate Demand

Aggregate demand is the relation between aggregate expenditures, or total spending, and the price level. Aggregate expenditures are the sum of expenditures of each sector of the economy: households (consumption), business firms (investment), government, and the rest of the world (net exports). Each sector of the economy has different reasons for spending; for instance, household spending depends heavily on household income, while business spending depends on the profits businesses expect to earn. Because each sector of the economy has a different reason for the amount of spending it undertakes, aggregate spending depends on all of these reasons. To understand aggregate demand, therefore, requires that we look at those factors that influence the expenditures of each sector of the economy.

2.a. Consumption

How much households spend depends on their income, their wealth, expectations about future prices and incomes, demographics like the age distribution of the population, and taxes.

- Income: If current income rises, households purchase more goods and services.
- Wealth: Wealth is different from income. It is the value of assets owned by a household, including homes, cars, bank deposits, stocks, and bonds. An increase in household wealth will increase consumption.
- Expectations: Expectations regarding future changes in income or wealth can affect consumption today. If households expect a recession and worry about job loss, consumption tends to fall. On the other hand, if households become more optimistic regarding future increases in income and wealth, consumption rises today.
- Demographics: Demographic change can affect consumption in several different ways. Population growth is generally associated with higher consumption for an economy. Younger households and older households generally consume more and save less than middle-aged households. Therefore, as the age distribution of a nation changes, so will consumption.
- Taxes: Higher taxes will lower the disposable income of households and decrease consumption, while lower taxes will raise disposable income and increase consumption. Government policy may change taxes and thereby bring about a change in consumption.

2.b. Investment

Investment is business spending on capital goods and inventories. In general, investment depends on the expected profitability of such spending, so any factor that could affect profitability will be a determinant of investment. Factors affecting the expected profitability of business projects include the interest rate, technology, the cost of capital goods, and capacity utilization.

- Interest rate: Investment is negatively related to the interest rate. The interest rate is the cost of borrowed funds. The greater the cost of borrowing, other things being equal, the fewer the investment projects that offer sufficient profit to be undertaken. As the interest rate falls, investment is stimulated as the cost of financing the investment is lowered.
- Technology: New production technology stimulates investment spending as firms are forced to adopt new production methods to stay competitive.
- Cost of capital goods: If machines and equipment purchased by firms rise in price, then the higher costs associated with investment will lower profitability and investment will fall.

■ Capacity utilization: The more excess capacity (unused capital goods) there is available, the more firms can expand production without purchasing new capital goods, and the lower investment is. As firms approach full capacity, more investment spending is required to expand output further.

2.c. Government Spending

Government spending may be set by government authorities independent of current income or other determinants of aggregate expenditures.

2.d. Net Exports

Net exports are equal to exports minus imports. We assume exports are determined by conditions in the rest of the world, like foreign income, tastes, prices, exchange rates, and government policy. Imports are determined by similar domestic factors.

Income   As domestic income rises and consumption rises, some of this consumption includes goods produced in other countries. Therefore, as domestic income rises, imports rise and net exports fall. Similarly, as foreign income rises, foreign residents buy more domestic goods, and net exports rise.

Prices   Other things being equal, higher (lower) foreign prices make domestic goods relatively cheaper (more expensive) and increase (decrease) net exports. Higher (lower) domestic prices make domestic goods relatively more expensive (cheaper) and decrease (increase) net exports.

Exchange Rates   Other things being equal, a depreciation of the domestic currency on the foreign exchange market will make domestic goods cheaper to foreign buyers and make foreign goods more expensive to domestic residents, so that net exports will rise. An appreciation of the domestic currency will have just the opposite effects.

Government Policy   Net exports may fall if foreign governments restrict the entry of domestic goods into their countries, reducing domestic exports. If the domestic government restricts imports into the domestic economy, net exports may rise.

2.e. Aggregate Expenditures

You can see how aggregate expenditures, the sum of all spending on U.S. goods and services, must depend on prices, income, and all of the other determinants discussed in the previous sections. As with the demand curve for a specific good or service, we want to classify the factors that influence spending into the price and the nonprice determinants for the aggregate demand curves as well. The components of aggregate expenditures that change as the price level changes will lead to movements along the aggregate demand curve—changes in quantity demanded—while changes in aggregate expenditures caused by nonprice effects will cause shifts of the aggregate demand curve—changes in aggregate demand. In the following section we look first at the price effects, or movements along an aggregate demand curve. Following that discussion, we focus on the nonprice determinants of aggregate demand.

1. Aggregate expenditures are the sum of consumption, investment, government spending, and net exports.
2. Consumption depends on household income, wealth, expectations, demographics, and taxation.
3. Investment depends on the interest rate, technology, the cost of capital goods, and capacity utilization.
4. Government spending is determined independent of current income.
5. Net exports depend on foreign and domestic incomes, prices, government policies, and exchange rates.

3. The Aggregate Demand Curve

When we examined the demand curves in Chapter 3, we divided our study into two parts: the movement along the curve—changes in quantity demanded—and the shifts of the curve—changes in demand. We take the same approach here in examining aggregate demand. We first look at the movements along the aggregate demand curve caused by changes in the price level. We then turn to the nonprice determinants of aggregate demand that cause shifts in the curve.

3.a. Why the Aggregate Demand Curve Slopes Downward

Aggregate demand curves are downward sloping just like the demand curves for individual goods that were shown in Chapter 3, although for different reasons. Along the demand curve for an individual good, the price of that good changes while the prices of all other goods remain constant. This means that the good in question becomes relatively more or less expensive compared to all other goods in the economy. Consumers tend to substitute a less expensive good for a more expensive good. The effect of this substitution is an inverse relationship between price and quantity demanded. As the price of a good rises, the quantity demanded falls. For the economy as a whole, however, it is not a substitution of a less expensive good for a more expensive good that causes the demand curve to slope down. Instead, the aggregate quantity demanded, or total spending, will change as the price level changes as a result of the wealth effect, the interest rate effect, and the international trade effect of a price-level change on aggregate expenditures. We will discuss each of these effects in turn.

3.a.1. The Wealth Effect Individuals and businesses own money, stocks, bonds, and other financial assets. The purchasing power of these assets is the quantity of goods and services that the assets can be exchanged for. When the level of prices falls, the purchasing power of these assets increases, allowing households and businesses to purchase more. When prices go up, the purchasing power of financial assets falls, which causes households and businesses to spend less. This is the **wealth effect** (sometimes called the *real-balance effect*) of a price change: a change in the real value of wealth that causes spending to change when the level of prices changes. *Real values* are values that have been adjusted for price-level changes. Here *real value* means "purchasing power." When the price level changes, the purchasing power of financial assets also changes. When prices rise, the real value of

wealth effect: a change in the real value of wealth that causes spending to change when the level of prices changes

When the price level changes, the purchasing power of financial assets changes.

assets and wealth falls, and aggregate expenditures tend to fall. When prices fall, the real value of assets and wealth rises, and aggregate expenditures tend to rise.

3.a.2. The Interest Rate Effect

When the price level rises, the purchasing power of each dollar falls, which means that more money is required to buy any particular quantity of goods and services (see Figure 4). Suppose that a family of three needs $100 each week to buy food. If the price level doubles, the same quantity of food costs $200. The household must have twice as much money to buy the same amount of food. Conversely, when prices fall, the family needs less money to buy food because the purchasing power of each dollar is greater.

When prices go up, people need more money. So they sell their other financial assets, like bonds, to get that money. The increase in the supply of bonds lowers bond prices and raises interest rates. Since bonds typically pay fixed-dollar interest payments each year, as the price of a bond varies, the interest rate (or yield) will change. For instance, suppose you pay $1,000 for a bond that pays $100 a year in interest. The interest rate on this bond is found by dividing the annual interest payment by the bond price, or $100/$1,000 = 10 percent. If the price of the bond

---

FIGURE 4

The Interest Rate Effect of Price-Level Changes on Aggregate Expenditures

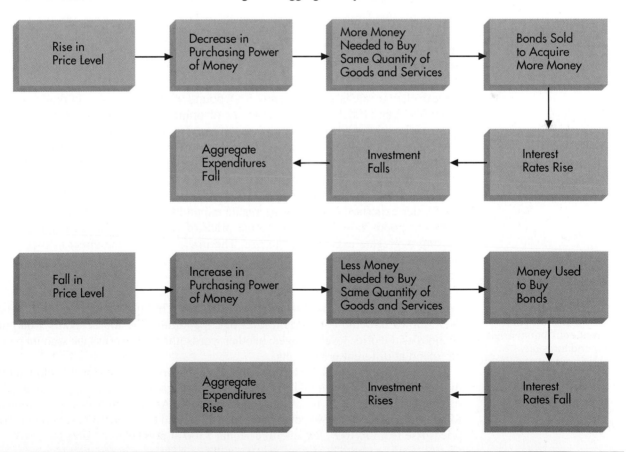

---

falls to $900, then the interest rate is equal to the annual interest payment (which remains fixed at $100 for the life of the bond) divided by the new price of $900: $100/$900 = 11 percent. When bond prices fall, interest rates rise, and when bond prices rise, interest rates fall.

If people want more money and they sell some of their bond holdings to raise the money, bond prices will fall and interest rates will rise. The rise in interest rates is necessary to sell the larger quantity of bonds, but it causes investment expenditures to fall, which causes aggregate expenditures to fall.

When prices fall, people need less money to purchase the same quantity of goods. So they use their money holdings to buy bonds and other financial assets. The increased demand for bonds increases bond prices and causes interest rates to fall. Lower interest rates increase investment expenditures, thereby pushing aggregate expenditures up.

interest rate effect: a change in interest rates that causes investment and therefore aggregate expenditures to change as the level of prices changes

Figure 4 shows the **interest rate effect,** the relationship among the price level, interest rates, and aggregate expenditures. As the price level rises, interest rates rise and aggregate expenditures fall. As the price level falls, interest rates fall and aggregate expenditures rise.

3.a.3. The International Trade Effect

The third channel through which a price-level change affects the quantity of goods and services demanded is called the **international trade effect.** A change in the level of domestic prices can cause net exports to change. If domestic prices rise while foreign prices and the foreign exchange rate remain constant, domestic goods become more expensive in relation to foreign goods.

international trade effect: a change in aggregate expenditures resulting from a change in the domestic price level that changes the price of domestic goods in relation to foreign goods

Suppose the United States sells oranges to Japan. If the oranges sell for $1 per pound and the yen-dollar exchange rate is 100 yen = $1, a pound of U.S. oranges costs a Japanese buyer 100 yen. What happens if the level of prices in the United States goes up 10 percent? All prices, including the price of oranges, increase 10 percent. Oranges in the United States sell for $1.10 a pound after the price increase. If the exchange rate is still 100 yen = $1, a pound of oranges now costs the Japanese buyer 110 yen (100 × 1.10). If the prices of oranges from other countries do not change, some Japanese buyers may buy oranges from those countries. The increase in the level of U.S. prices makes U.S. goods more expensive relative to foreign goods and causes U.S. net exports to fall; a decrease in the level of U.S. prices makes U.S. goods cheaper in relation to foreign goods, which increases U.S. net exports.

When the price of domestic goods increases in relation to the price of foreign goods, net exports fall, causing aggregate expenditures to fall. When the price of domestic goods falls in relation to the price of foreign goods, net exports rise, causing aggregate expenditures to rise. The international trade effect of a change in the level of domestic prices causes aggregate expenditures to change in the opposite direction.

3.a.4. The Sum of the Price-Level Effects

aggregate demand curve: a curve that shows the different equilibrium levels of expenditures on domestic output at different levels of prices

The **aggregate demand curve** (AD) shows how the equilibrium level of expenditures for the economy's output changes as the price level changes. In other words, the curve shows the amount people spend at different price levels.

Figure 5 displays the typical shape of the AD curve. The price level is plotted on the vertical axis, and real GDP is plotted on the horizontal axis. Suppose that initially the economy is at point A with prices at P_0. At this point, spending equals $500. If prices fall to P_1, expenditures equal $700 and the economy is at point C. If prices rise from P_0 to P_2, expenditures equal $300 at point B.

FIGURE 5

The Aggregate Demand Curve

The aggregate demand curve (*AD*) shows the level of expenditures at different price levels. At price level P_0, expenditures are \$500; at P_1, they are \$700; and at P_2, they are \$300.

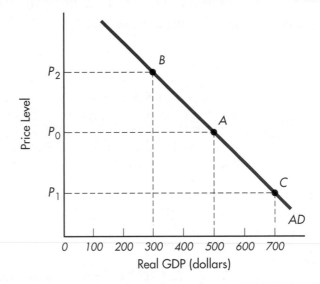

Because aggregate expenditures increase when the price level decreases and decrease when the price level increases, the aggregate demand curve slopes down. The aggregate demand curve is drawn with the price level for the *entire economy* on the vertical axis. A price-level change here means that, on average, *all prices in the economy change*; there is no relative price change among domestic goods. The negative slope of the aggregate demand curve is a product of the wealth effect, the interest rate effect, and the international trade effect.

A lower domestic price level increases consumption (the wealth effect), investment (the interest rate effect), and net exports (the international trade effect). As the price level drops, aggregate expenditures rise.

A higher domestic price reduces consumption (the wealth effect), investment (the interest rate effect), and net exports (the international trade effect). As prices rise, aggregate expenditures fall. These price effects are summarized in Figure 6.

3.b. Changes in Aggregate Demand: Nonprice Determinants

?

2. What causes the aggregate demand curve to shift?

The aggregate demand curve shows the level of aggregate expenditures at alternative price levels. We draw the curve by varying the price level and finding out what the resulting total expenditures are, holding all other things constant. As those "other things"—the nonprice determinants of aggregate demand—change, the aggregate demand curve shifts. The nonprice determinants of aggregate demand include all of the factors covered in the discussion of the components of expenditures—income, wealth, demographics, expectations, taxes, the interest rate (interest rates can change for reasons other than price-level changes), the cost of capital goods, capacity utilization, foreign income and price levels, exchange rates, and government policy. A change in any one of these can cause the *AD* curve to shift. In the discussions that follow, we will focus particularly on the effect of expectations and foreign income and price levels; we will also mention government policy, which will be examined in detail in Chapter 12. Figure 7 summarizes these effects, which are discussed next.

FIGURE 6

Why the Aggregate Demand Curve Slopes Downward

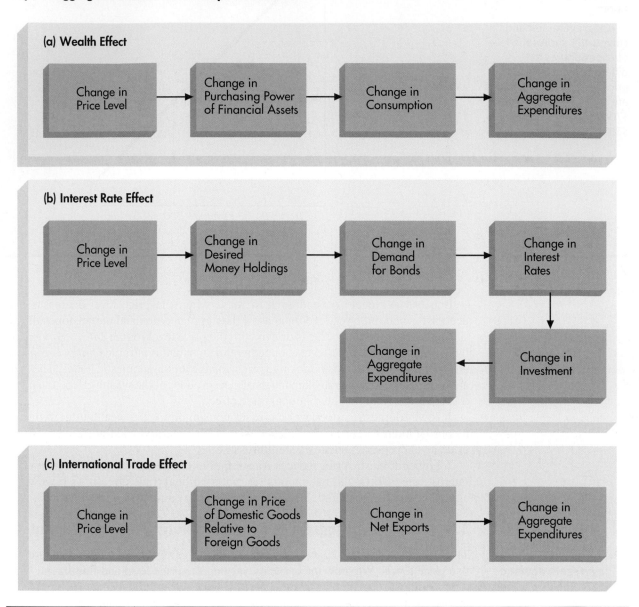

(a) Wealth Effect

Change in Price Level → Change in Purchasing Power of Financial Assets → Change in Consumption → Change in Aggregate Expenditures

(b) Interest Rate Effect

Change in Price Level → Change in Desired Money Holdings → Change in Demand for Bonds → Change in Interest Rates → Change in Investment → Change in Aggregate Expenditures

(c) International Trade Effect

Change in Price Level → Change in Price of Domestic Goods Relative to Foreign Goods → Change in Net Exports → Change in Aggregate Expenditures

3.b.1. Expectations Consumption and business spending are affected by expectations. Consumption is sensitive to people's expectations of future income, prices, and wealth. For example, when people expect the economy to do well in the future, they increase consumption today at every price level. This is reflected in a shift of the aggregate demand curve to the right, from AD_0 to AD_1, as shown in Figure 8. When aggregate demand increases, aggregate expenditures increase at every price level.

FIGURE 7

Nonprice Determinants: Changes in Aggregate Demand

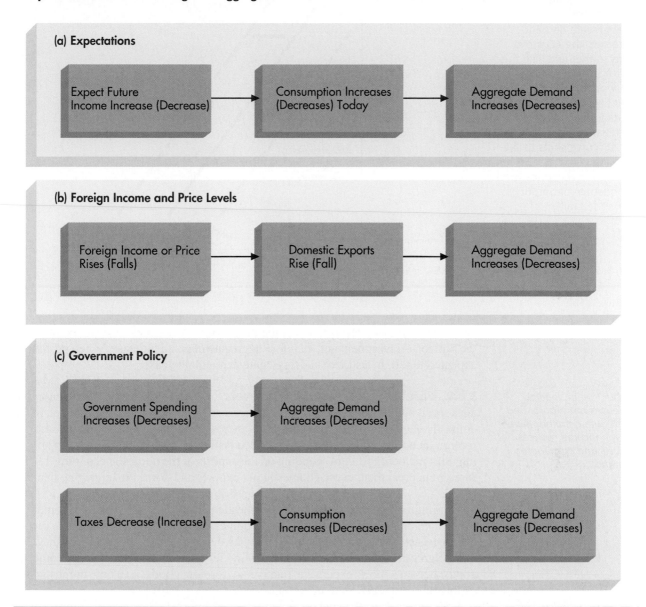

On the other hand, if people expect a recession in the near future, they tend to reduce consumption and increase saving in order to protect themselves against a greater likelihood of losing a job or a forced cutback in hours worked. As consumption drops, aggregate demand decreases. The AD curve shifts to the left, from AD_0 to AD_2. At every price level along AD_2, planned expenditures are less than they are along AD_0.

Expectations also play an important role in investment decisions. Before undertaking a particular project, businesses forecast the likely revenues and costs

FIGURE 8

Shifting the Aggregate Demand Curve

As aggregate demand increases, the *AD* curve shifts to the right, like the shift from AD_0 to AD_1. At every price level, the quantity of output demanded increases. As aggregate demand falls, the *AD* curve shifts to the left, like the shift from AD_0 to AD_2. At every price level, the quantity of output demanded falls.

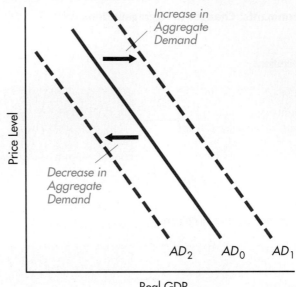

associated with that project. When the profit outlook is good—say, a tax cut is on the horizon—investment and therefore aggregate demand increase. When profits are expected to fall, investment and aggregate demand decrease.

Higher foreign income increases net exports and aggregate demand; lower foreign income reduces net exports and aggregate demand.

3.b.2. Foreign Income and Price Levels

When foreign income increases, so does foreign spending. Some of this increased spending is for goods produced in the domestic economy. As domestic exports increase, aggregate demand rises. Lower foreign income has just the opposite effect. As foreign income falls, foreign spending falls, including foreign spending on the exports of the domestic economy. Lower foreign income, then, causes domestic net exports and domestic aggregate demand to fall.

If foreign prices rise in relation to domestic prices, domestic goods become less expensive relative to foreign goods, and domestic net exports increase. This means that aggregate demand rises, or the aggregate demand curve shifts right, as the level of foreign prices rises. Conversely, when the level of foreign prices falls, domestic goods become more expensive relative to foreign goods, causing domestic net exports and aggregate demand to fall.

Changes in the level of foreign prices change domestic net exports and aggregate demand in the same direction.

Let's go back to the market for oranges. Suppose U.S. growers compete with Brazilian growers for the Japanese orange market. If the level of prices in Brazil rises while the level of prices in the United States remains stable, the price of Brazilian oranges to the Japanese buyer rises in relation to the price of U.S. oranges. What happens? Exports of U.S. oranges to Japan should rise while exports of Brazilian oranges to Japan fall.[1]

---

[1]This assumes no change in exchange rates. If the Brazilian currency were to depreciate in value as Brazilian prices rose, than the cheaper exchange rate would at least partially offset the higher price and reduce the impact of the price change on exports.

3.b.3. Government Policy One of the goals of macroeconomic policy is to achieve economic growth without inflation. For GDP to increase, either *AD* or *AS* would have to change. Government economic policy can cause the aggregate demand curve to shift. An increase in government spending or a decrease in taxes will increase aggregate demand; a decrease in government spending or an increase in taxes will decrease aggregate demand. We devote an entire chapter to fiscal policy, an examination of the effect of taxes and government spending on aggregate demand. In another chapter, on monetary policy, we describe how changes in the money supply can cause the aggregate demand curve to shift.

RECAP

1. The aggregate demand curve shows the level of aggregate expenditures at different price levels.

2. Aggregate expenditures are the sum of consumption, investment, government spending, and net exports.

3. The wealth effect, the interest rate effect, and the international trade effect are three reasons why the aggregate demand curve slopes down. These effects explain movements along a given *AD* curve.

4. The aggregate demand curve shifts with changes in the nonprice determinants of aggregate demand: expectations, foreign income and price levels, and government policy.

4. Aggregate Supply

aggregate supply curve: a curve that shows the amount of real GDP produced at different price levels

3. What factors affect aggregate supply?

The **aggregate supply curve** shows the quantity of real GDP produced at different price levels. The aggregate supply curve (*AS*) looks like the supply curve for an individual good, but, as with aggregate demand and the microeconomic demand curve, different factors are at work. The positive relationship between price and quantity supplied of an individual good is based on the change in the price of that good in relation to the prices of all other goods. As the price of a single good rises relative to the prices of other goods, sellers are willing to offer more of the good for sale. With aggregate supply, on the other hand, we are analyzing how the amount of all goods and services produced changes as the level of prices changes. The direct relationship between prices and national output is explained by the effect of changing prices on profits, not by relative price changes.

4.a. Why the Aggregate Supply Curve Slopes Upward

Along the aggregate supply curve, everything is held fixed except the price level and output. The price level is the price of output. The prices of resources, that is, the costs of production—wages, rent, and interest—are assumed to be constant, at least for a short time following a change in the price level.

If the price level rises while the costs of production remain fixed, business profits go up. As profits rise, firms are willing to produce more output. As the price level rises, then, the quantity of output firms are willing to supply increases. The result is the positively sloped aggregate supply curve shown in Figure 9.

FIGURE 9

Aggregate Supply

The aggregate supply curve shows the amount of real GDP produced at different price levels. The *AS* curve slopes up, indicating that the higher the price level, the greater the quantity of output produced.

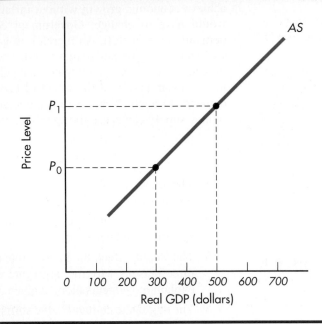

As the price level rises from P_0 to P_1 in Figure 9, real GDP increases from $300 to $500. The higher the price level, the higher are profits, everything else held constant, and the greater is the quantity of output produced in the economy. Conversely, as the price level falls, the quantity of output produced falls.

4.b. Short-Run Versus Long-Run Aggregate Supply

The curve in Figure 9 is a *short-run* aggregate supply curve because the costs of production are held constant. Although production costs may not rise immediately when the price level rises, eventually they will. Labor will demand higher wages to compensate for the higher cost of living; suppliers will charge more for materials. The positive slope of the *AS* curve, then, is a short-run phenomenon. How short is the short run? It is the period of time over which production costs remain constant. (In the long run, all costs change or are variable.) For the economy as a whole, the short run can be months or, at most, a few years.

4. Why does the short-run aggregate supply curve become steeper as real GDP increases?

4.b.1. Short-Run Aggregate Supply Curve
Figure 9 represents the general shape of the short-run aggregate supply curve. In Figure 10 you see a more realistic version of the same curve—its steepness varies. The steepness of the aggregate supply curve depends on the ability and willingness of producers to respond to price-level changes in the short run. Figure 10 shows the typical shape of the short-run aggregate supply curve.

Notice that as the level of real GDP increases in Figure 10, the *AS* curve becomes steeper. This is because each increase in output requires firms to hire more and more resources, until eventually full capacity is reached in some areas of the economy, resources are fully employed, and some firms reach maximum output. At this point, increases in the price level bring about smaller and smaller increases in output from firms as a whole. The short-run aggregate supply curve becomes increasingly steep as the economy approaches maximum output.

FIGURE 10

The Shape of the Short-Run Aggregate Supply Curve

The upward-sloping aggregate supply curve occurs when the price level must rise to induce further increases in output. The curve gets steeper as real GDP increases, since the closer the economy comes to the capacity level of output, the less output will rise in response to higher prices as more and more firms reach their maximum level of output in the short run.

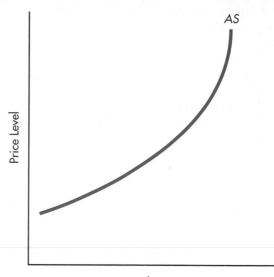

4.b.2. Long-Run Aggregate Supply Curve   Aggregate supply in the short run is different from aggregate supply in the long run (see Figure 11). That difference stems from the fact that quantities and costs of resources are not fixed in the long run. Over time, contracts expire and wages and other resource costs adjust to current conditions. The increased flexibility of resource costs in the long run has costs rising and falling with the price level and changes the shape of the aggregate supply curve. Lack of information about economic conditions in the short run also

Technological advance shifts the aggregate supply curve outward and increases output. An example of a technological advance that has increased efficiency in the airline industry is the self check-in kiosk. The photo shows customers at O'Hare International Airport checking in for flights without waiting in line at ticket counters. This allows the airlines to lower costs, as these customers do not require an airline employee for assistance.

How Lack of Information in the Short Run Affects Wages in the Long Run

Workers do not have perfect information. In other words, they do not know everything that occurs. This lack of information includes information about the price level. If workers form incorrect expectations regarding the price level in the short run, they may be willing to work for a different wage in the short run than in the long run. For example, if workers thought that the inflation rate would be 3 percent over the next year, they would want a smaller wage raise than if they believed that the inflation rate would be 6 percent. If, in fact, they base their wage negotiations on 3 percent inflation and accept a wage based on that inflation rate, but it turns out that the price level has increased by 6 percent, workers will then seek higher wages. In the long run, wages will reflect price-level changes.

If it cost nothing to obtain information, everyone who was interested would always know the current economic conditions. However, since there are costs of obtaining and understanding information about the economy, people will make mistakes in the short run. Both managers and employees make mistakes due to lack of information. Such mistakes are not due to stupidity but to ignorance—ignorance of future as well as of current economic conditions. In the long run, mistakes about the price level are realized and wages adjust to the known price level.

We now have two reasons why wages will be more flexible in the long run than in the short run: long-term contracts and lack of information in the short run. The same arguments could be made for other resources as well. Because of these two reasons, the short-run aggregate supply curve is generally upward sloping due to resource prices' being relatively fixed in the short run.

FIGURE 11

The Shape of the Long-Run Aggregate Supply Curve

In the long run, the *AS* curve is a vertical line at the potential level of real GDP, which indicates that there is no relationship between price-level changes and the quantity of output produced.

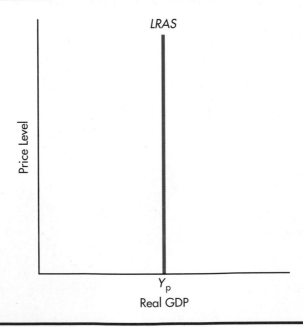

The aggregate supply curve shifts in response to changes in the price of resources, in technology, and in expectations.

contributes to the inflexibility of resource prices as compared to the long run. The Economic Insight "How Lack of Information in the Short Run Affects Wages in the Long Run" shows why this is true for labor, as well as for other resources.

The **long-run aggregate supply curve** (*LRAS*) is viewed by most economists as being a vertical line at the potential level of real GDP or output (Y_p), as shown in Figure 11. Remember that the potential level of real GDP is the income level that is produced in the absence of any cyclical unemployment, or when the natural rate of unemployment exists. In the long run, wages and other resource costs fully adjust to price changes. The short-run *AS* curve slopes up because we assume that the costs of production, particularly wages, do not change to offset changing prices. In the short run, then, higher prices increase producers' profits and stimulate production. In the long run, because the costs of production adjust completely to the change in prices, neither profits nor production increases. What we find here are higher wages and other costs of production to match the higher level of prices.

4.c. Changes in Aggregate Supply: Nonprice Determinants

The aggregate supply curve is drawn with everything but the price level and real GDP held constant. There are several things that can change and cause the aggregate supply curve to shift. The shift from AS_0 to AS_1 in Figure 12 represents an increase in aggregate supply. The AS_1 curve lies to the right of AS_0, which means that at every price level, production is higher on AS_1 than on AS_0. The shift from AS_0 to AS_2 represents a decrease in aggregate supply. The AS_2 curve lies to the left of AS_0, which means that at every price level, production along AS_2 is less than along AS_0. The nonprice determinants of aggregate supply are resource prices, technology, and expectations. Figure 13 summarizes the nonprice determinants of aggregate supply, discussed in detail next.

FIGURE 12

Changes in Aggregate Supply

The aggregate supply curve shifts with changes in resource prices, technology, and expectations. When aggregate supply increases, the curve shifts to the right, like the shift from AS_0 to AS_1, so that at every price level more is being produced. When aggregate supply falls, the curve shifts to the left, like the shift from AS_0 to AS_2, so that at every price level less is being produced.

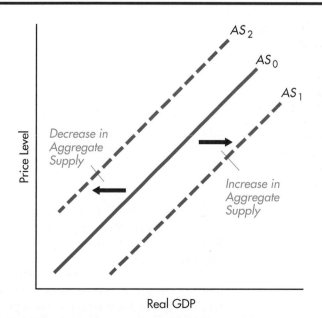

FIGURE 13

Determinants of Aggregate Supply Shift the *AS* Curve

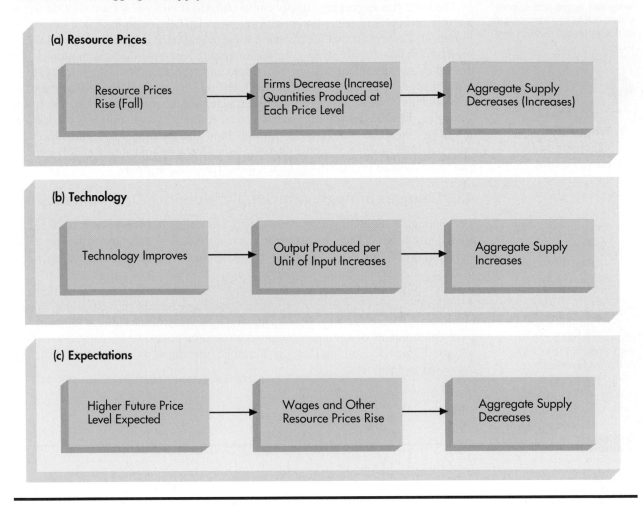

(a) Resource Prices

Resource Prices Rise (Fall) → Firms Decrease (Increase) Quantities Produced at Each Price Level → Aggregate Supply Decreases (Increases)

(b) Technology

Technology Improves → Output Produced per Unit of Input Increases → Aggregate Supply Increases

(c) Expectations

Higher Future Price Level Expected → Wages and Other Resource Prices Rise → Aggregate Supply Decreases

4.c.1. Resource Prices   When the price of output changes, the costs of production do not change immediately. At first, then, a change in profits induces a change in production. Costs eventually change in response to the change in prices and production, and when they do, the aggregate supply curve shifts. When the cost of resources—labor, capital goods, materials—falls, the aggregate supply curve shifts to the right, from AS_0 to AS_1 in Figure 12. This means that firms are willing to produce more output at any given price level. When the cost of resources goes up, profits fall and the aggregate supply curve shifts to the left, from AS_0 to AS_2. Here, at any given level of price, firms produce less output.

Remember that the vertical axis of the aggregate supply graph plots the price level for all goods and services produced in the economy. Only those changes in resource prices that raise the costs of production across the economy have an impact on the aggregate supply curve. For example, oil is an important raw material. If a new source of oil is discovered, the price of oil falls and aggregate supply increases.

Oil and Aggregate Supply

In the late winter of 2003, there was much talk about high oil prices leading to a fall in GDP for oil-importing countries. At the same time that the Bush administration was planning to invade Iraq, which would disrupt oil supplies from the Mideast, a strike by Venezuelan oil workers interrupted oil supplies from the world's fifth-largest producer. Oil prices rose dramatically, and the price of gasoline rose from about $1.60 per gallon to more than $2.00 per gallon. The higher oil prices rose, the more talk there was about recession. What is the link between oil prices and real GDP? A look back to recent history helps develop our understanding of this link.

In 1973 and 1974, and again in 1979 and 1980, the Organization of Petroleum Exporting Countries (OPEC) reduced the supply of oil, driving the price of oil up dramatically. For example, the price of Saudi Arabian crude oil more than tripled between 1973 and 1974, and more than doubled between 1979 and 1980. Researchers estimate that the rapid jump in oil prices reduced output by 17 percent in Japan, by 7 percent in the United States, and by 1.9 percent in Germany.*

Oil is an important resource in many industries. When the price of oil increases due to restricted oil output, aggregate supply falls. You can see this in the graph. When the price of oil goes up, the aggregate supply curve falls from AS_1 to AS_2. When aggregate supply falls, the equilibrium level of real GDP (the intersection of the AS curve and the AD curve) falls from Y_1 to Y_2.

Higher oil prices due to restricted oil output would decrease not only short-run aggregate supply and current equilibrium real GDP, as shown in the figure, but also potential equilibrium income at the natural rate of unemployment. Unless other factors change to contribute to economic growth, the higher resource (oil) price reduces the productive capacity of the economy.

There is evidence that fluctuations in oil prices have less effect on the economy today than in the past.[†] The amount of energy that goes into producing a dollar of GDP has declined over time, so that oil plays a less important role as a determinant of aggregate supply today than in the 1970s and earlier. This means that any given change in oil prices today will be

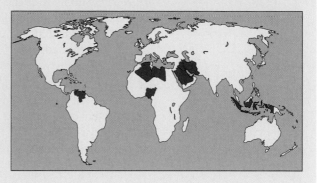

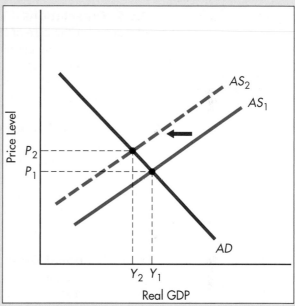

associated with smaller shifts in the AS curve than in earlier decades.

*These estimates were taken from "Energy Price Shocks, Aggregate Supply, and Monetary Policy: The Theory and the International Evidence," Robert H. Rasche and John A. Tatom, in *Carnegie-Rochester Conference Series on Public Policy,* Vol. 14, eds. Karl Brunner and Allan H. Meltzer (North-Holland, 1981), pp. 9–93.

†See "Oil Prices and the Economy," by Stephen P. A. Brown and Mine K. Yücel, Federal Reserve Bank of Dallas, *Southwest Economy,* July–August 2000.

However, if oil-exporting countries restrict oil supplies and the price of oil increases substantially, aggregate supply decreases, a situation that occurred when OPEC reduced the supply of oil in the 1970s (see the Global Business Insight "Oil and Aggregate Supply"). If the price of only one minor resource changed, then aggregate supply would be unlikely to change. For instance, if the price of land in Las Cruces, New Mexico, increased, we would not expect the U.S. aggregate supply curve to be affected.

4.c.2. Technology

Technological innovations allow businesses to increase the productivity of their existing resources. As new technology is adopted, the amount of output that can be produced by each unit of input increases, moving the aggregate supply curve to the right. For example, personal computers and word-processing software have allowed secretaries to produce much more output in a day than type-writers allowed.

4.c.3. Expectations

To understand how expectations can affect aggregate supply, consider the case of labor contracts. Manufacturing workers typically contract for a nominal wage based on what they and their employers expect the future level of prices to be. Because wages typically are set for at least a year, any unexpected increase in the price level during the year lowers real wages. Firms receive higher prices for their output, but the cost of labor stays the same. So profits and production go up.

If wages rise in anticipation of higher prices but prices do not go up, the cost of labor rises. Higher real wages caused by expectations of higher prices reduce current profits and production, moving the aggregate supply curve to the left. Other things being equal, anticipated higher prices cause aggregate supply to decrease; conversely, anticipated lower prices cause aggregate supply to increase. In this sense, expectations of price-level changes that shift aggregate supply actually bring about price-level changes.

4.c.4. Economic Growth: Long-Run Aggregate Supply Shifts

The vertical long-run aggregate supply curve, as shown in Figure 11, does not mean that the economy is forever fixed at the current level of potential real gross domestic product. Over time, as new technologies are developed and the quantity and quality of resources increase, potential output also increases, shifting both the short- and long-run aggregate supply curves to the right. Figure 14 shows long-run economic growth by the shift in the aggregate supply curve from $LRAS$ to $LRAS_1$. The movement of the long-run aggregate supply curve to the right reflects the increase in potential real GDP from Y_p to Y_{p1}. Even though the price level has no effect on the level of output in the long run, changes in the determinants of the supply of real output in the economy do.

1. The aggregate supply curve shows the quantity of output (real GDP) produced at different price levels.

2. The aggregate supply curve slopes up because, everything else held constant, higher prices increase producers' profits, creating an incentive to increase output.

3. The aggregate supply curve shifts with changes in resource prices, technology, and expectations. These are nonprice determinants of aggregate supply.

FIGURE 14

Shifting the Long-Run Aggregate Supply Curve

Changes in technology and the availability and quality of resources can shift the *LRAS* curve. For instance, a new technology that increases productivity would move the curve to the right, from *LRAS* to *LRAS*₁.

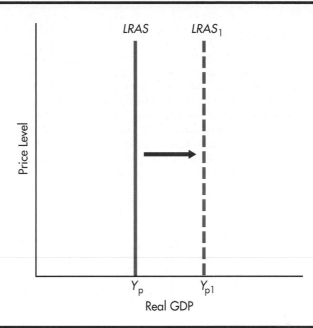

4. The short-run aggregate supply curve is upward sloping, showing that increases in production are accompanied by higher prices.

5. The long-run aggregate supply curve is vertical at potential real GDP because, eventually, wages and the costs of other resources adjust fully to price-level changes.

5. Aggregate Demand and Supply Equilibrium

7. What determines the equilibrium price level and real GDP?

Now that we have defined the aggregate demand and aggregate supply curves separately, we can put them together to determine the equilibrium price level and real GDP.

5.a. Short-Run Equilibrium

Figure 15 shows the level of equilibrium in a hypothetical economy. Initially the economy is in equilibrium at point 1, where AD_1 and AS_1 intersect. At this point, the equilibrium price level is P_1 and the equilibrium real GDP is $500. At price level P_1, the amount of output demanded is equal to the amount supplied. Suppose aggregate demand increases from AD_1 to AD_2. In the short run, aggregate supply does not change, so the new equilibrium is at the intersection of the new aggregate demand curve, AD_2, and the same aggregate supply curve, AS_1, at point 2. The new equilibrium price level is P_2, and the new equilibrium real GDP is $600. Note that in the short run, the equilibrium point on the short-run aggregate supply curve can lie to the right of the long-run aggregate supply curve (*LRAS*). This is because the *LRAS* represents the potential level of real GDP, not the capacity level. It is possible to

FIGURE 15

Aggregate Demand and Supply Equilibrium

The equilibrium price level and real GDP is at the intersection of the *AD* and *AS* curves. Initially equilibrium occurs at point 1, where the AD_1 and AS_1 curves intersect. Here the price level is P_1 and real GDP is $500. If aggregate demand increases, moving from AD_1 to AD_2 in the short run there is a new equilibrium at point 2, where AD_2 intersects AS_1. The price level rises to P_2, and the equilibrium level of real GDP increases to $600. Over time, as wages and the costs of other resources rise in response to higher prices, aggregate supply falls, moving AS_1 to AS_2. Final equilibrium occurs at point 3, where the AS_2 curve intersects the AD_2 curve. The price level rises to P_3, but the equilibrium level of real GDP returns to its initial level, $500. In the long run, there is no relationship between prices and the equilibrium level of real GDP because the costs of resources adjust to changes in the level of prices.

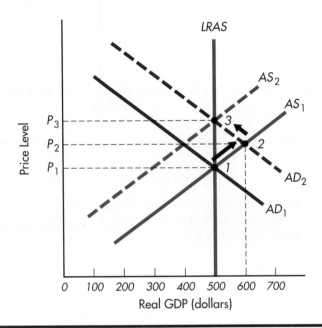

produce more than the potential level of real GDP in the short run when the unemployment rate falls below the natural rate of unemployment.

5.b. Long-Run Equilibrium

Point 2 is not a permanent equilibrium because aggregate supply decreases to AS_2 once the costs of production rise in response to higher prices. Final equilibrium is at point 3, where the price level is P_3 and real GDP is $500. Notice that equilibrium here is the same as the initial equilibrium at point 1. Points 1 and 3 both lie along the long-run aggregate supply curve (*LRAS*). The initial shock to or change in the economy was an increase in aggregate demand. The change in aggregate expenditures initially led to higher output and higher prices. Over time, however, as resource costs rise and profit falls, output falls back to its original value.

We are not saying that the level of output never changes. The long-run aggregate supply curve shifts as technology changes and new supplies of resources are obtained. But the output change that results from a change in aggregate demand is a temporary, or short-run, phenomenon. The price level eventually adjusts, and output eventually returns to the potential level.

An increase in aggregate demand increases real GDP only temporarily.

RECAP

1. The equilibrium price level and real GDP is at the point where the aggregate demand and aggregate supply curves intersect.
2. In the short run, a shift in aggregate demand establishes a temporary equilibrium along the short-run aggregate supply curve.
3. In the long run, the short-run aggregate supply curve shifts so that changes in aggregate demand affect only the price level, not the equilibrium level of output or real GDP.

Summary

❓ What factors affect aggregate demand?

1. Aggregate demand is the relation between aggregate expenditures and the price level. *§2*

2. Aggregate demand is the sum of consumption, investment, government spending, and net exports at alternative price levels. *§2.a, 2.b, 2.c, 2.d*

3. Aggregate expenditures change with changes in the price level because of the wealth effect, the interest rate effect, and the international trade effect. These cause a movement along the *AD* curve. *§3.a.1, 3.a.2, 3.a.3*

❓ What causes the aggregate demand curve to shift?

4. The aggregate demand (*AD*) curve shows the level of expenditures for real GDP at different price levels. *§3.a.4*

5. Because expenditures and prices move in opposite directions, the *AD* curve is negatively sloped. *§3.a.4*

6. The nonprice determinants of aggregate demand include expectations, foreign income and price levels, and government policy. *§3.b.1, 3.b.2, 3.b.3*

❓ What factors affect aggregate supply?

7. The aggregate supply curve shows the quantity of real GDP produced at different price levels. *§4*

❓ Why does the short-run aggregate supply curve become steeper as real GDP increases?

8. As real GDP rises and the economy pushes closer to capacity output, the level of prices must rise to induce increased production. *§4.b.1*

❓ Why is the long-run aggregate supply curve vertical?

9. The long-run aggregate supply curve is a vertical line at the potential level of real GDP. The shape of the curve indicates that there is no effect of higher prices on output when an economy is producing at potential real GDP. *§4.b.2*

❓ What causes the aggregate supply curve to shift?

10. The nonprice determinants of aggregate supply are resource prices, technology, and expectations. *§4.c.1, 4.c.2, 4.c.3*

❓ What determines the equilibrium price level and real GDP?

11. The equilibrium price level and real GDP is at the intersection of the aggregate demand and aggregate supply curves. *§5.a*

12. In the short run, a shift in aggregate demand establishes a new, but temporary, equilibrium along the short-run aggregate supply curve. *§5.a*

13. In the long run, the short-run aggregate supply curve shifts so that changes in aggregate demand determine the price level, not the equilibrium level of output or real GDP. *§5.b*

Key Terms

demand-pull inflation *§1.a*

cost-push inflation *§1.b*

wealth effect *§3.a.1*

interest rate effect *§3.a.2*

international trade effect *§3.a.3*

aggregate demand curve *§3.a.4*

aggregate supply curve *§4*

long-run aggregate supply curve (*LRAS*) *§4.b.2*

Exercises

1. How is the aggregate demand curve different from the demand curve for a single good, like hamburgers?

2. Why does the aggregate demand curve slope down? Give real-world examples of the three effects that explain the slope of the curve.

3. How does an increase in foreign income affect domestic aggregate expenditures and demand? Draw a diagram to illustrate your answer.

4. How does a decrease in foreign price levels affect domestic aggregate expenditures and demand? Draw a diagram to illustrate your answer.

5. How is the aggregate supply curve different from the supply curve for a single good, like pizza?

6. There are several determinants of aggregate supply that can cause the aggregate supply curve to shift.

   a. Describe those determinants and give an example of a change in each.

   b. Draw and label an aggregate supply diagram that illustrates the effect of the change in each determinant.

7. Draw a short-run aggregate supply curve that gets steeper as real GDP rises.

   a. Explain why the curve has this shape.

   b. Now draw a long-run aggregate supply curve that intersects a short-run *AS* curve. What is the relationship between short-run *AS* and long-run *AS*?

8. Draw and carefully label an aggregate demand and supply diagram with initial equilibrium at P_0 and Y_0.

   a. Using the diagram, explain what happens when aggregate demand falls.

   b. How is the short run different from the long run?

9. Draw an aggregate demand and supply diagram for Japan. In the diagram, show how each of the following affects aggregate demand and supply.

   a. The U.S. gross domestic product falls.

   b. The level of prices in Korea falls.

   c. Labor receives a large wage increase.

   d. Economists predict higher prices next year.

10. If the long-run aggregate supply curve gives the level of potential real GDP, how can the short-run aggregate supply curve ever lie to the right of the long-run aggregate supply curve?

11. What will happen to the equilibrium price level and real GDP if:

    a. Aggregate demand and aggregate supply both increase?

    b. Aggregate demand increases and aggregate supply decreases?

    c. Aggregate demand and aggregate supply both decrease?

    d. Aggregate demand decreases and aggregate supply increases?

12. During the Great Depression, the U.S. economy experienced a falling price level and declining real GDP. Using an aggregate demand and aggregate supply diagram, illustrate and explain how this could occur.

13. Suppose aggregate demand increases, causing an increase in real GDP but no change in the price level. Using an aggregate demand and aggregate supply diagram, illustrate and explain how this could occur.

14. Suppose aggregate demand increases, causing an increase in the price level but no change in real GDP. Using an aggregate demand and aggregate supply diagram, illustrate and explain how this could occur.

15. Use an aggregate demand and aggregate supply diagram to illustrate and explain how each of the following will affect the equilibrium price level and real GDP:

    a. Consumers expect a recession.

    b. Foreign income rises.

    c. Foreign price levels fall.

    d. Government spending increases.

e. Workers expect higher future inflation and negotiate higher wages now.

f. Technological improvements increase productivity.

16. In the boom years of the late 1990s, it was often said that rapidly increasing stock prices were responsible for much of the rapid growth of real GDP. Explain how this could be true, using aggregate demand and aggregate supply analysis.

17. In 2003, there was much concern that rising oil prices would contribute to a global recession. Use aggregate demand and supply analysis to explain how high oil prices could reduce real GDP.

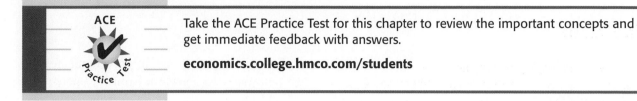

Take the ACE Practice Test for this chapter to review the important concepts and get immediate feedback with answers.

economics.college.hmco.com/students

The Conference Board's Consumer Confidence Index Plummets Nearly 15 Points

The Conference Board's Consumer Confidence Index declined sharply in February, the third consecutive monthly decline. The Index now stands at 64.0 (1985 = 100), down from 78.8 in January, an almost 15-point drop. The Expectations Index fell to 65.6 from 81.1. The Present Situation Index dropped to 61.6 from 75.3. The last time the Consumer Confidence Index was lower was in October of 1993 when it reached 60.5.

The survey by The Conference Board, a not-for-profit research organization, is released on the last Tuesday of every month at 10 AM (ET). It is based on a representative sample of 5,000 U.S. households. The monthly survey is conducted for The Conference Board by NFO WorldGroup, a member of The Interpublic Group of Companies (NYSE: IPG).

"Lackluster job and financial markets, rising fuel costs, and the increasing threat of war and terrorism appear to have taken a toll on consumers," says Lynn Franco, Director of The Conference Board's Consumer Research Center. "This month's confidence readings paint a gloomy picture of current economic conditions, with no apparent rebound on the short-term horizon."

Consumers' assessment of current conditions turned extremely bleak. Those rating current business conditions as "bad" rose to 30.7 percent from 26.7 percent. Those holding the opposite view declined to 13.2 percent from 15.0 percent.

Consumers' expectations for the next six months were also considerably more pessimistic than last month. Those anticipating that business conditions will worsen increased to 19.0 percent from 14.0 percent. Those antici-pating an improvement fell to 15.3 percent from 17.7 percent.

Jobs "hard to get" at a nine-year high

The employment outlook was grim. Consumers reporting jobs are hard to get rose to a nine-year high of 30.1 percent from 28.9 percent. Those claiming jobs are plentiful decreased to 11.2 per-cent from 14.5 percent.

Consumers anticipating fewer jobs to become available in the next six months surged to 28.4 percent from 21.2 percent. Those expecting more jobs fell to 12.7 percent from 14.2 percent. The proportion of consumers antici-pating an increase in their income dropped to 15.2 percent, an all-time low, from 18.4 percent.

Source: The Conference Board Consumer Confidence Index, February 2003, www.consumerresearchcenter.org/ consumer_confidence/index.htm.

The Conference Board/February 25, 2003.

Why would a business firm want to receive reports regarding consumer confidence in the U.S. economy? The answer lies in the role of expectations as a determinant of consumption spending and therefore aggregate demand. If households are confident that incomes will rise and prosperous times are ahead, they are much more likely to spend more than if they expect a recession. By monitoring consumer confidence in the economy, we can better understand consumer spending. Since consumption accounts for about two-thirds of GDP, changes in household spending can play a big role in business-cycle fluctuations.

In terms of aggregate demand and supply analysis, if households are more optimistic about the economy's performance, then the aggregate demand should shift to the right, like the shift from AD_0 to AD_1 in the accompanying figure. This would increase the equilibrium level of real GDP from Y_0 to Y_1. If households are less optimistic about the economy's performance, then the aggregate demand curve should shift to the left, like the shift from AD_0 to AD_2. This would decrease the equilibrium level of real GDP from Y_0 to Y_2.

Because of the implications of shifts in consumer confidence for business-cycle fluctuations, government officials, along with businesspeople, watch the consumer confidence measures to maintain a sense of what is happening in the typical household. The two best-known surveys, the University of Michigan and Conference Board surveys, ask questions like: "Six months from now do you think business conditions will be better, the same, or worse?" "Would you say that you are better off or worse off financially than you were a year ago?" The answers to these questions and others are used as inputs in constructing an index of consumer confidence, so that the press typically reports only how the overall index changes rather than the responses to any particular question.

Although the popular consumer confidence indexes fluctuate up and down every month, researchers have found that the monthly fluctuations are not very useful in predicting consumption or GDP. However, major shifts in the indexes or several months of rising or falling indexes may provide an early signal of forthcoming changes in consumption and GDP.

In early 2003, the news was mostly bad. The Conference Board's Consumer Confidence Index had fallen for three consecutive months and was reaching its lowest point since 1993. Business firms could not be optimistic about consumer spending based upon the outlook offered by the Consumer Confidence Index in early 2003.

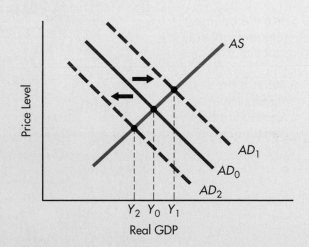

CHAPTER 10

Aggregate Expenditures

? **Fundamental Questions**

1. How are consumption and saving related?

2. What are the determinants of consumption?

3. What are the determinants of investment?

4. What are the determinants of government spending?

5. What are the determinants of net exports?

6. What is the aggregate expenditures function?

To understand why real GDP, unemployment, and inflation rise and fall over time, we must know what causes the aggregate demand and aggregate supply curves to shift. We cannot understand why the U.S. economy has experienced eleven recessions since 1945 or why in the 1990s and 2000s, we witnessed the longest peacetime business-cycle expansion in modern times unless we understand why the *AD* and *AS* curves shift. In this chapter, we examine in more detail the demand side of the economy.

Chapter 9 discussed how the price level affects aggregate expenditures through the interest rate, international trade, and wealth effects. This chapter examines in greater detail the nonprice determinants of spending and shifts in aggregate demand and assumes the price level is fixed. This assumption means that the aggregate supply curve is a horizontal line at the fixed-price level. This approach was used by John Maynard Keynes, who analyzed the macro economy during the Great Depression. A fixed price level, as shown in Figure 1, suggests a situation in which unemployment and excess capacity exist. Firms can hire from this pool of unemployed labor

FIGURE 1

The Fixed-Price Keynesian Model

The Keynesian assumption that the price level is fixed requires a horizontal aggregate supply curve. In this case, aggregate demand will determine the equilibrium level of real GDP.

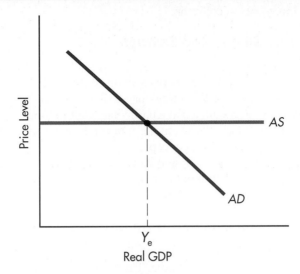

and increase their output at no extra cost and without any pressure on the price level. It is not surprising that Keynes would rely on such a model at a time when he was surrounded by mass unemployment. He was more interested in the determination of income and output than in the problem of inflation.

With a horizontal *AS* curve, as shown in Figure 1, the location of the *AD* curve will determine the equilibrium level of real GDP, Y_e. If we understand what determines aggregate demand—consumption, investment, government spending, and net exports—we will understand what determines real GDP.

We begin our detailed examination of aggregate expenditures by discussing consumption, which accounts for approximately 69 percent of total expenditures in the U.S. economy. We then look at investment (16 percent of total expenditures), government spending (18 percent of total expenditures), and net exports (−3 percent of total expenditures). ▪

1. How are consumption and saving related?

1. Consumption and Saving

Households can do three things with their income. They can spend it for the consumption of goods and services, they can save it, or they can pay taxes. Disposable income is what is left after taxes have been paid. It is the sum of consumption and saving:

$$\text{Disposable income} = \text{consumption} + \text{saving}$$

or

$$Yd = C + S$$

Disposable income is the income that households actually have available for spending after taxes. Whatever disposable income is not spent is saved.

Why are we talking about saving, which is not a component of total spending, in a chapter that sets out to discuss the components of total spending? Saving is simply "not consuming"; it is impossible to separate the incentives to save from the incentives to consume.

1.a. Saving and Savings

Before we go on, it is necessary to understand the difference between *saving* and *savings*. *Saving* occurs over a unit of time—a week, a month, a year. For instance, you might save $10 a week or $40 a month. Saving is a *flow* concept. *Savings* are an amount accumulated at a particular point in time—today, December 31, your sixty-fifth birthday. For example, you might have savings of $2,500 on December 31. Savings are a *stock* concept.

Like saving, GDP and its components are flow concepts. They are measured by the year or quarter of the year. Consumption, investment, government spending, and net exports are also flows. Each of them is an amount spent over a period of time.

1.b. The Consumption and Saving Functions

The primary determinant of the level of consumption over any given period is the level of disposable income. The higher the disposable income, the more households are willing and able to spend. This relationship between disposable income and consumption is called the **consumption function.** Figure 2 contains the consumption function for the United States over the long-run period from 1947 to 2002. For each quarter-year in this period, the value of disposable income and consumption are plotted in the figure. Note that Figure 2 also contains a 45-degree line. (A 45-degree line makes a graph easier to read because every point on the line represents the same value on both axes.) This line splits the area of the figure in half and shows all points at which the value of disposable income and consumption are equal. Since the actual consumption function lies below the 45-degree line, it can be seen that consumption is less than disposable income—but not much less. The consumption function in Figure 2 is a long-run consumption function. In the short run, like this year, the relationship between consumption and disposable income may be much flatter than that

consumption function: the relationship between disposable income and consumption

Consumption spending is the largest component of aggregate expenditures. Households in Chichicastenango, Guatemala, come to the produce market shown here to purchase food. Their expenditures on food will be counted in the consumption and the GDP of Guatemala. If the households decide to save less and spend more, then, other things being equal, the higher consumption will raise the GDP of Guatemala.

FIGURE 2

Consumption and Disposable Income, 1947–2002

The figure shows the long-run consumption function for the United States. The 45-degree line shows all points at which consumption and disposable income are equal. Note that the actual consumption function lies only slightly below the 45-degree line. This indicates that consumption is less than disposable income, but not much less.

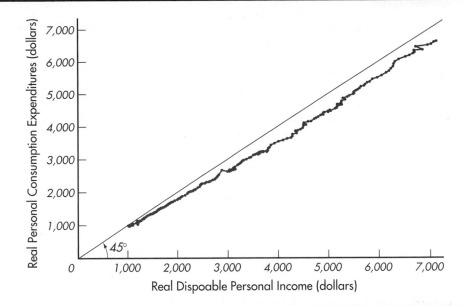

shown in Figure 2. We now turn to a deeper analysis of the consumption function to better understand this important relationship.

To focus on the relationship between income and consumption, we draw a new graph, Figure 3, with income on the horizontal axis and consumption on the vertical axis. Figure 3(a) shows a hypothetical consumption function. In this economy, when disposable income is zero, consumption is $30. As disposable income rises, consumption rises. For instance, when disposable income is $100, consumption is $100.

We use C to represent consumption and Yd to represent disposable income. The line labeled C in Figure 3(a) is the consumption function: it represents the relationship between disposable income and consumption. The other line in the figure creates a 45-degree angle with either axis. In Figure 3(a), as in Figure 2, the 45-degree line shows all the points where consumption equals disposable income.

The level of disposable income at which all disposable income is being spent occurs at the point where the consumption function (line C) crosses the 45-degree line. In the graph, C equals Yd when disposable income is $100. Consumers save a fraction of any disposable income above $100. You can see this in the graph. Saving occurs at any level of disposable income at which the consumption function lies below the 45-degree line (at which consumption is less than disposable income). The amount of saving is measured by the vertical distance between the 45-degree line and the consumption function. If disposable income is $600, consumption is $450 and saving is $150.

saving function: the relationship between disposable income and saving

The **saving function** is the relationship between disposable income and saving. Figure 3(b) plots the saving function (S). When the level of disposable income is at $100, consumption equals disposable income, so saving is zero. As disposable income increases beyond $100, saving goes up. In Figure 3(a), saving is the vertical distance between the 45-degree line and the consumption function. In Figure 3(b), we can read the level of saving directly from the saving function.

Notice that at relatively low levels of disposable income, consumption exceeds disposable income. How can consumption be greater than disposable income?

FIGURE 3

Consumption and Saving in a Hypothetical Economy

Figure 3(a) shows that consumption is a positive function of disposable income: it goes up as disposable income rises. The line labeled $C = Yd$ forms a 45-degree angle at the origin. It shows all points where consumption equals disposable income. The point at which the consumption function (line C) crosses the 45-degree line—where disposable income measures $100—is the point at which consumption equals disposable income. At lower levels of disposable income, consumption is greater than disposable income; at higher levels, consumption is less than disposable income. Figure 3(b) shows the saving function. Saving equals disposable income minus consumption. When consumption equals disposable income, saving is 0. At higher levels of disposable income, we find positive saving; at lower levels, we find negative saving, or dissaving.

(a) The Consumption Function

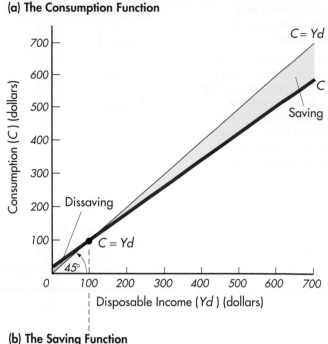

(b) The Saving Function

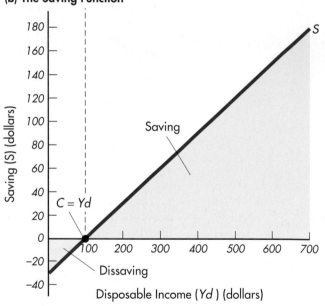

Disposable Income (Yd)	Consumption (C)	Saving (S)
$ 0	$ 30	-$ 30
$100	$100	$ 0
$200	$170	$ 30
$300	$240	$ 60
$400	$310	$ 90
$500	$380	$120
$600	$450	$150
$700	$520	$180

dissaving: spending financed by borrowing or using savings

When a household spends more than it earns in income, the household must finance the spending above income by borrowing or using savings. This is called **dissaving.** In Figure 3(a), dissaving occurs at levels of disposable income between 0 and $100, where the consumption function lies above the 45-degree line. Dissaving, like saving, is measured by the vertical distance between the 45-degree line and the consumption function, but dissaving occurs when the consumption function lies *above* the 45-degree line. In Figure 3(b), dissaving occurs where the saving function (line S) lies below the disposable income axis, at disposable income levels between zero and $100. For example, when disposable income is $0, dissaving (negative saving) is −$30.

Both the consumption function and the saving function have positive slopes: As disposable income rises, consumption and saving increase. Consumption and saving, then, are positive functions of disposable income. Notice that when disposable income equals zero, consumption is still positive.

autonomous consumption: consumption that is independent of income

There is a level of consumption, called **autonomous consumption,** that does not depend on income. (*Autonomous* here means "independent of income.") In Figure 3(a), consumption equals $30 when disposable income equals zero. This $30 is autonomous consumption; it does not depend on income but will vary with the non-income determinants of consumption that will soon be introduced. The intercept of the consumption function (the value of *C* when *Yd* equals zero) measures the amount of autonomous consumption. The intercept in Figure 3(a) is $30, which means that autonomous consumption in this example is $30.

1.c. Marginal Propensity to Consume and Save

Total consumption equals autonomous consumption plus the spending that depends on income. As disposable income rises, consumption rises. This relationship between *change* in disposable income and *change* in consumption is the **marginal propensity to consume (MPC).** The *MPC* measures change in consumption as a proportion of the change in disposable income:

marginal propensity to consume (MPC): the change in consumption as a proportion of the change in disposable income

$$MPC = \frac{\text{change in consumption}}{\text{change in disposable income}}$$

In Table 1, columns 1 and 2 list the consumption function data used in Figure 3. The marginal propensity to consume is shown in column 4. In our example, each time that disposable income changes by $100, consumption changes by $70. This means that consumers spend 70 percent of any extra income they receive.

$$MPC = \frac{\$70}{\$100}$$

$$= .70$$

TABLE 1

Marginal Propensity to Consume and to Save

Disposable Income (Yd)	Consumption (C)	Saving (S)	Marginal Propensity to Consume (MPC)	Marginal Propensity to Save (MPS)
$ 0	$ 30	−$ 30	—	—
$100	$100	$ 0	.70	.30
$200	$170	$ 30	.70	.30
$300	$240	$ 60	.70	.30
$400	$310	$ 90	.70	.30
$500	$380	$120	.70	.30
$600	$450	$150	.70	.30
$700	$520	$180	.70	.30

The *MPC* tells us how much consumption changes when income changes. The **marginal propensity to save (MPS)** defines the relationship between change in saving and change in disposable income. It is the change in saving divided by the change in disposable income:

$$MPS = \frac{\text{change in saving}}{\text{change in disposable income}}$$

The *MPS* in Table 1 is a constant 30 percent at all levels of income. Each time that disposable income changes by $100, saving changes by $30:

$$MPS = \frac{\$30}{\$100}$$

$$= .30$$

The *MPC* and the *MPS* will always be constant at all levels of disposable income in our examples.

Since disposable income will be either consumed or saved, the marginal propensity to consume plus the marginal propensity to save must total 1:

$$MPC + MPS = 1$$

The percentage of additional income that is not consumed must be saved. If consumers spend 70 percent of any extra income, they save 30 percent of that income.

The slope of the consumption function is the same as the MPC; the slope of the saving function is the same as the MPS.

The *MPC* and the *MPS* determine the rate of consumption and saving as disposable income changes. The *MPC* is the slope of the consumption function; the *MPS* is the slope of the saving function. Remember that the slope of a line measures change along the vertical axis that corresponds to change along the horizontal axis, the rise over the run (see the Appendix to Chapter 1). In the case of the consumption function, the slope is the change in consumption (the change on the vertical axis) divided by the change in disposable income (the change on the horizontal axis):

$$\text{Slope of consumption function} = \frac{\text{change in consumption}}{\text{change in disposable income}}$$

$$= MPC$$

The higher the *MPC,* the greater the fraction of any additional disposable income that consumers will spend. At .70, consumers spend 70 percent of any change in disposable income; at an *MPC* of .85, consumers want to spend 85 percent of any change in disposable income. The size of the *MPC* shows up graphically as the steepness of the consumption function. The consumption function with an *MPC* of .85 is a steeper line than the one drawn in Figure 3(a). In general, the steeper the consumption function, the larger the *MPC.* If the *MPC* is less than .70, the consumption function will be flatter than the one in the figure.

The slope of the saving function is the *MPS:*

$$\text{Slope of saving function} = \frac{\text{change in saving}}{\text{change in disposable income}}$$

$$= MPS$$

In general, the steeper the saving function, the greater the slope and the greater the *MPS.*

Figure 4(a) shows three consumption functions. Since all three consumption functions have the same intercept, autonomous consumption is the same for all. But each consumption function in Figure 4(a) has a different slope. Line C_1 has an MPC of .70. A larger MPC, .80, produces a steeper consumption function (line C_2). A smaller MPC, .60, produces a flatter consumption function (line C_3). The saving functions that correspond to these consumption functions are shown in Figure 4(b). Function S_1, with an MPS of .30, corresponds to consumption function C_1, with an MPC of .70 (remember: $MPS = 1 - MPC$). Function S_2 corresponds to C_2, and S_3 corresponds to C_3. The higher the MPC (the steeper the consumption function), the lower the MPS (the flatter the saving function). If people spend a greater fraction of extra income, they save a smaller fraction.

FIGURE 4

Marginal Propensity to Consume and Save

The MPC is the slope of the consumption function. The greater the MPC, the steeper the consumption function. The MPS is the slope of the saving function. The greater the MPS, the steeper the saving function. Because the sum of the MPC and the MPS is 1, the greater the MPC, the smaller the MPS. The steeper the consumption function, then, the flatter the saving function.

(a) Three Consumption Functions

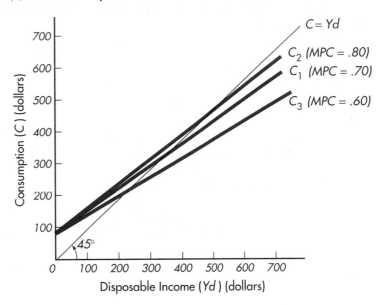

(b) Three Saving Functions

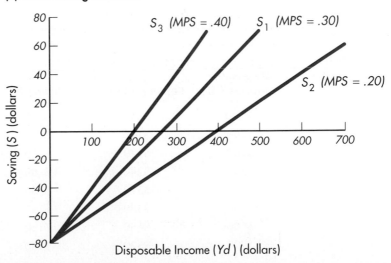

1.d. Average Propensity to Consume and Save

Suppose our interest is not the proportion of change in disposable income that is consumed or saved, but the proportion of disposable income that is consumed or saved. For this we must know the average propensity to consume and the average propensity to save.

The **average propensity to consume (APC)** is the proportion of disposable income that is spent for consumption:

average propensity to consume (APC): the proportion of disposable income spent for consumption

$$APC = \frac{\text{consumption}}{\text{disposable income}}$$

or

$$APC = \frac{C}{Yd}$$

average propensity to save (APS): the proportion of disposable income saved

The **average propensity to save (APS)** is the proportion of disposable income that is saved:

$$APS = \frac{\text{saving}}{\text{disposable income}}$$

or

$$APS = \frac{S}{Yd}$$

Table 2 uses the consumption and saving data plotted in Figure 3. The APC and APS are shown in columns 4 and 5. When disposable income is $100, consumption is also $100, so the ratio of consumption to disposable income (C/Yd) equals 1 ($100/$100). At this point, saving equals 0, so the ratio of saving to disposable income (S/Yd) also equals 0 (0/$100). We really do not have to compute the APS because we already know the APC. There are only two things to do with disposable income: spend it or save it. The percentage of income spent plus the percentage saved must add up to 100 percent of disposable income. This means that

$$APC + APS = 1$$

If the APC equals 1, then the APS must equal 0.

TABLE 2

Average Propensity to Consume and to Save

Disposable Income (Yd)	Consumption (C)	Saving (S)	Average Propensity to Consume (APC)	Average Propensity to Save (APS)
$ 0	$ 30	$ 30	—	—
$100	$100	$ 0	1.00	0
$200	$170	$ 30	.85	.15
$300	$240	$ 60	.80	.20
$400	$310	$ 90	.78	.22
$500	$380	$120	.76	.24
$600	$450	$150	.75	.25
$700	$520	$180	.74	.26

When disposable income equals $600, consumption equals $450, so the *APC* equals .75 ($450/$600) and the *APS* equals .25 ($150/$600). As always, the *APC* plus the *APS* equals 1. If households are spending 75 percent of their disposable income, they must be saving 25 percent.

Notice in Table 2 how the *APC* falls as disposable income rises. This is because households spend just a part of any change in income. In Figure 3(a), the consumption function rises more slowly than the 45-degree line. (Remember that consumption equals disposable income along the 45-degree line.) The consumption function tells us, then, that consumption rises as disposable income rises, but not by as much as income rises. Because households spend a smaller fraction of disposable income as that income rises, they must be saving a larger fraction. You can see this in Table 2, where the *APS* rises as disposable income rises. At low levels of income, the *APS* is negative, a product of dissaving (we are dividing negative saving by disposable income). As disposable income rises, saving rises as a percentage of disposable income; this means that the *APS* is increasing.

1.e. Determinants of Consumption

?

2. What are the determinants of consumption?

Disposable income is an important determinant of household spending. But disposable income is not the only factor that influences consumption. Wealth, expectations, demographics, and taxation (taxation effects will be considered in Chapter 12) are other determinants of consumption.

1.e.1. Disposable Income
Household income is the primary determinant of consumption, which is why the consumption function is drawn with disposable income on the horizontal axis. Household income usually is measured as current disposable income. By *current* we mean income that is received in the current period—the current period could be today, this month, this year, or whatever period we are discussing. Past income and future income certainly can affect household spending, but their effect is through household wealth or expectations, not income. Disposable income is after-tax income.

The two-dimensional graphs we have been using relate consumption only to current disposable income. A change in consumption caused by a change in disposable income is shown by *movement along* the consumption function. The effects of other variables are shown by *shifting* the intercept of the consumption function up and down as the values of these other variables change. All variables *except* disposable income change *autonomous* consumption.

Changes in taxes will affect disposable income. *If we assume that there are no taxes, then* Yd *equals* Y, *and consumption (and other expenditures) may be drawn as a function of real GDP rather than disposable income.* Chapter 12 is devoted to an analysis of government fiscal policy, including taxation. As a result, we put off our discussion of tax effects until then; this allows us to simplify our analysis of aggregate expenditures. The discussion of the components of aggregate expenditures in the remainder of this chapter and in later chapters will be related graphically to pretax real GDP rather than to disposable income.

wealth: the value of all assets owned by a household

1.e.2. Wealth
Wealth is the value of all the assets owned by a household. Wealth is a stock variable; it includes homes, cars, checking and savings accounts, and stocks and bonds, as well as the value of income expected in the future. As household wealth increases, households have more resources available for spending, so consumption increases at every level of real GDP. You can see this in Figure 5(a) as a shift of the consumption function from *C* to C_1. The autonomous increase

FIGURE 5

Autonomous Shifts in Consumption and in Saving

Autonomous consumption is the amount of consumption that exists when real GDP is 0. It is the intercept of the consumption function. The shift from C to C_1 is an autonomous increase in consumption of \$40; it moves the intercept of the consumption function from \$60 to \$100. The shift from C to C_2 is an autonomous decrease in consumption of \$40; it moves the intercept of the consumption function from \$60 to \$20. Autonomous saving is the amount of saving that exists when real GDP is 0. This is the intercept of the saving function. The shift from S to S_1 is an autonomous decrease in saving of \$40; it moves the intercept of the saving function from $-\$60$ to $-\$100$. The shift from S to S_2 is an autonomous increase in saving of \$40; it moves the intercept of the saving function from $-\$60$ to $-\$20$. Because disposable income minus consumption equals saving, an autonomous increase in consumption is associated with an autonomous decrease in saving, and an autonomous decrease in consumption is associated with an autonomous increase in saving.

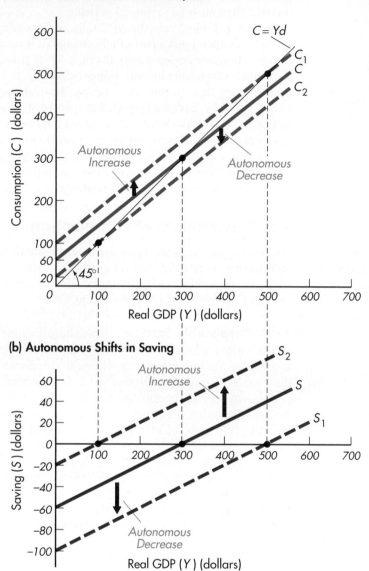

(a) Autonomous Shifts in Consumption

(b) Autonomous Shifts in Saving

in consumption shifts the intercept of the consumption function from \$60 to \$100, so consumption increases by \$40 at every level of real GDP. If households spend more of their current income as their wealth increases, they save less. You can see this as the downward shift of the saving function in Figure 5(b), from S to S_1. The higher level of wealth has households more willing to dissave at each income level than before. Dissaving now occurs at any level of income below \$500. During the long expansionary period of the 1990s, stock price increases made many households much wealthier and stimulated consumption.

A decrease in wealth has just the opposite effect. For instance, during the 1990–1991 recession, property values declined in most areas of the United States. Household wealth declined as the value of real estate fell, and spending fell as a result. Here you would see an autonomous drop in consumption, like the shift from C to C_2, and an autonomous increase in saving, like the shift from S to S_2. Now at every level of real GDP, households spend \$40 less than before and save \$40 more. The intercept of the consumption function is \$20, not \$60, and the intercept of the saving function is −\$20, not −\$60. The new consumption function parallels the old one; the curves are the same vertical distance apart at every level of income. So consumption is \$40 lower at every level of income. Similarly, the saving functions are parallel because saving is \$40 greater at every level of real GDP along S_2 compared to S.

1.e.3. Expectations

Another important determinant of consumption is consumer expectations about future income, prices, and wealth. When consumers expect a recession, when they are worried about losing jobs or facing cutbacks in hours worked, they tend to spend less and save more. This means an autonomous decrease in consumption and increase in saving, like the shift from C to C_2 and S to S_2 in Figure 5. Conversely, when consumers are optimistic, we find an autonomous increase in consumption and decrease in saving, like the shift from C to C_1 and S to S_1 in Figure 5.

Expectations are subjective opinions; they are difficult to observe and measure. This creates problems for economists looking to analyze the effect of expectations on consumption. The Conference Board surveys households to construct its *Consumer Confidence Index,* a measure of consumer opinion regarding the outlook for the economy. Economists follow the index in order to predict how consumer spending will change. Since consumption is the largest component of GDP, changes in consumption have important implications for business cycles.

Clearly the Consumer Confidence Index is not always a reliable indicator of expansion or recession. Still, economists' increasing use of this and other measures to better understand fluctuations in consumption underscores the importance of consumer expectations in the economy (see the Economic Insight "Permanent Income, Life Cycles, and Consumption").

1.e.4. Demographics

Other things being equal, economists expect the level of consumption to rise with increases in population. The focus here is on both the number of people in the economy and the composition of that population. The size of the population affects the position of the consumption function; the age of the population affects the slope of the consumption function. The greater the size of the population, other things equal, the higher the intercept of the consumption function. With regard to the effect of age composition on the economy, young households typically are accumulating durable consumer goods (refrigerators, washing machines, automobiles); they have higher *MPC*s than older households.

Permanent Income, Life Cycles, and Consumption

Studies of the consumption function over a long period of time find a function like the one labeled C_L in the graph, as we saw earlier in Figure 2. This function has a marginal propensity to consume of .90 and an intercept of 0. Consumption functions studied over a shorter period of time have lower *MPC*s and positive intercepts, like the function C_s in the graph, with an *MPC* of .60. How do we reconcile these two functions?

Economists offer two related explanations for the difference between long-run and short-run consumption behavior: the permanent income hypothesis and the life-cycle hypothesis. The basic idea is that people consume on the basis of their idea of what their long-run or permanent level of income is.

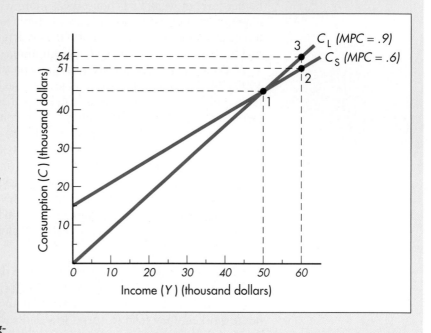

A substantial increase in income this month does not affect consumption much in the short run unless it is perceived as a permanent increase.

Let's use point 1 on the graph as our starting point. Here disposable income is $50,000 and consumption is $45,000. Now suppose household income rises to $60,000. Initially consumption increases by 60 percent, the short-run *MPC*. The household moves from point 1 to point 2 along the short-run consumption function (C_s). The short-run consumption function has a lower *MPC* than the long-run consumption function because households do not completely adjust their spending and saving habits with short-run fluctuations in income. Once the household is convinced that $60,000 is a permanent level of income, it moves from point 2 to point 3 along the long-run consumption function. At point 3, consumption has increased by 90 percent, the long-run *MPC*. In the long run, households adjust fully to changes in income, in the short run, a fluctuation in income does not cause as large a fluctuation in consumption.

When income falls below the permanent income level, the household is willing to dissave or borrow to support its normal level of consumption. When income rises above the permanent income level, the household saves at a higher rate than the long-run *MPS*. The lower *MPC* in the short run works to smooth out consumption in the long run. The household does not adjust current consumption to every up and down movement in household income.

To maintain a steady rate of consumption over time households follow a pattern of saving over the life cycle. Saving is low when current income is low relative to permanent income (during school years, periods of unemployment, or retirement). Saving is high when current income is high relative to the lifetime average, typically during middle age.

In the long run, households adjust fully to changes in income. In the short run, in order to smooth consumption over time, they do not. This explains both the difference between the long-run and short-run consumption functions and the stability of consumption over time.

1. It is impossible to separate incentives to save from incentives to consume.
2. Saving is a flow; savings is a stock.
3. Dissaving is spending financed by borrowing or using savings.
4. The marginal propensity to consume measures change in consumption as a proportion of change in disposable income.
5. The marginal propensity to save measures change in saving as a proportion of change in disposable income.
6. The *MPC* plus the *MPS* must equal 1.
7. Change in the *MPC* changes the slope of the consumption function; change in the *MPS* changes the slope of the saving function.
8. The average propensity to consume measures that portion of disposable income spent for consumption.
9. The average propensity to save measures that portion of disposable income saved.
10. The sum of the *APC* and the *APS* must equal 1.
11. The determinants of consumption include income, wealth, expectations, demographics, and taxation.
12. A change in consumption caused by a change in disposable income is shown by movement along the consumption function.
13. Changes in wealth, expectations, or population change autonomous consumption, which is shown as a shift of the consumption function.

2. Investment

Investment is business spending on capital goods and inventories. It is the most variable component of total spending. In this section of the chapter, we take a look at the determinants of investment and see why investment changes so much over the business cycle.

2.a. Autonomous Investment

In order to simplify our analysis of real GDP in the next chapter, we assume that investment is autonomous, that it is independent of current real GDP. This does not mean that we assume that investment is fixed at a constant amount. There are several factors that cause investment to change, but we assume that current real GDP is not one of them.

As a function of real GDP, autonomous investment is drawn as a horizontal line. This means that investment remains constant as real GDP changes. In Figure 6, the investment function (the horizontal line labeled I) indicates that investment equals $50 at every level of real GDP. As the determinants of investment change, the investment function shifts autonomously. As investment increases, the function shifts upward (for example, from I to I_1); as investment decreases, the function shifts downward (from I to I_2).

FIGURE 6

Investment as a Function of Income

Investment is assumed to be autonomous. Because it is independent of current real GDP, it is drawn as a horizontal line. An autonomous increase in investment shifts the function upward, from *I* to *I*₁. An increase could be the product of lower interest rates, optimism in business about future sales and revenues, technological change, an investment tax credit that lowers the cost of capital goods, or a need to expand capacity because of a lack of available productive resources. An autonomous decrease in investment moves the function down, from *I* to *I*₂. The same factors that cause investment to rise can also cause it to fall when they move in the opposite direction.

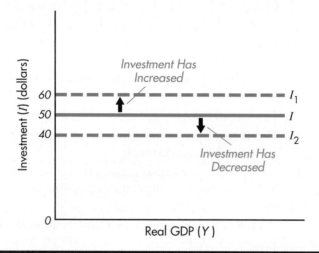

2.b. Determinants of Investment

3. What are the determinants of investment?

Investment is business spending on capital goods and inventories. Capital goods are the buildings and equipment that businesses need to produce their products. Inventories are final goods that have not been sold. Inventories can be planned or unplanned. For example, in the fall a retail department store wants to have enough sizes and styles of the new clothing lines to attract customers. Without a good-sized inventory, sales will suffer. The goods it buys are *planned* inventory, based on expected sales. But come February, the store wants to have as few fall clothes left unsold as possible. Goods not sold at this stage are *unplanned* inventory. They are a sign that sales were not as good as expected and that too much was produced last year.

Both types of inventories—planned and unplanned—are called investment. But only planned investment—capital purchases plus planned inventories—combines with planned consumer, government, and foreign-sector spending to determine the equilibrium level of aggregate expenditures, as we will see in the next chapter. Unplanned investment and unwanted inventories do not affect the equilibrium. They are simply the leftovers of what has recently gone on in the economy. What economists are interested in are the determinants of planned investment.

2.b.1. The Interest Rate   Business investment is made in the hopes of earning profits. The greater the expected profit, the greater the investment. A primary determinant of whether an investment opportunity will be profitable is the rate of interest. The interest rate is the cost of borrowed funds. Much of business spending is financed by borrowing. As the rate of interest goes up, fewer investment projects offer enough profit to warrant undertaking them. In other words, the higher the interest rate, the lower the rate of investment. As the interest rate falls, opportunities for greater profits increase and investment rises.

Let's look at a simple example. A firm can acquire a machine for $100 that will yield $120 in output. Whether the firm is willing to undertake the investment depends on whether it will earn a sufficient return on its investment. The return from an investment is the profit from an investment divided by its cost.

If the firm has to borrow $100 for the investment, it will have to pay interest to the lender. Suppose the lender charges 10 percent interest. The firm will have to pay 10 percent of $100, or $10, interest. This raises the cost of the investment to $110, the $100 cost of the machine plus the $10 interest. The firm's return from the investment is 9 percent:

$$\text{Return on investment} = \frac{(\$120 - \$110)}{\$110}$$

$$= .09$$

As the interest rate rises, the firm's cost of borrowing also rises and the return on investment falls. When the interest rate is 20 percent, the firm must pay $20 in interest, so the total cost of the investment is $120. Here the return is 0 ([$120 − $120]/$120). The higher interest rate reduces the return on the investment and discourages investment spending.

As the interest rate falls, the firm's cost of borrowing falls and the return from the investment rises. If the interest rate is 5 percent, the firm must pay $5 in interest. The total cost of the investment is $105, and the return is 14 percent ([$120 − $105]/$105). The lower interest rate increases the return from the investment and encourages investment spending.

2.b.2. Profit Expectations

Firms undertake investment in the expectation of earning a profit. Obviously, they cannot know exactly how much profit they will earn. So they use forecasts of revenues and costs to decide on an appropriate level of investment. It is their *expected* rate of return that actually determines their level of investment.

Many factors affect expectations of profit and, therefore, change the level of investment. Among them are new firms entering the market; political change; new laws, taxes, or subsidies from government; and the overall economic health of the country or world as measured by gross domestic product.

2.b.3. Other Determinants of Investment

Everything that might affect a firm's expected rate of return determines its level of investment. But three factors—technological change, the cost of capital goods, and capacity utilization—warrant special attention.

Technological Change Technological change is often a driving force behind new investment. New products or processes can be crucial to remaining competitive in an industry. The computer industry, for example, is driven by technological change. As faster and larger-capacity memory chips are developed, computer manufacturers must utilize them in order to stay competitive.

The impact of technology on investment spending is not new. For example, the invention of the cotton gin stimulated investment spending in the early 1800s, and the introduction of the gasoline-powered tractor in 1905 created an agricultural investment boom in the early 1900s. More recently, the development of integrated circuits stimulated investment spending in the electronics industry.

One measure of the importance of technology is the commitment to research and development. Data on spending for research and development across U.S. industries and across countries are listed in Table 3. The industries listed in the table are those that rely on innovation and the development of new technologies to remain competitive. Research and development is a multibillion-dollar commitment for these industries. The data on the four industrial countries indicate that these countries spend roughly the same percentage of GDP on research and development. The most obvious trend is the increase in Japanese spending since the mid-1960s. As Japan has grown to be an industrial giant, the role of technological innovation has become increasingly important there.

A commitment to research and development is a sign of the technological progress that marks the industrial nation. The countries listed in Table 3, along with other industrial nations, are the countries in which new technology generally originates. New technology developed in any country tends to stimulate investment

TABLE 3

Research and Development Expenditures

	In Selected U.S. Industries, 2000		
Industry	Expenditures (millions of dollars)	Expenditures as Percentage of Sales	Number of Researchers
Aircraft and missiles	9,640	7.3	40,200
Chemicals	19,542	5.9	82,000
Machinery	6,197	3.9	51,900

As a Percentage of GDP, Selected Years, 1965–2000				
Year	United States	France	Germany	Japan
1965	2.8	2.0	1.7	1.5
1968	2.8	2.1	2.0	1.6
1971	2.4	1.9	2.2	1.9
1974	2.2	1.8	2.1	2.0
1977	2.2	1.8	2.1	1.9
1980	2.3	1.8	2.4	2.2
1983	2.6	2.2	2.5	2.6
1985	2.8	2.3	2.7	2.9
1988	2.8	2.3	2.8	2.9
1991	2.7	2.4	2.8	3.0
1994	2.5	2.4	2.3	2.7
1997	2.6	2.2	2.3	2.9
2000	2.8	2.2	2.5	3.0

Source: Data are drawn from the *Statistical Abstract of the United States, 2002,* and the National Science Foundation website, www.nsf.gov/sbe/.

Research and development, as that carried out in this lab at Duke University, stimulates technological advance and shifts the aggregate supply curve to the right. Advances in technology make it possible to produce more output and lower costs of production.

spending across all nations as firms in similar industries are forced to adopt new production methods to keep up with their competition.

Cost of Capital Goods   The cost of capital goods also affects investment spending. As capital goods become more expensive, the rate of return from investment in them drops and the amount of investment falls. One factor that can cause the cost of capital goods to change sharply is government tax policy. The U.S. government has imposed and then removed investment tax credits several times in the past. These credits allow firms to deduct part of the cost of investment from their tax bill. When the cost of investment drops, investment increases. When the cost of investment increases, the level of investment falls.

Capacity Utilization   If its existing capital stock is being used heavily, a firm has an incentive to buy more. But if much of its capital stock stands idle, the firm has little incentive to increase that stock. Economists sometimes refer to the productive capacity of the economy as the amount of output that can be produced by businesses. In fact the Federal Reserve constructs a measure of capacity utilization that indicates how close the economy is to capacity output.

Figure 7 plots the rate of capacity utilization in the U.S. economy. During 1967 to 2003, U.S. industry operated at a high rate of 89.4 percent of capacity in 1967 and at a low rate of 70.8 percent of capacity in the recession year of 1982. We never expect to see 100 percent of capacity utilized for the same reasons that we never expect zero unemployment. There are always capital goods that are temporarily unused, as in the case of frictional unemployment of labor, and there are always capital goods that are obsolete because of technological change, similar to the case of structural unemployment of labor.

When the economy is utilizing its capacity at a high rate, there is pressure to increase the production of capital goods and expand productive capacity. When capacity utilization is low—when factories and machines sit idle—investment tends to fall.

FIGURE 7

Capacity Utilization Rates for Total U.S. Industry

The Federal Reserve estimates the rate at which capacity is utilized in U.S. industry. The higher the rate, the greater the pressure for investment to expand productive capacity.

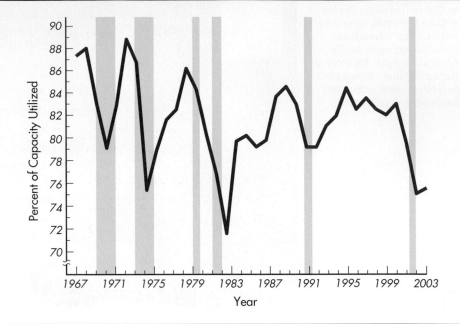

2.c. Volatility

We said that investment is the most variable component of total spending. What role do the determinants of investment play in that volatility?

Interest rates fluctuate widely. They are much more variable than income. Interest rates are a very important determinant of investment. Clearly the fact that they are so variable contributes to the variability of investment.

Expectations are subjective judgments about the future. Expectations can and often do change suddenly with new information. A rumor of a technological breakthrough, a speech by the president or a powerful member of Congress, even a revised weather forecast can cause firms to reexamine their thinking about the expected profitability of an investment. In developing economies, the protection of private property rights can have a large impact on investment spending. If a business expects a change in government policy to increase the likelihood of the government's expropriating its property, obviously it is not going to undertake new investments. Conversely, if a firm believes that the government will protect private property and encourage the accumulation of wealth, it will increase its investment spending. The fact that expectations are subject to large and frequent swings contributes to the volatility of investment.

Technological change proceeds very unevenly, making it difficult to forecast. Historically we find large increases in investment when a new technology is first developed and decreases in investment after the new technology is in place. This causes investment to move up and down unevenly through time.

Changes in tax policy occur infrequently, but they can create large incentives to invest or not to invest. Tax laws in the United States have swung back and forth on whether to offer an investment tax credit. A credit was first introduced in 1962. It was repealed in 1969, then readopted in 1971, and later revised in 1975, 1976, and 1981. In 1986, the investment tax credit was repealed again. Each of these changes had an impact on the cost of capital goods and contributed to the volatility of investment.

Finally, investment generally rises and falls with the rate of capacity utilization over the business cycle. As capacity utilization rises, some firms must add more factories and machines in order to continue increasing output and avoid reaching their maximum output level. As capacity utilization fluctuates, so will investment.

RECAP

1. As a function of real GDP, autonomous investment is drawn as a horizontal line.
2. The primary determinants of investment are the interest rate and profit expectations. Technological change, the cost of capital goods, and the rate of capacity utilization have an enormous impact on those expectations.
3. Investment fluctuates widely over the business cycle because the determinants of investment are so variable.

3. Government Spending

4. What are the determinants of government spending?

Government spending on goods and services is the second largest component of aggregate expenditures in the United States. In later chapters we examine the behavior of government in detail. Here we focus on how the government sector fits into the aggregate expenditures–income relationship. We assume that government spending is set by government authorities at whatever level they choose, independent of current income. In other words, we assume that government spending, like investment, is autonomous.

Figure 8 depicts government expenditures as a function of real GDP. The function, labeled G, is a horizontal line. If government officials increase government

FIGURE 8

Government Expenditures as a Function of Real GDP

Government spending is assumed to be autonomous and set by government policy. The government spending function is the horizontal line labeled G. Autonomous increases in government spending move the function upward (for example, from G to G_1); decreases move the function downward (for example, from G to G_2).

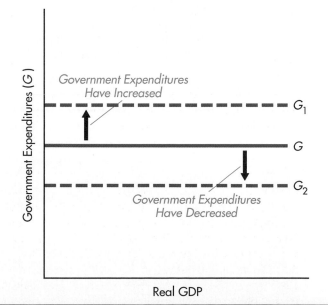

expenditures, the function shifts upward, parallel to the original curve, by an amount equal to the increase in expenditures (for example, from G to G_1). If government expenditures are reduced, the function shifts downward by an amount equal to the drop in expenditures (for example, from G to G_2).

4. Net Exports

5. What are the determinants of net exports?

The last component of aggregate expenditures is net exports, spending in the international sector. Net exports equal a country's exports of goods and services (what it sells to the rest of the world) minus its imports of goods and services (what it buys from the rest of the world). When net exports are positive, there is a surplus in the merchandise and services accounts. When net exports are negative, there is a deficit. The United States has had a net exports deficit since 1975. This is a relatively new phenomenon: the country had run surpluses throughout the post–World War II era until that time.

4.a. Exports

We assume that exports are autonomous. There are many factors that determine the actual value of exports, among them foreign income, tastes, prices, government trade restrictions, and exchange rates. But we assume that exports are not affected by current domestic income. You see this in the second column of Table 4, where exports are $50 at each level of real GDP.

As foreign income increases, foreign consumption rises—including consumption of goods produced in other countries—so domestic exports increase at every level of domestic real GDP. Decreases in foreign income lower domestic exports at every level of domestic real GDP. Similarly, changes in tastes or government restrictions on international trade or exchange rates can cause the level of exports to shift autonomously. When tastes favor domestic goods, exports go up. When tastes change, exports go down. When foreign governments impose restrictions on international trade, domestic exports fall. When restrictions are lowered, exports rise. Finally, as discussed in Chapter 7, when the domestic currency depreciates on the foreign exchange market (making domestic goods cheaper in foreign countries), exports rise. When the domestic currency appreciates on the foreign exchange market (making domestic goods more expensive in foreign countries), exports fall.

TABLE 4

Hypothetical Export and Import Schedule

Real GDP	Exports	Imports	Net Exports
$ 0	$50	$ 0	$50
$100	$50	$10	$40
$200	$50	$20	$30
$300	$50	$30	$20
$400	$50	$40	$10
$500	$50	$50	$ 0
$600	$50	$60	−$10
$700	$50	$70	−$20

4.b. Imports

Domestic purchases from the rest of the world (imports) are also determined by tastes, trade restrictions, and exchange rates. Here domestic income plays a role too. The greater domestic real GDP, the greater domestic imports. The import data in Table 4 show imports increasing with real GDP. When real GDP is 0, autonomous imports equal $0. As real GDP increases, imports increase.

marginal propensity to import (*MPI*): the change in imports as a proportion of the change in income

We measure the sensitivity of changes in imports to changes in real GDP by the marginal propensity to import. The **marginal propensity to import (*MPI*)** is the proportion of any extra income spent on imports:

$$MPI = \frac{\text{change in imports}}{\text{change in income}}$$

In Table 4, the *MPI* is .10, or 10 percent. Every time income changes by $100, imports change by $10.

How do other factors—tastes, government trade restrictions, and exchange rates—affect imports? When domestic tastes favor foreign goods, imports rise. When they do not, imports fall. When the domestic government tightens restrictions on international trade, domestic imports fall. When those restrictions are loosened, imports rise. Finally, when the domestic currency depreciates on the foreign exchange market (making foreign goods more expensive to domestic residents), imports fall. And when the domestic currency appreciates on the foreign exchange market (lowering the price of foreign goods), imports rise.

4.c. The Net Export Function

In our hypothetical economy in Table 4, net exports are listed in the last column. They are the difference between exports and imports. Because imports rise with domestic income, the higher that income, the lower net exports.

The higher domestic income, the lower net exports.

The net exports function, labeled *X*, is shown in Figure 9. The downward slope of the function (given by the *MPI*) indicates that net exports fall as real GDP

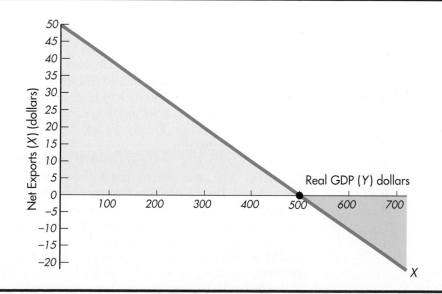

FIGURE 9

Net Exports as a Function of Real GDP

The net exports function is the downward-sloping line labeled *X*. Because exports are autonomous and imports increase with income, net exports fall as domestic real GDP rises. Notice that net exports can be positive or negative.

---

increases. Net exports are the only component of aggregate expenditures that can take on a negative value (saving can be negative, but it is not part of spending). Negative net exports mean that the domestic economy is importing more than it exports. The net exports function shifts with changes in foreign income, prices, tastes, government trade restrictions, and exchange rates. For example, as foreign income increases, domestic exports increase and the net exports function shifts upward.

RECAP

1. Net exports equal a country's exports minus its imports.
2. Exports are determined by foreign income, tastes, government trade restrictions, and exchange rates; they are independent of domestic real GDP.
3. Imports are a positive function of domestic real GDP; they also depend on tastes, domestic government trade restrictions, and exchange rates.
4. The marginal propensity to import measures the change in imports as a proportion of the change in domestic income.
5. Net exports fall as domestic real GDP rises.

5. The Aggregate Expenditures Function

6. What is the aggregate expenditures function?

The aggregate, or total, expenditures function is the sum of the individual functions for each component of planned spending. Aggregate expenditures (*AE*) equal consumption (*C*), plus investment (*I*), plus government spending (*G*), plus net exports (*X*):

$$AE = C + I + G + X$$

5.a. Aggregate Expenditures Table and Function

The table in Figure 10 lists aggregate expenditures data for a hypothetical economy. Real GDP is in the first column; the individual components of aggregate expenditures are in columns 2 through 5. Aggregate expenditures, listed in column 6, are the sum of the components at each level of income.

The aggregate expenditures function (*AE*) can be derived graphically by summing the individual expenditure functions (Figure 10) in a vertical direction. We begin with the consumption function (*C*) and then add autonomous investment, $50, to the consumption function at every level of income to arrive at the *C* + *I* function. To this we add constant government spending, $70, at every level of income to find the *C* + *I* + *G* function. Finally, we add the net exports function to find *C* + *I* + *G* + *X*, or the *AE* function.

Notice that the *C*, *C* + *I*, and *C* + *I* + *G* functions are all parallel. They all have the same slope, that determined by the *MPC*. This is because *I* and *G* are autonomous. The *AE* function has a smaller slope than the other functions because the slope of the net exports function is negative. By adding the *X* function to the *C* + *I* + *G* function, we are decreasing the slope of the *AE* function; the *C* + *I* + *G* + *X* function has a smaller, flatter slope than the *C* + *I* + *G* function.

The *X* function increases spending for levels of real GDP below $500 and decreases spending for levels of real GDP above $500. At $500, net exports equal 0 (see column 5). Because domestic imports increase as domestic income increases,

FIGURE 10

The Aggregate Expenditures Function

To find the aggregate expenditures function, we begin with the consumption function (labeled C) and add the investment function (I), to create the $C + I$ function. We then add the government spending function (G) to find the $C + I + G$ function. Notice that the C, $C + I$, and $C + I + G$ functions are all parallel. They have the same slope because investment and government spending are assumed to be autonomous. Because I and G do not change with income, the slope of the $C + I$ and $C + I + G$ functions is equal to the slope of the consumption function (the MPC). Net exports are added to the $C + I + G$ function to find the aggregate expenditures function, $C + I + G + X$. The aggregate expenditures function has a smaller slope than the other functions because the slope of the net exports function is negative.

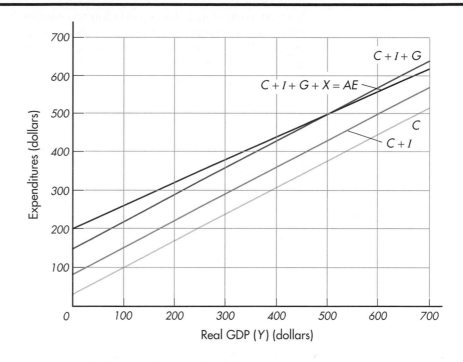

(1)	(2)	(3)	(4)	(5)	(6)
Y	C	I	G	X	AE
$ 0	$ 30	$50	$70	$50	$200
$100	$100	$50	$70	$40	$260
$200	$170	$50	$70	$30	$320
$300	$240	$50	$70	$20	$380
$400	$310	$50	$70	$10	$440
$500	$380	$50	$70	$ 0	$500
$600	$450	$50	$70	−$10	$560
$700	$520	$50	$70	−$20	$620

net exports fall as income rises. At incomes above $500, net exports are negative, so aggregate expenditures are less than $C + I + G$.

5.b. The Next Step

Though we have also been using *aggregate demand* to refer to total spending, you can see from Figure 10 that the aggregate expenditures line slopes up while the aggregate demand curve you saw in Figure 1 slopes down. In the next chapter we will explore the formal relationship between these two related concepts, when we go about determining the equilibrium level of real GDP using the AE function.

The concept of macroeconomic equilibrium points out the key role that aggregate expenditures play in determining output and income. As you will see, the equilibrium level of real GDP is that level toward which the economy automatically tends to move. Once that equilibrium is established, there is no tendency for real GDP to change unless a change in autonomous expenditures occurs. If aggregate expenditures rise, then the equilibrium level of real GDP rises. If aggregate expenditures fall, then the equilibrium level of real GDP falls. Such shifts in the *AE* function are associated with shifts in *C, I, G,* or *X.*

RECAP

1. Aggregate expenditures are the sum of planned consumption, planned investment, planned government spending, and planned net exports at every level of real GDP.

2. Assuming that *I* and *G* are autonomous, the *C, C + I,* and *C + I + G* functions are parallel lines.

3. Net exports increase aggregate expenditures at relatively low levels of domestic real GDP and decrease aggregate expenditures at relatively high levels of domestic real GDP.

Summary

? How are consumption and saving related?

1. Consumption and saving are the components of disposable income; they are determined by the same variables. *§1*

2. Dissaving occurs when consumption exceeds income. *§1.b*

3. The marginal propensity to consume (*MPC*) is change in consumption divided by change in disposable income; the marginal propensity to save (*MPS*) is change in saving divided by change in disposable income. *§1.c*

4. The average propensity to consume (*APC*) is consumption divided by disposable income; the average propensity to save (*APS*) is saving divided by disposable income. *§1.d*

? What are the determinants of consumption?

5. The determinants of consumption are income, wealth, expectations, demographics, and taxation. *§1.e.1, 1.e.2, 1.e.3, 1.e.4*

? What are the determinants of investment?

6. Investment is assumed to be autonomous, independent of current income. *§2.a*

7. The determinants of investment are the interest rate, profit expectations, technological change, the cost of capital goods, and the rate at which capacity is utilized. *§2.b.1, 2.b.2, 2.b.3*

8. Firms use the expected return on investment to determine the expected profitability of an investment project. *§2.b.1*

9. Investment is highly variable over the business cycle because the determinants of investment are themselves so variable. *§2.c*

? What are the determinants of government spending?

10. Government spending is set by government authorities at whatever level they choose. *§3*

? What are the determinants of net exports?

11. Net exports are the difference between what a country exports and what it imports; both exports and imports are a product of foreign or domestic income, tastes, foreign and domestic government trade restrictions, and exchange rates. *§4.a, 4.b*

12. Because imports rise with domestic income, the higher that income, the lower net exports. *§4.c*

13. The aggregate expenditures function is the sum of the individual functions for each component of spending. *§5*

14. The slope of the aggregate expenditures function is flatter than that of the consumption function because it includes the net exports function, which has a negative slope. *§5.a*

Key Terms

consumption function *§1.b*

saving function *§1.b*

dissaving *§1.b*

autonomous consumption *§1.b*

marginal propensity to consume (*MPC*) *§1.c*

marginal propensity to save (*MPS*) *§1.c*

average propensity to consume (*APC*) *§1.d*

average propensity to save (*APS*) *§1.d*

wealth *§1.e.2*

marginal propensity to import (*MPI*) *§4.b*

Exercises

1. Why do we study the consumption and saving functions together?

2. Explain the difference between a flow and a stock. Classify each of the following as a stock or a flow: income, wealth, saving, savings, consumption, investment, government expenditures, net exports, GDP.

3. Fill in the blanks in the following table:

Income	Consumption	Saving	MPC	MPS	APC	APS
$1,000	$ 400	_____			_____	.60
$2,000	$ 900	$1,100	_____	_____	_____	_____
$3,000	$1,400	_____	_____	.50	_____	_____
$4,000	_____	$2,100	_____	_____	_____	_____

4. Why is consumption so much more stable over the business cycle than investment? In formulating your answer, discuss household behavior as well as business behavior.

5. Assuming investment is autonomous, draw an investment function with income on the horizontal axis. Show how the function shifts if:

   a. The interest rate falls.
   b. An investment tax credit is repealed by Congress.
   c. A new president is expected to be a strong advocate of probusiness policies.
   d. There is a great deal of excess capacity in the economy.

6. Use the following table to answer these questions:

Y	C	I	G	X
$ 500	$500	$10	$20	$60
$ 600	$590	$10	$20	$40
$ 700	$680	$10	$20	$20
$ 800	$770	$10	$20	$ 0
$ 900	$860	$10	$20	−$20
$1,000	$950	$10	$20	−$40

   a. What is the *MPC*?
   b. What is the *MPS*?
   c. What is the *MPI*?
   d. What is the level of aggregate expenditures at each level of income?
   e. Graph the aggregate expenditures function.

7. Based on the table in exercise 6, what is the linear equation for each of the following functions?

   a. Consumption
   b. Investment
   c. Net exports
   d. Aggregate expenditures

8. Is the *AE* function the same thing as a demand curve? Why or why not?

9. What is the level of saving if:

   a. Disposable income is $500 and consumption is $450?

b. Disposable income is $1,200 and the *APS* is .9?

c. The *MPC* equals .9, disposable income rises from $800 to $900, and saving is originally $120 when income equals $800?

10. What is the marginal propensity to consume if:

a. Consumption increases by $75 when disposable income rises by $100?

b. Consumption falls by $50 when disposable income falls by $100?

c. Saving equals $20 when disposable income equals $100 and saving equals $40 when disposable income equals $300?

11. How can the *APC* fall as income rises if the *MPC* is constant?

12. Why would economies with older populations tend to have greater slopes of the consumption function?

13. Draw a diagram and illustrate the effects of the following on the net exports function for the United States:

a. The French government imposes restrictions on French imports of U.S. goods.

b. The U.S. national income rises.

c. Foreign income falls.

d. The dollar depreciates on the foreign exchange market.

14. Why is the slope of the $C + I + G$ function different from the slope of the $C + I + G + X$ function?

15. Suppose the consumption function is $C = \$200 + 0.8Y$.

a. What is the amount of autonomous consumption?

b. What is the marginal propensity to consume?

c. What would consumption equal when real GDP equals $1,000?

16. Explain why the consumption function is flatter in the short run than in the long run. Draw a diagram to illustrate your answer.

ACE

Take the ACE Practice Test for this chapter to review the important concepts and get immediate feedback with answers.

economics.college.hmco.com/students

Economically Speaking

U.S. Trade Deficit for 2002 Largest in History

The United States recorded the largest trade deficit in its history during 2002 as the American economy continued to demand foreign goods while U.S. exporters found weak overseas markets, according to figures released yesterday.

The U.S. trade deficit for goods and services reached $435.2 billion for 2002, up 21.5 percent from 2001, the U.S. Commerce Department said yesterday.

The record-breaking trade deficit reflects stronger growth in the United States than overseas.

The United States' major trade partners, with the exception of China, have seen poor economic growth. But they are still sending goods to the United States, even though they are buying less.

The U.S. trade deficit with the 15-nation European Union grew by 34 percent. And while Japan sent $5 billion less in goods to America last year, it bought $6 billion less.

U.S. Treasury Secretary John W. Snow said he would raise concerns about the lack of growth in Europe and Japan this weekend when he meets in Paris with finance ministers from the Group of Seven industrialized countries.

The Bush administration contends that trade spurs growth in overseas markets for U.S. goods and services, enhances opportunities for higher-paying American jobs, expands choices for American consumers, and promotes U.S. security interests.

Opponents of the free-trade policy contend it costs jobs.

U.S. sales of capital goods, mainly computer accessories, telecommunications equipment and semiconductors, fell by $31.1 billion from 2001. Exports of industrial supplies and consumer goods also tailed off, while those of vehicles increased.

U.S. imports of consumer goods, primarily pharmaceuticals, household goods, televisions, VCRs, furniture and apparel, increased the most. Food and beverage, and vehicle imports also jumped.

The U.S. recorded its biggest trade deficit with China. The gap reached $103.1 billion, even as U.S. exports to that country grew. U.S. firms sold more aircraft, semiconductors, fertilizers, industrial machines and chemicals to China, while China registered a surge in sales of computer accessories, toys, games, electronics and furniture.

The next biggest trade deficits were with Japan and Western Europe. The figures are likely to worsen if the U.S. economy recovers or at least continues to grow more quickly than those of our major trading partners, said Charles Pearson, head of the economics department at the Johns Hopkins School of Advanced International Studies.

"I think we're in a particularly vulnerable position with regard to foreign trade. We're at the bottom of the [economic] cycle and when recovery comes, that means sucking in more imports," he said.

While China's economy is growing steadily, Japan and Europe are faring poorly.

The U.S. economy grew slowly during the past three months of 2002, according to preliminary Commerce Department figures. The projected 0.7 percent annual growth rate for the fourth quarter is likely to be revised down because of the trade numbers, Mr. Levy said.

The United States pays for the trade deficit by importing capital; that is, foreigners have to invest in the United States.

JEFFREY SPARSHOTT

The Washington Times/February 21, 2003

Commentary

In this chapter, we saw how net exports contribute to aggregate expenditures. Merchandise exports bring money from the rest of the world, and higher net exports mean greater aggregate expenditures. Merchandise imports involve outflows of money to foreign countries, and lower net exports mean lower aggregate expenditures.

We saw in the chapter that higher domestic real GDP leads to higher imports and lower net exports. This article points out that the U.S. net export deficit is expected to grow if the U.S. economy "continues to grow more quickly than those of our major trading partners." As a result of the effect of net exports on aggregate expenditures, we often hear arguments for policy aimed at increasing exports and decreasing imports. Domestic residents are often resentful of foreign producers and blame foreign competitors for job losses in the home country. However, we must consider the circumstances and then ask if a policy aimed at increasing the national trade surplus (or decreasing the deficit) is really desirable.

Since one country's export is another's import, it is impossible for everyone to have surpluses—on a worldwide basis, the total value of exports equals the total value of imports. If someone must always have a trade deficit when others have trade surpluses, is it necessarily true that surpluses are good and deficits bad so that one country benefits at another's expense? In a sense, imports should be preferred to exports since exports represent goods that are no longer available for domestic consumption and will be consumed by foreign importers. In later chapters you will learn that the benefits of free international trade include more efficient production and increased consumption. Furthermore, if trade among nations is voluntary, it is difficult to argue that deficit countries are harmed while surplus countries benefit from trade.

In general, it is not obvious whether a country is better or worse off running merchandise surpluses rather than deficits. Consider the following simple example of a world with two countries, R and P. Country R is a rich creditor country that is growing rapidly and has a net exports deficit. Country P is a poor debtor country that is growing slowly and has positive net exports. Should we prefer living conditions in P to R based solely on the knowledge that P has a net exports surplus and R has a net exports deficit? Although this is indeed a simplistic example, there are real-world analogues of rich creditor countries with international trade deficits and poor debtor nations with international trade surpluses. The point is that you cannot analyze the balance of payments apart from other economic considerations. Deficits are not inherently bad, nor are surpluses necessarily good.

APPENDIX TO CHAPTER 10

An Algebraic Model of Aggregate Expenditures

Aggregate expenditures (AE) equal consumption (C) plus investment (I) plus government spending (G) plus net exports (X). If we can develop an equation for each component of spending, we can put them together in a single model.

Consumption   The consumption function can be written in general form as

$$C = C^a + cYd$$

where C^a is autonomous consumption and c is the MPC. The consumption function for the data in Chapter 10 is

$$C = \$30 + .70Yd$$

as shown in Figure 1.

Saving   The corresponding saving function is

$$S = -\$30 + .30Yd \text{ as illustrated in Figure 2.}$$

FIGURE 1

The Consumption Function

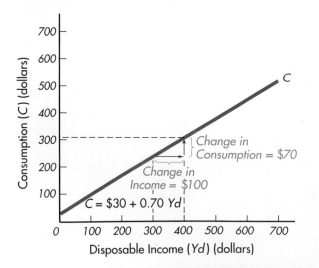

FIGURE 2

The Saving Function

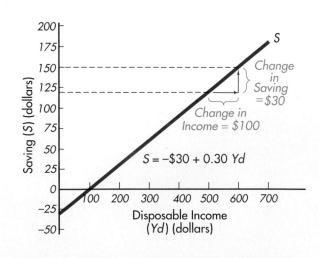

Investment   Investment is autonomous at I^a, which is equal to $50.

Government Spending   Government spending is autonomous at G^a, which is equal to $70.

Net Exports   Exports are autonomous at EX^a and equal to $50. Imports are given by the function

$$IM = IM^a + imY$$

where im is the *MPI*. Here, then,

$$IM = \$0 + .10Y$$

Net exports equal exports minus imports, or

$$X = \$50 - \$0 - .10Y$$
$$= \$50 - .10Y$$

as shown in Figure 3.

Aggregate Expenditures   Summing the functions for the four components (and ignoring taxes, so that Yd equals Y) gives

$$AE = C^a + cY + I^a + G^a + EX^a - IM^a - imY$$
$$= \$30 + .70Y + \$50 + \$70 + \$50 - \$0 - .10Y$$
$$= \$200 + .60Y$$

as shown in Figure 4.

In the Appendix to Chapter 11 we use the algebraic model of aggregate expenditures presented here to solve for the equilibrium level of real GDP.

FIGURE 3

The Net Exports Function

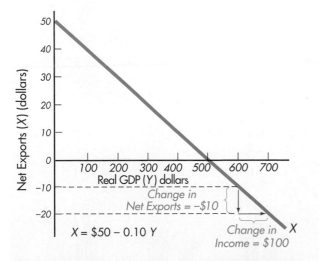

FIGURE 4

The Aggregate Expenditures Function

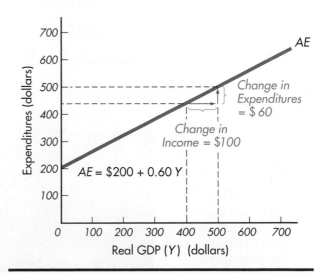

Income and Expenditures Equilibrium

? **Fundamental Questions**

W hat determines the level of income and expenditures, or real GDP? In Chapter 9 we used aggregate demand and aggregate supply to answer this question. Then in Chapter 10 we developed the components of aggregate expenditures in more detail to provide the foundation for an additional approach to answering the question "What determines the level of real GDP?" If you know the answer to this question, you are well on your way to understanding business cycles. Sometimes real GDP is growing and jobs are relatively easy to find; at other times real GDP is falling and large numbers of people are out of work. Macroeconomists use several models to analyze the causes of business cycles. Underlying all of the models is the concept of macroeconomic equilibrium.

Equilibrium here means what it did when we talked about supply and demand: a point of balance, a point from which there is no tendency to move. In macroeconomics, equilibrium is the level of income and expenditures that the economy tends to move toward and remain at until autonomous spending changes.

John Maynard Keynes

John Maynard Keynes (pronounced "canes") is considered by many to be the greatest economist of the twentieth century. His major work, *The General Theory of Employment, Interest, and Money,* had a profound impact on macroeconomics, both thought and policy. Keynes was born in Cambridge, England, on June 5, 1883. He studied economics at Cambridge University, where he became a lecturer in economics in 1908. During World War I, Keynes worked for the British treasury. At the end of the war, he was the treasury's representative at the Versailles Peace Conference. He resigned from the British delegation at the conference to protest the harsh terms being imposed on the defeated countries. His resignation and the publication of the *Economic Consequences of the Peace* (1919) made him an international celebrity.

In 1936, Keynes published *The General Theory.* It was a time of world recession (it has been estimated that around one-quarter of the U.S. labor force was unemployed at the height of the Depression), and policymakers were searching for ways to explain the persistent unemployment. In the book, Keynes suggested that an economy could come to equilibrium at less than potential GDP. More important, he argued that government policy could be altered to end recession. His analysis emphasized aggregate expenditures. If private expenditures were not sufficient to create equilibrium at potential GDP, government expenditures could be increased to stimulate income and output. This was a startling concept. Most economists of the time believed that government should not take an active role in the economy. With his *General Theory,* Keynes started a "revolution" in macroeconomics.

Economists have not always agreed on how an economy reaches equilibrium or on the forces that move an economy from one equilibrium to another. This last issue formed the basis of economic debate during the Great Depression of the 1930s. Before the 1930s, economists generally believed that the economy was always at or moving toward an equilibrium consistent with a high level of employed resources. The British economist John Maynard Keynes did not agree. He believed that an economy can come to rest at a level of real GDP that is too low to provide employment for all those who desire it. He also believed that certain actions are necessary to ensure that the economy rises to a level of real GDP consistent with a high level of employment. In particular, Keynes argued that government must intervene in the economy in a big way (see the Economic Insight "John Maynard Keynes").

To understand the debate that began during the 1930s and continues on various fronts today, it is necessary to understand the Keynesian view of how equilibrium real GDP is determined. This is our focus here. We have seen in Chapter 9 that the aggregate demand and supply model of macroeconomic equilibrium allowed the price level to fluctuate as the equilibrium level of real GDP changed. The Keynesian income-expenditures model assumes that the price level is fixed. It emphasizes aggregate expenditures without explicit consideration of the supply side of the economy. This is why we considered the components of spending in detail in Chapter 10—to provide a foundation for the analysis in this chapter. The Keynesian model may be viewed as a special fixed-price case of the aggregate demand and aggregate supply model. In later chapters we examine the relationship between equilibrium and the level of employed resources, and the effect of government policy on both of these elements. ■

1. **What does equilibrium mean in macroeconomics?**

2. **How do aggregate expenditures affect income, or real GDP?**

1. Equilibrium Income and Expenditures

Equilibrium is a point from which there is no tendency to move. People do not change their behavior when everything is consistent with what they expect. However, when plans and reality do not match, people adjust their behavior to make them match. Determining a nation's equilibrium level of income and expenditures is the process of defining the level of income and expenditures at which plans and reality are the same.

1.a. Expenditures and Income

We use the aggregate expenditures function described at the end of Chapter 10 to demonstrate how equilibrium is determined. Keep in mind that the aggregate expenditures function represents *planned* expenditures at different levels of income, or real GDP. We focus on planned expenditures because they represent the amount that households, firms, government, and the foreign sector expect to spend.

Actual expenditures always equal income and output because they reflect changes in inventories. That is, inventories automatically raise or lower investment expenditures so that actual spending equals income, which equals output, which equals real GDP. However, aggregate expenditures (which are planned spending) may not equal real GDP. What happens when planned spending and real GDP are not equal? When planned spending on goods and services *exceeds* the current value of output, the production of goods and services increases. Because output equals income, the level of real GDP also increases. This is the situation for all income levels below $500 in Figure 1. At these levels, total spending is greater than real GDP, which means that more goods and services are being purchased than are being produced. The only way this can happen is for goods produced in the past to be sold. When planned spending is greater than real GDP, business inventories fall. The change in inventories offsets the excess of planned expenditures over real GDP, so that actual expenditures (including the unplanned change in inventories) equal real GDP. You can see this in column 7 of the table in Figure 1, where the change in inventories offsets the excess of aggregate expenditures over real GDP (the difference between columns 6 and 1).

When aggregate expenditures exceed real GDP, real GDP rises.

What happens when inventories fall? As inventories fall, manufacturers increase production to meet the demand for products. The increased production raises the level of real GDP. *When aggregate expenditures exceed real GDP, real GDP rises.*

At real GDP levels above $500 in the table, aggregate expenditures are less than income. As a result, inventories are accumulating above planned levels—more goods and services are being produced than are being purchased. As inventories rise, businesses begin to reduce the quantity of output they produce. The unplanned increase in inventories is counted as a form of investment spending, so that actual expenditures equal real GDP. For example, when real GDP is $600, aggregate expenditures are only $560. The $40 of produced goods that are not sold are measured as inventory investment. The $560 of aggregate expenditures plus the $40 of unplanned inventories equal $600, the level of real GDP. As inventories increase, firms cut production; this causes real GDP to fall. *When aggregate expenditures are less than real GDP, real GDP falls.*

When aggregate expenditures are less than real GDP, real GDP falls.

The equilibrium level of real GDP is where aggregate expenditures equal real GDP.

There is only one level of real GDP in the table in Figure 1 where real GDP does not change. When real GDP is $500, aggregate expenditures equal $500. The equilibrium level of real GDP (or output) is that point at which aggregate expenditures equal real GDP (or output).

FIGURE 1

The Equilibrium Level of Real GDP

Macroeconomic equilibrium occurs where aggregate expenditures (*AE*) equal real GDP (*Y*). In the graph it is the point where the *AE* line crosses the 45-degree line, where expenditures and real GDP both equal $500. When aggregate expenditures exceed real GDP (as they do at a real GDP level of $400, for example), real GDP rises to the equilibrium level. When aggregate expenditures are less than real GDP (as they are at a real GDP level of $600, for example), real GDP falls back to the equilibrium level.

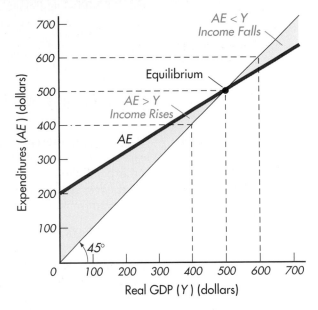

(1) Real GDP (Y)	(2) Consumption (C)	(3) Investment (I)	(4) Government Spending (G)	(5) Net Exports (X)	(6) Aggregate Expenditures (AE)	(7) Unplanned Change in Inventories	(8) Change in Real GDP
$ 0	$ 30	$50	$70	$ 50	$200	−$200	Increase
$100	$100	$50	$70	$ 40	$260	−$160	Increase
$200	$170	$50	$70	$ 30	$320	−$120	Increase
$300	$240	$50	$70	$ 20	$380	−$ 80	Increase
$400	$310	$50	$70	$ 10	$440	−$ 40	Increase
$500	$380	$50	$70	$ 0	$500	$ 0	No change
$600	$450	$50	$70	$−10	$560	$40	Decrease
$700	$520	$50	$70	$−20	$620	$80	Decrease

When aggregate expenditures equal real GDP, planned spending equals the output produced and the income generated from producing that output. As long as planned spending is consistent with real GDP, real GDP does not change. But if planned spending is higher or lower than real GDP, real GDP does change. Equilibrium is that point at which planned spending and real GDP are equal.

The graph in Figure 1 illustrates equilibrium. The 45-degree line shows all possible points where aggregate expenditures (measured on the vertical axis) equal real GDP (measured on the horizontal axis). The equilibrium level of real GDP, then, is simply the point where the aggregate expenditures line (*AE*) crosses the 45-degree line. In the figure, equilibrium occurs where real GDP and expenditures are $500.

When the *AE* curve lies above the 45-degree line—for example, at a real GDP level of $400—aggregate expenditures are greater than real GDP. What happens? Real GDP rises to the equilibrium level, where it tends to stay. When the *AE* curve lies below the 45-degree line—at a real GDP level of $600, for example—aggregate expenditures are less than real GDP; this pushes real GDP down. Once real GDP falls to the equilibrium level ($500 in our example), it tends to stay there.

1.b. Leakages and Injections

Equilibrium can be determined by using aggregate expenditures and real GDP, which represents income. Another way to determine equilibrium involves leakages from and injections into the income stream, the circular flow of income and expenditures.

Leakages reduce autonomous aggregate expenditures. There are three leakages in the stream from domestic income to spending: saving, taxes, and imports.

- The more households save, the less they spend. An increase in autonomous saving means a decrease in autonomous consumption, which could cause the equilibrium level of real GDP to fall (see the Economic Insight "The Paradox of Thrift").

- Taxes are an involuntary reduction in consumption. The government transfers income away from households. Higher taxes lower autonomous consumption, in the process lowering autonomous aggregate expenditures and the equilibrium level of real GDP.

- Imports are expenditures for foreign goods and services. They reduce expenditures on domestic goods and services. An autonomous increase in imports reduces net exports, causing autonomous aggregate expenditures and the equilibrium level of real GDP to fall.

For equilibrium to occur, these leakages must be offset by corresponding *injections* of spending into the domestic economy, through investment, government spending, and exports.

- Household saving generates funds that businesses can borrow and spend for investment purposes.

- The taxes collected by government are used to finance government purchases of goods and services.

- Exports bring foreign expenditures into the domestic economy.

There is no reason to expect that each injection matches its corresponding leakage—that investment equals saving, that government spending equals taxes, or that exports equal imports. But for equilibrium to occur, total injections must equal total leakages.

Figure 2 shows how leakages and injections determine the equilibrium level of real GDP. Column 5 of the table lists the total leakages from aggregate expenditures: saving (S) plus taxes (T) plus imports (IM). Saving and imports both increase when real GDP increases. We assume that there are no taxes, so the total amount of leakages ($S + T + IM$) increases as real GDP increases.

Column 9 lists the injections at alternative income levels. Because investment (I), government spending (G), and exports (EX) are all autonomous, total injections ($I + G + EX$) are constant at all levels of real GDP.

To determine the equilibrium level of real GDP, we compare leakages with injections. When injections exceed leakages, planned spending is greater than current income or output, so real GDP rises. In the table in Figure 2, this occurs for levels of real GDP under $500, so real GDP increases if it is under $500 (see the last

3. What are the leakages from and injections to spending?

Saving, taxes, and imports are leakages that reduce autonomous aggregate expenditures.

Investment, government spending, and exports are injections that increase autonomous aggregate expenditures.

The equilibrium level of real GDP occurs where leakages equal injections.

FIGURE 2

Leakages, Injections, and Equilibrium Income

Leakages equal saving (*S*), taxes (*T*), and imports (*IM*). Injections equal investment (*I*), government spending (*G*), and exports (*EX*). Equilibrium is that point where leakages equal injections. In the graph, equilibrium is the point at which the *S* + *T* + *IM* curve intersects the *I* + *G* + *EX* curve, where real GDP (*Y*) equals $500. At lower levels of income, injections exceed leakages, so *Y* rises. At higher levels of income, leakages exceed injections, so *Y* falls.

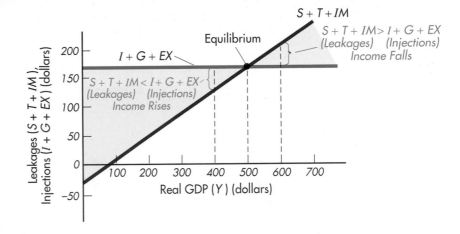

(1) Real GDP (*Y*)	(2) Saving (*S*)	(3) Taxes (*T*)	(4) Imports (*IM*)	(5) Leakages (*S* + *T* + *IM*)	(6) Investment (*I*)	(7) Government Spending (*G*)	(8) Exports (*EX*)	(9) Injections (*I* + *G* + *EX*)	(10) Change in Real GDP
$ 0	−$ 30	$0	$ 0	−$ 30	$50	$70	$50	$170	Increase
$100	$ 0	$0	$10	$ 10	$50	$70	$50	$170	Increase
$200	$ 30	$0	$20	$ 50	$50	$70	$50	$170	Increase
$300	$ 60	$0	$30	$ 90	$50	$70	$50	$170	Increase
$400	$ 90	$0	$40	$130	$50	$70	$50	$170	Increase
$500	$120	$0	$50	$170	$50	$70	$50	$170	No change
$600	$150	$0	$60	$210	$50	$70	$50	$170	Decrease
$700	$180	$0	$70	$250	$50	$70	$50	$170	Decrease

column). When leakages exceed injections, planned spending is less than current real GDP, so real GDP falls. In Figure 2, at all levels of real GDP above $500, real GDP falls. Only when leakages equal injections is the equilibrium level of real GDP established. When real GDP equals $500, both leakages and injections equal $170, so there is no pressure for real GDP to change. The equilibrium level of real GDP occurs where leakages (*S* + *T* + *IM*) equal injections (*I* + *G* + *EX*).

Figure 2 shows the interaction of leakages and injections graphically. The equilibrium point is where the *S* + *T* + *IM* and *I* + *G* + *EX* curves intersect, at a real GDP level of $500. At higher levels of real GDP, leakages are greater than injections (the *S* + *T* + *IM* curve lies above the *I* + *G* + *EX* curve). When leakages are greater than injections, real GDP falls to the equilibrium point. At lower levels of income, injections are greater than leakages (the *I* + *G* + *EX* curve lies above the *S* + *T* + *IM* curve). Here real GDP rises until it reaches $500. Only at $500 is there no pressure for real GDP to change.

The Paradox of Thrift

People generally believe that saving is good and that more saving is better. However, if every family increased its saving, the result could be less income for the economy as a whole. In fact, increased saving could actually lower savings for all households.

An increase in saving may provide an example of the *paradox of thrift*. A *paradox* is a true proposition that seems to contradict common beliefs. We believe that we will be better off by increased saving, but in the aggregate, increased saving could cause the economy to be worse off. The paradox of thrift is a *fallacy of composition:* the assumption that what is true of a part is true of the whole. It often is unsafe to generalize from what is true at the micro level to what is true at the macro level.

The graph illustrates the effect of higher saving. Initial equilibrium occurs where the $S_1 + T + IM$ curve intersects the $I + G + EX$ curve, at an income of $500. Suppose saving increases by $20 at every level of income. The $S_1 + T + IM$ curve shifts up to the $S_2 + T + IM$ curve. A new equilibrium is established at an income level of $400. The higher rate of saving causes equilibrium income to fall by $100.

Notice that the graph is drawn with a constant $I + G + EX$ line. If investment increases along with

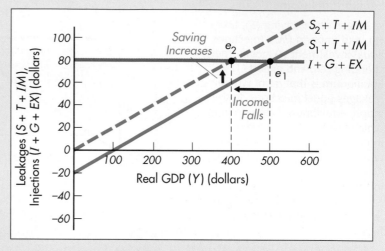

saving, equilibrium income will not necessarily fall. In fact, because saving is necessary before there can be any investment, we would expect a greater demand for investment funds to induce higher saving. If increased saving is used to fund investment expenditures, the economy should grow over time to higher and higher levels of income. Only if the increased saving is not injected back into the economy is there a paradox of thrift. The fact that governments do not discourage saving suggests that the paradox of thrift generally is not a real-world problem.

If you compare Figures 1 and 2, you can see that it does not matter whether we use aggregate expenditures or leakages and injections—the equilibrium level of real GDP is the same.

RECAP

1. Equilibrium is a point from which there is no tendency to move.
2. When aggregate expenditures exceed real GDP, real GDP rises.
3. When aggregate expenditures are less than real GDP, real GDP falls.
4. Saving, taxes, and imports are leakages of planned spending from domestic aggregate expenditures.
5. Investment, government spending, and exports are injections of planned spending into domestic aggregate expenditures.
6. Equilibrium occurs at the level of real GDP at which aggregate expenditures equal real GDP, and leakages equal injections.

2. Changes in Equilibrium Income and Expenditures

4. Why does equilibrium real GDP change by a multiple of a change in autonomous expenditures?

5. What is the spending multiplier?

Any change in autonomous expenditures is multiplied into a larger change in equilibrium real GDP.

Equilibrium is a point from which there is no tendency to move. But in fact the equilibrium level of real GDP does move. In the last section we described how aggregate expenditures push real GDP, representing the economy's income and output, up or down toward their level of equilibrium. Here we examine how changes in autonomous expenditures affect equilibrium. This becomes very important in understanding macroeconomic policy, the kinds of things government can do to control the business cycle.

2.a. The Spending Multiplier

Remember that equilibrium is that point where aggregate expenditures equal real GDP. If we increase autonomous expenditures, then we raise the equilibrium level of real GDP. But by how much? It seems logical to expect a 1-to-1 ratio: if autonomous spending increases by a dollar, equilibrium real GDP should increase by a dollar. Actually, equilibrium real GDP increases by *more* than a dollar. The change in autonomous expenditures is *multiplied* into a larger change in the equilibrium level of real GDP.

In Chapter 6 we used a circular flow diagram to show the relationship of expenditures to income. In that diagram we saw how one sector's expenditures become another sector's income. This concept helps explain the effect of a change in autonomous expenditures on the equilibrium level of income or real GDP. If A's autonomous spending increases, then B's income rises. Then B spends part of that income in the domestic economy (the rest is saved or used to buy foreign goods), generating new income for C. In turn C spends part of that income in the domestic economy, generating new income for D. And the rounds of increased spending and income continue. All of this is the product of A's initial autonomous increase in spending. And each round of increased spending and income affects the equilibrium level of income, or real GDP.

Let's look at an example, using Table 1. Suppose government spending goes up $20 to improve public parks. What happens to the equilibrium level of income? The autonomous increase in government spending increases the income of park employees by $20. As the income of the park employees increases, so does their consumption. For example, let's say they spend more money on hamburgers. In the process, they are increasing the income of the hamburger producers, who in turn increase their consumption.

Table 1 shows how a single change in spending generates further changes. Round 1 is the initial increase in government spending to improve public parks. That $20 expenditure increases the income of park employees by $20 (column 1). As income increases, those components of aggregate expenditures that depend on current income—consumption and net exports—also increase by some fraction of the $20.

Consumption changes by the marginal propensity to consume multiplied by the change in income; imports change by the marginal propensity to import multiplied by the change in income. To find the total effect of the initial change in spending, we must know the fraction of any change in income that is spent in the domestic economy. In the hypothetical economy we have been using, the *MPC* is .70 and the *MPI* is .10. This means that for each $1 of new income, consumption

TABLE 1

The Spending Multiplier Effect

	(1) Change in Income	(2) Change in Domestic Expenditures	(3) Change in Saving	(4) Change in Imports
Round 1	$20.00	$12.00	$ 6.00	$2.00
Round 2	12.00	7.20	3.60	1.20
Round 3	7.20	4.32	2.16	0.72
Round 4	4.32	2.59	1.30	0.43
	.	.	.	.
	.	.	.	.
	.	.	.	.
Totals	$50.00	$30.00	$15.00	$5.00

$$\text{Column 2} = \text{column 1} \times (MPC - MPI)$$
$$\text{Column 3} = \text{column 1} \times MPS$$
$$\text{Column 4} = \text{column 1} \times MPI$$

$$\text{Multiplier} = \frac{1}{MPS + MPI}$$
$$= \frac{1}{.30 + .10}$$
$$= \frac{1}{.40}$$
$$= 2.5$$

rises by $.70 and imports rise by $.10. Spending on *domestic* goods and services, then, rises by $.60. Because consumption is spending on domestic goods and services, and imports are spending on foreign goods and services, the percentage of a change in income that is spent domestically is the difference between the *MPC* and the *MPI*. If the *MPC* equals .70 and the *MPI* equals .10, then 60 percent of any change in domestic income ($MPC - MPI = .60$) is spent on domestic goods and services.

The percentage of a change in income that is spent domestically is the difference between the MPC and the MPI.

In round 1 of Table 1, the initial increase in income of $20 induces an increase in spending on domestic goods and services of $12 (.60 × $20). Out of the $20, $6 is saved because the marginal propensity to save is .30 ($1 - MPC$). The other $2 is spent on imports ($MPI = .10$). The park employees receive $20 more income. They spend $12 on hamburgers at a local restaurant, they save $6, and they spend $2 on imported coffee.

Only $12 of the workers' new income is spent on goods produced in the domestic economy, hamburgers. That $12 becomes income to the restaurant's employees and owner. When their income increases by $12, they spend 60 percent of that income ($7.20) on domestic goods (round 2, column 2). The rest of the income is saved or spent on imports.

Each time income increases, expenditures increase. But the increase is smaller and smaller in each new round of spending. Why? Because 30 percent of each change in income is saved and another 10 percent is spent on imports. These are leakages out of the income stream. This means that just 60 percent of the change in income is spent and passed on to others in the domestic economy as income in the next round.

To find the total effect of the initial change in spending of $20, we could keep on computing the change in income and spending round after round, and then sum the total of all rounds. The change in income and spending never reaches zero, but it becomes infinitely small.

Fortunately, we do not have to compute each round-by-round increase in spending to find the total increase. If we know the percentage of additional income that "leaks" from domestic consumption at each round, we can determine the total change in income, or real GDP, by finding its reciprocal. This measure is called the **spending multiplier.** The leakages are that portion of the change in income that is saved (the *MPS*) and that proportion of the change in income that is spent on imports (the *MPI*).

spending multiplier: a measure of the change in equilibrium income or real GDP produced by a change in autonomous expenditures

$$\text{Multiplier} = \frac{1}{\text{leakages}}$$

$$= \frac{1}{MPS + MPI}$$

When the *MPS* is .30 and the *MPI* is .10, the multiplier equals 2.5 (1/.4). An initial change in expenditures of $20 results in a total change in real GDP of $50, 2.5 times the original change in expenditures. The greater the leakages, the smaller the multiplier. When the *MPS* equals .35 and the *MPI* equals .15, the multiplier equals 2 (1/.50). The multiplier is smaller here because less new income is being spent in the domestic economy. The more people save, the smaller the expansionary effect on income of a change in spending. And the more people spend on imports, the smaller the expansionary effect on income of a change in spending. Notice that the multiplier would be larger in a *closed economy,* an economy that does not trade with the rest of the world. In that economy, because the *MPI* equals zero, the spending multiplier is simply equal to the reciprocal of the *MPS*.

2.b. The Spending Multiplier and Equilibrium

The spending multiplier is an extremely useful concept. It allows us to calculate how a change in autonomous expenditures affects real GDP. To better understand how changes in spending can bring about changes in equilibrium income, or real GDP, let's modify the example we used in Figure 1. In the table in Figure 3 we have increased government spending to $110. The autonomous increase in government spending raises aggregate expenditures by $40 at every level of income. Aggregate expenditures now equal real GDP at $600. The increase in government spending of $40 yields an increase in equilibrium real GDP of $100.

The graph in Figure 3 illustrates the multiplier effect and shows the change in equilibrium income when spending increases by $40. The original aggregate expenditures curve, AE_1, intersects the 45-degree line at a real GDP level of $500. A spending increase of $40 at every level of real GDP creates a new aggregate expenditures curve, AE_2, which lies $40 above the original curve. The curve AE_2 is parallel

FIGURE 3

A Change in Equilibrium Expenditures and Income

A change in aggregate expenditures (AE) causes a change in equilibrium real GDP (Y). Initially equilibrium is $500, the point at which the AE_1 curve intersects the 45-degree line. If autonomous expenditures increase by $40, the aggregate expenditures curve shifts up to AE_2. The new curve intersects the 45-degree line at a new equilibrium level of real GDP, $600. An increase in autonomous expenditures of $40, then, causes equilibrium real GDP to increase by $100.

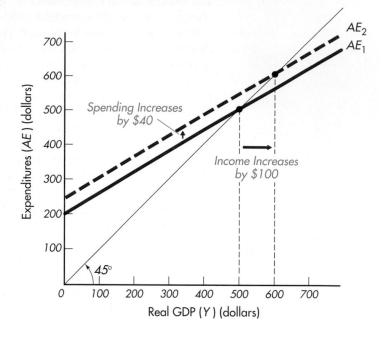

(1) Real GDP (Y)	(2) Consumption (C)	(3) Investment (I)	(4) Government Spending (G)	(5) Net Exports (X)	(6) Aggregate Expenditures (AE)	(7) Unplanned Change in Inventories	(8) Change in Real GDP
$ 0	$ 30	$50	$110	$50	$240	−$240	Increase
$100	$100	$50	$110	$40	$300	−$200	Increase
$200	$170	$50	$110	$30	$360	−$160	Increase
$300	$240	$50	$110	$20	$440	−$120	Increase
$400	$310	$50	$110	$10	$480	−$ 80	Increase
$500	$380	$50	$110	$ 0	$540	−$ 40	Increase
$600	$450	$50	$110	−$10	$600	$ 0	No change
$700	$520	$50	$110	−$20	$660	$ 40	Decrease

to AE_1 because the increase is in autonomous spending. The new curve, AE_2, intersects the 45-degree line at an income of $600.

In Chapter 8 we introduced the concept of the natural rate of unemployment—the unemployment rate that exists in the absence of cyclical unemployment. When the economy operates at the natural rate of unemployment, the corresponding level of output (and income) is called potential real GDP. However, equilibrium does not necessarily occur at potential real GDP. Equilibrium is any level of real GDP at which planned expenditures equal real GDP. Suppose that equilibrium real GDP is not at the level of potential real GDP and that government policymakers make the achievement of potential real GDP an important goal. In this case, government policy is addressed to closing the *GDP gap*, the difference between potential real GDP and actual real GDP. The nature of that policy depends on the value of the multiplier.

If we know the size of the GDP gap and we know the size of the spending multiplier, we can determine by how much spending needs to change in order to yield equilibrium at potential real GDP. Remember that the GDP gap equals potential real GDP minus actual real GDP:

$$\text{GDP gap} = \text{potential real GDP} - \text{actual real GDP}$$

When real GDP is less than potential real GDP, the GDP gap is the amount the GDP must rise to reach its potential. Suppose potential real GDP is $500 but the economy is in equilibrium at $300. The GDP must rise by $200 to reach potential real GDP. How much must spending rise? If we know the size of the spending multiplier, we simply divide the spending multiplier into the GDP gap to determine how much spending must rise to achieve equilibrium at potential real GDP. This required change in spending is called the **recessionary gap:**

$$\text{Recessionary gap} = \frac{\text{GDP gap}}{\text{spending multiplier}}$$

Figure 4 shows an economy in which equilibrium real GDP (Y_e) is less than potential real GDP (Y_p). The difference between the two—the GDP gap—is $200. It

6. What is the relationship between the GDP gap and the recessionary gap?

recessionary gap: the increase in expenditures required to reach potential GDP

The GDP Gap and the Recessionary Gap

In the graph, the GDP gap is $200, the difference between potential real GDP (Y_p) of $500 and equilibrium real GDP (Y_e) of $300. The GDP gap tells us that equilibrium real GDP must rise by $200 to reach equilibrium at the potential level of real GDP. The recessionary gap indicates the amount that autonomous expenditures must rise to close the GDP gap. The recessionary gap is the vertical distance between the 45-degree line and the *AE* curve at the potential level of real GDP, or $80. If autonomous expenditures are increased by $80, the *AE* curve will move up, intersecting with the 45-degree line at $500.

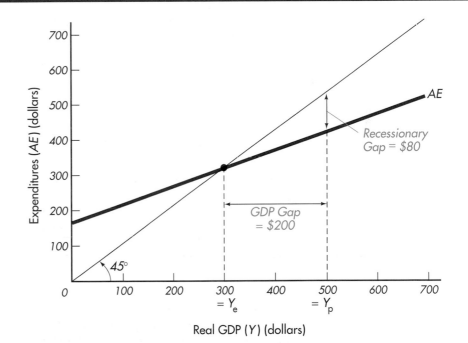

is the *horizontal* distance between equilibrium real GDP and potential real GDP. The amount that spending must rise in order for real GDP to reach a new equilibrium level of $500 is measured by the recessionary gap. The recessionary gap is the *vertical* distance between the aggregate expenditures curve and the 45-degree line at the potential real GDP level.

The recessionary gap in Figure 4 is $80:

$$\text{Recessionary gap} = \frac{\$200}{2.5}$$

$$= \$80$$

With a spending multiplier of 2.5, if aggregate expenditures rise by $80, equilibrium income rises by the $200 necessary to close the GDP gap. Government policy may be addressed to closing the gap, as an increase in government expenditures of $80 would move the economy to the potential level of real GDP in this example.

2.c. Real-World Complications

Our definition of the spending multiplier,

$$\frac{1}{MPS + MPI}$$

is a simplification of reality. Often other factors besides the *MPS* and *MPI* determine the actual multiplier in an economy. If prices rise when spending increases, the spending multiplier will not be as large as shown here. Also, taxes (which are ignored until Chapter 12, on fiscal policy) will reduce the size of the multiplier. Another factor is the treatment of imports. We have assumed that whatever is spent on imports is permanently lost to the domestic economy. For a country whose imports are a small fraction of the exports of its trading partners, this is a realistic assumption. But for a country whose imports are very important in determining the volume of exports of the rest of the world, this simple spending multiplier understates the true multiplier effect. To see why, let's examine how U.S. imports affect income in the rest of the world.

?

7. How does international trade affect the size of the multiplier?

2.c.1. Foreign Repercussions of Domestic Imports

When a resident of the United States buys goods from another country, that purchase becomes income to foreign residents. If Mike in Miami buys coral jewelry from Victor in the Dominican Republic, Mike's purchase increases Victor's income. So the import of jewelry into the United States increases income in the Dominican Republic.

Imports purchased by one country can have a large effect on the level of income in other countries. For instance, Canada and Mexico are very dependent on sales to the United States, since about 80 percent of their exports goes to the United States. South Africa, on the other hand, sells about 5 percent of its total exports to U.S. buyers. If U.S. imports from South Africa doubled, the effect on total South African exports and income would be small. But if imports from Canada or Mexico doubled, the effect on those countries' exports and income would be substantial.

Imports from the United States play a key role in determining the real GDP of the major U.S. trading partners. This is important because foreign income is a determinant of U.S. exports. As that income rises, U.S. exports rise (see Chapter 10). That is, foreign imports increase with foreign income, and some of those imports come

Next exports equal exports minus imports. These papayas being washed in Tapapulcha, Mexico, will be shipped to the United States. Once sold to a U.S. importer, the papayas represent Mexican exports and contribute to increased GDP in Mexico by means of higher net exports.

from the United States. And, of course, when foreign spending on U.S. goods increases, national income in the United States rises.

The simple spending multiplier understates the true multiplier effects of increases in autonomous expenditures because of the foreign repercussions of domestic spending. Some spending on imports comes back to the domestic economy in the form of exports. This means that the chain of spending can be different from that assumed in the simple spending multiplier. Figure 5 illustrates the difference.

Figure 5(a) shows the sequence of spending when there are no foreign repercussions from domestic imports. In this case, domestic spending rises, which causes domestic income, or real GDP, to rise. Higher domestic real GDP leads to increased spending on imports as well as further increases in domestic spending, which induce further increases in real GDP, and so on, as the multiplier process works itself out. Notice, however, that the imports are simply a leakage from the spending stream.

In Figure 5(b), the sequence of expenditures includes the foreign repercussions of domestic imports. As before, increases in domestic spending cause domestic income, or real GDP, to rise; this in turn leads to more domestic spending as well as greater domestic imports. Now, however, the greater imports increase foreign income, or real GDP, which increases foreign imports of goods produced in the domestic economy. As domestic exports rise, domestic real GDP rises. This is a more realistic view of how spending and income interact to create interdependencies among nations.

The diagrams in Figure 5 show why the multiplier effect is higher with foreign repercussions than without. Rather than complicate the multiplier definition, we continue to use the simple spending multiplier. But remember that (holding prices constant and ignoring taxes) our definition underestimates the true magnitude of the

FIGURE 5

The Sequence of Expenditures

If there are no foreign repercussions from changes in domestic income or real GDP, the simple spending multiplier holds. Increases in domestic spending increase domestic income or real GDP, which causes domestic spending—including spending on foreign goods—to rise further. Here higher expenditures on domestic imports do not have any effect on domestic exports to foreign countries.

If there are foreign repercussions from changes in domestic real GDP, the simple spending multiplier underestimates the actual effect of a change in autonomous expenditures on the equilibrium level of real GDP. As Figure 5(b) shows, increases in domestic spending increase domestic income, or real GDP, which causes domestic spending—including spending on foreign goods—to rise further. Here higher spending on foreign goods causes foreign real GDP to rise, and with it, spending on domestic exports. Higher domestic exports stimulate domestic real GDP further. The actual multiplier effect of an increase in domestic spending, then, is larger than it is when domestic imports have no effect on domestic exports.

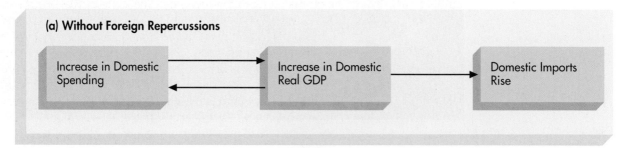

(a) Without Foreign Repercussions

Increase in Domestic Spending → Increase in Domestic Real GDP → Domestic Imports Rise

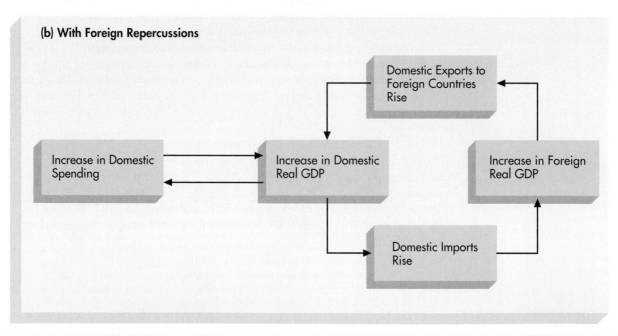

(b) With Foreign Repercussions

Increase in Domestic Spending → Increase in Domestic Real GDP → Domestic Imports Rise → Increase in Foreign Real GDP → Domestic Exports to Foreign Countries Rise → Increase in Domestic Real GDP

multiplier's effects in open economies. In fact, the foreign repercussions of domestic imports help explain the similarity in business cycles across countries. When the United States is booming, the economies of other countries that depend on exports to the U.S. market also boom. When the United States is in recession, income in these other countries tends to fall.

2.c.2. Multiplier Estimates

Many private and public organizations have developed models that are used to analyze current economic developments and to forecast future ones. A large number of these models include foreign repercussions. From these models we get a sense of just how much the simple multiplier can vary from the true multiplier.

An increase in U.S. autonomous expenditures has a multiplier of about 0.8. This means that if autonomous government expenditures increased by $25, U.S. equilibrium GDP would be $20 higher after one year. A multiplier less than 1 suggests important "leakages" in the operation of the economy. One such leakage stems from the openness of the U.S. economy. Thus, when there is an expansionary fiscal policy in the United States, the GDP of other countries is increased because some of that spending is on U.S. imports from the rest of the world. Estimates of spending multipliers indicate that the equilibrium level of GDP for the industrial countries taken as a whole increases by 0.4 times the change in U.S. expenditures. For developing countries, the multiplier effect is smaller, at 0.1. So increases in U.S. government spending have a bigger impact on the GDP of other industrial countries than on the GDP of developing countries. Because trade between industrial countries is much larger than the trade of industrial countries with developing countries, it is not surprising that increases in spending in one industrial country, like the United States, have a bigger impact on other industrial countries than on developing countries.

The multiplier examples we use in this chapter show autonomous government spending changing. It is important to realize that the multiplier effects apply to any change in autonomous expenditures in any sector of the economy.

RECAP

1. Any change in autonomous expenditures is multiplied into a larger change in the equilibrium level of real GDP.

2. The multiplier measures the change in equilibrium real GDP produced by a change in autonomous spending.

3. The multiplier equals

$$\frac{1}{\text{Leakages}} = \frac{1}{MPS + MPI}$$

4. The recessionary gap is the amount by which spending must increase in order to achieve equilibrium at potential real GDP; graphically, it is measured by the vertical distance between the 45-degree line and the aggregate expenditures curve at potential real GDP.

5. The true spending multiplier may differ from the simple spending multiplier [$1/(MPS + MPI)$] because of the foreign repercussions of domestic spending. Price changes and taxes cause the simple spending multiplier to overestimate the true multiplier.

3. Aggregate Expenditures and Aggregate Demand

The approach to macroeconomic equilibrium presented in this chapter focuses on aggregate expenditures and income. It is called the *Keynesian model*. This model of the economy can be very useful in explaining some real-world events, but it suffers from a serious drawback: the model assumes that the supply of goods and services in the economy always adjusts to aggregate expenditures, that there is no need for price changes. The Keynesian model is a *fixed-price model*.

In the real world, we find that shortages of goods and services often are met by rising prices, not just increased production. We also find that when supply increases in the face of relatively constant demand, prices may fall. In other words, prices as well as production adjust to differences between demand and supply. We introduced price as a component of macroeconomic equilibrium in Chapter 9, in the aggregate demand and supply model. You may recall that aggregate expenditures represent demand when the price level is constant. This can be demonstrated by using the income and expenditures approach developed in this chapter to derive the aggregate demand curve that was introduced in Chapter 9.

8. Why does the aggregate expenditures curve shift with changes in the price level?

3.a. Aggregate Expenditures and Changing Price Levels

As discussed in Chapter 9, the *AE* curve will shift with changes in the price level because of the wealth effect, interest rate effect, and international trade effect. Wealth is one of the nonincome determinants of consumption. Households hold part of their wealth in financial assets like money and bonds. As the price level falls, the purchasing power of money rises and aggregate expenditures increase. As the price level rises, the purchasing power of money falls and aggregate expenditures fall.

The interest rate is a determinant of investment spending. As the price level changes, interest rates may change as households and business firms change their demand for money. The change in interest rates will then affect investment spending. For instance, when the price level rises, more money is needed to buy any given quantity of goods and services. To acquire more money, households and firms sell their nonmonetary financial assets, like bonds. The increased supply of bonds will tend to raise interest rates to attract buyers. The higher interest rates will tend to lower investment spending and aggregate expenditures. Conversely, a lower price level will tend to be associated with lower interest rates, greater investment spending, and greater aggregate expenditures.

Net exports may change, causing aggregate expenditures to change, when the domestic price level changes. If domestic prices rise while foreign prices and the exchange rate are constant, then domestic goods become more expensive relative to foreign goods, and net exports and aggregate expenditures tend to fall. If domestic prices fall while foreign prices and the exchange rate are constant, then domestic goods become cheaper relative to foreign goods, and net exports and aggregate expenditures tend to rise.

3.b. Deriving the Aggregate Demand Curve

The aggregate demand curve (*AD*) shows how the equilibrium level of expenditures changes as the price level changes. In other words, the curve shows the amount people spend at different price levels. Let's use the example of Figure 6 to show how aggregate demand is derived from the shifting aggregate expenditures curve (*AE*).

FIGURE 6

Aggregate Expenditures and Aggregate Demand

Figure 6(a) shows how changes in the price level cause the AE curve to shift. The initial curve, AE_0, is drawn at the initial level of prices, P_0. On this curve, the equilibrium level of aggregate expenditures (where expenditures equal real GDP) is $500. If the price level falls to P_1, autonomous expenditures increase, shifting the curve up to AE_1, and moving the equilibrium level of aggregate expenditures to $700. If the price level rises to P_2, autonomous expenditures fall, shifting the curve down to AE_2 and moving the equilibrium level of aggregate expenditures to $300.

The aggregate demand curve *(AD)* in Figure 6(b) is derived from the aggregate expenditures curves. The AD curve shows the equilibrium level of aggregate expenditures at different price levels. At price level P_0, equilibrium aggregate expenditures are $500; at P_1, they are $700; and at P_2, they are $300.

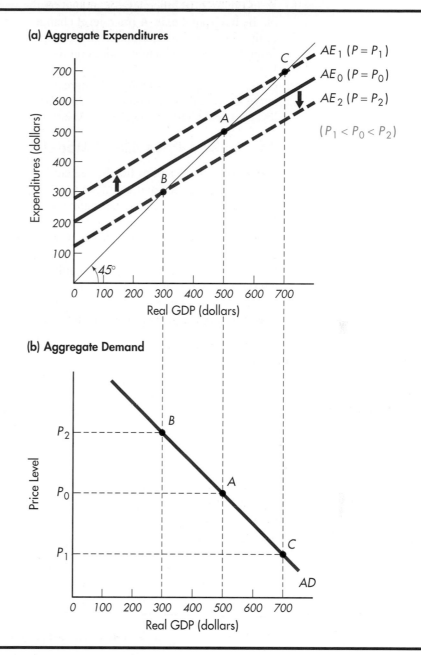

(a) Aggregate Expenditures

(b) Aggregate Demand

The aggregate demand curve is derived from the AE curve. Figure 6(a) shows three AE curves, each drawn for a different price level. Suppose that the initial equilibrium occurs at point A on curve AE_0 with prices at P_0. At this point, equilibrium real GDP and expenditures are $500. If prices fall to P_1, the AE curve shifts up to AE_1. Here equilibrium is at point C, where real GDP equals $700. If prices rise from P_0 to P_2, the AE curve falls to AE_2. Here equilibrium is at point B, where real GDP equals $300.

In Figure 6(b), price level is plotted on the vertical axis and real GDP is plotted on the horizontal axis. A price-level change here means that, on average, all prices in the economy change. The negative slope of the aggregate demand curve results from the effect of changing prices on wealth, interest rates, and international trade. If you move vertically down from points A, B, and C in Figure 6(a), you find corresponding points along the aggregate demand curve in Figure 6(b). The AD curve shows all of the combinations of price levels and corresponding equilibrium levels of real GDP and aggregate expenditures.

3.c. A Fixed-Price AD-AS Model

The Keynesian model is a fixed-price model.

The Keynesian model of fixed-price equilibrium may be considered a special case of the aggregate demand and aggregate supply equilibrium. We can define a horizontal segment of the aggregate supply curve as the Keynesian region of the curve. This represents an economy with substantial unemployment and excess capacity where real GDP and output may be increased without pressure on the price level. Figure 7 illustrates this case.

In Figure 7, the aggregate supply curve is horizontal at price level P_e. Throughout the range of the AS curve, the price level is fixed. Suppose aggregate expenditures increase for some reason other than a price-level change. For instance, consumers could expect future incomes to rise, so they increase consumption now; or business firms could expect sales to rise in the future, so they increase investment spending now; or government spending rises to improve the national highway system; or foreign prices rise so that net exports increase. If aggregate expenditures rise as a result of something other than a domestic price-level change, then the aggregate demand curve shifts to the right, like the shift from AD_1 to AD_2 in Figure 7. This increase in AD causes real GDP to rise to Y_2, yet the price level remains fixed at P_e.

FIGURE 7

A Fixed-Price AD-AS Model

If the AS curve is horizontal, then shifts in the AD curve will have no effect on the equilibrium level of prices but will change the equilibrium level of real GDP.

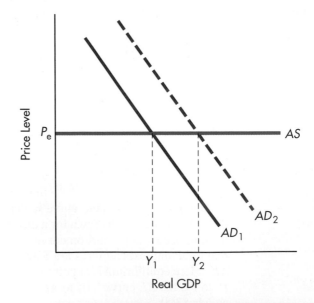

Because the fixed-price model of macroeconomic equilibrium requires a horizontal *AS* curve, many economists believe that this model is too restrictive and not representative of the modern economy. As a result, we will generally see the *AD-AS* model using upward-sloping *AS* curves so that price as well as real GDP fluctuates with shifts in aggregate demand.

R E C A P

1. As the price level rises (falls), aggregate expenditures fall (rise).
2. Aggregate demand is the equilibrium level of aggregate expenditures at alternative price levels.
3. The Keynesian fixed-price model is represented by a horizontal aggregate supply curve.

Summary

? What does equilibrium mean in macroeconomics?

1. Macroeconomic equilibrium is that point where aggregate expenditures equal real GDP. *§1.a*

? How do aggregate expenditures affect income, or real GDP?

2. When aggregate expenditures exceed income or real GDP, real GDP rises; when they are less than real GDP, real GDP falls. *§1.a*

? What are the leakages from and injections to spending?

3. Leakages are saving, taxes, and imports; injections are investment, government spending, and exports. *§1.b*

4. Equilibrium real GDP occurs where leakages equal injections. *§1.b*

? Why does equilibrium real GDP change by a multiple of a change in autonomous expenditures?

5. The effect of a change in autonomous spending is multiplied by a spiral of increased spending and income. *§2.a*

? What is the spending multiplier?

6. The spending multiplier equals the reciprocal of the sum of the *MPS* and the *MPI*. *§2.a*

? What is the relationship between the GDP gap and the recessionary gap?

7. The recessionary gap is the amount by which autonomous expenditures must change to eliminate the GDP gap and reach potential GDP. *§2.b*

? How does international trade affect the size of the spending multiplier?

8. The actual spending multiplier may be larger than the reciprocal of the sum of the *MPS* and the *MPI* because of the foreign repercussions of changes in domestic spending. *§2.c.1*

? Why does the aggregate expenditures curve shift with changes in the price level?

9. The *AE* curve shifts with changes in the price level because of the wealth effect, the interest rate effect, and the international trade effect. *§3.a*

10. The Keynesian model of fixed-price equilibrium is a special case of the *AD* and *AS* equilibrium. *§3.c*

Key Terms

spending multiplier *§2.a*

recessionary gap *§2.b*

Exercises

1. Explain the role of inventories in keeping actual expenditures equal to real GDP.

2. Rework Figure 1 assuming a closed economy (net exports equal zero at all levels of income). What is the equilibrium level of real GDP? What is the spending multiplier?

3. Draw a graph representing a hypothetical economy. Carefully label the two axes, the $S + T + IM$ curve, the $I + G + EX$ curve, and the equilibrium level of real GDP. Illustrate the effect of an increase in the level of autonomous saving.

4. Given the following information, what is the spending multiplier in each case?

   a. $MPC = .90, MPI = .10$
   b. $MPC = .90, MPI = .30$
   c. $MPC = .80, MPI = .30$
   d. $MPC = .90, MPI = 0$

5. Draw a graph representing a hypothetical economy in a recession. Carefully label the two axes, the 45-degree line, the AE curve, and the equilibrium level of real GDP. Indicate and label the GDP gap and the recessionary gap.

6. Explain the effect of foreign repercussions on the value of the spending multiplier.

7. Suppose the MPC is .80, the MPI is .10, and the income tax rate is 10 percent. What is the multiplier in this economy?

Use the information in the following table to do exercises 8–15:

Y	C	I	G	X
$100	$120	$20	$30	$10
$300	$300	$20	$30	−$10
$500	$480	$20	$30	−$30
$700	$660	$20	$30	−$50

8. What is the MPC?
9. What is the MPI?
10. What is the MPS?
11. What is the multiplier?
12. What is the equilibrium level of real GDP?
13. What is the value of autonomous consumption?
14. If government spending increases by $20, what is the new equilibrium level of real GDP?
15. What are the equations for the consumption, net exports, and aggregate expenditures functions?

16. Derive the aggregate demand curve from an aggregate expenditures diagram. Explain how aggregate demand relates to aggregate expenditures.

17. In Chapter 9, the aggregate supply (AS) curve was upward sloping. Now, in this chapter, we have a flat AS curve. What are the implications for equilibrium real GDP if AD shifts by some amount and the AS curve is perfectly flat in one economy and upward sloping in another?

ACE

Take the ACE Practice Test for this chapter to review the important concepts and get immediate feedback with answers.

economics.college.hmco.com/students

Mexico: Hostage to Its Neighbor's Troubles

Weak demand in the U.S. is becoming a big problem for Mexico's manufacturing sector.

Total Mexican industrial production in May was down 2.3% from a year ago. Construction and mining posted solid gains, but factory output fell 3.5%. The factory weakness reflects a drop-off in exports. Total manufactured exports so far in the second quarter are down 4.7% from a year ago, and most of the decline is due to falling exports to the U.S., Mexico's largest trading partner.

Two key problems are hurting Mexico's sales across the border. First, the peso has been rising against the dollar. Although it has fallen a bit from its high set in February, the peso is still 7.5% stronger than it was a year ago.

Second, Mexico's auto industry depends heavily on Detroit's Big Three, who have been losing U.S. market share. Research firm CreditSights Inc. says that in the second quarter of 2000, Mexico was exporting 125,000 vehicles per month, mostly to the U.S. and Canada. Now the monthly rate is down to 108,000, a drop of 14%.

Sagging exports are starting to fall back on the domestic economy. Retail sales edged up only 0.2% in the year ended in May. And banks are lending, but loan demand is weak despite historically low interest rates. That's because consumers and businesses are wary the economy will not rebound until the U.S. economy picks up significantly. Private analysts expect the Mexican economy will probably grow by 2% or less in 2003. Although that's better than the 0.9% gain in 2002, it will not be fast enough to keep the jobless rate from rising from June's official 3.2%.

Interest rates have been falling to levels more in line with U.S. rates, thanks in part to Mexico's continuing fiscal discipline. But any further government help will be delayed. Fiscal and labor reforms are all on the back burner until the newly elected lower house of Congress takes office in September. Expectations are that the U.S. economy will be stronger by then, allowing Mexico's export sector to boost economic growth and hiring plans.

JAMES C. COOPER and
KATHLEEN MADIGAN

Business Week/August 4, 2003

Commentary

This article reemphasizes a main point made in this chapter: countries are linked internationally, and so aggregate expenditure shifts in one country will have an impact on other nations. When other countries, like Mexico, sell goods to the United States, those exports increase Mexican GDP, since net exports is one of the components of GDP. Remembering that net exports increase with a country's GDP, we should expect net exports to vary over the business cycle. Since U.S. imports vary with U.S. GDP, slower growth in the United States tends to reduce U.S. imports, leading to lower GDP in the countries that export to the United States. Conversely, when the U.S. economy is booming, U.S. imports from Mexico will rise and stimulate GDP growth in Mexico.

The article discusses how a sluggish U.S. economy has reduced exports and economic growth for Mexico. The effect of a rapid decrease in U.S. growth will be felt more strongly in those countries that are most closely tied to the United States.

The United States had a recession in 1990 and 1991. Did the economies of the major trading partners of the United States have recessions around this time? There was a recession in Canada that roughly coincided with the U.S. recession. However, real GDP continued to grow in Germany until the fourth quarter of 1991. These numbers reflect the fact that the Canadian economy is much more integrated with that of the United States than the economy of Germany is.

We should also expect Mexico to be greatly affected by U.S. business cycles, since about 85 percent of Mexican exports go to the United States. Australia, South Africa, Sweden, and Turkey are likely to have business cycles that are more independent of U.S. influences, since their exports to the U.S. as a share of their total exports are less than 10 percent.

The international links between countries should grow over time as restrictions on international trade are removed and transportation and communication costs continue to fall. The future may be one in which national business cycles are increasingly interdependent and such interdependences will have to be given greater emphasis in national policymaking.

An Algebraic Model of Income and Expenditures Equilibrium

Continuing the example we began in the Appendix to Chapter 10, if we know the equations for each component of aggregate expenditures (*AE*), we can solve for the equilibrium level of real GDP (*Y*) for the economy represented in Figure 1 of the chapter:

$$C = \$30 + .70Y$$
$$I = \$50$$
$$G = \$70$$
$$X = \$50 - .10Y$$

Summing these components, we can find the aggregate expenditures function:

$$AE = \$30 + .70Y + \$50 + \$70 + \$50 - .10Y$$
$$= \$200 + .60Y$$

Given the *AE* function, we can solve for the equilibrium level of *Y*, where

$$Y = AE$$
$$= \$200 + .60Y$$
$$Y - .60Y = \$200$$
$$.40Y = \$200$$
$$.40Y/.40 = \$200/.40$$
$$Y = \$500$$

The Spending Multiplier   It is also possible to solve for the spending multiplier algebraically. We start by writing the general equations for each function, where C^a, I^a, G^a, EX^a, and IM^a represent autonomous consumption, investment, government spending, exports, and imports, respectively, and where *c* represents the *MPC* and *im* represents the *MPI*:

$$C = C^a + cY$$
$$I = I^a$$
$$G = G^a$$
$$X = EX^a - IM^a - imY$$

Now we sum the individual equations for the components of aggregate expenditures to get the aggregate expenditures function:

$$AE = C + I + G + X$$

$$= C^a + cY + I^a + G^a + EX^a - IM^a - imY$$

$$= (C^a + I^a + G^a + EX^a - IM^a) + cY - imY$$

We know that aggregate expenditures equal income. So

$$Y = (C^a + I^a + G^a + EX^a - IM^a) + cY - imY$$

Solving for Y, we first gather all of the terms involving Y on the left side of the equation:

$$Y[1 - (c - im)] = C^a + I^a + G^a + EX^a - IM^a$$

Next we divide each side of the equation by $[1 - (c - im)]$ to get an equation for Y:

$$Y = \frac{1}{1 - (c - im)} (C^a + I^a + G^a + EX^a - IM^a)$$

A change in autonomous expenditures causes Y to change by

$$\frac{1}{1 - (c - im)}$$

times the change in expenditures. Because c is the *MPC* and *im* is the *MPI*, the multiplier can be written

$$\frac{1}{1 - (MPC - MPI)}$$

or, since $1 - MPC = MPS$, then $1 - (MPC - MPI) = MPS + MPI$, and the spending multiplier equals

$$\frac{1}{MPS + MPI}$$

Part Three

Macroeconomic Policy

CHAPTER 12

Fiscal Policy

1. **How can fiscal policy eliminate a GDP gap?**

2. **How has U.S. fiscal policy changed over time?**

3. **What are the effects of budget deficits?**

4. **How does fiscal policy differ across countries?**

Macroeconomics plays a key role in national politics. When Jimmy Carter ran for the presidency against Gerald Ford in 1976, he created a "misery index" to measure the state of the economy. The index was the sum of the inflation rate and the unemployment rate, and Carter showed that it had risen during Ford's term in office. When Ronald Reagan challenged Carter in 1980, he used the misery index to show that inflation and unemployment had gone up during the Carter years. The implication is that presidents are responsible for the condition of the economy. If the inflation rate or the unemployment rate is relatively high coming into an election year, incumbent presidents are open to criticism by their opponents. For instance, many people believe that George Bush was defeated by Bill Clinton in 1992 because of the recession that began in 1990—a recession that was not announced as having ended in March 1991 until after the election. Clinton's 1992 campaign made economic growth a focus of its attacks on Bush, and his 1996 campaign emphasized the strength of the economy.

In 1996, a healthy economy helped Clinton defeat Bob Dole. And in the election of 2000, Gore supporters made the strong economic growth during the Clinton years a major focal point of their campaign against Bush. This was more than just campaign rhetoric, however. By law the government *is* responsible for the macroeconomic health of the nation. The Employment Act of 1946 states:

> It is the continuing policy and responsibility of the Federal Government to use all practical means consistent with its needs and obligations and other essential considerations of national policy to coordinate and utilize all its plans, functions, and resources for the purpose of creating and maintaining, in a manner calculated to foster and promote free competitive enterprise and the general welfare conditions under which there will be afforded useful employment opportunities, including self-employment for those able, willing, and seeking to work, and to promote maximum employment, production, and purchasing power.

Fiscal policy is one tool that government uses to guide the economy along an expansionary path. In this chapter we examine the role of fiscal policy—government spending and taxation—in determining the equilibrium level of income. Then we review the budget process and the history of fiscal policy in the United States. Finally we describe the difference in fiscal policy between industrial and developing countries. ■

1. Fiscal Policy and Aggregate Demand

1. How can fiscal policy eliminate a GDP gap?

The GDP gap is the difference between potential real GDP and the equilibrium level of real GDP. If the government wants to close the GDP gap so that the equilibrium level of real GDP reaches its potential, it must use fiscal policy to alter aggregate expenditures and cause the aggregate demand curve to shift.

Fiscal policy is the government's policy with respect to spending and taxation. Since aggregate demand includes consumption, investment, net exports, and government spending, government spending on goods and services affects the level of aggregate demand directly. Taxes affect aggregate demand indirectly by changing the disposable income of households, which alters consumption.

1.a. Shifting the Aggregate Demand Curve

By varying the level of government spending, policymakers can affect the level of real GDP.

Changes in government spending and taxes shift the aggregate demand curve. Remember that the aggregate demand curve represents combinations of equilibrium aggregate expenditures and alternative price levels. An increase in government spending or a decrease in taxes raises the level of expenditures at every level of prices and moves the aggregate demand curve to the right.

Figure 1 shows an increase in aggregate demand that would result from an increase in government spending or a decrease in taxes. Only if the aggregate supply curve is horizontal do prices remain fixed as aggregate demand increases. In Figure 1(a), equilibrium occurs along the horizontal segment (the Keynesian region) of the *AS* curve. If government spending increases and the price level remains constant, aggregate demand shifts from *AD* to AD_1; it increases by the horizontal distance from point *A* to point *B*. Once aggregate demand shifts, the AD_1 and *AS* curves intersect at potential real GDP, Y_p.

But Figure 1(a) is not realistic. The *AS* curve is not likely to be horizontal all the way to the level of potential real GDP; it should begin sloping up well before Y_p. And

FIGURE 1

Eliminating the Recessionary Gap: Higher Prices Mean Greater Spending

When aggregate demand increases from *AD* to *AD*₁ in Figure 1(a), equilibrium real GDP increases by the full amount of the shift in demand. This is because the aggregate supply curve is horizontal over the area of the shift in aggregate demand. In Figure 1(b), in order for equilibrium real GDP to rise from Y_e to Y_p aggregate demand must shift by more than it does in Figure 1(a). In reality, the aggregate supply curve begins to slope up before potential real GDP (Y_p) is reached, as shown in Figure 1(b) of the figure.

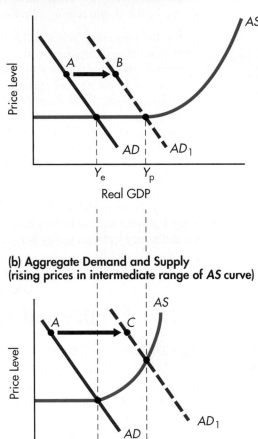

(a) Aggregate Demand and Supply
(constant prices in Keynesian range of *AS* curve)

(b) Aggregate Demand and Supply
(rising prices in intermediate range of *AS* curve)

once the economy reaches the capacity level of output, the *AS* curve should become a vertical line, as shown in Figure 1(b).

If the *AS* curve slopes up before reaching the potential real GDP level, as it does in Figure 1(b), expenditures have to go up by more than the amount suggested in Figure 1(a) for the economy to reach Y_p. Why? Because when prices rise, the effect of spending on real GDP is reduced. This effect is shown in Figure 1(b). To increase the equilibrium level of real GDP from Y_e to Y_p, aggregate demand must shift by the amount from point *A* to point *C*, a larger increase than that shown in Figure 1(a), where the price level is fixed.

1.b. Multiplier Effects

Changes in government spending may have an effect on real GDP that is a multiple of the original change in government spending; a $1 change in government spending may increase real GDP by more than $1. This is because the original $1 of expenditure is spent over and over again in the economy as it passes from person to person. The government spending multiplier measures the multiple by which an increase in government spending increases real GDP. Similarly, a change in taxes may have an effect on real GDP that is a multiple of the original change in taxes. (The appendix to this chapter provides an algebraic analysis of the government spending and tax multipliers.)

If the price level rises as real GDP increases, the multiplier effects of any given change in aggregate demand are smaller than they would be if the price level remained constant. In addition to changes in the price level modifying the effect of government spending and taxes on real GDP, there are other factors that affect how much real GDP will change following a change in government spending. One such factor is how the government pays for, or finances, its spending.

Government spending must be financed by some combination of taxing, borrowing, and creating money:

$$\text{Government spending} = \text{taxes} + \text{change in government debt} + \text{change in government-issued money}$$

In Chapter 14 we discuss the effect of financing government spending by creating money. As you will see, this source of government financing is relied on heavily in some developing countries. Here we talk about the financing problem relevant for industrial countries: how taxes and government debt can modify the expansionary effect of government spending on national income.

1.c. Government Spending Financed by Tax Increases

Suppose that government spending rises by $100 billion and that this expenditure is financed by a tax increase of $100 billion. Such a "balanced-budget" change in fiscal policy will cause equilibrium real GDP to rise. This is because government spending increases aggregate expenditures directly, but higher taxes lower aggregate expenditures indirectly, through consumption spending. For instance, if taxes increase by $100, consumers will not cut their spending by $100 but will cut it by some fraction, say 9/10, of the increase. If consumers spend 90 percent of a change in their disposable income, then a tax increase of $100 would lower consumption by $90. So the net effect of raising government spending and taxes by the same amount is an increase in aggregate demand, illustrated in Figure 2 as the shift from AD to AD_1. However, it may be incorrect to assume that the only thing that changes is aggregate demand. An increase in taxes may also affect aggregate supply.

Aggregate supply measures the output that producers offer for sale at different levels of prices. When taxes go up, workers have less incentive to work because their after-tax income is lower. The cost of taking a day off or extending a vacation for a few extra days is less than it is when taxes are lower and after-tax income is higher. When taxes go up, then, output can fall, causing the aggregate supply curve to shift to the left. Such supply-side effects of taxes have been emphasized by the so-called supply-side economists, as discussed in the Economic Insight "Supply-Side Economics and the Laffer Curve."

Figure 2 shows the possible effects of an increase in government spending financed by taxes. The economy is initially in equilibrium at point A, with prices at P_1 and real GDP at Y_1. The increase in government spending shifts the aggregate demand curve from AD to AD_1. If this was the only change, the economy would be in equilibrium at point B. But if the increase in taxes reduces output, the aggregate supply curve moves back from AS to AS_1, and output does not expand all the way to

FIGURE 2

The Effect of Taxation on Aggregate Supply

An increase in government spending shifts the aggregate demand curve from *AD* to *AD₁*, moving equilibrium from point *A* to point *B,* and equilibrium real GDP from Y_1 to Y_p. If higher taxes reduce the incentive to work, aggregate supply could fall from *AS* to *AS₁*, moving equilibrium to point *C* and equilibrium real GDP to Y_2, a level below potential real GDP.

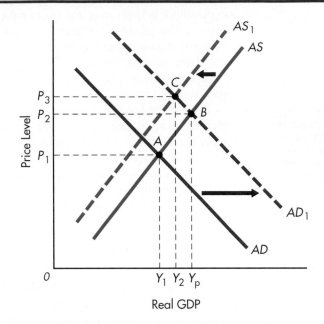

Y_p. The decrease in aggregate supply creates a new equilibrium at point *C*. Here real GDP is at Y_2 (less than Y_p) and the price level is P_3 (higher than P_2).

The standard analysis of government spending and taxation assumes that aggregate supply is not affected by the change in fiscal policy, leading us to expect a greater change in real GDP than may actually occur. If tax changes do affect aggregate supply, the expansionary effects of government spending financed by tax increases are moderated. The actual magnitude of the effect is the subject of debate

Fiscal policy includes government spending on the provision of goods and services. In this photo, firemen in Wertheim, Germany, are involved in rescue work following a major flood. Police and fire protection are typically provided by government and funded by taxpayers.

Supply-Side Economics and the Laffer Curve

The large budget deficits incurred by the U.S. government in the 1980s were in part a product of lower tax rates engineered by the Reagan administration. President Reagan's economic team took office in January 1981 hoping that lower taxes would stimulate the supply of goods and services to a level that would raise tax revenues even though tax rates as a percentage of income had been cut. These arguments were repeated in 1995 by members of Congress pushing for tax-rate cuts. This emphasis on greater incentives to produce created by lower taxes has come to be known as *supply-side economics.*

The most widely publicized element of supply-side economics was the *Laffer curve.* The curve is drawn with the tax rate on the vertical axis and tax revenue on the horizontal axis. When the rate of taxation is zero, there is no tax revenue. As the tax rate increases, tax revenue increases up to a point. The assumption here is that there is some rate of taxation that is so high that it discourages productive activity. Once this rate is reached, tax revenue begins to fall as the rate of taxation goes up. In the graph, tax revenue is maximized at R_{max} with a tax rate of t percent. Any increase in the rate of taxation above t percent produces lower tax revenues. In the extreme case—a 100 percent tax rate—no one is willing to work because the government taxes away all income.

Critics of the supply-side tax cuts proposed by the Reagan administration argued that lower taxes would increase the budget deficit. Supply-side advocates

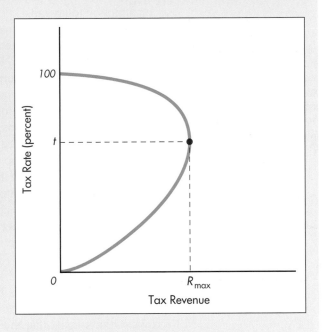

insisted that if the United States were in the backward-bending region of the Laffer curve (above t percent in the graph), tax cuts would actually raise, not lower, tax revenue. The evidence following the tax cuts indicates that the tax cuts did, however, contribute to a larger budget deficit, implying that the U.S. was not on the backward-bending portion of the Laffer curve.

among economists. Most argue that the evidence in the United States indicates that tax increases have a fairly small effect on aggregate supply.

1.d. Government Spending Financed by Borrowing

The standard multiplier analysis of government spending does not differentiate among the different methods of financing that spending. Yet you just saw how taxation can offset at least part of the expansionary effect of higher government spending. Borrowing to finance government spending can also limit the increase in aggregate demand.

A government borrows funds by selling bonds to the public. These bonds represent debt that must be repaid at a future date. Debt is, in a way, a kind of substitute for current taxes. Instead of increasing current taxes to finance higher spending, the government borrows the savings of households and businesses. Of course the debt will mature and have to be repaid. This means that taxes will have to be higher in the future in order to provide the government with the funds to pay off the debt.

Current government borrowing, then, implies higher future taxes. This can limit the expansionary effect of increased government spending. If households and businesses take higher future taxes into account, they tend to save more today so that they will be able to pay those taxes in the future. And as saving today increases, consumption today falls.

The idea that current government borrowing can reduce current nongovernment expenditures was suggested originally by the early-nineteenth-century English economist David Ricardo. Ricardo recognized that government borrowing could function like increased current taxes, reducing current household and business expenditures. *Ricardian equivalence* is the principle that government spending activities financed by taxation or borrowing have the same effect on the economy. If Ricardian equivalence holds, it doesn't matter whether the government raises taxes or borrows more to finance increased spending. The effect is the same: private-sector spending falls by the same amount today, and this drop in private spending will at least partially offset the expansionary effect of government spending on real GDP. Just how much private spending drops (and how far to the left the aggregate demand curve shifts) depends on the degree to which current saving increases in response to expected higher taxes. The less that people respond to the future tax liabilities arising from current government debt, the smaller the reduction in private spending.

Ricardian equivalence holds if taxation and government borrowing both have the same effect on spending in the private sector.

There is substantial disagreement among economists over the extent to which current government borrowing acts like an increase in taxes. Some argue that it makes no difference whether the government raises current taxes or borrows. Others insist that the public does not base current spending on future tax liabilities. If the first group is correct, we would expect government spending financed by borrowing to have a smaller effect than if the second group is correct. Research on the issue continues, with most economists questioning the relevance of Ricardian equivalence and a small but influential group arguing its importance.

1.e. Crowding Out

Expansionary fiscal policy can crowd out private-sector spending; that is, an increase in government spending can reduce consumption and investment. **Crowding out** is usually discussed in the context of government spending financed by borrowing rather than by taxing. We have just seen how future taxes can cause consumption to fall today, but investment can also be affected. Increases in government borrowing drive up interest rates. As interest rates go up, investment falls. This sort of indirect crowding out works through the bond market. The U.S. government borrows by selling Treasury bonds or bills. Because the government is not a profit-making institution, it does not have to earn a profitable return on the money it raises by selling bonds. A corporation does, however. When interest rates rise, fewer corporations offer new bonds to raise investment funds because the cost of repaying the bond debt may exceed the rate of return on the investment.

crowding out: a drop in consumption or investment spending caused by government spending

Crowding out, like Ricardian equivalence, is important in principle, but economists have never demonstrated conclusively that its effects can substantially alter spending in the private sector. Still, you should be aware of the possibility in order to understand the potential shortcomings of changes in government spending and taxation.

2. How has U.S. fiscal policy changed over time?

2. Fiscal Policy in the United States

Our discussion of fiscal policy assumes that policy is made at the federal level. In the modern economy, this is a reasonable assumption. This was not the case before the 1930s, however. Before the Depression, the federal government limited its activities largely to national defense and foreign policy, and left other areas of government policy to the individual states. With the growth in the importance of the federal government in fiscal policy has come a growth in the role of the federal budget process.

2.a. The Budget Process

Fiscal policy in the United States is the product of a complex process that involves both the executive and legislative branches of government (Figure 3). The fiscal year for the U.S. government begins October 1 of one year and ends September 30 of the next. The budget process begins each spring, when the president directs the federal agencies to prepare their budgets for the fiscal year that starts almost 18 months later. The agencies submit their budget requests to the Office of Management and Budget (OMB) by early September. The OMB reviews and modifies each agency's request and consolidates all of the proposals into a budget that the president presents to Congress in January.

Once Congress receives the president's budget, the Congressional Budget Office (CBO) studies it and committees modify it before funds are appropriated. The budget is evaluated in Budget Committee hearings in both the House of Representatives and the Senate. In addition, the CBO reports to Congress on the validity of the economic assumptions made in the president's budget. A budget resolution is passed by April 15 that sets out major expenditures and estimated revenues. (Revenues are estimated because future tax payments can never be known exactly.) The resolution is followed by *reconciliation,* a process in which each committee of Congress must coordinate relevant tax and spending decisions. Once the reconciliation process is completed, funds are appropriated. The process is supposed to end before Congress recesses for the summer, at the end of June. When one is talking about the federal budget, the monetary amounts of various categories of

The Taxpayer's Federal Government Credit Card Statement

Suppose the U.S. government's expenditures and revenues were accounted for annually to each individual income taxpayer like a credit card statement. For 2002, the statement would look like the table to the right.

Statement for 2002 Budget Year		
Previous balance (your average taxpayer share of the beginning-of-year national debt)		**$45,176.47**
New purchases during the year (your average taxpayer share)		
Social security	$3,440.65	
National defense	2,627.57	
Income security	2,355.85	
Medicare	1,740.29	
Commerce and housing credit	−2.90	
Health	1,481.65	
Education, training, and employment	531.79	
Veterans' benefits and services	384.34	
Transportation	466.34	
Natural resources and environment	222.04	
Science, space, and technology	156.59	
International affairs	168.54	
Agriculture	167.26	
Administration of justice	258.69	
General government	131.06	
Community and regional development	97.93	
Energy	3.64	
Payments received—Thank you (your average taxpayer share)		
Individual income and social security taxes		$11,753.26
Corporate income taxes		1,116.02
Other		1,100.80
Finance charge (your average taxpayer share of net interest on the national debt)	**$1,288.71**	
New balance due (your average taxpayer share of the end-of-year national debt)		**$46,726.43**

FIGURE 3

The Making of U.S. Fiscal Policy

The flow chart shows the policymaking process. Start with the president and follow the arrows in order. Although the dates are approximate, the process of

setting the federal budget involves these stages and participants.

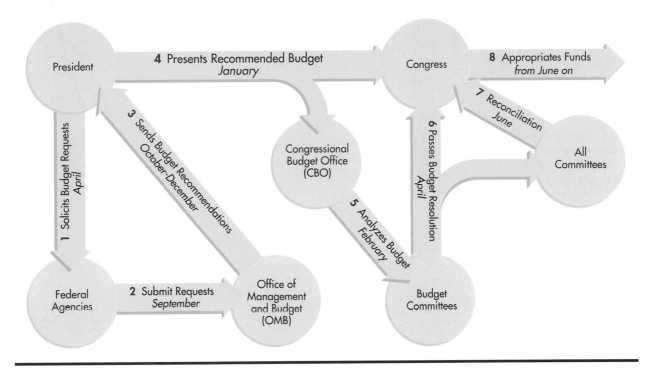

expenditures are so huge that they are often difficult to comprehend. But if you were to divide up the annual budget by the number of individual taxpayers, you'd come up with an average individual statement that might make more sense, as shown in the Economic Insight "The Taxpayer's Federal Government Credit Card Statement."

The federal budget is determined as much by politics as by economics. Politicians respond to different groups of voters by supporting different government programs regardless of the needed fiscal policy. It is the political response to constituents that tends to drive up federal budget deficits (the difference between government expenditures and tax revenues), not the need for expansionary fiscal policy. As a result, deficits have become commonplace.

2.b. The Historical Record

The U.S. government has grown dramatically since the early part of the century. Figure 4 shows federal revenues and expenditures over time. Note that expenditures were lower than revenues in the 1998–2001 period. Figure 5 places the growth of government in perspective by plotting U.S. government spending as a percentage of gross domestic product over time. Before the Great Depression, federal spending was approximately 3 percent of the GDP; by the end of the Depression, it had risen to about 10 percent. The ratio of spending to GDP reached its peak during World War II, when federal spending hit 44 percent of the GDP. After the war, the ratio fell

FIGURE 4

U.S. Government Revenues and Expenditures

Revenues are total revenues of the U.S. government in each fiscal year. Expenditures are total spending of the U.S. government in each fiscal year. The difference between the two curves equals the U.S. budget deficit (when expenditures exceed revenues) or surplus (when revenues exceed expenditures).
Source: Data are drawn from Economic Report of the President, 2003.

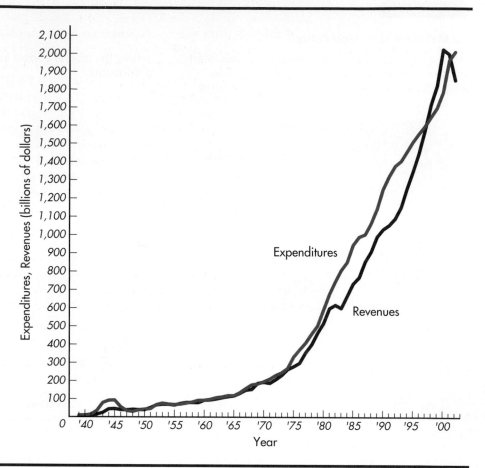

FIGURE 5

U.S. Government Expenditures as a Percentage of Gross Domestic Product

U.S. federal government spending as a percentage of the GDP reached a high of 44 percent in 1943 and 1944. Discounting wartime spending and cutbacks after the war, you can see the upward trend in U.S. government spending, which has constituted a larger and larger share of the GDP until the early 1980s.

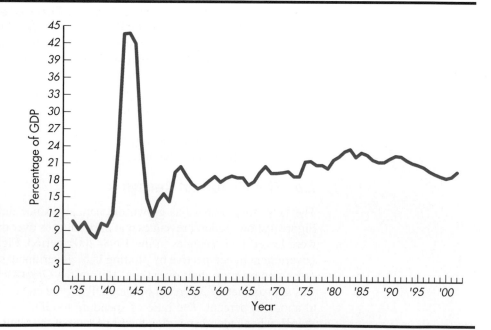

dramatically and then slowly increased to a peak of about 24 percent in 1983. In recent years, the ratio has been a little less than 20 percent.

Fiscal policy has two components: discretionary fiscal policy and automatic stabilizers. **Discretionary fiscal policy** refers to changes in government spending and taxation aimed at achieving a policy goal. **Automatic stabilizers** are elements of fiscal policy that automatically change in value as national income changes. Figures 4 and 5 suggest that government spending is dominated by growth over time. But there is no indication here of discretionary changes in fiscal policy, changes in government spending and taxation aimed at meeting specific policy goals. Perhaps a better way to evaluate the fiscal policy record is in terms of the budget deficit. Government expenditures can rise, but the effect on aggregate demand could be offset by a simultaneous increase in taxes, so that there is no expansionary effect on the equilibrium level of national income. By looking at the deficit, we see the combined spending and tax policy results that are missing if only government expenditures are considered.

Figure 6 illustrates the pattern of the U.S. federal deficit and the deficit as a percentage of GDP over time. Figure 6(a) shows that the United States ran close to a balanced budget for much of the 1950s and 1960s. There were large deficits associated with financing World War II, and then large deficits resulting from fiscal policy decisions in the 1970s, 1980s, and 1990s. By 1998, however, the first surplus since

discretionary fiscal policy: changes in government spending and taxation aimed at achieving a policy goal

automatic stabilizer: an element of fiscal policy that changes automatically as income changes

FIGURE 6

The U.S. Deficit

As Figure 6(a) shows, since 1940 the U.S. government has rarely shown a surplus. For much of the 1950s and 1960s, the United States was close to a balanced budget. Figure 6(b) shows the federal deficit as a percentage of GDP. The deficits during the 1950s and 1960s generally were small. The early 1980s were a time of rapid growth in the federal budget deficit, and this is reflected in the growth of the deficit as a percentage of GDP.

(a) Federal Surplus (+) or Deficit (−)

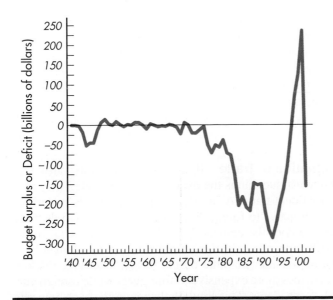

(b) Federal Deficit as a Percent of GDP (absolute value of deficit)

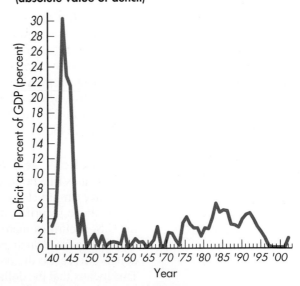

1969 was recorded. Figure 6(b) shows that the deficit as a percentage of GDP was much larger during World War II than in the 1980s and 1990s.

The deficit increase in the mid-1970s was a product of a recession that cut the growth of tax revenues. Historically, aside from wartime, budget deficits increase the most during recessions. When real GDP falls, tax revenues go down and government spending on unemployment and welfare benefits goes up. These are examples of automatic stabilizers in action. As income falls, taxes fall and personal benefit payments rise to partially offset the effect of the drop in income. The rapid growth of the deficit in the 1980s involved more than the recessions in 1980 and 1982, however. The economy grew rapidly after the 1982 recession ended, but so did the fiscal deficit. The increase in the deficit was the product of a rapid increase in government spending to fund new programs and enlarge existing programs while taxes were held constant. In the late 1990s the deficit decreased. This was the result of surprisingly large tax revenue gains, generated by strong economic growth, combined with only moderate government spending increases. The deficit is likely to reach all-time highs in the next few years, however, because the slowdown in U.S. economic growth will depress tax revenues while government spending for defense and homeland security rises.

2.c. Deficits and the National Debt

3. What are the effects of budget deficits?

The large federal deficits of the 1980s and 1990s led many observers to question whether a deficit can harm the economy. Figure 6 shows how the fiscal deficit has changed over time. One major implication of a large deficit is the resulting increase in the national debt, the total stock of government bonds outstanding. Table 1 lists data on the debt of the United States. Notice that the total debt doubled between 1981 ($994.8 billion) and 1986 ($2,120.6 billion), and then doubled again between 1986 and 1993. Column 3 shows debt as a percentage of GDP. In the late 1990s, the debt was falling as a percentage of GDP. During World War II, the debt was greater than the GDP for five years. Despite the talk of "unprecedented" federal deficits in the 1980s and 1990s, clearly the ratio of the debt to GDP was by no means unprecedented.

We have not yet answered the question of whether deficits are bad. To do so, we have to consider their potential effects.

2.c.1. Deficits, Interest Rates, and Investment Because government deficits mean government borrowing and debt, many economists argue that deficits raise interest rates. Increased government borrowing raises interest rates; this in turn can depress investment. (Remember that as interest rates rise, the rate of return on investment drops, along with the incentive to invest.) What happens when government borrowing crowds out private investment? Lower investment means fewer capital goods in the future. So deficits lower the level of output in the economy, both today and in the future. In this sense, deficits are potentially bad.

Through their effect on investment, deficits can lower the level of output in the economy.

2.c.2. Deficits and International Trade If government deficits raise real interest rates (the nominal interest rate minus the expected inflation rate), they also may have an effect on international trade. A higher real return on U.S. securities makes those securities more attractive to foreign investors. As the foreign demand for U.S. securities increases, so does the demand for U.S. dollars in exchange for Japanese yen, British pounds, and other foreign currencies. As the demand for dollars increases, the dollar *appreciates* in value on the foreign exchange market. This means that the dollar becomes more expensive to foreigners while foreign currency becomes cheaper to U.S. residents. This kind of change in the exchange rate

TABLE 1

Debt of the U.S. Government (dollar amounts in billions)

(1) Year	(2) Total Debt	(3) Debt/GDP (percent)	(4) Net Interest	(5) Interest/Government Spending (percent)
1958	$ 279.7	63	$ 5.6	6.8
1960	$ 290.5	57	6.9	7.5
1962	$ 302.9	55	6.9	6.5
1964	$ 316.1	50	$ 8.2	6.9
1966	$ 328.5	44	$ 9.4	7.0
1968	$ 368.7	43	$ 11.1	6.2
1970	$ 380.9	39	$ 14.4	7.4
1972	$ 435.9	38	$ 15.5	6.7
1974	$ 483.9	34	$ 21.4	8.0
1976	$ 629.0	37	$ 26.7	7.3
1978	$ 776.6	36	$ 35.4	7.9
1980	$ 909.1	34	$ 52.5	9.1
1981	$ 994.8	34	$ 68.8	10.5
1982	$1,137.3	36	$ 85.0	11.6
1983	$1,371.7	41	$ 89.8	11.2
1984	$1,564.7	42	$111.1	13.2
1985	$1,817.5	46	$129.5	13.6
1986	$2,120.6	50	$136.0	13.7
1987	$2,396.1	53	$138.7	13.8
1988	$2,601.3	54	$151.8	14.3
1989	$2,868.0	55	$169.3	14.8
1990	$3,206.6	56	$184.2	14.7
1991	$3,598.5	61	$194.5	14.7
1992	$4,002.1	65	$199.4	14.4
1993	$4,351.4	67	$198.8	14.1
1994	$4,643.7	66	$203.0	13.9
1995	$4,921.0	66	$232.2	15.3
1996	$5,181.9	66	$241.1	15.5
1997	$5,369.7	65	$244.0	15.2
1998	$5,478.7	63	$241.2	14.6
1999	$5,606.1	61	$229.7	13.5
2000	$5,628.7	57	$222.9	12.5
2001	$5,769.9	57	$206.2	11.1
2002	$6,198.4	59	$171.0	8.5

encourages U.S. residents to buy more foreign goods, and foreign residents to buy fewer U.S. goods. Ultimately, then, as deficits and government debt increase, U.S. net exports fall. Many economists believe that the growing fiscal deficits of the 1980s were responsible for the record decline in U.S. net exports during that period.

The U.S. federal budget deficit rose from $73.8 billion in 1980 to $212.3 billion in 1985. During this time, the dollar appreciated in value from 1.95 German marks per dollar to 3.32 marks per dollar and from 203 Japanese yen per dollar to 260 yen per dollar. These changes in the dollar exchange rate caused U.S. goods to rise in price to foreign buyers. For instance, a $1,000 IBM personal computer would sell for 1,950 German marks at the exchange rate of 1.95 marks per dollar. But at the rate of 3.32 marks per dollar, the $1,000 computer would sell for 3,320 marks. Furthermore, foreign currencies became cheaper to U.S. residents, making foreign goods cheaper in dollars. In 1980, one German mark sold for $.51. In 1985, one mark sold for $.30. At these prices, a Volkswagen wheel that sold for 100 marks would have changed in dollar price from $51 to $30 as the exchange rate changed. The combination of the dollar price of U.S. imports falling and the foreign currency price of U.S. exports rising caused U.S. net exports to fall dramatically at the same time that the fiscal deficit rose dramatically. Such foreign trade effects are another potentially bad effect of deficits.

2.c.3. Interest Payments on the National Debt   The national debt is the stock of government bonds outstanding. It is the product of past and current budget deficits. As the size of the debt increases, the interest that must be paid on the debt tends to rise. Column 4 of Table 1 lists the amount of interest paid on the debt; column 5 lists the interest as a percentage of government expenditures. The numbers in both columns have risen steadily over time and only recently started to drop.

The increase in the interest cost of the national debt is an aspect of fiscal deficits that worries some people. However, to the extent that U.S. citizens hold government bonds, we owe the debt to ourselves. The tax liability of funding the interest payments is offset by the interest income bondholders earn. In this case there is no net change in national wealth when the national debt changes.

Of course, we do not owe the national debt just to ourselves. The United States is the world's largest national financial market, and many U.S. securities, including government bonds, are held by foreign residents. Today, foreign holdings of the U.S. national debt amount to about 17 percent of the outstanding debt. Because the tax liability for paying the interest on the debt falls on U.S. taxpayers, the greater the payments made to foreigners, the lower the wealth of U.S. residents, other things being equal.

Other things are not equal, however. To understand the real impact of foreign holdings on the economy, we have to evaluate what the economy would have been like if the debt had not been sold to foreign investors. If the foreign savings placed in U.S. bonds allowed the United States to increase investment and its productive capacity beyond what would have been possible in the absence of foreign lending, then the country could very well be better off for selling government bonds to foreigners. The presence of foreign funds may keep interest rates lower than they would otherwise be, preventing the substantial crowding out associated with an increase in the national debt.

So while deficits are potentially bad as a result of the crowding out of investment, larger trade deficits with the rest of the world, and greater interest costs of the debt, we cannot generally say that all deficits are bad. It depends on what benefit the deficit provides. If the deficit spending allowed for greater productivity than would have occurred otherwise, the benefits may outweigh the costs.

2.d. Automatic Stabilizers

We have largely been talking about discretionary fiscal policy, the changes in government spending and taxing that policymakers make consciously. *Automatic stabilizers* are the elements of fiscal policy that change automatically as income changes. Automatic stabilizers partially offset changes in income: as income falls, automatic stabilizers increase spending; as income rises, automatic stabilizers decrease spending. Any program that responds to fluctuations in the business cycle in a way that moderates the effect of those fluctuations is an automatic stabilizer. Examples are progressive income taxes and transfer payments.

In our examples of tax changes, we have been using *lump-sum taxes*—taxes that are a flat dollar amount regardless of income. However, income taxes are determined as a percentage of income. In the United States, the federal income tax is a **progressive tax:** as income rises, so does the rate of taxation. A person with a very low income pays no income tax, while a person with a high income can pay more than a third of that income in taxes. Countries use different rates of taxation on income. Taxes can be *regressive* (the tax rate falls as income rises) or *proportional* (the tax rate is constant as income rises) as well as progressive. But most countries, including the United States, use a progressive tax, with which the percentage of income paid as taxes rises with taxable income.

progressive tax: a tax whose rate rises as income rises

Progressive income taxes act as an automatic stabilizer. As income falls, so does the average tax rate. Suppose a household earning $60,000 must pay 30 percent of its income ($18,000) in taxes, leaving 70 percent of its income ($42,000) for spending. If that household's income drops to $40,000 and the tax rate falls to 25 percent, the household has 75 percent of its income ($30,000) available for spending. But if the tax rate is 30 percent at all levels of income, the household earning $40,000 would have only 70 percent of its income ($28,000) to spend. By allowing a greater percentage of earned income to be spent, progressive taxes help offset the effect of lower income on spending.

All industrial countries have progressive federal income tax systems. For instance, the tax rate in Japan starts at 10 percent for low-income households and rises to a maximum of 40 percent for high-income households. In the United States, individual income tax rates start at 15 percent and rise to a maximum of 39.6 percent. In the U.K. tax system, rates rise from 10 percent to 40 percent, while tax rates in Germany rise from 23.9 to 53 percent and those in France, from 10.5 to 54 percent.

transfer payment: a payment to one person that is funded by taxing others

A **transfer payment** is a payment to one person that is funded by taxing others. Food stamps, welfare benefits, and unemployment benefits are all government transfer payments: current taxpayers provide the funds to pay those who qualify for the programs. Transfer payments that use income to establish eligibility act as automatic stabilizers. In a recession, as income falls, more people qualify for food stamps or welfare benefits, raising the level of transfer payments.

Unemployment insurance is also an automatic stabilizer. As unemployment rises, more workers receive unemployment benefits. Unemployment benefits tend to rise in a recession and fall during an expansion. This countercyclical pattern of benefit payments offsets the effect of business-cycle fluctuations on consumption.

RECAP

1. Fiscal policy in the United States is a product of the budget process.
2. Federal spending in the United States has grown rapidly over time, from just 3 percent of the GDP before the Great Depression to approximately 19 percent of the GDP at the end of the 1990s.
3. Government budget deficits can hurt the economy through their effect on interest rates and private investment, net exports, and the tax burden on current and future taxpayers.
4. Automatic stabilizers are government programs that are already in place and that respond automatically to fluctuations in the business cycle, moderating the effect of those fluctuations.

3. Fiscal Policy in Different Countries

4. How does fiscal policy differ across countries?

A country's fiscal policy reflects its philosophy toward government spending and taxation. In this section we present comparative data that demonstrate the variety of fiscal policies in the world.

3.a. Government Spending

Government spending has grown over time as a fraction of GNP in all industrial countries.

Our discussion to this point has centered on U.S. fiscal policy. But fiscal policy and the role of government in the economy can be very different across countries. Government has played an increasingly larger role in the major industrial countries over time. Table 2 shows how government spending has gone up as a percentage of output in five industrial nations. In every case, government spending accounted for a larger percentage of output in 2001 than it did 100 years earlier. For instance, in 1880, government spending was only 6 percent of the GNP in Sweden. By 1929 it had risen to 8 percent; and by 2001, to 26 percent.

Historically, in industrial countries, the growth of government spending has been matched by growth in revenues. But in the 1960s, government spending began to grow faster than revenues, creating increasingly larger debtor nations.

Developing countries have not shown the uniform growth in government spending found in industrial countries. In fact, in some developing countries (for instance, Chile, the Dominican Republic, and Peru), government spending is a smaller percentage of GDP today than it was twenty years ago. And we find a greater variation in the role of government in developing countries.

One important difference between the typical developed country and the typical developing country is that government plays a larger role in investment spending in the developing country. One reason for this difference is that state-owned enterprises account for a larger percentage of economic activity in developing countries than they do in developed countries. Also, developing countries usually rely more on government rather than the private sector to build their infrastructure—schools, roads, hospitals—than do developed countries.

How a government spends its money is a function of its income. Here we find differences not only between industrial and developing countries but also among developing countries. Figure 7 reports central government spending for the United States, an industrial country, and two large developing countries: Russia, a middle-income developing country, and China, a low-income developing country. It clearly illustrates the relative importance of social welfare spending in industrial and developing countries. Although standards of living are lowest in the poorest countries,

TABLE 2					
Share of Government Spending in GNP in Selected Industrial Countries, 1880, 1929, and 2001 (percent)	**Year**	**France**	**Germany**	**Sweden**	**United Kingdom**	**United States**

Year	France	Germany	Sweden	United Kingdom	United States
1880	15	10*	6	10	8
1929	19	31	8	24	10
2001	23	19	26	19	14

*1881

Source: Data are drawn from World Bank, *World Development Report 1996* and *2003*.

FIGURE 7

Central Government Spending by Functional Category

The charts show the pattern of government spending in an industrial country, the United States; a middle-income developing country, Russia; and a low-income developing country, China. Social programs (education, health, and housing, social security, and welfare) account for 55 percent of federal government expenditures in the United States, but only 37 percent in Russia and 6 percent in China. *Source: Data are drawn from International Monetary Fund,* Government Finance Statistics Yearbook, 2002.

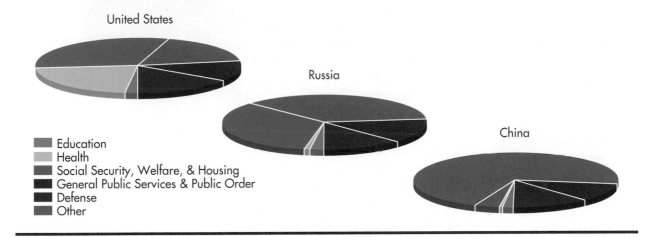

United States

Russia

China

- Education
- Health
- Social Security, Welfare, & Housing
- General Public Services & Public Order
- Defense
- Other

these countries do not have the resources to spend on social services (education, health, housing, social security, welfare). The United States spends 55 percent of its budget on social programs. Russia spends 37 percent of its budget on social programs, while a low-income developing country like China spends only 6 percent of its budgets on these programs.

3.b. Taxation

There are two different types of taxes: *direct taxes* (on individuals and firms) and *indirect taxes* (on goods and services). Figure 8 compares the importance of different sources of central government tax revenue across industrial countries and developing countries in Asia. The most obvious difference is that personal income taxes are much more important in industrial countries than in developing countries. Why? Because personal taxes are hard to collect in agricultural nations, where a large percentage of household production is for personal consumption. Taxes on businesses are easier to collect, and thus are more important in developing countries.

That industrial countries are better able to afford social programs is reflected in the great disparity in social security taxes between industrial countries and developing countries. With so many workers living near the subsistence level in the poorest countries, their governments simply cannot tax workers for retirement and health security programs.

Figure 8 also shows that taxes on international trade are very important in developing countries. Because goods arriving or leaving a country must pass through customs inspection, export and import taxes are relatively easy to collect compared to income taxes. In general, developing countries depend more heavily on indirect taxes on goods and services than do developed countries.

FIGURE 8

Central Government Tax Composition by Income Group

When we group countries by income level, the importance of different sources of tax revenue is obvious. Domestic income taxes account for roughly a third of government revenue in industrial and middle-income developing countries and a quarter of government revenue in developing countries. However, personal income taxes are more important in industrial countries, while business income taxes are more important in developing countries. Social security taxes are a major source of government revenue in industrial countries; they are less important in developing countries, which cannot afford social programs. International trade taxes represent just 1 percent of tax revenues in industrial countries; developing countries rely heavily on these taxes. (Note: Percentages do not total 100 because of rounding.) *Source: Data are drawn from* Government Finance Statistics, 2002.

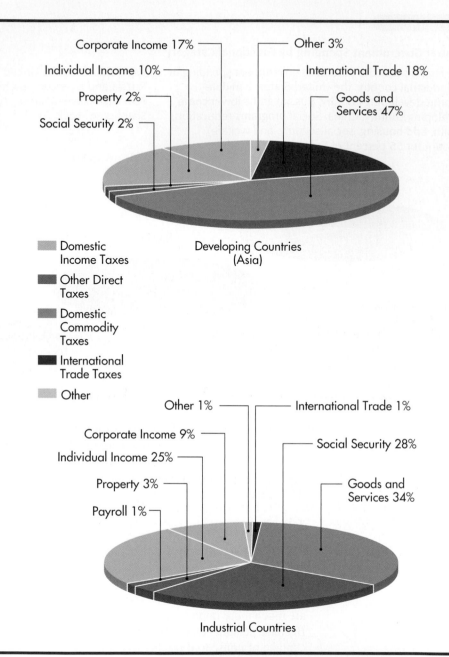

Corporate Income 17%
Individual Income 10%
Property 2%
Social Security 2%
Other 3%
International Trade 18%
Goods and Services 47%

Domestic Income Taxes
Other Direct Taxes
Domestic Commodity Taxes
International Trade Taxes
Other

Developing Countries (Asia)

Other 1%
Corporate Income 9%
Individual Income 25%
Property 3%
Payroll 1%
International Trade 1%
Social Security 28%
Goods and Services 34%

Industrial Countries

value-added tax (VAT): a general sales tax collected at each stage of production

Figure 8 lists "Goods and Services" taxes. Of these, 65 percent are **value-added taxes (VATs)** for industrial countries, while 61 percent of developing country commodity taxes come from value-added taxes. A value-added tax is an indirect tax imposed on each sale at each stage of production. Each seller from the first stage of production on collects the VAT from the buyer, then deducts any VATs it has paid in buying its inputs. The difference is remitted to the government. From time to time, Congress has debated the merits of a VAT in the United States, but it has never approved this kind of tax. The Global Business Insight "Value-Added Tax" provides further discussion.

Value-Added Tax

A value-added tax (VAT) is a tax levied on all sales of goods and services at each stage of production. As implied by the name, the tax applies only to the value added at each stage, and so a firm that pays value-added taxes will pay tax only on the value that it added to the good or service that it sells. If a firm sells melons at a fruit stand, the VAT it pays is based on the difference between the cost the firm paid for the melons and the sales price it charges to its customers who buy the fruit. Of course, the customers bear the cost of the VAT, as it is built into the price they must pay.

As the accompanying map indicates, VATs are very popular around the world. Many countries adopted VATs in the 1990s. It is clear that there are more countries that use VATs than that do not. Such a tax has its advantages. One important consideration is that a VAT is a tax on consumption. Anyone who buys goods and services will contribute to the government's VAT revenue. Thus, VATs are very powerful revenue generators. Those individuals who evade income taxes and pay less than their legal obligation will not escape the VAT. For instance, a criminal who earns income illegally and pays no tax on that income will be taxed

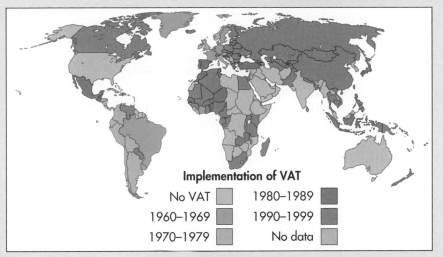

Implementation of VAT

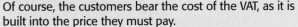

No VAT	1980–1989
1960–1969	1990–1999
1970–1979	No data

Source: From IMF Survey, International Monetary Fund, Fol. 29, No. 9, May 8, 2000, p. 156. Reprinted with permission of International Monetary Fund.

on all legal goods and services that he or she purchases. In this sense, there is a certain attractiveness to taxing consumption rather than income. But a VAT also acts as a regressive tax in that a poor person would tend to pay a higher fraction of income as VAT than a rich person. It is important to realize that no country relies strictly on a VAT for government revenue. VATs are part of an overall government tax policy that attempts to incorporate fairness along with a need to raise sufficient revenue to finance public expenditures.

RECAP

1. Over time, government spending has become more important in industrial countries.
2. Governments in developing countries typically play a larger role in investment spending in their economies than do the governments of developed countries.
3. Developing countries depend more on indirect taxes on goods and services as a source of revenue than on direct taxes on individuals and businesses.
4. Value-added taxes are general sales taxes that are collected at every stage of production.

Summary

❓ How can fiscal policy eliminate a GDP gap?

1. A GDP gap can be closed by increasing government spending or by cutting taxes. *§1*

2. Government spending affects aggregate expenditures directly; taxes affect aggregate expenditures indirectly, through their effect on consumption. *§1*

3. Aggregate expenditures must rise to bring equilibrium real GDP up to potential real GDP to eliminate the GDP gap. *§1*

4. An increase in government spending matched by an increase in taxes raises equilibrium spending and real GDP. *§1.c*

5. If the public expects to pay higher taxes as a result of government borrowing, then the expansionary effects of government deficits may be reduced. *§1.c*

6. Government borrowing can crowd out private spending by raising interest rates and reducing investments. *§1.e*

❓ How has U.S. fiscal policy changed over time?

7. Fiscal policy in the United States is a product of the budget process. *§2.a*

8. Federal government spending in the United States has increased from just 3 percent of the GDP before the Great Depression to a little less than 20 percent of the GDP today. *§2.b*

9. Fiscal policy has two components: discretionary fiscal policy and automatic stabilizers. *§2.b*

❓ What are the effects of budget deficits?

10. Budget deficits, through their effects on interest rates, international trade, and the national debt, can reduce investment, output, net exports, and national wealth. *§2.c.1, 2.c.2, 2.c.3*

11. Progressive taxes and transfer payments are automatic stabilizers, elements of fiscal policy that change automatically as national income changes. *§2.d*

❓ How does fiscal policy differ across countries?

12. Industrial countries spend a much larger percentage of their government budget for social programs than developing countries do. *§3.a*

13. Industrial countries depend more on direct taxes and less on indirect taxes than developing countries do. *§3.b*

Key Terms

crowding out *§1.e*

discretionary fiscal policy *§2.b*

automatic stabilizer *§2.b*

progressive tax *§2.d*

transfer payment *§2.d*

value-added tax (VAT) *§3.b*

Exercises

1. What is the role of aggregate demand in eliminating the GDP gap? How does the slope of the *AS* curve affect the fiscal policy actions necessary to eliminate the GDP gap?

2. Briefly describe the process of setting the federal budget in the United States. What is the time lag between the start of the process and the point at which the money is actually spent?

3. In what ways are government deficits harmful to the economy?

4. Define and give three examples of automatic stabilizers.

5. Briefly describe the major differences between fiscal policy in industrial countries and that in developing countries.

6. Why will real GDP tend to rise when government spending and taxes rise by the same amount?

7. How can a larger government fiscal deficit cause a larger international trade deficit?

8. Why do government budget deficits grow during recessions?

9. Taxes can be progressive, regressive, or proportional. Define each, and briefly offer an argument for why income taxes are usually progressive.

The following exercises are based on the appendix to this chapter.

Answer exercises 10–13 on the basis of the following information. Assume that equilibrium real GDP is $800 billion, potential real GDP is $900 billion, the MPC is .80, and the MPI is .40.

10. What is the size of the GDP gap?

11. How much must government spending increase to eliminate the GDP gap?

12. How much must taxes fall to eliminate the GDP gap?

13. If government spending and taxes both change by the same amount, how much must they change to eliminate the recessionary gap?

14. Suppose the *MPC* is .90 and the *MPI* is .10. If government expenditures go up $100 billion while taxes fall $10 billion, what happens to the equilibrium level of real GDP?

Use the following equations for exercises 15–17.

$$C = \$100 + .8Y$$

$$I = \$200$$

$$G = \$250$$

$$X = \$100 - .2Y$$

15. What is the equilibrium level of real GDP?

16. What is the new equilibrium level of real GDP if government spending increases by $100?

17. What is the new equilibrium level of real GDP if government spending and taxes both increase by $100?

ACE

Take the ACE Practice Test for this chapter to review the important concepts and get immediate feedback with answers.

economics.college.hmco.com/students

Economically Speaking

Brussels Takes Action Against France over Budget Deficit

Formal moves to discipline France for breaching European limits on government borrowing were ordered by Brussels yesterday, fuelling EU budget tensions.

After the EU's statistics office, Eurostat, confirmed that French state borrowing hit 3.1 per cent last year, breaching the 3 per cent ceiling under the Stability Pact, the European Commission said that it would begin a disciplinary process against Paris.

The Commission's spokesman, Gerassimos Thomas, said that it had no choice but to take action that could ultimately lead to the imposition on France of massive punitive fines.

Brussel's decision immediately to begin the Stability Pact procedures, designed to bring to heel member states that break the borrowing rules, could lead to a renewed confrontation between the Commission and the French Government.

Germany, whose budget deficit for last year rose to 3.6 per cent of GDP, is already facing action under the Pact's disciplinary codes.

But while Berlin has accepted censure by the Commission and pledged to take swift corrective action, Paris has defied calls to comply with the Pact's strictures and has stepped up pressure for changes to its tough budget regime.

"Given the situation, the Commission has no option but to start preparing a report under the excessive deficit procedure," Mr Thomas said. . . .

The Commission also underlined its continued determination to enforce the Stability Pact in its existing form when it said that it would now consider action against eurozone member states whose national debts break its limit of 60 per cent of GDP.

Until now, the Commission has concentrated on annual borrowing levels and has turned a blind eye to countries' accumulated debt.

While Belgium, for example, has a balanced budget, its national debt stands at 105 per cent of GDP. Italy's debt is now 106.7 per cent of GDP, yesterday's official data showed.

However, the Commission welcomed a drop in Portugal's deficit to 2.7 per cent of GDP last year, from 4.2 per cent in 2001.

GARY DUNCAN

Source: Copyright 2003 Times Newspapers Limited.

The Times (London)/March 18, 2003

Commentary

Government budget deficits are a global concern. While we usually think in terms of internal political and economic pressures on a nation to keep its government budget from generating large and unsustainable deficits, the article discusses the case of the European Union (EU), where member countries face multinational pressure to comply with the EU *stability pact*. When the euro was in the planning stage, it was decided that every country that wanted to use the euro as its currency would have to have a stable, sustainable fiscal policy. The EU created the stability pact to explicitly state the limits on national governments' flexibility with regard to debt and deficits. As stated in the article, the stability pact requires all euroland countries to maintain budget deficits of less than 3 percent of GDP and government debt of less than 60 percent of GDP. At the time this article was written, both Germany and France exceeded the 3 percent deficit limit, and the 60 percent debt limit was exceeded by Germany, Italy, Greece, Austria, and Belgium.

In the case of the countries that share the same currency, the euro, it makes sense that they maintain similar fiscal policies in order to maintain a stable value for the euro against external currencies like the dollar. However, should other countries that have their own national money, like the United States or Japan, worry about maintaining a small deficit?

You may have heard arguments concerning the effects of a budget deficit that proceed by means of an analogy between the government's budget and a family's budget. Just as a family cannot spend more than it earns, so the argument goes, the government cannot follow this practice without bringing itself to ruin. The problem with this analogy is that the government has the ability to raise money through taxes and bond sales, options that are not open to a family.

A more appropriate analogy is to compare the government's budget to that of a large corporation. Large corporations run persistent deficits that are never paid back. Instead, when corporate debt comes due, the corporations "roll over" their debt by selling new debt. Corporations are able to do this because they use their debt to finance investment that enables them to increase their worth. To the extent that the government is investing in projects like road repairs and building the nation's infrastructure, it is increasing the productive capacity of the economy, which widens the tax base and increases potential future tax receipts.

There are, of course, legitimate problems associated with a budget deficit. The government has two options if it cannot pay for its expenditures with tax receipts. One method of financing the budget deficit is by creating money. This is an unattractive option because it leads to inflation. Another method is to borrow funds by selling government bonds. A problem with this option is that the government must compete for scarce loanable funds. Unless saving increases at the same time, interest rates rise and government borrowing crowds out private investment. This results in a lower capital stock and diminished prospects for future economic growth.

So while the euroland countries face pressure, and potential fines, from the European Union if they exceed the limits of the stability pact, there are pressures from financial markets on all countries. The financial markets punish those countries that have excessive budget deficits. A country with big budget deficits will find its interest rates rising, as investors buying the bonds sold by a country that borrows ever larger amounts of money will demand a higher and higher return. Those countries that resort to printing money to finance a budget deficit end up with higher and higher inflation rates. Such a policy has brought down more than one government in the past. Good government, as measured by careful management of the budget, is rewarded with good economic conditions (other things equal) and political survival.

An Algebraic Examination of the Balanced-Budget Change in Fiscal Policy

What would happen if government spending and taxes went up by the same amount? We can analyze such a change by expanding the analysis begun in the Appendix to Chapter 11.

The spending multiplier is the simple multiplier defined in Chapter 11:

$$\text{Spending multiplier} = \frac{1}{MPS + MPI}$$

In the Chapter 11 example, because the *MPS* equals .30 and the *MPI* equals .10, the spending multiplier equals 2.5:

$$\text{Spending multiplier} = \frac{1}{MPS + MPI} = \frac{1}{.30 + .10}$$

$$= \frac{1}{.40} = 2.5$$

When government spending increases by $20, the equilibrium level of real GDP increases by 2.5 times $20, or $50.

We also can define a tax multiplier, a measure of the effect of a change in taxes on equilibrium real GDP. Because a percentage of any change in income is saved and spent on imports, we know that a tax cut increases expenditures by less than the amount of the cut. The percentage of the tax cut that actually is spent is the marginal propensity to consume (*MPC*) less the *MPI*. If consumers save 30 percent of any extra income, they spend 70 percent, the *MPC*. But the domestic economy does not realize 70 percent of the extra income because 10 percent of the extra income is spent on imports. The percentage of any extra income that actually is spent at home is the *MPC* minus the *MPI*. In our example, 60 percent (.70 − .10) of any extra income is spent in the domestic economy.

With this information, we can define the tax multiplier like this:

$$\text{Tax multiplier} = -(MPC - MPI)\frac{1}{MPS + MPI}$$

In our example, the tax multiplier is −1.5:

$$\text{Tax multiplier} = -(.70 - .10)\frac{1}{.30 + .10}$$

$$= -(.60)(2.5) = -1.5$$

A tax cut increases equilibrium real GDP by 1.5 times the amount of the cut. Notice that the tax multiplier is always a *negative* number because a change in taxes moves income and expenditures in the opposite direction. Higher taxes lower income and expenditures; lower taxes raise income and expenditures.

Now that we have reviewed the spending and tax multipliers, we can examine the effect of a balanced-budget change in fiscal policy, where government spending and taxes change by the same amount. To simplify the analysis, we assume that taxes are lump-sum taxes (taxpayers must pay a certain amount of dollars as tax) rather than income taxes (where the tax rises with income). We can use the algebraic model presented in the Appendix to Chapter 11 to illustrate the effect of a balanced-budget change in government spending. Here are the model equations.

$$C = \$30 + .70Y$$

$$I = \$50$$

$$G = \$70$$

$$X = \$50 - .10Y$$

Solving for the equilibrium level of Y (as we did in the Appendix to Chapter 11), Y equals \$500 where Y equals aggregate expenditures.

Now suppose that G increases by \$10 and that this increase is funded by taxes of \$10. The increase in G changes autonomous government spending to \$80. The increase in taxes affects the autonomous levels of C and X. The new model equations are

$$C = \$30 + .70(Y - \$10) = \$23 + .70Y$$

$$X = \$50 - .10(Y - \$10) = \$51 - .10Y$$

Using the new G, C, and X functions, we can find the new equilibrium level of real GDP by setting Y equal to AE $(C + I + G + X)$:

$$Y = C + I + G + X$$

$$Y = \$23 + .70Y + \$50 + \$80 + \$51 - .10Y$$

$$Y = \$204 + .60Y$$

$$Y - .60Y = \$204$$

$$.40Y = \$204$$

$$Y = \$510$$

Increasing government spending and taxes by \$10 each raises the equilibrium level of real GDP by \$10. A balanced-budget increase in G increases Y by the change in G. If government spending and taxes both fall by the same amount, then real GDP will also fall by an amount equal to the change in government spending and taxes.

CHAPTER 13

Money and Banking

U p to this point, we have been talking about aggregate expenditures, aggregate demand and supply, and fiscal policy without explicitly discussing money. Yet money is used by every sector of the economy in all nations and plays a crucial role in every economy. In this chapter we discuss what money is, how the quantity of money is determined, and the role of banks in determining this quantity. In the next chapter, we examine the role of money in the aggregate demand and supply model.

As you will see in the next two chapters, the quantity of money has a major impact on interest rates, inflation, and the amount of spending in the economy. Money is, then, important for macroeconomic policymaking, and government officials use both monetary and fiscal policy to influence the equilibrium level of real GDP and prices.

Banks and the banking system also play key roles, both at home and abroad, in the determination of the amount of money in circulation and the movement of money between nations. After we define money and its functions, we look at the

banking system. We begin with banking in the United States, and then discuss international banking. Someone once joked that banks follow the rule of 3-6-3: they borrow at 3 percent interest, lend at 6 percent interest, and close at 3 P.M. If those days ever existed, clearly they do not today. The banking industry in the United States and the rest of the world has undergone tremendous change in recent years. New technology and government deregulation are allowing banks to respond to changing economic conditions in ways that were unthinkable only a few years ago, and these changes have had dramatic effects on the economy. ■

1. What is money?

money: anything that is generally acceptable to sellers in exchange for goods and services

liquid asset: an asset that can easily be exchanged for goods and services

1. What is Money?

Money is anything that is generally acceptable to sellers in exchange for goods and services. The cash in your wallet can be used to buy groceries or a movie ticket. You simply present your cash to the cashier, who readily accepts it. If you wanted to use your car to buy groceries or a movie ticket, the exchange would be more complicated. You would probably have to sell the car before you could use it to buy other goods and services. Cars are seldom exchanged directly for goods and services (except for other cars). Because cars are not a generally acceptable means of paying for other goods and services, we don't consider them to be money. Money is the most liquid asset. A **liquid asset** is an asset that can easily be exchanged for goods and services. Cash is a liquid asset; a car is not. How liquid must an asset be before we consider it money? To answer this question, we must first consider the functions of money.

1.a. Functions of Money

Money serves four basic functions: it is a *medium of exchange,* a *unit of account,* a *store of value,* and a *standard of deferred payment.* Not all monies serve all of these functions equally well, as will be apparent in the following discussion. But to be money, an item must perform enough of these functions to induce people to use it.

1.a.1. Medium of Exchange
Money is a medium of exchange; it is used in exchange for goods and services. Sellers willingly accept money in payment for the products and services they produce. Without money, we would have to resort to *barter,* the direct exchange of goods and services for other goods and services.

For a barter system to work, there must be a *double coincidence of wants.* Suppose Bill is a carpenter and Jane is a plumber. In a monetary economy, when Bill needs plumbing repairs in his home, he simply pays Jane for the repairs, using money. Because everyone wants money, money is an acceptable means of payment. In a barter economy, Bill must offer his services as a carpenter in exchange for Jane's work. If Jane does not want any carpentry work done, Bill and Jane cannot enter into a mutually beneficial transaction. Bill has to find a person who can do what he wants and also wants what he can do—there must be a double coincidence of wants.

The use of money as a medium of exchange lowers transaction costs.

The example of Bill and Jane illustrates the fact that barter is a lot less efficient than using money. This means that the cost of a transaction in a barter economy is higher than the cost of a transaction in a monetary economy. The use of money as a medium of exchange lowers transaction costs.

The people of Yap Island highly value, and thus accept as their medium of exchange, giant stones. In most cultures, however, money must be *portable* in order to be an effective medium of exchange—a property the stone money of Yap Island clearly lacks. Another important property of money is *divisibility*. Money must be measurable in both small units (for low-value goods and services) and large units (for high-value goods and services). Yap stone money is not divisible, so it is not a good medium of exchange for the majority of goods that are bought and sold.

1.a.2. Unit of Account

Money is a unit of account: We price goods and services in terms of money. This common unit of measurement allows us to compare relative values easily. If whole-wheat bread sells for a dollar a loaf and white bread sells for 50 cents, we know that whole-wheat bread is twice as expensive as white bread.

The use of money as a unit of account lowers information costs.

Using money as a unit of account is efficient. It reduces the costs of gathering information on what things are worth. The use of money as a unit of account lowers information costs relative to barter. In a barter economy, people constantly have to evaluate the worth of the goods and services being offered. When money prices are placed on goods and services, their relative value is obvious.

1.a.3. Store of Value

Money functions as a store of value or purchasing power. If you are paid today, you do not have to hurry out to spend your money. It will still have value next week or next month. Some monies retain their value better than others. In colonial New England, fish and furs both served as money. But because fish does not store as well as furs, its usefulness as a store of value was limited. An important property of a money is its *durability,* its ability to retain its value over time.

Inflation plays a major role in determining the effectiveness of a money as a store of value. The higher the rate of inflation, the faster the purchasing power of money falls. In high-inflation countries, workers spend their pay as fast as possible because the purchasing power of their money is falling rapidly. It makes no sense to hold on to a money that is quickly losing value. In countries where the domestic money does not serve as a good store of value, it ceases to fulfill this function of money and people begin to use something else as money, like the currency of another nation. For instance, U.S. dollars have long been a favorite store of value in Latin American countries that have experienced high inflation. This phenomenon—**currency substitution**—has been documented in Argentina, Bolivia, Mexico, and other countries during times of high inflation.

currency substitution: the use of foreign money as a substitute for domestic money when the domestic economy has a high rate of inflation

1.a.4. Standard of Deferred Payment

Finally, money is a standard of deferred payment. Debt obligations are written in terms of money values. If you have a credit card bill that is due in 30 days, the value you owe is stated in monetary units—for example, dollars in the United States and yen in Japan. We use money values to state amounts of debt and use money to pay our debts.

credit: available savings that are lent to borrowers to spend

We should make a distinction here between money and credit. Money is what we use to pay for goods and services. **Credit** is available savings that are lent to borrowers to spend. If you use your Visa or MasterCard to buy a shirt, you are not buying the shirt with your money. You are taking out a loan from the bank that issued the credit card in order to buy the shirt. Credit and money are different. Money is an asset, something you own. Credit is *debt,* something you owe.

1.b. The U.S. Money Supply

The quantity of money available for spending is an important determinant of many key macroeconomic variables, since changes in the money supply affect interest rates, inflation, and other indicators of economic health. When economists measure

2. How is the U.S. money supply defined?

the money supply, they measure spendable assets. Identifying those assets, however, can be difficult. Although it would seem that *all* bank deposits are money, some bank deposits are held for spending, while others are held for saving. In defining the money supply, then, economists must differentiate among assets on the basis of their liquidity and the likelihood of their being used for spending.

The problem of distinguishing among assets has produced several definitions of the money supply: M1, M2, and M3. Economists and policymakers use all three definitions to evaluate the availability of funds for spending. Although economists have tried to identify a single measure that best influences the business cycle and changes in interest rates and inflation, research indicates that different definitions work better to explain changes in macroeconomic variables at different times.

1.b.1. M1 Money Supply

The narrowest and most liquid measure of the money supply is the **M1 money supply,** the financial assets that are immediately available for spending. This definition emphasizes the use of money as a medium of exchange. The M1 money supply consists of currency, travelers' checks, demand deposits, and other checkable deposits. Demand and other checkable deposits are **transactions accounts;** they can be used to make direct payments to a third party.

Surveys find that families use their checking account for about 30 percent of purchases. Cash transactions account for about 44 percent of purchases.

The components of the M1 money supply are used for about 74 percent of family purchases. This is one reason why the M1 money supply may be a useful variable in formulating macroeconomic policy.

- *Currency* includes coins and paper money in circulation (in the hands of the public). In 2003, currency represented 52 percent of the M1 money supply. A common misconception about currency today is that it is backed by gold or silver. This is not true. There is nothing backing the U.S. dollar except the confidence of the public. This kind of monetary system is called a *fiduciary monetary system.* Fiduciary comes from the Latin *fiducia,* which means "trust." Our monetary system is based on trust. As long as we believe that our money is an acceptable form of payment for goods and services, the system works. It is not necessary for money to be backed by any precious object. As long as people believe that a money has value, it will serve as money.

  The United States has not always operated under a fiduciary monetary system. At one time the U.S. government issued gold and silver coins and paper money that could be exchanged for silver. In 1967, Congress authorized the U.S. Treasury to stop redeeming "silver certificate" paper money for silver. Coins with an intrinsic value are known as *commodity money;* they have value as a commodity in addition to their face value. The problem with commodity money is that as the value of the commodity increases, the money stops being circulated. People hoard coins when their commodity value exceeds their face value. For example, no one would take an old $20 gold piece to the grocery store to buy $20 worth of groceries because the gold is worth much more than $20 today.

  The tendency to hoard money as its commodity value increases is called *Gresham's Law.* Thomas Gresham was a successful businessman and financial adviser to Queen Elizabeth I. He insisted that if two coins have the same face value but different intrinsic values—perhaps one is silver and the other brass— the cheaper coin will be used in exchange while the more expensive coin will be hoarded. People sometimes state Gresham's Law as "bad money drives out

M1 money supply: the financial assets that are the most liquid

transactions account: a checking account at a bank or other financial institution that can be drawn on to make payments

According to Gresham's Law, bad money drives out good money.

good money," meaning that the money with the low commodity value will be used in exchange while the money with the high commodity value will be driven out of hand-to-hand use and be hoarded.[1]

- *Traveler's checks.* Outstanding U.S. dollar–denominated travelers' checks issued by nonbank institutions are counted as part of the M1 money supply. There are several nonbank issuers, among them American Express and Cook's. (Travelers' checks issued by banks are included in demand deposits. When a bank issues its own traveler's checks, it deposits the amount paid by the purchaser in a special account that is used to redeem the checks. Because this amount is counted as part of demand deposits, it is not counted again as part of outstanding travelers' checks.) Travelers' checks account for less than 1 percent of the M1 money supply.

- *Demand deposits.* Demand deposits are checking account deposits at a commercial bank. These deposits pay no interest. They are called *demand deposits* because the bank must pay the amount of the check immediately on the demand of the depositor. Demand deposits accounted for 25 percent of the M1 money supply in 2003.

- *Other checkable deposits.* Until the 1980s, demand deposits were the only kind of checking account. Today there are many different kinds of checking accounts, known as *other checkable deposits (OCDs).* These OCDs are accounts at financial institutions that pay interest and give the depositor check-writing privileges. Among the OCDs included in the M1 money supply are the following:

  Negotiable orders of withdrawal (NOW) accounts are interest-bearing checking accounts offered by savings and loan institutions.

  Automatic transfer system (ATS) accounts are accounts at commercial banks that combine an interest-bearing savings account with a non-interest-bearing checking account. The depositor keeps a small balance in the checking account; anytime the checking account balance is overdrawn, funds automatically are transferred from the savings account.

  Credit union share draft accounts are interest-bearing checking accounts that credit unions offer their members.

  Demand deposits at mutual savings banks are checking account deposits at nonprofit savings and loan organizations. Any profits after operating expenses have been paid may be distributed to depositors.

1.b.2. M2 Money Supply The components of the M1 money supply are the most liquid assets, the assets most likely to be used for transactions. The M2 is a broader definition of the money supply that includes assets in somewhat less liquid forms. The M2 money supply includes the M1 money supply plus savings and small-denomination time deposits, and balances in retail money market mutual funds.

---

[1]Actually, Gresham was not the first to recognize that bad money drives out good money. A fourteenth-century French theologian, Nicholas Oresme, made the same argument in his book *A Treatise on the Origin, Nature, Law, and Alterations of Money,* written almost 200 years before Gresham was born.

- *Savings deposits* are accounts at banks and savings and loan associations that earn interest but offer no check-writing privileges.

- *Small-denomination time deposits* are often called *certificates of deposit*. Funds in these accounts must be deposited for a specified period of time. (*Small* means less than $100,000.)

- *Retail money market mutual fund balances* combine the deposits of many individuals and invest them in government Treasury bills and other short-term securities. Many money market mutual funds grant check-writing privileges but limit the size and number of checks.

1.b.3. M3 Money Supply

The M3 money supply equals the M2 money supply plus *large time deposits* (deposits in amounts of $100,000 or more), *repurchase agreements, Eurodollar deposits,* and *institution-only money market mutual fund balances* (which do not include the balances of individuals). These additional assets are less liquid than those found in the M1 or M2 money supply. Figure 1 summarizes the three definitions of the money supply.

- A *repurchase agreement (RP)* is an agreement between a bank and a customer under which the customer buys U.S. government securities from the bank one day and then sells them back to the bank later at a price that includes the interest earned overnight. Overnight RPs are used by firms that have excess cash one day that may be needed the next.

- *Eurodollar deposits* are deposits denominated in dollars but held outside the U.S. domestic bank industry.

3. How do countries pay for international transactions?

1.c. Global Money

So far we have discussed the money supply in a domestic context. Just as the United States uses dollars as its domestic money, every nation has its own monetary unit of account. Japan has the yen, Mexico the peso, Canada the Canadian dollar, and so on. Since each nation uses a different money, how do countries pay for transactions that involve residents of other countries? As you saw in Chapter 7, the foreign exchange market links national monies together, so that transactions can be made across national borders. If Sears in the United States buys a home entertainment system from Sony in Japan, Sears can exchange dollars for yen in order to pay Sony in yen. The exchange rate between the dollar and the yen determines how many dollars are needed to purchase the required number of yen. For instance, if Sony wants 1,000,000 yen for the component and the exchange rate is ¥100 = $1, Sears needs $10,000 (1,000,000/100) to buy the yen.

Sales contracts between developed countries usually are written (invoiced) in the national currency of the exporter. To complete the transaction, the importer buys the exporter's currency on the foreign exchange market. Trade between developing and developed nations typically is invoiced in the currency of the developed country, whether the developed country is the exporter or the importer, because the currency of the developed country is usually more stable and more widely traded on the foreign exchange market than the currency of the developing country. As a result, the currencies of the major developed countries tend to dominate the international medium-of-exchange and unit-of-account functions of money.

The currencies of the major developed countries tend to dominate the international medium-of-exchange and unit-of-account functions of money.

FIGURE 1

The U.S. Money Supply: M1, M2, M3 (billions of dollars)

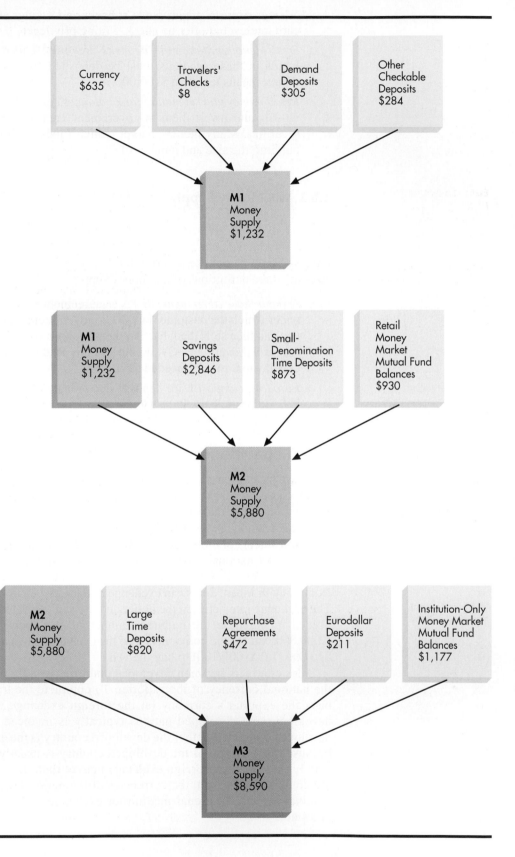

1.c.1. International Reserve Currencies Governments hold monies as a temporary store of value until money is needed to settle international debts. At one time gold was the primary **international reserve asset,** an asset used to settle debts between governments. Although gold still serves as an international reserve asset, its role is unimportant relative to that of currencies. Today national currencies function as international reserves. The currencies that are held for this purpose are called **international reserve currencies.**

Table 1 shows the importance of the major international reserve currencies over time. In the mid-1970s, the U.S. dollar made up almost 80 percent of international reserve holdings. By 1990 its share had fallen to less than 50 percent, but that share has risen again recently.

Prior to the euro, there was an artificial currency in Europe, the **European currency unit (ECU).** The industrial nations of western Europe used ECUs to settle debts between them. The ECU was a **composite currency;** its value was an average of the values of several different national currencies: the Austrian schilling, the Belgian franc, the Danish krone, the Finnish markkaa, the French franc, the German mark, the Greek drachma, the Irish pound, the Italian lira, the Luxembourg franc, the Netherlands guilder, the Spanish peseta, and the Portuguese escudo (the U.K. pound was withdrawn from the system in September 1992).

The ECU was not an actual money but an accounting entry transferred between two parties. It was a step along the way to a new actual money, the *euro,* which replaced the ECU and circulates throughout the member countries as a real European money.

Another composite currency used in international financial transactions is the **special drawing right (SDR).** The value of the SDR is an average of the values of the currencies of the major industrial countries: the U.S. dollar, the euro, the Japanese yen, and the U.K. pound. This currency was created in 1970 by the International Monetary Fund, an international organization that oversees the monetary relationships among countries. The SDRs are an international reserve asset; they are used to settle international debts by transferring governments' accounts held at the International Monetary Fund. We discuss the role of the International Monetary Fund in later chapters.

Prior to the actual introduction of the euro, there was much discussion about its potential popularity as a reserve currency. In fact, some analysts were asserting that

international reserve asset: an asset used to settle debts between governments

international reserve currency: a currency held by a government to settle international debts

European currency unit (ECU): a unit of account formerly used by western European nations as their official reserve asset

composite currency: an artificial unit of account that is an average of the values of several national currencies

special drawing right (SDR): a composite currency whose value is the average of the values of the U.S. dollar, the euro, the Japanese yen, and the U.K. pound

---

TABLE 1 ────────────────────────────────

International Reserve Currencies (percentage shares of national currencies in total official holdings of foreign exchange)

Year	U.S. Dollar	Pound Sterling	Deutsche Mark	French Franc	Japanese Yen	Swiss Franc	Netherlands Guilder	Euro	ECU	Unspecified Currencies
1976	78.8	1.0	8.7	1.5	1.9	2.1	0.8	—	—	5.2
1980	56.6	2.5	12.8	1.5	3.7	2.8	1.1	—	16.4	2.7
1990	47.8	2.8	16.5	2.2	7.7	1.2	1.0	—	9.7	11.1
2000	68.1	3.9	—	—	5.2	0.7	—	13.0	—	9.1

Source: Data are drawn from International Monetary Fund, *Annual Report,* various issues.

---

we should expect the euro to replace the U.S. dollar as the world's dominant currency. As Table 1 shows, the euro is now the second most popular reserve currency, but it has a much lower share of reserve currency use than the dollar does. The dominant world currency evolves over time as business firms and individuals find one currency more useful than another. Prior to the dominance of the dollar, the British pound was the world's most important reserve currency. As the U.S. economy grew in importance and U.S. financial markets developed to the huge size they now have, the growing use of the dollar emerged naturally as a result of the large volume of financial transactions involving the United States. Perhaps over time, the euro will some day replace the dollar as the world's dominant money.

RECAP

1. Money is the most liquid asset.
2. Money serves as a medium of exchange, a unit of account, a store of value, and a standard of deferred payment.
3. The use of money lowers transaction and information costs relative to barter.
4. To be used as money, an asset should be portable, divisible, and durable.
5. The M1 money supply is the most liquid definition of money and equals the sum of currency, travelers' checks, demand deposits, and other checkable deposits.
6. The M2 money supply equals the sum of the M1 money supply, savings and small-denomination time deposits, and retail money market mutual fund balances.
7. The M3 money supply equals the sum of the M2 money supply, large time deposits, repurchase agreements, Eurodollar deposits, and institution-only money market mutual fund balances.
8. International reserve currencies are held by governments to settle international debts.
9. Composite currencies have their value determined as an average of the values of several national currencies.

2. Banking

Commercial banks are financial institutions that offer deposits on which checks can be written. In the United States and most other countries, commercial banks are privately owned. *Thrift institutions* are financial institutions that historically offered just savings accounts, not checking accounts. Savings and loan associations, credit unions, and mutual savings banks are all thrift institutions. Prior to 1980, the differences between commercial banks and thrift institutions were much greater than they are today. For example, only commercial banks could offer checking accounts, and those accounts earned no interest. The law also regulated maximum interest rates. In 1980 Congress passed the Depository Institutions Deregulation and Monetary Control Act, in part to stimulate competition among financial institutions. Now thrift institutions and even brokerage houses offer many of the same services as commercial banks. In 1999 Congress passed the Gramm-Leach-Bliley Act, which allowed

Islamic Banking

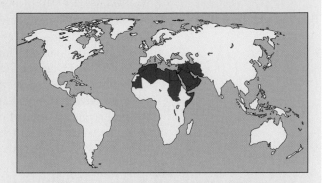

According to the Muslim holy book, the Koran, Islamic law prohibits interest charges on loans. Banks that operate under Islamic law still act as intermediaries between borrowers and lenders. However, they do not charge interest on loans or pay interest on deposits. Instead they take a predetermined percentage of the borrowing firm's profits until the loan is repaid, then share those profits with depositors.

Since the mid-1970s, over a hundred Islamic banks have opened, most in Arab nations. Deposits in these banks have grown rapidly. In fact, in some banks, deposits have grown faster than good loan opportunities, forcing the banks to refuse new deposits until their loan portfolio could grow to match available deposits. One bank in Bahrain claimed that over 60 percent of deposits during its first two years in operation were made by people who had never made a bank deposit before.

In addition to profit-sharing deposits, Islamic banks typically offer checking accounts, travelers' checks, and trade-related services on a fee basis. The return on profit-sharing deposits has fluctuated with regional economic conditions. In the late 1970s and early 1980s, when oil prices were high, returns were higher than they were in the mid-1980s, when oil prices were depressed.

Because the growth of deposits has usually exceeded the growth of local investment opportunities, Islamic banks have been lending money to traditional banks, to fund investments that satisfy the moral and commercial needs of both, such as lending to private firms. These funds cannot be used to invest in interest-bearing securities or in firms that deal in alcohol, pork, gambling, or arms. The growth of mutually profitable investment opportunities suggests that Islamic banks are meeting both the dictates of Muslim depositors and the profitability requirements of modern banking.

The potential for expansion and profitability of Islamic financial services has led major banks to create units dedicated to providing Islamic banking services. In addition, there are stock mutual finds that screen firms for compliance with Islamic law before buying their stock. For instance, since most financial institutions earn and pay large amounts of interest, such firms would tend to be excluded from an Islamic mutual fund.

The most popular instrument for financing Islamic investments is *murabaha*. This is essentially cost-plus financing, where the financial institution purchases goods or services for a client and then is repaid over time an amount that equals the original cost plus an additional amount of profit. Such an arrangement is even used for financing mortgages on property in the United States. A financial institution will buy a property and then charge a client rent until the rent payments equal the purchase price plus some profit. After the full payment is received, the title to the property is passed to the client.

Sources: Peter Koh, "The Shari'ah Alternative," *Euromoney* (October 2002). A good source of additional information is found on the website www.failaka.com/.

commercial banks to expand their business into other areas of finance, including insurance and selling securities. This will permit greater integration of financial products under one umbrella known as a financial holding company.

2.a. Financial Intermediaries

4. Why are banks considered intermediaries?

Both commercial banks and thrift institutions are *financial intermediaries*, middle-men between savers and borrowers. Banks accept deposits from individuals and firms, then use those deposits to make loans to individuals and firms. The borrowers are likely to be different individuals or firms from the depositors, although it is not uncommon for a household or business to be both a depositor and a borrower at the same institution. Of course, depositors and borrowers have very different interests. For instance, depositors typically prefer short-term deposits; they don't want to tie their money up for a long time. Borrowers, on the other hand, usually want more time for repayment. Banks typically package short-term deposits into longer-term loans. To function as intermediaries, banks must serve the interests of both depositors and borrowers.

A bank is willing to serve as an intermediary because it hopes to earn a profit from this activity. It pays a lower interest rate on deposits than it charges on loans; the difference is a source of profit for the bank. Islamic banks are prohibited by holy law from charging interest on loans; thus they use a different system for making a profit (see the Global Business Insight "Islamic Banking").

2.b. U.S. Banking

2.b.1. Current Structure
If you add together all the pieces of the bar graph in Figure 2, you see that there were 87,545 depository institution offices operating in the United States at the end of 2001. Roughly 85 percent of these offices were operated by banks and 15 percent by savings institutions.

Historically, U.S. banks were allowed to operate in just one state. In some states, banks could operate in only one location. This is known as *unit banking*. Today there are still many unit banks, but these are typically small community banks.

Over time, legal barriers have been reduced so that today almost all states permit entry to banks located out of state. In the future, banking is likely to be done on a national rather than a local scale. The growth of automated teller machines (ATMs) is a big step in this direction. The ATM networks give bank customers access to services over a much wider geographic area than any single bank's branches cover. These international networks allow a bank customer from Dallas to withdraw cash in Seattle, Zurich, or almost anywhere in the world. Today more

---

FIGURE 2

U.S. Depository Institutions

There are many more banks and bank branches than there are savings institutions and savings branches. *Source: Data are drawn from Federal Deposit Insurance Corporation,* Statistics on Banking, *www.fdic.gov.*

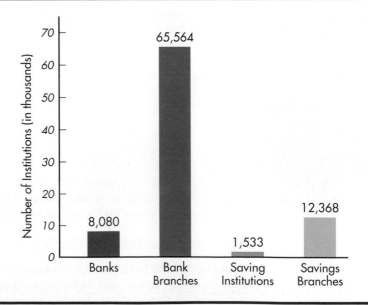

Part Three Macroeconomic Policy

than one-fourth of ATM transactions occur at banks that are not the customer's own bank.

2.b.2. Bank Failures

Banking in the United States has had a colorful history of booms and panics. Banking is like any other business. Banks that are poorly managed can fail; banks that are properly managed tend to prosper. Regional economic conditions are also very important. In the mid-1980s, hundreds of banks in states with large oil industries, like Texas and Oklahoma, and farming states, like Kansas and Nebraska, could not collect many of their loans as a result of falling oil and agricultural prices. Those states that are heavily dependent on the oil industry and farming had significantly more banks fail than did other states. The problem was not so much bad management as it was a matter of unexpectedly bad business conditions. The lesson here is simple: commercial banks, like other profit-making enterprises, are not exempt from failure.

A bank panic occurs when depositors become frightened and rush to withdraw their funds.

Federal Deposit Insurance Corporation (FDIC): a federal agency that insures deposits in commercial banks

At one time, a bank panic could close a bank. A bank panic occurs when depositors, fearing a bank's closing, rush to withdraw their funds. Banks keep only a fraction of their deposits on reserve, so bank panics often result in bank closings as depositors try to withdraw more money than the banks have on a given day. In the United States today, this is no longer true. The **Federal Deposit Insurance Corporation (FDIC)** was created in 1933. The FDIC is a federal agency that insures bank deposits in commercial banks so that depositors do not lose their deposits when a bank fails. Figure 3 shows the number of failed banks and the number without deposit insurance. In the 1930s, many of the banks that failed were not insured by the FDIC. In this environment, it made sense for depositors to worry about losing their money. In the 1980s, the number of bank failures increased dramatically, but none of the failed banks were uninsured. Deposits in those banks were protected by the federal government. Even though large banks have failed in recent times, the depositors have not lost their deposits.

FIGURE 3

Number of Failed and Uninsured Banks

The number of banks that went out of business in the 1980s was the highest it had been since the Depression. Unlike the banks that failed in the 1930s, however, the banks that closed in the 1980s were covered by deposit insurance, so depositors did not lose their money.
Source: Data are from Federal Deposit Insurance Corporation, Statistics on Banking, *www.fdic.gov.*

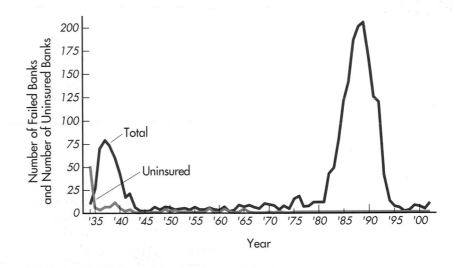

2.c. International Banking

Large banks today are truly transnational enterprises. International banks, like domestic banks, act as financial intermediaries, but they operate in a different legal environment. The laws regulating domestic banking in each nation are typically very restrictive, yet many nations allow international banking to operate largely unregulated. Because they are not hampered by regulations, international banks typically can offer depositors and borrowers better terms than could be negotiated at a domestic bank.

2.c.1. Eurocurrency Market

Eurocurrency market or offshore banking: the market for deposits and loans generally denominated in a currency other than the currency of the country in which the transaction occurs

Because of the competitive interest rates offered on loans and deposits, there is a large market for deposits and loans at international banks. For instance, a bank in London, Tokyo, or the Bahamas may accept deposits and make loans denominated in U.S. dollars. The international deposit and loan market often is called the **Eurocurrency market,** or **offshore banking.** In the Eurocurrency market, the currency used in a banking transaction generally is not the domestic currency of the country in which the bank is located. (The prefix *Euro-* is misleading here. Although the market originated in Europe, today it is global and operates with different foreign currencies; it is in no way limited to European currencies or European banks.) There are deposits and loans in Eurodollars, Euroyen, Euroeuro, and any other major currency.

In those countries that allow offshore banking, we find two sets of banking rules: restrictive regulations for banking in the domestic market and little or no regulation of offshore banking activities. Domestic banks are required to hold reserves against deposits and to carry deposit insurance; and they often face government-mandated credit or interest rate restrictions. The Eurocurrency market operates with few or no costly restrictions, and international banks generally pay lower taxes than domestic banks. Because offshore banks operate with lower costs, they are able to offer better terms to their customers than domestic banks.

Offshore banks are able to offer a higher rate on dollar deposits and a lower rate on dollar loans than their domestic competitors. Without these differences, the Eurodollar market probably would not exist, because Eurodollar transactions are riskier than domestic transactions in the United States, as a result of the lack of government regulation and deposit insurance.

There are always risks involved in international banking. Funds are subject to control by both the country in which the bank is located and the country in whose currency the deposit or loan is denominated. Suppose a Canadian firm wants to withdraw funds from a U.S. dollar-denominated bank deposit in Hong Kong. The transaction is subject to control in Hong Kong. For example, the government may not allow foreign exchange to leave the country freely. It is also subject to U.S. control. If the United States reduces its outflow of dollars, for instance, the Hong Kong bank may have difficulty paying the Canadian firm with U.S. dollars.

The Eurocurrency market exists for all of the major international currencies, but the value of activity in Eurodollars dwarfs the rest. Eurodollars account for about 60 percent of deposit and loan activity in the Eurocurrency market. This emphasizes the important role the U.S. dollar plays in global finance. Even deposits and loans that do not involve a U.S. lender or borrower often are denominated in U.S. dollars.

2.c.2. International Banking Facilities

The term *offshore banking* is somewhat misleading in the United States today. Prior to December 1981, U.S. banks were forced to process international deposits and loans through their offshore branches. Many of the branches in places like the Cayman Islands and the Bahamas were little more than "shells," small offices with a telephone. Yet these branches allowed U.S. banks to avoid the reserve requirements and interest rate regulations that restricted domestic banking activities.

international banking facility (IBF): a division of a U.S. bank that is allowed to receive deposits from and make loans to nonresidents of the United States without the restrictions that apply to domestic U.S. banks

In December 1981, the Federal Reserve Board legalized **international banking facilities (IBFs),** allowing domestic banks to take part in international banking on U.S. soil. The IBFs are not physical entities; they are bookkeeping systems set up in existing bank offices to record international banking transactions. The IBFs can receive deposits from and make loans to nonresidents of the United States or other IBFs. These deposits and loans must be kept separate from other transactions because IBFs are not subject to the reserve requirements, interest rate regulations, or FDIC deposit insurance premiums that apply to domestic U.S. banking. The goal of the IBF plan was to allow banking offices in the United States to compete with offshore banks without having to use offshore banking offices.

2.d. Informal Financial Markets in Developing Countries

In many developing countries, a sizable portion of the population has no access to formal financial institutions like banks. In these cases, it is common for informal financial markets to develop. Such markets may take many different forms. Sometimes they take the form of an individual making small loans to local residents. Sometimes groups of individuals form a self-help group where they pool their resources to provide loans to each other. To give some idea of the nature of these sorts of arrangements, a few common types are reviewed here.

ROSCA: a rotating savings and credit association

A common form of informal financial arrangement is rotating savings and credit associations, or **ROSCAs.** These tend to go by different names in different countries, such as, *tandas* in Mexico, *susu* in Ghana, *hui* in China, and *chits* in India. ROSCAs are like savings clubs; members contribute money every week or month into a common fund, and then each month one member of the group receives the full amount contributed by everyone. This usually operates for a cycle of as many months as there are members in the group. For instance, if there are 12 members in the group contributing $10 a month, then a cycle would last 12 months, and each month a different member of the group would receive the $120 available. Thus the ROSCA is a vehicle for saving in which only the last member of the group to receive the funds has saved over the full 12-month period before having the use of $120. The determination of who receives the funds in which month is typically made by a random drawing at the beginning of the cycle. So a ROSCA is a means of saving that allows all but one member in each cycle to receive funds faster than they could save on their own.

The informal market in many countries is dominated by individual lenders, who tend to specialize in a local area and make loans primarily for the acquisition of seeds, fertilizer, or mechanical equipment needed by farmers. Surveys in China indicate that about two-thirds of farm loans to poor rural households are made by informal lenders. Such informal lenders are distinct from friends and relatives, who can also be important in lending to poor households. The interest rate charged by informal lenders is typically significantly higher than that charged by banks or government lending institutions. The higher interest rates may reflect the higher risk associated with the borrower, who may have no collateral (goods or possessions that may be transferred to the lender if the borrower does not repay).

Informal loans among friends or relatives are typically one-time loans for purposes like financing weddings or home construction. If your cousin lends you money today in your time of need, then you are expected to lend to him at some later time if he has a need. Repeat loans, like those to a farmer in advance of the harvest each year, tend to be made by individuals who are unrelated to the borrower and are in the business of providing such financing.

A form of informal financial market that gained much publicity after the September 11, 2001, terrorist attacks on New York City's World Trade Center is the **hawala** network. In much of the developing world with heavy Muslim populations, people can send money all over the world using the hawala network. Let's say a Pakistani immigrant, working as a taxi driver in New York, wants to send money to a relative in a remote village of Pakistan. He can go to a hawala agent and give the money to the agent, who writes down the destination location and the amount of money to be sent. The agent then gives the taxi driver a code number and the location of an agent in Pakistan, which the driver passes along to his relative. The agent in the United States then calls a counterpart agent in Pakistan and informs that person of the amount of money and the code number. The Pakistani agent will pay the money to whoever walks in his door with the code number. Since no records of names or addresses for the source of the money or the recipient are kept, it is easy to see how such a network can be an effective source of financing for terrorist activities. For this reason, the hawala network was a source of much investigation following the 2001 terrorist attacks in the United States. Of course, such a network serves many more than just terrorists and is an important part of the informal financial market operating in many countries. For poor people without bank accounts, such informal markets allow some access to financial services.

hawala: an international informal financial market used by Muslims

RECAP

1. The Depository Institutions Deregulation and Monetary Control Act (1980) eliminated many of the differences between commercial banks and thrift institutions.
2. Banks are financial intermediaries.
3. The deregulation act also eliminated many of the differences between national and state banks.
4. Since the FDIC began insuring bank deposits in commercial banks, bank panics are no longer a threat to the banking system.
5. The international deposit and loan market is called the Eurocurrency market or offshore banking.
6. With the legalization of international banking facilities in 1981, the Federal Reserve allowed international banking activities on U.S. soil.
7. Informal financial markets play an important role in developing countries.

6. How do banks create money?

fractional reserve banking system: a system in which banks keep less than 100 percent of the deposits available for withdrawal

3. Banks and the Money Supply

Banks create money by lending money. They take deposits, then lend a portion of those deposits in order to earn interest income. The portion of deposits that banks keep on hand is a *reserve* to meet the demand for withdrawals. In a **fractional reserve banking system,** banks keep less than 100 percent of their deposits on reserve. If all banks hold 10 percent of their deposits as a reserve, for example, then 90 percent of their deposits are available for loans. When they loan these deposits, money is created.

FIGURE 4

First National Bank Balance Sheet, Initial Position

The bank has cash totaling $100,000 and loans totaling $900,000, for total assets of $1,000,000. Deposits of $1,000,000 make up its total liabilities. With a reserve requirement of 10 percent, the bank must hold required reserves of 10 percent of its deposits, or $100,000. Because the bank is holding cash of $100,000, its total reserves equal its required reserves. Because it has no excess reserves, the bank cannot make new loans.

First National Bank

Assets		Liabilities	
Cash	$100,000	Deposits	$1,000,000
Loans	900,000		
Total	$1,000,000	Total	$1,000,000

Total reserves = $100,000
Required reserves = 0.1 ($1,000,000) = $100,000
Excess reserves = 0

3.a. Deposits and Loans

Figure 4 shows a simple balance sheet for First National Bank. A *balance sheet* is a financial statement that records a firm's assets (what the firm owns) and liabilities (what the firm owes). The bank has cash assets ($100,000) and loan assets ($900,000). The deposits placed in the bank ($1,000,000) are a liability (they are an asset of the depositors).[2] Total assets always equal total liabilities on a balance sheet.

Banks keep a percentage of their deposits on reserve. In the United States the reserve requirement is set by the Federal Reserve Board (which will be discussed in detail in the next chapter). Banks can keep more than the minimum reserve if they choose. Let's assume that the reserve requirement is set at 10 percent and that banks always hold actual reserves equal to 10 percent of deposits. With deposits of $1,000,000, the bank must keep $100,000 (.10 × $1,000,000) in cash reserves held in its vault. This $100,000 is the bank's **required reserves,** as the Federal Reserve requires the banks to keep 10 percent of deposits on reserve. This is exactly what First National Bank has on hand in Figure 4. Any cash held in excess of $100,000 would represent **excess reserves.** Excess reserves can be loaned by the bank. A bank is *loaned up* when it has zero excess reserves. Because its total reserves equal its required reserves, First National Bank has no excess reserves and is loaned up.

required reserves: the cash reserves (a percentage of deposits) a bank must keep on hand or on deposit with the Federal Reserve

excess reserves: the cash reserves beyond those required, which can be loaned

$$\text{Excess reserves} = \text{total reserves} - \text{required reserves}$$

$$= \$100,000 - \$100,000$$

$$= 0$$

The bank cannot make any new loans.

What happens if the bank receives a new deposit of $100,000? Figure 5 shows the bank's balance sheet right after the deposit is made. Its cash reserves are now $200,000 and its deposits $1,100,000. With the additional deposit, the bank's total reserves equal $200,000. Its required reserves are $110,000 (.10 × $1,100,000). So its excess reserves are $90,000 ($200,000 − $110,000). Since a bank can lend its excess reserves, First National Bank can loan an additional $90,000.

---

[2]In our simplified balance sheet, we assume there is no net worth, or owner's equity. Net worth is the value of the owner's claim on the firm (the owner's equity) and is found as the difference between the value of assets and nonequity liabilities.

FIGURE 5

First National Bank Balance Sheet After $100,000 Deposit

A $100,000 deposit increases the bank's cash reserves to $200,000 and its deposits to $1,100,000. The bank must hold 10 percent of deposits, or $110,000, on reserve. The difference between total reserves ($200,000) and required reserves ($110,000) is excess reserves ($90,000). The bank now has $90,000 available for lending.

First National Bank

Assets		Liabilities	
Cash	$200,000	Deposits	$1,100,000
Loans	900,000		
Total	$1,100,000	Total	$1,100,000

Total reserves = $200,000
Required reserves = 0.1 ($1,100,000) = $110,000
Excess reserves = $90,000

Suppose the bank lends someone $90,000 by depositing $90,000 in the borrower's First National account. At the time the loan is made, the money supply increases by the amount of the loan, $90,000. By making the loan, the bank has increased the money supply. But this is not the end of the story. The borrower spends the $90,000, and it winds up being deposited in the Second National Bank.

Figure 6 shows the balance sheets of both banks after the loan is made and the money is spent and deposited at Second National Bank. First National Bank now has loans of $990,000 and no excess reserves (the required reserves of $110,000 equal total reserves). So First National Bank can make no more loans until a new deposit

FIGURE 6

Balance Sheets After a $90,000 Loan Made by First National Bank is Spent and Deposited at Second National Bank

Once First National Bank makes the $90,000 loan, its cash reserves fall to $110,000 and its loans increase to $990,000. At this point, the bank's total reserves ($110,000) equal its required reserves (10 percent of deposits). Because it has no excess reserves, the bank cannot make new loans.

Second National Bank receives a deposit of $90,000. It must hold 10 percent, or $9,000, on reserve. Its excess reserves equal total reserves ($90,000) minus required reserves ($9,000), or $81,000. Second National Bank can make a maximum loan of $81,000.

First National Bank

Assets		Liabilities	
Cash	$110,000	Deposits	$1,100,000
Loans	990,000		
Total	$1,100,000	Total	$1,100,000

Total reserves = $110,000
Required reserves = 0.1 ($1,100,000) = $110,000
Excess reserves = 0

Second National Bank

Assets		Liabilities	
Cash	$90,000	Deposits	$90,000
Total	$90,000	Total	$90,000

Total reserves = $90,000
Required reserves = 0.1 ($90,000) = $9,000
Excess reserves = $81,000

TABLE 2

The Effect on Bank Deposits of an Initial Bank Deposit of $100,000

Bank	New Deposit	Required Reserves	Excess Reserves (new loans)
First National	$ 100,000	$ 10,000	$ 90,000
Second National	90,000	9,000	81,000
Third National	81,000	8,100	72,900
Fourth National	72,900	7,290	65,610
Fifth National	65,610	6,561	59,049
Sixth National	59,049	5,905	53,144
⋮	⋮	⋮	⋮
Total	$1,000,000	$100,000	$900,000

is made. Second National Bank has a new deposit of $90,000 (to simplify the analysis, we assume that this is the first transaction at Second National Bank). Its required reserves are 10 percent of $90,000, or $9,000. With total reserves of $90,000, Second National Bank has excess reserves of $81,000. It can make loans up to $81,000.

Notice what has happened to the banks' deposits as a result of the initial $100,000 deposit in First National Bank. Deposits at First National Bank have increased by $100,000. Second National Bank has a new deposit of $90,000, and the loans it makes will increase the money supply even more. Table 2 shows how the initial deposit of $100,000 is multiplied through the banking system. Each time a new loan is made, the money is spent and redeposited in the banking system. But each bank keeps 10 percent of the deposit on reserve, lending only 90 percent. So the amount of money loaned decreases by 10 percent each time it goes through another bank. If we carried the calculations out, you would see that the total increase in deposits associated with the initial $100,000 deposit is $1,000,000. Required reserves would increase by $100,000, and new loans would increase by $900,000.

3.b. Deposit Expansion Multiplier

Rather than calculate the excess reserves at each bank, as we did in Table 2, we can use a simple formula to find the maximum increase in deposits given a new deposit. The **deposit expansion multiplier** equals the reciprocal of the reserve requirement:

deposit expansion multiplier: the reciprocal of the reserve requirement

$$\text{Deposit expansion multiplier} = \frac{1}{\text{reserve requirement}}$$

In our example, the reserve requirement is 10 percent, or .10. So the deposit expansion multiplier equals 1/.10, or 10. An initial increase in deposits of $100,000 expands deposits in the banking system by 10 times $100,000, or $1,000,000. This is because the new $100,000 deposit creates $90,000 in excess reserves and $10 \times \$90,000 = \$900,000$, which when added to the initial deposit of $100,000 equals $1,000,000. The maximum increase in deposits is found by multiplying the deposit expansion multiplier by the amount of the new deposit.

With no new deposits, the banking system can increase the money supply only by the multiplier times excess reserves:

$$\text{Deposit expansion multiplier} \times \text{excess reserves}$$
$$= \text{maximum increase in deposits}$$

The deposit expansion multiplier indicates the *maximum* possible change in total deposits when a new deposit is made. For the effect to be that large, all excess reserves must be loaned out and all of the money that is deposited must stay in the banking system.

If banks hold more reserves than the minimum required, they lend a smaller fraction of any new deposits; this reduces the effect of the deposit expansion multiplier. For instance, if the reserve requirement is 10 percent, we know that the deposit expansion multiplier is 10. If a bank chooses to hold 20 percent of its deposits on reserve, the deposit expansion multiplier equals 5 (1/.20).

If money (currency and coin) is withdrawn from the banking system and kept as cash, deposits and bank reserves are smaller and less money exists to loan out. This *currency drain*—removal of money—reduces the deposit expansion multiplier. The greater the currency drain, the smaller the multiplier. There is always some currency drain as people carry currency to pay for day-to-day transactions. However, during historical periods of bank panic, where people lost confidence in banks, large currency withdrawals contributed to declines in money supply.

Remember that the deposit expansion multiplier measures the *maximum* expansion of the money supply by the banking system. Any single bank can lend only its excess reserves, but the whole banking system can expand the money supply by a multiple of the initial excess reserves. Thus the banking system as a whole can increase the money supply by the deposit expansion multiplier times the excess reserves of the system. The initial bank is limited to its initial loan; the banking system generates loan after loan based on that initial loan. A new deposit can increase the money supply by the deposit expansion multiplier times the new deposit.

In the next chapter we discuss how changes in the reserve requirement affect the money supply and the economy. This area of policymaking is controlled by the Federal Reserve.

A single bank increases the money supply by lending its excess reserves; the banking system increases the money supply by the deposit expansion multiplier times the excess reserves of the system.

RECAP

1. The fractional reserve banking system allows banks to expand the money supply by making loans.

2. Banks must keep a fraction of their deposits on reserve; their excess reserves are available for lending.

3. The deposit expansion multiplier measures the maximum increase in the money supply given a new deposit; it is the reciprocal of the reserve requirement.

4. A single bank increases the money supply by lending its excess reserves.

5. The banking system can increase the money supply by the deposit expansion multiplier times the excess reserves in the banking system.

Summary

❓ What is money?

1. Money is anything that is generally acceptable to sellers in exchange for goods and services. *§1*

2. Money serves as a medium of exchange, a unit of account, a store of value, and a standard of deferred payment. *§1.a*

3. Money, because it is more efficient than barter, lowers transaction costs. *§1.a.1*

4. Money should be portable, divisible, and durable. *§1.a.1, 1.a.3*

❓ How is the U.S. money supply defined?

5. There are three definitions of money based on its liquidity. *§1.b*

6. The M1 money supply equals the sum of currency plus travelers' checks plus demand deposits plus other checkable deposits. *§1.b.1*

7. The M2 money supply equals the M1 money supply plus savings and small-denomination time deposits, and retail money market mutual fund balances. *§1.b.2*

8. The M3 money supply equals the M2 money supply plus large time deposits, repurchase agreements, Eurodollar deposits, and institution-only money market mutual fund balances. *§1.b.3*

❓ How do countries pay for international transactions?

9. Using the foreign exchange market, governments (along with individuals and firms) are able to convert national currencies to pay for trade. *§1.c*

10. The U.S. dollar is the world's major international reserve currency. *§1.c.1*

11. The European currency unit (ECU) was a composite currency whose value was an average of the values of several western European currencies. *§1.c.2*

❓ Why are banks considered intermediaries?

12. Banks serve as middlemen between savers and borrowers. *§2.a*

❓ How does international banking differ from domestic banking?

13. Domestic banking in most nations is strictly regulated; international banking is not. *§2.c*

14. The Eurocurrency market is the international deposit and loan market. *§2.c.1*

15. International banking facilities (IBFs) allow U.S. domestic banks to carry on international banking activities on U.S. soil. *§2.c.2*

16. Informal financial markets are important in developing countries. *§2.d*

❓ How do banks create money?

17. Banks can make loans up to the amount of their excess reserves, their total reserves minus their required reserves. *§3.a*

18. The deposit expansion multiplier is the reciprocal of the reserve requirement. *§3.b*

19. A single bank expands the money supply by lending its excess reserves. *§3.b*

20. The banking system can increase the money supply by the deposit expansion multiplier times the excess reserves in the system. *§3.b*

Key Terms

money *§1*

liquid asset *§1*

currency substitution *§1.a.3*

credit *§1.a.4*

M1 money supply *§1.b.1*

transactions account *§1.b.1*

international reserve asset *§1.c.1*

international reserve currency *§1.c.1*

European currency unit (ECU) *§1.c.2*

composite currency *§1.c.2*

special drawing right (SDR) *§1.c.2*

Federal Deposit Insurance Corporation (FDIC) *§2.b.2*

Eurocurrency market or offshore banking *§2.c.1*
international banking facility (IBF) *§2.c.2*
ROSCA *§2.d*
hawala *§2.d*

fractional reserve banking system *§3*
required reserves *§3.a*
excess reserves *§3.a*
deposit expansion multiplier *§3.b*

Exercises

1. Describe the four functions of money, using the U.S. dollar to provide an example of how dollars serve each function.

2. During World War II, cigarettes were used as money in prisoner of war camps. Considering the attributes a good money should possess, why would cigarettes emerge as money among prisoners?

3. What is a financial intermediary? Give an example of how your bank or credit union serves as a financial intermediary between you and the rest of the economy.

4. What is the Eurocurrency market, and how is banking in the Eurocurrency market different from domestic banking?

5. What are IBFs? Why do you think they were legalized?

6. First Bank has cash reserves of $200,000, loans of $800,000, and deposits of $1,000,000.

    a. Prepare a balance sheet for the bank.
    b. If the bank maintains a reserve requirement of 12 percent, what is the largest loan it can make?
    c. What is the maximum amount the money supply can be increased as a result of First Bank's new loan?

7. Yesterday bank A had no excess reserves. Today it received a new deposit of $5,000.

    a. If the bank maintains a reserve requirement of 2 percent, what is the maximum loan bank A can make?
    b. What is the maximum amount the money supply can be increased as a result of bank A's new loan?

8. "M2 is a better definition of the money supply than M1." Agree or disagree with this statement. In your argument, clearly state the criteria on which you are basing your decision.

9. The deposit expansion multiplier measures the maximum possible expansion of the money supply in the banking system. What factors could cause the actual expansion of the money supply to differ from that given by the deposit expansion multiplier?

10. What is liquidity? Rank the following assets in order of their liquidity: $10 bill, personal check for $20, savings account with $400 in it, stereo, car, house, travelers' check.

Use the following table on the components of money in a hypothetical economy to do exercises 11–13.

Money Component	Amount
Travelers' checks	$ 100
Currency	$ 2,000
Small-denomination time deposits	$ 3,500
Repurchase agreements	$ 2,000
Demand deposits	$ 5,000
Other checkable deposits	$ 9,000
U.S. Treasury bonds	$25,000
Large-denomination time deposits	$ 8,000
Retail money market mutual funds	$ 7,500

11. What is the value of M1 in the above table?

12. What is the value of M2 in the above table?

13. What is the value of M3 in the above table?

14. The deposit expansion multiplier has been defined as the reciprocal of the reserve requirement. Suppose that banks must hold 10 percent of their deposits in reserve. However, banks also lose 10 percent of their deposits through cash drains out of the banking system.

    a. What would the deposit expansion multiplier be if there were no cash drain?
    b. With the cash drain, what is the value of the deposit expansion multiplier?

ACE

Take the ACE Practice Test for this chapter to review the important concepts and get immediate feedback with answers.

economics.college.hmco.com/students

They Love Our Money

ISTANBUL—Every morning thousands of traders from the countries of the former Soviet bloc descend on the Aksaray district of this ancient Turkish seaport. Soon its narrow streets, where signs in Russian outnumber those in Turkish, are filled with visitors buying wholesale goods for resale to consumers back home: jewelry, eyeglasses, plumbing fixtures, and, most of all, clothing. "You want it in black?" asks the Russian-speaking owner of a store specializing in leather coats. "Come back tomorrow by 5 p.m. and we'll have it in black." Then he names the price: $150 per coat—in American cash, please.

While Istanbul's moneychangers can handle everything from Romanian lei to Kazakh tenge, the greenback reigns supreme. And that is true around the globe. Few Americans may realize it, but more U.S. currency is in circulation outside the United States than inside. Of the $450 billion in bills and coins now lining people's wallets, cash registers, bank vaults, and mattresses, about two-thirds—or $300 billion—is abroad.

That percentage is rising. The end of the cold war opened the former Soviet bloc to American currency, and restrictions on currency trading have been eliminated in much of Africa, Asia, and the Middle East. Joseph Botta, who tracks U.S. cash for the Federal Reserve Bank of New York, says that the amount of U.S. currency abroad has grown $15 billion to $20 billion a year for the past five years.

Big bills only, please. Roughly 80 percent of the American cash abroad is in the form of $100 bills. That contrasts sharply with cash at home, which circulates mainly in $20 bills (the denomination favored for use in automated teller machines). Says Botta: "The higher denominations are very popular outside the U.S., and that reflects what people there are using the currency for"—not small, daily purchases but savings and commercial transactions. In many countries, the local currency is ravaged by inflation or residents do not trust the banks.

The popularity of the dollar overseas benefits the United States in ways that go far beyond mere pride or ease of shopping for American tourists. From the point of view of the Federal Reserve Board, the $300 billion circulating abroad is like an interest-free loan to the U.S. government. Foreign producers have accepted the paper money in return for real goods and services. As long as the paper stays overseas, the United States does not have to redeem it for other goods or services, and it does not swell America's domestic money supply or contribute to inflation. The Fed estimates the annual savings at $15 billion to $20 billion—the bill that taxpayers would otherwise have to foot for the government's interest payments on $300 billion (a benefit that economists call seigniorage, a medieval French term for the right of a lord to coin money).

Source: "They Love Our Money," *U.S. News and World Report*, p. 28. Copyright 1998 *U.S. News and World Report*.

U.S. News and World Report/April 27, 1998

Commentary

There is considerable evidence that U.S. dollars are held in large amounts in many developing countries. Residents of these countries hold dollars because their domestic inflation rate is (or has been) very high, and by holding dollars, they can avoid the rapid erosion of purchasing power that is associated with holding domestic currency. This "dollarization" of a country begins with people's holding dollars rather than domestic currency as savings (the store of value function of money). But if high inflation continues, dollars, rather than domestic currency, come to be used in day-to-day transactions as the medium of exchange. In the late 1980s, as the Polish economy became heavily dollarized, a common joke in Poland was: "What do America and Poland have in common? In America, you can buy everything for dollars and nothing for zlotys [the Polish currency]. In Poland, it is exactly the same."

One implication of the demand for dollars in developing countries is that dollar currency leaves the United States. This currency drain will affect the size of the deposit expansion multiplier. In the chapter, the deposit expansion multiplier was defined as

$$\text{Deposit expansion multiplier} = \frac{1}{\text{reserve requirement}}$$

This definition was based on the assumption that when a bank receives a deposit, all of the deposit will be loaned except for the fraction the bank is required to keep by the legal reserve requirement set by the Federal Reserve. With a currency drain, some of the deposit is withdrawn from the banking system as cash. As a result, the deposit expansion multiplier is now

$$\text{Deposit expansion multiplier} = \frac{1}{\begin{array}{c}(\text{reserve requirement} \\ + \text{ currency drain})\end{array}}$$

For instance, if the reserve requirement equals 10 percent, our original definition of the deposit expansion multiplier would provide a multiplier equal to $1/.10 = 10$. But if people withdraw 10 percent of their deposits as cash, then the 10 percent currency drain is added to the 10 percent reserve requirement to yield a deposit expansion multiplier of $1/.20 = 5$. So the larger the currency drain, the smaller the money-creating potential of the banking system.

An additional interesting aspect of the foreign demand for dollars is the *seigniorage,* or revenue earned by the government from creating money. If it costs about 7 cents to print a dollar bill but the exchange value is a dollar's worth of goods and services, then the government earns about 93 cents for each dollar put into circulation. If foreigners hold U.S. currency, then the government earns a profit from providing a stable-valued dollar that people want to hold. However, we should not overestimate the value of this in terms of the U.S. government budget. Even if all the new currency issued by the U.S. government flowed out to the rest of the world, the seigniorage earned by the United States over the past decade would have averaged less than 1.7 percent of federal government revenue. Given the relatively insignificant revenue earned from seigniorage, it is not surprising that U.S. policy with regard to the dollarization of developing countries has largely been one of disinterest.

CHAPTER 14

Monetary Policy

? Fundamental Questions

1. What does the Federal Reserve do?

2. How is monetary policy set?

3. What are the tools of monetary policy?

4. What role do central banks play in the foreign exchange market?

5. What are the determinants of the demand for money?

6. How does monetary policy affect the equilibrium level of real GDP?

In the previous chapter, we saw how banks "create" money by making loans. However, that money must get into the system to begin with. Most of us never think about how money enters the economy. All we worry about is having money available when we need it. But there is a government body that controls the U.S. money supply, and in this chapter we will learn about this agency—the Federal Reserve system and the Board of Governors that oversees monetary policy.

The amount of money available for spending by individuals or businesses affects prices, interest rates, foreign exchange rates, and the level of income in the economy. Thus, having control of the money supply gives the Federal Reserve powerful influence over these important economic variables. As we learned in Chapter 12, fiscal policy, or the control of government spending and taxes, is one of two ways by which government can change the equilibrium level of real GDP. Monetary policy as carried out by the Federal Reserve is the other mechanism through which

attempts are made to manage the economy. In this chapter we will also explore the tools of monetary policy and see how changes in the money supply affect the equilibrium level of real GDP. ▪

1. The Federal Reserve System

The Federal Reserve is the central bank of the United States. A *central bank* performs several functions: accepting deposits from and making loans to commercial banks, acting as a banker for the federal government, and controlling the money supply. We discuss these functions in greater detail later on, but first we look at the structure of the Federal Reserve System, or the Fed.

1.a. Structure of the Fed

1. What does the Federal Reserve do?

Congress created the Federal Reserve System in 1913, with the Federal Reserve Act. Bank panics and failures had convinced lawmakers that the United States needed an agency to control the money supply and make loans to commercial banks when those banks found themselves without sufficient reserves. Because Americans tended to distrust large banking interests, Congress called for a decentralized central bank. The Federal Reserve System divides the nation into 12 districts, each with its own Federal Reserve bank (Figure 1).

1.a.1. Board of Governors Although Congress created a decentralized system so that each district bank would represent the special interests of its own region, in practice the Fed is much more centralized than its creators intended. Monetary policy is largely set by the Board of Governors in Washington, D.C. This board is made up of seven members, who are appointed by the president and confirmed by the Senate.

The most visible and powerful member of the board is the chairman. In fact the chairman of the Board of Governors has been called *the second most powerful person in the United States.* This individual serves as a leader and spokesperson for the board and typically exercises more authority in determining the course of monetary policy than do the other governors.

The chairman is appointed by the president to a four-year term: In recent years most chairmen have been reappointed to one or more additional terms (Table 1). The governors serve 14-year terms, with the terms staggered so that a new position comes up for appointment every two years. This system allows continuity in the policymaking process and is intended to place the board above politics. Congress created the Fed as an independent agency: monetary policy is supposed to be formulated independent of Congress and the president. Of course, this is impossible in practice because the president appoints and the Senate approves the members of the board. But because the governors serve 14-year terms, they outlast the president who appointed them.

1.a.2. District Banks Each of the Fed's 12 district banks is formally directed by a nine-person board of directors. Three directors represent commercial banks in the district, and three represent nonbanking business interests. These six individuals are elected by the Federal Reserve System member banks in the district. The three remaining directors are appointed by the Fed's Board of Governors. District bank

FIGURE 1

The Federal Reserve System

The Federal Reserve System divides the country into 12 districts. Each district has its own Federal Reserve bank, headquarters for Fed operations in that district. For example, the first district bank is in Boston; the twelfth is in San Francisco. There are also branch banks in Los Angeles, Miami, and other cities. *Source:* Federal Reserve Bulletin.

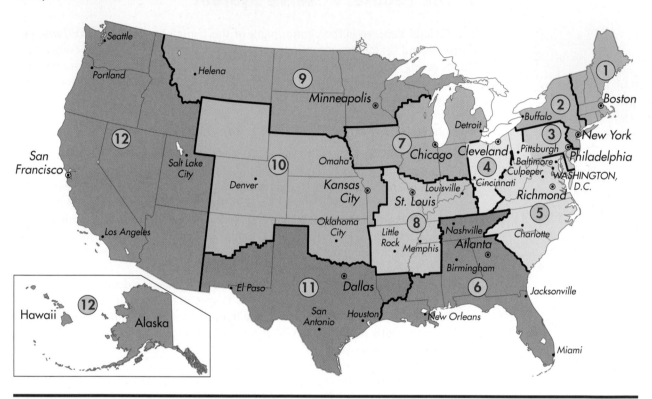

directors are not involved in the day-to-day operations of the district banks, but they meet regularly to oversee bank operations. They also choose the president of the bank. The president, who is in charge of operations, participates in monetary policy-making with the Board of Governors in Washington, D.C.

TABLE 1

Recent Chairmen of the Federal Reserve Board

Name	Age at Appointment	Term Began	Term Ended	Years of Tenure
William McChesney Martin	44	4/2/51	1/31/70	18.8
Arthur Burns	65	1/31/70	2/1/78	8.0
G. William Miller	52	3/8/78	8/6/79	1.4
Paul Volcker	51	8/6/79	8/5/87	8.0
Alan Greenspan	61	8/11/87		

What's on a 20-Dollar Bill?

The figure shows both sides of a twenty-dollar bill. We've numbered several elements for identification.

1. **Watermark**
A watermark, created during the paper-making process, depicts the same historical figure as the portrait. It is visible from both sides when held up to a light.

2. **Security thread**
An embedded polymer strip, positioned in a unique spot for each denomination, guards against counterfeiting. The thread itself, visible when held up to a bright light, contains microprinting—the letters *USA,* the denomination of the bill, and a flag. When viewed under ultraviolet light, the thread glows a distinctive color for each denomination.

3. **Color-shifting ink**
The ink used in the numeral in the lower right-hand corner on the front of the bill looks green when viewed straight on but copper when viewed at an angle.

4. **Serial number**
No two notes of the same kind, denomination, and series have the same serial number. This fact can be important in detecting counterfeit notes; many counterfeiters make large batches of a particular note with the same number.

Notes are numbered in lots of 100 million. Each lot has a different suffix letter, beginning with *A* and following in alphabetical order through *Z,* omitting *O* because of its similarity to the numerical zero.

Serial numbers consist of two prefix letters, eight numerals, and a one-letter suffix. The first letter of the prefix designates the series. The second letter of the prefix designates the Federal Reserve Bank to which the note was issued, with *A* designating the first district, or the Boston Fed, and *L,* the twelfth letter in the alphabet, designating the twelfth district, or the San Francisco Fed.

5. **"In God We Trust"**
Secretary of the Treasury Salmon P. Chase first authorized use of "In God We Trust" on U.S. money on the 2-cent coin in 1864. In 1955, Congress mandated the use of this phrase on all currency and coins.

Source: Federal Reserve Bank of Atlanta and Bureau of Engraving and Printing.

1.a.3. The Federal Open Market Committee

The **Federal Open Market Committee (FOMC)** is the official policymaking body of the Federal Reserve System. The committee is made up of the seven members of the Board of Governors plus five of the twelve district bank presidents. All of the district bank presidents, except for the president of the Federal Reserve Bank of New York, take turns serving on the FOMC. Because the New York Fed actually carries out monetary policy, that bank's president is always on the committee. In section 2 we talk more about the FOMC's role and the tactics it uses.

1.b. Functions of the Fed

The Federal Reserve System offers banking services to the banking community and the U.S. Treasury and supervises the nation's banking system. The Fed also regulates the U.S. money supply.

1.b.1. Banking Services and Supervision

The Fed provides several basic services to the banking community: it supplies currency to banks, holds their reserves, and clears checks. The Fed supplies U.S. currency (Federal Reserve notes) to the banking community through its 12 district banks. (See the Economic Insight "What's on a 20-Dollar Bill?") Commercial banks in each district also hold reserves in the form of deposits at their district bank. In addition, the Fed makes loans to banks. In this sense, the Fed is a *banker's bank.* And the Fed clears checks, transferring funds to the banks where checks are deposited from the banks on which the checks are drawn.

The Fed also supervises the nation's banks, ensuring that they operate in a sound and prudent manner. And it acts as the banker for the U.S. government, selling U.S. government securities for the U.S. Treasury.

1.b.2. Controlling the Money Supply

All of the functions the Federal Reserve carries out are important, but none is more important than managing the nation's money supply. Before 1913, when the Fed was created, the money supply did not change to meet fluctuations in the demand for money. These fluctuations can stem from changes in income or seasonal patterns of demand. For example, every year during the Christmas season, the demand for currency rises because people carry more money to buy gifts. During the holiday season, the Fed increases the supply of currency to meet the demand for cash withdrawals from banks. After the holiday season, the demand for currency drops and the public deposits currency in banks, which then return the currency to the Fed.

The Fed controls the money supply to achieve the policy goals set by the FOMC. It does this largely through its ability to influence bank reserves and the money-creating power of commercial banks that we talked about in Chapter 13.

RECAP

1. As the central bank of the United States, the Federal Reserve accepts deposits from and makes loans to commercial banks, acts as a banker for the federal government, and controls the money supply.
2. The Federal Reserve system is made up of the Board of Governors in Washington, D.C., and 12 district banks.
3. The most visible and powerful member of the Board of Governors is the chairman.

4. The governors are appointed by the president and confirmed by the Senate to serve 14-year terms.

5. Monetary policy is made by the Federal Open Market Committee, whose members include the seven governors and five of the twelve district bank presidents.

6. The Fed provides currency, holds reserves, clears checks, and supervises commercial banks.

7. The most important function the Fed performs is controlling the U.S. money supply.

2. Implementing Monetary Policy

2. How is monetary policy set?

Changes in the amount of money in an economy affect the inflation rate, the interest rate, and the equilibrium level of national income. Throughout history, monetary policy has made currencies worthless and toppled governments. This is why controlling the money supply is so important.

2.a. Policy Goals

The objective of monetary policy is economic growth with stable prices.

The ultimate goal of monetary policy is much like that of fiscal policy: economic growth with stable prices. *Economic growth* means greater output; *stable prices* mean a low, steady rate of inflation.

2.a.1. Intermediate Targets
The Fed does not control gross domestic product or the price level directly. Instead, it controls the money supply, which in turn affects GDP and the level of prices. The money supply, or the growth of the money supply, is an **intermediate target**, an objective that helps the Fed achieve its ultimate policy objective—economic growth with stable prices.

intermediate target: an objective used to achieve some ultimate policy goal

Using the growth of the money supply as an intermediate target assumes that there is a fairly stable relationship between changes in money and changes in income and prices. The bases for this assumption are the equation of exchange and the quantity theory of money. The **equation of exchange** is a definition that relates the quantity of money to nominal GDP:

equation of exchange: an equation that relates the quantity of money to nominal GDP

$$MV = PQ$$

where M = the quantity of money
V = the velocity of money
P = the price level
Q = the quantity of output, like real income or real GDP

This equation is true by definition: money times the velocity of money will always be equal to nominal GDP.

In Chapter 13 we said there are several definitions of the money supply: M1, M2, and M3. The **velocity of money** is the average number of times each dollar is spent on final goods and services in a year. If P is the price level and Q is real GDP (the quantity of goods and services produced in the economy), then PQ equals nominal GDP. If

velocity of money: the average number of times each dollar is spent on final goods and services in a year

$$MV = PQ$$

then
$$V = \frac{PQ}{M}$$

Suppose the price level is 2 and real GDP is $500; *PQ,* or nominal GDP, is $1,000. If the money supply is $200, then velocity is 5 ($1,000/$200). A velocity of 5 means that each dollar must be spent an average of 5 times during the year if a money supply of $200 is going to support the purchase of $1,000 worth of new goods and services.

quantity theory of money: the theory that with constant velocity, changes in the quantity of money change nominal GDP

The **quantity theory of money** uses the equation of exchange to relate changes in the money supply to changes in prices and output. If the money supply (M) increases and velocity (V) is constant, then nominal GDP (PQ) must increase. If the economy is operating at maximum capacity (producing at the maximum level of Q), an increase in M causes an increase in P. And if there is substantial unemployment, so that Q can increase, the increase in M may mean a higher price level (P) as well as higher real GDP (Q).

The Fed attempts to set money growth targets that are consistent with rising output and low inflation. In terms of the quantity theory of money, the Fed wants to increase M at a rate that supports steadily rising Q with slow and steady increases in P. The assumption that there is a reasonably stable relationship among M, P, and Q is what motivates the Fed to use money supply growth rates as an intermediate target to achieve its ultimate goal—higher Q with slow increases in P.

Of course, other central banks may have different goals. An example of a central bank that pursues inflation targeting is given in the Global Business Insight "The European Central Bank."

The FOMC used to set explicit ranges for money growth targets; however, in 2000 it stopped doing so. While no longer publicly announcing a range for money growth, the FOMC still monitors the money supply growth rates. This shift away from announced targets reflects the belief that in recent years, money growth has

The chairman of the Federal Reserve Board of Governors is sometimes referred to as the second most powerful person in the United States. At the time this book was written, Alan Greenspan was the Fed chairman. His leadership of the Fed has important implications for money and credit conditions in the United States.

The European Central Bank

The European Central Bank (ECB) began operations on June 1, 1998, in Frankfurt, Germany, and now conducts monetary policy for the euro-area countries. The national central banks like the Bank of Italy and the German Bundesbank are still operating and perform many of the functions they had prior to the ECB, such as bank regulation and supervision and facilitating payments systems in each nation. In some sense, they are like the regional banks of the Federal Reserve System in the United States. Monetary policy for the euro area is conducted by the ECB in Frankfurt, just as monetary policy for the United States is conducted by the Federal Reserve in Washington, D.C. Yet the national central banks of the euro area play an important role in each of the respective countries. The entire network of national central banks and the ECB is called the *European System of Central Banks.* Monetary policy for the euro area is determined by the *Governing Council* of the ECB. This council is composed of the heads of the national central banks of the euro-area countries plus the members of the ECB *Executive Board.* The board is made up of the ECB president and vice president and four others chosen by the heads of the governments of the euro-area nations.

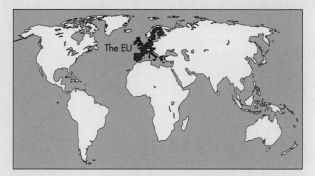

The ECB pursues a primary goal of price stability, defined as an inflation rate of less than 2 percent per year. Subject to the achievement of this primary goal, additional issues, such as economic growth, may be addressed. A benefit of a stated policy goal is that people can more easily form expectations of future ECB policy. This builds public confidence in the central bank and allows for greater stability than if the public were always trying to guess what the central bank really cares about and how policy will be changed as market conditions change.

become an unreliable indicator of monetary conditions as a result of unpredictable changes in velocity.

From the late 1950s to the mid-1970s, the velocity of the M1 money supply grew at a steady pace, from 3.5 in 1959 to 5.5 in 1975. Knowing that V was growing at a steady pace, the Fed was able to set a target growth rate for the M1 money supply, confident that it would produce a fairly predictable growth in nominal GDP. But when velocity is not constant, there can be problems with using money growth rates as an intermediate target. This is exactly what happened starting in the late 1970s. Figure 2 plots the velocity of the M1, M2, and M3 money supplies from 1959. Although the M2 and M3 velocities continued to indicate a stable pattern of growth, M1 velocity behaved erratically. With the breakdown of the relationship between the M1 money supply and GDP, the Fed shifted its emphasis from the M1 money supply, concentrating instead on achieving targeted growth in the M2 and M3 money supplies. More recently the velocities of M2 and M3 have also become less predictable.

Economists are still debating the reason for the fluctuations in velocity. Some argue that new deposits and innovations in banking have led to fluctuations in the money held in traditional demand deposits as bank customers switched to different types of financial assets. These unpredictable changes in financial asset holdings affect the various money supplies and their velocities.

FIGURE 2

Velocity of the M1, M2, and M3 Money Supplies

The velocity of money is the ratio of nominal gross domestic product to the money supply. The narrower the definition of money, the higher its velocity. So M1, the narrowest definition, has a higher velocity than M2 or M3. In recent years, the velocity of M1 has been much less stable than the velocity of the broader money definitions.

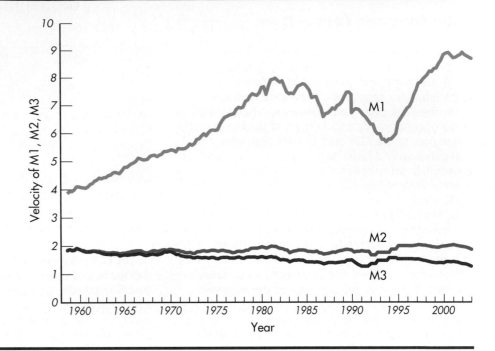

In addition to its interest in money growth, the Fed monitors other key variables that are used to indicate the future course of the economy. These include commodity prices, interest rates, and foreign exchange rates. The Fed may not set formal targets for all of them, but it considers them in setting policy. At the time of this edition, the FOMC just announced an explicit target for the *federal funds rate* of interest—the interest rate banks pay for borrowing overnight from other banks. We will discuss this interest rate in more detail in the next section.

2.a.2. Inflation Targeting Some countries have moved away from pursuing intermediate targets like money growth rates and have instead focused on an ultimate goal: a low inflation rate. In part, these countries realize that using monetary policy to support economic growth, low unemployment, and also low inflation has often resulted in an inflationary bias. The public generally likes to see policies supporting faster economic growth, like lower interest rates, whereas fighting inflation may mean unpopular higher interest rates and slower growth. Thus, a central bank may find it politically attractive to stimulate the economy so that inflation takes a secondary position. In addition, if the central bank always considers multiple goals like low unemployment and low inflation, the public may not be able to easily understand the central bank's decision-making process, with the result that there is great uncertainty regarding monetary policy, and business firms and households have more difficulty making economic plans for the future. Commitment to a target inflation rate greatly reduces that uncertainty.

Inflation targeting has been adopted in several countries, including New Zealand, Canada, the U.K., Australia, Switzerland, Chile, Korea, South Africa, and Europe (by the European Central Bank). It is important to realize that in order to use inflation targeting, a central bank must be independent from fiscal policy. It is not enough to announce a target for the inflation rate. The central bank must not be in the position of having to help finance government spending. Only with this independence can a central bank truly have a credible inflation target.

2.b. Operating Procedures

The FOMC sets federal funds rate targets and then implements them through the Federal Reserve Bank of New York. The mechanism for translating policy into action is an **FOMC directive.** Each directive outlines the conduct of monetary policy over the six-week period until the FOMC meets again to reconsider its targets and specify policy tools.

Figure 3 contains the directive issued by the FOMC meeting of January 29, 2003. The FOMC directed the bond traders at the Federal Reserve Bank of New York to buy or sell government bonds as needed to keep the **federal funds rate,** or the interest rate that one bank charges another for overnight lending, around 1-1/4 percent. If the rate starts to rise above 1-1/4 percent, then the New York Fed will buy bonds from bond dealers. The dealers are paid with funds drawn on the Federal Reserve, which are then deposited in the dealers' accounts in commercial banks. This will inject money into the banking system. It will increase bank excess reserves, giving the banks more money to lend; as a result the cost of these funds, the federal funds rate, will fall. If the rate drops below 1-1/4 percent, then the New York Fed will sell bonds to bond dealers. The dealers pay for the bonds with funds drawn on commercial banks. This drains money from the banking system. Bank excess reserves will fall, and since banks will have less money to lend, the cost of these funds, the federal funds rate, will rise. So the actual federal funds rate fluctuates about the target rate set by the FOMC directive.

FOMC directive: instructions issued by the FOMC to the Federal Reserve Bank of New York to implement monetary policy

federal funds rate: the interest rate a bank charges when it lends excess reserves to another bank

---

FIGURE 3

FOMC Directive and Policy Statement

The FOMC always issues a directive to guide the conduct of monetary policy between meetings. In addition, a press statement at the conclusion of the meeting indicates the committee's view regarding the likely course of policy in the near future. At the meeting of January 29, 2003, the directive and policy statement shown here were issued.

Directive
The Federal Open Market Committee seeks monetary and financial conditions that will foster price stability and promote sustainable growth in output. To further its long-run objectives, the Committee in the immediate future seeks conditions in reserve markets consistent with maintaining the federal funds rate at an average of around 1-1/4 percent.

Policy Statement
The Federal Open Market Committee decided today to keep its target for the federal funds rate unchanged at 1-1/4 percent.

Oil price premiums and other aspects of geopolitical risks have reportedly fostered continued restraint on spending and hiring by businesses. However, the Committee believes that as those risks lift, as most analysts expect, the accomodative stance of monetary policy, coupled with ongoing growth in productivity, will provide support to an improving economic climate over time.

In these circumstances, the Committee believes that, against the background of its long-run goals of price stability and sustainable economic growth and of the information currently available, the risks are balanced with respect to the prospects for both goals for the foreseeable future.

At the conclusion of each FOMC meeting, a policy statement is issued to the press. This statement informs the public of the committee's view regarding the likely course of the economy in the near term. This will also indicate the likely course of monetary policy. In Figure 3, the policy statement issued at the conclusion of the meeting held on January 29, 2003, is given. The key part of this statement is the last phrase: "the risks are balanced with respect to the prospects for both goals for the foreseeable future." The goals are stable prices and economic growth. A "balanced" view indicates that the FOMC cannot clearly see either mounting inflation pressures or recession pressures. If the FOMC was worried about rising inflation, then the public would expect that it might raise interest rates at its next meeting. If it was worried about recession, then the public would expect that it might lower interest rates at the next meeting. But the balanced view indicates that the FOMC is likely to make no changes in interest rates.

?

3. What are the tools of monetary policy?

2.b.1. Tools of Monetary Policy

The Fed controls the money supply and interest rates by changing bank reserves. There are three tools the Fed can use to change reserves: the *reserve requirement,* the *discount rate,* and *open market operations.* In the last chapter, you saw that banks can expand the money supply by a multiple of their excess reserves—the deposit expansion multiplier, the reciprocal of the reserve requirement.

Reserve Requirement   The Fed requires banks to hold a fraction of their transaction deposits on reserve. This fraction is the reserve requirement. *Transaction deposits* are checking accounts and other deposits that can be used to pay third parties. Large banks hold a greater percentage of deposits in reserve than small banks do (the reserve requirement increases from 0 for the first $6 million of deposits to 3 percent for deposits from $6 to $42.1 million, and then to 10 percent for deposits in excess of $42.1 million).

Remember from Chapter 13 that required reserves are the dollar amount of reserves that a bank must hold to meet its reserve requirement. There are two ways in which required reserves may be held: vault cash at the bank or a deposit in the Fed. The sum of a bank's *vault cash* (coin and currency in the bank's vault) and its deposit in the Fed is called its **legal reserves.** When legal reserves equal required reserves, the bank has no excess reserves and can make no new loans. When legal reserves exceed required reserves, the bank has excess reserves available for lending.

legal reserves: the cash a bank holds in its vault plus its deposit in the Fed

As bank excess reserves change, the lending and money-creating potential of the banking system changes. One way the Fed can alter excess reserves is by changing the reserve requirement. If it lowers the reserve requirement, a portion of what was previously required reserves becomes excess reserves, which can be used to make loans and expand the money supply. A lower reserve requirement also increases the deposit expansion multiplier. By raising the reserve requirement, the Fed reduces the money-creating potential of the banking system and tends to reduce the money supply. A higher reserve requirement also lowers the deposit expansion multiplier.

Consider the example in Table 2. If First National Bank's balance sheet shows vault cash of $100,000 and a deposit in the Fed of $200,000, the bank has legal reserves of $300,000. The amount of money that the bank can lend is determined by its excess reserves. Excess reserves (*ER*) equal legal reserves (*LR*) minus required reserves (*RR*):

$$ER = LR - RR$$

If the reserve requirement (*r*) is 10 percent (.10), the bank must keep 10 percent of its deposits (*D*) as required reserves:

$$RR = rD$$
$$= .10(\$1,000,000)$$
$$= \$100,000$$

In this case, the bank has excess reserves of $200,000 ($300,000 − $100,000). The bank can make a maximum loan of $200,000. The banking system can expand the money supply by the deposit expansion multiplier ($1/r$) times the excess reserves of the bank, or $2,000,000 ($1/.10 \times \$200,000$).

TABLE 2

The Effect of a Change in the Reserve Requirement

Balance Sheet of First National Bank

Assets		Liabilities	
Vault cash	$ 100,000	Deposits	$1,000,000
Deposit in Fed	200,000		
Loans	700,000		
Total	$1,000,000	Total	$1,000,000

Legal reserves (*LR*) equal vault cash plus the deposit in the Fed, or $300,000:

$LR = \$100,000 + \$200,000$
    $= \$300,000$

Excess reserves (*ER*) equal legal reserves minus required reserves (*RR*):

$ER = LR - RR$

Required reserves equal the reserve requirement (*r*) times deposits (*D*):

$RR = rD$

If the reserve requirement is 10 percent:

$RR = (.10)(\$1,000,000)$
    $= \$100,000$
$ER = \$300,000 - \$100,000$
    $= \$200,000$

First National Bank can make a maximum loan of $200,000.

The banking system can expand the money supply by the deposit expansion multiplier ($1/r$) times the excess reserves of the bank, or $2,000,000:

$(1/.10)(\$200,000) = 10(\$200,000)$
              $= \$2,000,000$

If the reserve requirement is 20 percent:

$RR = (.20)(\$1,000,000)$
    $= \$200,000$
$ER = \$300,000 - \$200,000$
    $= \$100,000$

First National Bank can make a maximum loan of $100,000.

The banking system can expand the money supply by the deposit expansion multiplier ($1/r$) times the excess reserves of the bank, or $500,000:

$(1/.20)(\$100,000) = 5(\$100,000)$
              $= \$500,000$

If the reserve requirement goes up to 20 percent (.20), required reserves are 20 percent of $1,000,000, or $200,000. Excess reserves are now $100,000, which is the maximum loan the bank can make. The banking system can expand the money supply by $500,000:

$$\frac{1}{.20}\,(\$100,000) = 5(\$100,000)$$
$$= \$500,000$$

By raising the reserve requirement, the Fed can reduce the money-creating potential of the banking system and the money supply. And by lowering the reserve requirement, the Fed can increase the money-creating potential of the banking system and the money supply.

Discount Rate   If a bank needs more reserves in order to make new loans, it typically borrows from other banks in the federal funds market. The market is called the *federal funds market* because the funds are being loaned from one commercial bank's excess reserves on deposit with the Federal Reserve to another commercial bank's deposit account at the Fed. For instance, if the First National Bank has excess reserves of $1 million, it can lend the excess to the Second National Bank. When a bank borrows in the federal funds market, it pays a rate of interest called the federal funds rate.

discount rate: the interest rate the Fed charges commercial banks when they borrow from it

At times, however, banks borrow directly from the Fed. The **discount rate** is the rate of interest the Fed charges banks. (In other countries, the rate of interest the central bank charges commercial banks is often called the *bank rate*.) Another way the Fed controls the level of bank reserves and the money supply is by changing the discount rate.

When the Fed raises the discount rate, it raises the cost of borrowing reserves, reducing the amount of reserves borrowed. Lower levels of reserves limit bank lending and the expansion of the money supply. When the Fed lowers the discount rate, it lowers the cost of borrowing reserves, increasing the amount of borrowing. As bank reserves increase, so do loans and the money supply.

There are actually two different discount rates. The rate on *primary credit* is for loans made to banks that are in good financial condition and is set above the federal funds target rate. At the time this edition was revised, the interest rate on primary credit was set at 1 percentage point above the federal funds rate. So if the FOMC sets the federal funds rate at 2 percent, then the discount rate on primary credit is 3 percent. In addition to the discount rate for primary credit loans, there is another discount rate for *secondary credit*. This rate is for banks that are having financial difficulties. At the time of this edition, the secondary credit rate was set at 1-1/2 percentage points above the federal funds rate. So if the federal funds target is set at 2 percent, the interest rate on secondary credit is 3-1/2 percent. Loans made at these discount rates are for very short terms, typically overnight.

open market operations: the buying and selling of government bonds by the Fed to control bank reserves, the federal funds rate, and the money supply

Open Market Operations   The major tool of monetary policy is the Fed's **open market operations,** the buying and selling of U.S. government bonds. Suppose the FOMC wants to increase bank reserves to lower the federal funds rate. The committee issues a directive to the bond-trading desk at the Federal Reserve Bank of New York to change the federal funds rate to a lower level. In order to accomplish this, the Fed buys bonds, with the results described earlier. If the higher reserves that result lead to increased bank lending to the public, then the new loans in turn expand the money supply through the deposit expansion multiplier process.

If the Fed wants to increase the federal funds rate, it sells bonds. As a result, the money supply decreases through the deposit expansion multiplier process.

To lower the federal funds rate and increase the money supply, the Fed buys U.S. government bonds. To increase the federal funds rate and decrease the money supply, it sells U.S. government bonds.

Its open market operations allow the Fed to control the federal funds rate and the money supply. To lower the federal funds rate and increase the money supply, the Fed buys U.S. government bonds. To raise the federal funds rate and decrease the money supply, it sells U.S. government bonds. The effect of selling these bonds, however, varies according to whether there are excess reserves in the banking system. If there are excess reserves, the money supply does not necessarily decrease when the Fed sells bonds. The open market sale may simply reduce the level of excess reserves, reducing the rate at which the money supply increases.

Table 3 shows how open market operations change bank reserves and illustrates the money-creating power of the banking system. First National Bank's initial balance sheet shows excess reserves of $100,000 with a 20 percent reserve requirement. Therefore the bank can make a maximum loan of $100,000. On the basis of

---

TABLE 3

The Effect of an Open Market Operation

Balance Sheet of First National Bank

Assets		Liabilities	
Vault cash	$ 100,000	Deposits	$1,000,000
Deposit in Fed	200,000		
Loans	700,000		
Total	$1,000,000	Total	$1,000,000

Initially legal reserves (LR) equal vault cash plus the deposit in the Fed, or $300,000:

$LR = \$100,000 + \$200,000$

$\quad = \$300,000$

If the reserve requirement (r) is 20 percent (.20), required reserves (RR) equal $200,000:

$.20(\$1,000,000) = \$200,000$

Excess reserves (ER), then, equal $100,000 ($300,000 − $200,000). The bank can make a maximum loan of $100,000. The banking system can expand the money supply by the deposit expansion multiplier ($1/r$) times the excess reserves of the bank, or $500,000:

$(1/.20)(\$100,000) = 5(\$100,000)$

$\quad\quad\quad\quad\quad\quad\quad = \$500,000$

Open market purchase:

The Fed purchases $100,000 worth of bonds from a dealer, who deposits the $100,000 in an account at First National. At this point the bank has legal reserves of $400,000, required reserves of $220,000, and excess reserves of $180,000. It can make a maximum loan of $180,000, which can expand the money supply by $900,000 [(1/.20)($180,000)].

Open market sale:

The Fed sells $100,000 worth of bonds to a dealer, who pays with a check drawn on an account at First National. At this point, the bank has legal reserves of $200,000, required reserves of $180,000 (its deposits now equal $900,000), and excess reserves of $20,000. It can make a maximum loan of $20,000, which can expand the money supply by $100,000 [(1/.20)($20,000)].

---

the bank's reserve position, the banking system can increase the money supply by a maximum of $500,000.

If the Fed purchases $100,000 worth of bonds from a private dealer, who deposits the $100,000 in an account at First National Bank, the excess reserves of First National Bank increase to $180,000. These reserves can generate a maximum increase in the money supply of $900,000. The open market purchase increases the excess reserves of the banking system, stimulating the growth of money and, eventually, nominal GDP.

What happens when an open market sale takes place? If the Fed sells $100,000 worth of bonds to a private bond dealer, the dealer pays for the bonds using a check drawn on First National Bank. First National's deposits drop from $1,000,000 to $900,000, and its legal reserves drop from $300,000 to $200,000. With excess reserves of $20,000, the banking system can increase the money supply by only $100,000. The open market sale reduces the money-creating potential of the banking system from $500,000 initially to $100,000.

2.b.2. FOMC Directives

When it sets monetary policy, the FOMC begins with its *ultimate goal:* economic growth at stable prices. It defines that goal in terms of GDP and inflation. Then it works backwards to identify its *intermediate target,* the rate at which the money supply must grow to achieve the wanted growth in GDP. Then it must decide how to achieve its intermediate target. In Figure 4, as is usually the case in real life, the Fed uses open market operations. But to know whether it should buy or sell bonds, the FOMC must have some indication of whether the money supply is growing too fast or too slowly. The committee relies on a *short-run operating target* for this information. The short-run target indicates how the money supply should change. Both the quantity of excess reserves in the banking system and the federal funds rate can serve as short-run operating targets.

The FOMC carries out its policies through directives to the bond-trading desk at the Federal Reserve Bank of New York. The directives specify a short-run operating target that the trading desk must use in its day-to-day operations. In recent years, the target has been the federal funds rate.

FIGURE 4

Monetary Policy: Tools, Targets, and Goals

The Fed primarily uses open market operations to implement monetary policy. The decision to buy or sell bonds is based on a short-run operating target, like the federal funds rate. The short-run operating target is set to achieve an intermediate target, a certain level of money supply. The intermediate target is set to achieve the ultimate goal, a certain level of gross domestic product and/or inflation.

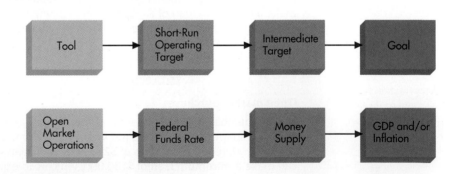

FIGURE 5

The Dollar-Yen Foreign Exchange Market

The demand is the demand for dollars arising out of the Japanese demand for U.S. goods and services. The supply is the supply of dollars arising out of the U.S. demand for Japanese goods and services. Initially, the equilibrium exchange rate is at the intersection of the demand curve (D_1) and the supply curve (S_1), where the exchange rate is ¥100 = $1. An increase in the U.S. demand for Japanese goods increases S_1 to S_2 and pushes the equilibrium exchange rate down to point B, where ¥90 = $1. If the Fed's target exchange rate is ¥100 = $1, the Fed must intervene and buy dollars in the foreign exchange market. This increases demand to D_2 and raises the equilibrium exchange rate to point C, where ¥100 = $1.

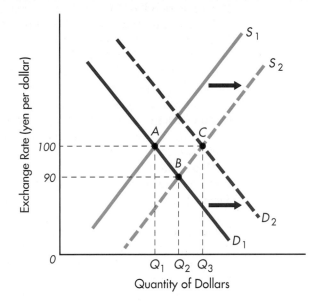

2.c. Foreign Exchange Market Intervention

4. What role do central banks play in the foreign exchange market?

In the mid-1980s, conditions in the foreign exchange market took on a high priority in FOMC directives. There was concern that the value of the dollar in relation to other currencies was contributing to a large U.S. international trade deficit. Furthermore, the governments of the major industrial countries decided to work together to maintain more stable exchange rates. This meant that the Federal Reserve and the central banks of the other developed countries had to devote more attention to maintaining exchange rates within a certain target band of values. While more recently exchange rates have had less of a role in FOMC meetings, it is still important to understand how central banks may intervene to change exchange rates.

foreign exchange market intervention: the buying and selling of currencies by a central bank to achieve a specified exchange rate

2.c.1. Mechanics of Intervention   Foreign exchange market intervention is the buying and selling of foreign exchange by a central bank in order to move exchange rates up or down. We can use a simple supply and demand diagram to illustrate the role of intervention. Figure 5 shows the U.S. dollar–Japanese yen exchange market. The demand curve is the demand for dollars produced by the demand for U.S. goods and financial assets. The supply curve is the supply of dollars generated by U.S. residents' demand for the products and financial assets of other countries. Here, the supply of dollars to the dollar-yen market comes from the U.S. demand to buy Japanese products.

The initial equilibrium exchange rate is at point A, where the demand curve (D_1) and the supply curve (S_1) intersect. At point A, the exchange rate is ¥100 = $1, and Q_1 dollars are exchanged for yen. Suppose that over time, U.S. residents buy more from Japan than Japanese residents buy from the United States. As the supply of dollars increases in relation to the demand for dollars, equilibrium shifts to point B. At point B, Q_2 dollars are exchanged at a rate of ¥90 = $1. The dollar has *depreciated* against the yen, or, conversely, the yen has *appreciated* against the dollar.

When the dollar depreciates, U.S. goods are cheaper to Japanese buyers (it takes fewer yen to buy each dollar). The depreciated dollar stimulates U.S. exports to Japan. It also raises the price of Japanese goods to U.S. buyers, reducing U.S. imports from Japan. Rather than allow exchange rates to change, with the subsequent changes in trade, central banks often seek to maintain fixed exchange rates because of international agreements or desired trade in goods or financial assets.

Suppose the Fed sets a target range for the dollar at a minimum exchange rate of ¥100 = $1. If the exchange rate falls below the minimum, the Fed must intervene in the foreign exchange market to increase the value of the dollar. In Figure 5, you can see that the only way to increase the dollar's value is to increase the demand for dollars. The Fed intervenes in the foreign exchange market by buying dollars in exchange for yen. It uses its holdings of Japanese yen to purchase $Q_3 - Q_1$ dollars, shifting the demand curve to D_2. Now equilibrium is at point C, where Q_3 dollars are exchanged at the rate of ¥100 = $1.

The kind of intervention shown in Figure 5 is only temporary because the Fed has a limited supply of yen. Under another intervention plan, the Bank of Japan would support the ¥100 = $1 exchange rate by using yen to buy dollars. The Bank of Japan could carry on this kind of policy indefinitely because it has the power to create yen. A third alternative is *coordinated intervention,* in which both the Fed and the Bank of Japan sell yen in exchange for dollars to support the minimum yen-dollar exchange rate.

Coordinated intervention involves more than one central bank in attempts to shift the equilibrium exchange rate.

2.c.2. Effects of Intervention

Intervention can be used to shift the demand and supply for currency and thereby change the exchange rate. Foreign exchange market intervention also has effects on the money supply. If the Federal Reserve wanted to increase the dollar price of the euro, it would create dollars to purchase euro. Thus when foreign exchange market intervention involves the use of domestic currency to buy foreign currency, it increases the domestic money supply. The expansionary effect of this intervention can be offset by a domestic open market operation, in a process called **sterilization.** If the Fed creates dollars to buy euro, for example, it increases the money supply, as we have just seen. To reduce the money supply, the Fed can direct an open market bond sale. The bond sale sterilizes the effect of the intervention on the domestic money supply.

sterilization: the use of domestic open market operations to offset the effects of a foreign exchange market intervention on the domestic money supply

RECAP

1. The ultimate goal of monetary policy is economic growth with stable prices.
2. The Fed controls GDP indirectly, through its control of the money supply.
3. The equation of exchange ($MV = PQ$) relates the quantity of money to nominal GDP.

4. The quantity theory of money states that with constant velocity, changes in the quantity of money change nominal GDP.

5. Every six weeks, the Federal Open Market Committee issues a directive to the Federal Reserve Bank of New York that defines the FOMC's monetary targets and policy tools.

6. The Fed controls the nation's money supply by changing bank excess reserves.

7. The tools of monetary policy are reserve requirements, the discount rate, and open market operations.

8. The money supply tends to increase (decrease) as the reserve requirement falls (rises), the discount rate falls (rises), and the Fed buys (sells) bonds.

9. Each FOMC directive defines its short-run operating target in terms of the federal funds rate.

10. Foreign exchange market intervention is the buying and selling of foreign exchange by a central bank to achieve a targeted exchange rate.

11. Sterilization is the use of domestic open market operations to offset the money supply effects of foreign exchange market intervention.

3. Monetary Policy and Equilibrium Income

To see how changes in the money supply affect the equilibrium level of real GDP, we incorporate monetary policy into the aggregate demand and supply model. The first step in understanding monetary policy is understanding the demand for money. If you know what determines money demand, you can see how monetary policy is used to shift aggregate demand and change the equilibrium level of real GDP.

3.a. Money Demand

5. What are the determinants of the demand for money?

Why do you hold money? What does it do for you? What determines how much money you will hold? These questions are addressed in this section. Wanting to hold more money is not the same as wanting more income. You can decide to carry more cash or keep more dollars in your checking account even though your income has not changed. The quantity of dollars you want to hold is your demand for money. By summing the quantity of money demanded by each individual, we can find the money demand for the entire economy. Once we understand what determines money demand, we can put that demand together with the money supply and examine how money influences the interest rate and the equilibrium level of income.

In Chapter 13 we discussed the functions of money, that is, what money is used for. People use money as a unit of account, a medium of exchange, a store of value, and a standard of deferred payment. These last functions help explain the demand for money.

transactions demand for money: the demand to hold money to buy goods and services

People use money for transactions, to buy goods and services. The **transactions demand for money** is a demand to hold money in order to spend it on goods and services. Holding money in your pocket or checking account is a demand for money. Spending money is not demanding it; by spending it, you are getting rid of it.

If your boss paid you the same instant that you wanted to buy something, the timing of your receipts and expenditures would match perfectly. You would not have to hold money for transactions. But because receipts typically occur much less often than expenditures, money is necessary to cover transactions between paychecks.

People also hold money to take care of emergencies. The **precautionary demand for money** exists because emergencies happen. People never know when an unexpected expense will crop up or when actual expenditures will exceed planned expenditures. So they hold money as a precaution.

Finally, there is a **speculative demand for money,** a demand created by uncertainty about the value of other assets. This demand exists because money is the most liquid store of value. If you want to buy a stock, but you believe the price is going to fall in the next few days, you hold the money until you are ready to buy the stock.

The speculative demand for money is not necessarily tied to a particular use of funds. People hold money because they expect the price of any asset to fall. Holding money is less risky than buying the asset today if the price of the asset seems likely to fall. For example, suppose you buy and sell fine art. The price of art fluctuates over time. You try to buy when prices are low and sell when prices are high. If you expect prices to fall in the short term, you hold money rather than art until the prices do fall. Then you use money to buy art for resale when the prices go up again.

3.a.1. The Money Demand Function
If you understand why people hold money, you can understand what changes the amount of money they hold. As you've just seen, people hold money in order to: (1) carry out transactions (transactions demand), (2) be prepared for emergencies (precautionary demand), and (3) speculate on purchases of various assets (speculative demand). The interest rate and nominal income (income measured in current dollars) influence how much money people hold in order to carry out these three activities.

The interest rate is the opportunity cost of holding money.

The Interest Rate
There is an inverse relationship between the interest rate and the quantity of money demanded (see Figure 6). The interest rate is the *opportunity cost* of holding money. If you bury a thousand dollar bills in your backyard, that cur-

---

The Money Demand Function

Money demand (*Md*) is a negative function of the rate of interest. The interest rate is the opportunity cost of holding money. The higher the interest rate, the lower the quantity of money demanded. At an interest rate of 9 percent, the quantity of money demanded is $600 billion. At an interest rate of 12 percent, the quantity of money demanded falls to $400 billion.

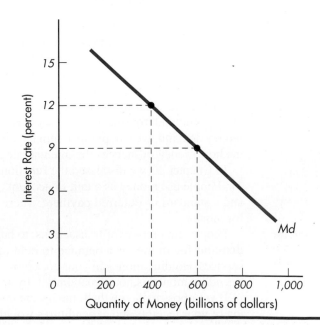

rency is earning no interest—you are forgoing the interest. At a low interest rate, the cost of forgone interest is small. At a higher interest rate, however, the cost of holding wealth in the form of money means giving up more interest. The higher the rate of interest, the greater the interest forgone by holding money, so the less money held. The costs of holding money limit the amount of money held.

Some components of the money supply pay interest to the depositor. Here the opportunity cost of holding money is the difference between the interest rate on a bond or some other nonmonetary asset and the interest rate on money. If a bond pays 9 percent interest a year and a bank deposit pays 5 percent, the opportunity cost of holding the deposit is 4 percent.

Figure 6 shows a money demand function, where the demand for money depends on the interest rate. The downward slope of the money demand curve (Md) shows the inverse relation between the interest rate and the quantity of money demanded. For instance, at an interest rate of 12 percent, the quantity of money demanded is $400 billion. If the interest rate falls to 9 percent, the quantity of money demanded increases to $600 billion.

The transactions demand for money rises with nominal income.

Nominal Income   The demand for money also depends on nominal income. Money demand varies directly with nominal income because as income increases, more transactions are carried out and more money is required for those transactions.

The greater nominal income, the greater the demand for money. This is true whether the increase in nominal income is a product of a higher price level or an increase in real income. Both generate a greater dollar volume of transactions. If the prices of all goods increase, then more money must be used to purchase goods and services. And as real income increases, more goods and services are being produced and sold and living standards rise; this means more money is being demanded to execute the higher level of transactions.

FIGURE 7

The Effect of a Change in Income on Money Demand

A change in real GDP, whatever the interest rate, shifts the money demand curve. Initially real GDP is Y_0; the money demand curve at that level of income is Md. At an interest rate of 9 percent, the quantity of money demanded is $600 billion. If income increases to Y_1, the money demand shifts to Md_1. Here $800 billion is demanded at 9 percent. If income falls to Y_2, the money demand curve falls to Md_2, where $400 billion is demanded at 9 percent.

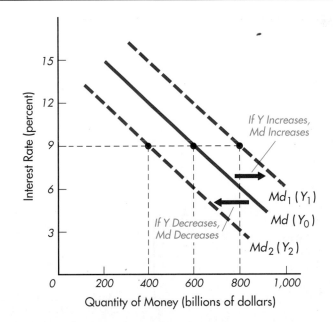

A change in nominal income changes the demand for money at any given interest rate. Figure 7 shows the effect of changes in nominal income on the money demand curve. If income rises from Y_0 to Y_1, money demand increases from Md to Md_1. If income falls from Y_0 to Y_2, money demand falls from Md to Md_2. When the money demand function shifts from Md to Md_1, the quantity of money demanded at an interest rate of 9 percent increases from \$600 billion to \$800 billion. When the money demand function shifts from Md to Md_2, the quantity of money demanded at 9 percent interest falls from \$600 billion to \$400 billion.

3.a.2. The Money Supply Function

The Federal Reserve is responsible for setting the money supply. The fact that the Fed can choose the money supply means that the money supply function is independent of the current interest rate and income. Figure 8 illustrates the money supply function (Ms). In the figure, the money supply is \$600 billion at all interest rate levels. If the Fed increases the money supply, the vertical money supply function shifts to the right. If the Fed decreases the money supply, the function shifts to the left.

3.a.3. Equilibrium in the Money Market

To find the equilibrium interest rate and quantity of money, we have to combine the money demand and money supply functions in one diagram. Figure 9 graphs equilibrium in the money market. Equilibrium, point e, is at the intersection of the money demand and money supply functions. In the figure the equilibrium interest rate is 9 percent and the quantity of money is \$600 billion.

What forces work to ensure that the economy tends toward the equilibrium rate of interest? Let's look at Figure 9 again to understand what happens if the interest rate is not at equilibrium. If the interest rate falls below 9 percent, there will be an excess demand for money. People will want more money than the Fed is supplying. But because the supply of money does not change, the demand for more money just

---

FIGURE 8

The Money Supply Function

The money supply function (*Ms*) is a vertical line. This indicates that the Fed can choose any money supply it wants, independent of the interest rate (and real GDP). In the figure, the money supply is set at \$600 billion at all interest rates. The Fed can increase or decrease the money supply, shifting the curve to the right or left, but the curve remains vertical.

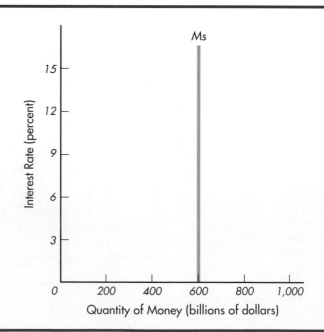

FIGURE 9

Equilibrium in the Money Market

Equilibrium is at point e, where the money demand and money supply curves intersect. At equilibrium, the interest rate is 9 percent and the money supply is $600 billion. An interest rate above 9 percent would create an excess supply of money because the quantity of money demanded falls as the interest rate rises. An interest rate below 9 percent would create an excess demand for money because the quantity of money demanded rises as the interest rate falls.

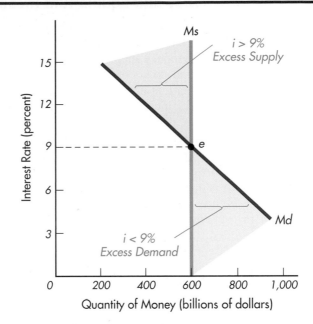

forces the interest rate to rise. How? Suppose people try to increase their money holdings by converting bonds and other nonmonetary assets into money. As bonds and other nonmonetary assets are sold for money, the interest rate goes up.

To understand the connection between the rate of interest and buying and selling bonds, you must realize that the current interest rate (yield) on a bond is determined by the bond price:

$$\text{Current interest rate} = \frac{\text{annual interest payment}}{\text{bond price}}$$

The numerator, the annual interest payment, is fixed for the life of the bond. The denominator, the bond price, fluctuates with supply and demand. As the bond price changes, the interest rate changes.

Suppose a bond pays $100 a year in interest and sells for $1,000. The interest rate is 10 percent ($100/$1,000). If the supply of bonds increases because people want to convert bonds to money, the price of bonds falls. Suppose the price drops to $800. At that price the interest rate equals 12.5 percent ($100/$800). This is the mechanism by which an excess demand for money changes the interest rate. As the interest rate goes up, the excess demand for money disappears.

Just the opposite occurs at interest rates above equilibrium. In Figure 9, any rate of interest above 9 percent creates an excess supply of money. Now people are holding more of their wealth in the form of money than they would like. What happens? They want to convert some of their money balances into nonmonetary assets, like bonds. As the demand for bonds rises, bond prices increase. And as bond prices go up, interest rates fall. This drop in interest rates restores equilibrium in the money market.

?

6. How does monetary policy affect the equilibrium level of real GDP?

3.b. Money and Equilibrium Income

Now we are ready to relate monetary policy to the equilibrium level of real GDP. We use Figure 10 to show how a change in the money supply affects real GDP. In Figure 10(a), as the money supply increases from Ms_1 to Ms_2, the equilibrium rate of interest falls from i_1 to i_2.

Remember that investment (business spending on capital goods) declines as the rate of interest increases. The interest rate is the cost of borrowed funds. As the interest rate rises, the return on investment falls, and with it the level of investment. As the interest rate falls, the return on investment rises, and with it the level of investment. In Figure 10(a), the interest rate falls. In Figure 10(b), you can see the effect of the lower interest rate on investment spending. As the interest rate falls from i_1 to i_2, investment increases from I_1 to I_2.

Figure 10(c) is the aggregate demand and supply equilibrium diagram. When investment spending increases, aggregate expenditures are higher at every price level, so the aggregate demand curve shifts to the right, from AD_1 to AD_2. The increase in aggregate demand increases equilibrium income from Y_1 to Y_2.

How does monetary policy affect equilibrium income? As the money supply increases, the equilibrium interest rate falls. As the interest rate falls, the equilibrium level of investment rises. Increased investment increases aggregate demand and equilibrium income. A decrease in the money supply works in reverse: as the interest rate rises, investment falls; as investment falls, aggregate demand and equilibrium income go down.

An excess supply of (demand for) money can increase (decrease) consumption as well as investment.

The mechanism we have just described is an oversimplification because the only element of aggregate expenditures that changes in this model is investment. But an excess demand for or supply of money involves more than simply selling or buying bonds. An excess supply of money probably would be reflected in increased consumption as well. If households are holding more money than they want to hold, they buy not only bonds but also goods and services, so that consumption increases.

FIGURE 10

Monetary Policy and Equilibrium Income

The three diagrams show the sequence of events by which a change in the money supply affects the equilibrium level of real GDP. In Figure 10(a), the money supply increases, lowering the equilibrium interest rate.

In Figure 10(b), the lower interest rate pushes the level of investment up. In Figure 10(c), the increase in investment increases aggregate demand and equilibrium real GDP.

(a) Money Supply Increases and Interest Rate Falls

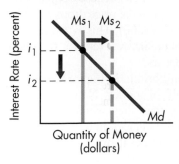

(b) Investment Spending Increases

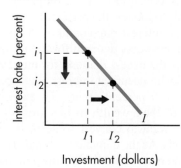

(c) Aggregate Demand and Equilibrium Income Increase

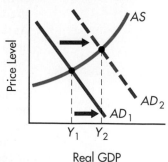

If they are holding less money than they want to hold, they will sell bonds and consume less. So the effect of monetary policy on aggregate demand is a product of a change in both investment and consumption. We discuss this in Chapter 15, where we also examine the important role expected policy changes can play.

RECAP

1. The transactions demand for money is a demand to hold money to buy goods and services.
2. The precautionary demand for money exists because not all expenditures can be planned.
3. The speculative demand for money is created by uncertainty about the value of other assets.
4. There is an inverse relationship between the interest rate and the quantity of money demanded.
5. The greater the nominal income, the greater the demand for money.
6. Because the Federal Reserve sets the money supply, the money supply function is independent of the interest rate and nominal income.
7. The current yield on a bond equals the annual interest payment divided by the price of the bond.
8. An increase in the money supply lowers the interest rate; this raises the level of investment, and this in turn increases aggregate demand and equilibrium income. A decrease in the money supply works in reverse.

Summary

? What does the Federal Reserve do?

1. The Federal Reserve is the central bank of the United States. *§1*
2. The Federal Reserve System is operated by 12 district banks and a Board of Governors in Washington, D.C. *§1.a*
3. The Fed services and supervises the banking system, acts as the banker of the U.S. Treasury, and controls the money supply. *§1.b*

? How is monetary policy set?

4. The Fed controls nominal GDP indirectly by controlling the quantity of money in the nation's economy. *§2.a.1*
5. The Fed uses the growth of the money supply as an intermediate target to help it achieve its ultimate goal—economic growth with stable prices. *§2.a.1*
6. Some countries have adopted inflation targeting to guide their monetary policy. *§2.a.2*

? What are the tools of monetary policy?

7. The three tools of monetary policy are the reserve requirement, the discount rate, and open market operations. *§2.b.1*
8. The Fed buys bonds to increase the money supply and sells bonds to decrease the money supply. *§2.b.1*
9. The Federal Open Market Committee (FOMC) issues directives to the Federal Reserve Bank of New York outlining the conduct of monetary policy. *§2.b.2*

? What role do central banks play in the foreign exchange market?

10. Central banks intervene in the foreign exchange market when it is necessary to maintain a targeted exchange rate. *§2.c*

❓ What are the determinants of the demand for money?

11. The demand for money stems from the need to buy goods and services, to prepare for emergencies, and to retain a store of value. *§3.a*

12. There is an inverse relationship between the quantity of money demanded and the interest rate. *§3.a.1*

13. The greater the nominal income, the greater the demand for money. *§3.a.1*

14. Because the Fed sets the money supply, the money supply function is independent of the interest rate and real GDP. *§3.a.2*

❓ How does monetary policy affect the equilibrium level of real GDP?

15. By altering the money supply, the Fed changes the interest rate and the level of investment, shifting aggregate demand and the equilibrium level of real GDP. *§3.b*

Key Terms

Federal Open Market Committee (FOMC) *§1.a.3*
intermediate target *§2.a.1*
equation of exchange *§2.a.1*
velocity of money *§2.a.1*
quantity theory of money *§2.a.1*
FOMC directive *§2.b*
federal funds rate *§2.b*
legal reserves *§2.b.1*

discount rate *§2.b.1*
open market operations *§2.b.1*
foreign exchange market intervention *§2.c.1*
sterilization *§2.c.2*
transactions demand for money *§3.a*
precautionary demand for money *§3.a*
speculative demand for money *§3.a*

Exercises

1. The Federal Reserve System divides the nation into 12 districts.
   a. List the 12 cities in which the district banks are located.
   b. Which Federal Reserve district do you live in?

2. Briefly describe the functions the Fed performs for the banking community. In what sense is the Fed a banker's bank?

3. Draw a graph showing equilibrium in the money market. Carefully label all curves and axes and explain why the curves have the slopes they do.

4. Using the graph you prepared for exercise 3, illustrate and explain what happens when the Fed decreases the money supply.

5. When the Fed decreases the money supply, the equilibrium level of income changes. Illustrate and explain how.

6. Describe the quantity theory of money, defining each variable. Explain how changes in the money supply can affect real GDP and the price level. Under what circumstances could an increase in the money supply have *no* effect on nominal GDP?

7. There are several tools the Fed uses to implement monetary policy.
   a. Briefly describe these tools.
   b. Explain how the Fed would use each tool in order to increase the money supply.

8. First Bank has total deposits of $2,000,000 and legal reserves of $220,000.
   a. If the reserve requirement is 10 percent, what is the maximum loan that First Bank can make, and what is the maximum increase in the money supply based on First Bank's reserve position?
   b. If the reserve requirement is changed to 5 percent, how much can First Bank lend, and how much can the money supply be expanded?

9. Suppose you are a member of the FOMC and the U.S. economy is entering a recession. Write a directive to the New York Fed about the conduct of monetary policy over the next two months. Your directive should address targets for the rate of growth of the M2 and M3 money supplies, the federal funds rate, the rate of inflation, and the foreign exchange value of the dollar versus the Japanese yen and euro. You may refer to the Board of Governors web site,

www.bog.frb.fed.us, for examples, since this site reports FOMC directives.

10. Suppose the Fed has a target range for the yen-dollar exchange rate. How would it keep the exchange rate within the target range if free market forces push the exchange rate out of the range? Use a graph to help explain your answer.

11. Why do you demand money? What determines how much money you keep in your pocket, purse, or bank accounts?

12. What is the current yield on a bond? Why do interest rates change when bond prices change?

13. If the Fed increases the money supply, what will happen to each of the following (other things being equal)?
    a. Interest rates
    b. Money demand
    c. Investment spending
    d. Aggregate demand
    e. The equilibrium level of national income

14. It is sometimes said that the Federal Reserve System is a nonpolitical agency. In what sense is this true?

Why might you doubt that politics have no effect on Fed decisions?

15. Suppose the banking system has vault cash of $1,000, deposits at the Fed of $2,000, and demand deposits of $10,000.
    a. If the reserve requirement is 20 percent, what is the maximum potential increase in the money supply given the banks' reserve position?
    b. If the Fed now purchases $500 worth of government bonds from private bond dealers, what are excess reserves of the banking system? (Assume that the bond dealers deposit the $500 in demand deposits.) How much can the banking system increase the money supply given the new reserve position?

16. What does ECB stand for? Where is the ECB located? In what way is central banking in the euro-area countries similar to the Federal Reserve System?

ACE

Take the ACE Practice Test for this chapter to review the important concepts and get immediate feedback with answers.

economics.college.hmco.com/students

Fed Leaves Rates Alone, but Message Needs Translation: Strange Statement Puzzles Economists

NEW YORK—Federal Reserve policy-makers held interest rates at 1961 lows yesterday, contending they could not gauge the economy's prospects because of uncertainties from the pending Iraqi war.

The Federal Open Market Committee's (FOMC) 12-0 decision left the federal-funds rate target for overnight loans between banks at 1.25 percent, where it has been since a hefty cut in November.

But the language of yesterday's bizarre policy statement from the Fed left market players scratching their heads and wondering if Alan Greenspan and his colleagues had outdone themselves on obtuseness. . . .

Not only did the Fed not change rates, it didn't even want to characterize the economy's risks, as it usually does in each statement after a policy-setting meeting.

Yet the Fed seemed to suggest it could cut interest rates in coming weeks if the economy is still struggling or badly hurt by a war. Maybe. . . .

The Fed said that due to the "unusually large uncertainties clouding the geopolitical situation in the short run," it could not tell how the economy is faring.

"The Committee does not believe it can usefully characterize the current balance of risks with respect to the prospects for its long-run goals of price stability and sustainable economic growth," the statement said.

"The language is very tortured," said Wayne Ayers, chief economist with FleetBoston Financial in Boston.

Most analysts had expected the Fed to say future economic weakness is the greatest risk, rather than its prior claim of the risks being balanced between stronger growth and weakness.

Also strangely worded was the Fed's phrase that "heightened surveillance is particularly informative," which seemed to indicate its willingness to cut rates if conditions deteriorate quickly.

All in all, those who follow the Fed's every utterance were befuddled at a time when investors are looking for something concrete to hang their hats on.

"It is a head-scratcher indeed. Unfortunately it's a bit of a reminder that policy-makers do not have a lock on knowledge," said Lara Rhame, an economist at Brown Brothers Harriman.

"It sounds as if they are as uncertain as we are."

Source: Copyright 2003 The Seattle Times Company.

The Seattle Times/March 19, 2003

Commentary

The Board of Governors of the Federal Reserve System sets the monetary policy for the country. If the Fed believes that economic growth is too slow and inflation is not likely to increase, then it tries to increase aggregate demand by increasing money growth. As we learned in this chapter, when the Fed increases the money supply, interest rates fall, aggregate demand rises, and real GDP growth increases.

The article discusses the controversy over Federal Reserve interest rate policy in early 2003. The controversy arose because the inflation rate had been quite low and many people expected the Fed's policy statement to say something about a weak economy. Instead, the statement suggested that there was a great deal of uncertainty, so that the Fed could not make a reasonable forecast of the short-term outlook.

It is important to realize that policymakers do not have very much information at the time they must make policy decisions. For instance, the consumer price index is available with a one-month lag, so our knowledge of inflation is always running a month behind the actual economy. The GDP is even worse.

The GDP data are available only quarterly, and we do not find out about GDP until well after a quarter ends, and even then substantial revisions to the numbers often occur many months after the quarter. The point is simply that the Federal Reserve (and other policymaking institutions) must formulate policy today on the basis of less than complete knowledge of the *current* situation and the policy must be addressed to their best guess of the *future* situation.

For these reasons, policymakers often find themselves the target of critics who dispute their current and future outlook on inflation and other key economic variables. Even though the inflation rate in 2003 was low and had been low for several years, the Fed was worried that military action in Iraq could lead to greater inflationary pressures. Yet at the same time, the economy was growing slowly, so there was also concern about a possible weakening of GDP growth.

The Fed wants to act in advance of rising inflation or slowing GDP growth to avoid bad economic outcomes. However, even central banks cannot always clearly determine the state of the economy and, consequently, the best course of action.

CHAPTER 15

Macroeconomic Policy: Tradeoffs, Expectations, Credibility, and Sources of Business Cycles

Macroeconomics is a dynamic discipline. Monetary and fiscal policies change over time. And so does our understanding of those policies. Economists debate the nature of business cycles—what causes them and what, if anything, government can do about them. Some economists argue that policies that lower the unemployment rate tend to raise the rate of inflation. Others insist that only unexpected inflation can influence real GDP and employment. If the latter economists are right, does government always have to surprise the public in order to improve economic conditions?

Some economists claim that politicians manipulate the business cycle to increase their chances of reelection. If they are right, we should expect economic growth just before national elections. But what happens after the elections? What are the long-term effects of political business cycles? Because of these issues, the material in this chapter should be considered somewhat controversial. In Chapter 16 we will examine the controversies in more detail, and it will be more apparent where the sources of controversy lie. ■

1. The Phillips Curve

In 1958 a New Zealand economist, A. W. Phillips, published a study of the relationship between the unemployment rate and the rate of change in wages in England. He found that over the period from 1826 to 1957 there had been an inverse relationship between the unemployment rate and the rate of change in wages: the unemployment rate fell in years when there were relatively large increases in wages and rose in years when wages increased relatively little. Phillips's study started other economists searching for similar relationships in other countries. In those subsequent studies, it became common to substitute the rate of inflation for the rate of change in wages.

Early studies in the United States found an inverse relationship between inflation and the unemployment rate. The graph that illustrates this relationship is called a **Phillips curve.** Figure 1 shows a Phillips curve for the United States in the 1960s. Over this period, lower inflation rates were associated with higher unemployment rates, as shown by the downward-sloping curve.

The slope of the curve in Figure 1 depicts an inverse relationship between the rate of inflation and the unemployment rate: As the inflation rate falls, the unemployment rate rises. In 1969 the inflation rate was relatively high, at 5.5 percent, while the unemployment rate was relatively low, at 3.5 percent. In 1967 an inflation rate of 3.1 percent was consistent with an unemployment rate of 3.8 percent; and in 1961, 1 percent inflation occurred with 6.7 percent unemployment.

The downward-sloping Phillips curve seems to indicate a tradeoff between unemployment and inflation. A country could have a lower unemployment rate by accepting higher inflation, or a lower rate of inflation by accepting higher unemployment. Certainly this was the case in the United States in the 1960s. But is the curve depicted in Figure 1 representative of the tradeoff over long periods of time?

Phillips curve: a graph that illustrates the relationship between inflation and the unemployment rate

---

FIGURE 1

A Phillips Curve, United States, 1961–1969

In the 1960s, as the rate of inflation rose, the unemployment rate fell. This inverse relationship suggests a tradeoff between the rate of inflation and the unemployment rate.

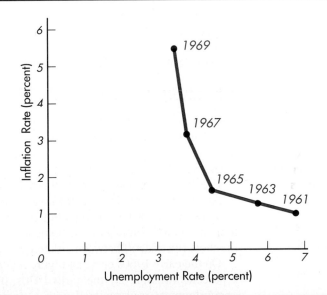

FIGURE 2

Unemployment and Inflation in the United States, 1955–2000

The data on inflation and unemployment rates in the United States between 1955 and 2000 show no particular relationship between inflation and unemployment over the long run. There is no evidence here of a downward-sloping Phillips curve.

1. Is there a tradeoff between inflation and the unemployment rate?

1.a. An inflation-Unemployment Tradeoff?

Figure 2 shows unemployment and inflation rates in the United States for several years from 1955 to 2000. The points in the figure do not lie along a downward-sloping curve like the one shown in Figure 1. For example, in 1955 the unemployment rate was 4.4 percent and the inflation rate was −0.4 percent. In 1960 the unemployment rate was 5.5 percent and the inflation rate was 1.7 percent. Both unemployment and inflation rates had increased since 1955. Moving through time, you can see that the inflation rate tended to increase along with the unemployment rate through the 1960s and 1970s. By 1980, the unemployment rate was 7.1 percent and the inflation rate was 13.5 percent.

The scattered points in Figure 2 show no evidence of a tradeoff between unemployment and inflation. A downward-sloping Phillips curve does not seem to exist over the long term.

1.b. Short-Run Versus Long-Run Tradeoffs

2. How does the tradeoff between inflation and the unemployment rate vary from the short to the long run?

Most economists believe that the downward-sloping Phillips curve and the tradeoff it implies between inflation and unemployment are short-term phenomena. Think of a series of Phillips curves, one for each of the points in Figure 2. From 1955 to 1980, the curves shifted out to the right. In the early 1980s, they shifted in to the left.

Figure 3 shows a series of Phillips curves that could account for the data in Figure 2. At any point in time, a downward-sloping Phillips curve indicates a tradeoff between inflation and unemployment. Many economists believe that this kind of tradeoff is just a short-term phenomenon. Over time, the Phillips curve shifts so that the short-run tradeoff between inflation and unemployment disappears in the long run.

On the early 1960s curve in Figure 3, 5 percent unemployment is consistent with 2 percent inflation. By the early 1970s, the curve had shifted up. Here 5 percent unemployment is associated with 6 percent inflation. On the late 1970s curve,

FIGURE 3

The Shifting Phillips Curve

We can reconcile the long-run data on unemployment and inflation with the downward-sloping Phillips curve by using a series of Phillips curves. (In effect, we treat the long run as a series of short-run curves.) The Phillips curve for the early 1960s shows 5 percent unemployment and 2 percent inflation. Over time, the short-run curve shifted out to the right. The early 1970s curve shows 5 percent unemployment and 6 percent inflation. And the short-run curve for the late 1970s shows 5 percent unemployment and 10 percent inflation. In the early 1980s, the short-run Phillips curve began to shift down toward the origin. By the late 1980s, 5 percent unemployment was consistent with 4 percent inflation.

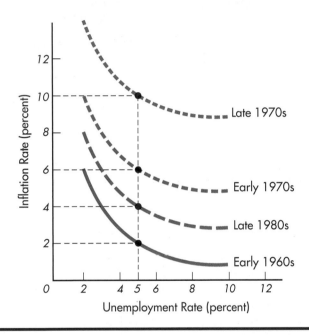

5 percent unemployment is consistent with 10 percent inflation. For more than two decades, the tradeoff between inflation and unemployment worsened as the Phillips curves shifted up, so that higher and higher inflation rates were associated with any given level of unemployment. Then in the 1980s, the tradeoff seemed to improve as the Phillips curve shifted down. On the late 1980s curve, 5 percent unemployment is consistent with 4 percent inflation.

The data indicate that the Phillips curve may have shifted out in the 1960s and 1970s and shifted in during the 1980s.

The Phillips curves in Figure 3 represent changes that took place over time in the United States. We cannot be sure of the actual shape of a Phillips curve at any time, but an outward shift of the curve in the 1960s and 1970s and an inward shift during the 1980s are consistent with the data. Later in this chapter we describe how changing government policy and the public's expectations about that policy may have shifted aggregate demand and aggregate supply and produced these shifts in the Phillips curves.

1.b.1. In the Short Run   Figure 4 uses the aggregate demand and supply analysis we developed in Chapter 9 to explain the Phillips curve. Initially the economy is operating at point 1 in both diagrams. In Figure 4(a), the aggregate demand curve (AD_1) and the aggregate supply curve (AS_1) intersect at price level P_1 and real GDP level Y_p, the level of potential real GDP. Remember that potential real GDP is the

FIGURE 4

Aggregate Demand and Supply and the Phillips Curve

The movement from point 1 to point 2 to point 3 traces the adjustment of the economy to an increase in aggregate demand. Point 1 is initial equilibrium in both diagrams. At this point potential real GDP is Y_p and the price level is P_1 in the aggregate demand and supply diagram, and the inflation rate is 3 percent with an unemployment rate of 5 percent (the natural rate) along short-run curve I in the Phillips curve diagram.

If the aggregate demand curve shifts from AD_1 to AD_2, equilibrium real GDP goes up to Y_2 and the price level rises to P_2 in the aggregate demand and supply diagram. The increase in aggregate demand pushes the inflation rate up to 6 percent and the unemployment rate down to 3 percent along Phillips curve I. The movement from point 1 to point 2 along the

curve indicates a tradeoff between inflation and the unemployment rate.

Over time the AS curve shifts in response to rising production costs at the higher rate of inflation. Along AS_2, equilibrium is at point 3, where real GDP falls back to Y_p and the price level rises to P_3. As we move from point 2 to point 3 in Figure 4(b), we shift to short-run Phillips curve II. Here the inflation rate remains high (at 6 percent), while the unemployment rate goes back up to 5 percent, the rate consistent with production at Y_p. In the long run, then, there is no tradeoff between inflation and unemployment. The vertical long-run aggregate supply curve at the potential level of real GDP is associated with the vertical long-run Phillips curve at the natural rate of unemployment.

(a) Aggregate Demand and Supply

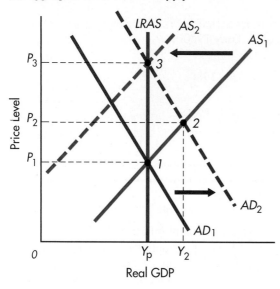

(b) Phillips Curve

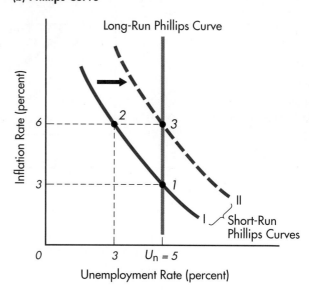

level of income and output generated at the natural rate of unemployment, the unemployment rate that exists in the absence of cyclical unemployment. In Figure 4(b), point 1 lies on Phillips curve I, where the inflation rate is 3 percent and the unemployment rate is 5 percent. We assume that the 5 percent unemployment rate at the level of potential real GDP is the natural rate of unemployment (U_n). A discussion of the natural rate of unemployment and its determinants is given in the Economic Insight "The Natural Rate of Unemployment."

What happens when aggregate demand goes up from AD_1 to AD_2? A new equilibrium is established along the short-run aggregate supply curve (AS_1) at point 2. Here the price level (P_2) is higher, as is the level of real GDP (Y_2). In part (b), the

The Natural Rate of Unemployment

The natural rate of unemployment is defined as the unemployment rate that exists in the absence of cyclical unemployment. As we discussed in Chapter 8, the natural rate of unemployment reflects the normal amount of frictional unemployment (people temporarily between jobs), structural unemployment (people who lost jobs because of technological change), and seasonal unemployment (people who lost jobs because the jobs are available only at certain times of the year). What factors determine the normal amount of frictional and structural unemployment?

One of the most important factors is demographic change. As the age, gender, and racial makeup of the labor force changes, the natural rate of unemployment also changes. For instance, when the baby boom generation entered the labor force, the natural rate of unemployment increased because new workers typically have the highest unemployment rates. Between 1956 and 1979, the proportion of young adults (ages sixteen to twenty-four) in the labor force increased, increasing the natural rate of unemployment. Since 1980, the average age of U.S. workers has been rising. As workers age, employers can more easily evaluate a worker's ability based upon that worker's job history. In addition, it is more likely that younger workers will have difficulty finding a good job match for their skills and so are likely to have higher frictional unemployment, whereas older workers are more likely to have a long-term job with a single employer. As the labor force ages, we should expect the natural rate of unemployment to fall.

In addition to the composition of the labor force, several other factors affect the natural rate of unemployment:

■ In the early 1990s, structural changes in the economy, such as the shift from manufacturing to service jobs and the downsizing and restructuring of firms throughout the economy contributed to a higher natural rate of unemployment. Related to these structural changes is a decline in the demand for low-skilled workers, so that rising unemployment is overwhelmingly concentrated among workers with limited education and skills.

■ Increases in the legal minimum wage tend to raise the natural rate of unemployment. When the government mandates that employers pay some workers a higher wage than a freely competitive labor market would pay, fewer workers are employed.

■ The more generous the unemployment benefits, the higher the natural rate of unemployment. Increased benefits reduce the cost of being out of work and allow unemployed workers to take their time finding a new job. For these reasons, we observe higher natural rates of unemployment in European countries, where unemployed workers receive higher benefits.

■ Income taxes can also affect the natural rate of unemployment. Higher taxes mean that workers keep less of their earned income and so have less incentive to work.

The effect of these factors on the unemployment rate is complex, so it is difficult to state what the natural rate of unemployment is exactly. But as these factors change over time, the natural rate of unemployment also changes.

One last thing. It is not clear that minimizing the natural rate of unemployment is a universal goal. Minimum wages, unemployment benefits, and taxes have other important implications besides their effect on the natural rate of unemployment. We cannot expect these variables to be set solely in terms of their effect on unemployment.

---

increase in price and income is reflected in the movement along Phillips curve I to point 2. At point 2, the inflation rate is 6 percent and the unemployment rate is 3 percent. The increase in expenditures raises the inflation rate and lowers the unemployment rate (because national output has surpassed potential output).

Notice that there appears to be a tradeoff between inflation and unemployment on Phillips curve I. The increase in spending increases output and stimulates employment, so that the unemployment rate falls. And the higher spending pushes the rate of inflation up. But this tradeoff is only temporary. Point 2 in both diagrams is only a short-run equilibrium.

1.b.2. In the Long Run   As we discussed in Chapter 9, the short-run aggregate supply curve shifts over time as production costs rise in response to higher prices. Once the aggregate supply curve shifts to AS_2, long-run equilibrium occurs at point 3, where AS_2 intersects AD_2. Here, the price level is P_3 and real GDP returns to its potential level, Y_p.

The shift in aggregate supply lowers real GDP. As income falls, the unemployment rate goes up. The decrease in aggregate supply is reflected in the movement from point 2 on Phillips curve I to point 3 on Phillips curve II. As real GDP returns to its potential level (Y_p), unemployment returns to the natural rate (U_n), 5 percent. In the long run, as the economy adjusts to an increase in aggregate demand and expectations adjust to the new inflation rate, there is a period in which real GDP falls and the price level rises.

Over time there is no relationship between the price level and the level of real GDP. You can see this in the aggregate demand and supply diagram. Points 1 and 3 both lie along the long-run aggregate supply curve (*LRAS*) at potential real GDP. The *LRAS* curve has its analogue in the long-run Phillips curve, a vertical line at the natural rate of unemployment. Points 1 and 3 both lie along this curve.

The long-run Phillips curve is a vertical line at the natural rate of unemployment.

> **R E C A P**
>
> 1. The Phillips curve shows an inverse relationship between inflation and unemployment.
> 2. The downward slope of the Phillips curve indicates a tradeoff between inflation and unemployment.
> 3. Over the long run that tradeoff disappears.
> 4. The long-run Phillips curve is a vertical line at the natural rate of unemployment, analogous to the long-run aggregate supply curve at potential real GDP.

2. The Role of Expectations

The data and analysis in the previous section indicate that there is no long-run tradeoff between inflation and unemployment. But they do not explain the movement of the Phillips curve in the 1960s, 1970s, and 1980s. To understand why the short-run curve shifts, you must understand the role that unexpected inflation plays in the economy.

2.a. Expected Versus Unexpected Inflation

3. What is the relationship between unexpected inflation and the unemployment rate?

Figure 5 shows two short-run Phillips curves like those in Figure 4. Each curve is drawn for a particular expected rate of inflation. Curve I shows the tradeoff between inflation and unemployment when the inflation rate is expected to be 3 percent. If the actual rate of inflation (measured along the vertical axis) is 3 percent, the economy is operating at point 1, with an unemployment rate of 5 percent (the natural rate). If the inflation rate unexpectedly increases to 6 percent, the economy moves

FIGURE 5

Expectations and the Phillips Curve

Short-run Phillips curve I shows the tradeoff between inflation and the unemployment rate as long as people expect 3 percent inflation. When the actual rate of inflation is 3 percent, the rate of unemployment (U_n) is 5 percent (point 1). Short-run Phillips curve II shows the tradeoff as long as people expect 6 percent inflation. When the actual rate of inflation is 6 percent, the unemployment rate is 5 percent (point 3).

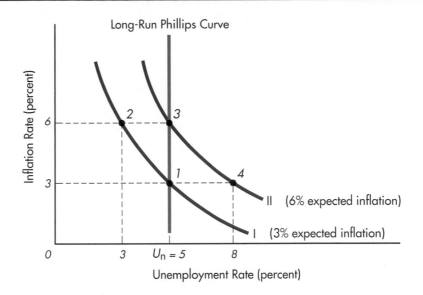

from point 1 to point 2 along Phillips curve I. Obviously, unexpected inflation can affect the unemployment rate. There are three factors at work here: wage expectations, inventory fluctuations, and wage contracts.

2.a.1. Wage Expectations and Unemployment   Unemployed workers who are looking for a job choose a **reservation wage,** the minimum wage they are willing to accept. They continue to look for work until they receive an offer that equals or exceeds their reservation wage.

reservation wage: the minimum wage a worker is willing to accept

Wages are not the only factor that workers take into consideration before accepting a job offer. A firm that offers good working conditions and fringe benefits can pay a lower wage than a firm that does not offer these advantages. But other things being equal, workers choose higher wages over lower wages. We simplify our analysis here by assuming that the only variable that affects the unemployed worker who is looking for a job is the reservation wage.

The link between unexpected inflation and the unemployment rate stems from the fact that wage offers are surprisingly high when the rate of inflation is surprisingly high. An unexpected increase in inflation means that prices are higher than anticipated, as are nominal income and wages. If aggregate demand increases unexpectedly, then prices, output, employment, and wages go up. Unemployed workers with a constant reservation wage find it easier to obtain a satisfactory wage offer during a period when wages are rising faster than the workers expected. This means that more unemployed workers find jobs, and they find those jobs quicker than they do in a period when the rate of inflation is expected. So the unemployment rate falls during a period of unexpectedly high inflation (Figure 6).

Consider an example. Suppose an accountant named Jason determines that he must find a job that pays at least $105 a day. Jason's reservation wage is $105.

FIGURE 6

Inflation, Unemployment, and Wage Expectations

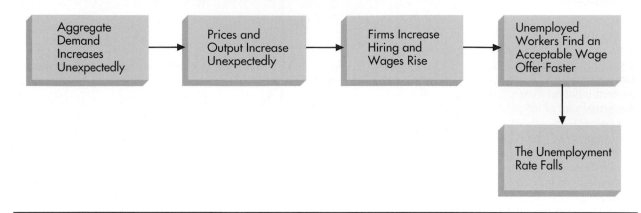

Furthermore, Jason expects prices and wages to be fairly stable across the economy; he expects no inflation. Jason looks for a job and finds that the jobs he qualifies for are offering wages of only $100 a day. Because his job offers are all paying less than his reservation wage, he keeps on looking. Let's say that aggregate demand rises unexpectedly. Firms increase production and raise prices. To hire more workers, they increase the wages they offer. Suppose wages go up 5 percent. Now the jobs that Jason qualifies for are offering 5 percent higher wages, $105 a day instead of $100 a day. At this higher wage rate, Jason quickly accepts a job and starts working. This example explains why the move from point 1 to point 2 in Figure 5 occurs.

The short-run Phillips curve assumes a constant *expected* rate of inflation. It also assumes that every unemployed worker who is looking for a job has a constant reservation wage. When inflation rises unexpectedly, then, wages rise faster than expected and the unemployment rate falls. The element of surprise is critical here. If the increase in inflation is *expected,* unemployed workers who are looking for a job will revise their reservation wage to match the expected change in the level of prices. If reservation wages go up with the rate of inflation, there is no tradeoff between inflation and the unemployment rate. Higher inflation is associated with the original unemployment rate.

If the reservation wage goes up with the rate of inflation, there is no tradeoff between inflation and the unemployment rate.

Let's go back to Jason, the accountant who wants a job that pays $105 a day. Previously we said that if wages increased to $105 unexpectedly because of an increase in aggregate demand, he would quickly find an acceptable job. However, if Jason knows that the price level is going to go up 5 percent, then he knows that a wage increase from $100 to $105 is not a real wage increase because he needs $105 in order to buy what $100 would buy before. The *nominal wage* is the number of dollars earned; the *real wage* is the purchasing power of those dollars. If the nominal wage increases 5 percent at the same time that prices have gone up 5 percent, it takes 5 percent more money to buy the same goods and services. The real wage has not changed. What happens? Jason revises his reservation wage to account for the higher price level. If he wants a 5 percent higher real wage, his reservation wage goes up to $110.25 (5 percent more than $105). Now if employers offer him $105, he refuses and keeps searching.

In Figure 5, an expected increase in inflation moves us from point 1 on curve I to point 3 on curve II. When increased inflation is expected, the reservation wage reflects the higher rate of inflation and there is no tradeoff between inflation and the unemployment rate. Instead the economy moves along the long-run Phillips curve, with unemployment at its natural rate. The clockwise movement from point 1 to point 2 to point 3 is the pattern that follows an unexpected increase in aggregate demand.

What if the inflation rate is lower than expected? Here we find a reservation wage that reflects higher expected inflation. This means that those people who are looking for jobs are going to have a difficult time finding acceptable wage offers, the number of unemployed workers is going to increase, and the unemployment rate is going to rise. This sequence is shown in Figure 5 as the economy moves from point 3 to point 4. When the actual inflation rate is 6 percent and the expected inflation rate is also 6 percent, the economy is operating at the natural rate of unemployment. When the inflation rate falls to 3 percent but workers still expect 6 percent inflation, the unemployment rate rises (at point 4 along curve II). Eventually, if the inflation rate remains at 3 percent, workers adjust their expectations to the lower rate and the economy moves to point 1 on curve I. The short-run effect of unexpected *disinflation* is rising unemployment. Over time the short-run increase in the unemployment rate is eliminated.

As long as the actual rate of inflation equals the expected rate, the economy operates at the natural rate of unemployment.

As long as the actual rate of inflation equals the expected rate, the economy remains at the natural rate of unemployment. The tradeoff between inflation and the unemployment rate comes from unexpected inflation.

2.a.2. Inventory Fluctuations and Unemployment

Businesses hold inventories based on what they expect their sales to be. When aggregate demand is greater than expected, inventories fall below targeted levels. To restore inventories to the levels wanted, production is increased. Increased production leads to increased employment. If aggregate demand is lower than expected, inventories rise above targeted levels. To reduce inventories, production is cut back and workers are laid off from their jobs until sales have lowered unwanted inventories. Once production increases, employment rises again.

When aggregate demand is higher than expected, inventories are lower than expected and prices are higher than expected, so the unemployment rate falls. When aggregate demand is lower than expected, inventories are higher than expected and prices are lower than expected, so the unemployment rate rises.

Inventory, production, and employment all play a part in the Phillips curve analysis (Figure 7). Expected sales and inventory levels are based on an expected level of aggregate demand. If aggregate demand is greater than expected, inventories fall and prices on the remaining goods in stock rise. With the unexpected increase in inflation, the unemployment rate falls as businesses hire more workers to increase output to offset falling inventories. This sequence represents movement along a

---

FIGURE 7

Inflation, Unemployment, and Inventories

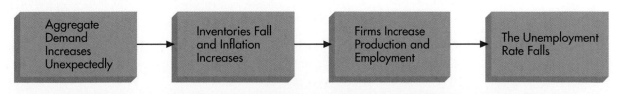

short-run Phillips curve because there is a tradeoff between inflation and the unemployment rate. We find the same tradeoff if aggregate demand is lower than expected. Here inventories increase and prices are lower than anticipated. With the unexpected decrease in inflation, the unemployment rate goes up as workers are laid off to reduce output until inventory levels fall.

2.a.3. Wage Contracts and Unemployment

Another factor that explains the short-run tradeoff between inflation and unemployment is labor contracts that fix wages for an extended period of time. When an existing contract expires, management must renegotiate with labor. A firm facing lower demand for its products may negotiate lower wages in order to keep as many workers employed as before. If the demand for a firm's products falls while a wage contract is in force, the firm must maintain wages; this means it is going to have to lay off workers.

For example, a pizza restaurant with $1,000 a day in revenues employs 4 workers at $40 a day each. The firm's total labor costs are $160 a day. Suppose revenues fall to $500 a day. If the firm wants to cut its labor costs in half, to $80, it has two choices: it can maintain wages at $40 a day and lay off 2 workers, or it can lower wages to $20 a day and keep all 4 workers. If the restaurant has a contract with the employees that sets wages at $40 a day, it must lay off 2 workers.

If demand increases while a wage contract is in force, a business hires more workers at the fixed wage. Once the contract expires, the firm's workers will negotiate higher wages, to reflect increased demand. For instance, suppose prices in the economy, including the price of pizzas, go up 10 percent. If the pizza restaurant can raise its prices 10 percent and sell as many pizzas as before (because the price of every other food also has gone up 10 percent), its daily revenues increase from $1,000 to $1,100. If the restaurant has a labor contract that fixes wages at $40 a day, its profits are going to go up, reflecting the higher price of pizzas. With its increased profits, the restaurant may be willing to hire more workers. Once the labor contract expires, the workers ask for a 10 percent wage increase to match the price level increase. If wages go up to $44 a day (10 percent higher than $40), the firm cannot hire more workers because wages have gone up in proportion to the increase in prices. If the costs of doing business rise at the same rate as prices, both profits and employment remain the same.

In the national economy, wage contracts are staggered; they expire at different times. Each year only 30 to 40 percent of all contracts expire across the entire economy. As economic conditions change, firms with expiring wage contracts can adjust *wages* to those conditions; firms with existing contracts must adjust *employment* to those conditions.

How do long-term wage contracts tie in with the Phillips curve analysis? The expected rate of inflation is based on expected aggregate demand and reflected in

FIGURE 8

Inflation, Unemployment, and Wage Controls

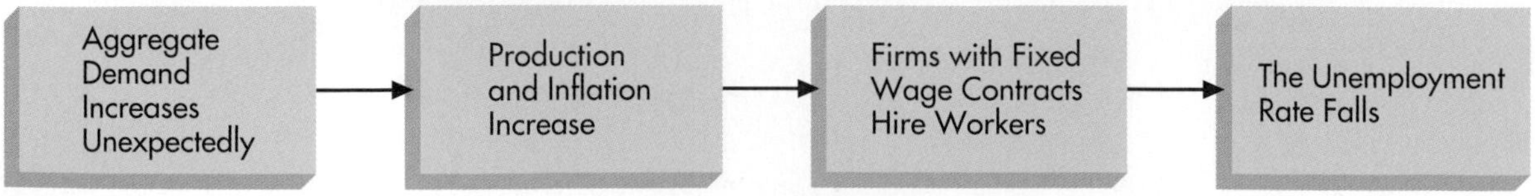

| Aggregate Demand Increases Unexpectedly | → | Production and Inflation Increase | → | Firms with Fixed Wage Contracts Hire Workers | → | The Unemployment Rate Falls |

Why Wages Don't Fall During Recessions

A look at macroeconomic data across countries reveals that when economies experience recessions, unemployment rates rise but wages fall very little, if at all. If we think of a supply and demand diagram for labor, we would think that as demand for labor falls in a recession, both the equilibrium quantity of labor and the equilibrium price, the wage rate, would fall. We do see the quantity effect as workers lose their jobs and the unemployment rate rises. Why don't we see wages falling also?

The text discusses long-term labor contracts as one reason why wages may be relatively inflexible over time. Beyond the presence of contracts, recent research points to human behavior as a contributing factor. Surveys of firms and workers indicate that worker morale is a major reason why wages are not reduced during recessions. Workers would view a wage cut as an indication that the firm does not value

their work as much, and they might, therefore, suffer lower morale, with the result being lower effort. When some workers are laid off, these workers suffer from the job loss, but they are no longer at the firm and cannot harm morale and work effort. Only in the case where the very survival of the firm is clearly at stake do wage cuts appear to be acceptable to workers.

So wages are "sticky downwards" because this promotes good worker effort and ensures that workers and firms share the same goals of efficient production and profit maximization. Rather than keep all workers when demand falls by paying lower wages to all, it may be better for the firm to lay off some workers and keep paying the remaining employees the same wage as before.

Sources: Truman F. Bewley, *Why Wages Don't Fall During a Recession* (Cambridge: Harvard University Press, 1999) and Peter Howitt, "Looking Inside the Labor Market: A Review Article," *Journal of Economic Literature,* March 2002.

the wage that is agreed on in the contract. When the actual rate of inflation equals the expected rate, businesses retain the same number of workers they had planned on when they signed the contract. For the economy overall, when actual and expected inflation rates are the same, the economy is operating at the natural rate of unemployment. That is, businesses are not hiring new workers because of an unexpected increase in aggregate demand, and they are not laying off workers because of an unexpected decrease in aggregate demand.

When aggregate demand is higher than expected, those firms with unexpired wage contracts hire more workers at the fixed wage, reducing unemployment (Figure 8). Those firms with expiring contracts have to offer higher wages in order to maintain the existing level of employment at the new demand condition. When aggregate demand is lower than expected, those firms with unexpired contracts have to lay off workers because they cannot lower the wage, while those firms with expiring contracts negotiate lower wages in order to keep their workers.

If wages were always flexible, unexpected changes in aggregate demand might be reflected largely in *wage* rather than *employment* adjustments. Wage contracts force businesses to adjust employment when aggregate demand changes unexpectedly. The Economic Insight "Why Wages Don't Fall During Recessions" addresses this issue further.

Wage contracts force businesses to adjust employment rather than wages in response to an unexpected change in aggregate demand.

4. How are macroeconomic expectations formed?

2.b. Forming Expectations

Expectations play a key role in explaining the short-run Phillips curve, the tradeoff between inflation and the unemployment rate. How are these expectations formed?

2.b.1. Adaptive Expectations

Expectations can be formed solely on the basis of experience. **Adaptive expectations** are expectations that are determined by what has happened in the recent past.

People learn from their experiences. For example, suppose the inflation rate has been 3 percent for the past few years. Based on past experience, then, people expect the inflation rate in the future to remain at 3 percent. If the Federal Reserve increases the growth of the money supply to a rate that produces 6 percent inflation, the public will be surprised by the higher rate of inflation. This unexpected inflation creates a short-run tradeoff between inflation and the unemployment rate along a short-run Phillips curve. Over time, if the inflation rate remains at 6 percent, the public will learn that the 3 percent rate is too low and will adapt its expectations to the actual, higher inflation rate. Once public expectations have adapted to the new rate of inflation, the economy returns to the natural rate of unemployment along the long-run Phillips curve.

2.b.2. Rational Expectations

Many economists believe that adaptive expectations are too narrow. If people look only at past information, they are ignoring what could be important information in the current period. **Rational expectations** are based on all available relevant information.

We are not saying that people have to know everything in order to form expectations. Rational expectations require only that people consider the information they believe to be relevant. This information includes their past experience along with what is currently happening and what they expect to happen in the future. For instance, in forming expectations about inflation, people consider rates in the recent past, current policy, and anticipated shifts in aggregate demand and supply that could affect the future rate of inflation.

If the inflation rate has been 3 percent over the past few years, adaptive expectations suggest that the future inflation rate will be 3 percent. No other information is considered. Rational expectations are based on more than the historical rate. Suppose the Fed announces a new policy that everyone believes will increase inflation in the future. With rational expectations, the effect of this announcement will be considered. Here, when the actual rate of inflation turns out to be more than 3 percent, there is no short-run tradeoff between inflation and the unemployment rate. The economy moves directly along the long-run Phillips curve to the higher inflation rate, while unemployment remains at the natural rate.

If we believe that people have rational expectations, we do not expect them to make the same mistakes over and over. We expect them to learn and react quickly to new information.

RECAP

1. Wage expectations, inventory fluctuations, and wage contracts help explain the short-run tradeoff between inflation and the unemployment rate.

2. The reservation wage is the minimum wage a worker is willing to accept.

3. Because wage expectations reflect expected inflation, when the inflation rate is surprisingly high, unemployed workers find jobs faster and the unemployment rate falls.

4. Unexpected increases in aggregate demand lower inventories and raise prices. To increase output (to replenish shrinking inventories), businesses hire more workers, which reduces the unemployment rate.

5. When aggregate demand is higher than expected, those businesses with wage contracts hire more workers at the fixed wage, lowering unemployment.

6. If wages were always flexible, unexpected changes in aggregate demand would be reflected in wage adjustments rather than employment adjustments.

7. Adaptive expectations are formed on the basis of information about the past.

8. Rational expectations are formed using all available relevant information.

3. Credibility and Time Inconsistency

The rate of inflation is a product of growth in the money supply. That growth is controlled by the country's central bank. If the Federal Reserve follows a policy of rapidly increasing the money supply, one consequence is rapid inflation. If it follows a policy of slow growth, it keeps inflation down.

To help the public predict the future course of monetary policy, Congress passed the Federal Reserve Reform Act (1977) and the Full Employment and Balanced Growth Act (1978). The Full Employment Act requires that the chairman of the Board of Governors of the Federal Reserve System testify before Congress semiannually about the Fed's targets for money growth along with other policy plans.

Of course, the Fed's plans are only plans. There is no requirement that the central bank actually follow the plans announced to Congress. During the course of the year, the Fed may decide that a new policy is necessary in light of economic developments. Changing conditions mean that plans can be **time inconsistent.** A plan is time inconsistent when it is changed over time in response to changed conditions.

time inconsistent: a characteristic of a policy or plan that changes over time in response to changing conditions

3.a. The Policymaker's Problem

Time inconsistency gives the Fed a credibility problem and the public the problem of guessing where monetary policy and the inflation rate are actually heading.

Figure 9 shows an example of how announced monetary policy can turn out to be time inconsistent. The Fed, like all central banks, always announces that it plans to follow a low-money-growth policy to promote a low rate of inflation. (It is unlikely that a central bank would ever state that it intends to follow an inflationary monetary policy.) Yet we know that the world is often characterized by higher rates of inflation. Because the actual inflation rate often ends up being higher than the intended inflation rate, low-inflation plans often are time inconsistent.

In Figure 9, labor contracts are signed following the central bank's announcement. The contracts call for either low wage increases or high wage increases. If everyone believes that the money supply is going to grow at the announced low rate, then the low-wage contracts are signed. However, if there is reason to believe that the announced policy is time inconsistent, the high-wage contracts are signed.

Over time, the central bank either follows the announced low-money-growth policy or implements a high-money-growth policy. If the low-wage contract is in force and the central bank follows the low-money-growth policy, the actual inflation rate will match the low rate that people expected and the unemployment rate will equal the natural rate. If the central bank follows a high-money-growth policy, the rate of inflation will be higher than expected and the unemployment rate will fall below the natural rate.

If the high-wage contract is in force and the low-money-growth policy is followed, the inflation rate will be lower than expected and the unemployment rate will

FIGURE 9

Time Inconsistency: An Example

Regardless of which labor contract is signed, the central bank achieves the lowest unemployment rate by following the high-money-growth policy—the opposite of its announced policy.

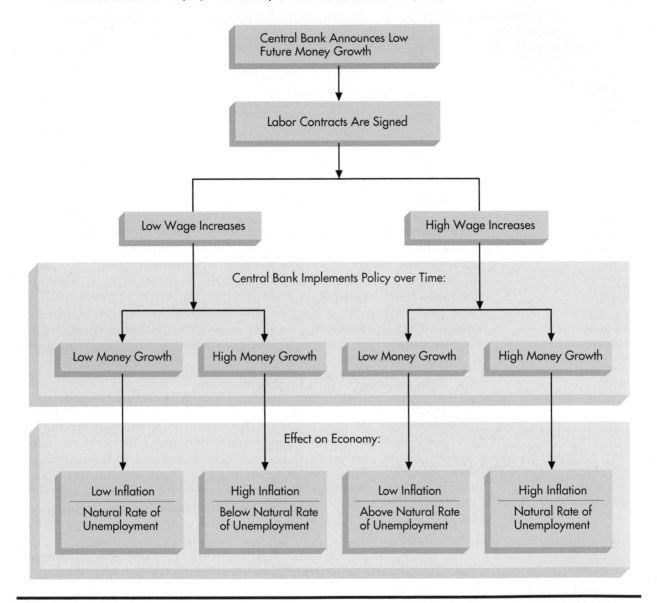

exceed the natural rate. If the high-money-growth policy is followed, the inflation rate will be as expected and the unemployment rate will be at the natural rate.

Look what happens to unemployment. Regardless of which labor contract is signed, if the central bank wants to keep unemployment as low as possible, it must deviate from its announced plan. The plan turns out to be time inconsistent. Because the public knows that unemployment, like the rate of inflation, is a factor in the Fed's policymaking, the central bank's announced plan is not credible.

3.b. Credibility

5. What makes government policies credible?

If the public does not believe the low-money-growth plans of the central bank, high-wage contracts will always be signed, and the central bank will always have to follow a high-money-growth policy to maintain the natural rate of unemployment. This cycle creates an economy in which high inflation persists year after year. If the central bank always followed its announced plan of low money growth and low inflation, the public would believe the plan, low-wage contracts would always be signed, and the natural rate of unemployment would exist at the low rate of inflation. In either case, high or low inflation, if the inflation rate is expected, the unemployment rate does not change. If the central bank eliminates the goal of reducing unemployment below the natural rate, the problem of inflation disappears. However, the public must be convinced that the central bank intends to pursue low money growth in the long run, avoiding the temptation to reduce the unemployment rate in the short run.

How does the central bank achieve credibility? One way is to fix the growth rate of the money supply by law. Congress could pass a law requiring that the Fed maintain a growth rate of, say, 3 to 5 percent a year. There would be problems defining the money supply, but this kind of law would give the Fed's policies credibility.

Another way for the Fed to establish credibility is to create incentives for monetary authorities to take a long-term view of monetary policy. In the long run, the economy is better off if policymakers do not try to exploit the short-run tradeoff between inflation and the unemployment rate. The central bank can achieve a lower rate of inflation at the natural rate of unemployment by avoiding unexpected increases in the rate at which money and inflation grow.

Reputation is a key factor here. If the central bank considers the effects of its actual policy on public expectations, it will find it easier to achieve low inflation by establishing a reputation for low-inflation policies. A central bank with a reputation for time-consistent plans will find labor contracts calling for low wage increases because people believe that the bank is going to follow its announced plans and generate a low rate of inflation. In other words, by maintaining a reputation for following through on announced policy, the Fed can earn the public confidence necessary to produce a low rate of inflation in the long run.

RECAP

1. A plan is time inconsistent when it changes over time in response to changing conditions.
2. If the public believes that an announced policy is time inconsistent, policymakers have a credibility problem that can limit the success of their plans.
3. Credibility can be achieved by fixing the growth rate of the money supply by law or by creating incentives for policymakers to follow through on announced plans.

4. Sources of Business Cycles

In Chapter 12 we examined the effect of fiscal policy on the equilibrium level of real GDP. Changes in government spending and taxes can expand or contract the economy. In Chapter 14 we described how monetary policy affects the equilibrium level of real GDP. Changes in the money supply also produce booms and recessions. Besides the policy-induced sources of business cycles covered in earlier chapters, there are other sources of economic fluctuations that economists have studied. One is the election campaign of incumbent politicians; when a business cycle results from this action, it is called a *political business cycle*. Macroeconomic policy may be used to promote the reelection of incumbent politicians. We also examine another source of business cycles that is not related to discretionary policy actions, the *real business cycle*.

4.a. The Political Business Cycle

6. Are business cycles related to political elections?

If a short-run tradeoff exists between inflation and unemployment, an incumbent administration could stimulate the economy just before an election to lower the unemployment rate, making voters happy and increasing the probability of reelection. Of course, after the election, the long-run adjustment to the expansionary policy would lead to higher inflation and move unemployment back to the natural rate.

Figure 10 illustrates the pattern. Before the election, the economy is initially at point 1 in Figure 10(a) and Figure 10(b). The incumbent administration stimulates the economy by increasing government spending or increasing the growth of the money supply. Aggregate demand shifts from AD_1 to AD_2 in Figure 10(a). In the short run, the increase in aggregate demand is unexpected, so the economy moves along the initial aggregate supply curve (AS_1) to point 2. This movement is reflected in Figure 10(b) of the figure, in the movement from point 1 to point 2 along short-run Phillips curve I. The pre-election expansionary policy increases real GDP and lowers the unemployment rate. Once the public adjusts its expectations to the higher inflation rate, the economy experiences a recession. Real GDP falls back to its potential level (Y_p) and the unemployment rate goes back up to the natural rate (U_n), as shown by the movement from point 2 to point 3 in both parts of the figure.

An unexpected increase in government spending or money growth temporarily stimulates the economy. If an election comes during the period of expansion, higher incomes and lower unemployment may increase support for the incumbent administration. The long-run adjustment back to potential real GDP and the natural rate of unemployment comes after the election.

Economists do not agree on whether a political business cycle exists in the United States. But they do agree that an effort to exploit the short-run tradeoff between inflation and the unemployment rate would shift the short-run Phillips curve out as shown in Figure 10(b).

The evidence of a political business cycle is not clear. If government macroeconomic policy is designed to stimulate the economy before elections and to bear the costs of rising unemployment and inflation after elections, we should see recessions regularly following national elections. Table 1 lists the presidential elections since 1948 along with the recessions that followed them. In six cases, a recession occurred the year after an election. A recession began before President Kennedy's election, and there was no recession during the Johnson, second Reagan, and Clinton administrations. Of course, just because recessions do not follow every election, there is no guarantee that some business cycles have not stemmed from political manipulation. If a short-run Phillips curve exists, the potential for a political business cycle exists as long as the public does not expect the government to stimulate the economy before elections.

FIGURE 10

The Political Business Cycle

Before the election, the government stimulates the economy, unexpectedly increasing aggregate demand. The economy moves from point 1 to point 2, pushing equilibrium real GDP above Y_p (Figure 10[a]) and the unemployment rate below U_n (Figure 10[b]). The incumbent politicians hope that rising incomes and lower unemployment will translate into votes. After the election comes adjustment to the higher aggregate demand, as the economy moves from point 2 to point 3. The aggregate supply curve shifts to the left, and equilibrium real GDP falls back to Y_p. Unemployment goes back up to U_n, and the rate of inflation rises.

(a) Aggregate Demand and Supply

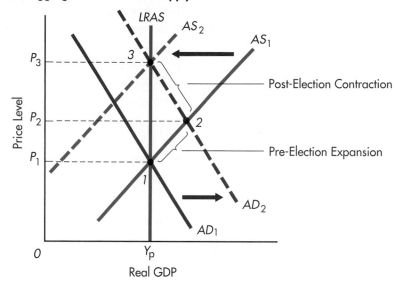

(b) Phillips Curve

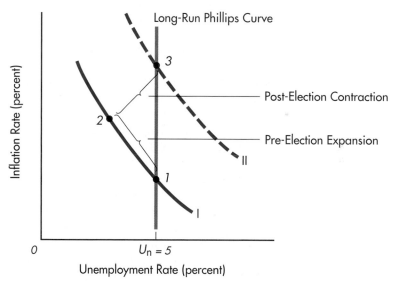

4.b. Real Business Cycles

shock: an unexpected change in a variable

In recent years economists have paid increasing attention to real **shocks**—unexpected changes—in the economy as a source of business cycles. Many believe that it is not only fiscal or monetary policy that triggers expansion or contraction in the economy but also technological change, change in tastes, labor strikes, weather, war, terrorism, or other real changes. A real business cycle is one that is generated by a change in one of those real variables.

TABLE 1

Presidential Elections and U.S. Recessions, 1948–2001

Presidential Election (Winner)	Next Recession
November 1948 (Truman)	November 1948–October 1949
November 1952 (Eisenhower)	June 1953–May 1954
November 1956 (Eisenhower)	June 1957–April 1958
November 1960 (Kennedy)	April 1960–February 1961
November 1964 (Johnson)	
November 1968 (Nixon)	October 1969–November 1970
November 1972 (Nixon)	December 1973–March 1975
November 1976 (Carter)	January 1980–July 1980
November 1980 (Reagan)	May 1981–November 1982
November 1984 (Reagan)	
November 1988 (G. H. W. Bush)	July 1990–March 1991
November 1992 (Clinton)	
November 1996 (Clinton)	
November 2000 (G. W. Bush)	March 2001–November 2001

7. How do real shocks to the economy affect business cycles?

Interest in the real business cycle was stimulated by the oil price shocks in the early 1970s and the important role they played in triggering the recession of 1973–1975. At that time, many economists were focusing on the role of unexpected changes in monetary policy in generating business cycles. They argued that these kinds of policy changes (changes in a nominal variable, the money supply) were responsible for the shifts in aggregate demand that led to expansions and contractions. When OPEC raised oil prices, it caused major shifts in aggregate supply. Higher oil prices in 1973 and 1974, and in 1979 and 1980, reduced aggregate supply, pushing the equilibrium level of real GDP down. Lower oil prices in 1986 raised aggregate supply and equilibrium real GDP.

An economywide real shock, like a substantial change in the price of oil, can affect output and employment across all sectors of the economy. Even an industry-specific shock can generate a recession or expansion in the entire economy if the industry produces a product used by a substantial number of other industries. For example, a labor strike in the steel industry would have major recessionary implications for the economy as a whole. If the output of steel fell, the price of steel would be bid up by all the industries that use steel as an input. This would shift the short-run aggregate supply curve to the left, as shown in Figure 11(a), and would move equilibrium real GDP from Y_1 down to Y_2.

Real shocks can also have expansionary effects on the economy. Suppose that the weather is particularly good one year and that harvests are surprisingly large. What happens? The price of food, cotton, and other agricultural output tends to fall, and the short-run aggregate supply curve shifts to the right, as shown in Figure 11(b), raising equilibrium real GDP from Y_1 to Y_2.

A business cycle can be the product of discretionary government policy or of real shocks that occur independent of government actions.

Real business cycles explain why national output can expand or contract in the absence of a discretionary macroeconomic policy that would shift aggregate demand. To fully understand business cycles, we must consider both policy-induced changes in real GDP, as covered in Chapters 12 and 14, and real shocks that occur independent of government actions.

FIGURE 11

The Impact of Real Shocks on Equilibrium Real GDP

A labor strike in a key industry can shift the aggregate supply curve to the left, like the shift from AS_1 to AS_2. This pushes equilibrium real GDP down from Y_1 to Y_2.

If good weather leads to a banner harvest, the aggregate supply curve shifts to the right, like the shift from AS_1 to AS_2, raising equilibrium real GDP from Y_1 to Y_2.

(a) A Labor Strike in the Steel Industry

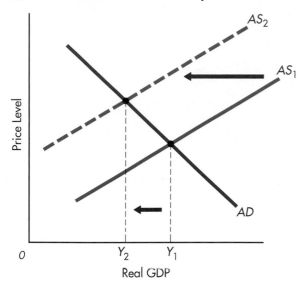

(b) A Surprisingly Large Agricultural Harvest

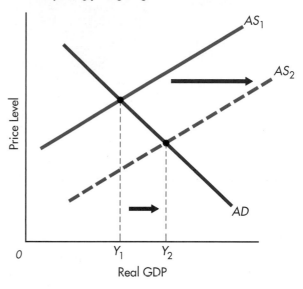

RECAP

1. The political business cycle is a short-term expansion stimulated by an administration before an election to earn votes. After the election comes the long-term adjustment (rising unemployment and inflation).

2. A real business cycle is an expansion and contraction caused by a change in tastes or technology, strikes, weather, or other real factors.

5. The Link Between Monetary and Fiscal Policies

In earlier chapters we have described how monetary and fiscal policies determine the equilibrium level of prices and national income. In our discussions we have talked about monetary policy and fiscal policy individually. Here we consider the relationship between them.

In some countries, monetary and fiscal policies are carried out by a single central authority. Even in the United States, where the Federal Reserve was created as an independent agency, monetary policy and fiscal policy are always related. The

Those who were around in the 1970s can remember the long lines and shortages at gas stations and the rapid increase in the price of oil that resulted from the oil embargo imposed by the Organization of Petroleum Exporting Countries. There was another effect of the oil price shock—the aggregate supply curve in the United States and other oil-importing nations shifted to the left, lowering the equilibrium level of real GDP while raising the price level. Such real sources of business cycles can explain why national output can rise or fall in the absence of any discretionary government macroeconomic policy.

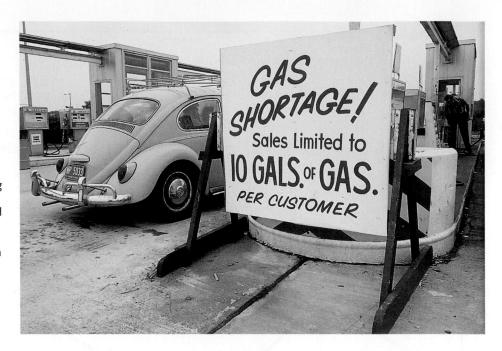

actions of the central bank have an impact on the proper role for fiscal policy, and the actions of fiscal policymakers have an impact on the proper role for monetary policy.

For example, suppose the central bank follows a monetary policy that raises interest rates. That policy raises the interest cost of new government debt, in the process increasing government expenditures. On the other hand, a fiscal policy that generates large fiscal deficits could contribute to higher interest rates. If the central bank has targeted an interest rate that lies below the current rate, the central bank could be drawn into an expansionary monetary policy. This interdependence between monetary and fiscal policy is important to policymakers as well as to businesspeople and others who seek to understand current economic developments.

5.a. The Government Budget Constraint

The *government budget constraint* clarifies the relationship between monetary and fiscal policies:

$$G = T + B + \Delta M$$

where

$$G = \text{government spending}$$

$$T = \text{tax revenue}$$

$$B = \text{government borrowing}$$

$$\Delta M = \text{the change in the money supply[1]}$$

?

8. **How is inflationary monetary policy related to government fiscal policy?**

---

[1]The M in the government budget constraint is government-issued money (usually called *base money* or *high-powered money*). It is easiest to think of this kind of money as currency, although in practice base money includes more than currency.

Extreme weather can be a source of real business cycle fluctuations. In this photo, damage caused by Hurricane Iris in Belize has destroyed some of the capital stock of the nation and would be associated with a temporary reduction in output.

The government budget constraint always holds because there are only three ways for the government to finance its spending: by taxing, by borrowing, and by creating money.

We can rewrite the government budget constraint with the change in M on the left-hand side of the equation:

$$\Delta M = (G - T) - B$$

In this form, you can see that the change in government-issued money equals the government fiscal deficit $(G - T)$ minus borrowing. This equation is always true. A government that has the ability to borrow at reasonable costs will not have the incentive to create rapid money growth and the consequent inflation that results in order to finance its budget deficit.

5.b. Monetary Reforms

In the United States and other industrial nations, monetary and fiscal policies are conducted by separate, independent agencies. Fiscal authorities (Congress and the president in the United States) cannot impose monetary policy on the central bank. But in typical developing countries, monetary and fiscal policies are controlled by a central political authority. Here monetary policy is often an extension of fiscal policy. Fiscal policy can impose an inflationary burden on monetary policy. If a country is running a large fiscal deficit and much of this deficit cannot be financed by government borrowing, monetary authorities must create money to finance the deficit.

Using money to finance fiscal deficits has produced very rapid rates of inflation in several countries. As prices reach astronomical levels, currency with very large face values must be issued. For instance, when Bolivia faced a sharp drop in the availability of willing lenders in the mid-1980s, the government began to create money to finance its fiscal deficit. As the money supply increased in relation to the output of goods and services, prices rose. In 1985 the government was creating

TABLE 2

Recent Monetary Reforms

Country	Old Currency	New Currency	Date of Change	Change
Angola	Readjusted kwanza	Kwanza	December 1999	1 kwanza = 1,000,000 readjusted kwanza
Argentina	Peso	Peso argentino	June 1983	1 peso argentino = 10,000 pesos
	Peso argentino	Austral	June 1985	1 austral = 1,000 pesos argentino
	Austral	Peso argentino	January 1992	1 peso argentino = 10,000 australes
Bolivia	Peso	Boliviano	January 1987	1 boliviano = 1,000,000 pesos
Brazil	Cruzeiro	Cruzado	February 1986	1 cruzado = 1,000 cruzeiros
	Cruzado	New cruzado	January 1989	1 new cruzado = 1,000 cruzados
	New cruzado	Cruzeiro	March 1990	1 cruzeiro = 1 new cruzado
	Cruziero	Real	July 1994	1 real = 2,700 cruzeiros
Chile	Peso	Escudo	January 1969	1 escudo = 1,000 pesos
	Escudo	Peso	September 1975	1 peso = 1,000 escudos
Congo, D.R.	New Zaire	Congolese franc	June 1998	1 Congolese franc = 100,000 new Zaire
Georgia	Kuponi	Lari	September 1995	1 lari = 1,000,000 kuponi
Israel	Pound	Shekel	February 1980	1 shekel = 10 pounds
	Old shekel	New shekel	September 1985	1 new shekel = 1,000 old shekels
Mexico	Peso	New peso	January 1993	1 new peso = 1,000 pesos
Peru	Sol	Inti	February 1985	1 inti = 1,000 soles
	Inti	New sol	July 1991	1 new sol = 1,000,000 intis
Poland	Zloty	New zloty	January 1995	1 new zloty = 10,000 zlotys
Russia	Ruble	New ruble	January 1998	1 new ruble = 1,000 rubles
Ukraine	Karbovanets	Hryvnia	September 1996	1 hryvnia = 100,000 karbovanets
Uruguay	Old peso	New peso	July 1975	1 new peso = 1,000 old pesos
Yugoslavia	Dinar	New dinar	January 1994	1 new dinar = 13,000,000 dinars

money so fast that the rate of inflation reached 8,170 percent. Lunch in a La Paz hotel could cost 10 million Bolivian pesos. You can imagine the problem of counting money and recording money values with cash registers and calculators. As the rate of inflation increased, Bolivians had to carry stacks of currency to pay for goods and services. Eventually the government issued a 1 million peso note, then 5 million and 10 million peso notes.

This extremely high inflation, or hyperinflation, ended when a new government introduced its economic program in August 1985. The program reduced government spending dramatically, which slowed the growth of the fiscal deficit. At the same time, a monetary reform was introduced. A **monetary reform** is a new monetary policy that includes the introduction of a new monetary unit. The central bank of Bolivia announced that it would restrict money creation and introduced a new currency, the boliviano, in January 1987. It set 1 boliviano equal to 1 million Bolivian pesos.

The new monetary unit, the boliviano, did not lower prices; it lowered the units in which prices were quoted. Lunch now cost 10 bolivianos instead of 10 million pesos. More important, the rate of inflation dropped abruptly.

Did the new unit of currency end the hyperinflation? No. The rate of inflation dropped because the new fiscal policy controls introduced by the government relieved the pressure on the central bank to create money in order to finance government spending. Remember the government budget constraint. The only way to reduce the amount of money being created is to reduce the fiscal deficit $(G - T)$ minus borrowing (B). Once fiscal policy is under control, monetary reform is possible. If a government introduces a new monetary unit without changing its fiscal policy, the monetary unit by itself has no lasting effect on the rate of inflation.

Table 2 lists monetary reforms enacted in recent years. Argentina had a monetary reform in June 1983. Yet by June 1985, another reform was needed. The inflationary problems that Argentina faced could not be solved just by issuing a new unit of currency. Fiscal reform also was needed, and none was made. In any circumstances of inflationary monetary policy, monetary reform by itself is not enough. It must be coupled with a reduction in the fiscal deficit or an increase in government borrowing to produce a permanent change in the rate of inflation.

Monetary policy is tied to fiscal policy through the government budget constraint. Although money creation is not an important source of deficit financing in developed countries, it has been and still is a significant source of revenue for developing countries, where taxes are difficult to collect and borrowing is limited.

monetary reform: a new monetary policy that includes the introduction of a new monetary unit

The introduction of a new monetary unit without a change in fiscal policy has no lasting effect on the rate of inflation.

RECAP

1. The government budget constraint $(G = T + B + \Delta M)$ defines the relationship between fiscal and monetary policies.

2. The implications of fiscal policy for the growth of the money supply can be seen by rewriting the government budget constraint this way:

$$\Delta M = (G - T) - B.$$

3. A monetary reform is a new monetary policy that includes the introduction of a new unit of currency.

4. A government can end an inflationary monetary policy only with a fiscal reform that lowers the fiscal deficit $(G - T)$ minus borrowing (B).

Summary

? Is there a tradeoff between inflation and the unemployment rate?

1. The Phillips curve shows the relationship between inflation and the unemployment rate. *§1*

? How does the tradeoff between inflation and the unemployment rate vary from the short to the long run?

2. In the long run, there is no tradeoff between inflation and the unemployment rate. *§1.b*

3. The long-run Phillips curve is a vertical line at the natural rate of unemployment. *§1.b.2*

? What is the relationship between unexpected inflation and the unemployment rate?

4. Unexpected inflation can affect the unemployment rate through wage expectations, inventory fluctuations, and wage contracts. *§2.a, 2.a.1, 2.a.2, 2.a.3*

? How are macroeconomic expectations formed?

5. Adaptive expectations are formed on the basis of past experience; rational expectations are formed on the basis of all available relevant information. *§2.b.1, 2.b.2*

? What makes government policies credible?

6. A policy is credible only if it is time consistent. *§3.b*

? Are business cycles related to political elections?

7. A political business cycle is created by politicians who want to improve their chances of reelection by stimulating the economy just before an election. *§4.a*

? How do real shocks to the economy affect business cycles?

8. Real business cycles are a product of an unexpected change in technology, weather, or some other real variable. *§4.b*

? How is inflationary monetary policy related to government fiscal policy?

9. The government budget constraint defines the relationship between monetary and fiscal policies. *§5.a*

10. When government-issued money is used to finance fiscal deficits, inflationary monetary policy can be a product of fiscal policy. *§5.b*

Key Terms

Phillips curve *§1*

reservation wage *§2.a.1*

adaptive expectation *§2.b.1*

rational expectation *§2.b.2*

time inconsistent *§3*

shock *§4.b*

monetary reform *§5.b*

Exercises

1. What is the difference between the short-run Phillips curve and the long-run Phillips curve? Use an aggregate supply and demand diagram to explain why there is a difference between them.

2. Give two reasons why there may be a short-run tradeoff between unexpected inflation and the unemployment rate.

3. "Unexpected increases in the money supply cause clockwise movements in the Phillips curve diagram; unexpected decreases in the money supply cause counterclockwise movements in the Phillips curve diagram." Evaluate this statement using a graph to illustrate your answer.

4. Economists have identified two kinds of macroeconomic expectations.

   a. Define them.
   b. What are the implications for macroeconomic policy of these two forms of expectations?

5. Write down the government budget constraint and explain how it can be used to understand the relationship between fiscal and monetary policies.

6. Using the government budget constraint, explain:

   a. Why some countries experience hyperinflation
   b. How fiscal policy must change in order to implement a noninflationary monetary policy

7. Parents, like governments, establish credibility by seeing to it that their "policies" (the rules they outline for their children) are time consistent. Analyze the potential for time consistency of these rules:

   a. If you don't eat the squash, you'll go to bed 30 minutes early tonight!
   b. If you get any grades below a C, you won't be allowed to watch television on school nights!
   c. If you don't go to my alma mater, I won't pay for your college education!
   d. If you marry that disgusting person, I'll disinherit you!

8. Suppose an economy has witnessed an 8 percent rate of growth in its money supply and prices over the last few years. How do you think the public will respond to an announced plan to increase the money supply by 4 percent over the next year if:

   a. The central bank has a reputation for always meeting its announced policy goals.
   b. The central bank rarely does what it says it will do.

9. What are the implications for the timing of business-cycle fluctuations over the years if all business cycles are:

   a. Manipulated by incumbent administrations
   b. A product of real shocks to the economy

10. Suppose the Federal Reserve System were abolished and the Congress assumed responsibility for monetary policy along with fiscal policy. What potential harm to the economy could result from such a change?

11. Suppose tax revenues equal $100 billion, government spending equals $130 billion, and the government borrows $25 billion. How much do you expect the money supply to increase given the government budget constraint?

12. If the government budget deficit equals $220 billion and the money supply increases by $100 billion, how much must the government borrow?

13. Discuss how each of the following sources of real business cycles would affect the economy.

   a. Farmers go on strike for six months.
   b. Oil prices fall substantially.
   c. Particularly favorable weather increases agricultural output nationwide.

14. Using an aggregate demand and aggregate supply diagram, illustrate and explain how a political business cycle is created.

15. Use a Phillips curve diagram to illustrate and explain how a political business cycle is created.

16. What is the natural rate of unemployment? What can cause it to change over time?

17. Many developing countries have experienced high money growth rates and, consequently, high inflation. Use the government budget constraint to explain how a poor country that wants to increase government spending can get into an inflationary situation.

Take the ACE Practice Test for this chapter to review the important concepts and get immediate feedback with answers.

economics.college.hmco.com/students

War Worries Hurting U.S. Markets: Fed Chief Alan Greenspan Warns of Further Interest Rate Cuts if Sluggishness Continues

WASHINGTON (AP)—Federal Reserve chairman Alan Greenspan said yesterday that shocks from falling stock prices and worries about war with Iraq are dimming business prospects, even though the economy has proven "remarkably resilient" over the past year.

Greenspan said the Fed's decision last week to cut interest rates by a surprisingly large half-point was the central bank's response to the growing dangers.

He also repeated the Fed's view in its rate cut announcement that the central bank believes the U.S. economy will soon pull out of the current weak period.

"The actions taken last week to ease monetary policy should prove helpful as the economy works its way through this current soft spot," Greenspan said.

In response to questions, he told the committee he believes that the most likely outcome for economic growth is "to come out of this soft spot and to start accelerating."

He said if this occurs, the central bank will be ready to reverse course quickly and start pushing interest rates higher to make sure inflation doesn't get out of control.

But if the Fed's expectations are wrong and the sluggish period gets worse, it will cut rates further, he said.

Bush Agrees

U.S. President George W. Bush said at the White House he agreed with Greenspan's view that the economy isn't as strong as it should be.

"He uses the words 'soft spot.' I use the words 'bumping along.' Both of us understand that our economy is not nearly as strong as it's going to be," Bush said. "Our job here in Washington is to create the environment necessary for people to feel confident about risking capital."

The president promised to consider "new ideas" for improving the economy once Congress comes back into session next year.

Greenspan told the Joint Economic Committee there was no doubt that a number of forces are holding back growth. He cited in particular the fallout from revelations about corporate accounting scandals, the continued reluctance of businesses to increase investment spending and "heightened geopolitical risks.

"Over the last few months, these forces have taken their toll on activity and evidence has accumulated that the economy has hit a soft patch," Greenspan told the panel.

He said all of those problems are creating uncertainty among consumers, who have been the driving force in the current recovery and among businesses.

"Households have become more cautious in their purchases, while business spending has yet to show any substantial vigour," Greenspan said.

Lowest in 41 Years

He said it was against this backdrop that the Fed's interest rate panel, the Federal Open Market Committee, decided last week to cut its target for the federal funds rate, the interest that banks charge on overnight loans, by a half-point to 1.25 per cent, the lowest level in 41 years.

Greenspan gave no hint in his prepared testimony about what the central bank might do next, but private economists believe if the economy continues to weaken, the Fed will cut rates again—either at its next meeting in December or at its first meeting of the new year in January.

Greenspan said that even with the current slowdown, the U.S. economy has proven its adaptability over the past year since the Sept. 11, 2001, terrorist attacks, managing to grow at an average rate of three per cent since the fourth quarter of 2001.

***The Halifax Daily News*/November 14, 2002**

Macroeconomic policy in the United States is determined by Congress, the presidential administration, and the Federal Reserve. The article reports comments by Federal Reserve Chairman Alan Greenspan and President George W. Bush that highlight some of the issues raised in this chapter.

The issue of government credibility is highlighted by President Bush's saying, "Our job here in Washington is to create the environment necessary for people to feel confident about risking capital." In other words, the public needs to believe that government economic policy will not be a source of uncertainty or business-cycle fluctuations, but rather will be a steadying influence. The public needs to believe that the government will follow policies that are consistent with low and stable inflation rates and steady economic growth. In such an environment, business investment spending will increase, as people will "feel confident about risking capital."

The source of business cycles is highlighted by Alan Greenspan's remarks that shocks from falling stock prices, worries about war with Iraq, and corporate accounting scandals have all contributed to households' becoming more uncertain about the future and more cautious in making spending decisions. The things Greenspan mentions are consistent with "real business cycles." Changes in consumer behavior resulting from war or accounting scandals reflect a lack of confidence in the economy because of uncertainty about the future. The article tells us that the Fed lowered the federal funds interest rate to its lowest level in 41 years to combat the slowdown in the economy, and that it stood ready to lower this rate further if necessary. Communicating the Fed's readiness to take further monetary policy action to stimulate the economy is intended to convince business firms and consumers that the Fed is standing watch and will not let the economy suffer a significant recession. If people believe that better economic times are ahead, then business investment spending will increase and consumers will be more willing to make new purchases.

Of course, there is no guarantee that government policy aimed at minimizing business-cycle fluctuations will be successful. Since the policy is taken today, yet is aimed at bettering economic conditions in the future, there is always a possibility that such an activist policy can aggravate business-cycle fluctuations rather than moderate them. For instance, suppose the Fed cut the federal funds rate today because of a belief that the economy needs to be stimulated in order to avoid a recession. Yet, if the economy is already starting to generate a recovery without the Fed's stimulus (perhaps because of some earlier Fed action), the new stimulus may cause spending to grow too fast and generate an inflation problem that otherwise would not have occurred. Economic policymaking is always done with some degree of uncertainty. While policymakers like Alan Greenspan and George Bush may support policy changes that are aimed at making the economy grow with low inflation, there is always a chance that their policies will have effects other than what was intended.

CHAPTER 16

Macroeconomic Viewpoints: New Keynesian, Monetarist, and New Classical

? Fundamental Questions

1. **What do Keynesian economists believe about macroeconomic policy?**

2. **What role do monetarists believe the government should play in the economy?**

3. **What is new classical economics?**

4. **How do theories of economics change over time?**

Economists do not all agree on macroeconomic policy. Sometimes disagreements are due to normative differences, or differences in personal values, regarding what the truly pressing needs are that should be addressed. Other disagreements are based on different views of how the economy operates and what determines the equilibrium level of real GDP.

It would be very easy to classify economists, to call them liberals or conservatives, for example. But an economist who believes that the government should not intervene in social decisions (abortion, censorship) may favor an active role for government in economic decisions (trade protection, unemployment insurance, welfare benefits). Another economist may support an active role for government in regulating the social behavior of individuals, yet believe that government should allow free markets to operate without interference.

In this chapter, an overview of important differences among schools of macroeconomic thought is presented. Most economists probably do not align themselves

solely with any one theory of macroeconomics, instead choosing to incorporate pieces of various schools of thought. But the three approaches we discuss in this chapter—Keynesian, monetarist, and new classical—have had enormous impact on macroeconomic thinking and policy. Economic thinking has evolved over time as economists develop new economic theories to fit the realities of a changing world. ■

1. What do Keynesian economists believe about macroeconomic policy?

1. Keynesian Economics

Keynesian macroeconomics (named after the English economist John Maynard Keynes) dominated the economics profession from the 1940s through the 1960s. Some economists today refer to themselves as "new Keynesians." The common thread that pervades Keynesian economics is an emphasis on the inflexibility of wages and prices. This leads many Keynesians to recommend an activist government macroeconomic policy aimed at achieving a satisfactory rate of economic growth.

1.a. The Keynesian Model

Keynesian economics grew out of the Great Depression, when inflation was no problem but output was falling. As a result, the Keynesian model of macroeconomic equilibrium assumes that prices are constant and that changes in aggregate expenditures determine equilibrium real GDP. In an aggregate demand and supply analysis, the simple Keynesian model looks like the graph in Figure 1. The aggregate supply curve is a horizontal line at a fixed level of prices, P_1. Changes in aggregate demand, such as from AD_1 to AD_2, cause changes in real GDP with no change in the price level.

Figure 1 reflects the traditional Keynesian emphasis on aggregate demand as a determinant of equilibrium real GDP. But no economist today would argue that the aggregate supply curve is always horizontal at every level of real GDP. More representative of Keynesian economics today is the aggregate supply curve shown in

---

FIGURE 1

The Fixed-Price Keynesian Model

In the simple Keynesian model, prices are fixed at P_1 by the horizontal aggregate supply curve, so that changes in aggregate demand determine equilibrium real GDP.

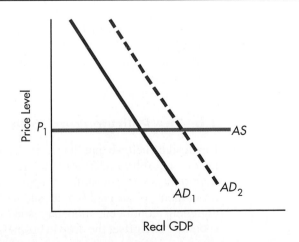

FIGURE 2

The Modern Keynesian Model

Modern Keynesians typically believe that the aggregate supply curve is horizontal only at relatively low levels of real GDP. As real GDP increases, more and more industries reach their capacity level of output, and the aggregate supply curve becomes positively sloped.

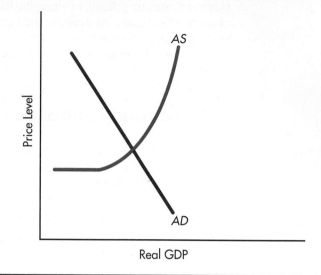

Figure 2. At low levels of real GDP, the curve is flat. In this region (the Keynesian region), increases in aggregate demand are associated with increases in output but not with increases in prices. This flat region of the aggregate supply curve reflects the Keynesian belief that inflation is not a problem when unemployment is high. As the level of real GDP increases, and more and more industries reach their capacity level of output, the aggregate supply curve becomes positively sloped.

The economic theories that John Maynard Keynes proposed in the 1930s have given way to new theories. Today **Keynesian economics** focuses on the role the government plays in stabilizing the economy by managing aggregate demand. *New Keynesians* believe that wages and prices are not flexible in the short run. They use their analysis of business behavior to explain the Keynesian region on the aggregate supply curve of Figure 2. They believe that the economy is not always in equilibrium. For instance, if the demand for labor falls, we would expect the equilibrium price of labor (the wage) to fall and, because fewer people want to work at a lower wage, the number of people employed to fall. New Keynesians argue that wages do not tend to fall, because firms choose to lay off workers rather than decrease wages. Businesses retain high wages for their remaining employees in order to maintain morale and productivity. As a result, wages are quite rigid. This wage rigidity is reflected in price rigidity in goods markets, according to new Keynesian economics.

Keynesian economics: a school of thought that emphasizes the role government plays in stabilizing the economy by managing aggregate demand

New Keynesian macroeconomists argue that wages and prices are not flexible in the short run.

1.b. The Policymakers' Role

Keynesians believe that the government must take an active role in the economy to restore equilibrium. Traditional Keynesians identified the private sector as an important source of shifts in aggregate demand. For example, they argued that investment is susceptible to sudden changes. If business spending falls, the argument continued, monetary and fiscal policies should be used to stimulate spending and offset the drop in business spending. Government intervention is necessary to offset private-sector shifts in aggregate demand and avoid recession. And if private spending increases, creating inflationary pressure, then monetary and fiscal policies should restrain spending, again to offset private-sector shifts in aggregate demand.

New Keynesian macroeconomics does not focus on fluctuations in aggregate demand as the primary source of the problems facing policymakers. Keynesian economists realize that aggregate supply shocks can be substantial. But whatever the source of the instability—aggregate demand or aggregate supply—they emphasize active government policy to return the economy to equilibrium.

RECAP

1. Keynesian economists today reject the simple fixed-price model in favor of a model in which the aggregate supply curve is relatively flat at low levels of real GDP and slopes upward as real GDP approaches its potential level.

2. Keynesians believe that the tendency for the economy to experience disequilibrium in labor and goods markets forces the government to intervene in the economy.

2. Monetarist Economics

The Keynesian view dominated macroeconomics in the 1940s, the 1950s, and most of the 1960s. In the late 1960s and the 1970s, Keynesian economics faced a challenge from **monetarist economics,** a school of thought that emphasizes the role that changes in the money supply play in determining equilibrium real GDP and prices. The leading monetarist, Milton Friedman, had been developing monetarist theory since the 1940s, but it took several decades before his ideas became popular. In part the shift was a product of the forcefulness of Friedman's arguments, but the relatively poor macroeconomic performance of the United States in the 1970s probably contributed to a growing disenchantment with Keynesian economics, creating an environment ripe for new ideas. The Economic Insight "Milton Friedman" describes how Friedman's monetarist theories became popular.

monetarist economics: a school of thought that emphasizes the role changes in the money supply play in determining equilibrium real GDP and price level

2.a. The Monetarist Model

Monetarists focus on the role of the money supply in determining the equilibrium level of real GDP and prices. In Chapter 14 we discussed monetary policy and equilibrium income. We showed that monetary policy is linked to changes in the equilibrium level of real GDP through changes in investment (and consumption). Keynesians traditionally assumed that monetary policy affects aggregate demand by changing the interest rate and, consequently, investment spending. Monetarists believe that changes in the money supply have broad effects on expenditures through both investment and consumption. An increase in the money supply pushes aggregate demand up by increasing both business and household spending and raises the equilibrium level of real GDP. A decrease in the money supply does the opposite.

Milton Friedman

Milton Friedman is widely considered to be the father of monetarism. Born in 1912 in New York City, Friedman spent most of his career at the University of Chicago. Early in his professional life, he recognized the importance of developing economics as an empirical science—that is, using data to test the applicability of economic theory.

In 1957, Friedman published *A Theory of the Consumption Function.* In the book, he discussed the importance of *permanent income,* rather than current income, in understanding consumer spending. His analysis of consumption won widespread acclaim, an acclaim that would be a long time coming for his work relating monetary policy to real output and prices.

In the 1950s, Keynesian theory dominated economics. Most macroeconomists believed that the supply of money in the economy was of little importance. In 1963, with the publication of *A Monetary History of the United States, 1867–1960* (coauthored with Anna Schwartz of the National Bureau of Economic Research), Friedman focused attention on the monetarist argument. Still Keynesian economics dominated scholarly and policy debate.

In the late 1960s and early 1970s, the rate of inflation and the rate of unemployment increased simultaneously. This was a situation that Keynesian economics could not explain. The timing was right for a new theory of macroeconomic behavior, and monetarism, with Milton Friedman its most influential advocate, grew in popularity. The new stature of monetarism was clearly visible in 1979, when the Fed adopted a monetarist approach to targeting the money supply.

In 1976, Milton Friedman was awarded the Nobel Prize for economics. By this time he had become a public figure. He wrote a column for *Newsweek* from 1966 to 1984 and in 1980 developed a popular public television series, *Free to Choose,* based on his book of the same title. Through the popular media, Friedman became the most effective and well-known supporter of free markets in the United States and much of the rest of the world. Many would argue that only Keynes has had as much influence on scholarly literature and public policy in economics as Milton Friedman.

Monetarists believe that accelerating inflation is a product of efforts to increase real GDP through expansionary monetary policy.

Monetarists believe that changes in monetary policy (or fiscal policy, for that matter) have only a short-term effect on real GDP. In the long run, they expect real GDP to be at a level consistent with the natural rate of unemployment. As a result, the long-run effect of a change in the money supply is fully reflected in a change in the price level. Attempts to exploit the short-run effects of expansionary monetary policy produce an inflationary spiral, in which the level of GDP increases temporarily, then falls back to the potential level while prices rise. This is the rightward shift of the Phillips curve we described in Chapter 15.

2.b. The Policymakers' Role

2. What role do monetarists believe the government should play in the economy?

Unlike Keynesian economists, monetarists do not believe that the economy is subject to a disequilibrium that must be offset by government action. Most monetarists believe that the economy tends toward equilibrium at the level of potential real GDP. Their faith in the free market (price) system leads them to favor minimal government intervention.

Monetarists often argue that government policy heightens the effects of the business cycle. This is especially true of monetary policy. To prove their point, monetarists link changes in the growth of the money supply to business-cycle fluctuations. Specifically, they suggest that periods of relatively fast money growth are followed by booms and inflation and that periods of relatively slow money growth are followed by recessions.

FIGURE 3

The Growth Rate of the U.S. Money Supply, Consumer Prices, and Real GDP

In general, the inflation rate follows the rate at which the money supply grows with a lag of one or two years. Growth in real GDP follows growth in the money supply with a lag of about one year. *Sources: Data are from the* Economic Report of the President, 2003; *Department of Commerce (www.bea.doc.gov/bea).*

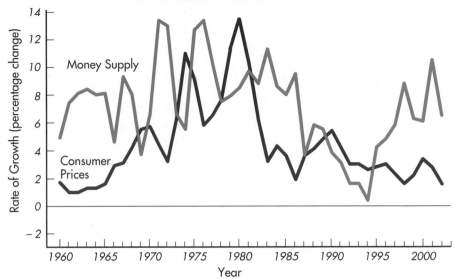

(a) Growth Rate of U.S. Money Supply and Consumer Prices

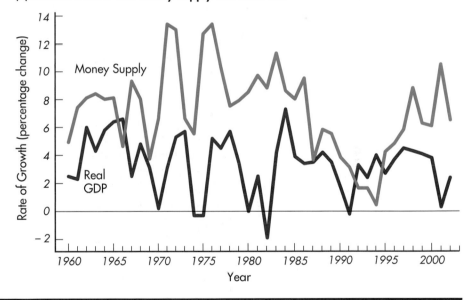

(b) Growth Rate of U.S. Money Supply and Real GDP

Figure 3 shows the rate at which the money supply, consumer prices, and real GDP grew in the United States in recent years. The inflation rate (consumer prices) seems to follow changes in the growth rate of the money supply with a lag of one or two years; GDP typically follows a change in the growth rate of the money supply by a year. The links between money growth and inflation and between money growth and GDP are by no means perfect. Sometimes there seem to be closer relationships than at other times. This makes it difficult to predict the effect of a particular change in monetary policy on prices or real GDP. In addition, a number of other variables influence GDP.

Economic policy operates with a long and variable lag.

Monetarists favor nonactivist government policy because they believe that the government's attempts to make the economy better off by aiming monetary and fiscal policies at low inflation and low unemployment often make things worse. Why? Because economic policy, which is very powerful, operates with a long and variable lag. First, policymakers have to recognize that a problem exists. This is the *recognition lag.* Then they must formulate an appropriate policy. This is the *reaction lag.* Then the effects of the policy must work through the economy. This is the *effect lag.*

When the Federal Reserve changes the rate of growth of the money supply, real GDP and inflation do not change immediately. In fact, studies show that as much as two years can pass between a change in policy and the effect of that change on real GDP. This means that when policymakers institute a change targeted at a particular level of real GDP or rate of inflation, the effect of the policy is not felt for a long time. And it is possible that the economy could be facing an entirely different set of problems in a year or two from those that policymakers are addressing today. But today's policy will still have effects next year, and those effects may aggravate next year's problems.

Because of the long and variable lag in the effect of fiscal and monetary policies, monetarists argue that policymakers should set policy according to rules that do not change from month to month or even year to year. What kinds of rules? A fiscal policy rule might be to balance the budget annually; a monetary policy rule might be to require that the money supply grow at a fixed rate over time or that the central bank commit to following an inflation target. These kinds of rules restrict policymakers from formulating discretionary policy. Monetarists believe that when discretionary shifts in policy are reduced, economic growth is steadier than it is when government consciously sets out to achieve full employment and low inflation.

RECAP

1. Monetarists emphasize the role that changes in the money supply play in determining equilibrium real GDP and the level of prices.

2. Monetarists do not believe that the economy is subject to disequilibrium in the labor and goods markets or that government should take an active role in the economy.

3. Because economic policy operates with a long and variable lag, attempts by government to stabilize the economy may, in fact, make matters worse.

4. Monetarists believe that formal rules, rather than the discretion of policymakers, should govern economic policymaking.

3. New Classical Economics

In the 1970s an alternative to Keynesian and monetarist economics was developed: new classical economics. But before we discuss the new classical theory, let's look at the old one.

classical economics: a school of thought that assumes that real GDP is determined by aggregate supply, while the equilibrium price level is determined by aggregate demand

Classical economics is the theory that was popular before Keynes changed the face of economics in the 1930s. According to classical economics, real GDP is determined by aggregate supply, while the equilibrium price level is determined by aggregate demand. Figure 4, the classical aggregate demand and supply diagram, shows the classical economist's view of the world. The vertical aggregate supply curve means that the equilibrium level of output (income) is a product only of the determinants of aggregate supply: the price of resources, technology, and expectations (see Chapter 9).

If the aggregate supply curve is vertical, then changes in aggregate demand, such as from AD_1 to AD_2, change only the price level; they do not affect the equilibrium level of output. Classical economics assumes that prices and wages are perfectly flexible. This rules out contracts that fix prices or wages for periods of time. It also rules out the possibility that people are not aware of all prices and wages. They know when prices have gone up and ask for wage increases to compensate.

Both Keynesians and monetarists would argue that information about the economy, including prices and wages, is not perfect. When workers and businesses negotiate wages, they may not know what current prices are, and they certainly do not know what future prices will be. Furthermore, many labor contracts fix wages for long periods of time. This means that wages are not flexible; they cannot adjust immediately to new price levels.

3.a. The New Classical Model

new classical economics: a school of thought that holds that changes in real GDP are a product of unexpected changes in the level of prices

New classical economics was a response to the problems of meeting economic policy goals in the 1970s. New classical economists questioned some of the assumptions on which Keynesian economics was based. For instance, new classical economists believe wages are flexible, while both traditional Keynesian and new Keynesian economists assume that wages can be fixed in the short run.

FIGURE 4

The Classical Model

The vertical aggregate supply curve indicates that equilibrium real GDP is determined strictly by the determinants of aggregate supply.

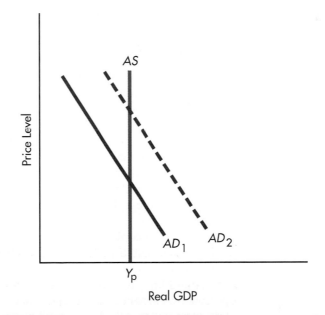

---

3. What is new classical economics?

New classical economics does not assume that people know everything that is happening, as the old theory did. People make mistakes because their expectations of prices or some other critical variable are different from the future reality. New classical economists emphasize rational expectations. As defined in Chapter 15, *rational expectations* are based on all available relevant information. This was a new way of thinking about expectations. Earlier theories assumed that people formed adaptive expectations—that their expectations were based only on their past experience. With rational expectations, people learn not only from their past experience, but also from any other information that helps them predict the future.

Suppose the chairman of the Federal Reserve Board announces a new monetary policy. Price-level expectations that are formed rationally take this announcement into consideration; those that are formed adaptively do not. It is much easier for policymakers to make unexpected changes in policy if expectations are formed adaptively rather than rationally.

Another element of new classical economics is the belief that markets are in equilibrium. Keynesian economics argues that disequilibrium in markets demands government intervention. For instance, Keynesian economists define a recession as a disequilibrium in the labor market—a surplus of labor—that requires expansionary government policy. New classical economists believe that because real wages are lower during a recession, people are more willing to substitute nonlabor activities (going back to school, early retirement, work at home, or leisure) for work. As the economy recovers and wages go up, people substitute away from nonlabor activities toward more working hours. The substitution of labor for leisure and leisure for labor, over time, suggests that much of observed unemployment is voluntary in the sense that those who are unemployed choose not to take a job at a wage below their reservation wage (see Chapter 15).

3.b. The Policymakers' Role

New classical economics emphasizes expectations. Its basic tenet is that changes in monetary policy can change the equilibrium level of real GDP only if those changes are *unexpected*. Fiscal policy can change equilibrium real GDP only if it *unexpectedly* changes the level of prices or one of the determinants of aggregate supply.

Figure 5 (which is the same as Figure 4 in Chapter 15) illustrates the new classical view of the effect of an unexpected increase in the money supply. Suppose initially the expected rate of inflation is 3 percent and the actual rate of inflation is also 3 percent. The economy is operating at point 1 in Figure 5(b), the Phillips curve diagram, with unemployment at 5 percent, which is assumed to be the natural rate of unemployment. At the natural rate of unemployment, the economy is producing the potential level of real GDP (Y_p) at price level P_1. If the central bank unexpectedly increases the money supply, pushing the inflation rate up from 3 percent to 6 percent, the economy moves from point 1 to point 2 along short-run Phillips curve I, which is based on 3 percent expected inflation. The unemployment rate is now 3 percent, which is less than the natural rate. In part (a), real GDP rises above potential income to Y_2.

Over time, people come to expect 6 percent inflation. They adjust to the higher inflation rate, and the economy moves back to the natural rate of unemployment. At the expected rate of inflation, 6 percent, the economy is operating at point 3 on short-run Phillips curve II. As the expected rate of inflation increases from 3 to 6 percent, workers negotiate higher wages and the aggregate supply curve shifts to the left, from AS_1 to AS_2. A new equilibrium exists at point 3 in the aggregate demand and supply diagram, and real GDP drops back to its potential level.

FIGURE 5

New Classical Economics

New classical economists believe that government-induced shifts in aggregate demand affect real GDP only if they are unexpected. In Figure 5(a), the economy initially is operating at point 1, with real GDP at Y_p, the potential level. An unexpected increase in aggregate demand shifts the economy to point 2, where both real GDP (Y_2) and prices (P_2) are higher. Over time, as sellers adjust to higher prices and costs of doing business, aggregate supply shifts from AS_1 to AS_2. This shift moves the economy to point 3. Here GDP is back at the potential level, and prices are even higher. In the long run, an increase in aggregate demand does not increase output. The long-run aggregate supply curve (LRAS) is a vertical line at the potential level of real GDP.

In Figure 5(b), if the expected rate of inflation is 3 percent and actual inflation is 3 percent, the economy is operating at point 1, at the natural rate of unemployment (U_n). If aggregate demand increases, there is an unexpected increase in inflation from 3 to 6 percent. This moves the economy from point 1 to point 2 along short-run Phillips curve I. Here the unemployment rate is 3 percent. As people learn to expect 6 percent inflation, they adjust to the higher rate and the economy moves back to the natural rate of unemployment, at point 3. If the increase in inflation is expected, then the economy moves directly from point 1 to point 3 with no temporary decrease in the unemployment rate.

(a) Aggregate Demand and Supply

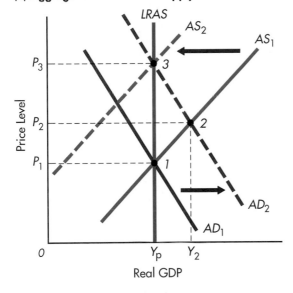

(b) Phillips Curve

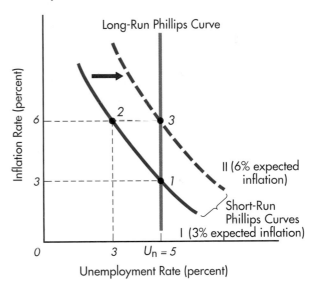

New classical economists believe that wages and prices are flexible and that people form expectations rationally, so that only unexpected changes in the price level can affect real GDP.

The analysis changes dramatically if the change in the money supply is expected. Now the economy moves not from point 1 to point 2 to point 3 but from point 1 directly to point 3. This is because the shift from point 1 to point 2 is temporary, based on unexpected inflation. If the inflation is expected, the economy is on short-run Phillips curve II, where inflation is 6 percent, unemployment is at the natural rate, and real GDP is at the potential level.

The lesson of new classical economics for policymakers is that managing aggregate demand has an effect on real GDP only if change is unexpected. Any predictable policy simply affects prices. As a result, new classical economists argue that monetary and fiscal policies should be aimed at maintaining a low, stable rate of inflation and should not attempt to alter real national output and unemployment. This brings new classical economists close to the monetarists, who would choose policy rules over discretionary policy.

1. New classical economics holds that wages are flexible and that expectations are formed rationally, so that only unexpected changes in prices have an effect on real GDP.

2. New classical economists believe that markets are always in equilibrium.

3. According to new classical economic theory, any predictable macroeconomic policy has an effect only on prices.

4. New classical economists argue that monetary and fiscal policies should try to achieve a low, stable rate of inflation rather than changes in real GDP or unemployment.

4. Comparison and Influence

4. How do theories of economics change over time?

The three theories of macroeconomics we have been talking about are often treated as though they are different in every way. Yet at times they overlap and even share conclusions. Moreover, as we mentioned at the beginning of the chapter, it is an oversimplification to categorize economists by a single school of thought. Many if not most economists do not classify themselves by economic theory. Typically they take elements of each, so that their approach to macroeconomics is more a synthesis of the various theories than strict adherence to any one theory.

Macroeconomic theories have developed over time in response to the economy's performance and the shortcomings of existing theories. Keynesian economics became popular in the 1930s because classical economics did not explain or help resolve the Great Depression. Monetarist economics offered an explanation for rising unemployment and rising inflation in the United States in the 1960s and 1970s. New classical economics suggested an alternative explanation for rising unemployment and inflation that the static Phillips curve analysis used by traditional Keynesians could not explain. Each of these theories, then, was developed or became popular because an existing theory did not answer pressing new questions.

All of these theories have influenced government policy. A by-product of Keynes's work in the 1930s was the wide acceptance and practice of activist government fiscal policy. Monetarist influence was dramatically apparent in the change in monetary policy announced by the Federal Reserve in 1979. Monetarists had criticized the Fed's policy of targeting interest rates. They argued that money-growth targets would stabilize income and prices. In October 1979, Chairman Paul Volcker announced that the Fed would concentrate more on achieving money-growth targets and less on controlling interest rates. This change in policy reflected the Fed's concern over rising inflation and the belief that the monetarists were right, that a low rate of money growth would bring about a low rate of inflation. The new policy led to an abrupt drop in the rate of inflation, from more than 13 percent in 1979 to less than 4 percent in 1982.

The new classical economists' emphasis on expectations calls for more information from policymakers to allow private citizens to incorporate government plans into their outlook for the future. The Federal Reserve Reform Act (1977) and the Full Employment and Balanced Growth Act (1978) require the Board of Governors to report to Congress semiannually on its goals and money targets for the next 12 months. New classical economists also believe that only credible government poli-

TABLE 1

Major Approaches to Macroeconomic Policy

Approach	Major Source of Problems	Proper Role for Government
New Keynesian	Disequilibrium in private labor and goods markets	To actively manage monetary and fiscal policies to restore equilibrium
Monetarist	Government's discretionary policies that increase and decrease aggregate demand	To follow fixed rules for money growth and minimize fiscal policy shocks
New classical	Government's attempt to manipulate aggregate demand, even though government policies have effect on real GDP only if unexpected	To follow predictable monetary and fiscal policies for long-run stability

cies can affect expectations. In the last chapter we discussed the time consistency of plans. For plans to be credible, to influence private expectations, they must be time consistent.

Table 1 summarizes the three approaches to macroeconomics, describing the major source of problems facing policymakers and the proper role of government policy according to each view. Only Keynesian economics supports an active role for government; the other two theories suggest that government should not intervene in the economy.

RECAP

1. Different economic theories developed over time as changing economic conditions pointed out the shortcomings of existing theories.

2. Keynesian, monetarist, and new classical economics have each influenced macroeconomic policy.

3. Only Keynesian economists believe that government should actively intervene to stabilize the economy.

Summary

1. Economists do not all agree on the determinants of economic equilibrium or the appropriate role of government policy. *Preview*

? What do Keynesian economists believe about macroeconomic policy?

2. Keynesian economists believe that the government should take an active role in stabilizing the economy by managing aggregate demand. *§1.a*

? What role do monetarists believe the government should play in the economy?

3. Monetarists do not believe that the economy is subject to serious disequilibrium, which means that they favor minimal government intervention in the economy. *§2.b*

4. Monetarists believe that a government that takes an active role in the economy may do more harm than

good because economic policy operates with a long and variable lag. §2.b

How do theories of economics change over time?

What is new classical economics?

5. New classical economics holds that only unexpected changes in policy can influence real GDP, so that government policy should target a low, stable rate of inflation. §3.b

6. New economic theories are a response to changing economic conditions that point out the shortcomings of existing theories. §4

Key Terms

Keynesian economics §1.a
monetarist economics §2

classical economics §3
new classical economics §3.a

Exercises

1. What is the difference between traditional Keynesian and new Keynesian economics?

2. Why does monetary policy operate with a long and variable lag? Give an example to illustrate your explanation.

3. What is the difference between old classical and new classical economics?

4. Draw an aggregate demand and supply diagram for each theory of macroeconomics. Use the diagrams to explain how the government can influence equilibrium real GDP and prices.

5. What, if any, similarities are there among the theories of economics discussed in this chapter regarding the use of fiscal and monetary policies to stimulate real GDP?

6. If unexpected increases in the growth rate of the money supply can increase real GDP, why doesn't the Fed follow a policy of unexpectedly increasing the money supply to increase the growth of real GDP?

7. "The popular macroeconomic theories have evolved over time as economic conditions have changed to reveal shortcomings of existing theory." Evaluate this quote in terms of the emergence of the three theories discussed in this chapter.

For exercises 8–15, tell which school of thought would most likely be associated with the following quotes:

8. "Changes in prices and wages are too slow to support the new classical assumption of persistent macroeconomic equilibrium."

9. "The best monetary policy is to keep the money supply growing at a slow and steady rate."

10. "Frictional unemployment is a result of workers voluntarily substituting leisure for labor when wages fall."

11. "A change in the money supply will affect GDP after a long and variable lag, so it is difficult to predict the effects of money on output."

12. "Government policymakers should use fiscal policy to adjust aggregate demand in response to aggregate supply shocks."

13. "The economy is subject to recurring disequilibrium in labor and goods markets, so government can serve a useful function of helping the economy adjust to equilibrium."

14. "Since the aggregate supply curve is horizontal, aggregate demand will determine the equilibrium level of real GDP."

15. "If everyone believed that the monetary authority was going to cut the inflation rate from 6 to 3 percent, such a reduction in inflation could be achieved without any significant increase in unemployment."

Take the ACE Practice Test for this chapter to review the important concepts and get immediate feedback with answers.

economics.college.hmco.com/students

The Ghosts of Christmas Past Haunt Economists

Financial crises have come back because policy makers fail to learn earlier lessons.

In Charles Dickens' great novel, *A Christmas Carol,* the soulless businessman Ebeneezer Scrooge is tormented by a visit from the Spirit of Christmas Past. Today, economists are similarly troubled by unwanted ghosts, as they ponder the reappearance of economic ills long thought buried and dead.

From Stephen Roach at Morgan Stanley to Paul Krugman at Princeton, to the governors of the US Federal Reserve and the senior staff at the European Central Bank, to almost everyone in Japan, economists all over the world are worrying about deflation. Their thoughts retrace the economic thinking of more than 50 years ago, a time when economists concluded that the thing to do with deflation was to avoid it like the plague.

Back in 1933 Irving Fisher— Milton Friedman's predecessor atop the US's monetarist school of economists—announced that governments could prevent deep depressions by avoiding deflation. Deflation—a steady, continuing decline in prices—gave businesses and consumers powerful incentives to cut spending and hoard cash.

It reduced the ability of businesses and banks to service their debt, and might trigger a chain of big bankruptcies that would destroy confidence in the financial system, providing further incentives to hoard. Such strong incentives to hoard rather than spend can keep demand low and falling, and unemployment high and rising, for a much longer time than even the most laissez-faire-oriented politician or economist had ever dared contemplate. Hence the Keynesian solution: use monetary policy (lower interest rates) and fiscal policy (expanded government spending and reduced taxes) to keep the economy from ever approaching the precipice where deflation becomes possible.

But if this is an issue solved more than 50 years ago, why is it haunting us now? Why is this menace a matter of grave concern in Japan today, and a threat worth worrying about in the US? . . .

The truth is that economic policy makers are juggling sets of potential disasters, exchanging the one that appears most threatening for a threat that seems more distant.

In the US, the Bush administration is sceptical of the stimulative power of monetary policy and wants bigger fiscal deficits to reduce unemployment, hoping that the future dangers posed by persistent deficits—low investment, slow growth, loss of confidence, uncontrolled inflation and exchange rate depreciation—can be finessed, or will not become visible until after the Bush team leaves office.

In Europe, the European Central Bank believes the danger of uncontrolled inflation following a loss of public confidence in its commitment to low inflation, outweighs the costs of European unemployment that is far too high. . . .

The ghosts of economics' past return because the lessons of the present are always oversold. Politicians and policy makers advance their approach to economics as the One True Doctrine. But what they are doing, however, is dealing with the biggest problem of the moment, but at the price of removing institutions and policies that policymakers before them had put into place to control problems they felt to be the most pressing.

Ebeneezer Scrooge's nocturnal visitors were able to convince him of the errors of his ways. Let us hope today's economists also learn the lessons of their unwanted ghosts.

J. BRADFORD DELONG

Africa News/January 10, 2003

Commentary

Macroeconomics has always been a lively field, filled with controversy over the proper approach to modeling the economy, the correct interpretation of experience, and the role that government policy can and should play. Indeed, debate in macroeconomics is as old as the field itself. The views of John Maynard Keynes, the founder of macroeconomics, were challenged by his colleague at Cambridge University, Arthur Pigou. This debate focused on the importance of the "real balance effect," whereby a fall in the price level raises real money balances (or the purchasing power of the money supply), increases wealth, and thus increases consumption. Like most debates in macroeconomics, this was more than an ivory-tower exercise, since the real balance effect provides a channel by which the economy can bring itself out of a slump without government intervention.

The article indicates that in early 2003, the issue of falling prices was back again as a policy concern. The Japanese economy had experienced deflation in recent years, and some were worried that the United States could also move from low inflation to deflation. The author claims that economists knew long ago that deflation could be avoided by expansionary fiscal and monetary policy. A monetarist-type solution would be central bank targeting of inflation. In the early 2000s, some economists were suggesting that this is what the central bank of Japan should do: Set an inflation target and aim monetary policy solely at the achievement of such a target. A Keynesian-type solution would be increasing government spending and/or reducing taxes. The Bush administration in the United States was proposing a Keynesian approach, with tax cuts to stimulate the U.S. economy. The European Central Bank was utilizing a monetarist approach of inflation targeting to achieve public confidence in its commitment to low inflation. Both of these policies may avoid deflation. However, we can never be sure of the effects of a tax cut on important variables like unemployment, interest rates, and real GDP, and the inflation target achieves only the inflation goal and may have undesirable consequences for unemployment and real GDP growth. In short, there is no magic economic solution that always provides the best mix of macroeconomic outcomes. This is a major reason for the debates that have raged in macroeconomics.

The debate between the Keynesians and the monetarists dominated the macroeconomic discourse of the 1950s and 1960s. During this period, those who identified themselves as Keynesians gave primacy to the role of fiscal policy and to the issue of unemployment; these economists had great faith in the ability of the government to fine-tune the economy through the proper application of policy, thereby ensuring stability and growth. Keynesians of this vintage also believed that changes in the money supply had little effect on the economy. In contrast, monetarists were very concerned about inflation, which they believed to be a purely monetary phenomenon. These economists also doubted that active government intervention could stabilize the economy, for they believed that policy operated only with long and variable lags. Today, you will often hear people refer to Democratic party advisers as Keynesians. Although none of these economists would necessarily subscribe to the philosophy of John Maynard Keynes, the term is popularly assigned to macroeconomists who emphasize that free markets don't always provide the best solutions, so there is a needed role for government activism to ensure that the economy provides for growth with low inflation. Those economists who support rules to be followed by policymakers tend to be identified as monetarists, yet few such economists would willingly agree to the label.

Although outside observers may view the debate within macroeconomics as evidence of confusion, a more accurate appraisal is that the debate is a healthy intellectual response to a world in which few things are certain and much is unknown—and perhaps unknowable. That there are differences between schools of thought masks the fact that there is a great deal of consensus about a number of issues in macroeconomics. This consensus is a product of lessons learned from past debates. In a similar fashion, the controversies of today will yield tomorrow's consensus, and our knowledge of the real workings of the economy will grow.

Part Four

Economic Growth and Development

CHAPTER 17

Economic Growth

? **Fundamental
Questions**

**1. What is economic
growth?**

**2. How are
economic growth
rates determined?**

**3. What is
productivity?**

**4. What explains
productivity
changes?**

Modern economies tend to raise living standards for the population generation after generation. This is economic growth. However, this was not always the case. Prior to the seventeenth century, economic activity involved a constant struggle to avoid starvation. Only in recent centuries has the idea of living standards being improved within a generation become common. An economist (Angus Maddison) estimated that GDP grew at about a rate of 0.1 percent per year between the years 500 and 1500. Yet since population growth was about the same 0.1 percent per year, there was no increase in GDP per capita. He estimates that between 1500 and 1700, growth of per capita GDP increased to 0.1 percent per year, and between 1700 and 1820, it increased to about 1.6 percent per year, not too different from recent growth rates for the major industrial countries. Understanding why and how economic growth happens is a very important part of macroeconomics.

Although much of macroeconomics is aimed at understanding business cycles—recurring periods of prosperity and recession—the fact is that over the long run,

most economies do grow wealthier. The long-run trend of real GDP in the United States and most other countries is positive. Yet the rate at which real GDP grows is very different across countries. Why? What factors cause economies to grow and living standards to rise?

In this chapter we focus on the long-term picture. We begin by defining economic growth and discussing its importance. Then we examine the determinants of economic growth, to understand what accounts for the different rates of growth across countries. ■

1. What is economic growth?

1. Defining Economic Growth

What do we mean by economic growth? Economists use two measures of growth—real GDP and per capita real GDP—to compare how economies grow over time.

1.a. Real GDP

economic growth: an increase in real GDP

Basically, **economic growth** is an increase in real GDP. As more goods and services are produced, the real GDP increases and people are able to consume more.

To calculate the percentage change in real GDP over a year, we simply divide the change in GDP by the value of GDP at the beginning of the year, and then multiply the quotient by 100. For instance, the real GDP of Singapore was approximately 160,853 million Singapore dollars in 2002 and approximately 157,319 million in 2001. So the economy grew 2.2 percent in 2002:

$$\text{Percentage change in real GDP} = \frac{\text{change over year}}{\text{beginning value}} \times 100$$

$$= \frac{160,853 - 157,319}{157,319} \times 100$$

$$= .022 \times 100$$

$$= 2.2$$

1.a.1. Compound Growth

From 1990 to 2001, the industrial countries of the world showed an average annual growth rate of real GDP of 2.5 percent. Over the same period, the average annual growth rate of real GDP for low-income developing countries was 3.4 percent. The difference between a growth rate of 2.5 percent and one of 3.4 percent may not seem substantial, but in fact it is. Growth is compounded over time. This means that any given rate of growth is applied every year to a growing base of real GDP, so any difference is magnified over time.

Small changes in rates of growth produce big changes in real GDP over a period of many years.

Figure 1 shows the effects of compounding growth rates. The upper line in the figure represents the path of real GDP if the economy grows at a rate of 3.4 percent a year. The lower line shows real GDP growing at a rate of 2.5 percent a year.

Suppose that in each case the economy originally is producing a real GDP of $1 billion. After five years, there is not much difference: a GDP of $1.13 billion at 2.5 percent growth versus $1.19 billion at 3.4 percent growth. The effect of compounding becomes more visible over long periods of time. After 40 years, the difference between 2.5 and 3.4 percent growth, a seemingly small difference, represents a substantial difference in output. A 2.5 percent rate of growth yields an output of $2.7 billion; at 3.4 percent, output is $3.9 billion. After 40 years, the level of output is more than 40 percent larger at the higher growth rate.

FIGURE 1

Comparing GDP Growth Rates of 2.5% and 3.4%

Between 1990 and 2001, real GDP in the industrial countries grew at an average annual rate of 2.5 percent, while real GDP in low-income developing countries grew at an average annual rate of 3.4 percent. The difference seems small, but the graph shows how even a small difference is compounded over time, producing a substantial difference in real GDP.

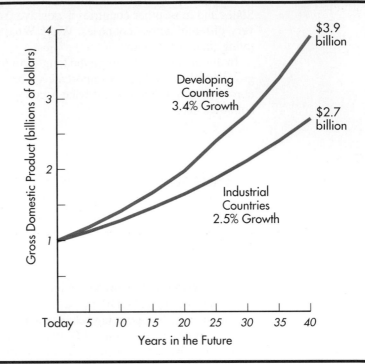

1.a.2. The Rule of 72 Compound growth explains why countries are so concerned about maintaining positive high rates of growth. If growth is maintained at a constant rate, we can estimate the number of years required for output to double by using the **rule of 72.** If we divide 72 by the growth rate, we find the approximate time it takes for any value to double.

rule of 72: the number of years required for an amount to double in value is 72 divided by the annual rate of growth

Suppose you deposit $100 in a bank account that pays a constant 6 percent annual interest. If you allow the interest to accumulate over time, the amount of money in the account grows at a rate of 6 percent. At this rate of interest, the rule of 72 tells us that your account will have a value of approximately $200 (double its initial value) after 12 years:

$$\frac{72}{6} = 12$$

The interest rate gives the rate of growth of the amount deposited if earned interest is allowed to accumulate in the account. If the interest rate is 3 percent, the amount would double in 24 (72/3) years.

The rule of 72 applies to any value. If real GDP is growing at a rate of 6 percent a year, then real GDP doubles every 12 years. At a 3 percent annual rate, real GDP doubles every 24 years.

Table 1 lists the average annual rate of growth of GDP between 1990 and 2001 and approximate doubling times for six countries. The countries listed have growth rates ranging from a high of 10 percent in China to a low of 1.3 percent in Japan. If these growth rates are maintained over time, it would take just 7.2 years for GDP in China to double and 55 years for the GDP in Japan to double.

TABLE 1

GDP Growth Rates and Doubling Times

Country	Average Annual Growth Rate (percent)*	Doubling Time (years)
China	10.0	7.2
South Korea	5.7	12.6
Bangladesh	4.9	14.7
Australia	4.0	18
United States	3.5	20.6
Japan	1.3	55

*Average annual growth rates from 1990 to 2001.
Source: Data are from World Bank, *World Development Report, 2003.*

1.b. Per Capita Real GDP

Economic growth is sometimes defined as an increase in per capita real GDP.

per capita real GDP: real GDP divided by the population

We've defined economic growth as an increase in real GDP. But, if growth is supposed to be associated with higher standards of living, our definition may be misleading. A country could show positive growth in real GDP, but if the population is growing at an even higher rate, output per person can actually fall. Economists, therefore, often adjust the growth rate of output for changes in population. **Per capita real GDP** is real GDP divided by the population. If we define economic growth as rising per capita real GDP, then growth requires a nation's output of goods and services to increase faster than its population.

The World Bank computes per capita GDP for countries as an indicator of economic development. From 2000 to 2001, per capita real GDP grew at an average annual rate of 2.4 percent in low-income developing countries and 0.6 percent in industrial countries. The difference in per capita real GDP growth between low-income developing and industrial countries is much smaller than the difference in real GDP growth. The difference in growth rates between the level of output and per capita output points out the danger of just looking at real GDP as an indicator of change in the economic well-being of the citizens in developing countries. Population growth rates are considerably higher in developing countries than they are in industrial countries, so real GDP must grow at a faster rate in developing countries than it does in industrial countries just to maintain a similar growth rate in per capita real GDP. Figure 2 depicts how average annual growth rates of GDP differ around the world. Eastern Europe and northern Asia experienced very low rates of economic growth.

1.c. The Problems with Definitions of Growth

Economic growth is considered to be good because it allows people to have a higher standard of living, to have more material goods. But an increase in real GDP or per capita real GDP does not tell us whether the average citizen is better off. One problem is that these measures say nothing about how income is distributed. The national economy may be growing, yet the poor may be staying poor while the rich get richer.

FIGURE 2

GDP Growth of the World's Economies

The figure illustrates how GDP growth differed over the period 1990–2000. Whereas some countries experienced strong economic growth, others had low or no growth. The latter is especially true of countries in eastern Europe and northern Asia.

Source: http: //nebula. worldbank.org/website/index. htm#.

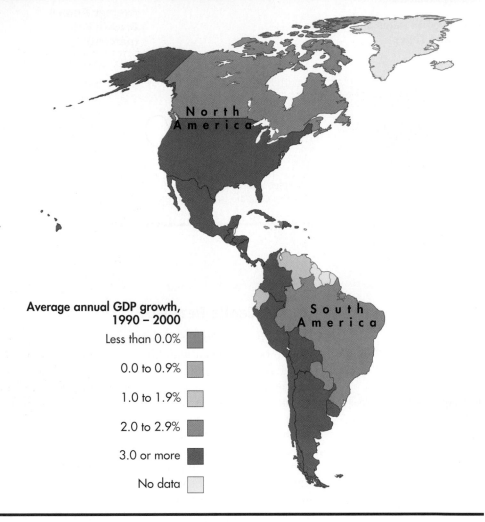

Average annual GDP growth, 1990 – 2000

Less than 0.0%

0.0 to 0.9%

1.0 to 1.9%

2.0 to 2.9%

3.0 or more

No data

The lesson here is simple. Economic growth may benefit some groups more than others. And it is entirely possible that despite national economic growth, some groups can be worse off than they were before. Clearly, neither per capita real GDP nor real GDP accurately measures the standard of living for all of a nation's citizens.

Another reason real GDP or per capita real GDP is misleading is that it says nothing about the quality of life. People have nonmonetary needs—they care about personal freedom, the environment, their leisure time. If a rising per capita GDP goes hand in hand with a repressive political regime or a rapidly deteriorating environmental quality, people are not going to feel better off. By the same token, a country could have no economic growth, yet reduce the hours worked each week. More leisure time could make workers feel better off, even though per capita GDP has not changed.

Once again, be careful in interpreting per capita GDP. Don't allow it to represent more than it does. Per capita GDP is simply a measure of the output produced divided by the population. It is a useful measure of economic activity in a country, but it is a questionable measure of the typical citizen's standard of living or quality of life.

Per capita real GDP is a questionable indicator of the typical citizen's standard of living or quality of life.

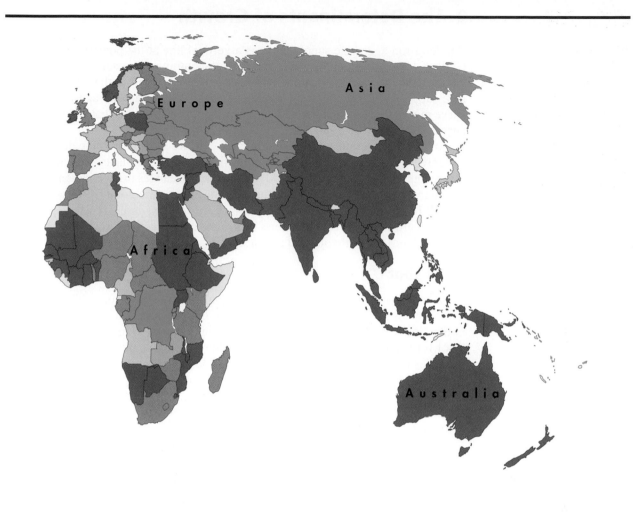

1. Economic growth is an increase in real GDP.

2. Because growth is compounded over time, small differences in rates of growth are magnified over time.

3. For any constant rate of growth, the time required for real GDP to double is 72 divided by the annual growth rate.

4. Per capita real GDP is real GDP divided by the population.

5. Per capita real GDP says nothing about the distribution of income in a country or the nonmonetary quality of life.

2. The Determinants of Growth

2. How are economic growth rates determined?

Economic growth raises the potential level of real GDP, shifting the long-run aggregate supply curve to the right.

The long-run aggregate supply curve is a vertical line at the potential level of real GDP (Y_p1). As the economy grows, the potential output of the economy rises. Figure 3 shows the increase in potential output as a rightward shift in the long-run aggregate supply curve. The higher the rate of growth, the farther the aggregate supply curve moves to the right. To illustrate several years' growth, we would show several curves shifting to the right.

To find the determinants of economic growth, we must turn to the determinants of aggregate supply. In Chapter 9, we identified three determinants of aggregate supply: resource prices, technology, and expectations. Changes in expectations can shift the aggregate supply curve, but changing expectations are not a basis for long-run growth in the sense of continuous rightward movements in aggregate supply. The long-run growth of the economy rests on growth in productive resources (labor, capital, and land) and technological advances.

2.a. Labor

Economic growth depends on the size and quality of the labor force. The size of the labor force is a function of the size of the working-age population (sixteen and older in the United States) and the percentage of that population in the labor force. The labor force typically grows more rapidly in developing countries than in industrial countries because birthrates are higher in developing countries. Figure 4 shows the annual growth rates of the population for selected developing and industrial countries, as well as average growth rates for all low-income countries and all industrial countries. Between 1990 and 2001, the population grew at an average annual rate of 2.0 percent in low-income countries and 0.7 percent in industrial countries.

FIGURE 3

Economic Growth

As the economy grows, the long-run aggregate supply curve shifts to the right. This represents an increase in the potential level of real GDP.

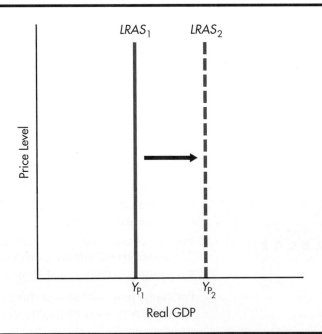

FIGURE 4

Average Annual Population Growth in Selected Countries (percent)

Population growth rates across countries vary considerably. Generally, population grows at a much higher rate in developing countries. *Source: Data are from World Development Report, 2003.*

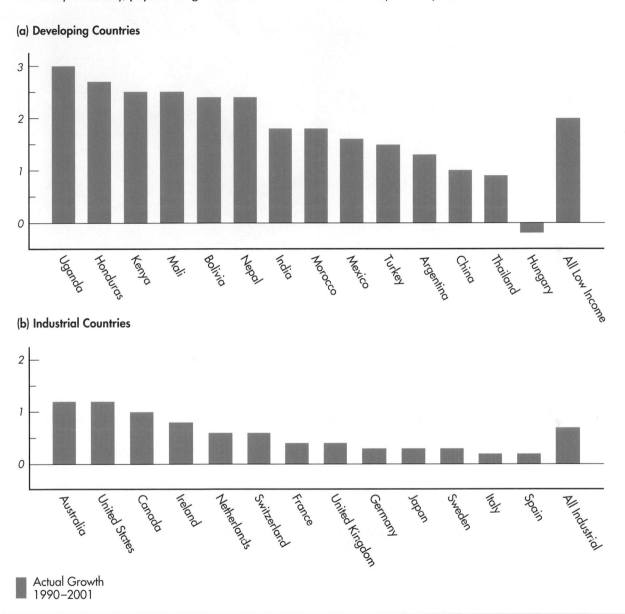

(a) Developing Countries

(b) Industrial Countries

■ Actual Growth
1990–2001

Based solely on growth in the labor force, it seems that developing countries are growing faster than industrial countries. But the size of the labor force is not all that matters; changes in productivity can compensate for lower growth in the labor force, as we discuss in section 3.

The U.S. labor force has changed considerably in recent decades. The most notable event of the post–World War II period was the baby boom. The children born

Developing countries are playing an increasing role in the "outsourcing" of labor for firms in the industrial world. Here, workers in Accra, Ghana process data for U.S. health insurance firms.

between the late 1940s and the early 1960s made up more than a third of the total U.S. population in the early 1960s and have significantly altered the age structure of the population. In 1950, 41 percent of the population was 24 years old or younger and 59 percent was 25 years old or older. By 1970, 46 percent of the population was in the younger group with 54 percent in the older group. By 1990 this bulge in the age distribution had moved to where about 36 percent of the U.S. population was 24 years or younger. Over time the bulge will be moving to older ranges of the population. By 2000, 35 percent of the population was 24 years or younger with 65 percent 25 years or older.

The initial pressure of the baby boom fell on school systems faced with rapidly expanding enrollments. Over time, as these children aged and entered the labor market, they had a large impact on potential output. The U.S. labor force grew at an average rate of about 2.5 percent a year in the 1970s, approximately twice the rate of growth experienced in the 1950s. The growth of the labor force slowed in the 1980s and 1990s, as the baby boom population aged. On the basis of the size of the labor force, the 1970s should have been a time of greater economic growth than the 1950s and 1960s or the 1980s and 1990s. It was not. More important than the size of the labor force is its productivity.

2.b. Capital

Labor is combined with capital to produce goods and services. A rapidly growing labor force by itself is no guarantee of economic growth. Workers need machines, tools, and factories in order to work. If a country has lots of workers but few machines, then the typical worker cannot be very productive. Capital is a critical resource in growing economies.

The ability of a country to invest in capital goods is tied to its ability to save. A lack of current saving can be offset by borrowing, but the availability of borrowing is limited by the prospects for future saving. Debt incurred today must be repaid by

Technological Advance:
The Change in the Price of Light

A particularly striking example of the role of technological change is provided by the change in the labor cost of providing light. An economist, William Nordhaus, estimated the effects of technological change on the labor cost of providing lighting.* Light can be measured in *lumen hours,* where a lumen is the amount of light provided by one candle. Nordhaus estimated the number of hours of work required to produce 1,000 lumen-hours of light. His estimates of the cost of providing 1,000 lumen hours of light are:

Time	Light Source	Labor Price
500,000 B.C.	Open fire	58 hours
1750 B.C.	Babylonian lamp	41.5 hours
1800	Tallow candle	5.4 hours
1900	Filament lamp	0.2 hour
1990	Filament lamp	0.0006 hour

The choice of light is appropriate, as the desirable service provided by light, illumination, is essentially unchanged over time. What has changed dramatically is the manner in which light is produced and the cost of production. The example shows not only how changing technology has increased the productivity of light production but also how the pace of technological advance has quickened in recent times.

The faster technology progresses, the faster the cost of production falls.

*William Nordhaus, "Do Real-Output and Real-Wage Measures Capture Reality? The History of Lighting Suggests Not," in *The Economics of New Goods,* ed. Timothy Bresnahan and Robert Gordon (Chicago: University of Chicago Press, 1997).

not consuming all output in the future. If lenders believe that a nation is going to consume all of its output in the future, they will not make loans today.

The lower the standard of living in a country, the harder it is to forgo current consumption in order to save. It is difficult for a population living at or near subsistence level to do without current consumption. This in large part explains the low level of saving in the poorest countries.

2.c. Land

Abundant natural resources are not a necessary condition for economic growth.

Land surface, water, forests, minerals, and other natural resources are called *land.* Land can be combined with labor and capital to produce goods and services. Abundant natural resources can contribute to economic growth, but natural resources alone do not generate growth. Several developing countries, like Argentina and Brazil, are relatively rich in natural resources but have not been very successful in exploiting these resources to produce goods and services. Japan, on the other hand, has relatively few natural resources but showed dramatic economic growth until a recession in the late 1990s. The experience of Japan makes it clear that abundant natural resources are not a necessary condition for economic growth.

2.d. Technology

A key determinant of economic growth is **technology,** ways of combining resources to produce goods and services. New management techniques, scientific discoveries, and other innovations improve technology. Technological advances allow the production of more output from a given amount of resources. This means that technological progress accelerates economic growth for any given rate of growth in the labor force and the capital stock. A particularly dramatic example of technological change is provided in the Economic Insight "Technological Advance: The Change in the Price of Light."

Technological change depends on the scientific community. The more educated a population, the greater its potential for technological advances. Industrial countries have better-educated populations than developing countries do. Education gives industrial countries a substantial advantage over developing countries in creating and implementing innovations. In addition, the richest industrial countries traditionally have spent 2 to 3 percent of their GNP on research and development, an investment that developing countries cannot afford. The greater the funding for research and development, the greater the likelihood of technological advances.

Impeded by low levels of education and limited funds for research and development, the developing countries lag behind the industrial countries in developing and implementing new technology. Typically these countries follow the lead of the industrial world, adopting new technology developed in that world once it is affordable and feasible, given their capital and labor resources. In the next chapter we discuss the role of foreign aid, including technological assistance, in promoting economic growth in developing countries.

RECAP

1. Economic growth raises the potential level of real GDP, shifting the long-run aggregate supply curve to the right.
2. The long-run growth of the economy is a product of growth in labor, capital, and natural resources and advances in technology.
3. The size of the labor force is determined by the working-age population and the percentage of that population in the labor force.
4. The post–World War II baby boom has created a bulge in the age distribution of the U.S. population.
5. Growth in capital stock is tied to current and future saving.
6. Abundant natural resources contribute to economic growth but are not essential to that growth.
7. Technology is the way in which resources are combined to produce output.
8. Hampered by low levels of education and limited financial resources, developing countries lag behind the industrial nations in developing and implementing new technology.

3. Productivity

3. What is productivity?

In the last section we described how output depends on resource inputs like labor and capital. One way to assess the contribution a resource makes to output is its productivity. *Productivity* is the ratio of the output produced to the amount of input. We can measure the productivity of a single resource—say labor or capital—or the overall productivity of all resources. **Total factor productivity (TFP)** is the term economists use to describe the overall productivity of an economy. It is the ratio of the economy's output to its stock of labor and capital.

3.a. Productivity and Economic Growth

Economic growth depends on both the growth of resources and technological progress. Advances in technology allow resources to be more productive. If the quantity of resources is growing and each resource is more productive, then output grows even faster than the quantity of resources. Economic growth, then, is the sum of the growth rate of total factor productivity and the growth rate of resources:

Economic growth = growth rate of *TFP* + growth rate of resources

The amount that output grows because the labor force is growing depends on how much labor contributes to the production of output. Similarly, the amount that output grows because capital is growing depends on how much capital contributes to the production of output. To relate the growth of labor and capital to the growth of output (we assume no change in natural resources), then, the growth of labor and the growth of capital must be multiplied by their relative contributions to the production of output. The most straightforward way to measure those contributions is to use the share of real GDP received by each resource. For instance, in the United States, labor receives about 70 percent (.70) of real GDP and capital receives about 30 percent (.30). So we can determine the growth of output by using this formula:

$$\%\Delta Y = \%\Delta TFP + .70(\%\Delta L) + .30(\%\Delta K)$$

where

$$\%\Delta = \text{percentage change in}$$
$$Y = \text{real GDP}$$
$$TFP = \text{total factor productivity}$$
$$L = \text{size of the labor force}$$
$$K = \text{capital stock}$$

The equation shows how economic growth depends on changes in productivity ($\%\Delta TFP$) as well as changes in resources ($\%\Delta L$ and $\%\Delta K$). Even if labor (L) and capital stock (K) are constant, technological innovation will generate economic growth through changes in total factor productivity (TFP).

For example, suppose *TFP* is growing at a rate of 2 percent a year. Then, even with labor and capital stock held constant, the economy grows at a rate of 2 percent a year. If labor and capital stock also grow at a rate of 2 percent a year, output grows by the sum of the growth rates of all three components (*TFP*, .70 times labor growth, and .30 times the capital stock growth), or 4 percent.

How do we account for differences in growth rates across countries? Because almost all countries have experienced growth in the labor force, percentage increases in labor forces have generally supported economic growth. But growth in the capital stock has been steadier in the industrial countries than in the developing countries, so differences in capital growth rates may explain some of the differences in economic growth across countries. Yet differences in resource growth rates alone cannot explain the major differences we find across countries. In recent years, those differences seem to be related to productivity.

3.b. Determinants of Productivity

Productivity in the United States has fluctuated considerably in recent years. From 1948 to 1965, *TFP* grew at an annual average rate of 2.02 percent. In the 1970s, *TFP* growth averaged 0.7 percent per year; in the 1980s, 0.6 percent; and by the late 1990s, 1 percent. If the pre-1965 rate of growth had been maintained, output in the United States would be an estimated 39 percent higher today than it actually is. What caused this dramatic change in productivity—first down in the 1970s and 1980s and then up in the 1990s? More generally, what determines the productivity changes for any country?

Several factors determine productivity growth. They include the quality of the labor force, technological innovations, energy prices, and a shift from manufacturing to service industries.

3.b.1. Labor Quality

Labor productivity is measured as output per hour of labor. Figure 5 shows how the productivity of labor in the United States and four other countries changed between 1979 and 2000. Although changes in the productivity of labor can stem from technological innovation and changes in the capital stock, they can also come from changes in the quality of labor. These changes may be a product of the level and quality of education, demographic change, and changing attitudes toward work.

Education Level The average level of education in the world has gone up over time. Table 2 lists three measures of education level for the United States. The first, median school years completed, increased from 8.6 years in 1940 to 12.9 years currently. In the same period, the percentage of adults with at least a high school education rose from 24.5 to 84.1, and the percentage of those with a college education

---

FIGURE 5

Average Annual Percentage Change in Output per Hour of Labor

Output per labor hour is a measure of productivity.
Source: Data from Bureau of Labor Statistics, www.bls.gov/fls/home.htm.

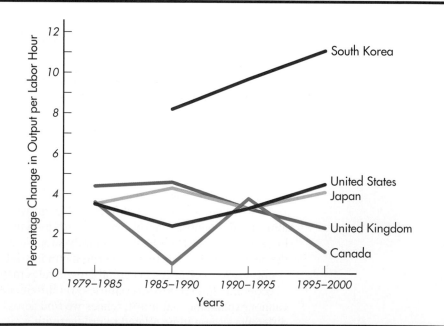

TABLE 2

The Average Level of Education, United States, 1940–2002*

	1940	1950	1960	1970	1980	1990	2000	2002
Median school years completed	8.6	9.3	10.6	12.1	12.5	12.7	12.9	N.A
People with at least a high school education (percent)	24.5	34.3	41.1	52.3	66.5	75.2	84.1	84.1
People with at least four years of college (percent)	4.6	6.2	7.7	10.7	16.2	20.3	25.6	26.7

*People 25 years of age and over.
Source: U.S. Census Bureau; www.census.gov/population/socdemo/education.

rose from 4.6 to 26.7. The figures seem to indicate that the level of education supports increases in U.S. productivity.

Demographic Change   Changes in the size and composition of the population have an impact on the labor market. As the baby boom generation entered the labor force in the late 1960s and early 1970s, a large pool of inexperienced, unskilled workers was created. The average quality of the labor force may have fallen at this time, as reflected in some large drops in output per hour of labor. In the 1980s, the baby boom segment of the labor force had more experience, skills, and education, thus pushing the quality of the labor force up.

Another important demographic change that has affected the quality of the labor force is the participation rates of women. As more and more women entered the labor force in the 1980s, the pool of untrained workers increased, probably reducing the average quality of labor. Over time, as female participation rates have stabilized, the average quality of labor should rise as the skills and experience of female workers rise.

Finally, immigration can play a role in labor force quality. For instance, the 1970s and 1980s saw a change in the pattern of U.S. immigration. Although many highly skilled professionals immigrate to the United States as part of the "brain drain" from developing countries, recent immigrants, both legal and illegal, have generally added to the supply of unskilled labor and reduced the average quality of the labor force.

3.b.2. Technological Innovation   New technology alters total factor productivity. Innovations increase productivity, so when productivity falls, it is natural to look at technological developments to see whether they are a factor in the change. The pace of technological innovation is difficult to measure. Expenditures on research and development are related to the discovery of new knowledge, but actual changes in technology do not proceed as evenly as those expenditures. We expect a long lag between funding and operating a laboratory and the discovery of useful technology. Still, a decline in spending on research and development may indicate less of a commitment to increasing productivity.

Productivity changes in service industries are difficult to measure. For instance, this tour bus in Madrid, Spain, offers guided trips through the city. How should we measure the productivity of the tour company? If it buys a more luxurious bus that seats fewer people and raises the price of tours, has productivity changed? While the company may serve fewer customers, this is not really a drop in productivity; instead, it is a change in the kind of service the company provides. Economists actively debate the appropriate measurement of productivity in services.

The most notable technological innovation in recent decades has been the widespread availability of cheaper and faster computers. The information technology (IT) revolution has played an important role in enhancing productivity. One may think of the purchase of computer hardware or software as investment. The capital stock increases with such purchases. However, researchers have also found that there are increases in total factor productivity associated with the development and spread of information technology. Such gains have not been realized by all countries. Poor countries lag far behind the rich in the implementation of IT. Table 3 provides data on the number of personal computers per 1,000 people in selected countries in 2000. Clearly the productivity-enhancing benefits of IT have been realized in industrial countries like the United States, Sweden, and Norway, where the number of personal computers per 1,000 people are 585, 507, and 490, respectively. However, in developing countries, the benefits of IT innovations are not being fully exploited as a result of poverty and lack of skills. For instance, Bangladesh, Cambodia, and Ethiopia have only 1.5, 1.1, and 0.9 personal computers per 1,000 people, respectively. This indicates an inability to implement IT widely across the economy. IT is just one example of how productivity may differ across countries as a result of differing uses of modern technology.

3.b.3. Other Factors We have seen how changing labor quality and technological innovation are related to changes in productivity. Other reasons have been offered to explain changes in productivity across countries and over time. We examine three of them: the cost of energy, the shift from a manufacturing- to a service-oriented economy, and the development of financial markets.

Energy Prices In 1973, 1974, and 1979, OPEC succeeded in raising the price of oil substantially. The timing of the dramatic increase in oil prices coincided with a drop in productivity growth in the United States. U.S. output per labor hour actually fell in 1974 and 1979. Higher energy prices due to restricted oil output should directly decrease aggregate supply because energy is an important input across

TABLE 3

The Number of Personal Computers per 1,000 People

Country	Personal Computers (per 1,000 people; 2000)	Country	Personal Computers (per 1,000 people; 2000)
Argentina	51.3	Jamaica	46.6
Australia	464.6	Japan	315.2
Austria	276.5	Jordan	22.5
Bangladesh	1.5	Kenya	4.9
Belgium	344.5	Korea, Rep.	237.9
Bolivia	16.8	Kuwait	130.6
Brazil	44.1	Lebanon	50.1
Bulgaria	43.9	Malaysia	103.1
Cambodia	1.1	Mexico	50.6
Cameroon	3.3	Morocco	12.3
Canada	390.2	Netherlands	394.1
Chile	82.3	New Zealand	360.2
China	15.9	Nigeria	6.6
Hong Kong, China	350.6	Norway	490.5
Colombia	35.4	Pakistan	4.2
Costa Rica	149.1	Peru	40.9
Cuba	10.7	Philippines	19.3
Czech Republic	122.0	Portugal	299.3
Denmark	431.5	Russian Federation	42.9
Ecuador	21.7	Saudi Arabia	60.2
Egypt, Arab Rep.	22.1	Senegal	16.8
El Salvador	19.1	Singapore	483.1
Ethiopia	0.9	South Africa	61.8
Finland	396.1	Spain	142.9
France	304.3	Sweden	506.7
Germany	336.0	Switzerland	499.7
Ghana	3.0	Thailand	24.3
Greece	70.5	Turkey	38.1
Guatemala	11.4	Uganda	2.7
Honduras	10.8	United Arab Emirates	153.5
India	4.5	United Kingdom	337.8
Indonesia	9.9	United States	585.2
Iran, Islamic Rep.	62.8	Uruguay	104.9
Ireland	359.1	Vietnam	8.8
Israel	253.6	Yugoslavia, Fed. Rep.	22.6
Italy	179.8	Zimbabwe	11.9

Source: Data from the World Bank, www.worldbank.org/data/databytopic/databytopic.html.

industries. As the price of energy increases, the costs of production rise and aggregate supply decreases.

Higher energy prices can affect productivity through their impact on the capital stock. As energy prices go up, energy-inefficient capital goods become obsolete. Like any other decline in the value of the capital stock, this change reduces economic growth. Standard measures of capital stock do not account for energy obsolescence, so they suggest that total factor productivity fell in the 1970s. However, if the stock of usable capital actually did go down, it was the growth rate of capital, not *TFP,* that fell.

Manufacturing Versus Services The industrial economies have, in recent decades, seen a shift away from manufacturing toward services. Some economists believe that productivity grows more slowly in service industries than in manufacturing, because of the less capital-intensive nature of providing services. Therefore, the movement into services reduces the overall growth rate of the economy.

Although a greater emphasis on service industries may explain a drop in productivity, we must be careful with this kind of generalization. It is more difficult to measure changes in the quality of services than changes in the quality of goods. If prices in an industry rise with no change in the quantity of output, it makes sense to conclude that the real level of output in the industry has fallen. However, if prices have gone up because the quality of the service has increased, then output actually has changed. Suppose a hotel remodels its rooms. In effect it is improving the quality of its service. Increased prices here would reflect this change in output.

Service industries—fast-food restaurants, airlines, hotels, banks—are not all alike. One way service firms compete is on the basis of the quality of service they provide. Because productivity is measured by the amount of output per unit of input, if we don't adjust for quality changes, we may underestimate the amount of output and so underestimate the productivity of the industry. The issue of productivity measurement in the service industries is an important topic of discussion among economists today.

Financial Market Development The evidence across countries suggests that economic growth is related to the development of financial markets. For any given amount of labor and capital, the more developed an economy's financial markets are, the more efficient should be the allocation of resources and, therefore, the greater the productivity. A nation may have a high rate of saving and investment and a sizable capital stock, but the key to efficient production is the allocation of resources to their best use.

Financial markets facilitate the allocation of resources. This occurs through the following mechanisms:

- Financial institutions act as intermediaries between savers and borrowers and screen borrowers so that the best projects are more likely to be funded.
- Financial institutions monitor the behavior of borrowers to ensure that the borrowed funds are used as intended.
- Financial institutions lower the risk of providing funds for investment purposes, as they provide loans to different individuals and firms and through this diversification of loans reduce the likelihood of suffering a catastrophic loss. If one borrower defaults on a loan, the financial institution does not fail, as it still has many other loans that are being repaid. This is a far different situation from the one that an individual making a single large loan may face. If you lend a large amount of your wealth to a single borrower and that borrower defaults

on the loan, your living standard may be at great risk. Because of the "risk sharing" that takes place in financial institutions, the cost of borrowed funds, the interest rate, will be lower than in an environment in which there is no such pooling of loan risks.

The more developed the financial sector of an economy, the more types of financing alternatives there are for funding investment. For instance, the typical poor country has a banking sector and a very limited stock market, if any at all. Firms in such a country must rely on bank loans. The governments in such countries often determine where banks are allowed to lend based on political considerations. As economies develop, the financial sector evolves so that alternatives to bank financing develop. Firms in economies with well-developed financial markets can raise funds by selling shares of ownership in the stock market, by issuing debt in the form of bonds to nonbank lenders, or by borrowing from banks. The more developed a country's financial markets, the more efficient the funding sources for borrowers and the more productive the economy.

3.c. Growth and Development

Economic growth depends on the growth of productivity and resources. Productivity grows unevenly, and its rate of growth is reflected in economic growth. Although the labor force seems to grow faster in developing countries than in industrial countries, lower rates of saving have limited the growth of the capital stock in developing countries. Without capital, workers cannot be very productive. This means that the relatively high rate of growth in the labor force in the developing world does not translate into a high rate of economic growth. We use this information on economic growth in Chapter 18 to explain and analyze the strategies used by developing countries to stimulate output and increase standards of living.

RECAP

1. Productivity is the ratio of the output produced to the amount of input.
2. Total factor productivity is the nation's real GDP (output) divided by its stock of labor and capital.
3. Economic growth is the sum of the growth of total factor productivity and the growth rate of resources (labor and capital).
4. Changes in productivity may be explained by the quality of the labor force, technological innovations, energy prices, a shift from manufacturing to service industries, and financial market development.

Summary

? What is economic growth?

1. Economic growth is an increase in real GDP. *§1.a*

2. Economic growth is compounded over time. *§1.a.1*

3. Per capita real GDP is real GDP divided by the population. *§1.b*

4. The definitions of economic growth are misleading because they do not indicate anything about the distribution of income or the quality of life. *§1.c*

5. The growth of the economy is tied to the growth of productive resources and technological advances. *§2*

6. Because their populations tend to grow more rapidly, developing countries typically experience faster growth in the labor force than do industrial countries. *§2.a*

7. The inability to save limits the growth of capital stock in developing countries. *§2.b*

8. Abundant natural resources are not necessary for rapid economic growth. *§2.c*

9. Technology defines the ways in which resources can be combined to produce goods and services. *§2.d*

? **What is productivity?**

10. Productivity is the ratio of the output produced to the amount of input. *§3*

11. Total factor productivity is the overall productivity of an economy. *§3*

12. The percentage change in real GDP equals the percentage change in total factor productivity plus the percentage changes in labor and capital multiplied by the share of GDP taken by labor and capital. *§3.a*

? **What explains productivity changes?**

13. Productivity changes with changes in the quality of the labor force, technological innovations, changes in energy prices, a shift away from manufacturing to service industries, and financial market development. *§3.b*

Key Terms

economic growth *§1.a*
rule of 72 *§1.a.2*
per capita real GDP *§1.b*

technology *§2.d*
total factor productivity (*TFP*) *§3*

Exercises

1. Why is the growth of per capita real GDP a better measure of economic growth than the growth of real GDP?

2. What is the level of output after four years if initial output equals $1,000 and the economy grows at a rate of 10 percent a year?

3. Use the data in the following table to determine the average annual growth rate for each country in terms of real GDP growth and per capita real GDP growth (real GDP is in billions of U.S. dollars, and population is in millions of people). Which country grew at the faster rate?

	1999		2001	
Country	**Real GDP**	**Population**	**Real GDP**	**Population**
Morocco	108.0	30.1	112.0	31.2
Australia	416.2	19.2	528.0	19.5

4. Suppose labor's share of GDP is 70 percent and capital's is 30 percent, real GDP is growing at a rate of 4 percent a year, the labor force is growing at 2 percent, and the capital stock is growing at 3 percent. What is the growth rate of total factor productivity?

5. Suppose labor's share of GDP is 70 percent and capital's is 30 percent, total factor productivity is growing at an annual rate of 2 percent, the labor force is growing at a rate of 1 percent, and the capital stock is growing at a rate of 3 percent. What is the annual growth rate of real GDP?

6. Discuss possible reasons for the slowdown in U.S. productivity growth that occurred in the 1970s and 1980s, and relate each reason to the equation for economic growth. (Does the growth of *TFP* or of resources change?)

7. How did the post–World War II baby boom affect the growth of the U.S. labor force? What effect is this

baby boom likely to have on the future U.S. labor force?

8. How do developing and industrial countries differ in their use of technological change, labor, capital, and natural resources to produce economic growth? Why do these differences exist?

9. How would an aging population affect economic growth?

10. If real GDP for China was 10,312 billion yuan at the end of 2002 and 9,593 billion yuan at the end of 2001, what is the annual rate of growth of the Chinese economy?

11. If Kenya's economy grew at a rate of 1 percent during 2002 and real GDP at the beginning of the year was 806 billion shillings, then what is real GDP at the end of the year?

12. Suppose a country has a real GDP equal to $1 billion today. If this economy grows at a rate of 5 percent a year, what will be the value of real GDP after five years?

13. Is the following statement true or false? Explain your answer. "Abundant natural resources are a necessary condition for economic growth."

14. What is the difference between total factor productivity and the productivity of labor? Why do you suppose that people often measure a nation's productivity using labor productivity only?

15. How would each of the following affect productivity in the United States?
   a. The quality of education increases in high schools.
   b. A cutback in oil production by oil-exporting nations raises oil prices.
   c. A large number of unskilled immigrant laborers move into the country.

16. How does the development of financial markets enhance the productivity of a country?

U.S. Updating Its Economic Measurements

It sounds like stuff only accountants could appreciate: This week the Commerce Department will change the way it measures the size and shape of the U.S. economy. . . .

The most important revisions represent Commerce's efforts to account for the information revolution. If the statisticians could ever agree on a way of doing this, it would do much to resolve the debate over whether America is enjoying a wondrous "new economy," in which the tedious old give-and-take between labor markets and inflation no longer applies. "New economy" theorists suggest that the increasing use of computers has led to such spectacular gains in productivity that bosses can hire more people than ever before, without having to pass on the resulting labor-cost increases to consumers. . . .

The problem is that there is no statistical evidence to prove the theory. Even as the information revolution has streamlined the way Americans do business, it has made a hash of the statistical methods used to measure the gains.

"We're like a tailor who's trying to take measurements for a suit from somebody who's running," says the Commerce Department's Moran, adding that things might be better if his agency's budget requests didn't always get shot down by Congress.

Most people assume that computers enhance productivity—otherwise why use them?—but when improvements finally appeared in official economic measurements, they were smaller and later than expected. This has led many analysts to fault the way productivity is measured, and indeed, there is much to find fault with. How to come up with a good gauge that includes the output per hour of both, say, a Bill Gates and a janitor? Is one schoolteacher twice as productive as another whose class is half as big?

Commerce has still not found a magic solution to this problem, but some of the forthcoming changes attempt to address it at least in part.

For one thing, Commerce is going to start counting software, when purchased by business, as an investment in plant and equipment. Until now, software has been treated as a raw material, like so much copper or rubber.

The category switch may sound like a technical triviality, but it makes a difference because raw materials aren't included in the most basic measure of U.S. economic output, the gross domestic product. Investments are.

Once Commerce starts adding in the software, the gross domestic product will rise. Commerce is making the revisions as far back as 1959, the dawn of the computer era, and the difference between the old and new figures should help solve at least some of the mystery about where the economic benefits of the computer revolution have been hiding all these years.

The trouble, economists say, is that the price of software keeps changing. "It's very difficult to know what to measure," warns Dean Baker, senior researcher at the Preamble Center, a Washington think tank. "If you make a mistake, it will be very costly."

Source: "U.S. Updating Its Economic Measurements," *Los Angeles Times,* October 25, 1999, p. A1. Copyright 1999 Times Mirror Company.

Los Angeles Times/October 25, 1999

Commentary

Measuring a nation's output has never been an easy task. As the Commerce Department spokesperson says in the article, trying to measure activity in an economy is "like a tailor who's trying to take measurements for a suit from somebody who's running." Since business and government policymakers make important decisions on the basis of the economic data provided by government, accurate measurement is crucial.

An example of the controversy related to the measurement problems is the issue of the "new economy." As discussed in the article, the new economy is thought to describe the modern economy, where technological advances in computers and information technology are driving increased productivity and output. While many analysts and reporters have written about the likely presence and effects of the new economy, it is much harder to find evidence in the official statistics. The Nobel prize–winning economist Robert Solow once said, "You can see the computer age everywhere but in the productivity statistics."

One possible key to this puzzle has been well argued by Daniel Sichel, who suggests that computers make up a relatively small part of the overall capital stock, so that the contribution of computers to overall growth may be correspondingly small.[*] Even though firms spend large amounts on computers each year, because of the rapid obsolescence of computers, much of this spending is aimed at updating old systems, so that the net addition to the capital stock is rather small.

To estimate the contribution of computers to growth, one can modify the growth equation presented in section 3.a of this chapter to allow computers to be treated apart from the rest of the capital stock:

$$\%\Delta Y = \%\Delta TFP + 0.70(\%\Delta L) + 0.29(\%\Delta K) + 0.01(\%\Delta COMP)$$

Note that this equation has computers accounting for 1 percent of the real GDP, and other capital for 29 percent.

The growth equation with computers treated apart from the rest of the capital stock allows us to estimate the effect of computers on growth (the product of their GDP share, 0.01, and the percentage change in the stock of computers). In the period of the late 1990s, computers contributed a growth rate of 0.35 percentage points per year, according to Sichel's estimates. This is more than twice their contribution to growth in the early 1990s and is also much larger relative to the contribution of other capital than in any earlier period. In addition, it is likely that the increasing spread of information technology associated with more widespread and better computer applications has contributed to the growth in productivity.

Another study, conducted by Dale Jorgensen, Mun Ho, and Kevin Stiroh,[†] estimated that *TFP* increased 0.51 percentage points as a result of IT in the 1995–2000 period, compared to 0.10 for 1959–1973 and 0.24 for 1973–1995. The U.S. evidence thus indicates a clear role for IT in increasing *TFP*.

[*]Daniel E. Sichel, "Computers and Aggregate Economic Growth: An Update," *Business Economics,* April 1999, 18–24.
[†]Dale W. Jorgensen, Mun S. Ho, and Kevin J. Stiroh, "Projecting Productivity Growth: Lessons from the U.S. Growth Resurgence," Federal Reserve Bank of Atlanta *Economic Review,* 3rd Quarter 2002, 1–44.

CHAPTER 18

Development Economics

Fundamental Questions

1. How is poverty measured?

2. Why are some countries poorer than others?

3. What strategies can a nation use to increase its economic growth?

4. How are savings in one nation used to speed development in other nations?

5. What microeconomic issues are involved in the transition from socialism?

6. What macroeconomic issues are involved in the transition from socialism?

There is an enormous difference between the standards of living in the poorest and richest countries in the world. In Botswana, the average life expectancy at birth is 39 years, 38 years less than in the United States. In Cambodia, only an estimated 30 percent of the population has access to safe water. In Ghana, 45 percent of the population exists on less than $1 per day. And in Chad, students average only 4 years of formal education.

The plight of developing countries is our focus in this chapter. We begin by discussing the extent of poverty and how it is measured across countries. Then we turn to the reasons why developing countries are poor and look at strategies for stimulating growth and development. The reasons for poverty are many, and the remedies often are rooted more in politics than in economics. Still, economics has much to say about how to improve the living standards of the world's poorest citizens. Finally we discuss the development problems of countries in the transition from socialism to capitalism. ■

1. The Developing World

Three-fourths of the world's population lives in developing countries. These countries are often called *less-developed countries (LDCs)* or *Third World countries.* "First World" countries are the industrialized nations of western Europe and North America, along with Australia, Japan, and New Zealand. "Second World" countries were the Communist countries of eastern Europe and the former Soviet Union. The Third World is made up of non-Communist developing countries, although people commonly use the term to refer to all developing countries.

The common link among developing countries is low per capita GNP or GDP, which implies a relatively low standard of living for the typical citizen. Otherwise the developing countries are a diverse group—with their cultures, their politics, even their geography varying enormously. Although we have used GDP throughout the text as the popular measure of a nation's output, in this chapter we frequently refer to GNP, as this is the measure used by the World Bank in classifying countries in terms of stage of development.

The developing countries are located primarily in South and East Asia, Africa, the Middle East, and Latin America (Figure 1). The total population of developing countries is over 5 billion people. Of this population, 25 percent live in China and 20 percent live in India. The next largest concentration of people is in Indonesia (4 percent), followed by Brazil, Pakistan, Bangladesh, and Nigeria. Except for Latin America, where 74 percent of the population lives in cities, most Third World citizens live in rural areas and are largely dependent on agriculture.

1.a. Measuring Poverty

1. How is poverty measured?

Poverty typically is defined in absolute terms.

Poverty is not easy to measure. Typically poverty is defined in an *absolute* sense: a family is poor if its income falls below a certain level. For example, the poverty level for a family of four in the United States in 2003 was an income of $18,244. The World Bank uses per capita GNP of $755 or less as its criterion for a low-income country. The countries in gold in Figure 1 meet this absolute definition of poverty.

Poverty is also a *relative* concept. Family income in relation to other incomes in the country or region is important in determining whether a family feels poor. The poverty level in the United States would represent a substantial increase in the living standard of most of the people in the world. Yet a poor family in the United States does not feel less poor because it has more money than poor families in other countries. In a nation where the median income of a family of four is more than $60,000, a family with an income of $18,244 clearly feels poorer.

Because poverty is also a relative concept, using a particular level of income to distinguish the poor from the not poor is often controversial. Besides the obvious problem of where to draw the poverty line, there is the more difficult problem of comparing poverty across countries with different currencies, customs, and living arrangements. Also, data are often limited and difficult to obtain because many of the poor in developing countries live in isolated areas. This makes it difficult to draw a comprehensive picture of the typical poor household in the Third World.

1.b. Basic Human Needs

Some economists and other social scientists, recognizing the limitations of an absolute definition of poverty (like the per capita GNP measure most commonly

FIGURE 1

The World by Stage of Development

This map of the world is colored to show each country's income level as measured by per capita GNP. *Source: World Bank, http://nebula.worldbank .org/website/GNIwdi/ viewer.htm.*

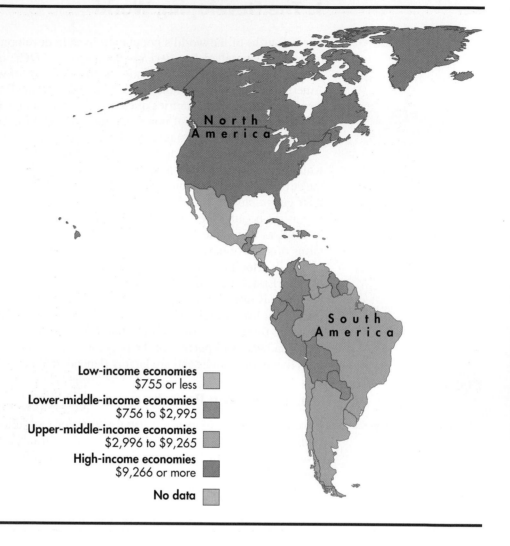

Low-income economies
$755 or less

Lower-middle-income economies
$756 to $2,995

Upper-middle-income economies
$2,996 to $9,265

High-income economies
$9,266 or more

No data

Basic human needs are a minimal level of caloric intake, health care, clothing, and shelter.

used), suggest using indicators of how basic human needs are being met. Although they disagree on an exact definition of *basic human needs,* the general idea is to set minimal levels of caloric intake, health care, clothing, and shelter.

Another alternative to per capita GNP is a physical *quality-of-life index* to evaluate living standards. One approach uses life expectancy, infant mortality, and literacy as indicators—a very narrow definition that ignores elements like justice, personal freedom, environmental quality, and employment opportunities. Nonetheless, these three indicators are, at least in theory, measures of social progress that allow meaningful comparisons across countries, whatever their social or political orientation.

Table 1 lists per capita GNP and indicators of human development for selected countries. The countries are listed in order of per capita GNP, beginning with the smallest. Generally there is a strong positive relationship between per capita GNP

and the other measures. But there are cases where higher per capita GNP does not mean higher quality of life. For instance, Namibia has a higher per capita GNP than China or the Philippines, but life expectancy and literacy are lower in Namibia than in the other two countries. Remember the limitations of per capita output: it is not a measure of everyone's standard of living in a particular country. However, as the table shows, it is a fairly reliable indicator of differences in living standards across countries. Ethiopia has the lowest per capita GNP and is clearly one of the world's poorest nations. Usually, as per capita GNP increases, living standards increase as well.

Per capita GNP and quality-of-life measures are not the only ways to determine a country's level of economic development—we could consider the number of households with running water, televisions, or any other good that varies with living standards. Recognizing that there is no perfect measure of economic development,

TABLE 1

Quality-of-Life Measures, Selected Countries

Country	Per Capita GNP*	Life Expectancy at Birth (years)	Literacy Rate[†]
Ethiopia	$ 100	42	57%
Bangladesh	$ 360	61	52%
India	$ 460	63	74%
China	$ 890	70	98%
Philippines	$ 1,030	69	99%
Namibia	$ 1,960	47	92%
El Salvador	$ 2,040	70	89%
Turkey	$ 2,530	70	97%
Mexico	$ 5,530	73	97%
Greece	$11,430	78	100%
United States	$34,280	77	100%

*2001 data measured in terms of U.S. dollars.
†Percentage of the population 15–45 years old that is literate.

Source: United Nations, http://uustats.un.org/unsd; and WorldBank, www.worldbank.org/data/.

economists and other social scientists often use several indicators to assess economic progress.

RECAP

1. Usually poverty is defined in an absolute sense, as a specific level of family income or per capita GNP or GDP.
2. Within a country or region, poverty is a relative concept.
3. Human development indexes based on indicators of basic human needs incorporate nonmonetary measures of well-being that are an alternative to per capita GDP for measuring economic development.

2. Obstacles to Growth

2. Why are some countries poorer than others?

Every country is unique. Each nation's history, both political and cultural, helps economists understand why poor nations have not developed and what policies offer the best hope for their development. Generally the factors that impede development are political or social. The political factors include a lack of administrative skills, instability, corruption, and the ability of special interest groups to block changes in economic policy. The social obstacles include a lack of entrepreneurs and rapid population growth.

2.a. Political Obstacles

2.a.1. Lack of Administrative Skills
Government support is essential to economic development. Whether support means allowing private enterprise to flourish and develop or actively managing the allocation of resources, a poorly organized or corrupt government can present an obstacle to economic growth. Some developing countries have suffered from well-meaning but inept government management. This is most obvious in countries with a long history of colonialization. For example, when Zaire won independence from Belgium, few of its native citizens were college educated. Moreover, Belgians had run most of the important government offices. Independence brought a large group of inexperienced and unskilled workers to important positions of power. And at first there was a period of "learning by doing."

2.a.2. Political Instability and Risk
One of the most important functions a government performs in stimulating economic growth is providing a political environment that encourages saving and investment. People do not want to do business in an economy weakened by wars, demonstrations, or uncertainty. For instance, since becoming an independent nation in 1825, Bolivia has had more than 150 changes in government. This kind of instability forces citizens to take a short-run view of the economy. Long-term planning is impossible without knowing the attitudes and policies of the government that is going to be in power next year or even next month.

A country must be able to guarantee the rights of private property if it is going to create an environment that encourages private investment.

The key issue here is *property rights.* A country that guarantees the right of private property encourages private investment and development. Where ownership rights may be changed by revolution or political decree, there is little incentive for private investment and development. People do not start new businesses or build new factories if they believe that a change in government or a change in the political will of the current government could result in the confiscation of their property.

expropriation: the government seizure of assets, typically without adequate compensation to the owners

This confiscation is called **expropriation.** Countries with a history of expropriating foreign-owned property without compensating the owners (paying them the property's market value) have difficulty encouraging foreign investment. An example is Uganda. In 1973 a successful revolution by Idi Amin was followed by the expropriation of over 500 foreign-owned (mostly British) firms. Foreign and domestic investment in Uganda fell dramatically as a result.

The loss of foreign investment is particularly important in developing countries. In Chapter 17 we pointed out that developing countries suffer from a lack of saving. If domestic residents are not able to save because they are living at or below subsistence level, foreign saving is a crucial source of investment. Without that investment, the economies of developing countries cannot grow.

2.a.3. Corruption
Corrupt practices by government officials have long reduced economic growth. Payment of money or gifts in order to receive a government service or benefit is quite widespread in many countries. Research shows that there is a definite negative relationship between the level of corruption in a country and both investment and growth.

Research also shows that corruption thrives in countries where government regulations create distortions between the economic outcomes that would exist with free markets and the actual outcomes. For instance, a country where government permission is required to buy or sell foreign currency will have a thriving black market in foreign exchange in which the black market exchange rate of a U.S. dollar will cost much more domestic currency than the official rate offered by the government.

This distortion allows government officials an opportunity for personal gain by providing access to the official rate.

Generally speaking, the more competitive a country's markets are, the fewer the opportunities for corruption. So policies aimed at reducing corruption typically involve reducing the discretion that public officials have in granting benefits or imposing costs on others. This may include greater transparency of government practices and the introduction of merit-based competition for government employment.

Corruption reduces growth most directly through government investment in projects with low productivity. The evidence indicates that corrupt governments spend more on capital goods than governments that are less corrupt, but that the investment projects of corrupt governments probably reduce the productivity of the country. In addition, those countries in which corrupt governments engage in large amounts of capital expenditures have relatively small amounts of private investment. Since private investment is aimed at earning a profit, such investment tends to increase the productivity of a nation. Private firms do not undertake risky projects unless they expect to earn a profit. It is possible, however, that a corrupt government may award large construction projects in order to receive financial rewards from the contractors hired. The projects chosen may turn out to be inefficient uses of government funds and retard economic growth rather than increase it.

2.a.4. Good Economics as Bad Politics
Every Third World politician wants to maximize economic growth, all things being equal. But all things are rarely equal. Political pressures may force a government to work toward more immediate objectives than economic growth.

For example, maximizing growth may mean reducing the size of government in order to lower taxes and increase investment. However, in many developing countries, the strongest supporters of the political leaders are those working for the current government. Obviously it's not good political strategy to fire those workers. So the government stays overstaffed and inefficient, and the potential for economic growth falls. The governments in developing countries often subsidize purchases of food and other basic necessities. Reducing government expenditures and moving toward free market pricing of food, energy, and other items make good economic sense. But the citizens who depend on those subsidies are not going to be happy if they stop.

In 1977 the Egyptian government lowered its food subsidies in order to use those funds for development. What happened? There was widespread rioting that ended only when the government reinstituted the subsidies. In 1989, Venezuela lowered government subsidies on public transportation and petroleum products. Public transit fares went up 30 percent, to the equivalent of 7 U.S. cents, and gasoline prices went from 16 to 26 cents a gallon. (One official said that the prices were raised "from the cheapest in the world to the cheapest in the world."[1]) The resulting rioting in Caracas led to 50 deaths, over 500 injuries, and more than 1,000 arrests. Lowering government expenditures and reducing the role of government in the economy can be politically and physically dangerous.

What we are saying here is that seemingly good economics can make for bad politics. Because some group is going to be hurt in the short run by any change in policy aimed at increasing growth, there always is opposition to change. Often the continued rule of the existing regime depends on not alienating a certain group. Only a government that is stabilized by military force (a dictatorship), popular support (a democracy), or party support (a Communist or socialist country) has the

---

[1]See "Venezuela Rumblings: Riots and Debt Crisis," *New York Times,* March 2, 1989, p. A13.

Economic Development in the Americas

It is not well known that at one time, the United States and Canada were not the richest countries of North and South America. The accompanying table shows how per capita GDP changed over time for several countries relative to that of the United States.

Per Capita GDP Relative to the United States (in percent)				
Country	1700	1800	1900	2000
Argentina	—	102	52	36
Barbados	150	—	—	44
Brazil	—	50	10	22
Chile	—	46	38	28
Cuba	167	112	—	—
Mexico	89	50	35	26
Peru	—	41	20	14
U.S. Real GDP per capita (1985 dollars)	550	807	3,859	34,260

One can see that some of what were then European colonies, such as Barbados and Cuba, were much richer in 1700 than the group of colonies in North America that were to eventually become the United States. Others, like Mexico, were about as rich as the colonies that became the United States. In 1800, Argentina was slightly richer than the United States, as was Cuba. But by 1900, per capita GDP had risen much faster in the United States than in the other countries. What happened?

As we have learned, abundant natural resources are not sufficient to ensure economic growth. The industrialization that occurred in the United States in the early 1800s was not duplicated in the Latin American countries. This became a point of divergence for the growth rates of the United States and Latin America. Researchers have suggested that an important difference contributing to the differential rates of development was the provision of government policies, including laws and institutions, in the United States and Canada that encouraged widespread participation in economic development.* Through investment in human capital via education and skills training, workers could experience upward mobility. By saving and investing, individual entrepreneurs could turn small businesses into large, successful enterprises.

In Latin America, institutions developed that blocked opportunities for economic advancement for a large portion of the population. The agriculture and mining industries of Latin America were conducted on a relatively large scale, so that there were few entrepreneurs and managers and many poor workers. Even after slavery was ended and these countries achieved their independence from their European colonizers, the institutions of Latin American countries worked against individual investment in human capital and upward mobility. The class of individual entrepreneurs found in Canada and the United States did not emerge in Latin America. The upwardly mobile workers of Canada and the United States provided the opportunities for mass-market consumer goods that drove the industrialization process. But in Latin America, such mass markets of consumers with income to spend did not emerge.

Most poor countries may be characterized as having a small number of very rich individuals and a large number of very poor people. The members of the rich elite want to maintain their position and so support institutions that restrict the opportunities for advancement of the masses of poor people. So the initial development of an environment with a few rich and many poor was carried forward through time. In this way we can see the importance of institutions and government policies for charting a path of high growth and rapid development or low growth and relative stagnation.

*Drawn from World Bank, *World Development Report, 2003*, and Stanley L. Engerman and Kenneth L. Sokoloff, "Factor Endowments, Institutions, and Differential Paths of Growth Among New World Economies: A View from Economic Historians of the United States," in Stephen H. Haber, ed., *How Latin America Fell Behind: Essays in the Economic Histories of Brazil and Mexico, 1800–1914* (Stanford, CA: Stanford University Press, 1997).

power to implement needed economic change. A government that lacks this power is handicapped by political constraints in its efforts to stimulate economic growth.

The Global Business Insight "Economic Development in the Americas," points out how history plays a role in shaping the institutions and economic framework in which development takes place. The more rapid development of Canada and the United States than of Latin America may be traced back to colonial times and the institutions that evolved from conditions that existed then.

2.b. Social Obstacles

Cultural traditions and attitudes can work against economic development. In traditional societies, children follow in their parents' footsteps. If your father is a carpenter, there is a good chance that you will be a carpenter. Moreover, production is carried out in the same way generation after generation. For an economy to grow, it must be willing to change.

2.b.1. Lack of Entrepreneurs

A society that answers the questions What to produce? How to produce? and For whom to produce? by doing things as they were done by the previous generation lacks a key ingredient for economic growth: entrepreneurs. Entrepreneurs are risk takers; they bring innovation and new technology into use. Understanding why some societies are better at producing entrepreneurs than others may help explain why some nations have remained poor while others have grown rapidly.

Entrepreneurs are more likely to develop among minority groups that have been blocked from traditional high-paying jobs.

One theory is that entrepreneurs often come from *blocked minorities*. Some individuals in the traditional society are blocked from holding prestigious jobs or political office because of discrimination. This discrimination can be based on race, religion, or immigrant status. Because discrimination keeps them from the best traditional occupations, these minority groups can achieve wealth and status only through entrepreneurship. The Chinese in Southeast Asia, the Jews in Europe, and the Indians in Africa were all blocked minorities, forced to turn to entrepreneurship to advance themselves.

Immigrants provide a pool of entrepreneurs who have skills and knowledge that often are lacking in the developing country.

In developing countries, entrepreneurship tends to be concentrated among immigrants, who have skills and experience that do not exist in poor countries. Many leaders of industry in Latin America, for example, are Italian, German, Arab, or Basque immigrants or the descendants of immigrants; they are not part of the dominant Spanish or native Indian population. The success of these immigrants is less a product of their being discriminated against than of their expertise in commerce. They know the foreign suppliers of goods. They have business skills that are lacking in developing regions. And they have the traditions—among them, the work ethic—and training instilled in their home country.

Motivation also plays a role in the level of entrepreneurship that exists in developing countries. In some societies, traditional values may be an obstacle to development because they do not encourage high achievement. A good example is provided by the tribal culture in Sub-Saharan Africa. In this tribal culture, economic success does not result in upward social mobility if the success is obtained outside of the tribe. Instead, it could result in the person's being shunned by the rest of the tribe. So incentives work against individual saving and investment or entrepreneurship. The social pressure is to share communally any riches that one obtains and not to rise above the group in any important way. In this sort of environment, development is hindered by the lack of incentives for wealth accumulation and risk taking.

Societies in which the culture supports individual achievement produce more entrepreneurs. It is difficult to identify the specific values in a society that account for a lack of motivation. In the past, researchers have pointed to factors that are not always valid across different societies. For instance, at one time many argued that the Protestant work ethic was responsible for the large number of entrepreneurs in the industrial world. According to this argument, some religions are more supportive of the accumulation of wealth than others. Today this argument is difficult to make because we find economic development in nations with vastly different cultures and religions.

2.b.2. Rapid Population Growth   Remember that per capita real GNP is real GNP divided by the population. Although labor is a factor of production, and labor force growth may increase output, when population rises faster than GNP, the standard of living of the average citizen does not improve. One very real problem for many developing countries is the growth of their population. With the exception of China and India (where population growth is controlled), population growth in the developing countries is proceeding at a pace that will double the Third World population every 25 years. In large part the rate at which the population of the Third World is growing is a product of lower death rates. Death rates have fallen, but birthrates have not.

Social scientists do not all agree on the effects of population growth on development. A growing labor force can serve as an important factor in increasing growth. But those who believe that population growth has a negative effect cite three reasons:

Capital shallowing   Rapid population growth may reduce the amount of capital per worker, lowering the productivity of labor.

Age dependency   Rapid population growth produces a large number of dependent children, whose consumption requirements lower the ability of the economy to save.

Investment diversion   Rapid population growth shifts government expenditures from the country's infrastructure (roads, communication systems) to education and health care.

Population growth may have had a negative effect on development in many countries, but the magnitude of the effect is difficult to assess. And in some cases, population growth probably has stimulated development. For instance, the fact that children consume goods and services and thus lower the ability of a nation to save ignores the fact that the children grow up and become productive adults. Furthermore, any investment diversion from infrastructure to education and health care is not necessarily a loss, as education and health care will build up the productivity of the labor force. The harmful effect of population growth should be most pronounced in countries where usable land and water are relatively scarce. Although generalizations about acceptable levels of population growth do not fit all circumstances, the World Bank has stated that population growth rates above 2 percent a year act as a brake on economic development.

The GNP can grow steadily year after year, but if the population grows at a faster rate, the standard of living of the average individual falls. The simple answer to reducing population growth seems to be education: programs that teach methods of birth control and family planning. But reducing birthrates is not simply a matter of education. People have to choose to limit the size of their families. It must be socially acceptable and economically advantageous for families to use birth control, and for many families it is neither.

Remember that what is good for society as a whole may not be good for the individual. Children are a source of labor in rural families and a support for parents in their old age. How many children are enough? That depends on the expected infant mortality rate. Although infant mortality rates in developing countries have fallen in recent years, they are still quite high relative to those in the developed countries. Families still tend to follow tradition, and so keep having lots of children.

RECAP

1. In some countries, especially those that have been colonies, economic growth has been slow because government officials lack necessary skills.
2. Countries that are unable to protect the rights of private property have difficulty attracting investors.
3. Expropriation is the seizure by government of assets without adequate compensation.
4. Corruption in government reduces investment and growth.
5. Often government officials know the right economic policies to follow but are constrained by political considerations from implementing those policies.
6. Immigrants are often the entrepreneurs in developing countries.
7. Rapid population growth may slow development because of the effects of capital shallowing, age dependency, and investment diversion.

3. What strategies can a nation use to increase its economic growth?

3. Development Strategies

Different countries follow different strategies to stimulate economic development. There are two basic types of development strategies: inward oriented and outward oriented.

3.a. Inward-Oriented Strategies

The typical developing country has a comparative advantage over other countries in the production of certain primary products. Having a comparative advantage means that a country has the lowest opportunity cost of producing a good. (We talked about comparative advantage in Chapter 2.) A **primary product** is a product in the first stage of production, which often serves as an input in the production of some other good. Agricultural produce and minerals are examples of primary products. In the absence of a conscious government policy that directs production, we expect countries to concentrate on the production of that thing in which they have a comparative advantage. For example, we expect Cuba to focus on sugar production, Colombia to focus on coffee production, and the Ivory Coast to focus on cocoa production—each country selling the output of its primary product to the rest of the world.

primary product: a product in the first stage of production, which often serves as an input in the production of another product

One of the "newly industrialized countries," or "NICs," is South Korea. This photo of a ship assembly line at Hyundai Heavy Industries is indicative of the importance of production for world markets, which lifted South Korea, Hong Kong, Taiwan, and Singapore from developing country to industrialized country status.

import substitution: the substitution of domestically produced manufactured goods for imported manufactured goods

Today many developing countries have shifted their resources away from producing primary products for export. Inward-oriented development strategies focus on production for the domestic market rather than exports of goods and services. For these countries, development means industrialization. The objective of this kind of inward-oriented strategy is **import substitution,** replacing imported manufactured goods with domestic goods.

Import-substitution policies dominate the strategies of the developing world. The basic idea is to identify domestic markets that are being supplied in large part by imports. Those markets that require a level of technology that is available to the domestic economy are candidates for import substitution. Industrialization goes hand in hand with tariffs or quotas on imports that protect the newly developing domestic industry from its more efficient foreign competition. As a result, production and international trade will not occur solely as a result of comparative advantages, but are affected primarily by these countries' import-substitution policy activities.

Because the domestic industry can survive only with protection from foreign competition, import-substitution policies typically raise the price of the domestically produced goods over the imported goods. In addition, the quality of the domestically produced goods may not be as high (at least at first) as the quality of the imported goods. Ideally, as the industry grows and becomes more experienced, price and quality become competitive with those of foreign goods. Once this happens, the import barriers are no longer needed, and the domestic industry may even become an export industry. Unfortunately, the ideal is seldom realized. The Third World is full of inefficient manufacturing companies that are unlikely ever to improve enough to be able to survive without protection from foreign competitors.

3.b. Outward-Oriented Strategies

The inward-oriented strategy of developing domestic industry to supply domestic markets is the most popular development strategy, but it is not the only one.

Beginning in the 1960s, a small group of countries (notably South Korea, Hong Kong, Singapore, and Taiwan) chose to focus on the growth of exports. These countries follow an outward-oriented strategy, utilizing their most abundant resource to produce those products that they can produce better than others.

export substitution: the use of resources to produce manufactured products for export rather than agricultural products for the domestic market

The abundant resource in these countries is labor, and the goods they produce are labor-intensive products. This kind of outward-oriented policy is called **export substitution.** The countries use labor to produce manufactured goods for export rather than agricultural products for domestic use.

Outward-oriented development strategies are based on efficient, low-cost production. Their success depends on being able to compete effectively with producers in the rest of the world. Here most governments attempt to stimulate exports. This can mean subsidizing domestic producers to produce goods for export rather than for domestic consumption. International competition is often more intense than the competition at home—producers face stiffer price competition, higher quality standards, and greater marketing expertise in the global marketplace. This means that domestic producers may have to be induced to compete internationally. Inducements can take the form of government assistance in international marketing, tax reductions, low-interest-rate loans, or cash payments.

Another inducement of sorts is to make domestic sales less attractive. This means implementing policies that are just the opposite of import substitution. The government reduces or eliminates domestic tariffs that keep domestic price levels above international levels. As profits from domestic sales fall, domestic industry turns to producing goods for export.

3.c. Comparing Strategies

Import-substitution policies are enacted in countries that believe that industrialization is the key to economic development. In the 1950s and 1960s, economists argued that specializing in the production and export of primary products does not encourage the rapid growth rates that developing countries are looking for. This argument—the *deteriorating-terms-of-trade argument*—was based on the assumption that the real value of primary products would fall over time. If the prices of primary products fall in relation to the prices of manufactured products, then countries that export primary products and import manufactured goods find the cost of manufactured goods rising in terms of the primary products required to buy them. The amount of exports that must be exchanged for some quantity of imports is often called the **terms of trade.**

terms of trade: the amount of an exported good that must be given up to obtain an imported good

The deteriorating-terms-of-trade argument in the 1950s and 1960s led policymakers in developing countries to fear that the terms of trade would become increasingly unfavorable. One product of that fear was the choice of an inward-oriented strategy, a focus on domestic industrialization rather than production for export.

At the root of the pessimism about the export of primary products was the belief that technological change would slow the growth of demand for primary products over time. That theory ignored the fact that if the supply of natural resources is fixed, those resources could become more valuable over time, even if demand grows slowly or not at all. And if the real value of primary products does fall over time, this does not necessarily mean that an inward-oriented policy is required. Critics of inward-oriented policies argue that nations should exploit their comparative advantage, that resources should be free to move to their highest-valued use. And they argue that market-driven resource allocation is unlikely to occur in an inward-oriented economy where government has imposed restrictions aimed at maximizing the rate of growth of industrial output.

Other economists believe that developing countries have unique problems that call for active government intervention and regulation of economic activity. These economists often favor inward-oriented strategies. They focus on the structure of developing countries in terms of uneven industrial development. Some countries have modern manufacturing industries paying relatively high wages that operate alongside traditional agricultural industries paying low wages. A single economy with industries at very different levels of development is called a **dual economy.** Some insist that in a dual economy, the markets for goods and resources do not work well. If resources could move freely between industries, then wages would not differ by the huge amounts observed in certain developing countries. These economists support active government direction of the economy in countries where markets are not functioning well, believing that resources in these countries are unlikely to move freely to their highest-valued use if free markets are allowed.

The growth rates of the outward-oriented economies are significantly higher than the growth rates of the inward-oriented economies. The success of the outward-oriented economies is likely to continue in light of a strong increase in saving in those economies. In 1963, domestic saving as a fraction of GDP was only 13 percent in the strongly outward-oriented economies. After more than two decades of economic growth driven by export-promotion policies, the rate of saving in these countries had increased to 31.4 percent of GDP. This high rate of saving increases investment expenditures, which increase the productivity of labor, further stimulating the growth of per capita real GDP.

Why are outward-oriented strategies more successful than inward-oriented strategies? The primary advantage of an outward orientation is the efficient utilization of resources. Import-substitution policies do not allocate resources on the basis of cost minimization. In addition, an outward-oriented strategy allows the economy to grow beyond the scale of the domestic market. Foreign demand creates additional markets for exports, beyond the domestic market.

dual economy: an economy in which two sectors (typically manufacturing and agriculture) show very different levels of development

The growth rates of outward-oriented economies are significantly higher than the growth rates of inward-oriented economies.

RECAP

1. Inward-oriented strategies concentrate on building a domestic industrial sector.
2. Outward-oriented strategies utilize a country's comparative advantage in exporting.
3. The deteriorating-terms-of-trade argument has been used to justify import-substitution policies.
4. Evidence indicates that outward-oriented policies have been more successful than inward-oriented policies at generating economic growth.

?

4. How are savings in one nation used to speed development in other nations?

4. Foreign Investment and Aid

Developing countries rely on savings in the rest of the world to finance much of their investment needs. Foreign savings may come from industrial countries in many different ways. In this section we describe the ways in which savings are transferred from industrial to developing countries and the benefits of foreign investment and aid to developing countries.

4.a. Foreign Savings Flows

Poor countries that are unable to save enough to invest in capital stock must rely on the savings of other countries to help them develop economically. Foreign savings come from both private sources and official government sources.

Private sources of foreign savings can take the form of direct investment, portfolio investment, commercial bank loans, and trade credit. **Foreign direct investment** is the purchase of a physical operating unit, like a factory, or an ownership position in a foreign country that gives the domestic firm making the investment ownership of more than 10 percent of the foreign firm. This is different from **portfolio investment,** which is the purchase of securities, like stocks and bonds. In the case of direct investment, the foreign investor may actually operate the business. Portfolio investment helps finance a business, but host-country managers operate the firm; foreign investors simply hold pieces of paper that represent a share of the ownership or the debt of the firm. **Commercial bank loans** are loans made at market rates of interest to either foreign governments or business firms. These loans are often made by a *bank syndicate,* a group of several banks, to share the risk associated with lending to a single country. Finally, exporting firms and commercial banks offer **trade credit,** allowing importers a period of time before payment is due on the goods or services purchased. Extension of trade credit usually involves payment in 30 days (or some other term) after the goods are received.

The relative importance of direct investment and bank lending have changed over time. In 1970, direct investment in developing countries was greater than bank loans. By the late 1970s and early 1980s, however, bank loans far exceeded direct investment. Bank lending gives the borrowing country greater flexibility in deciding how to use funds. Direct investment carries with it an element of foreign control over domestic resources. Nationalist sentiment combined with the fear of exploitation by foreign owners and managers led many developing countries to pass laws restricting direct investment. By the early 1990s, however, as more nations emphasized the development of free markets, direct investment was again growing in importance as

foreign direct investment: the purchase of a physical operating unit or more than 10 percent ownership in a foreign country

portfolio investment: the purchase of securities

commercial bank loan: a bank loan at market rates of interest, often involving a bank syndicate

trade credit: the extension of a period of time before an importer must pay for goods or services purchased

Multinational firms operate in developing countries, providing jobs and modern technology, and thereby aiding development.

a source of funds for developing countries, and by the late 1990s, it was the most important source of funds for developing countries.

4.b. Benefits of Foreign Investment

Not all developing countries discourage foreign direct investment. In fact, many countries have benefited from foreign investment. Those benefits fall into three categories: new jobs, new technology, and foreign exchange earnings.

4.b.1. New Jobs
Foreign investment should stimulate growth and create new jobs in developing countries. But the number of new jobs created directly by foreign investment is often limited by the nature of the industries in which foreign investment is allowed.

Usually foreign investment is invited in capital-intensive industries, like chemicals or mineral extraction. Because capital goods are expensive and often require advanced technology to operate, foreign firms can build a capital-intensive industry faster than the developing country can do so. One product of the emphasis on capital-intensive industries is that foreign investment often has little effect on employment in developing countries. A $.5 billion oil refinery may employ just a few hundred workers; yet the creation of these few hundred jobs, along with other expenditures by the refinery, will stimulate domestic income by raising incomes across the economy.

4.b.2. Technology Transfer
In Chapter 17 we said that economic growth depends on the growth of resources and technological change. Most expenditures on research and development are made in the major industrial countries. These are also the countries that develop most of the innovations that make production more efficient. For the Third World country with limited scientific resources, the industrial nations are a critical source of information, technology, and expertise.

The ability of foreign firms to utilize modern technology in a developing country depends in part on having a supply of engineers and technical personnel in the host country. India and Mexico have a fairly large number of technical personnel, which means that new technology can be adapted relatively quickly. Other countries, where a large fraction of the population has less than an elementary-level education, must train workers and then keep those workers from migrating to industrial countries, where their salaries are likely to be much higher.

4.b.3. Foreign Exchange Earnings
Developing countries expect foreign investment to improve their balance of payments. The assumption is that the multinational firms located inside the developing country increase exports and thus generate greater foreign currency earnings that can be used for imports or for repaying foreign debt. But this scenario does not unfold if the foreign investment is used to produce goods primarily for domestic consumption. In fact, the presence of a foreign firm can create a larger deficit in the balance of payments if the firm sends profits back to its industrial country headquarters from the developing country and the value of those profits exceeds the value of the foreign exchange earned by exports.

4.c. Foreign Aid

foreign aid: gifts of low-cost loans made to developing countries from official sources

Official foreign savings are usually available as either outright gifts or low-interest-rate loans. These funds are called **foreign aid.** Large countries, like the United States, provide much more funding in terms of the dollar value of aid than do small countries. However, some small countries—for example, the Netherlands and Norway—commit a much larger percentage of their GNP to foreign aid.

Foreign aid itself can take the form of cash grants or transfers of goods or technology, with nothing given in return by the developing country. Often foreign aid is used to reward political allies, particularly when those allies hold a strategic military location. Examples of this politically inspired aid are the former Soviet support of Cuba and U.S. support of Turkey.

bilateral aid: foreign aid that flows from one country to another

Foreign aid that flows from one country to another is called **bilateral aid.** Governments typically have an agency that coordinates and plans foreign aid programs and expenditures. The U.S. Agency for International Development (USAID) performs these functions in the United States. Most of the time bilateral aid is project oriented, given to fund a specific project (an educational facility, an irrigation project).

Food makes up a substantial portion of bilateral aid. After a bad harvest or a natural disaster (drought in the Sudan, floods in Bangladesh), major food-producing nations help feed the hungry. Egypt and Bangladesh were the leading recipients of food aid during the late 1980s. In the early 1990s, attention shifted to Somalia. The major recipients of food aid change over time, as nature and political events combine to change the pattern of hunger and need in the world.

The economics of food aid illustrates a major problem with many kinds of charity. Aid is intended to help those who need it without interfering with domestic production. But when food flows into a developing country, food prices tend to fall, pushing farm income down and discouraging local production. Ideally food aid should go to the very poor, who are less likely to have the income necessary to purchase domestic production anyway.

Foreign aid does not flow directly from the donors to the needy. It goes through the government of the recipient country. Here we find another problem: the inefficient and sometimes corrupt bureaucracies in recipient nations. There have been cases where recipient governments have sold products that were intended for free distribution to the poor. In other cases, food aid was not distributed because the recipient government had created the conditions leading to starvation. The U.S. intervention in Somalia in 1993 was aimed at helping food aid reach the starving population. In still other cases, a well-intentioned recipient government simply did not have the resources to distribute the aid, so the products ended up largely going to waste. One response to these problems is to rely on voluntary agencies to distribute aid. Another is to rely on multilateral agencies.

multilateral aid: aid provided by international organizations that are supported by many nations

Multilateral aid is provided by international organizations that are supported by many nations. The largest and most important multilateral aid institution is the World Bank. The World Bank makes loans to developing countries at below-market rates of interest and oversees projects it has funded in developing countries. As an international organization, the World Bank is not controlled by any single country. This allows the organization to advise and help developing countries in a nonpolitical way that is usually not possible with bilateral aid.

RECAP

1. Private sources of foreign savings include direct investment, portfolio investment, commercial bank loans, and trade credit.

2. Developing countries can benefit from foreign investment through new jobs, the transfer of technology, and foreign exchange earnings.

3. Foreign aid involves gifts or low-cost loans made available to developing countries by official sources.

4. Foreign aid can be provided bilaterally or multilaterally.

5. Economies in Transition from Socialism

As the world turned from the 1980s into the 1990s, the economies of the former Soviet Union and its eastern European satellites were leaving socialism behind and embracing capitalism as the road to future prosperity. The desire for change was motivated by low productivity and consumption, or, as Soviet workers were fond of saying, "We pretend to work and the state pretends to pay us." The transition road has not been easy; it has proven much more difficult to make the transition from socialism than many thought in 1990.

An economy in transition poses special development problems as it moves from socialism, with widespread government ownership of productive resources and massive government intervention in economic decision making, to a market-based economy, with an emphasis on private property and individual decision making. Since much is still being learned and there is no clearly established "best way," we focus on certain fundamentals that are required for a successful transition.

5.a. Microeconomic Issues

?

5. What microeconomic issues are involved in the transition from socialism?

privatize: to convert state-owned enterprises to private ownership

The transformation of a socialist economy into a capitalist economy requires the creation of markets. Resources that were formerly owned and allocated by government must be **privatized,** or converted from state ownership to private ownership. The state still has a role, since private property rights must be developed, recognized, and protected by government. Privately owned resources will then be allocated by the market system through prices set by supply and demand in a competitive environment with incomes that are based on productivity. Although it is easy to state where an economy should be in terms of free markets rather than central planning, getting there is easier said than done. The issue of privatization is the most obvious case.

Every nation has its local characteristics. This photo of production at the Budweiser Budvar brewery in the Czech Republic is indicative of the importance of pub life and beer in the Czech culture. The Czech Republic ranks first in the world in terms of per capita beer consumption.

5.a.1. Privatization

Socialist economies are characterized by many state-owned enterprises (SOEs). These enterprises are frequently large, technologically outdated, and unprofitable. The move to a market economy requires that these enterprises be privatized. How should SOEs be sold or otherwise converted to private ownership?

One alternative is to issue shares of ownership (like shares of stock) to the existing workers and managers in an enterprise. This method has the advantage of simplicity—the new private owners are easy to identify, and ownership is easy to transfer. The disadvantage is that some SOEs may be uncompetitive in a capitalist environment, so that ownership of such a firm is worthless, while other SOEs may be able to compete effectively, so that ownership may have considerable value. This privatization system would reward and penalize the working population on the basis of where they were previously assigned to work by the state rather than on the basis of individual investment and risk taking. Moreover, a simple change of ownership may not change the manner in which the firm operates.

Another alternative is to issue shares of ownership randomly to the public in a kind of lottery. You may have an equal chance of becoming one of the owners of a steel mill, a shoe factory, or a farm. In a truly random assignment of ownership, everyone has an equal chance of receiving a profitable share. This scheme does away with the unfortunate circumstance associated with those who have the misfortune to be employed by the state in an unproductive job when shares are issued only to existing employees of each firm. A problem with this scheme is that those who are interested in, or knowledgeable about, a particular firm or industry would have no better chance to be involved in that industry than would those who had no interest.

Yet another alternative is to auction ownership of SOEs to the highest bidder. In addition to raising revenue for the state, this method is quite straightforward to carry out. A common argument against this method is that those with enough wealth to make winning bids are likely to be former Communist party leaders or individuals who traded on black markets under the socialist regime. Such people are not favorably viewed by the masses, and as a result, auctions are controversial.

The privatization method chosen by Czechoslovakia (before its split into two nations) was a coupon giveaway to millions of citizens, who then used the coupons to buy stock in SOEs. The goal of this kind of plan was to create a broad-based democratic capitalism with millions of citizens holding ownership positions in productive firms. An advantage of this plan is that the government does not have to find buyers who are willing to exchange real money for SOEs. Since many SOEs have a questionable initial money value, by granting ownership to a wide group of citizens, the state pushes the burden of managing relatively unproductive firms to the general public.

There is no universal approach to converting SOEs into privately owned firms. Each nation has taken the approach that best seems to fit its particular political and economic system. In all cases, it has been relatively easy to privatize small, profitable firms but much more difficult to privatize large, unprofitable firms. One lesson learned from past privatizations is the importance of openness and transparency. To avoid corruption and cronyism in the privatization process, everyone must know how the process works and be able to observe the outcomes in terms of who the new owners are.

5.a.2. Price Reform

Under socialism, prices of goods and services are established by the state. These prices need not reflect economic costs or scarcity. But in a market-oriented economy, prices serve an important signaling role. If consumers

A market system requires that prices be free to fluctuate to reflect supply and demand fluctuations.

want more of a good or service, its price rises, and that induces producers to offer more for sale. If consumer tastes change, so that demand for a good or service falls, then the price should fall to induce producers to offer less for sale. If there is an excess supply of a good, its price falls, and that induces consumers to buy more. If there is an excess demand for a good, the price rises to induce consumers to buy less. A major problem with socialism is that prices are not free to serve this role of a signal to producers and consumers. Therefore, an important step in the transition from socialism to capitalism is the freeing of prices so that they may seek their free market levels.

Considering that there were around 25 million goods and services to be priced in the former Soviet Union, it was impossible for government officials to know the appropriate free market price for each item and then to plan a shift from the state-regulated price. However, there is a way to allow the correct prices to be set very quickly. There are existing prices for every good in the rest of the world. If the economy is opened to competition from foreign countries, foreign trade will force the domestic prices to be comparable to foreign prices. Of course, the presence of tariffs or quotas on foreign goods will distort the price comparisons, but the lower the restrictions on trade, the more domestic prices will conform to prices in the rest of the world. For goods that are not traded internationally and for many services, foreign trade will not set a domestic price. In this case, a free market may be allowed to adjust the price over time in response to the internal domestic pressures of supply and demand.

The normal response to a freeing of prices from state control is an increase in the availability of goods and services, although initially output may fall. However, the beneficial aspects of price reform require privatization of the economy. Price changes bring about profits and losses that induce profit-seeking producers to provide what buyers want. If production is still controlled by state-owned enterprises that have no profit incentive, then price reform will not have the desired effect of increasing output and efficiency.

While the transition from central planning to a market-based economy has created opportunities for enterprising individuals to earn living standards previously only available to high-ranking members of the socialist elite, it has also created large masses of disenfranchised people who have lost the income security that existed under socialism. A major problem associated with the early transition from socialism is providing a safety net to protect the disenfranchised.

It is important to realize that price reform has an initial shock effect on the economy. Prices under socialism are typically well below the true opportunity cost for most items considered to be necessities. As a result, nonprice rationing will determine who gets the scarce goods. One popular way of rationing when the money price is below equilibrium is simply first-come, first-served. But this creates long lines. One of the graduate students assisting with the preparation of this text tells of his Russian family spending five years on a waiting list for a new car. When their turn finally arrived, they bought the car from the state-owned dealer for 12,000 rubles, which was worth about 120 U.S. dollars at the time. While the ruble had been depreciating in value against the dollar so that rubles were worth only a fraction of their former dollar value, the car price was held fixed by the state. Since price was not being used to ration cars, the state did not feel a need to raise prices but, instead, allowed people to wait long periods of time for a new car. Price reform allows money price to serve the rationing function so that waiting in line is no longer needed. Speaking of price reform in Bulgaria, the Bulgarian National Bank's chief economist said, "One no longer has to get up at four or five A.M. to line up for bread and milk. Items that in the past might not even be available when one finally reached the counter now are available, but at ten times higher prices." This is a source of political conflict in taking an economy on the transition path from socialism to capitalism. People have to learn the new rules of the game, and the lessons are often quite harsh to those who have lived under socialism for decades.

5.a.3. Social Safety Net

Moving from socialism to capitalism will harm many people during the transition period as enterprises are closed and unemployment increases at the same time that prices of many goods and services rise. As a result, it is critical to have a program in place to provide a minimal standard of living for all citizens in order to avoid massive political unrest. Under socialism, the state provided for health care and took care of the disabled, aged, and unemployed. Moreover, many goods, such as housing and food, were heavily subsidized. Such widespread subsidies were inefficient because they were provided to everyone, even to those who could afford to pay higher prices. It is politically necessary that government subsidies continue, but they should be focused on the most needy groups. Over time, as more and more of the economy is privatized, government programs will have to be financed by explicit taxation of workers and firms. In other cases, user charges will be introduced, a phenomenon much less common under socialism.

The abandonment of socialism was due to populist sentiment in eastern Europe. The populations of these nations were tired of stagnant or declining standards of living and were ready for change. However, market-oriented economies operate in a democratic framework, and political unrest due to dissatisfaction with the operation of the economy can be demonstrated much more easily in a democratic setting than under the authoritarian rule of the centrally planned economy. A social safety net must be generous enough to buy time for the transition to capitalism to yield benefits for the majority of citizens. Otherwise, the movement toward capitalism may never survive the transition period.

5.b. Macroeconomic Issues

Good macroeconomic policy is aimed at providing steady income growth with low inflation. This is true whether we are talking about the United States, Japan, or Russia. Good macroeconomic policy, then, requires limited use of government budget deficits and tight control over monetary and credit growth. Although these features of good macroeconomic policy are universal, there are some macro issues that are unique to the transition from socialism to capitalism.

?

6. What macroeconomic issues are involved in the transition from socialism?

5.b.1. Monetary Policy Monetary policy in the transition economy must deal with issues not covered in the earlier monetary policy discussion of Chapter 14. When prices were strictly controlled in the earlier socialist regime, money could not be used to freely buy and sell goods as in market-oriented economies. As a result, the following special problems must be addressed as part of the transition from socialism to capitalism.

Monetary Overhang In many socialist countries, there is believed to be a substantial **monetary overhang,** which is the term used to describe the money that households have accumulated because there was nothing they could buy with it. With limited access to consumer goods, and with subsidized housing, food, and health care, the typical household had savings in the form of money building up over time that it would not have had if it had had access to more consumer goods.

> **monetary overhang:** the money accumulated by households because there was nothing available that they wanted to buy

The potential problem with a large monetary overhang is that inflation can result if goods become available and induce spending of the saved funds. How can the monetary overhang be eliminated? One way is for the state to decontrol prices suddenly and have prices rise sharply, thereby decreasing the purchasing power of the money held by households. The state basically imposes its own inflation tax on the purchasing power of the monetary overhang early in the transition period rather than let the households create their own inflation later in the transition period. Of course, it is critical that the one-time inflation not turn into a prolonged inflation if the economy is to enjoy long-term prosperity. Unfortunately, the early record suggests that high inflation has been difficult to reduce once it has been allowed to emerge.

An alternative way of reducing the monetary overhang is to privatize—that is, to sell state-owned property (like houses or land) to private households. Another alternative is to allow greater access to Western consumer goods so that households spend their excess money balances on such goods. Yet another alternative is to allow interest rates on household savings accounts to rise so that households willingly hold on to their accumulated money because of the higher interest they will earn.

> *During the transition from socialism, monetary policy should be aimed at achieving a low and stable inflation rate.*

Beyond the issue of monetary overhang, monetary policy will be primarily aimed at controlling inflation during the transition to capitalism. The early lesson of successful transition was that without low inflation, it is impossible to have the growth of saving and investment required for sustainable growth of GDP. By maintaining a steady and low rate of inflation, a nation will also realize stable exchange rates, which will contribute to its speedy integration into trade with the rest of the world.

Currency Convertibility Closely related to the issue of foreign trade and exchange rates is **currency convertibility.** The currency of the country must be freely convertible into other currencies if domestic prices are to be linked to (and disciplined by) foreign markets. One cannot compare the cost of a tractor in Romania with that of a tractor in Germany if the currency of Romania cannot be freely traded for the currency of Germany at a market-determined exchange rate.

> **currency convertibility:** the ease with which the domestic currency can be converted into foreign currency so that foreign exchange rates can properly reflect the domestic currency value of foreign prices

Socialist countries traditionally did not permit free exchange of their currencies for other currencies. Government controls on foreign exchange trading allowed the government to fix an official exchange rate value of the domestic currency that was often far from the true market value. As a result, international prices were unable to serve their purpose of increasing production of the goods that a country could produce relatively cheaply and increasing imports of those goods that could be produced more cheaply in the rest of the world. For instance, if the true value of Soviet rubles relative to the U.S. dollar was 30 rubles per dollar, yet the official exchange rate set by the Soviet Union was 3 rubles per dollar, then the ruble was officially overvalued. Suppose a computer monitor produced in the United States sold for $200. At the official exchange rate, the monitor was worth 600 rubles ($200 at 3 rubles per dollar). At the true market value of the currencies, the monitor was worth 6,000 rubles ($200 at 30 rubles per dollar). Since Soviet citizens were unable to buy foreign goods (all foreign trade was in the hands of the state), the official exchange rate was largely irrelevant. However, the absence of free trading in a ruble that was convertible into dollars meant that there was no way to identify which goods the Soviet Union could produce more cheaply than other nations. The absence of such relative cost information made specialization according to comparative advantage a difficult task. If a country cannot determine which goods it can produce more cheaply than others, it will not know which goods it should specialize in.

Under socialism, with central planning of production, the absence of relative price information was not as critical a problem as it is with capitalism. When private decision makers must decide which goods to produce, they must rely on relative prices to guide them. In international trade, this requires a currency that is convertible into other currencies at market-determined exchange rates.

Money and Credit   In industrial countries with well-developed financial markets, monetary policy is often aimed at changing interest rates in order to change aggregate demand. For instance, when the monetary authorities are concerned that inflation is a problem, money growth is slowed and interest rates tend to rise. The higher interest rates reduce investment and consumption spending and lower (or at least slow the growth of) aggregate demand, or total spending in the economy. In a socialist system that is just beginning the transformation toward capitalism, financial markets are generally undeveloped, since under socialism the state regulated interest rates and limited the saving and borrowing opportunities for citizens. Changes in the money supply may have little or no effect on interest rates. Therefore, the role of monetary policy in terms of money growth rates should be to maintain a low and steady rate of inflation. Any other effects of money growth on the economy are likely to be of secondary importance until further development of the economy occurs.

Under socialism, credit was often extended to enterprises on the basis of political connections or central planner preferences. A market economy requires that credit occur on the basis of productive potential. Firms that offer good prospects of earning a sufficient profit to repay debts should receive greater access to credit than firms that have little hope of competing profitably. The move toward a market economy must include the development of financial institutions like banks that are able to efficiently evaluate creditworthiness and allocate credit accordingly. The experience so far indicates that the development of the banking system requires a low and stable inflation rate. High inflation and uncertainty about future macroeconomic policy make it difficult for banks to evaluate the likely profitability of a firm and discourage lenders (as well as depositors) from committing funds for long periods.

The operation of an efficient and competitive financial system is aided by opening the economy to foreign financial institutions. In addition, a strict system of regulations and examinations applied to financial institutions will ensure that they operate in a prudent and safe manner.

5.b.2. Fiscal Policy   Reform of fiscal policy involves reducing government subsidies and reforming tax policy to avoid large budget deficits. Socialist countries have been characterized by subsidies to enterprises that produced a value of output less than the costs of production. Under a market system, firms that cannot operate at a profit should not be allowed to exist forever by continued subsidies from the government. It is for this reason that, as noted earlier, a safety net is necessary, since lower subsidies lead to transitional unemployment.

A socialist government does not rely on explicit or direct taxes on the public, since the state controls prices, wages, and production. By paying workers less than the value of their output, the state can extract the revenue needed to operate the government, so the workers pay an implicit tax. However, once private ownership and free markets have replaced central planning, the activities of government must be financed by explicit taxes. Reforming countries must implement income, value-added, and profit taxes to produce revenue for the remaining functions of government. Again, the goal should be to match government revenue and expenditures as closely as possible to avoid a large budget deficit.

The experience of transition economies in terms of implementing successful fiscal policies is quite mixed. The evidence so far suggests that those countries that have had major political changes have had opportunities to take more aggressive steps in establishing sound fiscal policies than the economies in which many of the remnants of the old socialist regime still linger. If major sectors of the economy are still dependent on government subsidies, or influential politicians cling to their power by offering support to old, inefficient enterprises, then fiscal deficit reduction will be much more difficult than in an environment where the population has clearly rejected the old ways along with the old politicians.

One problem that seems pervasive in the transition economy is collecting taxes. The largest of the old state-owned enterprises typically provided the largest amounts of tax revenue for the government. In many cases, these are now declining sectors of the economy and contribute less and less tax revenue. The newly emerging private sector, which should experience the fastest growth, is where tax collection has proved difficult. The problems include political pressures to provide tax exemptions or even ignore evasion of legally required taxes.

5.c. The Sequencing of Reforms

Considering all of the reforms necessary in the transition from socialism to capitalism, how should a country proceed? Are some measures needed before others can be undertaken? How rapidly should the changes be introduced? There are no certain answers to these questions, and there is an ongoing debate regarding the proper order of the reforms.

Some economists argue that all reforms should be undertaken simultaneously (or as nearly so as possible). Most tend to agree that macroeconomic stabilization is necessary for any serious conversion of the economy to a market system. Inflation must be stabilized at a reasonably low and steady rate, and the fiscal deficit must be brought to a level low enough to support a noninflationary monetary policy (so that the monetary authorities are not creating money to fund the budget deficit). Included in the macroeconomic stabilization is the development of a convertible currency.

Following the macroeconomic reform, micro reforms like privatization may proceed, along with the opening of the economy to foreign trade and competition. Then the foreign prices will guide the deregulation of industry in setting appropriate prices for domestic products. It is generally thought that the micro reforms are intertwined and support one another. In this case, they should be carried out simultaneously. Otherwise, each element will tend to be less effective than it otherwise would be. For instance, privately owned firms need deregulated prices and wages to respond to changing relative prices and produce what consumers want.

1. The transition from socialism to capitalism requires that state-owned enterprises be privatized.

2. A market system requires that prices fluctuate freely to allow producers and consumers to make efficient production and consumption decisions.

3. Since the transition from socialism will create unemployment and lower incomes for many, the government must provide a social safety net.

4. Since households could not buy all of the consumer goods they wanted, socialist economies often had a monetary overhang of excess money holdings.

5. The convertibility of the domestic currency into foreign currencies is necessary to link the domestic country with prices in the rest of the world.

6. The transition economy will aim monetary policy at the creation of a low and stable rate of inflation.

7. Credit must be available to firms on the basis of potential profitability rather than political relationships in order to increase productivity.

8. Fiscal policy should be reformed to reduce subsidies from government to firms and also to collect explicit taxes.

9. Macroeconomic reform must provide a stable, low-inflation environment for microeconomic reform to succeed.

10. Since microeconomic reforms tend to reinforce one another, they should generally be carried out simultaneously.

Summary

❓ How is poverty measured?

1. Poverty usually is defined in an absolute sense as the minimum income needed to purchase a minimal standard of living and is measured by per capita GNP or GDP. *§1.a*

2. Some economists and social scientists use a quality-of-life index to evaluate standards of living. *§1.b*

❓ Why are some countries poorer than others?

3. Both political obstacles (lack of skilled officials, instability, corruption, constraints imposed by special interest groups) and social obstacles (cultural attitudes that discourage entrepreneurial activity and encourage rapid population growth) limit economic growth in developing countries. *§2.a, 2.b*

❓ What strategies can a nation use to increase its economic growth?

4. Inward-oriented development strategies focus on developing a domestic manufacturing sector to produce goods that can substitute for imported manufactured goods. *§3.a*

5. Outward-oriented development strategies focus on producing manufactured goods for export. *§3.b*

6. The growth rates of outward-oriented economies are significantly higher than those of inward-oriented economies. *§3.c*

❓ How are savings in one nation used to speed development in other nations?

7. Private sources of foreign savings include direct investment, portfolio investment, commercial bank loans, and trade credit. *§4.a*

8. Foreign investment in developing countries can increase their economic growth by creating jobs, transferring modern technology, and stimulating exports to increase foreign exchange earnings. *§4.b*

9. Official gifts or low-cost loans made to developing countries by official sources are called foreign aid. *§4.c*

10. Foreign aid can be distributed bilaterally or multilaterally. *§4.c*

❓ What microeconomic issues are involved in the transition from socialism?

11. The move toward capitalism requires that state-owned enterprises be privatized. *§5.a*

12. Prices and incomes must be freed from state control if markets are to work efficiently. *§5.a.2*

13. Since many workers may be unemployed and incomes may fall during the transition, there must be a social safety net provided by the government. *§5.a.3*

❓ What macroeconomic issues are involved in the transition from socialism?

14. There may be a substantial monetary overhang as a result of limited opportunities to exchange money for goods under socialism. *§5.b.1*

15. Exchange rates can link economies together, but the currency must be freely convertible into other currencies if exchange rates are to indicate accurate price information. *§5.b.1*

16. Monetary policy should be aimed at providing a low and steady rate of inflation. *§5.b.1*

17. Credit must be allocated on the basis of productivity and profitability rather than political connections. *§5.b.1*

18. Fiscal policy must avoid large deficits and must raise explicit taxes. *§5.b.2*

19. Macroeconomic stabilization is generally necessary before microeconomic reforms are implemented. *§5.c*

Key Terms

expropriation *§2.a.2*

primary product *§3.a*

import substitution *§3.a*

export substitution *§3.b*

terms of trade *§3.c*

dual economy *§3.c*

foreign direct investment *§4.a*

portfolio investment *§4.a*

commercial bank loan *§4.a*

trade credit *§4.a*

foreign aid *§4.c*

bilateral aid *§4.c*

multilateral aid *§4.c*

privatize *§5.a*

monetary overhang *§5.b.1*

currency convertibility *§5.b.1*

Exercises

1. What are basic human needs? Can you list additional needs besides those considered in the chapter?

2. Per capita GNP or GDP is used as an absolute measure of poverty.
   a. What are some criticisms of using per capita GNP as a measure of standard of living?
   b. Do any of these criticisms also apply to a quality-of-life index?

3. In many developing countries there are economists and politicians who were educated in industrial countries. These individuals know the policies that would maximize the growth of their countries, but they do not implement them. Why not?

4. Suppose you are a benevolent dictator who can impose any policy you choose in your country. If

your goal is to accelerate economic development, how would you respond to the following problems?

a. Foreign firms are afraid to invest in your country because your predecessor expropriated many foreign-owned factories.

b. There are few entrepreneurs in the country.

c. The dominant domestic religion teaches that the accumulation of wealth is sinful.

d. It is customary for families to have at least six children.

5. What effect does population growth have on economic development?

6. Why have most developing countries followed inward-oriented development strategies?

7. Why is an outward-oriented development strategy likely to allocate resources more efficiently than an inward-oriented strategy?

8. Who benefits from an import-substitution strategy? Who is harmed?

9. If poverty is a relative concept, why don't we define it in relative terms?

10. "The poor will always be with us." Does this statement have different meanings depending on whether poverty is interpreted as an absolute or relative concept?

11. How do traditional societies answer the questions What to produce? How to produce? and For whom to produce?

12. What are the most important sources of foreign savings for developing countries? Why don't developing countries save more so that they don't have to rely on foreign savings for investment?

13. Private foreign investment and foreign aid are sources of savings to developing countries. Yet each has been controversial at times. What are the potential negative effects of private foreign investment and foreign aid for developing countries?

14. Why do immigrants often play an important role in developing the economies of poor nations?

15. How does a nation go about instituting a policy of import substitution? What is a likely result of such a policy?

16. Discuss the alternative ways in which state-owned enterprises can be privatized.

17. One problem associated with the transition from socialism to capitalism is deregulating prices of goods and services. How can government officials find the appropriate prices to use when ending the government regulation of prices?

18. What is monetary overhang, and how can government eliminate it?

19. Suppose the official exchange rate is set by the government at 10 rubles per dollar. If the government does not allow its citizens to freely trade rubles for dollars, what is the use of such an exchange rate? How would currency convertibility change things?

20. What is the proper role of monetary policy during the transition from socialism to capitalism?

21. Is there any particular order in which the reforms needed in the transition from socialism to capitalism should occur? If so, discuss why.

22. The social safety net necessary for easing the transition from socialism will require the government to continue many of its health and public welfare policies to protect the unemployed and avoid social and political unrest that threatens the transition. In what sense does the social safety net program also hinder the movement toward a market-based economy?

23. What is the proper role of fiscal policy during the transition from socialism to capitalism?

Take the ACE Practice Test for this chapter to review the important concepts and get immediate feedback with answers.

economics.college.hmco.com/students

Food Aid

1. More than 800 million people worldwide do not have enough food.

2. Every day, 29,000 children die from causes related to poverty and malnutrition.

3. Thirteen million people in six Southern African countries will need food aid over the next nine months. CARE is delivering food for hundreds of thousands of people and helping communities improve their prospects beyond the crisis.

4. In 2001, CARE provided food for more than 8 million people in 13 countries through Global Food for Education and food-for-work programs.

5. CARE's Kabul Widows Emergency Feeding Project assists in feeding more than 10,000 widows and their children in Afghanistan—60,000 people in all.

6. There is more than enough food produced in the world for everyone. Yet due to poverty, natural disasters, and lack of transportation and proper tools, malnutrition and hunger still afflict one out of every seven people on earth.

Source: www.careusa.org/getinvolved/advocacy/agenda/food/foodfacts.asp.

Commentary

The six statements regarding food aid indicate that hunger is a serious global problem. Yet simply delivering free food to countries suffering from famine may not be the best solution.

Famines do not necessarily imply a shortage of food. Instead, famines sometimes represent shortfalls in the purchasing power of the poorest sectors of society. In many cases, grants of income are a better means of alleviating famines than grants of food.

We can understand this argument using demand and supply analysis. In the following two diagrams we represent the demand for food and the supply of food in a famine-stricken country that is receiving aid. In each diagram, the demand curve D_1 intersects the supply curve S_1 at an equilibrium quantity of food Q_1, which represents a subsistence level of food consumption. The equilibrium depicted in each graph is one in which, in the absence of aid, a famine would occur.

The first graph illustrates the effects of providing aid in the form of food. The food aid increases the available supply of food, which is shown by an out-ward shift of the supply curve to S_2. The effect of this aid is to increase the equilibrium quantity of food (Q_2) and lower the equilibrium price (P_2). The lower price of food will adversely affect the income of domestic producers. Domestic producers will thus attempt to grow other crops or to search for sources of income other than growing food if they cannot receive enough money for their produce. As the amount of domestic food production falls, a country becomes more dependent on imports of food.

The second graph illustrates the effect of income aid for the famine-stricken country. The aid is depicted by a shift in the demand curve to D_2. As with food aid, this relief allows consumption to rise to a point above the subsistence level. The effects of this aid on domestic food producers, however, are quite different. The price of food rises, and thus domestic food producers are not hurt by the aid package. As a result, aid in the form of income does not cause disincentives for production. An increase in domestic food production also serves to make a country less dependent on food imports.

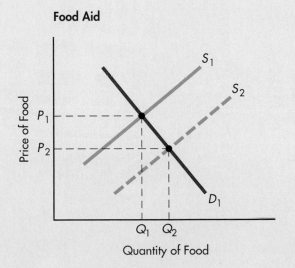

Food Aid

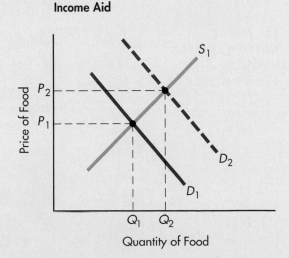

Income Aid

CHAPTER 19

Globalization

? Fundamental Questions

1. What is globalization?

2. What are the arguments against globalization?

3. What are the arguments in support of globalization?

4. How has globalization affected economic growth and poverty?

5. Can recent financial crises be linked to globalization?

In every chapter we have discussed the international aspects of the topics covered. However, we have not yet considered the implications of closer links between economies internationally. The so-called *globalization* of the world's economies has become an issue that is rich in controversy. Thousands have gathered to protest globalization in Washington, D.C. and Seattle in the United States; in Johannesburg, South Africa; in Davos, Switzerland; and in many other places. This chapter will provide an introduction to the potential costs and benefits of globalization and offer an analysis of the historical record regarding the effects of globalization.

It is important to recognize that the debate over globalization continues and involves political and social, as well as economic dimensions. Intelligent people disagree about the impact of globalization on rich as well as poor countries. The reader should keep in mind that the issue is unsettled and much can change in the coming years. ◾

1. The Meaning of Globalization

Globalization is characterized by an increased cross-border flow of trade in goods, services, and financial assets, along with an increased international mobility of technology, information, and individuals. As globalization progresses, countries become less isolated, so that we can think more in terms of a global economy and its implications for individuals and nations.

1.a. Globalization Is neither New nor Widespread

Globalization is not new. The forces that drive globalization have existed as long as humans have been around. Everyone has a natural desire to improve his or her well-being, so interest in trade has always existed. As we learned in earlier chapters, trade based on comparative advantage raises living standards. Even primitive societies engaged in trade so that their living standards would be higher than would otherwise have been possible. As circumstances permitted a greater range of travel, trade with more remote regions became possible. International trade is not a new phenomenon. World trade as a fraction of world GDP was about the same at the end of the nineteenth century as it is today. However, between World War I and World War II, the value of international trade plummeted. Then, in the postwar era, international trade rose substantially. Thus, the view that the growth of world trade is something new is true only in the shortsighted view of the world since the 1950s.

Globalization is not yet a truly global phenomenon. Some countries have remained largely closed to the rest of the world. These are mostly the world's poorest countries. If a government follows policies that work against economic integration with other countries, international trade and investment will not materialize.

The movement of people across international borders is greatly limited by government policies. There was much more immigration in the nineteenth and early twentieth centuries than there is in the present day. Barriers to immigration are high today, and workers generally cannot move freely from country to country. This was

Economic and political isolation is a sure recipe for poverty. This photo of the border fence separating North and South Korea is indicative of the isolation of the North Korean economy.

not always the case. In 1900, 14 percent of the U.S. population was born in a foreign country. Today that number is 8 percent. However, there are some multinational agreements that permit international movements of workers. An important example is the European Union (EU). Within the EU, there is free mobility of labor. Of course, this does not mean that there are widespread relocations of workers from, say, Germany to Italy. Family, language, and customs tie people to particular areas, so that the fact that people have the right to move does not mean that large numbers of them will actually do so. This is analogous to workers in the United States, who have the right to move anywhere in the country, but many of whom choose to stay in a particular area because they have personal ties to the area.

1.b. The Role of Technological Change

The pace of globalization has been driven by technological change. International trade and movement of people are facilitated by falling transportation costs. It is estimated that the real cost of ocean freight transport fell by 70 percent between 1920 and 1990.

International communication is enhanced by reductions in the cost of communications. Measured in 2000 U.S. dollars, a 3-minute telephone call from New York to London cost $60.42 in 1960 and $.40 in 2000. The reduction in communication costs has made possible global interactions that were at best a dream just a few decades ago.

The development of fast, modern computers allows information to be processed at speeds that were unimaginable just a generation ago. As a result, technology is shared more efficiently, so that management of business operations can extend more easily to far-flung locations, and complex transactions can be completed in a fraction of the time that was once required. Technological progress in the computer industry is truly amazing. A computer that would sell for $1,000 today would have cost $1,869,004 in 1960.

The fact that globalization has progressed at an uneven rate over time is due to the uneven pace of technological change, in addition to important events, such as war, that disrupt relationships among nations.

1.c. Measuring Globalization

There are many alternatives for measuring how globalized the world and individual nations are. One useful ranking is provided by *Foreign Policy* magazine. It ranks countries in terms of four broad categories:

- *Political engagement:* number of memberships in international organizations, U.N. Security Council missions in which the country participates, and foreign embassies that the country hosts
- *Technology:* number of Internet users, Internet hosts, and secure servers
- *Personal contact:* international travel and tourism, international telephone traffic, and cross-border income transfers
- *Economic integration:* international trade, foreign direct investment and portfolio capital flows, and income payments and receipts

Table 1 shows the *Foreign Policy* rankings for several countries. Note that the rankings for economic integration tend to penalize countries with a large domestic market, like the United States, Russia, and Japan. For these countries, international trade is a relatively small fraction of GDP. Note also that poor countries tend to rank low in terms of personal contact and technology. These countries have few foreign workers and relatively low amounts of international telephone use. They also have

TABLE 1

Globalization Rankings

Country	Overall Rank	Economic Integration	Personal Contact	Political Engagement	Technology
Ireland	1	1	1	22	17
Switzerland	2	5	2	49	7
Sweden	3	2	9	5	5
Singapore	4	4	3	53	6
Netherlands	5	3	6	28	10
Canada	7	17	7	6	3
United Kingdom	9	10	10	4	11
United States	11	50	33	2	1
France	12	12	17	1	21
Portugal	14	15	12	34	19
New Zealand	16	28	14	46	8
Germany	17	22	22	9	14
Malaysia	18	8	24	32	23
Israel	19	32	8	58	20
Spain	20	18	23	21	24
Australia	21	33	38	39	3
Italy	24	36	27	8	22
Greece	26	41	15	30	28
Korea, Rep.	28	40	42	33	15
Poland	32	43	29	16	30
Taiwan	34	29	30	62	17
Japan	35	56	52	26	12
South Africa	38	20	50	40	33
Senegal	41	39	36	31	52
Russian Federation	45	51	54	3	43
Argentina	48	53	57	13	32
Mexico	49	37	44	48	39
Pakistan	50	60	37	18	56
China	51	45	62	11	45
Philippines	52	26	56	51	46
Turkey	53	38	58	35	41
Bangladesh	54	62	39	24	59
India	56	61	49	14	54
Saudi Arabia	61	54	48	52	50

Source: Data are drawn from the *Foreign Policy* magazine website, www.foreignpolicy.com/issue_janfeb_2003/.

relatively low levels of Internet use, as a large segment of the population does not have access to computers or the training to use computers in daily life.

The more globalized an economy, the greater its links with the rest of the world. The aftermath of the terrorist attacks in the United States on September 11, 2001, showed how measures of globalization may be affected by important events. World trade fell after the attacks, as did global foreign direct investment. International travel and tourism dropped in 2002 for the first time since 1945. However, political engagement increased as a result of multinational efforts aimed at combating terrorism. The number of countries participating in U.N. peacekeeping missions increased. The volume of international telephone calls increased substantially. The increase in telephone use may partly be due to the drop in international travel. If people choose not to travel for personal or business reasons because of safety concerns, they may be more likely to have telephone conversations with the parties they otherwise would have visited in person. In addition, the number of Internet users grew 22 percent in 2002, with China alone adding 11 million new users. So major events like the terrorist attacks of September 2001 may suppress some measures of globalization while increasing others. This serves as a good reminder to take a broad view when measuring globalization rather than narrowly focusing on one or two measures.

RECAP

1. Globalization is characterized by an increased flow of trade in goods, services, and financial assets across national borders, along with increased international mobility of technology, information, and individuals.
2. The process of globalization is not new, but it accelerated after World War II.
3. Technological advance plays an important role in determining the pace of globalization.
4. Measuring globalization involves measurement of the international movements of goods, services, financial assets, people, ideas, and technology.

2. Globalization Controversy

Globalization has stimulated much controversy in recent years. Massive demonstrations have been held to coincide with meetings of the World Trade Organization (WTO), the International Monetary Fund (IMF), the World Bank, and other gatherings of government and business leaders dealing with the process of developing international trade and investment. Each side sees globalization in a very different light. On the one hand are the critics of globalization, who believe that free international trade in goods and financial assets does more harm than good. On the other hand are the supporters of free international trade, who believe that globalization holds the key to increasing the living standards of all the world's people. We will review the arguments on both sides.

2.a. Arguments Against Globalization

?

2. What are the arguments against globalization?

Critics view globalization as a vehicle for enriching corporate elites, to the detriment of poor people and the environment. In this view, the major international organizations are tools of corporations whose aim is to increase corporate profits at the

The World Trade Organization

The World Trade Organization (WTO) is an international organization with 146 member countries, established in 1995 and headquartered in Geneva, Switzerland. The job of the WTO is to provide a venue for negotiating international trade agreements and then to enforce these global rules of international trade. The WTO trade agreements are negotiated and signed by a large majority of the world's nations. These agreements are contracts for the proper conduct of international trade. An important role of the WTO is the settlement of trade disputes between countries. An example of such a dispute involved bananas and the European Union (EU). The EU restricted banana imports to bananas from only a few countries that were former European colonies. As a result, the price paid for bananas in European markets was about twice the price of bananas in the United States. The world's largest banana companies, Dole, Chiquita, and Del Monte, headquartered in the United States, complained that they were being harmed because their bananas,

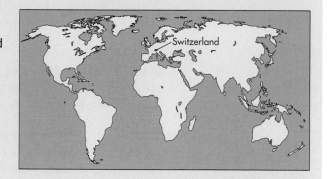

which came from other countries of Central and South America, were excluded from the EU system, which favored a few former colonies. The WTO ruled that the EU restrictions on banana imports were harmful and against the rules of trade to which all nations had agreed. This is but one example of the role of the WTO in promoting fair and free international trade.

expense of people and the environment. Rather than being a democratic system in which the majority of people are involved in economic decision making, globalization is seen by critics as a force that reduces the influence of people at the local level, with power being taken by the global elites, represented by rich corporations and their government supporters. A few specific criticisms associated with the antiglobalization movement follow.

2.a.1. "Fair," Not "Free," Trade   Critics argue that free trade agreements put people out of jobs. When goods are produced by the lowest-cost producer, people working in that industry in less competitive countries will no longer be employed. If foreign competition were limited, then these jobs would be saved. In addition, free trade may encourage governments to participate in a **"race to the bottom,"** with environmental safeguards and workers' rights being ignored in order to attract the investment and jobs that come from a concentration of production based upon comparative advantage. International trade agreements are seen as roadblocks to democratic decision making at the local level, as they transfer power away from local authorities to multinational authorities.

"race to the bottom": with globalization, countries compete for international investment by offering low or no environmental regulations or labor standards

2.a.2. International Organizations Serve Only the Interests of Corporations   An example of this argument is the assertion that the World Trade Organization, or WTO, is a tool of corporations, and that international trade agreements negotiated and enforced through the WTO are used to generate corporate profits against the interests of the citizens of the world. The Global Business Insight "The World Trade Organization" provides background information on the nature of the organization and its duties. International organizations like the WTO are used as platforms for instituting rules for international trade. Thus, an individual who is against free international trade would also be critical of organizations whose aim is the promotion of free trade. The WTO, the IMF, and the World Bank are viewed as undemocratic organizations that have assumed powers over economic decision making that rightly belong to local authorities.

2.a.3. Globalization Occurs at the Cost of Environmental Quality
As stated earlier, critics of globalization fear a "race to the bottom," in which governments block costly regulations related to environmental quality in order to provide a cheaper location for large global firms seeking manufacturing facilities. If the rich countries impose costly regulations on manufacturers, then these firms will shift production to poor countries that are willing to trade environmental degradation for jobs and higher money incomes. Related to this issue is World Bank financing for resource extraction projects, such as mining or oil and gas extraction. Such projects are seen as benefiting the corporations that receive contracts for work related to the projects, while environmental destruction is a little-considered by-product. World Bank funding for large dams is also seen as harmful, as these projects frequently involve the relocation of large numbers of poor people who lose what modest living arrangements they had.

2.a.4. Globalization Encourages Harmful Labor Practices
This argument is based upon a belief that multinational corporations will locate where wages are cheapest and workers' rights weakest. In these settings, on-the-job safety is ignored, and workers who are injured or ill are likely to be dismissed without any compensation. Furthermore, critics believe that globalization may result in the worst employment practices, such as child labor or prisoner labor. If such practices are allowed in poor countries, then the industrial countries will suffer follow-on effects as workers in rich countries lose their jobs to workers in countries where there are no regulations associated with worker protection, no minimum wages, and no retirement plans, and where employers must pay nothing more than the minimum necessary to attract an employee.

2.b. Arguments in Favor of Globalization

?

3. What are the arguments in support of globalization?

Globalization's supporters believe that free trade and international investment result in an increase in living standards in all countries. Of course, some individuals and firms are harmed by the globalization process. Those industries that exist in a country only as a result of protection from foreign competitors will suffer when that country's markets are opened to the rest of the world. Yet the few who suffer are small in number relative to the many who benefit from the advantages that globalization provides. This section will consider each of the criticisms mentioned in the prior section and present the alternative view of those who support globalization.

2.b.1. Free Trade Helps Developing Countries
As just discussed, opening markets to free trade will usually harm some individuals and firms. But supporters of globalization believe that the benefits of globalization for all consumers greatly outweigh the costs of providing a social safety net for those who lose their jobs as a result of opening markets to global competitors. Developing countries have much to gain from free trade. Restrictions on trade in the rich countries are often aimed at products that poor countries can produce most efficiently. For instance, textile imports are restricted by the United States, and this harms many developing countries that could

provide clothing and fabrics to the United States at a lower cost than U.S. producers can. The European Union restricts imports of agricultural products in order to increase the incomes of European farmers. If such restrictions were lifted, incomes in poor countries would rise substantially. Supporters of globalization believe that free trade agreements administered by the WTO can offer great benefits to the poor countries.

2.b.2. International Organizations Represent Governments and People
Globalization supporters argue that international organizations offer all countries a platform for expressing their dissatisfaction with economic and social conditions and provide a mechanism for change. Without organizations like the IMF, World Bank, United Nations, and WTO, there would be no opportunities for representatives of all nations to come together to discuss needed changes in the global economy. These organizations also provide for transfers of funds from rich to poor countries that would not occur in an ongoing manner in the absence of such organizations. International organizations are funded by governments, not corporations. Representatives of the government of each member nation participate in the decision making at each organization. This suggests that if international organizations have followed unwise policies, the most effective path to change would be putting political pressure on national governments to support policies that open markets for the goods of poor countries as well as rich countries.

2.b.3. The Connection Between Globalization and Environmental Harm Is Weak
Supporters of globalization argue that there is no evidence of a "race to the bottom" in which multinational firms move production to countries with lax environmental standards. Looking at the globalization rankings in Table 1, the countries at the top of the list have more stringent environmental regulations than do less open economies. Figure 1 plots the globalization rank against a ranking of environmental quality, where the environmental performance of a country is determined by its rankings in terms of the quality of its air and water, its protection of land, and its

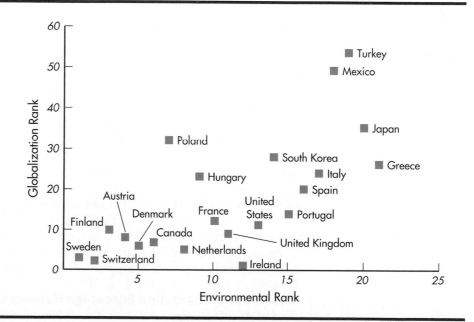

FIGURE 1

Globalization and Environmental Quality

Source: Globalization data are drawn from Foreign Policy *magazine website, www.foreignpolicy.com. Environmental quality rankings are the "Pilot Environmental Performance Index" from www.ciesin.columbia.edu/indicators/ESI.*

The high environmental quality in Sweden results in the leading city, Stockholm, being surrounded by water so clean that one can swim in it.

impact on climate change through carbon dioxide emissions. Only 21 countries have globalization rankings for which all environmental measures are available, and these are the countries illustrated in Figure 1. The lower the number for a country, the better its environmental ranking or the greater its globalization. The figure indicates that the more globalized the country, the better its environmental quality. For instance, Sweden is shown to have the highest ranking in terms of environmental quality, and it is the third most globalized economy. The scatter of the countries plotted in Figure 1 suggests that an upward-sloping line would represent the relationship between globalization and environmental quality well.

In addition, there are many cases of environmental degradation associated with countries that are closed to economic relations with the rest of the world. The former communist countries of eastern Europe had governments that displayed the greatest disregard of the environment of any group of nations in modern times. As these nations globalize as part of the transition away from socialism, they are attracting foreign direct investment from rich countries, which has transferred cleaner technology to eastern Europe and improved environmental quality.

One of the major assumptions made by critics of globalization is that multinational firms will locate production units in developing countries, employ local resources, and then sell the products in the rich countries. This may be typical of certain industries, such as the production of shoes or clothing. However, increasingly, multinational firms' production is aimed at supplying local markets. The U.S. Department of Commerce found that more than 60 percent of the production of U.S. firms' subsidiaries in developing countries was sold in the local market where the production occurred. One look at the global firms that have raced to invest in China indicates that the prospect of selling to the massive Chinese market is the attraction for much of the investment. In this setting, governments do not need to offer a lack of environmental standards in order to attract multinational firms.

2.b.4. Does Globalization Encourage Harmful Labor Practices?
Supporters of globalization argue that there is no evidence of a "race to the bottom" in labor

standards. In fact, multinational firms tend to pay higher wages than local firms and tend to provide greater benefits for workers than existed in the country prior to globalization. At a basic level, if a worker freely accepts employment, that worker must be better off than with the next best alternative. So even though wages in, for instance, Vietnam may be much lower than those in Western Europe or North America, this is not evidence of worker exploitation. The local wages across the Vietnamese economy are lower than those in, say, France or Canada. The workers who accept employment at a factory in Vietnam operated by a multinational firm prefer such work to working in agriculture at much lower wages. It is common to find long waiting lists of workers who want jobs at multinational firms' factories in developing countries. Rather than exploitation, this suggests that globalization is raising living standards and making people better off.

RECAP

1. Arguments against globalization include a concern that free trade is harmful to people, that international organizations serve only the interests of corporations, and that there is a "race to the bottom," with countries offering lax regulation of environmental quality and labor standards in order to offer multinational firms better opportunities for profit.

2. Supporters of globalization argue that trade based on comparative advantage raises living standards everywhere; that international organizations are funded by governments, not corporations, and provide a formal mechanism for all governments to be represented and to push for change; and that environmental quality and welfare of workers actually improve with globalization.

?

4. How has globalization affected economic growth and poverty?

Asian tigers: Hong Kong, Korea, Singapore, and Taiwan, countries that globalized in the 1960s and 1970s and experienced fast economic growth

NICs: newly industrialized countries

3. Globalization, Economic Growth, and Incomes

The increased integration of the world's economies has been associated with economic growth and reduction of poverty in most countries. The so-called **Asian tigers**—Hong Kong, Korea, Singapore, and Taiwan—underwent the process of opening their economies in the 1960s and 1970s and experienced rapid growth and dramatic increases in their living standards. Nowadays, these countries are sometimes referred to as "newly industrialized countries," or **NICs**. More recently several other countries have been through the globalization process since 1980. Figure 2 shows the NICs and the post-1980 globalizers. The 24 post-1980 globalizers are spread around the world. One World Bank study tracked the performance of all of these countries over time to measure how globalization has affected them.[1] The major conclusions of the study are:

- *Economic growth has increased with globalization.* Average growth of per capita GDP increased from 1.4 percent per year in the 1960s to 2.9 percent in

---

[1]David Dollar and Aart Kraay, "Trade, Growth, and Poverty," *World Bank Policy Research Department Working Paper No. 2615, 2001.* For additional evidence and discussion, see "Globalization: Threat or Opportunity," IMF Issues Brief, January 2002, and the references cited (available at www.imf.org/external/np/exr/ib/2000/041200.htm).

FIGURE 2

NICs and Post-1980 Globalizers

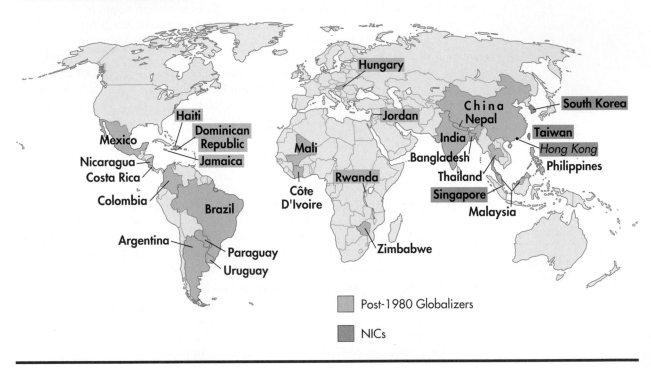

Post-1980 Globalizers

NICs

the 1970s to 3.5 percent in the 1980s to 5.0 percent in the 1990s. At the same time that these countries were increasing their growth rates, average annual per capita GDP growth in the rich countries fell from 4.7 percent in the 1960s to 2.2 percent in the 1990s. What makes this even more dramatic is the fact that nonglobalizing developing countries had average annual growth rates of only 1.4 percent during the 1990s.

■ *Income inequality has not increased.* The benefits of increased economic growth are widely shared in globalizing countries. An important exception to this finding is China, where income inequality has increased. However, government policies in China that resulted in moving to free markets from socialism while restricting internal migration may have played a much bigger role in causing changes in the Chinese income distribution than globalization did.

■ *The gap between rich countries and globalized developing countries has shrunk.* Some of the countries listed in Figure 2 were among the poorest countries in the world 25 years ago. The higher growth rates experienced by these countries have allowed them to gain ground on the rich countries.

■ *Poverty has been reduced.* The fraction of the very poor, those who live on less than $1 per day, declined in the newly globalized economies. For instance, between the 1980s and the 1990s, the fraction of the population living on less than $1 per day fell from 43 percent to 36 percent in Bangladesh, from 20 percent to 15 percent in China, and from 13 percent to 10 percent in Costa Rica.

The evidence from around the world indicates that the real losers in the globalization of the world economy are those countries that have not participated. They tend to be mired in a low-growth path, with enduring poverty and none of the benefits that globalization has conferred.

RECAP

1. Some studies have shown that globalization increases economic growth without increases in income inequality within nations.

2. Some studies have shown that globalization narrows the income gap between rich and poor nations and reduces poverty.

4. Financial Crises and Globalization

5. Can recent financial crises be linked to globalization?

The 1990s provided several dramatic episodes of financial crises in developing countries, in which investors in these countries were punished with substantial losses and local businesses also suffered. To understand the nature of the crises, we will first look at some data that illustrate the severity of the crises. Then we will analyze the reasons for the crises. It will be seen that globalization may have played a contributing role in these recent crises.

4.a. Crises of the 1990s

Table 2 provides summary data on some key economic indicators for countries that underwent severe crises. Crises occurred in Mexico in 1994–1995 and in Southeast

TABLE 2

Economic Conditions in Crisis Countries

Country	Short-Term External Debt/Reserves (year)	Bank Loans/GDP (year)	Stock Market Returns (%)	Exchange Rate
Mexico	230% (1993)	24% (1993)	−29%	3.88 (12/94); 6.71 (3/95)
Indonesia	226% (1996)	55% (1996)	−40%	2368 (1/97); 9743 (1/98)
Korea	300% (1996)	59% (1996)	−26%	850 (1/97); 1694 (1/98)
Malaysia	42% (1996)	93% (1996)	−57%	2.49 (1/97); 4.38 (1/98)
Philippines	126% (1996)	49% (1996)	−29%	26.3 (1/97); 42.7 (1/98)
Thailand	103% (1996)	99% (1996)	−30%	25.7 (1/97); 52.6 (1/98)

Note: Data on short-term debt/reserves and bank loans/GDP come from Steven B. Kamin, "The Current International Financial Crisis: How Much Is New?" *Journal of International Money & Finance,* August 1999. Stock market returns and exchange rates are drawn from Yahoo! Finance, yahoo.com. Stock market returns are calculated for the six-month period following the onset of the crisis in each country. Exchange rates are price of local currency per 1 U.S. dollar.

Asia—Indonesia, Korea, Malaysia, the Philippines, and Thailand—in 1997. The table shows that in the year prior to the crises, each of these countries except Malaysia owed substantial short-term debt to foreigners. Short-term debt is debt that is due in less than one year. The table lists short-term debt as a fraction of reserves. International reserves were discussed in Chapter 13, where it was stated that these are assets that countries hold that can be used to settle international payments. The primary international reserve asset is foreign currency, mainly U.S. dollars. So except for Malaysia, all the countries affected by these crises owed more short-term debt to foreigners than the value of their international reserves.

Table 2 also shows that bank loans were a sizable fraction of GDP in all the crisis countries except Mexico. This becomes a problem when business turns bad. If individuals and business firms have falling incomes, then they will be less able to repay their loans to banks. As a result, the banks are also in trouble, and the result may be an economic crisis.

In each country, the stock market dropped dramatically. This is seen in Table 2 as the percentage change in stock prices over the first 6 months following the onset of the crisis. Stock prices dropped by an amount ranging from 26 percent in Korea to 57 percent in Malaysia. Investors in each country lost huge amounts of wealth as a result of the rapid drop in the values of local firms.

Finally, Table 2 shows that the exchange rate against the U.S. dollar dropped substantially in each country. Exchange rates played a particularly large role in these financial crises and pointed out a vulnerability of small developing countries to globalization in terms of international capital flows.

4.b. Exchange Rates and Financial Crises

Each of the countries in Table 2 had a fixed exchange rate prior to the crisis period. Chapter 14 included a discussion of how central banks must intervene in the foreign exchange market to maintain a fixed exchange rate. Here we can apply the same analysis to understand how a fixed exchange rate may contribute to financial crises. Figure 3 illustrates the situation for Mexico. The demand in this figure is the demand for dollars arising out of the Mexican demand for U.S. goods, services, and financial assets. The supply is the supply of dollars arising out of the U.S. demand for Mexican goods, services, and financial assets. Initially, the equilibrium is located at point A, where the exchange rate is 4 pesos per dollar and $10 billion are traded for pesos each day. If there is concern that Mexican financial assets will fall in value, then investors will start to sell peso-denominated assets and will then sell their pesos for dollars in order to buy dollar-denominated assets. This shifts the demand curve for dollars from D_1 to D_2. The new equilibrium would then be at point B, with a depreciated peso exchange rate of 6 pesos per dollar and $15 billion per day being traded. To maintain a fixed exchange rate of 4 pesos per dollar and keep the private traders from shifting the equilibrium to point B, the central bank (Banco de Mexico) must intervene in the foreign exchange market by selling dollars equal to the private market demand for dollars in excess of the amount that would yield equilibrium at point A. In the figure, we see that the new equilibrium with central bank intervention is at point C, where the central bank is selling $10 billion per day ($20 − $10 billion) in order to maintain the exchange rate at 4 pesos per dollar.

If the shift in private investors' demand from D_1 to D_2 is not a temporary phenomenon, then there is a problem for the Banco de Mexico: It has a limited supply of international reserves, including U.S. dollars. The intervention to support the fixed exchange rate involves selling dollars and buying pesos. Eventually it will

FIGURE 3

Foreign Exchange Market Intervention with a Fixed Exchange Rate

The demand is the demand for dollars arising out of the Mexican demand for U.S. goods, services, and financial assets. The supply is the supply of dollars arising out of the U.S. demand for Mexican goods, services, and financial assets. Initially, the equilibrium is located at point A, where the exchange rate is 4 pesos per dollar and $10 billion are traded for pesos each day. If there is concern that Mexican financial assets will fall in value, then investors will start to sell peso-denominated assets and then will sell their pesos for dollars in order to buy dollar-denominated assets. This shifts the demand curve for dollars from D_1 to D_2. The new equilibrium would then be at point B, with a depreciated peso exchange rate of 6 pesos per dollar and $15 billion per day being traded. To maintain a fixed exchange rate of 4 pesos per dollar and avoid private traders' shifting the equilibrium to point B, the central bank (Banco de Mexico) must intervene in the foreign exchange market, selling dollars equal to the private market demand for dollars in excess of the amount that would yield an equilibrium at point A. In the figure, we see that the new equilibrium with central bank intervention is at point C, where the central bank is selling $10 billion per day ($20 − $10 billion) in order to maintain the exchange rate at 4 pesos per dollar.

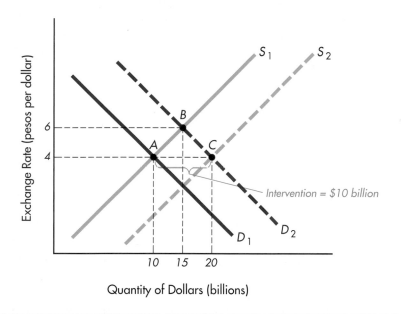

Quantity of Dollars (billions)

---

exhaust its supply of dollars, and it will then be forced to devalue the currency, letting the exchange rate adjust to the free market equilibrium of 6 pesos per dollar. Once speculators realize that the central bank is losing a substantial fraction of its international reserves, a **speculative attack** occurs. This is the term given to a situation in which private speculators start selling even more pesos for dollars, expecting that the central bank will be forced to devalue the currency. If a speculator sells pesos and buys dollars for a price of 4 pesos per dollar, and then the peso is devalued to 6 pesos per dollar, that speculator can turn around and sell the dollars for pesos, receiving $6 - 4 = 2$ pesos in profit for each dollar invested in the speculative activity. Of course, once the speculative attack occurs, the demand for dollars shifts out even further, and the central bank will have to spend even more of its international reserves to defend the fixed exchange rate.

speculative attack: a situation in which private investors sell domestic currency and buy foreign currency, betting that the domestic currency will be devalued

Each of the recent international financial crises has involved a fixed exchange rate. In each case, once it became clear that the domestic currency was overvalued relative to its true free market value, speculative attacks occurred and the central bank lost a sizable amount of its international reserves. With floating or flexible exchange rates, the exchange rate changes every day with the free market forces of supply and demand, so that countries are not forced to intervene and spend their international reserves to maintain a fixed exchange rate. In this situation, a speculative attack cannot occur.

Once the currency has been devalued, it is common for some local business firms to be driven into bankruptcy as a result of the effect of the devaluation on the value of their debt. This is because much borrowing is done in U.S. dollars. In Thailand, for instance, prior to the crisis of 1997, the Thai government had repeatedly stated that there was no way it would ever change the fixed exchange rate. Business firms, believing that the exchange rate between the Thai baht and the U.S. dollar would not change, borrowed in U.S. dollars, expecting that the dollars they borrowed and the dollars they would have to repay would be worth the same amount of baht. Imagine a firm that had a debt of $1 million. Prior to the financial crisis that started in the summer of 1997, the exchange rate was about 25 baht to 1 U.S. dollar. At this exchange rate, it would cost 25 million baht to repay $1 million. By January 1998, the exchange rate was about 52 baht per dollar. So the firm would find that the baht price of repaying $1 million had risen to 52 million baht. The cost of repaying the dollar loan had more than doubled as a result of the currency devaluation. Because of such exchange rate changes, the financial crises of the 1990s had devastating effects on local businesses in each country. As business firms in these countries lost value, foreign investors who had invested in these firms also suffered large losses. The 1990s financial crises imposed huge costs on the global economy.

4.c. What Caused the Crises?

The prior section showed how a fixed exchange rate could contribute to a crisis. The crises of the 1990s taught economists some lessons regarding exchange rates and other factors that increased the vulnerability of countries to crises. Considerable resources have been devoted to understanding the nature and causes of financial crises in hopes of avoiding future crises and forecasting those crises that do occur. Forecasting is always difficult in economics, and it is safe to say that there will always be surprises that no economic forecaster anticipates. Yet there are certain variables that are so obviously related to past crises that they may serve as warning indicators of potential future crises. The list includes the following:

- *Fixed exchange rates.* All of the countries involved in recent crises, including Mexico in 1993–1994, the southeast Asian countries in 1997, and Argentina in 2002, utilized fixed exchange rates prior to the onset of the crisis. Generally, these countries' macroeconomic policies were inconsistent with the maintenance of the fixed exchange rate, and when large devaluations ultimately occurred, domestic residents holding loans denominated in foreign currency suffered huge losses.

- *Falling international reserves.* The maintenance of fixed exchange rates may be no problem. One way to tell if the exchange rate is no longer an equilibrium rate is to monitor the country's international reserve holdings (largely the foreign currency held by the central bank and the treasury). If the stock of international reserves is falling steadily over time, that is a good indicator that the fixed-exchange-rate regime is under pressure and that there is likely to be a devaluation.

- *Lack of transparency.* Many crisis countries suffer from a lack of transparency in government activities and a lack of public disclosure of business conditions. Investors need to know the financial situation of firms in order to make informed investment decisions. If accounting rules allow firms to hide the financial impact of actions that would harm investors, then investors may not be able to adequately judge when the risk of investing in a firm rises. In such cases, a financial crisis may come as a surprise to all but the insiders in a troubled firm. Similarly, if the government does not disclose its international reserve position in a timely and informative manner, investors may be taken by surprise when a devaluation occurs. The lack of good information on government and business activities serves as a warning sign of potential future problems.

This short list of warning signs provides an indication of the sorts of variables an international investor must consider when evaluating the risks of investing in a foreign country. This list is also useful to international organizations like the International Monetary Fund when monitoring countries and advising them on recommended changes in policy.

So far we have not explicitly considered how globalization may contribute to crises. The analysis of Figure 3 provides a hint. If there is free trading in a country's currency and the country has globalized financial markets, so that foreign investors trade domestic financial assets, there is a greater likelihood of a crisis than in a country that is not globalized. The money that comes into the developing country from foreign investors can also flow back out. This points out an additional factor to be considered:

- *Short-term international investment.* The greater the amount of short-term money invested in a country, the greater the potential for a crisis if investors lose confidence in the country. So if foreigners buy large amounts of domestic stocks, bonds, or other financial assets, they can turn around and sell these assets quickly. These asset sales will depress the value of the country's financial markets, and as foreigners sell local currency for foreign currency, like U.S. dollars, the local currency will also fall in value. Too much short-term foreign investment may serve as another warning sign for a financial crises.

Of course, a country can always avoid financial crises by not globalizing—keeping its domestic markets closed to foreigners. However, such a policy costs more than it is worth. As discussed earlier in this chapter, globalization has paid off with faster economic growth and reductions in poverty. To avoid globalization in order to avoid financial crises is to remain in poverty as the rest of the world grows richer. We should think of globalization and financial crises in these terms: A closed economy can follow very bad economic policies for a long time, and the rest of the world will have no influence in bringing about change for the better. A country with a globalized economy will be punished for bad economic policy as foreign investors move money out of the country, contributing to financial market crises in that country. It is not globalization that brings about the crisis. Instead, globalization allows the rest of the world to respond to bad economic policies in a way that highlights the bad policy and imposes costs on the country for following such policies. In this sense, globalization acts to discipline countries. A country with sound economic policy and good investment opportunities is rewarded with large flows of savings from the rest of the world to lower the cost of developing the local economy.

RECAP

1. The 1990s saw financial crises in Mexico, Indonesia, Korea, Malaysia, the Philippines, and Thailand.
2. Fixed exchange rates encouraged speculative attacks and ultimate devaluations of the currencies of the countries involved in these crises.
3. Exchange rate devaluations raised the cost of debts that were denominated in foreign currency and imposed large losses on debtor firms.
4. Factors contributing to the financial crises included fixed exchange rates, falling international reserves, a lack of transparency to investors, and a high level of short-term international investment.

Summary

❓ What is globalization?

1. Globalization involves an increased cross-border flow of trade in goods, services, and financial assets, along with increased international mobility of technology, information, and individuals. *§1*
2. The process of globalization has always existed because of its potential to raise living standards. *§1.a*
3. The rapid pace of globalization in recent decades has been made possible by technological advances. *§1.b*

❓ What are the arguments against globalization?

4. Free trade increases corporate profits but harms people. *§2.a.1*
5. International organizations and the agreements they are associated with serve corporate interests and harm people. *§2.a.2*
6. Globalization occurs at the cost of environmental quality. *§2.a.3*
7. Globalization encourages harmful labor practices. *§2.a.4*

❓ What are the arguments in support of globalization?

8. Those who lose their jobs to more efficient producers in other countries will be harmed, but the benefits to all consumers far outweigh the losses of those firms and workers that are harmed by globalization. *§2.b.1*
9. International organizations are funded by governments, not firms, and such organizations serve the interests of all nations in that they provide a setting where grievances must be heard and policy changes can be implemented. *§2.b.2*
10. Globalization has not resulted in a "race to the bottom," in which labor practices suffer and environmental decay results. *§2.b.3, 2.b.4*

❓ How has globalization affected economic growth and poverty?

11. Globalizers have faster economic growth and less poverty than nonglobalizers. *§3*

❓ Can recent financial crises be linked to globalization?

12. Globalization allows for international financial flows that punish countries that follow bad economic policy. *§4.c*

Key Terms

"race to the bottom" *§2.a.1*
Asian tigers *§3*

NICs *§3*
speculative attack *§4.b*

Exercises

1. What is globalization?

2. Comment on the following statement: "Globalization is an event of the 1980s and 1990s. Prior to this time, we never had to worry about globalization and its effects."

3. Write a script for two speakers arguing about globalization and its effects. Give each speaker a name, and then write a script for a debate between the two. The debate should be no longer than two pages, double-spaced. Each speaker should make a few key points, and the other speaker should offer a reply to each point the first speaker makes.

4. Why has the pace of globalization quickened since the 1950s?

5. If you wanted to compare countries on the basis of how globalized they are, how could you construct some numerical measures that would allow a cross-country comparison?

6. What are the major arguments against globalization?

7. What are the major arguments in favor of globalization?

8. What is the difference between "fair" and "free" trade?

9. What is the WTO? Where is it located, and what does it do?

10. Suppose we find that multinational firms are paying much lower wages in some poor countries than they would have to pay in the United States. Would this be sufficient evidence that these firms are exploiting the workers in the poor countries? Why or why not?

11. How can globalization reduce poverty? What does the evidence suggest about globalization and poverty?

12. There were several major international financial crises in the 1990s. What role did globalization play in these crises?

13. Using a supply and demand diagram, explain how central banks maintain a fixed exchange rate. What can cause an end to the fixed exchange rate regime?

14. Using a supply and demand diagram, explain how speculative attacks occur in the foreign exchange market.

15. If you were forecasting the likelihood of a financial crisis for a major international bank, what key variables would you want to monitor for the countries you are studying? Why would you want to monitor these variables?

Take the ACE Practice Test for this chapter to review the important concepts and get immediate feedback with answers.

economics.college.hmco.com/students

Economically Speaking

Germans' Coziness Puts Nation at Risk

BERLIN—Economists say Germany is on the ropes. Polls show worried voters know pro-business reforms could get things moving again in Europe's biggest economy. Politicians promise change.

Yet nothing happens—because the crisis so far is in the economic numbers and not in the homes.

"I live well," says Klaus Holgart, 63, a retired sheet-metal worker. Forget the polls, he says. "People won't support reforms. Germans still live very, very well."

Average Germans don't feel the pinch because they live under a social safety net matched by few other nations. There's cradle-to-grave government health care, nursing care, welfare and education. The government collects taxes for the churches and for cleaning dog poop off the streets. It regulates everything from shopping hours (tight) to sex on television (not so tight).

The system helps satisfy a craving for what the German's call gemuetlichkeit, a word that translates roughly to "coziness." It's sitting on the sofa, secure and content and enjoying a beer. It's a feeling that people are loath to risk, even if it means that their country falls behind. Which, increasingly, appears to be the case.

Germany is "a prisoner of its status quo," says Deutsche Bank Chairman Josef Ackermann. Comfortable Germans can't see how weak the country has become.

Just a few years ago, Germany was the economic powerhouse driving Europe's newly unified market to challenge U.S. supremacy. Its model of business expertise combined with technical prowess and cooperation with government surely would be world-conquering, experts predicted.

Now, Germany is struggling to pull its own weight, and Europe and the U.S. increasingly worry that the world's third-largest economy is dragging everyone else down. . . .

Unemployment in December was 10.1%—or 4.2 million people—the highest level since Chancellor Gerhard Schroeder took office in 1998 promising more jobs.

Deutsche Bank, the nation's largest, and the other big financial firms have cut tens of thousands of jobs. Siemens, the huge electronics and appliance maker, has laid off 35,000 people in Germany and elsewhere in the past two years.

Economic growth has virtually stopped. Estimates are that the gross domestic product rose no more than 0.3% last year. That makes 2002 the worst year since the recession of 1993, when output shrank by 1.1%.

When the giant international construction firm Holzmann filed for bankruptcy protection, it was only the most notable of thousands of failures. "This is a new experience, because in former down-swings, big business was secure," says Horst Tomann, an economist at Berlin's Free University. One reason it's not now: Globalization means that German companies are more exposed than ever to competition. . . .

Pressure is increasing on Schroeder for reforms, all of which are likely to make Germans' lives less cozy. . . .

In interviews, average Germans agree that changes are needed. Yes, benefits are too high, they say. But they also are wary of the costs. And maintaining economic consensus is considered vital in a country where Hitler rose to power on a wave of economic discontent. . . .

Says photo-shop owner Gerd-Peter Huber, "People are just too spoiled."

STEVEN KOMAROW

***USA Today*/February 10, 2003**

Commentary

We normally hear critics of globalization stressing the harm to workers in poor countries when foreign producers want to come and "exploit" the workers and the environment of the developing world. The chapter discussed the realities of such assertions. What is subtler and less prone to open discussion is the effect of globalization on rich countries. In a globalized world, competition punishes the relatively unproductive or high-cost producers and rewards the relatively more productive or lower-cost producers. This means that in the industrial countries of western Europe, North America, and Asia, foreign competition will put some domestic firms out of business and some workers will lose their jobs. These workers typically do not find new jobs that pay as well as their old jobs.

The article indicates how German society values *gemuetlichkeit,* or coziness. Another way of expressing this is to say that people in Germany are comfortable with the social order and living standards provided by German laws affecting industry and labor. As a result, in the face of increasing competition from foreign firms, their initial response is to fight change. This typically is reflected in calls by labor unions and firms that are losing money for trade restrictions on foreign goods so that the local firms and workers can keep their jobs. Some of the international demonstrations against globalization have been supported by labor unions from rich countries. The goal is to slow or even stop the globalization process in order to protect jobs in the rich countries. This is one reason why officials in poor countries complain that so far the globalization process has not resulted in the large gains that could be realized if the rich countries truly opened their markets to the products that the developing countries produce best.

The rich countries are slow to open their markets to the poor countries because of political pressure at home to protect the workers and firms that would be displaced by the foreign competitors. Of course, the cost of such protection is lower living standards for all consumers in the country. The pressures of globalization will increasingly move countries such as Germany to become more efficient and reduce costly benefits that discourage production. However, as the article makes clear, such change comes slowly and is often subject to great political battles. One message is certain: globalization cannot be ignored. Those who choose not to participate will become poorer as the rest of the world becomes richer.

Part Five

Product Market Basics

CHAPTER 20

Elasticity: Demand and Supply

? **Fundamental Questions**

1. How do we measure how much consumers alter their purchases in response to a price change?

2. Why are measurements of elasticity important?

3. How does a business determine whether to increase or decrease the price of the product it sells in order to increase revenues?

4. Why might senior citizens or children receive price discounts relative to the rest of the population?

5. What determines whether consumers alter their purchases a little or a lot in response to a price change?

Let's begin by trying to gain some perspective on what we have been doing and what we will be doing in the next few chapters. In the previous five chapters we defined economics, opportunity costs, and the "economic way of thinking." The economic way of thinking is to recognize that people are self-interested and as a result do those things that they expect will make them happiest. We say that people compare the costs and benefits of some activity, but it is the incremental or marginal costs and marginal benefits that are important. It is the next minute, the next day, the next dollar, the next month's income that matter in people's decisions.

People compare marginal benefits and marginal costs. If the marginal benefits are larger than the marginal costs of some activity, then people do that activity. If the marginal benefits are less than the marginal costs, then people do not do that activity. One of the things people do is trade or exchange. But, as we discovered, they trade only if they believe that the trade will make them better off. This is what the gains from trade are all about; all parties to a trade can gain and have to think they will gain or else they will not trade.

6. How do we measure how much changes in income, changes in the prices of related goods, or changes in advertising expenditures affect consumer purchases?

7. How do we measure how much producers respond to a price change?

The interaction of traders—of buyers and sellers—is represented by demand and supply. A market is a situation or place where buyers and sellers interact—demand and supply. Within a market, demand and supply determine the market price—the price at which buyers and sellers agree to trade.

In the previous chapters we examined how markets work to allocate scarce goods, services, and resources. We need to do more, however, if we are to understand why the world is what it is. We have to have a more in-depth understanding of markets, of demand and supply. We begin that process here. In this and the following chapters, we examine demand. We delve into the incentives and motivations of consumers. We examine how consumers behave when the price of a good or service changes, when income changes, or, in general, when marginal benefits or marginal costs change. After examining consumer behavior in more detail, we turn to supply. Suppliers are firms of one form or another, so to understand supply, we have to examine how firms behave. We look at sales, revenue, costs, and profits and see what firms do to try to be successful. Businesses often say that they must "know their customer" if they are to be successful. By this they mean that they must know everything they can about demand. What they need to know is what we discuss in this chapter. ▪

1. How do we measure how much consumers alter their purchases in response to a price change?

1. The Price Elasticity of Demand

The manager of a local movie theater raised the price from $7.50 to $8.50 per movie in order to pay for a new sound system he had installed. He knew that the higher price would lower ticket sales, but he expected to more than make this up with the higher ticket price. He found that not only had ticket sales declined, but his revenue had fallen as well. What had the manager been thinking? He must have believed that his customers would not respond much to the price increase, that they would continue coming to the theater. The error he made was not knowing what the price elasticity of demand was.

1.a. The Definition of Price Elasticity

The price elasticity of demand is a measure of the magnitude by which consumers alter the quantity of some product they purchase in response to a change in the price of that product. The more price-elastic demand is, the more responsive consumers are to a price change—that is, the more they will adjust their purchases of a product when the price of that product changes. Conversely, the less price-elastic demand is, the less responsive consumers are to a price change.

price elasticity of demand: the percentage change in the quantity demanded of a product divided by the percentage change in the price of that product

The **price elasticity of demand,** e_d, is the percentage change in the quantity demanded of a product divided by the percentage change in the price of that product:

$$e_d = \frac{\%\Delta Q^D}{\%\Delta P}$$

For instance, if the quantity of videotapes that are rented falls by 3 percent whenever the price of a videotape rental rises by 1 percent, the price elasticity of demand for videotape rentals is 3.

According to the law of demand, whenever the price of a good rises, the quantity demanded of that good falls. Thus, the price elasticity of demand is always negative, which can be confusing when referring to a "very high elasticity"—actually, a large negative number—or to a "low elasticity"—a small negative number. To avoid this confusion, economists typically ignore the negative sign.

Demand can be elastic, unit-elastic, or inelastic. When the price elasticity of demand is greater than 1, demand is said to be *elastic*. For instance, the demand for videotape rentals, according to the example of $e_d = 3$, is elastic. When the price elasticity of demand is 1, demand is said to be *unit-elastic*. For example, if the price of private education rises by 1 percent and the quantity of private education purchased falls by about 1 percent, the price elasticity of demand is

$$e_d = 1\%/1\% = 1$$

When the price elasticity of demand is less than 1, demand is said to be *inelastic*. In this case, a 1 percent rise in price brings forth a smaller than 1 percent decline in quantity demanded. For example, if the price of gasoline rises by 1 percent and the quantity of gasoline purchased falls by .2 percent, the price elasticity of demand is

$$e_d = .2\%/1\% = .2$$

1.b. Demand Curve Shapes and Elasticity

perfectly elastic demand curve: a horizontal demand curve indicating that consumers can and will purchase all they want at one price

A **perfectly elastic demand curve** is a horizontal line that shows that consumers are willing and able to purchase any quantity at the single prevailing price. In Figure 1(a), a perfectly elastic demand curve represents the demand for the wheat harvested by a single farmer in Canada. The Canadian farmer is only one small producer of wheat who, because he is just one among many, is unable to charge a price that differs from the price of wheat in the rest of the world. If this farmer's wheat is even slightly more expensive than wheat elsewhere, consumers will shift their purchases away from this farmer and buy the wheat produced by other farmers in Canada and the rest of the world. A perfectly elastic demand means that even the smallest price change will cause consumers to change their consumption by a huge amount, in fact, totally switching purchases to the producer with the lowest prices.

Grocery shopping in many nations does not resemble the once-a-week trip to the supermarket typical of most households in the United States. In this market in Peru, people purchase their foodstuffs each day. Having more time to shop, only a small amount of money with which to purchase food, and many choices of local produce means the price elasticity of demand is high. A small price change would induce the shopper to switch to another farmer's produce or to purchase something else.

FIGURE 1

The Price Elasticity of Demand

Figure 1(a), a perfectly elastic demand curve, represents the demand for one farmer's wheat. Because there are so many other suppliers, buyers purchase wheat from the least expensive source. If this farmer's wheat is priced ever so slightly above other farmers' wheat, buyers will switch to another source. Also, because this farmer is just one small producer in a huge market, he can sell everything he wants at the market price. Figure 1(b), a perfectly inelastic demand curve, represents the demand for insulin by a diabetic. A certain quantity is necessary to satisfy the need regardless of the price. Figure 1(c) shows two straight-line demand curves, D_1 and D_3, and a curved demand curve, D_2. These demand curves are neither perfectly elastic nor perfectly inelastic.

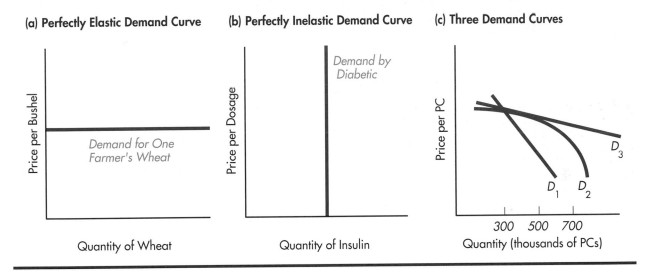

(a) Perfectly Elastic Demand Curve   **(b) Perfectly Inelastic Demand Curve**   **(c) Three Demand Curves**

perfectly inelastic demand curve: a vertical demand curve indicating that there is no change in the quantity demanded as the price changes

A **perfectly inelastic demand curve** is a vertical line illustrating the idea that consumers cannot or will not change the quantity of a good they purchase when the price of the product is changed. Perhaps insulin to a diabetic is a reasonably vivid example of a good whose demand is perfectly inelastic. Of course, this behavior holds only over a certain price range. Eventually, the price rises enough that even the diabetic will have to decrease the quantity demanded. Figure 1(b) shows a perfectly inelastic demand curve.

In between the two extreme shapes of demand curves are the demand curves for most products. Figure 1(c) shows two downward-sloping straight-line demand curves, D_1 and D_3, and one downward-sloping curved demand curve, D_2. Although demand curves can have virtually any shape—curve or straight line—the straight-line shape is used to illustrate the demand for most goods and services.

The price elasticity of demand declines as we move down a straight-line demand curve.

1.b.1 Price Elasticity Along a Straight-Line Demand Curve

The price elasticity of demand varies along a straight-line downward-sloping demand curve, declining as we move down the curve. The reason that elasticity changes along the straight-line demand curve is due to the way that elasticity is calculated, not to some intuitive economic explanation.

Along a straight-line demand curve, equal changes in price mean equal changes in quantity. For instance, if price changes by $1 in Figure 2, quantity demanded changes by 20 units; as price changes from $1 to $2, quantity demanded falls from

FIGURE 2

The Price Elasticity of Demand Varies Along a Straight-Line Demand Curve

Figure 2 shows that the price elasticity of demand varies along a straight-line demand curve. As we move down the demand curve, the price elasticity varies from elastic to unit-elastic to inelastic.

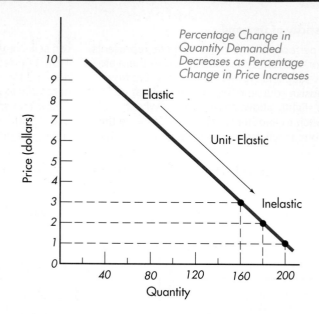

The terms elastic *and* inelastic *refer to a price range, not to the entire demand curve.*

200 to 180; as price changes from $2 to $3, quantity demanded falls from 180 to 160; and so on. Each $1 change in price means a 20-unit change in quantity demanded. But those same amounts (constant amounts of $1 and 20 units) do not translate into constant percentage changes.

A $1 change at the top of the demand curve is a significantly different percentage change from a $1 change at the bottom of the demand curve. A $1 change from $10 is a 10 percent change, but a $1 change from $2 is a 50 percent change. Thus, as we move down the demand curve from higher to lower prices, a given dollar change becomes a larger and larger percentage change in price. The opposite is true of quantity changes. As we move downward along the demand curve, the same change in quantity becomes a smaller and smaller percentage change. A 10-unit change from 20 is a 50 percent change, while a 10-unit change from 200 is a 5 percent change. As we move down the straight-line demand curve, the percentage change in quantity demanded declines while the percentage change in price increases. Because the price elasticity of demand is the ratio of the percentage change in quantity demanded to the percentage change in price, the price elasticity of demand moves close to zero as we move down the straight-line demand curve.

The downward-sloping straight-line demand curve is divided into three parts by the price elasticity of demand: the *elastic region,* the *unit-elastic point,* and the *inelastic region.* The demand is elastic from the top of the curve to the unit-elastic point. At all prices below the unit-elastic point, the price elasticity of demand lies between 1 and 0. This is the inelastic portion of the curve.

Elastic	$e_d > 1$
Unit-elastic	$e_d = 1$
Inelastic	$0 < e_d < 1$

1.c. The Price Elasticity of Demand Is Defined in Percentage Terms

By measuring the price elasticity of demand in terms of percentage changes, economists are able to compare how consumers respond to changes in the prices of different products. For instance, the impact of a 1 percent increase in the price of gasoline (measured in gallons) can be compared to the impact of a 1 percent change in the price of videotape rentals (measured in number of rentals). Or the impact of a 1 percent increase in the price of college tuition can be compared to the impact of a 1 percent rise in the price of a Big Mac.

Percentage changes ensure that we are comparing apples to apples, not apples to oranges. What sense could be made of a comparison between the effects on quantity demanded of a $1 rise in the price of college tuition, from $5,000 to $5,001, and a $1 rise in the price of Big Macs, from $2 to $3? The dollar change would mean that tuition increases by 0.02 percent and the hamburger price increases by 50 percent.

1.d. Calculating Elasticity

The formula used to calculate elasticity is

$$e_d = \frac{(Q_2 - Q_1)/[(Q_1 + Q_2)/2]}{(P_2 - P_1)/[(P_1 + P_2)/2]}$$

Let's use this formula to calculate an elasticity. At a price of $6 per ticket, the average moviegoer demands 2 tickets per month. At a price of $4 per ticket, the average moviegoer purchases 6 tickets per month. Thus,

$$P_1 = \$6 \quad Q_1 = 2$$
$$P_2 = \$4 \quad Q_2 = 6$$

The *change* in quantity demanded is $Q_2 - Q_1 = 6 - 2 = 4$. The *percentage change* is the change divided by the base. The base is the average, or midpoint between the two quantities, the sum of the two quantities divided by 2: $(Q_1 + Q_2)/2 = (6 + 2)/2 = 4$. With 4 as the base, the percentage change in quantity is 4/4, or 100 percent. We can say that the quantity of movie tickets sold rose by an average of 100 percent as the price of a ticket declined from $6 to $4.

The change in price is −$2, from $6 to $4, and the average price is $(P_1 + P_2)/2 = (\$6 + \$4)/2 = \$5$. The percentage change in price is −$2/$5 = −40 percent.

Because the numerator of the price elasticity of demand is 100 percent and the denominator is −40 percent, the price elasticity is

$$e_d = 100/-40 = -2.5 \text{ or just } 2.5$$

According to these calculations, the price elasticity of demand for movie tickets, over the price range from $6 to $4, is 2.5. We can say that demand is elastic over this price range.

RECAP

1. The price elasticity of demand is a measure of the degree to which consumers will alter the quantities of a product that they purchase in response to changes in the price of that product.

2. Because the quantity demanded always declines as price rises, the price elasticity of demand is always a negative number. To avoid confusion when discussing price elasticity of demand, the negative sign is ignored.

3. The price elasticity of demand is a ratio of the percentage change in the quantity demanded to the corresponding percentage change in the price.
4. When the price elasticity of demand is greater than 1, demand is said to be *elastic*. When the price elasticity of demand is equal to 1, demand is said to be *unit-elastic*. When the price elasticity of demand is less than 1, demand is said to be *inelastic*.
5. An elasticity is obtained by using average price and average quantity demanded.

2. The Use of Price Elasticity of Demand

The price elasticity of demand may be a manager's best friend. It informs her whether to raise or lower prices, whether to charge different customers different prices; whether to charge different prices at different times of the day; whether it is better to focus on prices or to advertise; or, in general, what strategies to employ.

2.a. Total Revenue and Price Elasticity of Demand

?

3. How does a business determine whether to increase or decrease the price of the product it sells in order to increase revenues?

total revenue (*TR*):
$TR = P \times Q$

A manager concerned with increasing revenue must know what the current price elasticity of demand is for the firm's product. There is a close relationship between price elasticity of demand and total revenue. **Total revenue (TR)** equals the price of a product multiplied by the quantity sold: $TR = P \times Q$. If P rises by 10 percent and Q falls by more than 10 percent, then total revenue declines as a result of the price rise. If P rises by 10 percent and Q falls by less than 10 percent, then total revenue rises as a result of the price rise. And if P increases by 10 percent and Q falls by 10 percent, total revenue does not change as the price changes. Thus, total revenue increases as price is increased if demand is inelastic, decreases as price is increased if demand is elastic, and does not change as price is increased if demand is unit-elastic.

Whenever the price elasticity of demand for a product is in the elastic region, the product supplier must decrease price in order to increase revenue. For instance, the price elasticity of demand for airline travel has been found to be near 2.4. This means that, over some price range, for each 1 percent increase in the price of an airline ticket, the quantity of tickets demanded will decline by 2.4 percent.

In the spring of 2003, a trip could be made from New York to Los Angeles for $250 each way, if you included a Saturday night stay. If the airlines had increased the fare by 10 percent, to $275 each way, they would have sold 24 percent (2.4 × 0.10) fewer tickets. As a result, their total revenue would have fallen. The revenue from selling 3,000 tickets per day for the trip between New York and Los Angeles at a fare of $250 was $750,000 per day. At a fare of $275, the quantity of tickets demanded would have declined by 720 to 2,280 per day (3,000 × 0.24 = 720), and revenue would have fallen to $627,000 per day. As long as the price elasticity of demand exceeds 1, total revenue is decreased if the price is increased.

As long as the price elasticity of demand exceeds 1, total revenue is decreased if the price is increased.

As long as demand is elastic, price must be decreased to increase total revenue. But by how much should the price be lowered? Since the price elasticity of demand declines as the price falls along a straight-line demand curve, eventually price reaches a point where demand becomes unit-elastic. Further price decreases at this stage would cause total revenue to fall. Thus, *total revenue* can be maximized by setting the price where demand is unit-elastic.

The table in Figure 3 is a demand schedule for airline tickets listing the price and quantity of tickets sold and the total revenue ($P \times Q$). Figure 3(a) shows a

FIGURE 3

Total Revenue and Price Elasticity

The demand schedule provides data for plotting the straight-line demand curve, Figure 3(a), and the total revenue curve, Figure 3(b). In the elastic region of the demand curve, a price decrease will increase total revenue. At the unit-elastic point, a price decrease will not change total revenue. In the inelastic region of the demand curve, a price decrease will decrease total revenue.

Price per Ticket	Quantity of Tickets Sold per Day	Total Revenue
$1,000	200	$200,000
$ 900	400	$360,000
$ 800	600	$480,000
$ 700	800	$560,000
$ 600	1,000	$600,000
$ 500	1,200	$600,000
$ 400	1,400	$560,000
$ 300	1,600	$480,000
$ 200	1,800	$360,000
$ 100	2,000	$200,000

(a) Air Travel Demand Curve

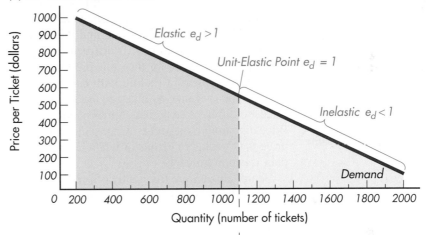

(b) Total Revenue for Airline

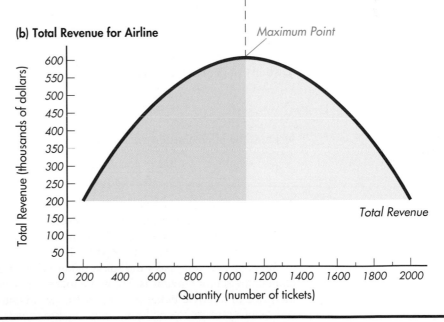

straight-line demand curve representing the demand for air travel. Total revenue is plotted in Figure 3(b), directly below the demand curve. You can see that total revenue rises as price falls in the elastic range of the demand curve, while in the inelastic range of the demand curve, total revenue declines as price falls. *The unit-elastic point is the price at which revenue is at a maximum.* Remember that this is revenue, not profit, we are discussing. A firm may or may not want to maximize revenue. To increase revenue:

1. If in the elastic range of demand, lower price.
2. If in the inelastic range of demand, raise price.

2.b. Price Discrimination

?

4. Why might senior citizens or children receive price discounts relative to the rest of the population?

Ads and marquees proudly proclaim that "Kids stay free" or that "Senior discounts apply," and it is well known that airlines sell vacation travelers tickets for significantly less than the business traveler pays. The price elasticity of demand might explain why firms will not always increase revenue if they lower their prices, but what explains why firms charge different customers different prices for the same product? It is exactly the same principle. When demand is elastic, a price decrease causes total revenue to increase; and when demand is inelastic, a price increase causes total revenue to rise. If different groups of customers have different price elasticities of demand for the same product and if the groups are easily identifiable and can be kept from trading with each other, then the seller of the product can increase total revenue by charging each group a different price. Charging different prices to different customers for the same product is called **price discrimination.** Price discrimination occurs when senior citizens purchase movie tickets at a lower price than younger citizens or when business travelers pay more for airline tickets than vacation travelers.

price discrimination:
charging different customers different prices for the same product

Senior citizens are frequently offered movie tickets at lower prices than younger people. The reason for the discount is that, on average, older people are more inclined than younger people to respond to a change in the price of admission to a movie.

Suppose that senior citizens will purchase 100 tickets per movie if the price is $8 and 300 tickets if the price is $6, while the rest of the population will purchase 150 tickets per movie at a price of $8 and 200 at a price of $6. The senior citizens are more responsive to price changes than is the rest of the population. The price elasticity of demand for senior citizens is

$$\frac{(300 - 100)/[(300 + 100)/2]}{(6 - 8)/[(6 + 8)/2]} = \frac{1}{.286} = 3.5$$

whereas the price elasticity of demand for the rest of the population is:

$$\frac{(200 - 150)/[(200 + 150)/2]}{(6 - 8)/[(6 + 8)/2]} = \frac{.286}{.286} = 1$$

The senior citizens are much more sensitive to a price change. Since their demand is elastic, the movie theater can raise revenue by lowering the price to them. But since the rest of the population has a unitary price elasticity of demand, revenue will not increase if the price they pay is lowered.

Suppose everyone pays the same ticket price of $5 and the price elasticity of demand by senior citizens is 2.0, while that by nonsenior citizens is 0.5. Lowering the price of a movie ticket by 10 percent would cause senior citizens to increase

Dumping

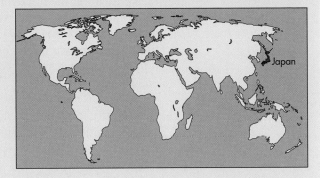

Price discrimination is a strategy used by many firms that sell their products in different countries. A derogatory name for this policy is *dumping.* Dumping occurs when an identical good is sold to foreign buyers for a lower price than is charged to domestic buyers. International dumping is a controversial issue. Producers in a country facing foreign competitors are likely to appeal to their domestic government for protection from the foreign goods being dumped in their market. Typically, the appeal for government assistance is based on the argument that the dumping firms are practicing *predatory dumping*—dumping intended to drive rival firms out of business. A successful predator firm raises prices after the rival is driven from the market.

Canadian electronics manufacturers might accuse Japanese firms of dumping if the Japanese firms are selling electronics in Canada for less than they charge in Japan. The Canadian manufacturers may appeal to the Canadian government, asserting that the Japanese firms are engaged in predatory dumping to drive the Canadian firms out of business and warning that the Japanese firms will then raise the price of electronics products in Canada without fear of competition by the domestic Canadian firms. Claims of predatory dumping are often emotional and stir up the nationalistic sympathy of the rest of the domestic economy.

The U.S. government frequently responds to charges of dumping brought against foreign firms by U.S. industry. The government has pursued claims of predatory dumping against South African manufacturers of steel plate; German, Italian, and French winemakers; Japanese manufacturers of semiconductors; Singapore manufacturers of typewriters; Korean shipbuilders; Chinese motor bike producers; and many other manufacturers.

One famous case involved Sony Corporation of Japan. In the United States, Sony was selling Japanese-made TV sets for $180 while charging buyers in Japan $333 for the same model. The U.S. television producers claimed that Sony was dumping TV sets in the U.S. market and seriously damaging U.S. television manufacturers. (Although U.S. producers disliked the low price of Japanese competitors, U.S. consumers benefited.) The U.S. government threatened to place high tariffs on Japanese television sets entering the United States unless Japan raised the price of Japanese televisions sold in the United States. The threat worked, and the price of Japanese TVs exported to the United States increased.

Charges of predatory dumping make good news stories, but it is also true that dumping is to be expected when producers with the ability to set prices face segmented markets that have different price elasticities of demand. Conceptually, dumping is no different from what happens when a car dealer charges one buyer a higher price than another for the same car. If both buyers were aware of the range of prices at which the dealer would sell the car, or if both buyers had exactly the same price elasticity of demand, they would pay exactly the same price.

The Japanese electronics manufacturer realizes that the electronics market in Japan is separate from the electronics market in Canada or the United States. If the price elasticity of demand for electronics is different in each country, the Japanese manufacturer will maximize profit by charging a different price in each country.

their purchases of movie tickets by 20 percent, but nonsenior citizens would increase their purchases by only 5 percent. Total revenue from senior citizens would rise, but that from nonsenior citizens would fall. It would make more sense for the theater to lower the price for senior citizens but not for younger people.

Airline discounts are constructed on the basis of the price elasticity of demand as well. Vacationers know their schedules well in advance and can take advantage of the least expensive means of travel. Business travelers are more constrained. They often do not know their schedules days in advance, and they usually want to travel on Monday through Friday. The airlines recognize that the demand for air travel by vacationers is much more elastic than the demand by business travelers. As a result, airlines offer discounts to travelers who purchase tickets well in advance and stay over a Saturday night. For instance, in the spring of 2003, a cross-country roundtrip fare was $840 unless the trip included an overnight stay on Saturday. Then the fare dropped to $360. If tickets were purchased two weeks in advance, the fare dropped to $240. Price discrimination can also be used when a country sells goods abroad, as the Global Business Insight box shows.

RECAP

1. If the price elasticity of demand is greater than 1, revenue and price changes move in the opposite direction. An increase in price causes a decrease in revenue, and a decrease in price causes an increase in revenue. If the price elasticity of demand is less than 1, revenue and price move in the same direction. If the price elasticity of demand is 1, revenue does not change as price changes.

2. When the price elasticity of demand for one product differs among different groups of easily identified customers, firms can increase revenues by charging each group a different price. The groups with elastic demands will receive lower prices than those with inelastic demands.

5. What determines whether consumers alter their purchases a little or a lot in response to a price change?

3. Determinants of the Price Elasticity of Demand

The degree to which the price elasticity of demand is inelastic or elastic depends on the following factors, which differ among products and among consumers:

- The existence of substitutes
- The importance of the product in the consumer's total budget
- The time period under consideration

3.a. The Existence of Substitutes

Consumers who can switch from one product to another without losing quality or some other attribute associated with the original product will be sensitive to a price change. Their demand will be elastic. Such consumers will purchase a substitute rather than the original product whenever the relative price of the original product rises.

A senior citizen discount is offered at movie theaters because of the different price elasticities of demand by senior citizens and nonsenior citizens. Why are their elasticities different? More substitutes may be available to senior citizens than to younger folks. Retirees have more time to seek out alternative entertainment activities than do people who are working full-time. Retirees can go to movies during the early part of the day or on weekdays when the theater runs a special.

The more substitutes there are for a product, the greater the price elasticity of demand.

In contrast, diabetics have no substitutes that replace insulin, and business travelers have few substitutes for the airlines. As a result, their demands are relatively inelastic. The more substitutes there are for a product, the greater the price elasticity of demand.

3.b. The Importance of the Product in the Consumer's Total Budget

Because a new car and a European vacation are quite expensive, even a small percentage change in their prices can take a significant portion of a household's income. As a result, a 1 percent increase in price may cause many households to delay the purchase of a car or vacation. Coffee, on the other hand, accounts for such a small portion of a household's total weekly expenditures that a large percentage increase in the price of coffee will probably have little effect on the quantity of coffee purchased. The demand for vacations is most likely quite a bit more elastic than the demand for coffee. The greater the portion of the consumer's budget a good constitutes, the more elastic is the demand for the good.

The greater the portion of the consumer's budget a good constitutes, the more elastic the demand for the good.

3.c. The Time Period Under Consideration

If we are speaking about a day or an hour, then the demand for most goods and services will have a low price elasticity. If we are referring to a year or to several years, then the demand for most products will be more price-elastic than in a shorter period. For instance, the demand for gasoline is very nearly perfectly inelastic over a period of a month. No good substitutes are available in so brief a period. Over a ten-year period, however, the demand for gasoline is much more elastic. The additional time allows consumers to alter their behavior to make better use of gasoline and to find substitutes for gasoline. The longer the period under consideration, the more elastic is the demand for any product.

The longer the period under consideration, the more elastic the demand for the good.

RECAP

1. The price elasticity of demand depends on how readily and easily consumers can switch their purchases from one product to another.
2. Everything else held constant, the greater the number of close substitutes, the greater the price elasticity of demand.
3. Everything else held constant, the greater the proportion of a householder's budget that a good constitutes, the greater is the householder's price elasticity of demand for that good.
4. Everything else held constant, the longer the time period under consideration, the greater is the price elasticity of demand.

4. Other Demand Elasticities

?

6. How do we measure how much changes in income, changes in the prices of related goods, or changes in advertising expenditures affect consumer purchases?

A price change leads to a movement along the demand curve. When something that affects demand, other than price, changes, the demand curve shifts. How far the demand curve shifts is measured by elasticity—elasticity of the variable whose value changes. As we saw in Chapter 3, "Markets, Demand and Supply, and the Price System," demand is determined by income, prices of related goods, expectations, tastes, number of buyers, and international effects. A change in any one of these will cause the demand curve to shift, and a measure of elasticity exists for each of these demand determinants. The *income elasticity of demand* measures the percentage change in demand caused by a 1 percent change in income, the *cross-price elasticity of demand* measures the percentage change in demand caused by a 1 percent change in the price of a related good, the *advertising elasticity of demand* measures the percentage change in demand caused by a 1 percent change in advertising expenditures (change in tastes), and so on.[1] Each elasticity is calculated by dividing the percentage change in demand by the percentage change in the variable under consideration.

4.a. The Cross-Price Elasticity of Demand

cross-price elasticity of demand: the percentage change in the quantity demanded for one good divided by the percentage change in the price of a related good, everything else held constant

The **cross-price elasticity of demand** measures the degree to which goods are substitutes or complements (for a discussion of substitutes and complements, see Chapter 3). The cross-price elasticity of demand is defined as the percentage change in the quantity demanded for one good divided by the percentage change in the price of a related good, everything else held constant:

$$\text{Cross-price elasticity of demand} = \frac{\text{percentage change in quantity demanded for good j}}{\text{percentage change in the price of good k}}$$

When the cross-price elasticity of demand is positive, the goods are substitutes, and when the cross-price elasticity of demand is negative, the goods are complements. If a 1 percent *increase* in the price of a movie ticket leads to a 5 percent *increase* in the quantity of videotapes that are rented, movies and videotapes are substitutes. If a 1 percent rise in the price of a movie ticket leads to a 5 percent *drop* in the quantity of popcorn consumed, movies and popcorn are complements.

In 2002, DVD and VHS rentals and sales were greater than movie ticket sales in the United States. As the price of a movie ticket increased from $7.50 to $8.50, the quantity of DVD and VHS rentals increased from 20,000 to 22,000 per month. The cross-price elasticity of demand between rentals and movies is

$$\frac{(22,000 - 20,000)/[(22,000 + 20,000)/2]}{(8.50 - 7.50)/[(8.50 + 7.50)/2]} = \frac{.095}{.125} = .76$$

The cross-price elasticity of demand is positive, telling us that the goods are substitutes and that for every 10 percent increase in movie ticket prices, the quantity of DVD and VHS rentals increases by 7.6 percent.

---

[1]Notice that we should define the cross-price elasticity as the percentage change in demand rather than the percentage change in quantity demanded because it is the entire demand curve that is changing. However, common usage defines the formula as the percentage change in quantity demanded. Thus for cross-price, income, and advertising elasticities, we follow the common usage.

4.b. The Income Elasticity of Demand

The income elasticity of demand measures the magnitude of consumer responsiveness to income changes. The **income elasticity of demand** is defined as the percentage change in quantity demanded for a product divided by the percentage change in income, everything else held constant:

income elasticity of demand: the percentage change in the quantity demanded for a good divided by the percentage change in income, everything else held constant

normal goods: goods for which the income elasticity of demand is positive

$$\text{Income elasticity of demand} = \frac{\text{percentage change in quantity demanded for good j}}{\text{percentage change in income}}$$

Goods whose income elasticity of demand is greater than zero are **normal goods.** Products that are often called necessities have lower income elasticities than products known as luxuries. Gas, electricity, health-oriented drugs, and physicians' services might be considered necessities. Their income elasticities are about 0.4 or 0.5. On the other hand, people tend to view dental services, automobiles, and private education as luxury goods. Their elasticities are 1.5 to 2.0.

A physician who was against smoking was arguing in front of the legislature that a subsidy should be provided to low-income households so that they would stop smoking. He pointed out that most smokers are lower income, so the subsidy policy would be very effective. An economist for the legislature tried to explain why the policy would be very expensive. He had carried out a study and found that an increase in average household income from $30,000 to $40,000 led to a reduction in smoking from 4 packs a day to 3.5 packs a day, on average. The income elasticity of demand for cigarettes was

$$\frac{(3.5 - 4)/[(3.5 + 4)/2]}{(40,000 - 30,000)/[(40,000 + 30,000)/2]} = \frac{.5/7.5}{10,000/35,000} = \frac{.066}{.287} = .209$$

With such a low income elasticity of demand, it is clear that incomes would have to rise a great deal to have an impact on smoking. For each 10 percent increase in income, there would be only a 2 percent reduction in smoking.

As incomes rise, people tend to purchase luxury items rather than basic, less expensive items. In this photo, women display new lines of mobile phones having the ability to take pictures and send them electronically to others. The quantity of mobile phones purchased as income rises is positive; the income elasticity of demand for mobile phones is positive. Not only is it positive, but it is larger than 1, indicating that as income rises by 10 percent, the quantity of phones purchased rises by more than 10 percent.

Consumers could have a negative income elasticity of demand for some goods: less of those goods would be consumed as income rose. Such goods are called **inferior goods.** Some people claim that potatoes, rice, and hamburger are inferior goods because people who have very low levels of income eat large quantities of these goods but give up those items and begin eating fruit, fish, and higher-quality meats as their incomes rise.

Air pollution is a problem throughout the world. Studies have shown that the air pollution in the poorest nations is much worse than that in the wealthiest nations. Air pollution in India, much of Africa, and China is so bad that associated health problems are epidemic. Isn't it logical that if these nations improved their air, they would improve the conditions of their populations considerably and thus contribute to economic growth?

It does seem logical, but the problem is that because they have little income, these nations would have to forgo other important things in order to devote resources to cleaning the air. And taking resources away from other areas of the economy, such as health care, could lead to more serious health problems than are caused by the pollution.

It turns out that a nation will not begin devoting resources to cleaning its air until its per capita income is about $8,000 to $15,000 per year. Given that China's per capita income is about $4,000 per year at best, and that of the other nations mentioned is less, spending money to solve pollution problems is not likely. The greater a nation's per capita income, the more likely it is that it can reduce air pollution. It is estimated that no money is devoted to reducing air pollution when per capita income levels are between $200 and $8,000. When per capita incomes range between $8,000 and $15,000, enough money is devoted air pollution to reduce it by 1 percent. And for every $1,000 rise in per capita income above $15,000, air pollution will be reduced by 2 percent. So, if per capita income was $20,000, air pollution would be reduced by 10 percent compared to the case where per capita incomes are less than $8,000. For a country with a per capita income of $600, the income elasticity of demand for reducing air pollution is

$$\frac{(\$20,000 - 600)/[(20,000 + 600)/2]}{.10} = \frac{19,400/10,300}{.10} = \frac{1.88}{.10} = 18.8$$

This huge income elasticity of demand tells us that the absence of air pollution is a **luxury good.** In light of this result, to demand that a poor country reduce its air pollution is not an economically logical demand.

RECAP

1. The cross-price elasticity of demand is the percentage change in the quantity demanded for one product divided by the percentage change in the price of a related product, everything else held constant. If the cross-price elasticity of demand is positive, the goods are substitutes. If the cross-price elasticity of demand is negative, the goods are complements.

2. The income elasticity of demand is the percentage change in the quantity demanded for one product divided by the percentage change in income, everything else held constant. If the income elasticity of a good is greater than zero, the good is called a *normal good.* If the income elasticity of a good is negative, the good is called an *inferior good.*

3. Elasticities can be calculated for any determinant of demand. Although income and related goods elasticities were calculated in the text, other elasticities like international development, service, quality, and expectations elasticities could have been calculated.

5. Supply Elasticities

7. How do we measure how much producers respond to a price change?

Elasticity is a measure of responsiveness. The response of buyers to price changes is measured by the price elasticity of demand. The response of sellers to price changes can also be measured by elasticity. The *price elasticity of supply* is a measure of how sellers adjust the quantity of a good that they offer for sale when the price of that good changes.

5.a. The Price Elasticity of Supply

price elasticity of supply: the percentage change in the quantity supplied divided by the percentage change in price, everything else held constant

The **price elasticity of supply** is the percentage change in the quantity supplied of a good divided by the percentage change in the price of that good, everything else held constant. The price elasticity of supply is usually a positive number because the quantity supplied typically rises when the price rises. Supply is said to be elastic over a price range if the price elasticity of supply is greater than 1 over that price range. It is said to be inelastic over a price range if the price elasticity of supply is less than 1 over that price range.

$$\text{Price elasticity of supply} = \frac{\text{percentage change in the quantity supplied}}{\text{percentage change in the price}}$$

Different shapes the supply curve may take are illustrated in Figure 4. Figure 4(a) is a vertical line, representing a product for which the quantity supplied cannot increase no matter the price. There are some special types of goods for which supply cannot change no matter the length of time allowed for change—land surface, Monet paintings, Beethoven symphonies. For such goods, the price elasticity of supply is zero. Figure 4(b) shows a perfectly elastic supply curve, a horizontal line. There are some goods for which the quantity supplied at the current price can be whatever anyone wants given sufficient time. The production of food, for instance, has increased tremendously during the past century while the price has remained about the same. For most goods, the supply curve lies between the perfectly inelastic and perfectly elastic extremes. In Figure 4(c), three supply curves are drawn illustrating different shapes that the supply curve might have. Curve S_1 is steeper than the others but less steep than a perfectly inelastic curve. Curve S_2 is a curved supply curve, and curve S_3 is flatter than the others but not as flat as the perfectly elastic curve.

For many consumer electronics items, in the first few years after the product is introduced, only a few people purchase it and only a very few firms supply it. But, once the product begins to catch on, a great deal more is supplied—prices actually decline over time. Examples include VHS, DVD, radios, TV, game consoles, PCs, CDs, and others. For these products, the price elasticity of supply is quite high, meaning that a small price increase can lead to a large increase in quantity supplied, everything else held constant. For example, in 2003, an increase in the price of DVDs from $12 apiece to $14 apiece increased the quantity supplied from 10,000

FIGURE 4

The Price Elasticity of Supply

There are some special types of goods for which supply cannot change no matter the length of time allowed for change. For such goods, the price elasticity of supply is zero and the supply curve is vertical, as shown in Figure 4(a). Figure 4(b) is a perfectly elastic supply curve, a horizontal line. A perfectly elastic supply curve says that the quantity supplied is unlimited at the given price; a small—infinitesimal—price change would lead to an infinite change in quantity supplied. For most goods, the supply curve lies between the perfectly inelastic and perfectly elastic extremes. In Figure 4(c) three supply curves are drawn. Curve S_1 is steeper than the others but less steep than a perfectly inelastic curve. Curve S_2 is a curved supply curve. Curve S_3 is flatter than the others but not as flat as the perfectly elastic curve.

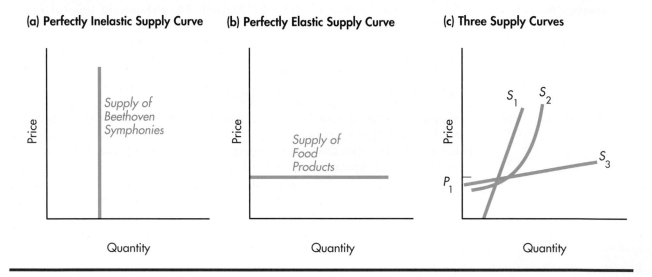

(a) Perfectly Inelastic Supply Curve   **(b) Perfectly Elastic Supply Curve**   **(c) Three Supply Curves**

per week to 15,000 per week in the United States. The price elasticity of supply in this case is

$$\frac{(10,000 - 15,000)/[(10,000 + 15,000)/2]}{(12 - 14)/[(12 + 14)/2]} = \frac{-5,000/15,000}{-2/13} = \frac{-.33}{-.15} = 2.2$$

Thus, for each 10 percent increase in price, the quantity supplied rose by 22 percent.

5.b. The Long and Short Runs

The shape of the supply curve depends primarily on the length of time being considered. Economists view time in terms of two distinct periods, the short run and the long run. The **short run** is a period of time long enough for existing firms to change the quantity of output they produce by changing the quantities of *some* of the resources used to produce their output, but not long enough for the firms to change the quantities of *all* of the resources. In the short run, firms are not able to build new factories or retrain workers. The **long run** is a period of time long enough for existing firms to change the quantities of all the resources they use and for new firms to begin producing the product. The chronological time for short and long runs varies from industry to industry. The long run for oil refining may be as long as seven to eight years; for personal computers, perhaps a year; for basket making, probably no longer than a day or two.

short run: a period of time short enough that the quantities of at least one of the resources cannot be varied

long run: a period of time long enough that the quantities of all resources can be varied

Usually, the greater the time period allowed, the more readily firms will increase their quantities supplied in response to a price change. Thus, supply curves applicable to shorter periods of time tend to be more inelastic than supply curves that apply to longer periods of time. If firms have to change their production techniques or switch from the production of one good to another in order to change the quantities they supply, they can respond to a price change less in a week than they could in a year. A baker who can switch from producing cupcakes to muffins within a day has large price elasticities of supply for cupcakes and for muffins; a small increase in the price of muffins relative to that of cupcakes will cause the bakery to significantly increase the quantity of muffins baked and reduce the quantity of cupcakes baked. An automobile manufacturing plant that requires several months or years to switch from one type of car to another, however, will have a relatively inelastic supply.

In Figure 4(c), supply curve S_1 represents a shorter-run supply curve. For a given price change, the quantity supplied would change by a small amount, shown by moving along S_1 from point P_1. Curve S_2 represents a firm that is able to increase quantity supplied substantially in the short run if it is currently producing a small amount. But, if it is producing a larger amount, it cannot increase output very much in the short run, perhaps because increased production would require an expansion of the current factory. Curve S_3 represents a longer-run supply curve. The change in output in response to a price change is greater along S_3 than along either of the other curves.

During 2002, the Mini-Cooper automobile produced by BMW was in short supply. The prices being charged were far above the manufacturer's suggested retail price of $20,000, reaching levels of $40,000 in some cases. Yet, the quantity of these cars supplied by BMW hardly changed. By the end of 2003, the situation had changed. BMW was able to increase its supplies by a third. What had happened? The answer is that the price elasticity of supply in the short run is different from that in the long run. In the short run, BMW was not able to change production processes, build additional factories, and increase the quantity supplied. But with time, it could increase production. Suppose that during one year a change in price from $20,000 to $40,000 brings only an additional 1,000 cars to market—from 20,000 to 21,000. The price elasticity of supply in the short run is

$$\frac{(21,000 - 20,000)/[(20,000 + 21,000)/2]}{(\$40,000 - \$20,000)/[(20,000 + 40,000)/2]} = \frac{1/41}{1/3} = \frac{.024}{.33} = .07$$

In the longer period, the $20,000 increase in price brought forth an increase of 10,000 automobiles. The price elasticity of supply in the long run is

$$\frac{(30,000 - 20,000)/[(20,000 + 30,000)/2]}{.33} = \frac{.04}{.33} = 1.2$$

The price elasticity of supply is much larger in the longer run, 1.2, than in the short run, .07. This is illustrated as a flatter supply curve.

5.c. Price Elasticities of Demand and Supply

It takes both demand and supply to determine the equilibrium price and quantity in a market. Similarly, it takes both the price elasticity of demand and the price elasticity of supply to determine the full effect of a price change. If the price elasticity of supply of an item is large and the demand for it is price-inelastic, then the firm can raise the price without losing revenue. In this case, the consumer will pay all price increases. We say that the firm can pass cost increases to the consumer. Conversely, if the price elasticity of supply is small and the price elasticity of demand is large, then it is the firm that will bear cost increases. Because the firm will lose revenue by raising price, the firm is reluctant to increase price, even as its costs rise.

Consider how this relationship between price elasticities of demand and supply affect tax policy. Suppose a good that is going to be taxed has a demand that is price-inelastic and a supply that is price-elastic. If the tax is levied on the firm, the firm simply raises its price; it is the consumer that pays the tax even though the tax is levied on the firm. But, if the price elasticity of demand is large and supply is price-inelastic, then a tax levied on the consumer will be borne by the firm; the firm will have to lower price to offset the tax increase in order to induce customers to keep purchasing the good.

tax incidence: a measure of who pays a tax

Regardless of whether the tax is imposed on the firm or on the consumer, when it is the consumer who actually pays the tax, we say that the **tax incidence** falls on the consumer. Consider cigarettes, for example. If smokers will buy the same quantity of cigarettes even if the price rises by 20 percent, then an 8 percent tax levied on cigarettes will not affect sales. Firms would not need to reduce price to keep sales the same.

In general, the more elastic the demand and the less elastic the supply, everything else held constant, the more the incidence of a tax falls on businesses and the less it falls on consumers.

RECAP

1. The price elasticity of supply is the percentage change in the quantity supplied of one product divided by the percentage change in the price of that product, everything else held constant. The price elasticity of supply increases as the time period under consideration increases.

2. The long run is a period of time just long enough that the quantities of all resources can be varied. The short run is a period of time just short enough that the quantity of at least some of the resources cannot be varied.

3. The interaction of demand and supply determines the price and quantity produced and sold; the relative size of demand and supply price elasticities determines how the market reacts to changes. For instance, the size of supply relative to demand price elasticities determines the incidence of a tax.

Summary

❓ How do we measure how much consumers alter their purchases in response to a price change?

1. The price elasticity of demand is a measure of the responsiveness of consumers to changes in price. It is defined as the percentage change in the quantity demanded of a good divided by the percentage change in the price of the good. *§1.a*

2. The price elasticity of demand is always a negative number because price and quantity demanded are inversely related. To avoid confusion about what

large or small elasticity means, the price elasticity of demand is calculated as the percentage change in the quantity demanded of a good divided by the percentage change in the price of the good, with the negative sign ignored. *§1.a*

3. As the price is lowered along a straight-line demand curve, the price elasticity of demand declines. *§1.b.1*

4. The straight-line demand curve consists of three segments: the top part, which is elastic; the unit-elastic region; and the bottom part, which is inelastic. *§1.b.1*

? Why are measurements of elasticity important?

5. Comparing the price elasticity of demand for various products/services allows economists to see how consumers respond to price changes. In other words, it can tell us how big a difference price makes in a particular purchasing decision.

? How does a business determine whether to increase or decrease the price of the product it sells in order to increase revenues?

6. If the price elasticity of demand is greater than 1, total revenue and price changes move in opposite directions. An increase in price causes a decrease in total revenue, and a decrease in price causes an increase in total revenue. If demand is inelastic, total revenue and price move in the same direction. *§2.a*

? Why might senior citizens or children receive price discounts relative to the rest of the population?

7. When the price elasticity of demand for one product differs among different groups of easily identifiable customers, firms can increase total revenue by resorting to price discrimination. The customers with the more elastic demands will receive lower prices than the customers with less elastic demands. *§2.b*

? What determines whether consumers alter their purchases a little or a lot in response to a price change?

8. Everything else held constant, the greater the number of close substitutes, the greater the price elasticity of demand. *§3.a*

9. Everything else held constant, the greater the proportion of a household's budget that a good constitutes, the greater the household's elasticity of demand for that good. *§3.b*

10. Everything else held constant, the longer the time period under consideration, the greater the price elasticity of demand. *§3.c*

? How do we measure whether changes in income, changes in the prices of related goods, or changes in advertising expenditures affect consumer purchases?

11. Elasticities can be calculated for any variable that affects demand. *§4*

12. The cross-price elasticity of demand is defined as the percentage change in the quantity demanded for one good divided by the percentage change in the price of a related good, everything else held constant. *§4.a*

13. The income elasticity of demand is defined as the percentage change in the quantity demanded of a good divided by the percentage change in income, everything else held constant. *§4.b*

? How do we measure whether producers respond to a price change?

14. The price elasticity of supply is defined as the percentage change in the quantity supplied of a good divided by the percentage change in the price of that good, everything else held constant. *§5.a*

15. The short run is a period of time short enough that the quantities of at least some of the resources cannot be varied. The long run is a period of time just long enough that the quantities of all resources can be varied. *§5.b*

16. The incidence of a tax depends on the price elasticities of demand and supply. In general, the more elastic the demand and the less elastic the supply, everything else held constant, the more the incidence falls on businesses and the less on consumers. *§5.c*

Key Terms

price elasticity of demand *§1.a*

perfectly elastic demand curve *§1.b*

perfectly inelastic demand curve *§1.b*

total revenue (*TR*) *§2.a*

price discrimination *§2.b*

cross-price elasticity of demand *§4.a*

income elasticity of demand *§4.b*

normal goods *§4.b*

inferior goods *§4.b*

luxury good *§4.b*

price elasticity of supply *§5.a*

short run *§5.b*

long run *§5.b*

tax incidence *§5.c*

Exercises

Use the following hypothetical demand schedule for movies to do exercises 1–4.

Quantity Demanded	Price	Elasticity
100	$ 5	
80	$10	
60	$15	
40	$20	
20	$25	
10	$30	

1. a. Determine the price elasticity of demand at each quantity demanded.
   b. Redo exercise 1a using price changes of $10 rather than $5.
   c. Plot the price and quantity data given in the demand schedule. Indicate the price elasticity value at each quantity demanded. Explain why the elasticity value gets smaller as you move down the demand curve.

2. Below the demand curve plotted in exercise 1, plot the total revenue curve, measuring total revenue on the vertical axis and quantity on the horizontal axis.

3. What would a 10 percent increase in the price of movie tickets mean for the revenue of a movie theater if the price elasticity of demand was 0.1, 0.5, 1.0, and 5.0?

4. Using the demand curve plotted in exercise 1, illustrate what would occur if the income elasticity of demand was 0.05 and income rose by 10 percent. If the income elasticity of demand was 3.0 and income rose by 10 percent, what would occur?

5. Which is easier: to list five substitutes for each of the products listed under the elastic portion of Table 1 or to list five substitutes for the goods listed under the inelastic portion? Explain.

6. Are the following pairs of goods substitutes or complements? Indicate whether their cross-price elasticities are negative or positive.
   a. Bread and butter
   b. Bread and potatoes
   c. Socks and shoes
   d. Tennis rackets and golf clubs
   e. Bicycles and automobiles
   f. Foreign investments and domestic investments
   g. Cars made in Japan and cars made in the United States

7. Suppose the price elasticity of demand for movies by teenagers is 0.2 and that by adults is 2.0. What policy would the movie theater implement to increase total revenue? Use hypothetical data to demonstrate your answer.

8. Explain how consumers will react to a job loss. What will be the first goods they will do without?

9. Explain why senior citizens can obtain special discounts at movie theaters, drugstores, and other businesses.

10. Calculate the income elasticity of demand from the following data (use the midpoint or average):

Income	Quantity Demanded
$15,000	20,000
$20,000	30,000

   a. Explain why the value is a positive number.
   b. Explain what would happen to a demand curve as income changes if the income elasticity was 2.0. Compare that outcome to the situation that would occur if the income elasticity of demand was 0.2.

11. The poor tend to have a price elasticity of demand for movie tickets that is greater than 1. Why don't you see signs offering "poor people discounts" similar to the signs offering "senior citizen discounts"?

12. Suppose a tax is imposed on a product that has a completely inelastic supply curve. Who pays the tax?

13. Explain why a 40 percent across-the-board tax on businesses might not benefit the consumers.

14. Explain what must occur for the strategies suggested by the following headlines to be successful:
   a. "Ford to go nationwide with plan for one-price selling of Escorts."
   b. "P. F. Flyers cut sneaker prices to $20 a pair in a move to triple 1999 sales to 10 million pairs."
   c. "Honda plans to launch a less expensive 'value-priced' Accord."
   d. "Procter & Gamble cuts prices of Dash detergent 30 to 40 percent."

15. Suppose the demand for insulin consists of two types of consumers, those who must have a dose each day and those who are able to go without the drug for several weeks. Suppose the price elasticity of demand for the first group is 0.01 and that for the second group is 4.0. Explain how the firms producing insulin might price the insulin.

Take the ACE Practice Test for this chapter to review the important concepts and get immediate feedback with answers.

economics.college.hmco.com/students

Higher Gas Prices Make Future Murky for Big SUVs: Impact of Rising Fuel Costs Could Be Bigger in Canada than U.S.

Fuel isn't the only liquid flowing at gasoline stations these days. It's joined by the teardrops of sport utility vehicle owners filling their tanks and paying some of the highest prices ever in Canada.

Sales of SUVs—the big, heavily marketed vehicles loved by many and scorned by others as gas guzzlers owned by fad-conscious drivers—rose significantly in the Canadian new vehicle market in 2002.

And this year, gasoline prices across the country have surpassed the 80-cents-a-litre mark and in some places are approaching 90 cents.

Industry experts generally agree that amid a public perception of SUVs as being environmentally unfriendly, their fuel economy has dramatically improved over the past few years. But the big vehicles—part of the light-truck segment, with car-like features—are still more expensive to fuel than a compact or mid-sized sedan.

That has analysts wondering if the two market trends of higher SUV sales and higher pump prices are destined to collide in a country where fuel economy is considered more important than it is in the United States. . . .

Higher gasoline prices in Canada haven't driven consumers away from the dozens of SUV models available. According to DesRosiers Automotive Consultants Inc., SUV sales rose 17.7 per cent in 2002, to nearly 270,000. . . .

But small cars still sold well in a country that embraces vehicles with better fuel economy. The top six sedans sold in Canada last year were all compact cars, led by the Honda Civic; the family-oriented Dodge Caravan led all vehicle sales, including the light-truck minivan segment.

"There comes a point in time where people say, 'I can't afford to spend that extra money on fuel every day if I'm commuting,'" says Jim Miller, vice-president of communications for Honda Canada. Honda boasted the top-selling sedan in Canada last year—the Civic—while its CR-V compact SUV placed eighth among all light trucks, a category that includes minivans and pickups.

"Is it 80 cents a litre? Is it 90 cents a litre? When do we hit that magic break point that changes people's buying habits?" Miller asks rhetorically. . . .

In the United States, gasoline prices—while vulnerable to price swings based on potential shortages amid war tension in the oil-rich Middle East—are generally lower. Plus, Americans have more disposable income and tend to use more of their available cash for bigger vehicles, favouring style and performance over economical concerns.

Environmental activists are pushing for the wider use of vehicles with cleaner, hybrid or fuel cell engines through new U.S. standards and under Canada's Kyoto commitments to reduce air pollution. But industry observers say those alternative engines are decades away from being used in the mass production of consumer vehicles.

Still, an anti-SUV movement is rising. American TV ads have suggested that owners of gas-guzzling SUVs are indirectly assisting terrorists who obtain financing in oil-exporting Middle East countries.

And a group of Christian ministers launched a "What Would Jesus Drive?" campaign, urging SUV owners to consider whether they could switch to more fuel-efficient vehicles to preserve the planet. . . .

STEVE ERWIN

Edmonton Journal/**February 25, 2003**

After September 11, 2001, some of the U.S. public and some of the media started a campaign against the sports utility vehicle, the SUV. As the article states, American TV ads have suggested that owners of gas-guzzling SUVs are indirectly assisting terrorists who obtain financing in oil-exporting Middle East countries, and a group of Christian ministers launched a "What Would Jesus Drive?" campaign, urging SUV owners to consider whether they could switch to more fuel-efficient vehicles to preserve the planet. However, while these campaigns may have changed some consumers' tastes, the real effect on consumers' demand for SUVs has come from the increased gas prices.

A question someone might ask is, why have higher gas prices affected purchases of SUVs rather than purchases of gasoline? It is the price of gasoline that has risen, not the price of SUVs. The answer is that in the short run, the price elasticity of gasoline is very inelastic and the cross-price elasticity of gasoline and SUVs is negative. The demand for gasoline is price-inelastic in the short run because there are no close substitutes. When the price increases, people do not reduce their consumption very much. In the long run, if the price of gasoline

should remain high, substitutes would become available. In fact, the article notes that people are finding more fuel-efficient means of transportation: purchasing crossover vehicles or smaller vehicles.

The cross-price elasticity is calculated by dividing the percentage change in the quantity of SUVs purchased by the percentage change in the price of gasoline. Gasoline prices in the United States rose from $1.30 per gallon in January 2003 to $1.90 per gallon in March 2003, a 46 percent increase. This increase has "hurt sales of SUVs," according to the article. If so, the percentage change in SUV sales would be a negative amount, perhaps 10 percent. Dividing $-.10$ by $.46$ is $-.217$; the cross-price elasticity is negative, indicating that the two products are complements.

An interesting aspect of the market for SUVs, according to the article, is that in 2002, SUV sales increased even as gas prices increased. This means that there was little relationship between the SUV purchase and gasoline prices when gasoline prices were low. But at some point, as the price of gasoline rose, the cross-price elasticity rose enough that the gas prices affected sales of SUVs.

CHAPTER 21

Consumer Choice

? **Fundamental Questions**

1. **How do consumers allocate their limited incomes among the billions of goods and services that exist?**

2. **Why does the demand curve slope down?**

3. **What is consumer surplus?**

Several students who had just completed their final exam in economics were joking that any lab animal could be trained to get an A in economics. It would only have to answer "demand and supply" to every question. The students' sarcasm demonstrated both their grasp and their lack of understanding of economics. There is no doubt that demand and supply are at the heart of economics, but unless you know why demand and supply behave as they do, can you be confident about what they imply? Can firms be sure that they will sell more if they lower the price of their product? Should producers confidently assume that when income grows, demand will increase?

In this chapter we go behind the scenes of demand. We examine how and why consumers make choices and what factors influence their choices. In the next chapter, "Supply: The Costs of Doing Business," we turn to the supply side and discuss what decisions and factors lie behind the relation between quantities supplied and price. ■

1. Decisions

Do we go to college or get a job? Do we get married or remain single? Do we live in the dorm, a house, or an apartment? "Decisions, decisions, decisions! Don't we ever get a break from the pressure of making choices?" Not unless scarcity disappears will we be freed of having to make choices. Although scarcity and choice are pervasive, how people make decisions is a question that has eluded scientific explanation. Some decisions seem to be based on feelings, or come from the heart, while others seem more calculated. Some are quick and impulsive, while others take months or years of research. Is it the appeal of the book cover that makes you decide to buy one book over another? Does a television commercial affect your decision? Are you more influenced by your spouse, your family, your friends, or your coworkers?

The answers to these questions depend on your values, on your personality, on where you were raised, on how others might react to your decision, and on many other factors. Although the important factors in a decision may vary from person to person, everyone makes decisions in much the same way. People tend to compare the perceived costs and benefits of alternatives and select those that they believe give them the greatest relative benefits. This is not to say that everyone walks around with a computer into which he or she continually feeds data and out of which comes the answer: "Buy this," or "Do that." Instead, whether the decision is made on the basis of emotion or on the basis of an accountant's balance sheet, people are comparing what they perceive at the time of the decision to be the costs and benefits to them of that decision. To explain how these comparisons are made, philosophers and economists of the nineteenth century developed a concept called *utility*. That concept can help us understand consumer decision making today.

1.a. Utility

How is success measured in the game of life? It is measured not as the bumper sticker says, "The one with the most toys at the end wins," but by happiness—how much fun you have along the way. The word *happiness* is used very generally here. It implies that whatever individuals' goals are—peace, serenity, religious devotion, self-esteem, or the well-being of others—the more one has of what one desires, the better off one is. **Utility** is the term economists and philosophers have used to capture this general concept of happiness. You are nourished by a good meal, entertained by a concert, proud of a fine car, and comforted by a nice home and warm clothing. Whatever feelings are described by *nourishment, entertainment, pride,* and *comfort* are captured in the term *utility*. Utility is another term for *satisfaction* or happiness.

Consumers make choices that give them the greatest utility; they maximize their utility. The utility you derive from experiencing some activity or consuming some good depends on your tastes and preferences. You may love opera and intensely dislike country and western music. You may have difficulty understanding how anyone can eat tripe, but you love hot chilies. We shall have little to say about why some people prefer country and western music and others classical music, although the issue is interesting; we simply assume that tastes and preferences are given and use those given tastes and preferences to describe the process of decision making.

1.b. Diminishing Marginal Utility

Utility is used to show why the law of demand is referred to as a law. To illustrate how utility maximization can be useful, we must create a hypothetical world in which we can measure the satisfaction that people receive from consuming goods and services.

utility: a measure of the satisfaction received from possessing or consuming goods and services

Individuals behave so as to maximize their utility.

Suppose that a consumer named Gabrielle can listen to as much country and western music as she wishes during the course of the day. Assume that Gabrielle is hooked up to a computer that measures satisfaction in units called *utils*. The utils that Gabrielle associates with each hour of listening are presented in Table 1.

Several important concepts associated with consumer choice can be observed in Table 1. First, each *additional* hour of music yields Gabrielle less satisfaction (fewer utils) than the previous hour. According to Table 1, the first hour yields 200 utils, the second 98, the third 50, the fourth 10, and the fifth none. Each additional hour of music, until the fifth hour, adds to total utility; but Gabrielle enjoys each additional hour just a little bit less than she enjoyed the prior hour. This relationship is called **diminishing marginal utility.**

Marginal utility is the change in total utility that occurs because one more unit of the good is consumed or acquired:

$$\text{Marginal utility} = \frac{\text{change in total utility}}{\text{change in quantity}}$$

According to the principle of diminishing marginal utility, the more of a good or service that someone consumes during a particular period of time, the less satisfaction another unit of that good or service provides that individual. Imagine yourself sitting down to a plate piled high with cake. The first piece is delicious, and the second tastes good but not as good as the first. The fourth piece doesn't taste very good at all, and the sixth piece nearly makes you sick. Instead of satisfaction, the sixth piece of cake yields dissatisfaction, or **disutility.**

Notice that we are speaking of diminishing *marginal* utility, not diminishing *total* utility. **Total utility,** the measure of the total satisfaction derived from consuming a quantity of some good or service, climbs until dissatisfaction sets in. For Gabrielle, total utility rises from 200 to 298 to 348 and reaches 358 with the fourth hour of music. From the fifth hour on, total utility declines. Marginal utility, however, is the additional utility gained from listening to another hour of music, and it declines from the first hour on.

To illustrate the relation between marginal and total utility, we have plotted the data from Table 1 in Figure 1(a). The total utility curve rises as quantity rises until the fifth hour of listening. After 5 hours, the total utility curve declines. The reason total utility rises at first is that each additional hour provides a little more utility. The marginal utility of the first hour is 200; the marginal utility of the second hour is 98; of the third, 50; of the fourth, 10; and of the fifth, zero. By the fifth hour, total utility is 200 + 98 + 50 + 10 + 0 = 358.

diminishing marginal utility: the principle that the more of a good that one obtains in a specific period of time, the less is the additional utility yielded by an additional unit of that good

marginal utility: the extra utility derived from consuming one more unit of a good or service

disutility: dissatisfaction

total utility: a measure of the total satisfaction derived from consuming a quantity of some good or service

TABLE 1			
The Utility of Listening to Country and Western Music	**Hours of Listening per Day**	**Util of Each Hour (marginal utility)**	**Total Utility**
	1	200	200
	2	98	298
	3	50	348
	4	10	358
	5	0	358
	6	−70	288
	7	−200	88

FIGURE 1

Total and Marginal Utility

Figure 1(a) shows the total utility obtained from listening to country and western music. Total utility reaches a maximum and then declines as additional listening becomes distasteful. For the first hour, the marginal and total utilities are the same. For the second hour, the marginal utility is the additional utility provided by the second unit. The total utility is the sum of the marginal utilities of the first and second units. The second unit provides less utility than the first unit, the third less than the second, and so on, in accordance with the law of diminishing marginal utility. But total utility, the sum of marginal utilities, rises as long as marginal utility is positive. Figure 1(b) shows marginal utility. When marginal utility is zero, total utility is at its maximum. When marginal utility is negative, total utility declines.

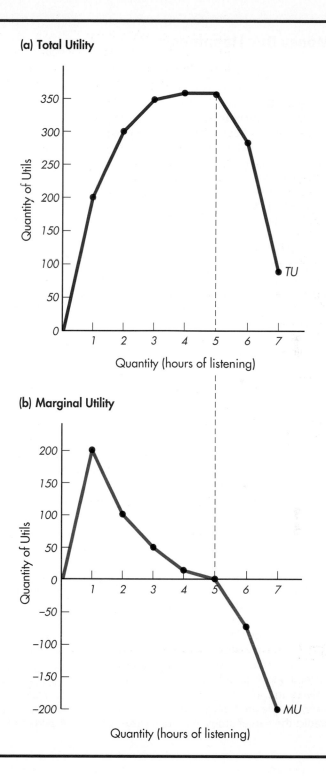

(a) Total Utility

(b) Marginal Utility

Does Money Buy Happiness?

Diminishing marginal utility affects consumer purchases of every good. Does diminishing marginal utility affect income as well? This question has been a topic of economic debate for years. The case for progressive taxation—the more income you have, the greater the percentage of each additional dollar that you pay in taxes—is based on the idea that the marginal utility of income diminishes. In theory, if each additional dollar brings less utility to a person, the pain associated with giving up a portion of each additional dollar will decline. And as a result of taxing the rich at a higher rate than the poor, the total pain imposed on society from a tax will be less than it would be if the same tax rate were applied to every dollar.

Source: Adapted from David G. Myers, *The Pursuit of Happiness* (New York: William Morrow, 1992).

Economists have attempted to confirm or disprove the idea of the diminishing marginal utility of income, but doing so has proved difficult. Experiments have even been carried out on the topic. In one experiment, laboratory rats were trained to work for pay. They had to hit a bar several times to get a piece of food or a drink of water. After a while, after obtaining a certain amount of food and water, the rats reduced their work efforts, choosing leisure instead of more food and water. Thus, the rats did react as if their "income"—food and water—had a diminishing marginal utility.

Economists have also turned to the literature of psychology. Psychologists have carried out many surveys to measure whether people are more or less happy under various circumstances. One survey back in the 1960s asked people in different income brackets whether they were unhappy, pretty happy, or very happy. The results indicated that the higher income is, the happier people are. More recent studies by David Myers and John Stossel of ABC News examine why people are happy and find some results that contradict the earlier study. Although citizens of the more wealthy nations tend to be happier than citizens of the less wealthy nations, this relationship is not very strong. More important than wealth is the history of democracy; the longer a nation has been democratic, the happier are its citizens. Within any one country, there is only a modest link between well-being and being well-off. "Once we're comfortable, more money therefore provides diminishing returns. The second helping never tastes as good as the first," says Myers. "The second fifty thousand dollars of income means much less than the first." Myers uses a figure something like the accompanying one to illustrate his findings. Notice how income and percentage who are happy both rise until a 1990 income level of about $7,000 per person after tax is reached. After that income level, as income rises, the percentage who are happy does not change much.

Sources: John Stossel, "The Mystery of Happiness: Who Has It and How to Get It," ABC News, April 15, 1996, and replayed since; David G. Myers, *The Pursuit of Happiness* (New York: William Morrow, 1992); and N. M. Bradbum and D. Caplovitz, *Reports on Happiness* (Chicago: Aldine, 1965), p. 9.

We have plotted marginal utility in Figure 1(b), directly below the total utility curve of Figure 1(a). Marginal utility declines with each successive unit, reaches zero, and then turns negative. As long as marginal utility is positive, total utility rises. When marginal utility becomes negative, total utility declines. Marginal utility is zero at the point where total utility is at its maximum (unit 5 in this case). Marginal utility is the slope of the total utility curve.

1.c. Diminishing Marginal Utility and Time

The concept of diminishing marginal utility makes sense only if we define the *period of time* during which consumption is occurring. If Gabrielle listened to the music over a period of several days, we would not observe diminishing marginal utility until she had listened more than 5 hours. Usually, the shorter the time period, the more quickly marginal utility diminishes. Once the time period has been defined, diminishing marginal utility will apply; it applies to everyone and to every good and service, except perhaps to income itself, as discussed in the Economic Insight "Does Money Buy Happiness?"

1.d. Consumers Are Not Identical

All consumers experience diminishing marginal utility, but the rate at which marginal utility declines is not identical for all consumers. The rate at which marginal utility diminishes depends on an individual's tastes and preferences. Gabrielle clearly enjoys country and western music. For a person who dislikes it, the first hour might yield disutility or negative utility.

1.e. An Illustration: "All You Can Eat"

The principle of diminishing marginal utility says something about "all you can eat" specials. It says that you will stop eating when marginal utility is zero. At some restaurants consumers who pay a fixed charge may eat as much as they desire. The only restriction is that the restaurant does not allow "doggy bags." Because diminishing marginal utility eventually sets in, all consumers eventually stop eating when their marginal utility is zero. This is the point at which their total utility is at a maximum: one more bite would be distasteful and would decrease utility. The restaurant must determine what fixed price to charge. Knowing that no consumer will eat forever—that each will stop when his or her marginal utility is zero—the restaurant must set a price that yields a profit from the average consumer.

RECAP

1. Utility is a concept used to represent the degree to which goods and services satisfy wants.
2. Total utility is the total satisfaction that a consumer obtains from consuming a particular good or service.
3. Marginal utility is the utility that an additional unit of a good or service yields.
4. Total utility increases until dissatisfaction sets in. When another unit of a good would yield disutility, the consumer has been filled up with the good—more will not bring greater satisfaction.
5. According to the principle of diminishing marginal utility, marginal utility declines with each additional unit of a good or service that the consumer obtains. When marginal utility is zero, total utility is at its maximum.

1. How do consumers allocate their limited incomes among the billions of goods and services that exist?

2. Utility and Choice

Can we simply conclude that people will consume goods until the marginal utility of each good is zero? No, we cannot, for we would be ignoring scarcity and opportunity costs. No one has enough income to purchase everything until the marginal utility of each item is zero. Because incomes are limited, purchasing one thing means not purchasing other things. Gabrielle, our country and western music fancier, might be able to get more utility by purchasing some other good than by buying more music to listen to.

2.a. Consumer Choice

To illustrate the effect of opportunity costs on consumption, let's turn again to Gabrielle. Gabrielle has a budget of $10 to spend on CDs, gasoline, and movies. She has found a place selling used CDs. She also goes to a discount gas station and a discount movie theater. We want to know how many units of each she will purchase. The answer is in Table 2.

The price (P) of each secondhand CD is $2; the price of each gallon of gas is $1; the price of each movie is $3. The marginal utility (MU) provided by each unit and the ratio of the marginal utility to the price (MU/P) are presented at the top of the table. In the lower part of the table are the steps involved in allocating income among the three goods.

The first purchase involves a choice among the first unit of each of the three goods. The first CD yields a marginal utility (MU) of 200 and costs $2; thus, per dollar of expenditure, the first CD yields 100 utils ($MU/P = 100$). The first gallon of gas yields a marginal utility per dollar of expenditure of 200. The first movie yields a marginal utility per dollar of expenditure of 50; it yields 150 utils and costs $3. Which does Gabrielle choose?

To find the answer, compare the ratios of the marginal utility per dollar of expenditure (MU/P), *not* the marginal utility of each good (MU). The ratio of marginal utility to price puts the goods on the same basis (utility per dollar) and allows us to make sense of Gabrielle's decisions. Looking only at marginal utilities would not do this. For instance, another diamond might yield 10,000 utils and another apple might yield only 100 utils; but if the diamond costs $100,000 and the apple costs $1, the marginal utility per dollar of expenditure on the apple is greater than the marginal utility per dollar of expenditure on the diamond, and thus a consumer is better off purchasing the apple.

As indicated in Table 2, Gabrielle's first purchase is the gallon of gas. It yields the greatest marginal utility per dollar of expenditure (she needs gas in her car to be able to go anywhere); and because it costs $1, Gabrielle has $9 left to spend.

The second purchase involves a choice among the first CD, the second gallon of gas, and the first movie. The ratios of marginal utility per dollar of expenditure are 100 for the CD, 150 for the gas, and 50 for a movie. Thus, Gabrielle purchases the second gallon of gas and has $8 left.

For the third purchase, Gabrielle must decide between the first CD, the first movie, and the third gallon of gas. Because the CD yields a ratio of 100 and both the gas and the movie yield ratios of 50, she purchases the CD. The CD costs $2, so she has $6 left to spend.

A utility-maximizing consumer like Gabrielle always chooses the purchase that yields the greatest marginal utility per dollar of expenditure. If two goods offer the same marginal utility per dollar of expenditure, the consumer will be indifferent

TABLE 2

The Logic of Consumer Choice

CD (P = $2)			Gas (P = $1)			Movie (P = $3)		
Units	*MU*	*MU/P*	Units	*MU*	*MU/P*	Units	*MU*	*MU/P*
1	200	100	1	200	200	1	150	50
2	98	49	2	150	150	2	90	30
3	50	25	3	50	50	3	60	20
4	10	5	4	30	30	4	30	10
5	0	0	5	0	0	5	9	3
6	−70	−35	6	−300	−300	6	0	0
7	−200	−100	7	−700	−700	7	−6	−2

Steps	Choices		Decision	Remaining Budget
1st purchase	1st CD:	$MU/P = 100$	Gas	$10 − $1 = $9
	1st gas:	$MU/P = 200$		
	1st movie:	$MU/P = 50$		
2nd purchase	1st CD:	$MU/P = 100$	Gas	$9 − $1 = $8
	2nd gas:	$MU/P = 150$		
	1st movie:	$MU/P = 50$		
3rd purchase	1st CD:	$MU/P = 100$	CD	$8 − $2 = $6
	3rd gas:	$MU/P = 50$		
	1st movie:	$MU/P = 50$		
4th purchase	2nd CD:	$MU/P = 49$	Gas	$6 − $1 = $5
	3rd gas:	$MU/P = 50$		
	1st movie:	$MU/P = 50$		
5th purchase	2nd CD:	$MU/P = 49$	Movie	$5 − $3 = $2
	4th gas:	$MU/P = 30$		
	1st movie:	$MU/P = 50$		
6th purchase	2nd CD:	$MU/P = 49$	CD	$2 − $2 = $0
	4th gas:	$MU/P = 30$		
	2nd movie:	$MU/P = 30$		

Note: Purchases made with $10: 2 CDs, 3 gallons of gas, and 1 movie ticket.

between the two—that is, the consumer won't care which is chosen. For example, Table 2 indicates that for the fourth purchase, either another gallon of gas or a movie would yield 50 utils per dollar. The consumer is completely indifferent between the two and so arbitrarily selects gas. The movie is chosen for the fifth purchase. With the sixth purchase, the total budget is spent. For $10, Gabrielle ends up with 2 CDs, 3 gallons of gas, and 1 movie.

In this example, Gabrielle is portrayed as a methodical, robotlike consumer who calculates how to allocate her scarce income among goods and services in a way that ensures that each additional dollar of expenditure yields the greatest marginal utility. This picture is more than a little far-fetched, but it does describe the result if not the process of consumer choice. People do have to decide which goods and services

2.b. Consumer Equilibrium

With $10, Gabrielle purchases 2 CDs, 3 gallons of gas, and 1 movie ticket. For the second CD, the marginal utility per dollar of expenditure is 49; for the third gallon of gas, it is 50; and for the first movie, it is 50. Is it merely a fluke that the marginal utility per dollar of expenditure ratios are nearly equal? No. *In order to maximize utility, consumers must allocate their limited incomes among goods and services in such a way that the marginal utilities per dollar of expenditure on the last unit of each good purchased will be as nearly equal as possible.* This is called the **equimarginal principle** and also represents **consumer equilibrium.** It is consumer equilibrium because the consumer will not change from this point unless something changes income, marginal utility, or price.

In our example, the ratios are not identical at consumer equilibrium—49, 50, and 50—but they are as close to equal as possible because Gabrielle (like all consumers) had to purchase whole portions of the goods. Consumers cannot spend a dollar on any good or service and always get the fractional amount that a dollar buys—one-tenth of a tennis lesson or one-third of a bottle of water. Instead, consumers have to purchase goods and services in whole units—1 piece or 1 ounce or 1 package—and pay the per unit price.

The equimarginal principle is simply common sense. Consumers spend an additional dollar on the good that gives the greatest satisfaction. At the prices given in Table 2, with an income of $10, and with the marginal utilities given, Gabrielle maximizes her utility by purchasing 2 CDs, 3 gallons of gas, and 1 movie ticket. Everything else held constant, no other allocation of the $10 would yield Gabrielle more utility.

Consumers are in equilibrium when they have no incentive to reallocate their limited budget or income. With MU standing for marginal utility and P for price, the general rule for consumer equilibrium is

$$\frac{MU_{CD}}{P_{CD}} = \frac{MU_{gas}}{P_{gas}} = \frac{MU_{movie}}{P_{movie}} = \cdots = \frac{MU_x}{P_x}$$

MU_x/P_x is the marginal utility per dollar of expenditure on any good other than CDs, gas, or movies. It represents the opportunity cost of spending $1 on CDs, gas, or movies.

to purchase with their limited incomes, and people do select the options that give them the greatest utility.

equimarginal principle or **consumer equilibrium:** to maximize utility, consumers must allocate their scarce incomes among goods so as to equate the marginal utilities per dollar of expenditure on the last unit of each good purchased

RECAP

1. To maximize utility, consumers must allocate their limited incomes in such a way that the marginal utilities per dollar obtained from the last unit consumed are equal among all goods and services; this is the equimarginal principle.

2. As long as the marginal utilities per dollar obtained from the last unit of all products consumed are the same, the consumer is in equilibrium and will not reallocate income.

3. Consumer equilibrium, or utility maximization, is summarized by a formula that equates the marginal utilities per dollar of expenditure on the last item purchased of all goods:

$$MU_a/P_a = MU_b/P_b = MU_c/P_c = MU_x/P_x$$

3. The Demand Curve Again

We have shown how consumers make choices—by allocating their scarce incomes among goods in order to maximize their utility. The next step is to relate consumer choices to the demand curve.

3.a. The Downward Slope of the Demand Curve

The demand curve or schedule can be derived from consumer equilibrium by altering the price of one good or service.

2. Why does the demand curve slope down?

Recall from Chapter 3 that as the price of a good falls, the quantity demanded of that good rises. This inverse relation between price and quantity demanded arises from diminishing marginal utility and consumer equilibrium.

Consumers allocate their income among goods and services in order to maximize their utility. A consumer is in equilibrium when the total budget is expended and the marginal utilities per dollar of expenditure on the last unit of each good are the same. A change in the price of one good will disturb the consumer's equilibrium; the ratios of marginal utility per dollar of expenditure on the last unit of each good will no longer be equal. The consumer will then reallocate her income among the goods in order to increase total utility.

In the example presented in Table 2, the price of a CD is $2, the price per gallon of gas is $1, and the price of a movie ticket is $3. Now suppose the price of the CD falls to $1 while the prices of gas and movies and Gabrielle's budget of $10 remain the same. Common sense tells us that Gabrielle will probably alter the quantities purchased by buying more CDs. To find out if she does—and whether the equimarginal principle holds—her purchases can be traced step by step as we did previously.

In Table 3, only the *MU/P* ratio for CDs is different from the corresponding figure at the top of Table 2. At the old consumer equilibrium of 2 CDs, 3 gallons of gas, and 1 movie, the marginal utility per dollar of expenditure (*MU/P*) on each good is

CD: 98/$1 = 98/$1   Gas: 50/$1 = 50/$1   Movie: 150/$3 = 50/$1

Clearly, the ratios are no longer equal. In order to maximize utility, Gabrielle must reallocate her budget among the goods. When all $10 is spent, Gabrielle finds that she has purchased 3 CDs, 4 gallons of gas, and 1 movie ticket. The lower price of

---

TABLE 3

A Price Change

CD (*P* = $1)			Gas (*P* = $1)			Movie (*P* = $3)		
Units	*MU*	*MU/P*	Units	*MU*	*MU/P*	Units	*MU*	*MU/P*
1	200	**200**	1	200	200	1	150	50
2	98	**98**	2	150	150	2	90	30
3	50	**50**	3	50	50	3	60	20
4	10	**10**	4	30	30	4	30	10
5	0	**0**	5	0	0	5	9	3
6	−70	**−70**	6	−300	−300	6	0	0
7	−200	**−200**	7	−700	−700	7	−6	−2

FIGURE 2

Consumer Surplus and the Demand for Used CDs

Gabrielle is willing and able to pay $3 for the first used CD. She is willing to pay $2 for the second used CD. If the market price of CDs is $2, she can buy both the first and the second used CDs for $2 each; and she receives a bonus on the first, paying less for it than she is willing and able to pay. This bonus, the consumer surplus, is indicated by the blue area. At a price of $1, the consumer surplus is both the blue and yellow areas.

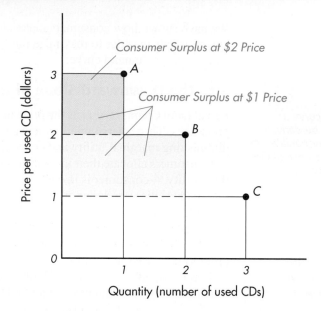

CDs has induced her to purchase an additional CD. Gabrielle's behavior illustrates what you already know: the quantity demanded of CDs increases as the price of the CD decreases.

If the price of the CD is increased to $3, we find that Gabrielle demands only 1 CD. The three prices and the corresponding quantities of CDs purchased give us Gabrielle's demand for CDs, which is shown in Figure 2. At $3 she is willing and able to buy 1 CD; at $2 she is willing and able to buy 2 CDs; and at $1 she is willing and able to buy 3 CDs.

3.b. Consumer Surplus

3. What is consumer surplus?

An individual's demand curve measures the value that the individual consumer places on each unit of the good being considered. For example, the value that Gabrielle places on the first CD she buys during the week is the price that she would be willing and able to pay for it. The price Gabrielle would be willing and able to pay for one used CD is $3, as shown in Figure 2. At a price of $2, Gabrielle purchases two CDs. She is willing to pay $3 for the first and $2 for the second, but she gets both for $2 each. She gets a bonus because the value she places on the first CD is higher than the price she has to pay for it. This bonus is called *consumer surplus.*

consumer surplus: the difference between what the consumer is willing and able to pay for a unit of a good and the price that the consumer actually has to pay

Consumer surplus is a measure of the difference between what a consumer is willing and able to pay and the market price of a good. At a market price of $2, Gabrielle's consumer surplus is equal to ($3 − $2) + ($2 − $2) = $1. At a price of $1, Gabrielle is willing and able to purchase 3 CDs, but only the third CD is worth only $1 to her. The first two are worth more than the $1 she has to pay for them. When she purchases the CDs, she gets a bonus of ($3 − $1) + ($2 − $1) + ($1 − $1) = $3.

3.c. Shifts of Demand and the Determination of Market Demand

Individual demand comes from utility maximization. Individuals allocate their scarce incomes among goods in order to get the greatest utility; this occurs when consumer equilibrium is reached, represented in symbols as $MU_a/P_a = MU_b/P_b = \cdots = MU_x/P_x$. As the price of a good or service is changed, consumer equilibrium is disturbed. In response to the price change, individuals alter their purchases so as to achieve maximum utility.

When the price of one good falls while everything else is held constant, two things occur: (1) other goods become relatively *more* expensive, so consumers buy more of the less expensive good and less of the more expensive goods, and (2) the good purchased prior to the price change now costs less, so the consumer can buy more of all goods.

When a good becomes relatively less expensive, it yields more satisfaction per dollar than before, so consumers buy more of it than before as they decrease their expenditures on other goods. This is the *substitution effect* of a price change.

Figure 3 shows that at the price of $2 per used CD, Gabrielle spends $4 on CDs. When the price falls to $1, she spends only $2 for those two CDs. As a result, Gabrielle can purchase more of all goods, including the good whose price has fallen. This is the *income effect* of a price change.

The process of changing the price of one good or service while income, tastes and preferences, and the prices of related goods are held constant defines the individual's demand for that good or service. Should income, tastes and preferences, or prices of related goods and services change, then the individual's demand will change. More or less income means that more or less goods and services can be purchased. A change in income affects the ratios of *MU/P* and disturbs consumer equilibrium. When the price of a related good changes, the ratio of marginal utility to price for that good changes, thus disturbing consumer equilibrium. And changes in

The substitution effect indicates that following a decrease in the price of a good or service, an individual will purchase more of the now less expensive good and less of other goods.

The income effect of a price change indicates that an individual's income can buy more of all goods when the price of one good declines, everything else held constant.

FIGURE 3

Gabrielle's Demand Curve for Used CDs

The demand curve shows that Gabrielle purchases 1 used CD at a price of $3, 2 used CDs at a price of $2, and 3 used CDs at a price of $1.

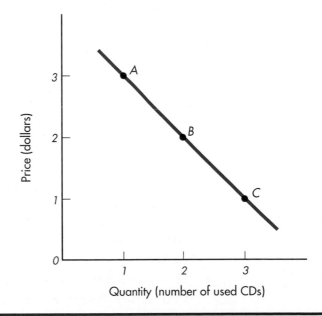

Halloween has changed from a child's holiday to the second most popular holiday in the United States. Spending on Halloween supplies exceeds spending for every holiday except Christmas. The increased tastes for Halloween fun have led to an increased demand for costumes. In terms of economic theory, marginal utility for each dollar of spending on Halloween costumes has risen.

Consumer equilibrium shows that the nonprice determinants of demand have their effects through the MUs or the prices of other goods and services.

tastes and preferences, represented as changes in the *MU*s, also alter consumer equilibrium. For each change in a determinant of demand, a new demand curve for a good or service is derived; the demand curve will have shifted.

The market demand curve is the sum of all the individual demand curves. This means that anything that affects the individual curves also affects the market curve. In addition, when we combine the individual demand curves into a market demand curve, the number of individuals to be combined determines the position of the market demand curve. Changes in the number of consumers alters the market demand curve. We thus say that the determinants of demand are tastes and preferences, income, prices of related goods, international effects, and number of consumers. Also, recall that diminishing marginal utility is defined for consumption during a specific period of time. Since consumer equilibrium and thus the demand curve depend on diminishing marginal utility, the demand curve is also defined for consumption over a specific period of time. Changes in the time period or changes in expectations will therefore also alter demand.

RECAP

1. The principle of diminishing marginal utility and the equimarginal principle account for the inverse relation between the price of a product and the quantity demanded.
2. Consumer surplus is the excess of the amount consumers are willing and able to pay for an item over the price they actually pay.
3. A price change triggers the substitution effect and the income effect.
4. The substitution effect occurs because once a good becomes less expensive, it yields more satisfaction per dollar than before and consumers buy more of it

than before. They do this by decreasing their purchases of other goods. The income effect of the price change occurs because a lower price raises real income (total utility) and the consumer purchases more of all goods.

5. The market demand curve is the summation of all individual demand curves.

6. Economists derive the market demand curve for a good by assuming that individual incomes are fixed, that the prices of all goods except the one in question are constant, that each individual's tastes remain fixed, that expectations do not change, that the number of consumers is constant, and that the time period under consideration remains unchanged. A change in any one of these determinants causes the demand curve to shift.

Summary

❓ How do consumers allocate their limited incomes among the billions of goods and services that exist?

1. Utility is a measure of the satisfaction received from possessing or consuming a good. *§1.a*

2. *Diminishing marginal utility* refers to the decline in marginal utility received from each additional unit of a good that is consumed during a particular period of time. The more of some good a consumer has, the less desirable is another unit of that good. *§1.b*

3. Even if a good is free a consumer will eventually reach a point where one more unit of the good would be undesirable or distasteful, and he or she will not consume that additional unit. *§1.e*

4. Consumer equilibrium refers to the utility-maximizing situation in which the consumer has allocated his or her budget among goods and services in such a way that the marginal utilities per dollar of expenditure on the last unit of any good are the same for all goods. It is represented in symbols as

$$MU_a/P_a = MU_b/P_b = \cdots = MU_x/P_x \qquad §2.b$$

❓ Why does the demand curve slope down?

5. The demand curve slopes down because of diminishing marginal utility and consumer equilibrium. *§3.a*

6. The income and substitution effects of a price change occur because of diminishing marginal utility and the equimarginal principle. When the price of one good falls while all other prices remain the same, it yields more satisfaction per dollar than before, so consumers buy more of it than before. *§3.b*

❓ What is consumer surplus?

7. The amount by which the market price is less than the price consumers are willing and able to pay for each quantity is consumer surplus. *§3.b*

8. Market demand is the summation of individual demands. *§3.c*

Key Terms

utility *§1.a*

diminishing marginal utility *§1.b*

marginal utility *§1.b*

disutility *§1.b*

total utility *§1.b*

equimarginal principle *§2.b*

consumer equilibrium *§2.b*

consumer surplus *§3.b*

Exercises

1. Using the following information, calculate total utility and marginal utility.

   a. Plot the total utility curve.

   b. Plot marginal utility directly below total utility.

   c. At what marginal utility value does total utility reach a maximum?

Number of utils for the 1st unit	300
Number of utils for the 2nd unit	250
Number of utils for the 3rd unit	220
Number of utils for the 4th unit	160
Number of utils for the 5th unit	100
Number of utils for the 6th unit	50
Number of utils for the 7th unit	20
Number of utils for the 8th unit	0
Number of utils for the 9th unit	−250

2. Is it possible for marginal utility to be negative and total utility positive? Explain.

3. Suppose Mary is in consumer equilibrium. The marginal utility of good A is 30 and the price of good A is $2.

   a. If the price of good B is $4, the price of good C is $3, the price of good D is $1, and the price of all other goods and services is $5, what is the marginal utility of each of the goods Mary is purchasing?

   b. If Mary has chosen to keep $10 in savings, what is the ratio of MU to P for savings?

4. Using the following utility schedule, derive a demand curve for pizza.

   a. Assume income is $10, the price of each slice of pizza is $1, and the price of each glass of beer is $2. Then change the price of pizza to $2 per slice.

   b. Now change income to $12 and derive a demand curve for pizza.

Slices of Pizza	Total Utility	Glasses of Beer	Total Utility
1	200	1	500
2	380	2	800
3	540	3	900
4	600	4	920
5	630	5	930

5. Using utility, explain the following commonly made statements:

   a. I couldn't eat another bite.

   b. I'll never get tired of your cooking.

   c. The last drop tastes as good as the first.

   d. I wouldn't eat broccoli if you paid me.

   e. My kid would eat nothing but junk food if I allowed her.

   f. Any job worth doing is worth doing well.

6. How would guests' behavior be likely to differ at a BYOB (bring your own bottle) party and one at which the host provides the drinks? Explain your answer.

7. A round of golf on a municipal golf course usually takes about 5 hours. At a private country club golf course, a round takes less than 4 hours. What accounts for the difference? Would the time spent playing golf be different if golfers paid only an admission fee (membership fee) and no monthly dues or if they paid only a charge per round and no monthly dues?

8. To increase marginal utility, you must decrease consumption (everything else held constant). This statement is correct, even though it sounds strange. Explain why.

9. Suppose that the marginal utility of good A is 4 times the marginal utility of good B, but the price of good A is only 2 times larger than the price of good B. Is this point consumer equilibrium? If not, what will occur?

10. Last Saturday you went to a movie and ate a large box of popcorn and two candy bars and drank a medium soda. This Saturday you went to a movie and ate a medium box of popcorn and one candy bar and drank a large soda. Your tastes and preferences did not change. What could explain the different combinations of goods that you purchased?

11. Peer pressure is an important influence on the behavior of youngsters. For instance, many preteens begin smoking because their friends pressure them into being "cool" by smoking. Using utility theory, how would you explain peer pressure?

12. Many people who earn incomes below some level receive food stamps from the government. Economists argue that these people would be better off if the government gave them the cash equivalent of the food stamps rather than the food stamps. What is the basis of the economists' argument?

13. Suppose you are in consumer equilibrium and have chosen to work 10 hours a day, leaving the other 14 hours each day for leisure activities (leisure includes sleeping and anything other than working on the job).

a. How might you change your behavior if your wage rate per hour rises?

b. What are the income and substitution effects of the price change?

c. What would occur if the income effect is larger than the substitution effect?

14. What is the impact on charitable giving of a reduction in the tax rate on income? Will the lower tax rate lead to more or to less charitable giving?

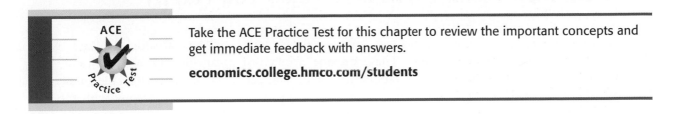

Economically Speaking

Why Sudden Wealth Will Not Make You Happy

Lotteries are booming as a way to generate income without taxation, a prime example being Hong Kong's newly introduced soccer betting draw. Big-prize quiz shows guarantee massive viewer ratings. E-commerce, property, the stock exchange, music, sports, publishing and other sectors are making people wealthy overnight. . . .

The world over, most ticket buyers—and therefore winners—are working-class people who live and work in modest neighbourhoods. When they win, their world turns upside down. They are ill-equipped to handle the new situation. They do not know whom to trust. Nor are they prepared for what is likely to happen in their relationships.

Not much information is available on this subject, and the newly rich are becoming increasingly secretive because of the consequences they fear, such as harassment by strangers, exploitation by swindlers or vilification in the press. Many receive so many requests for money for seemingly worthy causes that they are hounded from their homes. One now anonymous lottery-winning couple in Ohio, reports *Money*

magazine, was inundated with calls. They became frightened about robberies and stressed about managing their new wealth, and their children progressively lost all their old friends.

Choices expand and decisions are unavoidable. If lottery winners quit work and buy a new house in a fancy neighbourhood, they become alienated from their previous friends and family. They do not really fit in with their new neighbours, either. They can stay where they are and share their wealth. But then they are often relegated to the status of a free meal ticket and they begin to doubt the sincerity of those around them. Most studies of sudden wealth are limited to lottery winners who have volunteered to talk about their experiences, creating a sort of natural selection of the disgruntled and exploited.

But one study focused on customers of financial and legal consultants. These suddenly wealthy people were taking action to try to manage their new status and were not limited to lottery winners. Researcher Eileen Gallo's key finding was that "early money messages" made a big difference in how well people adapted to

sudden wealth. If told while growing up to save and only spend responsibly, the winner was likely to be happy with the new wealth, with a positive view as to how it affected their relationships. The vast majority of those with a negative experience with their new affluence had not received that message.

Dr. Gallo found that married people did far better than single people at handling sudden wealth. Perhaps marriage gives you at least one trustworthy person with whom you can talk. There was also a positive connection with altruism. Viewing sudden affluence as a good opportunity to help others corresponded with a more satisfactory overall adaptation. . . .

A big win or a sudden business success creates euphoria. One study suggests it takes at least HK$ 1 million to guarantee the effect, but that is certainly relative, too. In any case, the effect does not last. A windfall brings challenges and, in the long run, overall happiness is virtually unaffected.

JEAN NICOL

Source: Copyright 2003 South China Morning Post Ltd.

South China Morning Post (Hong Kong)/March 21, 2003

"The underlying assumption is that if you have all the money in the world, you'll be happy and fulfilled. That's simply not true." Does this contradict economics? Isn't the basic assumption in economics that more is better than less, that more money is better than less money? The answer is no, more is not always better than less. More disease, more filth, more garbage, more pollution, more of many things is not better than less. With respect to goods, we do assume that more is better than less as long as there is no problem in storing or keeping the goods and services and as long as our tastes do not change. The cake example used in the text, where our consumer ate so much that he or she got sick, illustrates nicely that more is preferred to less as long as there are no storage costs: it is simply impossible to "store" an infinite amount of cake, that is, to eat it. Eventually, more cake is not desired. This is the law of diminishing marginal utility in operation. It says that during a given period of time, as we get more of an additional good, the marginal amount of that good will provide us less additional happiness than a previous amount did.

In the Economic Insight "Does Money Buy Happiness?" it was shown that up to some income level, money and expressed happiness seem to rise together, but then as money continues to rise, happiness does not. The article says the same thing. People want more money—more money enables people to purchase more of everything—and so more money equates to more happiness. This seems to occur up to a point. Once someone has a bunch of money, however, additional amounts do not mean very much.

What does more income do? It shifts the budget constraint out; it enables people to purchase more of everything. The consumer equilibrium formula

$$MU_a/P_a = MU_b/P_b = MU_c/P_c = \cdots = MU_z/P_z$$

states that a consumer will purchase additional amounts of items until the consumer's budget is spent and the marginal utility of each dollar of expenditures is nearly equal across all purchases. With more income, more of everything can be purchased. The consumer still purchases by spending the budget on each good and service up to the point where the last dollar spent on each item yields the same additional utility. So the question is, do people also experience diminishing marginal utility with money? The answer has to be no as long as there are no costs to storage and tastes do not change.

The theme of the article is that people's attitudes toward sudden wealth change over time and that unless they are prepared for the sudden wealth, they may not be happier with the wealth than they were before they had it. For instance, those people who saved and spent responsibly were more likely to be happier with their new wealth than those who were not able to manage their finances. In addition, viewing sudden affluence as a good opportunity to help others seemed to make people with sudden wealth happier than those who were less altruistic. What this means is that the utility of each individual for the same item (money or any other item) is different; comparing one person's utility (happiness) to another's is not possible. How can you measure whether one person is happier than another?

Indifference Analysis

Indifference analysis is an alternative approach to utility theory for explaining consumer choice but does not require us to rely on the concept of utility.

1. Indifference Curves

In Figure 1, four combinations of CDs and gallons of gasoline are listed in the table and plotted in Figure 1(a). Preferring more to less, the consumer will clearly prefer C to the other combinations. Combination C is preferred to B because C offers one more gallon of gas than B and the same amount of CDs. Combination C is preferred to A because C offers 1 more CD and 1 more gallon of gas than A. And combination C is preferred to D because one more CD is obtained with no loss of gas. Combinations B and D are preferred to A; however, it is not obvious whether B is preferred to D or D is preferred to B.

Let's assume that the consumer has no preference between B and D. We thus say that the consumer is **indifferent** between combination B (2 CDs and 1 gallon of gas) and combination D (1 CD and 2 gallons of gas). Connecting points B and D, as in Figure 1(b), produces an indifference curve. An **indifference curve** shows all the combinations of two goods that the consumer is indifferent among, or, in other words, an indifference curve shows all the combinations of goods that will give the consumer the same level of total utility.

The quantity of goods increases as the distance from the origin increases. Thus, any combination lying on the indifference curve (like B or D) is preferred to any combination falling below the curve, or closer to the origin (like A). Any combination appearing above the curve, or farther from the origin (like C), is preferred to any combination lying on the curve.

1.a. The Shape of Indifference Curves

The most reasonable shape for an indifference curve is a downward slope from left to right, indicating that as less of one good is consumed, more of another good is consumed. Indifference curves are not likely to be vertical, horizontal, or upward sloping. They do not touch the axes, and they do not touch each other.

An indifference curve that is a vertical line, like the one labeled I_v in Figure 2(a), would mean that the consumer is indifferent to combinations B and A. For most goods this will not be the case because combination B provides more of one good with no less of the other good.

indifferent: lacking any preference

indifference curve: a curve showing all combinations of two goods that the consumer is indifferent among

FIGURE 1

Indifference Curve

Four combinations of two goods, CDs and gasoline, are presented to the consumer in Figure 1(a). Preferring more to less, the consumer will clearly prefer C to A, B, and D. Points B and D are preferred to A, but the consumer has no clear preference between B and D. The consumer is indifferent between B and D. Figure 1(b) shows that all combinations of goods among which the consumer is indifferent lie along an indifference curve.

Combination	CDs	Gallons of Gasoline
A	1	1
B	2	1
C	2	2
D	1	2

(a) Combinations of CDs and Gasoline

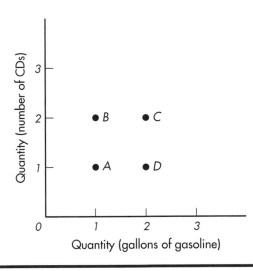

(b) Indifference Curve

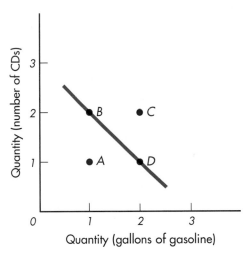

Similarly, horizontal indifference curves, such as line I_h in Figure 2(b), are ruled out for most goods. People are not likely to be indifferent between combinations A and B along the horizontal curve, since B provides more of one good with no less of the other good than A.

An upward-sloping curve, such as I_u in Figure 2(c), would mean that the consumer is indifferent between a combination of goods that provides less of everything and a combination that provides more of everything (compare points A and B). Rational consumers tend to prefer more to less.

1.b. The Slope of Indifference Curves

The slope, or steepness, of indifference curves is determined by consumer preferences. The amount of one good that a consumer must give up to get an additional unit of the other good and remain equally satisfied changes as the consumer trades off one good for the other. The less a consumer has of a good, the more the consumer values an additional unit of that good. This preference is shown by an indifference curve that bows in toward the origin, like the curve shown in Figure 3. A consumer who has 4 CDs and 1 gallon of gasoline (point D) may be willing to give up 2 CDs for 1 more gallon of gasoline, moving from D to E. But a consumer who has only

FIGURE 2

Unlikely Shapes of Indifference Curves

A vertical indifference curve, as in Figure 2(a), would violate the condition that more is preferred to less, as would a horizontal indifference curve, as in Figure 2(b), or an upward-sloping curve, as in Figure 2(c). Thus, indifference curves are not likely to have any of these shapes.

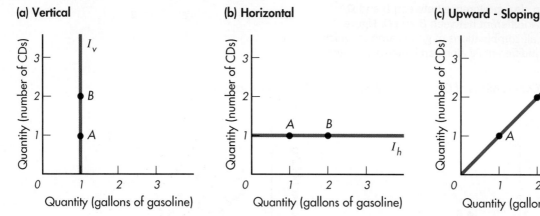

(a) Vertical

(b) Horizontal

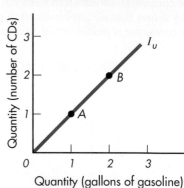

(c) Upward - Sloping

2 CDs may be willing to give up only 1 CD to get that additional gallon of gasoline. This preference is shown as the move from *E* to *F*.

1.c. Indifference Curves Cannot Cross

Indifference curves do not intersect. If the curves crossed, two combinations of goods that are clearly not equally preferred by the consumer would seem to be

FIGURE 3

Bowed-In Indifference Curve

Indifference curves slope down from left to right and bow in toward the origin. They bow in because consumers value a good relatively more if they have less of it, other things being equal. At the top of the curve, where a little gasoline and many CDs are represented by point *D,* the consumer is willing to give up 2 CDs to get 1 gallon of gasoline. But lower down on the curve, such as at point *E,* the consumer has more gasoline and fewer CDs than at point *D* and thus is willing to give up fewer CDs to get 1 more gallon of gasoline.

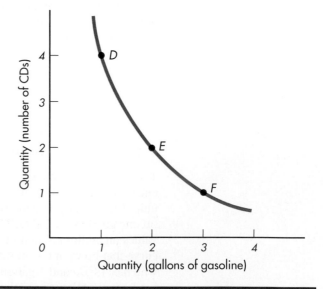

FIGURE 4 ———————————————— FIGURE 5 ————————————————

Indifference Curves Do Not Cross

If two indifference curves intersected, such as at point B, then the consumer would be indifferent to all points on each curve. But point C clearly provides more CDs than point A and no less gasoline, so the consumer will prefer C to A. If the consumer prefers more to less, the indifference curves will not cross.

Indifference Map

Indifference curves cover the entire positive quadrant. As we move away from the origin, more is preferred to less: I_5 is preferred to I_4, I_4 is preferred to I_3, and so on.

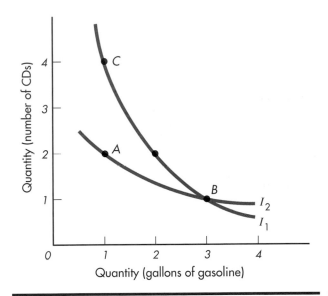

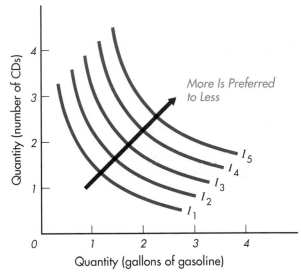

equally preferred. According to Figure 4, the consumer is indifferent between A and B along indifference curve I_2 and indifferent between B and C along indifference curve I_1. Thus, the consumer appears to be indifferent among A, B, and C. Combination C, however, offers more CDs and no less gasoline than combination A. Clearly, the consumer, preferring more to less, will prefer C to A. Thus, indifference curves are not allowed to cross.

1.d. An Indifference Map

indifference map: a complete set of indifference curves

An **indifference map,** located in the positive quadrant of a graph, indicates the consumer's preferences among all combinations of goods and services. The farther from the origin an indifference curve is, the more the combinations of goods along that curve are preferred. The arrow in Figure 5 indicates the ordering of preferences: I_2 is preferred to I_1; I_3 is preferred to I_2 and I_1; I_4 is preferred to I_3, I_2, and I_1; and so on.

2. Budget Constraint

The indifference map reveals only the combinations of goods and services that a consumer prefers or is indifferent among—what the consumer is *willing* to buy. It does not tell us what the consumer is *able* to buy. Consumers' income levels or

budget line: a line showing all the combinations of goods that can be purchased with a given level of income

budgets limit the amount that they can purchase. Let's suppose a consumer has allocated $6 to spend on gas and CDs. Figure 6 shows the **budget line,** a line giving all the combinations of goods that a budget can buy at given prices.

Anywhere along the budget line in Figure 6(a), the consumer is spending $6. When the price of CDs is $1 and the price of gas is $1 per gallon, the consumer can choose among several different combinations of CDs and gas that add up to $6. If only CDs are purchased, 6 CDs can be purchased (point A). If only gas is purchased, 6 gallons of gas can be purchased (point G). At point B, 5 CDs and 1 gallon of gas can be purchased. At point C, 4 CDs and 2 gallons of gas can be purchased. At point F, 1 CD and 5 gallons of gas can be purchased.

FIGURE 6

The Budget Line

In Figure 6(a), a budget line is drawn for a consumer with a $6 budget to be spent on CDs and gallons of gasoline costing $1 each. The consumer can purchase 6 CDs and no gas, 5 CDs and 1 gallon of gas, and so on. In Figure 6(b), the budget line shifts outward because the budget is increased from $6 to $7 and the consumer can purchase more. In Figure 6(c), the initial budget line (Y_1) runs from 6 to 6. When the price of CDs increases from $1 to $2, the budget line (Y_2) rotates down along the CD axis. Spending the entire $6 budget on CDs allows the consumer to buy only 3 CDs rather than the 6 that were obtained at the per unit price of $1.

(a) Initial Budget Line

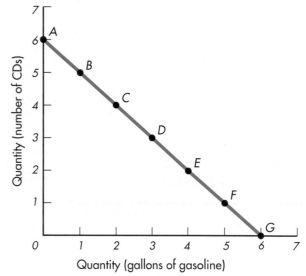

(b) Shift Due to Income Increase

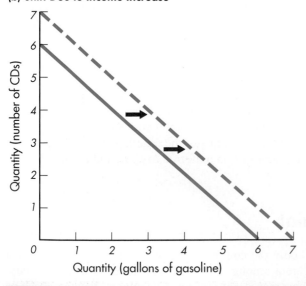

(c) Shift (Rotation) Due to Relative Price Change

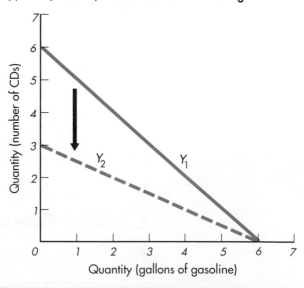

An increase in the consumer's income or budget is shown as an outward shift of the budget line. Figure 6(b) shows an increase in income from $6 to $7. The budget line shifts out to the line running from 7 to 7. A change in income or in the consumer's budget causes a parallel shift of the budget line.

A change in the price of one of the goods causes the budget line to rotate. For example, with a budget of $6 and the prices of both CDs and gas at $1, we have the budget line Y_1 of Figure 6(c). If the price of CDs rises to $2, only 3 CDs can be purchased if the entire budget is spent on CDs. As a result, the budget line (Y_2) is flatter, running from 3 on the vertical axis to 6 on the horizontal axis. Conversely, a rise in the price of gas would cause the budget line to become steeper.

3. Consumer Equilibrium

Putting the budget line on the indifference map allows us to determine the one combination of goods and services that the consumer is both *willing* and *able* to purchase. Any combination of goods that lies on or below the budget line is within the consumer's budget. Which combination will the consumer choose in order to yield the greatest satisfaction (utility)?

The budget line in Figure 7 indicates that most of the combinations along indifference curve I_1 and point C on indifference curve I_2 are attainable. Combinations along indifference curve I_3 are preferred to combinations along I_2, but the consumer is *not able* to buy combinations along I_3 because they cost more than the consumer's budget. Therefore, point C represents the maximum level of satisfaction, or utility, available to the consumer. Point C is the point where the budget line is tangent to (just touches) the indifference curve.

The demand curve for a good can be derived from indifference curves and budget lines by changing the price of one of the goods, leaving everything else the same, and finding the consumer equilibrium points. Budget line Y_1, running from 6 on the vertical axis to 6 on the horizontal axis in Figure 8(a), is the initial budget, in which

---

FIGURE 7

Consumer Equilibrium

The consumer maximizes satisfaction by purchasing the combination of goods that is on the indifference curve farthest from the origin but attainable given the consumer's budget. The combinations along I_1 are attainable, but so are the combinations that lie above, I_1. Combinations beyond the budget line, such as those along I_3, cost more than the consumer's budget. Point C, where the indifference curve I_2 just touches, or is tangent to, the budget line, is the chosen combination and the point of consumer equilibrium.

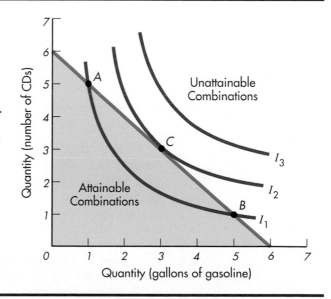

FIGURE 8

The Demand Curve

By changing the price of one of the goods and leaving everything else the same, we can derive the demand curve. Figure 8(a) shows that as the price of a gallon of gasoline increases from $1 to $2, the budget line rotates in toward the CD axis. Consumer equilibrium occurs at point E instead of at point C. The consumer is purchasing only 2 gallons of gasoline at the $2 per gallon price, whereas the consumer purchased 3 gallons of gasoline at the $1 per gallon price. Plotting the price of gasoline and the number of gallons of gasoline directly below, in Figure 8(b), yields the demand curve for gasoline.

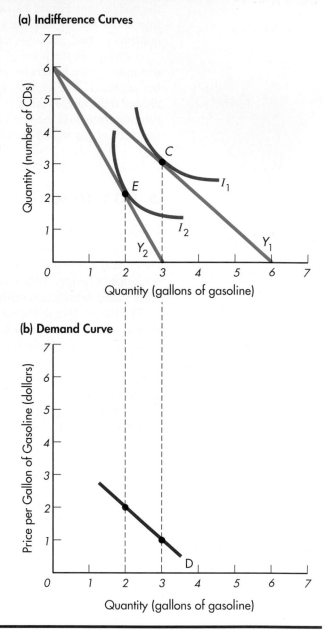

the price of each CD is $1 and the price of each gallon of gas is $1. We then increase the price of a gallon of gasoline to $2 and draw the second budget line, Y_2, running from 6 CDs to 3 gallons of gas. For each budget (income) line, we draw the indifference curve that is tangent. For Y_1 it is curve I_1; for Y_2 it is curve I_2. The original consumer equilibrium is point C, the tangency between the initial budget line and curve I_1. The point at which the new budget line is just tangent to an indifference curve is the new consumer equilibrium point. This is point E.

At point C, 3 gallons of gas are purchased; at point E, 2 gallons of gas are purchased. By plotting the combinations of price and quantity demanded below the indifference curves, as in Figure 8(b), we trace out the demand curve for gasoline.

Summary

1. Indifference curves show all combinations of two goods that give the consumer the same level of total utility. *§1*

2. An indifference map is a complete set of indifference curves filling up the positive quadrant of a graph. *§1.d*

3. The indifference curve indicates what the consumer is willing to buy. The budget line indicates what the consumer is able to buy. Together they determine the combination of goods that the consumer is willing and able to buy. *§1, 2*

4. Consumer equilibrium occurs at the point where the budget line just touches, or is tangent to, an indifference curve. *§3*

5. The demand curve can be derived from the indifference curves and budget lines. A change in the relative price causes the budget line to rotate and become tangent to an indifference curve at a different quantity of goods. As the price of one good rises relative to the price of another, the quantity demanded of the higher-priced good falls. *§3*

Key Terms

indifferent *§1*

indifference curve *§1*

indifference map *§1.d*

budget line *§2*

Exercises

1. Use these combinations for exercises a and b:

Combination	Clothes	Food
A	1 basket	1 pound
B	1 basket	2 pounds
C	1 basket	3 pounds
D	2 baskets	1 pound
E	2 baskets	2 pounds
F	2 baskets	3 pounds
G	3 baskets	1 pound
H	3 baskets	2 pounds
I	3 baskets	3 pounds

a. If more is preferred to less, which combinations are clearly preferred to other combinations? Rank the combinations in the order of preference.

b. Some clothes-food combinations cannot be clearly ranked. Why not?

2. Explain why two indifference curves cannot cross.

3. Using the data that follow, plot two demand curves for cake. Then explain what could have led to the shift of the demand curve.

I. Price of Cake	Quantity of Cake Demanded	II. Price of Cake	Quantity of Cake Demanded
$1	10	$1	14
$2	8	$2	10
$3	4	$3	8
$4	3	$4	6
$5	1	$5	5

CHAPTER 22

Supply: The Costs of Doing Business

? Fundamental Questions

1. **What is the law of diminishing marginal returns?**

2. **What is the relationship between costs and output in the short run?**

3. **What is the relationship between costs and output in the long run?**

In 1955, Akio Morita, the founder of Sony Corporation, began selling a small transistor radio in the United States. "I saw the United States as a natural market," he said. Morita showed the radio to Bulova, a large watch and appliance firm. Bulova offered to purchase a huge amount of radios but with one condition: Sony would have to put Bulova's name on the radio; Sony would be a so-called OEM (original equipment manufacturer) supplier. Morita refused, stating that in a few years the name Sony would be as well known as Bulova.

Morita soon received another large purchase offer, nearly 100,000 radios, from a chain store. He knew that Sony did not have the capacity to produce that many radios. "Our capacity was less than a thousand radios a month." An order of 100,000 would mean hiring and training new employees and expanding facilities even more. Morita sat down and drew a curve that looked something like the lopsided letter U shown in Figure 1. The cost for 5,000 would be the beginning of the curve. For 10,000 the costs would fall (and Sony could offer a lower price), and that was at the bottom of the U. For 30,000 the cost would begin to climb. For 50,000 the cost per

FIGURE 1

Morita's Cost Curve for Transistor Radios

Visualizing Sony's production capabilities, Akio Morita saw that per unit costs would fall initially and then rise quite rapidly.

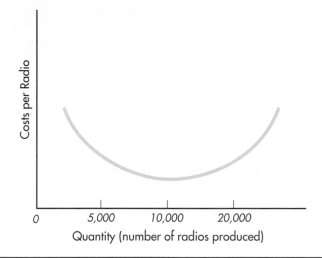

unit would be higher than for 5,000, and for 100,000 units, the cost would be much more per unit than for the first 5,000.

Morita explained to the chain store buyer, "If we had to double our production—more labor, more materials, etc.—to complete an order for 100,000 radios and if we could not get a repeat order the following year, we would be in big trouble." The buyer, initially stunned, was eventually persuaded and ended up buying 10,000 radios. But why couldn't Morita have simply increased the quantity produced? Would anyone forgo such huge sales?[1] ∎

1. Firms and Production

The terms *company, enterprise,* and *business* are used interchangeably with *firm.* Recall from Chapter 4 that firms can be organized as sole proprietorships, partnerships, or corporations and can be national or multinational companies. In our discussion of the costs of doing business, we use *firm* to refer to all types of business organizations. Thus, we speak of a firm as an institution in which resources—land, labor, and capital—are combined to produce a product or service. The terms *produce* and *production* are also used broadly; they refer not only to manufacturing but also to the retailer who buys goods from a wholesaler and offers the goods to the customers. We also refer to the *owner* of a company, no matter whether the company is public or private. A company whose owners are shareholders and whose shares of stock are bought and sold on a stock exchange is called a *public company.* The ownership of a *private company* is not traded on a stock exchange.

---

[1]Story paraphrased from Slomo Maital, *Executive Economics* (New York: Free Press, 1994), pp. 66–75; "The World's Best Brand," *Fortune,* May 31, 1993, p. 31; and "Sony Corp.: Globalization," *Harvard Business School Case Study 391–071,* 1990.

FIGURE 2

The Circular Flow

The flow of goods and services and money between the household and business sectors is pictured. Businesses sell goods and services to households. The money received is total revenue. The difference between total revenue and the payment for land, labor, and capital is profit. The resources—land, labor, and capital—flow from the household to the business sector. The payment for these resources flows from the business sector to the household sector.

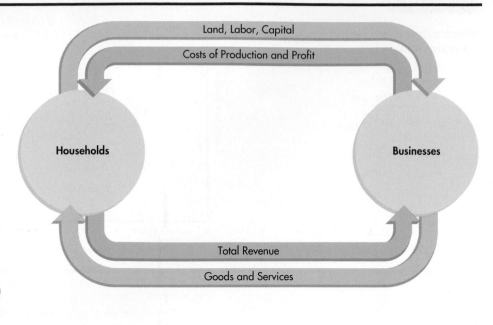

1.a. The Relationship Between Output and Resources

The simplest circular flow diagram from Chapter 4 is reproduced here as Figure 2. It shows that money flows from the household sector to the business sector in payment for goods and services. The flow of money from the household sector to the business sector is the firm's total revenue. In turn, money flows from the business sector to households as payment for the use of their resources—land, labor, and capital. After the owners of land, labor, and capital have been paid, the owner of the business receives what is left, the profit. Clearly, the amount of profit received by the owner of the business depends on the output produced by the firm and the quantities and costs of land, labor, and capital used by the firm to produce the output. Owners of businesses want to produce output at the lowest possible cost. Doing so requires a business owner to compare all combinations of resources (inputs) that can be used to produce output and select the least-cost combination.

Let's use a hypothetical firm, Pacific Western Airlines (PWA), to discuss the relationship between inputs and output. The number (in thousands) of passenger-miles that results when PWA employs alternative combinations of mechanics and airplanes during a specific period of time is shown in Table 1. One mechanic can generate 30 (thousand) passenger-miles if PWA has 5 airplanes, 100 (thousand) passenger-miles if PWA has 10 airplanes, 250 (thousand) passenger-miles if PWA has 15 airplanes, and so on. With a second mechanic, output is increased with each quantity of airplanes: 2 mechanics and 5 airplanes now generate 60 (thousand) passenger-miles, and so on.

Pacific Western Airlines could produce about the same amount, say 340 (thousand) to 360 thousand passenger-miles, with several different combinations of mechanics and airplanes—3 mechanics with 10 airplanes, 2 mechanics with 15 airplanes, or 1 mechanic with 20 airplanes. And several other output levels can be produced with a number of different combinations of mechanics and airplanes. Which combination does PWA choose?

TABLE 1

Alternative Quantities (in thousands) of Output That Can Be Produced by Different Combinations of Resources

Number of Mechanics	Capital (number of airplanes)						
	5	10	15	20	25	30	35
0	0	0	0	0	0	0	0
1	30	100	250	340	410	400	400
2	60	250	360	450	520	530	520
3	100	360	480	570	610	620	620
4	130	440	580	640	690	700	700
5	130	500	650	710	760	770	780
6	110	540	700	760	800	820	830
7	100	550	720	790	820	850	870
8	80	540	680	800	830	860	880

That depends on whether PWA is making choices for the short run or for the long run. In the long run, or planning period, the firm may consider any and all combinations of resources. In the short run, or production period, the choices open to the firm are limited. Recall that the short run is a period of time just short enough that at least one resource cannot be changed—it is fixed. Suppose that PWA had previously leased or purchased 10 airplanes and cannot change the number of planes for at least a year. In this case, the fixed resource is airplanes. The options open to PWA in the short run thus are only those under the column in Table 1 labeled "10" airplanes. Pacific Western Airlines can vary the number of mechanics but not the number of airplanes in the short run.

total physical product (TPP): the maximum output that can be produced when successive units of a variable resource are added to fixed amounts of other resources

The **total physical product** (*TPP*, also called total product) schedule and curve show how the quantity of the variable resource (mechanics) and the output produced are related for a certain quantity of the fixed resource. In Figure 3(a), columns 1 and 3 of Table 1 are reproduced and plotted. With total output measured on the vertical axis and the number of mechanics measured on the horizontal axis, the combinations of output and mechanics trace out the *TPP* curve. Both the table and the *TPP* curve in Figure 3(a) show that as additional units of the variable resource are used with a fixed amount of another resource, total output at first rises, initially quite rapidly and then more slowly, and then declines. As the first units of the variable resource (mechanics) are used, each additional mechanic can provide many passenger-miles for the airline. But at some point, there are "too many chefs stirring the broth" and each additional mechanic adds only a little to total passenger-miles flown and, eventually, actually detracts from the productivity of the other mechanics.

1.b. Diminishing Marginal Returns

law of diminishing marginal returns: when successive equal amounts of a variable resource are combined with a fixed amount of another resource, marginal increases in output that can be attributed to each additional unit of the variable resource will eventually decline

This relationship between quantities of a variable resource and quantities of output is called the **law of diminishing marginal returns.** According to the law of diminishing marginal returns, when successive equal amounts of a variable resource are combined with a fixed amount of another resource, output will initially accelerate, then decelerate, and eventually will usually decline. Looking at Table 1, you can see the law of diminishing marginal returns at each quantity of airplanes. Just increase the number of mechanics for any given quantity of airplanes and output will rise, at first rapidly, but then more slowly. Similarly, if you fix the quantity of mechanics and then vary the number of airplanes, you will also observe the law of diminishing marginal returns.

FIGURE 3

Total, Average, and Marginal Product

The table provides plotting data for the graphs. Total, average, and marginal product schedules and curves are shown. The total physical product schedule, shown in Figure 3(a), is derived from Table 1 by fixing one resource, airplanes, at 10.

The average and marginal physical product schedules are calculated from the total physical product schedule. Average is total output divided by number of mechanics; marginal is the change in the total output divided by the change in the number of mechanics.

Number of Mechanics	Total Output	Average Physical Product	Marginal Physical Product
0	0	—	—
1	100	100	100
2	250	125	150
3	360	120	110
4	440	110	80
5	500	100	60
6	540	90	40
7	550	78.6	10
8	540	675	−10

(a) The Total Physical Product Curve

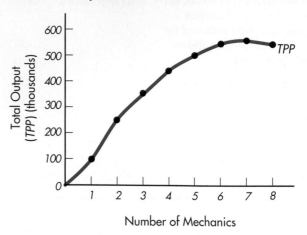

(b) The Average Physical Product Curve

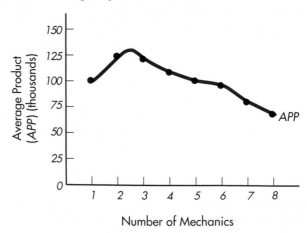

(c) The Marginal Physical Product Curve

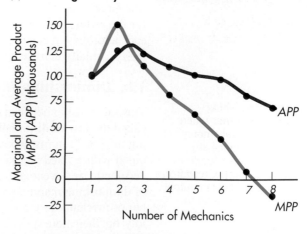

With 1 mechanic, for instance, as the number of airplanes is increased, output rises from 30 to 100 to 250 to 340, and so on. The first increases are large, but the output rises less rapidly and eventually declines as the number of airplanes is increased.

The law of diminishing marginal returns shows up more clearly with the average product and marginal product curves, also called **average physical product (APP)** and **marginal physical product (MPP)** curves. The average product schedule, shown in the third column of the table in Figure 3, is calculated by dividing total output by the number of mechanics:

$$APP = \frac{\text{total output}}{\text{number of mechanics}}$$

Plotting APP gives us Figure 3(b), a curve that rises quite rapidly and then slowly declines. The marginal product schedule is the change in total output divided by the change in the quantity of variable resources (the number of mechanics):

$$MPP = \frac{\text{change in output}}{\text{change in number of mechanics}}$$

The MPP schedule is column 4 in the table. Each row shows the additional output produced when one more mechanic is used. The graph of the MPP schedule is shown in Figure 3(c); it is drawn on top of the APP curve so that we can compare MPP and APP. The MPP curve rises initially more rapidly than APP, then falls more rapidly than APP, and eventually reaches zero. When MPP is zero or negative, the additional variable resources are actually detracting from the production of other resources, causing output to decline.

average physical product (APP): output per unit of resource

marginal physical product (MPP): the additional quantity that is produced when one additional unit of a resource is used in combination with the same quantities of all other resources

Business owners combine quantities of land, labor, and capital to produce goods and services in the most profitable way. Technological improvements help them produce a larger quantity of goods and services at lower cost, thereby increasing profitability. Here, an Egyptian woman supervises several automatic sewing machines. One woman can produce the same quantity with the automatic machines 100 times faster than when the sewing was done by hand. Employing more people may speed up production; eventually, however, employing more people will not speed up production and could actually retard production as the workers interfere with each other's tasks.

1. What is the law of diminishing marginal returns?

According to the law of diminishing marginal returns, when successive equal amounts of a variable resource are combined with a fixed amount of another resource, output will rise, initially accelerating but then decelerating, and eventually may decline. Diminishing marginal returns are not unique to the airline industry. In every instance where increasing amounts of one resource are combined with fixed amounts of other resources, the additional output that can be produced initially increases but eventually decreases.

For instance, diminishing marginal returns limit the effort to improve passenger safety during collisions by installing air bags in cars. The first air bag added to a car increases protection considerably. The second adds an element of safety, particularly for the front-seat passenger. But additional air bags provide little additional protection and eventually would lessen protection as they interfered with each other. As successive units of the variable resource, air bags, are placed on the fixed resource, the car, the additional amount of protection provided by each air bag declines.

The law of diminishing marginal returns also applies to studying. On a typical day, during the first hour you study a subject you probably get a great deal of information. During the second hour you may also learn a large amount of new material, but eventually another hour of studying will produce no benefits and could be counterproductive.

Diminishing marginal returns occur because the efficiency of variable resources depends on the quantity of the fixed resources. If the airline mechanics must stand around waiting for tools or for room to work on the jet engines, then an additional mechanic will allow few, if any, additional passenger-miles to be flown. The limited capacity of the fixed resources—the number of planes, tools, and hangar space—causes the efficiency of the variable resource—the mechanics—to decline. Similarly, we often see diminishing marginal returns at restaurants. We walk into a restaurant and see lots of empty tables, but we are told that there is a 15-minute wait to be seated. The problem is that the number of servers (the fixed resource) is not sufficient to provide quality service to all the tables (the variable resource). The restaurant gives each server one table to serve, then two, then three, and so on, until the quality of the service begins to decline. Without more servers, some tables will have to be left empty.

1.b.1. Average and Marginal

Average and marginal relationships behave the same way with respect to each other no matter whether they refer to physical product, cost, utility, grade points, or anything else. For instance, think of the grade point average (GPA) that you get each semester as your *marginal* GPA and your cumulative, or overall, GPA as your *average* GPA. You can see the relation between marginal and average by considering what will happen to your cumulative GPA if this semester's GPA is less than your cumulative GPA. Suppose your GPA this semester is 3.0 for 16 hours of classes and your cumulative GPA, not including this semester, is 3.5 for 48 hours of classes. Your marginal (this semester's) GPA will be less than your average GPA. Thus, when your marginal GPA is added to your average GPA, the average GPA falls, from 3.5 to 3.375. *As long as the marginal is less than the average, the average falls.* If your GPA this semester is 4.0 instead of 3.0, your average GPA will rise from 3.5 to 3.625. *As long as the marginal is greater than the average, the average rises.*

If the average is falling when marginal is below average and rising when marginal is above average, then marginal and average can be the same only when the average is neither rising nor falling. If your GPA this semester is 3.5 and your cumulative GPA up to this semester was 3.5, then your new GPA will be 3.5. Average and marginal are the same when the average is constant. This occurs only when the average curve is at its maximum or minimum point.

In Figure 4 the relationship between average physical product and marginal physical product is illustrated. You can see in both the table and the figure that as long as

Whenever marginal is less than average, the average is falling, and whenever marginal is greater than average, the average is rising.

FIGURE 4

Marginal and Average Physical Product

When the marginal is above the average, the average is rising; when the marginal is below the average, the average is falling. The *MPP* = *APP* at the maximum of the *APP*, between 2 and 3 mechanics.

Number of Mechanics	Total Output	Average Physical Product	Marginal Physical Product
0	0	—	—
1	100	100	100
2	250	125	150
3	360	120	110
4	440	110	80
5	500	100	60
6	540	90	40
7	550	78.6	10
8	540	67.5	−10

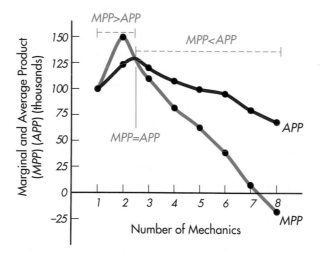

the *MPP* is greater than the *APP*, the *APP* is rising; whenever the *MPP* is less than the *APP*, the *APP* is falling. Thus, the *MPP* and the *APP* are equal at the peak or top of the *APP* curve. This occurs between 2 and 3 mechanics.

RECAP

1. According to the law of diminishing marginal returns, as successive units of a variable resource are added to the fixed resources, the additional output produced will initially rise but will eventually decline.
2. Diminishing marginal returns occur because the efficiency of variable resources depends on the quantity of the fixed resources.
3. As long as the marginal is less than the average, the average falls. As long as the marginal is greater than the average, the average rises.

2. From Production to Costs

Every firm (and every individual and nation as well) is faced with the law of diminishing marginal returns. The law is, in fact, a physical property, not an economic one, but is important to economics because it defines the relationship between costs and output in the short run.

2.a. The Calculation of Costs

The total, average, and marginal physical product schedules and curves show the relationship between quantities of resources (inputs) and quantities of output. To examine the costs of doing business rather than the physical production relationships, we must define the costs of each unit of resources. Suppose, in our airline example, that the cost per mechanic, the variable resource, is $1,000 per mechanic, and that this is the only cost PWA has. Then, the total costs are those listed in column 3 of the table in Figure 5, calculated by multiplying $1,000 by the number of mechanics necessary to produce the output listed in column 2.

The total cost schedule is plotted on a graph with output measured on the horizontal axis and total cost on the vertical axis, as shown in Figure 5(a). The total cost curve indicates that as output rises in the short run, costs rise, initially rapidly, then more slowly, and finally more and more rapidly.

Figure 5(b) is the total physical product curve of Figure 3(a). You might notice a resemblance between the total cost curve and the total physical product curve. In fact, they are like mirror images, both shaped by the law of diminishing marginal returns.[2]

Since total cost and total physical product have the same shape (except for being mirror images), then average physical product and average cost and marginal physical product and marginal cost should also have the same shapes except for being mirror images. **Average total cost (ATC)** is the per unit cost and is derived by dividing total cost by the quantity of output:

average total cost (ATC): per unit cost; total cost divided by the total output

$$ATC = \frac{\text{total cost}}{\text{total output}}$$

marginal cost (MC): the additional cost of producing one more unit of output

Marginal cost (MC) is the change in cost caused by a change in output and is derived by dividing the change in total cost by the change in the quantity of output:

$$MC = \frac{\text{change in total cost}}{\text{change in quantity of output}}$$

The average total cost schedule is listed in column 3 and the marginal cost schedule in column 4 of the table in Figure 6. Notice that these schedules are calculated with respect to output. It is the *relationship* between costs and output produced that is focused on with the cost schedules and curves.

2.b. The U Shape of Cost Curves

In Figure 6(a) the average cost schedule is plotted next to the *APP* curve of Figure 3(b). In Figure 6(b), the marginal cost schedule is plotted next to the *MPP* curve of Figure 3(c). Can you see the resemblances between the curves? Whereas the *MPP* and *APP* curves might be described as hump-shaped, the *MC* and *ATC* curves can

---

[2] You might see the resemblance more clearly if the total cost curve is rotated so that output is the vertical axis and cost the horizontal axis.

FIGURE 5

Total Costs

Figure 5(a) is the total cost curve, columns 2 and 3 of the table. Figure 5(b) is the total product curve, reproduced from Figure 3(a). Both curves illustrate diminishing marginal returns.

Number of Mechanics	Total Output (thousands)	Total Cost (thousands)
0	0	$ 0
1	100	$1,000
2	250	$2,000
3	360	$3,000
4	440	$4,000
5	500	$5,000
6	540	$6,000
7	550	$7,000
8	540	$8,000

(a) The Total Cost Curve

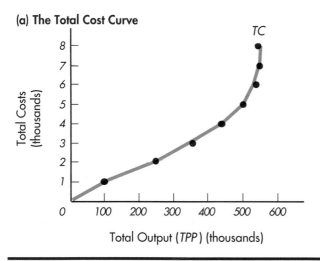

(b) The Total Product Curve

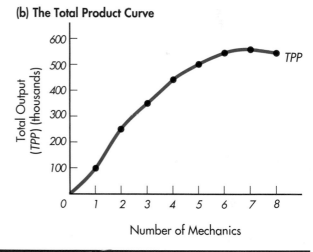

be described as U-shaped. In Figure 6(c), the MC and ATC curves are put on the same graph next to the MPP and APP curves of Figure 4. You can see that the relationship between marginal and average applies to both product and cost curves: whenever the marginal is above the average, the average is rising, and whenever the marginal is below the average, the average is falling; note also that $MPP = APP$ at the maximum point of the APP curve, while $MC = ATC$ at the minimum point on the ATC curve.

The purpose of comparing the product and cost curves is to emphasize the importance of the law of diminishing marginal returns to short-run costs. Diminishing returns defines the relationship between costs and output in the short run for every firm, no matter whether that firm is a billion-dollar-a-year corporation or a small proprietorship. Obviously, the size or scale of the companies will differ, but the U shape of the cost curves will not. *Every firm will face a U-shaped cost curve in the short run because of the law of diminishing marginal returns.*

?

2. What is the relationship between costs and output in the short run?

FIGURE 6

Average and Marginal Costs

Figure 6(a) shows the average total cost curve and the *APP* curve. Figure 6(b) shows the marginal cost curve and the *MPP* curve. The cost curves are described as U-shaped, the product curves as hump-shaped. The shapes of the curves are due to the law of diminishing marginal returns. Figure 6(c) shows the relationship between average and marginal curves.

Quantity of Output (thousands)	Total Cost (thousands)	Average Cost	Marginal Cost
100	$1,000	$10	$ 10
250	$2,000	$ 8	$ 6.7
360	$3,000	$ 8.33	$ 9.1
440	$4,000	$ 9	$ 12.5
500	$5,000	$10	$ 16.7
540	$6,000	$11.1	$ 25
550	$7,000	$12.7	$100

(a) Compare APP with ATC

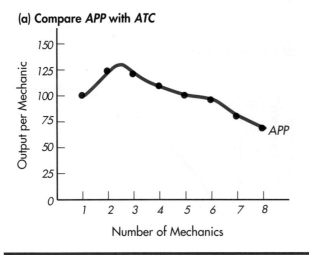

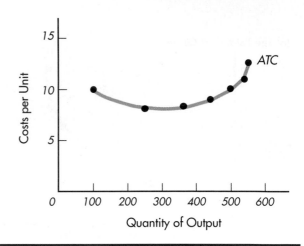

To this point we have used a very simplified situation to describe costs. We placed a cost on the mechanics but on nothing else. Everything has costs. For PWA, the leased airplanes are costs; the buildings, other employees, utilities, and so on are also costs. In the next section we turn to a more in-depth look at costs.

RECAP

1. Costs are derived by putting dollar figures on the resources used in production.
2. Average total cost is the cost per unit of output—total cost divided by the number of units of output produced.
3. Marginal cost is the change in costs divided by the change in output.
4. The relationship between costs and output in the short run is defined by the law of diminishing marginal returns.
5. The cost curves (*TC, ATC, MC*) and the product curves (*TPP, APP, MPP*) are like mirror images of each other, all reflecting the law of diminishing marginal returns.

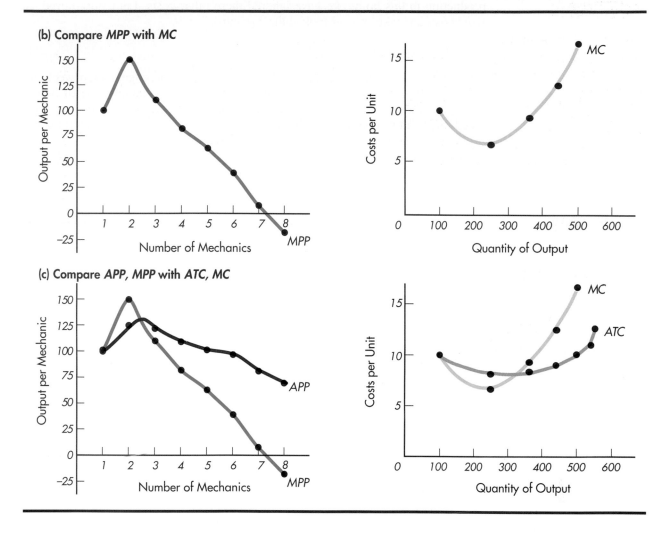

(b) Compare *MPP* with *MC*

(c) Compare *APP, MPP* with *ATC, MC*

6. The U shape of the cost curves indicates that as output is increased, a great deal of output can be produced by each additional unit of a variable resource initially. But eventually, the increase in output slows and may decline as more and more units of the variable resource are added.

7. The relationship between marginal and average applies to both product and cost curves. When marginal is above average, average is rising, and when marginal is below average, average is falling. The *MPP = APP* at the maximum of *APP; MC = ATC* at the minimum of *ATC*.

3. Cost Schedules and Cost Curves

A firm must pay for its variable resources, such as the mechanics for PWA, but it has other costs as well—it must pay for the fixed resource. In our discussion of costs and production to this point, we have ignored these other costs. Let's now introduce fixed costs and take another look at the cost curves.

3.a. An Example of Costs

Let's suppose that the costs for PWA of transporting passengers each week are shown in the table in Figure 7. Column 1 lists the total quantity (Q) of output produced (measured in hundred million passenger-miles). Notice that we have listed the data by equal increments of output, from 1 to 2 to 3 and so on (hundred millions of passenger-miles) to make it easier to focus on the relationship between output and costs.

FIGURE 7

The Marginal and Average Cost Curves

The table provides plotting data for the figure, which shows the average fixed, average variable, average total, and marginal costs. Average fixed costs (*AFC*) decline steadily from the first unit of output. Average variable costs (*AVC*) initially decline but then rise as output rises. Average total costs (*ATC*), the sum of average fixed and average variable costs, decline and then rise as output rises. The distance between the *ATC* and *AVC* curves is *AFC*. The *MC* curve crosses the *AVC* curve at its minimum point, point *A*, and crosses the *ATC* curve at its minimum, point *B*. (Note: Total output is measured in hundred million passenger-miles. The *TFC*, *TVC*, and *TC* are measured in thousands of dollars. The *AFC*, *AVC*, *ATC*, and *MC* are measured in thousands of dollars per hundred-million passenger-miles.)

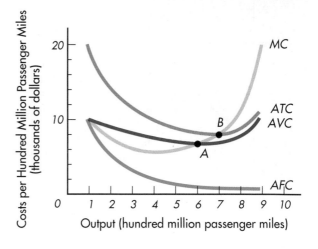

(1) Total Output (Q)	(2) Total Fixed Costs (TFC)	(3) Total Variable Costs (TVC)	(4) Total Costs (TC)	(5) Average Fixed Costs (AFC)	(6) Average Variable Costs (AVC)	(7) Average Total Costs (ATC)	(8) Marginal Costs (MC)	
0	$10	$ 0	$10					
1	$10	$10	$20	$10	$10	$20	$10	
2	$10	$18	$28	$ 5	$ 9	$14	$ 8	
3	$10	$25	$35	$ 3.33	$ 8.33	$11.6	$ 7	
4	$10	$30	$40	$ 2.5	$ 7.5	$10	$ 5	
5	$10	$35	$45	$ 2	$ 7	$ 9	$ 5	
6	$10	$42	$52	$ 1.66	$ 7	$ 8.66	$ 7	Point *A*
7	$10	$50.6	$60.6	$ 1.44	$ 7.2	$ 8.6	$ 8.6	Point *B*
8	$10	$60	$70	$ 1.25	$ 7.5	$ 8.75	$ 9.4	
9	$10	$80	$90	$ 1.1	$ 8.8	$10	$20	

Overhead

Economists classify costs as fixed or variable. Fixed costs do not change as the volume of production changes. Variable costs, on the other hand, depend on the volume of production. In business, costs are often classified into overhead and direct operating costs. Overhead costs are those that are not directly attributable to the production process. They include such items as taxes, insurance premiums, managerial or administrative salaries, paperwork, the cost of electricity not used in the production process, and others. Overhead costs can be either fixed or variable. Insurance premiums, taxes, and managerial salaries are fixed costs. They must be paid regardless of how much is produced. Electricity used to operate the production process is a variable cost, increasing as the quantity of output produced is increased.

Statements like "We need to spread the overhead" sound somewhat like the concept of declining average fixed costs—fixed cost per unit of output declines as output rises. But overhead may also include variable costs. Thus, the need to "spread the overhead" refers to reducing the total costs that are not directly attributable to the production process. The more a firm can keep its overhead costs the same and increase its volume of production, the more overhead costs look and act like fixed costs. The higher the percentage of overhead costs that are fixed, the more closely related the economists' and the business person's classifications will be. But the two are not—and are not meant to be—the same.

The different classifications provide different information. The economist is interested in the decision to produce, whether to produce, and how much to produce at all. This is the information provided by fixed and variable costs. The business-person is interested in attributing costs to different activities, that is, in determining whether the business is running as cost-efficiently as it can. The classification of costs into overhead and direct provides this information.

---

total fixed costs (*TFC*): costs that must be paid whether a firm produces or not

total variable costs (*TVC*): costs that rise or fall as production rises or falls

total costs (*TC*): the sum of total variable and total fixed costs

short-run average total cost (*SRATC*): the total cost of production divided by the total quantity of output produced when at least one resource is fixed

Column 2 lists the **total fixed costs (*TFC*),** costs that must be paid whether the firm produces or not. Fixed costs are $10,000—this is what must be paid whether 1 or 1 billion passenger-miles are produced. The fixed costs in this example might represent the weekly portion of the annual payment for the planes, which are the resource whose quantity is fixed. Column 3 lists the **total variable costs (*TVC*),** costs that rise or fall as production rises or falls. The costs of resources such as employees, fuel, water, and meals rise as output rises. **Total costs (*TC*),** the sum of total variable and total fixed costs, are listed in column 4. Although the distinction between variable and fixed costs is important to economists, many businesspeople focus more on overhead and direct costs. The relation between these concepts is discussed in the Economic Insight "Overhead." (Overhead is not the same as fixed costs. Overhead refers to costs that are not directly attributable to production, such as administrative costs. Overhead costs may vary, however. For instance, more production may bring with it more paperwork and administration.)

Average costs—average total, average fixed, and average variable costs—are derived by dividing the corresponding total costs by the quantity of output—number of passenger-miles. *Average fixed costs (AFC)* decline as output rises because the total fixed cost, $10,000, is divided by a larger and larger number as output rises. *Average variable costs (AVC)* and *average total costs (ATC)* first decline and then rise, according to the law of diminishing marginal returns. When there are fixed resources and fixed costs, the firm is operating in the short run. For this reason, average total cost is often referred to as the **short-run average total cost (*SRATC*).** Marginal costs (*MC*), the additional costs that come from producing an additional unit of output, are listed in column 8. Marginal costs initially fall and then rise as output rises.

The average and marginal cost schedules are plotted in Figure 7. The *AVC* curve reaches a minimum at the 5 to 6 hundred million passenger-mile level. The *ATC* curve lies above the *AVC* curve by the amount of the average fixed costs. The *ATC* curve declines until the 7 hundred million passenger-mile point and then rises. The *MC* curve begins below the *AVC* and *ATC* curves and declines until the 5 hundred million passenger-mile point, where it begins to climb. The *MC* curve passes through the *AVC* curve at the minimum value of the *AVC* curve and then continues rising until it passes through the *ATC* curve at the minimum point of the *ATC* curve. The marginal cost curve intersects the average cost curves at the minimum points of the average cost curves.

The MC *curve intersects the* AVC *curve at the minimum point of the* AVC *curve; the* MC *curve intersects the* ATC *curve at the minimum point of the* AVC *curve.*

The role of each of the three types of costs—fixed, variable, and marginal—should be relatively obvious. In the short run, firms can do nothing about fixed costs—they are fixed. It is variable costs that are important in the short run. Firms can alter their variable costs. Average variable costs are the per unit variable costs. Marginal costs play the most important role; they are the incremental costs, the change in costs resulting from a small decline or increase in output. They inform the executive whether the last unit of output produced—the last passenger carried on the plane—increased costs a huge amount, a small amount, or not at all. Thus, the executive can decide whether to produce that last unit. We will see how the costs come into play more clearly in the following chapters.

RECAP

1. Total fixed costs (*TFC*) are costs that do not vary as the quantity of goods produced varies. An example of a fixed cost is the rent on a building. Rent has to be paid whether or not the firm makes or sells any goods.

2. Total variable costs (*TVC*) are costs that change as the quantity of goods produced changes. The cost of materials is usually variable. For instance, the cost of leather for making boots or cloth for manufacturing clothing changes as the quantity produced changes. The fuel required to fly planes will increase as more passengers are transported.

3. Total costs (*TC*) are the sum of fixed and variable costs:

$$TC = TFC + TVC$$

4. Average total costs (*ATC*) are total costs divided by the total quantity of the good that is produced, *Q*:

$$ATC = \frac{TC}{Q}$$

5. Average fixed costs (*AFC*) are total fixed costs divided by the quantity produced:

$$AFC = \frac{TFC}{Q}$$

6. Average variable costs (*AVC*) are total variable costs divided by the quantity produced:

$$AVC = \frac{TVC}{Q}$$

7. Marginal costs (MC) are the incremental costs that come from producing one more or one less unit of output:

$$MC = \frac{\text{change in } TC}{\text{change in } Q}$$

8. Short-run average total cost ($SRATC$) is the total cost divided by the total quantity of output when at least one resource cannot be changed.

3. What is the relationship between costs and output in the long run?

4. The Long Run

A firm can choose to relocate, build a new plant, or purchase additional planes only in the long run, or planning stage. A manager can choose any size of plant or building and any combination of other resources when laying out the firm's plans because all resources are variable in the long run. In essence, during the long run the manager compares all short-run situations.

Table 2, which is based on Table 1, shows the quantities of output that can be produced by alternative combinations of mechanics and airplanes at our hypothetical airline, PWA. You may recall that we specified that PWA had leased 10 airplanes and thus had to constrain itself to producing those combinations under the column labeled "10" in the short run. In the long run, the firm faces no fixed resources—everything is variable. PWA has a choice of how many airplanes to lease and thus has the choice of any combination of resources shown in Table 2.

The law of diminishing marginal returns does not apply when all resources are variable. Diminishing returns applies only when quantities of variable resources are combined with a fixed resource. In the long run, everything is variable. Consider the combinations of resources and the resulting output levels shaded in Table 2. A single mechanic combined with 5 airplanes can produce 30 (thousand) passenger-miles. Doubling both mechanics and airplanes (to 2 mechanics and 10 airplanes) means that 250 (thousand) passenger-miles can be produced. Doubling both resources again, to 4 mechanics and 20 airplanes, means that 640 (thousand)

TABLE 2								
The Long Run or Planning Period (passenger-miles in thousands)	**Number of Mechanics**	**Capital (number of airplanes)**						
		5	**10**	**15**	**20**	**25**	**30**	**35**	**40**
	0	0	0	0	0	0	0	0	0
	1	30	100	250	340	410	400	400	390
	2	60	250	360	450	520	530	520	500
	3	100	360	480	570	610	620	620	610
	4	130	440	580	640	690	700	700	690
	5	130	500	650	710	760	770	780	770
	6	110	540	700	760	800	820	830	840
	7	100	550	720	790	820	850	870	890
	8	80	540	680	800	830	860	880	900

passenger-miles can be produced. Doubling the resources once again, to 8 mechanics and 40 airplanes, results in 900 (thousand) passenger-miles being flown. For the first few times the quantities of both resources were doubled, output rose by more than the resources. But eventually, the output increase was less than double as the resources were doubled. This need not have been the case. Output could have continued to rise more rapidly than the resources, or it could have risen at a constant amount, or it could have declined throughout. Unlike the short run, where the relationship between inputs and output is defined by the law of diminishing marginal returns, the long run is not guided by a physical law.

4.a. Economies of Scale and Long-Run Cost Curves

scale: size; all resources change when scale changes

When all resources are changed, we say that the scale of the firm has changed. **Scale** means size. In the long run, a firm has many sizes to choose from—those given in Table 2 for PWA, for instance. The short run requires that scale be fixed—only a variable resource is changed. For each size or scale, therefore, there is a set of short-run average- and marginal-cost curves. For each quantity of airplanes (each column in Table 2), PWA has a set of average and marginal U-shaped cost curves. Figure 8(a) shows several short-run cost curves along which a firm could produce. Each short-run cost curve is drawn for a particular quantity of the capital resource—that is, a specific column in Table 2. Once the quantity of the capital resource is selected, the firm brings together different combinations of the other resources with the fixed capital resource. If a small quantity of the capital resource is selected, the firm might operate along $SRATC_1$. If the firm selects a slightly larger quantity of the capital resource, then it will be able to operate anywhere along $SRATC_2$. With a still larger quantity, the firm can operate along $SRATC_3$, $SRATC_4$, $SRATC_5$, or some other short-run average total cost curve.

In the long run, the firm can choose any of the $SRATC$ curves. All it needs to do is choose the level of output it wants to produce and then select the least-cost combination of resources with which to reach that level. Least-cost combinations are represented in Figure 8(b) by a curve that just touches each $SRATC$ curve. This curve is the **long-run average-total-cost** curve (**LRATC**—the lowest cost per unit of output for every level of output when all resources are variable). If the firm had chosen to acquire or use a quantity of fixed resources indicated by $SRATC_3$ in Figure 8(b), then it could produce Q_4 only at point A. Only by increasing its quantity of fixed resources could the firm produce at point B on $SRATC_4$.

long-run average total cost (LRATC): the lowest-cost combination of resources with which each level of output is produced when all resources are variable

You can see in Figure 8(b) that the long-run average-total-cost curve does *not* connect the minimum points of each of the short-run average-cost curves ($SRATC_1$, $SRATC_2$, etc.). The reason is that the minimum point of a short-run average-total-cost curve is not necessarily the lowest-cost method of producing a given level of output. For instance, point A on $SRATC_3$ is much higher than point B on $SRATC_4$, but output level Q_4 could be produced at either A or B. When the quantities of all resources can be varied, the choices open to the manager are much greater than when only one or a few of the resources are variable.

economies of scale: the decrease in per unit costs as the quantity of production increases and all resources are variable

The long-run average-total-cost curve gets its shape from economies and diseconomies of scale. If producing each unit of output becomes less costly as the amount of output produced rises, there are **economies of scale**—unit costs decrease as the quantity of production increases and all resources are variable. If the cost per unit rises as output rises, there are **diseconomies of scale**—unit costs increase as the quantity of production increases and all resources are variable. Economies of scale account for the downward-sloping portion of the long-run average-cost curve. Diseconomies of scale account for the upward-sloping portion.

diseconomies of scale: the increase in per unit costs as the quantity of production increases and all resources are variable

FIGURE 8

The Short-Run and Long-Run Average-Cost Curves

The long-run average-cost curve represents the lowest costs of producing any level of output when all resources are variable. Short-run average-cost curves represent the lowest costs of producing any level of output in the short run, when at least one of the resources is fixed. Figure 8(a) shows the possible SRATC curves facing a firm. Figure 8(b) shows the LRATC curve, which connects the minimum cost of producing each level of output. Notice that the SRATC curves need not indicate the lowest costs of producing in the long run. If the short run is characterized by $SRATC_3$, then quantity Q_4 can be produced at point A. But if some of the fixed resources are allowed to change, managers can shift to $SRATC_4$ and produce at point B.

(a) Short-Run Average-Total-Cost Curves

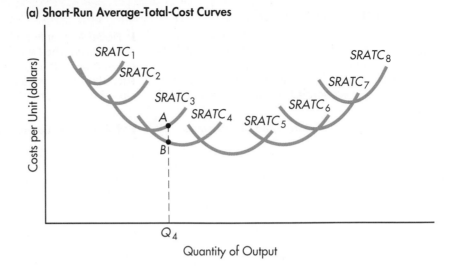

(b) Long-Run Average-Total-Cost Curve

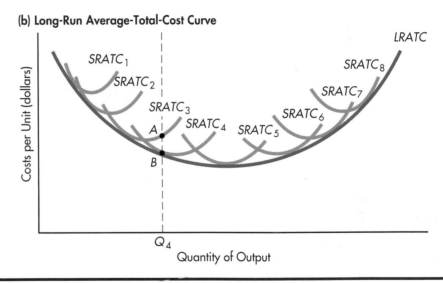

constant returns to scale: unit costs remain constant as the quantity of production is increased and all resources are variable

If the cost per unit of output is constant as output rises, there are **constant returns to scale.** Figures 9(a), 9(b), and 9(c) show three possible shapes of a long-run average-cost curve. Figure 9(a) is the usual U shape, indicating that economies of scale are followed by constant returns to scale and then diseconomies of scale. Figure 9(b) is a curve indicating only economies of scale. Figure 9(c) is a curve indicating only constant returns to scale. Each of these long-run average-total-cost curves would connect several short-run average-total-cost curves, as shown in Figure 9(d), 9(e), and 9(f).

4.b. The Reasons for Economies and Diseconomies of Scale

Firms that can specialize more as they grow larger may be able to realize economies of scale. Specialization of marketing, sales, pricing, and research, for example, allows some employees to focus on research while others focus on marketing and still others focus on sales and on pricing. For instance, when Mrs. Fields Cookies

FIGURE 9

Long-Run and Short-Run Cost Curves

In Figure 9(a), a U-shaped *LRATC* curve is shown. The downward-sloping portion is due to economies of scale, the horizontal portion to constant returns to scale, and the upward-sloping portion to diseconomies of scale. In Figure 9(b), only economies of scale are experienced.

In Figure 9(c), only constant returns to scale are experienced. The *LRATC* curve connects the lowest cost for each level of output given by the *SRATC* curves. Three such short-run cost curves for each *LRATC* curve are illustrated in Figure 9(d), 9(e), and 9(f).

(a) Economies, Constant Returns, and Diseconomies

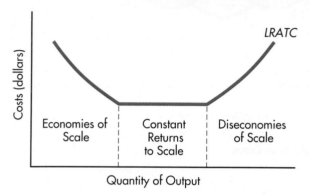

(d) Economies, Constant Returns, and Diseconomies

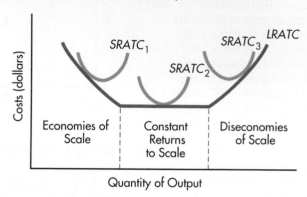

(b) Economies of Scale

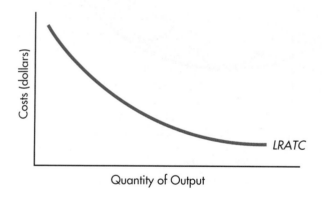

(e) Economies of Scale

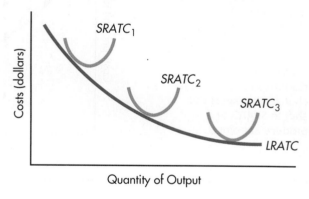

(c) Constant Returns to Scale

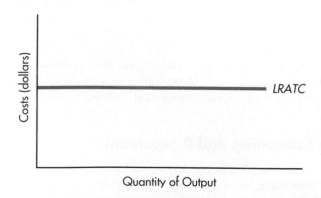

(f) Constant Returns to Scale

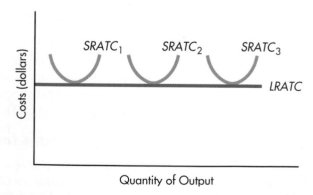

was just starting out, it was a one-person operation in northern California. When it moved to Park City, Utah, it was a multiperson operation with cookie outlets throughout most of the western United States. As it grew, the company was able to experience economies of scale. Its employees could specialize more in just one activity, its advertising did not have to increase as its size increased, and larger machinery enabled it to produce a larger quantity of dough in a shorter period of time.

In 2001 and 2002, oil companies merged—Exxon and Mobil, Chevron and Texaco. The firms resulting from these combinations became two of the largest companies in the world. The reason for merging given by the chief executive officers of these companies was to achieve economies of scale. They believed that having larger oil fields and more refining capability would enable their employees to specialize more and their drilling and refining equipment to be more fully utilized.

Economies of scale may also result from the use of large machines that are more efficient than small ones. Large blast furnaces can produce more than twice as much steel per hour as smaller furnaces, but they do not cost twice as much to build or operate. Large electric-power generators are more efficient (more output per quantity of resource) than small ones.

Size, however, does not automatically improve efficiency. The specialization that comes with large size often requires the addition of specialized managers. A 10 percent increase in the number of employees may require an increase greater than 10 percent in the number of managers. A manager to supervise the other managers is needed. Paperwork increases. Meetings are held more often. The amount of time and labor that are not devoted to producing output grows. In other words, the overhead increases. In addition, it becomes increasingly difficult for the CEO to coordinate the activities of all the division heads and for the division heads to communicate with one another. In this way, size can cause diseconomies of scale.

Again consider what happened to Mrs. Fields Cookies. As the company continued to add more and more outlets, its CEO could not keep track of everything. Assistant managers, vice presidents, and other executives were hired. The company had experienced economies of scale by utilizing larger equipment in its central location in Park City. But as more and more outlets were added at greater distances from Park City, the distribution of the cookie dough became more and more costly. At some size, most companies reach a point where diseconomies of scale set in. Mrs. Fields Cookies went beyond that point and eventually was sold, dismantled, and reorganized.

4.c. The Minimum Efficient Scale

The law of diminishing marginal returns applies to every resource, every firm, and every industry. Whether there are economies of scale, diseconomies of scale, constant returns to scale, or some combination of these depends on the industry under consideration. No law dictates that an industry will have economies of scale eventually followed by diseconomies of scale, although that seems to be the typical pattern. Theoretically, it is possible for an industry to experience only diseconomies of scale, only economies of scale, or only constant returns to scale.

Most industries experience both economies and diseconomies of scale. As we noted earlier, Mrs. Fields Cookies was able to achieve economies of scale as it grew from one location to 700. But the company faced diseconomies because the cookie dough was produced at one location and distributed to the outlets in premixed packages. The dough factory could be large, but the distribution of dough produced diseconomies of scale that worsened as outlets were opened farther and farther away from the factory.

If the long-run average-total-cost curve reaches a minimum, the level of output at which the minimum occurs is called the **minimum efficient scale (MES).** The *MES* varies from industry to industry; it is significantly smaller, for instance, in the production of shoes than it is in the production of cigarettes. A shoe is made by stretching leather around a mold, sewing the leather, and fitting and attaching the soles and insoles. The process requires one worker to operate just two or three machines at a time. Thus, increasing the quantity of shoes made per hour requires more building space, more workers, more leather, and more machines. The cost per shoe declines for the first few shoes made per hour, but rises thereafter. Cigarettes, on the other hand, can be rolled in a machine that can produce several thousand per hour. Producing 100 cigarettes an hour is more costly per cigarette than producing 100,000 per hour.

4.d. The Planning Horizon

The long run is referred to as a planning horizon because the firm has not committed to a fixed quantity of any resource and has all options available to it. In determining the size or scale to select, the manager must look at expected demand and expected costs of production and then select the size that appears to be the most profitable. Once a scale is selected, the firm is operating in the short run, since at least one of the resources is fixed. Sony, for instance, was constrained to a rather small production facility for transistor radios back in the 1950s, as discussed in the Preview. This means that it was operating along a specific short-run average-cost curve. To produce 100,000 radios would have meant moving far up the right side of the U, so that per unit costs would have been extremely high. If Akio Morita had anticipated several more huge purchase orders in future years, he might have committed to produce 100,000 radios and increased the scale of Sony. Expanding the scale of Sony would have meant moving down along the long-run average-cost curve, perhaps from the current position of $SRATC_1$ in Figure 10 to $SRATC_5$. Once having committed to the scale of $SRATC_5$, Sony would again be operating in the short run. Increases and decreases in production would be a move along $SRATC_5$. You can see what Morita was worried about. Suppose that production dropped back to the 10,000 radios per year level. Then, being constrained to operate along $SRATC_5$, Sony would have experienced huge per unit costs.

FIGURE 10

Morita's Problem

Had Sony chosen to produce at $SRATC_5$, it would have been constrained to operate along $SRATC_5$ in the short run. A decrease in production to 10,000 units would have meant rising up the short-run cost curve and producing at very high per unit costs.

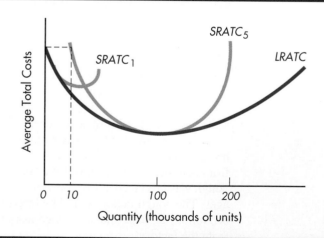

1. Many industries are characterized by U-shaped long-run average-cost curves but need not be. There is no law dictating a U-shaped *LRATC* curve.

2. The long-run average-total-cost curve gets its U shape from economies and diseconomies of scale, unlike the short-run cost curves, which get their U shape from diminishing marginal returns.

3. The minimum efficient scale (*MES*) is the size of a firm that is at the minimum point of a long-run average-cost curve.

4. The *MES* varies from industry to industry. Some industries, like the electric-power distribution industry, have large economies of scale and a large *MES*. Other kinds of industries, like the fast-food industry, have a relatively small *MES*.

5. Economies of scale may result from specialization and technology. Diseconomies of scale may occur because coordination and communication become more difficult as size increases.

Summary

1. A firm is a business organization that brings together land, labor, capital, and business ownership to produce a product or service. *§1*

2. The short run is a period of time just short enough that the quantity of at least one of the resources cannot be altered. *§1.a*

3. The total physical product curve is a picture of the short-run relationship between resources (inputs) and output when one resource is variable. *§1.a*

? **What is the law of diminishing marginal returns?**

4. According to the law of diminishing marginal returns, when successive equal amounts of a variable resource are combined with a fixed amount of another resource, there will be a point beyond which the extra or marginal product that can be attributed to each additional unit of the variable resource will decline. *§1.a, 1.b*

? **What is the relationship between costs and output in the short run?**

5. The shapes of the *TC, TPP, MC, MPP,* and *APP* curves are due to the law of diminishing marginal returns. *§2.a, 2.b*

6. Fixed costs are costs that do not vary as the quantity of goods produced varies. *§3.a*

7. Variable costs rise as the quantity of goods produced rises. *§3.a*

8. Total costs are the sum of fixed and variable costs. *§3.a*

9. Average total costs are the costs per unit of output—total costs divided by the quantity of output produced. *§3.a*

10. Average costs fall when marginal costs are less than average and rise when marginal costs are greater than average. *§3.a.1*

11. The U shape of the short-run average-total-cost curve is due to the law of diminishing marginal returns. *§2.b, 3.b*

? **What is the relationship between costs and output in the long run?**

12. The U shape of the long-run average-total-cost curve is due to economies and diseconomies of scale. *§4.a*

13. Economies of scale result when increases in output lead to decreases in unit costs and the quantities of all resources are variable. *§4.a*

14. Diseconomies of scale result when increases in output lead to increases in unit costs and the quantities of all resources are variable. *§4.a*

15. Constant returns to scale occur when increases in output lead to no changes in unit costs and the quantities of all resources are variable. *§4.a*

16. The minimum efficient scale (*MES*) occurs at the minimum point of the long-run average-total-cost curve. *§4.c*

17. The long run is the planning horizon where all resources are variable. Once a size or scale is selected, the firm is operating in the short run. *§4.d*

Key Terms

total physical product (*TPP*) *§1.a*
law of diminishing marginal returns *§1.b*
average physical product (*APP*) *§1.b*
marginal physical product (*MPP*) *§1.b*
average total cost (*ATC*) *§2.a*
marginal cost (*MC*) *§2.a*
total fixed costs (*TFC*) *§3.a*
total variable costs (*TVC*) *§3.a*

total costs (*TC*) *§3.a*
short-run average total cost (*SRATC*) *§3.a*
scale *§4.a*
long-run average total cost (*LRATC*) *§4.a*
economies of scale *§4.a*
diseconomies of scale *§4.a*
constant returns to scale *§4.a*
minimum efficient scale (*MES*) *§4.c*

Exercises

1. Use the following information to list the total fixed costs, total variable costs, average fixed costs, average variable costs, average total costs, and marginal costs.

Output	Costs	TFC	TVC	AFC	AVC	ATC	MC
0	$100						
1	$150						
2	$225						
3	$230						
4	$300						
5	$400						

2. Use the following table to answer the questions listed below.

Output	Cost	TFC	TVC	AFC	AVC	ATC	MC
0	$ 20						
10	$ 40						
20	$ 60						
30	$ 90						
40	$120						
50	$180						
60	$280						

a. Calculate the total fixed costs, total variable costs, average fixed costs, average variable costs, average total costs, and marginal costs.
b. Plot each of the cost curves.

c. At what quantity of output does marginal cost equal average total cost and average variable cost?

3. Use Table 2 in the chapter to demonstrate the law of diminishing marginal returns. Where does the law apply if there are 20 airplanes in the short run? What occurs if there are only 10 airplanes? Plot the *APP* curve for 20 airplanes and for 10 airplanes.

4. Use Table 2 in the chapter to demonstrate the law of diminishing marginal returns if the fixed resource is mechanics. Plot the *APP* curve for 1 mechanic and for 4 mechanics.

5. Describe some conditions that might cause large firms to experience inefficiencies that small firms would not experience.

6. What is the minimum efficient scale? Why would different industries have different minimum efficient scales?

7. Describe the relation between marginal and average costs. Describe the relation between marginal and average fixed costs and between marginal and average variable costs.

8. Explain why the *APP* curve rises when *MPP* is greater than *APP* and falls when *MPP* is less than *APP*.

9. Explain why the short-run marginal-cost curve must intersect the short-run average-total-cost and average-variable-cost curves at their minimum

points. Why doesn't the marginal-cost curve also intersect the average-fixed-cost curve at its minimum point?

10. Explain the relationship between the shapes of the production curves and the cost curves. Specifically, compare the marginal-physical-product curve and the marginal-cost curve, and the average-physical-product curve and the average-total-cost curve.

11. Consider a firm with a fixed-size production facility as described by its existing cost curves.

   a. Explain what would happen to those cost curves if a mandatory health insurance program is imposed on all firms.

   b. What would happen to the cost curves if the plan required the firm to provide a health insurance program for each employee worth 10 percent of the employee's salary?

   c. How would that plan compare to one that requires each firm to provide a $100,000 group program that would cover all employees in the firm no matter the number of employees?

12. Explain the fallacy of the following statement: "You made a real blunder. The $600 you paid for repairs is worth more than the car."

13. Explain the statement "We had to increase our volume to spread the overhead."

14. Three college students are considering operating a tutoring business in economics. This business would require that they give up their current jobs at the student recreation center, which pay $6,000 per year. A fully equipped facility can be leased at a cost of $8,000 per year. Additional costs are $1,000 a year for insurance and $.50 per person per hour for materials and supplies. Their services would be priced at $10 per hour per person.

   a. What are fixed costs?
   b. What are variable costs?
   c. What is the marginal cost?
   d. How many students would it take to break even?

15. Express Mail offers overnight delivery to customers. It is attempting to come to some conclusion on whether to expand its facilities or not. Currently its fixed costs are $2 million per month and its variable costs are $2 per package. It charges $12 per package and has a monthly volume of 2 million packages. If it expands, its fixed costs will rise by $1 million and its variable costs will fall to $1.50 per package. Should it expand?

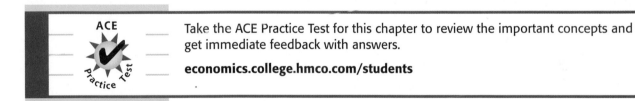

ACE

Take the ACE Practice Test for this chapter to review the important concepts and get immediate feedback with answers.

economics.college.hmco.com/students

Merge or Die

Tanker operators were yesterday urged to merge or pool resources in order to survive in a market where oil companies are looking for economies of scale in leasing.

Charterers of tankers and product carriers seeking to lower their risks need high quality tonnage, owned by large companies with low-risk profiles. For smaller family-operated tanker owners there is the choice of evolving or being eaten. To evolve they can merge with other smaller players or join one of many vessel-pool organisations. Alex Papachristidis-Bove, president and chartering manager of Seatramp Tankers, told London's Tanker Operator conference yesterday: "Big fleets rule! Oil companies need high quality tonnage so large stable companies will continue to lead the market.

"Large companies have lower risk so show accountability and quality. They can grow because they are attractive to investment."

He believed this highly fragmented market was moving towards consolidation because the oil industry had already gone through the process.

He said Scandinavian companies—Bergesen, Fredriksen, Stolt-Nielsen and Moller—were leading the market, with strong evidence that Greek players and US companies were building fleets through acquisition.

Joining forces meant "optimising vessel utilisation to satisfy a broader market base" and it provided a "stronger asset base for accessing capital and renewing fleets," he said.

Mr. Papachristidis-Bove also thought consolidation led to economies of scale and "profitability from service rather than opportunistic sale and purchase activity." But if tanker owners wanted to stay independent they could benefit from economies of scale through vessel pools.

"Small companies need to pool resources," added Alex Staring, director of operations of Tanker International, a pool of 44 very large crude carriers owned by Moller, Euronav, Oldendorff and OSG.

Some of the advantages included improved cash flow, as earnings were distributed across pool members, and lower voyage waiting times, which could reduce waiting costs to Dollars 400 per journey.

MARTYN WINGROVE

Lloyd's List/February 12, 2003

erge or die? What does this mean? According to the article, oil shippers need to experience economies of scale, and to do this the smaller companies must get larger. A quick way to get larger is to merge with another firm. Why is it necessary to be large? If, as the article states, there are economies of scale, then the larger firms will have a cost advantage over the smaller firms. Consider the figure shown here, which shows a long-run average-total-cost curve with economies of scale and two short-run average-total-cost curves, one for a smaller firm, $SRATC_S$, and one for a larger firm, $SRATC_L$. The larger firm has experienced economies of scale and therefore can offer a price significantly below the price that the smaller firm can offer. The larger firm's lowest price would be P_L, whereas the smaller firm's best price would be P_S.

The article notes that if smaller companies want to remain independent, they can form vessel pools. This type of sharing arrangement is common;

high-tech firms located in Silicon Valley because other high-tech firms were there, and so the firms had a large supply of highly skilled labor available. The firms achieved economies of scale without being large themselves. If the transport firms can pool vessels so that each firm can become more specialized, then the vessel pools may result in economies of scale.

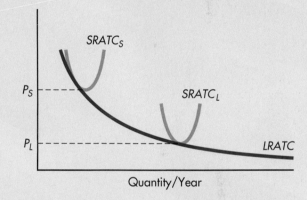

Part Six

Product Markets

CHAPTER 23

Profit Maximization

1. **What is the role of economic profit in allocating resources?**

2. **Why do economists and accountants measure profit differently?**

3. **How do firms decide how much to supply?**

4. **What is a market structure?**

5. **What are price makers and price takers?**

A firm is a combination of resources used to produce a good or service. The firm adds value to the resources it uses if it pays the resources for their use and still has something left over. In 2003 Microsoft bought materials worth $5 billion. Its wage and salary bill was around $13 billion, and the cost of the capital that the company used—premises, factories, machinery, and equipment—was about $4 billion. Thus, it cost Microsoft $22 billion to produce its output. Sales were $32 billion—$10 billion more than it cost to produce the output. This figure of $10 billion is a measure of the value that Microsoft added, the difference between the value of its output and the full cost of its inputs. ■

1. Profit Maximization

The objective of a for-profit firm is to maximize profit. The purpose of a charitable organization, university, or tennis or golf club is to maximize the benefits it provides. For instance, St. Mary's Food Bank is a nonprofit firm whose wage and salary bill was $2.8 million and whose cost of capital was $1.4 million in 2003. Its charitable contributions were $4.2 million, exactly the cost of the resources it used. Its value was the amount by which the value of the services it provided exceeded the cost of inputs.

1.a. Economic Profit

Profit is what remains of the value of output once the costs of the inputs used in the organization have been fully accounted for. Inputs consist of three general groups: land, labor, and capital.

The cost of each is an opportunity cost—the amount necessary to keep the owners of the resource from moving it to an alternative use. For instance, if a landowner can rent her land to another firm at a higher rate, then she will. She has to be paid the opportunity cost of the land. Similarly, if you could earn more for doing the same job somewhere else, you would take that job. An employee must be paid at least what he could earn elsewhere.

The cost of capital is also an opportunity cost. Capital is aquired through loans (**debt**) and sales of ownership rights (shares of stock—**equity**—for a publicly traded company). The cost of debt is the interest that is paid on the debt. The cost of equity is the alternative returns that the investors (owners) could have gotten had they not chosen to invest in this particular activity or company—the investors' opportunity cost. For instance, since shareholders of Microsoft could do something else with the money, the cost of investing in Microsoft is the highest return that any of the alternative uses of the money would have been expected to generate. Microsoft must pay these shareholders at least what they expect to get from alternative investments, or the shareholders will take their money elsewhere.

The return to shareholders (or owners) that exceeds the return they expected to get from an alternative investment is **economic profit.** The profit figure reported in annual reports, income statements, and other financial statements is **accounting profit,** not economic profit. Accounting profit is the value of output less the cost of inputs, but *not including* the opportunity cost of the owner's (shareholder's) capital. Economic profit is the difference between the value of output and the opportunity cost of all inputs *including* the opportunity cost of the owner's or shareholder's capital.[1]

$$\text{Accounting profit} = \text{revenue} - \text{cost of land} - \text{cost of labor} - \text{cost of debt capital}$$

$$\text{Economic profit} = \text{accounting profit} - \text{cost of equity capital}$$

Wal-Mart, for instance, reported a profit of $6,671 million for 2002. This is Wal-Mart's accounting profit. To get Wal-Mart's economic profit, we have to subtract Wal-Mart's cost of capital from its accounting profit. Wal-Mart's cost of capital was $5,534 million, so its economic profit was $1,134 million, only 17 percent of its accounting profit.

1. What is the role of economic profit in allocating resources?

debt: loans

equity: shares of stock

2. Why do economists and accountants measure profit differently?

economic profit: total revenue less total costs, including all opportunity costs

accounting profit: total revenue less total costs except for the opportunity cost of capital

---

[1]If the firm is a private firm, then the equity capital includes the owner's own dollars put into the business and the uncompensated time the owner puts into the business.

Coca-Cola had $3.9 billion in accounting profits in 2002. The economic profit for Coca-Cola in 2002 was

$$\text{Economic profit} = \text{accounting profit} - \text{opportunity cost of capital}$$
$$= \$3.9 \text{ billion} - \$1.7 \text{ billion} (.10)$$
$$= \$3.9 \text{ billion} - \$1.7 \text{ billion}$$
$$= \$2.2 \text{ billion}[2]$$

1.a.1. Negative Economic Profit

negative economic profit: total revenue is less than total costs when total costs include all opportunity costs

Economists refer to a firm that subtracts value (whose cost of equity capital is greater than its accounting profit) as having **negative economic profit.** Negative economic profit means that the resources would have a higher value in another use. A firm that continually subtracts value will not exist in the long run. Suppose you were an investor in General Motors Corporation (GM). Having experienced 4 percent annual returns over the last ten years, lower returns than you anticipated, you look at your alternatives. You realize that you could have earned more by selling your shares of stock in GM and purchasing shares in another firm. If many GM shareholders did this, GM could no longer acquire the use of resources. It would have to go out of business. Why has GM not gone out of business? Because not enough investors have decided that they could do better investing in another firm. However, for more than 1 percent of the total firms in the United States each year, investors choose to invest elsewhere and the firms do go out of business. For a short period, firms can earn negative economic profit and remain in business. In 2000, such well-known companies as AOL, Hewlett-Packard, Pepsico, Walt Disney, Motorola, and Boeing had negative economic profit. If their owners anticipated a continuing pattern of negative economic profit, they would take their money elsewhere.

1.a.2. Zero Economic Profit

zero economic profit: total revenue is equal to total costs when total costs include all opportunity costs

normal accounting profit: zero economic profit

A firm that neither adds value nor subtracts it is a firm whose revenue is sufficient to pay the cost of inputs, but with nothing left over after paying those inputs. Economists refer to this as **zero economic profit** or **normal accounting profit.** If Microsoft had revenue of $8.75 billion and costs of $6.75 billion, it would have an accounting profit of $2 billion. But if the shareholders could have earned 10 percent in an alternative activity and they have invested $20 billion in Microsoft, then Microsoft's economic profit would be zero; its added value would be zero.

Zero economic profit might sound bad, but it is not. A zero economic profit simply means that the owners could not have expected to have done better elsewhere; the firm is earning a positive accounting profit. The investors have no incentive to sell Microsoft and purchase something else, since they would expect to earn no more than they are earning with Microsoft.

1.a.3. Positive Economic Profit

positive economic profit: total revenue is greater than total costs when total costs include all opportunity costs

If a firm is returning more to its owners than the owners' opportunity cost, the firm is said to be earning **positive economic profit.** Positive economic profit is a powerful signal in the marketplace. Whenever other investors see the positive economic profit, they want to get in on it as well. As a result, they take their funds from whatever use they are currently in and invest them in existing and new firms that will compete with the profitable firm. Recall the

---

[2]Coca-Cola reports its economic profit as part of its financial data. See p. 186 of its 2002 annual statement.

A cab driver in Tokyo dusts the rear seat of his cab prior to picking up passengers. Taxicabs are tightly regulated in Japan, having to serve specific districts and maintain specified quality standards. A particular company may have a government-created monopoly in a certain part of the city. Nevertheless, each cab company attempts to compete with other cab and limousine companies by providing extra service. Cleanliness and order are emphasized. Many cab drivers wear white gloves; others use feather dusters on the seats before each customer enters the cab; still others provide special music and other services.

scenario of the bottled water that was carried to the top of a hiking trail and sold to thirsty hikers. The profit earned as more hikers showed up than there were water bottles available induced the owner of the stand to increase supplies and others to open their own water stands. With additional firms producing the good or service, the supply increases; this will lower the price of that good or service and reduce the positive economic profit. The entry of new firms will stop once economic profit is zero.

1.a.4. Role of Economic Profit

Economic profit serves as a beacon, attracting resources when it is positive and directing resources to other uses when it is negative. When a firm earns a positive economic profit, it is making enough to pay the opportunity cost of all the resources it uses, including the opportunity cost of the investors. The investors are doing better than they would have expected to do in any other investment. Resources flow to where they will earn more. Conversely, when a firm earns a negative economic profit, the investors are not being paid their opportunity cost, and they will take their investments elsewhere. When economic profit is zero, the firm is earning just enough to pay all the resources their opportunity costs. Thus, investors are getting as much as they would have expected to get in any other investment. The firm earning zero economic profit will neither drive investors away nor attract additional investors.

1.b. Accountants and Economic Profit

Accountants do not present economic profit in income statements and balance sheets. Why not? Partly because they have not been convinced it is necessary, but more importantly because of the difficulty of calculating the cost of capital.

The cost of equity capital is the amount that the investors would have to be paid to keep them from moving their funds to another firm, that is, the opportunity cost to investors of leaving their money with a particular firm. That amount is sure to vary from investor to investor. My opportunity cost is not the same as yours. But even ignoring this problem and focusing on the average investor, the cost of capital is not

Brisk Business in Measuring Economic Profit

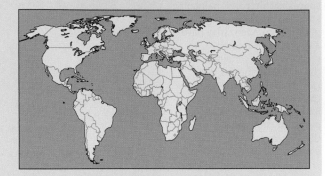

The recognition that it is the economic profit that matters has led to a brisk business in management consulting. Spurred by lucrative fees, consultants are scrambling to help companies install new performance measures to replace the old standbys such as earnings per share (EPS) and return on equity (ROE). The dominant firm in this business is Stern-Stewart, promoting its Economic Value Added (EVA). Another major firm in the business is the Boston Consulting Group, whose experts combine cash flow return on investment (CFROI) with a concept that they call Total Business Return. McKinsey uses the term *economic profit,* while the LEK/Alcar Group pushes for Shareholder Value Added (SVA). These are far from the only consulting firms in the business, but they are the dominant ones.

The value of measuring economic profit as well as accounting profit has become increasingly clear to executives in recent years. A change in focus from accounting profit to economic profit has altered the behavior of many firms.* Before Quaker Oats adopted economic profit as its measure of performance, the manager of Quaker's granola bar plant in Danville, Illinois, used long production runs to turn out the various sizes of bars in order to minimize downtime and setup costs. This bolstered operating profits, but also resulted in huge inventories of bars that sat in a warehouse until they were shipped to customers. Inventory is not free, however, since money is tied up in that inventory. Thus, when the company charged

the manager for the inventory—that is, for the money tied up in inventory—he switched to short production runs, which reduced net operating profits but increased economic profit. Prior to focusing on economic profit, the Coca-Cola Company shipped its soft drink syrup to bottlers in stainless steel cans that could be used over and over. The problem was that the steel cans were expensive; they required significant amounts of capital. When the company began focusing on economic profit, it sold off the stainless steel cans and used cardboard. The cardboard increased operating costs, but by less than the cost of capital declined. As a result, economic profit rose.

*These examples are from Al Ehrbar, *EVA: The Real Key to Creating Wealth* (New York: John Wiley and Sons, 1999), p. 141.

easily measured. As a result, few firms report economic profits along with their accounting profits. But, more and more firms are beginning to offer investors some information on economic profit, as the Global Business Insight "Brisk Business in Measuring Economic Profit" shows.

RECAP

1. Economic profit refers to the difference between the value of output and the full cost of inputs.
2. Accounting profit is total revenue less total costs. It does not include the opportunity cost of the owner's capital.
3. Economic profit is accounting profit less the opportunity cost of the owner's capital.

4. Economic profit can be positive, negative, or zero. A positive economic profit means that the revenue exceeds the full cost of inputs, that is, that inputs are earning more than their opportunity cost. A negative economic profit means that the inputs are not earning their opportunity costs. A zero economic profit means that the inputs are just earning their opportunity costs.

5. Economic profit is not straightforward to measure because the opportunity cost of capital depends on investors' alternatives.

6. The cost of capital is the amount that a firm has to pay investors in order to have them invest in this firm rather than another.

2. Marginal Revenue and Marginal Cost

A firm's decision to supply a good or service depends on expected profit. An entrepreneur or manager of a firm looks at the demand for the firm's product and at its costs of doing business and determines whether a profit potential exists. To analyze the firm's decisions, we must put the demand for the firm's product together with the firm's costs.

2.a. Demand and Cost Curves

?

3. How do firms decide how much to supply?

Consider Figure 1, in which the average-total-cost and marginal-cost curves, derived in the previous chapter, are drawn along with a downward-sloping demand curve. We are talking about one firm and all the consumers of that firm's goods and services. The firm may be just one of many in the market, or it may be the only firm in the market. Whatever the case, the cost curves in Figure 1 are those of one firm, and the demand curve is the demand for that single firm's goods and services. The demand curve could also be horizontal or vertical. The shape of the demand curve characterizes the environment in which the firm is selling.

With the downward-sloping demand curve, the firm knows that total revenue first rises and then declines as price is lowered down along the demand curve. Maximum revenue is the point where the price elasticity of demand is 1. But this point is not necessarily the profit-maximizing point. How do we find the profit-maximizing point?

Profit is the difference between total revenue and total costs. Consider the profit the firm shown in Figure 1 earns at price P_1 selling output Q_1. Total revenue is price times quantity, or $P_1 \times Q_1$, the rectangle $ABCD$. At quantity Q_1 total cost is given by $ABEF$, found by determining the average total cost (cost per unit of output) at Q_1 and multiplying that by the quantity Q_1. Profit at quantity Q_1, then, is the difference between the rectangle $ABCD$ and the rectangle $ABEF$. Profit at Q_1 is given by $ABCD - ABEF = FECD$.

The profit given by the rectangle $FECD$ in Figure 1 is the profit the firm would earn by producing and selling quantity Q_1. The area $FECD$ is not necessarily the maximum profit—the firm might earn more by producing more or less than Q_1. To find the quantity at which profit is maximized, we could compare total revenue and total cost for each output level. There is an easier way, however: to find the quantity of output at which profit is a maximum, simply compare marginal cost and marginal revenue.

2.b. Profit Maximum: Marginal Revenue Equals Marginal Cost

Marginal cost is the additional cost of producing one more unit of output. *Marginal revenue* is the additional revenue obtained from selling one more unit of output. If

FIGURE 1

Revenue, Cost, and Profit

In Figure 1 the demand curve is drawn along with the average-total-cost and marginal-cost curves. A point of output, Q_1, is arbitrarily chosen to illustrate what total costs, total revenue, and total profit would be at that output point. The price, P_1, is given by the demand curve, tracing Q_1 up to the demand curve. Total revenue, $P_1 \times Q_1$, is given by the rectangle labeled *ABCD*. The total costs are given by seeing how much it costs per unit of output to produce Q_1. That quantity, *BE*, multiplied by the total quantity *AB*, provides the total cost area, *ABEF*. Total profit is total revenue minus total costs, $ABCD - ABEF = FECD$.

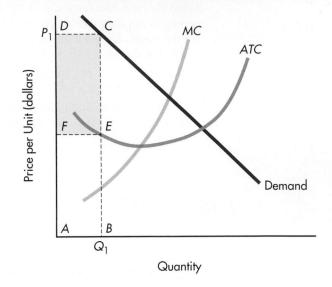

the production of one more unit of output increases costs less than it increases revenue—that is, if marginal cost is less than marginal revenue—then producing (and selling) that unit will increase profit. Conversely, if the production of one more unit costs more than the revenue obtained from the sale of the unit, then producing that unit will decrease profit. When marginal revenue is greater than marginal cost, producing more will increase profit. Conversely, when marginal revenue is less than marginal cost, producing more will lower profit. Thus, *profit is at a maximum when marginal revenue equals marginal cost.*

Profit is maximized at the output level where marginal revenue and marginal cost are equal (MR = MC).

The profit-maximizing rule, $MR = MC$, is illustrated in Table 1, which lists output, total revenue, total cost, marginal revenue, marginal cost, and profit for an individual firm selling custom-made mountain bicycles. The first column is the total quantity (Q) of bikes produced. In column 2 is the total revenue (TR) generated by selling each quantity, and in column 3 is the total cost (TC) of producing each quantity. Fixed costs, the costs the firm encounters even when it produces nothing, amount to $1,000, as listed in column 3, row 1. Marginal revenue (MR), the change in total revenue that comes with the production of an additional bike, is listed in the fourth column. The marginal revenue of the first bike produced is the change in revenue that the firm receives for increasing its production and sales from zero to 1 unit; the marginal revenue of the first bike is listed in the row of bike number 1. The marginal revenue of the second bike produced is the change in revenue that the firm receives for increasing its production and sales from 1 to 2 bikes; the marginal

TABLE 1

Profit Maximization

(1) Total Output (Q)	(2) Total Revenue (TR)	(3) Total Cost (TC)	(4) Marginal Revenue (MR)	(5) Marginal Cost (MC)	(6) Profit (TR − TC)
0	$ 0	$1,000			−$1,000
1	$ 1,700	$2,000	$1,700	$1,000	−$ 300
2	$ 3,300	$2,800	$1,600	$ 800	$ 500
3	$ 4,800	$3,500	$1,500	$ 700	$1,300
4	$ 6,200	$4,000	$1,400	$ 500	$2,200
5	$ 7,500	$4,500	$1,300	$ 500	$3,000
6	$ 8,700	$5,200	$1,200	$ 700	$3,500
7	$ 9,800	$6,000	$1,100	$ 800	$3,800
8	$10,800	$7,000	$1,000	$1,000	$3,800
9	$11,700	$9,000	$ 900	$2,000	$2,700

revenue of that second bike is listed in the row of bike number 2. Marginal cost (MC), the additional cost of producing an additional bike, is listed in column 5. The marginal cost of the first bike is the additional cost of producing the first bike; the marginal cost of the second bike is the increase in costs that results from increasing production from 1 to 2 bikes. Total profit, the difference between total revenue and total cost (TR − TC), is listed in the last column.

The first bike costs $2,000 to produce ($1,000 of fixed costs and $1,000 of variable costs); the marginal cost (additional cost) of the first bike is $1,000. When sold, the bike brings in $1,700 in revenue, so the marginal revenue is $1,700. Since marginal revenue is greater than marginal cost, the firm is better off producing that first bike than not producing it.

The second bike costs an additional $800 (column 5) to produce and brings in an additional $1,600 (column 4) in revenue. With the second bike, marginal revenue exceeds marginal cost. Thus the firm is better off producing 2 bikes than none or 1.

Supply rule: Produce and offer for sale the quantity at which marginal revenue equals marginal cost (MR = MC).

Profit continues to rise as production rises until the eighth bike is produced. The marginal cost of producing the seventh bike is $800, and the marginal revenue from selling the seventh bike is $1,100. The marginal cost of producing the eighth bike is $1,000, and the marginal revenue from selling that eighth bike is also $1,000. The marginal cost of producing the ninth bike, $2,000, exceeds the marginal revenue obtained from the ninth bike, $900. Profit declines if the ninth bike is produced. The firm increases profit by producing the seventh bike and reduces profit by producing the ninth bike. Thus, the firm can maximize profit by producing 8 bikes, the quantity at which marginal revenue and marginal cost are equal.[3]

---

[3]You might notice that profit is at the maximum level for quantities of 7 and 8 bikes. This occurs because we are dealing with integers, 1, 2, 3, and so on, when discussing output. There would be a unique quantity for which profit is at its maximum level if we could divide the quantities into small units instead of having to deal with integers. That unique quantity would be where MR = MC. Thus, we always choose the quantity at which marginal revenue and marginal cost are the same as the profit-maximizing quantity.

2.b.1. The Marginal-Revenue Curve The example of the mountain bikes shows us that the only thing we need to add to Figure 1 to be able to point out the profit-maximizing point is the marginal-revenue curve. Drawing the marginal-revenue curve is really quite simple. The first step is to recognize that the demand curve is also the average-revenue curve; it shows the revenue per unit. Thus, the marginal-revenue curve and the demand curve are related to each other in the same way any average and marginal curves are related. That is, when the average is declining, the marginal is also declining and lies below the average. Thus, when the demand curve is downward sloping, the marginal-revenue curve is also downward sloping but lies below the demand curve.

The steeper the demand curve, the steeper the marginal-revenue curve; the marginal-revenue curve for a perfectly inelastic demand curve is the same vertical line as the demand curve. The flatter the demand curve, the flatter the marginal-revenue curve; the marginal-revenue curve for the perfectly elastic demand curve is the same as the demand curve. In between these two extremes, the marginal-revenue curve lies below the demand curve and slopes down.

For the downward-sloping demand curve, we can be more specific in drawing the marginal-revenue curve than simply noting that it slopes down and lies below the demand curve. Recall that the marginal-revenue curve is positive as long as total revenue is rising and is negative as total revenue declines. Since total revenue rises in the price-elastic region of the demand curve, marginal revenue is positive in that region. Total revenue reaches its peak at the unit-elastic point of the demand curve and then turns down; marginal revenue is zero at the unit-elastic point. And total revenue declines in the inelastic region of the demand curve, so marginal revenue must be negative in the inelastic region. Thus, the marginal-revenue curve slopes down and crosses the horizontal axis at the quantity where the demand curve is unit-elastic.

FIGURE 2

Profit Maximum with MR = MC

The demand, *ATC*, and *MC* curves from Figure 1 are redrawn. In addition, the *MR* curve is added. The curve *MR* is drawn by recognizing that demand is average revenue, and since average revenue is falling, marginal revenue must also be falling and lie below the average. In addition, marginal revenue crosses the horizontal axis at the output level at which the price elasticity of demand is unity. Profit is then found where *MR* = *MC*. This is quantity Q_m and price P_m. Total profit is the rectangle *GHIJ*.

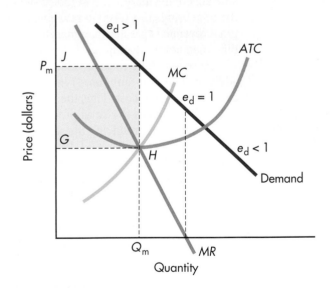

In Figure 2 we have redrawn Figure 1 and added the marginal-revenue curve. Now we can easily find the profit-maximizing point. It is the point at which $MR = MC$. In Figure 2, the profit-maximizing point is given by price P_m and the quantity Q_m, and total profit is given by the rectangle *GHIJ*.

RECAP

1. The average- and marginal-cost curves and the demand and marginal-revenue curves together characterize the producing and selling environments of a firm.
2. The demand curve is also the average-revenue curve. Thus, the marginal-revenue and demand curves are related to each other, as are any average and marginal curves. When demand declines, marginal revenue declines and lies below demand.
3. The profit-maximizing rule is to produce where marginal revenue equals marginal cost.

3. Selling Environments or Market Structure

We know that every firm, no matter what its size, no matter what its location, and no matter what it does, has a relationship in the short run between costs and output dictated by the law of diminishing marginal returns. Thus, the cost curves can have only one shape—the U shape. Demand is another matter. Every single firm has a unique demand curve for its goods and services. But the similarities of the shapes of the demand curves for similar types of firms enable us to identify just four very general selling environments—perfect competition, monopolistic competition, oligopoly, and monopoly—although perfect competition and monopoly are used more as extremes (bookends) to what occurs in the real world. At one end, there are many firms selling an identical product—perfect competition—and at the other end there is just one firm—monopoly. In between these extremes are most firms, firms that operate in a monopolistically competitive or oligopolistic selling environment.

3.a. Characteristics of the Market Structures

? 4. What is a market structure?

To represent all real-world selling environments, economists have derived four models. A model is a representation or simplification of the real world that enables scientists to organize their thoughts. A computer simulation of the galaxies is a model of the galaxies. A model can illustrate aspects of the real world but is not intended to capture every aspect. Good economic models are those that explain or predict the real world well. Few if any industries fit neatly into one selling environment or another. Economists use the four models to describe how firms might behave under certain conditions. They can then modify the models to improve their understanding of how firms behave in real life.

The selling environment in which a firm produces and sells its product, called a *market structure,* is defined by three characteristics:

■ The number of firms that make up the market
■ The ease with which new firms may enter the market and begin producing the good or service
■ The degree to which the products produced by the firms are different

TABLE 2

Summary of Market Structures and Predicted Behavior

Market Structure	Characteristics			Behavior	
	Number of Firms	Entry Condition	Product Type	Price Strategy	Promotion Strategy
Perfect competition	Very large number	Easy	Standardized	Price taker	None
Monopoly	One	No entry possible	Only one product	Price maker	Little
Monopolistic competition	Large number	Easy	Differentiated	Price maker	Large amount
Oligopoly	Few	Impeded	Standardized or differentiated	Interdependent	Little or large amount

In some industries, such as agriculture, there are millions of individual firms. In others, such as the photofinishing supplies industry, there are very few firms. It is relatively easy and inexpensive to enter the desktop publishing business, but it is much more costly and difficult to start a new airline.

3.b. Market Structure Models

Table 2 summarizes the characteristics of the four market structures. An economic model uses assumptions to simplify the real world. Assumptions are things that are taken for granted or accepted as true without proof. One of the most commonly used assumptions in economics is *everything else held constant,* referred to quite often in its Latin form, ***ceteris paribus.*** When we describe the real world of competition with the perfectly competitive model, we are assuming that firms and their products are indistinguishable, that consumers can easily (costlessly) switch from buying at one store to buying at another, and that new firms may begin selling the identical product at any time and existing firms may quit the business at any time.

ceteris paribus: Latin for "everything else held constant"

3.b.1. Perfect Competition   Perfect competition is a market structure characterized by a very large number of firms, so large that whatever any *one* firm does has no effect on the market; firms that produce an identical (standardized or nondifferentiated) product; and easy entry. Because of the large number of firms, consumers have many choices of where to purchase the good or service, and there is no cost to the consumer of going to a different store. Because the product is standardized, consumers do not prefer one store to another or one brand to another. In fact, there are no brands—only identical, generic products. Because each firm is such a small part of the market, each is unable to do anything other than choose how much to sell at the prevailing market price. In other words, the demand curve for the individual firm in perfect competition is a horizontal line, as shown in Figure 3(a).

3.b.2. Monopoly   Monopoly is a market structure in which there is just one firm and entry by other firms is not possible. Because there is only one firm, consumers have only one place to buy the good, and there are no close substitutes.

FIGURE 3

The Demand Curve Facing an Individual Firm

The demand curve for the individual firm in perfect competition is a horizontal line at the market price, as shown in Figure 3(a).

Figure 3(b) shows the market demand, which is the demand curve faced by the monopoly firm. The firm is the only supplier and thus faces the entire market demand.

Figure 3(c) shows the downward-sloping demand curve faced by the firm in monopolistic competition. The curve slopes downward because of the differentiated nature of the products in the industry.

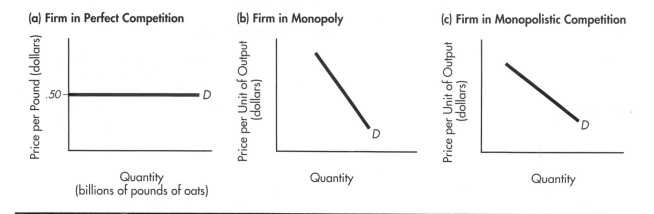

(a) Firm in Perfect Competition   (b) Firm in Monopoly   (c) Firm in Monopolistic Competition

5. What are price makers and price takers?

price maker, price setter, or **price searcher:** a firm that sets the price of the product it sells

The demand curve facing the single firm in a monopoly is the market demand because the firm is the only supplier in the market. Figure 3(b) shows the demand curve facing the firm in a monopoly. Being the only producer, the firm in a monopoly must carefully consider what price to charge. Unlike a price increase in a perfectly competitive market, a price increase in a monopoly will not drive every customer to another producer. But if the price is too high, revenue will decline as consumers decide to forgo the product supplied by that one firm. A firm operating in any market but perfect competition is not a price taker. Economists have used different names to refer to a firm that is not a price taker, sometimes using **price maker,** other times **price setter,** and still other times **price searcher.** All three terms are meant to imply the same thing: that the firm determines the quantity it produces and the price at which it sells the products.

3.b.3. Monopolistic Competition A monopolistically competitive market structure is characterized by a large number of firms, easy entry, and differentiated products. Product differentiation distinguishes a perfectly competitive market from a monopolistically competitive market (in both, entry is easy and there are a large number of firms).

Even though there are many firms in a monopolistically competitive market structure, the demand curve faced by *any one firm* slopes downward, as in Figure 3(c). Because each product is slightly different from all other products, each firm is like a minimonopoly—the only producer of that specific product. The greater the differentiation among products, the less price-elastic the demand.

3.b.4. Oligopoly In an oligopoly, there are few firms—more than one but few enough so that each firm alone can affect the market. Automobile producers constitute one oligopoly, steelmakers another. Entry into an oligopoly is more difficult than entry into a perfectly competitive or monopolistically competitive market, but in contrast to monopoly, entry can occur. The products offered by the firms in an oligopoly may be differentiated or nondifferentiated. Oligopolistic firms are *interdependent,* and this interdependence distinguishes oligopoly from the other market structures.

The oligopolist faces a downward-sloping demand curve, but the shape of the curve depends on the behavior of competitors. Oligopoly is the most complicated of the market structure models to examine because there are so many behaviors that firms might display. Because of its diversity, many economists describe oligopoly as the most realistic of the market structure models.

3.c. Demand and Profit Maximization

Does a perfectly competitive firm maximize profit in a different manner from a monopolist or a monopolistically competitive firm? The answer is not really. Each firm maximizes profit by finding the quantity where marginal revenue equals marginal cost ($MR = MC$) and then setting the price according to demand. For the perfectly competitive firm, the only decision is what quantity to produce because the individual firm has no control over price; price is determined by the entire market (all firms and all consumers). The output choice of the perfectly competitive firm is shown in Figure 4(a). As with all firms, the perfectly competitive firm chooses to produce and offer for sale the amount where the MC curve crosses the MR curve. The difference is that for the perfectly competitive firm, marginal revenue, demand, and price are identical. For firms in all other selling environments, the process of maximizing profit is what we described earlier: the firm finds the quantity where $MR = MC$ and then determines what price consumers are willing and able to pay to purchase the quantity of output offered by the firm [indicated by tracing a vertical line up to demand, shown in Figure 4(b)]. That price is the profit-maximizing price, P^*.

FIGURE 4

Profit-Maximizing Price and Quantity for Price Taker and Price Maker

Figure 4(a) shows the profit-maximizing quantity Q^* and price P^* for the price taker, while Figure 4(b) shows the profit maximizing quantity Q^* and price P^* for the price maker. In both cases, the quantity is determined by finding where $MC = MR$ and the price is determined by demand at that quantity.

(a) Price Taker

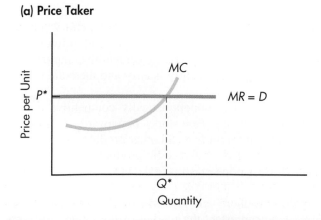

(b) Price Maker

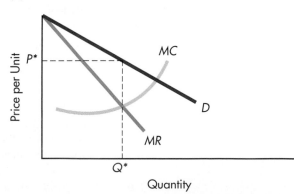

TABLE 3

Marginal Revenue and Marginal Cost

Output	MC	MR
0		
1	$ 30	$100
2	$ 50	$ 90
3	$ 80	$ 80
4	$120	$ 70
5	$170	$ 60

Once again note that when $MR = MC$, the firm can't do better; it is maximizing its profit. Consider the data shown in Table 3. Column 1 is output, column 2 is the marginal cost of each output level, and column 3 is the marginal revenue.

The first unit of output costs $30 but, when sold, brings in $100, so the firm earns a profit of $70 on the first suit. The second unit costs another $50 but brings in another $90 when sold, so the second unit increases profit by $40. The third unit costs an additional $80 and brings in an additional $80 when sold. The third unit neither increases nor decreases profit. The fourth unit costs another $120 but brings in only $70 when sold, and the fifth unit costs $110 more than the revenue the firm obtains by selling it. The firm makes additional profit by producing and selling units 1 and 2 and makes no additional profit but loses nothing by producing and selling the third unit. The fourth and fifth units take profit away. The firm clearly will produce and sell either 2 or 3 units. If the firm produced 2 and saw the additional profit from that second unit, it would produce the third unit. When the firm sees that the additional profit from the third unit is zero, it knows that to produce the fourth unit would reduce profit. Thus, the firm produces 3 units. Notice that this is also the quantity where $MR = MC$. In fact, a firm will be willing and able to supply the quantity given by $MR = MC$; that is, the MC curve is the firm's supply curve.

Now that we understand the profit-maximization process, we'll discuss firm behavior in each of the market structures in more detail. We'll begin in the next chapter with perfect competition and then turn to monopoly, monopolistic competition, and finally oligopoly.

RECAP

1. Economists have identified four market structures: perfect competition, monopoly, monopolistic competition, and oligopoly.

2. Perfect competition is a market structure in which many firms are producing a nondifferentiated product and entry is easy.

3. Monopoly is a market structure in which only one firm supplies the product and entry cannot occur.

4. Monopolistic competition is a market structure in which many firms are producing differentiated products and entry is easy.

5. Oligopoly is a market structure in which a few firms are producing either standardized or differentiated products and entry is possible but not easy. The distinguishing characteristic of oligopoly is that the firms are interdependent.

Summary

? What is the role of economic profit in allocating resources?

1. Economic profit indicates whether resources will remain in their current activity or will be distributed to a different activity. When economic profit is positive, all resources including the firm's investors and owners are getting paid more than what they could have expected to get in another activity. Others seeing this will redirect their time and investments to that activity. Conversely, when economic profit is negative, all resources are not getting paid their opportunity costs. Resource owners will take their resources and place them into an activity promising to pay more. *§1.a*

? Why do economists and accountants measure profit differently?

2. The basic assumption about the behavior of firms is that firms maximize profit. Although some firms may deviate from profit maximization, the assumption of profit maximization is a useful simplification of reality. *§1*

3. Accountants measure only the direct costs. Economists measure all opportunity costs. *§1.a*

4. Normal profit is a zero economic profit. Above-normal profit is positive economic profit. Below-normal profit is a negative economic profit. *§1.a.1*

? How do firms decide how much to supply?

5. The supply rule for all firms is to supply the quantity at which the firm's marginal revenue and marginal cost are equal. This means that each firm's supply curve is its marginal cost curve. *§2.b*

? What is a market structure?

6. A market structure is a model of the producing and selling environments in which firms operate. The three characteristics that define market structure are the number of firms, the ease of entry, and whether the products are differentiated. *§3.a*

7. A perfectly competitive market is a market in which a very large number of firms are producing an identical product and entry is easy. *§3.b.1*

8. A monopoly is a market in which there is only one firm and entry by others cannot occur. *§3.b.2*

9. A monopolistically competitive market is a market in which a large number of firms are producing differentiated products and entry is easy. *§3.b.3*

10. The demand curve facing a monopolistically competitive firm is downward sloping because of the differentiated nature of the products offered by the firm. *§3.b.3*

11. An oligopoly is a market in which a few firms are producing either differentiated or nondifferentiated products and entry is possible but not easy. *§3.b.4*

12. The demand curve facing a firm in an oligopoly is downward sloping. The elasticity depends on the actions and reactions to price changes by fellow oligopolists in the industry. *§3.b.4*

? What are price makers and price takers?

13. The demand curve facing a perfectly competitive firm is a horizontal line at the market price. The firm takes the price determined in its market as its price. *§3.b.1*

14. A firm that determines the quantity it produces and the price at which it sells the products, is a price maker. *§3.b.2*

15. The marginal-revenue curve for all firms except those in perfect competition is downward sloping and lies below the demand curve. The marginal-revenue curve for the perfectly competitive firm is the same as the demand curve, a horizontal or perfectly elastic curve. *§3.c*

Key Terms

debt *§1.a*

equity *§1.a*

economic profit *§1.a*

accounting profit *§1.a*

negative economic profit *§1.a.1*

zero economic profit *§1.a.2*

normal accounting profit *§1.a.2*

positive economic profit *§1.a.3*

ceteris paribus *§3.1*

price maker, price setter, or price searcher *§3.b.2*

Exercises

1. Can accounting profit be positive and economic profit negative? Can accounting profit be negative and economic profit positive? Explain.

2. Use the following information to calculate accounting profit and economic profit.

   Sales $100
   Employee expenses $40
   Inventory expenses $20
   Value of owner's labor in any other enterprise $40

3. Calculate accounting profit and economic profit for each of the following firms (amounts are in millions of dollars).

	General Motors	Barclay's Bank	Micro-soft
Sales	$50,091	$5,730	$2,750
Wages and salaries	$29,052	$3,932	$ 400
Cost of capital—equity	$12,100	$ 750	$ 35
Interest on debt	$ 7,585	$ 275	$ .5
Cost of materials	$ 6,500	$ 556	$1,650

4. Which type of market characterizes most businesses operating in the United States today?

5. Since a firm in monopoly has no competitors producing close substitutes, does the monopolist set exorbitantly high prices?

6. Advertising to create brand preferences is most common in what market structures?

7. Draw a perfectly elastic demand curve on top of a standard U-shaped average-total-cost curve. Now add in the marginal-cost and marginal-revenue curves. Find the profit-maximizing point, $MR = MC$. Indicate the firm's total revenues and total cost.

8. Give ten examples of differentiated products. Then list as many nondifferentiated products as you can.

9. Describe profit maximization in terms of marginal revenue and marginal cost.

10. Use the information in the table to calculate total revenue, marginal revenue, and marginal cost.

Indicate the profit-maximizing level of output. If the price was $3 and fixed costs were $5, what would variable costs be? At what level of output would the firm produce?

Output	Price	Total Costs	Total Revenue ($P \times Q$)
1	$5	$10	
2	$5	$12	
3	$5	$15	
4	$5	$19	
5	$5	$24	
6	$5	$30	
7	$5	$45	

11. If agriculture is an example of perfect competition, why are there so many brands of dairy products at the grocery store?

12. Using demand curves, illustrate the effect of product differentiation on the part of haircutters.

13. Why might society prefer perfect competition over monopoly?

14. Try to classify the following firms into one of the four market structure models. Explain your choice.

   a. Rowena's Gourmet Foods (produces and sells a line of specialty foods)
   b. Shasta Pool Company (swimming pool and spa building)
   c. Merck (pharmaceuticals)
   d. America West Airlines
   e. UDC Homebuilders
   f. Legal Seafoods (restaurant chain)

15. Draw two sets of cost curves. For the first set, assume fixed costs are huge and there are large economies of scale (large *MES*). For the second set, assume fixed costs are small and the economies of scale are small (small *MES*). Now, on each set of cost curves place a downward-sloping demand curve. Find the profit-maximizing point in each case.

ACE

Take the ACE Practice Test for this chapter to review the important concepts and get immediate feedback with answers.

economics.college.hmco.com/students

Economically Speaking

Business Ethics Guarantee Value to All Interested Parties

The shock of the Enron and WorldCom scandals inflicted serious damage on the pride of corporate America. Before their onset, nobody really dared to doubt the superiority of the United States economy, completely trusting its transparency, accountability, and integrity. Corporate America's rules were thus regarded as the global standard, which is why Korea accepted them unconditionally, especially in the wake of the Asian financial crisis. The recent accounting mishaps in the U.S., however, proved that the system alone will not warrant everything, and that in order for it to function efficiently, the right ethics need to be in place.

The same goes for Korea. Before and even after the financial crisis in 1997, the Korean government implemented a series of reforms to regulate the domestic business sector and guide it under the principles of transparency, global standards and accountability. Noted for its relatively tight regulatory framework, Korea is sometimes dubbed as the "kingdom of regulation," but despite the high-handed regulations, corruption does not seem to show any signs of dwindling. Political corruptions stemming from ruling politicians and the president's own family continue to plague the nation, along with those in the economy involving venture companies. There are too many to even recollect, showing how futile the regulatory framework is when not coupled with the right business ethics. . . .

Most people automatically assume that business ethics simply symbolize righteousness or virtue, but actually, they are the natural result of the process in seeking to maximize the profit of a company. The management and owners and other shareholders adhere to ethical management practices not because they are people with such high moral standards and believe in contributing to society, but because pursuing them leads to increased profits.

For instance, by removing corrupted connections within a company, such as between the firm's suppliers and the firm itself, the company can benefit by cutting away the additional costs it had been bearing due to the corruption. Ethical business management can also work to improve a company's reputation, which in turn would enhance its price competitiveness to ultimately boost its sales. Thus, in order to survive in the market today, companies have to ensure customers that they are clean and ethical. Consumers, stock holders and creditors don't hesitate to punish unethical companies and boycott their products, meaning that in the end, only the ethical companies will remain in the market. . . .

The market is already globalized so that no product nor company that fails to meet the global standards in any way survives even in the local or regional markets. As a result, corporate ethics have become not an option, but an indispensable way to do business in order for a company to avoid government regulations and pursue a competitive edge in the international markets. . . .

KIM SUK-JOONG

Source: Copyright 2003 The Korea Herald.

The Korea Herald/January 24, 2003

Commentary

It is often claimed that striving for profits means not caring about ethics. During the corporate scandals of 2000–2003, excesses on the part of many executives were discovered and reported. The chief executive of Tyco used the company as his personal bank account. The top executives of Enron lived lavish lifestyles using company resources. Martha Stewart was indicted for insider trading and misleading investigators. The list of wrongdoers seems to go on and on. But, notice two things: first, that it is these examples of unethical behaviors that make the headlines, and second, that for the most part these executives and their companies were harshly punished. Martha Stewart's company has lost over $80 million in value; Enron has been decimated; Tyco is valued significantly lower than it was prior to 2001.

As noted in this article, ethics and profit are not contradictory; they are instead complementary. If the public wants ethical behavior on the part of firms, the public will get such behavior. A company that fails to follow an ethical path will find itself without many customers and with a lower stock market value than a comparable company that follows the ethical path.

In this chapter we discussed profit maximization. Profit is the difference between revenue and costs. If a firm loses customers, it loses revenue. Everything else the same, profits will decline. Similarly, if a firm's costs rise, everything else the same, its profits will decline. Unethical behavior could reduce revenue because the public will not purchase the firm's goods and services. Unethical behavior could also raise costs—the firm would have to do more advertising and more lobbying of government and make more payments to ensure that its behavior is not discovered. These increase costs and reduce profit.

The author of the article notes: "The market is already globalized so that no product nor company that fails to meet the global standards in any way survives even in the local or regional markets. As a result, corporate ethics have become not an option, but an indispensable way to do business in order for a company to avoid government regulations and pursue a competitive edge in the international markets." This statement emphasizes that a firm must meet not only the standards of the nation in which it is located, but the standards in all nations with which it does business and from which stockholders come—in general, those of almost everywhere. A company that operates to maximize profit while minimizing ethics or a social conscience will fail to maximize profit.

CHAPTER **24**

Perfect Competition

? **Fundamental Questions**

1. **What is perfect competition?**

2. **What does the demand curve facing the individual firm look like, and why?**

3. **How does the firm maximize profit in the short run?**

4. **At what point does a firm decide to suspend operations?**

5. **When will a firm shut down permanently?**

6. **What is the break-even price?**

7. **What is the firm's supply curve in the short run?**

8. **What is the firm's supply curve in the long run?**

9. **What are the long-run equilibrium results of a perfectly competitive market?**

The market structure of perfect competition is a model intended to capture the behavior of firms when there are a great many competitors offering a virtually identical product. Among real-life markets that come close to fitting into the model of perfect competition, we could include most agricultural products and most commodities such as gold and silver, as well as aspects of crude oil shipping and hard drives for personal computers. ■

570

1. The Perfectly Competitive Firm in the Short Run

We begin our analysis of perfect competition by taking the viewpoint of an individual firm that is currently in business, having already procured the necessary land, tools, equipment, and employees to operate the firm. After we discuss how much the firm produces and at what price it sells its products, we discuss the entry and the exit processes. We examine how someone begins a business and how someone leaves or exits the business. We then alter our perspective and look at the market as a whole. Let's start our discussion by reviewing the characteristics of a perfectly competitive market.

1.a. The Definition of Perfect Competition

1. What is perfect competition?

A market that is perfectly competitive exhibits the following characteristics:

1. There are many sellers. No one firm can have an influence on market price. Each firm is such a minute part of the total market that however much the firm produces—nothing at all, as much as it can, or some amount in between—it will have no effect on the market price.

Perfect competition is a firm behavior that occurs when many firms produce identical products and entry is easy.

2. The products sold by the firms in the industry are identical. The product sold by one firm can be substituted perfectly for the product sold by any other firm in the industry. Products are not differentiated by packaging, advertising, or quality.

3. Entry is easy, and there are many potential entrants. There are no huge economies of scale relative to the size of the market. Laws do not require producers to obtain licenses or pay for the privilege of producing. Other firms cannot take action to keep someone from entering the business. Firms can stop producing and can sell or liquidate the business without difficulty.

4. Buyers and sellers have perfect information. Buyers know the price and quantity at each firm. Each firm knows what the other firms are charging and how they are behaving.

1.b. The Demand Curve of the Individual Firm

2. What does the demand curve facing the individual firm look like, and why?

A firm in a perfectly competitive market structure is said to be a *price taker* because the price of the product is determined by market demand and supply, and the individual firm simply has to accept that price. In 2003 the world market price of corn was about $1 per bushel, and nearly 20 billion bushels were produced worldwide. Approximately 46 percent of all the corn harvested in the world comes from the United States. Nevertheless, the average farm in the United States produces an extremely small percentage of the total quantity harvested each year.

What would occur if one U.S. farmer decided to set the price of corn at $1.20 per bushel when the market price was $1 per bushel? According to the model of a perfectly competitive market, no one would purchase the higher-priced corn because the identical product could be obtained without difficulty elsewhere for $1 per bushel. In this instance, what the model predicts is what actually occurs in the real-world corn market. The grain silo owner who buys the farmers' grain would simply pass on that farm's grain and move to the next truckful of grain at $1 per bushel. By setting a price above the market price, the individual farmer may sell nothing.

Is an individual farmer likely to set a price of $.80 per bushel when the market price is $1 per bushel? Not in a perfectly competitive market. All of the produce from a single farm can be sold at the market price. Why would a farmer sell at $.80 per bushel when he or she can get $1 per bushel? The individual farm is a price taker because it cannot charge more than the market price and it will not charge less.

You could think of price takers as being the sellers in a big auction. The potential buyers bid against each other for the product until a price is determined. The product is then sold at that price. The seller has no control over the price.

Market demand and supply are shown in Figure 1(a). The demand curve of a single firm is shown in Figure 1(b). The horizontal line at the market price is the demand curve faced by an individual firm in a perfectly competitive market structure. It shows that the individual firm is a price taker—that the demand curve is perfectly elastic. The question facing the individual firm in a perfectly competitive industry is how much to produce, not what price to charge.

1.c. Profit Maximization

3. How does the firm maximize profit in the short run?

We know that profit is maximized when $MR = MC$. Profit rises when the revenue brought in by the sale of one more unit (one more bushel) is greater than the cost of producing that unit. Conversely, if the cost of producing one more unit is greater than the amount of revenue brought in by selling that unit, profit declines with the

---

FIGURE 1

Market Demand and Supply and Single-Firm Demand for Corn

Market demand and supply are shown in Figure 1(a). The equilibrium price is $1 per bushel, and 20 billion bushels are produced and sold. The equilibrium price defines the horizontal, or perfectly elastic, demand curve faced by the individual perfectly competitive firm in Figure 1(b).

(a) Market

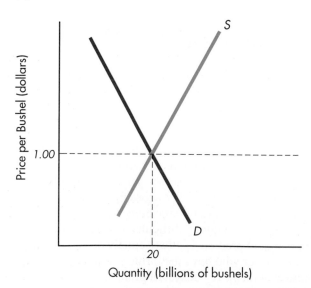

(b) Individual Firm

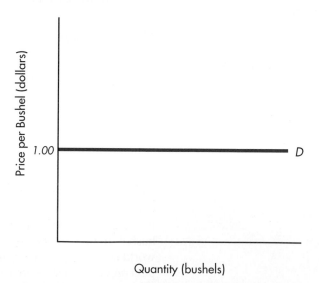

Profit maximization occurs at the output level where MR = MC.

4. At what point does a firm decide to suspend operations?

MR = MC is the profit-maximizing or loss-minimizing output level.

5. When will a firm shut down permanently?

production of that unit. Only when marginal revenue and marginal cost are the same is profit at a maximum, as illustrated in Figure 2.[1]

With a price of $1 per bushel, the individual farm maximizes profit by producing 9 bushels. We can illustrate how much profit the individual firm in perfect competition earns, or whether it makes a loss, by calculating total costs at the quantity where $MR = MC$ and comparing that with total revenue.

In Figure 2, the price per bushel of $1 exceeds the cost per bushel (average total cost, $.8733) by the distance BC ($.1267) when 9 bushels are produced. This amount ($.1267) is the profit per bushel. The total profit is the rectangle $ABCD$ (highlighted in the table).

Figure 3 illustrates what occurs to the individual firm in a perfectly competitive market as the market price changes. The only curve in Figure 3 that changes as a result of the price change is the perfectly elastic demand curve (which is also the price line and the marginal-revenue curve). Let's assume that the market price changes to $.70 per bushel, so that the individual farm's demand curve shifts down. Whether the firm is making a profit is determined by finding the new quantity at which the new marginal-revenue curve, MR_2, *equals the marginal-cost curve, at point F,* and then tracing a vertical line from point F to the ATC curve at point G. The distance FG is the profit or loss per unit of output. If the demand curve is above the ATC curve at that point, the firm is making a profit. If the ATC curve exceeds the price line, as is the case in Figure 3, the firm is suffering a loss.

A profit cannot be made as long as the price is less than the average-cost curve, because the cost per bushel (ATC) exceeds the revenue per bushel (price). At a price of $.70 per bushel, marginal revenue and marginal cost are equal as the sixth bushel is produced (see Figure 3 and the highlighted bar in the table), but the average total cost is greater than the price. The cost per bushel (ATC) is $.8667, which is higher than the price or revenue per bushel of $.70. Thus, the firm makes a loss, shown as the rectangle $EFGH$ in Figure 3.

Recall that an economic loss means that opportunity costs are not being covered by revenues; that is, the owners could do better in another line of business. An economic loss means that a firm is confronted with the choice of whether to continue producing, shut down temporarily, or shut down permanently. The decision depends on which alternative has the lowest opportunity cost.

1.d. Short-Run Break-Even and Shutdown Prices

In the short run, certain costs, such as rent on land and equipment, must be paid whether or not any output is produced. These are the firm's fixed costs. If a firm has purchased equipment and buildings but does not produce, the firm still has to pay for the equipment and buildings. Thus, the decision about whether to produce or to

---

[1] Marginal revenue and marginal cost could be equal at small levels of production and sales, such as with the first bushel, but profit would definitely not be at its greatest level. The reason is that marginal cost is falling with the first unit of production—the marginal cost of the second unit is less than the marginal cost of the first unit. Since marginal revenue is the same for both the first and second units, profit actually rises as quantity increases. Profit maximization requires both that marginal revenue equal marginal cost *and that marginal cost be rising.* Since marginal revenue and marginal cost are the same for the ninth bushel and marginal cost is *rising,* the ninth bushel is the profit-maximizing level of output.

FIGURE 2

Profit Maximization

The profit-maximization point for a single firm is shown for a price of $1 per bushel. Marginal revenue and marginal cost are equal at the profit-maximization point, 9 bushels. At quantities less than 9 bushels, marginal revenue exceeds marginal cost, so increased production would raise profits. At quantities greater than 9, marginal revenue is less than marginal cost, so reduced production would increase profits. The point at which profit is maximized is shown by the highlighted row in the table. The profit per unit is the difference between the price line and the average-total-cost curve at the profit-maximizing quantity. Total profit ($1.14) is the rectangle ABCD, an area that is equal to the profit per unit times the number of units.

Total Output (Q)	Price (P)	Total Revenue (TR)	Total Cost (TC)	Total Profit (TR − TC)	Marginal Revenue (MR)	Marginal Cost (MC)	Average Total Cost (ATC)
0	$1	$ 0	$ 1.00	−$1.00			
1	$1	$ 1	$ 2.00	−$1.00	$1	$1.00	$2.00
2	$1	$ 2	$ 2.80	−$.80	$1	$ .80	$1.40
3	$1	$ 3	$ 3.50	−$.50	$1	$ .70	$1.1667
4	$1	$ 4	$ 4.00	$ .00	$1	$ .50	$1.00
5	$1	$ 5	$ 4.50	$ .50	$1	$ .50	$ .90
6	$1	$ 6	$ 5.20	$ .80	$1	$ .70	$ .8667
7	$1	$ 7	$ 6.00	$1.00	$1	$ .80	$ .8571
8	$1	$ 8	$ 6.86	$1.14	$1	$ .86	$ .8575
9	$1	$ 9	$ 7.86	$1.14	$1	$1.00	$ .8733
10	$1	$10	$ 9.36	$ .64	$1	$1.50	$ .936
11	$1	$11	$12.00	−$1.00	$1	$2.64	$1.09

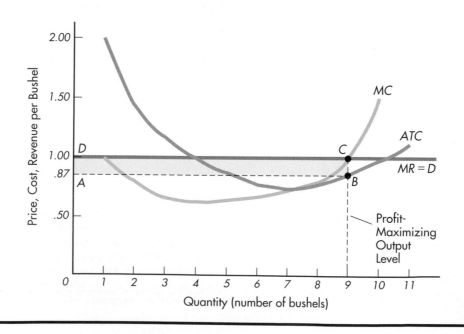

FIGURE 3

Loss Minimization

In Figure 3 the price changed from $1 per bushel to $.70 per bushel. The profit-maximization, or loss-minimization, point is the level of output where $MR = MC$. If, at this output level, the price is less than the corresponding average-cost curve, the firm makes a loss. At a price of $.70 per bushel, a loss is incurred—the loss-minimizing level of output is 6 bushels, as shown by the highlighted bar in the table. The total loss is the rectangle $EFGH$.

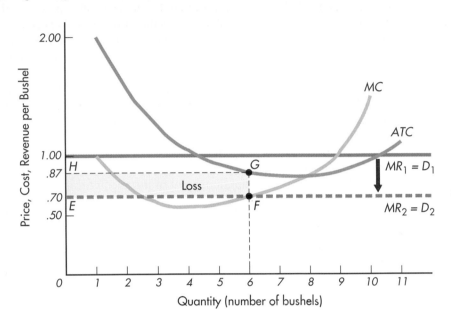

Total Output (Q)	Price (P)	Total Revenue (TR)	Total Cost (TC)	Total Profit (TR − TC)	Marginal Revenue (MR)	Marginal Cost (MC)	Average Total Cost (ATC)
0	$.70	$ 0	$ 1.00	−$1.00			
1	$.70	$ .70	$ 2.00	−$1.30	$.70	$1.00	$2.00
2	$.70	$1.40	$ 2.80	−$1.40	$.70	$ .80	$1.40
3	$.70	$2.10	$ 3.50	−$1.40	$.70	$ .70	$1.1667
4	$.70	$2.80	$ 4.00	−$1.20	$.70	$ .50	$1.00
5	$.70	$3.50	$ 4.50	−$1.00	$.70	$ .50	$ .90
6	$.70	$4.20	$ 5.20	−$1.00	$.70	$ .70	$ .8667
7	$.70	$4.90	$ 6.00	−$1.10	$.70	$ .80	$ .8571
8	$.70	$5.60	$ 6.86	−$1.26	$.70	$ .86	$ .8575
9	$.70	$6.30	$ 7.86	−$1.56	$.70	$1.00	$ .8733
10	$.70	$7.00	$ 9.36	−$2.36	$.70	$1.50	$ .936
11	$.70	$7.70	$12.00	−$4.30	$.70	$2.64	$1.09

temporarily suspend operations depends on which option promises the lesser costs. In order to continue producing in the short run, the firm must earn sufficient revenue to pay all of the *variable* costs (the costs that change as output changes), because then the excess of revenue over variable costs will enable the firm to pay some of its fixed costs. If the variable costs cannot all be paid for out of revenue, then the firm should suspend operations temporarily because by continuing to produce, the firm must pay its fixed costs as well as those variable costs in excess of revenue.

Does suspending operations mean quitting the business altogether—shutting down permanently? It may, but it need not. The decision depends on the long-term outlook. If the long-term outlook indicates that revenue will exceed costs, then production is warranted. However, if the outlook is for continued low prices and inability to cover costs, a firm would be better off quitting the business altogether.

To see how producing at a loss can at times be better than not producing at all, let's return to the individual farm in Figure 4. At a price of $.70 per bushel, the output at which $MR = MC$ is 6 bushels, as shown by the highlighted bar in the table. At 6 bushels, total revenue is $4.20 and total cost is $5.20. The farm loses $1 by producing 6 bushels. The question is whether to produce at all. If production is stopped, the fixed cost of $1 must still be paid. Thus, the farmer is indifferent between producing 6 bushels and losing $1 or shutting down and losing $1. Should the price be less than the minimum point of the average-variable-cost curve (AVC), as would occur at any price less than $P = $.70 per bushel, the farm is not earning enough to cover its variable costs (see Figure 4 and accompanying table). By continuing to produce, the farm will lose more than it would lose if it suspended operations or shut down until the outlook improved. The minimum point of the average-variable-cost curve is the **shutdown price.** If the market price is less than the minimum point of the AVC curve, then the firm will incur fewer losses if it does not produce than if it continues to produce in the short run.

At prices above the minimum point of the average-variable-cost curve, the excess of revenue over variable cost means that some fixed costs can be paid. A firm is better off producing than shutting down because by producing it is able to earn enough revenue to pay all the variable costs and some of the fixed costs. If the firm does not produce, it will still have to pay all of the fixed costs. When the price equals the minimum point of the average-total-cost curve, the firm is earning just enough revenue to pay for all of its costs, fixed and variable. This point is called the **break-even price.** At the break-even price, economic profit is zero—all costs are being covered, including opportunity costs. Because costs include the opportunity costs of the resources already owned by the entrepreneur—his or her own labor and capital—zero economic profit means that the entrepreneur could not do better in another activity. Zero economic profit is normal profit, profit just sufficient to keep the entrepreneur in this line of business.

The shutdown price is the price that is equal to the minimum point of the AVC curve. The break-even price is the price that is equal to the minimum point of the ATC curve.

In the examples just discussed, the firm continues to operate at a loss because variable costs are being covered and the long-term outlook is favorable. Many firms decide to operate for a while at a loss, then suspend operations temporarily, and finally shut down permanently. A firm will shut down permanently if all costs cannot be covered in the long run. In the long run, the minimum point of the ATC curve is the permanent shutdown point. Price must exceed the minimum point of the ATC curve in the long run if the firm is to remain in business. Of the 80,000 businesses that shut down permanently in 1997, most went through a period in which they continued to operate even though variable costs were not being covered by revenue.

shutdown price: the minimum point of the average-variable-cost curve

6. What is the break-even price?

break-even price: a price that is equal to the minimum point of the average-total-cost curve

FIGURE 4

Shutdown Price

When the firm is making a loss, it must decide whether to continue producing or to suspend operations and not produce. The decision depends on which alternative has higher costs. When the price is equal to or greater than the minimum point of the average-variable-cost curve, $.70, the firm is earning sufficient revenue to pay for all of the variable costs. When the price is less than the

minimum point of the average-variable-cost curve, the firm is not covering all of its variable costs. In that case the firm is better off shutting down its operations. For this reason, the minimum point of the *AVC* curve is called the *shutdown price*. The *break-even price* is the minimum point of the *ATC* curve because at that point all costs are being paid.

Total Output (Q)	Price (P)	Total Revenue (TR)	Total Cost (TC)	Total Profit (TR – TC)	Marginal Revenue (MR)	Marginal Cost (MC)	Average Total Cost (ATC)	Average Variable Cost (AVC)
0	$.70	$ 0	$ 1.00	−$1.00				
1	$.70	$ .70	$ 2.00	−$1.30	$.70	$1.00	$2.00	$1.00
2	$.70	$1.40	$ 2.80	−$1.40	$.70	$ .80	$1.40	$ .90
3	$.70	$2.10	$ 3.50	−$1.40	$.70	$ .70	$1.1667	$ .833
4	$.70	$2.80	$ 4.00	−$1.20	$.70	$ .50	$1.00	$ .75
5	$.70	$3.50	$ 4.50	−$1.00	$.70	$ .50	$ .90	$ .70
6	$.70	$4.20	$ 5.20	−$1.00	$.70	$ .70	$ .8667	$ .70
7	$.70	$4.90	$ 6.00	−$1.10	$.70	$ .80	$ .8571	$ .714
8	$.70	$5.60	$ 6.86	−$1.26	$.70	$ .86	$ .8575	$ .7325
9	$.70	$6.30	$ 7.86	−$1.56	$.70	$1.00	$ .8733	$ .7622
10	$.70	$7.00	$ 9.36	−$2.36	$.70	$1.50	$ .936	$ .836
11	$.70	$7.70	$12.00	−$4.30	$.70	$2.64	$1.09	$1.00

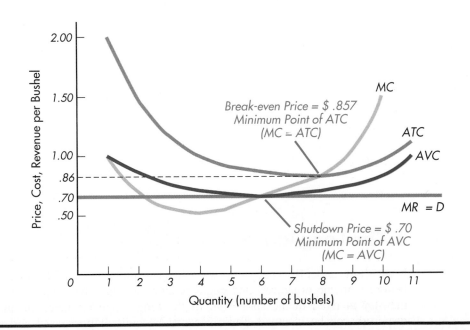

1.e. The Firm's Supply Curve in the Short Run

As long as revenue equals or exceeds variable costs, an individual firm will produce the quantity at which marginal revenue and marginal cost are equal. This means that the individual firm's supply curve is the portion of the *MC* curve that lies above the *AVC* curve. An individual firm's supply curve shows the quantity that a firm will produce and offer for sale at each price. When the price is less than the minimum point of the *AVC* curve, a firm incurs fewer losses from not producing than from producing. The firm thus produces and supplies nothing, and there is no supply curve. When the price is greater than the minimum point of the *AVC* curve, the firm will produce and offer for sale the quantity yielded at the point where the *MC* curve and the *MR* line intersect for each price. The supply curve is thus the *MC* curve. The portion of the *MC* curve lying above the minimum point of the *AVC* curve is the individual firm's supply curve in the short run.

In our example of an individual farm illustrated in Figure 4, nothing is produced at a price of $.50 per bushel. At $.70 per bushel, the farm produces 6 bushels in the short run; at $1 per bushel, the farm produces 9 bushels. The higher the price, the greater the quantity produced and offered for sale.

A firm may continue to produce and offer its products for sale even if it is earning a negative economic profit, as long as it earns enough revenue to pay its variable costs and expects revenue to grow enough to pay all costs eventually. If the business does not improve and losses continue to pile up, the firm will shut down permanently. In the long run, the firm must be able to earn enough revenue to pay all of its costs. If it does not, the business will not continue to operate. If the firm does earn enough to pay its costs, the firm will produce and offer for sale the quantity of output yielded at the point where $MR = MC$. This means that the firm's supply curve is the portion of its *MC* curve that lies above the minimum point of the *ATC* curve.

8. What is the firm's supply curve in the long run?

RECAP

1. The firm maximizes profit or minimizes losses by producing at the output level at which *MR* and *MC* are equal.

2. In order to remain in business, the firm must earn sufficient revenue to pay for all of its variable costs. The shutdown price is the price that is just equal to the minimum point of the *AVC* curve.

3. The firm's break-even price is the price that is just equal to the minimum point of the *ATC* curve.

4. The portion of the marginal-cost curve lying above the minimum point of the *AVC* curve is the firm's short-run supply curve.

5. The portion of the marginal-cost curve lying above the minimum point of the *ATC* curve is the firm's long-run supply curve.

2. The Long Run

In the short run, at least one of the resources *cannot* be altered. This means that new firms cannot be organized and begin producing. Thus the supply of firms in an industry is fixed in the short run. In the long run, of course, all quantities of resources can be changed. Buildings can be built or purchased and machinery accumulated and placed into production. New firms may arise as entrepreneurs not currently in the industry see that they could earn more than they are currently earning and decide to expand into new businesses.

Exit and entry are long-run phenomena.

Entry and exit can both occur in the long run. On average, 4.5 percent of the total number of farms in the United States go out of business each year, and more than half of them file for bankruptcy.

How does exit occur? Entrepreneurs may sell their businesses and move to another industry, or they may use the bankruptcy laws to exit the industry. In the United States, a sole proprietor or partnership may file Chapter 13 personal bankruptcy; a corporation may file Chapter 7 bankruptcy or a Chapter 11 reorganization; a farmer may file Chapter 12. From the mid-1970s to the present, the average birthrate for all industries (the percent of total businesses that begin during a year) has been just over 11.2 percent, and the average death rate (the percent of total businesses that disappear during a year) has been 9.6 percent.

Bankruptcy laws in the developed nations are similar to those in the United States. Although most nations have some type of laws regarding going out of business, the laws are not enforced or used in many emerging-market nations.

2.a. The Market Supply Curve and Exit and Entry

When additional firms enter the industry and begin producing the product, the market supply curve shifts out.

When firms leave the industry, the market supply curve shifts in.

Recall from Chapter 3 that the market supply curve shifts when the number of suppliers changes. The market supply curve is the sum of all the individual firms' supply curves. In the corn-producing business, when new farms enter the market, the total quantity of corn supplied at each price increases. In other words, entry causes the market supply curve to shift out to the right.

Conversely, exit means fewer producers and lower quantities supplied at each price, and a leftward or inward shift of the market supply curve. Suppose some existing farms are not covering their costs and believe the future is not bright enough to warrant continued production. As a result, they shut down their operations and sell their equipment and land. As the number of farms in the industry declines,

The price taker can do nothing but accept the market price and sell at that price. When times are bad, the market price may be so low that some of the price takers must exit the market. In this photo, farmers are gathered at an auction as several must liquidate and leave the business. Others attend the auction to purchase equipment at bargain basement prices.

everything else held constant, the market supply curve shifts to the left—as long as those remaining in the business produce the same quantity as they did before the farms exited, or less.

2.b. Normal Profit in the Long Run

One of the principal characteristics of the perfectly competitive market structure is that entry and exit can occur easily. Thus, entry and exit occur whenever firms are earning more or less than a *normal profit* (zero economic profit). When a normal profit is being earned, there is no entry or exit. This condition is the long-run equilibrium.

The process of establishing the long-run position is shown in Figure 5. The market demand and supply curves for corn are shown in Figure 5(a), and the cost and revenue curves for a representative firm in the industry are shown in Figure 5(b). Let's assume that the market price is $1. Let's also assume that at $1 per bushel, the demand curve facing the individual farm (the price line) is equal to the minimum point of the *ATC* curve. The quantity produced is 9 bushels. The individual farm and the industry are in equilibrium. There is no reason for entry or exit to occur, and there is no reason for individual farms to change their scale of operation.

FIGURE 5

Economic Profit in the Long Run

Market demand and supply determine the price and the demand curve faced by the single perfectly competitive firm. At a price of $1 per bushel, the individual farm is earning normal profit. After an agricultural disaster in Russia increases the demand for U.S. corn, the price rises to $1.50. At $1.50 per bushel, the single farm makes a profit equal to the yellow rectangle. Above-normal profits induce new farms to begin raising corn and existing farms to increase their production.

(a) Market

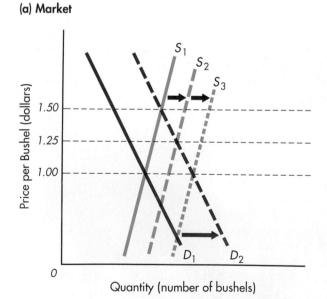

(b) Individual Firm

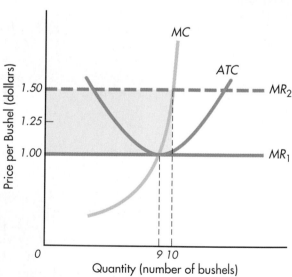

To illustrate how the process of reaching the long-run equilibrium occurs in the perfectly competitive market structure, let's begin with the market in equilibrium at $S_1 = D_1$. Then let's suppose a major agricultural disaster strikes Russia and Russia turns to the United States to buy agricultural products. As a result of the increased Russian demand, the total demand for U.S. corn increases, as shown by the rightward shift of the demand curve to D_2 in Figure 5(a). In the short run, the market price rises to $1.50 per bushel, where the new market demand curve intersects the initial market supply curve, S_1. This raises the demand curve for the individual farm to the horizontal line at $1.50 per bushel. In the short run, the individual farms in the industry increase production (by adding variable inputs) from 9 bushels to 10 bushels, the point in Figure 5(b) where $MC = MR_2 = \$1.50$, and earn economic profit of the amount shown by the yellow rectangle.

The above-normal profit attracts others to the farming business. The result of the new entry and expansion is a rightward shift of the market supply curve. How far does the market supply curve shift? It shifts until the market price is low enough that firms in the industry earn normal profit.

Let us suppose that the costs of doing business do not rise as the market expands. Then, if the market supply curve shifts to S_2, the new market price, $1.25, is less than the former price of $1.50 but still high enough for firms to earn above-normal profits. These profits are sufficient inducement for more firms to enter, causing the supply curve to shift farther right. The supply curve continues to shift until there is no incentive for additional firms to enter—that is, until firms are earning the normal profit, where price is equal to the minimum ATC, shown as S_3 in Figure 5(a). When the adjustment stops, firms are just earning the normal profit.

In the long run, perfectly competitive firms earn normal profits.

9. What are the long-run equilibrium results of a perfectly competitive market?

2.c. The Predictions of the Model of Perfect Competition

According to the model of perfect competition, whenever above-normal profits are earned by existing firms, entry occurs until a normal profit is earned by all firms. Conversely, whenever economic losses occur, exit takes place until a normal profit is made by all remaining firms.

It is so important to keep in mind the distinctions between economic and accounting terms that we repeatedly remind you of them. A *zero economic profit* is a *normal accounting profit*, or just *normal profit*. It is the profit that is just sufficient to keep a business owner or investors in a particular line of business, the point where revenue exactly equals total opportunity costs. Business owners and investors earning a normal profit are earning enough to cover their opportunity costs—they could not do better by changing—but they are not earning more than their opportunity costs. A *loss* refers to a situation where revenue is not sufficient to pay all of the opportunity costs. A firm can earn a positive accounting profit and yet be experiencing a loss, not earning a normal profit.

Perfect competition results in economic efficiency.

The long-run equilibrium position of the perfectly competitive market structure shows firms producing at the minimum point of their long-run average-total-cost curves. If the price is above the minimum point of the ATC curve, then firms are earning above-normal profit and entry will occur. If the price is less than the minimum of the ATC curve, exit will occur. Only when price equals the minimum point of the ATC curve will neither entry nor exit take place.

Producing at the minimum of the ATC curve means that firms are producing with the lowest possible costs. They could not alter the way they produce and produce less expensively. They could not alter the resources they use and produce less expensively.

FIGURE 6

Producer and Consumer Surpluses

Since the firm is willing to sell the product at the marginal cost and since the firm receives the market price, the difference between the two is a bonus to the firm, a bonus of market exchange. This bonus is producer surplus. Figure 6 illustrates total producer surplus in a competitive market, the sum of the producer surplus received by each firm in the market. Producer surplus is the area below the price line and above the supply curve. Also pictured is total consumer surplus. Recall that consumer surplus is the difference between what the consumer would be willing to pay for a good, the demand curve, and the price actually paid. The sum of producer and consumer surplus represents the total benefits that come from exchange in a market: benefits that accrue to the consumer plus those that accrue to the firm.

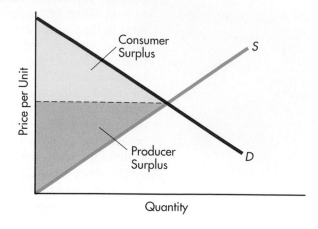

Firms produce at a level where marginal cost and marginal revenue are the same. Since marginal revenue and price are the same in a perfectly competitive market, firms produce where marginal cost equals price. This means that firms are employing resources until the marginal cost to them of producing the last unit of a good just equals the price of the last unit. Moreover, since price is equal to marginal cost, consumers are paying a price that is as low as it can get; the price just covers the marginal cost of producing that good or service. There is no waste—no one could be made better off without making someone else worse off. Economists refer to this result as **economic efficiency.**

economic efficiency: when the price of a good or service just covers the marginal cost of producing that good or service and people are getting the goods they want

2.c.1. Consumer and Producer Surplus
Efficiency is the term economists give to the situation where firms are producing with as little cost as they can (minimum point of the *ATC* curve) and consumers are getting the products they desire at a price that is equal to the marginal cost of producing those goods. To say that a competitive market is efficient is to say that all market participants get the greatest benefits possible from market exchange.[2]

We measure the benefits from market exchange as the sum of the consumer surplus and the producer surplus. Consumer surplus is the difference between what consumers would be willing and able to pay for a product and the price they actually have to pay to buy the product. **Producer surplus** is the difference between the price firms would have been willing and able to accept for their products and the price they actually receive.

producer surplus: the difference between the price firms would have been willing to accept for their products and the price they actually receive

[2]Economists have classified efficiency into several categories. *Productive efficiency* refers to the firm's using the least-cost combination of resources to produce any output level. This output level may not be the goods consumers want, however. *Allocative efficiency* is the term given to the situation where firms are producing the goods consumers most want and consumers are paying a price just equal to the marginal cost of producing the goods. Allocative efficiency may occur when firms are not producing at their most efficient level. Economic efficiency exists when both productive and allocative efficiency occur.

FIGURE 7

Rent Control and Market Efficiency

The market for rental apartments is pictured in this graph; the market solution would yield a monthly rent of $400. The consumer surplus would be the area *ABC*; the producer surplus would be the area *ABD*. Now, suppose the city imposes rent control at $300 per month. The producer surplus changes to area *EFD* while the consumer surplus changes to *EFHC*. The total surplus has been reduced by the rent control.

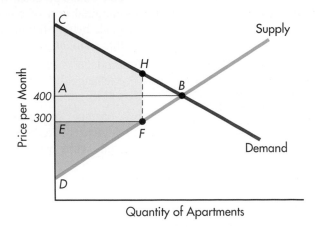

Since the firm is willing to sell the product at the marginal cost, as long as marginal cost is greater than average variable cost, and since the firm receives the market price, the difference between the two is a bonus to the firm, a bonus resulting from market exchange. This bonus is producer surplus.

Consumer surplus = area above equilibrium price and
below the demand curve

Producer surplus = area below equilibrium price and
above the supply curve

Figure 6 illustrates consumer and producer surplus in a competitive market. The sum of producer and consumer surplus represents the total benefits that come from exchange in a market: the benefits that accrue to the consumer plus those that accrue to the firm.

The primary result of perfect competition is that things just do not get any better: total consumer and producer surplus is at a maximum. Any interference with the market exchange reduces the total surplus. Consider rent control on apartments, for instance. The market for rental apartments is pictured in Figure 7. As shown in Figure 7, the market solution would yield a monthly rent of $400. The consumer surplus would be the area *ABC;* the producer surplus would be the area *ABD.* Now, suppose the city imposes a rent control at $300 per month. The producer surplus changes to area *EFD* while the consumer surplus changes to *EFHC.* Clearly the total surplus has been reduced. The question policymakers must decide is whether the additional benefits to consumers offset the additional losses to producers. We will discuss this further in the chapter "Government and Market Failure."

RECAP

1. Entry occurs when firms are earning above-normal profit or positive economic profit.
2. A temporary shutdown occurs when firms are not covering their variable costs in the short run. In the long run, exit occurs when firms are not covering all costs.
3. The short-run market supply curve is the horizontal sum of the supply curves of all individual firms in the industry.

4. In a perfectly competitive market, firms produce goods at the least cost, and consumers purchase the goods they most desire at a price that is equal to the marginal cost of producing the good. There is no waste—no one could be made better off without making someone else worse off. Economists refer to this result as economic efficiency.

5. Producer surplus is the benefit the firm receives for engaging in market exchange; it is the difference between the price the firm would be willing to sell its goods for and the price the firm actually receives.

6. Consumer surplus is the area below the demand curve and above the equilibrium price; producer surplus is the area above the supply curve and below the equilibrium price.

Summary

❓ What is perfect competition?

1. Perfect competition is a market structure in which there are many firms that are producing an identical product and where entry and exit are easy. *§1.a*

❓ What does the demand curve facing the individual firm look like, and why?

2. The demand curve of the individual firm is a horizontal line at the market price. Each firm is a price taker. *§1.b*

❓ How does the firm maximize profit in the short run?

3. The individual firm maximizes profit by producing at the point where $MR = MC$. *§1.c*

❓ At what point does a firm decide to suspend operations?

4. A firm will shut down operations temporarily if price does not exceed the minimum point of the average-variable-cost curve. *§1.c*

❓ When will a firm shut down permanently?

5. A firm will shut down operations permanently if price does not exceed the minimum point of the average-total-cost curve in the long run. *§1.d*

❓ What is the break-even price?

6. The firm breaks even when revenue and cost are equal—when the demand curve (price) just equals the minimum point of the average-total-cost curve. *§1.d*

❓ What is the firm's supply curve in the short run?

7. The firm's short-run supply curve is the portion of its marginal-cost curve that lies above the minimum point of the average-variable-cost curve. *§1.e*

❓ What is the firm's supply curve in the long run?

8. The firm produces at the point where marginal cost equals marginal revenue, as long as marginal revenue exceeds the minimum point of the average-total-cost curve. Thus, the firm's long-run supply curve is the portion of its marginal-cost curve that lies above the minimum point of the average-total-cost curve. *§1.e*

❓ What are the long-run equilibrium results of a perfectly competitive market?

9. In the long run, all firms operating in perfect competition will earn a normal profit by producing at the lowest possible cost, and all consumers will buy the goods and services they most want at a price equal to the marginal cost of producing the goods and services. *§2.c*

10. Producer surplus is the difference between what a firm would be willing to produce and sell a good for and the price the firm actually receives for the good. Consumer surplus is the difference between what an individual would be willing to pay for a good and what the individual actually has to pay. Total consumer and producer surpluses are at a maximum in a perfectly competitive market. *§2.c.1*

Key Terms

shutdown price §1.d
break-even price §1.d

economic efficiency §2.c
producer surplus §2.c.1

Exercises

1. Cost figures for a hypothetical firm are given in the following table. Use them for the exercises below. The firm is selling in a perfectly competitive market.

Out-put	Fixed Cost	AFC	Variable Cost	AVC	Total Cost	ATC	MC
1	$50		$ 30				
2	$50		$ 50				
3	$50		$ 80				
4	$50		$120				
5	$50		$170				

   a. Fill in the blank columns.
   b. What is the minimum price needed by the firm to break even?
   c. What is the shutdown price?
   d. At a price of $40, what output level would the firm produce? What would its profits be?

2. Label the curves in the following graph.

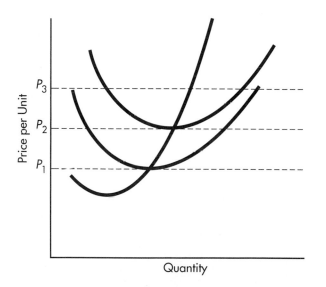

   a. At each market price, P_1, P_2, and P_3, what output level would the firm produce?

   b. What profit would be earned if the market price was P_1?
   c. What are the shutdown and break-even prices?

3. Why might a firm continue to produce in the short run even though the market price is less than its average total cost?

4. Explain why the demand curve facing the individual firm in a perfectly competitive industry is a horizontal line.

5. Explain what occurs in the long run in a constant-cost industry, an increasing-cost industry, and a decreasing-cost industry when the market demand declines (shifts in).

6. What can you expect from an industry in perfect competition in the long run? What will price be? What quantity will be produced? What will be the relation between marginal cost, average cost, and price?

7. Assume that the market for illegal drugs is an example of a perfectly competitive market structure. Describe what the perfectly competitive market model predicts for illegal drugs in the long run. What is likely to be the impact of the U.S. government's war on drugs in the short run? In the long run?

8. If no real-life industry meets the conditions of the perfectly competitive model exactly, why do we study perfect competition? What is the relevance of the model to a decision to switch careers? Why might it shed some light on pollution, acid rain, and other social problems?

9. Using the model of perfect competition, explain what it means to say, "Too much electricity is generated," or "Too little education is produced." Would the firm be producing at the bottom of the ATC curve if too much or too little was being produced?

10. Private swimming pools can be dangerous. There are serious accidents each year in those areas of the United States where backyard pools are common. Should pools be banned? In other words, should the market for swimming pools be eliminated? Answer this in terms of producer and consumer surplus.

11. Discuss whether the following are examples of perfectly competitive industries.

   a. The U.S. stock market
   b. The automobile industry
   c. The consumer electronics market
   d. The market for college students

12. Macy's was making millions of dollars in profits when it declared bankruptcy. Explain Macy's decision.

13. Entry and exit of firms occur in the long run but not in the short run. Why? What is meant by the long run and the short run? Would you say that entry is more or less difficult than exit?

14. Use the following data for the exercises below.

Price	Quantity Supplied	Quantity Demanded
$20	30	0
$18	25	5
$16	20	10
$14	15	15
$12	10	20
$10	5	25
$ 8	0	30

   a. What is the equilibrium price and quantity?

   b. Draw the demand and supply curves. If this represents perfect competition, are the curves individual-firm or market curves? How is the quantity supplied derived?

   c. Show the consumer surplus. Show the producer surplus.

   d. Suppose that a price ceiling of $12 was imposed. How would this change the consumer and producer surplus? Suppose a price floor of $16 was imposed. How would this change the consumer and producer surplus?

15. Explain the following statement: "The market can better determine the value of polluting than the politicians. Rather than assign an emission fee to a polluting firm, simply allow firms to purchase the rights to pollute."

ACE

Take the ACE Practice Test for this chapter to review the important concepts and get immediate feedback with answers.

economics.college.hmco.com/students

Avoid "Commoditization"

From advanced telecommunications gear to raw chemicals, the "commoditization" of products continues unabated.

How can companies differentiate themselves? Unfortunately, many companies have cut back on one tool at their disposal: marketing. Companies that sell commodities often view marketing as an unnecessary expense. This strategic miscalculation perpetuates, and even accelerates, shrinking margins and smaller profits. Strategic marketing programs that promote your "universe of value" will create a competitive edge.

Your universe of value is more than quality products; it encompasses the total value that you provide to customers. It includes benefits that improve customers' buying experiences, eliminate administrative burdens and improve operational efficiency. These benefits are delivered at every point of contact with customers.

The first step is to strategically identify your real-world differentiating factors. Don't rely exclusively on sales personnel for feedback from the field. Survey customers to determine the benefits that you are delivering.

Perhaps your company has an online ordering system. The value to your customer is that the system significantly reduces inefficient administrative tasks to lower order processing costs. Make customers aware of this intrinsic value.

Technical services may provide another marketing opportunity. Failure to effectively market these services can diminish their inherent value.

Innovative packaging can also be a differentiating factor. Take rock salt, for example. Little difference exists between rock salt products. But companies that incorporate "easy-to-carry handles" into bulk packaging can drive brand preference.

Once differentiating factors have been identified, brand them. Simply branding for the sake of brand awareness is worthless (think about Pets.com).

The goal is not simply to develop new names and creative logos. Brands represent your company. They convey value. Most important, they help to promote the benefits that your products and services deliver to customers.

Promote your differentiating factors through strategic publicity, advertising and other marketing tactics. Develop return on investment tools that quantify value. Use testimonials to demonstrate how customers achieved specific results.

By marketing your universe of value, you begin to differentiate your company from the competition. Remember to heed one key principle: market brand value.

Customers will begin to see that the services you provide are more valuable than the penny discount they typically ask for.

KELLY HOWARD

Crain Communications Inc./October 14, 2002

A new product is introduced, such as the cell phone. The firm introducing the product earns a nice profit. The profit is shown in the figure below. Everyone wants to get in on a good thing, and other firms introduce their own cell phones. As more and more phones are introduced, consumers have many choices of virtually identical products. This is shown by the demand curve becoming more and more price-elastic, as shown in the figures that follow.

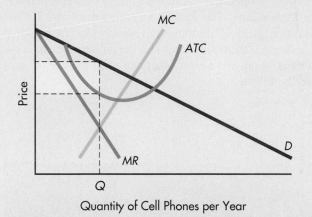

Quantity of Cell Phones per Year

The price elasticity finally approaches infinity—where the demand curve is a horizontal line. This is what the article means by "commoditization." The product has many substitutes that are essentially identical. When this occurs, the market is perfectly competitive, and the demand seen by any one firm is a horizontal line at the market price.

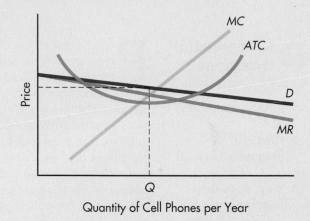

Quantity of Cell Phones per Year

Notice what happens to the firm's ability to raise price and to its profits. The firm cannot raise its price without losing most or all of its customers. The firm's profits decline to the point where it earns a zero economic profit. This is why business advisers consider commoditization bad.

The article goes on to advise firms to differentiate their products, to somehow make the demand curve less price-elastic. Distinctive packaging, brand names, and advertising can all help create a difference in the consumer's mind between one firm's product and the similar products.

CHAPTER 25

Monopoly

? Fundamental Questions

1. **What is monopoly?**

2. **How is a monopoly created?**

3. **What does the demand curve for a monopoly firm look like, and why?**

4. **Why would someone want to have a monopoly in some business or activity?**

5. **Under what conditions will a monopolist charge different customers different prices for the same product?**

6. **How do the predictions of the models of perfect competition and monopoly differ?**

Perfect competition captures the behavior of individual firms when there are a great many firms selling an identical product. To find out how a firm's behavior would be different in the opposite situation—that is, when there is just one firm—economists use the model of monopoly. In this chapter, we'll discuss how behavior changes when there is just one firm selling a good or service that has no close substitutes. While the market structure of monopoly is a model and intended to be used as a contrast to perfect competition, there are aspects of some real-life businesses that are called as monopolies. The Justice Department of the United States found Microsoft Corporation guilty of attempting to *monopolize* the personal computer operating system and applications market. The postal services in most nations are monopolies, and there is only one entity that can print money in most countries. What does a monopoly do? ■

1. The Market Structure of Monopoly

1. What is monopoly?

Does a monopolist earn unseemly profits by charging outrageously high prices? Does a monopolist go its own way no matter what customers want? What is the relation between the Parker Brothers game Monopoly and the economic model of monopoly? We'll discuss these questions in this chapter, and we'll begin by defining what a monopolist is.

1.a. Market Definition

monopoly: a market structure in which there is a single supplier of a product

monopoly firm (monopolist): a single supplier of a product for which there are no close substitutes

Monopoly is a market structure in which there is a single supplier of a product. A **monopoly firm (monopolist)** may be large or small, but whatever its size, it must be the *only supplier* of the product. In addition, a monopoly firm must sell a product for which there are *no close substitutes*. The greater the number of close substitutes for a firm's products, the less likely it is that the firm has a monopoly.

You purchase products from monopoly firms every day, perhaps without realizing it. Congress created the U.S. Postal Service to provide first-class mail service. No other firm is allowed to provide that service. The currency you use is issued and its quantity is controlled by a government entity known as the Federal Reserve. It is illegal for any organization or individual other than the Federal Reserve to issue currency.

1.b. The Creation of Monopolies

2. How is a monopoly created?

The pharmaceutical firm Glaxo-Wellcome's profits doubled in the three years following the introduction of AZT. Glaxo-Wellcome was a monopoly supplier of AZT, a drug to slow down AIDs, and it was earning above-normal profits. But if a product is valuable and the owners are getting rich from selling it, won't others develop substitutes and also enjoy the fruits of the market? Yes, unless something impedes entry. The name given to that something is **barrier to entry.** There are three general classes of barriers to entry:

barrier to entry: anything that impedes the ability of firms to begin a new business in an industry in which existing firms are earning positive economic profits

- Natural barriers, such as economies of scale
- Actions on the part of firms that create barriers to entry
- Governmentally created barriers

1.b.1. Economies of Scale   Economies of scale can be a barrier to entry. There are economies of scale in the generation of electricity. The larger the generating plant, the lower the cost per kilowatt-hour of electricity produced. A large generating plant can produce each unit of electricity much less expensively than several small generating plants. Size thus constitutes a barrier to entry, since to be able to enter the market and compete with existing large-scale public utilities, a firm needs to be large so that it can produce each kilowatt-hour as inexpensively as the large-scale plants.

1.b.2. Actions by Firms   Entry is barred when one firm owns an essential resource. The owners of the desiccant clay mine in New Mexico had a monopoly position because they owned the essential resource, clay. Inventions and discoveries are essential resources, at least until others develop close substitutes. Microsoft owned the important resource known as Windows. Was Microsoft a monopoly?

1.b.3. Government Barriers to entry are often created by governments. The U.S. government issues patents, which provide a firm a monopoly on certain products, inventions, or discoveries for a period of 17 years. Such is the case with the Glaxo-Wellcome monopoly. The company was granted a patent on AZT and thus was, by law, the only supplier of the drug. Domestic government policy also restricts entry into many industries. The federal government issues broadcast licenses for radio and television and grants airlines landing rights at certain airports. City governments limit the number of taxi companies that can operate, the number of cable television companies that can provide service, and the number of garbage collection firms that can provide service. State and local governments issue liquor licenses and restrict the number of electric utility companies. These are just a few examples of government-created monopolies in the United States.

1.c. Types of Monopolies

natural monopoly: a monopoly that arises from economies of scale

The word *monopoly* is often associated with other terms such as *natural monopoly, local monopoly, regulated monopoly, monopoly power,* and *monopolization.* A **natural monopoly** is a firm that has become a monopoly because of economies of scale and demand conditions. The adjective *natural* indicates that the monopoly arises from cost and demand conditions, not from government action. If costs decline as the quantity produced rises, only very large producers will be able to stay in business. Their lower costs will enable them to force smaller producers, who have higher costs, out of business. Large producers can underprice smaller producers, as illustrated in Figure 1. The larger firm, operating along ATC_2, can set a price anywhere between P_1 and P_2 and thereby drive the smaller firm, operating along ATC_1, out of business. If the market can support only one producer or if the long-run average-total-cost curve continually slopes downward, the monopoly that results is said to be natural. Electric utilities are often considered to be natural monopolies because there are large economies of scale in the generation of electricity. One large power plant

---

FIGURE 1

Economies of Scale

A large firm producing along ATC_2 can produce output much less expensively per unit than a small firm operating along ATC_1. The large firm, therefore, can set a price that is below the minimum point of the small firm's average-total-cost curve yet still earn profit. Any price between P_1 and P_2 will provide a profit for the large firm and a loss for the small firm.

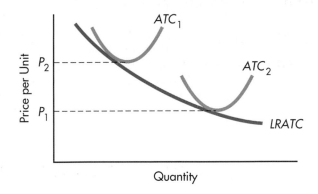

---

can generate electricity at a lower per-kilowatt-hour cost than can several small power plants. The transmission of electricity is different, however. There are diseconomies of scale in the transmission of electricity. The farther electricity has to be transmitted, the higher the per-kilowatt-hour costs. Together, generation and transmission imply an MES (minimum efficient scale) that is sufficiently large for a local monopoly but not for a national or international monopoly.

local monopoly: a monopoly that exists in a limited geographic area

A **local monopoly** is a firm that has a monopoly within a specific geographic area. An electric utility may be the sole supplier of electricity in a municipality or local area. A taxicab company may have a monopoly for service to the airport or within a city. Cable TV companies may have monopolies within municipalities. An airline may have a monopoly over some routes.

regulated monopoly: a monopoly firm whose behavior is monitored and prescribed by a government entity

A **regulated monopoly** is a monopolist whose prices and production rates are controlled by a government entity. Electric utility companies, telephone companies, cable TV companies, and water companies are or have been regulated monopolies. A state corporation or utility commission sets their rates, determines the costs to be allowed in the production of their services, and restricts entry by other firms.

monopoly power: market power, the ability to set prices

Monopoly power is market power, the ability to set prices. It exists whenever the demand curve facing the producer is downward sloping. Monopolies exercise monopoly power, but so do all firms except those operating in perfectly competitive markets. A firm that has monopoly power is a price maker rather than a price taker.

monopolization: an attempt by a firm to dominate a market or become a monopoly

Monopolization refers to the attempt by a firm to take over a market—that is, the attempt to become the only supplier of a good or service. As we'll discuss in the chapter "Antitrust and Regulation," the law forbids monopolization even though it does not always forbid monopolies.

RECAP

1. A monopoly firm is the sole supplier of a product for which there are no close substitutes.

2. A monopoly firm remains the sole supplier because of barriers to entry.

3. Barriers to entry may be economic, such as economies of scale; they may be due to the exclusive ownership of an essential resource; or they may be created by government policy.

4. A natural monopoly is a monopoly that results through economies of scale. A regulated monopoly is a monopoly whose pricing and production are controlled by the government. A local monopoly is a firm that has a monopoly in a specific geographic region.

5. Monopoly power, or market power, is the ability to set prices.

3. What does the demand curve for a monopoly firm look like, and why?

2. The Demand Curve Facing a Monopoly Firm

In any market, the industry demand curve is a downward-sloping line because of the law of demand. Although the industry demand curve is downward sloping, the demand curve facing an individual firm in a perfectly competitive market is a horizontal line at the market price. This is not the case for the monopoly firm. Because a monopoly firm is the sole producer, it *is* the industry, so its demand curve is the industry demand curve.

2.a. Marginal Revenue

The demand curve facing the monopoly firm is the industry demand curve.

In the early 1990s, a small U.S. company introduced a wireless VCR that could operate from more than one television set and didn't even have to be placed in the same room as the television. For a few years, this company had a monopoly on the wireless VCR. Let's consider the pricing and output decisions of the firm, using hypothetical cost and revenue data.

Suppose a wireless VCR sells for $1,500, and at that price the firm is selling 5 VCRs per day, as shown in Figure 2. If the monopoly firm wants to sell more, it must move down the demand curve. Why? Because of the law of demand. People will do without the wireless VCR rather than pay more than they think it's worth. As the price declines, sales increase. The table in Figure 2 shows that if the monopoly firm lowers the price to $1,350 per unit from $1,400, it will sell 8 VCRs per day instead of 7.

What is the firm's marginal revenue? To find marginal revenue, the total revenue earned at $1,400 per VCR must be compared to the total revenue earned at $1,350 per VCR—the change in total revenue must be calculated. At $1,400 apiece, 7 VCRs are sold each day and total revenue each day is

$$\$1,400 \text{ per VCR} \times 7 \text{ VCRs} = \$9,800$$

At $1,350 apiece, 8 VCRs are sold and total revenue is

$$\$1,350 \text{ per VCR} \times 8 \text{ VCRs} = \$10,800$$

Public utilities supply some basic good or service like electricity and water and are regulated monopolies in the United States or government-run enterprises in some other countries. Until the 1990s, utilities in the United States were guaranteed by government regulation not to have losses, but they had to provide electricity at prices dictated by government. Beginning around 1992, many state governments began deregulating electric utilities. The deregulation process has been a bumpy ride, however. In some states, no changes were made; in other states, the generation was partially or completely deregulated so that firms could compete in selling electricity. But the transmission of electricity has not been deregulated for fear that private firms would not invest sufficiently in building transmission wires. As a result, the transmission system in the United States is outdated and unable to handle the volume of demand, and blackouts have occurred in all parts of the country.

FIGURE 2

Demand Curve for a Monopolist

As the VCR price is reduced, the quantity demanded increases. But because the price is reduced on all quantities sold, not just on the last unit sold, marginal revenue declines faster than price.

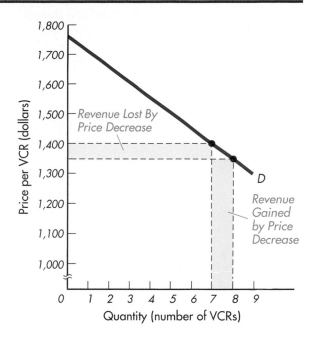

Quantity per Day	Price	Total Revenue	Marginal Revenue
1	$1,700	$ 1,700	$1,700
2	$1,650	$ 3,300	$1,600
3	$1,600	$ 4,800	$1,500
4	$1,550	$ 6,200	$1,400
5	$1,500	$ 7,500	$1,300
6	$1,450	$ 8,700	$1,200
7	$1,400	$ 9,800	$1,100
8	$1,350	$10,800	$1,000
9	$1,300	$11,700	$ 900

The difference, change in total revenue, is $1,000. Thus, marginal revenue is

$$\frac{\Delta TR}{\Delta Q} = \frac{\$1,000}{1 \text{ VCR}} = \$1,000$$

The change in revenue is the difference between the increased revenue due to increased quantity sold, the yellow area in Figure 2, and the decreased revenue due to a lower price, the blue area in Figure 2.

Marginal revenue is less than price for a monopoly firm.

The price is $1,350 per VCR, but marginal revenue is $1,000 per VCR. Price and marginal revenue are not the same for a monopoly firm. This is a fundamental difference between a monopolist and a perfect competitor. For a perfect competitor, price and marginal revenue are the same.

Marginal revenue is less than price and declines as output rises because the monopolist must lower the price in order to sell more units. When the price of a VCR is $1,400, the firm sells 7 VCRs. When the price is dropped to $1,350, the firm sells 8 units. The firm does not sell the first 7 VCRs for $1,400 and the eighth one for $1,350. It might lose business if it tried to do that. The customer who purchased the good at $1,350 could sell the product for $1,375 to a customer who was about to pay $1,400, and the firm would lose the $1,400 sale. Customers who would have paid $1,400 could decide to wait until they too can get the $1,350 price. As long as customers know about the prices paid by other customers and as long as the firm cannot easily distinguish among customers, the monopoly firm is not able to charge a different price for each additional unit. All units are sold at the same price, and in order to sell additional units, the monopolist must lower the price on all units. As a result, marginal revenue and price are not the same.

2.a.1. Marginal and Average Revenue
Recall from the chapter "Elasticity: Demand and Supply" that whenever the marginal is greater than the average, the average rises, and whenever the marginal is less than the average, the average falls. Average revenue is calculated by dividing total revenue by the number of units of output sold:

$$AR = \frac{P \times Q}{Q} = P$$

At a price of $1,500 per VCR, average revenue is

$$\frac{\$7,500}{5} = \$1,500$$

Average revenue at a price of $1,450 per VCR is

$$\frac{\$8,700}{6} = \$1,450$$

Average revenue is the same as price; in fact, *the average-revenue curve is the demand curve.* Because of the law of demand, where quantity demanded rises as price falls, average revenue (price) always falls as output rises (the demand curve slopes downward). Because average revenue falls as output rises, marginal revenue must always be less than average revenue. For the monopolist (or any firm facing a downward-sloping demand curve), marginal revenue always declines as output increases, and the marginal-revenue curve always lies below the demand curve.

Also recall from previous chapters that the marginal-revenue curve is positive in the elastic region of the demand curve ($e_d > 1$), is zero at the output level where the demand curve is unit-elastic ($e_d = 1$), and is negative in the inelastic portion of the demand curve ($e_d < 1$).[1] This is illustrated in Figure 3.

RECAP

1. The demand curve facing a monopoly firm is the market demand curve.
2. For the monopoly firm, price is greater than marginal revenue. For the perfectly competitive firm, price and marginal revenue are equal.
3. As price declines, total revenue increases in the elastic portion of the demand curve, reaches a maximum at the unit-elastic point, and declines in the inelastic portion.
4. The marginal-revenue curve of the monopoly firm lies below the demand curve.
5. For both the perfectly competitive firm and the monopoly firm, price = average revenue = demand.

---

[1]The slope of the demand curve is one-half the slope of the marginal-revenue curve. Consider the demand formula $P = a - bQ$; total revenue is $PQ = aQ - bQ^2$, so marginal revenue is $MR = a - 2bQ$.

FIGURE 3

Downward-Sloping Demand Curve and Revenue

The straight-line downward-sloping demand curve in Figure 3(a) shows that the price elasticity of demand becomes more inelastic as we move down the curve. In the elastic region, revenue increases as price is lowered, as shown in Figure 3(b); in the inelastic region, revenue decreases as price is lowered. The revenue-maximizing point, the top of the curve in Figure 3(b), occurs where the demand curve is unit-elastic, shown in Figure 3(a).

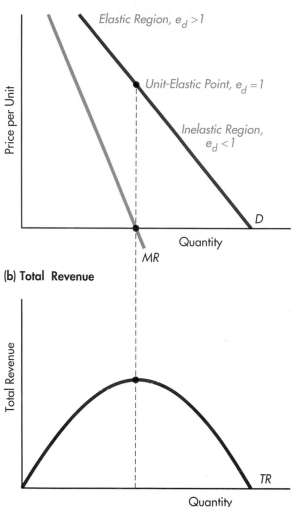

(a) Demand and Price Elasticity

Elastic Region, $e_d > 1$

Unit-Elastic Point, $e_d = 1$

Inelastic Region, $e_d < 1$

Price per Unit

Quantity

MR

D

(b) Total Revenue

Total Revenue

Quantity

TR

3. Profit Maximization

The objective of the monopoly firm is to maximize profit. Where does the monopolist choose to produce, and what price does it set? Recall from the chapter "Profit Maximization" that all profit-maximizing firms produce at the point where marginal revenue equals marginal cost.

3.a. What Price to Charge?

A schedule of revenues and costs for the wireless VCR producer accompanies Figure 4. Total revenue (*TR*) is listed in column 3; total cost (*TC*), in column 4. Total profit (*TR − TC*), shown in column 5, is the difference between the entries in

FIGURE 4

Profit Maximization for the VCR Producer

The data listed in the table are plotted in Figure 4(a). The firm produces where $MR = MC$, 8 units; charges a price given by the demand curve directly above the production of 8 units, a price of $1,350 per VCR; and earns a profit (yellow rectangle). In Figure 4(b), the firm is shown to be operating at a loss (blue rectangle). It produces output Q at price P, but the average total cost exceeds the price.

(1) Total Output (Q)	(2) Price (P)	(3) Total Revenue (TR)	(4) Total Cost (TC)	(5) Total Profit (TR−TC)	(6) Marginal Revenue (MR)	(7) Marginal Cost (MC)	(8) Average Total Cost (ATC)
0	$1,750	$ 0	$1,000	−$1,000			
1	$1,700	$ 1,700	$2,000	−$ 300	$1,700	$1,000	$2,000
2	$1,650	$ 3,300	$2,800	$ 500	$1,600	$ 800	$1,400
3	$1,600	$ 4,800	$3,500	$1,300	$1,500	$ 700	$1,167
4	$1,550	$ 6,200	$4,000	$2,200	$1,400	$ 500	$1,000
5	$1,500	$ 7,500	$4,500	$3,000	$1,300	$ 500	$ 900
6	$1,450	$ 8,700	$5,200	$3,500	$1,200	$ 700	$ 867
7	$1,400	$ 9,800	$6,000	$3,800	$1,100	$ 800	$ 857
8	$1,350	$10,800	$7,000	$3,800	$1,000	$1,000	$ 875
9	$1,300	$11,700	$9,000	$2,700	$ 900	$2,000	$1,000

(a) Making a Profit

(b) Operating at a Loss

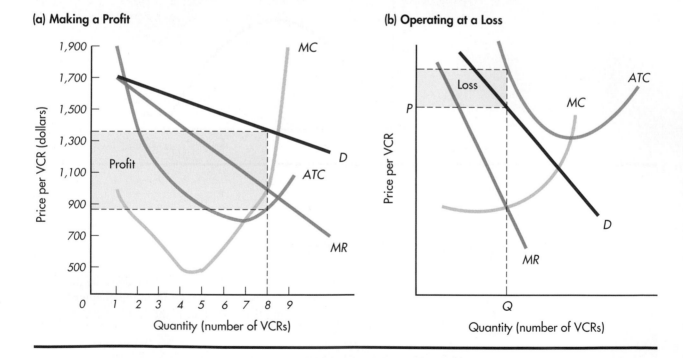

column 3 and those in column 4. Marginal revenue (*MR*) is listed in column 6, marginal cost (*MC*) in column 7, and average total cost (*ATC*) in column 8.

The quantity of output to be produced is the quantity that corresponds to the point where *MR* = *MC*. How high a price will the market bear at that quantity? The market is willing and able to purchase the quantity given by *MR* = *MC* at the corresponding price on the demand curve. As shown in Figure 4(a), the price is found by drawing a vertical line from the point where *MR* = *MC* up to the demand curve and then extending a horizontal line over to the vertical axis. That price is $1,350 when output is 8.

3.b. Monopoly Profit and Loss

?

4. **Why would someone want to have a monopoly in some business or activity?**

The profit that the monopoly firm generates by selling 8 VCRs at a price of $1,350 is shown in Figure 4(a) as the colored rectangle. The vertical distance between the *ATC* curve and the demand curve, multiplied by the quantity sold, yields total profit.

Just like any other firm, a monopoly firm could experience a loss. A monopoly supplier of sharpeners for disposable razor blades probably would not be very successful, and the U.S. Postal Service has failed to make a profit in five of the last ten years. Unless price exceeds average costs, the firm loses money. A monopolist producing at a loss is shown in Figure 4(b)—the price is less than the average total cost.

Like a perfectly competitive firm, a monopolist will suspend operations in the short run if its price does not exceed the average variable cost at the quantity the firm produces. And, like a perfectly competitive firm, a monopolist will shut down permanently if revenue is not likely to equal or exceed all costs in the long run (unless the government subsidizes the firm, as it does in the case of the U.S. Postal Service). In contrast, however, if a monopolist makes a profit, barriers to entry will keep other firms out of the industry. As a result, the monopolist can earn above-normal profits in the long run.

A monopolist can earn above-normal profits in the long run.

3.c. Supply and the Monopoly Firm

For the firm in perfect competition, the supply curve is that portion of the marginal-cost curve that lies above the average-cost curve, and the market supply curve is the sum of all the individual firms' supply curves. The supply curve for the firm selling in any of the other market structures is not as straightforward to derive, and, therefore, neither is the market supply curve. The reason is that firms selling in market structures other than perfect competition are price makers rather than price takers. This means that the hypothetical experiment of varying the price of a product and seeing how the firm selling that product reacts makes no sense.

In the case of the monopolist, the firm supplies a quantity determined by setting marginal revenue equal to marginal cost, but it also sets the price to go along with this quantity. Varying the price will not change the decision rule, since the firm will choose to produce its profit-maximizing output level and set the price accordingly. There is, therefore, only one quantity and price at which the monopolist will operate. There is a supply point, not a supply curve. Moreover, because the monopolist is the only firm in the market, its supply curve (or supply point) is also the market supply curve (or point).

The complications of the price makers do not alter the supply rule: a firm will produce and offer for sale a quantity that equates marginal revenue with marginal cost. This supply rule applies to all firms, regardless of the market structure in which the firm operates.

3.d. Monopoly Myths

There are a few myths about monopoly that we have debunked here. The first myth is that a monopolist can charge any price it wants and will reap unseemly profits by continually increasing the price. We know that a monopolist maximizes profit by producing the quantity that equates marginal revenue and marginal cost. We also know that a monopolist can price and sell only the quantities given by the demand curve. If the demand curve is very inelastic, as would be the case for a lifesaving pharmaceutical, then the price the monopolist will charge will be high. Conversely, if demand is very price-elastic, the monopolist will experience losses by charging exorbitant prices. A second myth is that a monopolist is not sensitive to customers. The monopolist can stay in business only if it earns at least a normal profit. Ignoring customers, producing a good no one will purchase, setting prices that all customers think are exorbitant, and providing terrible service or products that customers do not want will not allow a firm to remain in business for long. The monopolist faces a demand curve for its product and must search for a price and quantity that are dictated by that demand curve. The third myth is that the monopolist cannot make a loss. A monopolist is no different from any other firm in that it has costs of doing business and it must earn sufficient revenues to pay those costs. If the monopolist sets too high a price or provides a product that few want, revenues may be less than costs and losses may result.

RECAP

1. Profit is maximized at the output level where $MR = MC$.

2. The price charged by the monopoly firm is the point on the demand curve that corresponds to the quantity where $MR = MC$.

3. A monopoly firm can make profits or experience losses. A monopoly firm can earn above-normal profit in the long run.

4. The monopoly firm will shut down in the short run if all variable costs aren't covered. It will shut down in the long run if all costs aren't covered.

5. The amount a firm is willing and able to supply depends on marginal revenue and marginal cost. A firm will produce and offer for sale a quantity that equates marginal revenue and marginal cost.

4. Market Power and Price Discrimination

Firms that have a demand curve that is downward sloping are said to have *market* or *monopoly power*. This merely means that the firm has some control over the price it charges; it is not like the perfectly competitive firm, which is a price taker. With market power, a firm can choose to charge more and sell less or to charge less and sell more. Under certain conditions, a firm with market power is able to charge different customers different prices. This is called **price discrimination**. Figure 5 shows the demand curve facing a firm with market power. Notice that the demand curve tells us that at price P_1, consumers are willing and able to purchase quantity Q_1. If the price is P_2, they are willing and able to purchase Q_2. If the firm sells to everyone at the same price, say P_2, it does not make as much money as it would if it could charge some customers, those who were willing and able to pay a higher price, P_1 and other

price discrimination: charging different customers at different prices for the same product

FIGURE 5

Price Discrimination

If the firm can charge a price equal to what each person is willing and able to pay, the firm essentially collects the consumer surplus instead of the consumer. In this figure, the firm is charging one set of customers price P_1 and another set of customers price P_2.

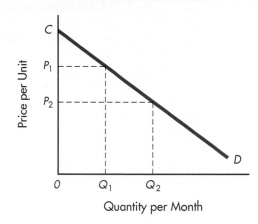

customers P_2. It could sell quantity Q_1 at price P_1 and quantity $Q_2 - Q_1$ at price P_2. What would be even better for the firm would be to charge each customer what that customer was willing and able to pay. Price discrimination enables the firm to capture consumer surplus for itself.

4.a. Necessary Conditions for Price Discrimination

5. Under what conditions will a monopolist charge different customers different prices for the same product?

You read in section 2.a that the monopoly firm has to sell all of its products at a uniform price; otherwise, one customer could sell to another, thereby reducing the monopoly firm's profit. However, if customers do not come into contact with each other or are somehow separated by the firm, the firm may be able to charge each customer the exact price that he or she is willing to pay.

When different customers are charged different prices for the same product or when customers are charged different prices for different quantities of the same product, price discrimination is occurring. Price discrimination occurs when price changes result not from cost changes, but from the firm's attempt to extract more of the consumer surplus. Certain conditions are necessary for price discrimination to occur:

- The firm cannot be a price taker (perfect competitor).
- The firm must be able to separate customers according to price elasticities of demand.
- The firm must be able to prevent resale of the product.

4.b. Examples of Price Discrimination

Examples of price discrimination are not hard to find. Senior citizens often pay a lower price than the general population at movie theaters, drugstores, and golf courses. It is relatively easy to identify senior citizens and to ensure that they do not resell their tickets to the general population.

Tuition at state schools is different for in-state and out-of-state residents. It is not difficult to find out where a student resides, and it is very easy to ensure that in-state students do not sell their places to out-of-state students.

Airlines discriminate between business passengers and others. Passengers who do not fly at the busiest times, who purchase tickets in advance, and who can stay at their destination longer than a day pay lower fares than business passengers, who cannot make advance reservations and who must travel during rush hours. It is relatively easy for the airlines to separate business from nonbusiness passengers and to ensure that the latter do not sell their tickets to the former.

Electric utilities practice a form of price discrimination by charging different rates for different quantities of electricity used. The rate declines as the quantity purchased increases. A customer might pay $.07 per kilowatt-hour for the first 100 kilowatt-hours, $.06 for the next 100, and so on. Many utility companies have different rate structures for different classes of customers as well. Businesses pay less per kilowatt-hour than households.

Grocery coupons, mail-in rebates, trading stamps, and other discount strategies are also price-discrimination techniques. Shoppers who are willing to spend time cutting out coupons and presenting them receive a lower price than those who are not willing to spend that time. Shoppers are separated by the amount of time they are willing to devote to coupon clipping. Is it possible that the popcorn at the movies is also a price-discrimination tactic? If the excess price of the popcorn and other foodstuffs at the movies was simply translated to an admission ticket, the movie theater would lose those customers who do not purchase popcorn. By charging a high price for the popcorn, the movie theater is distinguishing those customers who have a lower price elasticity of demand for the entire package of the movie and the popcorn from those with a higher elasticity of demand.

4.c. The Theory of Price Discrimination

How does price discrimination work? Suppose there are two classes of buyers for movie tickets, senior citizens and everybody else, and each class has a different price elasticity of demand. The two classes are shown in Figure 6. Profit is maximized when $MR = MC$. Because the same firm is providing the goods in two submarkets, MC is the same for senior citizens and the general public, but the demand curves differ. Because the demand curves of the two groups differ, there are two MR curves: MR_{sc} for senior citizens, in Figure 6 (a), and MR_{gp} for the general population, in Figure 6 (b). Profit is maximized when $MR_{sc} = MC$ and when $MR_{gp} = MC$. The price is found by drawing a vertical line from the quantities where $MR = MC$ up to the respective demand curves, D_{sc} and D_{gp}.

Notice that the price to the general population, P_{gp}, is higher than the price to the senior citizens, P_{sc}. The reason is that the senior citizens' demand curve is more elastic than the demand curve of the general population. Senior citizens are more sensitive to price than is the general population, so to attract more of their business, the merchant has to offer them a lower price.

By discriminating, a monopoly firm makes greater profits than it would make by charging both groups the same price. If both groups were charged the same price, P_{gp}, the monopoly firm would lose sales to senior citizens who found the price too high, Q_{sc} to Q_2. And if both groups were charged P_{sc}, so few additional sales to the general population would be made that revenues would fall. A firm with market power could collect the entire consumer surplus if it could charge each customer exactly the price that that customer was willing and able to pay. This is called *perfect price discrimination*.

FIGURE 6

Price Discrimination in Action

There are two classes of buyers for the same product. Figure 6(a) shows the elasticity of demand for senior citizens. Figure 6(b) shows the elasticity of demand for the general population. The demand of the senior citizens is more elastic than that of the general population. As a result, faced with the same marginal cost, the firm charges senior citizens a lower price than it charges the rest of the population. The quantity sold to senior citizens is Q_{sc}, the intersection between MC and MR_{sc}, and the price charged is P_{sc}. The quantity sold to the general population is Q_{gp}, and the price charged is P_{gp}.

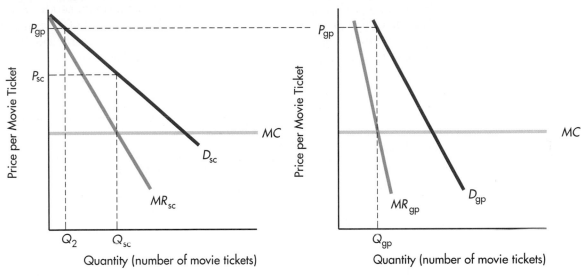

(a) Senior Citizens

(b) General Population (other than senior citizens)

RECAP

1. Price discrimination occurs when a firm charges different customers different prices for the same product or charges different prices for different quantities of the same product.

2. Three conditions are necessary for price discrimination to occur: (1) the firm must have some market power, (2) the firm must be able to separate customers according to price elasticities of demand, and (3) the firm must be able to prevent resale of the product.

?

6. How do the predictions of the models of perfect competition and monopoly differ?

5. Comparison of Perfect Competition and Monopoly

Because perfect competition and monopoly are bookends—opposites that are intended to surround all business behavior—it is useful to compare the outcome of the two.

5.a. Costs of Monopoly: Inefficiency

In the long run, the perfectly competitive firm operates at the minimum point of the long-run average-total-cost curve and the firm's price is equal to its marginal cost. Profit is at the normal level. A monopolist does not operate at the minimum point of the average-total-cost curve and does not set price equal to marginal cost. Because entry does not occur, a monopoly firm may earn above-normal profit in the long run.

Figure 7(a) shows a perfectly competitive market. The market demand curve is D; the market supply curve is S. The market price determined by the intersection of D and S is P_{pc}. At P_{pc} the perfectly competitive market produces Q_{pc}. Consumers are able to enjoy the consumer surplus indicated by the triangle $P_{pc}BA$ by purchasing the quantity Q_{pc} at the price P_{pc}. Firms receive the producer surplus indicated by triangle OBP_{pc} by producing the quantity Q_{pc} and selling that quantity at price P_{pc}.

To compare these results to monopoly, we must assume that all of the firms in a perfectly competitive industry are merged into a single monopoly firm and that the monopolist does not close or alter plants and does not achieve any economies of

---

FIGURE 7

Monopoly and Perfect Competition Compared

Figure 7(a) shows a perfectly competitive industry; it produces at the point where industry demand, D, and industry supply, S, intersect. The quantity produced by the industry is Q_{pc}; the price charged is P_{pc}. Consumer surplus is the triangle $P_{pc}BA$. Figure 7(b) shows what happens if the industry is monopolized. The single firm faces the industry demand curve, D, and has the marginal-revenue curve MR. The intersection of the marginal-cost curve and the marginal-revenue curve

indicates the quantity that will be produced, Q_m. The price charged for Q_m is P_m. Thus, the monopoly firm produces less and charges more than the perfectly competitive industry. Consumer surplus, shown as the triangle P_mCA, is smaller in the monopoly industry. The area $P_{pc}ECP_m$ is the consumer surplus in perfect competition that is transferred from consumer to producer. The producer surplus is area $OFCP_m$. The deadweight loss is the area CFB.

(a) The Perfectly Competitive Market

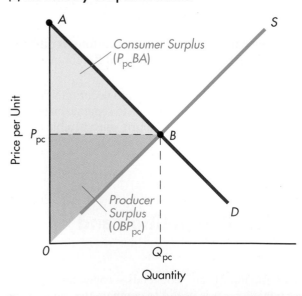

(b) Monopoly

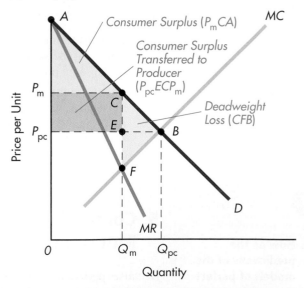

---

scale. In other words, what would occur if a perfectly competitive industry is transformed into a monopoly—just one firm determines price and quantity produced? The industry demand curve becomes the monopoly firm's demand curve, and the industry supply curve becomes the monopoly firm's marginal-cost curve. Recall that a firm's marginal-cost curve (above the average-variable-cost curve) is that firm's supply curve. This is illustrated in Figure 7(b).

The monopoly firm restricts quantity produced to Q_m, where $MR = MC$, and charges a price P_m as indicated on the demand curve shown in Figure 7(b). *The monopoly firm thus produces a lower quantity than does the perfectly competitive market, Q_m compared to Q_{pc}, and sells that smaller quantity at a higher price, P_m compared to P_{pc}.* In addition, the consumer surplus in monopoly is the triangle P_mCA, which is smaller than the consumer surplus under perfect competition, $P_{pc}BA$. The rectangle $P_{pc}ECP_m$ is part of consumer surplus in perfect competition. In monopoly, that part of consumer surplus is transferred to the firm. The total producer surplus is area $OFCP_m$.

Thus, firms are better off (more producer surplus) while consumers are worse off (less consumer surplus) under monopoly compared to perfect competition. Consumers are worse off by area $P_{pc}BCP_m$, and firms are better off by area $P_{pc}ECP_m$ less area EFB. The consumer and producer surplus represented by triangle CFB is lost by both consumers and firms and goes to no one. This loss is the reduction in consumer surplus and producer surplus that is not transferred to the monopoly firm or to anyone else; it is called a **deadweight loss.**

deadweight loss: the reduction of consumer surplus without a corresponding increase in profit when a perfectly competitive firm is monopolized

---

RECAP

1. A monopoly firm produces a smaller quantity and charges a higher price than a perfectly competitive industry if the two industries have identical costs.

2. The consumer surplus is smaller if an industry is operated by a monopoly firm than it is if an industry is operated by perfectly competitive firms. Profits are larger in the monopoly case.

3. The costs to society that result when a perfectly competitive industry becomes a monopoly are a reduction of consumer surplus and producer surplus that is not transferred to anyone. This loss is called a *deadweight loss.*

Summary

❓ What is monopoly?

1. Monopoly is a market structure in which there is a single supplier of a product. A monopoly firm, or monopolist, is the only supplier of a product for which there are no close substitutes. *§1.a*

❓ How is a monopoly created?

2. Natural barriers to entry (such as economies of scale), barriers erected by firms in the industry, and barriers erected by government may create monopolies. *§1.b, 1.b.1, 1.b.2, 1.b.3*

3. The term *monopoly* is often associated with natural monopoly, local monopoly, regulated monopoly, and monopoly power. *§1.c*

❓ What does the demand curve for a monopoly firm look like, and why?

4. Because a monopolist is the only producer of a good or service, the demand curve facing a monopoly firm is the industry demand curve. *§2*

5. Price and marginal revenue are not the same for a monopoly firm. Marginal revenue is less than price. *§2.a*

6. The average-revenue curve is the demand curve. *§2.a.1*

7. A monopoly firm maximizes profit by producing the quantity of output yielded at the point where marginal revenue and marginal cost are equal. *§3.a*

8. A monopoly firm sets a price that is on the demand curve and that corresponds to the point where marginal revenue and marginal cost are equal. *§3.a*

? Why would someone want to have a monopoly in some business or activity?

9. A monopoly firm can make above-normal or normal profit or even a loss. If it makes above-normal profit, entry by other firms does not occur and the monopoly firm can earn above-normal profit in the long run.

Exit occurs if the monopoly firm cannot cover costs in the long run. *§3.b*

? Under what conditions will a monopolist charge different customers different prices for the same product?

10. Price discrimination occurs when the firm is not a price taker, can separate customers according to their price elasticities of demand for the firm's product, and can prevent resale of the product. *§4.a*

? How do the predictions of the models of perfect competition and monopoly differ?

11. A comparison of monopoly and perfectly competitive firms implies that monopoly imposes costs on society. These costs include less output being produced and that output being sold at a higher price. *§5.a*

Key Terms

monopoly *§1.a*

monopoly firm (monopolist) *§1.a*

barrier to entry *§1.b*

natural monopoly *§1.c*

local monopoly *§1.c*

regulated monopoly *§1.c*

monopoly power *§1.c*

monopolization *§1.c*

price discrimination *§4*

deadweight loss *§5.a*

Exercises

1. About 85 percent of the soup sold in the United States is Campbell's brand. Is Campbell Soup Company a monopoly firm?

2. Price discrimination is practiced by movie theaters, motels, golf courses, drugstores, and universities. Are they monopolies? If not, how can they carry out price discrimination?

3. Why is it necessary for the seller to be able to keep customers from reselling the product in order for price discrimination to occur? There are many products for which you get a discount for purchasing large quantities. For instance, most liquor stores will provide a discount on wine if you purchase a case. Is this price discrimination? If so, what is to keep one customer from purchasing cases of wine and then reselling single bottles at a price above the case price but below the liquor store's single-bottle price?

4. Many people have claimed that there is no good for which substitutes are not available. If so, does this mean there is no such thing as monopoly?

5. Suppose that at a price of $6 per unit, quantity demanded is 12 units. Calculate the quantity demanded when the marginal revenue is $6 per unit. (*Hint:* The price elasticity of demand is unity at the midpoint of the demand curve.)

6. In the following figure, if the monopoly firm faces ATC_1, which rectangle measures total profit? If the monopoly firm faces ATC_2, what is total profit? What information would you need in order to know whether the monopoly firm will shut down or continue producing in the short run? In the long run?

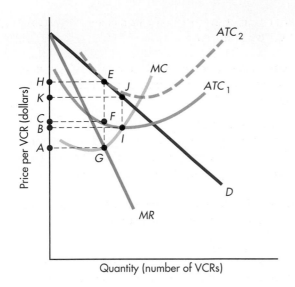

Price per VCR (dollars) vs Quantity (number of VCRs)

7. In recent years, U.S. car manufacturers have charged lower car prices in western states in an effort to offset the competition by Japanese cars. This two-tier pricing scheme has upset many car dealers in the eastern states. Many have called it discriminatory and illegal. What conditions are necessary for this pricing scheme to be profitable to the U.S. companies?

8. Consider the following demand schedule. Does it apply to a perfectly competitive firm? Compute marginal and average revenue.

Price	Quantity	Price	Quantity
$100	1	$ 70	5
$ 95	2	$ 55	6
$ 88	3	$ 40	7
$ 80	4	$ 22	8

9. Suppose the marginal cost of producing the good in question 8 is a constant $10 per unit of output. What quantity of output will the firm produce?

10. Do you agree or disagree with this statement: "A monopoly firm will charge an exorbitant price for its product"? Explain your answer.

11. Do you agree or disagree with this statement: "A monopoly firm will run a much less safe business than a perfect competitor"? Explain your answer.

12. State colleges and universities have two levels of tuition or fees. The less expensive is for residents of the state, the more expensive for nonresidents. Assume that the universities are profit-maximizing monopolists and explain their pricing policy. Now, explain why the colleges and universities give student aid and scholarships.

13. Several electric utilities are providing customers with a choice of billing procedures. Customers can select a time-of-day meter that registers electric usage throughout the day, or they can select a regular meter that registers total usage at the end of the day. With the time-of-day meter, the utility is able to charge customers a much higher rate for peak usage than for nonpeak usage. The regular meter users pay the same rate for electric usage no matter when it is used. Why would the electric utility want customers to choose the time-of-day meter?

14. Suppose that a firm has a monopoly on a good with the following demand schedule:

Price	Quantity	Price	Quantity
$10	0	$4	6
$ 9	1	$3	7
$ 8	2	$2	8
$ 7	3	$1	9
$ 6	4	$0	10
$ 5	5		

a. What price and quantity will the monopolist produce at if the marginal cost is a constant $4?

b. Calculate the deadweight loss from having the monopolist produce, rather than a perfect competitor.

ACE

Take the ACE Practice Test for this chapter to review the important concepts and get immediate feedback with answers.

economics.college.hmco.com/students

Conflict Diamonds

This is a story about diamonds— "conflict diamonds." These stones come from war-ravaged Angola, Sierra Leone and Congo. Far from being anyone's best friend, they have proven a powerful enemy of the innocent thousands killed, wounded and maimed in those wars.

Why is this of concern to Americans? Because Americans buy 65 percent of all retail diamonds. Because if Americans begin to insist on proof that those diamonds are not washed with African blood, they can become a powerful force for bringing peace to these horribly brutalized peoples.

Rep. Tony Hall, D-Ohio, has introduced legislation that would require certificates on all diamonds, detailing their place of origin. The United Nations and the British government are pushing for tighter controls as well. Opinions differ on whether Hall's approach is practical, but his legislation sends a strong message to the diamond industry: Find ways to clean up your trade or we will.

"Diamonds are forever," says diamond cartel DeBeers. But human lives and human limbs aren't. Consider Maria, an 8-month-old baby girl in Sierra Leone. In an act of unfathomable cruelty, her arm was hacked off by the "rebel" terrorists of the Revolutionary United Front (RUF). The RUF mob has sought to impose its will on Sierra Leone by chopping off thousands of civilian hands, feet and ears. Thousands more people have simply been slaughtered and left to rot in village streets. Men, women, children, civilian, soldier; it makes no difference to the RUF.

What's the diamond connection? The RUF has kept itself well supplied with arms, vehicles, food and other supplies by mining and smuggling hundreds of millions of dollars worth of illicit diamonds into a world market that is determined to see no evil.

It's the same in Angola, where illicit diamonds have funded the 25-year-old war waged by Jonas Savimbi and his UNITA forces. By one estimate, UNITA earned $4 billion from its illegal sales of diamonds between 1992 and 1998. It used that money to undermine the Angola peace process and to purchase new arms.

The international diamond industry has taken several steps to stop the trade in illicit diamonds, but they are puny steps. Much more could be done, beginning with an acknowledgment of responsibility.

Take the DeBeers cartel. It mines 50 percent of the world's diamonds and purchases about 80 percent of those offered for sale on open markets. More than $4 billion in diamonds are stockpiled in DeBeers offices; it buys and sells in quantities designed to keep diamond prices at an artificially high rate. All told, it controls 85 percent of the world trade. (Where is trust buster Joel Klein when we need him?)

DeBeers insists it is impossible to tell where uncut diamonds originate (others disagree) but simultaneously insists it buys no conflict diamonds. How can those statements both be true? Well, DeBeers says, it has closed its offices in the controversial areas of Angola, Sierra Leone and Congo.

But here's how it works. The Ivory Coast diamond industry closed down in the 1980s, but Belgium recorded imports of more than 1.5 million carats in gemstones from the Ivory Coast annually in the mid-'90s. Those stones were most likely smuggled to the Ivory Coast from Angola and Sierra Leone.

Liberia produces about 100,000 carats a year. But between 1994 and 1998, more than 31 million carats were exported to the world diamond center in Antwerp. These too were smuggled stones, fueling not only the violence in their countries of origin, but in Liberia.

Sierra Leone officially exported only 8,500 carats in 1998, but Belgium recorded 770,000 carats coming from that country. You've got to ask: Why did Belgium take them, and where did they go?

The answers seem pretty straightforward: Belgium let them in because Antwerp is afraid of losing market share to Tel Aviv and Mumbai (formerly Bombay). And it's impossible to believe many of those stones didn't end up with DeBeers. Otherwise, the price would have tumbled.

If this trade in illicit diamonds caused harm only to soldiers, it would be bad enough. But for every soldier killed in these African wars, death and injury comes to scores of innocents like baby Maria.

What can you do? Push Congress and this year's crop of congressional candidates to put pressure on the international diamond trade. Because the United States is the premier retail market for diamonds, it has the clout to force a cleanup. Belgium and the major diamond trading companies seem determined to turn a blind eye. The United States must force that eye open.

Source: Copyright 2000 *Star Tribune.*

Star Tribune (Minneapolis, MN)/June 12, 2000

One of the most famous monopolies is DeBeers, the diamond suppliers. DeBeers is not actually a monopolist—the only seller—but it has been the dominant firm in the diamond market for nearly 70 years. The South African company controls over 60 percent of the $7 billion a year global market for uncut diamonds. Over the years, it has used its dominance of the industry to drive up the price of diamonds by buying up surplus diamonds. The policy dates back to 1934, when the Great Depression caused a slump in diamond prices and the chairman then of DeBeers, Sir Ernest Oppenheimer, offered to buy all the rough stones on the market. Had prices continued to fall, the move would have probably led to DeBeers's bankruptcy. But the price recovered and Sir Ernest's gamble laid the foundation for the company's dominance of the diamond industry for the remainder of the century. DeBeers spent billions of dollars to accumulate a large stockpile of diamonds that were never sold. At the end of 1999, the DeBeers's diamond mountain, hoarded in its London vaults, was worth around $4 billion. The diamonds were used to maintain or manipulate the price. But that practice is changing. DeBeers has announced that it is giving up its traditional role of buyer of last resort of every stone on the market. The reason given for the change is what are called conflict diamonds, diamonds sold by various forces in Africa to fuel civil wars. DeBeers announced that it will not purchase or trade in conflict diamonds.

While the policy might have some emotional or ethical appeal, the real reason DeBeers is ending its buyer of last resort strategy is to reduce its declining economic profits. DeBeers knows that if conflict, or blood, diamonds become an emotional consumer issue, they could trigger a public opinion backlash similar to the one that crippled the fur trade. Moreover, rivals such as BHP, the Australian group, and Rio Tinto of the United Kingdom are gaining more and more market share. DeBeers's strategy is two-pronged: one to attempt to reduce the supply of diamonds and one to increase the demand.

DeBeers's strategy on conflict diamonds is most likely motivated by more than just fears of a consumer boycott. If DeBeers can position itself as a producer and distributor of clean diamonds, it will keep a tight grip on the market without the expense of maintaining a stockpile. The company is proposing measures that will make it the only buyer of rough diamonds that are licensed. Moreover, by reducing the supply of licensed stones, DeBeers will be able to sell its stockpile without disrupting prices. On the demand side, DeBeers spent $170 million last year to advertise the gems under its famous slogan, "A diamond is forever," and it has begun to place a certificate of guarantee on the stones that they are not from rebel-controlled areas. It has asked its buyers to join in the advertising campaign and to support its efforts at restricting the supply of diamonds from war-torn Africa.

It is difficult for a monopolist to give up its monopoly power and positive economic profits. DeBeers doesn't plan to do so without a fight.

CHAPTER 26

Monopolistic Competition and Oligopoly

? Fundamental Questions

1. What is monopolistic competition?

2. What behavior is most common in monopolistic competition?

3. What is oligopoly?

4. In what form does rivalry occur in an oligopoly?

5. Why does cooperation among rivals occur most often in oligopolies?

To understand how most firms behave, one or more of the characteristics of perfect competition and monopoly must be altered. These alterations give us the models of monopolistic competition and oligopoly.

Monopolistic competition is like perfect competition in that there are many firms and new firms may enter easily, but it differs from perfect competition in that each firm produces a slightly different product. Monopolistic competition is like monopoly in that each firm in monopolistic competition has some market power.

Oligopoly captures all marked structures not included in perfect competition, monopolistic competition, and monopoly. There are a few firms in an oligopoly—not a large number and not just one.

We'll discuss monopolistic competition in the first part of this chapter and oligopoly in the second part. ■

?

1. What is monopolistic competition?

1. Monopolistic Competition

Monopolistic competition is a market structure in which (1) there are a large number of firms, (2) the products produced by the firms are differentiated, and (3) entry and exit occur easily. The definitions of *monopolistic competition* and *perfect competition* overlap. In both structures, there are a large number of firms. The difference is that each firm in monopolistic competition produces a product that is slightly different from all other products, whereas in perfect competition the products are standardized. The definition of *monopolistic competition* also overlaps with that of *monopoly*. Because each firm in monopolistic competition produces a unique product, each has a "mini" monopoly over its product. Thus, like a monopolist, the firm in a monopolistically competitive market structure has a downward-sloping demand curve, marginal revenue is below the demand curve, and price is greater than marginal cost. What distinguishes monopolistic competition from monopoly is ease of entry. Any time firms in monopolistic competition are earning above-normal profit, new firms enter and entry continues until firms are earning normal profit. In monopoly, a firm can earn above-normal profit in the long run. Table 1 summarizes the differences among perfect competition, monopoly, and monopolistic competition.

1.a. Profits and Entry

Monopolistically competitive firms produce differentiated products.

Firms in monopolistic competition tend to use product differentiation more than price to compete. They attempt to provide a product for each market niche. Even though the total market may not be expanding, they divide the market into smaller and smaller segments by introducing variations of products. You can think of a market demand curve for clothes, but within that market there are many niches and many demand curves. In fact, there are separate demand curves for each firm and for each product the firm sells. Each individual demand curve is quite price-elastic because of the existence of many close substitutes.

1.a.1. In the Short Run
Figure 1(a) shows the cost and revenue curves of a monopolistically competitive firm providing a single product in the short run. As with all profit-maximizing firms, production occurs at the quantity where $MR = MC$. The price the firm charges, P_1, is given by the demand curve at the quantity where $MR = MC$. Price P_1 is above average total cost, as indicated by

TABLE 1

Summary of Perfect Competition, Monopoly, and Monopolistic Competition

	Perfect Competition	Monopoly	Monopolistic Competition
Number of firms	Many	One	Many
Type of product	Undifferentiated	One	Differentiated
Entry conditions	Easy	Difficult or impossible	Easy
Demand curve for firm	Horizontal (perfectly elastic)	Downward sloping	Downward sloping
Price and marginal cost	$MC = P$	$MC < P$	$MC < P$
Long-run profit	Zero	Yes	Zero

FIGURE 1

A Monopolistically Competitive Firm

A monopolistically competitive firm faces a downward-sloping demand curve. The firm in Figure 1(a) maximizes profit by producing Q_1, where $MR = MC$, and charging a price, P_1, given by the demand curve above Q_1. Profit is the rectangle $CBAP_1$. In Figure 1(b), the firm is earning a normal profit because where $MR = MC$, price is P_1 on the demand curve above Q_1 and is equal to average total cost. In Figure 1(c) the firm is earning the loss of rectangle P_1BAC. At the profit-maximizing (loss-minimizing) output level, Q_1, average total cost exceeds price.

(a) Above Normal Profit

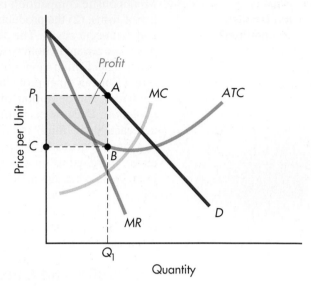

(b) Normal Profit

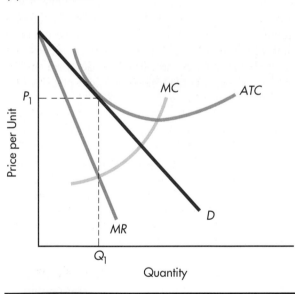

(c) Economic Loss

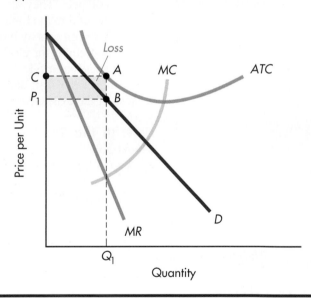

the distance AB. Thus, the firm is earning above-normal profit, shown as the rectangle $CBAP_1$.

In Figure 1(b), the firms in a monopolistically competitive market are earning normal profit. The price is the same as the average total cost at Q_1, so a normal profit is obtained. If the firm is earning a loss, then the average-total-cost curve lies above the demand curve at the quantity produced, as shown in Figure 1(c). At Q_1, the firm is earning a loss, the rectangle P_1BAC. The firm must decide whether to temporarily suspend production of that product or to continue producing because the outlook is favorable. The decision depends on whether revenue exceeds variable costs.

Monopolistic competition and some oligopolies compete more with differentiation than with price. The Hummer is an excellent example. Manufactured and sold by General Motors, the big SUV gets about five miles per gallon, costs upwards of $60,000, and rides like a very rough truck. Yet, the Hummer has been the largest-selling SUV during the past few years. The Hummer is significantly larger and wider than other SUVs. Its image is one of tough, macho soldiers; the Hummer was first developed and used by the military.

1.a.2. In the Long Run

Whenever existing firms in a market structure without barriers to entry are earning above-normal profit, new firms enter the business and, in some cases, existing firms expand until all firms are earning the normal profit. In a perfectly competitive industry, the new firms supply a product that is identical to the product being supplied by existing firms. *In a monopolistically competitive industry, entering firms produce a close substitute, not an identical or standardized product.*

As the introduction of new products by new or existing firms occurs, the demand curves for existing products shift in until a normal profit is earned. For each firm and each product, the demand curve shifts in, as shown in Figure 2, until it just touches the average-total-cost curve at the price charged and output produced, P_2 and Q_2. When profit is at the normal level, expansion and entry cease.

When firms are earning a loss on a product and the long-run outlook is for continued losses, the firms will stop producing that product. Exit means that fewer differentiated products are produced, and the demand curves for the remaining products shift out. This continues until the remaining firms are earning normal profits.

1.b. Monopolistic Competition Versus Perfect Competition

Figure 3 shows both a perfectly competitive firm in long-run equilibrium and a monopolistically competitive firm in long-run equilibrium. The perfectly competitive firm, shown as the horizontal demand and marginal-revenue curve, $MR_{pc} = D_{pc}$ produces at the minimum point of the long-run average-total-cost curve at Q_{pc}; and the price, marginal cost, marginal revenue, and average total costs are P_{pc}. The long-run equilibrium for a monopolistically competitive firm is shown with the demand curve D_{mc} and marginal-revenue curve MR_{mc}. The monopolistically competitive firm produces at Q_{mc}, where $MR_{mc} = MC$, and charges a price determined by drawing a vertical line up from the point where $MR_{mc} = MC$ to the demand curve. That price is just equal to the point where the long-run average-total-cost curve touches the demand curve, P_{mc}. In other words, at Q_{mc} the monopolistically competitive firm is just earning the normal profit.

FIGURE 2

Entry and Normal Profit

In the long run, the firm in monopolistic competition earns a normal profit. Entry shifts the firm's demand curve in from D_1 to D_2. Entry, which takes the form of a differentiated product, continues to occur as long as above-normal profits exist. When the demand curve just touches the average-total-cost curve, as at P_2 and Q_2, profit is at the normal level.

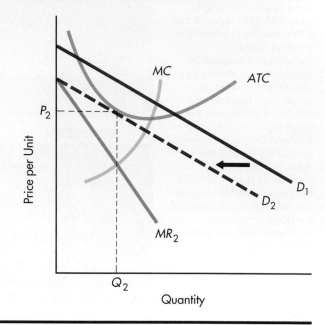

FIGURE 3

Perfect and Monopolistic Competition Compared

The perfectly competitive firm produces at the point where the price line, the horizontal MR curve, intersects the MC curve. This is the bottom of the ATC curve in the long run, quantity Q_{pc} at price P_{pc}. The monopolistically competitive firm also produces where $MR = MC$. The downward-sloping demand curve faced by the monopolistically competitive firm means that the quantity produced, Q_{mc} is less than the quantity produced by the perfectly competitive firm, Q_{pc}. The price charged by the monopolistically competitive firm is also higher than that charged by the perfectly competitive firm, P_{mc} versus P_{pc}. In both cases, however, the firms earn only a normal profit.

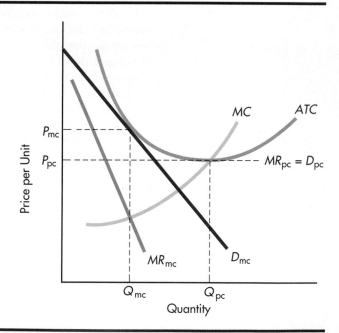

Monopolistically competitive firms produce less and charge a higher price than perfectly competitive firms.

The difference between a perfectly competitive firm and a monopolistically competitive firm is clear in Figure 3. Because of the downward-sloping demand curve facing the monopolistically competitive firm, the firm does not produce at the minimum point of the long-run average-total-cost curve, Q_{pc}. Instead, it produces a smaller quantity of output, Q_{mc}, at a higher price, P_{mc}. The difference between P_{mc} and P_{pc} is the additional amount consumers pay for the privilege of having differentiated products. If consumers placed no value on product choice—if they desired generic products—they would not pay anything extra for product differentiation, and the monopolistically competitive firm would not exist.

Monopolistic competition does not yield economic efficiency because consumers are willing and able to pay for variety.

Even though price does not equal marginal cost and the monopolistically competitive firm does not operate at the minimum point of the average-total-cost curve, the firm does earn normal profit in the long run. And although the monopolistically competitive firm does not strictly meet the conditions of economic efficiency (since price is not equal to marginal cost), the inefficiency is not due to the firm's ability to restrict quantity and increase price, but instead results directly from consumers' desire for variety. It is hard to argue that society is worse off with monopolistic competition than it is with perfect competition, since the difference is due solely to consumer desires. Yet variety is costly, and critics of market economies argue that the cost is not worthwhile. Would the world be a better place if we had a simpler array of products to choose from, if there was a simple generic product—one type of automobile, say—for everyone?

2. What behavior is most common in monopolistic competition?

1.c. Nonprice Competition

A firm in a monopolistically competitive market structure attempts to differentiate its product from the products offered by its rivals. Differentiation means that in the consumer's mind, this product is not the same as another product. Successful product differentiation reduces the price elasticity of demand. The demand curve, shown as the rotation from D_1 to D_2 in Figure 4, becomes steeper.

Numerous characteristics may serve to differentiate products: quality, color, style, safety features, taste, packaging, purchase terms, warranties, and guarantees. A firm might change its hours of operation—for example, a supermarket might offer service 24 hours a day—to call attention to itself. Firms can also use location to

---

FIGURE 4

Advertising, Prices, and Profits

A successful differentiation program will reduce the price elasticity of demand, shown as a steeper demand curve, D_2, compared to D_1. The successful differentiation enables the firm to charge a higher price.

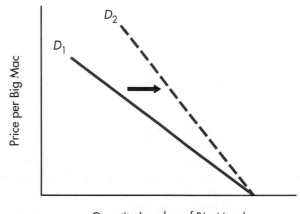

Quantity (number of Big Macs)

FIGURE 5

Location Under Monopolistic Competition

Five customers—A, B, C, D, and E—reside along a straight line. Customer C is in the middle, equidistant from B and D and from A and E. McDonald's decides to locate a restaurant at the spot that is closest to all five customers. This is the median position, where consumer C resides.

Other fast-food firms locate nearby because any other location will increase the total distance of some consumers from the fast-food restaurant, thereby causing some customers to go elsewhere.

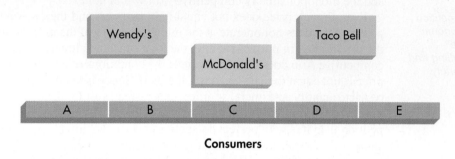

Consumers

differentiate their products. A firm may locate where traffic is heavy and the cost to the consumer of making a trip to the firm is minimal. If location is used for differentiation, however, why do fast-food restaurants tend to group together? Where you find a McDonald's, you usually find a Taco Bell or a Wendy's nearby. The model of monopolistic competition explains this behavior. Suppose that five identical consumers—A, B, C, D, and E—are spread out along a line as shown in Figure 5. Consumer C is the median consumer, residing equidistantly from consumers B and D and equidistantly from consumers A and E. Assume that the five consumers care about the costs incurred in getting to a fast-food restaurant and are indifferent between the food offered. McDonald's is the first fast-food provider to open near these five consumers. Where does it locate? It locates as close to consumer C as possible because that location minimizes the total distance of all five consumers from McDonald's.

Taco Bell wants to open in the same area. If it locates near consumer D, then Taco Bell will pull customers D and E from McDonald's but will have no chance to attract A, B, or C. Conversely, if it locates near consumer A, only A will go to Taco Bell. Only if Taco Bell locates next door to McDonald's will it have a chance to gather a larger market share than McDonald's. As other fast-food firms enter, they too will locate close to McDonald's.

Being able to earn positive economic profits is what drives firms to differentiate their goods and services. Every firm—producer, fabricator, seller, broker, agent, or merchant—tries to distinguish its offering from all others. The reason that firms try to differentiate themselves or their products is to make it more difficult for competitors to take away business.

Successful differentiation reduces the price elasticity of demand and gives the firm more market power. What does this mean for a firm? It means that the firm can raise the price of the good or service it sells without incurring the loss of revenue that would result if the elasticity were higher. For years Intel was able to charge more for its microchips than competitors could charge for essentially the same microchip. Intel was able to do that because of its successful campaign to differen-

Starbucks stores are popping up everywhere—it seems that you can't go a block without seeing a Starbucks sign. When firms do not compete with lower prices, they compete with differentiation, location, service, or some other dimension. Starbucks has successfully differentiated itself with its coffee and other products and with its locations.

tiate itself—"Intel Inside." Intel was able to shift the demand curve for its products out and make it more inelastic.

How does a firm differentiate its good or service? The obvious way is to create a physical difference. But often, nonphysical differences are created. One of the most important differentiating factors is brand name. A brand name means that demand for the brand-name good will be less price-elastic than that for a nonbranded good. Where does a brand name come from? How is it created?

Most goods have many different attributes—look, feel, taste, sensation, reliability, performance, and so on. Some of these attributes are revealed by search, some emerge immediately upon consumption, and others are discovered through long-term experience with the good. In other words, people don't know with perfect certainty if a good or service tastes good or works well or is healthy.

When people do not have complete and perfect information, economists say that information is costly or that consumers have to search for information (perusing magazines, going from store to store to compare products, trying out certain types of products, or purchasing the advice of experts). Searching takes time and, in some cases, money.

A brand name can reduce consumers' search costs and thereby differentiate the good or service. How is a brand name created? Typically a positive brand name emerges after consumers have had positive experiences with the good or service. Thus, a firm has to get people to try its goods or services. There are many ways this can be done. For instance, a firm that wants the public to believe that it is stable and likely to be around for some time may devote resources to a large building or beautiful offices or large billboards. A clothing store in a mall appears to be more stable than a vendor on the street corner, even if the mall location is just being rented. For some products, a guarantee or warranty is an important signal that the product is of high quality.

Reliability is the important differentiator for some goods and services. But for customers to know that the product is reliable, they must first try the product. A firm may advertise that its product "tastes great" or "refreshes you." Goods may be advertised by showing groups of people having fun on a beach or in the mountains—such as with Coors beer, for example. The goods may be placed in a setting of upper class or wealth—Grey Poupon being requested by a passenger in a limousine, for instance. These advertisements are intended to get people to try the good or service.

Reliability may be represented by the consistent flavor of a McDonald's hamburger, the infrequency with which a machine breaks down, or the soundness of the opinions of a professional adviser. The consumer has to experience these products and services over a relatively long period of time before reliability is established. Once a consumer has had a positive experience with a good, the price elasticity of demand for that good typically decreases—the consumer becomes loyal to the product. For instance, Coke and Pepsi drinkers are usually loyal to one of the two brands—Coke and Pepsi—even though the products are similar. Prudential Insurance shows "the rock" and Allstate shows the "good hands" to illustrate their reliability. Although these symbols have nothing to do with the actual service, they promote an aspect of the service that consumers find valuable—the idea that the service will continue to be offered in the future, so that an experience now can be used to evaluate the service in the future. Lawyers and financial advisers need to present an image of success. Who wants to use an unsuccessful attorney or financial adviser? Thus, attorneys and financial advisers typically have richly appointed offices located in large central-city buildings. They dress in expensive clothes and carry expensive briefcases.

Many people claim that marketing and advertising create phony or artificial distinctions among products and that the benefits conferred by brand names are illusory. These critics note that there may be no difference between Tide laundry detergent and the generic detergent sold under the grocery store's label, that Ralph Lauren's Polo brand shirts may be constructed of exactly the same fabric and knit design as several less-expensive brands, and that aspirin is aspirin whether or not it is Bayer. Nonetheless, consumers are often willing to pay a higher price for a brand-name product than for a similar product without a brand name. Why? Because the brand name signals something valuable—reliability, confidence, assurance.

The objective of creating a brand name is to increase consumer loyalty and thus reduce the price elasticity of demand. The greater the consumer's reluctance to shift brands, the lower the price elasticity of demand. Consumers who are loyal to a brand or to a firm will purchase that brand or purchase from that firm even if the prices are above those of competing brands.

We have just discussed the fact that a brand name can be based only on the provision of high quality in repeated trials—that is, after consumers experience the good or service. Because it takes a long time to establish such a reputation, some firms attempt to rent a reputation that has been established in one market and use it in a new market. Endorsement by famous personalities is a clear example. Everyone knows that when celebrities endorse a product, it is not because the celebrities have scoured the market for the best product, but rather because they have canvassed potential sponsors to see who will offer the highest fee. So why are consumers influenced by the endorsement? Because the endorser is, to some degree, putting his or her reputation at risk. If the product is of low quality, the celebrity's reputation and value to other sponsors can be damaged. For the manufacturer, payment of the endorsement fee is a demonstration of its commitment to the market. Willingness to pay the endorsement fee is therefore actually a measure of product quality.

Firms will sometimes use their established reputation in one market to enter a new market. BMW's reputation for producing cars reinforces its reputation for producing motor bikes, and vice versa. BMW also endorses a range of "Active Line" sportswear. Caterpillar has a line of clothing, "CAT," that provides the image of tough, no-nonsense fashions. There is little reason to believe that the capabilities that distinguish BMW cars or CAT equipment are applicable to the manufacture of clothes. But it would clearly be foolish for the companies to attach their name to poor-quality clothes.

Guarantees and warranties can also serve as ways to get people to experience a good or service. When Japanese automobile companies first entered the U.S. market in the 1960s, they faced the problem of convincing consumers of the quality of the cars. Although the manufacturers knew that their products were of high quality, their potential customers did not. In fact, many believed that Japanese goods were shoddy imitations of western products. "Made in Japan" had become synonymous with cheap and crummy. Accordingly, Japanese manufacturers offered more extensive warranties than had been usual in the market.

Guarantees are difficult to fake. A low-quality product will break down frequently, making the guarantee quite costly for the firm. Thus, the higher the quality of the product, the better the guarantee offered by the firm.

If a firm establishes a warranty policy, then other firms have to either follow or admit to having a lower-quality product. If another firm is unable to imitate its rivals' existing warranties, it may decide not to enter the market in the first place. This is what the Japanese auto producers did to the U.S. auto producers in the 1970s. U.S. auto producers did not offer as extensive warranties as the Japanese auto producers. As a result, customers soon came to see that "Made in Japan" meant quality. A similar event has been occurring in the late 1990s and early 2000s with respect to the Korean-manufactured Hyundai. Hyundai offered a 100,000-mile full warranty at a time when other manufacturers were offering 36,000-mile warranties.

The key aspect of firms in monopolistic competition is that they devote considerable resources to differentiating their goods and services. But, since entry is easy, does that differentiation do the firm any good?

An innovation or successful differentiation in any area—style, quality, location, service—leads initially to above-normal profit but eventually brings in copycats that drive profit back down to the normal level. In a monopolistically competitive market structure, innovation and above-normal profit for one firm are followed by entry and normal profit. Differentiation and above-normal profit then occur again. They induce entry, which again drives profit back to the normal level. The cycle continues until product differentiation no longer brings above-normal profit.

Although an above-normal profit attracts competitors, even a short-lived period of above-normal profit is better than no positive economic profit. That is why firms in monopolistic competition devote so many resources to differentiating their products.

RECAP

1. The market structure called *monopolistic competition* is an industry in which many sellers produce a differentiated product and entry is easy.

2. In the short run, a firm in monopolistic competition can earn above-normal profit.

3. In the long run, a firm in a monopolistically competitive market structure will produce at a higher cost and lower output than a firm in a perfectly competitive market structure will. In both market structures, firms earn only a normal profit.

4. Monopolistic competitors may engage more in nonprice competition than in price differentiation.

5. The key aspect of monopolistic competition is differentiation.

6. As a firm successfully differentiates its product and earns a positive economic profit, other firms will mimic the successful firm and reduce the differentiation. As a result, the positive economic profit will be competed down toward a normal economic profit.

2. Oligopoly and Interdependence

3. What is oligopoly?

Oligopoly is a market structure characterized by (1) few firms, (2) either standardized or differentiated products, and (3) difficult entry. Oligopoly may take many forms. It may consist of one dominant firm coexisting with many smaller firms or a group of giant firms (two or more) that dominate the industry coexisting with other small firms. Whatever the number of firms, the characteristic that describes oligopoly is *interdependence;* an individual firm in an oligopoly does not decide what to do without considering what the other firms in the industry will do. When a large firm in an oligopoly changes its behavior, the demand curves of the other firms are affected significantly.

In monopolistically competitive and perfectly competitive markets, what one firm does affects each of the other firms so slightly that each firm essentially ignores the others. Each firm in an oligopoly, however, must closely watch the actions of the other firms because the action of one can dramatically affect the others. This interdependence among firms leads to actions not found in the other market structures.

2.a. Oligopoly and Strategic Behavior

4. In what form does rivalry occur in an oligopoly?

strategic behavior: the behavior that occurs when what is best for A depends on what B does, and what is best for B depends on what A does

game theory: a description of oligopolistic behavior as a series of strategic moves and countermoves

Because of the great variety of behavior possible under oligopoly, economists have been unable to agree on a single description of how oligopolistic firms behave. The only uniform description of the behavior of oligopolistic firms is *strategic.*

Strategic behavior occurs when what is best for A depends on what B does and what is best for B depends on what A does. It is much like a card game—bridge, say—where strategies are designed depending on the cards the players are dealt. Underbidding, overbidding, bluffing, deceit, and other strategies are carried out. In fact, the analogy between games and firm behavior in oligopoly is so strong that economists have applied **game theory** to their analyses of oligopoly. Game theory, developed in the 1940s by John von Neumann and Oskar Morgenstern, describes oligopolistic behavior as a series of strategic moves and countermoves. In this section we briefly discuss some of the theories of oligopolistic behavior.

Oligopolistic behavior includes both competition and cooperation. Competition does not just mean that firms lower their prices. In oligopoly, firms typically compete more on other dimensions than they do on price. In the real world, we observe as much competition through innovation as we do through price. In computer hardware and software, firms race to see which will be the first to come out with a new product or which can obtain the patent on an innovation. Consumers are constantly being presented with upgrades and improvements to existing products as well as with brand new products. Pharmaceutical companies race to create new drugs. They don't compete on price, but rather on innovation. Such competition can take many forms. To analyze all of the behaviors we find in oligopoly would be too much of an undertaking here. What we want to do is to get a flavor of how firms in an oligopoly might behave. To do that, we'll consider two rather simple models—the kinked demand curve and the prisoner's dilemma.

2.a.1. The Kinked Demand Curve

All firms know the law of demand. Thus, they know that sales will rise if price is lowered because people will purchase more of all goods (the income effect) and will substitute away from the more expensive goods to purchase more of the less expensive goods (the substitution effect). But the firms in an oligopoly may not know the shape of the demand curve for their product because the shape depends on how the rivals react to one another. They have to predict how their competitors will respond to a price change in order to know what their demand curve looks like.

Let's consider the auto industry. Suppose General Motors's costs have fallen (its marginal-cost curve has shifted down) and the company is deciding whether to lower the prices on its cars. If GM did not have to consider how the other car companies would respond, it would simply lower the price in order to be sure that the new MC curve intersected the MR curve, as illustrated in Figure 6(a). But GM

FIGURE 6

The Kinked Demand Curve

If competitors do not follow price changes, the demand curve faced by an oligopolistic firm is the curve D_1 in Figures 6(a) and 6(b). If competitors do follow price changes, the demand curve faced by the firm is D_2 in 6(b). If competitors match price decreases but not price increases, then the firm faces a combination of the two demand curves. If competitors do not follow a price increase, then above the current price, P_1, the relevant demand curve is D_1. If competitors do follow a price decrease, then below price P_1 the relevant demand curve is D_2. The demand curve is the shaded combinations of the two demand curves; it has a kink at the current price. The resulting marginal-revenue curve is also a combination of the two marginal-revenue curves. The marginal-revenue curve is MR_1 to the left of the kink in the demand curve and MR_2 to the right of the kink. Between the two marginal-revenue curves is a gap. The firm produces where $MR = MC$. If the MC curve intersects the MR curve in the gap, the resulting price is P_1 and the resulting quantity produced is Q_1. If costs fall, as represented by a downward shift of MC_1 to MC_2, the price and quantity produced do not change.

(a) Competitors Do Not Follow Price Changes

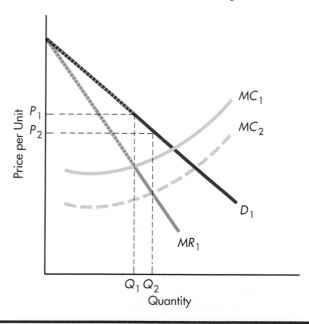

(b) Competitors Follow Price Changes

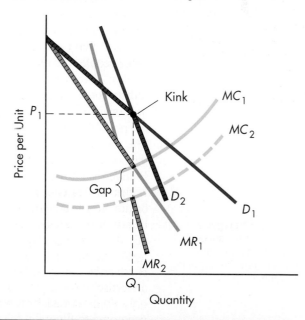

suspects that the demand and marginal-revenue curves in Figure 6(a) do not represent its true market situation. Instead GM believes that if it lowers the prices on its cars from their current level of P_1, the other auto companies will follow suit. If they also lower the price on their cars, the substitution effect for the GM cars does not occur; sales of GM cars might increase a little, but only because of the income effect. In other words, GM does not capture the market as indicated in Figure 6(b) by D_1 but finds the quantity demanded increasing along D_2 (below price P_1). Also, GM suspects that should it increase the price of its cars, none of the other auto companies would raise theirs. In this case, the price increase would mean substantially reduced sales because of both the income and substitution effects. The quantity demanded decreases, as indicated along D_1. Consequently, the demand curve for GM is a combination of D_1 and D_2. It is D_1 above P_1 and D_2 below P_1, a demand curve with a *kink*.

What should GM do? It should price where $MR = MC$. But the resulting marginal-revenue curve is given by a combination of MR_1 and MR_2. The MR_1 curve slopes down gently until reaching the quantity associated with the kink. As we move below the kink, the MR_2 curve becomes the appropriate marginal-revenue curve. Thus, the shaded portions of the two marginal-revenue curves combine to give the firm's marginal-revenue curve. Notice how GM's marginal-cost curves, MC_1 and MC_2, intersect the combined MR curves at the same price and quantity, P_1 and Q_1. Thus, GM's strategy is to do nothing: *not* to change price even though costs have changed.

The kinked demand curve is a very simplified model of real life. Nevertheless, it suggests how oligopolistic firms might behave. Because there are just a few firms and what one does significantly affects its rivals, firms tend not to change price very often. This is what the kink sort of tells us—that firms are reluctant to change price. The implication is that firms in an oligopoly compete on dimensions other than price. We see how this type of behavior might occur in the next model we consider, the prisoner's dilemma. The firms in an oligopoly might avoid price competition altogether and devote resources to nonprice competition. Even with nonprice competition, however, strategic behavior comes into play, as noted in the next section.

Game theory can illustrate ways in which oligopolistic firms interact. Game theory considers each firm a participant in a game where the winners are the firms with the greatest profit.

2.a.2. Prisoner's Dilemma

Consider the situation in which firms must decide whether to devote more resources to advertising. When a firm in any given industry advertises its product, its demand increases for two reasons. First, people who had not used that type of product before learn about it, and some will buy it. Second, other people who already consume a different brand of the same product may switch brands. The first effect boosts sales for the industry as a whole, while the second redistributes existing sales within the industry.

Consider the cigarette industry as an example and assume that Figure 7 illustrates the possible actions that two firms might undertake and the results of those actions. The top left rectangle represents the payoffs, or results, if both A and B advertise; the bottom left is where A advertises but B does not; the top right is the payoffs when B advertises but A does not; and the bottom right is the payoffs if neither advertises. If firm A can earn higher profits by advertising than by not advertising, whether or not firm B advertises, then firm A will surely advertise. This is referred to as a **dominant strategy**—a strategy that produces the best results no matter what strategy the opposing player follows. Firm A compares the left side of the matrix to the right side and sees that it earns more by advertising no matter what firm B does. If B advertises and A advertises, then A earns 70, but if B advertises and A does not advertise, it earns 40. If B does not advertise, then A earns 100 by advertising and only 80 by not advertising. The dominant strategy for firm A is to advertise. And according to Figure 7, the dominant strategy for firm B also is to advertise. Firm B

dominant strategy: a strategy that produces better results no matter what strategy the opposing firm follows

FIGURE 7

Prisoner's Dilemma

Figure 7 illustrates the dominant strategy game. The dominant strategy for firm A is to advertise. No matter what firm B does, firm A is better off advertising. If firm B does not advertise, firm A earns 80 not advertising and 100 advertising. If firm B does advertise, firm A earns 40 not advertising and 70 advertising. Similarly, firm B is better off advertising no matter what firm A does. Both A and B have dominant strategies—advertise.

	Firm A	
	Advertise	Not Advertise
Firm B Advertise	Firm A 70 Firm B 80	Firm A 40 Firm B 100
Not Advertise	Firm A 100 Firm B 50	Firm A 80 Firm B 90

will earn 80 by advertising and 50 by not advertising if A advertises. Firm B will earn 100 advertising, but only 90 not advertising if A does not advertise. But notice that both firms would be better off if neither advertised; firm A would earn 80 instead of 70, and firm B would earn 90 instead of 80. Yet, the firms cannot afford to *not* advertise because they would lose more if the other firm advertised and they didn't. This situation is known as the prisoner's dilemma; see the Economic Insight "The Prisoner's Dilemma" for a more complete description of why it has this name.

None of the cigarette manufacturers wants to do much advertising, for example. Yet strategic behavior suggests that they must. Firm A advertises, so firm B does also. Each ups the advertising ante. How can this expensive advertising competition be controlled? Each firm alone has no incentive to do it, since unilateral action will mean a significant loss of market share. But if they can ban advertising together or if the government passes a law banning cigarette advertising, all of the cigarette companies will be better off. In fact, a ban on cigarette advertising on television has been in effect since January 1, 1971. The ban was intended by the government as a means of reducing cigarette smoking—of helping the consumer. Yet who does this ban really benefit?

2.b. Cooperation

5. Why does cooperation among rivals occur most often in oligopolies?

If the firms in an oligopoly cooperate, they may all be better off. Because there are only a few firms in an oligopoly, the firms can communicate more easily than the many firms in a perfectly competitive or monopolistically competitive industry. This allows the oligopolistic firms to cooperate instead of competing.

Acting jointly allows firms to earn more profits than if they act independently or against each other. To avoid the destruction of strategic behavior, the few firms in an oligopoly can collude, or come to some agreement about price and output levels. Typically these agreements provide the members of the oligopoly higher profits and

The Prisoner's Dilemma

Strategic behavior characterizes oligopoly. Perhaps the most well-known example of strategic behavior occurs in what is called the prisoner's dilemma.

Two people have been arrested for a crime, but the evidence against them is weak. The sheriff keeps the prisoners separated and offers each a special deal. If one prisoner confesses, that prisoner can go free as long as only he confesses, and the other prisoner will get ten or more years in prison. If both prisoners confess, each will receive a reduced sentence of two years in jail. The prisoners know that if neither confesses, they will be cleared of all but a minor charge and will serve only two days in jail. The problem is that they do not know what deal the other is offered or if the other will take the deal.

The options available to the two prisoners are shown in the four cells of the figure. Prisoner B's options are shown along the horizontal direction and prisoner A's along the vertical direction. In the upper left cell is the result if both prisoners confess. In the lower left is the result if prisoner A does not confess but prisoner B does; in the upper right cell is the result of A's confessing but prisoner B's not

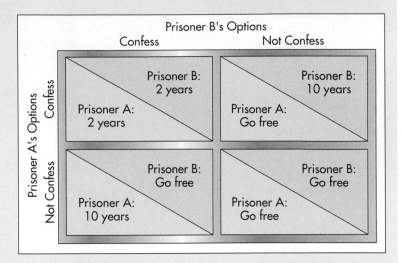

confessing; and in the lower right cell is the result when neither prisoner confesses. The dominant strategy for both prisoners is to confess and to receive two years of jail time.

If the prisoners had been loyal to each other, each would have received a much smaller penalty. Because both chose to confess, each is worse off than would have been the case if each had known what the other was doing. Yet, in the context of the interdependence of the decisions, each made the best choice.

---

thus raise prices to consumers. Collusion, which leads to secret cooperative agreements, is illegal in the United States, although it is acceptable in many other nations.

2.b.1. Price-Leadership Oligopoly   One way for firms to communicate without illegally colluding is to allow one firm to be the leader in changes in price or advertising activities. Once the leader makes a change, the others duplicate what the leader does. This action enables all firms to know exactly what their rivals will do. It eliminates a kink in the demand curve because both price increases and price decreases will be followed, and it avoids the prisoner's dilemma situation where excessive expenses are made on advertising or other activities. This type of oligopoly is called a *price-leadership oligopoly*.

The steel industry in the 1960s is an example of a dominant-firm price-leadership oligopoly. For many years, steel producers allowed U.S. Steel to set prices for the entire industry. The cooperation of the steel companies probably led to higher profits than would have occurred with rivalry. However, the absence of rivalry is said to be one reason for the decline of the steel industry in the United States. Price leadership removed the need for the firms to compete by maintaining and upgrading equipment and materials and by developing new technologies. As a result, foreign firms that chose not to behave as price followers emerged as more-sophisticated producers of steel than U.S. firms.

For many years airlines also relied on a price leader. In many cases the price leader in the airlines was not the dominant airline but instead one of the weaker or new airlines. In recent years, airlines have communicated less through a price leader and more through their computerized reservation system, according to the Justice Department.

cartel: an organization of independent firms whose purpose is to control and limit production and maintain or increase prices and profits

2.b.2. Cartels and Other Cooperative Mechanisms

A **cartel** is an organization of independent firms whose purpose is to control and limit production and maintain or increase prices and profits. A cartel can result from either formal or informal agreement among members. Like collusion, cartels are illegal in the United States. The cartel most people are familiar with is the Organization of Petroleum Exporting Countries (OPEC), a group of nations rather than a group of independent firms. During the 1970s, OPEC was able to coordinate oil production in such a way that it drove the market price of crude oil from $1.10 a barrel to $32 a barrel. For nearly eight years, each member of OPEC agreed to produce a certain, limited amount of crude oil as designated by the OPEC production committee. Then in the early 1980s, the cartel began to fall apart as individual members began to cheat on the agreement. Members began to produce more than their allocation in an attempt to increase profit. As each member of the cartel did this, the price of oil fell, reaching $12 per barrel in 1988.

OPEC has attempted to set oil prices at a level that will earn the member countries significant profits but not so high that oil exploration and production will be dramatically increased, but it has often found its policies subverted by world events. When Iraq invaded Kuwait in 1990, oil prices shot up but then were reduced as the other OPEC countries increased production and the Kuwaiti oil fields were repaired and brought back into production. Then in 2002, in anticipation of and during the U.S. and U.K. invasion of Iraq, oil prices rose again. In late 2003, oil production resumed and oil prices returned to earlier levels. Most of the fluctuations in oil prices of recent years have been due to the vagaries of world events, but some continue to be the result of policies of the OPEC nations.

Production quotas are not easy to maintain among different firms or different nations. Most cartels do not last very long because the members chisel on the agreements. If each producer thinks that it can increase its own production, and thus its profits, without affecting what the other producers do, all producers end up producing more than their assigned amounts; the price of the product declines and the cartel falls apart.

Economists have identified certain conditions that make it likely that a cartel will be stable. A cartel is likely to remain in force when:

- There are few firms in the industry.
- There are significant barriers to entry.
- An identical product is produced.
- There are few opportunities to keep actions secret.
- There are no legal barriers to sharing agreements.

2.b.3. The Theory of Cartels

In 1998, the U.S. Justice Department showed that ten firms held meetings is places as disparate as Vienna and Tokyo to set the price of the food additive sorbate in the global market and to allocate market shares. Federal officials said that the conspiracy affected $1 billion in sales made between 1979 and 1997. Although ten firms produce and sell sorbate, let's assume that there

FIGURE 8

Behavior of a Cartel

In Figure 8(a), the firms agree to act as a monopolist, setting the price where the monopolist would maximize profit and then sharing the resulting profits. When the cartel members act alone, as shown in Figure 8(b), they maximize profit by setting a lower price and selling to fewer customers than was the case when they acted as monopolists. The result is a lower profit.

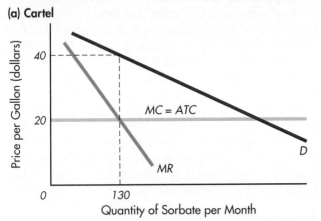

(a) Cartel

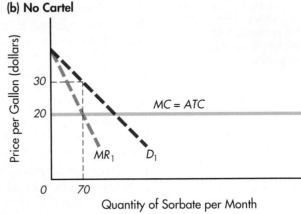

(b) No Cartel

are just two in order to show how and why the firms might fix prices. In Figure 8, we've drawn the market demand curve, D, and we've drawn the marginal and average costs as being constant. If the two firms were a monopolist rather than being two firms, the monopolist's marginal-revenue curve would be as shown in Figure 8(a), intersecting the marginal-cost curve at a quantity of 130 and a price of $40. If the two companies act as one, they will select the monopoly price of $40 and quantity of 130 and then split the market, with each having 65. The average cost is $20, so each firm earns a profit of $1,300 ($20 × 65).

If instead the two firms compete with each other, then their demand curves will lie inside the market or monopoly demand curve. Figure 8(b) shows the demand and marginal revenue for firm 1. Firm 2 is identical to firm 1. As a result of competition, each firm sets a lower price and serves more customers. The profit each firm makes is $700 ($10 × 70). When the two firms compete, their combined profits are $1,400; when they collude by fixing the price and setting the quantities each will produce, their profits are $1,300 each or $2,600 combined.

The extra profits from collusion create an incentive for firms to cheat on their agreements. Suppose that one of the firms decides to sell more than its allotted quantity of 65. The higher quantity will be sold only if the price is lower or if the other firm serves fewer customers. Either case hurts at least one of the colluding firms, and the cartel breaks apart.

Because there is a strong incentive for firms who are members of a cartel or who are colluding to cheat on agreements, a way to stop cheaters, to penalize them, must be found if the cartel is to remain in place. In most cartels, the strongest member takes over and polices it. In OPEC, it is Saudi Arabia that serves as police. When a member does not adhere to the prescribed quantity, Saudi Arabia opens its valves and floods the market with petroleum. Saudi Arabia can do this because it is the nation with the largest supply of petroleum. The flooded market means a lower price and thus lower profits for all countries. With the drug cartels of Colombia and Mexico, one family will police the agreement; cheaters typically end up dead. Without a policing authority, the cartel will fall apart.

Even though cartels are illegal in the United States, a few have been sanctioned by the government. The National Collegiate Athletic Association (NCAA) is a cartel of colleges and universities. It sets rules of behavior and enforces those rules through a governing board. Member schools are placed on probation or their programs are dismantled when they violate the agreement. The citrus cartel, composed of citrus growers in California and Arizona, enforces its actions through its governing board. Sunkist Growers Inc., a cooperative of many growers, represents more than half of the California and Arizona production and also plays an important role in enforcing the rules of the cartel.

2.b.4. Facilitating Practices

facilitating practices: actions by oligopolistic firms that can contribute to cooperation and collusion even though the firms do not formally agree to cooperate

cost-plus/markup pricing: a pricing policy whereby a firm computes its average costs of producing a product and then sets the price at some percentage above this cost

most-favored customer (MFC): a customer who receives a guarantee of the lowest price and all product features for a certain period of time

Actions by firms can contribute to cooperation and collusion even though the firms do not formally agree to cooperate. Such actions are called **facilitating practices.** Pricing policies can leave the impression that firms are explicitly fixing prices, or cooperating, when in fact they are merely following the same strategies. For instance, the use of **cost-plus/markup pricing** tends to bring about similar if not identical pricing behavior among rival firms. If firms set prices by determining the average cost of an item and adding a fixed markup to the cost, they would be engaging in cost-plus pricing. If all firms face the same cost curves, then all firms will set the same prices. If costs decrease, then all firms will lower prices the same amount and at virtually the same time. Such pricing behavior is common in the grocery business.

Another practice that leads to implicit cooperation is the most-favored-customer policy. Often the time between purchase and delivery of a product is quite long. To avoid the possibility that customer A purchases a product at one price and then learns that customer B purchased the product at a lower price or benefited from product features that were unavailable to customer A, a producer will guarantee that customer A will receive the lowest price and all features for a certain period of time. Customer A is thus a **most-favored customer (MFC).**

The most-favored-customer policy actually gives firms an incentive not to lower prices even in the face of reduced demand. A firm that lowers the price of its product must then give rebates to all most-favored customers, which forces all other firms with most-favored-customer policies to do the same. In addition, the MFC policy allows a firm to collect information on what its rivals are doing. Customers will return products for a rebate when another firm offers the same product for a lower price.

Consider the behavior of firms that produced antiknock additives for gasoline from 1974 to 1979. Lead-based antiknock compounds had been used in the refining of gasoline since the 1920s. From the 1920s until 1948, the Ethyl Corporation was the sole domestic producer of the compounds. In 1948, DuPont entered the industry. Then PPG Industries followed in 1961, and Nalco in 1964. Beginning in 1973, the demand for lead-based antiknock compounds decreased dramatically. However, because each company had most-favored-customer clauses, high prices were maintained even as demand for the product declined.

A most-favored-customer policy discourages price decreases because it requires producers to lower prices retroactively with rebates. If all rivals provide all buyers with most-favored-customer clauses, a high price is likely to be stabilized in the industry.

1. Oligopoly is a market structure in which there are so few firms that each must take into account what the others do, entry is difficult, and either undifferentiated or differentiated products are produced.
2. Interdependence and strategic behavior characterize an oligopolistic firm.
3. The shape of the demand curve and the marginal-revenue curve facing an oligopolist depends on how rival firms react to changes in price and product.
4. The kinked demand curve is one example of how oligopolistic firms might react to price changes. The kink occurs because rivals follow price cuts but not price increases.
5. The prisoner's dilemma is an example of how competition among firms that are interdependent can result in an outcome that is not the best for the competing firms.
6. Oligopolistic firms have incentives to cooperate. In a price-leadership oligopoly, one firm determines the price and quantity, knowing that all other firms will follow suit. The price leader is usually the dominant firm in the industry.
7. Collusion, making a secret cooperative agreement, is illegal in the United States. Cartels, also illegal in the United States, rest on explicit cooperation achieved through formal agreement.
8. The incentive for cartel members to cheat typically leads to the collapse of the cartel. To minimize cheating, one member must police the others.
9. Facilitating practices implicitly encourage cooperation in an industry.

3. Summary of Market Structures

We have now discussed each of the four market structures in some detail. Table 2 summarizes the characteristics of each model and the main predictions yielded by

TABLE 2

Summary of Perfect Competition, Monopoly, Monopolistic Competition, and Oligopoly

	Perfect Competition	Monopoly	Monopolistic Competition	Oligopoly
Number of firms	Many	One	Many	Few
Type of product	Undifferentiated	One	Differentiated	Undifferentiated or differentiated
Entry conditions	Easy	Difficult or impossible	Easy	Difficult
Demand curve for firm	Horizontal (perfectly elastic	Downward sloping	Downward sloping	Downward sloping
Price and marginal cost	$MC = P$	$MC < P$	$MC < P$	$MC < P$
Long-run profit	Zero	Yes	Zero	Depends on whether entry occurs

that model. The model of perfect competition predicts that firms will produce at a point where price and marginal cost are the same (at the bottom of the average-total-cost curve) and profit will be zero in the long run. The model of monopoly predicts that price will exceed marginal cost and that the firm can earn positive economic profit in the long run. With monopolistic competition, price will exceed marginal cost and the firm will not produce at the bottom point of the average-total-cost curve, but this is due to the consumer's desire for product differentiation. In the long run, the firm in monopolistic competition will earn a normal profit. In oligopoly, a firm may be able to earn above-normal profit for a long time—as long as entry can be restricted. In oligopoly, price exceeds marginal cost, and the firm does not operate at the bottom of the average-total-cost curve.

Under perfect competition, consumers purchase products at the lowest possible price; there is no advertising, no excessive overhead, and no warranties or guarantees. Under monopoly, people purchase a single product and advertising is virtually nonexistent. With monopolistic competition and oligopoly, advertising commonly plays an important role.

Summary

❓ What is monopolistic competition?

1. Monopolistic competition is a market structure in which many firms are producing a slightly different product and entry is easy. *§1*

2. Monopolistically competitive firms will earn a normal profit in the long run. *§1.a.2*

❓ What behavior is most common in monopolistic competition?

3. Entry occurs in monopolistically competitive industries through the introduction of a slightly different product. *§1.a*

4. A monopolistically competitive firm will produce less output and charge a higher price than an identical perfectly competitive firm if demand and costs are assumed to be the same. *§1.b*

❓ What is oligopoly?

5. Oligopoly is a market structure in which a few large firms produce identical or slightly different products and entry is difficult but not impossible. The firms are interdependent. *§2*

❓ In what form does rivalry occur in an oligopoly?

6. The prisoner's dilemma illustrates an outcome where competition among interdependent firms results in an outcome that is less than the best for each firm. *§2.a.2*

7. Strategic behavior characterizes oligopoly. Each oligopolist must watch the actions of other oligopolists in the industry. *§2.b*

8. The kinked demand curve results when firms follow a price decrease but do not follow a price increase. *§2.b.1*

❓ Why does cooperation among rivals occur most often in oligopolies?

9. The small number of firms in oligopoly and the interdependence of these firms creates the situation where the firms are better off if they cooperate (as in the prisoner's dilemma). *§2.b.2, 2.c*

10. Price leadership is another type of strategic behavior. One firm determines price for the entire industry. All other firms follow the leader in increasing and decreasing prices. The dominant firm in the industry is most likely to be the price leader. *§2.c.1*

11. Practices like collusion and cartels minimize profit-reducing rivalry and ensure cooperation. Both are illegal in the United States but acceptable in many other nations. *§2.c.2*

12. Cost-plus pricing ensures that firms with the same costs will charge the same prices. The most-favored-customer policy guarantees a customer that the price he or she paid for a product will not be lowered for another customer. Cost-plus pricing and the most-favored-customer policy are facilitating practices. *§2.c.3*

Key Terms

strategic behavior *§2.a*

game theory *§2.a*

dominant strategy *§2.a.2*

cartel *§2.b.2*

facilitating practices *§2.b.4*

cost-plus/markup pricing *§2.b.4*

most-favored customer (MFC) *§2.b.4*

Exercises

1. Disney, Universal, and MGM, among others, have movie studios in Hollywood. Each of these major studios also has one or several subsidiary studios. Disney, for example, has Touchstone. What market structure best describes these movie production companies? Why would each studio have subsidiary studios? Consider the movies that have come out under Disney and those that have come out under Touchstone. Are they different?

2. Suppose that Disney was experiencing above-normal profits. If Disney is a member of a monopolistically competitive industry, what would you predict would occur over time to its demand curve (the demand curve for Disney movies)? Suppose that Disney is a member of an oligopoly. How would this change your answer?

3. Why is the monopolistically competitive industry said to be inefficient? Suppose that you counted the higher price the consumer pays for the monopolistically competitive firm's product as part of consumer surplus. Would that change the conclusion regarding the efficiency of monopolistic competition?

4. Why might some people claim that the breakfast cereal industry is monopolistically competitive but that the automobile industry is an oligopoly? In both cases, about eight to ten firms dominate the industry.

5. The graph that follows shows an individual firm in long-run equilibrium. In which market structure is this firm operating? Explain. Compare the long-run quantity and price to those of a perfectly competitive firm. What accounts for the difference? Is the equilibrium price greater than, equal to, or less than marginal cost? Why, or why not?

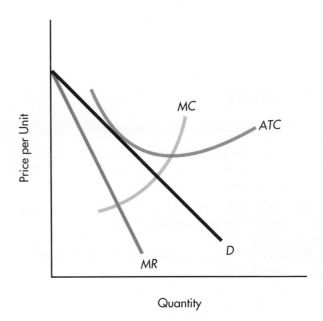

6. Explain what is meant by strategic behavior. How does the kinked demand curve describe strategic behavior?

7. The NCAA is described as a cartel. In what way is it a cartel? What is the product being produced? How does the cartel stay together?

8. Almost every town has at least one funeral home even if the number of deaths could not possibly keep the funeral home busy. What market structure does the funeral home best exemplify? Use the firm's demand and cost curves and long-run equilibrium position to explain the fact that the funeral home can handle more business than it has. (*Hint:* Is the firm operating at the bottom of the average-total-cost curve?)

9. What is the cost to a firm in an oligopoly that fails to take rivals' actions into account? Suppose the firm operates along demand curve D_1, shown below, as if no firms will follow its lead in price cuts or price rises. In fact, however, other firms do follow the price cuts and the true demand curve below price P_1 lies below D_1. If the firm sets a price lower than P_1, what happens?

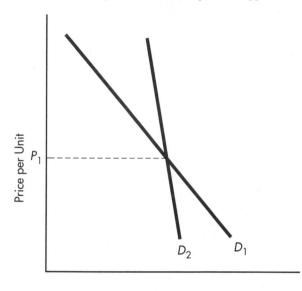

10. Suppose the following demand schedule exists for a firm in monopolistic competition. Suppose the marginal cost is a constant $70. How much will the firm produce? Is this a long- or short-run situation? Suppose the firm is earning above-normal profit. What will occur to this demand schedule?

Price	Quantity	Price	Quantity
$100	1	$ 70	5
$ 95	2	$ 55	6
$ 88	3	$ 40	7
$ 80	4	$ 22	8

11. The cement industry is an example of an undifferentiated oligopoly. The automobile industry is a differentiated oligopoly. Which of these two is most likely to advertise? Why?

12. The South American cocaine industry consists of several "families" that obtain the raw material, refine it, and distribute it in the United States. There are only about three large families, but there are several small families. What market structure does the industry most closely resemble? What predictions based on the market-structure models can be made about the cocaine business? How do you explain the lack of wars among the families?

13. Use the payoff matrix below for the following exercises. The payoff matrix indicates the profit outcome that corresponds to each firm's pricing strategy.

		Firm A's Price	
		$20	**$15**
	$20	Firm A earns $40 profit. Firm B earns $37 profit.	Firm A earns $35 profit. Firm B earns $39 profit.
Firm B's Price			
	$15	Firm A earns $49 profit. Firm B earns $30 profit.	Firm A earns $38 profit. Firm B earns $35 profit.

a. Firms A and B are members of an oligopoly. Explain the interdependence that exists in oligopolies using the payoff matrix facing the two firms.

b. Assuming that the firms cooperate, what is the solution to the problem facing the firms?

c. Given your answer to part b, explain why cooperation would be mutually beneficial and then explain why one of the firms might cheat.

14. What would occur if any maker of aspirin could put a Bayer Aspirin label on its product?

Take the ACE Practice Test for this chapter to review the important concepts and get immediate feedback with answers.

economics.college.hmco.com/students

Authorities Gather to Combat Warring Drug Cartels

Hundreds of special anti-drug forces have converged on northern Mexico to patrol what has become a bloody battleground in a war between powerful drug cartels just south of the Texas border.

Members of the Mexican Federal Preventive Police Force—Mexico's version of the U.S. National Guard—began arriving from Mexico City about a week ago in response to 67 gangland-style killings in the region since January.

The victims were workers and confidantes, group leaders and financiers, of the drug cartels, police say.

The power play ricochets almost daily between the region's two key trade cities, Monterrey and Nuevo Laredo, in the Mexican states of Taumalipas and Nuevo Leon, both of which border Texas.

Police say gangs from Juarez and Matamoros are pushing into Monterrey and Nuevo Laredo—and smaller groups from those cities are pushing back.

That, officials say, has led to the largest escalation of violence this region has seen in years.

To combat it, almost 200 armed federal soldiers and intelligence agents are patrolling the streets of Nuevo Laredo across the Rio Grande from Laredo. The city has seen 45 killings attributed to the cartel wars since January.

About 130 miles to the south, 300 more soldiers are in Monterrey, the capital of Nuevo Leon—where 10 men were assassinated in August alone and at least 22 have been slain since January.

The two cities have taken on the look of police states. Soldiers in gray fatigues and black vests stand guard on corners and ride in the backs of pick-ups, armed with assault rifles.

Federal intelligence officers don black ski masks and raid houses searching for marijuana, heroin and cocaine operations.

The officers are working with U.S. Drug Enforcement Administration agents, officials said.

"One thing that we're doing better now than we ever have before is working jointly with our Mexican counterparts," said Will Glaspy, spokesman for the DEA in Washington.

Authorities expect the soldiers to stay in Nuevo Laredo and Monterrey at least for the next month.

"It's starting to calm down a little," said Martin Gutierrez Gomez, who heads the federal prosecutor's office in Nuevo Laredo. "They're working directly with us, and they are everywhere."

One Nuevo Laredo curio-shop owner, a lifelong resident who asked not to be named, said the feeling of battle in the air is palpable.

"There have been a lot of things happening here lately," he said, "but it's between them. If you're not involved, you're not in any real danger."

The main aggressor, according to Mexican and U.S. agents, is the Osiel Cardenas–led group known as the Gulf Coast Cartel, based in Matamoros across the river from Brownsville, Texas.

Cardenas has a $2 million bounty on his head by the DEA, federal drug and assault charges in both countries, and is on Mexico's 10 most-wanted list.

Experts say Cardenas is moving into Monterrey and Nuevo Laredo because the cities are in strategic locations and have yet to be taken over by larger cartels.

KAREN BROOKS

Source: Copyright 2002 Knight Ridder/ Tribune News Service.

Fort Worth Star-Telegram/October 5, 2002

Commentary

The article describes a bloody battleground in a drug war—67 gangland-style killings since January, where the victims were workers and confidantes, group leaders and financiers, of the drug cartels. Why are illegal drug suppliers referred to so often as cartels? Why would competing cartels go to war? A cartel is a way for competitive firms to obtain more profits. The firms combine to form a monopoly and agree to divide the profits.

In the chapter, we discussed the theory of cartels and showed why interdependent firms might want to form a cartel. Let's use that discussion to answer the questions posed above.

The accompanying figure shows the market demand curve, D, along with the market supply curve. We'll assume that there are only two groups supplying the drugs. The firms compete to gain profits. Each of the firms has a demand that lies to the left of the market demand, D_1. This means the quantity produced is determined where $MR = MC$ and the price is set according to demand, $Q = 100$ and $P = \$20$.

If the two groups combine into a cartel rather than competing, they will select the monopoly price, \$30, and quantity, 150, and then split the market. By colluding or forming a cartel, the two groups earn more profit than they do if they act independently and compete with each other.

Having colluded and earned more profits than if they had competed, the drug cartel members may think that by selling even more drugs, their profits

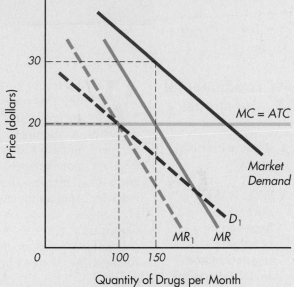

will rise more. Suppose that one of the cartel members decides to sell more than its allotted quantity of 75. The higher quantity will be sold only if the price is lower or the other members reduce their sales. Either case hurts at least one of the cartel members, and the cartel breaks apart.

Because there is strong incentive for firms that are members of the drug cartel to cheat on agreements, a way to stop cheaters must be found. With the drug cartels of Colombia and Mexico, one family will do the policing. This policing is what results in the gangland-style violence and drug wars.

CHAPTER 27

Antitrust and Regulation

? Fundamental Questions

1. **What is antitrust policy?**

2. **What is the difference between economic regulation and social regulation?**

W hy would government intervene in the operation of a business? One reason that government might intervene would be to promote competitive behavior. It is illegal for businesses in the United States (and many other countries) to attempt to monopolize an industry or to conspire with other firms to compete "unfairly." Companies engage in monopolistic behavior when they try to dominate a market, perhaps by forcing competitors out of business or by restricting entry into a market. The government's *antitrust policy* is aimed at controlling this behavior. Another tool available to the government to control the behavior of firms is *economic regulation*—price and output guidelines for individual industries. Government also uses *social regulation* to establish health and safety standards for the workplace and products, and environmental regulations for protecting the environment. We discuss these policies in this chapter. ■

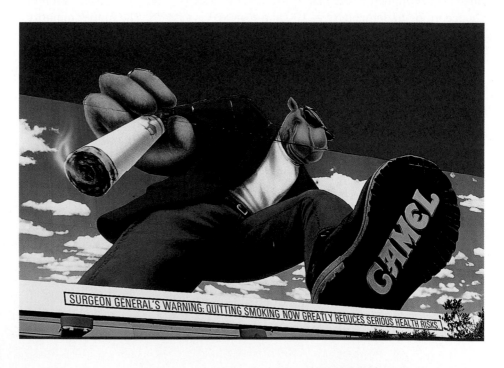

1. Antitrust Policy

In section 5.a of the chapter "Monopoly," we compared the outcome of monopoly with that of a perfectly competitive market. We found that in the long run, while the perfectly competitive firm operates at the minimum point of the long-run average-total-cost curve (the most efficient point of production) and price is the lowest it can be, the monopolist produces less than the most efficient output and charges a higher price. This inefficiency on the part of the monopolist results in a transfer of social surplus from the consumer to the producer and a reduction in total surplus by the amount of the deadweight loss. In section 2 of the chapter "Monopolistic Competition and Oligopoly," we discussed how cartels may form. A cartel is an attempt on the part of a few firms to join forces and act as if they were a monopolist. The cartel, like the monopolist, results in output and price that are not efficient. The inefficiencies of monopoly and cartels are what lead to government policies to limit and restrict the activities of large firms. The principal approach that governments use to address monopolization is antitrust.

antitrust policy: government policies and programs designed to control the growth of monopoly and enhance competition

Antitrust policy is the term used to describe government policies and programs designed to control the growth of monopoly and prevent firms from engaging in undesirable practices.

1.a. Antitrust and Business Activities

As noted in Table 1, three laws define the government's approach to antitrust policy—the Sherman, Clayton, and Federal Trade Commission Acts. These antitrust laws are intended to limit the creation and behavior of *trusts,* or combinations of independent firms. Today we refer to the process of combining firms as *mergers* and the resulting firms as large firms or corporations. Antitrust policy limits what these large firms can do. For instance, the firms cannot together decide to fix prices, they cannot restrict competition, and they cannot combine or become trusts if the resulting firm would have too great an influence in the market.

TABLE 1

Antitrust Acts

Sherman Antitrust Act (1890)
Section 1 outlaws contracts and conspiracies in restraint of trade.
Section 2 forbids monopolization and attempts to monopolize.

Clayton Antitrust Act (1914)
Section 2, as amended by the Robinson-Patman Act (1936), bans price discrimination that substantially lessens competition or injures particular competitors.
Section 3 prohibits certain practices that might keep other firms from entering an industry or competing with an existing firm.
Section 7, as amended by the Celler-Kefauver Act (1950), outlaws mergers that substantially lessen competition.

Federal Trade Commission Act (1914)
Section 5, as amended by the Wheeler-Lea Act (1938), prohibits unfair methods of competition and unfair or deceptive acts.

1.b. Interpretation

Antitrust policy is the responsibility of two government agencies, the Antitrust Division of the Department of Justice and the Federal Trade Commission. These agencies try to distinguish beneficial from harmful business practices by focusing on *unreasonable* monopolistic activities. What is unreasonable? The answer has varied as the interpretation of the statutes by the courts and government authorities has changed. There have been several distinct phases of antitrust policy in the United States, as illustrated in Figure 1. The first began with passage of the Sherman Antitrust Act in 1890 and lasted until about 1914. In this period, litigation was infrequent. The courts used a **rule of reason** to judge firms' actions: being a monopoly or attempting to monopolize was not in itself illegal; to be illegal, an action had to be unreasonable in a competitive sense, and the anticompetitive effects had to be demonstrated.

The second phase of antitrust policy began in 1914 with the passage of the Clayton Antitrust Act and the Federal Trade Commission Act. Operating under these two acts, the courts used the **per se rule** to judge firms' actions: activities that were potentially monopolizing tactics were illegal; the mere existence of these activities was sufficient evidence to lead to a guilty verdict.

Although the courts define the standard to be applied to antitrust cases, the administration in office appoints judges and defines the degree to which antitrust policy will be enforced. In the 1980s and through the Reagan and George H. W. Bush administrations, the courts returned to the looser rule-of-reason standard. The only tactic that was deemed illegal was price fixing—rival firms could not determine prices by agreement; they had to allow prices to be set by demand and supply. Other than that, firms could do just about anything to enhance their profitability. When Clinton became president, an attempt was made to return to the tighter standards. More money was allocated to antitrust enforcement, more lawyers were hired, and more cases were brought.

rule of reason: the rule that to be illegal, an action must be unreasonable in a competitive sense and the anticompetitive effects must be demonstrated

per se rule: actions that could be anticompetitive are intrinsically illegal

---

FIGURE 1

Phases of Antitrust Interpretation

The degree to which antitrust law has been enforced has varied over the years. With the Sherman Act of 1890, the government formally began antitrust policy. But enforcement was lax, based on a rule of reason, until about 1914. Between 1914 and the early 1980s, strict enforcement based on a per se rule was used. With the Reagan and Bush administrations, enforcement was relaxed again to the rule-of-reason standard. The Clinton administration tightened enforcement.

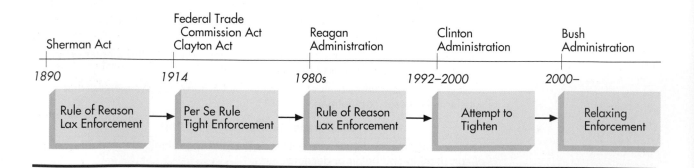

With the election of George W. Bush, the use of antitrust reverted to the approach taken in the Reagan administration. Standards were loosened and antitrust actions reduced. But, after the corporate scandals of 2000–2002 involving Enron, WorldCom, Tyco, and other companies, the government's actions toward large businesses were scrutinized more carefully, particularly by the Securities and Exchange Commission (SEC), which is responsible for financial dealings involving public companies in the United States. (We discuss the SEC in section 3.)

1.c. Procedures

Action against alleged violators of the antitrust statutes may be initiated by the U.S. Department of Justice, by the Federal Trade Commission (FTC), or by private plaintiffs. The Justice Department focuses on the Sherman Antitrust Act. The FTC focuses on the Federal Trade Commission and Clayton Antitrust Acts. Private plaintiffs (consumers and businesses) may sue on the basis of any of the statutes except the Federal Trade Commission Act. Since 1941, the FTC and the Justice Department together have filed nearly 2,800 cases, and since 1970, private suits have far outnumbered those filed by the Justice Department and the FTC combined.

1.d. Remedies

Private plaintiffs who prove their injuries can receive compensation up to three times the amount of the damages caused by the action. The Justice Department and the FTC do not obtain treble damages but can impose substantial penalties. They can force firms to break up through dissolution or divestiture, and criminal actions can be filed by the Justice Department for violations of the Sherman Act. A guilty finding can result in fines and prison sentences.

1.e. Demonstration of Antitrust Violations

Price fixing is by definition illegal—there is no justification for it. Other aspects of the antitrust statutes are not as clear-cut and are, therefore, difficult to prove. For instance, Section 2 of the Sherman Act outlaws "monopolization" but does not forbid monopolies. Monopoly itself is allowed. *To monopolize* or *to attempt to monopolize* constitutes a violation. If the firm attempts to preserve its monopoly by activities that restrict entry, then the firm may be guilty of a Section 2 violation.

The first step in enforcing an antitrust policy is to define market concentration. Government regulations often apply only to large businesses, and antitrust policies are typically directed toward large firms. The basis for the focus on large firms comes from the four market structure models—perfect competition, monopolistic competition, oligopoly, and monopoly—which suggest that the fewer the number of firms controlling the production in an industry, the greater the chance of collusive activity and other behavior designed to monopolize a market. And under monopoly and oligopoly, it is likely that consumers will pay more and firms produce less and earn greater profits than they would if the firms were small, perfect competitors. So the government focuses on larger firms and cases in which a few firms dominate an industry. Measures of size and influence are intended to provide information about market structures.

The most commonly used measure of size and influence is called the **Herfindahl index.** The Herfindahl index is a measure of **concentration**—the degree to which a

Herfindahl index: a measure of concentration calculated as the sum of the squares of the market share of each firm in an industry

concentration: the degree to which a few firms control the output and pricing decisions in a market

few firms control the output and pricing decisions in a market.[1] The Herfindahl index of concentration is defined as the sum of the squared market shares of each firm in the industry:

$$\text{Herfindahl index} = (S_1)^2 + (S_2)^2 + \cdots + (S_n)^2$$

where S refers to the market share of the firm, the subscripts refer to the firms, and there are n firms. The higher the Herfindahl index number, the more concentrated the industry.

An industry in which each of five firms has 20 percent of the market would have a Herfindahl index value of 2,000:

$$(20)^2 + (20)^2 + (20)^2 + (20)^2 + (20)^2 = 2,000$$

If the largest firm had 88 percent of the market and each of the others 3 percent, the Herfindahl index value would be 7,780:

$$(88)^2 + (3)^2 + (3)^2 + (3)^2 + (3)^2 = 7,780$$

The higher number indicates a much more concentrated market. As you can see from these examples, the Herfindahl index takes into account the size distribution of the firms in an industry. The idea is that an industry in which there is one dominant firm will be quite different from one in which there are several firms of equal size.

In 1982, 1984, and 1992, the Justice Department issued guidelines on market concentration and competition to inform businesses where the government would be especially likely to scrutinize activities. It stated that industries with Herfindahl indexes below 1,000 are considered *highly competitive;* those with indexes between 1,000 and 1,800 are *moderately competitive;* and those with indexes above 1,800 are *highly concentrated.*

Using the Herfindahl index to gauge the extent to which a few firms dominate a market sounds simple, but it is not. Before the concentration of an industry can be calculated, there must be some definition of the market. In a $100 billion market, an $80 billion firm would have an 80 percent market share. But in a $1,000 billion market, an $80 billion firm would have only an 8 percent market share. The Herfindahl index for the former would exceed 2,000, but for the latter it would be less than 1,000. Obviously, antitrust plaintiffs (those accusing a firm of attempting to monopolize a market) would want the market defined as narrowly as possible so that the alleged monopolizer would be seen to have a large market share. Conversely, defendants (those accused of monopolization) would argue for broadly defined markets in order to give the appearance that they possess a very small market share.

For example, Coca-Cola, Dr Pepper, PepsiCo, and Seven-Up are usually identified as producers of carbonated soft drinks (CSD). These firms provide bottlers with the concentrate that is used to make the drinks. Would CSD be the appropriate market in which to assess the competitive consequences of a merger, or should the market be more widely defined—perhaps to encompass all potable liquids (fruit juices, milk, coffee, tea, etc.)? In an actual merger case, the market definition was determined through interviews with CSD company executives. The executives indicated that they believed their primary competitors were other CSD producers. Their pricing and marketing strategies were made with other CSD producers in mind—not, as claimed by the defendant, by considering how the sellers of all potable drinks would

---

[1]The four-firm concentration ratio is another commonly used measured of concentration, but it has come under criticism because it does not account for the size distribution of firms. It merely divides the total output of the four largest firms by the total market output.

react. The interviews also revealed that many CSD industry executives thought that they could collectively raise the retail prices of carbonated soft drinks by as much as 10 percent with no fear of consumers switching to other beverages. That argument had implications for the definition of the market. If sellers can collectively raise the price by 10 percent without causing consumers to switch to other products, then those sellers represent the lion's share of the market. However, if consumers switch as a result of the price increase, then the market must be more broadly defined to include the substitutes that consumers move to.

When the market and market shares have been defined, the next task is to establish intent. The ease or difficulty with which intent can be established depends on whether the per se rule or the rule-of-reason standard is being used.

1.f. Concentration and Business Policy from a Global Perspective

Concentration measures and the Justice Department guidelines are often defined for production only within the United States, and this can present a misleading picture. For instance, the Herfindahl index in the United States for automobiles is very high, but if it took foreign competition into account, it would be significantly lower. In Sweden, two cars are produced, Volvo and Saab, and the Herfindahl index is greater than 5,000. That figure is also misleading, however, for Volvo and Saab account for only about 30 percent of all automobiles sold in Sweden. An appropriate policy measure must take into account all close substitutes, whether or not they are domestically produced. In addition, it must account for firms producing in more than one nation, the multinationals. The Herfindahl index may not provide a good indication of the competitive situation prevailing in an industry if it does not account for these factors or for the different ways in which governments treat their businesses—actions that are legal in one country may be illegal in another, for instance. Governments also restrict the imports of some goods and services, thereby affecting the number of substitutes available to domestic consumers. The definition of a market did not include worldwide factors until the early 1980s. From then until the early 1990s, market definition could include worldwide factors, but the United States would not apply antitrust sanctions against some action or restrict mergers unless they were deemed to harm U.S. consumers. In 1992, the United States extended its policies to include harm to either U.S. consumers or U.S. firms.

Compared to other countries, the United States is quite restrictive in terms of allowing certain types of business behavior and quite unrestrictive in placing limits on the importation of goods and services. When the per se rule was emerging in the United States during the 1920s and 1930s, most European nations had no antitrust laws at all, and cartels flourished. Today, many nations support cartels and cooperative behavior that is illegal in the United States. Some of these same nations are very restrictive in the importation of goods. Japan, for instance, allows, even supports, systems of cartels domestically while limiting the inflow of foreign-produced goods and services relative to the United States.

RECAP

1. Antitrust policy in the United States is based on the Sherman, Clayton, and Federal Trade Commission Acts.

2. The enforcement of antitrust policy has evolved through several phases. The first followed the Sherman Act in 1890 and extended to 1914. During this period, the rule-of-reason standard dictated policy. The second phase started

with the Clayton and Federal Trade Commission Acts in 1914 and lasted through the 1970s. During this period, the per se rule dictated policy. In the 1980s, most practices were considered to be part of the competitive process. In the early 1990s, an attempt was made to return to stricter enforcement.

3. Antitrust policy encompasses business actions such as pricing, advertising, restraint of trade, supplier relationships, and mergers.

4. If two or more rivals combine, it is called a merger.

5. Antitrust policy in the United States is stricter than that in other nations.

2. Regulation

2. What is the difference between economic regulation and social regulation?

The justification given for antitrust policy is that it should enhance the competitive environment—that is, it should create a "level playing field" on which firms may compete. When the competitive environment cannot be enhanced, such as in the case of a natural monopoly, where cost conditions lead to a sole supplier, then regulation is used to ensure that price and output are more beneficial for consumers than the levels that the monopolist would set without government influence. Regulation of natural monopolies is far from the only type of government regulation that occurs, however. Regulation of industries that are not natural monopolies is also widespread in the United States. This regulation has a number of different rationales, ranging from the protection of the health and safety of the general public to the protection of the health of a particular industry.

There are two categories of regulation, economic and social regulation. **Economic regulation** refers to the prescribing of prices and output levels for both natural monopolies and industries that are not natural monopolies. Economic regulation is specific, applying to a particular industry or line of business. **Social regulation** refers to prescribed performance standards, workplace health and safety standards, emission levels, and a variety of output and job standards that apply across several industries.

economic regulation: the prescription of price and output for a specific industry

social regulation: the prescribing of health, safety, performance, and environmental standards that apply across several industries

2.a. Regulation of Monopoly

Monopoly is inefficient; perfect competition is efficient. This comparison between monopoly and perfect competition has provided the basis for attempting to make monopolies behave more like perfectly competitive firms. Most natural monopolies are regulated by some level of government. In particular, the prices or rates that public utilities such as telephone companies, natural gas companies, and electricity suppliers can charge is determined by a federal, state, or local regulatory commission or board.

Figure 2 shows the demand, marginal-revenue, long-run average-total-cost, and long-run marginal-cost curves for a natural monopoly. The huge economies of scale mean that it would be inefficient to have many small firms supply the product. Yet producing at $MR = MC$ and setting a price of P_m from the demand curve yields too little output and too much profit for the firm, in comparison to the perfectly competitive result. In addition, since price is greater than marginal cost, resources are not being allocated efficiently. In fact, too few resources are devoted to this product—too few because if more was produced, MC would equal price. Can regulation solve this problem?

FIGURE 2

Natural Monopoly and Regulation

The demand, marginal-revenue, and long-run average-total-cost and marginal-cost curves for a natural monopoly are shown. The huge economies of scale mean that it would be inefficient to have many small firms supply the product. Yet, producing at $MR = MC$ and setting a price of P_m from the demand curve yields too small an output and too much profit for the firm, in comparison to the perfectly competitive result. Too few resources are devoted to this product—too few because if more was produced, MC would equal price. To achieve allocative efficiency (giving consumers the goods they most want), the regulatory agency must attempt to have the monopolist set a price equal to marginal cost. This price would be P_r. The monopolist would then produce at quantity Q_r. The problem with the regulated price P_r is that the revenues do not cover average costs. The fair-rate-of-return price is set to allow the monopolist a normal profit. The price corresponding to the normal profit is the one where demand and average total costs are equal, P_f.

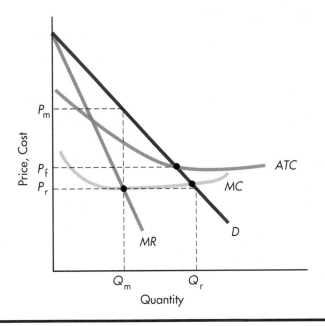

If the objective of the regulatory commission is to achieve allocative efficiency (giving consumers the goods they most want), the commission must attempt to have the monopolist set a price equal to marginal cost. This price would be P_r in Figure 2. The monopolist would then produce at quantity Q_r.

The problem with the regulated price P_r is that the regulated firm could actually make a loss. You can see in Figure 2 that revenues do not cover average costs. Figure 2 illustrates a fairly common situation with public utility companies because these companies' costs are large. Most public utilities must acquire sufficient resources (generating capacity or telephone-linking capacity, for example) to supply the *peak* demands. But because the peak periods are only a small portion of daily sales, the revenue generated overall is not sufficient to pay for the total resources required. For instance, air conditioning is used most heavily during the 5 to 9 P.M. time period during the summer months. To meet the demands during this peak period, the electric company has to acquire nearly double the generating capacity it would need in order to satisfy only the nonpeak demand. Thus, the regulated price equal to marginal cost is not sufficient to provide the revenue to pay for the large costs.

fair rate of return: a price
that allows a monopoly firm
to earn a normal profit

Regulatory commissions quickly moved away from setting price equal to marginal cost and have allowed for a **fair rate of return.** The fair-rate-of-return price is set to allow the monopolist a normal profit. The price corresponding to the normal profit is one where demand and average total costs are equal, P_f.

When price is set in order to achieve the most efficient allocation of resources ($P = MC$), the regulated firm is likely to suffer losses. Survival of the firm would then require subsidies from the public. On the other hand, the fair-return price ($P = ATC$) allows the monopolist to cover its costs, but it does not solve the misallocation of resources problem, since price is greater than marginal cost.

Fair-rate-of-return regulation can create another inefficiency on the part of the regulated firm. Since the firm is allowed to set the price as a percentage of average costs, the firm has an incentive to increase costs. The regulated firm thus ends up with "too much" capital as it attempts to acquire more costs.

2.b. Deregulation and Privatization in the United States

Over time it became evident that many regulated companies lacked incentives to keep costs under control and to be responsive to consumer demands. When they were regulated, the airlines competed in terms of schedules, movies, food, and size of aircraft because the Civil Aeronautics Board (CAB) did not allow price competition. Nonprice competition led to a much more rapid increase in the number of flights and expansion of aircraft capacity than was demanded by passengers. As a result, the load factor (the average percentage of seats filled) fell to less than 50 percent in the early 1970s.

Price competition among truckers was also stifled by regulation. The Interstate Commerce Commission (ICC) had a complex rate schedule and restrictions affecting whether trucks could be full or less than full and the routes trucks could take. As a result, by the mid-1970s, 36 percent of all truck-miles were logged by empty trucks.

These problems initiated a change. Trucking was deregulated in 1980. Trucks can now haul what they want, where they want, at rates set by the trucking companies. In air transportation, deregulation meant the end of government control of entry and prices. Deregulation of route authority and fares was completed by 1982, and the CAB was disbanded.

Much of the telecommunications industry was deregulated in 1984, when an antitrust suit against AT&T, filed by the Department of Justice in 1974, was finally settled. As part of the settlement, AT&T agreed to divest itself of the local portions of the 22 Bell operating companies. They were restructured into seven separate regulated monopolies known as the Baby Bells or Regional Bell Operating Companies (RBOCs). The seven new operating firms were excluded from long-distance service and from manufacturing terminal equipment. So AT&T continued to provide long-distance service and telephone equipment, but other suppliers could compete in both spheres, and customers could choose any supplier they wished.

The long-distance telephone market is deregulated. Although four firms have the dominant share of the market, there are about 500 providers of services, and it is relatively easy for virtually anyone who is interested in entering the industry to do so. Prior to 1984, the long-distance telephone market was a monopoly. What has occurred since 1984 is illustrative of the benefits of moving from monopoly to competition. Prices have declined about 80 percent since the creation of competition in the long-distance telephone market, from 52 cents per minute in 1985 to about 12 cents per minute. Services have risen significantly; consumer choice is widely expanded; innovation and technological change are increasing at extraordinary rates.

Global Business Insight

The California Debacle

In many countries, electric power has been deregulated without difficulty. That was not the case in California. Beginning in 1998, California utilities operated within a system that was unlike any other in the world. They could buy power only in the shortest-term market imaginable, paying prices for their next day's energy that varied hour by hour. They were prohibited from using longer-term contracts. In the summer of 2000, almost everything that could raise wholesale prices happened at once. Hot weather in the Southwest and low water levels in the Northwest cut importable power. Natural gas prices spiked, and the price of the pollution permits rose from $4 to $40. In addition, because of public objections to the construction of major power plants, none had been built in 15 years, while the growth of the silicon economy had raised demand to very high levels. Unethical behavior on the part of suppliers to the electrical utilities drove prices even higher. Enron, for instance, bought and sold gasoline supplies to itself through hidden companies (a practice called *round-trip trading*) in order to drive the price upward.

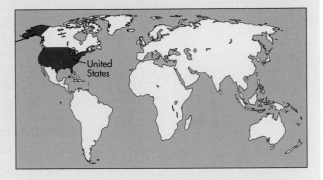

The California utilities had no choice but to pay the higher prices.

Although the utilities faced high wholesale prices, the rates they could charge customers were still frozen. Thus, by February 2000 their estimated net cash shortfalls were over $6 billion and rising, and analysts had downgraded their bonds to junk status. PG&E declared bankruptcy. The so-called deregulation experiment in California was finished.

The local market also is changing but continues to be dominated by just a few firms.

privatization: transferring a publicly owned enterprise to private ownership

Another form of deregulation is privatization. **Privatization** is the term for changing from a government-run business to a privately owned and run business. Advocates of privatization claim that private firms can, in many instances, provide better services at reduced costs. Cities and local governments in the United States have **contracted out** (privatized) many services in recent years. Local governments are now allowing private firms to provide garbage services, water services, and even road building and maintenance. Rural/Metro Company in Scottsdale, Arizona, has been running a private fire department for several decades. It is now purchasing contracts to run fire departments and emergency medical services throughout Arizona and in other states. Corrections Corporation of America in Nashville, Tennessee, and California Private Transportation Company in Anaheim, California, are building prisons and toll roads. Many members of Congress are looking at the U.S. Postal Service and arguing that private firms could deliver mail better and less expensively.

contracting out: the process of enlisting a private firm to provide a product or service for a government entity

stranded assets: assets acquired by a firm when regulated that have little value when deregulated

Deregulation is a politically difficult thing to accomplish. The formerly regulated companies argue that competition will cost too much because of their **stranded assets.** Electric and phone companies argue that once they are deregulated, they will be stuck with costly assets, such as inefficient nuclear power plants and obsolete telephone switches, on which no returns will be possible. The utilities argue that they invested for the public good on the assumption that their monopolies would be preserved, and that to now tell them that they aren't guaranteed a return on these assets is not right; exposing them to competition without compensating them for their previous investments amounts to an unconstitutional "taking" of their property. The public is wary of deregulation because of the possibility of price fluctuations. Even though economic theory tells us that changing from a monopoly market to one in which there is competition will lead to lower prices, the regulated market tends to have high but stable prices. With competition, prices will fluctuate as demand and supply fluctuate. These issues create a real dilemma for political bodies that are attempting to bring about deregulation. If it is not carried out correctly, the process of deregulation can lead to a worse situation than that created by regulation. See the Global Business Insight "The California Debacle" for more details. Nevertheless, the process of electric-power deregulation has continued in the United States, even if distorted and distracted. By September 2001, 23 states and the District of Columbia had passed deregulation laws, as shown in Figure 3. The problem with this picture is that many of the deregulation efforts stopped well before the industry was actually free. Arizona, for instance, has capped prices and restricted the activities of the primary electric utilities, even though it is considered to be one of the deregulated states.

FIGURE 3

Deregulation in the United States, Status as of September 2001.

Several nations are ahead of the United States in the deregulation process. Argentina, Australia, Canada, Chile, and the United Kingdom (UK) are among those countries that are at the forefront of deregulation.

Source: U.S. Department of Energy, Energy Information Administration, at http://www.eia.doe.gov/cneaf/electricity/chg_str/regmap.html.

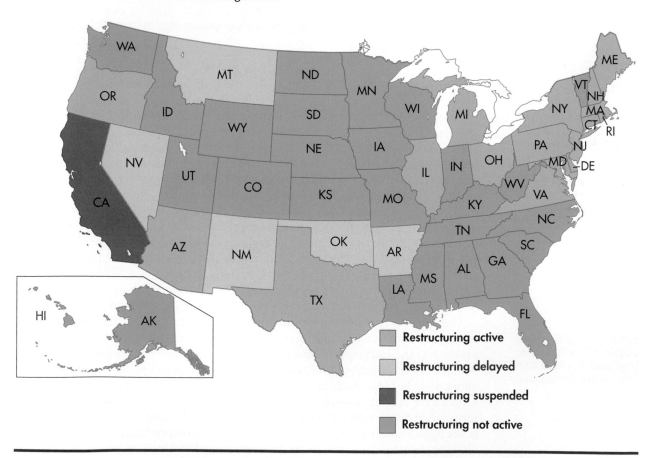

Restructuring active

Restructuring delayed

Restructuring suspended

Restructuring not active

2.c. Social Regulation

Although economists debate the costs and benefits of regulation, the amount of regulation has grown steadily since the Great Depression. Most of this growth has been in the form of social regulation.

Social regulation is concerned with the conditions under which goods and services are produced and the impact of these goods on the public. The following government agencies are concerned with social regulation:

- The Occupational Safety and Health Administration (OSHA), which is concerned with protecting workers against injuries and illnesses associated with their jobs
- The Consumer Product Safety Commission (CPSC), which specifies minimum standards for the safety of products
- The Food and Drug Administration (FDA), which is concerned with the safety and effectiveness of food, drugs, and cosmetics
- The Equal Employment Opportunity Commission (EEOC), which focuses on the hiring, promotion, and discharge of workers
- The Environmental Protection Agency (EPA), which is concerned with air, water, and noise pollution

Social regulation is often applied across all industries. For instance, while the ICC focuses on trucking and railroads, the EPA enforces emission standards related to all businesses.

Social regulation has grown since the early 1970s, as illustrated by the number of rules and regulations imposed by the federal government shown in Figure 4. This figure shows the number of telephone-book-sized pages in the *Federal Register*. The *Federal Register* is a chronicle of all regulations proposed and enacted by federal agencies. The number of pages rose rapidly and steadily until about 1980 when the

---

FIGURE 4

The number of telephone-book-sized pages required to list the rules and regulations of the federal government number 80,000. The number of regulations grew until the Reagan years of 1980 to 1985 and then grew again during the George H. W. Bush and Clinton administrations but declined during George W. Bush's first year in office (and rose thereafter).

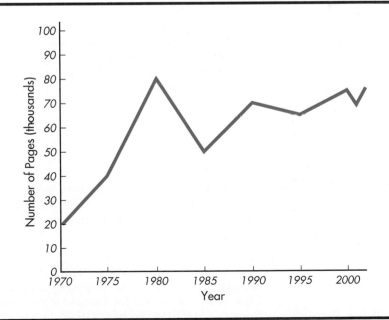

FIGURE 5

Regulatory Costs

The firm producing at Q_1 with costs of C_1 and selling at price P_1 is required to implement changes in production in order to meet pollution requirements. The increased costs of the regulation are illustrated as upward shifts of the *ATC* and *MC* curves, leading to less output being produced, Q_2 rather than Q_1, at higher costs, C_2 rather than C_1, and thus being sold at higher prices, P_2 rather than P_1.

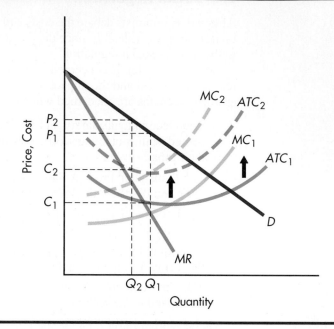

Whether an action should be undertaken can be determined by comparing the costs of a certain action to the benefits of that action.

Reagan Administration attempted to reduce the numbers of regulations enacted. Beginning in the George H. W. Bush administration, the number of pages began to rise again, and that continued during the Clinton administration. In the first year of the George W. Bush administration, 2001, the number declined by 13 percent, but then rose dramatically following that. The costs of these federal regulatory activities exceed $860 billion per year, according to some studies. According to others, the full costs of regulations are greater than $860 billion because of the increasing number of "mandates" (laws that force state and local governments to comply with federal rules and regulations).[2]

Added to the direct costs of regulations are the opportunity costs. For instance, the lengthy FDA process for approving new biotechnology has stymied advances in agriculture. Regulatory restrictions on the telecommunications industry have resulted in the United States lagging behind Japan in the development of fiber optics and high-definition television. The total cost imposed on the U.S. economy by federal government regulations is estimated to be more than $600 billion a year, or $6,000 per household.

The impact of social regulation on a business is illustrated in Figure 5. The firm is producing quantity Q_1 at a cost of C_1 and selling at a price of P_1. The firm, an automobile company, is told that it must increase the fuel efficiency of its fleet of cars. The requirement means that the company must modify its manufacturing plants and alter the parts it uses in its autos. The result is an increase in the company's fixed and variable costs, shown as an upward shift of the *ATC* and *MC* curves.

---

[2]Cato Institute, news release, July 28, 2003, "Under Bush, Federal Regulators Are Breaking Records: To control regulation, Congress needs to be held accountable for agencies' rulemaking"; Clyde Wayne Crews, Jr., "Ten Thousand Commandments: An Annual Snapshot of the Federal Regulatory State," Cato Institute, 2003.

The regulation causes the firm to bear increased costs, illustrated as upward shifts of the ATC and MC curves, leading to less output being produced, Q_2 rather than Q_1, at higher costs, C_2 rather than C_1, and the output being sold at higher prices, P_2 rather than P_1. In virtually every case of regulation, consumers pay higher prices for the goods and services sold by the regulated firm. How much more does the consumer pay? The answer depends on the price elasticities of demand and supply.

If the price elasticity of demand is low—demand is inelastic—then the consumer will not be very likely to switch to a substitute good or service as the price rises. In such a case, the firm will be able to pass along a larger portion of the increased costs to the consumer in the form of higher prices than it will if the price elasticity of demand is high. On the other hand, the firm is likely to have to bear a greater portion of the increased costs if it has a low price elasticity of supply. The low price elasticity of supply means that the firm is not able to easily switch its production and sales from the now more regulated and more costly good or service to a less regulated and less costly good or service. You can see this in Figure 6, where we've simplified Figure 5 by drawing just a demand curve that is more elastic and a demand curve that is very much less elastic. From point A the regulation is

FIGURE 6

Who Pays the Cost of Regulation?

In Figure 6(a), an elastic demand is compared to a less elastic demand. When demand is price-elastic, an increase in regulatory costs and a reduction in quantities supplied result in a price increase from P_1 to P_2. When demand is less elastic, the increase in regulatory costs results in a price increase from P_1 to P_3. In Figure 6(b), the effect of increased regulatory costs with a less elastic supply (marginal-cost) curve is compared to the effect with a more elastic supply curve. The straight-line marginal costs are less elastic than the curved ones. The vertical difference between the straight-line curves is the same as that between the more elastic curves; the resulting price increase is from P_1 to P_2.

(a) Different Demand Elasticity

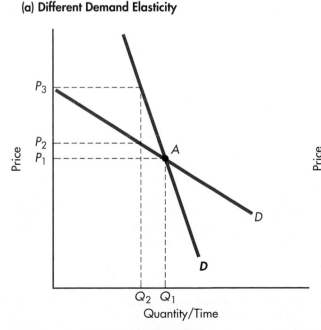

(b) Different Supply Elasticity

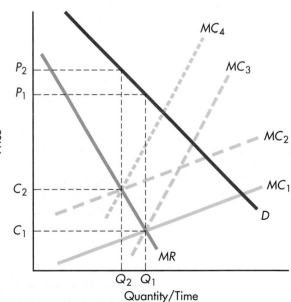

imposed and costs rise. The result is that marginal revenue and marginal cost intersect at a lower quantity. Then the firm passes on some of its increased costs to the consumer in the form of higher prices. On the more elastic demand curve, price increases to P_3, which is much higher than the price increase, to P_2, with the less elastic demand curve.

In Figure 6(b) we have drawn two price-elastic marginal-cost curves, MC_1 and MC_2, along with two price-inelastic marginal cost curves, MC_3 and MC_4, to illustrate what the regulation does to supply in the two cases. The marginal-cost curves MC_1 and MC_2 and MC_3 and MC_4 are the same vertical distance apart, C_1 to C_2, as those in Figure 5, where the vertical difference represents the increase in marginal costs caused by the regulation. But with MC_3 and MC_4, the less elastic marginal-cost curves mean that the firm will change its quantity supplied less in response to a cost change, and so the firm will increase the price to consumers by less. The price increases from P_1 to P_2 in Figure 6, which is much smaller than the increase in Figure 5. The less elastic the supply and the more elastic the demand, the more of a regulatory cost that is borne by the firm.

2.c.1. Cost-Benefit Calculations

Several studies have estimated the costs of regulations on the economy. These range from about $400 billion to over $800 billion, depending on what is included as a cost.[3] No matter the amount, there is no doubt that regulations impose costs on consumers and businesses. But are these costs worth the benefits the regulations create?

Since prices are higher and costs are higher as a result of regulation, both producers and consumers lose benefits—consumer and producer surplus is reduced. How are we to measure whether these costs are offset by the benefits of the regulation? A cost-benefit calculation has to be carried out. Consider Figure 7(a), in which the demand and supply curves for the market for automobiles are illustrated. Consumer surplus is shown as triangle ABP_1, and producer surplus is shown as triangle ACP_1. Total societal surplus is thus the area outlined as ABC. Autos pollute, and the cost of the pollution to society is shown as the area FGQ_1H.

A regulation is imposed on auto producers. The regulation causes the supply curve (the sum of the MC curves of each of the automobile firms) to shift in, as shown in Figure 7(b). This reduces consumer surplus to the area EBP_2 and producer surplus to EJP_2. The area $CAEJ$ has been lost. This area is the cost of the regulation. What are the benefits? The benefits are the cost of the pollution that is no longer created by the automobiles. This is shown as the smaller rectangle GIQ_2Q_1. Thus, we must compare the gain in benefits from the regulation to the costs created by the regulation.

The cost-benefit calculation indicates whether a regulation benefits society or not. If the costs exceed the benefits, then, according to economic theory, the regulation should not be imposed. If a regulation is to be imposed, the amount or restrictiveness of the regulation should be at a level where marginal benefits equal marginal costs. Carrying out cost-benefit analyses on regulations is an approach that has been agreed to in principle by the U.S. federal government's Office of Management and Budget and by the main financial agencies of most industrial countries. In many instances, the cost-benefit calculation is done in terms of lives saved and lives lost.

---

[3]Clyde Wayne Crews, Jr., "Ten Thousand Commandments: An Annual Snapshot of the Federal Regulatory State," Cato Institute, 2003.

FIGURE 7

Costs and Benefits of Regulation

Figure 7(a) shows the market prior to regulation, and Figure 7(b) shows the effects of regulation. The regulation causes the supply curve (the sum of the *MC* curves of each of the automobile firms) to shift up. This reduces consumer surplus to the area EBP_2 and producer surplus to EJP_2. The area $CAEJ$ is the cost of the regulation. The benefits of the regulation are the costs of the pollution that is no longer created by the automobiles, area GIQ_2Q_1.

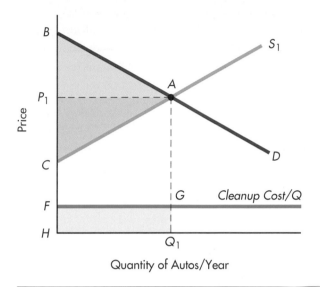

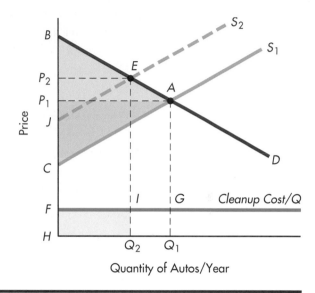

The role of government in the United States economy has grown during the past several decades—primarily as a result of social regulation. The Environmental Protection Agency is one of the most active promulgators of rules and regulations. In this photo, contaminated water is being pumped out of an area called a *superfund site.* Superfund sites are those polluted areas scheduled to be cleaned up using federal government funds. The EPA seldom carries out a cost-benefit calculation to select which sites are most in need of cleanup—that is, which would create the most benefits relative to costs. Instead, sites are often chosen as a result of lobbying on the part of special interest groups.

TABLE 2

The Cost of Regulation

Regulation Of	Saves	At a Cost per Life Of
Grain dust	4.00 lives/year	$5.3 million
Uranium mines	1.10 lives/year	6.9 million
Benzene	3.80 lives/year	17.1 million
Glass plants	0.11 life/year	19.2 million
Ethylene oxide	2.80 lives/year	25.6 million
Copper smelters	0.06 life/year	26.5 million
Uranium mill tailings, active	2.10 lives/year	53 million
Low-arsenic copper	0.08 life/year	764 million
Land disposal	2.52 lives/year	3,500 million
Formaldehyde	0.01 life/year	72,000 million

Source: U.S. Office of Management and Budget, Office of Information and Regulatory Affairs, *Report to Congress on the Costs and Benefits of Federal Regulations,* 1998.

For example, a program to detect and treat breast cancer among women over the age of 50 has been estimated to cost less than $15,000 per life-year saved, while the cost per life-year saved of a regulation to reduce airborne exposure to benzene is approximately $5,000,000. According to the federal government, the cost of some environmental regulations is high, as shown in Table 2.

Regulations may not just be costly in terms of dollars, but they could also cost lives. The argument, according to economists, is that regulations are costly to implement and conform to, and so reduce income. When people are poorer, they spend less on health care and safety measures and engage in riskier behavior. For example, they buy smaller cars and visit the doctor less often. Hence, regulations that reduce people's incomes can increase fatalities from other causes. A cost-benefit calculation for a regulation that is intended to save lives would compare the number of lives saved and the number of lives lost as a result of the regulation.

Studies have shown that any regulation costing more than about $8.4 million for each life saved is likely to cause overall fatalities to rise. Looking at the cost of regulations suggests that many do the opposite of their intended objective. Most of the Federal Aviation Administration's regulations cost less than $8.4 million per life saved, and thus arguably yield a net saving of lives. The same is true for most of the National Highway Traffic Safety Administration's rules. The record of the Occupational Safety and Health Administration (OSHA) is not so good. OSHA regulations are about evenly divided between those that are cheap enough to save lives on balance and those (such as OSHA's ethylene dibromide and formaldehyde rules) that are so costly that they have no doubt killed far more people than would have died in the absence of the regulations. The Environmental Protection Agency's (EPA) regulations are almost all more costly in terms of lives lost than they are beneficial in terms of lives saved. The arsenic standard, for example, costs almost $27 million per life saved, according to the official numbers. This income loss leads to about three added fatalities from other causes for each life saved. Similarly, the EPA asbestos standard was supposed to save ten lives each year. However, its cost per life saved (about $144 million) suggests that 18 people will die each year to save those ten.[4]

A cost-benefit test would limit regulations to those that create greater benefits than they cost. But as shown by the examples presented in Table 2, many regulations do not pass a cost-benefit test but are still implemented. Why? Many economists argue that a number of these regulations are implemented to benefit special interest groups rather than to solve problems resulting from market failure. We will discuss such issues further in the chapter "Government and Market Failure."

2.d. Regulation and Deregulation in Other Countries

In most European nations, nationalization rather than regulation was the traditional solution to natural monopoly. With nationalization, the government takes over and operates an industry. Privatization is the opposite of nationalization. Privatization, as discussed earlier, is the transfer of public-sector activities to the private sector. Privatization may take one of three forms: *wholesale privatization,* in which an entire publicly owned firm is transferred to private ownership; *contracting out,* in which a specific aspect of a government operation is carried out by a private firm; and *auctioning,* in which the rights to operate a government enterprise go to the highest private-sector bidder.

While the United States was deregulating, the rest of the world was privatizing. Chile, Argentina, Colombia, the United Kingdom, and 15 other nations now allow workers to invest their social security payroll deductions in privately managed funds. The Netherlands offered 25 percent of the Dutch postal and telephone system for private ownership in 1994. Britain has privatized its airlines, telephones, steel, and electric and gas utilities.

Since 1980, more than eighty countries have launched ambitious efforts to privatize their state-owned enterprises (SOEs). More than 2,000 SOEs have been privatized in developing countries, and more than 7,000 worldwide. State-owned enterprises are chronically unprofitable, partly because they are told to increase employment and locate so as to help the local population rather than to maximize efficiency. Governments provide SOEs with a variety of subsidies, such as reduced prices for resources and guarantees to cover operating losses. Privatization is intended to substitute the single objective of profit maximization for all these other objectives. Subjecting the newly privatized firms to the tests of the market and competition forces the companies to cut costs and increase efficiency or to get out of business altogether. At first glance, this would seem to indicate that the firms will have to cut employment. Interestingly, the experience has been that the privatized firms do perform much more efficiently, but that they also increase both output and employment relative to the SOEs. Employment in privatized firms has risen by about 10 percent relative to the SOEs.

2.e. Multinationals, International Regulation, GATT, and the WTO

International regulation occurs at two levels, one in which a specific government regulates the activities of individual firms operating within the country, and another

<hr>

[4]Ulf-G. Gerdtham and Magnus Johannesson, "Do Life-Saving Regulations Save Lives?" *Journal of Risk and Uncertainty* Vol. 24, 231–249, 2002; John F. Morrall, III, "A Review of the Record," *Regulation,* November/December 1986, 25–34. Daniel K. Benjamin, "Killing Us with Kindness," *PERC Reports,* Vol. 20, No. 3, September 2002, perc@perc.org.

in which several nations are involved. The General Agreement on Tariffs and Trade (GATT) is a form of the latter. In April 1947, delegates from the United States, Asia, Europe, and Latin America traveled to Geneva. Aware of the effects of trade restrictions on economic health that had been experienced during the Great Depression, they all sought to liberalize trade, reduce barriers, and create an environment in which economies would prosper. The first global trade agreement resulted, called GATT. Today the successor to GATT is called the World Trade Organization (WTO). Its 132 member nations have agreed to settle trade disputes in the WTO courts rather than raise barriers, impose tariffs, or otherwise restrict trade. The WTO was created on January 1, 1995, and since has dealt with more trade disputes than GATT did during its entire fifty-year history. Another global regulatory agreement is currently being developed by the industrial nations. This one deals with multinational corporations. It is called the Multilateral Agreement on Investment (MAI). The principal aim of MAI is to have nations treat multinational companies exactly as they treat their own companies. There would be no investment required in local projects or companies, no uncompensated expropriation, no limit of capital movement, and all disputes would be settled by a global organization, either one under the WTO or a separate organization.

RECAP

1. Economic regulation means that the government dictates the price a firm may charge and/or the quantity a firm must supply.

2. Economic regulation typically applies to an entire industry.

3. Since the mid-1970s, deregulation has occurred in airlines, trucking, railroads, and communications.

4. Social regulation deals with workplace safety, product safety, the environment, and other aspects of doing business; it applies to all industries.

5. A cost-benefit calculation measures whether the benefits of a rule or regulation exceed the costs. Economists assert that only those regulations that create more benefits than costs should be implemented.

6. The costs of a rule or regulation include the reduction in output produced, higher costs of production, and higher prices. They also include the lost consumer and producer surplus. The benefits of the rule or regulation are the reductions in the costs of cleaning up wastes and reductions in the risk to human life.

7. In other countries, nationalization occurred instead of regulation. In those countries, deregulation means privatization.

8. Attempts to increase trade among nations have led to the creation of GATT and then the WTO.

3. The Securities and Exchange Commission

After the stock market crash of 1929, President Roosevelt, the business community, and other government leaders believed that they needed to do something to restore faith in the financial markets and in the U.S. economy. What they came up with in 1934 was a government agency called the Securities and Exchange Commission

(SEC). The Securities and Exchange Commission regulates the financial activities of public companies (those whose shares of stock are traded on a stock exchange). The aim of the SEC is to protect investors from fraudulent and questionable public companies and from dishonest and scrupulous individuals dealing within financial markets. The SEC requires that companies provide it with prudent and truthful financial and material information, and all material information, whether it will positively or negatively affect the company, is provided to investors by the SEC. Today, this information is provided electronically through the SEC's EDGAR database. The problem is that the SEC does not have the resources to examine every document that is required to be submitted to it. It has to rely on the work of auditors, investment bankers, and others who have incentives to ensure that firms are reporting appropriate and accurate information. In the late 1990s, this reliance proved to be a disaster.

3.a. Auditors

Auditors are accountants who act like detectives, examining a company's books, inventories, and other areas of operation to determine whether what is being reported is accurate. The auditors are employed by an auditing or accounting company, such as PWC or KPMG. These accounting firms are separate entities from—and are supposed to be independent of—the firm being audited. In the 1990s, however, many accounting firms began providing business consulting services to the same firms they were auditing. This created a conflict of interest in which the auditors found it difficult to give a negative report about a firm while at the same time soliciting its consulting business. The conflict became evident in the late 1990s, when Arthur Andersen Company was found to be providing misleading auditing reports regarding Enron Corporation. The demise of Arthur Andersen Company was due to the lawsuits and other penalties resulting from its actions regarding Enron.

3.b. Investment Banks

Investment banks are companies that help a firm raise funds by issuing stocks or bonds, assisting in mergers and acquisitions, or performing other financial services. Investment banks also provide advice to investors about individual companies and stocks through *analyst recommendations*. This creates a conflict of interest; analysts could find it difficult to provide a negative opinion on a firm from which the analyst's company was providing investment banking services. The conflict came to roost in the late 1990s, as investment banking companies began to seek an increasing amount of business. For instance, Credit Suisse First Boston, Citigroup, and JP Morgan Chase helped design Enron's hidden partnerships and owned shares of stock in Enron at the same time their analysts were recommending that the general public buy Enron stock. The banks made money not only from their investments in Enron stock, but also from the services they provided to Enron.

3.c. The Sarbanes-Oxley Act

The public outcry as a result of Enron and the activities of other firms was so loud that Congress immediately enacted a law restricting many activities engaged in by auditors, investment banks, and the CEOs of companies. The Sarbanes-Oxley Act, passed by Congress in 2002, requires that auditing and consulting services be provided by different firms. No longer can one company, like Arthur Andersen, provide both auditing and consulting services to one client. To limit the possibility of fraud on the part of investment banks, analysts, and companies, the act requires the CEOs of corporations to sign and verify the accuracy of the financial statements; in essence, the CEO must take personal responsibility for the statements.[5] In the scandals of the early 2000s, CEOs typically said that they had no knowledge of any fraud, that it was the people who worked under them who had broken the law.

3.d. Financial Regulations in Other Countries

Financial instruments—stocks, bonds, mutual funds, etc.—trade within the regulatory structure that exists in each country. Regulations from country to country have many common features as well as many rules and regulations that are unique to a particular country. But since the six largest exchanges (New York, Nasdaq, Tokyo, London, Frankfurt, and Paris) account for 90 percent of all securities transactions in the world, their rules and regulations essentially determine who may offer stocks to the public, what information companies must provide to the public, and how all parties must behave.

RECAP

1. The Securities and Exchange Commission (SEC) regulates the equity market in the United States. It requires firms to submit documents regarding the firm's financial activities each quarter.

2. The SEC must rely on the work of auditors and others to ensure that firms comply with rules and regulations.

3. Auditors are accountants employed by accounting firms who peruse the financial statements of companies to ensure that what is being reported is the truth.

4. Investment banks provide firms with the tools and advice they need in order to issue stocks and carry out other financial activities.

5. Stock analysts are specialists who study firms and make recommendations to the investing public as to whether to purchase or sell a firm's stock.

6. In some of the scandals of the late 1990s, auditors failed to do their jobs, investment banks acted improperly, and stock analysts gave misleading recommendations.

Summary

❓ What is antitrust policy?

1. Antitrust policy is an attempt to enhance competition by restricting certain activities that could be anticompetitive. *§1.b*

2. The antitrust statutes include Sections 1 and 2 of the Sherman Antitrust Act, which forbid conspiracies and monopolization; Sections 2, 3, and 7 of the Clayton Antitrust Act, which prohibit anticompetitive pricing and nonprice restraints; and Section 5 of the Federal Trade Commission Act, which prohibits deceptive and unfair acts. *§1.b, Table 1*

3. Interpretation of the antitrust statutes has gone through several phases. In the early years, a rule of reason prevailed; acts had to be unreasonable to be a violation of the statutes. Between 1914 and 1980, a per se rule applied more often. Under this policy, the mere existence of actions that could be used anticompetitively was a violation. In the early 1980s, the

---

[5]For more information on the various laws that govern the securities industry, visit www.sec.gov/about/laws.shtml.

interpretations returned to the rule-of-reason standard. In the early 1990s, another attempt to tighten enforcement was made. *§1.b*

4. The Herfindahl index is used to measure size and influence; industries with a Herfindahl index above 1,800 are considered highly concentrated. *§1.e*

5. Antitrust laws are more rigorously enforced in the United States than elsewhere. *§1.f*

❓ What is the difference between economic regulation and social regulation?

6. Economic regulation refers to the prescription of price and output for a particular industry. Social regulation refers to the setting of health and safety standards for products and the workplace, and environmental and operating procedures for all industries. *§2*

7. Because monopoly is inefficient and perfect competition efficient, governments have attempted to regulate the natural monopolies to make them more like perfect competitors. The huge economies of scale rule out breaking up the natural monopolies into small firms. Instead, price has been set at a fair rate of return, $P = ATC$. *§2.a*

8. Social regulation has increased even as economic regulation has decreased. *§2.c*

9. Regulations create costs and provide benefits. The economist's view is that a regulation should be implemented only if its benefits exceed its costs. *§2.c.1*

10. Deregulation in other developed countries took the form of privatization: the selling, auctioning, or contracting out of a government enterprise to private interests. *§2.d*

11. The WTO is intended to lower tariffs and increase trade. *§2.e*

12. The SEC regulates the financial dealings of public companies; its purpose is to protect the public from fraudulent activities in the financial markets. *§3*

Key Terms

antitrust policy *§1*

rule of reason *§1.b*

per se rule *§1.b*

Herfindahl index *§1.e*

concentration *§1.e*

economic regulation *§2*

social regulation *§2*

fair rate of return *§2.a*

privatization *§2.b*

contracting out *§2.b*

stranded assets *§2.b*

Exercises

1. Using demand and cost curves, demonstrate why a typical monopolistically competitive firm might want to create a barrier to entry.

2. Using the demand and cost curves of an individual firm in oligopoly, demonstrate what the effects of each of the following are:
   a. The Clean Air Act
   b. The Nutrition and Labeling Act
   c. A ban on smoking inside the workplace
   d. A sales tax

3. Kodak has developed an important brand name through its advertising, innovation, and product quality and service. Suppose Kodak sets up a network of exclusive dealerships, and one of the dealers decides to carry Fuji and Mitsubishi as well as Kodak products. If Kodak terminates the dealership, is it acting in a pro- or anticompetitive manner?

4. Explain why a market in which broadcast licenses could be purchased might be more efficient than having the FCC assign licenses on some basis designed by the FCC.

5. Which of the three types of government policies—antitrust, social regulation, and economic regulation—is the basis for each of the following?
   a. Beautician education standards
   b. Certified Public Accounting requirements
   c. Liquor licensing
   d. Justice Department guidelines

e. The Clean Air Act

f. The Nutrition and Labeling Act

6. Some airline executives have called for reregulation. Why might an executive of an airline prefer to operate under a regulated environment?

7. Suppose the Herfindahl index for domestic production of televisions is 5,000. Does this imply a very competitive or a noncompetitive environment?

8. Discuss the claim that social regulation is unnecessary. Does the claim depend on whether the industrial structure of an industry is composed primarily of perfect competition or primarily of oligopoly?

9. Suppose a monopolist is practicing price discrimination and a lawsuit against the monopolist forces an end to the practice. Is it possible that the result is a loss in efficiency? Explain.

10. The Justice Department sued several universities for collectively setting the size of scholarships offered. Explain why the alleged price fixing on the part of universities might be harmful to students.

11. The FDA is considering the adoption of a higher standard of success in clinical trials for any pharmaceutical the agency will permit to be sold in the United States. Explain how a cost-benefit calculation would be carried out.

12. Suppose that in exercise 11, the benefits of the regulation were 1,000 lives saved per year. Would you support adoption of the regulation? Explain.

13. Explain what the costs of the regulation are in the scenario in exercises 11 and 12.

14. What does a loss of consumer surplus mean? In the case of exercises 11–13, exactly how do the losses of consumer surplus occur?

15. The scandals of the 2000–2003 period involving companies like Enron occurred even though the SEC was supposed to prevent fraudulent activities. Explain how such behavior by the executives of firms could occur under the eyes of a government watchdog like the SEC.

ACE

Take the ACE Practice Test for this chapter to review the important concepts and get immediate feedback with answers.

economics.college.hmco.com/students

Economically Speaking

Don't Let It Happen Again; Why Didn't the Post-'65 Fixes Stop This Blackout?

It will be days, at best, before blame for the sweeping power blackout that left 50 million people in the United States and Canada without electricity can be definitively assigned. But there's no question about the extent of the disruption to business, to public transportation systems, to cell phone and conventional telephone networks—to any of the myriad activities that rely on electricity to work.

In a modern, high-tech society, electric power touches nearly every aspect of life. It is vast amounts of power that help make this country the success that it is—and the largest consumer of energy per capita of any nation in the world. But, says former Energy Secretary Bill Richardson, "We are a major superpower with a third-world electrical grid ... It needs serious modernization."

His description may be overwrought, but his broad prescription is correct. The nation must respond with constructive action.

It's far from clear whether the cascading power failures were caused by weaknesses in the transmission system that links the electrical grid of New York with those of other sections of the eastern United States.

But that is one of several issues that will have to be examined in the wake of the largest blackout in North American history. And although it's increasingly certain that terrorism was not a cause of the power outage, its rapid spread and the dislocation and inconvenience in its wake show how vulnerable the nation is to a terrorist attack on its power delivery system.

After the massive 1965 blackout that swept much of the Northeast, the utility industry took steps that, it said, would prevent such a thing from happening again. One was formation of the North American Electric Reliability Council, which describes itself as "a voluntary organization, relying on reciprocity, peer pressure and the mutual self-interest of all those involved ... to make the North American bulk electric system the most reliable in the world."

The obvious question now is whether such voluntary measures are adequate to bring the nation's power grid up to major superpower standards, or whether government should be taking a more active role in controlling and modernizing the electric system. . . .

Since New York deregulated its electric system, in hopes of gaining new efficiencies from competition, it has depended on private energy companies to build new generating plants. But in the wake of the failure of Enron Corp., those companies have had difficulty financing new projects. A Not-in-My-Backyard climate makes building any major energy project dicey. And a streamlined state system for approving sites for new power plants has been allowed to lapse by the State Legislature. As a result of such factors, few new power plants have been built or even started in New York in recent years.

And deregulation makes it harder to plan when and where to bolster the state's transmission system, since it's unclear where new plants will be built.

That's a full plate for the power industry and federal and state officials to confront. But America was promised, after the 1965 blackout that darkened the Northeast, that this kind of thing would never happen again. Now it has, and there's no reason to think it couldn't be repeated. The industry and its regulators must redeem that promise.

Source: Copyright 2003 Newsday, Inc.

***Newsday* (New York)/August 17, 2003**

Commentary

In August 2003, electrical power to a large section of the United States and parts of Canada suddenly stops. People are stuck in elevators and subways, drinking water is unavailable in Cleveland and Detroit, cell phones won't work, and transportation comes to a stop. How could something like this happen? According to the article, the problem stems from the electrical grid. Throughout the United States, electricity generation stations—fueled by coal, oil, gas, water, wind, or nuclear fission—are interconnected in a system called power grids. Power from over 6,000 power generating units is moved around the country on almost a half-million miles of bulk transmission lines that carry high-voltage charges of electricity. At more than 100 control centers, officials direct the transmission and monitor the distribution of power, rerouting electricity from areas of low demand to areas of high demand.

The idea of the electrical grid is to ensure that areas in which demand is higher than normal are able to meet that demand. Electricity cannot be stored, and supply must always either equal demand or be less than it. These facts induced states and the federal government to try to share power. Conceptually, if New York City has a heat wave and requires large amounts of power to run air conditioners at the same time that Cleveland is using less power, then sending the power from Cleveland to New York City benefits everyone. The practical problem with this conceptually good idea is that the system consists of outdated and deteriorating transmission lines.

According to the article, the blackout was due to a bad combination of deregulation and regulation. The reason this combination exists relates to the structure of the electrical power industry. Electricity is generated in one location and then must be transmitted to users—homes and businesses. Although many different companies can build generating plants and compete to send power, transmission does not seem to lend itself to competition, at least according to government regulators who argue that transmission is a natural monopoly. With a natural monopoly, the first firm to build power lines would experience economies of scale (the more lines it provided the lower the cost per foot of line provided), so only one firm would end up owning the lines. As a result, the government regulators decided to deregulate generation and allow virtually anyone to generate power, while continuing to control transmission. Many firms believed that they could earn a profit by building generating plants and selling the electricity. No one thought a profit could be made building transmission lines because federal and state governments controlled the lines and the prices that could be charged to the users of those lines. The result has been an increasing and improving number of generation plants connected through a deteriorating set of transmission lines.

The article states that neither generating plants nor transmission lines have been built in the past several years. This isn't true nationwide. Although it did become more difficult to raise the money with which to build plants and it is true that people do not want the plants near their homes, many new plants have been built in the United States in the past five or six years; in fact, the amount of potential new electrical power that can be generated in the United States is nearly enough to supply half of Europe. The problem is that because transmission has remained under government control, there has been no incentive for companies to build additional transmission lines or to upgrade existing lines. Thus, even with greater generating capacity, the U.S. electrical power system is severely limited and susceptible to power failures.

CHAPTER 28

Government and Market Failure

? Fundamental Questions

1. **What are externalities?**

2. **Why did the hippie communes established in the 1960s disappear?**

3. **Why do governments create, own, and run national parks?**

4. **What is the reason the government requires the listing of ingredients on food packaging?**

5. **Is government the best way to solve market failure problems?**

In the previous chapter, we saw how the government intervenes in the economy to control the behavior of large firms. This response to the behavior of large firms is but one small way in which the government gets involved in the economy. The government also establishes speed limits and other traffic rules, requires the use of seat belts, specifies that the list of ingredients on packaged foods be readily available, provides public education, runs national parks, and carries out many, many other activities. In fact, the government has become an increasingly large player in the U.S. economy. This may be somewhat surprising, given that economic theory shows that free markets are more efficient, lead to increasing standards of living, and ensure that resources flow to where they are most highly valued. But, no matter how one measures government's influence in the United States and most other industrial countries, that influence has grown significantly over the past 20 or so years.

Why would the government be called upon to intervene in free markets? One reason that government intervenes in free markets is what economists call market

market failure: a situation in which resources are not allocated to their highest-valued use

failures. Economists, like the general public, may not agree with the outcomes of the market or may think that some outcomes are unfair, but that is not what economists consider to be a market failure. When economists refer to a market failure, they are speaking of it as a positive issue, that is, an efficiency issue. A **market failure** occurs when the market outcome is not the socially efficient outcome, that is, when resources are not allocated to their highest value. When the market provides an outcome that we don't like, this does not mean that a market failure has occurred. Not agreeing with an outcome is a normative issue, someone's personal opinion. In this chapter we examine the positive aspects of what are called market failures, and in so doing examine further the role of government in a market economy. ■

1. What are externalities?

private costs: costs that are borne solely by the individuals involved in the transaction that created the costs

1. Externalities

A business firm knows how much it costs to employ workers, and it knows the costs of purchasing materials or constructing buildings. An individual who buys a new car or pays for a pizza knows exactly what the cost of the purchase is. Such costs are **private costs:** they are costs that are borne solely by the individuals involved in the transaction that created the costs. In the case where the costs of an individual's actions are not borne directly and solely by that individual, the market cannot determine the efficient amount of the good or service to produce and consume. For instance, when a firm pollutes the air or water or when a tourist leaves trash in a park, the cost of the action is not borne by the individual or firm who performs it. This situation represents a market failure because the price of the good and the equilibrium quantity produced and consumed do not reflect the full costs of producing or consuming the good. In this sense, "too much" or "too little" is produced. If the firm that polluted had to pay to clean up its waste, it would have an incentive to consume or produce less of the product and thus pollute less.

Consider an oil tanker that runs aground and dumps crude oil into a pristine ocean area teeming with wildlife, people that litter a public beach, the constant barking of your neighbor's dog, secondhand smoke, and people who leave their cups, used papers, and food wrappers on the floor of your classrooms. A cost is involved in these actions: the crude oil may kill wildlife and ruin fishing industries, the trash may discourage families from using the beach and lower property values near the beach, the barking dog may disrupt your study or leisure time, the secondhand smoke may reduce your enjoyment of some activity or even cause health problems, and the trash in the classroom may distract from the discussions and lectures. But in none of these cases is the cost of the action borne solely by the individuals or firms who took the action. Instead, some or all of the cost is borne by people who were not participants in the activity. The fishermen did not spill the oil, yet they have to bear the cost. The beachgoers who encounter trash and broken bottles and the local property owners were not the litterers, yet they must bear the cost. It was not your dog that was barking, but you must bear the cost. You do not smoke, and yet you have to put up with secondhand smoke. Many students and professors do not litter, and yet they must wade through the trash. The cost is external to the activity and is thus called an **externality.**

externality: the cost or benefit of a transaction that is borne by someone not directly involved in the transaction

Externalities may be negative or positive. The examples just given are *negative externalities*. A *positive externality* may result when the benefits of an activity are received by consumers or firms that are not directly involved in the activity. For instance, inoculations for mumps, measles, and other communicable diseases provide benefits to all of society. If some people get a flu shot, you may have less chance of getting the flu even though you did not get a flu shot. You receive a positive externality from those who were vaccinated. The total cost of a transaction, the private cost plus the external cost, is called the **social cost.**

social cost: the total cost of a transaction, the private cost plus the external cost

$$\text{Social cost} = \text{private cost} + \text{value of externality}$$

If all the costs of a transaction are borne by the participants in that transaction, the private costs and the social costs are the same. When private costs differ from social costs, the full opportunity cost of using a scarce resource is borne not by the producer or the consumer, but by society in general. When you don't have to pay the full cost of a good or service, you will consume more than you would if you had to pay the full cost. In this sense, "too much" of the good or service is consumed.

1.a. Externalities and Market Failure

When there is a divergence between social costs and private costs, the result is either *too much* or *too little* production and consumption. In either case, resources are not being used in their highest-valued activity. For instance, those who pollute do not bear the entire costs of the pollution and therefore pollute more than they otherwise would. Those who smoke do not pay a cost for secondhand smoke and therefore tend to smoke more than they otherwise would. Those who get flu shots provide some protection for those who do not get the shots, so that fewer people get inoculations than otherwise would. These are cases of market failure, as can be illustrated using a typical market diagram.

Consider a gas station selling gasoline with pumps that have no emission-control equipment. Each time a consumer pumps gas, a certain quantity of pollutants is released into the air. Consumers are willing and able to purchase gasoline at various prices, as shown by the demand curve, D, in Figure 1. Gas is supplied according to the supply curve S_p. The equilibrium price and quantity are P_p and Q_p. The pollution

---

FIGURE 1

Negative Externalities

When a private transaction imposes costs on society that are not paid by the private transactors, a negative externality exists. With a negative externality, the supply of a product that is provided, S_p, is greater than it would be if the suppliers had to pay the externality, as shown by S_s.

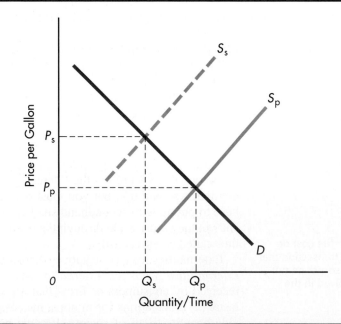

FIGURE 2

Positive Externalities

When a private transaction creates benefits for society that exceed those involved in the private transaction, positive externalities exist. D_p represents the demand for inoculations against a communicable disease when there is no externality. D_s represents the demand with an externality. Fewer people get the inoculations than would be desired by society.

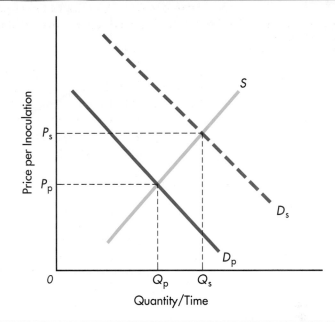

imposes costs on society, but neither those selling the gas nor those buying the gas pay these costs. If sellers did have to account for the pollution costs, their costs of supplying the gas would rise. The supply of gas would be given by the supply curve S_s. With higher costs, firms are willing and able to supply less at each price. The social equilibrium is when demand and supply intersect at price P_s and quantity Q_s. In other words, society would like the price to be set at P_s rather than P_p and the quantity purchased to be Q_s rather than Q_p. According to society's willingness and ability to pay, "too much" gasoline is purchased.

In contrast to negative externalities, private costs exceed social costs when external benefits are created. Figure 2 represents the market for inoculations against some communicable disease. People would be willing and able to purchase the inoculations according to D_s if there were no externalities. However, because some people in society can benefit from the inoculations without purchasing them, the demand for the inoculations is less, or D_p. This means that fewer people receive the inoculations than would be preferred by society. Society would prefer that Q_s get the inoculations, but the smaller number Q_p actually do—"too little" of the good is purchased.

1.b. Solutions to the Externality Problem

The solution to the externality problem is to ensure that all the costs of a transaction, private and social, are borne by those involved in the transaction. This will generate the "optimal" level of production. Many people argue that it is the government's responsibility to reduce the externality problem. One approach that the government uses is to impose a tax on or provide a subsidy to those creating the externality.

1.b.1. Pollution Tax
Suppose a firm is creating an externality by polluting as it produces its product. If the government imposed a tax on that company based on the amount of pollution the firm created, the firm would have to consider the extra cost

FIGURE 3

Pollution Tax

A tax on a firm that creates a negative externality reduces the quantity supplied and thus forces the firm to internalize the externality. Q_s is produced rather than Q.

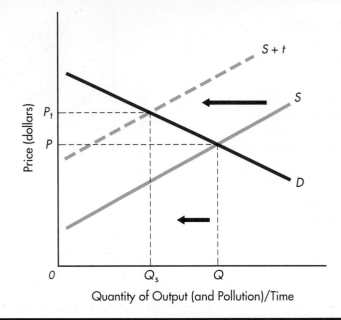

when deciding whether to increase output (and thereby pollution). This is shown in Figure 3 as the supply curve $S + t$, the supply curve plus the tax. The tax reduces the amount produced from Q to Q_s, and thereby reduces the amount of pollution created by the firm. The tax is a way in which the government can force the polluter to *internalize* the externality, that is, to pay for it rather than have society pay for it.

The firm can avoid the tax by either reducing the amount it produces or purchasing pollution abatement equipment—equipment that will reduce the amount of pollution created. With less pollution, the firm will pay fewer taxes. Either choice, paying the tax or buying the equipment, means the externality is internalized by the firm.

In the case of a positive externality, the government might provide a subsidy rather than impose a tax. Suppose each person getting an inoculation is given some money. More people would be willing to be inoculated, as shown in Figure 4. The subsidy, s, induces buyers to increase the quantities that they are willing and able to buy at each price. The total amount produced and consumed rises from Q to Q_s.

The problem with taxes and subsidies is that those setting the taxes and subsidies (the government in most cases) must guess at what the socially optimal level would be. A tax that is too high will create an inefficiency of too little production; a tax that is not high enough will do the opposite.

1.b.2. Command Rather than imposing a tax, the government could simply require or command that the company not create waste. For instance, the government could tell a copper mining operation to produce no more than 3 gallons of waste per ton of copper. The firm will then have no choice; it will have to reduce the amount of waste it produces or go out of business. However, the command approach provides no incentive for the firm to utilize any new technology that might reduce waste beyond the mandated amount. With the pollution tax, the firm is taxed only on the waste it produces—if it can reduce waste, it can reduce its taxes.

FIGURE 4

Subsidy

A subsidy to people getting inoculated increases the demand for inoculations, leading to more inoculations being obtained, Q_s.

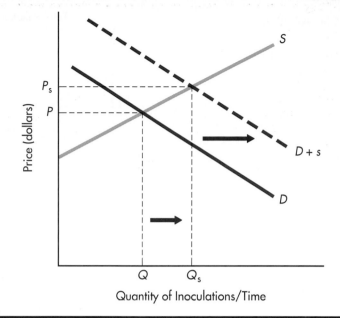

With a positive externality, the government might dictate who must use or consume the beneficial activity. For instance, by mandating that all children under the age of 6 be inoculated, the government is using a command approach: it is forcing the children to be inoculated. But by forcing everyone to be inoculated, the government is not selecting the socially optimal amount of inoculations. As a result, more than the socially optimal number of people get inoculations, and the costs of the inoculations are higher than would be necessary.

1.b.3. Marketable Pollution Permits Realizing that a command system is inefficient—it doesn't create incentives to reduce the problem—and that taxes and subsidies may not be set at the efficient levels, the government has attempted to establish a market for the right to create some externalities, such as air pollution. The government specifies that a certain quantity of pollutants will be permitted in a particular area. It then issues permits that enable the owners of the permits to pollute. For example, if the target pollution level in the Los Angeles basin is 400 billion particulates per day, the government could issue a total of 400 permits, each permitting 1 billion particulates per day. The government sells the permits. Demanders, typically firms, purchase the permits, allowing them to pollute up to the amount specified by the permits they own; if a firm purchased 20 permits, it could emit up to 20 billion particulates per day. If that firm implemented a cleaner technology or did not use all of its permits, it could sell them to other firms.

The marketable permit idea is illustrated in Figure 5. The pollution target set by the Environmental Protection Agency is indicated by the vertical supply curve for pollution rights in Figure 5 labelled "1." The demand for permits to pollute is shown by the downward-sloping demand curve, D. With a price, P_1, for pollution rights determined, firms choose whether to pollute the amount they have purchased, to not

FIGURE 5

The Market for Pollution Permits

The government establishes the amount of pollution to be permitted. It then issues permits, each allowing a certain amount of pollution. To be able to pollute, a firm, individual, or group must have a permit. The price of permits is determined by demand and supply. As the government reduces the amount of pollution allowed, the price of the permits increases.

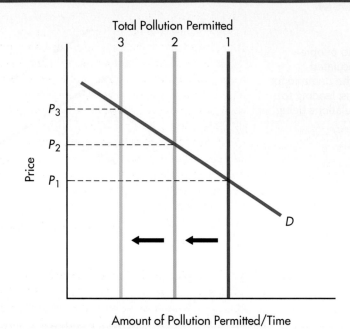

produce as much and sell the excess permits, or to adopt cleaner technology and thus be able to sell the permits they don't use.

If the government decides to reduce pollutants more than it has in the past, it will reduce its pollution target. This is shown in Figure 5 as an inward shift of the total pollution permitted line. Demanders will bid for the now fewer pollution permits, driving the price of the permits up. As the price rises, some firms will decide not to purchase the permits, but instead to purchase new pollution abatement equipment or to reduce the amount they produce.

The higher price gives firms an incentive to adopt more efficient pollution abatement equipment. The permit market also enables others to influence the total amount of pollution created. Anyone can purchase permits. Some might speculate that in the future the price of the permits will rise. If the price rises, the owners of the permits will be able to sell them for a gain. Some environmental groups, such as the Nature Conservancy and the Sierra Club, have purchased permits simply to reduce the total amount of pollution that can occur in a specific area or industry. By purchasing the permits and taking them out of circulation, they essentially reduce the total number of permits and the total amount of pollution permitted.

1.c. The Coase Theorem

Coase theorem: the idea that if people can negotiate with one another at no cost over the right to perform activities that cause externalities, they will always arrive at an efficient solution

Is government intervention the only way to solve an externality problem? Ronald Coase, a professor at the University of Chicago, said no. He was the first to see that if people can negotiate with one another at no cost over the right to perform activities that cause externalities, they will always arrive at an efficient solution. Professor Coase was awarded the 1991 Nobel Prize in economics for this insight, which is called the **Coase theorem.**

To illustrate the Coase theorem, consider the following situation. Suppose a mine can not discharge waste without permission from the city. The mine will have to negotiate with the city to figure out the price that the mine will pay the city. If the city says that there can be no pollution, then the mine shuts down and the city loses the entire consumer and producer surplus. This will make the city worse off. If the city says that it will be willing to allow the mine to discharge waste if the city bears no costs, then the mine will have to pay the $2 per gallon waste treatment. The result is the socially optimal amount of waste. Conversely, suppose the mine owns the right to discharge waste. The city will come to the mine and attempt to come to an agreement about how much waste is to be discharged. The city will offer the mine any amount up to $2 per gallon of waste not to pollute, since it will save the $2 per gallon of waste that it spends for cleanup. The mine will agree to reduce output. In both cases, when the mine has the right to discharge waste and when the city has the right to decide how much waste will be discharged, the socially optimal level of pollution results, if the parties can negotiate freely.

1.c.1. Outcomes When Negotiation Is Not Efficient

Efficient solutions to externalities will occur whenever the affected parties can negotiate with one another at no cost. But negotiation is not always practical or free. A motorist with a polluting automobile imposes costs on others—everyone who breathes the air—yet all these people can't practically stop the motorist and offer him a compensation payment to fix his car. The Coase theorem doesn't work. As a result, most governments simply require that cars meet certain emission standards.

Why do speed limits exist? Why are there other traffic laws, such as no-passing zones, right-of-way rules, and stop and go signals? What accounts for zoning laws? One answer is that these laws solve the externality problem when negotiation is not practicable.

RECAP

1. An externality occurs when the costs and/or benefits of a private transaction are borne by those who are not involved in that private transaction.

2. A positive externality is a situation in which a private transaction creates benefits for members of society who are not involved in the transaction. In the case of positive externalities, not enough of the good or service is produced and consumed.

3. A negative externality is a situation in which a private transaction creates costs for members of society who are not involved in the transaction. In the case of a negative externality, too much of the good or service is produced and consumed.

4. The government may attempt to minimize the problems of negative externalities by imposing taxes, dictating behavior, or creating a market in permits to internalize the externality.

5. The government may attempt to minimize the ill effects of positive externalities by subsidizing the beneficial activity or supplying the activity itself.

6. The Coase theorem says that if private parties are able to negotiate, the parties will resolve externality problems.

2. Private Property Rights

A market failure may result because of the absence of well-defined private property rights. A private property right is the right to claim ownership of an item—to do what you wish with that item. The private property right is well defined if there is a clear owner and if the right is recognized and enforced by society.

2.a. Market Failure and the Problem of Common Ownership

?

2. Why did the hippie communes established in the 1960s disappear?

Suppose you have purchased a pizza to be delivered to your house. If you have a well-defined property right in that pizza, only you decide who can enjoy the pizza. However, if you do not have a well-defined private property right in the pizza, anyone can simply run over and begin eating the pizza. You can see that if there were no private property right, no one would spend the money to buy a pizza. That's no problem with pizzas because there are private property rights. But with some goods and services, the ownership is not so clear-cut. Consider the pollution caused by auto emissions in your area of residence. Each driver of a car is imposing an externality on you. The problem is that neither you nor the driver owns the airspace in which the emissions occur. If you owned the airspace, you could restrict the driving activity or you could charge the driver a price that would pay for the externality. If the driver owned the airspace, you would have to pay the driver not to drive and pollute. In either case, the externality would no longer be external; it would be part of the private costs.

To illustrate why common ownership is a problem, let's consider why most of the communes established during the hippie days of the late 1960s have disappeared. Suppose a commune has five residents and each has $100. The $100 could be deposited in a bank account and over one year would earn $10. With the $100, each member could also purchase a lamb and raise it for a year. Lambs are allowed to graze on a small grass field called the commons. The price the lamb will sell for after one year depends on the amount of weight gained during the year, which in turn depends on the number of lambs sent onto the commons, as shown in Table 1.

If just one lamb grazes on the field, it will sell for $130, a gain of $30, or 30 percent for the year. This is three times the interest rate earned on the savings. Clearly, one lamb will be purchased and sent out to graze. With two lambs, the sale price is $120 each, so the total income for each owner is $20, for a return of 20 percent. With three lambs, the sale price is $112 each, so each owner receives a 12 percent return. With four lambs, the return to each owner is the same as putting the money in the bank, 10 percent. And with five lambs, the owners of the lambs are worse off than they would have been if they had simply put the money in the bank. So, four lambs

---

TABLE 1

Lambs on the Commons

Number of Lambs	Price After One Year	Income/Year
1	$130	$30
2	$120	$20
3	$112	$12
4	$110	$10
5	$109	$9

The *tragedy of the commons* is the name given to the problem created when something is owned commonly rather than privately. Fish, for instance, are overfished because no one owns them. Because there are no private property rights, everyone can catch the fish and no one has an incentive to ensure that enough fish are left to propagate. In Zanzibar, a string of people with nets slowly walks through the stream so that no fish are missed.

use the commons. Each lamb returns $10 profit at the end of the year. Thus, with $40 from the lambs and $10 from interest, the total commune income is $50, exactly what it would be if no lambs had been raised and the money had just been put in the bank.

Suppose the commune had decided to charge rent for using the commons. Would things have turned out differently? What is the most that one person would pay to allow her lamb to graze on the commons? The opportunity cost of the $100 used to purchase the lamb was $10 (what could have been earned from the bank), so the economic profit from the single lamb is $20 ($30 from the sale of the lamb − $10 opportunity cost). But with rent, the situation changes. A single commune member would pay no more than $10 to rent the land, since with that rent the total return is just $10 ($30 from the sale of the lamb − $10 opportunity cost − $10 rent). At a rent of $10, just one lamb would use the commons. Total village income would be the rent plus the $10 return per resident, or $60. When someone owns the commons—when there are private property rights—utilization is reduced and the benefits to society rise.

However, the issue of who is to use the commons nearly destroys the commune because each member blames the others for lowering the price of the lambs. The problem is that when no one owns the commons, too many people use it; no one takes into account the costs that each additional user imposes on others. This is what led to the demise of most of the communes established in the 1960s and early 1970s. Having common ownership led to overutilization and a lack of incentive for anyone to improve things.

The lack of private property ownership or rights is a common problem in the natural resources area. No one has a private property right to the ocean; no one owns the fish in the sea; no one owns the elephants that roam the African plains; and during the past one hundred years, no one owned the American buffalo or bald eagle. Since no one owns them, a "too rapid" rate of use or harvest occurs; the "commons" is overutilized.

We encounter the commons or common ownership with many items. Consider the African elephant. Without ownership of the elephant, no one has an incentive to protect the animal and ensure that it multiplies. Consider a forest. If the forest is

Why Aren't Cows and Chickens on the Endangered Species List?

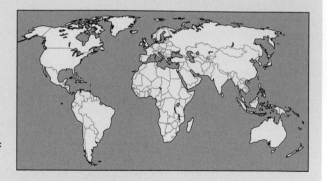

There are plenty of cows and chickens—and although they are consumed in huge numbers, their populations are not declining. Other species are experiencing declining numbers.

The *Red List of Threatened Species,* compiled by the World Conservation Union, gives details of 11,167 animals and plants that are known to be at risk of extinction. The ten animals that are of most concern because of their commercial value include the Hawksbill sea turtles, which are threatened because of the demand for their beautiful shells: the species is the sole source of "tortoiseshell" used to make curios and jewelry. Among the three species of Asian rhinos, the Sumatran rhino is the most threatened, as a result of both habitat loss and poaching for rhino horn, which is used in traditional Chinese medicine. A keystone species for Amazon rainforests, big-leaf mahogany, is highly prized for furniture in the United States, which is the world's leading importer of the wood. Marketed under the more appealing name of "Chilean sea bass," the toothfish has suffered for its popularity among seafood lovers in the United States and Japan. Yellow-headed Amazon parrots are in demand as pets. There are 32 known species of seahorses, and at least 20 are threatened by the unregulated trade in both live seahorses for aquariums and dried seahorses, which are sold as curios and as treatments in traditional Chinese medicine. Whale sharks are the world's largest fish—growing as long as 50 feet—and are found in tropical and warm temperate seas. They have been overfished

for their meat, fins, liver, cartilage, and skin. The Malayan giant turtle, along with dozens of other Asian tortoises and freshwater turtles, is threatened largely by unsustainable collection for food, primarily in China.

What is the difference between cows and chickens and these endangered species? Private ownership. When a species is privately owned, it will flourish because the owner will ensure that the numbers are at the levels that will earn the owner the most income. When a species is commonly owned—or not owned—no one has an incentive to ensure that the species endures. The command approach defines the endangered species list. Once a species is placed on the list, there are bans on hunting it, fishing for it, or otherwise endangering it. But, unless the bans carry huge penalties and are easily enforced, the hunting and fishing will continue.

privately owned, the owner will harvest the trees at a rate that ensures that more trees are available for harvesting in the future.

Common ownership fails to create an incentive for people to produce and consume the best amount for society. This is why communism failed. Under communism, no one has a private property right to anything, including his or her own labor. As a result, no one has an incentive to improve his or her human capital—to increase the value of personal skills and training—and no one has an incentive to ensure that companies are run efficiently. In China prior to 1990, people could not own the apartments in which they lived. All urban living took place in government-owned buildings. Since no one had a private property right to a home, no one had an incentive to take care of it. The buildings became dilapidated, the hallways were filthy, and the landscaping was nonexistent. When the Chinese leaders allowed some private property ownership of apartments, those that were privately owned immediately became much improved. The hallways became clean, the landscaping reappeared, and the apparent quality of the buildings changed virtually overnight. In China's rural areas, farmers were allowed to produce on very small portions of the farms on which they labored and use the output as they wanted. As a result, the privately owned produce accounted for nearly 90 percent of the total produce, even though it was generated on less than 10 percent of the acreage devoted to farming.

2.b. Solutions to Lack of Private Property Rights

The solution to the lack of private property rights seems pretty straightforward: create and enforce private property rights. This has occurred in some instances where what was considered to be a common good became privately owned; the result was less utilization of the commons. For instance, in many nations in which elephants reside, no one owns the elephants. The result is that they are *overutilized*—they are becoming extinct. In most nations with elephants, large national parks have been created in which hunting is forbidden. But, even in the face of these bans on hunting, the reduction in the number of elephants has continued. A decade ago, Africa's elephant population was more than a million; it has now fallen to less than half of that.

In contrast to the common ownership strategy, the governments of Botswana, Zimbabwe, and South Africa created private property rights by allowing individuals to own elephants. These elephant farmers ensure that the elephants breed and reproduce so that they can be sold for their tusks, for hunting in special hunting parks, or to zoos in developed nations. This has led to a revival of the elephant population in these nations.

Thousands of acres of Amazon forest are burned each year to provide land for Brazil's ranchers and subsistence farmers and to extract woods for use elsewhere. No one owns the rainforest, leading it to be overutilized. If the Brazilian government created private property rights to the forest, it would be taken care of. Consider what has happened in Sweden and neighboring Finland. Sweden and Finland have more standing forest today than at any time in the past. Unlike the situation in Canada, where the forest is dwindling, most of the forest land in Sweden is privately owned. Private owners do not cut at a loss and do not cut to maintain employment levels or for other political reasons. They cut at a rate that yields them the greatest return. If they simply razed their forests or sold off all their animals, they would have no income in coming years. So they cut or harvest at rates that ensure viable populations.

It is not always easy to establish private property rights. What occurs in cases where private property cannot be created, such as with ocean fish? Without private ownership, the oceans will be overutilized and species of fish will become extinct. The response of governments has been to restrict fishing around their shores, but this does not solve the problem. Instead, as the cost of fishing rises—as it becomes increasingly more difficult to find the fish—alternatives such as fish farms begin to arise. Private property rights arise to solve the commons problem.

RECAP

1. Private property rights enable someone to own an item, that is, to dispose of, destroy, share, give away, or do anything that the person wants with the item.
2. When there are no private property rights to an item, that item cannot be bought or sold. No one has an incentive to produce the item or to purchase it.
3. When something is commonly owned, that something is overutilized.
4. The solution to a lack of private property rights is to create such rights. Sometimes the creation of private property rights is not straightforward.

3. Public Goods

According to the **principle of mutual exclusivity,** the owner of private property is entitled to enjoy the consumption of that property *privately.* The principle of mutual exclusivity refers to a well-defined private property right. It says that if you own a good, I cannot use it or consume it without your permission; and if I own a good, you cannot use it or consume it unless I grant permission. When I purchase a pizza, it is mine to consume as I wish. You have no right to the pizza unless I provide that right. If the principle of mutual exclusivity does not apply to a particular good or service, then anyone can use or consume that good or service.

If the principal of mutual exclusivity does not apply and if the use of the good by one person does not diminish the quantity or quality available for other consumers, then the good is called a **public good.** The TV airwaves illustrate the characteristics of a public good quite well. A television station broadcasts on a certain frequency, and anyone can pick up that station. It doesn't matter whether one person or 1 million people tune in to the station—the signal is the same, and additional users do not deprive others of any of the good. If your neighbor tunes in to the channel you are watching, you don't receive a weaker signal.

3.a. The Problem

When goods are public, an individual has an incentive to be a **free rider**—a consumer or producer who enjoys the benefits of a good or service without paying for that good or service. As an example, suppose that national defense was not provided by the government and paid for with tax money, and that you would not be protected by the armed forces unless you paid a fee. A problem would arise because national defense is a public good; you would be protected whether or not you paid for it as long as others paid. Of course, since each person has an incentive not to pay for it, few will voluntarily do so, and the quantity of the good produced will be "too small" from society's viewpoint.

A private good comes in units that can be purchased by individuals, and once the good is purchased, the individual owns it and can decide how to consume it. A public good, in contrast, is not divisible into units that can be purchased and owned. Once the good is produced, the producer is unable to exclude nonpayers from consuming it. Since they can enjoy the good without paying for it, many will not pay. As a result, a demand curve for the public good may not exist.

Suppose that there are two people in society, Jesse and Rafael, whose willingness to pay for different quantities of a public good—public radio—is shown in Table 2. Jesse would be willing to pay as much as $5 for one day of radio programming,

TABLE 2			
The Demand for a Public Good	**Quantity**	**Willingness to Pay per Unit**	
		Jesse	Rafael
	1	$5	$3
	2	$4	$2
	3	$3	$1
	4	$2	$0

FIGURE 6

The Lack of Demand for a Public Good

D represents the willingness and ability to buy a good. When the good is public, no one has to pay, but some people do pay, represented as D_{PG}.

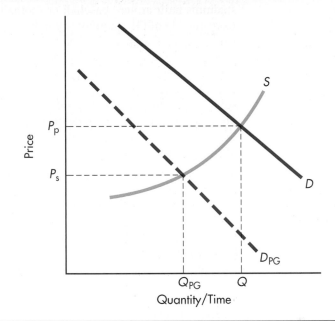

while Rafael would be willing to pay $3. Jesse would be willing to pay just $4 each for two days of programming and Rafael only $2 per day. Thus, in Table 2 we can see society's willingness to pay for different quantities of the public good. However, willingness to pay and actually paying are different things; since neither Jesse nor Rafael has to pay for any quantity, each may choose to listen without paying anything. There would then be no demand for the radio programming.

Figure 6 illustrates the case of a public good. The willingness and ability to pay for various quantities are shown by the demand curve, D. However, the actual amount of money spent to purchase the public good depends on how many people pay even though they would not have to. If the public good were private, the market for it would be supply curve S and demand curve D. But, since the good is public, fewer people are willing to pay for the good. The demand is less, if it exists at all. As a result, *too few* public goods are provided.

Examples of public goods that are often noted are national defense, lighthouses, fire protection, and police protection. If one rich person established a missile defense system on her property, all her neighbors would enjoy the protection without paying anything. Lighthouses signal landmasses to passing ships. Since any ship can see the light and heed the warning, none of them has an incentive to pay for the service. If my neighbors subscribe to fire or police protection services, then I can enjoy the benefit without having to subscribe myself. There is a market failure: too few resources are devoted to the production of the public good.

3.b. Solutions to Public Good Problems

?

3. Why do governments create, own, and run national parks?

The organization Defenders of Wildlife collects money from its members and uses the money to pay landowners who allow wolves to live on their properties. The host landowner receives a payment of $5,000 for each litter of pups reared by wolves. As a result of this program, the population of wolves in the Yellowstone Basin has risen. Other attempts have been made to turn public goods into private goods. Large stadiums built around baseball or football fields restrict the viewing of the games from outside of the stadiums—you have to purchase a ticket to see the contest. The Rural Metro Company of Scottsdale, Arizona, provides private subscription fire protection to residents of Scottsdale, Fountain Hills, and surrounding communities. The company will put out fires for subscribers at no cost, but will put out fires for nonsubscribers for a price that equals Rural Metro's cost. In general, however, the solution for the free-rider problems of public goods is to have the government produce the good. National defense, wildlife reserves in Kenya, wilderness areas in the United States, and the park system in every country are government provisions of public goods.

3.b.1. Government Provision of Public Goods
A public good requires only a means of financing the production. It need not be the government that produces the good. Why the government produces the good rather than simply financing its production is a topic of some controversy. John Lott, an economist, argues that public education is government-provided not because it is a public good nor because of its positive externalities, but because having the government provide it forces every student to learn what the government wants students to learn; in other words, public education is a way to brainwash the public.

Another argument for government provision of public goods is that a private company would have difficulty recovering its cost of production. In other words, no private company would provide the good. In many cases of what are called public goods, private for-profit firms can provide the good more efficiently than can the government. Private for-profit firms offer emergency vehicle service (ambulances) in some cities, offer wastewater management and drinking water in some cities, offer fire protection in some cities, offer highways in some areas, and so on. But, if the good is a public good, how can the private company collect for its services? The government has to tax either the public or the users of the good and compensate the private company.

The mere fact that a good is a public good does not necessarily mean that government ought to provide it. Government provision of a public good makes sense only if there is no other, less costly way of providing it. Even if private companies do not provide the good or service, it may be more efficient for a benevolent society—a charity—to provide the good or service. In 2002, Americans donated almost $200 billion to private charities, many of which provide public goods to their communities.

RECAP

1. A public good is one for which the principle of mutual exclusivity does not hold, and when one person uses the item, that use does not reduce the quantity available for others.

2. Since a public good can be used without paying for it, people have no incentive to purchase the item. A free-rider problem arises.

3. A free-rider problem occurs when someone can contribute less to an activity than that person can get back in return because that person relies on others to make up the difference. The problem is that if many people free-ride, the item or activity is not produced.

4. A solution to the public good problem is to turn the public good into one that is privately provided.

5. The government solution to the public good problem is to supply the good or to finance a private company so that it will supply the good.

4. What is the reason the government requires the listing of ingredients on food packaging?

4. Asymmetric Information

When people engage in a transaction, buying or selling a good or service, they are reasonably sure of what that good or service is. But, what happens when one party to the exchange knows a lot more about the good or service than the other party? Exchange that occurs under such conditions is called *exchange with asymmetric information*.

4.a. Adverse Selection

When you purchase a used car, you are probably unsure of the car's quality. You could hire a mechanic to look at the car before you buy it, but because that procedure is quite expensive, you probably choose to forgo it. Most people assume that cars offered for sale by private individuals are defective in some way, and they are not willing to pay top dollar for such a car. In Figure 7, the market for high-quality used cars and that for low-quality used cars is shown. People offer their cars for sale as shown along the supply curve. But, although demand for high-quality used cars would be D_{HQ} if demanders could differentiate high- from low-quality used cars, the actual demand is D_A. Thus, people who do have high-quality used cars for sale cannot obtain the high price that they deserve. The result is that low-quality cars continue to be sold in the secondhand market, but high-quality cars do not. This result of the good being driven out of a market by the bad is called **adverse selection.** Adverse selection occurs when unobservable qualities are misvalued because of a lack of information.

adverse selection: the problem that occurs when higher-quality consumers or producers are driven out of the market because unobservable qualities are misvalued

Adverse selection can occur in many different markets. For instance, banks do not always know which people who are applying for loans will default and which will pay on time. How can a bank distinguish among loan applicants? If the bank increases the interest rate in an attempt to drive high-risk applicants out of the market, adverse selection increases. As the bank raises the interest rate on loans, high-risk applicants continue to apply for loans, but low-risk applicants do not. As a result, only high-risk applicants remain in the market.

Adverse selection may occur in insurance markets as well. People purchase automobile or health insurance even if they are excellent drivers and enjoy good health. As the cost of insurance rises, the good drivers and healthy people may reduce their coverage, while the poor drivers and unhealthy people maintain their coverage. As a result, high-risk applicants take the place of more desirable low-risk applicants in the market for insurance.

4.b. Moral Hazard

When information is costly to obtain, monitoring the behavior of the other party to an exchange may be difficult. People who discover that they have a serious illness and then purchase health insurance are taking advantage of the insurance company's

FIGURE 7

Adverse Selection

High-quality cars should be priced at P_{HQ}. Because potential buyers cannot distinguish between high- and low-quality cars, the actual price of high-quality cars is P_A. The result is that only low-quality cars remain in the used-car market.

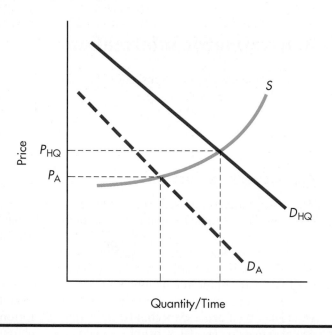

Quantity/Time

lack of information and creating a moral hazard. A person who drives much less carefully after obtaining car insurance is creating a moral hazard. A person who takes less care to be healthy after obtaining health insurance is creating a moral hazard. When verification of trades or contracts is difficult and when people can change their behavior from what was anticipated when a trade or contract was made, a **moral hazard** exists.

moral hazard: the problem that arises when people change their behavior from what was expected of them when they engaged in a trade or contract

4.c. Solutions to the Asymmetric Information Issue

Why can't someone with a high-quality used car simply tell the buyer about the car's condition? The reason is that the seller has an incentive to exaggerate the condition of the car and the buyer has an incentive to believe that it is of lower quality than it is. The problem can be resolved privately if the seller can credibly demonstrate the high quality of the car. A seller must provide credible information about the quality of the good. One approach is to devote considerable resources—to spend money—to demonstrate that the seller is credible. Consider the case of a sidewalk vendor who sells neckties on the street corner. If such a "firm" tells customers that it will guarantee the quality of its ties, customers will certainly question the validity of the guarantee. Think about it: the seller can pick up and leave with virtually no cost. It has no headquarters, no brand name, no costly equipment, no loyal customers to worry about. In short, a firm with no obvious stake in its future has a difficult time persuading potential customers that it will make good on its promises.

The incentives are different for a firm that has devoted significant resources to items that have no liquidation value, such as advertising campaigns or specific symbols like McDonald's golden arches. Firms that have done this have reputations to protect and want repeat business. And, knowing that, buyers can place greater trust in such firms' promise of a high-quality product. Businesses purchase advertising time and space on television, on radio, and in the newspapers. They construct elaborate signs, build fancy storefronts, and attempt to locate in places where they are visible and accessible. They also package their products in carefully designed boxes and wrappings. All of these expenditures are intended to convince people that their products, identified by brand names, are quality products.

Another way to inform consumers of the quality of the product is to provide a guarantee against product defects. Guarantees are difficult to fake. A low-quality product will break down frequently, making the guarantee quite costly for the firm. Thus, the higher the quality of the product, the better the guarantee offered by the firm.

What about the used-car market or the market for insurance or loans—how can individuals or firms spend enough to provide quality assurance or provide guarantees that buyers will believe? Many argue that they cannot, and that that is why government rules and regulations are necessary. The Federal Trade Commission restricts advertising, requiring that claims be demonstrable. Many state governments and the federal government require a time period after an exchange has occurred during which the buyer can change his mind; if before two days are up I decide that I don't want the product, I can return it and get my money back. In the case of insurance and loans, government rules and regulations indicate who is eligible for loans and whether different customers can be charged different rates.

4.c.1. Copayments and Deductibles

Sometimes a moral hazard problem can be reduced by having the person or firm creating the hazard and the person or firm being taken advantage of share in the costs. This is a reason that insurance companies require a deductible and banks and other lending institutions require a down payment: so that the company and the customer share in the expenses and risks. You are more likely to drive carefully and safeguard your health if you have to pay some of the costs of an accident or illness. Similarly, if you must pay a copayment, you are less likely to behave in a way that causes you to bear a large number of such copayments. And finally, insurance companies will often cancel a contract after a few claims have been made in a certain period of time. After two or three claims, the company believes that the moral hazard problem has occurred and that resolution requires canceling the contract. In many instances, when someone cannot get insurance, the government steps in to subsidize the insurance or to provide the insurance through government agencies.

RECAP

1. Adverse selection occurs when buyers have less information than sellers; a situation can arise in which high-quality products are driven out of the market, leaving only low-quality products.

2. Moral hazard occurs when one party in a transaction alters his behavior with regard to that item once he has purchased it. For instance, once someone is insured, that person may act differently, undertaking more risk.

3. Adverse selection and moral hazard problems are often resolved privately through copayments, deductibles, and other arrangements that reduce the incentives to change behavior or not reveal information.

4. The government is often called upon to intervene by requiring that information be provided and by subsidizing the activity in which a moral hazard exists.

5. Government Failure

5. Is government the best way to solve market failure problems?

While it is one thing to argue that a market failure cannot be resolved privately, it is quite another to argue that the inefficiency created by the failure is worse than the inefficiency of having the government try to solve the problem. At least this is what James Buchanan, who received the 1986 Nobel Prize in economics, argues. In many countries, expenditures on public goods, tax policy, and laws regulating behavior are determined by the votes of democratically elected representatives. Inefficiencies often arise not because legislators are incompetent or ignorant, but because of problems with individual incentives. We can illustrate some of these incentives with a simple story that you may have experienced.

Herb and nine friends are having dinner at Chimichangas in Phoenix. To simplify the task of paying for their meal, they have agreed in advance to split the cost of their meal equally, with each paying one-tenth of the total check. Herb recognizes that if he can order more expensive items than the others, he will be gaining at the expense of his nine friends. So he orders appetizers, the most expensive entree, and then the most exorbitant dessert and drinks. The problem is that each of his nine friends recognizes the same thing. Each orders far more than he would if he were dining alone. As a result, the total bill rises.

This example illustrates one of the inefficiencies of the political process. Legislators will support one another's pork-barrel programs, causing the total government spending to rise significantly. Consider a voter in a congressional district that contains one one-hundredth of the country's taxpayers. Suppose that district's representative is able to deliver a public project that generates benefits of $100 million for the district but that costs the government $150 million. Since the district's share of the tax bill for the project will be only $150 million/100 = $1.5 million, residents of the district are $98.5 million better off with the project than without it. And that explains why so many voters favor legislators who have a successful record of "bringing home the bacon."

Why would legislator A support such a project in legislator B's home district? After all, B's project will cause A's constituents' taxes to rise by a small amount, while they get absolutely no benefit. The answer is that if A does not support B's project, then B will not support A's. The practice of legislators supporting one another's projects is called **logrolling.**

Another source of inefficiency in government occurs because the gains from government projects are often concentrated in the hands of a few beneficiaries, while the costs are spread among many. This means that the beneficiaries have an incentive to organize and lobby in favor of their projects. Individual taxpayers, in contrast, have little at stake in any public project and therefore have little incentive to incur the cost of mobilizing themselves in opposition. This is called **rent seeking.** Rent seeking is an activity that consumes resources not for producing something, but merely for transferring wealth from one sector of society to another.

logrolling: an inefficiency in the political process in which legislators support one another's projects in order to ensure support for their own

rent seeking: the use of resources simply to transfer wealth from one group to another without increasing production or total wealth

Nobel laureate Milton Friedman has said that no bureaucrat spends taxpayers' money as carefully as the taxpayers themselves would have. Beyond the fact that the legislative process often results in pork-barrel programs, we must worry that government employees may not have incentives to get the most for what the government spends. Since the government is not a profit-maximizing entity, it has no incentive to minimize costs. The incentive of the government employees is to complete the task, no matter what the cost.

Because of the inefficiencies of the government, many economists have asked which is worse, market failure or government failure. Nevertheless the debate continues: how much should the government intervene in the market? What should the government do?

RECAP

1. The government is inefficient, and having the government resolve market failure problems may impose greater costs on society than if the government did not try to resolve the problems.

2. Government inefficiencies result from the legislative process, from the incentives of government employees, and from rent seeking.

3. The question asked by many economists is, which is worse, market failure or government failure?

Summary

? What are externalities?

1. A market failure occurs when the market is not able to reach the equilibrium that is most efficient, when resources are not allocated to their highest-valued use. *Preview*

2. The government is often called upon to resolve market failures. *Preview*

3. A freely functioning market results in resources being allocated to their highest-valued use. When something occurs that leads resources not to be so allocated, we say that a market failure has resulted. *Preview*

4. Private benefits of a transaction are the gains from trade that the individuals involved in the transaction achieve. Private costs are the opportunity costs that the individuals involved in the transaction must bear. *§1*

5. Social costs and benefits are the total costs and benefits created by a transaction. When some costs are borne by those who are not involved in the private transaction, a negative externality occurs, so that social costs exceed private costs. When some benefits are received by those who are not involved in the

private transaction, a positive externality occurs, so that social benefits exceed private benefits. *§1*

6. When social costs and benefits are not equal to private costs and benefits, the market outcome is either overutilization or underutilization: resources are not allocated to their most highly valued use. *§1.a*

7. There are several approaches to reducing the inefficiencies created by externalities. One approach is to impose a tax on the individual or institutions creating the externality. In another approach, the government requires or commands that those creating negative externalities reduce the amount created or that more production of positive externalities occur. In yet another, the government creates a market for the negative externalities by establishing ownership of the right to create the negative externality and allowing that ownership to be exchanged. *§1.b.1–§1.b.3*

8. The Coase theorem states that as long as private property rights can be established, private individuals will be able to solve an externality problem without government intervention. *§1.c*

9. Private ownership was abolished in the communes; the idea was that everyone would own everything and that all would contribute what they could. *§2.a*

10. Common ownership results in a market failure. Too much of the commonly owned good is consumed, and not enough is produced. *§2.a*

11. The solution to a common ownership problem is to create private property rights in any case where such rights can be created. *§2.c.1*

? **Why do governments create, own, and run national parks?**

12. One approach taken to resolve common ownership problems is for the government to claim ownership of the common good and to provide it as the government defines. *§3.a*

13. Private property rights provide ownership. In order to buy or sell something, one must be able to decide how that something is to be used. *§3.a*

14. Without private property rights, anyone can claim partial ownership of an item and thereby consume that item. Without private ownership, no one would be willing to purchase an item, since others could consume that item. *§3.a*

15. Free riding means that one person will contribute less than what that person expects to get in return because the person expects others to make up the difference. *§3.a*

16. People free-ride because they can—their self-interest tells them to get the most for the least. *§3.a*

17. The problem with free riding is that if many people or everyone free-rides, nothing gets done. *§3.a*

18. Solutions to public good problems include private provision of the public good and government provision of the good. *§3.b*

? **What is the reason the government requires the listing of ingredients on food packaging?**

19. When buyers have less information than sellers, a situation can arise in which high-quality products are driven out of the market, leaving just low-quality products. This is called *adverse selection*. *§4.a*

20. When buyers have more information than sellers about a particular item, buyers may alter their behavior with regard to that item once they have purchased it. For instance, once someone is insured, that person may act differently, taking on more risk. This is called moral hazard. *§4.b*

21. Problems of adverse selection and moral hazard are often resolved privately through copayments, deductibles, and other such arrangements that reduce the incentives to change behavior or not reveal information. *§4.c*

? **Is government the best way to solve market failure problems?**

22. Since the government has no competition, it is generally less efficient than the private market. *§5*

23. Government failures may result from logrolling and rent seeking. *§5*

Key Terms

market failure *Preview*

private costs *§1*

externality *§1*

social cost *§1*

Coase theorem *§1.c*

principle of mutual exclusivity *§3*

public good *§3*

free rider *§3.a*

adverse selection *§4.a*

moral hazard *§4.b*

logrolling *§5*

rent seeking *§5*

Exercises

1. The three following demand schedules constitute the total demand for a particular good.

   a. Determine the market demand schedule for the good if it is a private good.
   b. Determine the market demand schedule for the good if it is a public good.

Bob		Sally		Rafael	
P	Q_d	*P*	Q_d	*P*	Q_d
$6	0	$6	0	$6	1
$5	1	$5	0	$5	2
$4	2	$4	1	$4	3
$3	3	$3	2	$3	4
$2	4	$2	3	$2	5
$1	5	$1	4	$1	6

2. Using the public good described in exercise 1 and the following supply schedule, determine the optimal quantity of the good. Explain how you determined this quantity.

P	Q_s
$10	15
$ 9	11
$ 7	9
$ 6	8
$ 4	7
$ 2	4
$ 1	3

3. Use the following information to answer these questions:

   a. What is the external cost per unit of output?
   b. What level of output will be produced?
   c. What level of output should be produced to achieve economic efficiency?
   d. What is the value to society of correcting the externality?

Quantity	Private Cost	Social Cost	Benefit
1	$ 2	$ 4	$12
2	$ 6	$10	$22
3	$12	$18	$30
4	$20	$28	$36
5	$30	$40	$40

4. What level of tax would be appropriate to internalize the externality in exercise 3?

5. If, in exercise 3, the Private Cost and Social Cost columns were reversed, you would have an example of what? Would too much or too little of the good be produced? How would the market failure be resolved, by tax or by subsidy?

6. What is meant by the term *overfishing?* What is the fundamental problem associated with overfishing of the oceans? What might lead to *underfishing?*

7. Explain why the optimal amount of pollution is not a zero amount. Use the same explanation to discuss the amount of health and safety that the government should require in the workplace.

8. Suppose the following table describes the marginal costs and marginal benefits of waste (garbage) reduction. What is the optimal amount of garbage? What is the situation if no garbage is allowed to be produced?

Percentage of Waste Eliminated	Marginal Costs (millions of dollars)	Marginal Benefits (millions of dollars)
10%	10	1,000
20%	15	500
30%	25	100
40%	40	50
50%	70	20
60%	110	5
70%	200	3
80%	500	2
90%	900	1
100%	2,000	0

9. Elephants eat 300 pounds of food per day. They flourished in Africa when they could roam over huge areas of land, eating the vegetation in one area and then moving on so that the vegetation could renew itself. Now, the area over which elephants can roam is declining. Without some action, the elephants will become extinct. What actions might save the elephants? What are the costs and benefits of such actions?

10. What can explain why the value of pollution permits in one area of the country is rising 20 percent per year, while in another it is unchanged from year to year? What would you expect to occur as a result of this differential?

11. Smokers impose negative externalities on nonsmokers. Suppose the airspace in a restaurant is a resource owned by the restaurant owner.

    a. How would the owner respond to the negative externalities of smokers?

    b. Suppose that the smokers owned the airspace. How would that change matters?

    c. How about if the nonsmokers owned the airspace?

    d. Finally, consider what would occur if the government passed a law banning all smoking. How would the outcome compare with the outcomes described above?

12. Discuss the argument that education should be subsidized because it creates a positive externality.

13. If the best solution to solving the positive externality problem of education is to provide a subsidy, explain why education systems in all countries are nationalized, that is, are government entities.

Take the ACE Practice Test for this chapter to review the important concepts and get immediate feedback with answers.

economics.college.hmco.com/students

Bates College Students Retire Air Pollution Permit Worth a Ton of Sulfur Dioxide

For the third year, students in the 200-level Environmental Economics course at Bates College have successfully bid on and purchased a government permit for the atmospheric release of a ton of sulfur dioxide [SO_2], a pollutant that causes acid rain.

The 50 students in the two sections of the course each put $5 toward a bid for the U.S. Environmenal Protection Agency's 11th annual SO_2-permit auction, hosted by the Chicago Board of Trade. As it has each year, the class will retire its permit.

"We're not going to resell it, so that ton of sulfur dioxide will never be emitted into the atmosphere," says Lynne Lewis, associate professor of economics at Bates and the originator of the college's annual bidding effort.

The auction, held every March, is a mechanism in the EPA's Acid Rain Program, which uses a market-based "cap and trade" approach to curtail air pollution. "It's always sort of cool to see the theory applied in real life," says senior biology major Mark Thomson, of Minneapolis, who took the course with Lewis.

"There's something very tangible about seeing Bates' name on the actual auction," says Thomson. "And the fact that we obtained a permit is excellent, because you study different market-based incentive programs to reduce pollution, but to actually do it—and to say that we're willing to pay because we don't want acid rain in Maine—is a great opportunity."

Lewis came to Bates in 2000 and initiated the bid process in 2001. "One of the exciting parts of this program is that anyone can buy a permit," she says. "It's fairly straightforward."

[The EPA website offers ample information about the process, with a good starting point being the "Acid Rain Program SO_2 Allowances Fact Sheet" page at http://www.epa.gov/airmarkt/arp/allfact.html.]

This year's "clearing price" per permit—that is, the lowest successful bid—was $171.80. The Ohio-based American Electric Power, the nation's largest electrical supplier, won 99.9 percent of the 125,000 permits on offer. Bates' bid was $185.50, fourth-lowest of the 20 successful bids.

Determining how much to bid, Lewis says, is "the challenging part of the exercise, but also makes it fun to do with my class."

She divided her students into teams and assigned each to research the bid history for the auction, suggest a bid, and offer a defense of the amount. The final bid was the average of all bids. Student contributions left over were donated to the Acid Rain Retirement Fund, a program at the University of Southern Maine that was the only other Maine bidder this year.

Tradable permits "are something that economists have been touting for a long time as a good thing," Lewis says. "With economic incentives for pollution control, you can achieve an environmental standard at a lower cost, which is good for everybody." . . .

Source: Copyright 2003 AScribe Inc.

AScribe Newswire/April 24, 2003

The United States was the first nation to create a market for the buying and selling of rights to pollute water and air, but it is not alone. Several governments have proposed the creation of a market system to control air and water pollution. Why would a government create such a market? Why doesn't the government simply forbid firms from polluting the air and water?

A command system will reduce the amount of pollution created, but at what costs? As discussed in the chapter, by requiring firms to emit some restricted amount of pollution, the government is not allowing resources to be allocated to their most valuable use. In some cases, a firm might have to shut down because it can't meet the government's restrictions. In other cases, a firm could increase the amount of pollution it creates because it was emitting a smaller quantity than that permitted by the government. In no case does a firm have a choice or an incentive to meet the government's requirements in an efficient manner.

We discussed how such a market system is created. Essentially, the government specifies an amount of allowable pollution for a particular area or in a particular water system and then sells permits that allow firms to pollute. A firm compares the price of an additional permit to the cost of reducing pollution by the amount specified on the permit. If the price of the permit is greater than the cost of reducing pollution, the firm will choose to reduce the pollutants it emits. In other words, firms compare marginal benefits (MB) and marginal costs (MC)

and purchase additional permits until $MB = MC$. Thus, the market system provides an incentive for firms to use a cleaner technology when the price of the permits becomes more expensive than the purchase of new, cleaner technology.

As described in the chapter, the price of a permit is determined by demand and supply. As the government reduces the number of permits supplied, the price of the permits rises, *ceteris paribus*. As the price rises, the quantity demanded declines, and more firms choose to reduce their emissions rather than purchase additional permits.

An important aspect of the market approach to minimizing the externality problem it that it is the firm's choice as to when it is best to switch to the new technology. This ensures that resources are used in their most efficient manner—that is, where they have the highest value. The command approach does not do this. There is an additional aspect of the market system approach: it allows anyone interested in reducing pollution to bid for the permits. This drives the price up and induces more firms to adopt the more efficient or less polluting technologies more quickly. For instance, groups like the Sierra Club, the Nature Conservancy, Greenpeace, the Czech Republic's Children of the Earth, and even a group of college students such as at Bates College could raise funds to purchase permits and then simply not use them. With fewer permits available, the price of the permits rises and the quantity of pollution created is reduced.

Part Seven

Resource Markets

CHAPTER 29

Resource Markets

1. **Who are the buyers and sellers of resources?**

2. **How are resource prices determined?**

3. **How does a firm allocate its expenditures among the various resources?**

Do you recycle? Are you concerned with global warming, saving the rain forest, and reducing pollution? Perhaps you've noted the number of homeless people on the streets and wondered why they are homeless and what can be done about homelessness. Have you ever been discriminated against because of your age, race, or sex? Have you been touched by illegal drugs—gang wars, drive-by shootings, crime? In the following chapters we discuss some aspects of these issues as we examine the resource markets. Remember that resource markets provide the resources, or ingredients, for producing goods and services. They include the markets for labor, capital, and land in general terms, but more specifically they involve people and their jobs, physical and financial capital, and natural resources. In this chapter we'll look at how firms choose their resources and how firms draw on economic theory to help them decide what resources and how much of a given resource to use. In the chapters that follow, we'll look at each market more closely, examining some of the societal questions and issues that arise in the process. ■

1. Buyers and Sellers of Resources

1. Who are the buyers and sellers of resources?

resource market: a market that provides one of the resources for producing goods and services: labor, capital, and land

There are three general types of **resource markets:** those for land, labor, and capital. The price and quantity of each resource are determined in its resource market. Rent and the quantity of land used are determined in the land market. The wage rate and the number of people employed are determined in the labor market. The interest rate and the quantity of capital used are determined in the capital market. Although each of these markets is somewhat unique, they are all markets and thus simply involve the demand for and supply of that particular resource. Although these markets are actually no different from the other markets that we have examined to this point, the fact that they are markets for goods and services that are used to create and sell other goods and services complicates matters just a little.

1.a. The Resource Markets

To understand the resource markets, you need to realize that the roles of firms and households are reversed from what they are in the product markets. Figure 1 is the simplest circular flow diagram you saw in Chapter 4. It illustrates the roles of firms and households in the product and resource markets. The product market is represented by the top lines in the figure. Households buy goods and services from firms, as shown by the line going from firms to households; and firms sell goods and services and receive revenue, as shown by the line going from households to firms. The resource market is represented by the bottom half of the diagram in Figure 1. Households are the sellers of resources, and firms are the buyers of resources. Households sell resources, as shown by the line going from households to firms; and firms pay households income, as shown by the line going from firms to households.

Resources are wanted not for themselves but for what they produce. A firm uses resources in order to produce goods and services. Thus, the demand for a resource by a firm depends on the demand for the goods and services that the firm produces.

FIGURE 1

The Market for Resources

The buyers of resources are firms that purchase resources in order to produce goods and services. The sellers of resources are households that supply resources in order to obtain income with which to purchase goods and services.

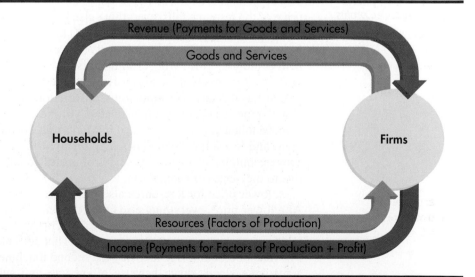

---

derived demand: demand stemming from what a resource can produce, not demand for the resource itself

For this reason, the demand for resources is often called a **derived demand:** an automobile manufacturer uses land, labor, and capital to produce cars; a retail T-shirt store uses land, labor, and capital to sell T-shirts; a farmer uses land, labor, and capital to produce agricultural products.

Households supply resources in order to earn income. By offering to work, individuals supply their labor; by purchasing stocks, bonds, and other financial capital, households supply firms with the ability to acquire capital; by offering their land and the minerals, trees, and other natural resources associated with it, households supply land.

RECAP

1. Resource markets are classified into three types: those for land, labor, and capital.
2. The price of each type of resource—rent, wages, and interest—and the quantity of each resource used are determined in the resource markets.
3. The buyers of resources are firms; the suppliers are households.

2. The Market Demand for and Supply of Resources

2. How are resource prices determined?

Firms demand resources and households supply resources. Except for this reversal in buyers and sellers, the supply and demand curves for resource markets look just like the supply and demand curves for product markets. The market demand curve slopes downward, and the market supply curve slopes upward. In resource markets, as in product markets, equilibrium defines the price and quantity. Changes in demand or supply cause the equilibrium price and quantity to change.

2.a. Market Demand

A firm chooses inputs in order to maximize profits.

The demand curve for a resource slopes down, as shown in Figure 2, because as the price of the resource falls, everything else held constant, producers are more *willing* and more *able* to use (to purchase or rent) that resource. If the price of the resource falls, that resource becomes relatively less expensive than other resources that the firm could use. Firms will substitute this now relatively less expensive resource for other now relatively more expensive resources. Thus substitution occurs in production just as it does in consumption. Construction firms switch from copper tubing to plastic pipe as copper becomes relatively more expensive than plastic. Firms move from Manhattan to Dallas as land in Manhattan becomes relatively more expensive than land in Dallas. Economists may be hired to teach finance, management, and even accounting classes as the wages of professionals in those other fields rise relative to the wages of economists.

A lower price for a resource also increases a firm's *ability* to hire that resource. At a lower price, everything else held constant, firms can purchase more resources for the same total cost. If the price of a machine drops by 50 percent, the firm can buy two machines at the old cost for one. This does not mean that the firm will buy two machines, but it is able to buy the second machine. Thus, the demand curve for a resource slopes down because of income and substitution effects just as the

FIGURE 2

Resource Market Demand and Market Supply

The demand curve for a resource slopes down, reflecting the inverse relation between the price of the resource and the quantity demanded. The supply curve for a resource slopes up, reflecting the direct relation between the price of the resource and the quantity supplied. Equilibrium occurs where the two curves intersect; the quantities demanded and supplied are the same at the equilibrium price. If the resource price is greater than the equilibrium price, a surplus of the resource arises and drives the price back down to equilibrium. If the resource price is less than the equilibrium price, a shortage occurs and forces the price back up to equilibrium.

demand curve for a product slopes down because of income and substitution effects, as you learned in the chapter on consumer choice.

2.a.1. The Elasticity of Resource Demand

The amount by which firms will alter their use of a resource when the price of that resource changes is measured by the price elasticity of resource demand. The price elasticity of the demand for a resource, e_r, is defined in exactly the same way as the price elasticity of demand—

In recent years, the textile industry in the United States has been relocated to other countries. The cost of doing business in the United States is much higher than the costs in Vietnam, China, Laos, and other nations because the cost of labor is so much higher. As the demand for textile workers in Vietnam and other nations increases, the wages of those workers rise. As the demand for textile workers in the United States declines, the wages of those workers decline—and jobs disappear.

as the percentage change in the quantity demanded of a resource divided by the percentage change in the price of the resource:

$$e_r = \frac{\text{percentage change in quantity demanded of resource } j}{\text{percentage change in price of resource } j}$$

If the price of lumber rises by 10 percent and the quantity demanded falls by 5 percent, the price elasticity of demand for lumber is 0.5. If the rental rate of office space falls by 5 percent and the quantity demanded increases by 20 percent, the price elasticity of demand for office space is 4. The price elasticity of demand for a resource depends on:

- The price elasticity of demand for the product the resource is used to produce
- The proportion of total costs constituted by the resource
- The number of substitutes for the resource
- The time period under consideration

Price Elasticity of the Product   The price elasticity of demand for a resource depends on the price elasticity of demand for the product the resource is being used to produce. For instance, if the price elasticity of demand for newspapers is very high and the price of newspapers increases, the quantity demanded of newspapers will fall by a "great deal." As a result, a similarly "great deal" fewer resources are needed. Suppose, then, that the price of one of these resources, ink, rises. If the higher ink cost leads to a rise in the price of newspapers, then the quantity of newspapers demanded will decline by a significant amount and cause the quantity of ink purchased to decline by a significant amount. Everything else the same, we can say that the larger the price elasticity of demand for a product, the larger the price elasticity of demand for the resources used to produce that product. The reverse is true as well.

Proportion of Total Costs   The larger one resource's proportion of the total costs of producing a good, the higher the price elasticity of demand for that resource. If airplanes constitute 60 percent of the total costs of running an airline, the price elasticity of demand for airplanes will be high. A small increase in the price of an airplane will tend to raise the airline's costs significantly, and this is likely to increase the price of tickets. The higher price for tickets will reduce the quantity demanded and thereby reduce the number of airplanes demanded.

Number of Substitutes   The number of substitutes for a resource affects the price elasticity of demand for that resource. For instance, if copper tubing, plastic tubing, steel tubing, or corrugated aluminum tubing can be used in construction equally well, the price elasticity of demand for any one of these types of tubing will be relatively high. Even a small increase in the price of copper tubing will cause firms to switch immediately to other types of tubing.

Time Period   The time period is also important in determining the price elasticity of demand. The longer the period of time under consideration, the greater the price elasticity of demand for a resource. A longer period of time enables firms to discover other substitutes and to move relatively immobile resources into or out of use.

The price elasticity of resource demand varies according to the four factors just mentioned. The price elasticity of resource demand also varies along a straight-line resource demand curve, going from elastic to inelastic as we move down the demand curve, just as is the case with a product demand curve (see the chapter on demand and supply elasticities).

2.a.2. Shifts in the Demand for a Resource

The demand curve for a resource will shift when one of the *nonprice* determinants of demand changes. Nonprice determinants of demand for a resource include:

- The price of the product the resource is used to produce
- The productivity of a resource
- The number of buyers of the resource
- The prices of related resources
- The quantities of other resources

Price of the Product   When the price of copper rises, the demand for copper miners increases—the demand curve shifts out to the right. Mining firms hire more workers at each wage rate in order to produce more copper and earn the higher revenues.

Productivity   When a resource becomes more productive—that is, when each unit of the resource can produce more output—the firm will use more of the resource. For instance, if new printing presses are able to produce twice as much in the same amount of time as existing presses, the demand for new printing presses will rise. The demand curve for printing presses will shift out to the right.

Number of Buyers   When new firms enter an industry, they require resources. The demand curve for resources will shift out to the right. For instance, when Wal-Mart builds a store in a small town, it must hire workers and acquire land, capital, buildings, and other supplies. The demand for workers, for capital, for land, and for the other supplies increases with the entry of Wal-Mart—the demand curves shift out to the right.

Substitutes   A change in the price of substitute resources will affect the demand for a resource. For instance, if labor and machines are substitutes in the production of iron ore, then when the price of labor rises, the demand for machines increases— the demand curve for machines shifts out to the right. Conversely, if copper and plastic are substitutes in construction, then when the price of plastic declines, the demand for copper decreases—the demand curve for copper shifts in.

Quantity of Other Resources   A restaurant using only 10 of its 60 tables requires only one waiter. If the other 50 tables are also used, the restaurant needs more wait-ers. With a bigger pot and more soil, the quantity of flowers grown with each addi-tional amount of fertilizer applied will be larger than it would be with a smaller pot and less soil. More capital tends to increase the demand for labor; more land tends to increase the demand for tractors. In other words, the demand for a resource depends on how many of the other resources are available.

2.b. Market Supply

A household supplies resources in order to maximize utility.

Individuals act so as to maximize their utility. They receive utility when they con-sume goods and services, but they need income to purchase the goods and services. To acquire income, households must sell the services of their resources. They must give up some of their leisure time and go to work or offer their other resources in order to acquire income. The quantity of resources that are supplied depends on the wages, rents, interest, and profits offered for those resources. If, while everything else is held constant, people can get higher wages, they will offer to work more hours; if they can obtain more rent for their land, they will offer more of their land for use, and so on. The quantity supplied of a resource rises as the price of the resource rises.

2.b.1. The Elasticity of Resource Supply

The amount by which resource owners alter the quantity they offer for use when the price of the resource changes is measured by the price elasticity of resource supply, e_r^s. The price elasticity of supply for a resource is defined as the percentage change in the quantity supplied divided by the percentage change in the price of the resource:

$$e_r^s = \frac{\text{percentage change in quantity of resource supplied}}{\text{percentage change in price of resource}}$$

The price elasticity of resource supply depends on the number of substitute uses for a resource and the time period under consideration. Some resources have no substitutes. For instance, there are few if any substitutes for a rocket scientist; as a result, the price elasticity of supply for the rocket scientist is very low. Typically, the longer the period under consideration, the more likely it is that substitutes for a resource can be discovered. Given a few years, even an economist could be trained to be a rocket scientist. For a month or two, the quantity of oil that can be pulled from the ground is relatively fixed; given a year or so, new wells can be drilled and new supplies discovered. The price elasticity of resource supply increases as the time period increases.

When a resource has a perfectly inelastic supply curve, its pay or earnings is called **economic rent.** If a resource has a perfectly elastic supply curve, its pay or earnings is called **transfer earnings.** For upward-sloping supply curves, resource earnings consist of both transfer earnings and economic rent. Transfer earnings is what a resource could earn in its best alternative use (its opportunity cost). It is the amount that must be paid to get the resource to "transfer" to another use. Economic rent is earnings in excess of transfer earnings. It is the portion of a resource's earnings that is not necessary to keep the resource in its current use. A movie star can earn more than $1 million per movie but probably could not earn that kind of income in another occupation. Thus, the greatest part of the earnings of the movie star is economic rent.

There are two different meanings for the term *rent* in economics. The most common meaning refers to the payment for the use of something, as distinguished from payment for ownership. In this sense, you purchase a house but rent an apartment; you buy a car from Chrysler but rent cars from Avis. The second use of the term *rent* is to mean payment for the use of something that is in fixed—that is, perfectly inelastic—supply. The total quantity of land is fixed; payment for land is economic rent.

2.b.2. Shifts in the Supply of a Resource

The supply of a resource will change—increase or decrease at every price—if:

- Tastes change.
- The number of suppliers changes.
- The prices of other uses of the resource change.

economic rent: the portion of earnings above transfer earnings

transfer earnings: the amount that must be paid to a resource owner to get him or her to allocate the resource to another use

Suppose it suddenly becomes more prestigious to be a lawyer. The supply of people entering law schools will increase—the supply curve of lawyers will shift up or out to the right. The shift will occur because of a change in tastes (more prestige), not because of a change in the wage rate of lawyers.

An increase in the number of suppliers means that the supply curve shifts out to the right. For instance, the discovery of oil in a country that is not currently an oil producer would mean an increase in the supply of oil—at each price a greater quantity of oil would be supplied. Immigration increases the supply of labor. More producers of bulldozers increase the supply of bulldozers.

The supply curve of a resource will shift if the price of related resources changes. If the wage rate of professionals in finance rises, economists and others may offer their services in the finance market. The supply curve of finance professionals will shift out. If the rental rate of land used for production of wheat rises, everything else held constant, land that is currently being used to produce alfalfa will be switched over to wheat—the supply curve of land used in the production of wheat will shift out to the right.

2.c. Equilibrium

The intersection between the market demand and supply curves determines the price and quantity of a resource. If the demand curve shifts out, everything else held constant, the price rises; if the supply curve shifts out, everything else held constant, the price decreases. If the price rises above the equilibrium price, then a surplus exists and the price is forced back to equilibrium; if the price falls below the equilibrium level, then a shortage arises and the price is forced back up to equilibrium.

2.c.1. Price Ceilings and Floors
A resource market will move toward its equilibrium price and quantity as long as nothing interferes with the market adjustment. There are many instances where floors or ceilings are placed on the resource price, however. Consider the impact of a price floor in the labor market and a price ceiling in the steel market.

Figure 3(a) shows a labor market, with the quantity of labor in hours along the horizontal axis and the hourly wage rate along the vertical axis. The equilibrium wage determined in the market would be $W_e = \$3.50$. The minimum wage is $5.15 per hour, so the actual wage paid would be $W_m = \$5.15$, a price floor. At the minimum wage, the quantity of hours that people are willing and able to work is Q_s, while the quantity of hours that firms are willing and able to pay for is Q_d. The difference between Q_s and Q_d is the number of hours that people would like to work at the minimum wage but for which there is no work.

A price ceiling works in just the opposite way from a price floor. The price ceiling creates a shortage. For instance, suppose the government requires foreign steel producers to sell their steel to U.S. manufacturers for no more than P_m in Figure 3(b). The quantity of steel demanded rises from Q_s to Q_d, whereas the quantity that the steel suppliers are willing to provide for sale at P_m is Q_s. The difference between Q_d and Q_s represents the shortage of steel.

RECAP

1. Firms purchase resources in such a way that they maximize profits. Households sell resources in order to maximize utility.

2. Transfer earnings is the portion of total earnings required to keep a resource in its current use.

FIGURE 3

Price Ceilings and Price Floors

Figure 3(a) is a labor market showing the quantity of labor in hours along the horizontal axis and the hourly wage rate along the vertical axis. The equilibrium wage determined in the market would be W_e = $3.50, but because a minimum wage of $5.15 per hour has been imposed, the actual wage paid is W_m = $5.15, a wage floor. At the minimum wage, the quantity of hours that people are willing and able to work is Q_s, while the quantity of hours that firms are willing and able to pay

for is Q_d. The difference between Q_s and Q_d is the number of hours that people would like to work but for which there is no work.

Figure 3(b) represents the market for steel. The equilibrium price is P_e, but because the government has implemented a program whereby foreign steel producers cannot sell their steel for more than P_m, the equilibrium price plays no role. A shortage is created equal to Q_d less Q_s.

(a) Labor Market

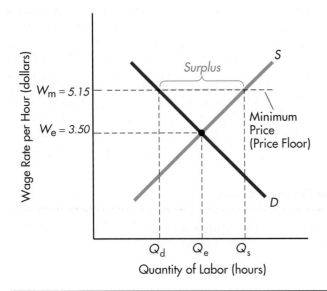

(b) Steel Market

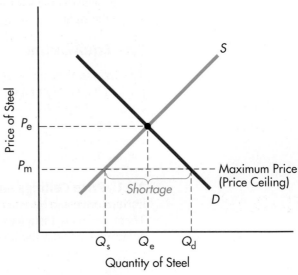

3. Economic rent is earnings in excess of transfer earnings.

4. Equilibrium in a resource market defines the price (wages, rent, interest, profit) of that resource as long as the price and quantity are free to adjust. Price ceilings lead to shortages; price floors lead to surpluses.

?

3. How does a firm allocate its expenditures among the various resources?

3. How Firms Decide What Resources to Buy

The market demand for a resource consists of the demands of each firm that is willing and able to pay for that resource. An electric utility firm in Iowa demands engineers, as does a construction firm in Minnesota. The market demand for engineers consists of the demands of the Iowa utility and the Minnesota construction firm. Each firm's demand depends on separate and distinct factors, however. The electric utility firm hires more engineers to modernize its plant; the construction firm hires more engineers to fulfill its contracts with the state government to build bridges. Yet all firms have the same decision-making process for hiring or acquiring resources.

3.a. Individual Firm Demand: Marginal Revenue Product

How do you decide how much you are willing to pay for something? Don't you decide how much it is worth to you? This is what businesses do when they decide how much to pay a worker or to pay for a machine. A firm uses the quantity of each resource that will enable the firm to maximize profit. Firms maximize profit when they operate at the level where marginal revenue (MR) equals marginal cost (MC). Thus, firms acquire additional resources until $MR = MC$. If the acquisition of a resource will raise the firm's revenues more than it will increase its costs—that is, if MR will be greater than MC—the firm will hire the resource. Conversely, if the acquisition of a resource will raise costs more than it will raise revenue—that is, if MR will be less than MC—then the firm will not hire the resource.

A firm will purchase the services of another unit of a resource if that additional unit adds more to the firm's revenue than it costs. Recall from the chapter on the costs of doing business that the additional output that an extra unit of a resource produces is called the marginal physical product (MPP) of that resource. The MPP of tax accountants for a CPA firm is the number of tax returns that additional tax accountant can complete; the MPP is listed in column 3 of the table in Figure 4, and the MPP curve is drawn in the accompanying graph. The MPP curve initially rises and then declines according to the law of diminishing marginal returns.

The value of this additional output to the firm is the additional revenue that the output generates—the marginal revenue. Multiplying marginal physical product by

---

FIGURE 4

The *MPP* Curve

The value of a resource to a firm depends on the additional output that the resource produces. This additional output is the marginal physical product of the resource. The marginal physical product of accountants measured in number of tax returns per day is listed in the table. The marginal physical product is drawn as a curve in the graph.

(1) Number of Accountants	(2) Number of Tax Returns per Day	(3) *MPP*
1	6	6
2	19	13
3	25	6
4	29	4
5	31	2
6	32	1
7	32	0

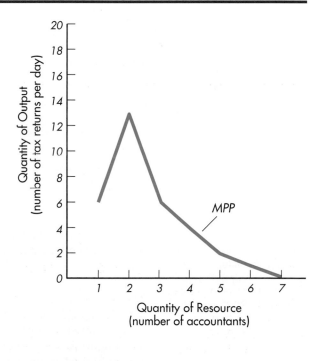

FIGURE 5

The Marginal Revenue Product

The marginal physical product multiplied by the
marginal revenue yields the marginal revenue product.
The *MPP* curve from Figure 4 is multiplied by the marginal revenue and plotted in Figure 5 as the *MRP* curve.
The information from Figure 4 is listed in columns 1 to 3
of Figure 5. The output price is listed in column 4, the
total revenue, $P \times Q$, is listed in column 5, and marginal
revenue is calculated in column 6. Multiplying column 6
by column 3 yields the *MRP*, listed in column 7.

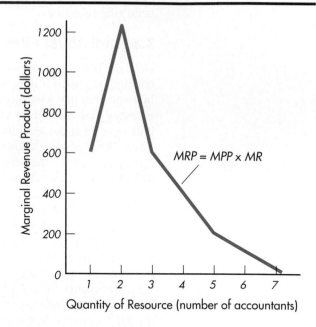

(1) Number of Accountants	(2) Number of Tax Returns per Day	(3) *MPP*	(4) Output Price (per tax return)	(5) Total Revenue	(6) Marginal Revenue	(7) *MRP* (*MPP* × *MR*)
1	6	6	$100	$ 600	$100	$ 600
2	19	13	$100	$1,900	$100	$1,300
3	25	6	$100	$2,500	$100	$ 600
4	29	4	$100	$2,900	$100	$ 400
5	31	2	$100	$3,100	$100	$ 200
6	32	1	$100	$3,200	$100	$ 100
7	32	0	$100	$3,200	$ 0	$ 0

**marginal revenue product
(MRP):** the value of the
additional output that an
extra unit of a resource can
produce, *MPP* × *MR;* the
value to the firm of an
additional resource

marginal revenue yields the value of an additional unit of a resource to the firm,
which is called the **marginal revenue product (MRP):**

$$MRP = MPP \times MR$$

The MRP *of a resource, such as labor, is a measure of how much the additional output generated by the last worker is worth to the firm.* The marginal-revenue-product
curve is drawn in Figure 5. The information from Figure 4 is listed in columns 1 to
3 of Figure 5. Marginal revenue is calculated in column 6 of the table in Figure 5
and multiplied by the *MPP* to arrive at the *MRP* in column 7. You can see that after
rising initially, the *MRP* curve slopes downward.

3.b. Marginal Factor Costs

The *MRP* measures the value of an additional resource to a firm. To determine the quantity of a resource that a firm will hire, the firm must know the cost of each additional unit of the resource. The cost of an additional unit of a resource depends on whether the firm is purchasing resources in a market with many suppliers or in a market with one or only a few suppliers.

3.b.1. Hiring Resources in a Perfectly Competitive Market

If the firm is purchasing resources in a market where there is a very large number of suppliers of an identical resource—a perfectly competitive resource market—the price of each additional unit of the resource to the firm is constant. Why? Because no seller is large enough to individually change the price. A firm can hire as much of the resource as it wants without affecting either the quantity available or the price of that resource. This situation is shown in Figures 6(a) and 6(b) for the market for accountants. The market wage is defined by the market demand and market supply, as shown in Figure 6(a), and that wage translates to a horizontal supply curve for the individual firm, as shown in Figure 6(b).

Let's assume that the market wage for accountants is $150 per day. The firm can hire as many accountants as it wants at $150 per day without influencing the price. How many accountants will the firm hire? It will hire additional accountants as long

---

FIGURE 6

The Perfectly Competitive Resource Market and the Individual Firm

The demand for and supply of a resource determine the price of the resource, as shown in Figure 6(a). This market price is the price the individual firm must pay to obtain any units of the resource. As shown in Figure 6(b), the individual firm is a price taker.

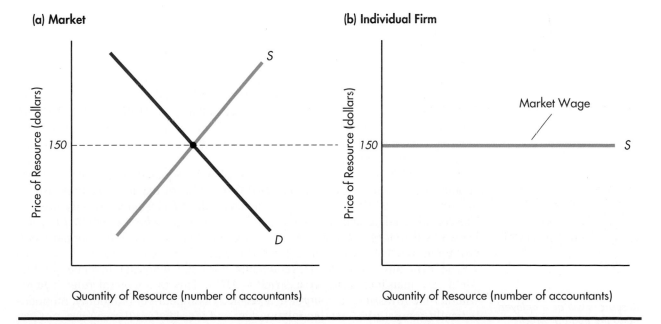

(a) Market

(b) Individual Firm

FIGURE 7

The Employment of Resources

The marginal revenue product and the marginal factor cost together indicate the number of accountants the individual firm would hire. The *MRP* and the *MFC* for an individual firm are listed in the table. The *MRP* curve and the *MFC* curve are shown in the graph. The marginal revenue product exceeds the marginal factor cost (wage rate) until after the fifth accountant is hired. The firm will not hire more than five, for then the costs would exceed the additional revenue produced by the last accountant hired.

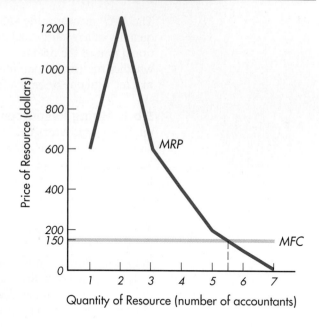

(1) **Number of Accountants**	(2) ***MRP***	(3) ***MFC***
1	$600	$150
2	$1,300	$150
3	$600	$150
4	$400	$150
5	$200	$150
6	$100	$150
7	$0	$150

as the additional revenue brought in by the last accountant hired is no less than the additional cost of that accountant.

Let's use the information in Figure 7, which combines Figures 5 and 6, to see how many accountants the firm would hire. The first accountant hired has a marginal revenue product of $600 per day and costs $150 per day. It is profitable to hire her. A second accountant, bringing in an additional $1,300 per day and costing $150 per day, is also profitable. The third accountant brings in $600 per day, the fourth $400 per day, the fifth $200 per day, the sixth $100 per day, and the seventh nothing. Thus, the third, fourth, and fifth accountants are profitable, but the sixth and seventh aren't. At $150 per day, the firm hires five accountants. You can see in the graph that the marginal revenue product lies above the wage rate until after the fifth accountant is hired.

The firm hires additional accountants until *MRP* is equal to the cost to the firm of another accountant. Remember, the *MRP* is the value of the additional resource to the firm; thus, the firm wants to be sure that the value of a resource exceeds its costs. The cost of an additional unit of a resource is the **marginal factor cost (*MFC*),** also known as the *marginal resource cost* or *marginal input cost*. The marginal factor cost for accountants is listed as column 3 in Figure 7.

The firm hires additional accountants until the marginal revenue product equals the marginal factor cost, *MRP* = *MFC*. This is a general rule; it holds whether the firms sells its output in a perfectly competitive, monopoly, monopolistically competitive, or oligopoly market; and it holds for all resources, not just accountants.

marginal factor cost (*MFC*): the additional cost of an additional unit of a resource

Resources will be employed up to the point at which MRP = MFC

The Company Town

Early in his career, Milton Friedman, the Nobel Prize–winning economist, served as an instructor for the navy. His assignment was in Hershey, Pennsylvania, where he stayed at the Hershey Hotel, on the corner of Cocoa Avenue and Chocolate Boulevard; across the street from the Hershey Junior College, down the street from the Hershey Department Store. Friedman describes Hershey as a benevolent company town, but not all the company towns that arose in the early 1900s were so benevolent. Workers who were employed in factories or mines located far from large cities were often required to live in company housing and buy their food and other supplies at company stores. In many cases the prices at the company store were very high, because the stores were local monopolies.

By the 1940s, most company towns and stores had disappeared but a few still exist today. Documented and undocumented aliens who work in the agricultural areas of the Southwest often must pay their employers for their sleeping quarters, their food and drinks, and other items. The workers are paid in kind rather than cash and often end up owing more to the company store than they receive in wages.

Sources: Andrew Gulliford, *Boomtown Blues: Colorado Oil Shale, 1885–1985* (Boulder University Press of Colorado, 1990); Dennis Farney, "Price of Progress," *Wall Street Journal,* April 3, 1990, pp. 1, A14; Milton Friedman, "The Folly of Buying Health Care at the Company Store," *Wall Street Journal,* February 3, 1993, p. A14.

monopsonist: a firm that is the only buyer of a resource

3.b.2. Hiring Resources as a Monopoly Buyer

If only one firm is bidding for a resource or a product, that firm is called a **monopsonist.** In the early days of mining in the United States, it was not uncommon for firms to create entire towns in order to attract a readily available supply of labor. The sole provider of jobs in the town was the mining company. Thus, when the company hired labor, it affected the prices of all workers, not just the worker it recently hired. In the 1970s along the Alaskan pipeline, and in the 1980s in foreign countries where U.S. firms were hired to carry out specialized engineering projects or massive construction jobs, small towns dependent on a single U.S. firm were created. There are cases where a monopsony exists even though a company town was not created. For instance, many universities in small communities are monopsonistic employers—they are the primary employer in the town. When these universities hire a mechanic, they affect the wage rates of all mechanics in the town. Also, automobile companies have market power when it comes to purchasing supplies. The companies that provide parts and supplies to the auto companies are so numerous that they have virtually no market power. And, because there are only a few automobile manufacturing companies, the companies are able to dictate the prices that they will pay for the parts and supplies. Other examples of monopsonies are discussed in the Economic Insight box.

A monopsony firm will pay resources less than their marginal revenue products. Suppose, for example, that a large semiconductor firm in a small town is the primary employer in the town and that the firm is in the process of hiring accountants. As shown in the table in Figure 8, at a wage of $25 per day, only 1 person is willing and able to work. If the firm pays $50 per day, it can hire 2 accountants. However, the firm isn't able to hire the first at $25 and the second at $50; it must pay both $50. Otherwise, the first will quit and then be rehired at $50 per day (only 2 were willing and able to work for $50). As a result, the total cost (called *total factor cost*) of two accountants is $100, not $75, and the additional, or marginal, factor cost is $75 rather than the $50 wage of the second accountant. If the firm offers $150 per day, it can hire 4 accountants; its total factor cost will be $600 and its marginal factor cost

FIGURE 8

The Monopsonist

When the firm is a monopsonistic buyer of resources, it faces a marginal-factor-cost curve that lies above the supply curve. Each time the firm purchases a unit of the resource, the price of all units of the resource is driven up. As a result, the cost of one additional unit of the resource exceeds the price that must be paid for that additional unit of the resource. This is shown in columns 8 through 10 of the table; columns 8 and 10 are plotted in the graph.

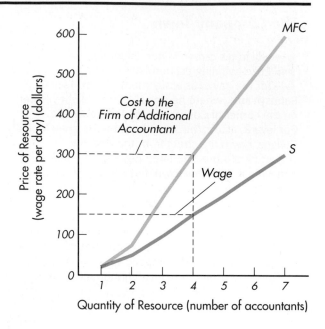

(1)	(2) Number of Tax Returns per Day	(3) MPP	(4) Product Price (per tax return)	(5) Total Revenue	(6) MR	(7) MRP	(8) Wage per Day	(9) Total Factor Cost of Accountants	(10) MFC
Number of Accountants									
1	6	6	$100	$ 600	$100	$ 600	$ 25	$ 25	$ 25
2	19	13	$100	$1,900	$100	$1,300	$ 50	$ 100	$ 75
3	25	6	$100	$2,500	$100	$ 600	$100	$ 300	$200
4	29	4	$100	$2,900	$100	$ 400	$150	$ 600	$300
5	31	2	$100	$3,100	$100	$ 200	$200	$1,000	$400
6	32	1	$100	$3,200	$100	$ 100	$250	$1,500	$500
7	32	0	$100	$3,200	$100	$ 0	$300	$2,100	$600

Note: Marginal revenue is the change in total revenue divided by the change in output. In this case, it is the change in total revenue divided by the change in the number of tax returns produced.

$300. This is shown in columns 8, 9, and 10 of the table. Column 8 is the wage per day, column 9 is the total factor cost (column 1 times column 8), and column 10 is the marginal factor cost.

The graph in Figure 8 shows the marginal factor cost and the supply curve for accountants in the small town. The *MFC* curve is plotted from the data in column 10 of the table, and the supply curve is plotted from the data in column 8. For a monopsonist, the *MFC* curve lies above the supply curve. The reason is that the cost of each additional accountant to the firm is the additional accountant's wage *plus* the additional wages paid to all of the other accountants.

The rising marginal factor cost means that the accountants would be paid less than their marginal revenue product. The firm would hire 4 accountants, since the fifth accountant costs the firm $400 ($MFC$) but brings in only $200 ($MRP$). The fourth accountant produces $400 of additional revenue for the firm (MRP), costs the firm an additional $300 ($MFC$), but is paid only $150.

As long as resource services are purchased by other than a monopsonist, they are paid their marginal revenue products. A monopsonist pays less than the marginal revenue product.

3.c. Hiring When There Is More than One Resource

To this point we've examined the firm's hiring decision for one resource, everything else, including the quantities of all other resources, held constant. However, a firm uses several resources and makes hiring decisions regarding most of them all the time. How does the firm decide what combinations of resources to use? Like the consumer deciding what combinations of goods and services to purchase, the firm will ensure that the benefits of spending one more dollar are the same no matter which resource the firm chooses to spend that dollar on.

You may recall that the consumer maximizes utility when the marginal utility per dollar of expenditure is the same on all goods and services purchased:

$$MU_{CDs}/P_{CDs} = MU_{gas}/P_{gas} = \cdots = MU_n/P_n$$

A similar rule holds for the firm that is attempting to purchase resource services in order to maximize profit and minimize costs. The firm will be maximizing profit when its marginal revenue product per dollar of expenditure on all resources is the same:

$$MRP_{land}/MFC_{land} = MRP_{labor}/MFC_{labor} = \cdots = MRP_n/MFC_n$$

As long as the marginal factor cost of a resource is less than its marginal revenue product, the firm will increase profit by hiring more of the resource. If a dollar spent on labor yields less marginal revenue product than a dollar spent on capital, the firm will increase profit more by purchasing the capital than if it purchases the labor.[1]

If a resource is very expensive relative to other resources, then the expensive resource must generate a significantly larger marginal revenue product than the other resources. For instance, for a firm to remain in Manhattan, it must generate a significantly larger marginal revenue product than could be obtained in Dallas or elsewhere, because rents are so much higher in Manhattan. The price of land in Tokyo is so high that its use requires a very high marginal revenue product.

A firm will streamline its work force when the last dollar of expenditures on labor generates less marginal revenue product than if that dollar were spent on another resource; a firm will streamline by reducing its middle management if the last dollar spent on middle management generates less return (lower MRP) than if that dollar were spent on other labor or another resource. During the early 1990s, many U.S. firms decided that their expenditures on middle management particularly, but also on their entire labor force, were not generating the same return that expenditures on other resources would yield. As a result, firms reduced their work force; they dismissed many middle-management employees. The media referred to this process as downsizing, but it was part of the ongoing

---

[1]This equimarginal rule can also be written as $MPP_{land}/MFC_{land} = MPP_{labor}/MFC_{labor} = \cdots$, since $MRP = MFC$ or $MRP/MFC = 1$ and since $MRP = MPP \times MR$, $MPP/MFC = 1/MR$ for all resources.

process by firms to ensure that the last dollar of expenditure on each resource generated the same *MRP.*

A firm in equilibrium in terms of allocating its expenditures among resources will alter the allocation only if the cost of one of the resources rises relative to the others. For instance, if government-mandated medical or other benefits mean that labor costs rise while everything else remains constant, then firms will tend to hire less labor and use more of other resources. Everything else the same, if the costs of doing business in the United States rise, firms will locate offices or plants in other countries.

3.d. Product Market Structures and Resource Demand

Firms purchase the types and quantities of resource services that allow them to maximize profit; each firm equates the *MRP* per dollar of expenditure on all resource services used. The *MRP* depends on the market structure in which the firm sells its output. A perfectly competitive firm produces more output and sells that output at a lower price than a firm operating in any other market, everything else the same. Since the perfectly competitive firm produces more output, it must use more resources. Thus, everything else the same, the demand curve for a resource by a perfectly competitive firm will lie above the demand curve for a resource by a firm selling in monopoly, oligopoly, or monopolistically competitive markets.

For the perfectly competitive firm, price and marginal revenue are the same, $P = MR$. Thus, the marginal revenue product, $MRP = MR \times MPP$, for the perfectly competitive firm can be written as $P \times MPP$. Sometimes this is called the value of the marginal product, *VMP,* to distinguish it from the marginal revenue product.

$$MRP = MR \times MPP$$

$$VMP = P \times MPP$$

The demand for a resource by a single firm is the *MRP* of that resource, no matter whether it sells its goods and services as a monopolist or as a perfect competitor (for the perfectly competitive firm, $VMP = MRP$, so that *MRP* is its resource demand as well). However, since for the firms that are not selling in a perfectly competitive market, price is greater than marginal revenue, *VMP* would be greater than *MRP,* which indicates that the perfectly competitive firm's demand curve for a resource lies above (or is greater than) the demand curve for a resource by a monopoly firm, an oligopoly firm, or a monopolistically competitive firm.

3.e. A Look Ahead

In the next few chapters, we will examine some interesting features of resource markets. We'll look at labor markets and discuss why different people receive different wages, why firms treat employees the way they do, the impact of labor laws, and the causes and results of discrimination. We'll discuss financial markets and physical and financial capital and explore why firms carry out research and development. We'll look at the markets for land and natural resources. Selling resource services creates income, so we'll examine who has income and why. And we'll look at how the government gets involved in providing needed human services such as health care and social security.

1. The *MRP* of a resource is a measure of how much the additional output generated by the last unit of the resource is worth to the firm.
2. Resources are hired up to the point at which *MRP* = *MFC*.
3. In a perfectly competitive resource market, resources are paid an amount equal to their marginal revenue product. In a monopsonistic resource market, resources are paid less than their marginal revenue product.
4. A firm will allocate its budget on resources up to the point where the last dollar spent yields an equal marginal revenue product no matter on which resource the dollar is spent.
5. A perfectly competitive firm will hire and acquire more resources than firms selling in monopoly, oligopoly, or monopolistically competitive product markets, everything else the same.

Summary

? Who are the buyers and sellers of resources?

1. The term *resource markets* refers to the buyers and sellers of three classes of resources: land, labor, and capital. *Preview*
2. The buyers of resources are firms that purchase resources in order to produce goods and services. *§1.a*
3. The sellers of resources are households that supply resources in order to obtain income with which to purchase goods and services. *§1.a*

? How are resource prices determined?

4. Equilibrium in each resource market defines the rate of pay of the resource and the quantity used. *§2*
5. The rate of pay of a resource consists of two parts: transfer earnings and economic rent. Transfer earnings are the rate of pay necessary to keep a resource in its current use. Economic rent is the excess of pay above transfer earnings. *§2.b.1*

? How does a firm allocate its expenditures among the various resources?

6. A single firm's demand for a resource is the downward-sloping portion of the marginal-revenue-product curve for that resource. *§3.a*
7. A firm purchasing resources in a perfectly competitive resource market will hire resources up to the point that *MRP* = *MFC*. A firm that is one of only a few buyers or the only buyer of a particular resource (a monopsonist) will face a marginal-factor-cost curve that is above the supply curve for that resource. As a result, the resource is paid less than its marginal revenue product. *§3.b.1, 3.b.2*
8. A firm will allocate its budget on resources in such a way that the last dollar spent will yield the same marginal revenue product no matter on which resource the dollar is spent. *§3.c*

Key Terms

resource market *§1*

derived demand *§1.a*

economic rent *§2.b.1*

transfer earnings *§2.b.1*

marginal revenue product (*MRP*) *§3.a*

marginal factor cost (*MFC*) *§3.b.1*

monopsonist *§3.b.2*

Exercises

1. What does it mean to say that the demand for resources is a derived demand? Is the demand for all goods and services a derived demand?

2. Using the information in the following table, calculate the marginal revenue product ($MRP = MPP \times MR$).

Units of Resources	Total Output	Output Price	Resource Price
1	10	$5	$10
2	25	$5	$10
3	35	$5	$10
4	40	$5	$10
5	40	$5	$10

3. Using the data in exercise 2, determine how many units of resources the firm will want to acquire.

4. Suppose the output price falls from $5 to $4 to $3 to $1 in exercise 2. How would that change your answers to exercises 2 and 3?

5. Using the data in exercise 2, calculate the marginal factor cost.

6. Suppose the resource price rises from $10 to $12 to $14 to $18 to $20 as resource units go from 1 to 5. How would that change your answer to exercise 5? How would it change your answer to exercise 3?

7. Using exercise 6, calculate the transfer earnings and economic rent of the third unit of the resource when four units of the resource are employed. Do the same calculations when only three units of the resource are employed. How do you account for the different answers?

8. Do resources earn their marginal revenue products? Demonstrate under what conditions the answer is yes.

9. What is a monopsonist? How does a monopsonist differ from a monopolist?

10. Supposedly Larry Bird once said that he would play basketball for $10,000 per year. Yet he was paid over $1 million per year. If the quote is correct, how much were Bird's transfer earnings? How much was his economic rent?

11. In 1989 the Japanese spent more than $14 billion to buy 322 foreign companies, half of them in the United States, and $100 billion to buy foreign stocks and bonds. Why was Japanese money flowing so heavily out of Japan and into other parts of the world?

12. Early in her journalistic career, Gloria Steinem posed as a Playboy Bunny to examine the inside of a Playboy Club. Steinem discovered that the Bunnies had to purchase their costumes from the club, pay for the cleaning, purchase their food from the club, and so on. This "company store" exploited the employees (the Bunnies), according to Steinem. Explain what Steinem meant by exploitation.

13. Explain the idea behind the lyrics "You load 16 tons, and what do you get? You get another day older and deeper in debt. Saint Peter, don't you call me, 'cause I can't go. I owe my soul to the company store."

14. The Glaxo-Wellcome Company had a monopoly on AZT, a pharmaceutical that delays the onset of AIDS after someone has become HIV positive. The demand for that pharmaceutical was virtually perfectly price-inelastic. Explain how that might affect the demand for employees by the Glaxo-Wellcome Company.

ACE

Take the ACE Practice Test for this chapter to review the important concepts and get immediate feedback with answers.

economics.college.hmco.com/students

Agent: Eagles, McNabb Agree to Deal Worth up to $115 Million

Donovan McNabb can spend the rest of his NFL career in a city that originally didn't want him.

McNabb and the Philadelphia Eagles agreed to a new 12-year contract Friday that could be worth up to a record $115 million.

The total potential value would be the highest in NFL history, topping the 10-year, $103 million contract Drew Bledsoe signed with the New England Patriots in March 2001.

McNabb's deal runs through 2013, and includes a $20.5 million signing bonus, said his agent, Fletcher Smith. McNabb will receive $13.5 million of that bonus up front and the rest after next season. Including the bonus, he'll get $30 million over the next three years, leaving $9.5 million in base salary over that span. "It means a lot," McNabb said. "You see great players, Hall of Fame players that didn't stay with their team. To know that I'll be pretty much locked in to the Philly area is a wonderful feeling for me, my family, where I can continue to get better and better and know that I'll be wearing the wonderful green."

McNabb didn't get a positive welcome to Philadelphia when the Eagles selected him with the No. 2 overall pick in the 1999 draft. He was booed loudly by a group of Eagles fans who wanted the team to select running back Ricky Williams.

But McNabb quickly won them over with his strong arm and exceptional scrambling ability, the increasingly preferred style for pro quarterbacks.

"We all know it started out pretty shaky early on," McNabb said. "With the help of the guys that are here on the team, in the organization, as well as in the community, we were all able to stay focused and do our jobs."

McNabb, a two-time Pro Bowl selection was in the fourth year of a seven-year contract under which he received a signing bonus of $11.3 million, the highest ever given by the Eagles.

He was scheduled to make $3 million this year, $6.2 million in 2003, and $7.5 million and $8.2 million the following two seasons.

The Eagles can void the new contract at any time. McNabb can opt out of the final three seasons by reaching certain performance incentives.

"The obvious advantage is he gets the up-front money now and gets to put it in his pocket now as opposed to waiting two or three years," Smith said. . . .

McNabb emerged as one of the league's top players in just his second season, leading the Eagles to an 11-5 record in 2000 and into the second round of the playoffs. He finished second to St. Louis Rams running back Marshall Faulk in NFL MVP voting that season.

McNabb again led the Eagles to 11 wins last season, and helped them reach the NFC championship game.

"Donovan is not only a great football player, he's a great leader," Eagles coach Andy Reid said. "That's very important, especially in the huddle to get people to listen.

"With Donovan, it's like I have a coach out on the field that can take control and get the offense in the right direction. Not only that, he's very unique because he's respected by all positions. Sometimes quarterbacks can alienate themselves from other members of the team. He doesn't do that. He makes his way around the locker room and gets everybody together. That's a very unique characteristic."

ROB MAADDI

The Associated Press/September 28, 2002

How can anyone be worth $115 million over 12 years or $9.6 million per year? How can we justify paying a quarterback on a football team $9.55 million more per year than a schoolteacher? Something must be wrong.

Well, is it? According to economic theory, resources are paid their *MRP,* or their value to the firm. The more revenue a resource generates for a firm, the more valuable that resource is. Demand and supply determine the value of resources. The greater the demand relative to the supply, the higher the price of the resource, and, conversely, the lower the demand relative to the supply, the lower the price of the resource. Schoolteachers are plentiful; nearly anyone with a college degree can be a schoolteacher. One merely needs to obtain a certificate. But to be a quarterback on a professional football team, one must have very special skills. There are very few people who can be quarterbacks on professional teams.

Nevertheless, why would the scarcity of quarterbacks relative to teachers create the huge distortion in salaries? The answer is that the quarterback brings in more revenue to the owners of the football team than the teacher does to the school district or school. Society is willing to pay high prices to attend football games, and the better the team, the higher the prices the owners can charge. So, McNabb is expected to attract many ticket buyers at high prices; the firm

expects to sell many more high-priced tickets with McNabb as quarterback than it did previously.

The accompanying figure shows the marginal revenue products of the quarterback, MRP_Q, and a schoolteacher, MRP_T. The huge difference in compensation is due to society's demands. Society demands the quarterback and is willing to pay; society has little demand for the teacher. Moreover, the supply of teachers is huge compared to the supply of quarterbacks.

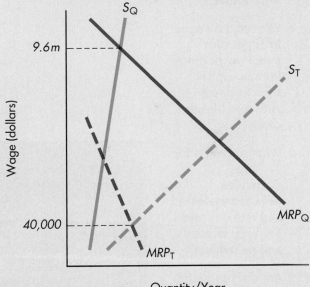

CHAPTER 30

The Labor Market

? **Fundamental Questions**

1. **Are people willing to work more hours for higher wages?**

2. **What are compensating wage differentials?**

3. **Why might wages be higher for people with more human capital than for those with less human capital?**

4. **What accounts for earnings disparities between males and females and between whites and nonwhites?**

5. **Are discrimination and freely functioning markets compatible?**

6. **Why do CEOs, movie stars, and professional athletes make so much money?**

Older workers tend to earn higher wages than younger workers; males earn more than females; whites earn more than African Americans and Hispanics; and unionized workers earn more than nonunionized workers. Yet, as we learned in the previous chapter, a worker will be paid his or her marginal revenue product (except in a monopsonistic firm). Does this mean that older workers are more productive than younger ones, males more productive than females, whites more productive than people of other ethnic backgrounds, and so on, or is there something missing in our theory of the labor market? In this chapter we delve more deeply into the labor market. ■

1. The Supply of Labor

1. Are people willing to work more hours for higher wages?

The supply of labor comes from individual households. Each member of a household must determine whether to give up a certain number of hours each day to work. That decision is the individual's labor supply decision and is called the *labor-leisure tradeoff.*

1.a. Individual Labor Supply: Labor-Leisure Tradeoff

People can allocate their time to work or to leisure.

There are only twenty-four hours in a day, and people have to decide how to allocate this scarce time. They really have only two options: they can spend their time (1) working for pay or (2) not working. *Any* time spent not working is called *leisure time.* Leisure time includes being a "couch potato," serving as a volunteer coach for your daughter's first-grade soccer team, volunteering to serve food at St. Jude's food bank, or participating in any other activity except working at a paying job. People want leisure time. Although most people enjoy aspects of their jobs, most would rather have more leisure time and less work time. However, people must purchase the desired good, leisure, by forgoing the wages they could earn by working. As wages increase, the cost of leisure time increases, causing people to purchase less leisure. Purchasing less leisure means working more.

The number of hours that people are willing and able to work rises as the wage rate rises, at least until people say, "I have enough income; perhaps I'll enjoy a little more leisure." When the price of leisure increases—in other words, when the wage rate increases—people choose to work more. But, as the wage rate increases, some people choose to enjoy more leisure time. They now have more income with which they can purchase all goods and services, including leisure time. Thus, a wage increase has two opposing effects: one leads to increased hours of work, and one leads to decreased hours. This means that the quantity of labor supplied may rise or fall as the wage rate rises.

The labor supply curve shown in Figure 1 is what the labor supply curve for an individual usually looks like. It rises as the wage rate rises until the wage is sufficiently high that people begin to choose more leisure; then the curve begins to turn backward. This is called the **backward-bending labor supply curve.**

backward-bending labor supply curve: a labor supply curve indicating that a person is willing and able to work more hours as the wage rate increases until, at some sufficiently high wage rate, the person chooses to work fewer hours

1.a.1. Do People Really Trade Off Labor and Leisure?
As discussed in the Economic Insight "The Overworked American?" not all economists agree with the idea that people trade off work and leisure. There is no doubt that few people have the luxury of deciding each minute whether to work or to take leisure time. Some might be able to choose between part-time and full-time work, but full-time work usually means eight hours a day, and part-time work typically means lower-quality jobs and much less pay per hour than a full-time job. Most people, then, are unable to choose how much to work on a day-to-day basis depending on their preferences for leisure that day. But over a month, a year, or several years, people do choose to put in more or less time on the job. Some people choose occupations that enable them to have more flexibility; many prefer to be self-employed in order to be able to choose whether to put in more or less time on the job. People can also *moonlight,* that is, work an additional job or put in extra hours after the full-time job is completed.

1.b. From Individual to Market Supply

When you enter the labor market, you offer various levels of services at various wage rates. The decision about whether to offer your labor services for employment

The Overworked American

The average employed person in the United States is now on the job an additional 163 hours, or the equivalent of an extra month a year, as compared to 1969.[1] What accounts for the increased hours devoted to work and thus the fewer hours devoted to leisure?

In European nations, the average workweek is by law no more than 30 to 35 hours. In 2001 the average American worked 1,978 hours—up from 1,942 hours in 1990. That represents an increase of almost a week of work. Americans are working longer hours than Canadians, Germans, Japanese, and other workers. The average Australian, Canadian, Japanese, or Mexican worker was on the job roughly 100 hours less than the average American in a year—that's almost 2 1/2 weeks less. Brazilians and British employees worked some 250 hours, or more than 5 weeks, less than Americans. Germans worked roughly 500 hours, or 12 1/2 weeks, less than careerists in the United States. Of countries classified as "developing" or "in transition," only South Korea and the Czech Republic tracked workers putting in more hours than American laborers. The Koreans logged almost 500 hours more annually than Americans, and the Czechs are doing some 100 hours more work than U.S. workers on average.[2] Why are Americans devoting so much more time to the job than are Europeans? The answer for the European nations is that laws have dictated the number of hours an individual can work. But in the United States, there are no such laws; people are devoting more time to work each year.

The view of most economists is that people choose to work more in order to acquire more income. People trade off leisure for more work and thus more income.

Not all economists agree with the view that people can trade off work and leisure. Many argue that individuals have no choice, that leisure time is simply being squeezed out by the necessity of working and the demands of firms. A group of economists known as *institutionalists* argue that the modern industrial state does not give workers the flexibility that economists seem to imply in their labor demand and labor supply model. The institutional economists argue that firms set the hours they require of their employees and that employees must either accept them or accept significantly lower standards of living. They point to studies that have asked people about their work habits and found that people did not have a choice of hours; they had a choice of either no job or a job at hours that were not those they would choose.[3] In a popular book, *The Overworked American; The Unexpected Decline of Leisure,* author Juliet Schor argues that consumer-workers become indoctrinated by firms into consuming, which requires more income and thus more hours devoted to work. According to Schor, workers can't really trade off work and leisure, but if they could their indoctrination to consume would constrain them; they must work more and more to be able to consume more and more.[4]

The economists opposing the institutionalists' view point out that workers can change occupations or jobs because hours worked vary considerably from occupation to occupation and that workers can also moonlight (work extra jobs or hours) or retire in order to alter their hours.[5] They also point to surveys where it was found that people preferred their current number of hours and pay to working fewer hours at the same rate of pay or more hours at the same rate of pay.[6] Like most issues in economics, unanimity of opinion on this issue does not exist.

[1] Juliet B. Schor, *The Overworked American: The Unexpected Decline of Leisure* (New York: Basic Books, 1991); Philip L. Rones, Randy E. Ig, and Jennifer M. Gardner, "Trends in Hours of Work Since the Mid 1970s," *Monthly Labor Review,* April 1997, pp. 3–14.

[2] "U.S. Employees Put In Most Hours," August 31, 1991, retrieved May 2003 from www.cnn.com/career.

[3] Shulamit Kahn and Kevin Lang, "Constraints on the Choice of Work Hours: Agency vs. Specific Capital," *National Bureau of Economic Research Working Paper* 2238, May 1987, p. 14; Robert Moffit, "The Tobit Model, Hours of Work, and Institutional Constraints," *Review of Economics and Statistics* 64, August 1982, pp. 510–515.

[4] Schor, *The Overworked American.*

[5] Joseph Altonji and Christina H. Paxson, "Labor Supply Preferences, Hours Constraints, and Hour-Wage Tradeoffs," *Journal of Labor Economics* 6, no. 2 (1988), pp. 254–276.

[6] Susan E. Shank, "Preferred Hours of Work and Corresponding Earnings," *Monthly Labor Review,* November 1986, p. 41, Table 1.

FIGURE 1

The Individual's Labor Supply Curve

As the wage rate rises, people are willing and able to supply more labor, at least up to some high wage rate. A higher wage rate means that the opportunity cost of leisure time increases, so that people will purchase less leisure (will work more). Conversely, as the wage rate rises and people's incomes rise, more of all goods are purchased, including leisure time. As a result, fewer hours are supplied for work. Which of these opposing effects is larger determines whether the labor supply curve slopes upward or downward. The most commonly shaped labor supply curve is one that slopes upward until the wage rate reaches some high level and then, as people choose more leisure time, begins to bend backward.

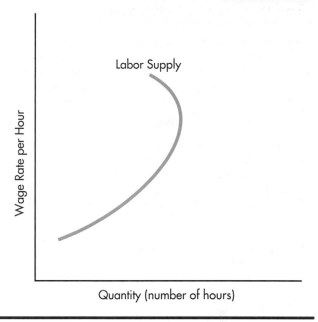

labor force participation:
entering the work force

is a decision about **labor force participation.** In the United States, people over the age of sixteen who are actively seeking a job are said to be members of the labor force. These are the people who have chosen to offer their labor services for employment at specific wage rates. As the wage rate increases, the number of people participating in the labor force increases.

Figure 2(a) shows the labor *market* supply curve. It consists of the horizontal sum of all individual labor supply curves, such as the sum of the individual labor supply curves shown in Figures 2(b) and 2(c). If the labor supply curve for each individual slopes upward, then the market supply curve, the sum of each individual supply curve, slopes upward. Even if the individual labor supply curve bends backward at some high wage, it is unlikely that all of the curves will bend backward at the same wage. Not everyone has the same tradeoffs between labor and leisure; not all offer to work at the same wage rate; not all want the same kind of job. As the wage rate rises, some people who chose not to participate in the labor market at lower wages are induced to offer their services for employment at a higher wage. You can see in Figure 2(b) that Mary chooses not to enter the labor force at wages below $20 per hour. Helen, in Figure 2(c), enters the labor force for any wage above $5 per hour. Thus, the labor market supply curve slopes up because the number of people willing and able to work rises as the wage rate rises and because the number of hours that each person is willing and able to work rises as the wage rate rises, at least up to some high wage rate.

1.c. Equilibrium

The labor market consists of the labor demand and labor supply curves. We've just discussed labor supply. Labor demand is based on the firms' marginal revenue product curves, as discussed in the previous chapter. The intersection of the labor demand and labor supply curves determines the equilibrium wage, W_e, and the quantity of hours people work at this equilibrium wage, Q_e, as shown in Figure 3.

FIGURE 2

The Labor Market Supply Curve

Figure 2(a) shows the labor market supply curve, obtained by adding the individual labor supply curves of Figures 2(b) and 2(c). Figure 2(a) indicates that as the wage rate rises, the number of hours each person is willing and able to work increases, at least up to some high wage rate, and the number of people willing and able to supply hours of work increases.

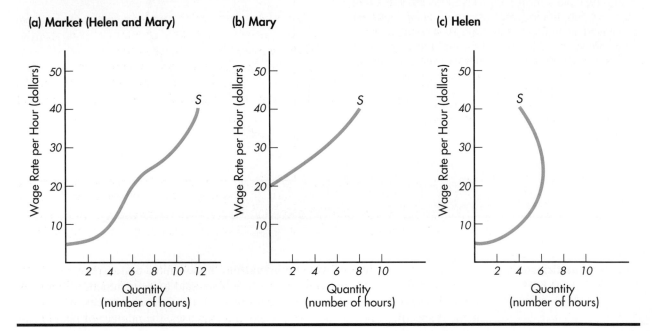

(a) Market (Helen and Mary)   (b) Mary   (c) Helen

FIGURE 3

Labor Market Equilibrium

If all workers are the same to firms—that is, if a firm doesn't care whether it hires Bob, Ray, Kate, or Allie—and if all firms and jobs are the same to workers—that is, if a worker doesn't care whether a job is with IBM or Ted's Hot Dog Stand—then one demand curve and one supply curve define the labor market. The intersection of the two curves is the labor market equilibrium at which the wage rate is determined.

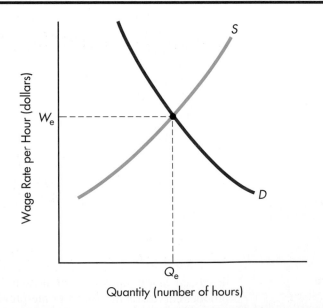

The labor market pictured in Figure 3 suggests that as long as workers are the same and jobs are the same, there will be one equilibrium wage. In fact, workers are not the same, jobs are not the same, and wages are definitely not the same. College-educated people earn more than people with only a high school education, and people with a high school education earn more than those with only a grammar school education. Older workers earn more than younger workers. Men earn more than women. Whites earn more than nonwhites. Unionized workers tend to earn more than nonunionized workers.

The labor market model also suggests that workers will be paid their marginal revenue products. The more productive a worker is, the higher his or her compensation will be, and vice versa. This relationship does not always hold in the real world, however. There are large salary differences for people with similar levels of productivity, and people who are vastly different in terms of productivity are paid the same. Some explanations for these wage differentials are given in the remainder of this chapter.

2. Wage Differentials

If people were identical, if jobs were identical, and if information were perfect, there would be no wage differentials.

If all workers are the same to a firm—that is, if a firm doesn't care whether it hires Bob, Ray, Kate, or Allie—and if all firms and jobs are the same to workers—that is, if IBM is no different from Ted's Hot Dog Stand to individual workers—then the one demand for labor and the one supply of labor define the one equilibrium wage. However, if firms do differentiate among workers and if workers do differentiate among firms and jobs, then there is more than one labor market and more than one equilibrium wage level. In this case, wages may differ from job to job and from person to person. The reasons for wage differences include compensating wage differentials and differences in individual levels of productivity.

2.a. Compensating Wage Differentials

2. What are compensating wage differentials?

Some jobs are quite unpleasant because they are located in undesirable locations or are dangerous or unhealthy. In most market economies, enough people voluntarily choose to work in unpleasant jobs that the jobs get filled. People choose to work in

compensating wage differentials: wage differences that make up for the higher risk or poorer working conditions of one job over another

unpleasant occupations because of **compensating wage differentials**—wage differences that make up for the high risk or poor working conditions of a job. Workers mine coal, clean sewers, and weld steel beams fifty stories off the ground because, compared to alternative jobs for which they could qualify, these jobs pay well.

Figure 4 illustrates the concept of compensating differentials. There are two labor markets, one for a risky occupation and one for a less risky occupation. At each wage rate, fewer people are willing and able to work in the risky occupation than in the less risky occupation. Thus, if the demand curves are identical, the supply curve of the risky occupation will be above (to the left of) the supply curve of the less risky occupation. As a result, the equilibrium wage rate is higher in the risky occupation ($10) than in the less risky occupation ($5). The difference between the wage in the risky occupation ($10 per hour) and the wage in the less risky occupation ($5 per hour) is an *equilibrium differential*—the compensation a worker receives for undertaking the greater risk.

Commercial deep-sea divers are exposed to the dangers of drowning and several physiological disorders as a result of compression and decompression. They choose this job because they earn about 90 percent more than the average high school graduate. Coal miners in West Virginia or in the United Kingdom are exposed to coal

---

FIGURE 4

Compensating Wage Differentials

Figure 4(a) shows the market for a risky occupation. Figure 4(b) shows the market for a less risky occupation. At each wage rate, fewer people are willing and able to work in the risky occupation than in the less risky occupation. Thus, the supply curve of the risky occupation is higher (supply is less) than the supply curve of the less risky occupation. As a result, the wage in the risky occupation ($10 per hour) is higher than the wage ($5

per hour) in the less risky occupation. The differential ($10 − $5 = $5) is an equilibrium differential—the amount necessary to induce enough people to fill the jobs. If the differential were any higher, more people would flow to the risky occupation, driving wages there down and wages in the less risky occupation up. If the differential were any lower, shortages would prevail in the risky occupation, driving wages there up.

(a) Risky Occupation

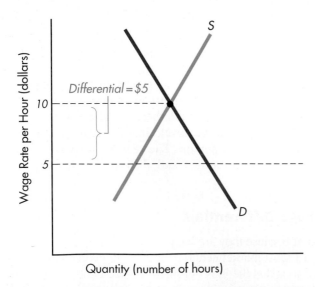

(b) Less Risky Occupation

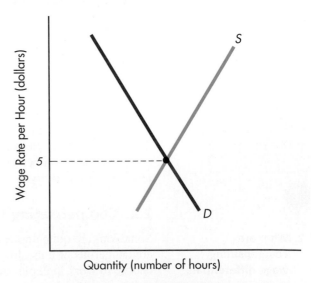

dust, black lung disease, and cave-ins. They choose to work in the mines because the pay is twice what they could earn elsewhere. Wage differentials ensure that deep-sea diving jobs, coal-mining jobs, and other risky occupations are filled.

Any characteristic that distinguishes one job from another may result in a compensating wage differential. A job that requires a great deal of travel and time away from home usually pays more than a comparable job without the travel requirements because most people find extensive travel and time away from home to be costly. If people were indifferent between extensive travel and no travel, there would be no compensating wage differential.

2.b. Human Capital

?

3. Why might wages be higher for people with more human capital than for those with less human capital?

People differ with respect to their training and abilities. These differences influence the level of wages for two reasons: (1) skilled workers have higher marginal productivity than unskilled workers, and (2) the supply of skilled workers is smaller than the supply of unskilled workers because it takes time and money to acquire training and education. Because of greater productivity and smaller supply, then, skilled labor will generate higher wages than less-skilled labor. For instance, in Figure 5, the skilled-labor market generates a wage of $15 per hour, and the unskilled-labor market generates a wage of $8 per hour. The difference exists because the demand for skilled labor relative to the supply of skilled labor is greater than the demand for unskilled labor relative to the supply of unskilled labor.

human capital: skills and training acquired through education and on-the-job training

The expectation of higher income induces people to acquire **human capital**— skills and training acquired through education and job experience. People go to college or vocational school or enter training programs because they expect the training to increase their future income. When people purchase human capital, they are said to be *investing in human capital.* Like investments in real capital (machines and equipment), education and training are purchased in order to generate output and income in the future.

Some jobs are more dangerous than others. Since fewer people are willing to work in the dangerous jobs if they pay the same as less dangerous jobs, it is necessary for the employers to pay more for the dangerous jobs. To induce people to climb tall buildings to wash windows, to construct skyscrapers, or to paint the Golden Gate Bridge, the pay must be increased. Some of the employees undertaking risky jobs earn more in two months than they could in a year undertaking a less risky job.

FIGURE 5

Human Capital

Two labor markets are pictured. Figure 5(a) shows the market for skilled labor. Figure 5(b) shows the market for unskilled labor. The smaller supply in the skilled- labor market results in a higher wage there. The equilibrium differential between the wages in the two markets is the return to human capital.

(a) Skilled-Labor Market

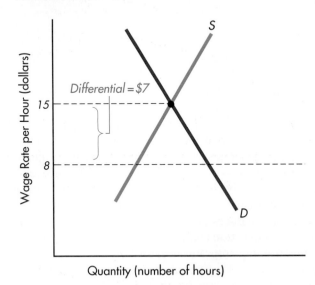

(b) Unskilled-Labor Market

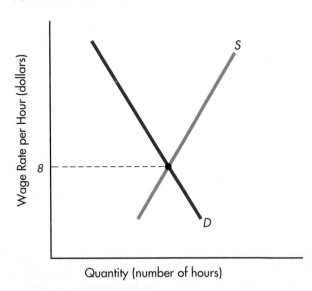

2.b.1. Investment in Human Capital   Individuals who go to college or obtain special training expect the costs of going to college or obtaining the training to be more than offset by the income and other benefits they will obtain in the future. Individuals who acquire human capital reap the rewards of that human capital over time. Figure 6(a) is an example of what the income profiles of a worker with a college degree and a worker without a college degree might look like. We might expect the income of the worker without the degree to increase rapidly from the early working years until the worker gets to be about fifty; then income might rise more slowly until the worker reaches retirement age. Until around age thirty, the worker without the college degree clearly enjoys more income than the college-educated worker. The shaded areas represent estimated income lost to the college-educated worker while he or she is attending classes and then gaining work experience. It may take several years after entering the labor market for a college-degree recipient to achieve and then surpass the income level of a worker without a degree, but on average a college-educated person does earn more than someone without a college education, as shown in Figure 6(b). Figure 6(b) shows the ratios of the median income of college- to high school–educated workers. This is called the college income premium. As mentioned in Chapter 1, college-educated people earn more over their lifetimes than people without a college degree.

The decision about whether to attend college depends on whether the benefits exceed the costs. Over the course of a lifetime, will the income and other benefits of a college degree offset the loss of income during the early years? Individuals who answer *yes* choose to attend college. This economic model of the decision to attend

FIGURE 6

Income Profiles and Educational Level

Income rises rapidly until age fifty, then rises more slowly until retirement. Figure 6 compares the income earned by the worker without a degree with the income earned by a college graduate. Figure 6(a) suggests what the actual pattern looks like. Initially, the college graduate gives up substantial income in the form of direct costs and forgone earnings to go to college. Eventually, however, the income of the college graduate exceeds that of the high school–educated worker. Figure 6(b) illustrates the college income premium, the ratio of median income of college-educated to median income of non-college-educated individuals.
Sources: Statistical Abstract of the United States, 2003; Economic Report of the President, 2003.

(a) Profiles

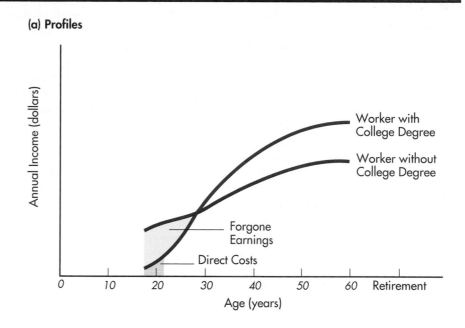

(b) College Income Premium

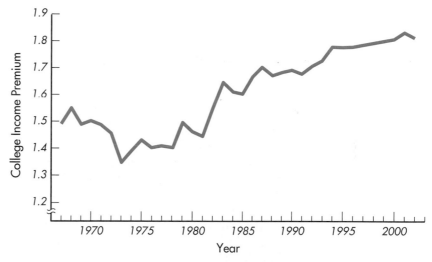

college does not suggest that every high school senior carries out a series of calculations regarding the expected costs and benefits of attending college. What it does suggest is that these people behave *as if* they carried out these calculations. As we discussed in Chapter 1, for many high school students, the decision to attend college was made long before they were in high school—there simply was no other alternative considered. For many, it was taken for granted by all friends and family members that college followed high school. This is the pattern for many families. Such patterns do not occur by accident. There is a reason why so many young adults go to college, and the economic model of labor suggests what that reason is: college-educated people have better-paying jobs and jobs with greater benefits and security than non-college-educated people.

2.b.2. Choice of a Major

If you decide to attend college, you must then decide what field to major in. Your decision depends on the opportunity costs that you face. If your opportunity costs of devoting a great deal of time to a job are high, you will choose to major in a field that is not overly time-consuming. For instance, for several years after college, men and women who have studied to become medical doctors, lawyers, and accountants face long training periods and very long workdays, and they have to devote significant amounts of time each year to staying abreast of new developments in their profession. If you think that you are not likely to undertake and complete a four- or five-year apprenticeship after college in order to reap the rewards from your expenditure of time and money, then it would be very costly for you to be a premed student or to major in accounting or law. Your choice of a college major and an occupation reflects the opportunity costs you face. The greater the opportunity costs of any one occupation, the smaller the number of people who will select that occupation, everything else the same. For instance, it takes more time, money, and effort to become a medical doctor than to become a teacher in the K–12 schools. For this reason, many more people choose to become teachers than choose to become doctors. As a result, a wage differential between the two fields exists that is sufficient to compensate those who become doctors for the extra opportunity costs of the medical career.

2.b.3. Changing Careers

It is estimated that one in three people in the United States's labor force today will change careers at least once during their work lives. People choose a major and thus a career on the basis of information they have at their disposal, family influences, and other related factors. People acquire additional information once they are involved in their occupation, and sometimes their tastes change. They decide to embark on another career path. Who will make such a change? What types of occupations might see more changes?

Relying on the labor market model, we can suggest some answers to these questions. There might be a temptation to say that those who devoted the most effort, time, and money to their first occupation would be the least likely to change. But it is the marginal cost that matters; the effort, time, and money that have been devoted to that first career are gone, whether one remains in the first occupation or moves to another. In the words of the chapter on monopolistic competition and oligopoly, these are sunk, or unrecoverable, costs. Thus, we would expect people who have the greatest expected net gains to make a change. Those who see that they are in dead-end positions or in occupations whose outlook for future income increases is not as good as other occupations would be more likely to move to a new career. We might expect people not to remain in or enter those professions where the marginal costs of remaining in the profession are high. For instance, those occupations that require continuous time and/or financial commitments if their members are to remain productive, such as the high-tech occupations, the hard sciences, engineering, accounting, or law, might lose relatively more people to areas that do not require similar time and money expenditures, such as management and administration.

RECAP

1. Compensating wage differentials are wage differences that make up for the higher risk or poorer working conditions of one job over another. Risky jobs pay more than risk-free jobs, and unpleasant jobs pay more than pleasant jobs.

2. Human capital is the education, training, and experience embodied in an individual.

3. An individual's choice of an occupation reflects a tradeoff between expected opportunity costs and expected benefits. An individual is likely to choose an occupation in which expected benefits outweigh expected opportunity costs.

4. What accounts for earnings disparities between males and females and between whites and nonwhites?

3. Discrimination

The United States is not alone in having differentials based on race and sex. In fact, there seem to be differentials among certain groups in nearly every country. "Colored" workers in Britain earn only about 60 percent of white workers' incomes. There are differentials in Israel between the Oriental Sephardic Jews and Ashkenazic Jews and in other nations between different groups based on color or religion. And in all countries women earn less than men. The Scandinavian countries, France, Australia, and New Zealand have female-to-male hourly pay ratios of 80 to 90 percent, while other countries in western Europe have pay ratios of 65 to 75 percent.

3.a. Definition of Discrimination

Is discrimination present when there is prejudice or just when prejudice has harmful results? Consider a firm with two branch offices. One office employs only African Americans; the other, only whites. Workers in both branches are paid the same wages and have the same opportunities for advancement. Is discrimination occurring?

Is a firm that provides extensive training to employees discriminating when it prefers to hire young workers who are likely to stay with the firm long enough for it to recoup the training costs? Is an economics department that has no African American faculty members guilty of discrimination if African American economists constitute only 1 percent of the profession? Would your answer change if the department could show that it advertised job openings widely and made the same offers to African Americans and whites? Clearly, discrimination is a difficult subject to define and measure.

From an economist's viewpoint, a worker's value in the labor market depends on the factors affecting the marginal revenue product. When a factor that is unrelated to marginal revenue product acquires a positive or negative value in the labor market, **discrimination** is occurring. In Figure 7, if D_M is the demand for males and D_F is the demand for females, and if males and females have identical marginal revenue products, then the resulting wage differences can be attributed to discrimination. Race, gender, age, physical handicaps, religion, sexual preference, and ethnic heritage may be factors that take on positive or negative values in the labor market and yet are unrelated to marginal revenue products.

discrimination: prejudice that occurs when factors unrelated to marginal revenue product affect the wages or jobs that are obtained

5. Are discrimination and freely functioning markets compatible?

3.b. Theories of Discrimination

Wage differentials due to race or gender pose a theoretical problem for economists because the labor market model attributes differences in wages to demand and supply differences that depend on productivity and the labor-leisure tradeoff. How can economists account for different pay scales for men and women, or for one race versus another, in the absence of marginal productivity differences between sexes or races? They identify discrimination as the cause of the differences, even though they find discrimination difficult to rationalize because it is costly to those who discriminate.

FIGURE 7

Discrimination

The curve D_M is the demand for males, and D_F is the demand for females. The two groups of workers are identical except in gender. The greater demand and the higher wage rate for males, even though males and females are equally productive, are due to discrimination.

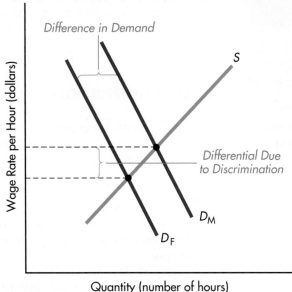

In the freely functioning labor market, there is a profit to be made from *not* discriminating; therefore, discrimination should not exist. But, because discrimination does exist, economists have attempted to find plausible explanations for it. They have identified two sources of labor market discrimination. The first is *personal prejudice:* employers, fellow employees, or customers dislike associating with workers of a given race or sex. The second is *statistical discrimination:* employers project certain perceived group characteristics onto individuals. Economists tend to argue that personal prejudice is not consistent with a market economy but have acknowledged that statistical discrimination can coexist within a market economy.

Discrimination might occur as employers attempt to hire only certain kinds of workers, as employees attempt to work only with certain kinds of coworkers, or as customers attempt to purchase goods and services from certain kinds of workers.

3.b.1. Personal Prejudice   Certain groups in a society could be precluded from higher-paying jobs or from jobs that provide valuable human capital by personal prejudice on the part of employers, fellow workers, or customers.

Employer Prejudice   If two workers have identical marginal revenue products and one worker is less expensive than the other, firms will want to hire the lower-cost worker. Otherwise, profits will be lower than they need to be. Suppose white males and others are identically productive, but managers prefer white males. Then the white males will be more expensive than women and minorities, and hiring white males will lower profits.

Discrimination is costly in that less productive employees or more expensive but not more productive employees are used.

Under what conditions will lower profits as a result of personal prejudice be acceptable? Perhaps a monopoly firm can forgo some of its monopoly profit in order to satisfy the manager's personal prejudices, or perhaps firms that do not maximize profits can indulge in personal preferences. However, for profit-maximizing firms selling their goods in the market structures of perfect competition, monopolistic competition, or oligopoly, personal prejudice will mean a loss of profit unless all rivals also discriminate. Could firms form a cartel to discriminate? Recall from the discussion of oligopoly that cartels do not last long—there is an incentive to cheat—unless an entity like the government sanctions and enforces the cartel.

In the United States, well-meaning legislation intended to protect women actually created a situation in which women were denied access to training and education and thus were not able to gain the human capital necessary to compete for high-skill, high-paying jobs. Until the 1960s, women were barred from jobs by legislation that attempted to protect them from heavy labor or injury. In reality, this legislation precluded women from obtaining certain kinds of human capital. Without the human capital, a generation or more of women were unable to obtain many high-paying jobs.

Worker Prejudice   Workers may not want to associate with other races or sexes. White males may resist taking orders from females or sharing responsibility with a member of a minority group. White male workers who have these discriminatory preferences will tend to quit employers who employ women or minorities on a nondiscriminatory basis.

The worker prejudice explanation of discrimination assumes that white males are willing to accept lower-paying positions in order to avoid working with anyone other than a white male. Such discrimination is costly to those who discriminate.

Consumer Prejudice   Customers may prefer to be served by white males in some situations and by minorities or women in others. If their preferences for white males extend to high-paying jobs such as physician and lawyer and their preferences for women and minorities are confined to lower-paying jobs like maid, nurse, and flight attendant, then women and minorities will be forced into occupations that work to their disadvantage.

This explanation of discrimination assumes that consumers are willing to pay higher prices to be served by a person of a specific race or gender. In certain circumstances and during certain periods of time, this may occur; but over wide geographic areas or across different nations and over long periods of time, consumer prejudice does not appear to be a very likely explanation of discrimination.

Be sure you recognize that economists are not saying that discrimination never occurs. They are saying that when it does occur, it costs the person doing the discriminating.

3.b.2. Statistical Discrimination
Discrimination not related to personal prejudices can occur because of a lack of information. Employers must try to predict the potential productivity of job applicants, but rarely do they know what a worker's actual productivity will be. Often, the only information available when they hire someone is information that may be imperfectly related to productivity in general and may not apply to a particular person at all. Reliance on indicators of productivity such as education, experience, age, and test scores may keep some very good people from getting a job and may result in the hiring of some unproductive people. This is called **statistical discrimination.**

statistical discrimination: discrimination that results when an indicator of group performance is incorrectly applied to an individual member of the group

Suppose two types of workers apply for a word-processing job: those who can process 80 words per minute and those who can process only 40 words per minute. The problem is that these actual productivities are unknown to the employer. The employer can observe only the results of a five-minute word-processing test given to all applicants. How can the employer decide who is lucky or unlucky on the test and who can actually process 80 words per minute? Suppose the employer discovers that applicants from a particular vocational college, the DeVat School, are taught to perform well on preemployment tests, but that their overall performance as employees is the same as that of the rest of the applicants—some do well and some do not. The employer might decide to reject all applicants from DeVat because the good and bad ones can't be differentiated. Is the employer discriminating against DeVat? The answer is yes. The employer is using statistical discrimination.

Let's extend this example to race and gender. Suppose that, on average, minorities with a high school education are discovered to be less productive than white males with a high school education because of differences in the quality of the schools they attend. An employer using this information when making a hiring decision might prefer to hire a white male. Statistical discrimination can cause a systematic preference for one group over another even if some individuals in each group have the same measured characteristics.

3.c. Occupational Segregation

crowding: forcing a group into certain kinds of occupations

occupational segregation: the separation of jobs by sex

Statistical discrimination and imperfect information can lead to **crowding**—forcing women and minorities into occupations where they are unable to obtain the human capital necessary to compete for high-paying jobs. Today, even in the industrial nations, some occupations are considered women's jobs and other occupations are considered men's jobs. This separation of jobs by sex is called **occupational segregation.**

Occupational segregation exists in the United States and other industrialized nations. One reason for occupational segregation is differences in the human capital acquired by males and females. Much of the human capital portion of the discrepancy between men and women is due to childbearing. Data suggest that marriage and children handicap women's efforts to earn as much as men. Many women leave the labor market during pregnancy, at childbirth, or when their children are young. These child-related interruptions are damaging to subsequent earnings because three out of four births occur to women before the age of thirty, the period in which men are gaining the training and experience that lead to higher earnings later in life. Second, even when mothers stay in the labor force, responsibility for children frequently constrains their choice of job: they accept lower wages in exchange for shorter or more flexible hours, location near home, limited out-of-town travel, and the like. Third, women have a disproportionate responsibility for child care and often have to make sacrifices that men do not make. For instance, when a young child is present, women are more likely than men to be absent from work, even when the men and women have equal levels of education and wages.

Perhaps most important of all, because most female children are expected to be mothers, they have been less likely than male children to acquire marketable human capital while in school. In the past, this difference was reflected in the choice of a curriculum in primary and secondary schools, in a college major, and in the reluctance of females to pursue graduate school training or to undergo the long hours and other rigors characteristic of apprenticeships in medicine, law, business, and other financially rewarding occupations. Females were channeled into languages, typing, and home economics, while males were channeled into mechanical drawing, shop, chemistry, and physics. This situation is changing, but the remnants of the past continue to influence the market. Since the late 1970s, about half of all law school classes and about one-third of medical school classes have been female. Nonetheless, mostly females major in languages, literature, education, and home economics, while mostly males major in physics, mathematics, chemistry, and engineering.

If new female entrants into the labor force have human capital equal to the human capital of new male entrants and thus greater than the human capital of females already in the labor force, then the average human capital and wages of females will rise. But even while the wage gap between males and females is decreasing, a gap will continue to exist because the average male in the labor force has more marketable human capital than the average female. The average rate of pay of males will continue to exceed that of females.

3.d. CEO Pay Packages

6. Why do CEOs, movie stars, and professional athletes make so much money?

Chief executive officers (CEOs) earn more than 200 times as much as the average worker. In 2002, the median salary of CEOs in companies listed in the Standard & Poor's 500 stock market index was $7 million. This is down from the peak of the stock market boom in 1999, when the top 100 CEOs earned an average of $37.5 million while the average worker earned $35,864. How could anyone justify such huge salaries and such incredible differences between the pay of top CEOs and that received by the average worker?

One answer that is often given is that the market for CEOs failed. The owners of firms, thousands of shareholders, exert little influence over the day-to-day activities of the manager and have little influence over the manager's pay. As a result, CEOs basically do what they want, including getting paid huge salaries, without regard to the desires of the firms' owners. Another answer given is that CEO pay is the result of a conspiracy involving other CEOs and friends of the CEO who, as members of the firm's board of directors, fail to listen to investors or look at the firm's performance, but instead simply provide the types of compensation that they themselves want to receive. A third explanation is that CEO pay makes sense from an economic efficiency perspective.

Workers receive the bulk of their compensation through salary, although many also invest in 401(k) plans and receive modest stock options. That was once true for CEOs as well. In 1970, the top 100 CEOs derived 84.66 percent of their income from salary and just 15.34 percent from stock options (the right to purchase a stock in the future at a price set now) and other compensation.[1] In 1999, salary accounted for just 9.73 percent of the compensation of top CEOs. Stock options provided 58.52 percent, and other compensation accounted for 31.76 percent. The change was due partly to corporate taxes. Because corporations could deduct only the first $1 million of CEO pay from their taxes, it became financially preferable to use other ways to provide compensation. In addition, it seemed that providing stock options provided a link between a firm's performance and that firm's rewards to its CEO. But what looked like a link was not one in practice. A stock option is typically provided on the basis of being priced above the current stock price. When the stock price rises, the CEO can purchase the stock at the price the stock option was granted at and then sell the stock at its current selling price. If a stock option has a price of $30 and the stock is selling at $35, the CEO earns $5 per share by exercising (cashing in) the option. Thus, as long as the stock market rises, CEO stock options also rise in value. In the stock market boom of the 1990s, stock prices rose for almost all companies, irrespective of their absolute or relative performance. In that situation, stock options provided CEOs the opportunity to cash in quickly and reap large incomes.

The declining stock market caused the total compensation received by CEOs to decline by double digits for two years in a row in 2001 and 2002. As the stock market declined, stock options had little value. As a result, CEO pay was about the same as it had been in 1996—a decline of 43 percent.[2] To avoid the problems associated with stock options in declining markets, CEO compensation has changed again.

[1] Emmanuel Saez, "Income Inequality in the U.S.," National Bureau of Economic Research, September 2001.

[2] Louis Lavell, Frederick F. Jespersen, Spencer Ante, and Jim Kerstetter, "Executive Pay," special report, *Business Week,* April 21, 2003, p. 86.

During 2001–2003, a greater proportion of compensation took place through stock grants (not options, but outright grants of shares of stock) and guaranteed deferred compensation in pension plans. Thus, median salaries of CEOs began to rise in 2003 even as the stock market struggled along.

Is CEO pay out of line? To place the pay of CEOs in perspective, let's look at the salaries of some professional athletes and movie stars. In 2002–2003, professional basketball's top earners were Kevin Garnett of Minnesota ($25,200,000), Shaquille O'Neal of the Los Angeles Lakers ($24,000,000), and Alonzo Mourning of Miami ($20,600,000). The average salary for all players exceeded $4 million. In football, the top earners in 2001 were Jonathan Ogden with $16.5 million, Keyshawn Johnson at $13.5 million, and Joey Galloway at $13 million. The average salary for all players exceeded $1 million. In baseball, the average salary exceeded $1.5 million and top earners received more than $14 million. Professional hockey paid about the same, with the average salary exceeding $1.6 million. Among celebrities, top earners include Tom Cruise ($105 million for *Mission Impossible II*), Tom Hanks ($40 million for *Saving Private Ryan*), and Mel Gibson ($25 million plus another $30 million or so [20 percent of the take] for *The Patriot*). Some of these stars earned double the listed amounts, as they had more than one movie released during the year. George Lucas pulled down $100 million, Steven Spielberg $100 million, Tiger Woods $69 million, and Tom Clancy $450 million. Television personalities earn substantial amounts as well. Oprah Winfrey is on top at $150 million, while Larry King earns about $14 million, Katie Couric $15 million, Matt Lauer $8 million, and Tom Brokaw, Peter Jennings, and Dan Rather between $9 and $14 million.

CEO pay does not seem so excessive when placed next to that of athletes or celebrities. But this comparison actually raises the question of why any of these people earn such huge salaries.

If someone were generating a huge income for you, you'd be willing to pay them a high salary to keep them working for you. Similarly, if an athlete is bringing in fans or a newscaster is increasing the numbers of viewers, the owners of the firms will willingly pay high salaries to keep the athlete or the newscaster. And, if a CEO were creating huge profits for shareholders, the shareholders would willingly pay a huge salary to the CEO. But there are cases where the CEO's compensation is rising at the same time the company is earning a loss. Although there are cases of outright theft by CEOs, most compensation is paid because owners value the CEO or because the compensation sends a signal to others that might create benefits in the future. Some economists argue that huge salaries provide an incentive for those who haven't yet attained these heights to work harder and better. They look at success in the business world as analogous to a tournament. In a tournament, the larger the first prize and the larger the difference between the first prize and all other prizes, the more productive the contestants. Thus, if we consider the labor market as a contest in which the first prize is the CEO position, a large first prize induces more effort and higher productivity from all contestants. An extremely high pay package for the CEO induces both that individual and all other employees (current and future) to exert extra effort during their working lives. So even if the company is not currently earning a profit, the huge compensation could serve as a signal that employees must be more productive and must contribute to the performance of the firm if they are to ever have a chance to earn such a huge salary.

Another possible economic explanation for the large salaries is called the economics of superstars. Sometimes small differences in ability translate into huge differences in compensation. Consider that the playing ability of the top tennis players or golfers is not much better than the playing ability of the players ranked between forty and fifty. Nonetheless, the compensation differences are incredibly large. The

Tiger Woods may turn out to be the greatest golfer of all time, surpassing Jack Nicklaus, Arnold Palmer, and Bobby Jones. For sure, Tiger Woods is a superstar. When he appears at a tournament, the crowds increase exponentially. The crowds do not disperse around the tournament watching each player but focus on Tiger. Hundreds of thousands struggle to get a glimpse of Tiger while other players are playing almost without anyone watching.

average income of the top ten tennis players and golfers is many hundreds of times higher than that of the next ten players. If their productivity differences are so small, why are their compensation differences so large?

Because most consumers have limited time, they choose to watch or follow the top players. A tennis match between the fortieth and forty-first players might be nearly as good as one between the first and second players. Yet, given the limited time to allocate between the two, nearly everyone would choose to watch the first and second players. At golf tournaments, huge throngs surround the top players, while lesser-known players play the game without the attention of adoring fans. In a similar manner, people choosing among television shows must select one over others, so if Katie Couric draws thousands more viewers than a competing personality, Katie Couric will receive substantially more compensation than the competing personality. These differences mean that the demand for the top players or personalities is huge relative to the demand for the lesser-ranked players or personalities. The sports franchises (the New York Yankees, for example) and the firms selling tickets to sporting events will be able to earn significantly higher revenues if the ranked players are included in the activity, and the television shows with greater numbers of viewers will generate substantially more advertising revenue than less-watched shows.

superstar effect: the situation in which people with small differences in abilities or productivity receive vastly different levels of compensation

The **superstar effect** occurs outside of sports. You might, for example, observe two lawyers of relatively equal ability earning significantly different fees, or two economic consultants with apparently similar abilities earning vastly different consulting fees. Consider the economist who offers advice to lawyers in cases involving firm behavior. A lawsuit filed against a firm might means billions of dollars won or lost. Even if there are very small differences between economists, if hiring the better economist means a win, then the better economist will receive huge compensation relative to the lesser economist. A $40 billion victory means that the value of the better economist is significantly greater than the value of the lesser economist.

While the tournament explanation or the superstar effect might explain the huge salaries of many CEOs, athletes, celebrities, and television personalities, not every case can be attributed to these effects. There are surely instances in which compensation is high because of unethical behavior on the parts of CEOs, boards of directors, auditors, and others. But, these are the exception rather than the rule, and the penalties for such actions are often severe. Between 2000 and 2003, many corporate executives were fired, lost huge sums of money, were indicted, and were jailed as a result of unethical behavior. The Tyco executives who stole from the firm were indicted and faced long jail terms. The American Airlines CEO who attempted to provide secret large sums of money to top executives while at the same time asking for pay cuts from all other employees was forced to resign. Martha Stewart, who was accused of insider trading (taking advantage of private information that the price of a company's stock was going to decline), lost about $80 million in the value of her company.

RECAP

1. Discrimination occurs when factors unrelated to marginal physical product acquire a positive or negative value in the labor market.
2. Earnings disparities may exist for a number of reasons, including personal prejudice, statistical discrimination, and human capital differentials. Human capital differentials may exist because of occupational choice, statistical discrimination, or unequal opportunities to acquire human capital.
3. There are two general classes of discrimination theories: prejudice theory and statistical theory. Prejudice theory claims that employers, workers, and consumers express their personal prejudices by, respectively, earning lower profits, accepting lower wages, and paying higher prices. Statistical discrimination theory asserts that firms have imperfect information and must rely on general indicators of marginal physical product to pay wages and hire people and that reliance on these general indicators may create a pattern of discrimination.
4. Occupational segregation is the separation of jobs by sex. Some jobs are filled primarily by women, and other jobs are filled primarily by men.
5. The high pay of the chief executive of a company might be explained as the CEO being the winner of an extensive tournament in which being in first place has a huge reward compared to being in second place or below.
6. Superstar effects occur when there is an all-or-nothing aspect to the market and result in situations in which individuals with small productivity differences receive vastly different compensation. High CEO pay could also be described as a superstar effect.

4. Wage Differentials and Government Policies

Not until the 1960s did wage disparities and employment practices become a major public policy issue in the United States. In 1963 the Equal Pay Act outlawed separate pay scales for men and women performing similar jobs, and Title VII of the 1964 Civil Rights Act prohibited all forms of discrimination in employment.

4.a. Antidiscrimination Laws

Since the 1930s, about thirty states have enacted fair employment practice laws prohibiting discrimination in employment on the basis of race, creed, color, or national origin. Under state fair employment practice legislation, it is normally illegal for an organization to refuse employment, to discharge employees, or to discriminate in compensation or other terms of employment because of race.

These state laws did not apply to women, however. In fact, prior to the 1960s, sex discrimination was officially sanctioned by so-called protective labor laws, which limited the total hours that women were allowed to work and prohibited them from working at night, lifting heavy objects, and working during pregnancy.

With the Civil Rights Act of 1964, however, it became unlawful for any employer to discriminate on the basis of race, color, religion, sex, or national origin. Unions also were forbidden from excluding anyone on the basis of those five categories. Historically, it had been very difficult for racial minorities to obtain admission into unions representing workers in the skilled trades. This exclusion prevented minorities from obtaining the human capital necessary to compete for higher-paying jobs.

The Civil Rights Act applied only to actions after the effective date of July 1, 1965. It also permitted exceptions in cases where religion, sex, or national origin is a bona fide occupational qualification reasonably necessary to the normal operation of a business. This qualification might apply to certain jobs in religious organizations, for example. In addition, the act permits an employer to differentiate wages and other employment conditions on the basis of a bona fide seniority system, provided that such differences are not the result of an intention to discriminate. As a result of these exceptions, the Civil Rights Act has had neither as large nor as quick an impact on wage and job differentials as many had anticipated. It has, however, led to a clearer definition of discrimination.

Two standards, or tests, of discrimination have evolved from court cases: disparate treatment and disparate impact. **Disparate treatment** means treating individuals differently because of their race, sex, color, religion, or national origin. The difficulty created by this standard is that personnel policies that appear to be neutral because they ignore race, gender, and so on, may nevertheless continue the effects of past discrimination. For instance, a seniority system that fires first the last person hired will protect those who were historically favored in hiring and training practices. Alternatively, a standard of hiring by word of mouth will perpetuate past discrimination if current employees are primarily of one race or sex.

The concern with perpetuating past discrimination led to the second standard, **disparate impact.** Under this standard, it is the result of different treatment, not the motivation, that matters. Thus, statistical discrimination is illegal under the impact standard even though it is not illegal under the treatment standard.

disparate treatment: different treatment of individuals because of their race, sex, color, religion, or national origin

disparate impact: an impact that differs according to race, sex, color, religion, or national origin, regardless of the motivation

4.b. Comparable Worth

The persistent wage gap between men and women in particular, but also between white males and minorities, has prompted well-meaning reformers to seek a new remedy for eliminating the gap—laws requiring companies to offer equal pay for jobs of comparable worth. **Comparable worth** is a catchword for the idea that pay ought to be determined by job characteristics rather than by supply and demand and that jobs with comparable requirements should receive comparable wages.

To identify jobs of comparable worth, employers would be required to evaluate all of the different jobs in their firms, answering questions such as these: What level

comparable worth: the idea that pay ought to be determined by job characteristics rather than by supply and demand and that jobs with comparable requirements should receive comparable wages

of formal education is needed? How much training is necessary? Is previous experience needed? What skills are required? How much supervision is required? Is the work dangerous? Are working conditions unpleasant? By assigning point values to the answers, employers could create job classifications based on job characteristics and could pay comparable wages for jobs with comparable "scores." A firm employing secretaries and steelworkers, for example, would determine the wages for these jobs by assessing job characteristics. If the assessment shows secretaries' work to be comparable to that of steelworkers, then the firm would pay secretaries and steelworkers comparable wages.

Proponents of comparable worth claim that market-determined wages are inappropriate because of the market's inability to assess marginal products as a result of statistical discrimination, team production, and personal prejudice. They argue that mandating a comparable worth system would minimize wage differentials that are due to statistical discrimination and occupational segregation, and they charge that a freely functioning market will continue to misallocate pay.

FIGURE 8

Comparable Worth

Two markets are shown, a market for computer science professors and a market for English professors. Demand and supply conditions determine that the wages for computer science professors are higher than the wages for English professors. Proponents of comparable worth might argue that the wages of both groups of professors should be equal to the higher wages of computer science professors, since the requirements and responsibilities of the two jobs are virtually identical. However, the effect of imposing a higher wage in the market for English professors, W_{CS}, is to create a surplus of English professors, $QE_2 - QE_1$. In addition, the higher wage sends the signal to current college students that majoring in English will generate the same expected income as majoring in computer science. Students who might have studied computer science turn to English. In the future, an excess of English professors remains and even grows, while the number of computer science professors shrinks.

(a) Market for Computer Science Professors

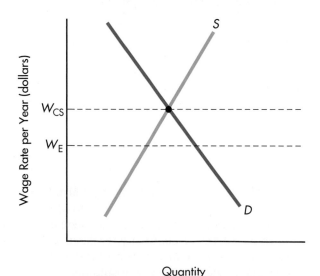

(b) Market for English Professors

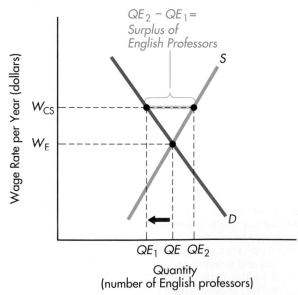

Opponents of comparable worth argue that interference with the functioning of the labor market will lead to shortages in some occupations and excess supplies in others. For instance, Figure 8 shows two markets for university professors, a market for computer science professors and a market for English professors. The supply and demand conditions in each market determine a wage for English professors that is less than the wage for computer science professors. The wage differential exists even though professors in both disciplines are required to have a Ph.D. and have essentially the same responsibilities.

Advocates of comparable worth would say that the two groups of professors should earn the same wage, the wage of the computer science professors, W_{CS}. But at this wage there would be a surplus of English professors, $QE_2 - QE_1$. The higher wage would cause the university to reduce the number of English professors it employs, from QE to QE_1. The net effect of comparable worth would be to reduce the number of English professors employed but to increase the wages of those who are employed. The policy would also have a detrimental effect in the future. The wage would send an incorrect signal to current college students. It would tell students to remain in English instead of forgoing English for computer science.

Comparable worth has not fared well in U.S. courtrooms. On the whole, U.S. federal courts have not accepted the notion that unequal pay for comparable jobs violates existing employment discrimination law. Perhaps not surprisingly, therefore, the concept has made little headway in the private sector. Greater success has occurred in the public sector at the local and state levels. In Colorado Springs, San Jose, and Los Angeles and in Iowa, Michigan, New York, and Minnesota, pay adjustments have been made on the basis of comparable worth. More than two-thirds of the state governments have begun studies to determine whether the compensation of state workers reflects the worth of their jobs. Why has comparable worth had more success in the government sector? State governments suffer from the problem of team production, and if personal prejudice is to occur, it is more likely to occur in nonprofit organizations such as government where firms do not employ to the profit-maximizing point where $MFC = MRP$. Thus, it is in the state, local, and federal governments that comparable worth can be an effective policy. Comparable worth was adopted nationwide in Australia in the early 1970s, and aspects of it have arisen in parts of the United Kingdom.

RECAP

1. The first national antidiscrimination law was the Civil Rights Act of 1964. It forbade firms from discriminating on the basis of sex, race, color, religion, or national origin.

2. Two tests of discrimination have evolved from court cases. According to the disparate treatment standard, it is illegal to intentionally treat individuals differently because of their race, sex, color, religion, or national origin. According to the disparate impact standard, it is the result, not the intention, of actions that is illegal.

3. Comparable worth is the idea that jobs should be evaluated on the basis of a number of characteristics and all jobs receiving the same evaluation should receive the same pay regardless of demand and supply conditions. Proponents argue that comparable worth is a solution to a market failure problem. Opponents argue that it will create surpluses and shortages in labor markets.

SUMMARY

❓ Are people willing to work more hours for higher wages?

1. The individual labor supply curve is backward bending because at some high wage, people choose to enjoy more leisure rather than to earn additional income. *§1.a*

❓ What are compensating wage differentials?

2. Equilibrium in the labor market defines the wage and quantity of hours worked. If all workers and all jobs were identical, then one wage would prevail. However, because jobs and workers differ, there are differential wages. *§1.c*

3. A compensating wage differential exists in situations where a higher wage is determined in one labor market than in another because of differences in job characteristics. *§2.a*

❓ Why might wages be higher for people with more human capital than for those with less human capital?

4. Human capital is the training, education, and skills that people acquire. Human capital increases productivity. Because acquiring human capital takes time and money, the necessity of obtaining human capital for some jobs reduces the supply of labor to those jobs. *§2.b*

❓ What accounts for earnings disparities between males and females and between whites and nonwhites?

5. Earnings disparities may result from discrimination, occupational choice, human capital differences, educational opportunity differences, age, and immigration. *§3.a, 3.c, 3.d*

6. Discrimination occurs when some factor not related to marginal revenue product affects the wage rate someone receives. *§3.a*

❓ Are discrimination and freely functioning markets compatible?

7. There are two general types of discrimination—personal prejudice and statistical discrimination. *§3.b*

8. Personal prejudice is costly to those who demonstrate the prejudice and should not last in a market economy. For it to last, some restrictions on the functioning of markets must exist. *§3.b.1*

9. Statistical discrimination is the result of imperfect information and can occur as long as information is imperfect. *§3.b.2*

10. Occupational segregation exists when some jobs are held mainly by one group in society and other jobs by other groups. A great deal of occupational segregation exists between males and females in the United States. *§3.c*

❓ Why do CEOs, movie stars, and professional athletes make so much money?

11. Incentives may explain why the best executives, movie stars, and athletes have much higher income than lesser executives, movie stars, and athletes. The greater the disparity between the best and the second-best, the greater the incentive for the second-best to improve. *§3.d*

12. The superstar effect may also explain why the best executives, movie stars, and athletes earn so much more than the second-best, third-best, and so on. The marginal revenue product of the best is much higher than the marginal revenue products of the second-best, third-best, and so on. *§3.d*

KEY TERMS

backward-bending labor supply curve *§1.a*

labor force participation *§1.b*

compensating wage differentials *§2.a*

human capital *§2.b*

discrimination *§3.a*

statistical discrimination *§3.b.2*

crowding *§3.c*

occupational segregation *§3.c*

superstar effect *§3.d*

disparate treatment *§4.a*

disparate impact *§4.a*

comparable worth *§4.b*

EXERCISES

1. What could account for a backward-bending labor supply curve?

2. What is human capital? How does a training program such as Mrs. Fields Cookie College affect human capital? Is a college degree considered to be human capital?

3. Define equilibrium in the labor market. Illustrate equilibrium on a graph. Illustrate the situation in which there are two types of labor, skilled and unskilled.

4. Describe how people choose a major in college. If someone majors in English literature knowing that the starting salary for English literature graduates is much lower than the starting salary for accountants, is the English literature major irrational?

5. Explain what is meant by discrimination, and explain the difference between personal prejudice and statistical discrimination.

6. Explain why occupational segregation by sex might occur. Can you imagine any society in which you would not expect to find occupational segregation by sex? Explain. Would you expect to find occupational segregation by race in most societies?

7. Why are women's wages only 60 to 80 percent of men's wages, and why has this situation existed for several decades? Now that women are entering college and professional schools in increasing numbers, why doesn't the wage differential disappear?

8. Why do economists say that discrimination is inherently inefficient and therefore will not occur in general?

9. Demonstrate, using two labor markets, what is meant by comparable worth. What problems are created by comparable worth? Under what conditions might comparable worth make economic sense? Explain.

10. There is a great deal of talk in the United States about providing more job flexibility for families. Why is it necessary for the government to provide this flexibility through the Family and Medical Leave Act and other programs? Why doesn't the private market provide this flexibility?

11. Consider the decision of a working woman or man who has young children or elderly relatives to take care of. Explain in terms of the labor supply curve how this person's decision to work is affected by the presence of dependents. What happens to the opportunity cost of working? How is the labor supply curve affected?

12. The 2003 PGA paid $1.2 million for first place, $600,000 for second place, and only $35,000 for eighth place. Explain what the difference might be if the differential between first-place prize money was only $10,000 greater than eighth-place prize money.

13. How could it be possible or ethical for a chief executive officer to receive several million dollars in compensation when the value of the company is declining? Is there an economic rationale for why this situation could actually benefit the company?

14. What would be the outcome if a firm paid a CEO only 10 times the lowest-paid employee, a movie producer paid the star only 10 times more than the lowest paid actor in the movie, and a sports franchise paid its star player no more than 10 times the lowest-paid player?

ACE

Take the ACE Practice Test for this chapter to review the important concepts and get immediate feedback with answers.

economics.college.hmco.com/students

Higher Apathy

A survey of college freshmen confirms what professors and administrators said they have been sensing, that students are increasingly disengaged and view higher education less as an opportunity to expand their minds and more as a means to increase their income.

The annual nationwide poll by researchers at the University of California at Los Angeles shows that two suggested goals of education—"to be very well off financially" and "to develop a meaningful philosophy of life"—have switched places in the last three decades.

In the survey taken at the start of the fall semester, 74.9 percent of freshmen chose being well off as an essential goal and 40.8 percent chose developing a philosophy. In 1968, the numbers were reversed, with 40.8 percent selecting financial security and 82.5 percent citing the importance of developing a philosophy.

It is using education more as a means to an end, rather than valuing what is being learned, said Linda Sax, director of the survey, first taken 32 years ago, at the Higher Education Research Institute at UCLA.

Now: Reasonable men can—and unreasonable men do—debate the nature and purposes of higher education. Cardinal Newman, for instance, had some ideas relating to the subject. And others might wonder if a year such as 1968 should serve as a benchmark for anything but rampant silliness. Nevertheless, the survey probably dismays the dwindling band believing colleges and universities ought to be devoted to higher education, not to mere training.

The researchers also found increased levels of "academic and political disengagement" among young scholars. (The less charitable might remark on the students' blasé ignorance.) Numerous reasons could explain the survey's results. . . .

The colleges themselves have degraded the liberal arts. Deconstructionism (a.k.a. destructionism) and the others isms and fads to which the professoriat is prone generate indifference among students preferring knowledge to ideology. Russia and its former satellites have gotten the message; the academy has not. The enemies of the liberal arts lie within the ivied walls. If students consider history, English, and philosophy irrelevant, then perhaps it is because their professors treat the humanities as though they were. Why should students respect the so-called canon, when noisemakers inside the academy treat it with contempt? . . .

Source: Reprinted by permission of the *Richmond Times Dispatch,* January 25, 1998.

Richmond Times Dispatch/January 25, 1998

Education and training account for a significant amount of the income differences among individuals. Generally, the more education one has, the higher one's lifetime income. In recent years the importance of education in determining income has risen. While the average worker's real income has been broadly flat for most of the decade, those at the top have gained considerably. The factor generally credited with this widening inequality is the changing demand for labor. As globalization has sent lower-skilled jobs overseas, the U.S. economy has restructured toward higher-skilled, higher-paid jobs.

The transformation has been remarkable. Professional, technical, and managerial jobs accounted for just one-sixth of the U.S. work force in 1950. By 1995, that proportion had risen to one-third. This demand for skilled labor has placed a much higher premium on educational attainment. As a result, more people are going to college and acquiring the necessary skills. The following table summarizes the role of education and wages; it shows the change in wages for each level of education for males and females over the period 1984 to 1995 (from the Urban Institute, as reported in the *Financial Times*, January 12, 1998, p. 9).

Education	All	Male	Female
High school dropout	−1.5	−3.2	2.0
High school graduate	4.2	− .3	11.9
Some college	2.1	− .6	19.7
College graduate	8.5	7.0	18.4
Postcollege education	13.7	10.6	20.0

Given these facts, why should anyone be surprised that students are in school to acquire skills that translate into more income and a better life? The real surprise would be if people were attending college simply to develop a philosophy. The pressures of the labor market are such that quality education is necessary; the human capital developed must have value in the labor market. Firms will pay for the human capital acquired in college.

CHAPTER 31

Financial Markets: Institutions and Recent Events

? **Fundamental Questions**

1. **What are stocks? How are stocks bought and sold?**

2. **What does a stock index represent?**

3. **What causes stock prices to rise and fall?**

4. **What causes bond prices to rise and fall?**

A firm must have money in order to hire labor, rent land, and purchase structures and equipment. Its sales or revenues provide money that can be used to pay operating expenses. These funds can be used to provide wages, salaries, and benefits to employees; make rent payments for land and offices; make interest payments on debt; and provide owners with a return on the funds they have invested in the company. But revenue is typically not sufficient to purchase buildings, structures, and equipment; these are huge expenditures that are purchased at one time but used over a long period of time. To acquire the funds necessary to purchase capital, a firm must sell shares of ownership and/or take out large loans. Where do these funds come from? From households.

On average, a family with income of around $45,000 will spend about $40,500 on goods, services, and taxes, using the remaining $4,500 to save. What happens to savings? Some is placed into accounts in banks, credit unions, and savings and loan institutions—the financial intermediaries—and some is used to purchase stocks, bonds, and mutual funds. Stocks represent ownership of a firm, bonds represent a

debt owed by a firm to the bondholder, and a mutual fund pools the money of many investors to purchase large amounts of stocks and/or bonds. Figure 1 shows how income earned by households goes to spending and to saving. (This is the circular flow diagram from Chapter 5.) The financial intermediaries, stocks, bonds, and mutual funds play an extremely important role in the economy by helping to channel savings from the household sector to the business sector. Without these funds, businesses would not be able to expand, purchase new buildings, or create new goods and services.

The flow of funds from households to firms occurs in the financial markets. In this chapter, we discuss the financial markets. The discussion will delve not only into how stock and bond prices are determined but also into why events like the 2000 stock market meltdown and the Enron scandal occur and what they mean for firms and for society in general. We begin with a look at the stock market. ■

1. What are stocks? How are stocks bought and sold?

shares, equity, stock: ownership of a piece of a company

common and **preferred stock:** the two main types of stock

dividend: the amount paid to shareholders on each share of stock owned

1. Equity

Whether you say **shares, equity,** or **stock** doesn't matter; these terms all mean the same thing—ownership of a piece of a company. Technically, owning a share of stock means that you own a share of everything the firm owns—every item of furniture, every piece of equipment, every building. In actuality, you are entitled only to a share of the company's earnings; you can't walk into the company's headquarters and walk out with a chair. There are two main types of stock: **common** and **preferred stock.** When people talk about stocks in general, they are referring to common stock. Preferred shares usually guarantee a fixed annual payment, or **dividend.** Common stock may or may not provide such a payment; that choice is at the discretion of the company.

1.a. Stock Exchanges

Stocks are bought and sold on stock exchanges. Some stock exchanges are physical locations where transactions are carried out on a trading floor. Others are virtual, composed of a network of computers where trades are made electronically. Firms have to meet stringent requirements and pay hefty fees to be "listed" on an exchange. Each firm is listed on just one exchange.

1.a.1. The New York Stock Exchange The New York Stock Exchange (NYSE), founded in 1792, is located on Wall Street in Manhattan and is the largest stock exchange in the world. There are about 3,000 firms listed on the NYSE. Each stock listed on the NYSE is allocated to a *specialist,* who is responsible for maintaining an orderly market in the stock. This person has a specific location on the floor of the exchange known as a **trading post.** The trading post is the location where the auction of a particular firm's stock takes place. A floor trader representing buyers and sellers will go to the trading post to learn about the current price for a security. The trader will call out an offer to buy or sell (traders jump up and down trying to get the attention of the specialist, making the whole thing look like a chaotic mess). The specialist will consider a trade to be completed when another trader is willing to sell or buy at that price.

trading post: a location on the floor of the NYSE where firms' stock is auctioned

1.a.2. The Nasdaq The second type of exchange is the virtual sort, of which the Nasdaq is the largest. Virtual markets have no central location or floor brokers.

FIGURE 1

The Circular Flow: Income and Spending

The circular flow diagram shows how income earned by households goes to spending and to saving. The financial intermediaries and stocks, bonds, and mutual funds channel savings from the household sector to the business sector. With these funds, businesses are able to expand, purchase new buildings and equipment, or create new goods and services. The market for the savings includes markets for stocks, bonds, and mutual funds.

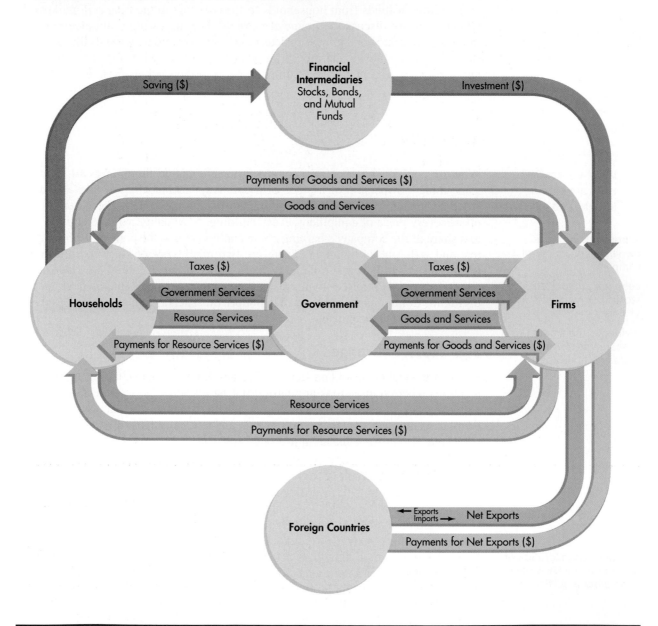

FIGURE 2

Stock Exchanges Around the World

Stocks can be traded literally 24 hours a day. The day opens with Hong Kong; then, as Hong Kong is ready to shut down, London opens up, followed later by New York.

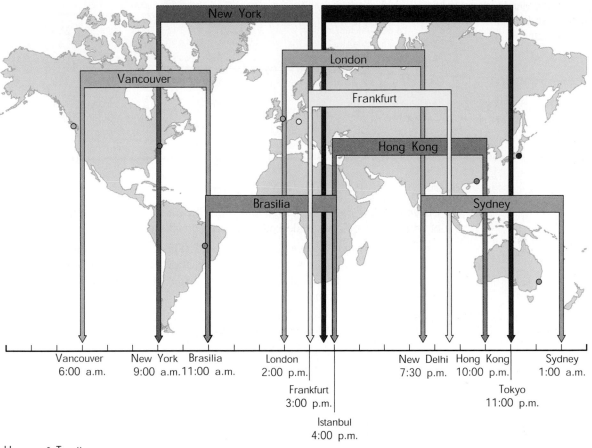

Hours of Trading
(9:00 a.m. Eastern Time)

Trading takes place through computers. Buyers and sellers submit orders electronically, and there are no specialists like those on the NYSE.

1.a.3. Other Exchanges The third largest exchange in the United States is the American Stock Exchange (AMEX). Almost all the firms listed on the AMEX are small firms. In addition to the various U.S. stock exchanges, many other countries have stock exchanges. In fact, trading takes place somewhere in the world 24 hours a day. Figure 2 shows how trading begins each day in Hong Kong, moves west to London, and then moves on to New York.

1.b. How to Read a Stock Table/Quote

Most newspapers report stock prices. The reports look something like Figure 3 and include the columns listed on the next page.

FIGURE 3

Stock Market Listing

Stocks are listed in newspapers in a standard form, showing annual highs and lows, dividends, P/E ratios, and daily volume and activity.

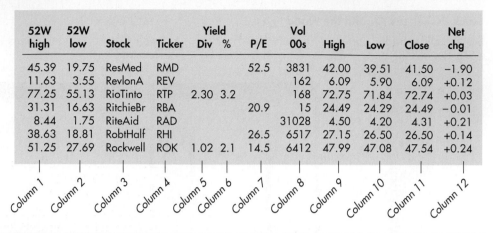

52W high	52W low	Stock	Ticker	Yield Div	%	P/E	Vol 00s	High	Low	Close	Net chg
45.39	19.75	ResMed	RMD			52.5	3831	42.00	39.51	41.50	−1.90
11.63	3.55	RevlonA	REV				162	6.09	5.90	6.09	+0.12
77.25	55.13	RioTinto	RTP	2.30	3.2		168	72.75	71.84	72.74	+0.03
31.31	16.63	RitchieBr	RBA			20.9	15	24.49	24.29	24.49	−0.01
8.44	1.75	RiteAid	RAD				31028	4.50	4.20	4.31	+0.21
38.63	18.81	RobtHalf	RHI			26.5	6517	27.15	26.50	26.50	+0.14
51.25	27.69	Rockwell	ROK	1.02	2.1	14.5	6412	47.99	47.08	47.54	+0.24

Column 1   Column 2   Column 3   Column 4   Column 5   Column 6   Column 7   Column 8   Column 9   Column 10   Column 11   Column 12

Columns 1 and 2: 52-week high and low. These are the highest and lowest prices at which the stock has traded over the previous 52 weeks (one year).

Column 3: Company name and type of stock. This column gives the name of the company. If there are no special symbols or letters following the name, the stock is common stock. Different symbols imply different classes of shares. For example, "pf" means that the shares are preferred stock.

Column 4: Ticker symbol. This is the unique alphabetic name that identifies the stock. If you are looking for stock quotes online, you use the ticker symbol.

Column 5: Dividend per share. This indicates the annual dividend payment per share. If this space is blank, the company does not currently pay out dividends.

Column 6: Dividend yield. This gives the percentage return provided by the dividend. It is calculated as annual dividends per share divided by price per share.

Column 7: Price/earnings ratio. This is calculated by dividing the current stock price by the earnings per share for the last four quarters.

Column 8: Trading volume. This figure gives the total number of shares traded for the day, in hundreds. To get the actual number traded, add "00" to the end of the number listed.

Columns 9 and 10: High and low for the day. This indicates the price range within which the stock has traded that day.

Column 11: Close. The close is the last trading price recorded when the market closed for the day. If the closing price is up or down more than 5 percent from the previous day's close, the entire listing for that stock is given in bold type.

Column 12: Net change. This is the dollar value change in the stock price from the previous day's closing price.

Stock quotes are also available on the Internet and are reported in the same way that the newspapers report them.

1.c. Stock Indexes

2. What does a stock index represent?

A stock index is a measure of the price movements of a group of stocks. The number of stocks in the group may vary; for example, there are 30 stocks in the Dow

Jones Industrial Average and 6,500 in the Wilshire Index. Since the prices of individual stocks do not necessarily go up or down at the same time, the importance or weight of a single stock in an index will vary. Most indexes weight companies based on **market capitalization (market cap),** which is the stock price multiplied by the number of shares of that stock that are outstanding. If a company's market cap is $1,000,000 and the value of all stocks in the index is $100,000,000, then the company has a weight of 1 percent of the index. An exception to weighting stocks by market cap is the Dow Jones Industrial Average, which uses the stock price relative to the sum of the prices of all the stocks in the index.

The most popular indexes are the Dow Jones Industrial Average (DJIA), the Standard & Poor's 500 (S&P 500), the Wilshire 5000, and the Nasdaq Composite Index. The DJIA contains 30 companies, the S&P 500 includes 500 companies, the Nasdaq Composite includes all companies listed on the Nasdaq stock exchange, and the Wilshire 5000 contains more than 6,500 stocks (the 5000 in the name is misleading). The S&P 500 tries to represent all major areas of the U.S. economy. It does not use the 500 largest companies, but rather includes 500 companies that are widely owned and represent all sectors of the economy. The stocks in the index are chosen by the S&P Index Committee, which typically makes between 25 and 50 changes every year. Non-U.S. companies were included in the past, but today, and in the future, only U.S. companies are included. The Nasdaq Composite Index represents all the stocks that are traded on the Nasdaq stock market. Most are technology and Internet-related, although there are financial, consumer, biotech, and industrial companies as well. The Wilshire 5000 Index contains more than 6,500 stocks that trade in the United States. It includes all of the stocks on the New York Stock Exchange and most of the Nasdaq and Amex issues. Another index, the Russell 2000, measures the performance of smaller stocks (small-cap stocks), which are often excluded from the big indexes. The average market capitalization in the Russell 2000 is approximately $530 million. To put that into perspective, Microsoft alone had a market capitalization of over $300 billion in 2002.

These well-known indexes are only a few among many indexes; every major country has an index that represents its stock exchange.

1.d. Mutual Funds

More than 80 million people, or half of the households in the United States, invest in mutual funds. A **mutual fund** is a group of stocks of individual firms that are placed into one investment pool by an investment company. For instance, one of the larger mutual fund investment companies is the Vanguard Group, which has many different mutual funds. One of its mutual funds is focused on high-tech firms, another on manufacturing firms, another on international firms, and so on. Individual investors are thus able to purchase a large set of stocks by simply purchasing shares of a mutual fund. There are more than 10,000 mutual funds offered to investors in the United States.

There are three general types of mutual funds: equity funds (made up of stocks), fixed-income funds (composed of corporate and government bonds), and money market funds (made up mostly of short-term U.S. government securities, but also including some corporate bonds).

If a fund includes international investments, it is called a **global fund** or an international fund. Some mutual funds focus on a specific sector of the economy, such as financial, technology, or health-care stocks, while others focus on a specific area of the world, say Latin America, or an individual country, such as Mexico. These are called **specific funds. Socially responsible funds** invest only in companies that

market capitalization (market cap): the stock price multiplied by the number of shares of stock that are outstanding

mutual fund: an investment tool that aggregates many different individual stocks into one entity

global fund: a mutual fund that includes international investments

specific fund: a mutual fund that focuses on a particular industry or a particular part of the world

socially responsible fund: a group of stocks or bonds of companies that meet the requirements of ethical behavior or environmental behavior

index fund: a mutual fund that tries to match the performance of a broad market index

load: the fees paid to the manager of a mutual fund

front-end load: a fee that you pay when you purchase a mutual fund

back-end load: a fee that you pay if you sell a mutual fund within a certain time frame

no-load fund: a mutual fund that sells its shares without a commission or sales charge

meet certain criteria. Most socially responsible funds don't invest in companies producing such things as tobacco, alcoholic beverages, weapons, or nuclear power. An **index fund** attempts to mimic the performance of a broad market index, such as the S&P 500 or the Dow Jones Industrial Average. These mutual funds purchase shares of stock in those companies that are included in the index and weight them so as to create as close a copy of the index as possible.

Funds may be load or no-load. **Load** refers to fees paid to a fund manager. With a **front-end load,** you pay a fee when you purchase the fund. If you invest $1,000 in a mutual fund with a 5 percent front-end load, $50 will pay for the sales charge, and $950 will be invested in the fund. With a **back-end load,** you pay the fee if you sell the fund within a certain time frame. For example, a fund may have a 5 percent back-end load that decreases to 0 percent in the sixth year. The load is 5 percent if you sell in the first year, 4 percent if you sell in the second year, and so on. If you don't sell the mutual fund until the sixth year, you don't have to pay the back-end load at all. A **no-load fund** sells its shares without a commission or sales charge (fees are typically paid by clients on a prearranged basis).

1.d.1. How to Read a Mutual Fund Table A typical newspaper report on mutual funds looks like Figure 4. The columns in the mutual fund table provide the following information:

Columns 1 and 2: 52-week high and low. These columns show the highest and lowest asset values the mutual fund has experienced over the previous 52 weeks (one year). This typically does not include the previous day's price.

Column 3: Fund name. This column gives the name of the mutual fund. The name of the company that manages the fund is written above the funds that the company manages in bold type.

Column 4: Fund specifics. Different letters and symbols have various meanings. For example, "N" means no load, "F" means front-end load, and "B" means that the fund has both front- and back-end fees.

FIGURE 4

The Reporting of Mutual Funds

Financial newspapers report on mutual fund performance in a standard manner, showing annual and weekly activity.

52W high	52W low	Fund	Spec.	Fri. NAVPS $chg	%chg	Wkly NAVPS high	low	cls	$chg	%chg
Montrusco Bolton Funds										
11.71	10.12	Bal Plus	*N	−0.08	−0.76	10.58	10.50	10.50	0.02	0.15
12.50	10.25	Growth Plus	*N	−0.10	−0.96	10.89	10.78	10.78	0.02	0.22
31.39	24.78	Quebec Growth	*FR	0.05	0.17	26.97	26.75	26.97	0.43	1.61
13.78	7.24	RSP Intl Growth	*N	−0.08	−1.01	7.45	7.36	7.36	−0.03	−0.41
11.16	9.09	Value Plus	*N	−0.07	−0.75	9.39	9.32	9.32	0.01	0.14
9.65	8.90	World Inc	*N	−0.04	−0.40	9.52	9.39	9.48	0.04	0.43
Montrusco Select Funds CS(a)										
12.87	10.49	Balanced	*N	−0.04	−0.37	10.85	10.80	10.81	0.05	0.45
16.32	12.11	Balanced+	*N	−0.05	−0.43	12.57	12.52	12.52	0.06	0.45
10.36	9.86	Bond Index+	X*N	−0.03	−0.32	10.35	10.30	10.30	0.04	0.37

Column 1   Column 2   Column 3   Column 4   Column 5   Column 6   Column 7   Column 8   Column 9   Column 10   Column 11

Column 5: Dollar change. This states the dollar change in the asset value of the mutual fund from the close of the previous day's trading. NAVPS stands for net asset value per share, the value of the mutual fund divided by the number of shares of the fund.

Column 6: Percentage change. This states the percentage change in the asset value of the mutual fund from the close of the previous day's trading.

Column 7: Week high. This is the highest asset value at which the fund was sold during the past week.

Column 8: Week low. This is the lowest asset value at which the fund was sold during the past week.

Column 9: Close. The asset value of the fund at the end of the trading day is shown in this column.

Column 10: Week's dollar change. This represents the dollar change in the asset value of the mutual fund from the previous week.

Column 11: Week's percentage change. This shows the percentage change in the asset value of the mutual fund from the previous week.

1.e. ADRs: American Depositary Receipts

Suppose you want to purchase the stock of a foreign company, one that is listed on the London Stock Exchange. You need to convert your dollars to pounds and then get a broker to purchase that stock for you. When you have the broker sell the stock, you have to pay whatever taxes are required in the U.K. and then convert the pounds back to dollars. Or suppose you run a Scottish firm that needs a large sum of money in order to enter Asian markets. You know that the United States provides more funds to businesses than any other country, so you want to sell stock in the United States. To do so, you would have to go through the process of meeting all requirements in the United States and then finding an exchange on which you could list your company, translating your currency to dollars and converting all your accounting statements to dollars. In addition to these difficulties, certain countries have regulations limiting foreign ownership (e.g., China, South Korea, Taiwan, and India) or controls on the movement of financial capital (e.g., Malaysia from 1998 to 2001) that make owning stock in a company in these nations difficult for U.S. investors. In the past these transactions were very difficult, and so few U.S. investors owned stock in foreign companies and few foreign businesses raised money in the United States. **American Depositary Receipts (ADRs)** allow easy access to non-U.S. stocks for

American Depositary Receipt (ADR): a stock that trades in the United States but represents shares of a foreign corporation

U.S. investors.

An ADR is a stock that trades in the United States but represents a specified number of shares in a foreign corporation. ADRs are bought and sold on American markets just like regular stocks, and are issued or sponsored in the United States by a bank or brokerage. A U.S. bank purchases shares of a company, say Sainsbury in England. The bank then issues ADRs representing ownership of the shares of Sainsbury stock and sells them in the United States as a Sainsbury ADR. Each ADR is backed by a specific number of the issuer's local shares; for instance, 1 Sainsbury ADR = 1.5 Sainsbury shares in the United Kingdom.

ADRs offer U.S. investors a convenient, easy-to use avenue for owning international stocks. And for foreign companies, ADRs are an easy way to raise money from U.S. investors. Today, ADRs are used by approximately 2,200 non-U.S. issuers from more than 80 countries. Of the 2,200 ADRs, approximately 600 are listed on U.S. stock exchanges. The remainder are sold "over the counter." A stock that is not traded on an exchange is said to trade over the counter.

1. Shares, equity, and stock mean the same thing—ownership of a piece of a company.
2. There are two main types of stock: common and preferred stock.
3. A stock index is a measure of the price movements of a group of stocks.
4. A mutual fund is an entity that invests money in stocks, bonds, and other securities for groups of people.
5. American Depository Receipts (ADRs) trade in the United States just like any U.S. stock but represent a specified number of shares in a foreign corporation.

3. What causes stock prices to rise and fall?

2. The Equity Market

The prices of stocks vary from day to day, and even minute to minute. What causes stock prices to rise or fall? It is the same thing that affects prices in any other market—demand and supply. The demand for stocks comes from investors—individuals, mutual funds, and other institutions like insurance companies—who are looking for the highest return on their investments. The return to a shareholder is the dividend the stock pays and the appreciation in the price of the stock. If a firm pays no dividends, then the return to a shareholder is just the appreciation in the stock, that is, the increase in the price of a share of stock between the time when the shareholder purchases the stock and the time when the shareholder sells it. Suppose, for instance, you purchased Microsoft at $5 per share in 1990 and then sold it for $100 per share in 2000. Your appreciation would have been $95 per share over the ten-year period. Since Microsoft paid no dividends during this period, your total return would have been the appreciation.

The demand curve for the shares of a company's stock slopes downward, since the higher the price of the stock, everything else the same, the lower the quantity of stock demanded. Demand depends on the prices of other companies' stocks and other possible investments, expectations regarding stock price movements, income, and tastes and preferences. When one of the determinants of demand for a firm's stock changes, the demand curve shifts. For instance, if the expectations investors have for the future price of the stock change so that the expected future price is higher than had previously been expected, demand will increase, as illustrated by the demand curve shifting out in Figure 5.

The supply of a stock comes from current shareholders who want to sell their shares of stock and from firms issuing additional shares.[1] The supply curve of a company's stock slopes upward, indicating that the higher the price, the greater the quantity offered for sale, everything else the same. The supply depends on the prices of related stocks and other investments and on the expectations of shareholders. When one of the determinants of supply changes, the supply curve shifts. For instance, if current shareholders begin to believe that the future price of the stock

---

[1]The *primary* market refers to the market in which a firm issues stock for the very first time—an IPO, the initial public offering of stocks by a firm—or issues additional stock. The *secondary* market is what we are typically referring to when we speak of the stock market. This is the market in which outstanding shares are bought and sold.

FIGURE 5

The Equity Market

Demand for stocks comes from investors looking to acquire wealth; the quantity demanded of a stock rises when the price of the stock declines. Supply of stocks comes from investors wanting to obtain money. The quantity supplied rises as the price of the stock rises. Demand shifts when the determinants of demand change; supply shifts when the determinants of supply shift.

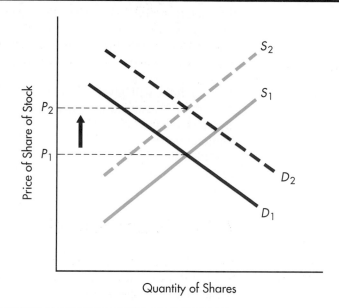

will be higher than they had previously believed, then they will tend to hold on to their shares, that is, to offer less for sale, and the supply curve will shift to the left, as illustrated in Figure 5.

You can see in Figure 5 that the effect of expectations about the likelihood of the price of a stock rising in the future leads to an increase in the price of the stock today from P_1 to P_2. Buyers want to purchase more shares now, so demand increases from D_1 to D_2, and sellers are offering less for sale, so supply decreases from S_1 to S_2. The result is a higher price today, P_2.

For one investor to sell a share of a particular company's stock to another investor, the buyer has to expect that the purchase of this stock will return more than any other comparable purchase, and the seller has to expect that the purchase of other financial assets, goods, or services with the money obtained from the sale of this stock will generate more satisfaction than holding onto the shares of this stock. An important point here is that buyers and sellers are comparing all possible investments and seeking the one that they think will give them the best return. Buyers and sellers evaluate the firm's stock on the basis of a comparison with all other comparable investments. A **comparable investment** is an investment that has the same features, such as risk and ease of selling (called liquidity), as the one being considered.

comparable investment: a stock that has the same features, such as risk and liquidity, as the one that buyers and sellers are evaluating

2.a. Risk

Risk is an important aspect of financial markets. What is risk? It is the possibility that some unexpected event will occur that will change the prices of stocks or bonds—for instance, something that will make an investment do better or worse than expected. Suppose you have two alternative investments. With the first, you know with certainty that you will get your money back plus an additional payment—the return on the investment. With the second, you may get a positive return, but you also may get nothing. To be equally willing to give either alternative $20,000 of your money, you would require a higher possible return from the second alternative than from the first. For instance, suppose you are looking at a biotech start-up company as a possible investment. This investment in a new firm with no history could return several times your initial investment, but it could also yield nothing. The other option you are considering is an established firm, such as Intel. Intel has been providing a steady stream of returns, and it is very unlikely that an investment in Intel will give you nothing back. Clearly, the biotech firm is a much more risky investment than Intel, and so the biotech firm will have to offer most investors a chance at a payoff that will provide a substantial premium over what Intel would provide.

Rather than investing in the risky biotech firm or the less risky Intel, investors could decide not to take any risk at all. By not taking any risk, investors would expect to receive a return that is even lower than the return that an established firm like Intel would provide. Thus, if an investor is to take on more risk, the investor must anticipate a greater return. There is, then, a trade-off between risk and return.

2.b. Stock Price Changes

Stock prices change every day because of supply and demand. If more people want to buy a stock (demand) than want to sell it (supply), then the price moves up. Conversely, if more people want to sell a stock than want to buy it, the price will fall. What causes the stock price to rise or fall? When investors change their expectations so that they now expect the price of the stock to rise more than they previously did, then more investors will want to buy and fewer will want to sell. As illustrated in Figure 6, demand will increase, supply will decrease, and price will rise from P_1 to P_2 when expectations are revised upward. When expectations are revised downward, fewer investors want to buy and more want to sell. In this case, supply will increase (shift right), demand will decrease (shift down), and price will fall from P_2 to P_1.

FIGURE 6

Revisions of Expectations

When a firm earns more than it had been expected to earn, investors in that firm's stock are likely to change their expectations of what the future may bring. This will induce investors to purchase more shares of the stock and sell fewer—an increase in demand and a decrease in supply.

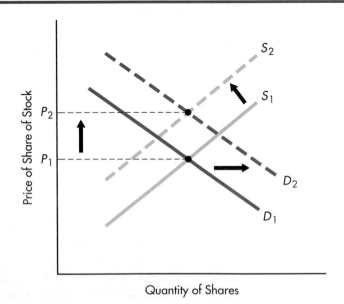

The P/E Ratio

How does a potential buyer decide which stocks to purchase? How does the buyer know when is a good time to buy? One method used is to see if the stock price is appropriately related to the firm's earnings. The P/E ratio is an indicator of this relationship. The P/E ratio is the ratio of a company's share price (P) to its earnings per share (E). To calculate the P/E, you divide the current stock price of a company by its earnings per share (EPS). Most of the time the P/E is calculated using the EPS from the last four quarters (known as the trailing P/E). Occasionally, however, you will see earnings expected over the next four quarters (known as the leading P/E) used as EPS.

Theoretically, a stock's P/E tells us how much investors are willing to pay for each dollar of earnings. For this reason, it's also called the *multiple* of a stock. In other words, a P/E ratio of 20 suggests that investors in the stock are willing to pay $20 for every $1 of earnings that the company generates during the period (leading or lagging). If a company has a P/E higher than the market or industry average, this is interpreted as meaning that the market is expecting that the company will have better performance over the next few months or years than the average firm in the market or industry. But you can't just compare the P/Es of two different companies to determine which is a better value, because the companies may have very different growth rates. If two companies have a P/E of 20, but one is growing twice as fast as the other, then the faster-growing firm is undervalued relative to the slower-growing one. Finally, a low P/E ratio could mean that the market believes that the company is headed for trouble in the near future. If earnings are expected to come in lower than forecast in the future, this won't be reflected in a trailing P/E ratio, as the future performance may differ greatly from the past.

Firms are required to report earnings (accounting profit) each quarter (for most companies, the end of March, June, September, and December). These quarterly reports are used by stock market analysts and investors to evaluate how well their previous forecasts of the firm's performance match what has actually been happening. When the quarterly results are not consistent with the investors' forecasts or expectations, then the investors will revise their expectations of future performance up or down. If the earnings reports indicate lower earnings than had been expected, the forecasts will be revised downward and the stock price will decline. When a firm does better than it had been expected to do, the forecasts will be revised upward and the stock price will rise.

As an illustration, consider Cisco's stock price movements in the 1990s. Cisco is a large company that manufacturers high-tech equipment. From the mid-1990s through 2000, Cisco generated very substantial economic profit, a value that was reflected in the high price of its shares. Since expectations were that Cisco would generate large profits, it would have been difficult for the company to have done better than those expectations. In fact, from March to June 2000, Cisco's performance did not meet expectations and its stock price declined, from a high of $80 per share to about $50 per share, even though Cisco was earning a profit.

2.c. Market Efficiency

There are hundreds of millions of people who own shares of stock. Some of these people analyze all available information about companies, and some don't even know which stocks they own. It would seem that those people who study the stock markets would be so much better informed than the average investor that they would be able to reap large returns relative to the average investor. But this is not necessarily so. To see why, suppose a particular investor gains a reputation as a stock

Stock Market Booms and Busts

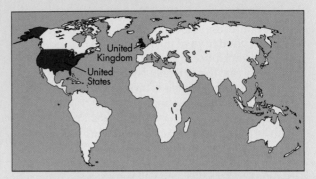

The stock market decline from 2000 to 2003 produced a dramatic decrease in investor wealth, especially after the boom of the 1990s. But this stock market decline was not an isolated event in history. Stock market booms and busts are a recurrent feature of developed economies. In the United States there have been 13 market crashes since 1800, and in the United Kingdom there have been 10. The patterns of booms and busts for the United States and the United Kingdom are noted in the accompanying table. The greatest declines in percentage terms occurred during the 1929–1932 period in the United States and the 1909–1920 period in the United Kingdom. The 2000–2002 decline ranked as the sixth greatest decline in the United States and the ninth in the United Kingdom.

Crashes—United States			Crashes—United Kingdom		
Peak	Trough	% Change	Peak	Trough	% Change
1809	1814	−37.8	1808	1812	−54.5
1835	1842	−46.6	1824	1826	−33.6
1853	1859	−53.4	1829	1831	−27
1863	1865	−22.5	1835	1839	−39.1
1875	1877	−26.8	1844	1847	−30.5
1881	1885	−22.2	1865	1867	−24.5
1892	1894	−16.4	1874	1878	−19.7
1902	1904	−19.4	1909	1920	−80.5
1906	1907	−22.3	1928	1931	−55.4
1916	1918	−42.5	1936	1940	−59.9
1919	1921	−24.5	2000	2002	−26.7
1929	1932	−66.5			
1936	1938	−27			
2000	2002	−30.8			

Source: *World Economic Outlook,* International Monetary Fund, April 2003, pp. 64–66.

market guru—a very successful investor—and that investor's activities are easily observed by others. What will happen? As with any market that does not have significant barriers to entry, when some firm (some person) begins making positive economic profits, others mimic that firm (that person) and compete with it. As others copy the initial investor's strategy and mimic every move, the initial investor's returns drop—economic profit is driven down to zero. This view of the behavior of the stock markets suggests that no investor can continually outperform the market.

Another way this suggestion is characterized is the idea that one can do as well at picking stocks by throwing darts as by picking them in any other way.[2] If there were one best way to pick stocks, then everyone would focus on that method and the price would reflect all such information. There would be no way to do better than everyone else.

Consider a hypothetical situation in which investors are considering buying the stocks of two firms, A and B. Investors know with certainty that the CEO for firm A is going to carry out an activity that will increase profits next year but lead to losses in the following years, and that the CEO for firm B is looking to the long term and wants to increase profits each year. The result of this is that firm B will not increase profits next year as much as firm A does.

Knowing the directions in which the two CEOs are taking their firms, investors think to themselves, "I want to own firm A's stock only next year. I don't want to be holding it after that. But I don't want to be the last to sell. In fact, I want to be the first to sell and then the first to own firm B, so that when everyone else tries to buy firm B, I will make a large profit. So I should sell firm A's stock before the end of the year—perhaps in month 11. But others will expect me to do that and they will sell in month 10. So I will have to sell before that—month 9, 8 . . . ?"

The process of moving the time of sale forward will continue until the investor realizes that the only way to gain is not to buy stock in firm A at all, but instead to buy stock in firm B now. As other investors do the same thing, the stock price of firm A decreases now, not next year, and that of firm B rises now, not next year. The stock price reflects all available information about the expected long-term economic profit stream.

A story about economists illustrates the idea that obvious profitable opportunities cannot exist for very long. Two economists are walking down the street. One sees a $20 bill lying on the sidewalk and leans over to pick it up. The other says, "Don't bother. If that were really a $20 bill, it would already have been picked up." The point is that stock prices will incorporate and reflect all relevant information instantaneously once that information appears. Thus, even though investors possess widely differing amounts of information, there is no way in which one investor can continually make above-normal profits or "beat the market." Of course there are some investors who seem to do better than others, but in few cases does a single investor continually do better than others. The basic idea of efficient markets is that there are no sure profits. As the Global Business Insight "Stock Market Booms and Busts" shows, investing is a risky business, as prices continually adjust to new information and circumstances.

2.d. Behavioral Economics and the Stock Market

The idea that you can't beat the market has met with considerable opposition, both from people whose livelihood stems from picking stocks (brokers, analysts, money managers) and from economists who say that people don't behave perfectly rationally. Consider the stock market crash of October 1987 and the stock market boom of the late 1990s. In both of these cases, many people were selling simply because others were selling and because the market had declined yesterday or, conversely, buying because others were buying and because the market had risen yesterday.

How can we explain such apparent irrationality? A field of study that blends psychology and economics, called **behavioral economics,** tries to explain why individuals don't always seem to be perfectly rational and why it makes sense for

behavioral economics: a field of study that blends psychology and economics

---

[2]This statement was made in a 1973 book by Burton Malkiel, *A Random Walk Down Wall Street* (W. W. Norton and Company).

individuals to behave this way. An individual is neither an automaton like Data in *StarTrek Generations* nor an imbecile, but rather a person who has to make complex decisions in a limited amount of time and with limited information, using a brain that is wired to operate in a certain way. This means that people do the best they can with the information they have, but that what they do may not, in hindsight, have been the best thing they could have done.

Using laboratory experiments, economists have found that people behave in certain regular ways that appear, on the surface, not to be rational. Yet these very actions enable individuals to achieve what they want with the least opportunity cost—in other words, they appear to be pretty rational overall. For instance, people tend to think that what occurred in the past will happen in the future. This is a lot easier than trying to figure out what else might occur. People also tend to put too much weight on recent, spectacular, or personal experiences in assessing the probability of events occurring. Think about the question as to whether there are more suicides or murders in New York City each year. The fact is that there are many more suicides, but because murders make headlines, people tend to think that there are more murders. Adding to these behaviors is the fact that people require less information to predict a desirable event than to predict an undesirable one—they engage in wishful thinking.

If you consider these tendencies in terms of the stock market, you can see why stock prices may rise or fall unreasonably—that is, why stock prices are not linked as closely to corporate profits as economic theory says they should be. During the 1997–2000 dot.com stock price surge, some companies, such as Amazon.com, had very high stock prices even though they had never made a profit. Perhaps some of that stock price was based on expectations of future profits, but a great deal of it was due to investors gambling or speculating on the basis of wishful thinking and the publicity given to great success stories like Microsoft. People would hear about the secretary of a start-up company becoming a millionaire, and so they would start purchasing stocks in start-up companies so that they too would become rich. Moreover, when the market was booming in the late 1990s, most people ignored negative information and kept predicting rising stock prices.

The problem is that wishful thinking cannot by itself drive stock prices up for very long. Eventually a firm must earn positive economic profits. The stock market collapsed in 2000 because it became evident that firms were not earning economic profits that were high enough to support the inflated stock prices. In the short run, psychological propensities may drive stock prices, but over the long run, stock prices will reflect economic profit.

RECAP

1. The equity market is the market in which stocks are bought and sold.

2. The demand for equities comes from investors who are seeking the greatest return on their savings.

3. The supply of equities comes from stock owners who want to sell their stock and purchase something else.

4. Demand depends on expectations, income, and the prices of and returns on other investments. Supply depends on expectations and the prices of and returns on other investments. A change in one of these determinants of demand and/or supply will cause the curve to shift. If buyers want to buy more stock (demand) than sellers want to sell (supply), then the price will move up. Conversely, if sellers want to sell more of a stock than buyers want to buy, the price will fall.

5. The equity market is said to be an efficient market in the sense that it is difficult for an investor to continually earn above-normal profits. If there were a secret formula for becoming rich in the stock market, everyone would soon learn that formula, and it would no longer be an effective strategy.

6. Some disagree with the notion of an efficient market, arguing that people just don't behave perfectly rationally. Behavioral economists have noted that people behave in certain regular ways that do not seem, in hindsight, to have been rational. In the short run, these tendencies can affect the prices of stocks; in the long run, however, it is the performance of the firm that determines stock price.

3. Fraud and Accounting Shenanigans

Figure 7 shows the dramatic run-up and then collapse of stock prices in the 1990s. The run-up was due in part to technological change and in part to speculation. The Internet revolution had created many new opportunities for businesses and allowed firms to reduce costs and increase revenues. Stock prices began rising in 1992, and as the market continued up, people began to feel that it would rise forever and that if they didn't purchase stocks, they would be left behind. This drove the market up more and more rapidly. Shareholders were demanding that companies grow faster and generate increasingly higher accounting profits. Companies that reported higher earnings saw their stocks rise in price, and executives in these companies saw their own wealth increase. It was in this setting that several high-profile corporate scandals occurred.

FIGURE 7

Stock Market Performance

The S&P 500 Index shows how the market rose steadily until about 1996, then accelerated until about 2000. After 2000, the market dropped by at least 33 percent. Between 2003 and 2004, it rose 30 percent.

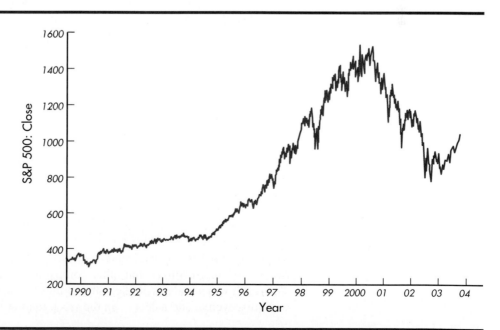

3.a. Enron Corporation

The best-known corporate scandal involved Enron Corporation. Enron originally was a gas pipeline and electricity-generating and electricity-transmission company—what most people considered to be a staid old electric utility. It was turned into a company that traded power—bought and sold it rather than producing it—and generated staggering profits in doing so. None of this got Enron into trouble. It was what Enron executives did with respect to the company's financial accounts and its relationships with auditors and investment banks that led to disaster. Enron executives made it appear that the company was earning more profits than it actually was. They did this by not accounting for many costs and overstating revenues. Enron's accountants hid costs by reporting them as costs not of Enron but of different entities—partnerships that were not directly part of the Enron Corporation. These accounting shenanigans were not all that the executives did in order to drive Enron's stock price higher. Enron used some unscrupulous means to convince stock analysts that Enron was in excellent shape and these analysts then recommended the purchase of Enron stock to their clients. This process continued until Enron's true situation could no longer be hidden. Once the seventh largest company in the world, Enron had virtually disappeared by 2002.

3.b. WorldCom, Tyco, and Others

Tyco and WorldCom also used aggressive accounting that was intended to increase current earnings above what they would have been under a more conservative treatment. WorldCom had grown into a telecommunications giant by acquiring or merging with more than 65 other companies, including MCI. Because of accounting maneuvers, each new acquisition allowed WorldCom to report higher per share profits, even when its business was doing poorly. To keep the momentum going, WorldCom needed larger and larger deals. The biggest and last was a $145 billion bid for Sprint. When the Justice Department decided not to allow this merger to proceed, WorldCom's ability to delude investors came to an end. Unable to continue hiding its costs through accounting maneuvers associated with acquisitions, the reality that WorldCom was losing money became widely known. The company declared bankruptcy in 2000.

These scandals contributed to the collapse of the stock market. Investors sold stock, fearing that more scandals involving other firms might occur. The resulting stock sales drove prices down. By 2003, the stock market had declined 33 percent from its 2000 high.

RECAP

1. By manipulating their financial statements, several companies were able to mislead the investing public about their performance. This helped to fuel the booming stock market in the late 1990s.

2. Enron was the best-known instance of misleading and deceptive practices on the part of its executives, but other companies engaged in similar practices. The result was a collapse in the value of these companies once their practices were discovered, and a decline in the stock market in general.

Country Bond Ratings

Governments issue bonds in order to raise money. Government bonds are rated in terms of risk much like corporate bonds are. The following are ratings provided by Moody's as of January 2003.

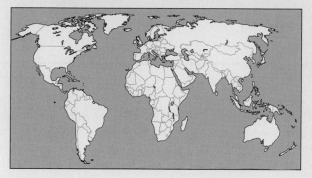

Country	Long-Term Bond Rating
Argentina	Ca
Australia	Aa
Brazil	B
Canada	Aa
Chile	Baa
China	A
Hong Kong	A
Hungary	A
India	Ba
Indonesia	B
Japan	Aa
Korea	Baa
Malaysia	Baa
Mexico	Baa
Pakistan	Caa
Philippines	Ba
Russia	Ba
Singapore	Aa
South Africa	Baa
Taiwan	Aa
Thailand	Baa
Turkey	B
UK	Aaa
USA	Aaa
Vietnam	B

4. Bonds

Firms can raise cash by selling ownership rights (shares of stock—equity—in the case of a public company), by retaining earnings in the firm (not allocating them to owners in the form of dividends), and by selling bonds or taking out loans (debt). A **bond** (sometimes called a fixed-income security or debt security) is an IOU issued by a borrower to a lender. When you buy a newly issued bond, you are lending money to the borrower. When you purchase a bond that is not a new issue, you are buying that bond not from the issuing firm but from an investor or lender that initially provided the loan. You are choosing to own a portion of the debt obligation of a company because you think the return on that bond exceeds what else you might have done with the money used to purchase the bond. The seller of the bond has

bond: an IOU issued by a borrower to a lender

FIGURE 8

Bond Ratings

Rating agencies provide measures of the amount of risk associated with particular bonds.

Bond Rating		Grade	Risk
Moody's	*Standard & Poor's*		
Aaa	AAA	Investment	Lowest risk
Aa	AA	Investment	Low risk
A	A	Investment	Low risk
Baa	BBB	Investment	Medium risk
Ba, B	BB, B	Junk	High risk
Caa/Ca/C	CCC/CC/C	Junk	Highest risk
C	D	Junk	In default

maturity date: the specified time at which the issuer of a bond will repay the loan

face or **par value:** the amount that the lender will be repaid when a bond matures

coupon: the fixed amount that the issuer of a bond agrees to pay the bondholder each year

decided that it is better off selling that debt and thus receiving money now rather than waiting for the debtor (the issuing firm) to pay off the loan.

There is a specified time at which the borrower will repay your loan; this is the **maturity date.** In most cases the bond's **face** or **par value** is $1,000; this is the amount that the lender will be repaid once the bond matures. The borrower pays the lender a fixed amount, called a **coupon,** each year. These interest payments are usually made every 6 months until the bond matures. The rate of interest that must be paid—that is, the *coupon rate*—depends on how risky the borrower is. The chart in Figure 8 illustrates the different bond rating scales from the two major rating agencies, Moody's and Standard & Poor's, their associated grades, and the risk levels the ratings indicate.

U.S. government bonds are considered no-risk investments because it is so unlikely that the United States will default on its obligations. Corporations must offer a higher yield than the government in order to entice lenders to purchase corporate bonds because corporate bonds are more risky. AAA corporate bonds are the lowest-risk corporate bonds—often referred to as blue chip bonds. The highest-risk corporate bonds are called junk bonds. Junk bonds are typically rated at BB/Ba or less. On average, a bond carries less risk than a share of stock because in the event of the firm's collapse, the shareholders cannot get anything until all debtholders have been paid.

4.a. Reading a Bond Table

In every financial newspaper there are bond tables similar to the one shown in Figure 9. The columns in the bond table provide the following information:

Column 1: Issuer. This is the company, state (or province), or country that issued the bond.

Column 2: Coupon. The coupon refers to the fixed interest rate that the issuer pays to the lender. The coupon rate varies by bond.

Column 3: Maturity date. This is the date when the borrower will pay the lenders (investors) their principal back. Typically only the last two digits of the year are quoted: 25 means 2025, 04 is 2004, and so on.

Column 4: Bid price. This is the price that someone is willing to pay for the bond. It is quoted in relation to 100, no matter what the par value is. Think of the bond price as a percentage: a bid of $93 means that the bond is trading at 93 percent of its par value.

FIGURE 9

Reading a Bond Table

Bonds are reported in financial newspapers and on the Internet in a standard manner.

	Coupon	Mat. Date	Bid $	Yld%
Corporate				
AGT Lt	8.800	Sep 22/25	100.46	8.75
Air Ca	6.750	Feb 02/04	94.00	9.09
AssCap	5.400	Sep 04/01	100.01	5.38
Avco	5.750	Jun 02/03	100.25	5.63
Bell	6.250	Dec 01/03	101.59	5.63
Bell	6.500	May 09/05	102.01	5.95
BMO	7.000	Jan 28/10	106.55	6.04
BNS	5.400	Apr 01/03	100.31	5.24
BNS	6.250	Jul 16/07	101.56	5.95
CardTr	5.510	Jun 21/03	100.52	5.27
Cdn Pa	5.850	Mar 30/09	93.93	6.83
Clearn	0.000	May 15/08	88.50	8.61
CnCrTr	5.625	Mar 24/05	99.78	5.68
Coke	5.650	Mar 17/04	99.59	5.80

Column 1   *Column 2*   *Column 3*   *Column 4*   *Column 5*

Column 5: Yield. The yield indicates the annual return until the bond matures. Yield is calculated as the amount of interest paid on a bond divided by the price; it is a measure of the income generated by a bond. If the bond is callable, the yield will be given as "c—," where the "—" is the year in which the bond can be called. For example c10 means that the bond can be called as early as 2010.

You will hear some bonds referred to as bills or notes. The name indicates the length of time until the bond matures. *Bills* are debt securities maturing in less than one year. *Notes* are debt securities maturing in one to ten years. *Bonds* are debt securities maturing later than ten years. A bond that provides no interest payments but instead is issued at a value that is lower than its face value is called a **zero-coupon bond.**

zero-coupon bond: a bond that provides no interest payments but is issued at a value lower than its face value

4. **What causes bond prices to rise and fall?**

4.b. The Bond Market

The market for bonds is not very different from the stock market, and the two are closely linked. Bond demanders are investors who are looking for the best return on their savings. They will purchase a bond when the return on the bond is expected to be greater than the return on other comparable investments—for instance, better than the return on stocks adjusted for risk. Consider a $100 bond maturing in one year that pays a 5 percent rate of interest, or coupon rate. The bondholder receives $5 per year in interest until the bond matures. If the price of the bond is $100, the same as the face value, then the yield is 5 percent ($5/$100). But if the price of the bond is lower than the face value, say $95, the yield is $10/$95 = 10.52 percent. Thus, for a bond paying 5 percent coupon, as the price rises, everything else the same, the quantity demanded will decline, so the demand curve slopes down. The demand for bonds depends on the coupon, the prices of and interest rates on other bonds and other investments, expectations of investors, income, and other factors. When one of the determinants of demand other than the bond's own price changes,

FIGURE 10

The Bond Market

The demand for bonds comes from lenders—investors who want to earn interest on their savings. The supply of bonds comes from the holders of bonds—firms and governments that are attempting to borrow and bond owners that are offering to sell. The quantity demanded of a bond paying a fixed coupon declines as the price of the bond rises; the quantity supplied of a bond paying a fixed coupon rises as the price of the bond rises. Demand and supply together determine the price of the bond. If expectations or interest rates on other investments, or something else other than the price of the bond, changes, the demand for the bond and/or the supply of the bond will change—the curves will shift.

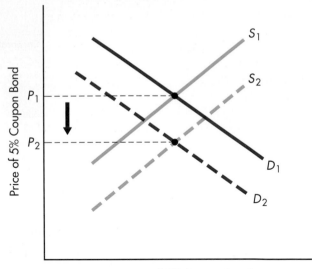

the demand curve shifts. For instance, in Figure 10, an increase in interest rates on other investments will cause the demand for a bond offering a 5 percent coupon to decline—the demand curve shifts down from D_1 to D_2.

The suppliers of bonds are the companies, governments, and other institutions offering new issues of IOUs and investors owning previously issued bonds who want to sell. The supply curve slopes upward, illustrating the idea that as the price of an IOU rises, everything else the same, the quantity offered for sale rises. The supply depends on the prices of other bonds and investments, interest rates on other bonds and investments, and expectations of bond sellers. If interest rates on other investments rise, the quantity of bonds offering a 5 percent coupon that suppliers are willing and able to sell will rise—the supply curve shifts out, and the bond price falls.

As illustrated in Figure 10, the result of an increase in interest rates, everything else the same, is to cause the price on a 5 percent coupon bond to fall. This illustrates the fact that bond prices and interest rates are inversely related. Everything else the same, when interest rates rise, bond prices fall.

Bonds and stocks are often substitute goods, meaning that as the price of stocks rise, the demand for bonds rises. The reason for this is that investors sell their shares of stock and purchase bonds when interest rates are higher than the expected return on stocks. Suppose that investors are expecting stock prices to decline in the future. Then current shareholders will offer to sell more stock. The supply of shares of stock increases and demand drops, forcing stock prices down. Expecting stock prices to drop, investors purchase bonds and other assets, driving the price of bonds up. As the price of bonds rises, the interest rate declines (remember the inverse relationship between interest rate and bond price).

In some cases, bonds and stocks are complementary goods. An investor will purchase both stocks and bonds when both are expected to yield better returns than other investments and when the investor wants to diversify his or her portfolio—to not put all his or her eggs in one basket. Thus, we can't always say that when stock prices rise, bond prices will fall, and vice versa. In some circumstances, both bond and stock prices will rise and fall together.

From 2000 until early 2003, stock prices fell while bond prices rose. The stock market collapse caused investors to sell their shares of stock and look for higher yielding investments. Many turned to the bond market and purchased bonds, hoping for a safe, stable return. But as military conflict in Iraq became a more and more likely possibility, investors looked for even safer returns. They continued to sell shares of stock, but they also sold bonds. Prices of both stocks and bonds declined as investors purchased gold and other commodities, believing that owning something real and physical was the safest way to invest their money. The price of gold rose from $240 per ounce in 1999 to $345 per ounce in 2002. From early in 2003 to late 2003, bond prices fell as stock prices rose very slightly.

RECAP

1. Bonds are IOUs provided by a lender or issuer of the bond to the purchaser of the bond.

2. The demanders of bonds are individuals and mutual funds seeking the highest return given a certain amount of risk.

3. The suppliers of bonds are the original issuers or borrowers—corporations and governments—and bond owners choosing to sell bonds they own.

4. The market for a bond consists of the demand for and supply of that bond. The price of the bond is determined by demand and supply.

Summary

? What are stocks? How are stocks bought and sold?

1. Shares, equity, and stock mean the same thing—ownership of a piece of a company. *§1*

2. There are two main types of stocks: common and preferred stock. *§1*

3. Stocks are bought and sold on a stock exchange. A company will complete specified requirements and pay fees to have its stock listed on a particular exchange. Typically, the NYSE lists larger, well-known companies; Nasdaq lists high-tech and biotech companies; and the AMEX lists small-cap stocks. Non-U.S. companies are listed on stock exchanges in their own countries, although ADR, which represent foreign companies, are listed on U.S. stock exchanges. *§1.a*

? What does a stock index represent?

4. A stock index is a measure of the price movements of a group of stocks. The best-known indexes are the Dow Jones Industrial Average, the S&P 500, the

Nasdaq Composite, and the Wilshire 5000, but there are other indexes for U.S. companies and indexes for every stock exchange in the world. *§1.c*

5. A mutual fund is a group of stocks or bonds of individual companies or governments placed into one investment pool. *§1.d, 4.b*

? What causes stock prices to rise and fall?

6. The equity market is the market in which stocks are bought and sold. *§2*

7. The demand for equities comes from investors who are seeking the greatest return on their savings—individuals, mutual funds, and institutions like insurance companies. *§2*

8. The supply of equities comes from stock owners who want to sell their stock and purchase something else. This is known as the secondary market. The primary market is the market for new issues—stocks that had not previously been sold by the firms. It is the secondary market that people are referring to when they speak of the stock market. *§2*

9. Demand depends on expectations, income, and prices of and returns on other investments. Supply depends on expectations and on prices of and returns on other investments. A change in one of these determinants of demand and/or supply will cause demand and/or supply to change. *§2.b*

10. If buyers want to buy more stock (demand) than sellers want to sell (supply), then the price will move up. Conversely, if sellers want to sell more of a stock than buyers want to buy, the price will fall. *§2.b*

11. The equity market is said to be an efficient market in the sense that it is difficult for an investor to continually earn above-normal profits. If there were a secret formula for becoming rich in the stock market, everyone would soon learn that formula, and it would no longer be an effective strategy. *§2.c*

12. Some disagree with the notion of an efficient market, arguing that people just don't behave perfectly rationally. Behavioral economists have noted that people behave in certain regular ways that do not seem, in hindsight, to have been rational. In the short run, these tendencies can affect the prices of stocks; in the long run, it is the performance of the firm that determines stock price. *§2.c*

❓ What causes bond prices to rise and fall?

13. Bonds are IOUs provided by a lender or issuer of the bond to the purchaser of the bond. *§4.b*

14. The demanders of bonds are individuals and mutual funds that are seeking the highest return given a certain amount of risk. *§4.b*

15. The suppliers of bonds are corporations and governments attempting to borrow money and the owners of previously issued bonds who choose to sell their bonds. *§4.b*

16. The market for a bond consists of the demand for and supply of that bond. As with the stock market, demand depends on the prices of and expected returns on other investments, income, and investor expectations; supply depends on the prices of and expected returns on other investments and supplier (bond issuer) expectations. *§4.b*

17. The price of a bond is determined by demand and supply. *§4.b*

18. There is an inverse relationship between bond prices and interest rates. As the interest rate rises, bond prices fall, and vice versa. *§4.b*

Key Terms

shares, equity, stock *§1*

common and preferred stock *§1*

dividend *§1*

trading post *§1.a.1*

market capitalization (market cap) *§1.c*

mutual fund *§1.d*

global fund *§1.d*

specific fund *§1.d*

socially responsible fund *§1.d*

index fund *§1.d*

load *§1.d*

front-end load *§1.d*

back-end load *§1.d*

no-load fund *§1.d*

American Depositary Receipt (ADR) *§1.e*

comparable investment *§2*

behavioral economics *§2.d*

bonds *§4*

maturity date *§4*

face or par value *§4*

coupon *§4*

zero-coupon bond *§4.a*

Exercises

1. What is saving? What role does it play in financial markets?

2. Investors know for sure that the CEO of firm A will undertake an investment that will yield $100 million profit next year and then $2 million each year after that for ten years. They also know for sure that the CEO of firm B will undertake an investment that will yield nothing for two years and then a profit of $20

million per year for ten years. Which company will have the higher stock price today, next year, the second year, the third year?

3. The investors in exercise 2 are surprised by firm B's performance in year 5. Instead of being $20 million, the firm's profits are $40 million. What happens to firm B's stock price in years 6 and 7?

4. Nova Corporation has just announced that it has had a record good year. It's earnings have increased nearly 10 percent. Explain how this announcement can lead to a decline in the price of Nova Corporation's stock.

5. The Benly Company needs to raise funds for a major expansion. The company is debating whether to issue stock or to issue bonds. If the company issues bonds, then its debts will increase and it will be under additional stress to ensure that its revenues can cover the costs of its debt. If it issues stock, the current owners will lose power and influence. What should the company do? Explain your answer.

6. The Federal Reserve has just lowered interest rates. Explain the effect of that on bond prices.

7. In exercise 6, not only bond prices but also stock prices are affected. Explain why.

8. Suppose the price elasticity of demand for stocks is 1.5. This means that for every 10 percent increase in stock prices, the quantity demanded will decline by

15 percent. Does this price elasticity make sense? Explain.

9. Suppose the cross-price elasticity of demand between stocks and bonds is negative 1.2. If stock prices are expected to rise by 10 percent, what is expected to happen to bond prices? Does this make sense? Explain.

10. Which would you expect bonds and stocks to be, substitutes or complements? Explain.

11. From 2000 to 2003, stock prices declined by about 33 percent. Explain why this occurred. If stocks have been falling for a period of time, what would have to happen to get stock prices to turn around and begin rising again?

12. The price of a stock is determined by the demand for and supply of that stock. Both demand and supply depend on investors' expectations of the future performance—future economic profits—of the firm. Explain what happens to a firm's stock when the company earns less than investors had expected.

13. IBM recently announced that its earnings declined during the past quarter, yet its stock price rose. How could this occur?

14. During the second quarter of 2003, both bond prices and stock prices fell. Explain why this occurred.

15. Explain why bond prices might decline when stock prices rise.

ACE

Take the ACE Practice Test for this chapter to review the important concepts and get immediate feedback with answers.

economics.college.hmco.com/students

Accountants Figure Law to Benefit Them

"The Sarbanes-Oxley Act might as well be called the Enron-Andersen Act," says attorney Peggy Zagel.

The law, which Congress adopted in July in the wake of corporate scandals at Enron, WorldCom, Tyco, and other prominent companies, is intended to make corporate fraud more difficult to commit and conceal.

The law probably will have some potent side effects, too. Many Chicago area businesses—including law, accounting, and consulting firms—see the new accounting and financial reporting rules mandated by Sarbanes-Oxley as an opportunity to boost revenue.

"It can almost be seen as the Lawyer and Accountant Full Employment Act," wisecracked Zagel, who recently was hired by Chicago law firm Altheimer & Gray to generate business by helping companies comply with Sarbanes-Oxley.

Another Chicago-based company, Parson Consulting, is licking its chops over the opportunities presented by the law.

"This is a radical transformation of corporate governance," said Dan Weinfurter, president of Parson Consulting.

Among the main provisions of Sarbanes-Oxley:

- Top management must certify corporate financial results.
- Deadlines were tightened for filing results.
- Regulations were tightened regarding potential conflicts of interest for accounting firms. For instance, an auditor of record is now barred from handling work other than tax and auditing responsibilities for a single client.
- Financial resources must be provided to key board committees so they can hire outside counsel to advise on issues such as compensation and audit functions.

Weinfurter sees an opportunity for Parson Consulting, a firm that specializes in financial and accounting consulting, in helping corporations adhere to the law. Companies will need help not only in setting up programs to comply with the law, but in executing those programs on a daily basis.

"Our focus has been on Fortune 1000 companies," he said. "We feel that we're very well positioned. We don't do tax and audit work for anyone. We're completely conflict-free."

Additionally, Weinfurter pointed out that the accelerated filing deadlines with the SEC probably will force many companies to rely on consultants, rather than adding employees, to process the welter of complex financial data more quickly. Processes will also have to be updated, Weinfurter said. "When you're used to closing your books in 45 days, and you now have to get that down to 20, you can't just work harder. You have to fundamentally change the process," he said.

It is too early to gauge the exact impact the new law will have on the company's revenues, Weinfurter said, but what he has seen so far is encouraging.

"We've noticed a big change in our corporate clients," he said. Chief financial officers who were difficult to reach in the past now return calls, he said.

SEAN CALLAHAN

***Chicago Sun-Times*/November 18, 2002**

Commentary

The Sarbanes-Oxley Act of 2002 was intended to reform the practices of accounting firms, corporation boards, and Wall Street stock analysts and thereby protect the small investor and consumer from unethical practices and fraud. The major provisions of the Act are:

1. Companies must disclose whether a board's audit committee has at least one "financial expert" and, if not, the reason for the absence.

2. It is generally unlawful for an accounting firm to provide any major nonaudit service (bookkeeping, for example) to a client while completing that company's audit.

3. The CEO and CFO must swear to the accuracy of the company's quarterly and annual financial reports. An officer who certifies a report that does not conform to the requirements of Sarbanes-Oxley faces a fine of not more than $1 million and a sentence of not more than ten years in jail, or both.

4. The act established the Public Company Accounting Oversight Board, or PCAOB—nicknamed Peekaboo.

5. New rules separate Wall Street's stock analysis from its deal-making side and punish companies that retaliate against analysts who criticize them.

6. The act makes tampering with corporate records a crime. The maximum penalty for mail and wire fraud has increased from five to ten years.

Economics is the study of unintended consequences; economists judge whether a public policy (rules, regulations, laws) is beneficial—that is, if it creates more benefits than costs. The Sarbanes-Oxley Act was aimed at protecting investors by forcing public companies to stand behind their financial reports. But although the six major provisions of the Act listed above may seem like they benefit small investors and consumers, there are some unintended consequences of the Act that suggest a different interpretation. One unintended effect is that firms have to bear higher costs of doing business. Firms are hiring more lawyers, accountants, and consultants specializing in corporate governance and are allocating more resources to internal staffs who focus on the Act. Where do the resources come from that are used to comply with the Sarbanes-Oxley Act? They are taken from any or all other uses of resources by each firm. As a result of taking resources away from other uses, the firm may be less efficient or may have lower profits than was the case prior to the Act.

Some of the additional costs will be passed along to consumers; the amount depends on the price elasticities of demand and supply (as discussed in the chapter Elasticity: Demand and Supply). In addition, lower profits mean lower stock prices; because the additional costs imposed on firms are not the same for every firm, some will be affected more than others. Some investors may be harmed by the Act in that their stocks will not rise in value as much as otherwise would have been the case.

So, how should we evaluate whether the Sarbanes-Oxley Act benefits society? The answer depends on whether these unintended consequences have greater costs than the benefits of the Act. This comparison of costs and benefits will determine whether the Act is good public policy.

CHAPTER 32

The Land Market and Natural Resources

? Fundamental Questions

1. **What is the difference between the land market and the markets for uses of land?**

2. **What is the difference between renewable and nonrenewable natural resources?**

3. **What is the optimal rate of use of natural resources?**

Global warming, the destruction of the rain forest, the depletion of the ozone, the extinction of animal species, and other environmental issues are of great concern to many people. So are the costs that people have to pay in the name of the environment: higher prices on cars as a result of emission controls, annual fees to test for emissions from cars, higher gas prices because of refining requirements, higher taxes to pay for cleaning up the environment, and so on. In this chapter we examine the market for land and natural resources. ■

1. Land

The category of resources that we call "land" refers not just to the land surface but to everything associated with the land—the natural resources. Natural resources are the nonproduced resources with which a society is endowed. A market exists for each type of natural resource and for each use of land.

1.a. Fixed Supply of Land

1. **What is the difference between the land market and the markets for uses of land?**

economic rent: the portion of earnings above transfer earnings

transfer earnings: the amount that must be paid to a resource owner to get him or her to allocate the resource to another use

The market for land is, in the most general terms, a market with a fixed supply. There is only so much land available. Obviously land is used in many different ways—cities and housing, parks, wilderness areas, agricultural areas, and on and on. For each use of land, there is a market in which the typical demand and supply curves apply. For instance, the market for land on which to put housing has a demand curve that slopes down and a supply curve that slopes up. As the price of land available for housing rises, the quantity of land demanded for housing declines and the quantity of land available increases. But, in the general market for land, where there is a fixed supply of land, we have a downward-sloping demand curve but a perfectly inelastic supply curve.

Recall from the chapter "Resource Markets" that when a resource has a perfectly inelastic supply curve, its earnings are called **economic rent.** If a resource has a perfectly elastic supply curve, its earnings are called **transfer earnings.** For resources with upward-sloping supply curves, earnings consist of both transfer earnings and economic rent. Transfer earnings are what a resource could earn in its best alternative use. This is the amount that must be paid to get the resource owner to "transfer" the resource to another use. Economic rent is earnings in excess of transfer earnings. It is the portion of a resource's earnings that is not necessary to keep the resource in its current use.

You've seen that there are two different meanings for the term *rent* in economics. The most common meaning refers to the payment for the use of something—the rent on an apartment, for instance. The second use of the term *rent* is to mean payment for something whose quantity is fixed—that is, that has a perfectly inelastic supply. The total quantity of land is fixed, so payment for land is economic rent.

The reason that the earnings of a good, service, or resource whose supply is fixed are called economic rent is to distinguish the result of changes in rent from changes in the price of a good, service, or resource that is not fixed in quantity. When the price of a good increases, everything else the same, the quantity supplied will increase. But, when economic rent increases, quantity supplied cannot increase. So an increase in economic rent is simply a transfer from the buyer to the seller without any change in quantity.

As we saw in the chapter "Government and Market Failure," the term *rent seeking* is used to distinguish the result of actions designed to gain additional income or wealth by seeking profits and the result of actions designed to do so by seeking rents. An increase in profits will bring on additional production and increased quantities supplied; an increase in rents simply transfers income from buyers to sellers. Rent seeking is not a productive activity; profit seeking is. Thus, economists refer to lobbying by individuals or groups to gain favors from the government as rent seeking. The resources devoted to the lobbying will not increase productive activities and quantities supplied; they merely transfer income and wealth from one individual or group to another. Rent seeking does not increase an economy's growth and improve its standards of living; profit seeking does.

1.b. Uses of Land

When we break the market for land into markets for uses of land, then the supplies are not fixed and prices and profits function as in any other market: they allocate land to alternative uses. For instance, an increase in the demand for housing will drive the price of land used for housing up, inducing landowners to offer more of their land in the housing market. The land has to come from somewhere, so an increase in land devoted to housing means less land devoted to parks or agriculture or wilderness. The use of land is shifted to where the land has the highest value.

R E C A P

1. The total supply of land is fixed.
2. The payment to landowners is economic rent because there are no transfer payments that serve to allocate resources.
3. The amount of land in any given use is not fixed. The use of land depends on the demand for and supply of that use.

?

2. What is the difference between renewable and nonrenewable natural resources?

nonrenewable (exhaustible) natural resources: natural resources whose supply is fixed

2. Nonrenewable Resources

Nonrenewable (exhaustible) natural resources can be used only once and cannot be replaced. Examples include coal, natural gas, and oil. The market for nonrenewable natural resources consists of the demand for and supply of these resources. Supply depends on the amount of the resource in existence, and the supply curve is perfectly inelastic. Only a fixed amount of oil or coal exists, so the more that is used in any given year, the less that remains for future use. This means that an upward-sloping supply curve exists for a particular period of time, such as a year. The quantity that resource owners are willing to extract and offer for sale during any particular year depends on the price of the resource. The supply curve in Figure 1(a) is upward sloping to reflect the relationship between the price of the resource today and the amount extracted and offered to users today. Resource owners are willing to extract more of a resource from its natural state and offer it for sale as the price of the resource increases.

As some of the resource is used today, less is available next year. The supply curve of the resource in the future shifts up, as shown in Figure 1(b) by the move from S_1 to S_2. The shift occurs because the cost of extracting any quantity of the resource rises as the amount of the resource in existence falls. The first amounts extracted come from the most accessible sources, and each additional quantity then comes from a less accessible source. For instance, in the late 1800s, oil became an important resource. At first, it was extracted with small pumps that gathered up oil seeping out of the ground. Once that extremely accessible source was gone, wells had to be dug. Overtime, wells had to be deeper and be placed in progressively more difficult terrain. From land, to the ocean off California, to the rugged waters off Alaska, to the wicked North Sea, the search for oil has progressed. As more and more is extracted, the marginal cost of extracting any given amount increases, and the supply curve shifts up.

If 200 billion barrels of crude oil are extracted this year, then in the future the extraction of another 200 billion barrels will be more difficult—more expensive—

FIGURE 1

The Market for Nonrenewable Resources

The demand curve slopes down, and the supply curve slopes up. The intersection of demand and supply determines the quantity used today and the price at which the quantity was sold, as shown in Figure 1(a). As quantities are used today, less remains for the future. Because the available quantities come from increasingly more expensive sources, the supply curve shifts in over time, as shown in Figure 1(b). The curve S_1 represents the quantities supplied in 1890 at $1 per barrel, and S_2 represents the quantities supplied today at $34 per barrel.

(a) Demand and Supply

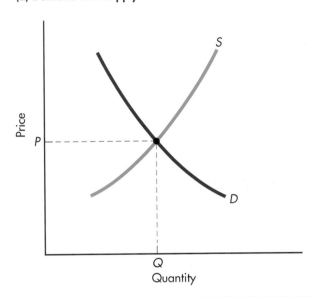

(b) Costs of Extraction Rise Over Time

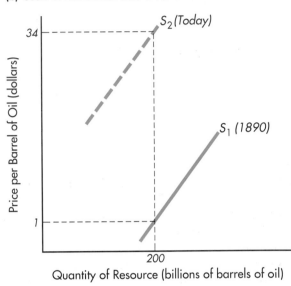

than the extraction of the 200 billion barrels was this year. This increase is illustrated by an upward shift of the supply curve in Figure 1(b).

The demand for a nonrenewable natural resource is determined in the same way as the demand for any other resource. It is the marginal revenue product of the resource. Thus, anything that affects the *MRP* of the nonrenewable resource will affect the demand for that resource.

Equilibrium occurs in the market for a nonrenewable natural resource when the demand and supply curves intersect, as shown in Figure 2. The equilibrium price, $15, and quantity, 200 billion barrels, represent the price and quantity today. Extracting and selling the equilibrium quantity of 200 billion barrels today reduces the quantity available tomorrow by 200 billion barrels. This means that extracting the resource tomorrow is probably going to be more costly than extracting it today. Thus, the supply curve for the resource in the future lies above the supply curve for today, S_2 rather than S_1, if any of the resource is being consumed today. With a higher supply curve and the same demand, the price is higher, $20 rather than $15. Thus, the price in the future is likely to be higher than the price today if some of the resource is extracted and sold today.

The resource owner must decide whether to extract and sell the resource today or leave it in the ground for future use. Suppose that by extracting and selling the oil

FIGURE 2

Price Today and in the Future

Equilibrium occurs in the market for an exhaustible natural resource when the demand and supply curves intersect. The equilibrium price, $15, and quantity, 200 billion barrels, represent the price and quantity of the resource used today. Selling the equilibrium quantity of 200 billion barrels today reduces the quantity available tomorrow by 200 billion barrels. With a smaller and probably less accessible quantity, extracting the resource tomorrow is probably going to be more costly than extracting it today. Thus, the supply curve for the resource in the future lies above the supply curve for today, S_2 rather than S_1, if any of the resource is being consumed today. With a higher supply curve, the price is higher, $20 rather than $15. Thus, the price in the future is likely to be higher than the price today.

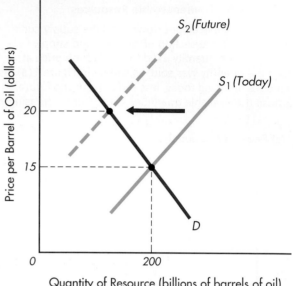

that lies below the land today, a landowner can make a profit of $10 per barrel after all costs of extraction have been paid. With that $10 the owner could buy stocks or bonds or put the money into a savings account or use it to acquire education or marketable skills. If the interest rate is 10 percent, the owner could realize $11 one year from now from the $10 profit obtained today. Should the oil be extracted today? The answer depends on how much profit the resource owner expects to earn on the oil one year from now, and this depends on what the price of oil and the cost of extraction are one year from now.

If the owner expects to obtain a profit of $13 a barrel one year from now, the oil should be left in the ground. If the profit on the oil one year from now is expected to be only $10.50, the oil should be extracted and the proceeds used to buy stocks, bonds, or savings accounts. The more that a simple bank account or interest-bearing investment yields, the more oil is extracted and sold. As the interest rate rises, more is extracted and sold today and less is left for the future.

Because suppliers and potential suppliers continually calculate whether to extract now or in the future and how much to extract, an equilibrium arises where the year-to-year rate of return of the resource equals the rate of interest on alternative uses of the funds. If the rate of interest is 10 percent a year, everything else held constant, the resource price will rise at a rate of about 10 percent a year (the rate of return must be 10 percent).

Suppose the interest rate rises above the current rate of return on the nonrenewable resource, oil. The higher interest rate means that producers will pump more oil out of the ground today and purchase stocks, bonds, or savings accounts with the money they get from selling the oil. More extraction means that the supply curve today shifts out and today's price falls. At the same time, the supply curve in the future shifts in (since less will be available in the future) and the future price rises. This will occur until the rate of return on leaving the oil in the ground equals the interest rate—that is, until the value of pumping the oil and selling it is the same as the value of the oil left in the

?

3. **What is the optimal rate of use of natural resources?**

ground. A higher interest rate implies the use of more resources today. Conversely, a lower interest rate implies the use of fewer resources today.

RECAP

1. Nonrenewable natural resources are natural resources whose supply is fixed.
2. The market's role is to ensure that resources are allocated across time to where they are most highly valued. If more is used today, the return for saving it for future use rises.
3. The higher the interest earning potential on financial investments, the more of the nonrenewable resource is extracted today.
4. The more a nonrenewable resource is consumed today, the less it is available in the future and the higher its price is in the future.

3. Renewable Resources

renewable (nonexhaustible) natural resources: natural resources whose supply can be replenished

Renewable (nonexhaustible) natural resources can be used repeatedly without depleting the amount available for future use. Examples include the land, sea, rivers, and lakes. Plants and animals are classified as nonexhaustible natural resources because it is possible for them to renew themselves and thus replace those used in production and consumption activities. The prices of renewable resources and the quantities used are determined in the markets for renewable resources. The role of the market is to determine a price at which the quantity of the resource used is just sufficient to enable the resource to renew itself at a rate that best satisfies society's wants.

Owners of forest lands could harvest all their trees in one year and reap a huge profit. But if they did so, several years would pass before the trees would have grown enough to be cut again. The rate at which the trees are harvested depends on the interest rate. A large harvest one year means fewer trees available in the future and a longer time for renewal to occur. This would suggest a lower price today and a higher price in the future. If the interest rate rises, everything else held constant, owners will want to increase harvesting in order to get more money with which to purchase stocks and bonds. This means more trees now and fewer in the future, thereby driving up the price of the trees that are not cut today. If the interest rate falls, owners will want to harvest fewer trees today. This means that today's price will rise and the future price will fall. As was the case with the nonrenewable resources, the market adjusts so that the resources are allocated to their highest-valued use now and in the future. The timing of the use of resources depends on the rate of interest.

Suppose you raise beef cattle and you want to remain in that business for most of your lifetime and eventually to pass it along to your children. You would sell only enough of your herd each year to ensure that you can have a herd to raise next year, the year after, and so on. If you sell more than that in any one year, the size of your herd next year will be smaller. If you sell the entire herd, you will have nothing in the future. What you want to do is to maximize your economic profit over the time periods you and your family remain in the business of cattle raising. Thus, you allocate the sale of your cattle over the various time periods. If the price of beef cattle increases rapidly one year due to mad cow disease in Britain, then you would sell

This sea of red tile roofs is the result of new homes built in Las Vegas, Nevada, the fastest growing city in the United States. The demand for new housing means a demand for land on which to put new housing. Because the use of land for housing is more valuable than the use of the land as open desert, the land is reallocated. Water is a different matter. Las Vegas has no natural supply of water; instead, water is brought in from the Colorado River. Yet, there is a huge demand for the water to be used in swimming pools. As the population of Las Vegas continues to grow, the demand for water will continue to rise. Eventually, water prices will begin rising, to match demand and supply.

more of your herd that year. Conversely, if the price of beef cattle falls substantially one year due to reports that eating beef causes heart disease, then you would sell fewer cattle that year. But, although your herd size varies with the price of cattle and the interest earning potential of other financial investments, you don't sell off your entire herd unless you plan to get out of the cattle business. You retain enough cattle so that they can propogate and replenish the herd.

The same principle applies to any renewable resource that is privately owned. The owner has the incentive to ensure that sufficient supplies exist in the future to maximize profits over all time periods. Some people argue that forests should not be privately owned because logging firms would raze or clear cut the forests, thereby leaving nothing for the future. But this makes no sense. No logging company that owns and logs its own forests would sell off all its forests unless it plans to get out of the logging business. When renewable resources are privately owned, the market ensures that resources are allocated between the current period and the future so that resources are used in the most valuable manner. The private owners want to maximize their profit over the current and future periods.

A problem arises in the current use of a resource, whether renewable or nonrenewable, when the resource is not privately owned. Recall from the chapter "Government and Market Failure" that private property rights are necessary for markets to work. When common ownership exists, the common property is overused. Many natural resources are overused because they are not privately owned. For instance, many fish are overfished; some are nearly extinct. Many animals are overhunted; some are nearly extinct. Many forests are razed; these are owned commonly (by a government). Air, lakes, streams, and oceans are often overused or polluted because they are not privately owned.

In summary, the markets for nonrenewable and renewable resources operate to ensure that current and future wants are satisfied in the least costly manner and that resources are used in their highest-valued alternative now and in the future. When a nonrenewable resource is being rapidly depleted, its future price rises and the value of using the resource in the future rises, so that less of the resource is used today. When a renewable resource is being used at a rate that does not allow the resource to replenish itself, the future price rises and the value of the future use rises, so that less of the resource is used today.

RECAP

1. Renewable natural resources are natural resources that can be replenished.
2. The rate of use of renewable resources in a functioning market system is one that equalizes the rate of return on the resource and the return on comparable investments.
3. A problem arises in the current use of resources, whether they are renewable or nonrenewable, when the resource is not privately owned. When common ownership exists, the common property is overused. Many natural resources are overused because they are not privately owned.

Summary

? What is the difference between the land market and the markets for uses of land?

1. The total amount of land is fixed. *§1.a*
2. Changes in the price of land do not change the quantity supplied. *§1.a*
3. There are many uses of land, and how much land is allocated to each use depends on the demand for and supply of land for each use. *§1.b*

? What is the difference between renewable and nonrenewable natural resources?

4. Nonrenewable natural resources are inert resources—coal, oil, and so on—that are fixed in supply. *§2*

5. Renewable natural resources are resources that can regenerate, such as wildlife, flora, and fauna. *§3*

? What is the optimal rate of use of natural resources?

6. The optimal rate of use of nonrenewable resources is not zero. It is the rate at which the nonrenewable resource can satisfy society's wants now and in the future. *§2*

7. The optimal rate of use of renewable resources is the rate that equates the expected return from using the resources and the expected return from not using them. *§3*

Key Terms

economic rent *§1.a*
transfer earnings *§1.a*

nonrenewable (exhaustible) natural resources *§2*
renewable (nonexhaustible) natural resources *§3*

Exercises

1. The market for some good or service is shown by the demand and supply curves below.

   a. Illustrate what transfer earnings and economic rent are.

   b. Explain what would occur if the demand for the good or service were to increase.

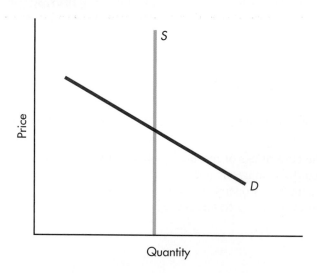

2. The market for some good or service is shown as the demand and supply curves shown below.

   a. Illustrate what transfer earnings and economic rent are.

   b. Explain what would occur if the demand for the good or service increased.

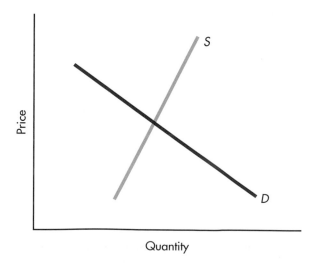

3. In its June 9, 2003, issue, the *Economist* magazine discussed the possibility that the real estate market might be in what is called a speculative bubble. A speculative bubble refers to the idea that prices are rising because buyers are "speculating," or betting that prices will continue to rise. How might the *Economist*'s article be illustrated using the land market in general? How might the article be illustrated using different markets for different uses of land, such as the housing market and the commercial office space market?

4. It is often stated that an artist is not famous until after he or she dies. Why do artists' works rise in price much more rapidly after the artist is dead than during the artist's life? How does this relate to the land market?

5. How would you describe economic rent in the case of a movie star earning millions of dollars each year?

6. If the world's population is rising and the quantity of land is not changing, won't the world eventually run out of room? Explain, using the market for land.

7. Will the world ever run out of a nonrenewable resource? Explain.

8. Suppose the supply of oil that had not been used yet was suddenly lost as a result of a rupture in the earth. What would occur?

9. The difference between a renewable and a nonrenewable resource is that the renewable resource can be replenished. Is there a difference between the markets for the two types of resources? What is the "optimal" rate of use of either renewable or nonrenewable resources?

10. In 2003, Alan Greenspan, chairman of the Federal Reserve, convinced the Open Market Committee to reduce the interest rate to near zero percent in an attempt to stimulate spending in the economy and increase the growth of income and employment. What might this policy do to the use of natural resources? Explain.

11. Urban sprawl is described as the establishment of housing and commercial development increasingly far from the city center. What might be the effect on sprawl if it was the policy of a city to build the infrastructure—sewers, power, and other essential services—to these developments at the average cost to the city? If it built the infrastructure at the marginal cost to the city?

12. If a city's political leaders decided to limit sprawl by restricting residential and commercial development to an area within a prescribed distance from the city center, what would be the effect on land prices in the areas—inside the development boundary and outside the development boundary?

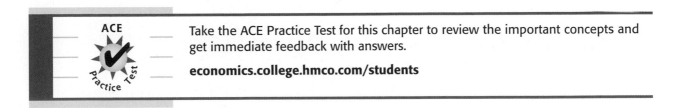

ACE

Take the ACE Practice Test for this chapter to review the important concepts and get immediate feedback with answers.

economics.college.hmco.com/students

Debate: Is Anti-Sprawl Really "Smart" Growth?

Imagine Durham as bread and housing growth as peanut butter.

If you spread the peanut butter across the bread in one smooth stroke that would be suburban sprawl, said Frank Duke, director for the City/County Planning Department, trying to put the complicated issues of population growth, the environment and anti-sprawl efforts into layman's terms.

But with anti-sprawl ordinances or what is often called "smart growth" the peanut butter is spread out in chunks, where sensitive areas and different community resources are protected, Duke said.

Currently, Durham has a traditional land-use plan. It treats all areas the same and ends up encouraging suburban sprawl, Duke said.

Durham is in the process of defining a unified development ordinance to guide growth and deter sprawl, Duke said. The plan would prohibit housing developments in environmentally sensitive areas and promote cluster developments, where housing units are grouped together so that other areas can remain undeveloped.

But smart growth has its downside, said David Almasey of the National Center for Public Policy and Research.

A recent report commissioned by the center claims that anti-growth policies hurt the poor and minorities by increasing housing costs and decreasing housing options. The center is a Washington-based conservative foundation that researches public policy.

The study, "Smart Growth and Its Effects on Housing Markets: The New Segregation," examined restricted growth policies in Portland, Ore., said Almasey, who spoke at a Triangle Community Coalition luncheon this week. The Triangle Community Coalition's stated mission is to promote public policy that supports a balance between economic growth, environment and protects the rights and interests of property owners.

The study examined what would happen to housing costs if Portland's policies were applied nationwide.

It found more than 1 million disadvantaged families—260,000 of them minority families—would have been unable to buy homes because the cost of the average home would have risen $7,000. The study found the cost of renting would have risen 6 percent.

Instead of restricting growth, the anti-sprawl policies caused housing prices in restricted areas to rise and people who could not afford the costs to move, Almasey said.

But anti-sprawl efforts are more than site restrictions, said Cara Crisler, executive director of the N.C. Smart Growth Alliance, which is based in Carrboro. The center's report was a misrepresentation about what "smart growth" is, she said.

Duke, who wasn't familiar with the report or the organization, said "any zoning and land development regulation that is not approached with sensitivity will adversely affect affordable housing."

Durham's current ordinances promote segregation, said Duke, who added that he's working to create anti-sprawl policies that will not inhibit growth but instead will recognize that different regulations are needed to protect distinct areas.

Durham County Commissioner Joe Bowser, who was recently elected the president of the Durham chapter of the NAACP, said the civil rights organization hasn't taken a position on "smart growth" but plans to talk about it in the future.

Bowser questioned whether "smart growth" really "ends up pitting community against homebuilders" by raising housing costs. He said it would be more appropriate to link lack of home ownership with lack of job-training opportunities rather than anti-sprawl efforts.

VIRGINIA BRIDGES

The Herald-Sun (Durham, N.C.)/March 29, 2003

"Sprawl" refers to a situation in which the distance from city center to outermost suburbs in a metropolitan area is increasing. Many people find sprawl unsightly and unpleasant. They want to restrict growth and sprawl and increase the density in which people live. In many cities, boundaries have been placed around urban areas, beyond which no housing and commercial development may occur.

In this article, one of the cities that is considering reducing sprawl is Durham, North Carolina, which currently treats all areas the same and ends up encouraging sprawl. What is the economic rationale for sprawl? Why do people move farther and farther from the city center? Primarily because land prices are lower the farther from the city you live. Open space and agricultural areas have a lower price per acre than land that is used for housing or commercial development. As open space or agricultural land becomes more valuable as housing property, landowners will sell the land to housing developers. The developers, who are able to acquire land more inexpensively than if they were purchasing land in the city center, then build housing that is relatively inexpensive compared to similar housing closer to the city center. People choose to purchase the housing that is less expensive even though it often means longer commutes. This increases the price of housing and drives development further away from the city center. This process has occurred in many metropolitan areas.

A few metropolitan areas have attempted to alter the economic process of sprawl. For example, Portland, Oregon, placed a boundary around the city and forbade development outside that boundary. What is the effect of such restrictions?

In the figure, the situation in Portland prior to the growth restrictions is shown by the supply curve without growth restrictions. The price is P_1. Now suppose that the city planners decide to impose a growth boundary equal to the current amount of land used for housing and commercial buildings. Nothing would change as long as demand did not change. But, if demand increases, such as to Demand$_2$, additional land cannot be shifted from open space or agricultural uses to housing and commercial uses. As a result, the price rises considerably more than it would without growth restrictions.

This is what the study noted in the article concludes. It found that if such antigrowth policies had been imposed nationwide, the cost of the average home would have risen $7,000, and the cost of renting would have risen 6 percent. Another aspect of the study is to point out just which group in society would be harmed by this policy. More than 1 million disadvantaged families—260,000 of them minority families—would have been unable to buy homes because of the restriction on land use, according to the study.

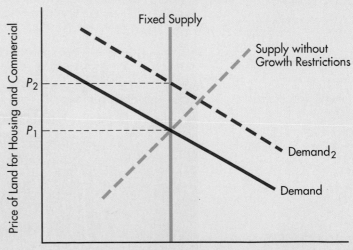

CHAPTER 33

Aging, Social Security, and Health Care

? **Fundamental Questions**

1. **Why worry about social security?**

2. **Why is health care heading the list of U.S. citizens' concerns?**

The population of the United States is aging rapidly. Currently, more than 12 percent of the population is retired—living off pensions, savings, and social security. By the year 2030, 21 percent of the population will be older than 65. The aging of the population is likely to have a dramatic effect on living standards. For instance, the types of goods and services produced will increasingly be influenced by the elderly. In particular, expenditures on health care will continue to rise. Already, people in the United States allocate more than 14 percent of their income to medical care. Is there a limit to how much they are willing to commit? The aging of the population also means that an increasing percentage of people will be retired and a smaller percentage will be producing goods and services and paying taxes. What are the implications for social security and for productivity? In this chapter, we look at the impact of an aging population on medical care and social security. ■

1. Aging and Social Security

The oldest population of the United States, persons 65 years or older, numbered 36 million in 2000 and represented more than 12.5 percent of the U.S. population, about one in every eight Americans. The oldest group itself is getting older. In 2000, the 65 to 74 age group was 8 times larger than in 1900, but the 75 to 84 group was 12 times larger and the 85-plus group was 22 times larger. The median age in 1850 was 18.9. It is now 40.

The pattern of aging is clearly visible in Figure 1, which shows the age of the U.S. population at three points of time: 1970, 1990, and what is anticipated for 2010. The pattern has been described as a python swallowing a pig: the pig represents the baby boom generation working its way up the age scale, the python.

The growth of the older population in the United States has brought several issues to the forefront of political debate. Among them are social security and health care.

1.a. Social Security

1. Why worry about social security?

An aging population means that the concerns of the aged will dominate national concerns. Retirement and security for the aged is one such concern. Old-Age, Survivors, and Disability Insurance (OASDI), also known as social security, had

---

FIGURE 1

Aging Patterns in the United States

The age distribution of the U.S. population at three points of time: 1970, 1990, and what is anticipated for 2010. The pattern has been described as a python swallowing a pig. The pig represents the baby boom generation working its way up the age scale, the python. *Source: U.S. Bureau of the Census.*

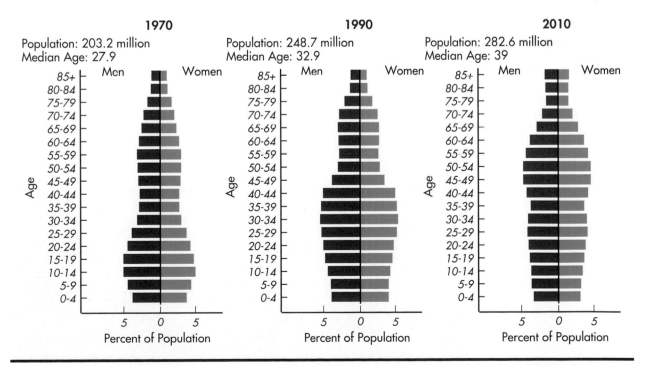

---

been established in 108 countries by the beginning of 1975. Some of the oldest plans are those of Germany (1889), the United Kingdom (1908), France (1910), Sweden (1913), and Italy (1919). The United States did not enact a national retirement program until 1935.

The social security system in the United States, which covers both Old-Age, Survivors, and Disability Insurance (commonly referred to as social security) and hospital insurance (Medicare), is financed by a payroll tax, Federal Insurance Corporation of America (FICA), levied in equal portions on the employer and the employee. The initial FICA tax rate was 1 percent of the first $3,000 of wage income paid by both parties. By 2003, this had risen to a tax rate of 7.65 percent (6.2 percent on the first $87,000 of earnings for the social security contribution and 1.45 percent on all earnings for the Medicare contribution), for each employee and employer.

1.b. The Viability of Social Security

Social security was intended to supplement the retirement funds of individuals.

The social security taxes that the working population pays today are used to provide benefits for current retirees. As a result, the financial viability of the system depends on the ratio of those working to those retired. The age distribution of the United States population has affected this viability. The consequence is a change in the ratio of workers to social security beneficiaries (see Figure 2). The ratio has declined from 16.5 in 1950 to about 3 today and is expected to decline to 2 by 2030. The situation in the United States is not any different from that in other parts of the world, as noted in the Global Business Insight "The World Is Aging." This trend means that the source of social security benefits is getting relatively smaller. The viability of the system depends on whether the trends of recent years continue. If birthrates remain low and if people continue to live longer, then the obligations to people who will retire in twenty-five years will be large relative to the income of the working population at that time.

The social security tax has risen more rapidly in the past two decades than any other tax. Social security tax revenues were less than 5 percent of personal income

---

FIGURE 2

Social Security Viability

The ratio of workers to social security beneficiaries is shown. The ratio has declined from 16.5 in 1950 to about 3 today and is expected to decline to 2 or less by 2030. This trend means that the source of social security benefits is getting relatively smaller. The viability of the system depends on whether the trends of recent years continue. *Source: Social Security Administration.*

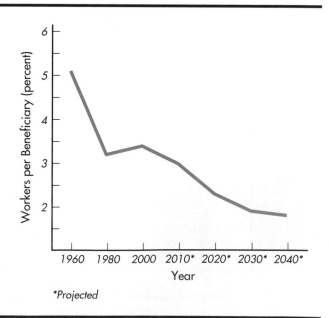

*Projected

The World Is Aging

Global Business Insight

The United States is not the only country whose population is growing older. Most of the developed nations in the world are experiencing the same aging of their populations. As seen in the accompanying figure, the elderly population constituted about 12 percent in the United States in 1985 but nearly 17 percent in Sweden. Although three-quarters of the world's population resides in developing areas, these areas contain only about 50 percent of the world's elderly. The developed countries are aging because the birthrates in these countries have decreased and life expectancy has increased. Japan's life expectancy of 77 years is the highest among the major countries, but life expectancies in most developed nations approach 75 years. In contrast, Bangladesh and some African nations south of the Sahara have life expectancies of 49 years.

As longevity has increased and families have had fewer children, the ratio of persons 65 and older to persons age 20 to 64 has risen in most of the developed countries. These elderly support ratios will rise modestly over the next fifteen years because the large number of people born between 1946 and 1961 will still be in the labor force. But as the large working-age population begins to retire after 2005, the elderly support ratio will rise sharply.

Source: U.S. Department of Commerce, U.S. Bureau of the Census, *International Population Reports*.

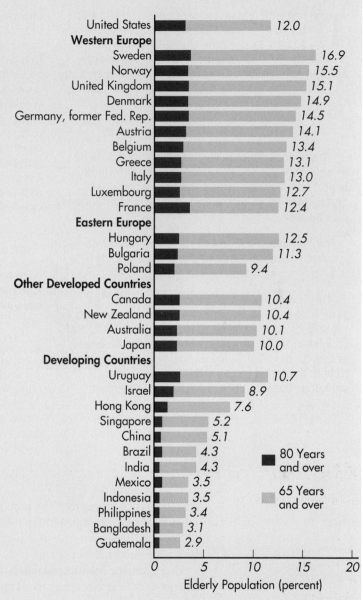

in 1960 and currently exceed 11 percent of personal income. The revenues from the personal income tax were 3.4 percent of personal income in 1940 and rose to the current amount of more than 15 percent in the early 1980s. Social security expenditures also have risen more rapidly than any other government program. Social security outlays currently constitute 7 percent of GDP, whereas national defense is less than 5.5 percent, and education and training expenditures are less than 1 percent. From 1979 to 1990, national defense expenditures rose 53.6 percent, education and

Myths About Social Security

The first recipient of social security in the United States was Ida Mae Fuller in 1940. Her check was for $22.45. By the time she died, shortly after her one hundredth birthday, she had collected about $20,000 in benefits, a large return considering that she had paid in a total of $22.

We've contributed to that fund all our lives! It's our money! It's not the government's money!

This is one of the most strongly and widely held myths about the social security system. In fact, the typical retiree collects more than twice the amount represented by employer and employee contributions plus interest.

The benefits of the system are determined by a scientific formula designed to ensure that the fund remains viable.

This is another myth about social security. The system of annually adjusting social security benefits as the cost of living increases dates only from 1975, and it came about as the result of political machinations, not foresight. In 1975, the annual benefits were about $7,000. Attempting to hold the line on federal spending, President Nixon proposed a 5 percent

increase in social security benefits and threatened a veto of anything higher. Democrats saw an opportunity to embarrass the president. They decided to pass a 10 percent increase and force Nixon to make an unpopular veto. The 10 percent increase was introduced in the Senate, but then rumors that Nixon would doublecross them and sign the bill anyway began circulating. So Congress increased the benefits to 20 percent, knowing that this huge increase would be vetoed. Nixon, however, signed the bill and proudly boasted of how well he had taken care of the elderly. Congress, irritated at being outflanked, passed the cost-of-living adjustment program to show that it, too, cared about the elderly.

Social Security ensures that only the elderly poor are cared for.

In fact, there are at least a million individuals currently collecting social security benefits who also have incomes exceeding $100,000 per year.

Sources: Jack Anderson, "Why Should I Pay for People Who Don't Need It?" *Parade Magazine,* February 21, 1993, p. 4; Eric Blac, "Social Security: Myths, Facts," *Arizona Republic,* February 21, 1993, p. F1.

training expenditures rose 0.8 percent, GDP grew 30.2 percent, and social security grew 70.9 percent, adjusted for inflation. From 1980 to 2000, Social Security rose 13 percent, Medicare rose 109 percent, national defense declined 29 percent, and education declined 34 percent.

If the system was funded solely by the revenues collected from the social security tax and if those revenues could be used for no other purpose than to provide benefits to social security recipients, then the worries about the system's viability would be much smaller. However, the social security system is included in the federal government's budget, and its revenues are used to pay for general government expenditures. This means that the excess of social security taxes over social security benefits is used to pay for other government programs; the funds are not deposited in a trust fund and allowed to accumulate for future years.

If the amount paid into the social security system by an individual was equal, on average, to the amount received by that individual in retirement benefits, the worries about the viability of the system would also be less. But people who retired in the 1980s, after working since the age of 21 at the minimum wage level, recovered all social security taxes paid, including employer and employee shares, in less than

4 years; at the maximum taxable amount each year, the employee recovered the total contributions in only 5 years. Retirees in the 1990s recovered the total contributions and interest earnings in 7 years. At an age of 82, the average worker who retired at age 65 will have received more than twice his and his employer's contributions to social security. Other social security issues are noted in the Economic Insight "Myths About Social Security."

So what's the alternative? There have been many proposals—increasing taxes, increasing the eligibility age, means testing, and holding down cost-of-living increases. The eligibility age, the age at which individuals can start collecting Social Security, was increased from 59 to 67 for those born in 1960 or later. Means testing has been resisted but is under serious consideration. Means testing would put a limit on the income one could earn and still collect Social Security.

One of the more controversial proposals has been to privatize the system. This is what Chile, Australia, Turkey, Sweden, Italy, Argentina, Mexico, the Philippines, Great Britain, and several other nations have done. Privatization allows individuals to choose among an approved list of possible investments rather than giving the money to the government. What the individual earns on those investments would be the individual's retirement funds. Unlike the government program, which is a pay-as-you-go system and which provides defined benefits for contributors, the private system will pay what individual investments earn. Some systems, like Chile's, are fully privatized: workers are required to save a portion of their own salary for retirement but give no money directly to the government. Others, like Great Britain's, are partially privatized: workers still contribute payroll taxes, but only part of this money is used to support a government-run system of basic pensions; the rest may be used for a private plan chosen by the worker. In Australia, workers are required to contribute 9 percent of their income to a fund of their choice.

Those who are critical of privatization note that with private investments there's no guaranteed return. Who would want to risk their life savings in the stock market? Social security, in contrast, is a sure thing. Most of the privatization plans have met this criticism by ensuring that no one contributing to the new plan will earn less than what would have been received under the former government-run plan.

The form of privatization differs from country to country, but the results have been uniformly positive. In every case, the returns individuals have received exceed those of the government system. In addition, the national savings rates have increased and government borrowing and debt creation have decreased.

RECAP

1. The U.S. population is aging as a result of lower birthrates, higher life expectancy, and the impact of the baby boom generation.
2. Social security, otherwise known as Old-Age, Survivors, and Disability Insurance, is financed by a tax imposed on employers and employees.
3. Social security is funded to provide benefits to the current retirees by the current working population's contributions. As the population ages, the ratio of contributors to beneficiaries declines.
4. Solutions to the social security problem include means testing, increasing eligibility age, and privatization.

2. Why is health care
heading the list of
U.S. citizens'
concerns?

2. Health Economics

Spending for health care in the United States amounts to nearly $1 trillion. Figure 3 shows that health-care expenditures were only 5.9 percent of GDP in 1965 but were 14 percent in 2003. What are the reasons that health-care expenditures have risen so dramatically over that time?

2.a. Overview

Figure 4 shows where the nation's health-care dollar is spent and where the money comes from. Figure 4(a) shows that expenditures for hospital services constitute 39 cents of every dollar, or 39 percent of the nation's health-care bill; nursing-home expenditures, 8 percent; spending for physicians' services, 20 percent; and spending for other personal health-care services (dental care, other professional services, drugs and other nondurables, durable medical products, and miscellaneous personal-care services), 21 percent. The remaining 12 percent of national health expenditures goes for medical research, construction of medical facilities, government public health services, and the administration of private health insurance.

Figure 4(b) shows the sources of payment for these expenditures. Of the $1 trillion spent on health care, 54 percent comes from private sources: private insurance and direct payments. Private health insurance, the single largest payer for health care, accounts for 33 cents of every dollar of national health expenditures, or 33 percent. Private direct payments account for 21 percent. Direct payments consist of out-of-pocket payments made by individuals, including copayments and deductibles required by many third-party payers (third-party payers are insurance companies and government).

Medicare: a federal health-care program for the elderly and the disabled

Medicaid: a joint federal-state program that pays for health care for poor families, the neediest elderly, and disabled persons

Government spending on health care constitutes 45 percent of the total; the federal government pays about 70 percent of this. **Medicare,** the largest publicly sponsored health-care program, funds health-care services for about 35 million aged and disabled enrollees. The Medicare program pays for 20 percent of all national health expenditures. **Medicaid,** a jointly funded federal and state program, finances 16 percent of all health care, covering the costs of medical care for poor families,

---

FIGURE 3

The Growth of U.S. Health-Care Spending

As a percentage of gross domestic product, health-care expenditures have risen from about 6 percent in 1965 to over 14 percent in 2003 and are projected to be about 16 percent by 2010. *Sources:* Health Care Financing Review, *May 2001; Office of National Health Statistics, Office of the Actuary, www.hcfa.gov/.*

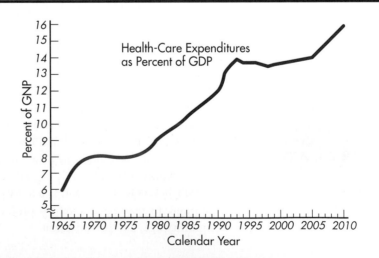

FIGURE 4

The U.S. Health Dollar

Figure 4(a) shows expenditures on health care by source; Figure 4(b) shows sources of payment for health expenditures. *Source:* Health Care Financing Review, 2003, *www.hhs.gov.*

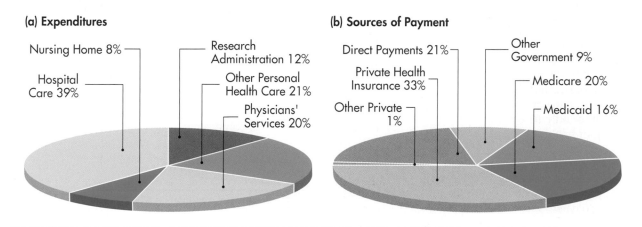

(a) Expenditures

Nursing Home 8%

Hospital Care 39%

Research Administration 12%

Other Personal Health Care 21%

Physicians' Services 20%

(b) Sources of Payment

Direct Payments 21%

Private Health Insurance 33%

Other Private 1%

Other Government 9%

Medicare 20%

Medicaid 16%

the neediest elderly, and disabled persons who are eligible for social security disability benefits. Other government programs pay for 9 percent.

Health-care spending varies tremendously among various groups in the U.S. population. Figure 5 illustrates how health-care expenditures vary across the economy. If each person spent the same amount on health care, the line of perfect equality shown in Figure 5 would describe the distribution of spending. In fact, the distribution of health expenditures is heavily skewed. The top 1 percent of persons ranked by health-care expenditures account for almost 30 percent of total health expenditures, and the top 5 percent incur 55 percent of all health expenditures. The bottom 50 percent of the population account for only 4 percent of all expenditures, and the bottom 70 percent account for only 10 percent of costs.

The high-cost segment of the population is older now than it was in the 1980s. Figure 6 shows that the distribution of spending for hospital care and for nursing homes is heavily dominated by the elderly. The top curve in Figure 6 represents the cumulative percentage of the population in each age group. As the age rises from under 5 to 10 to 20, and so on, there are increasing numbers of people. Eventually 100 percent of the population has been accounted for. The bottom curve represents the cumulative percentage of nursing home expenditures accounted for by people in each age group. Similarly, the middle line represents the cumulative percentage of expenditures on hospitals accounted for by each age group.

2.b. The Market for Medical Care

Health-care costs have risen because the demand for health care has risen relative to supply.

Rising costs or expenditures mean that the demand for medical care has risen relative to supply (Figure 7). The initial demand for medical care is D_1, and the supply of medical care is S_1. The intersection determines the price of medical care, P_1, and the total expenditures, P_1 times Q_1. An increase in demand relative to supply is shown as the outward shift of the demand curve, from D_1 to D_2. As a result, the price of medical care rises, from P_1 to P_2, as do the total expenditures on medical care, from P_1 times Q_1 to P_2 times Q_2. What accounts for the rising demand relative to supply?

FIGURE 5

The Inequality of U.S. Health-Care Spending

High-cost users of health care account for most health-care spending. The top 1 percent account for 30 percent of expenditures, and the top 5 percent for 55 percent of expenditures, while the bottom 70 percent account for only 10 percent of health-care expenditures. *Source: Steven A. Garfinkel et al., "High-Cost Users of Medical Care,"* Health Care Financing Review, *Summer 1988, pp. 41–50.*

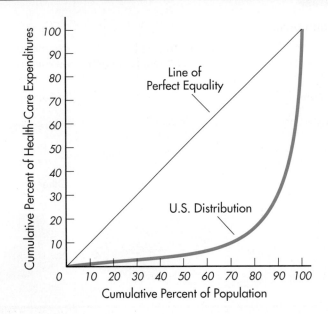

FIGURE 6

Age and Health-Care Spending

The high-cost users are increasingly the elderly. Nursing-home expenditures are predominantly made for people older than 70. The use of hospitals is also primarily by the aged. *Source:* Health Care Financing Review, *www.hcfa.gov/ (various issues).*

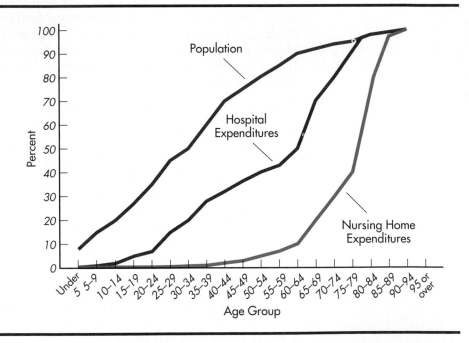

2.b.1. Demand Increase: The Aging Population

The aging of the population stimulates the demand for health care. The elderly consume four times as much health care per capita as the rest of the population. About 90 percent of the expenditures for nursing-home care are for persons 65 or over, a group that constitutes only 12 percent of the population. The aged (65 or older) currently account for 35 percent of hospital expenditures. In contrast, the young, although they constitute

FIGURE 7

The Market for Medical Care: A Demand Shift

The demand for and supply of health care determine the price of medical care, P_1, and the total expenditures, P_1 times Q_1. Rising health-care expenditures may be due to increased demand. A larger demand, D_2, means a higher price and a greater total quantity of expenditures, P_2 times Q_2.

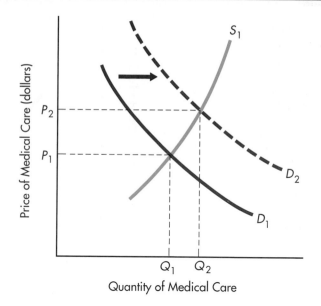

29 percent of the population, consume only 11 percent of hospital care. Per capita spending on personal health care for those 85 years of age or over is 2.5 times that for people age 65 to 69 years. For hospital care, per capita consumption is twice as great for those age 85 or over as for those age 65 to 69; for nursing-home care, it is 23 times as great.

2.b.2. Demand Increase: The Financing Mechanism For demand to increase, the aged must be both *willing* to buy medical care and *able* to pay for it. The emergence of Medicare and Medicaid in 1966 gave many elderly the ability. Medicare covers the cost of the first 100 days of hospital or nursing-home care for the elderly and disabled, providing benefits to 32 million people. Like social security, Medicare is funded by payroll taxes and is available on the basis of age (or disability), *not* need. By contrast, Medicaid helps only the neediest people, including many elderly people whose Medicare benefits have run out. As a result, Medicaid is considered the program most associated with long-term health care (such as for people living in nursing homes).

The effect of the Medicare and Medicaid programs has been to increase the demand for services and to decrease the price elasticity of demand because individuals do not pay for much of their health care. Private sources pay for about 55 percent of personal health care for the general population, and Medicare and Medicaid pick up most of the remainder. Private sources, however, pay for 74 percent of care for people under age 65. For the elderly, the private share of spending is only 15 percent for hospital care, 36 percent for physicians' services, and 58 percent for nursing-home care.[1] Medicaid spending for those 85 or over is seven times the spending for people age 65 to 69 and three times greater than the spending for people age 75 to 79. This difference is attributable to the heavy concentration of Medicaid money

---

[1]*Health Care Financing Review,* various issues.

FIGURE 8

The Market for Medical Care: A Supply Shift

The rising cost of medical care may be caused by an increase in the costs of supplying medical care. The supply curve shifts up, from S_1 to S_2, and the price of medical care rises, from P_1 to P_2.

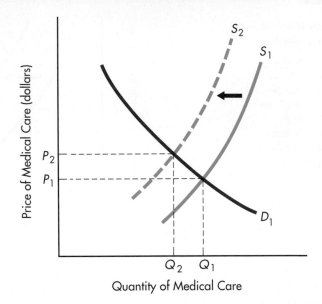

2.b.3. Demand Increase: New Technologies

New medical technologies provide the very sick with increased opportunities for survival. Everyone wants the latest technology to be used when their life or the lives of their loved ones are at stake. But because these technologies are cost-increasing innovations and because costs are not paid by the users, the increased technology increases demand.

2.b.4. Supply

Even if the demand curve for medical care was not shifting out rapidly, the cost of medical care could be forced up by a leftward shift of the supply curve, as shown in Figure 8. The supply curve, composed of the marginal-cost curves of individual suppliers of medical care, shifts up, from S_1 to S_2, if the cost of producing medical care is rising—that is, if resource prices are rising or if diseconomies of scale are being experienced. The three largest resources in the medical industry in terms of total expenditures are hospitals (39 percent), physicians (20 percent), and nursing homes (8 percent).

Hospitals   The original function of hospitals was to provide the poor with a place to die. Not until the twentieth century could wealthy individuals who were sick find more comfort, cleanliness, and service in a hospital than in their own homes. As technological changes in medicine occurred, the function of the hospital changed: the hospital became the doctor's workshop.

The cost of hospital care is attributable in large part to the way current operations and capital purchases are financed. Only a small fraction of the cost of hospital care is paid for directly by patients; the bulk comes from *third parties,* of which the government is the most important. The term *third-party payers* refers to insurance companies and government programs: neither the user (the patient) nor the supplier (the physician or hospital) pays.

Hospital size is typically measured in numbers of beds; efficiency, in expenditures per case or expenditures per patient-day. To make precise determinations of the effect of size on efficiency is difficult because hospitals that differ in size are likely to differ also with respect to location, kind of patient admitted, services provided, and other characteristics. Hospitals that do not provide a large number of complex services need not be very large to be efficient. But if hospitals do provide a large number of services, it is very inefficient for them to be small. A hospital of 200 beds can efficiently provide most of the basic services needed for routine short-term care. If that hospital grows to 600 beds yet still provides only the same basic services, inefficiencies are likely to develop because of increasing difficulties of administrative control. What is more likely to happen, however, is that specialized services will be introduced—services that could not have been provided at a reasonable cost when the hospital had only 200 beds.

In the past twenty years, the average number of beds per hospital increased by 50 percent, inpatient days declined by about 10 percent, lengths of stay declined by about 10 percent, and occupancy rates declined by nearly 20 percent. The problem that more beds per hospital and shorter stays creates for the hospital is that the occupancy rate is only about 66 percent while the efficient occupancy rate is between 80 and 88 percent.

Physicians   Physicians affect the cost of medical care not only through their impact on the operation of the hospital but also through their fees. Expenditures on physicians' services rose more rapidly than any other medical-care expenditure category in the 1980s and 1990s. Is the increased cost of physicians due to a shortage of doctors? The answer is not necessarily yes. From 1966 to 1997, the supply of physicians increased 100 percent while the U.S. population increased about 25 percent. As a result, the ratio of active physicians per 100,000 people increased substantially, from 169 in 1975 to 240 in 1997.

Medical care in the United States is expensive, but it is technologically superior to that available in any other nation. The advanced technology offers higher-quality care than could be obtained elsewhere, but it also means a higher cost of care. If patients do not have to pay the higher cost, they are willing and able to purchase it. The government and third-party payers such as insurance companies enable patients to obtain the advanced care and thus increase the demand for that care.

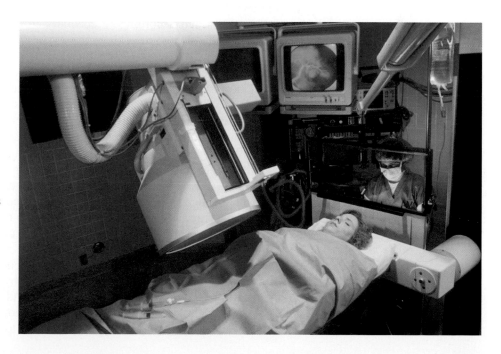

TABLE 1

Median Compensation of Specialists and Primary Care Physicians: The Five-Year Picture

Median Compensation for:	1997	1998	1999	2000	2001	Change 2000–2001	Change 1997–2001
Primary care*	$135,791	$139,244	$143,970	$147,232	$149,009	1.2%	9.7%
Specialists	$220,476	$231,993	$245,910	$256,494	$263,254	2.6%	19.4%
Consumer Price Index						1.6%	9.5%

*Includes internal medicine, family practice without obstetrics, and pediatric/adolescent medicine.
Source: *Physician Compensation and Production Survey,* Medical Group Management Association, 2002; *Statistical Abstract of the United States, 2003.*

The factors that have led to rising physicians' fees include an increase in demand relative to the supply of certain types of physicians, the ability of physicians to restrict price competition, and the payment system. The number of physicians per population has risen in many areas of the country. Yet, because the American Medical Association restricts advertising by physicians, consumers are unable to obtain complete information about prices or professional quality, and physicians are less likely to compete through advertising or lower prices. Moreover, the restrictions on advertising enable established physicians to keep new, entering physicians from competing for their customers by charging lower prices.

The payment system influences physicians' fees and the supply of physicians. Over 31 percent of all physicians' fees are set by the government. More than 75 percent are set by third-party providers. The physicians are reimbursed on the basis of procedures and according to specialty. A gynecologist would have to examine 275 women a week to achieve the income earned by a cardiac surgeon doing two operations per week. More than 60 percent of all physicians in the United States are specialists. The payment system has induced more physicians to specialize in those areas than would have occurred otherwise. Table 1 indicates the difference between the net income of those physicians who specialize and those who provide primary care. Income varies widely among specialties as well. Cardiac surgeons tend to earn more than other specialists, for instance.

The costs of doing business have risen for physicians. For instance, the cost of malpractice insurance has increased about 25 percent a year during the past two decades. Although only about 1 percent of health-care expenditures can be directly attributed to malpractice suits, there are some implicit costs associated with the fear of such suits. This fear has caused an increase in both the number of tests ordered by physicians and the quantity of medical equipment purchased by them.

Prescription Drugs The fastest-growing health expenditure category is prescription medicines. Prescription drug expenditures grew by 19.7 percent in 1999, by 16.4 percent in 2000, and by 15.7 percent in 2001. As shown in the table in the Global Business Insight "Health-Care Spendingin Various Nations," U.S. spending on prescription medications is the highest in the world. The United States is the

Health-Care Spending in Various Nations

How do other countries compare with the United States in regard to health-care spending and spending on pharmaceuticals? The following tables indicate that the United States spends more per capita than any other country, and also spends more on pharmaceuticals than any other country.

Health Spending in OECD Countries, 2000

	GDP per Capita, 2000*	Spending per Capita, 2000*
Australia	$26,497	$2,211
Austria	26,864	2,162
Belgium	26,049	2,269
Canada	27,963	2,535
Czech Republic	14,236	1,031
Denmark	29,050	2,420
Finland	25,078	1,664
France	24,847	2,349
Germany	25,936	2,748
Greece	16,950	1,399
Hungary	12,423	841
Iceland	29,323	2,608
Ireland	29,066	1,953
Italy	25,206	2,032
Japan	25,937	2,012
Korea	15,045	893
Luxembourg	46,960	2,701[c]
Mexico	9,136	490
Netherlands	27,675	2,246
New Zealand	20,262	1,623
Norway	30,195	2,362
Poland	9,580	576[c]
Portugal	17,638	1,441
Slovakia	11,650	690
Spain	20,297	1,556
Sweden	24,845	1,847[d]
Switzerland	30,098	3,222
Turkey	6,439	320[d]
United Kingdom	24,323	1,763
United States	35,657	4,631

Spending On Pharmaceuticals in Selected OECD Countries, 2000

	As Percent of GDP, 2000	Spending per Capita, 2000*
Australia	1.0%[a]	$252[a]
Belgium	1.4[b]	352[b]
Canada	1.4	385
Czech Republic	1.0	260
Denmark	0.8	223
Finland	1.0	259
France	1.9	473
Germany	1.4	375
Greece	1.5	258
Hungary	1.8[b]	193[b]
Iceland	1.3[e]	382[c]
Ireland	0.6	187
Italy	1.8	459
Japan	1.2[e]	313[e]
Korea	0.8[e]	110[e]
Luxembourg	0.7[e]	317[e]
Mexico	1.1[e]	93[e]
Netherlands	1.0	264
New Zealand	1.1[b]	210[b]
Norway	0.7[b]	217[b]
Portugal	2.0[a]	334[a]
Spain	1.4[b]	264[b]
Sweden	1.0[b]	244[b]
Switzerland	1.1	346
United Kingdom	1.1[b]	253[b]
United States	1.6	556

Source: Data for tables from Organization for Economic Cooperation and Development, *OECD Health Data 2002* (Paris: OECD, 2002). Printed in Gerard F. Anderson, Uwe E. Reinhardt, Peter S. Hussey, and Varduhi Petrosyan, "It's the Prices, Stupid: Why the United States Is So Different from Other Countries," *Health Affairs* (Project HOPE) 22, no. 3 (2003), pp. 89–105.
*In U.S. dollars, adjusted for purchasing power differences.
[a]1998. [b]1997. [c]1990–1997. [d]1991–1997. [e]1999.

world's leader in biomedical research: in public-sector spending through the National Institutes of Health and other government agencies; in private-sector research and development; in the scientific discoveries that this research has produced; and in manufacturing the drugs, diagnostics, and medical devices that apply these innovations to improving human health. It has, however, become increasingly difficult to bring these beneficial new medical products to the market. The only way a company can begin to sell a new drug or device is to get permission from the Federal Drug Administration (FDA). The FDA has a very strong incentive to keep unsafe products off the market, even if in doing so it may block beneficial new products. As a result, the FDA has made it increasingly more difficult to bring a new drug to market. The time required to bring a new drug to market, including preclinical testing, clinical development, and regulatory review, has increased from a low of 6.3 years in 1963–1965 to 16.1 years. This delay means that the percentage of drugs that are first available in the United States is low. While more than 60 percent of biopharmaceutical products approved in the United States, Europe, or Japan originated in the United States, less than 18 percent were first marketed in the United States. The latest estimate of the cost to develop a new drug and bring it to market exceeds $800 million; in 1987 the cost was $231 million.[2] This increased cost results in higher prices for these medications than occurs elsewhere (see Global Business Insight).

2.c. HMOs and PPOs

The increased costs of medical care and the increased supply of physicians have led to new medical-care delivery systems, the health maintenance organization and the preferred provider organization. A **health maintenance organization (HMO)** provides comprehensive medical care, including preventive, diagnostic, outpatient, and hospital services, in return for a fixed, prepaid amount of money from the enrollees.

There are four basic types of HMOs: staff, medical group, independent practice associations (IPAs), and networks. *Staff HMOs,* such as the Group Health Cooperative of Puget Sound in Seattle and ANCHOR Health Plan in Chicago, hire physicians as salaried employees. *Group HMOs* function as a medical group practice. Several physicians operating as a partnership or corporation contract with HMO management and an insurance plan to provide services and pool and redistribute income according to a predetermined formula. *Independent practice associations* are separate legal entities that contract with individual physicians practicing in a traditional office setting. *Networks* are organizations that franchise operations, in the same way that McDonald's and Pizza Hut are franchised operations. For instance, Blue Cross/Blue Shield is the main company, and local HMOs are franchises of Blue Cross/Blue Shield.

A **preferred provider organization (PPO)** is a group of physicians who contract with a firm to provide services at a price discount in hopes of increasing their volume of business or a firm that contracts with a group of physicians. A general practitioner serves as a member's primary-care provider and refers patients to specialists as needed. Instead of contacting a specialist directly, a patient must be referred to a specialist by the primary-care provider. Specialists are reimbursed out of the fees paid to the PPO plan by the firms that contract with it. The general practitioners have an incentive to reduce total costs because they split a portion of the

health maintenance organization (HMO): an organization that provides comprehensive medical care to a voluntarily enrolled consumer population in return for a fixed, prepaid amount of money

preferred provider organization (PPO): a group of physicians who contract to provide comprehensive medical services at a price discount

---

[2]Denise Myshko, "Pricing—The Cost of Doing Business," *PharmaVOICE*, March 1, 2002 (www.websterconsultinggroup.com/pharmapricing_030102.html#head1).

fixed fees that remain at the end of the year. As a result, the use of specialists and special tests is lower than in health-care plans that permit patients to select the specialists. Many hospitals are organizing PPOs in hopes of better managing hospital utilization and offsetting declining revenues.

Because HMOs and PPOs provide comprehensive coverage, they alter incentives for the patient. Patients who belong to an HMO or PPO are less likely to seek hospitalization for diagnostic work and other care that can be provided on an outpatient basis than are patients whose health insurance coverage is limited to care provided in the hospital. An HMO also alters incentives for physicians. Because their income is determined by annual payments, they are not likely to provide or order unnecessary care as a way of boosting their incomes.

2.d. Do the Laws of Economics Apply to Health Care?

Rising health-care costs have led many people to claim that or act as if health care is different: the laws of economics do not apply to it. People tend to look at health care as a right, something that everyone is entitled to regardless of costs. You may recall our survey and discussion about allocation mechanisms in Chapter 3; most people look on health care as something different from other goods and services. They do not want the market system to determine who gets the health care and who doesn't.

Is health care a scarce good? The answer is a clear yes; at a zero price, more people want health care than there is health care available, the definition of a scarce good. Scarcity means that choices must be made, that there is an opportunity cost for choosing to purchase the scarce good. The choice is made on the basis of rational self-interest. These principles of economics suggest that health care is an economic good and subject to the laws of economics.

The demand curve for medical care looks like any other demand curve; it slopes down because the higher the price, the lower the quantity demanded. The demand curve is probably quite inelastic, but it does slope downward. There also is a standard-looking supply curve. Physicians, hospitals, and medical firms offer an increasing quantity of medical care for sale as the price rises. As shown in Figures 7 and 8 and repeated in Figure 9, the demand and supply curves look no different from the curves representing a market in any other economic good.

In Figure 9, the price for medical care is the level at which the demand and supply curves intersect, the point of equilibrium. At price P_1, the quantity of medical care demanded is equal to the quantity supplied. Those people who are willing and able to pay price P_1 (all those lying along the demand curve from A to B) get the medical care. Those who are not willing and able to pay the price (all those lying along the demand curve from B to C) do not get the health care.

"Repealing the laws of economics" in the case of health care means that the demand for and supply of health care do not determine the price or quantity and that it is not just those who are willing and able to pay who get the care.

The problems that arise in the health-care market are due not to a repeal of the laws of economics, but instead to the nature of the product. People believe that they and others have an inalienable right to medical care, that it is not right to ignore those people making up the demand curve from B to C on D_1. As a result, government programs such as Medicare and Medicaid have been created. These programs, along with private insurance programs, mean that most of the payments for medical care are made by third parties, as described earlier in this chapter. The third-party payment system allows many of those who would not otherwise be willing and able to purchase health care, those lying along the demand curve from B to C, to be able to purchase the care. This shifts the demand curve out, which drives health-care costs up, as shown by the shift from D_1 to D_2 in Figure 9.

The government and private insurance programs thus face ever-rising health-care costs. Each new equilibrium means that some are unable to afford the care; if their

FIGURE 9

Do the Laws of Economics Apply to Health Care?

The price of medical care is the level at which the demand and supply curves intersect, the point of equilibrium. At price P_1, the quantity of medical care demanded is equal to the quantity supplied. Those people who are willing and able to pay price P_1 (all those lying along demand curve D_1 from A to B) get the medical care. Those who are not willing and able to pay the price (all those lying along the demand curve from B to C) do not get the medical care.

The third-party payment system allows many who would not otherwise be willing and able to purchase health care (those lying along the demand curve from B to C) to be able to purchase the care. This shifts the demand curve out and drives health-care costs up, as shown by the shift in the demand curve from D_1 to D_2.

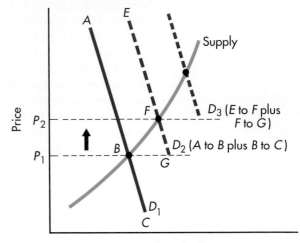

demand is covered, the demand curve shifts out again, to D_3. This continues as long as someone is willing and able to pay the price. That someone has been the government, principally through Medicare, and private employers through employee benefit plans. The result has been double-digit price increases for health care for over a decade.

2.d.1. The Market for Human Organs Many respected doctors, lawyers, economists, and ethicists argue that a legal and open market in kidneys, hearts, or livers could help cure the chronic organ shortage that is gripping transplant medicine. If the price is right and the seller is willing, why should someone not be allowed to sell a kidney? The debate over the issue is intense. Many who are against an open and free market in organs argue that it will result in the exploitation of the poor. They point to cases in which black market activity has occurred, such as in India's poorest sectors, where, for about $1,500, poor Indians have sold a kidney. Although the $1,500 is about three times India's per capita income, it does not seem to help the poorest of the poor. Within a year these donors are back in poverty, with huge debts and with one less kidney. Supporters of a free and open market argue that it would increase supplies of transplant organs and save many lives. In the United States alone, there are 50,000 people on dialysis waiting for a donor kidney. If you live in Toronto, Canada, and you're on dialysis, your wait is probably the longest in North America, about five to eight years. Typically, one-third of patients who are eligible for transplants will die while waiting. These long, often fruitless waits have driven many to the black market, but have caused more to die.

How would the legal market work? One part of the market would be the purchase of organs from living individuals. A person would offer a kidney or a part of a liver (since only pieces of livers, not whole livers, are needed for transplant) for a price. The price would be set by demand and supply. A second part of the market would be organs harvested from people who die suddenly, such as those killed in accidents. These people would have sold their organs, such as lungs, hearts, and kidneys, in what can be called a "futures" market. The rights to these organs harvested after death could be purchased from donors while they were still living, at prices set by supply and demand. Donors would be paid for future rights to their

FIGURE 10

The Market for Human Organs

The demand for transplant organs would be quite price-inelastic, since people who are awaiting a donor organ would be willing and able to pay nearly any price to save their lives. The demand and supply would determine the equilibrium price and quantity.

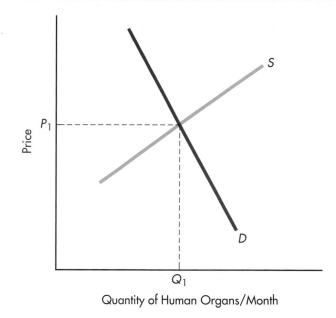

organs. So you could sell the rights to your kidneys once you die and receive the payment today.

What would the outcome of such a market be? Let's use Figure 10 to illustrate the market for organs. The demand for organs would be price-inelastic, since those who need the organs are willing to pay just about anything they are able to pay to get them. The supply of organs is expected to be price-elastic, at least once the price reaches some threshold level. For instance, a 10 percent increase in the price, say from $100,000 to $110,000, would induce more than a 10 percent increase in the number of organs offered for sale. And if a futures market developed, the supply would be price-elastic, since everyone who now volunteers to donate organs would continue to do so and many others would also do so because they would receive some income for almost no cost. The market for human organs would look something like Figure 10, where the equilibrium price would be P_1 and the equilibrium quantity Q_1. What would the price be? In the United States, a kidney was auctioned on eBay sometime in 2000. The auction was terminated by the government after only a few hours, but when it was stopped, the price had reached $5 million. At the other end of the price range, the black market (illegal market) price of a kidney was about three times average annual income, $1,500 in India.

A black market arises when an item that some people are willing and able to buy and others are willing and able to supply cannot be legally traded. Black markets are less efficient or more costly than legal markets simply because traders have to be discreet, cannot openly meet buyers and sellers, and have no means to enforce agreements. As a result, the number of traders in the market is less than it would be in a legal market. Most of the evidence available regarding human organs is that the market would be immensely larger if it were legal than the black market in human organs currently is.

The problem most people have with the idea of a market in human organs is the potential for what they call exploitation. They point out that the organs would be going one way—from poor people to rich people, from Third World to First World or to rich people in the Third World. This is the way markets work—from those who are willing and able to sell to those who are willing and able to buy. Arguing that this result is bad is a normative argument, not a positive one. Similarly, the counterargument that a father who is desperate to provide a plate of rice for his starving family should be entitled to sell one of his kidneys on the open market is a normative argument. No matter what the normative viewpoints, there is a market for human organs; transplant surgery is a business driven by the simple market principle of supply and demand. The positive aspect of the issue is not who would gain and who would lose in a free, open market, since both buyers and sellers gain as measured by consumer and producer surplus, but instead, how does the current black market situation compare with a free, open, legal market?

RECAP

1. Health care is the fastest-growing portion of total national expenditures. It is rising primarily because of the rising cost of physician services, nursing homes, and hospital services.

2. The demand for medical care has risen at a very rapid rate. One reason for the increase is the introduction of Medicare and Medicaid and private insurance plans that make demand relatively inelastic. The aging of the population has also increased the demand for medical care.

3. The cost of providing medical care has risen because of increases in hospital costs and physicians' fees. Rising hospital costs are partly a result of the reimbursement plans of third-party providers and partly a result of the control of the operation of hospitals by physicians.

4. Physicians' fees have risen even though the supply of physicians has risen. The demand for medical services does not match the supply; reimbursement methods have led to higher rates of return in certain specialties and thus have drawn an increasing number of physicians to those specialties.

5. The laws of economics do apply to the medical arena. They apply even in the case of markets for human organs.

SUMMARY

❓ Why worry about social security?

1. Social security is a government-mandated pension fund. In the United States it is funded by a tax on employer and employee. The current tax collections are used to provide benefits to current retirees. *§1.a*

❓ Why is health care heading the list of U.S. citizens' concerns?

2. The rapidly rising costs of medical care result from increases in demand relative to supply. *§2.a*

3. The increasing demand results from the aging of the population and from payment systems that decrease the price elasticity of demand. *§2.b.1, 2.b.2*

4. The reduced supply (higher costs of producing medical care) results from inefficiencies in the allocation of physicians among specialties and inefficiencies in the operation and organization of hospitals. *§2.b.4*

5. The percentage of income allocated to health care varies tremendously from country to country. The United States spends more per capita for health care than any other nation. *§2.b.4*

6. The health industry is changing in response to rapidly rising costs. Alternative methods of providing health care, such as HMOs and PPOs, have arisen. *§2.c*

KEY TERMS

Medicare *§2.a*

Medicaid *§2.a*

health maintenance organization (HMO) *§2.c*

preferred provider organization (PPO) *§2.c*

EXERCISES

1. What is social security? What is Medicare? What is the economic role of these government policies?

2. Why have medical-care expenditures risen more rapidly than expenditures on any other goods and services?

3. Explain how both the supply of physicians and physicians' fees can increase at the same time.

4. Why are there more medical specialists and fewer general practitioners in the United States now than was the case 50 years ago?

5. What is the economic logic of increasing social security benefits?

6. What does it mean to say that people have a right to a specific good or service? Why do people believe that they have a right to medical care but do not believe that they have a right to a 3,000-square-foot house?

7. Suppose the objective of government policy is to increase an economy's growth and raise citizens' standards of living. Explain in this context the roles of retirement, social security, and Medicare.

8. Explain why the U.S. system of payment for medical procedures leads to higher health costs than a system of payment for physicians' services.

9. Analyze the following solutions to the problem of social security.

   a. The retirement age is increased to 70.

   b. The FICA tax is increased.

   c. The income plus social security payments cannot exceed the poverty level.

   d. The total amount of social security benefits received cannot exceed the amount paid in by employer and employee plus the interest earnings on those amounts.

10. Oregon proposed a solution to the health costs problem that was widely criticized. The solution would allow the state to pay only for common medical problems. Special and expensive problems would not be covered. Using the market for medical care, analyze the Oregon plan.

11. What would be the impact of a policy that did away with Medicare and Medicaid and instead provided each individual with the amount that he or she had contributed to the Medicare program during his or her working life?

12. Why is a third-party payer a problem? Private insurance companies are third-party payers, and yet they want to maximize profit. So wouldn't they ensure that the allocation of dollars was efficient?

13. "We must recognize that health care is not a commodity. Those with more resources should not be able to purchase services while those with less do without. Health care is a social good that should be available to every person without regard to his or her resources." Evaluate this statement.

Take the ACE Practice Test for this chapter to review the important concepts and get immediate feedback with answers.

economics.college.hmco.com/students

Many Travel a Painful Circuit for Their Managed Health Care

Some hobble with injured legs across town for X rays before returning to their doctor, who could have taken the pictures in the first place. Others find themselves pressured to leave one hospital for another, even when their conditions are fragile. And some are referred back to their doctor's office for blood tests, tests that could have been done at the same lab where they had just undergone other screenings. Consumers in the Philadelphia area have discovered that health care under managed care can be a frustrating experience. While some patients are paying less out-of-pocket for well-coordinated care, others are finding unanticipated quirks and limitations that seem to complicate treatment rather than ease it. Managed care is not supposed to be a maze. Its goals include making medical care more accessible for consumers and less expensive for employers by overseeing who receives treatment, how much they get, and where they go for it. Until now, the Philadelphia area has lagged in replacing traditional indemnity plans—patients pick doctors,

insurers pay bill—with managed care. But, that's changing, as employers and consumers alike face rising health-care costs. One estimate indicates that nearly 4 to 10 people in the region belong to a health maintenance organization, one type of managed care. Among them are Sonya and Gus Pappas of Swarthmore, whose experiences under managed care could not have been more different, even though both were treated last year under the same insurance plan.

Gus Pappas, 32, an accountant, said he had been swaddled in the best health care imaginable from the moment he collapsed on his way to his doctor's office last March, through surgery for colon cancer, and nearly a year of follow-up chemotherapy. And he never saw a bill. By contrast, his wife, 28, a fund-raiser, encountered a bureaucratic morass as she sought treatment for infertility. Rather than travel to the lab to which the insurer directed her for tests, she paid hundreds of dollars a month out-of-pocket to use the lab at her doctor's office.

"You feel trapped," said Sonya Pappas, who sees patients as

caught in a riptide of change racing through health care. "It is almost like you don't know what everyone's role is and where they stand."

Some observers say the insurers seem to use their advantage to direct patients to services with low rates, even if they weren't user-friendly. Consequently, doctors and patients complain about inefficiencies, delays, higher costs, and even compromised care. "In searching for the best price, they fragment the system," said Alan Zuckerman, executive vice president in Philadelphia for Chi Systems, a health-care consulting firm.

"Our position is that we have more comprehensive benefits, high-quality delivery systems and better prices," said John Daddis, the Philadelphia insurer's senior vice president for managed care. "There are some trade-offs on choice. But that's inherent in the whole concept."

Source: Marian Uhlman, "Many Travel a Painful Circuit for Their Managed Health Care," *Philadelphia Inquirer*, February 1, 1995, p. 1. Reprinted by permission.

Philadelphia Inquirer/February 1, 1995

Rationing of one kind or another is inevitable with a scarce good. For the vast majority of goods, people have chosen rationing by price. Many have difficulty with applying that same choice to medical care, however. Moreover, because of the way that firms have provided medical-care benefits to employees, there has been little regard to the price of medical care over the past twenty years. Since patients do not pay directly for care, they have no incentive to be price-conscious. They encourage doctors to carry out additional tests and to provide the most technologically advanced medical care. This, combined with the government provision of medical care for the elderly, drove up the prices of medical care and medical insurance at accelerating rates during the 1970s and 1980s.

To reduce their costs, firms began to look for alternative ways to provide their employees medical insurance benefits. What evolved was managed care—a firm enlists physicians and other medical experts to provide services to enrollees. Some firms hire the physicians directly, while others contract with the physicians to provide services at a certain fee. Most physicians accept the conditions because the demand for their services on a fee-for-service basis is rapidly declining. To reduce costs, the managing firm allocates patients among doctors so that workloads are about equal. The managing firm also provides only the basic types of medical procedures. Fertility, plastic surgery, and certain high-technology or experimental procedures, like bone-marrow transplants, are not covered by the managed care. If enrollees want to go outside of the firm or network for care, then they must pay out of pocket. This is what Sonya Pappas decided to do.

As shown in the accompanying diagram, with a rise in demand—the demand curve shifts out—the price of medical care rises. Managed care is an attempt to reduce the rate at which the demand curve shifts out—shown as the smaller shifts from D_3 to D_4 to D_5. It also is an attempt to reduce the cost of supplying medical care, causing the supply curve to shift down—shown as the shift from S_1 to S_2. If successful, the managed care approach would lead to an equilibrium at a lower price and higher quantity.

As the article noted, there are tradeoffs involved. If people are willing and able to pay the price, then they can get any medical care they want. If they are not willing or able to pay the price, they must take what is available at the lower price. In other words, rationing the care in some way other than price occurs. In some cases, services are not available—are not supplied. In other cases, they are available on a first-come, first-served basis; those coming into the office first get served first. Lines and waiting in offices result. In still other cases, the patient is shuffled from place to place and medical facility to medical facility—time and convenience allocate the scarce goods.

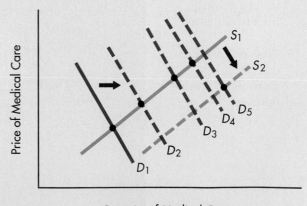

CHAPTER 34

Income Distribution, Poverty, and Government Policy

1. Are incomes distributed equally in the United States?

2. How is poverty measured, and does poverty exist in the United States?

3. Who are the poor?

4. What are the determinants of poverty?

5. Do government programs intended to reduce poverty benefit the poor?

6. Why are incomes unequally distributed among nations?

Income is what resource owners receive as payment for the use of their resources. A resource receives in compensation an amount determined by the marginal revenue product and the supply of the resource. Resource owners have incentives to increase the value of their resources—that is, to increase their income. When a resource is not being used in its highest-value alternative, resource owners will increase their income by shifting the use of the resource to the highest-value alternative. When an expenditure on the resource today will enhance the value of the resource in the future, the expenditure will be made when the resource value is increased by more than the expenditure. In other words, resource owners will innovate and adopt the latest technology in order to enhance the value of capital. They will invest in human capital, acquiring additional skills and education, in order to increase the value of human resources. They will redirect their land from agricultural uses to commercial uses when they gain from so doing, and they will make improvements to their land to enhance its value. The objective of resource owners is to ensure that they are receiving the highest value for the use of their resources, now and in the future.

In every society, different people own different resources and differently valued resources. This means that incomes vary from person to person. Half a million Americans will spend today living on city streets or in temporary shelters, and more than a million will do so over the next year. The trickle of people surviving on city streets a decade ago has become a steady stream—men, women, children, white, African American, Hispanic, mentally healthy, mentally ill. *Homeless* used to describe people who were transient, poor, socially isolated, and living in the cheap hotels and flophouses on skid row. They had housing, but they didn't have homes. Today, the homeless are "houseless" too.

Even the poor in the United States are better off than the entire populations of other nations, however. In Bolivia, the average life expectancy is only 53 years, a full 20 years less than in the United States. In Burma, only about one-fourth of the population has access to safe water. In Burundi, less than one-fourth of the urban houses have electricity. In Chad, less than one-third of the children reach the sixth grade. In Ethiopia, the per capita income is $120, sixty times lower than in the United States.

What accounts for the inequality among nations and among households within a nation? Who are the poor and the rich? Is the inequality of incomes something that can or should be corrected? These questions are the topic of this chapter. Previous chapters have discussed how the market system works to ensure that resources flow to their highest-valued uses, that output is produced in the least-cost manner, and that people get what they want at the lowest possible price. But the market does not produce equal incomes. Markets ensure that goods and services are allocated to those with the ability to pay, not necessarily to those with needs and not equal amounts to everyone. ■

1. Income Distribution and Poverty

In a market system, incomes are distributed according to the ownership of resources. Those who own the most highly valued resources have the highest incomes. One consequence of a market system, therefore, is that incomes are distributed unequally.

1.a. A Measure of Income Inequality

1. Are incomes distributed equally in the United States?

Lorenz curve: a curve measuring the degree of inequality of income distribution within a society

In the United States, as in every country, there are rich and there are poor. Incomes are not distributed equally, and the degree of inequality varies widely from country to country. In order to compare income distributions, economists need a measure of income inequality. The most widely used measure is the **Lorenz curve,** which provides a picture of how income is distributed among members of a population.

Equal incomes among members of a population can be plotted as a 45-degree line that is equidistant from the axes (see Figure 1). The horizontal axis measures the total population in cumulative percentages. As we move along the horizontal axis, we are counting a larger and larger percentage of the population. The numbers end at 100, which designates 100 percent of the population. The vertical axis measures total real gross domestic product (GDP) in cumulative percentages. As we move up the vertical axis, the percentage of total real GDP being counted rises to 100 percent. The 45-degree line splitting the distance between the axes is called the *line of income equality*. At each point on the line, the percentage of total population and the percentage of total real GDP are equal. The line of income equality indicates that

FIGURE 1

The U.S. Lorenz Curve

The farther a Lorenz curve lies from the line of income equality, the greater the inequality of the income distribution. The bottom 20 percent of the U.S. population receives 3.6 percent of total real GDP income, seen at point A. The Lorenz curve is plotted by successively adding 20 percent of the population and each group's percentage of total income.
Source: www.census.gov/hhes/www/incineq.html; http://ferret.bls.census.gov.

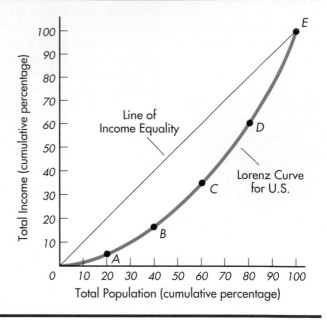

10 percent of the population earns 10 percent of the income, 20 percent of the population earns 20 percent of the income, and so on, until we see that 90 percent of the population earns 90 percent of the income and 100 percent of the population earns 100 percent of the income.

Points off the line of income equality indicate an income distribution that is unequal. Figure 1 shows the line of income equality and a curve that bows down below the income-equality line. The bowed curve is a Lorenz curve. The Lorenz curve in Figure 1 is for the United States. It shows that the bottom 20 percent of the population receives 3.6 percent of total real GDP income, seen at point A. The second 20 percent accounts for another 9.6 percent of real GDP income, shown as point B. The third 20 percent accounts for another 15.7 percent of real GDP income, so point C is plotted at a population of 60 percent and an income of 28.9 (3.6 + 9.6 + 15.7) percent. The fourth 20 percent accounts for another 23.4 percent of the national income, shown as point D. The richest 20 percent accounts for the remaining 47.7 percent of real GDP income, shown as point E. With the last 20 percent of the population and the last 47.7 percent of real GDP income, 100 percent of population and 100 percent of real GDP income are accounted for. Point E, therefore, is plotted where both income and population are 100 percent.[1]

The farther the Lorenz curve bows down, away from the line of income equality, the greater the inequality of the distribution of income. In Chapter 4 it was noted that on average, in developed countries, the richest 20 percent of households receive about 40 percent of household income and the poorest 20 percent receive only about 5 or 6 percent of household income. That distribution, however, is much more equal than the distribution found in developing countries. In developing countries, the

---

[1]A Lorenz curve for wealth could also be shown. It would bow down below the Lorenz curve for income, indicating that wealth is more unequally distributed than income. Wealth and income are different and should be kept distinct. Wealth is the stock of assets. Income is the flow of earnings that results from the stock of assets.

FIGURE 2

Lorenz Curves for Mexico and the United States

Based on data for the United States and Mexico, the two Lorenz curves show that total real GDP income in Mexico is distributed among Mexican citizens much more unequally than total real GDP income in the United States is distributed among citizens of the United States. *Source: Data are from* World Development Report, 2003.

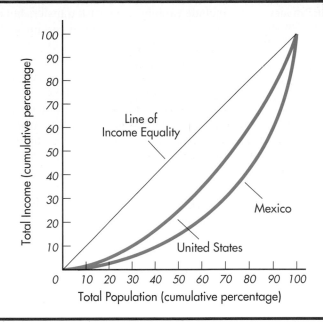

richest 20 percent of the population receive more than 50 percent of total household income, and the poorest 20 percent receive less than 4 percent of total household income. Figure 2 shows two Lorenz curves, one for the United States and one for Mexico. The curve for Mexico bows down far below the curve for the United States, indicating the greater inequality in Mexico.

1.b. Measuring Poverty

?

2. How is poverty measured, and does poverty exist in the United States?

A Lorenz curve does not indicate who the poor are or what their quality of life is. It is a relative measure. On the other hand, an absolute measure such as per capita income does not necessarily indicate how people feel about their income status or whether they enjoy good health and a decent standard of living. Those who are comfortable in one country could be impoverished in another. The poverty level in the United States would represent a substantial increase in living standards in many other nations. Yet members of a poor family in the United States would probably not feel less poor if they knew that their income level exceeded the median income in other countries.

1.c. The Definition of Poverty

If income or per capita income is to be used as a measure of poverty, then the proper definition of *income* must be used. Economists can measure income before any government intervention affecting the distribution of income, after accounting for government cash transfers, or after accounting for government cash transfers and assistance like food or shelter.

The first of these measurements indicates what people would earn from the market system in the absence of government intervention. To obtain a good measure of this income figure is virtually impossible because the government is such an important part of the economic system in almost all countries, including the United States. The U.S. government transfers over $400 billion annually from taxpayers to various groups.

Poverty statistics published by the federal government are based on incomes that include earnings from cash transfers but often not in-kind transfers. **Cash transfers** are unearned funds given to certain sectors of the population. They include some social security benefits, disability pensions, and unemployment compensation to those who are temporarily out of work. **In-kind transfers,** or noncash transfers, are services or products provided to certain sectors of society. They include food purchased with food stamps and medical services provided under Medicaid. Although economists agree that these in-kind transfers increase the economic well-being of those who receive them, there is much debate over how they should be accounted for and the extent to which they should be added to money income for the purpose of defining *poverty*. The official poverty rate measure does not account for in-kind transfers. If it did, the official poverty rate would be significantly lower.

The U.S. government uses after-transfers income to measure poverty, but does not include all such transfers. It adds market earnings, the cash equivalent of non-cash transfers, and cash transfers to calculate family incomes. But it does not include food stamps or housing subsidies. In sum, the poverty measure is arbitrary. It is an arbitrary level of income, and income is an arbitrary measure of the ability to purchase necessities.

Table 1 lists the average poverty levels of income for a nonfarm family of four since 1959. Families with incomes above the cutoffs would be above the poverty level, in the eyes of the federal government.

Where does the arbitrary poverty income level come from? A 1955 study found that the average family in the United States spent about one-third of its income on

TABLE 1

Average Income Poverty Cutoffs for a Nonfarm Family of Four in the United States, 1959–2002

Year	Poverty Level	Year	Poverty Level
1959	$2,973	1987	$11,611
1960	$3,022	1988	$12,090
1966	$3,317	1989	$12,675
1969	$3,743	1990	$13,359
1970	$3,968	1991	$13,924
1975	$5,500	1992	$13,950
1976	$5,815	1993	$14,764
1977	$6,191	1994	$15,200
1978	$6,662	1995	$15,600
1979	$7,412	1996	$16,036
1980	$8,414	1997	$16,400
1981	$9,287	1998	$16,660
1982	$9,862	1999	$16,895
1983	$10,178	2000	$17,463
1984	$10,609	2001	$17,960
1985	$10,989	2002	$18,244
1986	$11,203		

Source: www.census.gov/hhes/www/poverty.html.

food, so when the government decided to begin measuring poverty in the 1960s, it calculated the cost to purchase meals that met a predetermined nutritional standard for a year and multiplied that cost by 3. That is where it drew the poverty line. Since then, the official poverty-line income has been adjusted for inflation each year.

1.d. Poverty Distribution and Economic Trends

How many Americans fall below the poverty line? Figure 3 compares the number of people living in poverty and the percentage of the total population living in poverty (the incidence of poverty) for each year. From 1960 to the late 1970s, the incidence of poverty declined rapidly. From the late 1970s until the early 1980s, the incidence of poverty rose; it then began to decline again after 1982. Small upswings in the incidence of poverty occurred in 1968 and 1974, and a large rise occurred between 1978 and 1982. It then fell until 1990, when the United States once again dipped into recession. It continued to rise even as the economy grew in 1993 and then declined through 2000. It rose again in 2001 and 2002 as the United States entered another recession.

The health of the economy is a primary determinant of the incidence of poverty.

A major factor accounting for the incidence of poverty is the health of the economy. People are generally made better off by economic growth. Economic stagnation and recession throw the relatively poor out of their jobs and into poverty.

FIGURE 3

The Trends of Poverty Incidence

The number of people classified as living in poverty is measured on the left vertical axis. The percentage of the population classified as living in poverty is measured on the right vertical axis. The number and the percentage declined steadily throughout the 1960s, rose during the recessions of 1969, 1974, 1981, and 1990, and fell between 1982 and 1990 and again from 1992 to 2000. They then rose until 2003.
Source: www.census.gov/ hhes/www/poverty.html.

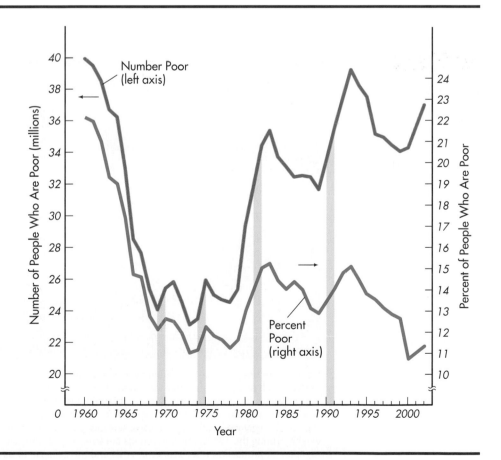

Economic growth increases the number of jobs and draws people out of poverty and into the mainstream of economic progress.

Four recent recessions have had important impacts on the numbers of people thrown into poverty. The recession of 1969–1970 was relatively mild. Between 1969 and 1971, the unemployment rate rose from 3.4 to 5.8 percent, and the total number of people unemployed rose from 2,832,000 to 5,016,000. This recession halted the decline in poverty rates for two years. When the economy once again began to expand, the poverty rates dropped. The 1974 recession brought on another bout of unemployment that threw people into poverty. The 1974 recession was relatively serious, causing the unemployment rate to rise to 8.3 percent by 1975 and the number of unemployed to rise to 7,929,000. Once again, however, the poverty rate declined as the economy picked up after 1975. The recession of 1980–1982 threw the economy off track again. In 1979, the total number of people unemployed was 6,137,000; by 1982, 10,717,000 were without jobs. As the economy came out of this recession, the poverty rate began to decline, and it continued to decline as the economy grew throughout the 1980s. The poverty rate then rose as the economy fell into recession in 1990 and struggled into 1992. The poverty rate of 14.2 percent in 1991 was the highest level in nearly three decades; the number of people living in poverty grew to 35.7 million. Somewhat surprising was that the number of people in poverty and the incidence of poverty both grew in 1993 and 1994, years of economic growth. The poverty rate and number in poverty declined throughout the 1990s. As the economy again entered a recession in 2000, the number of people in poverty began to

Incomes are unequally distributed in every nation. In developing countries, the distinction between rich and poor is greater than in the industrial nations, although the per capita income is significantly less in the developing countries. For instance, although the per capita income in Nigeria is only 7 percent of the per capita income in the United States, the wealthy in Lagos, Nigeria, live very well, with large houses, servants, expensive clothes, and other accouterments of wealth. During the 1970s, many Nigerians became very wealthy as the price of oil surged and Nigerian oil production rose. Economic crisis and the collapse of oil prices since the late 1970s have led to a decline in Nigeria that has wiped out the gains of the previous twenty years.

rise. Obviously, whether the economy is growing or in a recession significantly affects the poverty rate and the number of people in poverty.

There are many controversies over the poverty measure. Some argue that the poverty rate is really not nearly as high as these figures indicate; that government transfers and programs are not properly taken into account. Also, the poverty measure makes no distinction between the needs of a 3-month-old and a 14-year-old or between a rural family in a cold climate and an urban family in the subtropics. It draws no distinction between income and purchasing power. A welfare mom living on $400 a month is treated identically to a graduate student who earns $400 a month at a part-time job and borrows an additional $1,500 from her parents. Nor does it consider the problem of income from the underground economy—the income that is not reported or measured in income statistics. Nevertheless, the measure is used to determine how federal government money is to be allocated among states and regions.

RECAP

1. The Lorenz curve shows the degree to which incomes are distributed equally in a society.
2. The Lorenz curve bows down below the line of equality for all nations.
3. There are two ways to measure poverty: with an absolute measure and with a relative measure. The Lorenz curve is a relative measure. Per capita income is an absolute measure.
4. Per capita income after cash and in-kind transfers is used by the U.S. government to define a poverty level of income.
5. Recessions increase the incidence of poverty; economic growth reduces the incidence of poverty.

3. Who are the poor?

2. The Poor

Poverty is not a condition that randomly strikes women and men, and white, African American, and Hispanic families equally. Nor does it strike the educated and well trained in the same way it strikes the uneducated. The incidence of poverty itself is unequally distributed among sectors of the society.

2.a. Temporary and Permanent Poverty

If those who are poor at any one time are poor only temporarily, then their plight is only temporary. If people in poverty are able to improve their situation while others slip into poverty temporarily, the problem of poverty for society is not as serious as it is if poverty is a permanent condition once a person has slipped into it.

Studies indicate that approximately 25 percent of all Americans fall below the poverty line at some time in their lives. Many of these spells of poverty are relatively short; nearly 45 percent last less than a year. However, more than 50 percent of those in poverty at a particular time remain in poverty for at least ten years.

One major determinant of an individual's income is age. A young person or a senior citizen has a much greater chance of suffering a low income than a person who is between 30 and 60 years old. Figure 4 shows the percentage of the population

FIGURE 4

Age and Poverty

The percent of people who have income below the poverty line varies according to age. Younger and older people have the highest percentage in poverty. Middle-aged people (45–54) have the lowest percentage in poverty. *Source:* Statistical Abstract of the United States, 2002. *www.census.gov.*

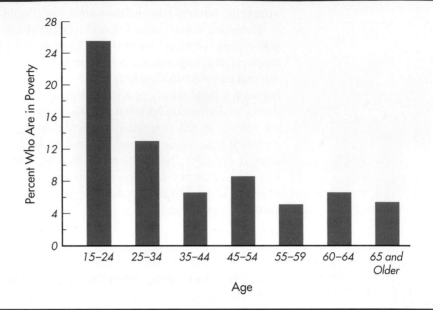

below the poverty level by age in 2002. The highest incidence of poverty by age occurs among those under 15 years. The second highest occurs among those between 15 and 24. The third highest occurs among those 25 to 34.

Poverty does not affect all racial and all age groups equally. As Figure 5 shows, the percentages of the population of different groups that fall below the poverty level each year are not equal. African Americans and Hispanics carry a much heavier burden of poverty relative to the size of their populations than do whites.

FIGURE 5

The Incidence of Poverty by Race and Hispanic Origin

The incidence of poverty is higher for African Americans and Hispanics than it is for whites. Good times help whites more than they help other races, and bad times harm whites less than they harm other races. *Source:* Statistical Abstract of the United States, 2002. *www.census.gov.*

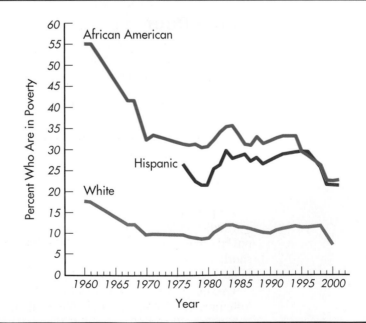

4. What are the determinants of poverty?

The primary characteristic of those who fall below the poverty line is the lack of a job.

The less education a person has, the greater his or her chance of experiencing poverty.

Poverty does not affect males and females equally, either. Approximately 35 percent of all families headed by a female have poverty-level incomes. Only 8 percent of all families headed by a male have incomes so low. More than 55 percent of households with a female head and children are living in poverty.

2.b. Causes of Poverty

The primary characteristic of those who fall below the poverty line is the lack of a job—the elderly, the young, and nonworking students. People who fall below the poverty line may have jobs but work less than full-time, or their jobs may pay so little that their income does not exceed the poverty cutoff. For instance, a job paying the minimum wage for 40 hours a week and 50 weeks a year yields an income that is more than $6,000 below the poverty level.

Place of residence also affects a person's ability to earn income. The metropolitan poverty rate differs greatly between the central city and the suburbs. In 2002, the average rates were 16.7 percent and 8.9 percent respectively. The poverty rate in rural areas was 14.2 percent.

The less education an individual has, the lower the income that that individual earns, and the greater the chance that that individual will experience poverty. A significant percentage of those in poverty have less than eight years of education. Fully 25 percent of the people with less than eight years of education fall below the poverty level of income. Only 4 percent of those with one or more years of college fall below the poverty cutoff. Lack of education prevents people from securing well-paying jobs. Without the human capital obtained from education or training programs, finding a job that is stable and will not disappear during a recession is very difficult. Even someone who has the desire to work but has no exceptional abilities and has not acquired the skills necessary for a well-paying job is unlikely to escape poverty completely. Minorities and women, the young, the disabled, and the old have disproportionately less education than the rest of the population and as a result have a higher likelihood of falling into poverty.

RECAP

1. Many people experience poverty only temporarily. Nearly 45 percent of the spells of poverty last less than a year. However, nearly 50 percent of those in poverty remain there for at least ten years.
2. The highest rates of poverty occur among people under 21 or over 65.
3. The incidence of poverty is much higher among African Americans and Hispanics than it is among whites.
4. A poor person may be poor because of age, lack of a job, lack of education, or place of residence.

3. Government Antipoverty Policies

Why are economists and others concerned with income inequality and poverty? One reason might be normative. People might have compassion for those who have less than they do, or people might not like to see the squalid living conditions endured by some in poverty. In other words, the existence of poverty may mean lower levels of utility for members of society who are not in poverty. If increases in poverty mean decreases in utility, then people will want less poverty. They will be willing and able to purchase less poverty by allocating portions of their income or their time to alleviating the problem.

Another reason for concern about income inequality and poverty might be positive, or not dependent on value judgments. Perhaps the inequality is a result of inefficiency, and a correction of the situation that creates the inefficiency will improve the functioning of the economy. For instance, if education provides benefits for society that are not taken into account in individual decisions to acquire education, then too few people will acquire education. People who would have acquired education if the positive benefits for society had been subsidized, but did not, are wasted resources. These people would have earned more income, fewer would have fallen into poverty, and the distribution of income might have been more equal. In this sense, the number of people in poverty and the existence of income inequality provide indications that allocative efficiency has failed to occur.

The government is often called on to resolve market failures. If poverty is distasteful to society, then citizens, by paying taxes and through their votes, may ask the government to reduce poverty. Whatever the rationale, positive or normative, the fact is that the government is involved in antipoverty programs and in the attempt to reduce income inequality. Given the fact that incomes are distributed unequally, if society does not want such inequality, what can be done? One approach—the most common—would be to take from the wealthy and give to the poor—a transfer of incomes. We'll look at this approach next.

3.a. Tax Policy

If people are provided with enough income to bring them above the poverty level, the number of people in poverty would be reduced. Funds used to supplement the incomes of the poor must come from somewhere. Many societies adopt a Robin Hood approach, taxing the rich to give to the poor. Income taxes can influence income distribution through their impact on after-tax income. Taxes may be progressive, proportional, or regressive.

progressive income tax: a tax whose rate increases as income increases

A **progressive income tax** is a tax that rises as income rises—the marginal tax rate increases as income increases. If someone with an annual income of $20,000 pays $5,000 in taxes while someone else with an annual income of $40,000 pays $12,000 in taxes, the tax rate is progressive. The first person is paying a 25 percent rate, and the second is paying a 30 percent rate.

proportional tax: a tax whose rate does not change as the tax base changes

A **proportional tax** is a tax whose rate does not change as the tax base changes. The rate of a proportional income tax remains the same at every level of income. If the tax rate is 20 percent, then all individuals pay 20 percent, whether they earn $10,000 or $100,000.

regressive tax: a tax whose rate decreases as the tax base changes

A **regressive tax** decreases as the tax base increases. The social security tax is regressive; a specified rate is paid on income up to a specified level. On income beyond that level, no social security taxes are paid. In 2003, the cutoff level of income was $87,000 and the tax rate was 6.2 percent. A person earning $300,000 paid no more social security taxes than someone earning $90,000.

A progressive tax rate tends to reduce income inequality; a proportional tax does not affect income distribution; and a regressive tax increases inequality. The progressive tax takes larger percentages of income from high-income members of society than it takes from low-income members. This tends to equalize after-tax incomes. In the United States, the federal income tax is progressive. The tax rate rises from zero to 36 percent as income rises (39 percent for incomes above $1 million).

3.b. Transfers

Once funds are collected, how are they transferred to the poor?

The main transfer programs are social insurance, cash welfare or public assistance, in-kind transfers, and employment programs. Social security—officially known as Old Age, Survivors, and Disability Insurance (OASDI) and listed as FICA on your paycheck stubs—is the largest social insurance program. It helps a family replace income that is lost when a worker retires, becomes severely disabled, or dies. Coverage is nearly universal, so the total amount of money involved is immense—nearly $200 billion annually. Two-thirds of the aged rely on social security for more than half of their income.

Unemployment insurance provides temporary benefits to regularly employed people who become temporarily unemployed. Funded by a national tax on payrolls levied on firms with eight or more workers, the system is run by state governments. Benefits normally amount to about 50 percent of a worker's usual wage.

Supplemental Security Income (SSI) ranks first among cash welfare programs. Fully 65 percent of the SSI population is blind or otherwise disabled. The rest are over age 65. Unlike social security recipients, who are *entitled* to receive benefits because they are a certain age or otherwise qualify, recipients of SSI must meet certain disability requirements or be of a certain age and must have incomes below about $4,500 per year.

About 60 percent of all poor households receive in-kind transfers. The largest of these programs is Medicaid (for a discussion of Medicaid and the medical-care industry, see the chapter "Aging, Social Security, and Health Care"). Medicaid provides federal funds to states to help them cover the costs of long-term medical and nursing-home care. Second in magnitude is the food stamp program, which gives households coupons that are redeemable at grocery stores. The amounts vary with income and household size. Other programs include jobs and training directed toward disadvantaged workers and the Head Start program, an education program available to poor children. Total government outlays for social service (welfare) programs run more than $700 billion annually.

3.c. The Effectiveness of Welfare Programs

5. Do government programs intended to reduce poverty benefit the poor?

In 1964, President Lyndon Johnson declared "unconditional war on poverty." In 1967, total transfers were about $10 billion. After nearly a quarter-century of increasing outlays to reduce poverty, is the war being won? Unfortunately, there is no easy or straightforward answer to that question. In fact, there is disagreement about whether antipoverty programs have reduced or increased poverty. Some people maintain that without the programs, income inequality and poverty would have been much more severe. Others argue that welfare has been a drag on the economy and may have made poverty and inequality worse than they otherwise would have been.

It is impossible to compare what did happen with what would have happened in the absence of the government's programs. All economists can do is look at what actually occurred.

Gini ratio: a measure of the dispersion of income ranging between 0 and 1; 0 means that all families have the same income; 1 means that one family has all of the income

The **Gini ratio** is a measure of the dispersion of income; the ratio measures the difference between the Lorenz curve and the line of perfect equality. It is a measure of the area between the Lorenz curve and the line of perfect equality divided by the total area if one family had all of the income. A Gini of 0 would occur if every family had the exact same amount of income; a Gini of 1 would occur if all income accrued to only one family. Figure 6 shows that the dispersion of income fell gradually from 1947 to 1968 but has risen since.

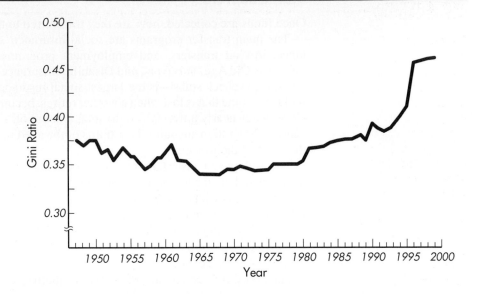

FIGURE 6

The Gini Ratio

The Gini ratio is a measure of the dispersion of income that ranges between 0 and 1. A lower value indicates less dispersion in the income distribution: a Gini of 0 would occur if every family had the exact same amount of income, while a Gini of 1 would occur if all income accrued to only one family. Figure 6 shows that from 1947 to 1968, the dispersion of income fell gradually. Since then the dispersion has risen slowly. *Source:* Economic Report of the President, 2000.

Figure 7 shows the annual expenditures on poverty programs along with the incidence of poverty from 1960. The incidence-of-poverty curve is taken from Figure 3. During the 1960s, as transfers and spending increased, the incidence of poverty fell. Since the early 1970s, transfers and spending have increased much more rapidly than in the previous decade, but the incidence of poverty has changed little, and in fact, it rose during the recessions of the early 1980s and the early 1990s, and again in 2000–2003.

In 1996, Congress passed the Personal Responsibility and Work Opportunity Reconciliation Act. This legislation ended the program known as Aid to Families with Dependent Children (AFDC) and replaced it with a program called Temporary Assistance for Needy Families (TANF). Under TANF, welfare assistance is no longer an entitlement program. Welfare benefits are time-limited and are closely tied to work requirements that are intended to move welfare recipients off welfare and into the labor force. TANF was supposed to reduce expenditures on welfare and shift a great deal of spending from the federal to the state governments. Expenditures are continuing to rise, however. Spending on TANF rose by 35 percent between 1998 and 2001. The Personal Responsibility and Work Opportunity Reconciliation Act of 1996 (PRWORA) also scaled back the food stamp program. Food stamp costs declined by $9 billion between 1996 and 2001.

3.c.1. Incentives and Government Income Transfer Programs Taxes are one method of collecting revenues with which antipoverty or welfare programs can be paid for. Taxes affect those who pay the taxes; they may lead to less labor being supplied. As we discussed in the chapter "The Labor Market," the supply of labor comes from the decisions that individuals make regarding the number of hours of work they are willing and able to perform at each wage. The individual trades off labor and leisure, essentially buying leisure time—giving up the income gained by working. Thus, when the cost of leisure to an individual is decreased, individuals

FIGURE 7

Spending and Poverty

Curves representing total government spending in real (1987) billions of dollars on poverty programs since 1960 and the incidence of poverty since 1960 are shown. Total expenditures on antipoverty programs in equal purchasing power terms (real terms) are measured on the left vertical axis, and the percent of the population in poverty is shown on the right vertical axis. During the 1960s, the incidence of poverty decreased as spending increased. Since then, spending has continued to increase, but the incidence of poverty has not declined. *Source: Department of Commerce, 1999. www.census.gov/ hhes/www/poverty.html.*

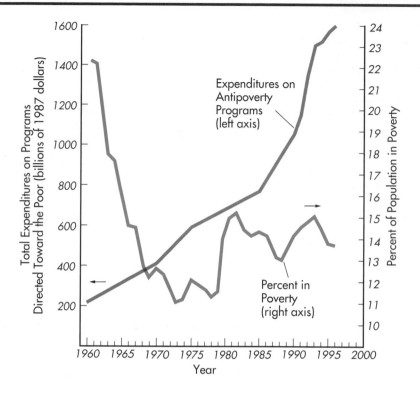

will buy more leisure; that is, they will work less. A tax increases the cost of working or, conversely, decreases the cost of leisure. It should be expected that people will choose the now less expensive leisure time over the now more costly work time. This will affect the cost of labor to firms. In Figure 8, suppose the equilibrium in the labor market prior to a tax on labor is Q_1. Now, suppose a tax of rate t on each hour of time worked (each dollar of income earned) is imposed on the worker. As a result of the tax, the worker decides to supply less labor at every wage rate, shown as an inward shift of supply, to $S + t$. The number of hours worked declines to Q_2. The tax has led to fewer hours worked and thus less income earned.

In Figure 8, the tax increases the wage rate, but not by the full amount of the pre-tax wage plus the tax. This means that the tax is partially paid by workers and partially paid by firms. In other words, if workers do receive some additional wages but not enough to pay the tax, then post-tax, workers have less disposable income than they did pre-tax. If workers receive no additional wages, then the workers pay the entire tax; their disposable income decreases by the amount of the tax.

The percentage of the tax paid for by businesses and by workers depends on the price elasticities of demand and supply, in the same way that the percentage of cost increases paid for by firms and by consumers depends on the price elasticities of demand and supply. In the extreme case where the labor supply curve is backward bending at some point, a tax on wages would lead those who are on the backward-bending part of the supply curve to actually increase the quantity of hours they

FIGURE 8

Taxes and Jobs

If a tax per hour of work is imposed on the worker, the individual will choose to supply less labor at each wage rate. The supply curve shifts in, and the number of hours worked decreases.

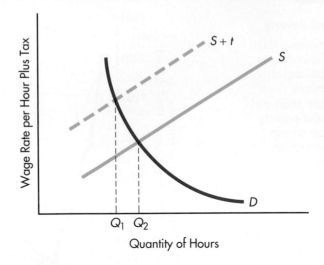

would be willing and able to supply. Looking at the backward-bending labor supply curve, you can see that if this effect occurs, it occurs at high wages or high income levels. There is some evidence that the labor supply curve does bend backward at some very high income level for some people. Some people who receive large inheritances or win the lottery stop working; this suggests that the backward-bending labor supply curve is valid at very high income levels. But for most people, most of the time, the labor supply curve is upward sloping. This means that the firm and the worker share in paying the tax, even though it is imposed on the worker.

When funds are distributed to the unemployed or to those who are employed but at low-paying jobs, it affects the incentives of these individuals to work. As a low-income individual receives a transfer payment, that individual has less of an incentive to forgo leisure time for work time. This raises the question about whether welfare leads to a permanent dependency on welfare and an unwillingness to work.

3.c.2. Disincentives Created by the Welfare System
Those who argue that welfare programs are a drag on the economy and may make poverty and income inequality worse typically focus on the disincentives created by the transfers. Incentives for both the rich and the poor to work hard and increase their productivity may be reduced by programs that take from the rich and give to the poor. Those who are paying taxes may ask themselves, "Why should I work an extra hour every day if all the extra income does is pay additional taxes?" Someone who gets to keep only 60 cents out of the next dollar earned has less incentive to earn that dollar than someone who gets to keep it all.

Those who receive benefits may lose the incentive to change their status. Why should someone take a job paying $6,000 per year when he or she can remain unemployed and receive $8,000? Someone who is out of work might wonder, "Why should I spend eight hours a day in miserable working conditions when I can relax every day and bring home nearly the same amount of income?" If incentives to work are weak, then the total income created in the economy is less than it otherwise would be. Less income and lower economic growth mean more people in poverty.

3.d. The Negative Income Tax and Family Allowance Plans

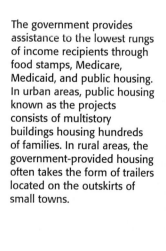

negative income tax (NIT): a tax system that transfers increasing amounts of income to households earning incomes below some specified level as their income declines

The solution to the welfare system problems most often proposed by economists is the **negative income tax (NIT)**—a tax system that transfers increasing amounts of income to households earning incomes below some specified level. The lower the income, the more that is transferred. As income rises above the specified level, a tax is applied. Economists like the NIT because, at least in theory, it attacks the distribution of income and reduces poverty without causing too many distortions in the economy.

Suppose policymakers determine that a family of four is to be guaranteed an income of $10,000. If the family earns nothing, then it will get a transfer of $10,000. If the family earns some income, it will receive $10,000 less a tax on the earned income. If the tax rate is 50 percent, then for each dollar earned, $.50 will be taken out of the $10,000 transfer.

With a 50 percent tax rate, there would always be some incentive to work under the NIT system because each additional dollar of earnings would bring the recipient of the transfer $.50 in additional income. At some income level, the tax taken would be equal to the transfer of $10,000. This level of income is referred to as the *break-even income level.* The break-even income level in the case of a $10,000 guaranteed income and a 50 percent tax rate is $20,000. Once a family of four earns more than $20,000, its taxes exceed the transfer of $10,000.

The government provides assistance to the lowest rungs of income recipients through food stamps, Medicare, Medicaid, and public housing. In urban areas, public housing known as the projects consists of multistory buildings housing hundreds of families. In rural areas, the government-provided housing often takes the form of trailers located on the outskirts of small towns.

The break-even level of income is determined by the income floor and the tax rate:

$$\text{Break-even income} = \frac{\text{income floor}}{\text{negative income tax rate}}$$

If the guaranteed income floor is $13,000 and the tax rate is 50 percent, then the break-even income would be $26,000. If the guaranteed income floor is $13,000 but the tax rate is 33 percent, then the break-even income would be $39,000.

In order for the negative income tax to eradicate poverty, the guaranteed level of income has to be equal to the poverty level, $18,244 in 2002. But if the tax rate is less than 100 percent, the break-even income level will be above the poverty level and families who are not officially considered "poor" will also receive benefits. At a guaranteed income level of $18,244 and a 33 percent tax rate, the break-even income level is $55,285. All families of four earning less than $55,285 would receive some income benefits.

For people now covered by welfare programs, the negative income tax would increase the incentive to work, and that is what proponents of the negative income tax like. However, for people who are too well off to receive welfare but who would become eligible for NIT payments, the negative income tax might create work disincentives. It provides these families with more income, and they may choose to buy more leisure.

The possibility of disincentive effects worried both social reformers and legislators, so in the late 1960s the government carried out a number of experiments to estimate the effect of the negative income tax on the supply of labor. Families from a number of U.S. cities were offered negative-income-tax payments in return for allowing social scientists to monitor their behavior. A matched set of families who were not given NIT payments were also observed. The idea was to compare the behavior of the families receiving NIT payments with that of the families who did not receive them. The experiments lasted about a decade and showed pretty clearly that the net effects of the negative income tax on labor supply were quite small.

Even though disincentive effects did not seem to occur to any great extent, the negative income tax has not gained political acceptability. One reason is the high break-even income level. Politicians are not very supportive of programs that may provide income transfers to a family earning significantly more than the poverty income level. Another reason is the transfer of dollars rather than in-kind benefits (food and medical care). Policymakers do not look favorably on the idea of giving a family cash that the family can use as it pleases.

While politicians focus on poverty and government expenditures on programs and support for the poor rise, the poor remain. In a market system, some people will have high incomes and others low incomes. So if those with low incomes are considered poor, there will always be the poor in a market economy. An important question, however, is whether the poor in a market economy are better or worse off than people in other systems. Are the poor in the United States better or worse off than the high income earners in Rwanda, Peru, or China? Studies of the poor in the United States indicate that people in poverty have, on average, a home or apartment, a television, a refrigerator, an air conditioner, a telephone, and other items that many people in the world just dream about. Nevertheless, few in the United States would argue that there are no poor people. So what conclusions can be drawn? One is that the poor will always exist in a market economy if poor is defined as those in the lower levels of income distribution. Incomes are not distributed equally in a market system.

1. Government policies designed to change the distribution of income to one that is more equal involve taking from the rich and giving to the poor—a Robin Hood approach.

2. A tax may be progressive, proportional, or regressive. A progressive tax is one with a marginal tax rate that increases as income rises. A proportional tax is one that rises as income rises, but with the marginal tax rate remaining constant. A regressive tax is one whose marginal tax rate decreases as income increases.

3. Transfer mechanisms include social security, welfare, and unemployment programs.

4. The incentives created by transfer programs may make the costs greater than the benefits. These programs may make those who receive assistance less willing to work and lead those who are taxed to support the transfer program to work less.

5. The negative income tax is a proposal to provide transfers, but in a way that minimizes disincentives.

4. Income Distribution Among Nations

Incomes differ greatly from one nation to another as well as within nations. Mexico's income distribution is less equal than that of the United States, but income levels in Mexico are also significantly lower than in the United States. The per capita annual income in Mexico is $8,981, while in the United States it exceeds $28,000. Figure 9 shows the per capita incomes of several countries. The figure illustrates

Per Capita Real Gross Domestic Product

Levels of income vary tremendously among nations; for instance, per capita income in Switzerland is the highest; that in Ethiopia, the lowest. *Source: www.un.org/pubs/cyberschoolbus.*

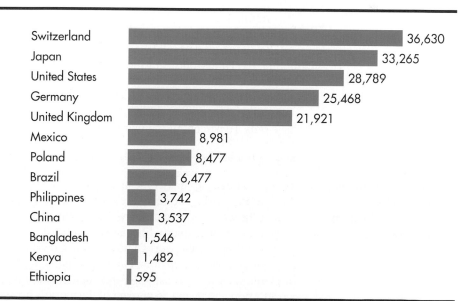

Switzerland	36,630
Japan	33,265
United States	28,789
Germany	25,468
United Kingdom	21,921
Mexico	8,981
Poland	8,477
Brazil	6,477
Philippines	3,742
China	3,537
Bangladesh	1,546
Kenya	1,482
Ethiopia	595

Economic Development and Happiness

A nation's standard of living influences the attitudes of the nation's population toward life in general, although it is not the only factor. Using subjective measures of happiness or satisfaction with life, researchers find that year after year, the Danes, Swiss, Irish, and Dutch feel happier and more satisfied with life than do the French, Greeks, Italians, and Germans. Whether they are German-, French-, or Italian-speaking, the Swiss rank very high on life satisfaction—much higher than their German, French, and Italian neighbors. People in the Scandinavian countries generally are both prosperous and happy. However, the link between national affluence and well-being isn't consistent. Germans, for instance, average more than double the per capita income of the Irish, but the Irish are happier. Similarly, although the developed nations all had higher per capita incomes than the Mexicans, the Mexicans stated a higher satisfaction with life than the populations of many of the developed nations. The overall pattern does show that wealthier nations tend to show higher levels of life satisfaction than poorer ones, but income and wealth are not the only factors influencing happiness. Related to wealth is the type of

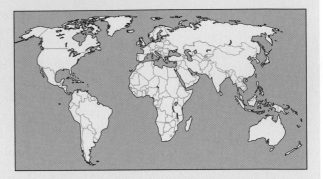

government under which citizens live. The most prosperous nations have enjoyed stable democratic governments, and there is a link between a history of stable democracy and national well-being. The thirteen nations that have maintained democratic institutions continuously since 1920 all enjoy higher life satisfaction levels than do the eleven nations whose democracies developed after World War II.

Source: Bruno Frey and Alois Stutzer, *Happiness and Economics* (Princeton University Press, 2002).

how great the differences in per capita income are. The Global Business Insight "Economic Development and Happiness" suggests that the feeling of well-being of a population generally depends on the level of per capita income.

The distribution of total world income among nations is very unequal, as shown in Figure 10. Three-fourths of the world's population lives in developing countries, but the income earned by the people in these countries—the lowest 90 percent of the population in terms of income—is only about 20 percent of the total world income, shown as point *A*. The richest countries, earning nearly 80 percent of total world income, have only 10 percent of the world's population, the difference between *A* and *B*.

?

6. Why are incomes unequally distributed among nations?

4.a. World Income Distribution

There is a huge gap in income and wealth distribution between the "haves" and "have nots" in the world, and there are indications that this gap is widening. About 80 percent of the world's population live below what countries in North America and Europe consider to be the poverty line, and the poorest 10 percent of Americans are better off than two-thirds of the world's population. Low-income countries represented 40 percent of the world's population but only 11 percent of the world's gross national income in 1999. In sharp contrast, high-income countries represented only 15 percent of the world's population and 56 percent of the world's gross national income. Data from the World Bank's *2001 World Development Indicators* are presented in Figure 11.

FIGURE 10

World Lorenz Curve

The Lorenz curve is typically used to illustrate the income distribution within countries. In this figure, a Lorenz curve is drawn to compare how world income is distributed across countries. The bottom 90 percent of the world's population, residing in the less developed countries, accounts for 20 percent of the world's income, shown as point *A*. The richest 10 percent of the population, residing in the developed countries, accounts for 80 percent of total income, shown as point *B*. *Source: Data are from* World Development Report, 1999 *and* 2000.

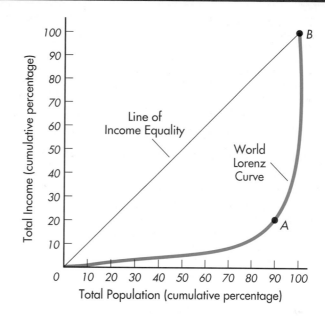

FIGURE 11

Lorenz Curve for Nations

The distribution of income among nations is very unequal. Low-income countries represent 40 percent of the world's population but receive only 11 percent of the world's gross national income, and high-income countries represent only 15 percent of the world's population and receive 56 percent of the world's gross national income. *Source: World Bank,* 2001 World Development Indicators.

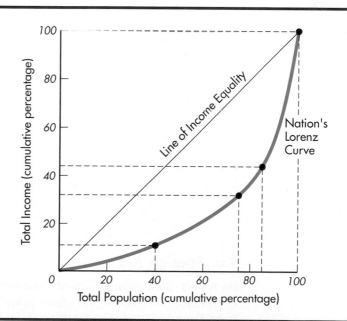

TABLE 2

Gini Coefficients for
Selected Countries

Country	Survey Year	Gini Index
Brazil	1997	59.1
Canada	1994	31.5
China	1998	40.3
India	1997	37.8
Japan	1993	24.9
Mexico	1996	51.9
Russian Federation	1998	48.7
South Africa	1994	59.3
United Kingdom	1991	36.1
United States	1997	40.8

Source: World Bank, *2001 World Development Indicators.*

The Gini coefficient for the diagram in Figure 11 is approximately 55, indicating a relatively significant degree of inequality in global income distribution. (Recall that the higher the Gini coefficient, the more unequal the distribution.) This Gini coefficient reflects the unequal distribution of income among countries but does not reflect the unequal distribution within countries. Table 2 shows Gini coefficient estimates for ten selected countries. The Gini coefficients indicate that income is distributed unequally within nations. Thus, when you measure the income distribution among families throughout the world rather than just within a nation or among nations, the Gini coefficient is closer to 66 than 55.

Why are income and wealth so unequally distributed among nations? The rate of growth of gross domestic product (and income) is the difference. Suppose one nation was growing at a rate of 4 percent per year and another nation was growing at a rate of 2 percent per year. How long would it take the two countries to double their income? Using the rule of 72, where dividing the growth rate into 72 yields the number of time periods until the item that is growing doubles, we find that an economy with a 4 percent growth rate doubles every 18 years, while one with a 2 percent growth rate doubles every 36 years. So, if the two countries started with $100, in a 36-year time period, the country growing at 2 percent per year would have $200, while the country growing at 4 percent per year would have $400. Thus, if all nations started out with the same level of income and some grew faster than others, it would not take long before incomes were widely unequal among nations. Thus, a major question that must be answered in order to explain why nations have different levels of income is why they grow at different rates. One of the answers that economists have provided is that the freer the economic and political systems are, the greater is the rate of economic growth.

How should the unequal distribution among nations that exists today be dealt with? One approach is welfare—transferring income from the rich countries to the poor countries. Another is to try to increase the growth rates of the poor countries.

4.b. Foreign Aid

On April 1, 2002, rich nations pledged more aid to poor nations at the International Conference on Financing for Development held in Monterrey, Mexico. *Foreign aid* is the name given to programs that transfer income from rich nations to poor nations.

The questions about foreign aid include all the questions regarding welfare within the United States—what are the incentives on recipients and on donors, and how much of the aid reaches those who are needy. But, foreign aid also involves issues such as whether the aid will spur economic growth. It is possible that the aid actually hinders growth, because it creates the wrong incentives.

Another approach to the inequality issue that creates positive incentives for economic growth has been the focus of Hernando de Soto, a Peruvian economist. He has suggested that if the institutions of private property in the poorer nations were comparable to those in the industrial nations, rapid economic growth would take place. He argues that poor countries have to reform their political and legal systems to allow poor people to establish clear title to assets, so they can more easily borrow money against those assets. He believes that bringing the poor into the legal economy would help them start more businesses. In Mexico, for instance, DeSoto notes that the assets for which there are no legal property rights include over 11 million houses, 137 million hectares of land (338.4 acres), and 6 million unregistered micro, small, and medium-sized businesses. About 78 percent of the population of Mexico is involved in that side of the economy. These assets are worth about $315 billion, which is equivalent to 31 times all foreign direct investment in Mexico for all time. According to DeSoto, the poor are really the largest potential capital that Mexico has.

But what has to be done to free that capital? The judicial system must ensure private property rights and do so much more efficiently than is currently the case. In poor nations, the legal system exists for a privileged elite but is cumbersome and costly for most of the population. For example, creating a mortgage in Mexico takes a buyer 24 months, working eight hours a day. Foreclosing on a mortgage takes 43 months. Selling a house, if you're among the 78 percent of Mexicans that are poor and you want to do it legally, takes 24 months working eight hours a day. Obtaining legal access for a business—that is to say, setting up a limited liability corporation, or whatever other form allows you to have shareholders—takes 17 months working eight hours a day and 126 contacts with government.

The creation and enforcement of private property rights is a necessary prelude to the functioning of markets, and an economy without markets does not grow very rapidly. Markets do not work when there are no private property rights or when private property rights are not widely available and enforced. As we'll discover in the next chapter, other approaches to enhancing economic growth have been tried. But these policies as a whole have not worked. Poor nations that have not established private property rights remain poor.

RECAP

1. The world has a great deal of income inequality—both within individual nations and among nations.
2. The poor nations are poor at least partly because of their lack of assurance and enforcement of private property rights.
3. One approach used to improve the conditions of people in poor nations is foreign aid—a transfer of income from rich nations to poor nations.
4. The incentives created by foreign aid are analogous to the incentives created by welfare systems and so might not be conducive to economic growth.
5. An approach to stimulate economic growth is to provide the population of a country, particularly its poor, the legal means to establish and maintain private property.

Summary

❓ Are incomes distributed equally in the United States?

1. The Lorenz curve illustrates the degree of income inequality. *§1.a*

2. If the Lorenz curve corresponds with the line of income equality, then incomes are distributed equally. If the Lorenz curve bows down below the line of income equality, then income is distributed in such a way that more people earn low incomes than earn high incomes. *§1.a*

❓ How is poverty measured, and does poverty exist in the United States?

3. Poverty is a measure of how well basic human needs are being met. Poverty is both a relative and an absolute concept. *§1.b*

4. Income consists of resource earnings and transfers. Transfers may be in cash or in kind. The distribution of income in the United States is more unequal when only market earnings are considered than it is when transfers as well as market earnings are considered. *§1.c*

5. The incidence of poverty decreases as the economy grows and increases as the economy falls into recession. *§1.d*

❓ Who are the poor?

6. Many people fall below the poverty line for a short time only. However, a significant core of people remain in poverty for at least ten years. *§2.a*

7. The poor are primarily those without jobs (the youngest and oldest members of society), those residing in the centers of large cities and in rural areas, and those without education. *§2.b*

❓ What are the determinants of poverty?

8. Age, a lack of education, and a lack of a full-time or well-paying job are the primary determinants of poverty. *§2.b*

❓ Do government programs intended to reduce poverty benefit the poor?

9. Tax policies that are progressive could reduce the incentives to acquire more income. *§3.c.1*

10. Government programs often reduce individuals' incentives to climb out of poverty. *§3.c.2*

11. Subsidies could offset incentives to work or produce. *§3.c.2*

❓ Why are incomes unequally distributed among nations?

12. As a rule, incomes are distributed more unequally in developing countries than in developed countries. *§4*

13. A fundamental reason that standards of living differ among nations is the different growth rates that the economies of these nations have experienced over time. *§4.a*

14. Free markets and political freedom lead to economic growth. *§4.a*

15. The creation and enforcement of private property rights is a necessity if a nation's economy is to grow. *§4.b*

Key Terms

Lorenz curve *§1.a*

cash transfers *§1.c*

in-kind transfers *§1.c*

progressive income tax *§3.a*

proportional tax *§3.a*

regressive tax *§3.a*

Gini ratio *§3.c*

negative income tax (NIT) *§3.d*

Exercises

1. What is a Lorenz curve? What would the curve look like if income were equally distributed? Could the curve ever bow upward above the line of income equality?

2. Why does the health of the economy affect the number of people living in poverty?

3. What would it mean if the poverty income level of the United States were applied to Mexico?

4. What positive arguments can be made for reducing income inequality? What normative arguments are made for reducing income inequality?

5. What does it mean to say that poverty is a luxury good?

6. Are people who are poor today in the United States likely to be poor for the rest of their lives? Under what conditions is generational poverty likely to exist?

7. Use the following information to plot a Lorenz curve.

Percent of Population	Percent of Income
20	5
40	15
60	35
80	65
100	100

8. If the incidence of poverty decreases during periods when the economy is growing and increases during periods when the economy is in recession, what government policies might be used to reduce poverty most effectively?

9. If the arguments for reducing income inequality and poverty are normative, why rely on the government to reduce the inequality? Why doesn't the private market resolve the problem?

10. How could transfer programs (welfare programs) actually increase the number of people in poverty?

11. What is the difference between in-kind and cash transfers? Which might increase the utility of the recipients the most? Why is there political resistance to the negative income tax?

12. Is it possible to eradicate poverty? The government's definition of poverty is a family of four with reported income less than $18,244. According to a recent study by the Heritage Foundation, this figure does not include the housing that 40 percent of those in poverty own or the cars that 62 percent own. Nor does it consider how the poorest 20 percent of households manage to consume twice as much as they earn. Is poverty a relative concept or an absolute concept?

13. Consider the following three solutions offered to get rid of homelessness and discuss whether any would solve the problem. First, provide permanent housing for all who are homeless. Second, provide free hospital care for the one-third of homeless who are mentally ill. Third, provide subsidies for the homeless to purchase homes.

14. What is the relationship between the Gini coefficient and the Lorenz curve? Illustrate your answer using exercise 7.

15. Why would Hernando DeSoto's suggestions, if implemented, stimulate economic growth?

Take the ACE Practice Test for this chapter to review the important concepts and get immediate feedback with answers.

economics.college.hmco.com/students

Zimbabwe: Income Distribution and Policy

With the exception of Zimbabwe, which continues to face a sustained decline in output, global output has been rising, save for the temporary recession-propelled setback that started in 2000 and was worsened by the terrorist attacks on the United States on September 11, 2001.

However, accompanied by the increase in global output, there has been an increase in income disparities in both developed and developing countries. Resultantly, one of the most pressing issues facing policy makers today is how to respond to this trend. . . .

Much of the debate about income distribution has centered on wage earnings.

For instance, in Zimbabwe an Earnings Survey done by PriceWaterHouseCoppers for the period 1995 and 2000 shows serious disparities between unskilled, skilled and managerial employees.

As a result, the ZCTU has used this analysis as its basis for wage negotiations. At a policy level, the government should look beyond wages if it wants to address the general problem of income inequalities in Zimbabwe.

The distribution of wealth (and, by implication, capital income) is more concentrated than labour income. For instance, in Africa and Latin America, unequal ownership of land has been identified as an important factor in the overall distribution of income. In fact, in recent years, there has been a shift from labour to capital income in many countries.

In transition economies, this shift has been due primarily to the privatisation of state-owned assets, and the government's act of warehousing some of the shares through a trust fund on behalf of the low-income groups is a welcome income redistribution gesture.

Furthermore, pension funds and other financial institutions receive a sizeable portion of capital income, and the share of capital income in total household income typically changes over the life cycle of the individuals in the household.

But is income inequality bad? The following are some of the reasons for addressing income inequalities.

Some societies view equity as a worthy goal because of its moral implications and its link with fairness and social justice. Policies that promote equity can help, directly and indirectly, to reduce poverty.

Another issue is the increase in the awareness about the discrimination suffered by certain groups on the basis of their gender, race, or ethnic origin, which has focused attention on the need to ensure that these groups have access to government services and receive fair treatment in the labour market.

Another factor is that many of today's policies will affect the welfare of future generations, which raises the issue of intergenerational equity.

Another reason why governments are concerned with equity issues is that policies that promote equity can boost social cohesion and reduce political conflict. . . .

Source: Copyright 2003 AllAfrica, Inc.

Africa News/May 7, 2003

Commentary

The article raises several interesting points. The first is that income inequality in Zimbabwe has increased in the last several years. The second is that income inequality is relatively less important than wealth inequality. The third point the article makes is that the government has a responsibility for reducing inequality. What should we make of these arguments?

Income inequality does indeed seem to have increased since 1990. One outcome of a market economy is income inequality; those with the most valued resources gain the most income. During periods when economies are growing and more and more countries are embracing a market economy as opposed to a government economy, income inequality will widen. A growing economy with growing income inequality does not mean that the rich get richer and the poor get poorer. The poor also get richer; it is just that their income increases may be less than the increases experienced by the rich.

The article notes that wealth is more "concentrated" or more unequally distributed than "labour income." What does this mean? Labor income is generated by someone only for long as that person works. Wealth can be created by that person, by following generations, and essentially forever, if the wealth can be passed on from generation to generation (inherited). If everyone had the same wealth but different incomes, how long would it take for wealth to be distributed unequally? Wealth is created with income that is saved: if incomes are not sufficiently high for individuals to save, then it is difficult to create wealth. Thus, if incomes are unequally distributed and if only the upper 50 percent can save, then fewer will have wealth than have income.

The article suggests that government measures to reduce inequality are necessary because inequality is linked to "fairness and social justice." Whether this justification is valid is not within the purview of economics to say; economists argue that fairness and social justice are in the eye of the beholder, or are normative judgments. Economists attempt to focus on the positive rather than the normative. The article also notes that inequality can increase political conflict and reduce social cohesion. Evidence does not necessarily support this statement. There are cases where social unrest occurs when inequality is large, but it also arises under totalitarian governments even when inequality is minor.

The primary point of the article is that inequality of incomes and wealth among and within countries exists and is unlikely to ever disappear. Moreover, the argument that inequality is bad is not necessarily an economic one; some inequality is necessarily the result of a booming economy. If all of a nation's citizens are better off or their standards of living are higher, does it matter whether economic inequality exists? Is someone who is poor in the United States worse or better off than the average citizen in sub-Saharan Africa?

Part Eight

Issues in International Trade and Finance

CHAPTER 35 | World Trade Equilibrium

? Fundamental Questions

1. **What are the prevailing patterns of trade between countries? What goods are traded?**

2. **What determines the goods a nation will export?**

3. **How are the equilibrium price and the quantity of goods traded determined?**

4. **What are the sources of comparative advantage?**

The United States's once-dominant position as an exporter of color television sets has since been claimed by nations like Japan and Taiwan. What caused this change? Is it because Japan specializes in the export of high-tech equipment? If countries tend to specialize in the export of particular kinds of goods, why does the United States import Heineken beer at the same time it exports Budweiser? This chapter will examine the volume of world trade and the nature of trade linkages between countries. As you saw in Chapter 2, trade occurs because of specialization in production. No single individual or country can produce everything better than others can. The result is specialization of production based on comparative advantage. Remember that comparative advantage is in turn based on relative opportunity costs: a country will specialize in the production of those goods for which its opportunity costs of production are lower than the costs in other countries. Nations then trade what they produce in excess of their own consumption to acquire other things that they want to consume. In this chapter, we will go a step further and discuss the sources of comparative advantage. We will look at why one country has

a comparative advantage in, say, automobile production, while another country has a comparative advantage in wheat production.

The world equilibrium price and quantity traded are derived from individual countries' demand and supply curves. This relationship between the world trade equilibrium and individual country markets will be utilized in the chapter on "International Trade Restrictions" to discuss the ways in which countries can interfere with free international trade to achieve their own economic or political goals. ■

1. An Overview of World Trade

?

1. **What are the prevailing patterns of trade between countries? What goods are traded?**

Trade occurs because it makes people better off. International trade occurs because it makes people better off than they would be if they could consume only domestically produced products. Who trades with whom, and what sorts of goods are traded? These are the questions we consider first, before investigating the underlying reasons for trade.

1.a. The Direction of Trade

Table 1 shows patterns of trade between two large groups of countries: the industrial countries and the developing countries. The industrial countries include all of western Europe, Japan, Australia, New Zealand, Canada, and the United States. The developing countries are, essentially, the rest of the world. Table 1 shows the dollar values and percentages of total trade between these groups of countries. The vertical column at the left lists the origin of exports, and the horizontal row at the top lists the destination of imports.

Trade between industrial countries accounts for the majority of international trade.

As Table 1 shows, trade between industrial countries accounts for the bulk of international trade. Trade between industrial countries is a little more than $2.8 trillion in value and amounts to 46 percent of world trade. Exports from industrial countries to developing countries represent 18 percent of total world trade. Exports from developing countries to industrial countries account for 21 percent of total trade, while exports from the developing countries to other developing countries currently represent only 15 percent of international trade.

Table 2 lists the major trading partners of selected countries and the percentage of total exports and imports accounted for by each country's top ten trading partners. For instance, 23 percent of U.S. exports went to Canada, and 10 percent of U.S.

TABLE 1

The Direction of Trade (in billions of dollars and percentages of world trade)

Origin	Destination	
	Industrial Countries	Developing Countries
Industrial countries	$2,806	$1,079
	46%	18%
Developing countries	$1,270	$926
	21%	15%

Source: Table is created from data found in International Monetary Fund, *Direction of Trade Statistics Quarterly,* March 2003.

TABLE 2

Major Trading Partners of Selected Countries

United States							
Exports		Imports					
Canada	23%	Canada	17%				
Mexico	14%	China	12%				
Japan	8%	Mexico	11%				
U.K.	5%	Japan	10%				
Germany	4%	Germany	5%				

Canada			
Exports		Imports	
U.S.	86%	U.S.	67%
Japan	3%	China	5%
U.K.	2%	Japan	4%
China	1%	Mexico	3%
France	1%	U.K.	2%

Germany			
Exports		Imports	
U.S.	10%	Netherlands	12%
France	10%	France	10%
U.K.	8%	Italy	7%
Italy	7%	U.K.	6%
Netherlands	7%	U.S.	6%

Mexico			
Exports		Imports	
U.S.	86%	U.S.	70%
Canada	3%	Germany	4%
Spain	1%	Japan	3%
Japan	1%	China	2%
Germany	1%	Korea	2%

Japan			
Exports		Imports	
U.S.	28%	China	18%
China	10%	U.S.	17%
Korea	7%	Korea	4%
Hong Kong	6%	Indonesia	4%
Singapore	3%	Australia	4%

United Kingdom			
Exports		Imports	
U.S.	16%	Germany	14%
Germany	12%	U.S.	11%
France	9%	France	8%
Ireland	7%	Netherlands	6%
Netherlands	7%	Belgium	5%

Source: Data for all countries from International Monetary Fund, *Direction of Trade Statistics Quarterly,* March 2003.

imports came from Japan. From a glance at the other countries listed in Table 2, it is clear that the United States is a major trading partner for many nations. This is true because of the size of the U.S. economy and the nation's relatively high level of income. It is also apparent that Canada and Mexico are very dependent on trade with the United States: 86 percent of Canada's exports and 67 percent of its imports, and 86 percent of Mexico's exports and 70 percent of its imports involve the United States. The dollar value of trade among the three North American nations is shown in Figure 1.

1.b. What Goods Are Traded?

The volume of trade in motor vehicles exceeds that of any other good.

Because countries differ in their comparative advantages, they will tend to export different goods. Countries also have different tastes and technological needs, and thus tend to differ in what they will import. Some goods are more widely traded than others, as Table 3 shows. Motor vehicles is the most heavily traded good in the

FIGURE 1

Merchandise Trade Flows in North America (billions of dollars)

In 2001, the United States exported $164 billion worth of goods to Canada and imported $220 billion of goods from Canada. The same year, U.S. merchandise exports to Mexico were $102 billion, while merchandise imports from Mexico were $133 billion.

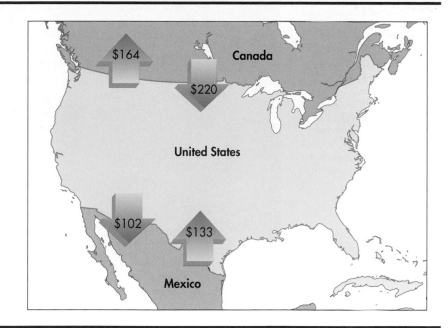

world, accounting for 5.33 percent of the total volume of world trade. Motor vehicles is followed by crude petroleum, transistors and valves, and data processing equipment. The top ten exported products, however, represent only 30 percent of world trade. The remaining 70 percent is distributed among a great variety of products. The importance of petroleum and motor vehicles in international trade should not obscure the fact that international trade involves all sorts of products from all over the world.

TABLE 3

Top Ten Exported Products (in millions of dollars and percentages of world exports)

Product Category	Value	Percentage of World Trade
Motor vehicles	$283,085	5.33%
Crude petroleum	$204,803	3.86%
Transistors, valves, etc.	$200,461	3.77%
Data processing equipment	$165,785	3.12%
Special transactions	$155,157	2.92%
Telecom equipment, parts	$149,807	2.82%
Motor vehicle parts	$129,347	2.44%
ADP machine parts	$117,477	2.21%
Aircraft	$109,921	2.07%
Medicinal, pharmaceutical products	$98,766	1.86%

Source: Data from U.N. Conference on Trade and Development, *Handbook of International Trade and Development Statistics, 2001* (TD/STAT.24), p. 158.

Comparative advantage is based on what a country can do relatively better than other countries. This photo shows a woman in Sri Lanka picking tea leaves. Sri Lanka is one of the few countries that export a significant amount of tea. Because of favorable growing conditions (a natural resource), these countries have a comparative advantage in tea production.

RECAP

1. Trade between industrial countries accounts for the bulk of international trade.
2. The most important trading partners of the United States are Canada, Mexico, and Japan.
3. Motor vehicles is the most heavily traded good in the world, in terms of value of exports.
4. World trade is distributed across a great variety of products.

2. An Example of International Trade Equilibrium

The international economy is very complex. Each country has a unique pattern of trade, in terms both of trading partners and of goods traded. Some countries trade a great deal, and others trade very little. We already know that countries specialize and trade according to comparative advantage, but what are the fundamental determinants of international trade that explain the pattern of comparative advantage?

The answer to this question will in turn provide a better understanding of some basic questions about how international trade functions: What goods will be traded? How much will be traded? What prices will prevail for traded goods?

2.a. Comparative Advantage

2. What determines the goods a nation will export?

Comparative advantage is found by comparing the relative costs of production in each country. We measure the cost of producing a particular good in two countries in terms of opportunity costs—what other goods must be given up in order to produce more of the good in question.

TABLE 4	Output per Worker per Day in Either Wheat or Cloth	
An Example of Comparative Advantage	U.S.	India
Wheat	8	4
Cloth	4	3

Table 4 presents a hypothetical example of two countries, the United States and India, that both produce two goods, wheat and cloth. The table lists the amounts of each good that could be produced by each worker. This example assumes that labor productivity differences alone determine comparative advantage. In the United States, a worker can produce either 8 units of wheat or 4 units of cloth. In India, a worker can produce 4 units of wheat or 3 units of cloth.

absolute advantage: an advantage derived from one country having a lower absolute input cost of producing a particular good than another country

The United States has an **absolute advantage**—greater productivity—in producing both wheat and cloth. Absolute advantage is determined by comparing the absolute productivity of producing each good in different countries. Since one worker can produce more of either good in the United States than in India, the United States is the more efficient producer of both goods.

It might seem that since the United States is the more efficient producer of both goods, there would be no need for trade with India. But absolute advantage is not the critical consideration. What matters in determining the benefits of international trade is comparative advantage, as originally discussed in Chapter 2. To find the **comparative advantage**—the lower opportunity cost—we must compare the opportunity cost of producing each good in each country.

comparative advantage: an advantage derived from comparing the opportunity costs of production in two countries

The opportunity cost of producing wheat is what must be given up in cloth using the same resources, like one worker per day. Look again at Table 4 to see the production of wheat and cloth in the two countries. Since one U.S. worker can produce 8 units of wheat or 4 units of cloth, if we take a worker from cloth production and move him to wheat production, we gain 8 units of wheat and lose 4 units of cloth. The opportunity cost of producing wheat equals $4/8$, or $1/2$, unit of cloth:

$$\frac{\text{Output of cloth given up}}{\text{Output of wheat gained}} = \begin{array}{l}\text{opportunity cost of} \\ \text{producing 1 unit of wheat} \\ \text{(in terms of cloth given up)}\end{array}$$

$$4/8 = 1/2$$

Applying the same thinking to India, we find that one worker can produce 4 units of wheat or 3 units of cloth. The opportunity cost of producing 1 unit of wheat in India is $3/4$ unit of cloth.

A comparison of the domestic opportunity costs in each country will reveal which one has the comparative advantage in producing each good. The U.S. opportunity cost of producing 1 unit of wheat is $1/2$ unit of cloth; the Indian opportunity cost is $3/4$ unit of cloth. Because the United States has a lower domestic opportunity cost, it has the comparative advantage in wheat production and will export wheat. Since wheat production costs are lower in the United States, India is better off trading for wheat rather than trying to produce it domestically.

The comparative advantage in cloth is found the same way. Taking a worker in the United States from wheat production and putting her in cloth production, we gain 4 units of cloth but lose 8 units of wheat per day. So the opportunity cost is

$$\frac{\text{Output of wheat given up}}{\text{Output of cloth gained}} = \begin{array}{l}\text{opportunity cost of}\\ \text{producing 1 unit of cloth}\\ \text{(in terms of wheat given up)}\end{array}$$

$$8/4 = 2$$

In India, moving a worker from wheat to cloth production means that we gain 3 units of cloth but lose 4 units of wheat, so the opportunity cost is $4/3$, or $1\frac{1}{3}$ units of wheat for 1 unit of cloth. Comparing the U.S. opportunity cost of 2 units of wheat with the Indian opportunity cost of $1\frac{1}{3}$ units, we see that India has the comparative advantage in cloth production and will therefore export cloth. In this case, the United States is better off trading for cloth rather than producing it, since India's costs of production are lower.

In international trade, as in other areas of economic decision making, it is opportunity cost that matters—and opportunity costs are reflected in comparative advantage. Absolute advantage is irrelevant, because knowing the absolute number of labor hours required to produce a good does not tell us if we can benefit from trade. We benefit from trade if we are able to obtain a good from a foreign country by giving up less than we would have to give up to obtain the good at home. Because only opportunity cost can allow us to make such comparisons, international trade proceeds on the basis of comparative advantage.

Countries export goods in which they have a comparative advantage.

2.b. Terms of Trade

On the basis of comparative advantage, India will specialize in cloth production and the United States will specialize in wheat production. The two countries will then trade with each other to satisfy the domestic demand for both goods. International trade permits greater consumption than would be possible from domestic production alone. Since countries trade when they can obtain a good more cheaply from a foreign producer than they can obtain it at home, international trade allows all traders to consume more. This is evident when we examine the terms of trade.

terms of trade: the amount of an exported good that must be given up to obtain an imported good

The **terms of trade** are the amount of an exported good that must be given up to obtain one unit of an imported good. The Global Business Insight "The Dutch Disease" provides a popular example of a dramatic shift in the terms of trade. As you saw earlier, comparative advantage dictates that the United States will specialize in wheat production and export wheat to India in exchange for Indian cloth. But the amount of wheat that the United States will exchange for a unit of cloth is limited by the domestic tradeoffs. If a unit of cloth can be obtained domestically for 2 units of wheat, the United States will be willing to trade with India only if the terms of trade are less than 2 units of wheat for a unit of cloth.

India, in turn, will be willing to trade its cloth for U.S. wheat only if it can receive a better price than its domestic opportunity costs. Since a unit of cloth in India costs $1\frac{1}{3}$ units of wheat, India will gain from trade if it can obtain more than $1\frac{1}{3}$ units of wheat for its cloth.

The limits of the terms of trade are determined by the opportunity costs in each country:

1 unit of cloth for more than $1\frac{1}{3}$ but less than 2 units of wheat

The Dutch Disease

The terms of trade are the amount of an export that must be given up to obtain a certain quantity of an import. The price of an import will be equal to its price in the foreign country of origin multiplied by the exchange rate (the domestic-currency price of foreign currency). As the exchange rate changes, the terms of trade will change. This can have important consequences for international trade.

A problem can arise when one export industry in an economy is booming relative to others. In the 1970s, for instance, the Netherlands experienced a boom in its natural gas industry. The dramatic energy price increases of the 1970s resulted in large Dutch exports of natural gas. Increased demand for exports from the Netherlands caused the Dutch currency to appreciate, making Dutch goods more expensive for foreign buyers. This situation caused the terms of trade to worsen for the Netherlands. Although the natural gas sector boomed, Dutch manufacturing was finding it difficult to compete in the world market.

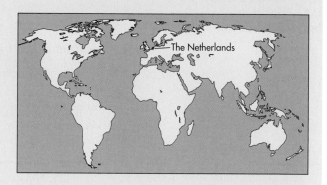

The phenomenon of a boom in one industry causing declines in the rest of the economy is popularly called the Dutch Disease. It is usually associated with dramatic increases in the demand for a primary commodity and can afflict any nation experiencing such a boom. For instance, a rapid rise in the demand for coffee could lead to a Dutch Disease problem for Colombia, where a coffee boom would be accompanied by decline in other sectors of the economy.

Within this range, the actual terms of trade will be decided by the bargaining power of the two countries. The closer the United States can come to giving up only $1\frac{1}{3}$ units of wheat for cloth, the better the terms of trade for the United States. The closer India can come to receiving 2 units of wheat for its cloth, the better the terms of trade for India.

Though each country would like to push the other as close to the limits of the terms of trade as possible, any terms within the limits set by domestic opportunity costs will be mutually beneficial. Both countries benefit because they are able to consume goods at a cost less than their domestic opportunity costs. To illustrate the *gains from trade,* let us assume that the actual terms of trade are 1 unit of cloth for $1\frac{1}{2}$ units of wheat.

Suppose the United States has 2 workers, one of whom goes to wheat production and the other to cloth production. This would result in U.S. production of 8 units of wheat and 4 units of cloth. Without international trade, the United States can produce and consume 8 units of wheat and 4 units of cloth. If the United States, with its comparative advantage in wheat production, chooses to produce only wheat, it can use both workers to produce 16 units. If the terms of trade are $1\frac{1}{2}$ units of wheat per unit of cloth, the United States can keep 8 units of wheat and trade the other 8 for $5\frac{1}{3}$ units of cloth (8 divided by $1\frac{1}{2}$). By trading U.S. wheat for Indian cloth, the United States is able to consume more than it could without trade. With no trade and half its labor devoted to each good, the United States could consume 8 units of wheat and 4 units of cloth. After trade, the United States consumes 8 units of wheat and $5\frac{1}{3}$ units of cloth. By devoting all its labor hours to wheat production and trading wheat for cloth, the United States gains $1\frac{1}{3}$ units of cloth. This is the gain from trade—an increase in consumption, as summarized in Table 5.

The gain from trade is increased consumption.

TABLE 5

Hypothetical Example of U.S. Gains from Specialization and Trade

Without International Trade
1 worker in wheat production: produce and consume 8 wheat
1 worker in cloth production: produce and consume 4 cloth

With Specialization and Trade
2 workers in wheat production: produce 16 wheat and consume 8; trade 8 wheat for 5 ⅓ cloth
Before trade: consume 8 wheat and 4 cloth
After trade: consume 8 wheat and 5 ⅓ cloth; gain 1 ⅓ cloth by specialization and trade

2.c. Export Supply and Import Demand

The preceding example suggests that countries benefit from specialization and trade. Realistically, however, countries do not completely specialize. Typically, domestic industries satisfy part of the domestic demand for goods that are also imported. To understand how the quantity of goods traded is determined, we must construct demand and supply curves for each country and use them to create export supply and import demand curves.

The proportion of domestic demand for a good that is satisfied by domestic production and the proportion that will be satisfied by imports are determined by the domestic supply and demand curves and the international equilibrium price of a good. The international equilibrium price and quantity may be determined once we know the export supply and import demand curves for each country. These curves are derived from the domestic supply and demand in each country. Figure 2 illustrates the derivation of the export supply and import demand curves.

Figure 2(a) shows the domestic supply and demand curves for the U.S. wheat market. The domestic equilibrium price is $6, and the domestic equilibrium quantity is 200 million bushels. (The domestic no-trade equilibrium price is the price that exists prior to international trade.) A price above $6 will yield a U.S. wheat surplus. For instance, at a price of $9, the U.S. surplus will be 200 million bushels. A price below equilibrium will produce a wheat shortage: at a price of $3, the shortage will be 200 million bushels. The key point here is that the world price of a good may be quite different from the domestic no-trade equilibrium price. And once international trade occurs, the world price will prevail in the domestic economy.

If the world price of wheat is different from a country's domestic no-trade equilibrium price, the country will become an exporter or an importer. For instance, if the world price is above the domestic no-trade equilibrium price, the domestic surplus can be exported to the rest of the world. Figure 2(b) shows the U.S. **export supply curve.** This curve illustrates the U.S. domestic surplus of wheat for prices above the domestic no-trade equilibrium price of $6. At a world price of $9, the United States would supply 200 million bushels of wheat to the rest of the world. The export supply is equal to the domestic surplus. The higher the world price above the domestic no-trade equilibrium, the greater the quantity of wheat exported by the United States.

export supply curve: a curve showing the relationship between the world price of a good and the amount that a country will export

FIGURE 2

The Import Demand and Export Supply Curves

Figures 2(a) and 2(c) show the domestic demand and supply curves for wheat in the United States and India, respectively. The domestic no-trade equilibrium price is $6 in the United States and $12 in India. Any price above the domestic no-trade equilibrium prices will create domestic surpluses, which are reflected in the export supply curves in Figures 2(b) and 2(d). Any price below the domestic no-trade equilibrium prices will create domestic shortages, which are reflected in the Import demand curves in Figures 2(b) and 2(d).

(a) U.S. Domestic Wheat Market

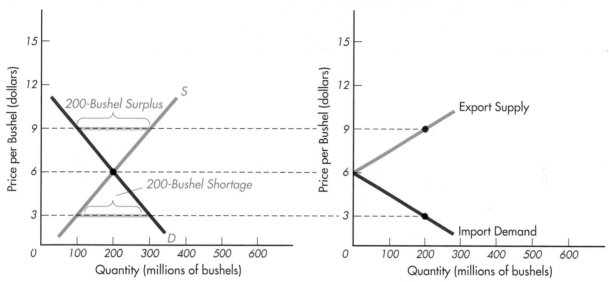

(b) U.S. Import Demand and Export Supply

(c) Indian Domestic Wheat Market

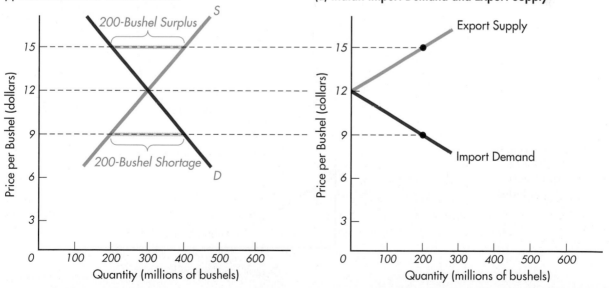

(d) Indian Import Demand and Export Supply

import demand curve:
a curve showing the relationship between the world price of a good and the amount that a country will import

If the world price of wheat is below the domestic no-trade equilibrium price, the United States will import wheat. The **import demand curve** is the amount of the U.S. shortage at various prices below the no-trade equilibrium. In Figure 2(b), the import demand curve is a downward-sloping line, indicating that the lower the price below the domestic no-trade equilibrium of $6, the greater the quantity of wheat imported by the United States. At a price of $3, the United States will import 200 million bushels.

The domestic supply and demand curves and the export supply and import demand curves for India appear in Figures 2(c) and (d). The domestic no-trade equilibrium price in India is $12. At this price, India would neither import nor export any wheat because the domestic demand would be satisfied by the domestic supply. The export supply curve for India is shown in Figure 2(d) as an upward-sloping line that measures the amount of the domestic surplus as the price level rises above the domestic no-trade equilibrium price of $12. According to Figure 2(c), if the world price of wheat is $15, the domestic surplus in India is equal to 200 million bushels. The corresponding point on the export supply curve indicates that at a price of $15, 200 million bushels will be exported. The import demand curve for India reflects the domestic shortage at a price below the domestic no-trade equilibrium price. At $9, the domestic shortage is equal to 200 million bushels: the import demand curve indicates that at $9, 200 million bushels will be imported.

2.d. The World Equilibrium Price and Quantity Traded

3. **How are the equilibrium price and the quantity of goods traded determined?**

The international equilibrium price of wheat and the quantity of wheat traded are found by combining the import demand and export supply curves for the United States and India, as in Figure 3. International equilibrium occurs if the quantity of imports demanded by one country is equal to the quantity of exports supplied by the other country. In Figure 3, this equilibrium occurs at the point labeled *e*. At this point, the import demand curve for India indicates that India wants to

---

FIGURE 3

International Equilibrium Price and Quantity

The international equilibrium price is the price at which the export supply curve of the United States intersects the import demand curve of India. At the equilibrium price of $9, the United States will export 200 million bushels to India.

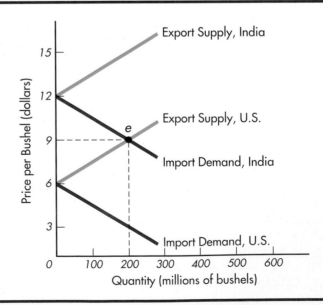

International equilibrium
occurs at the point where
the quantity of imports
demanded by one country
is equal to the quantity of
exports supplied by the
other country.

import 200 million bushels at a price of $9. The export supply curve for the United
States indicates that the United States wants to export 200 million bushels at a
price of $9. Only at $9 will the quantity of wheat demanded by the importing
nation equal the quantity of wheat supplied by the exporting nation. So the equilibrium world price of wheat is $9 and the equilibrium quantity of wheat traded is
200 million bushels.

RECAP

1. Comparative advantage is based on the relative opportunity costs of producing goods in different countries.

2. A country has an absolute advantage when it can produce a good more efficiently than can other nations.

3. A country has a comparative advantage when the opportunity cost of producing a good, in terms of forgone output of other goods, is lower than that of
   other nations.

4. The terms of trade are the amount of an export good that must be given up to
   obtain one unit of an import good.

5. The limits of the terms of trade are determined by the domestic opportunity
   costs of production in each country.

6. The export supply and import demand curves measure the domestic surplus
   and shortage, respectively, at different world prices.

7. International equilibrium occurs at the point where one country's import
   demand curve intersects with the export supply curve of another country.

**4. What are the
   sources of
   comparative
   advantage?**

3. Sources of Comparative Advantage

We know that countries specialize and trade in accordance with comparative
advantage, but what gives a country a comparative advantage? Economists have
suggested several theories of the source of comparative advantage. Let us review
these theories.

3.a. Productivity Differences

The example of comparative advantage earlier in this chapter showed the United
States to have a comparative advantage in wheat production and India to have
a comparative advantage in cloth production. Comparative advantage was determined by differences in the labor hours required to produce each good. In this example, differences in the *productivity* of labor accounted for comparative advantage.

Comparative advantage
due to productivity
differences between
countries is often called the
Ricardian model of
comparative advantage.

For over two hundred years, economists have argued that productivity differences
account for comparative advantage. In fact, this theory of comparative advantage is
often called the *Ricardian model,* after David Ricardo, a nineteenth-century English
economist who explained and analyzed the idea of productivity-based comparative
advantage. Variation in the productivity of labor can explain many observed trade
patterns in the world.

Although we know that labor productivity differs across countries—and that this can help explain why countries produce the goods they do—there are factors other than labor productivity that determine comparative advantage. Furthermore, even if labor productivity were all that mattered, we would still want to know why some countries have more productive workers than others. The standard interpretation of the Ricardian model is that technological differences between countries account for differences in labor productivity. The countries with the most advanced technology would have a comparative advantage with regard to those goods that can be produced most efficiently with modern technology.

3.b. Factor Abundance

Goods differ in terms of the resources, or factors of production, required for their production. Countries differ in terms of the abundance of different factors of production: land, labor, capital, and entrepreneurial ability. It seems self-evident that countries would have an advantage in producing those goods that use relatively large amounts of their most abundant factor of production. Certainly countries with a relatively large amount of farmland would have a comparative advantage in agriculture, and countries with a relatively large amount of capital would tend to specialize in the production of manufactured goods.

Comparative advantage based on differences in the abundance of factors of production across countries is described in the Heckscher-Ohlin model.

The idea that comparative advantage is based on the relative abundance of factors of production is sometimes called the *Heckscher-Ohlin model,* after the two Swedish economists, Eli Heckscher and Bertil Ohlin, who developed the original argument. The original model assumed that countries possess only two factors of production: labor and capital. Thus, researchers have examined the labor and capital requirements of various industries to see whether labor-abundant countries export goods whose production is relatively labor-intensive, and capital-abundant countries export goods that are relatively capital-intensive. In many cases, factor abundance has served well as an explanation of observed trade patterns. However, there remain cases in which comparative advantage seems to run counter to the predictions of the factor-abundance theory. In response, economists have suggested other explanations for comparative advantage.

3.c. Other Theories of Comparative Advantage

New theories of comparative advantage have typically come about in an effort to explain the trade pattern in some narrow category of products. They are not intended to serve as general explanations of comparative advantage, as do factor abundance and productivity. These supplementary theories emphasize human skills, product life cycles, and preferences.

Human Skills This approach emphasizes differences across countries in the availability of skilled and unskilled labor. The basic idea is that countries with a relatively abundant stock of highly skilled labor will have a comparative advantage in producing goods that require relatively large amounts of skilled labor. This theory is similar to the factor-abundance theory, except that here the analysis rests on two segments (skilled and unskilled) of the labor factor.

The human-skills argument is consistent with the observation that most U.S. exports are produced in high-wage (skilled-labor) industries and most U.S. imports are products produced in relatively low-wage industries. Since the United States has a well-educated labor force, relative to many other countries, we would expect the United States to have a comparative advantage in industries requiring a large amount of skilled labor. Developing countries would be expected to have a comparative advantage in industries requiring a relatively large amount of unskilled labor.

Product Life Cycles   This theory explains how comparative advantage in a specific good can shift from one country to another over time. This occurs because goods experience a *product life cycle.* At the outset, development and testing are required to conceptualize and design the product. For this reason, the early production will be undertaken by an innovative firm. Over time, however, a successful product tends to become standardized, in the sense that many manufacturers can produce it. The mature product may be produced by firms that do little or no research and development, specializing instead in copying successful products invented and developed by others.

Manufactured goods have life cycles. At first they are produced by the firm that invented them. Later, they may be produced by firms in other countries that copy the technology of the innovator.

The product-life-cycle theory is related to international comparative advantage in that a new product will first be produced and exported by the nation in which it was invented. As the product is exported elsewhere and foreign firms become familiar with it, the technology is copied in other countries by foreign firms seeking to produce a competing version. As the product matures, comparative advantage shifts away from the country of origin if other countries have lower manufacturing costs using the now-standardized technology.

The history of color television production shows how comparative advantage can shift over the product life cycle. Color television was invented in the United States, and U.S. firms initially produced and exported color TVs. Over time, as the technology of color television manufacturing became well known, countries like Japan and Taiwan came to dominate the business. Firms in these countries had a comparative advantage over U.S. firms in the manufacture of color televisions. Once the technology is widely available, countries with lower production costs, due to lower wages, can compete effectively against the higher-wage nation that developed the technology.

Preferences   The theories of comparative advantage we have looked at so far have all been based on supply factors. It may be, though, that the demand side of the market can explain some of the patterns observed in international trade. Different producers' goods are seldom exactly identical. Consumers may prefer the goods of one firm to those of another firm. Domestic firms usually produce goods to satisfy domestic consumers. But since different consumers have different preferences, some consumers will prefer goods produced by foreign firms. International trade allows consumers to expand their consumption opportunities.

Consumers who live in countries with similar levels of development can be expected to have similar consumption patterns. The consumption patterns of consumers in countries at much different levels of development are much less similar. This would suggest that firms in industrial countries will find a larger market for their goods in other industrial countries than in developing countries.

As you saw earlier in this chapter, industrial countries tend to trade with other industrial countries. This pattern runs counter to the factor-abundance theory of comparative advantage, which would suggest that countries with the most dissimilar endowments of resources would find trade most beneficial. Yet rich countries, with large supplies of capital and skilled labor forces, trade more actively with other rich countries than they do with poor countries. Firms in industrial countries tend to produce goods that relatively wealthy consumers will buy. The key point here is that

FIGURE 4

Theories of Comparative Advantage

Several theories exist that explain comparative advantage: labor productivity, factor abundance, human skills, product life cycles, and preferences.

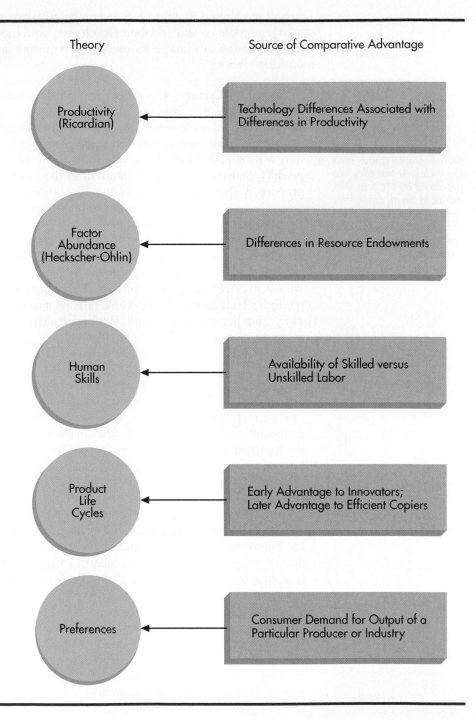

Theory

Source of Comparative Advantage

Productivity (Ricardian) — Technology Differences Associated with Differences in Productivity

Factor Abundance (Heckscher-Ohlin) — Differences in Resource Endowments

Human Skills — Availability of Skilled versus Unskilled Labor

Product Life Cycles — Early Advantage to Innovators; Later Advantage to Efficient Copiers

Preferences — Consumer Demand for Output of a Particular Producer or Industry

we do not live in a world based on simple comparative advantage, in which all cloth is identical, regardless of the producer. We inhabit a world of differentiated products, and consumers want choices between different brands or styles of a seemingly similar good.

Another feature of international trade that may be explained by consumer preference is **intraindustry trade,** a circumstance in which a country both exports and imports goods in the same industry. The fact that the United States exports Budweiser beer and imports Heineken beer is not surprising when preferences are taken into account. Supply-side theories of comparative advantage rarely provide an explanation of intraindustry trade, since they would expect each country to export only those goods produced in industries in which a comparative advantage exists. Yet the real world is characterized by a great deal of intraindustry trade.

We have discussed several potential sources of comparative advantage: labor productivity, factor abundance, human skills, product cycles, and preferences. Each of these theories, which are summarized in Figure 4, has proven useful in understanding certain trade patterns. Each has also been shown to have limitations as a general theory applicable to all cases. Once again we are reminded that the world is a very complicated place. Theories are simpler than reality. Nevertheless, they help us to understand how comparative advantage arises.

intraindustry trade: the simultaneous import and export of goods in the same industry by a particular country

RECAP

1. Comparative advantage can arise because of differences in labor productivity.

2. Countries differ in their resource endowments, and a given country may enjoy a comparative advantage in products that intensively use its most abundant factor of production.

3. Industrial countries may have a comparative advantage in products requiring a large amount of skilled labor. Developing countries may have a comparative advantage in products requiring a large amount of unskilled labor.

4. Comparative advantage in a new good initially resides in the country that invented the good. Over time, other nations learn the technology and may gain a comparative advantage in producing the good.

5. In some industries, consumer preferences for differentiated goods may explain international trade flows, including intraindustry trade.

Summary

❓ What are the prevailing patterns of trade between countries? What goods are traded?

1. International trade flows largely between industrial countries. *§1.a*

2. International trade involves many diverse products. *§1.b*

❓ What determines the goods a nation will export?

3. Comparative advantage is based on the opportunity costs of production. *§2.a*

4. Domestic opportunity costs determine the limits of the terms of trade between two countries—that is, the

amount of exports that must be given up to obtain imports. *§2.b*

5. The export supply curve shows the domestic surplus and amount of exports available at alternative world prices. *§2.c*

6. The import demand curve shows the domestic shortage and amount of imports demanded at alternative world prices. *§2.c*

? How are the equilibrium price and the quantity of goods traded determined?

7. The international equilibrium price and quantity of a good traded are determined by the intersection of the

export supply of one country with the import demand of another country. *§2.d*

? What are the sources of comparative advantage?

8. The productivity-differences and factor-abundance theories of comparative advantage are general theories that seek to explain patterns of international trade flow. *§3.a, 3.b*

9. Other theories of comparative advantage aimed at explaining trade in particular kinds of goods focus on human skills, product life cycles, and consumer preferences. *§3.c*

Key Terms

absolute advantage *§2.a*

comparative advantage *§2.a*

terms of trade *§2.b*

export supply curve *§2.c*

import demand curve *§2.c*

intraindustry trade *§3.c*

Exercises

1. Why must voluntary trade between two countries be mutually beneficial?

Use the following table for exercises 2–6.

Amount of Beef or Computers Produced by One Worker in a Day

	Canada	Japan
Beef	6	5
Computers	2	4

2. Which country has the absolute advantage in beef production?

3. Which country has the absolute advantage in computer production?

4. Which country has the comparative advantage in beef production?

5. Which country has the comparative advantage in computer production?

6. What are the limits of the terms of trade? Specifically, when is Canada willing to trade with Japan, and when is Japan willing to trade with Canada?

7. Use the following supply and demand schedule for two countries to determine the international equilibrium price of shoes. How many shoes will be traded?

Demand and Supply of Shoes (1,000s)

	Mexico		Chile	
Price	Qty. Demanded	Qty. Supplied	Qty. Demanded	Qty. Supplied
$10	40	0	50	0
$20	35	20	40	10
$30	30	40	30	20
$40	25	60	20	30
$50	20	80	10	40

8. How would each of the following theories of comparative advantage explain the fact that the United States exports computers?
   a. Productivity differences
   b. Factor abundance
   c. Human skills
   d. Product life cycle
   e. Preferences

9. Which of the theories of comparative advantage could explain why the United States exports computers to Japan at the same time that it imports computers from Japan? Explain.

10. Developing countries have complained that the terms of trade they face are unfavorable. If they voluntarily engage in international trade, what do you suppose they mean by "unfavorable terms of trade"?

11. If two countries reach equilibrium in their domestic markets at the same price, what can be said about their export supply and import demand curves and about the international trade equilibrium?

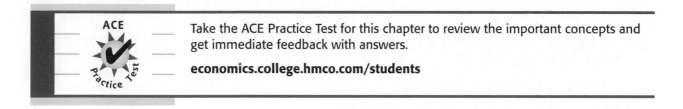

Take the ACE Practice Test for this chapter to review the important concepts and get immediate feedback with answers.

economics.college.hmco.com/students

China Trade Will Come Back to Haunt Us

I don't know who came first in the recent race in Buffalo, but the winner, clearly, was China. Practically all of the people who ran were clad in footwear that was "Made in China." . . .

It is increasingly difficult to find hard goods that are not made in China. The list would include all toys, nearly all hand tools, kitchen utensils, small kitchen appliances, some furniture, cameras, TV sets and air conditioners.

Barbie, the little girls' icon, used to be an American. No longer. Barbie is now a naturalized American—an immigrant from China. But "the unkindest cut of all" was my discovery that Lionel electric trains, as American as apple pie, are now being made in China. Is nothing sacred?

In the recent fuss at the World Trade Organization meeting in Seattle, organized labor was a prominent portion of the opposition to China's admission to the WTO. Isn't there a bit of hypocrisy here? How did all those boxes from China get unloaded from the ships onto the wharves? Then how did they move into tractor-trailers and into the distribution warehouses in the nation's interior? The answer: The "almighty buck" rules. So long as the price is right, merchants will stock these items and consumers will take them from the shelves. And China will flourish at the expense of American workers.

I've been through this before. I suppose it's useless to tell people to take a long look at the consequences of their actions. It seems it's the immediate future that counts most.

China is a threat. Let's not fund that nation. It's too late to boycott the stores that sell items "made in China"—there are practically no alternatives. An embargo is the only real solution.

Source: "China Trade Will Come Back to Haunt Us," *Buffalo News*, August 15, 2000, p. 3B. Copyright 2000. *Buffalo News.*

Buffalo News/August 15, 2000

There is no lack of stories in the U.S. media on the threat of foreign economic domination. As this article indicates, many people point to the large U.S. trade deficit with China as evidence that a problem exists.

However, the bilateral trade accounts provide little, if any, information on such issues. Indeed, it is easy to think of an example in which a country has a persistent trade deficit with one of its trading partners but has its overall trade account in balance. Suppose there are three countries that trade among themselves, which we will call countries A, B, and C. The people of each country produce only one type of good and consume only one other type of good. The people of country A produce apples and consume bananas, the people of country B produce bananas and consume cucumbers, and the people of country C produce cucumbers and consume apples. Even when the trade account of each country is balanced, each has a deficit with one of its trading partners and a surplus with the other. Furthermore, a larger trade deficit between countries A and B (with each country retaining balanced trade) implies that the people of country A are better off, since they are consuming more. If the government of country A tried to impose a law forcing bilateral trade balance with country B, citizens of country A could not consume as many bananas as before and would be forced to attempt to sell apples to the uninterested citizens of country B.

This simple example demonstrates that the U.S. trade deficit with China should not in itself be a

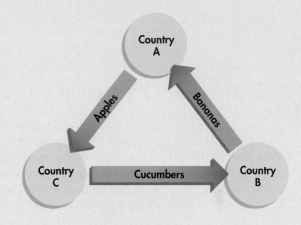

cause for concern. The United States could have a persistent trade deficit with China and yet maintain an overall balanced trade account. In fact, any country would be expected to have a trade deficit with some countries and a trade surplus with others. This reflects comparative advantage. Trade between countries makes both the exporting and the importing countries better off.

This is not to say that concern about the overall trade deficit is not well founded. An overall trade deficit indicates that a country is consuming more than it is producing. At any particular time, a country may want to run a trade deficit or a trade surplus, depending on the circumstances it faces. But regardless of the overall trade account of a country, we should expect bilateral trade imbalances among trading partners.

CHAPTER 36

International Trade Restrictions

1. Why do countries restrict international trade?

2. How do countries restrict the entry of foreign goods and promote the export of domestic goods?

3. What sorts of agreements do countries enter into to reduce barriers to international trade?

The Japanese government once announced that foreign-made skis would not be allowed into Japan because they were unsafe. Japanese ski manufacturers were active supporters of the ban. The U.S. government once imposed a tax of almost 50 percent on imports of motorcycles with engines larger than 700 cc. The only U.S.-owned motorcycle manufacturer, Harley-Davidson, produced no motorcycles with engines smaller than 1,000 cc and so did not care about the small-engine market. In the mid-1980s, Britain began replacing the distinctive red steel telephone booths that were used all through the country with new booths. Many U.S. residents were interested in buying an old British phone booth to use as a decorative novelty, so the phone booths were exported to the United States. However, when the phone booths arrived, the U.S. Customs Service impounded them because there was a limit on the amount of iron and steel products that could be exported from Britain to the United States. The phone booths would be allowed to enter the country only if British exports of some other iron and steel products were reduced. The British exporters protested the classification of the phone booths as iron and steel products

and argued that they should be considered antiques (which have no import restrictions). The phone booths were not reclassified, and as a result, few have entered the United States, and prices of old British phone booths have been in the thousands of dollars. There are many examples of government policy influencing the prices and quantities of goods that are traded internationally.

International trade is rarely determined solely by comparative advantage and the free market forces of supply and demand. Governments often find that political pressures favor policies that at least partially offset the prevailing comparative advantages. Government policy aimed at influencing international trade flows is called **commercial policy.** This chapter first examines the arguments in support of commercial policy and then discusses the various tools of commercial policy employed by governments. ■

commercial policy: government policy that influences international trade flows

1. **Why do countries restrict international trade?**

1. Arguments for Protection

Governments restrict foreign trade to protect domestic producers from foreign competition. In some cases the protection may be justified; in most cases it harms consumers. Of the arguments used to promote such protection, only a few are valid. We will look first at arguments that are widely considered to have little or no merit, and then at those that may sometimes be valid.

International trade on the basis of comparative advantage maximizes world output and allows consumers access to better-quality products at lower prices than would be available in the domestic market alone. If trade is restricted, consumers pay higher prices for lower-quality goods, and world output declines. Protection from foreign competition imposes costs on the domestic economy as well as on foreign producers. When production does not proceed on the basis of comparative advantage, resources are not expended on their most efficient uses. Whenever government restrictions alter the pattern of trade, we should expect someone to benefit and someone else to suffer. Generally speaking, protection from foreign competition benefits domestic producers at the expense of domestic consumers.

Protection from foreign competition generally benefits domestic producers at the expense of domestic consumers.

1.a. Creation of Domestic Jobs

If foreign goods are kept out of the domestic economy, it is often argued, jobs will be created at home. This argument holds that domestic firms will produce the goods that otherwise would have been produced abroad, thus employing domestic workers instead of foreign workers. The weakness of this argument is that only the protected industry will benefit in terms of employment. Since domestic consumers will pay higher prices to buy the output of the protected industry, they will have less to spend on other goods and services, which could cause employment in other industries to drop. If other countries retaliate by restricting the entry of U.S. exports, the output of U.S. firms that produce for export will fall as well. Typically, restrictions to "save domestic jobs" simply redistribute jobs by creating employment in the protected industry and reducing employment elsewhere.

Table 1 shows estimates of consumer costs and producer gains associated with protection in certain Japanese and U.S. industries. The first column lists the total cost to domestic consumers, in terms of higher prices paid, for each industry. For instance, the consumer cost of protecting the U.S. food and beverage industry is $2,947 million. The second column lists the cost to consumers of saving one job in each industry (found by dividing the total consumer cost by the number of jobs

TABLE 1

Benefits and Costs of Protection from Foreign Competition in Japan and the United States

	Consumer Costs		Producer Gains
	Total (million U.S. dollars)	Per Job Saved (U.S. dollars)	(million U.S. dollars)
Japan			
Food and beverages	58,394	762,000	43,210
Textiles and light industry	8,979	485,000	3,341
Metals	5,162	974,000	2,546
Chemical products	15,500	2,385,000	8,466
Machinery	21,587	287,000	12,286
United States			
Food and beverages	2,947	488,000	1,775
Textiles and light industry	26,443	148,000	12,242
Chemical products	484	942,000	222
Machinery	542	348,000	157

Sources: Data are drawn from Yoko Sazanimi, Shujiro Urata, and Hiroki Kawai, *Measuring the Costs of Protection in Japan* (Institute for International Economics, Washington, D.C., 1995); Gary C. Hulbauer and Kimberly Ann Elliott, *Measuring the Costs of Protection in the United States* (Institute for International Economics, Washington, D.C., 1994).

Saving domestic jobs from foreign competition may cost domestic consumers more than it benefits the protected industries.

saved by protection). In food and beverages, each job saved costs U.S. consumers $488,000. The gain to U.S. producers appears in the third column. Government protection of food and beverage firms allowed them to gain $1,775 million. This gain is less than the costs to consumers of $2,947 million. Note that this table reports data from studies in the mid 1990s. These are the most recent comprehensive studies of this subject, and the basic principle remains true today—restricting international trade may impose large costs on an economy.

Table 2 shows the annual cost to the United States of import restrictions in terms of reduced GDP as estimated by an agency of the U.S. government. The total estimated amount of $14,350 million means that U.S. GDP would be over $14 billion higher without import restrictions.

Tables 1 and 2 demonstrate the very high cost per job saved by protection. If the costs to consumers are greater than the benefits to the protected industries, you may wonder why government provides any protection aimed at saving jobs. The answer, in a word, is politics. Protection of the U.S. textile industry means that all consumers pay a higher price for clothing. But individual consumers do not know how much of the price they pay for clothes is due to protection, and consumers rarely lobby their political representatives to eliminate protection and reduce prices. Meanwhile, there is a great deal of pressure for protection. Employers and workers in the industry know the benefits of protection: higher prices for their output, higher profits for

TABLE 2

Annual Gain in U.S. GDP if U.S. Import Restrictions Were Eliminated

Sector	GDP Gain (million dollars)
Simultaneous liberalization of all restraints	14,350
Individual liberalization	
Textiles and apparel	13,040
Maritime transport (Jones Act)	656
Dairy	109
Sugar	420
Peanuts	2
Footwear	109
Ball and roller bearings, and parts	10
Costume jewelry and costume novelties	3
Frozen fruit, fruit juices, and vegetables	11
Ceramic wall and floor tile	3
Watches, clocks, watch cases, and parts	10
Table- and kitchenware	5

Source: *The Economic Effects of Significant U.S. Imports Restraints* (U.S. International Trade Commission, Washington, D.C., 2002), p. xviii.

owners, and higher wages for workers. As a result, there will be active lobbying for protection against foreign competition.

1.b. Creation of a "Level Playing Field"

Special interest groups sometimes claim that other nations that export successfully to the home market have unfair advantages over domestic producers. Fairness, however, is often in the eye of the beholder. People who call for creating a "level playing field" believe that the domestic government should take steps to offset the perceived advantage of the foreign firm. They often claim that foreign firms have an unfair advantage because foreign workers are willing to work for very low wages. "Fair trade, not free trade" is the cry that this claim generates. But advocates of fair trade are really claiming that production in accordance with comparative advantage is unfair. This is clearly wrong. A country with relatively low wages is typically a country with an abundance of low-skilled labor. Such a country will have a comparative advantage in products that use low-skilled labor most intensively. To create a "level playing field" by imposing restrictions that eliminate the comparative advantage of foreign firms will make domestic consumers worse off and undermine the basis for specialization and economic efficiency.

Calls for "fair trade" are typically aimed at imposing restrictions to match those imposed by other nations.

Some calls for "fair trade" are based on the notion of reciprocity. If a country imposes import restrictions on goods from a country that does not have similar restrictions, reciprocal tariffs and quotas may be called for in the latter country in order to stimulate a reduction of trade restrictions in the former country. For instance, it has been claimed that U.S. construction firms are discriminated against in Japan, because no U.S. firm has had a major construction project in Japan since the 1960s. Yet Japanese construction firms do billions of dollars' worth of business in the United States each year. Advocates of fair trade could argue that U.S. restrictions should be imposed on Japanese construction firms.

One danger of calls for fairness based on reciprocity is that calls for fair trade may be invoked in cases where, in fact, foreign restrictions on U.S. imports do not exist. For instance, suppose the U.S. auto industry wanted to restrict the entry of imported autos to help stimulate sales of domestically produced cars. One strategy might be to point out that U.S. auto sales abroad had fallen and to claim that this was due to unfair treatment of U.S. auto exports in other countries. Of course, there are many other possible reasons why foreign sales of U.S. autos might have fallen. But blaming foreign trade restrictions might win political support for restricting imports of foreign cars into the United States.

1.c. Government Revenue Creation

Developing countries often justify tariffs as an important source of government revenue.

Tariffs on trade generate government revenue. Industrial countries, which find income taxes easy to collect, rarely justify tariffs on the basis of the revenue they generate for government spending. But many developing countries find income taxes difficult to levy and collect, while tariffs are easy to collect. Customs agents can be positioned at ports of entry to examine all goods that enter and leave the country. The observability of trade flows makes tariffs a popular tax in developing countries, whose revenue requirements may provide a valid justification for their existence. Table 3 shows that tariffs account for a relatively large fraction of government revenue in many developing countries, and only a small fraction in industrial countries.

1.d. National Defense

Industries that are truly critical to the national defense should be protected from foreign competition if that is the only way to ensure their existence.

It has long been argued that industries that are crucial to the national defense, like shipbuilding, should be protected from foreign competition. Even though the United States does not have a comparative advantage in shipbuilding, a domestic shipbuilding industry is necessary, since foreign-made ships may not be available during war. This is a valid argument as long as the protected industry is genuinely critical to the national defense. In some industries, like copper or other basic metals,

TABLE 3		
Tariffs as a Percentage of Total Government Revenue	**Country**	**Tariffs as Percentage of Government Revenue**
	United Kingdom	0
	United States	1.0%
	Japan	1.2%
	Costa Rica	4.6%
	Ghana	26.8%
	Dominican Republic	42.8%
	Lesotho	47.7%

Source: International Monetary Fund, *Government Finance Statistics Yearbook,* Washington, D.C., 2002.

it might make more sense to import the crucial products during peacetime and store them for use in the event of war; these products do not require domestic production in order to be useful. Care must be taken to ensure that the national-defense argument is not used to protect industries other than those that are truly crucial to the nation's defense.

1.e. Infant Industries

Countries sometimes justify protecting new industries that need time to become competitive with the rest of the world.

Nations are often inclined to protect new industries on the basis that the protection will give those industries adequate time to develop. New industries need time to establish themselves and to become efficient enough that their costs are no higher than those of their foreign rivals. An alternative to protecting young and/or critical domestic industries with tariffs and quotas is to subsidize them. Subsidies allow such firms to charge lower prices and to compete with more-efficient foreign producers, while permitting consumers to pay the world price rather than the higher prices associated with tariffs or quotas on foreign goods.

Protecting an infant industry from foreign competition may make sense, but only until the industry matures. Once the industry achieves sufficient size, protection should be withdrawn, and the industry should be made to compete with its foreign counterparts. Unfortunately, such protection is rarely withdrawn, because the larger and more successful the industry becomes, the more political power it wields. In fact, if an infant industry truly has a good chance to become competitive and produce profitably once it is well established, it is not at all clear that government should even offer protection to reduce short-run losses. New firms typically incur losses, but they are only temporary if the firm is successful.

1.f. Strategic Trade Policy

strategic trade policy: the use of trade restrictions or subsidies to allow domestic firms with decreasing costs to gain a greater share of the world market

increasing-returns-to-scale industry: an industry in which the costs of producing a unit of output fall as more output is produced

Government can use trade policy as a strategy to stimulate production by a domestic industry capable of achieving increasing returns to scale.

There is another view of international trade that regards the description of comparative advantage presented in the previous chapter as misleading. According to this outlook, called **strategic trade policy,** international trade largely involves firms that pursue economies of scale—that is, firms that achieve lower costs per unit of production the more they produce. In contrast to the constant opportunity costs illustrated in the example of wheat and cloth in the chapter "World Trade Equilibrium," opportunity costs in some industries may fall with the level of output. Such **increasing-returns-to-scale industries** will tend to concentrate production in the hands of a few very large firms, rather than many competitive firms. Proponents of strategic trade policy contend that government can use tariffs or subsidies to allow domestic firms with decreasing costs an advantage over their foreign rivals.

A monopoly exists when there is only one producer in an industry and no close substitutes for the product exist. If the average costs of production decline with increases in output, then the larger a firm is, the lower its per unit costs will be. One large producer will be more efficient than many small ones. A simple example of a natural-monopoly industry will indicate how strategic trade policy can make a country better off. Suppose that the production of buses is an industry characterized by increasing returns to scale and that there are only two firms capable of producing buses: Volkswagen in Germany and General Motors in the United States. If both firms produce buses, their costs will be so high that both will experience losses. If only one of the two produces buses, however, it will be able to sell buses both at home and abroad, creating a level of output that allows the firm to earn a profit.

Assume further that a monopoly producer will earn $100 million and that if both firms produce, they will each lose $5 million. Obviously, a firm that doesn't produce earns nothing. Which firm will produce? Because of the decreasing-cost nature of the industry, the firm that is the first to produce will realize lower costs and be able to preclude the other firm from entering the market. But strategic trade policy can alter the market in favor of the domestic firm.

Suppose Volkswagen is the world's only producer of buses. General Motors does not produce them. The U.S. government could offer General Motors an $8 million subsidy to produce buses. General Motors would then enter the bus market, since the $8 million subsidy would more than offset the $5 million loss it would suffer by entering the market. Volkswagen would sustain losses of $5 million once General Motors entered. Ultimately, Volkswagen would stop producing buses to avoid the loss, and General Motors would have the entire market and earn $100 million plus the subsidy.

Strategic trade policy is aimed at offsetting the increasing-returns-to-scale advantage enjoyed by foreign producers and at stimulating production in domestic industries capable of realizing decreasing costs. One practical problem for government is the need to understand the technology of different industries and to forecast accurately the subsidy needed to induce domestic firms to produce new products. A second problem is the likelihood of retaliation by the foreign government. If the U.S. government subsidizes General Motors in its attack on the bus market, the German government is likely to subsidize Volkswagen rather than lose the entire bus market to a U.S. producer. As a result, taxpayers in both nations will be subsidizing two firms, each producing too few buses to earn a profit.

RECAP

1. Government restrictions on foreign trade are usually aimed at protecting domestic producers from foreign competition.

2. Import restrictions may save domestic jobs, but the costs to consumers may be greater than the benefits to those who retain their jobs.

3. Advocates of "fair trade," or the creation of a "level playing field," call for import restrictions as a means of lowering foreign restrictions on markets for domestic exports.

4. Tariffs are an important source of revenue in many developing countries.

5. The national-defense argument in favor of trade restrictions is that protection from foreign competition is necessary to ensure that certain key defense-related industries continue to produce.

6. The infant-industries argument in favor of trade restriction is to allow a new industry a period of time in which to become competitive with its foreign counterparts.

7. Strategic trade policy is intended to provide domestic increasing-returns-to-scale industries with an advantage over their foreign competitors.

2. Tools of Commercial Policy

? 2. How do countries restrict the entry of foreign goods and promote the export of domestic goods?

Commercial policy makes use of several tools, including tariffs, quotas, subsidies, and nontariff barriers like health and safety regulations that restrict the entry of foreign products. Since 1945, barriers to trade have been reduced. Much of the progress toward free trade may be linked to the *General Agreement on Tariffs and Trade,* or *GATT,* which began in 1947. In 1995, the *World Trade Organization (WTO)* was

Smoot-Hawley Tariff

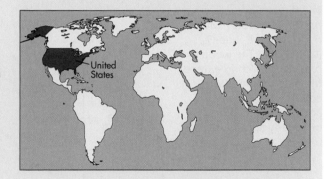

Many economists believe that the Great Depression of the 1930s was at least partly due to the Smoot-Hawley Tariff Act, signed into law by President Herbert Hoover in 1930. Hoover had promised that, if elected, he would raise tariffs on agricultural products to raise U.S. farm income. Congress began work on the tariff increases in 1928. Congressman Willis Hawley and Senator Reed Smoot conducted the hearings.

In testimony before Congress, manufacturers and other special interest groups also sought protection from foreign competition. The resulting bill increased tariffs on over 12,000 products. Tariffs reached their highest levels ever, about 60 percent of average import values. Only twice before in U.S. history had tariffs approached the levels of the Smoot-Hawley era.

Before President Hoover signed the bill, 38 foreign governments made formal protests, warning that they would retaliate with high tariffs on U.S. products. A petition signed by 1,028 economists warned of the harmful effects of the bill. Nevertheless, Hoover signed the bill into law.

World trade collapsed as other countries raised their tariffs in response. Between 1930 and 1931, U.S. imports fell 29 percent, but U.S. exports fell 33 percent. By 1933, world trade was about one-third of its 1929 level. As the level of trade fell, so did income and prices. In 1934, in an effort to correct the mistakes of Smoot-Hawley, Congress passed the Reciprocal Trade Agreements Act, which allowed the president to lower U.S. tariffs in return for reductions in foreign tariffs on U.S. goods. This act ushered in the modern era of relatively low tariffs. In the United States today, tariffs are about 5 percent of the average value of imports.

Many economists believe that the collapse of world trade and the Depression were linked by a decrease in real income caused by abandoning production based on comparative advantage. Few economists argue that the Great Depression was caused solely by the Smoot-Hawley tariff, but the experience serves as a lesson to those who support higher tariffs to protect domestic producers.

---

formed to incorporate the agreements under GATT into a formal permanent international organization to oversee world trade. The WTO has three objectives: to help global trade flow as freely as possible, to achieve reductions in trade restrictions gradually through negotiation, and to provide an impartial means of settling disputes. Nevertheless, restrictions on trade still exist, and this section will review the most commonly used restrictions.

2.a. Tariffs

tariff: a tax on imports or exports

A **tariff** is a tax on imports or exports. Every country imposes tariffs on at least some imports. Some countries also impose tariffs on selected exports as a means of raising government revenue. Brazil, for instance, taxes coffee exports. The United States does not employ export tariffs, which are forbidden by the U.S. Constitution.

Tariffs are frequently imposed in order to protect domestic producers from foreign competition. The dangers of imposing tariffs are well illustrated in the Global Business Insight "Smoot-Hawley Tariff." The effect of a tariff is illustrated in Figure 1, which shows the domestic market for oranges. Without international trade, the domestic equilibrium price, P_d, and the quantity demanded, Q_d, are determined by the intersection of

FIGURE 1

The Effects of a Tariff

The domestic equilibrium price and quantity with no trade are P_d and Q_d, respectively. The world price is P_w. With free trade, therefore, imports will equal $Q_2 - Q_1$. A tariff added to the world price reduces imports to $Q_4 - Q_3$.

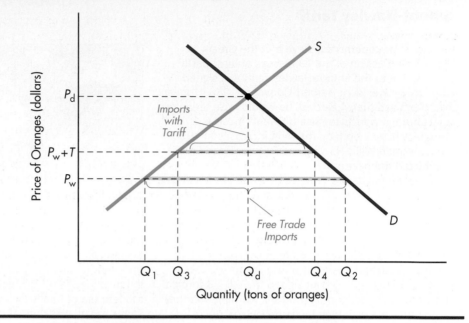

the domestic demand and supply curves. If the world price of oranges, P_w, is lower than the domestic equilibrium price, this country will import oranges. The quantity imported will be the difference between the quantity Q_1 produced domestically at a price of P_w and the quantity Q_2 demanded domestically at the world price of oranges.

When the world price of the traded good is lower than the domestic equilibrium price without international trade, free trade causes domestic production to fall and domestic consumption to rise. The domestic shortage at the world price is met by imports. Domestic consumers are better off, since they can buy more at a lower price. But domestic producers are worse off, since they now sell fewer oranges and receive a lower price.

Suppose a tariff of T (the dollar value of the tariff) is imposed on orange imports. The price paid by consumers is now $P_w + T$, rather than P_w. At this higher price, domestic producers will produce Q_3 and domestic consumers will purchase Q_4. The tariff has the effect of increasing domestic production and reducing domestic consumption, relative to the free trade equilibrium. Imports fall accordingly, from $Q_2 - Q_1$ to $Q_4 - Q_3$.

Domestic producers are better off, since the tariff has increased their sales of oranges and raised the price they receive. Domestic consumers pay higher prices for fewer oranges than they would with free trade, but they are still better off than they would be without trade. If the tariff had raised the price paid by consumers to P_d, there would be no trade, and the domestic equilibrium quantity, Q_d, would prevail.

The government earns revenue from imports of oranges. If each ton of oranges generates tariff revenue of T, the total tariff revenue to the government is found by multiplying the tariff by the quantity of oranges imported. In Figure 1, this amount is $T \times (Q_4 - Q_3)$. As the tariff changes, so do the quantity of imports and the government revenue.

2.b. Quotas

quantity quota: a limit on the amount of a good that may be imported

value quota: a limit on the monetary value of a good that may be imported

Quotas are limits on the quantity or value of goods imported and exported. A **quantity quota** restricts the physical amount of a good. For instance, for 2003, the United States allowed only 1.1 million tons of sugar to be imported. Even though the United States is not a competitive sugar producer compared to other nations like the Dominican Republic or Cuba, the quota allowed U.S. firms to produce about 6 percent of the world's sugar output. A **value quota** restricts the monetary value of a good that may be traded. Instead of a physical quota on sugar, the United States could have limited the dollar value of sugar imports.

Quotas are used to protect domestic producers from foreign competition. By restricting the amount of a good that may be imported, they increase the price of that good and allow domestic producers to sell more at a higher price than they would with free trade. For example, one effect of the U.S. sugar quota is a higher sugar price for U.S. consumers. In 2003, the world price of sugar was about $.07 per pound, but the U.S. price was about $.21 per pound.

Figure 2 illustrates the effect of a quota on the domestic orange market. The domestic equilibrium supply and demand curves determine the equilibrium price and quantity without trade to be P_d and 250 tons, respectively. The world price of oranges is P_w. Since P_w lies below P_d, this country will import oranges. The quantity of imports is equal to the amount of the domestic shortage at P_w. The quantity demanded at P_w is 400 tons, and the quantity supplied domestically is 100 tons, so imports will equal 300 tons of oranges. With free trade, domestic producers sell 100 tons at a price of P_w.

But suppose domestic orange growers convince the government to restrict orange imports. The government then imposes a quota of 100 tons on imported oranges. The effect of the quota on consumers is to shift the supply curve to the right by the

---

FIGURE 2

The Effects of a Quota

The domestic equilibrium price with no international trade is P_d. At this price, 250 tons of oranges would be produced and consumed at home. With free trade, the price is P_w and 300 tons will be imported. An import quota of 100 tons will cause the price to be P_q, where the domestic shortage equals the 100 tons allowed by the quota.

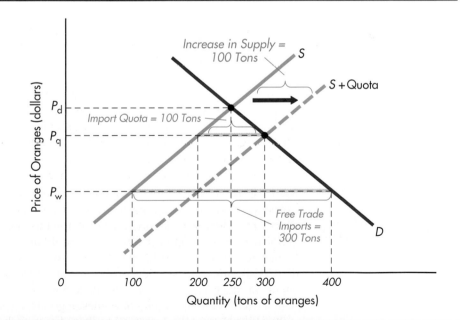

amount of the quota, 100 tons. Since the quota is less than the quantity of imports with free trade, the quantity of imports will equal the quota. The domestic equilibrium price with the quota occurs at the point where the domestic shortage equals the quota. At price P_q, the domestic quantity demanded (300 tons) is 100 tons more than the domestic quantity supplied (200 tons).

Quotas benefit domestic producers in the same way that tariffs do. Domestic producers receive a higher price (P_q instead of P_w) for a greater quantity (200 instead of 100) than they do under free trade. The effect on domestic consumers is also similar to that of a tariff: they pay a higher price for a smaller quantity than they would with free trade. A tariff generates government tax revenue; quotas do not (unless the government auctions off the right to import under the quota). Furthermore, a tariff raises the price of the product only in the domestic market. Foreign producers receive the world price, P_w. With a quota, both domestic and foreign producers receive the higher price, P_q, for the goods sold in the domestic market. So foreign producers are hurt by the reduction in the quantity of imports permitted, but they receive a higher price for the amount they do sell.

2.c. Other Barriers to Trade

Tariffs and quotas are not the only barriers to the free flow of goods across international borders. There are three additional sources of restrictions on free trade: subsidies, government procurement, and health and safety standards. Though often enacted for reasons other than protection from foreign competition, a careful analysis reveals their import-reducing effect.

Before discussing these three types of barriers, let us note the cultural or institutional barriers to trade that also exist in many countries. Such barriers may exist independently of any conscious government policy. For instance, Japan has frequently been criticized by U.S. officials for informal business practices that discriminate against foreigners. Under the Japanese distribution system, goods typically pass through several layers of middlemen before appearing in a retail store. A foreign firm faces the difficult task of gaining entry to this system to supply goods to the retailer. Furthermore, a foreigner cannot easily open a retail store. Japanese law requires a new retail firm to receive permission from other retailers in the area in order to open a business. A firm that lacks contacts and knowledge of the system cannot penetrate the Japanese market.

In the fall of 1989, the U.S. toy firm Toys "R" Us announced its intent to open several large discount toy stores in Japan. However, local toy stores in each area objected to having a Toys "R" Us store nearby. The U.S. government has argued that the laws favoring existing firms are an important factor in keeping Japan closed to foreign firms that would like to enter the Japanese market. Eventually, Toys "R" Us opened stores in Japan.

export subsidies:
payments made by government to domestic firms to encourage exports

2.c.1. Export Subsidies   **Export subsidies** are payments by a government to an exporter. These subsidies are paid in order to stimulate exports by allowing the exporter to charge a lower price. The amount of a subsidy is determined by the international price of a product relative to the domestic price in the absence of trade. Domestic consumers are harmed by subsidies in that their taxes finance the subsidies. Also, since the subsidy diverts resources from the domestic market toward export production, the increase in the supply of export goods could be associated with a decrease in the supply of domestic goods, causing domestic prices to rise.

Subsidies may take forms other than direct cash payments. These include tax reductions, low-interest loans, low-cost insurance, government-sponsored research funding, and other devices. The U.S. government subsidizes export activity through the U.S. Export-Import Bank, which provides loans and insurance to help U.S. exporters sell their goods to foreign buyers. Subsidies are more commonplace in Europe than in Japan or the United States.

2.c.2. Government Procurement

Governments are often required by law to buy only from local producers. In the United States, a "buy American" act passed in 1933 required U.S. government agencies to buy U.S. goods and services unless the domestic price was more than 12 percent above the foreign price. This kind of policy allows domestic firms to charge the government a higher price for their products than they charge consumers; the taxpayers bear the burden. The United States is by no means alone in the use of such policies. Many other nations also use such policies to create larger markets for domestic goods. The World Trade Organization has a standing committee working to reduce discrimination against foreign producers and open government procurement practices to global competition.

2.c.3. Health and Safety Standards

Government serves as a guardian of the public health and welfare by requiring that products offered to the public be safe and fulfill the use for which they are intended. Government standards for products sold in the domestic marketplace can have the effect (intentional or not) of protecting domestic producers from foreign competition. These effects should be considered in evaluating the full impact of such standards.

As mentioned in the Preview, the government of Japan once threatened to prohibit foreign-made snow skis from entering the country for reasons of safety. Only Japanese-made skis were determined to be suitable for Japanese snow. Several western European nations once announced that U.S. beef would not be allowed into Europe because the U.S. government had approved the feeding of hormones to U.S. beef cattle. In the late 1960s, France required tractors sold there to have a maximum speed of 17 miles per hour; in Germany, the permissible speed was 13 miles per hour, and in the Netherlands, it was 10 miles per hour. Tractors produced in one country had to be modified to meet the requirements of the other countries. Such modifications raise the price of goods and discourage international trade.

Product standards may not eliminate foreign competition, but standards different from those of the rest of the world do provide an element of protection to domestic firms.

RECAP

1. The World Trade Organization works to achieve reductions in trade barriers.
2. A tariff is a tax on imports or exports. Tariffs protect domestic firms by raising the prices of foreign goods.
3. Quotas are government-imposed limits on the quantity or value of an imported good. Quotas protect domestic firms by restricting the entry of foreign products to a level less than the quantity demanded.
4. Subsidies are payments by the government to domestic producers. Subsidies lower the price of domestic goods to foreign buyers.
5. Governments are often required by law to buy only domestic products.
6. Health and safety standards can also be used to protect domestic firms.

---

3. Preferential Trade Agreements

In an effort to stimulate international trade, groups of countries sometimes enter into agreements to abolish most barriers to trade among themselves. Such arrangements between countries are known as preferential trading agreements. The European Union and the North American Free Trade Agreement (NAFTA) are examples of preferential trading agreements.

3.a. Free Trade Areas and Customs Unions

free trade area: an organization of nations whose members have no trade barriers among themselves but are free to fashion their own trade policies toward nonmembers

customs union: an organization of nations whose members have no trade barriers among themselves but impose common trade barriers on nonmembers

Two common forms of preferential trade agreements are **free trade areas** (FTAs) and **customs unions** (CUs). These two approaches differ with regard to the treatment of countries outside the agreement. In an FTA, member countries eliminate trade barriers among themselves, but each member country chooses its own trade policies toward nonmember countries. Members of a CU agree to eliminate trade barriers among themselves and to maintain common trade barriers against nonmembers.

The best-known CU is the European Union (EU), formerly known as the European Economic Community (EEC), created in 1957 by France, West Germany, Italy, Belgium, the Netherlands, and Luxembourg. The United Kingdom, Ireland, and Denmark joined in 1973, followed by Greece in 1981 and Spain and Portugal in 1986. In 1992 the EEC was replaced by the EU with an agreement to create a single market for goods and services in western Europe. At the time this edition of the text was prepared, the following countries had applied to become members of the EU in the next round of enlargement: Bulgaria, Cyprus, Czech Republic, Estonia, Hungary, Latvia, Lithuania, Malta, Poland, Romania, Slovakia, Slovenia, and Turkey. Besides free trade in goods, European financial markets and institutions will eventually be able to operate across national boundaries. For instance, a bank in any EU country will be permitted to operate in any or all other EU countries.

In 1989, the United States and Canada negotiated a free trade area. The United States, Canada, and Mexico negotiated a free trade area in 1992 that became effective on January 1, 1994. Under the North American Free Trade Agreement

The North American Free Trade Agreement stimulates trade among Mexico, Canada, and the United States. In coming years, there will be more and more container ships from Mexico unloading their cargo at U.S. docks. Similarly, freight from Canada and the United States will increase in volume at Mexican ports.

(NAFTA), tariffs are lowered on 8,000 different items, and each nation's financial market is opened to competition from the other two nations. The NAFTA does not eliminate all barriers to trade among the three nations, but it is a significant step in that direction.

3.b. Trade Creation and Diversion

Free trade agreements provide for free trade among a group of countries, not worldwide. As a result, a customs union or free trade area may make a nation better off or worse off compared to the free trade equilibrium.

Figure 3 illustrates the effect of a free trade area. With no international trade, the U.S. supply and demand curves for oranges would result in an equilibrium price of $500 per ton and an equilibrium quantity of 425 tons. Suppose there are two other orange-producing countries, Israel and Brazil. Israel, the low-cost producer of oranges, is willing to sell all the oranges the United States can buy for $150 per ton, as represented by the horizontal supply curve S_I. Brazil will supply oranges for a price of $200 per ton, as represented by the horizontal supply curve S_B.

With free trade, the United States would import oranges from Israel. The quantity demanded at $150 is 750 tons, and the domestic quantity supplied at this price is 100 tons. The shortage of 650 tons is met by imports from Israel.

Now suppose a 100 percent tariff is imposed on orange imports. The price that domestic consumers pay for foreign oranges is twice as high as before. For oranges from Israel, the new price is $300, twice the old price of $150. The new supply curve

---

FIGURE 3

Trade Creation and Trade Diversion with a Free Trade Area

With no trade, the domestic equilibrium price is $500 and the equilibrium quantity is 425 tons. With free trade, the price is $150, and 650 tons would be imported, as indicated by the supply curve for Israel, S_I. A 100 percent tariff on imports would result in imports of 350 tons from Israel, according to the supply curve S_I + Tariff. A free trade agreement that eliminates tariffs on Brazilian oranges only would result in a new equilibrium price of $200 and imports of 550 tons from Brazil, according to supply curve S_B.

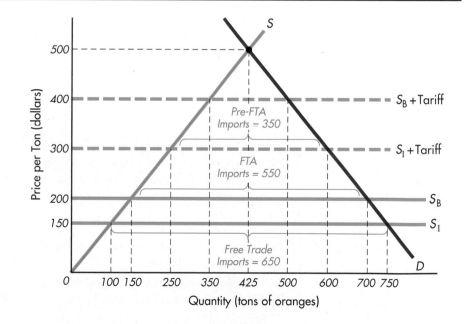

---

for Israel is represented as S_I + Tariff. Oranges from Brazil now sell for $400, twice the old price of $200; the new supply curve for Brazil is shown as S_B + Tariff. After the 100 percent tariff is imposed, oranges are still imported from Israel. But at the new price of $300, the domestic quantity demanded is 600 tons and the domestic quantity supplied is 250 tons. Thus only 350 tons will be imported. The tariff reduces the volume of trade relative to the free trade equilibrium, at which 650 tons were imported.

Now suppose that the United States negotiates a free trade agreement with Brazil, eliminating tariffs on imports from Brazil. Israel is not a member of the free trade agreement, so imports from Israel are still covered by the 100 percent tariff. The relevant supply curve for Brazil is now S_B, so oranges may be imported from Brazil for $200, a lower price than Israel's price including the tariff. At a price of $200, the domestic quantity demanded is 700 tons and the domestic quantity supplied is 150 tons; 550 tons will be imported.

The effects of the free trade agreement are twofold. First, trade was diverted away from the lowest-cost producer, Israel, to the FTA partner, Brazil. This **trade-diversion** effect of an FTA reduces worldwide economic efficiency, since production is diverted from the country with the comparative advantage. Oranges are not being produced as efficiently as possible. The other effect of the FTA is that the quantity of imports increases relative to the effect of a tariff applicable to all imports. Imports rise from 350 tons (the quantity imported from Israel with the tariff) to 550 tons. The FTA thus has a **trade-creation** effect as a result of the lower price available after the tariff reduction. Trade creation is a beneficial aspect of the FTA: the expansion of international trade allows this country to realize greater benefits from trade than would be possible without trade.

Countries form preferential trade agreements because they believe that FTAs will make each member country better off. The member countries view the trade-creation effects of such agreements as benefiting their exporters by increasing exports to member countries and as benefiting consumers by making a wider variety of goods available at a lower price. From the point of view of the world as a whole, preferential trade agreements are more desirable the more they stimulate trade creation to allow the benefits of trade to be realized and the less they emphasize trade diversion, so that production occurs on the basis of comparative advantage. This principle suggests that the most successful FTAs or CUs are those that increase trade volume but do not change the patterns of trade in terms of who specializes and exports each good. In the case of Figure 3, a more successful FTA would reduce tariffs on Israeli as well as Brazilian oranges, so that oranges would be imported from the lowest-cost producer, Israel.

trade diversion: an effect of a preferential trade agreement, reducing economic efficiency by shifting production to a higher-cost producer

trade creation: an effect of a preferential trade agreement, allowing a country to obtain goods at a lower cost than is available at home

RECAP

1. Countries form preferential trade agreements in order to stimulate trade among themselves.

2. The most common forms of preferential trade agreement are free trade areas (FTAs) and customs unions (CUs).

3. Preferential trade agreements have a harmful trade-diversion effect when they cause production to shift from the nation with a comparative advantage to a higher-cost producer.

4. Preferential trade agreements have a beneficial trade-creation effect when they reduce prices for traded goods and stimulate the volume of international trade.

Summary

❓ Why do countries restrict international trade?

1. Commercial policy is government policy that influences the direction and volume of international trade. *Preview*

2. Protecting domestic producers from foreign competition usually imposes costs on domestic consumers. *§1*

3. Rationales for commercial policy include saving domestic jobs, creating a fair-trade relationship with other countries, raising tariff revenue, ensuring a domestic supply of key defense goods, allowing new industries a chance to become internationally competitive, and giving domestic industries with increasing returns to scale an advantage over foreign competitors. *§1.a–1.f*

❓ How do countries restrict the entry of foreign goods and promote the export of domestic goods?

4. Tariffs protect domestic industry by increasing the price of foreign goods. *§2.a*

5. Quotas protect domestic industry by limiting the quantity of foreign goods allowed into the country. *§2.b*

6. Subsidies allow relatively inefficient domestic producers to compete with foreign firms. *§2.c.1*

7. Government procurement practices and health and safety regulations can protect domestic industry from foreign competition. *§2.c.2, 2.c3*

❓ What sorts of agreements do countries enter into to reduce barriers to international trade?

8. Free trade areas and customs unions are two types of preferential trade agreements that reduce trade restrictions among member countries. *§3.a*

9. Preferential trade agreements have harmful trade-diversion effects and beneficial trade-creation effects. *§3.b*

Key Terms

commercial policy *Preview*

strategic trade policy *§1.f*

increasing-returns-to-scale industry *§1.f*

tariff *§2.a*

quantity quota *§2.b*

value quota *§2.b*

subsidies *§2.c.1*

free trade area *§3.a*

customs union *§3.a*

trade diversion *§3.b*

trade creation *§3.b*

Exercises

1. What are the potential benefits and costs of a commercial policy designed to pursue each of the following goals?
   a. Save domestic jobs.
   b. Create a level playing field.
   c. Increase government revenue.
   d. Provide a strong national defense.
   e. Protect an infant industry.
   f. Stimulate exports of an industry with increasing returns to scale.

2. For each of the goals listed in exercise 1, discuss what the appropriate commercial policy is likely to be (in terms of tariffs, quotas, subsidies, etc.).

3. Tariffs and quotas both raise the price of foreign goods to domestic consumers. What is the difference between the effects of a tariff and the effects of a quota on the following?
   a. The domestic government
   b. Foreign producers
   c. Domestic producers

4. Would trade-diversion and trade-creation effects occur if the whole world became a free trade area? Explain.

5. What is the difference between a customs union and a free trade area?

6. Draw a graph of the U.S. automobile market in which the domestic equilibrium price without trade is P_d and the equilibrium quantity is Q_d. Use this graph to illustrate and explain the effects of a tariff if the United States were an auto importer with free trade. Then use the graph to illustrate and explain the effects of a quota.

7. If commercial policy can benefit U.S. industry, why would any U.S. resident oppose such policies?

8. Suppose you were asked to assess U.S. commercial policy to determine whether the benefits of protec-

tion for U.S. industries are worth the costs. Do Tables 1 and 2 provide all the information you need? If not, what else would you want to know?

9. How would the effects of international trade on the domestic orange market change if the world price of oranges were above the domestic equilibrium price? Draw a graph to help explain your answer.

10. Suppose the world price of kiwi fruit is $20 per case and the U.S. equilibrium price with no international trade is $35 per case. If the U.S. government had previously banned the import of kiwi fruit but then imposed a tariff of $5 per case and allowed kiwi imports, what would happen to the equilibrium price and quantity of kiwi fruit consumed in the United States?

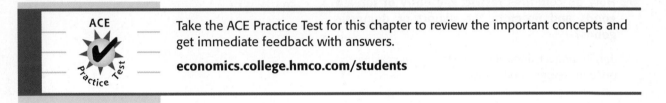

ACE

Take the ACE Practice Test for this chapter to review the important concepts and get immediate feedback with answers.

economics.college.hmco.com/students

Bull in a China Shop

Under a U.S. trade statute reserved for China, the president must decide whether to restrict imports of a product used to adjust the height of mobility scooter seats, which are used by those who are physically disabled.

Unless Bush exercises his discretion to deny restrictions, he will send a terrible signal to other industries that face Chinese competition—and also to China as it struggles to open its economy to foreign competition.

Last October, the U.S. International Trade Commission [ITC] determined that, in accordance with Section 421 of the Trade Act of 1974, imports of pedestal actuators from China are causing "market disruption" to U.S. producers of the same merchandise. The ITC also recommended that the president impose quotas.

This is the first case brought under this China-specific statute. The president's decision will set a precedent and could undermine U.S.–China trade relations at a delicate stage of the ongoing World Trade Organization negotiations.

The facts of this case are intriguing. It turns out that the petitioning "industry" is Motion Systems Corp., the only U.S. company that manufactures pedestal actuators. One of its largest customers, Electric Mobility [EMC], a producer of mobility scooters, ended its relationship with Motion Systems for a variety of reasons. EMC requested bids from other producers around the world—there are no other viable U.S. sources—and chose a Chinese manufacturer, CCL Industrial Motor [CIM], with whom it had cultivated a successful relationship purchasing other parts since 1998.

When Motion Systems was EMC's supplier, imports of pedestal actuators from China were nonexistent. Imports from China increased only after Electric Mobility terminated its contract with MSC and commenced business with CIM. "If Motion Systems had been more responsive to our needs, we would not have made the decision to stop purchasing from them—a decision that was made prior to our decision to purchase actuators from the Chinese," wrote EMC's president.

A private dispute between a company and its supplier has thus been transformed into an international trade dispute. Yet, three ITC commissioners concluded that imports from China are causing a market disruption in the United States. . . .

The ITC is at odds over this case, and possibly with the statute itself. How this case comports with Congress' intent that Section 421 be used only in extraordinary circumstances is difficult to comprehend. It is imperative that the president deny relief to the domestic industry, which in this case is one company whose financial well-being appears largely dependent upon the customer it seeks to punish.

Statutorily, to deny relief, the president must conclude that granting it would be contrary to the national economic or national security interest of the United States. And it is contrary to the national economic interest "only if the president finds that the taking of such action would have an adverse impact on the United States economy clearly greater than the benefits of such action." That case can be made.

The cost of mobility scooters dropped from $4,100 to $3,800 after Electric Mobility switched to the Chinese supplier of pedestal actuators. By impeding this supply chain, the remedy would have a direct, adverse impact on the physically disabled, as well as the country's ailing health care insurance industry. No wonder that leading representatives of the disabled community filed comments with the USTR opposing the quotas. . . .

DAN IKENSON

Source: Copyright 2003 News World Communications, Inc.

The Washington Times/January 13, 2003

This article shows how domestic firms may seek protection from international competition even though domestic consumers will be harmed by the action. In this case, a device that moves seats up and down on scooters used by the handicapped is available for a better price from a Chinese producer than from the only producer of the product in the United States. One could hardly argue that protecting the U.S. producer from foreign competition is clearly in the national interest of the people of the United States. However, the domestic producer wants to force the U.S. manufacturer of scooters to purchase its product, with no competition allowed. This is not a unique situation; it is a familiar story worldwide as firms threatened with foreign competition seek government protection from that competition. The protectionist measure of imposing quotas or tariffs on imports saves jobs in the domestic import-competing industries, but at a great cost to consumers.

The effect of reducing domestic competition with quotas can be understood using supply and demand analysis. Let's analyze the case of quotas on textile imports into the United States. In the diagram, S_1 is the domestic supply of textiles, S_2 is the sum of the domestic supply and the foreign supply allowed in by the quotas, and D is the demand for textiles. Under the quota system, the price of textiles in the United States is represented by P_q and the quantity of textiles consumed is Q_q. If the quotas were removed, the price of textiles in the United States would equal the world price of P_w, and this lower price would be associated with an increase in the consumption of textiles to Q_w. The quota represents a cost to society in terms of a loss of consumer welfare as well as a loss from the inefficient use of resources in an industry in which this country has no comparative advantage, just as Maine has no comparative advantage in the production of pineapples.

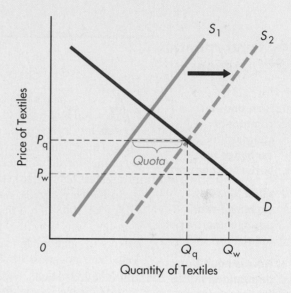

Given the costs to society of these quotas, why is there such strong support for them in Congress? An important political aspect of protectionist policies is that their benefits are concentrated among a relatively small number of people, while their costs are diffuse and spread across all consumers. Each individual import-competing producer faces very large losses from free trade, while the cost to each consumer of a protectionist policy is less dramatic. It is also easier to organize a relatively small number of manufacturers than to mobilize a vast population of consumers. These factors explain the strong lobby for the protection of industries like textiles and the absence of a legislative lobby that operates specifically in the interest of textile consumers.

Industrial arguments for trade protection should be seen for what they are: an attempt by an industry to increase its profits at the expense of the general public.

CHAPTER 37

Exchange Rates and Financial Links Between Countries

1. How does a commodity standard fix exchange rates between countries?

2. What kinds of exchange-rate arrangements exist today?

3. How is equilibrium determined in the foreign exchange market?

4. How do fixed and floating exchange rates differ in their adjustment to shifts in supply and demand for currencies?

5. What are the advantages and disadvantages of fixed and floating exchange rates?

6. How does a change in the exchange rate affect the prices of goods traded between countries?

7. Why don't similar goods sell for the same price all over the world?

An exchange rate is the link between two nations' monies. The value of a U.S. dollar in terms of Japanese yen or European euro determines how many dollars a U.S. resident will need in order to buy goods that are priced in yen or euro. Thus changes in exchange rates can have far-reaching implications. Exchange rates may be determined in free markets, through government intervention in the foreign exchange market, or even by law.

In the early 1990s, one U.S. dollar was worth about 125 Japanese yen. By the spring of 1995, the dollar was worth 83 yen. By April 2003, 120 yen would buy 1 dollar. Why does the dollar fluctuate in value relative to the yen? What are the effects of such changes? Should governments permit exchange rates to change? What can governments do to discourage changing exchange rates? These are all important questions, and this chapter will help to answer them.

The chapter begins with a review of the history of exchange-rate systems. It follows with an overview of exchange-rate practices in the world today, and how exchange rates provide a link between prices and interest rates across countries.

8. **How do we find the domestic currency return on a foreign bond?**

9. **What is the relationship between domestic and foreign interest rates and changes in the exchange rate?**

1. **How does a commodity standard fix exchange rates between countries?**

gold standard: a system whereby national currencies are fixed in terms of their value in gold, thus creating fixed exchange rates between currencies

A commodity money standard exists when exchange rates are fixed based on the values of different currencies in terms of some commodity.

The Bretton Woods agreement established a system of fixed exchange rates.

Along the way, it introduces terminology and institutions that play a major role in the evolution of exchange rates. ■

1. Past and Current Exchange-Rate Arrangements

1.a. The Gold Standard

In ancient times, government-produced monies were made of precious metals such as gold. Later, when governments began to issue paper money, that money was usually convertible into a fixed amount of gold. Ensuring the convertibility of paper money into gold was a way to maintain confidence in the currency's value, both at home and abroad. If a unit of currency was worth a fixed amount of gold, its value could be stated in terms of its gold value. The countries that maintained a constant gold value for their currencies were said to be on a **gold standard.**

Some countries had backed their currencies with gold long before 1880; however, the practice became widespread around 1880, so economists typically date the beginning of the gold standard to this period. From roughly 1880 to 1914, currencies had fixed values in terms of gold. For instance, the U.S. dollar's value was fixed at $20.67 per ounce of gold. Any other currency that was fixed in terms of gold also had a fixed exchange rate against the dollar. A simple example will illustrate how this works.

Suppose the price of an ounce of gold is $20 in the United States and £4 in the United Kingdom. The pound is worth five times the value of a dollar, since it takes five times as many dollars as pounds to buy one ounce of gold. Because 1 pound buys five times as much gold as 1 dollar, the exchange rate is £1 = $5. Since currency values are linked by gold values, as the supply of gold fluctuates, there will be pressure to alter the prices of goods and services. The gold standard fixes only the current price of gold. As the stock of gold increases, everything else held constant, the gold and currency prices of goods and services will tend to rise (as would occur when the money supply increases).

A gold standard is only one possible *commodity money standard.* Any other highly valued commodity (silver, for instance) could serve as a standard linking monies in a fixed-exchange-rate system.

The gold standard ended with the outbreak of World War I. The war was partially funded by increases in the money supplies of the hostile nations. A gold standard would not permit such a rapid increase in the money supply unless the stock of gold increased dramatically, which it did not. As money supplies grew faster than gold supplies, the link between money and gold had to be broken. During the war years and the Great Depression of the 1930s, and on through World War II, there was no organized system for setting exchange rates. Foreign trade and investment shrank as a result of the war, obviating the need for a well-functioning method of determining exchange rates.

1.b. The Bretton Woods System

At the end of World War II, there was widespread political support for an exchange-rate system linking all monies in much the same way as the gold standard had. It was believed that a system of fixed exchange rates would promote the growth of world trade. In 1944, delegates from 44 nations met in Bretton Woods, New Hampshire, to discuss the creation of such a system. The agreement reached at this conference has had a profound impact on the world.

The IMF and the World Bank

The International Monetary Fund (IMF) and the World Bank were both created at the Bretton Woods conference in 1944. The IMF oversees the international monetary system, promoting stable exchange rates and macroeconomic policies. The World Bank promotes the economic development of the poor nations. Both organizations are owned and directed by their 182 member countries.

The IMF provides loans to nations that are having trouble repaying their foreign debts. Before the IMF lends any money, however, the borrower must agree to certain conditions. The IMF *conditionality* usually requires that the country meet targets for key macroeconomic variables like money-supply growth, inflation, tax collections, and subsidies. The conditions attached to IMF loans are aimed at promoting stable economic growth.

The World Bank assists developing countries by providing long-term financing for development projects and programs. The Bank also provides expertise in many areas in which poor nations lack expert knowledge: agriculture, medicine, construction, and education, as well as economics. The IMF primarily employs economists to carry out its mission.

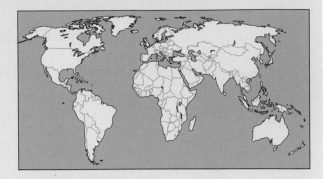

The diversity of World Bank activities results in the employment of about 6,500 people. The IMF has a staff of approximately 1,700. Both organizations post employees around the world, but most work at the organizations' headquarters in Washington, D.C.

World Bank funds are largely acquired by borrowing on the international bond market. The IMF receives its funding from member-country subscription fees, called quotas. A member's quota determines its voting power in setting IMF policies. The United States, whose quota accounts for the largest fraction of the total, has the most votes.

---

gold exchange standard: an exchange-rate system in which each nation fixes the value of its currency in terms of gold, but buys and sells the U.S. dollar rather than gold to maintain fixed exchange rates

The exchange-rate arrangement that emerged from the Bretton Woods conference is often called a **gold exchange standard.** Each country was to fix the value of its currency in terms of gold, just as it had under the gold standard. The U.S. dollar price of gold, for instance, was $35 an ounce. However, there were fundamental differences between this system and the old gold standard. The U.S. dollar, rather than gold, served as the focal point of the system. Instead of buying and selling gold, countries bought and sold U.S. dollars to maintain a fixed exchange rate with the dollar. Since the United States had the world's largest financial market and the strongest economy, its currency was the dominant world currency. The United States had the productive capacity to supply much-needed goods to the rest of the world, and these goods were priced in dollars.

reserve currency: a currency that is used to settle international debts and is held by governments to use in foreign exchange market interventions

The U.S. dollar was the **reserve currency** of the system. International debts were settled with dollars, and international trade contracts were often denominated in dollars. In effect, the world was on a dollar standard following World War II.

1.c. The International Monetary Fund and the World Bank

Two new organizations also emerged from the Bretton Woods conference: the International Monetary Fund and the World Bank. The **International Monetary Fund (IMF)** was created to supervise the exchange-rate practices of member countries and to encourage the free convertibility of any national money into the monies of other countries. The IMF also lends money to countries that are experiencing problems meeting their international payment obligations. The funds available to the IMF come from the annual membership fees (called *quotas*) of the 182 member countries of the IMF. The U.S. quota, for instance, is almost $48 billion. (The term *quota* has a different meaning in this context from the one it has in international trade.)

The **World Bank** was created to help finance economic development in poor countries. It provides loans to developing countries at more favorable terms than are available from commercial lenders and also offers technical expertise. The World Bank obtains the funds it lends by selling bonds. It is one of the world's major borrowers. See the Global Business Insight "The IMF and the World Bank" for an explanation of how these institutions work.

1.d. The Transition Years

The Bretton Woods system of fixed exchange rates required countries to actively buy and sell dollars in order to maintain fixed exchange rates when the *free market equilibrium* in the foreign exchange market differed from the fixed rate. The free market equilibrium exchange rate is the rate that would be established in the absence of government intervention. Governmental buying and selling of currencies to achieve a target exchange rate is called **foreign exchange market intervention.** The effectiveness of such intervention is limited to situations in which free market pressure to deviate from the fixed exchange rate was temporary. For instance, suppose a country has a bad harvest and earns less foreign exchange than usual. This may be only a temporary situation if the next harvest is plentiful and the country resumes its typical export sales. During the period of reduced exports, it will be necessary for the government of this country to intervene to avoid a depreciation of its domestic currency. In the 1960s, however, there were several episodes of permanent rather than temporary changes that called for changes in exchange rates rather than government foreign exchange market intervention.

The Bretton Woods system officially dissolved in 1971, at a meeting of the finance ministers of the leading world powers at the Smithsonian Institution in Washington, D.C. The Smithsonian agreement changed the exchange rates set during the Bretton Woods era. One result was a **devaluation** of the U.S. dollar. (A currency is said to be devalued when its value is officially lowered.)

Under the Smithsonian agreement, countries were to maintain fixed exchange rates at newly defined values. It soon became clear, however, that the new exchange rates were not **equilibrium exchange rates** that could be maintained without government intervention and that government intervention could not maintain the disequilibrium fixed exchange rates forever. The U.S. dollar was devalued again in February 1973, when the dollar price of gold was raised to $42.22. This new exchange rate was still not an equilibrium rate, and in March 1973 the major industrial countries abandoned fixed exchange rates.

1.e. Today

When fixed exchange rates were abandoned by the major industrial countries in March 1973, the world did not move to purely free market–determined floating exchange rates. Under the system that has been in existence since that time, the major industrial countries intervene to keep their currencies within acceptable ranges, while many smaller countries maintain fixed exchange rates.

The world today consists of some countries with fixed exchange rates, whose governments keep the exchange rates between two or more currencies constant over

TABLE 1

Exchange Rate Arrangements

Crawling Pegs (4)	Exchange Rates Within Crawling Bands (6)	Managed Floating with No Preannounced Path for Exchange Rate (42)	Independently Floating (40)
Bolivia	Belarus	Algeria	Afghanistan
Costa Rica	Honduras	Angola	Albania
Nicaragua	Israel	Azerbaijan	Armenia
Solomon Islands	Romania	Burundi	Australia
	Uruguay	Cambodia	Brazil
	Venezuela	Croatia	Canada
		Dominican Rep.	Chile
		Ethiopia	Colombia
		Ghana	Congo, Dem. Rep. of the
		Guatemala	Czech Rep.
		Guinea	Gambia, The
		Guyana	Georgia
		India	Haiti
		Indonesia	Iceland
		Iraq	Japan
		Jamaica	Korea
		Kazakhstan	Liberia
		Kenya	Madagascar
		Kyrgyz Rep.	Malawi
		Lao P.D.R.	Mexico
		Mauritania	Moldova
		Mauritius	Mozambique
		Mongolia	New Zealand
		Myanmar	Norway
		Nigeria	Papua New Guinea
		Pakistan	Peru
		Paraguay	Philippines
		Russia	Poland
		Rwanda	Sierra Leone
		São Tomé and Principe	Somalia
		Singapore	South Africa
		Slovak Rep.	Sweden
		Slovenia	Switzerland
		Sri Lanka	Tajikistan
		Thailand	Tanzania
		Trinidad and Tobago	Turkey
		Tunisia	Uganda
		Ukraine	United Kingdom
		Uzbekistan	United States
		Vietnam	Yemen
		Yugoslavia	
		Zambia	

Exchange Arrangements with No Separate Legal Tender (40)	Currency Board Arrangements (8)	Other Conventional Fixed Peg Arrangements (Including De Facto Peg Arrangements Under Managed Floating) (41)	Exchange Rates Within Horizontal Bands (5)
Another currency as legal tender	Argentina	***Against a single currency (31)***	***Within a cooperative arrangement ERM II (1)***
Ecuador	Bosnia and Herzegovina	Aruba	Denmark
El Salvador	Brunei Darusalam	Bahamas	***Other band arrangements (4)***
Kiribati	Bulgaria	Bahrain	Cyprus
Marshall Islands	Djibouti	Bangladesh	Egypt
Micronesia	Estonia	Barbados	Hungary
Palau	Hong Kong SAR	Belize	Tonga
Panama	Lithuania	Bhutan	
San Marino		Cape Verde	
CFA franc zone		China	
WAEMU		Comoros	
Benin		Eritrea	
Burkina Faso		Iran, Islamic Rep. of	
Côte d'Ivoire		Jordan	
Guinea-Bissau		Lebanon	
Mali		Lesotho	
Niger		Macedonia, FYR	
Senegal		Malaysia	
Togo		Maldives	
CAEMC		Namibia	
Cameroon		Nepal	
Central African Rep.		Netherlands Antilles	
Chad		Oman	
Congo, Rep. of		Qatar	
Equatorial Guinea		Saudi Arabia	
Gabon		Sudan	
Euro Area		Suriname	
Austria		Swaziland	
Belgium		Syrian Arab Republic	
Finland		Turkmenistan	
France		United Arab Emirates	
Germany		Zimbabwe	
Greece		***Against a composite (10)***	
Ireland		Botswana	
Italy		Fiji	
Luxembourg		Kuwait	
Netherlands		Latvia	
Portugal		Libyan A.J.	
Spain		Malta	
ECCU		Morocco	
Antigua and Barbuda		Samoa	
Dominica		Seychelles	
Grenada		Vanuatu	
St. Kitts and Nevis			
St. Lucia			
St. Vincent and the Grenadines			

Sources: IMF staff reports: International Monetary Fund, *Annual Report of the Executive Board of Directors for the Fiscal Year Ended April 30, 2002.*

time; other countries with floating exchange rates, which shift on a daily basis according to the forces of supply and demand; and still others whose exchange-rate systems lie somewhere in between. Table 1, which lists the exchange-rate arrangements of over 180 countries, illustrates the diversity of exchange-rate arrangements currently in effect.

We provide a brief description of each:

Crawling pegs   The exchange rate is adjusted periodically by small amounts at a fixed, preannounced rate or in response to certain indicators (such as inflation differentials against major trading partners).

Crawling bands   The exchange rate is maintained within certain fluctuation margins around a central rate that is periodically adjusted at a fixed, preannounced rate or in response to certain indicators.

Managed floating   The monetary authority (usually the central bank) influences the exchange rate through active foreign exchange market intervention with no preannounced path for the exchange rate.

Independently floating   The exchange rate is market determined, and any intervention is aimed at moderating fluctuations rather than determining the level of the exchange rate.

No separate legal tender   Either another country's currency circulates as the legal tender, or the country belongs to a monetary union where the legal tender is shared by the members (like the euro).

Currency board   A fixed exchange rate is established by a legislative commitment to exchange domestic currency for a specified foreign currency at a fixed exchange rate. New issues of domestic currency are typically backed in some fixed ratio (like 1-to-1) by additional holdings of the key foreign currency.

Fixed peg   The exchange rate is fixed against a major currency or some basket of currencies. Active intervention may be required to maintain the target pegged rate.

Horizontal bands   The exchange rate fluctuates around a fixed central target rate. Such target zones allow for a moderate amount of exchange-rate fluctuation while tying the currency to the target central rate.

Under "Exchange Rates with No Separate Legal Tender" in Table 1 we see the euro area. The countries listed in this section all use a common currency, the *euro*. The euro, the new European currency, made its debut on January 1, 1999. The symbol is €.

Table 2 lists the end-of-year exchange rates for several currencies versus the U.S. dollar beginning in 1950. For most of the currencies, there was little movement in the 1950s and 1960s, the era of the Bretton Woods agreement. In the early 1970s, exchange rates began to fluctuate. More recently, there has been considerable change in the foreign exchange value of a dollar, as Table 2 illustrates.

RECAP

1. Under a gold standard, each currency has a fixed value in terms of gold. This arrangement provides for fixed exchange rates between countries.

2. At the end of World War II, the Bretton Woods agreement established a new system of fixed exchange rates. Two new organizations—the International Monetary Fund (IMF) and the World Bank—also emerged from the Bretton Woods conference.

TABLE 2

Exchange Rates of Selected Countries (currency units per U.S. dollar)

Year	Canadian Dollar	Japanese Yen	French Franc	German Mark	Italian Lira	British Pound	Euro
1950	1.06	361	3.50	4.20	625	.36	—
1955	1.00	361	3.50	4.22	625	.36	—
1960	1.00	358	4.90	4.17	621	.36	—
1965	1.08	361	4.90	4.01	625	.36	—
1970	1.01	358	5.52	3.65	623	.42	—
1975	1.02	305	4.49	2.62	684	.50	—
1980	1.19	203	4.52	1.96	931	.42	—
1985	1.40	201	7.56	2.46	1,679	.69	—
1990	1.16	134	5.13	1.49	1,130	.52	—
1995	1.36	103	4.90	1.43	1,584	.65	—
1997	1.43	130	5.95	1.78	1,744	.60	—
1998	1.53	116	5.62	1.67	1,653	.60	—
1999	1.44	102	—	—	—	.62	1.00
2000	1.49	114	—	—	—	.67	1.06
2002	1.58	118	—	—	—	.62	.95

Source: End-of-year exchange rates from International Monetary Fund, *International Financial Statistics,* Washington, D.C., various issues, and www.oanda.com.

3. Fixed exchange rates are maintained by government intervention in the foreign exchange market; governments or central banks buy and sell currencies to keep the equilibrium exchange rate steady.

4. The governments of the major industrial countries adopted floating exchange rates in 1973. In fact, the prevailing system is characterized by managed floating—that is, by occasional government intervention—rather than being a pure free market–determined exchange-rate system.

5. Some countries choose floating exchange rates; others peg their currencies to a single currency or a composite.

2. Fixed or Floating Exchange Rates

Is the United States better off today with floating exchange rates than it was with the fixed exchange rates of the post–World War II period? The choice of an exchange-rate system has multiple implications for the performance of a nation's economy and, therefore, for the conduct of macroeconomic policy. As with many policy issues in economics, economists often disagree about the merits of fixed versus flexible exchange rates. Let us look at the characteristics of the different exchange-rate systems.

2.a. Equilibrium in the Foreign Exchange Market

An exchange rate is the price of one money in terms of another. Equilibrium is determined by the supply of and demand for the two currencies in the foreign exchange market. Figure 1 contains two supply and demand diagrams for the U.S. dollar–euro foreign exchange market. The downward-sloping demand curve indicates that the higher the dollar price of euro, the fewer euro will be demanded. The upward-sloping supply curve indicates that the higher the dollar price of euro, the more euro will be supplied.

Equilibrium in the foreign exchange market occurs at the point where the foreign exchange demand and supply curves intersect.

In Figure 1(a), the initial equilibrium occurs at the point where the demand curve D_1 intersects the supply curve. At this point, the equilibrium exchange rate is \$1.00 (1 euro costs \$1.00) and the quantity of euro bought and sold is Q_1.

Suppose U.S. residents increase their demand for French wine. Because euro are needed to pay for the wine, the greater U.S. demand for French wine generates a

---

FIGURE 1

The Supply of and Demand for Foreign Exchange

This figure represents the foreign exchange market for euro traded for dollars. The demand curve for euro is based partly on the U.S. demand for French products, and the supply curve of euro is based partly on the French demand for U.S. products: an increase in demand for French wine causes demand for euro to increase from D_1 to D_2. This shift causes an increase from Q_1 to Q_2 in the equilibrium quantity of euro traded and causes the euro to appreciate to \$1.03 from the initial equilibrium exchange rate of \$1.00. A decrease in demand for French wine causes the demand for euro to

fall from D_1 to D_3. This shift leads to a fall in the equilibrium quantity traded to Q_3 and a depreciation of the euro to \$.97. If the French demand for U.S. tractors falls, fewer euro are supplied for exchange for dollars, as illustrated by the fall in supply from S_1 to S_3. This shift causes the euro to appreciate to \$1.03 and the equilibrium quantity of euro traded to fall to Q_3. If the French demand for U.S. tractors rises, then more euro are supplied for dollars and the supply curve increases from S_1 to S_2. This causes the euro to depreciate and the equilibrium quantity of euro traded to rise to Q_2.

(a) A Change in the U.S. Demand for French Wine

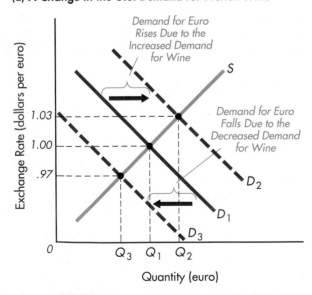

(b) A Change in the French Demand for U.S. Tractors

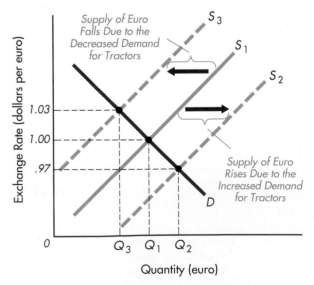

greater demand for euro by U.S. citizens, who hold dollars. The demand curve in Figure 1(a) thus shifts from D_1 to D_2. This increased demand for euro causes the euro to appreciate relative to the dollar. The new exchange rate is $1.03, and a greater quantity of euro, Q_2, is bought and sold.

If the U.S. demand for French wine falls, the demand for euro also falls, as illustrated by the shift from D_1 to D_3 in Figure 1(a). The decreased demand for euro causes the euro to depreciate relative to the dollar, so that the exchange rate falls to $.97.

So far, we have considered how shifts in the U.S. demand for French goods affect the dollar-euro exchange rate. We can also use the same supply and demand diagram to analyze how changes in the French demand for U.S. goods affect the equilibrium exchange rate. The supply of euro to the foreign exchange market partly originates with French residents who buy goods from the rest of the world. If a French importer buys a tractor from a U.S. firm, the importer must exchange euro for dollars to pay for the tractor. As French residents' demand for foreign goods and services rises and falls, the supply of euro to the foreign exchange market changes.

Suppose the French demand for U.S. tractors increases. This brings about a shift of the supply curve: as euro are exchanged for dollars to buy the U.S. tractors, the supply of euro increases. In Figure 1(b), the supply of euro curve shifts from S_1 to S_2. The greater supply of euro causes the euro to depreciate relative to the dollar, and the exchange rate falls from $1.00 to $.97. If the French demand for U.S. tractors decreases, the supply of euro decreases from S_1 to S_3, and the euro appreciates to $1.03.

Foreign exchange supply and demand curves are affected by changes in tastes and technology and by changing government policy. As demand and supply change, the equilibrium exchange rate changes. In fact, continuous shifts in supply and demand cause the exchange rate to change as often as every day, on the basis of free market forces. Now let us consider how fixed exchange rates differ from floating exchange rates.

2.b. Adjustment Mechanisms Under Fixed and Flexible Exchange Rates

4. How do fixed and floating exchange rates differ in their adjustment to shifts in supply and demand for currencies?

appreciate: when the value of a currency increases under floating exchange rates—that is, exchange rates determined by supply and demand

depreciate: when the value of a currency decreases under floating exchange rates

Figure 2 shows the dollar-euro foreign exchange market. The exchange rate is the number of dollars required to buy 1 euro; the quantity is the quantity of euro bought and sold. Suppose that, initially, the equilibrium is at point A, with quantity Q_1 euro traded at $1.00 per euro.

Suppose French wine becomes more popular in the United States, and the demand for euro increases from D_1 to D_2. With flexible exchange rates (as in Figure 1), a new equilibrium is established at point B. The exchange rate rises to $1.03 per euro, and the quantity of euro bought and sold is Q_2. The increased demand for euro has caused the euro to **appreciate** (rise in value against the dollar) and the dollar to **depreciate** (fall in value against the euro). This is an example of a freely floating exchange rate, determined by the free market forces of supply and demand.

Now suppose the Federal Reserve is committed to maintaining a fixed exchange rate of $1.00 per euro. The increase in demand for euro causes a shortage of euro at the exchange rate of $1.00. According to the new demand curve, D_2, the quantity of euro demanded at $1.00 is Q_3. The quantity supplied is found on the original supply curve S_1, at Q_1. The only way to maintain the exchange rate of $1.00 is for the Federal Reserve to supply euro to meet the shortage of $Q_3 - Q_1$. In other words, the

FIGURE 2

Foreign Exchange Market Equilibrium Under Fixed and Flexible Exchange Rates

Initially, equilibrium is at point *A;* the exchange rate is $1.00 and Q_1 euro are traded. An increase in demand for French wine causes the demand for euro to increase from D_1 to D_2. With flexible exchange rates, the euro appreciates in value to $1.03 and Q_2 euro are traded; equilibrium is at point *B.* If the government is committed to maintaining a fixed exchange rate of $1.00, the supply of euro must be increased to S_2 so that a new equilibrium can occur at point *C.* The government must intervene in the foreign exchange market and sell euro to shift the supply curve to S_2.

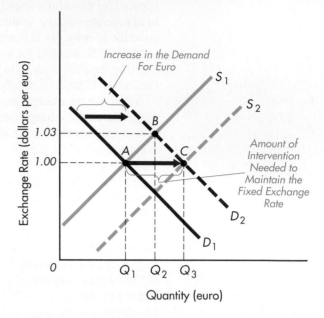

An increase in demand for a currency will cause an appreciation of its currency, unless governments intervene in the foreign exchange market to increase the supply of that currency.

fundamental disequilibrium: a permanent shift in the foreign exchange market supply and demand curves such that the fixed exchange rate is no longer an equilibrium rate

speculators: people who seek to profit from an expected shift in an exchange rate by selling the currency that is expected to depreciate and buying the currency that is expected to appreciate, then exchanging the appreciated currency for the depreciated currency after the exchange-rate adjustment

Fed must sell $Q_3 - Q_1$ euro to shift the supply curve to S_2 and thus maintain the fixed exchange rate.

If the increased demand for euro is temporary, the Fed can continue to supply euro for the short time necessary. However, if the increased demand for euro is permanent, the Fed's intervention will eventually end when it runs out of euro. This situation—a permanent change in supply or demand—is referred to as a **fundamental disequilibrium.** The fixed exchange rate is no longer an equilibrium rate. Under the Bretton Woods agreement, a country was supposed to devalue its currency in such cases.

Suppose that the shift to D_2 in Figure 2 is permanent. In this case, the dollar should be devalued. A devaluation to $1.03 per euro would restore equilibrium in the foreign exchange market without requiring further intervention by the government. Sometimes, however, governments try to maintain the old exchange rate ($1.00 per euro, in this case) even though most people believe the shift in demand to be permanent. When this happens, **speculators** buy the currency that is in greater demand (euro, in our example) in anticipation of the eventual devaluation of the other currency (dollars, in Figure 2). A speculator who purchases euro for $1.00 prior to the devaluation and sells them for $1.03 after the devaluation earns $.03 per euro purchased.

Speculation puts greater devaluation pressure on the dollar: the speculators sell dollars and buy euro, causing the demand for euro to increase even further. Such speculative activity contributed to the breakdown of the Bretton Woods system of fixed exchange rates. Several countries intervened to support exchange rates that were far out of line with free market forces. The longer a devaluation was put off, the more obvious it became that devaluation was forthcoming and the more speculators entered the market. In 1971 and 1973, speculators sold dollars for yen and

German marks. They were betting that the dollar would be devalued; both times they were correct. The speculative activity of the early 1970s drew attention to the folly of efforts to maintain fixed exchange rates in the face of a change in the fundamental equilibrium exchange rate.

2.c. Constraints on Economic Policy

?

5. What are the advantages and disadvantages of fixed and floating exchange rates?

Fixed exchange rates can be maintained over time only between countries with similar economic policies and similar underlying economic conditions. As prices rise within a country, the domestic value of a unit of its currency falls, since the currency buys fewer goods and services. In the foreign exchange market too, the value of a unit of domestic currency falls, since it buys relatively fewer goods and services than the foreign currency does. A fixed exchange rate thus requires that the purchasing power of the two currencies change at roughly the same rate over time. Only if two nations have approximately the same inflation experience will they be able to maintain a fixed exchange rate. This condition was a frequent source of problems in the Bretton Woods era of fixed exchange rates. In the late 1960s, for instance, the U.S. government was following a more expansionary macroeconomic policy than was Germany. U.S. government expenditures on the war in Vietnam and domestic antipoverty initiatives led to inflationary pressures that were not matched in Germany. Between 1965 and 1970, price levels rose by 23.2 percent in the United States but by only 12.8 percent in Germany. Since the purchasing power of the dollar was falling faster than that of the mark, the fixed exchange rate could not be maintained. The dollar had to be devalued.

One of the advantages of floating exchange rates is that countries are free to pursue their own macroeconomic policies without worrying about maintaining an exchange-rate commitment. If U.S. policy produces a higher inflation rate than Japanese policy, the dollar will automatically depreciate in value against the yen. The United States can choose the macroeconomic policy it wants, independently of other nations, and let the exchange rate adjust if its inflation rate differs markedly from that of other nations. If the dollar were fixed in value relative to the yen, the two nations couldn't follow independent policies and expect to maintain the exchange rate.

It became obvious in the late 1960s that many governments considered other issues more important than maintenance of a fixed exchange rate. A nation that puts a high priority on reducing unemployment will typically stimulate the economy to try to increase income and create jobs. This initiative may cause the domestic inflation rate to rise and the domestic currency to depreciate relative to other currencies. If one goal or the other—lower unemployment or a fixed exchange rate—must be given up, it is likely that the exchange-rate goal will be sacrificed.

Floating exchange rates allow countries to formulate their macroeconomic policies independently of other nations. Fixed exchange rates require the economic policies of countries linked by the exchange rate to be similar.

Floating exchange rates allow countries to formulate domestic economic policy solely in response to domestic issues; attention need not be paid to the economic policies of the rest of the world. For residents of some countries, this freedom may be more of a problem than a benefit. The freedom to choose a rate of inflation and let the exchange rate adjust itself can have undesirable consequences in countries whose politicians, for whatever reason, follow highly inflationary policies. In these countries a fixed-exchange-rate system would impose discipline, since maintenance of the exchange rate would not permit policies that diverged sharply from those of its trading partner.

1. Under a fixed-exchange-rate system, governments must sometimes intervene in the foreign exchange market to maintain the exchange rate. A fundamental disequilibrium requires a currency devaluation.

2. Fixed exchange rates can be maintained only between countries with similar macroeconomic policies and similar underlying economic conditions.

3. Fixed exchange rates serve as an anchor to constrain inflationary government policies.

?

6. How does a change in the exchange rate affect the prices of goods traded between countries?

3. Prices and Exchange Rates

An exchange rate, as you learned in Chapters 3 and 7, is the price of one money in terms of another. The exchange rate doesn't enter into the purchase and sale of Chryslers in Michigan and California because each state uses the U.S. dollar. But for goods and services traded across national borders, the exchange rate is an important part of the total price. We will assume that currencies are traded freely for each other and that foreign exchange markets respond to supply and demand without government intervention.

Let's look at an example. A U.S. wine importer purchases 1,000,000 euro (€1,000,000) worth of wine from France. The importer demands euro in order to pay the French wine seller. Suppose the initial equilibrium exchange rate is $1 = €1. At this rate, the U.S. importer needs 1,000,000 euro at $1 apiece, or $1,000,000.

3.a. Appreciation and Depreciation

When the exchange rate between two currencies changes, we say that one currency *depreciates* while the other *appreciates.* Suppose the exchange rate goes from $1 = €1 to $1.10 = €1. The euro is now worth $1.10 instead of $1. The dollar has depreciated in value in relation to the euro; dollars are worth less in terms of euro. At the new equilibrium exchange rate, the U.S. importer needs $1,100,000 ($1.10 × 1,000,000) to buy €1,000,000 worth of wine.

Instead of saying that the dollar has depreciated against the euro, we can say that the euro has *appreciated* against the dollar. If the dollar is depreciating against the euro, the euro must be appreciating against the dollar. Whichever way we describe the change in the exchange rate, the result is that euro are now worth more in terms of dollars. The price of a euro has gone from $1 to $1.10.

As exchange rates change, the prices of goods and services traded in international markets also change. Suppose the dollar appreciates against the euro. This means that a euro costs fewer dollars; it also means that French goods cost U.S. buyers less. If the exchange rate falls to $.90 = €1, then €1,000,000 costs $900,000 ($.90 × 1,000,000). The French wine has become less expensive to the U.S. importer.

- When the domestic (home) currency *depreciates,* foreign goods become *more expensive* to domestic buyers.

- When the domestic currency *appreciates,* foreign goods become *less expensive* to domestic buyers.

Let's look at the problem from the French side. When the dollar price of the euro rises, the euro price of the dollar falls; and when the dollar price of the euro falls, the euro price of the dollar rises. If the dollar price of the euro (\$/€) is originally \$1, the euro price of the dollar (€/\$) is the reciprocal (1/1), or €1. If the dollar depreciates against the euro to \$1.10, then the euro appreciates against the dollar to 1/1.10, or €.91. As the euro appreciates, U.S. goods become less expensive to French buyers. If the dollar appreciates against the euro to \$.90, then the euro depreciates against the dollar to 1/.90, or €1.11. As the euro depreciates, U.S. goods become more expensive to French buyers.

- When the domestic currency *depreciates,* domestic goods become *less expensive* to foreign buyers.

- When the domestic currency *appreciates,* domestic goods become *more expensive* to foreign buyers.

When the dollar depreciates, U.S. goods become less expensive to foreign buyers; as the dollar appreciates, those goods become more expensive.

The exchange rate is just one determinant of the demand for goods and services. Income, tastes, the prices of substitutes and complements, expectations, and the exchange rate all determine the demand for U.S. wheat, for example. As the dollar depreciates in relation to other currencies, the demand for U.S. wheat increases (along with foreign demand for all other U.S. goods), even if all the other determinants do not change. Conversely, as the dollar appreciates, the demand for U.S. wheat falls (along with foreign demand for all other U.S. goods), even if all the other determinants do not change.

3.b. Purchasing Power Parity

Within a country, where prices are quoted in terms of a single currency, all we need to know is the price in the domestic currency of an item in two different locations to determine where our money buys more. If Joe's bookstore charges \$20 for a book and Pete's bookstore charges \$30 for the same book, the purchasing power of our money is greater at Joe's than it is at Pete's.

International comparisons of prices must be made using exchange rates because different countries use different monies. Once we cross national borders, prices are quoted in different currencies. Suppose Joe's bookstore in New York City charges \$20 for a book and Pierre's bookstore in Paris charges €30. To compare the prices, we must know the exchange rate between dollars and euro.

purchasing power parity (PPP): the condition under which monies have the same purchasing power in different markets

If we find that goods sell for the same price in different markets, our money has the same purchasing power in those markets, which means that we have **purchasing power parity (PPP).** The PPP reflects a relationship among the domestic price level, the exchange rate, and the foreign price level:

$$P = EP^{\text{F}}$$

where

P = the domestic price

E = the exchange rate (units of domestic currency per unit of foreign currency)

P^{F} = the foreign price

If the dollar-euro exchange rate is .67 (\$.67 = €1), then a book priced at €30 in Pierre's store in Paris costs the same as a book priced at \$20 in Joe's New York store:

$$P = EP^{\text{F}}$$

$$= \$.67 \times 30$$

$$= \$20$$

The domestic price (we are assuming that the U.S. dollar is the domestic currency) equals the exchange rate times the foreign price. Because the dollar price of the book in Paris is $20 and the price in the United States is $20, PPP holds. The purchasing power (value) of the dollar is the same in both places.

Realistically, similar goods don't always sell for the same price everywhere. Actually they don't even sell for the same price within a country. If the same textbook is priced differently at different bookstores, it is unrealistic to expect the price of the book to be identical worldwide. There are several reasons why PPP does not hold. The most important are that goods are not identical, that information is costly, that shipping costs affect prices, and that tariffs and legal restrictions on trade affect prices. If these factors did not exist, we would expect that anytime a price was lower in one market than in another, people would buy in the low-price market (pushing prices up) and simultaneously sell in the high-price market (pushing prices down). This activity, known as *arbitrage,* would ensure that PPP holds.

RECAP

1. When the exchange rate between two currencies changes, one currency depreciates while the other appreciates.
2. Purchasing power parity means that money has the same purchasing power in different markets.
3. Similar goods do not sell for the same price all over the world because goods are not identical, information is costly, shipping costs affect prices, and tariffs and legal restrictions on international trade affect prices.

4. Interest Rates and Exchange Rates

Exchange rates are used to compare international prices of goods and services. They are also used to compare the return on foreign currency–denominated stocks and bonds to the return on domestic assets. For example, suppose you have a choice of buying a U.S. or a U.K. bond. The U.S. bond is denominated in dollars and pays 15 percent interest; the U.K. bond is denominated in British pounds and pays 10 percent interest. Because you are a U.S. resident and you ultimately want dollars for household spending, you must compare the dollar return from holding each bond.

4.a. The Domestic Currency Return from Foreign Bonds

The U.S. bond is denominated in dollars, so the 15 percent interest is a dollar return. The U.K. bond, on the other hand, promises to pay 10 percent in terms of British pounds. If you buy the U.K. bond, you exchange dollars for pounds at the time the bond is purchased. When the bond matures, you exchange the principal and interest (the proceeds), trading pounds for dollars. If the exchange rate remains the same, the return on the U.K. bond is 10 percent. But if the exchange rate changes between the time you buy the bond and the time it matures, your return in dollars may be more or less than 10 percent.

FIGURE 3

A U.S. Resident Buys a One-Year U.K. Bond

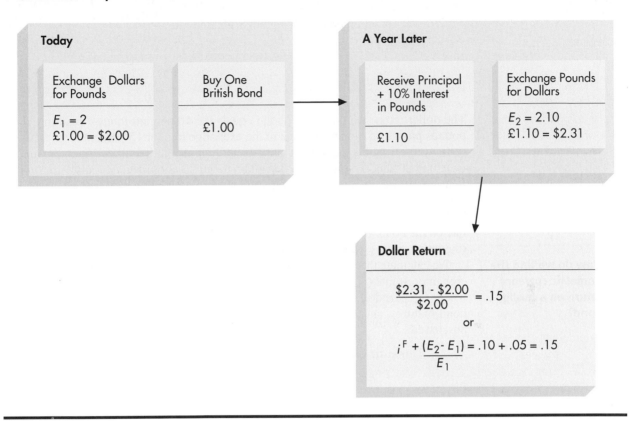

Figure 3 shows what happens when a U.S. resident buys a one-year U.K. bond. Suppose the exchange rate is $2 = £1 when the bond is purchased, and the bond sells for £1. The U.S. resident needs $2 to buy the bond. A year later the bond matures. The bondholder receives the principal of £1 plus 10 percent interest (£.10). Now the U.S. resident wants to convert the pounds into dollars. If the exchange rate has gone up from $2 = £1 to $2.10 = £1, the £1.10 proceeds from the bond are converted into dollars at the rate of 2.10 dollars per pound. The *dollar value* of the proceeds is $2.31 (the exchange rate [2.10] multiplied by the pound proceeds [£1.10]). The *dollar return* from the U.K. bond is the percentage difference between the dollar proceeds received after one year, and the initial dollar amount invested, or approximately 15 percent:

$$\text{Dollar return} = \frac{\$2.31 - \$2}{\$2}$$

$$= \frac{\$.31}{\$2}$$

$$= .15$$

We can also determine the dollar return from the U.K. bond by adding the U.K. interest rate to the percentage change in the exchange rate. The percentage change in the exchange rate is 5 percent:

$$\text{Percentage change in exchange rate} = \frac{\$2.10 - \$2}{\$2}$$

$$= \frac{\$.10}{\$2}$$

$$= 0.05$$

The dollar return from the U.K. bond equals the 10 percent interest paid in British pounds plus the 5 percent change in the exchange rate, or 15 percent.

In our example, the pound appreciates against the dollar. When the pound increases in value, foreign residents holding pound-denominated bonds earn a higher return on those bonds than the pound interest rate. If the pound depreciates against the dollar, so that the pounds received at maturity are worth less than the pounds originally purchased, then the dollar return from the U.K. bond is lower than the interest rate on the bond. If the pound depreciates 5 percent, the dollar return is just 5 percent (the interest rate [10 percent] *minus* the exchange rate change [5 percent]).

We calculate the domestic currency return from a foreign bond by adding the foreign interest rate (i^F) plus the percentage change in the exchange rate [$(E_2 - E_1)/E_1$], where E_2 is the dollar price of a unit of foreign currency in the next period, when the bond matures, and E_1 is the exchange rate in the current period, when the bond is purchased:

$$\text{Domestic currency return} = \text{foreign interest rate}$$
$$+ \text{percentage change in exchange rate}$$

$$= i^F + \frac{E_2 - E_1}{E_1}$$

4.b. Interest Rate Parity

Because U.S. residents can hold U.S. bonds, U.K. bonds, or the bonds or other securities of any country they choose, they compare the returns from the alternatives when deciding what assets to buy. Foreign investors do the same thing. One product of the process is a close relationship among international interest rates. Specifically, the return, or interest rate, tends to be the same on similar bonds when returns are measured in terms of the domestic currency. This is called **interest rate parity (IRP).**

Interest rate parity is the financial asset version of purchasing power parity. Similar financial assets have the same percentage return when that return is computed in terms of one currency. Interest rate parity defines a relationship among the domestic interest rate, the foreign interest rate, and the expected change in the exchange rate:

$$\text{Domestic interest rate} = \text{foreign interest rate}$$
$$+ \text{expected change in exchange rate}$$

In our example, the U.S. bond pays 15 percent interest; the U.K. bond offers 10 percent interest in pounds. If the pound is expected to appreciate 5 percent, the U.K. bond offers U.S. residents an expected dollar return of 15 percent. Interest rate parity holds in this case. The domestic interest rate is 15 percent, which equals the foreign interest rate (10 percent) plus the expected change in the exchange rate (5 percent).

8. **How do we find the domestic currency return on a foreign bond?**

interest rate parity (IRP): the condition under which similar financial assets have the same interest rate when measured in the same currency

9. **What is the relationship between domestic and foreign interest rates and changes in the exchange rate?**

Interest rate parity is the product of arbitrage in financial markets. If U.S. bonds and U.K. bonds are similar in every respect except the currency used to pay the principal and interest, then they should yield similar returns to bondholders. If U.S. investors can earn a higher return from buying U.K. bonds, they are going to buy more U.K. bonds and fewer U.S. bonds. This tends to raise the price of U.K. bonds, pushing U.K. interest rates down. At the same time, the price of U.S. bonds drops, raising U.S. interest rates. The initial higher return on U.K. bonds and resulting greater demand for U.K. bonds increases the demand for pounds, increasing the value of the pound versus the dollar today. As the pound appreciates today, if investors expect the same future exchange rate as they did before the current appreciation, the expected appreciation over the future falls. The change in the exchange rate and interest rates equalizes the expected dollar return from holding a U.S. bond or a U.K. bond. U.K. bonds originally offered a higher return than U.S. bonds, but the increase in demand for U.K. bonds relative to U.S. bonds lowers U.K. interest rates and the expected appreciation of the pound, so that the bond returns are equalized.

RECAP

1. The domestic currency return from a foreign bond equals the foreign interest rate plus the percentage change in the exchange rate.

2. Interest rate parity exists when similar financial assets have the same interest rate when measured in the same currency or when the domestic interest rate equals the foreign interest rate plus the expected change in the exchange rate.

Summary

? How does a commodity standard fix exchange rates between countries?

1. Between 1880 and 1914, a gold standard provided for fixed exchange rates among countries. §1.a

2. The gold standard ended with World War I, and no established international monetary system replaced it until after World War II, when the Bretton Woods agreement created a fixed-exchange-rate system. §1.b

? What kinds of exchange-rate arrangements exist today?

3. Today some countries have fixed exchange rates, others have floating exchange rates, and still others have managed floats or other types of systems. §1.e

? How is equilibrium determined in the foreign exchange market?

4. Foreign exchange market equilibrium is determined by the intersection of the demand and supply curves for foreign exchange. §2.a

? How do fixed and floating exchange rates differ in their adjustment to shifts in supply and demand for currencies?

5. Under fixed exchange rates, central banks must intervene in the foreign exchange market to keep the exchange rate from shifting. §2.b

? What are the advantages and disadvantages of fixed and floating exchange rates?

6. Floating exchange rates permit countries to pursue independent economic policies. A fixed exchange rate requires a country to adopt policies similar to those of the country whose currency it is pegged to. A fixed exchange rate may serve to prevent a country from pursuing inflationary policies. §2.c

? How does a change in the exchange rate affect the prices of goods traded between countries?

7. When the domestic currency depreciates against other currencies, foreign goods become more expensive to

domestic buyers and domestic goods become less expensive to foreign buyers. *§3.a*

8. When the domestic currency appreciates against other currencies, foreign goods become less expensive to domestic buyers and domestic goods become more expensive to foreign buyers. *§3.a*

9. Purchasing power parity exists when monies have the same value in different markets. *§3.b*

? Why don't similar goods sell for the same price all over the world?

10. Deviations from PPP arise because goods are not identical in different countries, information is costly, shipping costs affect prices, and tariffs and restrictions on trade affect prices. *§3.b*

? How do we find the domestic currency return on a foreign bond?

11. The domestic currency return from holding a foreign bond equals the foreign interest rate plus the percentage change in the exchange rate. *§4.a*

? What is the relationship between domestic and foreign interest rates and changes in the exchange rate?

12. Interest rate parity exists when the domestic interest rate equals the foreign interest rate plus the expected change in the exchange rate, so that similar financial assets yield the same return when measured in the same currency. *§4.b*

Key Terms

gold standard *§1.a*

gold exchange standard *§1.b*

reserve currency *§1.b*

International Monetary Fund (IMF) *§1.c*

World Bank *§1.c*

foreign exchange market intervention *§1.d*

devaluation *§1.d*

equilibrium exchange rates *§1.d*

appreciate *§2.b*

depreciate *§2.b*

fundamental disequilibrium *§2.b*

speculators *§2.b*

purchasing power parity (PPP) *§3.b*

interest rate parity (IRP) *§4.b*

Exercises

1. Under a gold standard, if the price of an ounce of gold is 400 U.S. dollars and 500 Canadian dollars, what is the exchange rate between U.S. and Canadian dollars?

2. What were the three major results of the Bretton Woods conference?

3. What is the difference between the IMF and the World Bank?

4. How can Mexico fix the value of the peso relative to the dollar when the demand for and supply of dollars and pesos changes continuously? Illustrate your explanation with a graph.

5. Draw a foreign exchange market supply and demand diagram to show how the yen-dollar exchange rate is determined. Set the initial equilibrium at a rate of 100 yen per dollar.

6. Using the diagram in exercise 5, illustrate the effect of a change in tastes that prompts Japanese residents to buy more goods from the United States. If the exchange rate is floating, what will happen to the foreign exchange market equilibrium?

7. Using the diagram in exercise 5, illustrate the effect of the change in Japanese tastes if exchange rates are fixed. What will happen to the foreign exchange market equilibrium?

8. When and why should exchange rates change under a fixed-exchange-rate system?

9. Suppose you just returned home from a vacation in Mazatlán, Mexico, where you exchanged U.S. dollars for Mexican pesos. How did your trip to Mexico affect the supply and demand for dollars and the exchange rate (assume that all other things are equal)?

10. What does it mean to say that a currency appreciates or depreciates in value? Give an example of each and briefly mention what might cause such a change.

11. How does a currency speculator profit from exchange-rate changes? Give an example of a profitable speculation.

12. Find the U.S. dollar value of each of the following currencies at the given exchange rates:
    a. $1 = C$1.20 (Canadian dollars)
    b. $1 = ¥140 (Japanese yen)
    c. $1 = A$0.5 (Australian dollars)
    d. $1 = SKr6 (Swedish krona)
    e. $1 = SF1.5 (Swiss francs)

13. You are a U.S. importer who buys goods from many different countries. How many U.S. dollars do you need to settle each of the following invoices?
    a. 1,000,000 Australian dollars for wool blankets (exchange rate: A$1 = $.769)
    b. 500,000 British pounds for dishes (exchange rate: £1 = $1.5855)
    c. 100,000 Indian rupees for baskets (exchange rate: Rs1 = $.0602)
    d. 150 million Japanese yen for stereo components (exchange rate: ¥1 = $.0069)
    e. 825,000 euro for German wine (exchange rate: € = $1.05)

14. What is the dollar value of the invoices in exercise 13 if the dollar:
    a. Depreciates 10 percent against the Australian dollar
    b. Appreciates 10 percent against the British pound
    c. Depreciates 10 percent against the Indian rupee
    d. Appreciates 20 percent against the Japanese yen
    e. Depreciates 100 percent against the euro

15. Explain purchasing power parity and why it does not hold perfectly in the real world.

16. Write an equation that describes purchasing power parity and explain the equation.

17. Write an equation that describes interest rate parity and explain the equation.

18. If the interest rate on one-year government bonds is 5 percent in Germany and 8 percent in the United States, what do you think is expected to happen to the dollar value of the euro? Explain your answer.

19. In 1960 a U.S. dollar sold for 620 Italian lire. If PPP held in 1960, what would the PPP value of the exchange rate have been in 1987 if Italian prices rose 12 times and U.S. prices rose 4 times between 1960 and 1987?

ACE

Take the ACE Practice Test for this chapter to review the important concepts and get immediate feedback with answers.

economics.college.hmco.com/students

The European Union

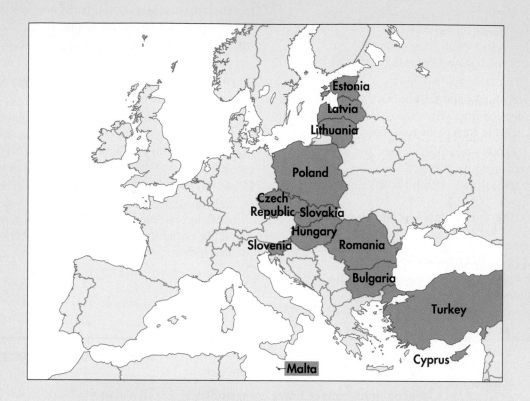

After successfully growing from 6 to 15 members, the European Union is now preparing for its biggest enlargement ever in terms of scope and diversity. 13 countries have applied to become new members: 10 of these countries—Cyprus, the Czech Republic, Estonia, Hungary, Latvia, Lithuania, Malta, Poland, the Slovak Republic, and Slovenia—are set to join on 1st May 2004. They are currently known by the term "acceding countries."

Bulgaria and Romania hope to do so by 2007, while Turkey is not currently negotiating its membership.

In order to join the Union, they need to fulfill the economic and political conditions known as the "Copenhagen criteria," according to which a prospective member must:

- Be a stable democracy, respecting human rights, the rule of law, and the protection of minorities;

- Have a functioning market economy;

- Adopt the common rules, standards and policies that make up the body of EU law.

The EU assists these countries in taking on EU laws, and provides a range of financial assistance to improve their infrastructure and economy.

Source: Europa website, http://europa.eu .int/comm/enlargement/enlargement.htm.

Commentary

The expansion of the European Union to include the countries from eastern Europe holds much promise for the economic development of these countries. Once in the EU, these countries would be able to trade freely with the other EU countries, just as the states of the United States trade freely with one another. Just as the U.S. states all share a common money to help facilitate interstate trade, it is likely that the eastern European countries would also welcome the adoption of the euro as their money to further solidify the links between their economies and those of the rest of the EU.

A fixed-exchange-rate system represents an agreement among countries to convert their individual currencies from one to another at a given rate. The adoption of one money for Europe is the strongest possible commitment to fixed exchange rates among the EU countries. If every nation uses the same currency, the euro, then all will be linked to the same inflation rate and there will be no fluctuation of the value of the currency across the EU nations using the currency—just as each state in the United States uses the same money, the U.S. dollar. The adoption of a single currency requires that economic policies be similar across EU countries. This means that individual countries must subjugate their monetary policies to the goals of the European Central Bank. If each nation insists on exercising its own monetary and fiscal policies and chooses different interest and inflation rates, there can never be one money.

A convergence in inflation rates is necessary for the smooth operation of any fixed exchange rate. Persistent inflation differentials across the members of a fixed-exchange-rate system affect the competitiveness of each member's exports in the world market. Though a fixed-exchange-rate system maintains stable *nominal exchange rates* (the rate observed in the foreign exchange market), the competitiveness of a currency is represented by the *real exchange rate*. The real exchange rate is the nominal exchange rate adjusted for the price level at home compared to the price level abroad:

$$\text{Real exchange rate} = \frac{\text{nominal exchange rate} \times \text{foreign price level}}{\text{domestic price level}}$$

The disruptive changes in competitiveness caused by persistent inflation differentials require a realignment of a fixed-exchange-rate system that adjusts nominal exchange rates to keep real exchange rates from drifting too far from their correct value. For instance, if the Italian price level starts to rise faster than German prices, Italian goods will be priced out of the German market unless there is an Italian currency that depreciates on the foreign exchange market. According to the equation just presented, if Italy is the domestic country and its price level rises, the real exchange rate falls and Italian goods are, therefore, relatively more expensive unless the nominal exchange rate rises to offset the higher domestic price level. The need for similar inflation rates within a fixed exchange-rate system indicates that a country can successfully join the fixed-exchange-rate system or a region with one money only when its inflation rate falls to a level close to that of other European countries.

Any countries seeking to join the euro area must align their economic policies with those of the other member countries.

Glossary

absolute advantage   an advantage derived from one country having a lower absolute input cost of producing a particular good than another country (35)

accounting profit   total revenue less total costs except for the opportunity cost of capital (23)

adaptive expectation   an expectation formed on the basis of information collected in the past (15)

adverse selection   the problem that occurs when higher-quality consumers or producers are driven out of the market because unobservable qualities are misvalued (28)

aggregate demand curve   a curve that shows the different equilibrium levels of expenditures on domestic output at different price levels (9)

aggregate supply curve   a curve that shows the amount of real GDP produced at different price levels (9)

American Depositary Receipt (ADR)   a stock that trades in the United States but represents shares of a foreign corporation (31)

antitrust policy   government policies and programs designed to control the growth of monopoly and enhance competition (27)

appreciate   when the value of a currency increases under floating exchange rates—that is, exchange rates determined by supply and demand (37)

Asian tigers   Hong Kong, Korea, Singapore, and Taiwan, countries that globalized in the 1960s and 1970s and experienced fast economic growth (19)

association as causation   the mistaken assumption that because two events seem to occur together, one causes the other (1)

automatic stabilizer   an element of fiscal policy that changes automatically as income changes (12)

autonomous consumption   consumption that is independent of income (10)

average physical product (*APP*)   output per unit of resource (22)

average propensity to consume (*APC*)   the proportion of disposable income spent for consumption (10)

average propensity to save (*APS*)   the proportion of disposable income saved (10)

average total cost (*ATC*)   per unit cost; total cost divided by the total output (22)

back-end load   a fee that you pay if you sell a mutual fund within a certain time frame (31)

backward-bending labor supply curve   a labor supply curve indicating that a person is willing and able to work more hours as the wage rate increases until, at some sufficiently high wage rate, the person chooses to work fewer hours (30)

balance of payments   a record of a country's trade in goods, services, and financial assets with the rest of the world (7)

balance of trade   the balance on the merchandise account in a nation's balance of payments (7)

barrier to entry   anything that impedes the ability of firms to begin a new business in an industry in which existing firms are earning positive economic profits (25)

barter   the direct exchange of goods and services without the use of money (3)

base year   the year against which other years are measured (6)

behavioral economics   a field of study that blends psychology and economics (31)

bilateral aid   foreign aid that flows from one country to another (18)

bond   an IOU issued by a borrower to a lender (31)

break-even price   a price that is equal to the minimum point of the average-total-cost curve (24)

budget line   a line showing all the combinations of goods that can be purchased with a given level of income (21 App.)

budget deficit   the shortage that results when government spending is greater than revenue (5)

budget surplus   the excess that results when government spending is less than revenue (5)

business cycle   fluctuations in the economy between growth (expressed in rising real GDP) followed by stagnation (expressed in falling real GDP) (5, 8)

business firm   a business organization controlled by a single management (4)

capital   products such as machinery and equipment that are used in production (1)

capital account   the record in the balance of payments of the flow of financial assets into and out of a country (7)

capital consumption allowance   the estimated value of depreciation plus the value of accidental damage to capital stock (6)

cartel   an organization of independent firms whose purpose is to control and limit production and maintain or increase prices and profits (26)

cash transfers   money allocated away from one group in society to another (34)

centrally planned economy   an economic system in which the government determines what goods and services are produced and the prices at which they are sold (5)

ceteris paribus   Latin for "everything else held constant" (23)

chain-type real GDP growth the mean of the growth rates found using beginning and ending year prices (6)

circular flow diagram a model showing the flow of output and income from one sector of the economy to another (4)

classical economics a school of thought that assumes that real GDP is determined by aggregate supply, while the equilibrium price level is determined by aggregate demand (16)

Coase theorem the idea that if people can negotiate with one another at no cost over the right to perform activities that cause externalities, they will always arrive at an efficient solution (28)

coincident indicator a variable that changes at the same time that real output changes (8)

commercial bank loan a bank loan at market rates of interest, often involving a bank syndicate (18)

commercial policy government policy that influences international trade flows (36)

common and preferred stock the two main types of stock (31)

comparable investment a stock that has the same features, such as risk and liquidity, as the one that buyers and sellers are evaluating (31)

comparable worth the idea that pay ought to be determined by job characteristics rather than by supply and demand and that jobs with comparable requirements should receive comparable wages (30)

comparative advantage the ability to produce a good or service at a lower opportunity cost than someone else (2, 35)

compensating wage differentials wage differences that make up for the higher risk or poorer working conditions of one job over another (30)

complementary goods goods that are used together; as the price of one rises, the demand for the other falls (3)

composite currency an artificial unit of account that is an average of the values of several national currencies (13)

concentration the degree to which a few firms control the output and pricing decisions in a market (27)

constant returns to scale unit costs remain constant as the quantity of production is increased and all resources are variable (22)

consumer equilibrium or **equimarginal principle** to maximize utility, consumers must allocate their scarce incomes among goods so as to equate the marginal utilities per dollar of expenditure on the last unit of each good purchased (21)

consumer price index (CPI) a measure of the average price of goods and services purchased by the typical household (6)

consumer sovereignty the authority of consumers to determine what is produced through their purchases of goods and services (4)

consumer surplus the difference between what the consumer is willing and able to pay for a unit of a good and the price that the consumer actually has to pay (21)

consumption household spending (4)

consumption function the relationship between disposable income and consumption (10)

contracting out the process of enlisting a private firm to provide a product or service for a government entity (27)

corporation a legal entity owned by shareholders whose liability for the firm's losses is limited to the value of the stock they own (4)

cost of living adjustment (COLA) an increase in wages that is designed to match increases in prices of items purchased by the typical household (6)

cost-plus markup pricing a pricing policy whereby a firm computes its average costs of producing a product and then sets the price at some percentage above this cost (26)

cost-push inflation inflation caused by rising costs of production (9)

coupon the fixed amount that the issuer of a bond agrees to pay the bondholder each year (31)

credit available savings that are lent to borrowers to spend (13)

cross-price elasticity of demand the percentage change in the quantity demanded for one good divided by the percentage change in the price of a related good, everything else held constant (20)

crowding forcing a group into certain kinds of occupations (30)

crowding out a drop in consumption or investment spending caused by government spending (12)

currency convertibility the ease with which the domestic currency can be converted into foreign currency so that foreign exchange rates can properly reflect the domestic currency value of foreign prices (18)

currency substitution the use of foreign money as a substitute for domestic money when the domestic economy has a high rate of inflation (13)

current account the sum of the merchandise, services, income, and unilateral transfers accounts in the balance of payments (7)

customs union an organization of nations whose members have no trade barriers among themselves but impose common trade barriers on nonmembers (36)

deadweight loss the reduction of consumer surplus without a corresponding increase in profit when a perfectly competitive firm is monopolized (25)

debt loans (23)

deficit in a balance of payments account, the amount by which debits exceed credits (7)

demand the amount of a product that consumers are willing and able to buy at each possible price during a given period of time, everything else held constant (3)

demand curve a graph of a demand schedule that measures price on the vertical axis and quantity demanded on the horizontal axis (3)

demand-pull inflation inflation caused by increasing demand for output (9)

demand schedule a table or list of the prices and the corresponding quantities demanded of a particular good or service (3)

dependent variable a variable whose value depends on the value of the independent variable (1 App.)

deposit expansion multiplier the reciprocal of the reserve requirement (13)

depreciation (of capital) a reduction in the value of capital goods over time due to their use in production (6)

depreciate (a currency) when the value of a currency decreases under floating exchange rates (37)

depression a severe, prolonged economic contraction (8)

derived demand demand stemming from what a resource can produce, not demand for the resource itself (29)

determinants of demand factors other than the price of the good that influence demand—income, tastes, prices of related goods and services, expectations, and number of buyers (3)

determinants of supply factors other than the price of the good that influence supply—prices of resources, technology and productivity, expectations of producers, number of producers, and the prices of related goods and services (3)

devaluation a deliberate decrease in the official value of a currency (37)

diminishing marginal utility the principle that the more of a good that one obtains in a specific period of time, the less is the additional utility yielded by each additional unit of that good (21)

direct, or **positive, relationship** the relationship that exists when the values of related variables move in the same direction (1 App.)

discount rate the interest rate the Fed charges commercial banks when they borrow from it (14)

discouraged workers workers who have stopped looking for work because they believe that no one will offer them a job (8)

discretionary fiscal policy changes in government spending and taxation aimed at achieving a policy goal (12)

discrimination prejudice that occurs when factors unrelated to marginal revenue product affect the wages or jobs that are obtained (30)

diseconomies of scale the increases in per unit costs as the quantity of production increases and all resources are variable (22)

disequilibrium a point at which quantity demanded and quantity supplied are not equal at a particular price (3)

disparate impact an impact that differs according to race, sex, color, religion, or national origin, regardless of the motivation (30)

disparate treatment different treatment of individuals because of their race, sex, color, religion, or national origin (30)

disposable personal income (DPI) personal income minus personal taxes (6)

dissaving spending financed by borrowing or using savings (10)

disutility dissatisfaction (21)

dividend the amount paid to shareholders on each share of stock owned (31)

dominant strategy a strategy that produces better results no matter what strategy the opposing firm follows (26)

double coincidence of wants the situation that exists when A has what B wants and B has what A wants (3)

double-entry bookkeeping a system of accounting in which every transaction is recorded in at least two accounts and in which the debit total must equal the credit total for the transaction as a whole (7)

dual economy an economy in which two sectors (typically manufacturing and agriculture) show very different levels of development (18)

economic bad any item for which we would pay to have less (1)

economic efficiency a situation where no one in society can be made better off without making someone else worse off (5, 24)

economic good any item that is scarce (1)

economic growth an increase in real GDP (17)

economic profit total revenue less total costs, including all opportunity costs (23)

economic regulation the prescription of price and output for a specific industry (27)

economic rent the portion of earnings above transfer earnings (29, 32)

economies of scale the decrease in per unit costs as the quantity of production increases and all resources are variable (22)

equation of exchange an equation that relates the quantity of money to nominal GDP (14)

equilibrium the price and quantity at which quantity demanded and quantity supplied are equal (3)

equilibrium exchange rates the exchange rates that are established in the absence of government foreign exchange market intervention (37)

equimarginal principle or **consumer equilibrium** to maximize utility, consumers must allocate their scarce incomes among goods so as to equate the marginal utilities per dollar of expenditure on the last unit of each good purchased (21)

equity shares of stock; ownership of a piece of a company (23, 31)

Eurocurrency market or **offshore banking** the market for deposits and loans generally denominated in a currency other than the currency of the country in which the transaction occurs; also called offshore banking (13)

European Currency Unit (ECU) a unit of account formerly used by western European nations as their official reserve asset (13)

excess reserves the cash reserves beyond those required, which can be loaned (13)

exchange rate the rate at which monies of different countries are exchanged (3, 7)

export substitution the use of resources to produce manufactured products for export rather than agricultural products for the domestic market (18)

export supply curve a curve showing the relationship between the world price of a good and the amount that a country will export (35)

exports products that a country sells to other countries (4)

expropriation the government seizure of assets, typically without adequate compensation to the owners (18)

externality the cost or benefit of an action that is borne by someone who is not directly involved in the transaction (5, 28)

face or **par value** the amount that the lender will be repaid once a bond matures (31)

facilitating practices actions by oligopolistic firms that can contribute to cooperation and collusion even though the firms do not formally agree to cooperate (26)

factors of production goods used to produce other goods, i.e., land, labor, capital, and entrepreneurial ability (1)

fair rate of return a price that allows a monopoly firm to earn a normal profit (27)

fallacy of composition the mistaken assumption that what applies in the case of one applies to the case of many (1)

Federal Deposit Insurance Corporation (FDIC) a federal agency that insures deposits in commercial banks (13)

federal funds rate the interest rate a bank charges when it lends excess reserves to another bank (14)

Federal Open Market Committee (FOMC) the official policymaking body of the Federal Reserve System (14)

Federal Reserve the central bank of the United States (5)

financial intermediaries institutions that accept deposits from savers and make loans to borrowers (4)

fiscal policy the policy directed toward government spending and taxation (5)

FOMC directive instructions issued by the FOMC to the Federal Reserve Bank of New York to implement monetary policy (14)

foreign aid gifts or low-cost loans made to developing countries from official sources (18)

foreign direct investment the purchase of a physical operating unit or more than 10 percent investment in a foreign country (18)

foreign exchange currency and bank deposits that are denominated in foreign money (7)

foreign exchange market a global market in which people trade one currency for another (7)

foreign exchange market intervention the buying and selling of currencies by a central bank to achieve a specified exchange rate (14, 37)

fractional reserve banking system a system in which banks keep less than 100 percent of the deposits available for withdrawal (13)

free good a good for which there is no scarcity (1)

free ride the enjoyment of the benefits of a good by a producer or consumer without having to pay for the good (5)

free rider a consumer or producer who enjoys the benefits of a good or service without paying for that good or service (28)

free trade area an organization of nations whose members have no trade barriers among themselves but are free to fashion their own trade policies toward nonmembers (36)

front-end load a fee that you pay when you purchase a mutual fund (31)

fundamental disequilibrium a permanent shift in the foreign exchange market supply and demand curves such that the fixed exchange rate is no longer an equilibrium rate (37)

game theory a description of oligopolistic behavior as a series of strategic moves and countermoves (26)

GDP price index a broad measure of the prices of goods and services included in the gross domestic product (6)

Gini ratio a measure of the dispersion of income ranging between 0 and 1: 0 means that all families have the same income; 1 means that one family has all of the income (34)

global fund a mutual fund that includes international investments (31)

gold exchange standard an exchange-rate system in which each nation fixes the value of its currency in terms of gold, but buys and sells the U.S. dollar rather than gold to maintain fixed exchange rates (37)

gold standard a system whereby national currencies are fixed in terms of their value in gold, thus creating fixed exchange rates between currencies (37)

gross domestic product (GDP) the market value of all final goods and services produced in a year within a country (6)

gross investment total investment, including investment expenditures required to replace capital goods consumed in current production (6)

gross national product (GNP) gross domestic product plus receipts of factor income from the rest of the world minus payments of factor income to the rest of the world (6)

hawala an informal financial market used by Muslims (13)

health maintenance organization (HMO) an organization that provides comprehensive medical care to a voluntarily enrolled consumer population in return for a fixed, prepaid amount of money (33)

Herfindahl index a measure of concentration calculated as the sum of the squares of the market share of each firm in an industry (27)

household one or more persons who occupy a unit of housing (4)

human capital skills and training acquired through education and on-the-job training (30)

hyperinflation an extremely high rate of inflation (8)

import demand curve a curve showing the relationship between the world price of a good and the amount that a country will import (35)

import substitution the substitution of domestically produced manufactured goods for imported manufactured goods (18)

imports products that a country buys from other countries (4)

income elasticity of demand the percentage change in the quantity demanded for a good divided by the percentage change in income, everything else held constant (20)

increasing-returns-to-scale industry an industry in which the costs of producing a unit of output fall as more output is produced (36)

independent variable a variable whose value does not depend on the values of other variables (1 App.)

index fund a mutual fund that tries to match the performance of a broad market index (31)

indifference curve a curve showing all combinations of two goods that the consumer is indifferent among (21 App.)

indifference map a complete set of indifference curves (21 App.)

indifferent   lacking any preference (21 App.)

indirect business tax   a tax that is collected by businesses for a government agency (6)

inferior goods   goods for which demand decreases as income increases (3, 20)

inflation   a sustained rise in the average level of prices (8)

in-kind transfers   the allocations of goods and services from one group in society to another (34)

inputs   goods used to produce other goods (1)

interest rate effect   a change in interest rates that causes investment and therefore aggregate expenditures to change as the level of prices changes (9)

interest rate parity (IRP)   the condition under which similar financial assets have the same interest rate when measured in the same currency (37)

intermediate good   a good that is used as an input in the production of final goods and services (6)

intermediate target   an objective used to achieve some ultimate policy goal (14)

international banking facility (IBF)   a division of a U.S. bank that is allowed to receive deposits from and make loans to nonresidents of the United States without the restrictions that apply to domestic U.S. banks (13)

International Monetary Fund (IMF)   an international organization that supervises exchange-rate arrangements and lends money to member countries that are experiencing problems meeting their external financial obligations (37)

international reserve asset   an asset used to settle debts between governments (13)

international reserve currency   a currency held by a government to settle international debts (13)

international trade effect   a change in aggregate expenditures resulting from a change in the domestic price level that changes the price of domestic goods in relation to foreign goods (9)

intraindustry trade   the simultaneous import and export of goods in the same industry by a particular country (35)

inventory   the stock of unsold goods held by a firm (6)

inverse, or **negative, relationship**   the relationship that exists when the values of related variables move in opposite directions (1 App.)

investment   spending on capital goods to be used in producing goods and services (4)

Keynesian economics   a school of thought that emphasizes the role government plays in stabilizing the economy by managing aggregate demand (16)

labor   the physical and intellectual services of people, including the training, education, and abilities of the individuals in a society (1)

labor force participation   entering the work force (30)

lagging indicator   a variable that changes after real output changes (8)

land   all natural resources, such as minerals, timber, and water, as well as the land itself (1)

law of demand   the quantity of a well-defined good or service that people are willing and able to purchase during a particular period of time decreases as the price of that good or service rises and increases as the price falls, everything else held constant (3)

law of diminishing marginal returns   when successive equal amounts of a variable resource are combined with a fixed amount of another resource, marginal increases in output that can be attributed to each additional unit of the variable resource will eventually decline (22)

law of supply   the quantity of a well-defined good or service that producers are willing and able to offer for sale during a particular period of time increases as the price of the good or service increases and decreases as the price decreases, everything else held constant (3)

leading indicator   a variable that changes before real output changes (8)

legal reserves   the cash a bank holds in its vault plus its deposit in the Fed (14)

liquid asset   an asset that can easily be exchanged for goods and services (13)

load   the fees paid to the manager of a mutual fund (31)

logrolling   an inefficiency in the political process in which legislators support one another's projects in order to ensure support for their own (21)

local monopoly   a monopoly that exists in a limited geographic area (25)

long run   a period of time long enough that the quantities of all resources can be varied (20)

long-run aggregate supply curve (LRAS)   a vertical line at the potential level of GDP (9)

long-run average total cost (LRATC)   the lowest-cost combination of resources with which each level of output is produced when all resources are variable (22)

Lorenz curve   a curve measuring the degree of inequality of income distribution within a society (34)

luxury goods   goods or services that will be purchased only when income is high (20)

M1 money supply   the financial assets that are the most liquid (13)

macroeconomics   the study of the economy as a whole (1)

marginal benefit   additional benefit (2, 32)

marginal cost (MC)   the additional cost of producing one more unit of output (2, 22)

marginal factor cost (MFC)   the additional cost of an additional unit of a resource (29)

marginal opportunity cost   the amount of one good or service that must be given up to obtain one additional unit of another good or service, no matter how many units are being produced (2)

marginal physical product (MPP)   the additional quantity that is produced when one additional unit of a resource is used in combination with the same quantities of all other resources (22)

marginal propensity to consume (*MPC*) the change in consumption as a proportion of the change in disposable income (10)

marginal propensity to import (*MPI*) the change in imports as a proportion of the change in income (10)

marginal propensity to save (*MPS*) the change in saving as a proportion of the change in disposable income (10)

marginal revenue product (*MRP*) the value of the additional output that an extra unit of a resource can produce, $MPP \times MR$; the value to the firm of an additional resource (29)

marginal utility the extra utility derived from consuming one more unit of a good or service (21)

market a place or service that enables buyers and sellers to exchange goods and services (3)

market capitalization (market cap) the stock price multiplied by the number of shares of stock that are outstanding (31)

market failure a situation in which resources are not allocated to their highest-valued use (28)

market imperfection a lack of efficiency that results from imperfect information in the marketplace (5)

maturity date the specified time at which the issuer of a bond will repay the loan (31)

Medicaid a joint federal-state program that pays for health care for poor families, the neediest elderly, and disabled persons (33)

Medicare a federal health-care program for the elderly and the disabled (33)

microeconomics the study of economics at the level of the individual (1)

minimum efficient scale (*MES*) the minimum point of the long-run average-cost curve; the output level at which the cost per unit of output is the lowest (22)

monetarist economics a school of thought that emphasizes the role changes in the money supply play in determining equilibrium real GDP and price level (16)

monetary overhang the money accumulated by households because there was nothing available that they wanted to buy (18)

monetary policy policy directed toward control of money and credit (5)

monetary reform a new monetary policy that includes the introduction of a new monetary unit (15)

money anything that is generally acceptable to sellers in exchange for goods and services (13)

monopolization an attempt by a firm to dominate a market or become a monopoly (25)

monopoly a market structure in which there is a single supplier of a product (5, 25)

monopoly firm (monopolist) a single supplier of a product for which there are no close substitutes (25)

monopoly power market power, the ability to set prices (25)

monopsonist a firm that is the only buyer of a resource (29)

moral hazard the problem that arises when people change their behavior from what was expected of them when they engaged in a trade or contract (28)

most-favored customer (MFC) a customer who receives a guarantee of the lowest price and all product features for a certain period of time (26)

multilateral aid aid provided by international organizations that are supported by many nations (18)

multinational business a firm that owns and operates producing units in foreign countries (4)

mutual fund an entity that invests money in stocks and bonds for groups of people (31)

national income (NI) net national product minus indirect business taxes (6)

national income accounting the process that summarizes and categorizes the level of production in an economy over a specific period of time, typically a year (6)

natural monopoly a monopoly that arises because of economies of scale (25)

natural rate of unemployment the unemployment rate that would exist in the absence of cyclical unemployment (8)

negative economic profit total revenue that is less than total costs when total costs include all opportunity costs (23)

negative income tax (NIT) a tax system that transfers increasing amounts of income to households earning incomes below some specified level as their income declines (34)

net exports the difference between the value of exports and the value of imports (4)

net investment gross investment minus capital consumption allowance (6)

net national product (NNP) gross national product minus capital consumption allowance (6)

new classical economics a school of thought that holds that changes in real GDP are a product of unexpected changes in the level of prices (16)

NICs newly industrialized countries (19)

no-load fund a mutual fund that sells its shares without a commission or sales charge (31)

nominal GDP a measure of national output based on the current prices of goods and services (6)

nominal interest rate the observed interest rate in the market (8)

nonrenewable (exhaustible) natural resources natural resources whose supply is fixed (32)

normal accounting profit zero economic profit (23)

normal goods goods for which demand increases as income increases (3, 20)

normative analysis analysis of what ought to be (1)

occupational segregation the separation of jobs by sex (30)

open market operations the buying and selling of government bonds by the Fed to control bank reserves, the federal funds rate, and the money supply (14)

opportunity costs the highest-valued alternative that must be forgone when a choice is made (2)

partnership a business with two or more owners who share the firm's profits and losses (4)

per capita real GDP real GDP divided by the population (17)

per se rule actions that could be anticompetitive are intrinsically illegal (27)

perfectly elastic demand curve a horizontal demand curve indicating that consumers can and will purchase all they want at one price (20)

perfectly inelastic demand curve a vertical demand curve indicating that there is no change in the quantity demanded as the price changes (20)

personal income (PI) national income plus income currently received but not earned, minus income currently earned but not received (6)

Phillips curve a graph that illustrates the relationship between inflation and the unemployment rate (15)

portfolio investment the purchase of securities (18)

positive analysis analysis of what is (1)

positive economic profit total revenue is greater than total costs when total costs include all opportunity costs (23)

potential real GDP the output produced at the natural rate of unemployment (8)

precautionary demand for money the demand for money to cover unplanned transactions or emergencies (14)

preferred provider organization (PPO) a group of physicians who contract to provide services at a price discount (33)

price ceiling a situation in which the price is not allowed to rise above a certain level (3)

price discrimination charging different customers different prices for the same product (20, 25)

price elasticity of demand the percentage change in the quantity demanded of a product divided by the percentage change in the price of that product (20)

price elasticity of supply the percentage change in the quantity supplied divided by the percentage change in price, everything else held constant (20)

price floor a situation in which the price is not allowed to decrease below a certain level (3)

price index a measure of the average price level in an economy (6)

price maker a firm that sets the price of the product it sells (23)

price searcher a firm that sets the price of the product it sells (23)

price setter a firm that sets the price of the product it sells (23)

primary product a product in the first stage of production, which often serves as an input in the production of another product (18)

principle of mutual exclusivity the rule that an owner of private property is entitled to enjoy the consumption of that property privately (28)

private costs costs that are borne solely by the individuals involved in the transaction that created the costs (28)

private property right the limitation of ownership to an individual (5)

private sector households, businesses, and the international sector (4)

privatization transferring a publicly owned enterprise to private ownership (19, 27)

privatize to convert state-owned enterprises to private ownership (18)

producer price index (PPI) a measure of average prices received by producers (6)

producer surplus the difference between the price firms would have been willing to accept for their products and the price they actually receive (24)

production possibilities curve (PPC) a graphical representation showing the maximum quantity of goods and services that can be produced using limited resources to the fullest extent possible (2)

productivity the quantity of output produced per unit of resource (3)

progressive tax (progressive income tax) a tax whose rate rises as income rises (12, 34)

proportional tax a tax whose rate does not change as the tax base changes (34)

public choice the study of how government actions result from the self-interested behaviors of voters and politicians (5)

public good a good whose consumption by one person does not diminish the quantity or quality available for others (5, 28)

public interest theory the theory that government should intervene in business actions to improve the well-being of the general public (28)

public sector the government (4)

purchasing power parity (PPP) the condition under which monies have the same purchasing power in different markets (37)

quantity demanded the amount of a product that people are willing and able to purchase at a specific price (3)

quantity quota a limit on the amount of a good that may be imported (36)

quantity supplied the amount sellers are willing and able to offer at a given price during a given period of time, everything else held constant (3)

quantity theory of money the theory that with constant velocity, changes in the quantity of money change nominal GDP (14)

"race to the bottom" with globalization, countries compete for international investment by offering low or no environmental regulations or labor standards (19)

rational expectation an expectation that is formed using all available relevant information (15)

rational self-interest the means by which people choose the options that give them the greatest amount of satisfaction (1)

real GDP a measure of the quantity of final goods and services produced, adjusted for price changes (6)

real interest rate the nominal interest rate minus the rate of inflation (8)

recession a period in which real GDP falls (8)

recessionary gap the increase in expenditures required to reach potential GDP (11)

regressive tax a tax whose rate decreases as the tax base changes (34)

regulated monopoly a monopoly firm whose behavior is monitored and prescribed by a government entity (25)

relative price the price of one good expressed in terms of the price of another good (3)

renewable (nonexhaustible) natural resources natural resources whose supply can be replenished (32)

rent seeking the use of resources simply to transfer wealth from one group to another without increasing production or total wealth (5, 28)

required reserves the cash reserves (a percentage of deposits) a bank must keep on hand or on deposit with the Federal Reserve (13)

reservation wage the minimum wage a worker is willing to accept (15)

reserve currency a currency that is used to settle international debts and is held by governments to use in foreign exchange market interventions (37)

resource market a market that provides one of the resources for producing goods and servces: labor, capital, and land (29)

resources goods used to produce other goods, i.e., land, labor, capital, and entrepreneurial ability (1)

ROSCA a rotating savings and credit association (13)

rule of reason the rule that to be illegal, an action must be unreasonable in a competitive sense and the anticompetitive effects must be demonstrated (27)

rule of 72 the number of years required for an amount to double in value is 72 divided by the annual rate of growth (17)

saving function the relationship between disposable income and saving (10)

scale size; all resources change when scale changes (22)

scarcity the shortage that exists when less of something is available than is wanted at a zero price (1)

shares ownership of a piece of a company (31)

shock an unexpected change in a variable (15)

short run a period of time short enough that the quantities of at least one of the resources cannot be varied (20)

short-run average total cost (*SRATC*) the lowest-cost combination of resources with which each level of output is produced when the quantity of at least one resource is fixed (22)

shortage a quantity supplied that is smaller than the quantity demanded at a given price; it occurs whenever the price is less than the equilibrium price (3)

shutdown price the minimum point of the average-variable-cost curve (24)

slope the steepness of a curve, measured as the ratio of the rise to the run (1 App.)

social cost the total cost of a transaction, the private plus the external cost (28)

social regulation the prescribing of health, safety, performance, and environmental standards that apply across several industries (27)

socially responsible fund a group of stocks or bonds of companies that meet the requirements of ethical behavior or environmental behavior (31)

sole proprietorship a business owned by one person, who receives all the profits and is responsible for all the debts incurred by the business (4)

special drawing right (SDR) an artificial unit of account created by averaging the values of the U.S. dollar, euro, Japanese yen, and British pound (13)

specific fund a mutual fund that focuses on a particular industry or a particular part of the world (31)

speculative attack a situation in which private investors sell domestic currency and buy Foreign currency, betting that the domestic currency will be devalued (19)

speculative demand for money the demand for money created by uncertainty about the value of other assets (14)

speculators people who seek to profit from an expected shift in an exchange rate by selling the currency that is expected to depreciate and buying the currency that is expected to appreciate, then exchanging the appreciated currency for the depreciated currency after the exchange rate adjustment (37)

spending multiplier a measure of the change in equilibrium income or real GDP produced by a change in autonomous expenditures (11)

statistical discrimination discrimination that results when an indicator of group performance is incorrectly applied to an individual member of the group (30)

sterilization the use of domestic open market operations to offset the effects of a foreign exchange market intervention on the domestic money supply (14)

stock ownership of a piece of a company (31)

stranded assets assets acquired by a firm when regulated that have little value when deregulated (27)

strategic behavior the behavior that occurs when what is best for A depends on what B does, and what is best for B depends on what A does (26)

strategic trade policy the use of trade restrictions or subsidies to allow domestic firms with decreasing costs to gain a greater share of the world market (36)

subsidies payments made by government to domestic firms to encourage exports (36)

substitute goods goods that can be used in place of each other; as the price of one rises, the demand for the other rises (3)

superstar effect the situation in which people with small differences in abilities or productivity receive vastly different levels of compensation (30)

supply the amount of a good or service that producers are willing and able to offer for sale at each possible price during a period of time, everything else held constant (3)

supply curve a graph of a supply schedule that measures price on the vertical axis and quantity supplied on the horizontal axis (3)

supply schedule a table or list of prices and corresponding quantities supplied of a particular good or service (3)

surplus a quantity supplied that is larger than the quantity demanded at a given price; it occurs whenever the price is greater than the equilibrium price (3)

surplus (in a balance of payments account) the amount by which credits exceed debits (7)

tariff a tax on imports or exports (36)

tax incidence a measure of who pays a tax (20)

technical efficiency producing at a point on the PPC (5)

technology ways of combining resources to produce output (17)

terms of trade the amount of an exported good that must be given up to obtain an imported good (18, 35)

time inconsistent a characteristic of a policy or plan that changes over time in response to changing conditions (15)

total costs (*TC*) the sum of total variable and total fixed costs (22)

total factor productivity (*TFP*) the ratio of the economy's output to its stock of labor and capital (17)

total fixed costs (*TFC*) costs that must be paid whether a firm produces or not (22)

total physical product (*TPP*) the maximum output that can be produced when successive units of a variable resource are added to fixed amounts of other resources (22)

total revenue (*TR*) $TR = P \times Q$ (20)

total utility a measure of the total satisfaction derived from consuming a quantity of some good or service (21)

total variable costs (*TVC*) costs that rise or fall as production rises or falls (22)

trade creation an effect of a preferential trade agreement, allowing a country to obtain goods at a lower cost than is available at home (36)

trade credit the extension of a period of time before an importer must pay for goods or services purchased (18)

trade deficit the situation that exists when imports exceed exports (4)

trade diversion an effect of a preferential trade agreement, reducing economic efficiency by shifting production to a higher-cost producer (36)

tradeoff the giving up of one good or activity in order to obtain some other good or activity (2)

trade surplus the situation that exists when imports are less than exports (4)

trading post a location on the floor of the NYSE where firms' stock is auctioned (31)

transaction costs the costs involved in making an exchange (3)

transactions account a checking account at a bank or other financial institution that can be drawn on to make payments (13)

transactions demand for money the demand to hold money to buy goods and services (14)

transfer earnings the amount that must be paid to a resource owner to get him or her to allocate the resource to another use (29)

transfer payment the income transferred by the government from one citizen, who is earning income, to another citizen; a payment to one person that is funded by taxing others. (5, 6, 12)

underemployment the employment of workers in jobs that do not utilize their productive potential (8)

unemployment rate the percentage of the labor force that is not working (8)

utility a measure of the satisfaction received from possessing or consuming goods and services (21)

value added the difference between the value of output and the value of the intermediate goods used in the production of that output (6)

value-added tax (*VAT*) a general sales tax collected at each stage of production (12)

value quota a limit on the monetary value of a good that may be imported (36)

velocity of money the average number of times each dollar is spent on final goods and services in a year (14)

wealth the value of all assets owned by a household (10)

wealth effect a change in the real value of wealth that causes spending to change when the level of prices changes (9)

World Bank an international organization that makes loans and provides technical expertise to developing countries (37)

zero-coupon bond a bond that provides no interest payments but is issued at a value lower than its face value (31)

zero economic profit total revenue is equal to total costs when total costs include all opportunity costs (23)

Text Credits

Economically Speaking

Chapter

1   From "Choice of Major, Years of College Influence Student Debt," Wichita, Kansas, October 16, 2002. Reprinted with permission of Wichita State University.

2   From "Guns and Butter," by Kevin Libin, *Canadian Business,* October 14, 2002. Reprinted with permission.

3   From "A Sleuth for Landlords with Eviction in Mind," by Corey Kilgannon, *New York Times,* March 26, 2000. Copyright © 2000 by the New York Times Co. Reprinted with permission.

4   From "Report: Ramsey Friend Sold Information to National Enquirer," The Associated Press, November 28, 2002. Reprinted with permission of The Associated Press.

5   *Los Angeles Times,* July 26, 2000, p. 9. Copyright 2000 Times Mirror Company.

6   From "Hiding in the Shadows: The Growth of the Underground Economy," by Friedrich Schneider and Dominik Enste, March 2002, International Monetary Fund. Reprinted with permission.

7   From "High Gas Prices, Weak Euro Result in Room Availability, Less-Crowded Facilities at Popular U.S. National Parks," The Associated Press, July 24, 2002. Reprinted with permission of The Associated Press.

8   From "Things Are Really Tight at Most Levels of Job Market," by Allison Linn, *Rocky Mountain News,* March 1, 2003. Reprinted with permission of the Rocky Mountain News.

9   From "The Conference Board's Consumer Confidence Index Plummets Nearly 15 Points," The Conference Board, Consumer Research Center, News Release, February 25, 2003. Reprinted with permission.

10   From "U.S. Trade Deficit for 2002 Largest in History," by Jeffrey Sharshott, *The Washington Times,* February 21, 2003. Copyright © 2003 Newsworld Communications, Inc. Reprinted with permission of The Washington Times.

11   Reprinted from August 4, 2003 issue of *Business Week* by special permission. Copyright © 2003 by The McGraw-Hill Companies, Inc.

12   From "Brussels Takes Action Against France over Budget Deficit," by Gary Duncan, *The Times* (London), March 18, 2003. Reprinted with permission.

13   From "They Love Our Money," *U.S. News & World Report,* April 27, 1998. Copyright © 1998 U.S. News & World Report, L.P. Reprinted with permission.

14   Copyright © 2003 Reuters. Reuters content is the intellectual property of Reuters. Any copying, republication, or redistribution of Reuters content is expressly prohibited. Reuters shall not be liable for any errors or delays in content, or for any act.

15   From "War Worries Hurting U.S. Markets: Fed Chief Alan Greenspan Warns of Further Interest Rate Cuts if Sluggishness Continues," The Associated Press, November 14, 2002. Reprinted with permission of The Associated Press.

16   From "The Ghost of Christmas Past Haunts Economists," by J. Bradford DeLong, January 10, 2003 *Business Day* (Johannesburg). Reprinted with permission.

17   From "U.S. Updating Its Economic Measurements," by Mary Williams Walsh, *Los Angeles Times,* October 25, 1999. Copyright © 1999 Los Angeles Times. Reprinted with permission.

18   Information from World Health Organization and International Food Policy Research Institute.

19   From "Germans' Coziness Puts Nation at Risk," by Steven Komarow, *USA Today,* February 10, 2003. Copyright © 2003 USA Today. Reprinted with permission.

20   From "Higher Gas Prices Make Future Murky for Big SUVs: Impact of Rising Fuel Costs Could Be Bigger in Canada Than U.S.," by Steve Erwin, *Edmonton Journal,* February 25, 2003. Reprinted with permission of The Canadian Press.

21   From "Why Sudden Wealth Will Not Make You Happy," by Jean Nicol, *South China Morning Post* (Hong Kong), March 21, 2003. Copyright © 2003 South China Morning Post.

22   From "Merge or Die, Operators Are Told as Economy of Scale Becomes Crucial," by Martyn Wingrove, *Lloyd's List,* March 12, 2003. Copyright © 2003 Lloyd's List. Reprinted with permission.

23   From "Business Ethics Guarantee Value to All Interested Parties," by Kim Suk-joong, *The Korea Herald,* January 24, 2003. Reprinted with permission.

24   From "Avoid Commoditization," by Kelly Howard, *BtoB Magazine,* October 14, 2002. Reprinted with permission of BtoB Magazine.

25   From "Conflict Diamonds: Americans Can Limit the Damage They Do," *Star Tribune* (Minneapolis, MN), June 12, 2000, p. 10A. Copyright 2000 Star Tribune.

26   From "Authorities Gather to Combat Warning Drug Cartels," by Karen Brooks, October 5, 2002. Copyright © 2002, Knight Ridder/Tribune Media Services. Reprinted with permission.

27   From "Don't Let It Happen Again: Why Didn't the Post-'65 Fixes Stop This Blackout?," Newsday, August 17, 2003. Distributed by Tribune Media Services. Copyright © 2003 Newsday. Reprinted with permission.

28   From "Bates College Students Retire Air Pollution Permit Worth a Ton of Sulfur Dioxide," April 24, 2003, Bates College, Lewiston, Maine. Reprinted with permission.

29   From "Agent: Eagles, McNabb Agree to Deal Worth up to $115 Million," by Rob Maaddi, The Associated Press, September 27, 2002. Reprinted with Permission of The Associated Press.

30   Reprinted by permission of the *Richmond Times Dispatch,* January 25, 1998.

31   From "Accountants Figure Law to Benefit Them," by Sean Callahan, *Chicago Sun-Times,* November 18, 2002. Reprinted with special permission from the Chicago Sun-Times, Inc. Copyright © 2002.

32   From "Debate: Is Anti-Sprawl Really 'Smart' Growth? As Durham Mulls Plan, Groups Differ on Effects on Poor," by Virginia Bridges,

Economic Insight

Chapter

U.S. Macroeconomic Data for Selected Years, 1929–2003

Year	Real GDP	Consumption	Investment	Government Spending	Net Exports	Chain-Type Real GDP Index	GDP Growth Rate
			$ billions			index	%
1929	822.20	625.70	93.60	110.10	-10.50	10.52	n/a
1933	603.30	511.00	17.50	118.00	-11.00	7.72	-1.40
1939	903.50	689.00	79.60	179.70	-5.50	11.56	8.10
1945	1693.30	851.80	69.00	1041.00	-28.70	21.67	-1.20
1950	1686.60	1090.90	232.50	367.40	-10.20	21.59	8.70
1955	2099.50	1310.40	262.10	580.40	-16.10	26.87	7.10
1960	2376.70	1510.80	272.80	661.30	-20.50	30.42	2.50
1965	3028.50	1897.60	402.00	791.10	-26.40	38.76	6.40
1970	3578.00	2317.50	436.20	931.10	-63.80	45.80	0.20
1971	3697.70	2405.20	485.80	913.80	-74.60	47.33	3.30
1972	3898.40	2550.50	543.00	914.90	-87.80	49.90	5.40
1973	4123.40	2675.90	606.50	908.30	-62.00	52.78	5.80
1974	4099.00	2653.70	561.70	924.80	-35.60	52.46	-0.60
1975	4084.40	2710.90	462.20	942.50	-7.50	52.28	-0.40
1976	4311.70	2868.90	555.50	943.30	-40.40	55.19	5.60
1977	4511.80	2992.10	639.40	952.70	-65.30	57.75	4.60
1978	4760.60	3124.70	713.00	982.20	-66.40	60.93	5.50
1979	4912.10	3203.20	735.40	1001.10	-45.50	62.87	3.20
1980	4900.90	3193.00	655.30	1020.90	10.00	62.73	-0.20
1981	5021.00	3236.00	715.60	1030.00	5.20	64.26	2.50
1982	4919.30	3275.50	615.20	1046.00	-14.60	62.96	-2.00
1983	5132.30	3454.30	673.70	1081.00	-63.80	65.69	4.30
1984	5505.20	3640.60	871.50	1118.40	-128.40	70.46	7.30
1985	5717.10	3820.90	863.40	1190.50	-149.10	73.17	3.80
1986	5912.40	3981.20	857.70	1255.20	-165.10	75.67	3.40
1987	6113.30	4113.40	879.30	1292.50	-156.20	78.24	3.40
1988	6368.40	4279.50	902.80	1307.50	-112.10	81.51	4.20
1989	6591.80	4393.70	936.50	1343.50	-79.40	84.37	3.50
1990	6707.90	4474.50	907.30	1387.30	-56.50	85.85	1.80
1991	6676.40	4466.60	829.50	1403.40	-15.80	85.45	-0.50
1992	6880.00	4594.50	899.80	1410.00	-19.80	88.06	3.00
1993	7062.60	4748.90	977.90	1398.80	-59.10	90.39	2.70
1994	7347.70	4928.10	1107.00	1400.10	-86.60	94.04	4.00
1995	7543.80	5075.60	1140.60	1406.40	-78.40	96.55	2.70
1996	7813.20	5237.50	1242.70	1421.90	-88.90	100.00	3.60
1997	8159.50	5423.90	1393.30	1455.40	-113.30	104.43	4.40
1998	8515.70	5678.70	1566.80	1486.40	-221.00	108.99	4.40
1999	8875.80	5978.80	1669.70	1536.10	-322.30	113.60	4.20
2000	9318.50	6294.30	1839.80	1579.20	-412.40	119.27	5.00
2001	9214.60	6377.20	1574.60	1640.40	-415.90	109.42	0.00
2002	9439.90	6575.80	1589.60	1712.80	-488.60	110.66	*0.03
2003*	9590.70	6702.40	1604.35	1754.65	-528.20	112.04	0.02

*2003 data are an average of the first two quarters of the year only.